Developing Technology–Rich Teacher Education Programs:

Key Issues

Drew Polly
University of North Carolina at Charlotte, USA

Clif Mims
University of Memphis, USA

Kay A. Persichitte
University of Wyoming, USA

Information Science
REFERENCE

Managing Director:	Lindsay Johnston
Senior Editorial Director:	Heather Probst
Book Production Manager:	Sean Woznicki
Development Manager:	Joel Gamon
Development Editor:	Michael Killian
Acquisitions Editor:	Erika Gallagher
Typesetters:	Mackenzie Snader
Print Coordinator:	Jamie Snavely
Cover Design:	Nick Newcomer, Greg Snader

Published in the United States of America by
Information Science Reference (an imprint of IGI Global)
701 E. Chocolate Avenue
Hershey PA 17033
Tel: 717-533-8845
Fax: 717-533-8661
E-mail: cust@igi-global.com
Web site: http://www.igi-global.com

Library of Congress Cataloging-in-Publication Data

Developing technology-rich teacher education programs: key issues / Drew Polly, Clif Mims, and Kay A. Persichitte, editors.
   p. cm.
 Includes bibliographical references and index.
 Summary: "This book offers professional teacher educators a rare opportunity to harvest the thinking of pioneering colleagues spanning dozens of universities, and to benefit from the creativity, scholarship, hard work, and reflection that led them to the models they describe"--Provided by publisher.
 ISBN 978-1-4666-0014-0 (hardcover) -- ISBN 978-1-4666-0015-7 (ebook) -- ISBN 978-1-4666-0016-4 (print & perpetual access) 1. Teachers--Training of--Curricula--United States. 2. Educational technology--Study and teaching (Higher)--United States. I. Polly, Drew, 1977- II. Mims, Clif, 1971- III. Persichitte, Kay A., 1954-
 LB1715.D484 2012
 370.71'1--dc23
                    2011043978

British Cataloguing in Publication Data
A Cataloguing in Publication record for this book is available from the British Library.

All work contributed to this book is new, previously-unpublished material. The views expressed in this book are those of the authors, but not necessarily of the publisher.

Editorial Advisory Board

Table of Contents

Section 1
Frameworks for Technology Integration

Chapter 1

Punya Mishra, Michigan State University, USA
Matthew J. Koehler, Michigan State University, USA
Andrea Zellner, Michigan State University, USA
Kristen Kereluik, Michigan State University, USA

Chapter 2

Priscilla Norton, George Mason University, USA
Dawn Hathaway, George Mason University, USA

Chapter 3

Timothy J. Frey, Kansas State University, USA
E. Ann Knackendoffel, Kansas State University, USA

Chapter 4

Minchi C. Kim, Purdue University, USA

Section 2
Integration of Web 2.0 Tools into Teacher Education Programs

Section 3
Integration of Technology into Teacher Education Courses

Section 4
Technology Integration across the Content Areas

Section 5
Technology-Rich Clinical and Student Teaching Experiences

Section 6
Supporting Faculty in Technology-Rich Teacher Education Programs

Detailed Table of Contents

Section 1
Frameworks for Technology Integration

Chapter 1

Punya Mishra, Michigan State University, USA
Matthew J. Koehler, Michigan State University, USA
Andrea Zellner, Michigan State University, USA
Kristen Kereluik, Michigan State University, USA

In this chapter, the authors describe the design and implementation of the Master's program in Educational Technology at Michigan State University (MSU) as an example of an institution's attempts to improve their facility to incorporate technology into the classroom practice. They briefly define the concept of the TPACK and how that theoretical model is important in thinking about technology with teacher practitioners, and how it helped to focus the design of the Educational Technology program at MSU. They then outline central TPACK themes that run through each of the stages of this program, and how each level, in turn, informs the others. Finally, they offer concrete examples of TPACK in practice at each stage of the Master's program in Educational Technology.

Chapter 2

Priscilla Norton, George Mason University, USA
Dawn Hathaway, George Mason University, USA

The authors' years of experience experimenting with and studying teacher education at the graduate, inservice level have led to a set of design strategies recommended as guides to making robust decisions about technology-rich preservice teacher education. This chapter is divided into three sections. The first section presents a brief discussion of preservice teacher technology education and the Integration of Technology in Schools (ITS) advanced studies graduate program. The second presents five guiding design strategies to inform the continuous process of technology-rich teacher education. The chapter concludes with a third section that discusses the implications of those design strategies for preservice teacher education.

Today's K-12 classrooms are learning environments that present teachers with the challenge of meeting the diverse needs of learners. Utilizing technology and the principles of Universal Design for Learning (UDL) can help teachers to meet the exceptional needs of learners in a variety of areas. This chapter presents ideas and strategies to utilize technology to facilitate the implementation of UDL principles (using multiple means of representation, engagement, and expression in the design of instruction) in teacher education and K-12 classrooms. Each principle of UDL is described, and examples of technology that can support implementation of the principle are shared. The chapter concludes with considerations for teacher education programs including providing modeling of UDL instruction and designing instruction with UDL in mind.

Promoting student utilization of technology has been a challenging and persistent theme in education for the past twenty years. Many teachers find it difficult to interpret and transform their daily routines to incorporate new pedagogies to promote such skills. Given the emergence of new technologies including social network, Web 2.0, simulations and games, and pedagogical frameworks to support learning and teaching with technologies, teachers are expected to use technology not only as a assistive tool to accomplish certain objectives but also a well-coordinated stage where students can learn more meaningfully and authentically. The purpose of this chapter is to discuss definitions, frameworks, and examples of technology integration and to elaborate on four key principles of technology integration: authenticity, collaboration, inquiry, and scaffolding.

Section 2
Integration of Web 2.0 Tools into Teacher Education Programs

This chapter presents and evaluates a Web 2.0 Learning Design Framework that can be used to develop pre-service teachers' learning design capabilities. The framework integrates the TPACK model of educational practice, Anderson and Krathwohl's Taxonomy of Learning, Teaching and Assessing, different types of constructive and negotiated pedagogies, with a range of contemporary Web 2.0 based learning technologies. Pre-service teachers in a second year learning technology subject felt that the framework helped them to better understand the relationship between technology, pedagogy and content, as well as create more effective learning designs for their students. Examples of student learning designs are used to illustrate the way that pre-service teachers applied the framework.

This chapter introduces readers to a category of interactive technology instruments called visualization tools and how these tools can be used to stimulate generative learning. Examples are provided, and criticisms of text visualization tools are also carefully considered. Readers are challenged to explore new uses for and the impact of visualization tools.

Recent educational reform movements have advocated for teacher educators to embrace learning communities as a way to prepare and support new teachers. Considering the current student population in schools of education and their affinity for digital communication, social networking can be used to foster online learning communities where preservice teachers' development can be supported. This chapter examines social networking and outlines recent research related to its use in the support of teacher education. The chapter concludes with design considerations for teacher educators who wish to develop social networks to foster their own online learning communities.

This chapter presents and analyzes an instructional practice developed in an Instructional Technology course required of Education students at Fordham University. The practice was employed to ensure a high level of engagement by assigning students the hands-on development of Web-based, instructional resources suitable for use with their own public school classes. Discussed in detail are the attitudes and understandings about Instructional Technology of the students, the Web 2.0 tools and content items they selected for use in their projects, the ways they applied them to the instructional resources they developed, and how those satisfied their needs as teachers.

    Stephanie A. Jones, Georgia Southern University, USA
    Lucilia Green, Georgia Southern University, USA
    Charles B. Hodges, Georgia Southern University, USA
    Kathryn Kennedy, Georgia Southern University, USA
    Elizabeth Downs, Georgia Southern University, USA
    Judi Repman, Georgia Southern University, USA
    Kenneth F. Clark, Georgia Southern University, USA

This chapter describes how and why Web 2.0 tools are being used in a completely online M.Ed. program in Instructional Technology. Examples of specific tools and their implementation are provided along with the theoretical or pragmatic bases for their use. McGee and Diaz's (2007) categories for Web 2.0 tools, documentative, communicative, generative, interactive, and collaborative, are used to structure the examples. A description of the evolution of the M.Ed. program and reasons for supplementing learning management systems with Web 2.0 tools are given.

    Janice W. Butler, University of Texas at Brownsville, USA

Technology is not a panacea for educational reform, but the use of technology in the classroom can enable teachers to engage today's students in learning content. While some believed that new, young teachers would bring technology to the PK-12 classroom, this clearly has not happened. Since teacher educators generally do not model technology integration and instead use primarily teacher-centered instruction, many new teachers do not know how to integrate technology, particularly Web 2.0 technologies, into instruction. To encourage teacher educators to learn about these easy-to-use technologies, this chapter examines wikis as a low-threshold Web 2.0 tool. This chapter will discuss the power of using these technology tools.

Section 3
Integration of Technology into Teacher Education Courses

    Anne T. Ottenbreit-Leftwich, Indiana University, USA

The objective of this chapter is to describe a case study of an educational technology course that uses subject-specific contexts to address preservice teachers' development of TPACK. This course uses various workouts and cases to develop preservice teachers' technology abilities within the context of their future classrooms. Through these activities, preservice teachers showed improvement in technology knowledge (TK), technological pedagogical knowledge (TPK), and technological pedagogical and content knowledge (TPACK). Recommendations are made to other teacher educators on how to apply such principles within their own educational technology courses.

This chapter discusses several challenges and recommendations in obtaining the desired outcome from technology-rich teacher education programs: a novice teacher prepared to make decisions supporting students' subject-area learning with technology. The authors of this chapter shape their discussion using select findings from two studies of preservice teachers enrolled in a technology-rich teacher education program at a U.S. university. They discuss the importance of the modeling relationship between instructors' and preservice teachers' experiences with digital technologies and describe productivity software's enduring grip as the most used digital technologies among preservice teachers during teacher education – even in technology-rich teacher education programs. The authors argue that teacher education's overemphasis on productivity tools is not adequately preparing new teachers for the knowledge society in which people live, work, and educate.

This chapter describes the results of a curriculum redesign of a course in technology integration in an initial licensure undergraduate program. While all students are held accountable to the same course objectives, multiple options are provided for learners to choose a path to meet those objectives. Rather than requiring all students to participate in the same activities, students are allowed to select activities and content related to their individual content areas and skill levels. Allowing students choices helps alleviate problems in delivering content to students with different majors and background knowledge.

This chapter is organized around shifting paradigms of information literacy, instructional literacy, and technology literacy. Information literacy focuses on the questions of what is knowledge management. The authors explore the impact of these shifts on the role of teacher, student, and content to promote knowledge creation (learning). The authors also discuss technology literacy as the merging the two constructs -- teaching and using technology.

This case study of EDM310 at the University of South Alabama covers the transition of the class from a group of face to face courses which covered Microsoft Office to face to face classes of 20 students taught by different teachers which emphasized, to varying degrees, the use of Web 2.0 tools, blogging, commenting on blogs; then to a set of face to face courses all delivering instruction using Web 2.0 tools, blogs and commenting on blogs. A detailed description is provided, showing how projects are used as a central learning tool; how blogging and comments on blogs play a critical role in the course; how students react to these new instructional approaches. The case study also contains specific suggestions on how to organize such a course and how it was implemented at the University of South Alabama with great success.

Chapter 16

Kelly L. Unger, Wayne State University, USA
Monica W. Tracey, Wayne State University, USA

Many teacher education (TED) faculty and professional development (PD) providers are now encouraged or required at a minimum to incorporate an online learning component into courses. Not only are they teaching the required course content to pre- and in-service teachers in an online environment, but are also modeling the use of that environment to teachers who will ultimately be required to design, develop, and provide online instruction to their future students. The purpose of this chapter is to discuss: (1) transitioning instruction from face-to-face to an online learning environment, (2) examples of learning activities to implement with the Web 2.0 social networking tool NING, and (3) implications the NING has for those instructing pre- and in-service teachers.

Chapter 17

Albert D. Ritzhaupt, University of Florida, USA
Michele A. Parker, University of North Carolina Wilmington, USA
Abdou Ndoye, Qatar University, Qatar

Though ePortfolios have grown in acceptance by teacher education programs across the United States, there still remain many questions regarding whether the tools are meeting student and teacher education program needs. This chapter will address this concern by first describing ePortfolios within teacher education. Next, the chapter will present a stakeholder interaction model and identify the individuals involved in an ePortfolio system. Then, a series of integration questions will be highlighted from a teacher education perspective. Two teacher education programs' ePortfolio initiatives are evaluated using the Electronic Portfolio Student Perspective Instrument (EPSPI) (Ritzhaupt, Singh, Seyferth, & Dedrick, 2008) in relation to several integration characteristics. Finally, recommendations to teacher education programs are made.

Section 4
Technology Integration across the Content Areas

Chapter 18

In this chapter, the author explains how a theory of Multiliteracies helped to shape the development of a graduate course which, in turn, initiated changes in an undergraduate content-area literacy course in a teacher education program. Both courses are described, and ways in digital technologies changed the way the instructor and students collaborated, worked, and learned, are discussed. Service learning aspects of these courses are explored with examples of how pre- and inservice teachers engaged with K-12 students and teachers in the community. Implications for teacher education faculty and students are presented as well as the need to implement Multiliterate pedagogies across the K-12 spectrum.

Chapter 19

In this chapter, the author explores three questions: 1.) How is the practice of writing in K-12 classrooms influenced by this era of new technologies? 2.) In what ways can we bring online technologies into the classroom so students can understand that they read and write everyday in digital forms? 3.) In what ways can teachers create technology-rich experiences to support 21st century writers? To answer these questions, the author briefly examines the theoretical foundation of the process model for writing and how online technologies have impacted this model in classrooms. Next, the author describes three Web 2.0 tools that are available to teachers to use in their classrooms during writing: digital portfolios, wikis, and digital storytelling. The author explains how he uses these tools within his own college classroom.

Chapter 20

The purpose of this chapter is to outline how changes related to technology integration in Early Childhood Education may occur within the context of national standards and policies, pedagogy and beliefs, curricular transformations, impact on children, and special tools. The author suggests re-conceptualizing the content and delivery of college courses to support and inspire teachers to take the road less traveled. Additionally, teachers need ongoing and recurrent support for continued progress in their educational technology usage.

Chapter 21

Technology, pedagogy, and content knowledge (TPACK) is the knowledge that teachers rely on for teaching content with appropriate digital technologies. What preparation do mathematics teachers need in order to develop this knowledge needed for integrating appropriate digital technologies as teaching and learning tools? The challenges of understanding TPACK and identifying appropriate educational programs for pre-service mathematics teachers call for thoughtful attention toward the development of the knowledge, skills, and dispositions that support the dynamic nature embedded within the TPACK construct.

Chapter 22

Chandra Hawley Orrill, University of Massachusetts Dartmouth, USA
Drew Polly, University of North Carolina at Charlotte, USA

This chapter describes Technology Integration in Mathematics (TIM), an iterative professional development model that focused on integrating technology into elementary school mathematics instruction. Grounded in the American Psychological Association's Learner-Centered Principles, the program provided teachers with ownership of their own learning and situated teachers' learning of technology in the context of learning mathematics. The authors provide design principles, a description of the project, examples, and challenges from their work.

Chapter 23

Darci J. Harland, Illinois State University, USA
Ydalisse Pérez, Illinois State University, USA
Cheri Toledo, Illinois State University, USA

The purpose of this chapter is to provide teacher education faculty, specifically mathematics and science methods instructors, with a variety of approaches for integrating technology into their courses. Practical strategies are provided to assist faculty with effective uses of technology for delivering content and scaffolding student collaboration. Sample assignments are provided to assist faculty in encouraging their students (future teachers) to look beyond the textbook for teaching resources and learning assessments.

Chapter 24

John H. Curry, Morehead State University, USA
David L. Buckner, Brigham Young University – Hawaii, USA

This chapter provides a resource to practitioners not only about what types of technologies can be integrated into Social Studies instruction, but also provides resources by Social Studies content area (U.S. History, World History, Government, Civics, Economics, Geography, Anthropology, Sociology, and Psychology). The intended audience is the Social Studies teacher who wants ideas on how to improve their instructional delivery and learning environment through the integration of technology. Differing levels of technology integration are defined. Major types of technologies covered in the chapter include audio, video, simulations, and interactive whiteboards. Implications include the opportunities for Social Studies educators to provide students content in more readily understandable ways and in richer learning environments.

Chapter 25

Susan Gibson, University of Alberta, Canada

Preparing new teachers for teaching with technology is a multi-faceted process. The study reported in this chapter examined the impact that immersion in two technology-enriched, pre-service social studies pedagogy courses had on the way beginning teachers approached technology use in their teaching of social studies. The study took place over two years and tracked education students through their social studies pedagogy course experiences and their practice teaching as part of their teacher preparation program then into their first year of teaching. The findings identified that the pre-service pedagogy courses did assist in increasing the education students' understanding of a variety of ways to approach the use of various technology tools as well as their willingness to use them in their teaching.

Chapter 26

Kristen G. Taggart, University of Delaware, USA

Hybrid classrooms, or blended instruction, blend the traditional face-to-face instruction model with newer technologies of online learning. This chapter explores the possibility and effectiveness of utilizing hybrid-learning environments at the high school level. This will be accomplished through review of the literature, an evaluation of the educational objectives met through the implementation of hybrid learning, addressing the obstacles to implementation, and suggesting methods of improvement for teacher preparation programs, state departments of education, and local education authorities to improve the technical skills of teachers.

Chapter 27

Joanne Leight, Slippery Rock University, USA
Randall Nichols, Slippery Rock University, USA

Technology is changing the way Physical Education is taught. From heart rate monitors and pedometers to podcasting, exergaming, and desktop applications, tomorrow's teachers need to know how to infuse technology into their teaching. The use of technology in Physical Education can increase both student learning and teacher productivity. Courses in a comprehensive PETE (Physical Education Teacher Education) program can be divided into the following categories: Fitness related courses, Activity courses, Assessment courses, and Methods courses (including field experiences and student teaching). This chapter will describe how to prepare future physical educators to utilize the myriad of technological options available in the field.

Section 5
Technology-Rich Clinical and Student Teaching Experiences

Chapter 28

Amy J. Good, University of North Carolina at Charlotte, USA
Drew Polly, University of North Carolina at Charlotte, USA

Preparing teacher candidates to move from the methods course to K-12 classrooms is not an easy task. This project builds on previous research related to tele-observation by presenting an observation scheme while capturing a "live case" of social studies instruction prior to the practicum experience with the help of videoconference capabilities. The research questions guiding this study include: a) In what way (s) could videoconference be part of the process of bridging theory to practice? And b) In what way (s) will teacher candidates pack up the concepts from the methods course and take them to their own practicum experience? Data sources include a three part tele-observation survey and the context of the live case is shared. Teacher candidates report teaching strategies and management strategies they use in the classroom following the tele-observation experience.

Chapter 29

Teresa M. Petty, University of North Carolina at Charlotte, USA
Richard Hartshorne, University of Central Florida, USA
Tina L. Heafner, University of North Carolina at Charlotte, USA

In this chapter, unexpected challenges, "lessons learned," as well as the best practices that have resulted during the implementation of a program involving the remote observation of graduate interns (ROGI), are addressed. More specifically, best practices and lessons learned related to a series of logistical, pedagogical, and technological issues encountered during both the pilot and full implementation of the ROGI process are presented. Logistical best-practices and lessons-learned address gaining school- and district-level approval to conduct remote observations; communication, verification, and documentation of the remote observations; gaining university supervisor, and student intern buy-in; and e-documentation involved in the ROGI process.

Chapter 30

Ann C. Cunningham, Wake Forest University, USA
Adam M. Friedman, Wake Forest University, USA

This chapter presents a technology integration model designed to help teacher candidates recognize the value of collaboration, inquiry-based instruction, and the use of technology to capture and sustain student engagement. Faculty from three courses collaborated to scaffold an instructional experience that included a field-based collaborative teaching component for early stage elementary teacher candidates. Using a Collaborative Recursive Model (CRM), which involved faculty teaching social studies methodology, instructional design, and a field experience course, candidates worked in teams to design a lesson that incorporated a digital video anchor created specifically to engage elementary students in the lesson. In addition to the technology-enhanced teaching experience, candidates learned how to create their own digital video resources. Results from teacher candidate reflections indicated that the CRM was an effective method for promoting candidates' appreciation of collaboration as well as supporting the development of content and pedagogical knowledge.

Chapter 31

Adriana L. Medina, University of North Carolina at Charlotte, USA
Maryann Tatum Tobin, Nova Southeastern University, USA
Paola Pilonieta, University of North Carolina at Charlotte, USA
Lina Lopez Chiappone, Nova Southeastern University, USA
William E. Blanton, University of Miami, USA

Computer-mediated communication (CMC) is becoming common place in the preparation of teachers. This chapter will focus on the application of CMC and will provide insight on how technology can be used in P-12 classrooms and potentially impact student learning. The purpose of the chapter is to: (a) describe the development, implementation, outcomes, and sustainability of a pre-service teacher (PST) supervision model arranged around digital technology and telecommunications, providing supervision and support for PSTs engaged in a student teaching internship and (b) to discuss how the technology utilized may later be utilized by participating PSTs in their future classrooms (specifically videoconferencing, instant messaging, video sharing, and the critical analysis and reflection of current practices). The authors created a virtual-geographical third space in the form of a Teaching Lab that was mediated with a multimedia platform and designed around the principle of Cultural-Historical Activity Theory (CHAT).

Chapter 32

Michael K. Barbour, Wayne State University, USA

Online learning at the K-12 level is growing exponentially. Students learning in supplemental virtual schools and full-time cyber schools, using a variety of delivery models that include and sometimes combine independent, asynchronous, and synchronous instruction, in almost every state in the U.S. In some instances the knowledge, skills, and abilities required by teachers in this technology-mediated environment are consistent with what they learned about face-to-face teaching in their teacher education programs; while in many instances, the two are quite different. Presently the lack of empirical research into effective K-12 online teaching limits teacher education programs. However, teacher education programs still need to better prepare pre-service and in-service teachers to design, deliver, and support students engaged virtual schooling.

Section 6
Supporting Faculty in Technology-Rich Teacher Education Programs

Chapter 33

This chapter reveals the significant and authentic challenges that methods' faculty face as they step into a zone of uncertainty when integrating computer technology into lessons, classroom teaching, and student learning. While faculty may perceive that current instructional strategies are successful as measured by classroom scores, a look into the student perceptions of classroom practices, students' preferences for learning efficiently using technology, demonstrates how they are undernourished and dissatisfied with current instructional strategies. The lack of modeling of technology use in higher education is a problem as new teachers leave the academic venue and venture into the classrooms of today. In this chapter, several themes are explored including challenges faced by faculty, significance of non-integrated technology, pathways to implementation, overcoming wait-long-enough attitudes, effective mentoring-coaching models for success, and conditions to begin a successful technology integration process.

Chapter 34

In this chapter, "lessons learned" and best practices that have resulted from the implementation of technology-focused professional learning community in a College of Education, as well as recommendations for future implementations, are addressed. The Technology & Teaching Professional Learning Community, which was created by faculty in the College of Education at UNC Charlotte, provided professional development to faculty engaged in teaching hybrid and online courses. This was one of several professional development efforts at UNC Charlotte, but one, the authors suggest, that created a safe and effective space for scaffolding instructors less familiar with online learning technologies and tools.

Foreword

A common bit of wisdom shared broadly across the Internet (which has been attributed to many different sources) proposes, **"Technology will not replace teachers, but teachers who use technologies well will replace those who do not."** I agree. Technologies have an incredibly important role to play in education, and the pressure is on for educators to deliver students who are capable and who will be successful in a dynamic, challenging, demanding future. That's not going to happen without modern technologies in the capable hands of well-prepared teachers and students.

Unfortunately, the pairing of teachers and technologies doesn't result in a magical transformation that delivers this power. Only when teachers understand, reflect on, and "grow into" the new opportunities that technologies offer can they acquire the knowledge, skills, and perspectives that allow the technologies to make teachers stronger, more effective, better informed, and better connected to their students and parents. Think of it as an equation in which a teacher's pedagogical skills (PS), interpersonal skills (IPS), and their educational technology skills and knowledge (ETSK) are all multiplied together to produce teaching effectiveness (TE), something like this…

$$PS \times IPS \times ETSK = TE$$

While we can be sure that that equation is oversimplified (there are likely to be more variables, and they are not all of equal power) it points out that if any of these values is low, it can pull down the overall result. Technologies can't make weak teachers strong, but they can enhance the performance of solid teachers, making them teachers that students will never forget.

Teacher preparation institutions have a series of crucial roles to play in this developmental process. Teacher educators accept an immense responsibility to produce teachers who will serve their students, their communities, and their nation. The importance of this mission and the perceived gap between expectations and students performance has led to a stream of calls for reform of teacher education. Considering ways to make teacher preparation more effective, it will be wise to consider the advice contained in this book, the contents of which span 32 different institutions in four nations.

Section one, *Frameworks for Technology Integration*, offers advice on integrating technology, pedagogy, and content knowledge; offers design strategies to consider when building technology-rich teacher education programs; and advocates using technology and the principles of Universal Design for Learning (UDL) to prepare teachers to meet the needs of exceptional learners.

The second section, *Integration of Web 2.0 Tools into Teacher Education Programs*, offers a framework for developing pre-service teachers' capabilities in designing Web 2.0 learning experiences; counsel on the use of Web 2.0 visualization tools to stimulate generative learning; and advice on the use of social networking and Web 2.0 tools to supplement learning management systems and to prepare school technology leaders.

Section three goes deeper, providing a series of discussions ranging from broad discussions of the integration of technology into teacher education courses and modeling effective technology use in teacher preparation programs, to focused discussions on the use of social networking, e-portfolios, creating content-centric learning environments, productivity software, and student choice. A case study of the transformation from a course originally designed to prepare teachers to use Microsoft Office to one that teaches and is based in Web 2.0 tools offers an opportunity to reflect on how one might move from what is to what might be.

In the fourth section, *Technology Integration Across the Content Areas*, content area specific chapters propose effective uses of technologies in preparing teachers of early childhood education, writing, mathematics, science, social studies, and physical education, and conceptual chapters cause reflection on the key questions related to technology integration in the content areas and how hybrid classrooms might be implemented.

Technology-Rich Clinical and Student Teaching Experiences, the fifth section, offers two different perspectives on the use technologies in the remote observation of teachers, insights into the use of digital video to promote reflection in the preparation of teachers, and an opportunity to consider the similarities and differences between preparing teachers to effectively teach in face-to-face and in online school settings.

The final section, *Supporting Faculty in Technology-Rich Teacher Education Programs*, helps us consider different ways to mentor higher education faculty as they learn to integrate technologies in their courses and shares lessons learned during the implementation of a technology-focused professional learning community designed to be a "safe and effective space for scaffolding instructors less familiar with online learning technologies and tools."

This book offers professional teacher educators a rare opportunity to harvest the thinking of pioneering colleagues spanning dozens of universities, and to benefit from the creativity, scholarship, hard work, and reflection that led them to the models they describe. Teacher educators are, indeed, fortunate to have this opportunity to make informed decisions that will transform teacher education at this important moment in the history of education.

Kyle L. Peck
Penn State University, USA

Kyle L. Peck *is Associate Dean for Outreach, Technology, and International Programs, and Professor of Education at Penn State University, and is also Director of the Regional Educational Lab for the mid-Atlantic region. He is the former Head of the Learning and Performance Systems Department and was Co-Founder of the innovative "Centre Learning Community Charter School."*

Preface

OVERVIEW

Teacher education programs, more than ever before, are under severe scrutiny from national and state government, policy, and accreditation organizations. Teacher education programs are being asked to provide evidence of their impact on teacher candidates, as well as the indirect impact of teacher education programs on PK-12 students. Reforms in teacher education programs focus on the integration of 21st century skills, which include knowledge and skills related to information technology, creativity, collaboration, critical thinking, and communication (Partnership for 21st Century Skills, 2004). Technology is an essential component of these 21st Century reforms.

The focus of teacher education programs is to prepare teacher candidates to effectively teach in 21st Century learning environments. These classrooms have access to Internet-connected educational technologies, including computers, hand-held, or portable devices (U.S. Department of Education, 2010). As a result of the technology-rich nature of PK-12 schools, it is critical for teacher education programs to examine their effectiveness related to preparing teacher candidates to effectively use educational technologies to support teaching and learning processes.

The construct of Technological Pedagogical and Content Knowledge (TPACK) has explicated the knowledge and skills related to technology integration. Candidates develop the knowledge and skills related to technology integration through educational technology courses, methods courses, and technology-rich field experiences (Schrum, 1999). In this book, contributors address all of those contexts and provide examples of how technology-rich teacher education programs have developed TPACK and related skills in teacher candidates and faculty.

The purpose of this book is to provide examples and frameworks related to creating effective models of infusing technology into teacher education programs. This book is intended for faculty and others associated with teacher education programs as a resource of creating technology-rich teacher education programs. As a result, each chapter has clear directions and implications for adopting their ideas into teacher education programs. Further, the ever-changing landscape of what constitutes *current* educational technologies, has led the editors to focus this book on examples and models that address current educational technologies, but are likely to be relevant over the next decade or two as well.

The book is divided into six sections, which focus on: Frameworks for Technology Integration, Web 2.0 technologies, Teacher Education Courses, Integrating Technology across Content Areas, Field Experiences, and Ways to Support Teacher Education Faculty.

SECTION 1: FRAMEWORKS FOR TECHNOLOGY INTEGRATION

In the first chapter, Mishra, Koehler, Zellner, and Kereluik use the TPACK framework to describe the design and implementation of the Master's program in Educational Technology at Michigan State University. The authors discuss how the theoretical model of TPACK supported their views of thinking about technology with practicing teachers (their students), and how TPACK helped focus the design of the program. Mishra et al. also provide examples from their program.

In Chapter 2, Norton and Hathaway lay out five design strategies that are applicable to the design of technology-rich teacher education programs. The first section presents a brief discussion of preservice teacher technology education and the Integration of Technology in Schools (ITS) advanced studies graduate program. The second presents five guiding design strategies to inform the continuous process of technology-rich teacher education. The chapter concludes with a third section that shares the implications of those design strategies for preservice teacher education.

In Chapter 3, Frey and Knackendoffel advance the principles of Universal Design for Learning (UDL) as a framework for integrating technology with exceptional students. This chapter presents ideas and strategies to utilize technology to facilitate the implementation of UDL principles (using multiple means of representation, engagement, and expression in the design of instruction) in teacher education and K-12 classrooms. The authors elaborate on each principle of UDL with examples of how technology can support implementation of the principle. The chapter concludes with implications on how teacher education programs can employ UDL principles.

In Chapter 4, Kim provides a critical analysis of technology integration by focusing on four key principles: authenticity, collaboration, inquiry, and scaffolding. The author provides examples of how contemporary technologies, such as social networks, Web 2.0 tools, and games align with these principles, and highlights implications for support teachers' integration of technology.

SECTION 2: INTEGRATION OF WEB 2.0 TOOLS INTO TEACHER EDUCATION PROGRAMS

In Chapter 5, Bower proposes a framework for developing teacher candidates' skills with Web 2.0 tools. The framework integrates the TPACK model of educational practice, Anderson and Krathwohl's Taxonomy of Learning, Teaching, and Assessing, different types of constructive and negotiated pedagogies, with a range of contemporary Web 2.0 based learning technologies. Examples of student learning designs are used to illustrate the way that pre-service teachers applied the framework.

In Chapter 6, Banas and Brown analyze and describe Web 2.0 visualization tools and share how teacher education programs can employ these tools to stimulate generative learning. The authors provide examples and criticisms of text visualization tools, as well as implications for the use of these tools in teacher education programs.

In Chapter 7, Dreon and Marcum-Dietrich examine social networking and outline recent research related to its use in teacher education programs. The authors share considerations and implications for designing social networking activities with pre-service teachers, and how social networking can support online learning communities in teacher education programs.

In Chapter 8, Gura analyzes pedagogies used in an instructional technology course at Fordham University. Gura describes the specific use of Web 2.0 tools, projects, and the impact of the experiences on teacher candidates' attitudes and knowledge of instructional technology.

In Chapter 9, Jones, Green, Hodges, Kennedy, Downs, Repman, & Clark share how Web 2.0 tools were employed to enhance the online Instructional Technology graduate program at Georgia Southern University. The authors describe specific uses of the technologies, and offer recommendations for infusing Web 2.0 tools into other teacher education programs.

In Chapter 10, Butler advances wikis as a low-threshold, easy adaptable Web 2.0 tool for PK-12 teachers to use in their classroom. Butler shares examples of how wikis can be used in PK-12 classrooms and teacher education programs.

SECTION 3: INTEGRATION OF TECHNOLOGY INTO TEACHER EDUCATION COURSES

In Chapter 11, Ottenbriet-Leftwich describes how subject-specific contexts in an educational technology course deepened teachers' TPACK. Through the course, preservice teachers showed improvement in technology knowledge (TK), technological pedagogical knowledge (TPK), and technological pedagogical and content knowledge (TPACK). The author provides recommendations on how to apply these principles within their own educational technology courses.

In Chapter 12, Hughes, Dholakia, Wen, & Yoon analyze challenges related to preparing novice teachers to make effective decisions related to subject-specific teaching with technology. The authors share findings from two studies of teacher candidates and discuss the importance of modeling and the issues with overemphasizing productivity software.

In Chapter 13, Jones and Harris describe a buffet model to an educational technology course, where teacher candidates chose which technologies and projects they completed. By allowing students to have choices, the authors contend that teacher candidates participated in effective learning experiences despite varied majors and background knowledge.

In Chapter 14, Samuel and Hinson analyze paradigm shifts of environments, information literacy, instructional literacy, and technology literacy. The authors propose the notion of integrating technology through content-centric learning environments that focus first on the content before considering how technology can support the teaching and learning of the content.

In Chapter 15, Strange elaborately describes the educational technology course at the University of South Alabama. The author describes how the course's project-based focus employs Web 2.0 tools and blogs to prepare teacher candidates to deepen their knowledge and skills related to technology integration. He provides suggestions about how to begin the process of integrating Web 2.0 tools into educational technology courses.

In Chapter 16, Unger and Tracey describe how teacher education faculty can utilize the social networking tool, NING, to support online courses or enhance face-to-face courses. The authors provide examples of learning activities to implement with the Web 2.0 social networking tool NING, and highlight implications the NING has for faculty.

In Chapter 17, Ritzhaupt, Parker, and Ndoye, provide findings from a research study on ePortfolio use in teacher education programs. The authors propose a stakeholder interaction model and provide findings from the evaluation of two teacher education programs' ePortfolio using the authors' Electronic Portfolio Student Perspective Instrument (EPSPI).

SECTION 4: TECHNOLOGY INTEGRATION ACROSS THE CONTENT AREAS

In Chapter 18, Taylor advances the theory of multiliteracies and explains how the construct helped the revision of a graduate and an undergraduate literacy course. The author describes how digital technologies changed the way the instructor and students collaborated, worked, and learned during the course.

In Chapter 19, Kissel examines how online technologies can support writing in digital forms. The author describes and gives examples about how three Web 2.0 tools were used in a literacy methods course for elementary education students.

In Chapter 20, Swaminathan outlines how changes related to technology integration in Early Childhood Education may occur within the context of national standards and policies, pedagogy and beliefs, curricular transformations, impact on children, and special tools. The author suggests re-conceptualizing the content and delivery of courses in Early Childhood Education to support and inspire teachers to take the road less traveled.

In Chapter 21, Neiss examines pre-service mathematics teachers' preparation through the lens of TPACK. Neiss critically analyzes the knowledge, skills, and dispositions needed to effectively integrate technology into mathematics teaching, and provides implications for supporting the dynamic nature embedded within the TPACK construct.

In Chapter 22, Orrill and Polly describe Technology Integration in Mathematics (TIM), an iterative professional development model that focused on integrating technology into elementary school mathematics instruction. The authors provide design principles, a description of the project, examples, challenges, and implications for supporting both pre-service and inservice elementary school teachers related to technology integration in mathematics teaching.

In Chapter 23, Harland, Pérez, and Toledo, provide mathematics and science education faculty with a variety of approaches for integrating technology into their courses. The authors provide samples and practical strategies to assist faculty with effective uses of technology for delivering content and scaffolding student collaboration.

In Chapter 24, Curry and Buckner provide provides a resource to practitioners not only about what types of technologies can be integrated into Social Studies instruction, but also provides resources by Social Studies content area (U.S. History, World History, Government, Civics, Economics, Geography, Anthropology, Sociology, and Psychology). The authors include a robust range of technologies, including audio and video-based tasks, simulations, and interactive whiteboard activities.

In Chapter 25, Gibson provides findings from a study that examined the impact that immersion in two technology-enriched, pre-service social studies pedagogy courses had on the way beginning teachers approached technology use in their teaching of social studies. The findings identified that the pre-service pedagogy courses did assist in increasing the education students' understanding of a variety of ways to approach the use of various technology tools as well as their willingness to use them in their teaching.

In Chapter 26, Taggart gives an overview of hybrid high school classrooms and describes the promises and challenges of offering these types of learning experiences to students. The author argues that hybrid learning has potential to address challenges of face-to-face instruction and also provides implications for teacher education programs and state departments of education.

In Chapter 27, Leight and Nichols discuss the need to infuse more technology into Physical Education Teacher Education programs. The authors provide examples of how heart rate monitors, exergaming, podcasts, and other technologies can be infused into methods courses, and also provides field experiences to support teaching and learning.

SECTION 5: TECHNOLOGY-RICH CLINICAL AND STUDENT TEACHING EXPERIENCES

In Chapter 28, Good and Polly describe a tele-observation project in which pre-service teachers viewed a "live case" of social studies instruction in a methods course prior to their field experience. After the experience, teacher candidates reported teaching strategies and management strategies they use in the classroom following the tele-observation experience.

In Chapter 29, Petty, Hartshorne, and Heafner provide an overview of their Remote Observation of Graduate Interns (ROGI) project. The authors share a description of the project as well as lessons learned related to a series of logistical, pedagogical, and technological issues encountered during both the pilot and full implementation of the ROGI process are presented.

In Chapter 30, Cunningham and Friedman propose a collaborative recursive model for integrating collaborative, technology-rich, inquiry-based instruction in social studies methods courses. During the project, teacher candidates created digital video resources and explored how to best incorporate them into an elementary school social studies lesson. The authors share suggestions on how to incorporate digital video into other methods courses.

In Chapter 31, Medina, Tobin, Pilonieta, Chiappone, and Blanton describe how computer-mediated communication can support teacher candidates, specifically during the student teaching semester. The authors given an overview of the virtual Teaching Lab that was mediated with a multimedia platform and designed around the principle of Cultural-Historical Activity Theory (CHAT).

In Chapter 32, Barbour describes the increase in virtual school experiences for secondary education students in the world. He contends that secondary education teacher education programs should attend to the need to prepare virtual school teachers and incorporate experiences that prepare secondary education teachers to teach effectively in virtual learning environments.

SECTION 6: SUPPORTING FACULTY IN TECHNOLOGY-RICH TEACHER EDUCATION PROGRAMS

In Chapter 33, Jackson addresses the challenges of methods faculty attempting to integrate technology into their courses for the first time. The author addresses faculty's perception that change is not needed as well as a lack of effective models at the university level as barriers to integrating more technology in methods courses. In this chapter, several themes are explored, including challenges faced by faculty, significance of non-integrated technology, pathways to implementation, overcoming wait-long-enough attitudes, effective mentoring-coaching models for success, and conditions to begin a successful technology integration process.

In Chapter 34, Taylor, Hartshorne, Eneman, Wilkins, and Polly share "lessons learned" and effective practices from a professional learning community (PLC) in a College of Education focused on integrating more technology into courses. A group of faculty in the College of Education provided professional development and facilitated discussions to one another on a series of topics. The authors also share suggestions for creating PLCs to support technology-rich teacher education programs.

Acknowledgment

The work of this book is truly a collaborative effort between the authors and the editors. As the editorial team, we would like to sincerely thank the authors for contributing to this work. We are proud of this product and feel that the chapters in this book provide an empirical and practical look at issues related to infusing technology into teacher education programs. Lastly, we would like to thank IGI Global for their support through the publication process.

Section 1
Frameworks for Technology Integration

Chapter 1
Thematic Considerations in Integrating TPACK in a Graduate Program

Punya Mishra[1]
Michigan State University, USA

Matthew J. Koehler
Michigan State University, USA

Andrea Zellner
Michigan State University, USA

Kristen Kereluik
Michigan State University, USA

ABSTRACT

The integration of technology into classrooms is an increasingly important issue in America's schools, and at the core of this integration is the training of teachers. Teacher educators seeking to impact teachers' use of technology should recognize the needs of these learners as well as their knowledge as practitioners, in order to expand their knowledge and help them think about technology in creative ways. In this chapter, the authors describe the design and implementation of the Master's program in Educational Technology at Michigan State University (MSU) as an example of an institution's attempts to improve their facility to incorporate technology into the classroom practice. The authors briefly define the concept of the TPACK and how that theoretical model is important in thinking about technology with teacher practitioners, and how it helped to focus the design of the Educational Technology program at MSU. The authors then outline central TPACK themes that run through each of the stages of this program, and how each level, in turn, informs the others. Finally, the chapter offers concrete examples of TPACK in practice at each stage of the Master's program in educational technology.

DOI: 10.4018/978-1-4666-0014-0.ch001

INTRODUCTION

The professional development of teachers has historically focused on the development of teachers' knowledge of content along with pedagogical moves that might be implemented (Lawless & Pelligrino, 2007; Wilson & Berne, 1999). As computers, the Internet, video games, and other newer technologies have been infused into the lives of students, so too have they been added into the educational repertoire of schools and other educational institutions. As new technologies have emerged, educators have sought the best path towards implementation, both in terms of the educational value gained by the learner as well as the development of a teaching force that is able to fluently navigate this changing educational landscape (Lawless & Pelligrino, 2007).

In some cases, that path to implementation has been met with resistance on the part of teachers unfamiliar with the technology and thus unwilling to utilize the full potential of the tools (Bauer & Kenton, 2005; Cuban, Kirkpatrick & Peck, 2001; Ertmer, 2005; Keengwe, Onchwari & Wachira, 2008). Administrators, support staff, and IT professionals have had a role as well, as they have often been unwilling or unable to offer the support and infrastructure necessary for the success of these initiatives. As a consequence, technology integration plans ranging from Interactive Whiteboards to 1-to-1 laptop initiatives have floundered. It is not the technology itself that is at issue, but rather the theoretical grounding of the implementations. In the end, the infusion of technological tools and innovations into the classroom must be firmly situated to both intersect and inform the teachers' existing pedagogical and content knowledge.

Why TPACK for Professional Development of Teachers?

The TPACK framework (American Association of Colleges of Teacher Education, 2008; Koehler & Mishra; 2008; Mishra & Koehler, 2006), initially

described by Mishra and Koehler (2006), helps to conceptually ground technology-integration initiatives by anchoring the issues in the context of teacher knowledge. Building on the work of Lee Shulman (1986) on Pedagogical Content Knowledge (PCK), the framework conceptualizes how teachers' pedagogical and content knowledge interacts with technology.

In this framework (see Figure 1) three areas of teachers' knowledge are depicted: content knowledge (CK), pedagogical knowledge (PK), and technology knowledge (TK). What is most important about the framework is the ways in which these areas intersect and inform one another, so that one might focus on teachers' technological pedagogical knowledge (TPK), or the ways in which the knowledge of best practices and the knowledge of the technology combine so that a teacher implements the technology in a way sure to impact student learning, for example. When all three are combined for TPACK, what we have is a framework in which the teacher's knowledge is combined to produce strong teaching of the content that utilizes technology in a way to ideally produce and enhance student learning (Harris, Mishra & Koehler, 2009; Koehler & Mishra, 2008; Koehler & Mishra, 2010; Mishra & Koehler, 2006; Mishra & Koehler, 2008; Mishra & Koehler, 2009).

The Master's program in Educational Technology at MSU has been designed with TPACK in mind in two key ways. First, the program allows teacher practitioners an opportunity to grow in their own TPACK. Second, the TPACK framework inspires the design of the courses themselves, so that the instruction models the very ideas that we would like the teachers to utilize in their own practices. In this way, TPACK is both part of the learning outcomes and the way in which those outcomes are met. This mutually informative cycle not only improves the ways in which the teachers gain TPACK, but also meets their needs as adult learners in a graduate program.

Figure 1. The standard representation of The Technological Pedagogical Content Knowledge (TPACK) Framework. Figure retrieved from http://www.tpack.org

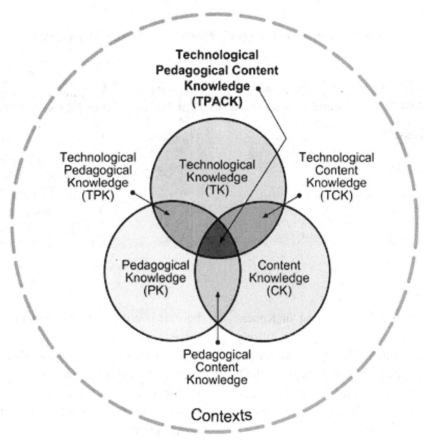

The Master's Degree Program in Educational Technology at MSU

Michigan State University's land-grant status enables outreach and support unlike that of other institutions. The College of Education is additionally uniquely situated: a leader in the nation, the college also trains and places the top-teaching candidates in the state. As part of the certification process, students are enrolled in Masters level courses, which, in turn, puts them on the road to earning their Masters degree as part of their re-certification process, moving from the early-career certification, known as the Provisional Certificate, to a Professional teaching certificate. Furthermore, the State of Michigan encourages

the procurement of subsequent endorsements. In response to the need for teachers to advance their education in order to remain certified, the Masters of Ed Tech program developed multiple pathways in order to best meet these types of requirements for Michigan's teachers. While there are many entry points to the pathway (see Figure 2) generally one can conceptualize the program as beginning with the Certificate program and advancing through to the Ph.D.

The program offers multiple delivery styles with which the students might engage. First, there are traditional, on-campus face-to-face cohorts. Additionally, there is the hybrid option: a month of face-to-face instruction either on Michigan State's campus or at satellites (for instance, this

Figure 2. The structure and relationship between various programs offered by the Educational Psychology and Educational Technology program offered by the College of Education

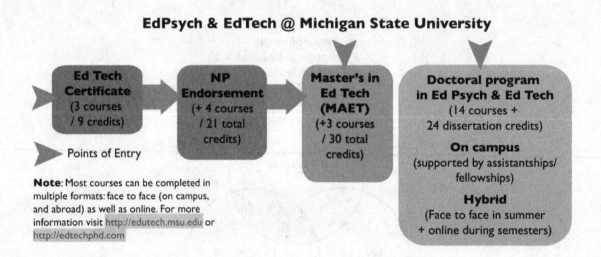

past summer saw a cohort meeting in Rouen, France). Finally, students may opt for an entirely online experience both for the certificate and for the Masters. This flexibility carries into the Ph.D. program, for students who pursue that degree, so that there are hybrid and face-to-face cohorts at the doctoral level as well.

TPACK THEMES RUNNING THROUGHOUT THE ED TECH MASTER'S PROGRAM

In terms of both the implementation and modeling of TPACK throughout the Educational Technology program, a number of themes emerge that run through each of the courses at every level, from certificate to doctoral level courses. In essence the program seeks to *go beyond technocentrism,* to helping teachers think creatively about *repurposing technology* for educational purposes through a process of *design* instantiated in a *spiral curriculum* that culminates on their *reflecting* on their experience to become better professionals. While these themes are discussed as distinct

here, it is not true that in practice they are also distinct. The themes not only inform one another, but also are interwoven throughout the program sequence. Each of these themes developed from the theoretical grounding in TPACK, and together these themes provide coherence to the courses in the program.

Theme 1: Beyond Techno-Centrism

Certainly, when discussing teachers' implementation of technology into their practice, it is important that teachers have some fluency with particular technologies and tools (Hew & Brush, 2007; Mishra & Koehler, 2006). It is our view, however, that the lack of strong technology integration in classrooms is caused, in part, by the over-reliance of techno-centric based professional development: workshops and programs which never move beyond the "how-tos" of the technology in question. When the focus becomes on the on the technology and tools, to the exclusion of all other considerations, the true potential of the integration is lost. This fetishization of technology, whether it be laser discs or Twitter, results in narrow implementation of technology, if it is implemented at all (Koehler, Mishra, & Kereluik, 2009). When the shine wears off of the new tool, it is abandoned and those who were skeptical have reason to resist future efforts to implement the next, shiny tool.

By presenting the technology as it influences, and is influenced by, pedagogy and content, helps teachers consider technology in relation to pedagogy and content. The following questions all help de-emphasize the tool itself, and instead focus on more important issues: "How might I introduce this tool my students?"; "How might advocate to my administrators and to parents that this tool will enhance the learning?"; and "What tool best complements my existing pedagogy and meets the content goals for my learners?" The real danger, of course, in techno-centrism is that the tools are constantly evolving, being replaced, or disappear altogether. At that point, the goal of the Ed Tech program is for the teachers to be theoretically nimble enough to adapt to the ever-shifting technological landscape.

There are a variety of ways in which the master's program is designed to go beyond a techno-centric approach. For example, at the core of the MAET program is a set of courses that focus on the psychological and developmental aspects of learning. The key here is to understand that the use of technology in educational settings need to be framed within a deeper knowledge of theories of learning and development, the kinds of misconceptions students have and how these can be addressed pedagogically. One assignment that captures our approach is the "Understanding Understanding" project. This project pushes our teachers to develop an awareness of the kinds of entrenched, well-developed naïve conceptions and knowledge structures that learners have and how these can often interfere with what they are taught in school. Groups of in-service teachers, on a topic of their choosing: (1) Examine prior research of the common conceptions or alternate conceptions of their topic; (2) Develop research

questions and an interview protocol; (3) Select and interview a variety of students to demonstrate understanding and misunderstanding from different ages and perspectives; (4) Edit a video to demonstrate a variety of understandings about the topic; and (5) Create a web page for the project, along with a summary of what they learned. The project follows a very specific design process in its unfolding, in order to encourage the in-service teachers to do the same with their own teaching. At the same time, we emphasize creative construction of a Web-based summary of the project as well as creative editing of the video clips. The project highlights various affordances of digital video that make the final presentations more easily understood and compelling to its viewers.

During this project, groups have interviewed a variety of subjects on a range of topics: where shadows come from, thunder, the color of blood, and how people view money. For instance, in the project about shadows, eight people were interviewed, ranging in age from 2 to 29 years. Interviewees answered questions for the camera, and also drew pictures of their own understanding (or misunderstanding) of the concept of shadows. They were asked: Where do shadows come from? Do objects/things have shadows all the time? Do you have a shadow at night? How about in a dark room? Can you touch or step on your shadow? They were then asked to draw a picture showing how a shadow works, and to explain their thought process while drawing. Based on these interviews, an engaging and informative video was constructed to demonstrate the concepts of misconception and contradiction. In this video, it was clear that students between the ages of 2 and 7 were able to contradict themselves regularly in their explanations, a development the group determined to be an invaluable lesson for teaching this age group. Another recent project took on the rather common misconception people have about our sense of taste. This video showed how the idea of "dedicated taste areas on our tongue" is a historical myth and yet one that remained in textbooks even today.

Here the technology is used as a tool to get at the deeper goal of understanding the students' understanding, or seeking patterns in what is found and representing it in an engaging and effective manner. There is little direct instruction about the technology (audio and video editing software, website authoring platforms, etc.) as most of the discussion in class is about the development of research protocols to get students' understanding of the selected topic.

Theme 2: Repurposing/Creativity

One fundamental human trait is the ways in which we are constantly changing and adapting the environment to our needs. People use (or re-use) everyday things for purposes they were never intended for. Be it a piece of red tape to mark a glass door so that people don't slam into the glass or use a chair to prop open a door—these are examples of everyday creativity. This phenomenon can be described in different ways (particularly in the context of educational technology), everything from situational creativity to repurposing to *jugaad*. In brief, there is no such thing as an educational technology. What we have are a range of technologies that we can repurpose, re-see, and re-envision as being educational technologies. Be it using an audio editing tool such as Audacity as a data analysis tool or a GPS device to teach mathematics, teachers are designers of experiences for their students. Teachers are designing experiences that allow students to engage with the world, gaining deep knowledge of the content in the process. But these technologies don't come as a given, with their pedagogical purpose stamped all over them. Educators have to work on "reseeing" them for their own educational purposes (Koehler, Mishra, & Kereluik, 2009).

The idea of creative repurposing is important because most technologies that teachers use have not been typically designed for educational pur-poses. Technologies including standard productive or office software, blogs, wikis, and GPS systems were not designed for teachers, and as such, teachers must re-purpose them for use in educational contexts. Such repurposing is possible only when the teacher knows the rules of the game, and is fluent enough to know which rules to bend, which to break, and which to leave alone. This requires a deep experiential understanding, developed through training and deliberate practice of all the aspects of the TPACK framework and how they interact with each other.

In the Master's program, we try to make these experiences with repurposing technologies both implicit and explicit ones for teachers. For instance, students in our program are explicitly asked to learn about technologies and then repurpose them for educational ends. One example is when students in our program have explored the use of micro-blogging in the classroom Microblogging (Twitter is a good example) involves participants sharing short messages (often less than 150 characters) with each other using a website or some other micro-blogging specific tool. We have found that using a system like this is a wonderful complement to face-to-face discussions in a classroom where everybody has a laptop. It is interesting to note here that whether or not students should have access to laptops (and the Internet) in class has been quite controversial. There are many professors who have banned them from their classrooms arguing that access to these technologies is distracting to students. In contrast, we have found that micro-blogging (within an appropriate pedagogical frame) can enhance the classroom in useful and engaging ways. We have tried this in both doctoral seminars and in undergraduate classrooms with various levels of success. The important thing to remember here, particularly given the TPACK framework, is that a technology such as micro-blogging does not exist in a vacuum. Its appropriate use has to be scaffolded by specific pedagogical instructions and guidelines. For instance, in an undergraduate classroom, providing specific goals, and times when and for how long to micro-blog were found to be useful. In a doctoral seminar on the other hand setting such boundaries was less of an issue. What *was* important in both contexts was constructing a "space" within the class-time where these student-generated comments could be discussed. Without this the micro-blogging activity remains divorced from the actual class routines and thus can be relatively ineffective.

Another student generated example has to do with using specialized search engines (particularly visual search engines such as Viewzi, Cuil, or Clusty) to help students understand the idea of intertextuality—i.e. that texts often refer to each other in complex and intricate ways to create webs of meaning. Students use these search engines to find webpages containing a target phrase they have chosen—a famous line (such as "daggers in men's smiles" from *Macbeth*), an adapted famous line (such as "method to his madness," adapted from a line in *Hamlet*), the words of a book title (such as Joseph Conrad's *Heart of Darkness*), or a character's name (such as Grendel from the epic poem *Beowulf*). As students explore their search results, they see first-hand how words and phrases are borrowed, re-combined, and re-circulated, and they reflect on how the same words can mean different things in different contexts. As they crisscross the Web, students also begin to formulate hypotheses about vectors of influence, processes of transformation, and dynamics of popularity. Of course this could be as easily be done with a standard search engine such as Google, but the advantage of some of these visual search engines is the manner in which these links are represented. These engines offer represent search results, not in the text based series of links as Google commonly does, but with tag-clouds or visual icons. Similar search "hits" are often clustered together allowing students to view at a glance how citations can cluster together, thus scaffolding a students developing understanding about how certain texts "work together." Combing

such a search with freely available bookmarking tools such as iBreadcrumbs allows students to not just record their navigation through hyperspace but also annotate them. These itineraries and annotations can then be shared with others and the teacher and be the basis for further discussion about the nature of intertextuality (and also offer interesting possibilities for student assessment).

There are many more examples we could provide here, such as an innovative use of Google Translation to teach foreign language, where the often error-ridden nature of computer translation is actually used to help students develop better understanding of grammar and metaphor. What is important here is to note that in each of these cases, the technology was not constructed for educational purposes. Making it an educational technology required creative input from the teacher to re-design, or maybe even subvert the original intentions of the software programmer. This would not be possible without a deep, complex, fluid and flexible knowledge of the technology, the content to be covered and an appropriate pedagogy. Teachers need a to develop a willingness to play with technologies and ideas, and an openness to the construction of new experiences for students.

Viewing teachers' use of technology in this manner emphasizes the role of the teacher as a producer (a designer), away from the traditional conceptualization of teachers as consumers (users) of these tools. When teachers are able to flexibly navigate the landscape of technology, pedagogy, and content, they become responsible for the total curriculum, the Total PACKage (TPACK) as it were, and thus help achieve the full educational potential of these cool tools.

Theme 3: Design

The idea of learning by design is key to the development of TPACK. Though we do have direct instruction on TPACK (more now than before) our overall guiding principle is to have people engage in authentic design activities with push them to understand the transactional dynamic between T, P & C. micro AND macro design activities. Design also represents the complex reality of practice with more fidelity than top-down approaches. Like teaching with technology, design requires a balancing act between a wide-range of factors that often work against each other (features vs. cost, ease of use vs. advanced features, time to market vs. product quality, etc.). It requires the application of a wide array of knowledge, including algorithms, understanding of users, rules of thumb, scientific "facts," and multidisciplinary connections.

For example, in order for teachers to come to understand the value of design, we have had teachers work in groups to make two *iVideos* (idea-based videos) to communicate an important educational idea (Wong, Mishra, Koehler, & Siebenthal, 2007). Topics for the videos included: the role of technology in the library sciences, affective communication on-line, and appropriate uses of technology. Instead of learning the de-contextualized skill of creating and editing digital video, the teachers had to learn the technology within the context of communicating their understanding of larger ideas that form the basis of their profession.

Students spent most of their time in groups discussing or debating their idea, storyboarding, filming, digitizing, editing, revising, and soliciting feedback. The instructors scheduled regular times for the whole class to preview the participants' work in progress and receive feedback. Versions of their iVideos were posted to a web site so that feedback from other masters' level courses could also serve as an impetus to change and re-design. Once the movies were complete, they were shown to an audience of approximately 80 other people involved in the summer session, and were posted to the web site so that people outside the summer school could also participate in the viewing and feedback.

The design approach often results in classrooms that look and feel quite different than traditional university offerings. This was especially true in this case. The teachers were never all in one place, and spread to other rooms of the school, the hallway, outside, and any other place they could find room to talk, film, edit, storyboard, discuss, screen, and preview video. These activities went well beyond class time, teachers worked late into the night in the lab, in their dorms, and through the weekends.

Given that there was no list of skills teachers needed to learn, nor was their grade based on learning specific skills, the list of technologies that were learned was impressive. These included skills such as, learning to operate digital cameras (still and video); learning to use video and image editing software (such as iMovie, Adobe Premiere and Adobe Photoshop), learning to conduct internet searches as well as uploading and downloading files (through FTP or other means); and learning to design web pages using software such as Dreamweaver or FrontPage. Apart from these specific skills, teachers also learned key concepts in information technology, such as internet protocols, file formats and structure, video compression technologies (CoDecs) and so on.

More important than the individual technology skills was their learning about the subtleties and relationships between and among tools, actors, and contexts. Technology was learned in the context of expressing educational ideas and metaphors. Teachers learned a lot about how to focus a message down to just two minutes of video, how to let images and symbolism convey ideas in an effective manner, how to inspire audiences, work together in groups, give and receive feedback, and communicate with audiences.

Theme 4: Spiraling

The idea of spiraling, or that each concept is considered and engaged at each level of the program, is core to the philosophy of the Ed Tech program. For example, the idea of online collaborative composition might be taken up in the first few courses of the program (the Certificate level) by introducing various tools to facilitate the collaboration and ensuring that the students are able to engage and fully manipulate the tool. Later in the program, the idea of collaborative composition would be revisited in terms of the theoretical and pedagogical reasoning behind engaging with such a tool and students would be encouraged to view the tool in terms of the way it might inform and enhance the teaching of the content. In this way, teachers are exposed to the technologies in way that allows them to play and engage with the tool as well as provide them an understanding and language for *why* the technology might be beneficial for their own students' learning. Additionally, this type of spiral recurrence of the idea both honors the TPACK that the teachers bring as well as growing that knowledge in a way that respects their individual grade assignments and content areas.

One example is an assignment known as the "55-word short story." Students are instructed to write and post a short story in 55 words. They are then to read and respond to their classmates' fiction. It is seen mostly as a quick, fun activity in which students practice interacting online. The end of the course culminates in a web design project, a project that involves many hours of creation and revision. As the students are refining their web design project, students revisit the purposes behind the short story: that choices within the confines of a web site or a short story are made with similar considerations. Re-reading the purposes behind the short story in light of the web design project show students the ways in which ideas inform and influence each other, and how all of these theories, tools, and practices are inter-related.

Theme 5: Reflection

Reflection projects are a chance for students to bring together their experience with all the different assignments and courses they have been doing in an integrated fashion so as to allow them to reflect on their own learning and think

of ways to apply their developing understanding of TPCK to their own classroom contexts. Thus these assignments go beyond helping students focus on specific course-related tasks and move them towards stepping back and reflect on the total PACKage. In these projects students look backwards *and* forwards, reflecting on their learning and developing strategies to continue to learn and explore even after the course or program is over.

For example, in one assignment called the *TPACK related DreamIT grant proposal*, teachers in the program identify a problem of practice, use the TPACK framework to address the problem, and create a web-based experience that presents his/her problem and solution to his/her peers as well as explains the thinking process that led the student to the solution as opposed to others. Hence, there are two goals of the project: (a) have students tackle a specific, authentic problem and practice and consider a plan for a solution, and (b) share their problem, plan, and the thinking that went into it with a larger audience (i.e., represent it on the Web).

Students come up with very divergent authentic problems of practice and very creative projects both in terms of applying the TPACK model to their problem of practice and their Web-based ways of representing their problems and "solutions". For example, John (not his real name) sought to address how he could help students engage in higher order thinking in an English class when students' educational conditioning focused on memorization and the idea that an answer is either right or wrong. In applying the TPACK model, John initially began with searching for how technology could be a solution to this problem. However, John had already integrated a great deal of technology into his teaching. Hence, he concluded he needed to change his pedagogy to work within his context, with this curriculum, and with the technology he was already implementing. In contrast, another student, Liz also arrived at technology as a solution to her problem of practice – teaching social studies in a way that makes it come alive and challenges just what is written in textbooks. Specifically, she chose to focus on Christopher Columbus for her TPACK project. Using an inquiry-based approach, Liz felt her technology options were limited, but eventually found an appropriate WebQuest that aligned with her pedagogy and curriculum.

The goal in these larger reflections on the Total PACKage projects is to develop the kinds of deep situated knowledge that is an essential characteristic of mastery. Clearly the work the students do in these projects does not guarantee mastery but it does set them up to look deeply into the ingrained patterns of teaching subject matter with technology, to play with these ideas and their relationships with each other, develop possible solutions and reflect both on their effectiveness and on their personal evolution as teachers. It is through this iterative process of play and design with Technology, Pedagogy and Content, and the contexts within which they are embedded that our teachers develop their TPACK.

IMPLICATIONS AND SUGGESTIONS FOR OTHER PROGRAMS

The thematic considerations described here are intentionally flexible and reflect the dynamic nature of the technologies themselves. This model is both unique and replicable, both reflecting the local MSU context at the same time as global enough to work across varieties of communities, countries, and delivery methods.

Indeed, it is this combination of consideration of the local context while maintaining universal flexibility that makes these thematic considerations ideal for other programs looking to strengthen TPACK within their own graduate programs. Whether it be a strictly teacher education/professional development program (as the one at MSU) or even one more tightly focused on a particular content area, the five themes outlined in this chapter can be instructive for any program

seeking to improve the technological knowledge of their students. As every content area experiences its digitization, teachers and pre-service teachers need to successfully navigate the attending transformation of how they do science, or math, or history within that changing technological context. By grounding teacher development in the ideas of TPACK and executing programs with similar thematic considerations, the specific content area demands can also be met in light of technological change. As technology integration becomes more and more seamless, the expectation will be that professionals will already have the tools to utilize their knowledge within these digital realms.

Graduate programs would do well to consider how they encourage thinking beyond techno-centrism, how they encourage an ability to repurpose technology in ways that support the goals of the program and the learners, and how the program deals with issues of design. Additionally, by spiraling these various ideals throughout the duration of the program and supporting student reflection, graduate programs can readily enhance their own students' TPACK.

CONCLUSION

The five themes of TPACK weaving throughout the masters program, while discussed distinctly here, mutually inform one another and, in practice, are not generally seen or implemented on their own. When TPACK is both the theoretical model on which instructional decisions are based as well as the content understanding that the students achieve as they progress through the program, the result is the dynamic interaction between these five themes.

Because the Master's program in Educational Technology at Michigan State University is aimed at helping expert teachers, with their own important set of professional understandings of the interaction of technology, pedagogy and content knowledge in the classroom, our program finds itself engaged in different types of conversations than if we were dealing with strictly theoretical concerns. It is our goal that that teachers enrolled in our program will learn and interact with an idea or a technology and immediately incorporate that into their classrooms, sometimes the very next day.

With professional knowledge also comes professional entrenchment, and it is the ways in which creativity and reflection is fostered that breaks that entrenchment. It is a familiar refrain heard from those working with professional teachers: that's a nice idea, but that won't work with my students. The balance between honoring teachers' professional knowledge and lived experiences and also pushing teachers to move beyond the boundaries of their current practice is a delicate one. It is through the thoughtful implementation of TPACK and the resulting themes that we find that balance in the Master's in Educational Technology program at MSU.

ACKNOWLEDGMENT

The authors would like to thank all the instructors in the MAET program without whose creativity, initiative and effort none of this work would have been possible. We would like to specifically thank Leigh Graves Wolf, coordinator of the program for embodying in practice much of what we speak about in theory.

REFERENCES

American Association of Colleges of Teacher Education (Ed.). (2008). *The handbook of technological pedagogical content knowledge (TPCK) for educators*. Mahwah, NJ: Lawrence Erlbaum Associates.

Bauer, J., & Kenton, J. (2005). Toward technology integration in the schools: Why it isn't happening. *Journal of Technology and Teacher Education, 13*(4), 519–546.

Cuban, L., Kirkpatrick, H., & Peck, C. (2001). High access and low use of technologies in high school classrooms: Explaining an apparent paradox. *American Educational Research Journal, 38*(4), 813–834. doi:10.3102/00028312038004813

Ertmer, P. A. (2005). Teacher pedagogical beliefs: The final frontier in our quest for technology integration? *Educational Technology Research and Development, 53*(4), 25–39. doi:10.1007/BF02504683

Harris, J., Mishra, P., & Koehler, M. J. (2009). Teachers' technological pedagogical content knowledge and learning activity types: Curriculum-based technology integration reframed. *Journal of Research on Technology in Education, 41*(4).

Hew, K. F., & Brush, T. (2007). Integrating technology in K-12 teaching and learning: Current knowledge gaps and recommendations for future research. *Educational Technology Research and Development, 55*(3), 223–252. doi:10.1007/s11423-006-9022-5

Keengwe, J., Onchwari, G., & Wachira, P. (2008). Computer technology integration and student learning: Barriers and promise. *Journal of Science Education and Technology, 17*(6), 560–565. doi:10.1007/s10956-008-9123-5

Koehler, M. J., & Mishra, P. (2008). Introducing TPCK. AACTE Committee on Innovation and Technology (Ed.), *The handbook of technological pedagogical content knowledge (TPCK) for educators* (pp. 3-29). Mahwah, NJ: Lawrence Erlbaum Associates.

Koehler, M. J., & Mishra, P. (2010). What is technological pedagogical content knowledge? *Contemporary Issues in Technology & Teacher Education, 9*(1), 60–70.

Koehler, M. J., & Mishra, P. (2010, June 1). *TPCK-Technological pedagogical content knowledge*. Retrieved from tpack.org

Koehler, M. J., Mishra, P., & Kereluik, K. (2009). Looking back to the future of educational technology. *TechTrends*, *53*, 48–53. doi:10.1007/s11528-009-0325-3

Lawless, K. A., & Pellegrino, J. W. (2007). Professional development in integrating technology into teaching and learning: Knows, unknowns, and ways to pursue better questions and answers. *Review of Educational Research*, *77*, 575–614. doi:10.3102/0034654307309921

Mishra, P., & Koehler, M. J. (2006). Technological pedagogical content knowledge: A new framework for teacher knowledge. *Teachers College Record*, *108*(6), 1017–1054. doi:10.1111/j.1467-9620.2006.00684.x

Mishra, P., & Koehler, M. J. (2008, March). *Introducing technological pedagogical content knowledge*. Paper presented the Annual Meeting of the American Educational Research Association, New York, March 24-28. (Conference Presentation)

Mishra, P., & Koehler, M. J. (2009). Too cool for school? No way! Using the TPACK framework: You can have your hot tools and teach with them, too. *Learning and Leading with Technology*, *36*(7), 14–18.

Shulman, L. (1986). Those who understand: Knowledge growth in teaching. *Educational Researcher*, *15*(2), 4–14.

Wilson, S. M., & Berne, J. (1999). Teacher learning and the acquisition of professional knowledge: An examination of research on contemporary professional development. *Review of Research in Education*, *24*, 173–209.

Wong, D., Mishra, P., Koehler, M. J., & Siebenthal, S. (2007). Teacher as filmmaker: iVideos, technology education, and professional development. In Girod, M., & Steed, J. (Eds.), *Technology in the college classroom*. Stillwater, OK: New Forums Press.

ENDNOTE

[1]   Contributions of the first two authors to this article were equal. We rotate the order of authorship in our writing.

Chapter 2

Lessons from the ITS Program:
Five Design Strategies on Which to Build Technology-Rich Teacher Education

Priscilla Norton
George Mason University, USA

Dawn Hathaway
George Mason University, USA

ABSTRACT

Educators concerned with building technology-rich preservice teacher education seek inspiration in many places. Looking to successful graduate programs might serve to inform those who seek a foundation on which to build successful programs. With years of experience experimenting and studying teacher education at the graduate, inservice level have led to a set of design strategies the authors recommend as guides to making robust decisions about technology-rich preservice teacher education. This chapter is divided into three sections. The first section presents a brief discussion of preservice teacher technology education and the Integration of Technology in Schools (ITS) advanced studies graduate program. The second presents five guiding design strategies to inform the continuous process of technology-rich teacher education. The chapter concludes with a third section that discusses the implications of those design strategies for preservice teacher education.

THE STATE OF PRESERVICE TECHNOLOGY TEACHER EDUCATION

Concerns about the inclusion of technology considerations in preservice teacher education and the role that technology might play in teacher preparation are long standing. "Extensive time

and money has been spent developing strategies and programs to help preservice teachers use technology effectively" (Kay, 2006, p. 392). This is evidenced by the more than 400 demonstration projects funded between 1999 and 2003 by the federal government's Preparing Tomorrow's Teachers to Use Technology (PT3) initiative authorized under Title II of the *No Child Left Behind Act* (NCLB; U.S. Congress, 2001). Over $750 million was allocated under Part B/

DOI: 10.4018/978-1-4666-0014-0.ch002

Section 221 to develop new methods for preparing "prospective teachers to use advanced technology to prepare all students to meet challenging state and local academic content and student academic achievement standards; and to improve the ability of institutions of higher education to carry out such programs."

In their review and analysis of over 100 preservice programs, Ottenbreit-Leftwich, Glazewski, and Newby (2010) identified six basic approaches to preservice technology teacher education, similar to those in previous reviews (Kay, 2006; Mims, Polly, Sheppard, & Inan, 2006). These approaches included information delivery of technology integration content, hands-on technology skill building, practice with technology integration in the field, technology integration observation or modeling sessions, authentic technology integration experiences, and technology integration reflections. They concurred with Kay (2006) that technology integration within teacher education programs should incorporate multiple approaches and added that "formats and levels of emphasis placed on these different approaches can vary depending on program restraints and opportunities. . ." (Ottenbreit-Leftwich et al., 2010, p. 28).

As the stated purpose of the Ottenbreit-Leftwich et al. (2010) study was to develop a conceptual design process guide for preservice teacher technology experiences, the authors recommended a four step process. The first step is analysis of the broader context to include curricular and instructional formats, resources, and skill sets. The second step recommends clear articulation of technology content goals to be followed by the third step which matches one of the six approaches with each technology content goal. The final and fourth step in their model focuses on creating a sequence of activities where appropriate tools, assignments, and student activities are selected. They concluded, "it is important to consistently reevaluate technology content goals and select appropriate approaches to best prepare teachers to use technology in their classrooms" (p. 28).

While we understand the need and value of consistent re-evaluation of goals and approaches, the design model suggested by Ottenbreit-Leftwich et al. (2010) seems incomplete. It does not present guidance in deciding what curricular or instructional formats are appropriate (Step 1), what technology content goals are necessary and desirable (Step 2), what principles might guide the process of matching approach with goal (Step 3), or how to select or sequence appropriate activities (Step 4). In our work with the Integration of Technology in Schools (ITS) advanced studies graduate program, we have come to understand these concerns are addressed when we recognize that our most important role as teacher educators is as designer. We may, at times, be directors, facilitators, guides, evaluators, counselors, or mentors. But through it all, we are designers, crafting learning opportunities for teacher-learners. By inventing or appropriating design principles and processes, identifying design patterns, and integrating them with programmatic, curricular, and instructional decisions, we have been able to engage in an iterative program of development and decision making within a stable and continuous program structure.

The ITS Program

Our design playground is the ITS program, an advanced studies graduate program for practicing teachers. During the fifteen years since its inception, we have added additional tools-oriented courses, additional research practicum experiences, and a teacher leadership and technology course. The program was originally structured to be completed in four semesters. Increased attention to additional and emerging technologies, design-based research, and technology teacher leadership, however, suggested the need to spread the density of concepts and practices over more time. Today, the ITS curriculum is five semesters and includes investigation of curriculum and learning theory as well as technology affordances and applications.

The 36 graduate credit hour program includes five tools courses (15 credit hours), four curriculum and instruction courses (12 credit hours), one leadership course (3 credit hours), and two design-based research practicum courses (6 credit hours). These design-based research practicums bridge the work of the cohort and the teacher-learners' individual contexts as they implement and assess technology-rich instructional designs created within the structure of the program into their classrooms. Although students register for discrete courses, topics remain interwoven within the work of the group using a master schedule not a course structure.

Researching such an evolving program has been a challenge with few research models available as guides. While existing research is informative, much of the research examining teacher education programs consists mainly of case studies of individual programs and has little or no evaluative data concerning which teacher education approaches are most effective in promoting technology integrating teachers (Kay, 2006). In addition, research often fails to follow teachers into the field to investigate the relationship between methods of preparation and practice in the field (Brush & Appelman, 2003). Finally, reviews of existing evaluation reports related to the impact of technology implementation in teacher education programs demonstrate a lack of attention to cross-institutional and/or longitudinal studies (Pellegrino, Goldman, Bertenthal, & Lawless, 2007).

Some of our research has attempted to address these limitations, following program graduates into the field and looking at graduates in longitudinal ways. Program review data has consistently identified shifts in attitudes and practice among program graduates. A 2001 study of program graduates (Norton & Farrell, 2001), for instance, found shifts in pre-post attitudes from a profile of nonusers to one more consistent with users. The study revealed changes in practice that included more frequent and realistic use of technology, technology use primarily directed at

teaching and learning opportunities for students rather than teacher use, increases in discussions with colleagues about technology use to support learning, increases in the number of assignments integrating technology, and the use of a variety of applications. The study concluded, "As attitudes become more positive, there are positive changes in practice" (p. 963). In another study, Norton and Schell (2001) compared program graduates with graduates of an abbreviated certificate program (12 credit hours as opposed to 36 credit hours) and found significant differences in practice between the two groups. They concluded that teacher education to promote changes that fully integrate technology in support of teaching and learning must be extensive, consistent, and long term. The study found that short term teacher education did little to advance the power inherent in technology to change teaching and learning. Wrote the Norton and Schell, "Those who are in teacher education must understand that they are in it for the long haul" (p. 964).

Program review data has consistently demonstrated that program graduates assume leadership roles in their schools. In a 2008 accreditation review of the program, graduates from 19 cohorts (375 graduates) who completed their program between 1999 and 2007 were surveyed. Eight graduates had completed PhD programs, six graduates were currently in the dissertation phase of their PhD studies, and six were participating in PhD studies. At least seven program graduates were serving in system-level technology leadership roles to include Director of Instructional Technology, Coordinator of Elementary Technology Staff Development, three system-level technology-instruction liaison positions, Director of 24-7 Learning, and project director for special technology initiatives at the system level. Other graduates had assumed leadership roles in their content field. Two graduates served as Curriculum Supervisor for their school division in English and Science respectively. Four graduates were Assistant Principals. Finally, many graduates had assumed site-based leadership in the role of technology resource teacher (a full time funded position). In the six school districts neighboring the university, the percent of program graduates holding one of the system's site-based technology resource teacher positions was 80%, 52%, 48%, 33%, 13%, and 11% respectively.

Cenzon (2009) surveyed 318 program participants who had graduated between 1999 and 2008 with 232 graduates responding. First, his study sought to describe program graduates' technology integration attitudes and practices. Findings revealed participants had relatively high positive levels of attitudes, beliefs, and practice. Second, the study investigated whether the length of time from completion of the program had any effect on technology integration attitudes or practice. No statistically significant differences in technology integration attitudes or practice between early (graduating between 1999 and 2003) and recent graduates (graduating between 2003 and 2008) were identified. Cenzon concluded there was no attrition in program graduates' attitudes about or practice of technology integration over time. He wrote, "Well above average use of technology tools and use of technology-enhanced instructional strategies by all participants provides positive evidence of the consistency of the ITS program. In addition, results of the study suggest that the length of time graduating from the program does not significantly influence participants' beliefs and practices in technology integration" (p. 107).

These studies were confirmatory but not particularly helpful. The shape of today's program is not the result of these general and broad approaches to program evaluation and research, focusing on program outcomes or student learning or implications for practice. As Heraclitus (n. d.) wrote centuries ago, "No man ever steps in the same river twice, for it's not the same river and he's not the same man." The same can be said of the ITS program for the program is not a fixed solution; it is a process. Thus, the program as it exists today is recognized by graduates as the ITS program (the river) but they constantly tell us how different today's program is from the "river" they experienced. Programs by their nature ought to be in constant flux, reflecting the changing world of technology, society, and our understanding of teaching and learning. It is unlikely that the "perfect" program is possible or even desirable. Rather, derived from our scholarship and experience, we offer five guiding design strategies to inform the continuous process of technology-rich teacher education whether offered at the preservice or the inservice level.

FIVE DESIGN STRATEGIES

Teacher educators who seek to design learning opportunities for teachers that promote technology-rich classrooms need to focus on robust principles and processes to guide their designs not on program structures or narrowly defined activities or assignments. Thus, while the central goals of the ITS program and university structures have remained constant, how these goals translate to practice is continually evolving. How technology-rich teacher education manifests itself in the structure of activity, culture, and tool and how its deeper meaning has shaped understanding and practice has evolved through systematic attention to design.

Anything that is not naturally occurring is in some way designed. If the principles and processes that guide the design are robust, flexible, grounded in theory and practice, articulated, and reusable, the design has applicability and usability and presents a positive solution to a problem. As Nussbaum (2005) wrote, "When people talk about innovation in this decade, they really mean design." Design demands the union of design principles and design processes. It demands a robust and flexible solution that adheres to the goals and needs of the context in which it serves.

Those involved in the act of design recognize that design is a complex, yet practical journey. Design is often referred to as selection of tradeoffs in decision-making, where the constraints are continually changing and need to be considered and reconsidered in relation to the overall problem and proposed solution (Preece, Rogers, & Sharp, 2002). Designers are tasked with the dual challenge of attempting to make meaning through deliberately causing things to happen through the act of design and development while also trying to find meaning in analyzing the consequences of that action to generate knowledge about teaching and learning. Thus, designers consider the characteristics of their learners, the demands of their contexts, the complexities of learning goals and outcomes, and the ways in which learning resources and tools can be leveraged – all in the service of designing solutions. They learn not *what* to do but *how* to do it. We offer below five design strategies we have found effective in guiding the design of robust technology-rich teacher education.

Designers as Collaborators

The ITS program was originally conceptualized by Norton (1994) and recognized that "teacher education about technology is really teacher education for change and demands new approaches" (p. 163). The program had as its central goal the attempt to restructure the teacher education experience as a process rather than a collection of courses. It proposed creating a teacher education experience formulated as a thought community within the frame of an integrated, transdisciplinary approach to curriculum and a vision of collaboration. It was hoped that a program thus framed would promote "the dialectic of idea and action grounded in informed practice" (p. 165). The program set out to transcend the course by course, subject-matter based disciplinary lines of traditional study by focusing on technology impacts on social contexts, knowledge forms, the learning process, and educational goals. Recognizing that no clear strategies existed for such an approach, the program embraced a vision of collaboration

in which individuals come together to dialogue, study, and shape plans for future action. Despite the potentials of such an approach and the possibilities that might be derived from an integrated, transdisciplinary approach set within a collaborative vision, it was still necessary to contextualize the program within the administrative structures of a university. Thus, students registered for courses but attended not to the course but to the work of the group.

Each Fall semester up to 24 cohort members are admitted to graduate study as an intact group from which members rarely withdraw and to which new members are never added. The notion of cohort is more than an administrative convenience although the cohort structure makes it easy to advise and manage the program. Instead, the cohort becomes a thought community. Effort is made from the beginning to build group identity and cohesion. Cohort members soon learn that solving problems, teaching and helping others, and responsibility for the integrity of conversation and thought do not reside solely with the instructors but are part of the responsibilities of all cohort members.

The journey toward professional growth, school reform, and an educational response to the challenges of technology integration is often a lonely one. Even when teachers (prospective or veteran) seek to confront technology challenges and work toward changing and refining educational practice, peers, parents, and sometimes even students view them as outsiders, non-conformists, and somehow "different." In the face of feelings of isolation or separateness, it is often easiest to return to more traditional practices. One solution is to design professional development experiences that are organized around cohorts. Structuring study as a cohort process facilitates the formation of a group that shares a common area of inquiry and is bound by a common question. Starting at the same time and proceeding together over a period of time facilitates the development of a shared set of experiences, knowledge, readings, activities, and support systems. The graduate classroom becomes an organism rather than a sequence of meetings. Academic study within the frame of a cohort process supports the redefinition of roles where all participants become learners, teachers, and practitioners.

Research on the program suggests that teachers shift their stages of concern from informational and personal to concerns relating to the consequences of technology for practice and collaboration. Several studies found that participants in the cohort process increase their levels of confidence, change their teaching practice, and became more actively involved in school and district level technology decision-making (Norton, 1995; Norton & Sprague, 1996; Norton & Sprague, 1999). Shared responsibility for learning, building interpersonal relationships with classmates, help and support from group members, and shared knowledge/ ideas/expertise emerged as themes related directly to the power of the cohort to support the difficult process of learning and changing (Norton & Sprague, 1999).

Together, these studies informed our decision to maintain the cohort structure as an integral part of program design. Participants' reflections on the cohort structure of the ITS Program over time suggest that combining this structure with ongoing study about the ways in which technology can support K-12 teaching and learning facilitates change. Participants come to understand learning and educational change as a group effort that depends on shared responsibility, shared knowledge and vision, and the help and support of colleagues. They learn to work with peers, developing and pursuing common goals and alternating between leadership and supportive roles. They learn to cope with inequalities in expertise and effort. The process of working with and within a group supports development of the skills and dispositions necessary for educational change whether personal, professional, or institutional. Technology-rich teacher education structured by a cohort process is a design strategy that works.

A Designer's Vision of Technology

How will teachers learn the operations of technology tools? How much time should be dedicated to teaching teachers to use various software applications? Will teachers be able to integrate technology with their instructional practices if they are not expert at using the technology? These are frequent and persistent questions asked by those who seek to plan technology-rich teacher education. Yet, we have found that focus on operations associated with a range of tools emphasizes the tool not the design of learning opportunities for students. What matters is not the mechanics of tool operation but the ways in which tools can amplify human ability to reach its goals.

The concept that best centers a discussion of technology's role in teaching and learning is the notion of affordance. The term affordance was introduced by Gibson (1986) and refers to the relation between an organism and an object with the object perceived in relation to the needs of the organism. Thus, an affordance is an emergent property realized at the intersection of organism and object, presenting both opportunity and constraint. Wrote Hammond (2009), the contribution of the notion of affordance is that "it suggests a way of seeing the world as a meaning laden environment offering countless opportunities for action and countless constraints on actions. The world is full of potential, not of things" (p. 206). Designs based primarily on the features of a technology can be innovative. Such practice is often anecdotal but rarely sustained and integrated practice. Conversely, designs based primarily on current articulated needs often overlook potential innovations and leave some affordances unrecognized. "We must understand the needs and abilities of perspective users. But equally, we must understand the capabilities and limitations of technologies in order to know the possibilities they offer for design" (Gaver, 1991, p. 79). A designer's vision of technology then is one that puts the principle of affordance at the center of design for technology-rich teacher education.

For instance, when we understood that it was time to redesign the ITS curriculum to include Web 2.0 tools, we discovered there was scant literature that focused on K-12 integration of Web 2.0 with classroom practice. Much of what targeted K-12 settings reflected teaching about the tools rather than providing direction for using the tools to support learning goals. What was available was predominantly anecdotal in nature. Thus, until a literature base could be built, we needed to support teachers' ability to create applications that capitalize on their clear understanding of the affordances of these tools. As Guzdial, Rick, and Kehoe (2001) found in their research, Web 2.0 tools are "an example of a kind of application in which teachers actively invent their own uses" (p. 6). But how could we support teachers to invent their own uses?

Understanding the power of affordances as a designer's strategy, we began with the need to clearly understand the affordances of these tools and quickly recognized that each tool affords a unique aspect to the whole. Blogs center on personal knowledge construction with the blog's owner setting the agenda – the "all about me" technology. Wikis, on the other hand, are more collaborative in nature, with multiple users joining together to construct knowledge in a dynamic interaction – the "all about us" technology. Podcasts focus on the sending and/or receiving of information as either an audio or video file and are less interactive and collaborative – the "broadcasting and sharing" technology.

Using the notion of affordance as a central design strategy for promoting technology-rich teacher education, we designed the ITS curriculum to focus on engagement with the Web 2.0 tools and the ways in which they might afford K-12 learning goals. We chose to design the course so that the Web 2.0 tools were embedded in teacher-learner activity and discussion of design. Little time was spent teaching the tool; the majority of

time was spent using the tool to support learning other course content, specifically leadership and advocacy. Yet, as was expected, tool use promoted teacher-learner understanding of the affordances of each tool and the ways in which it might be used to meet K-12 learning goals. In their survey responses, teacher-learners supported the notion that focusing on the affordances of the Web 2.0 tools scaffolded their ability to build bridges with their classroom practice. More powerful evidence of attention to affordance as a design strategy came from teacher-learners' reports of the ways they were "inventing" uses of Web 2.0 tools to support classroom learning (Norton & Hathaway, 2008a). We had centered our design decisions using the concept of affordances; our students appropriated the concept of affordances to guide the design of their practice.

Learning about Design by Experiencing Design

The art in teacher education depends on the complex interplay between theory and practice and finds its most important expression in the bridge between the two. This bridge is ever more problematic as "state-of-the art" knowledge about technology integration moves farther and farther from most observable educational practice. Thus, although practice with technology integration in the field and technology integration observation or modeling sessions comprise two of the six approaches identified by Ottenbreit-Leftwich et al. (2010), problems with identifying and/or providing appropriate modeling of powerful technology integration is one of the most challenging dilemmas facing those who seek to promote technology-rich teacher education. The difficulties of providing models of strong technology integration were driven home to one of authors in 2002 when the opportunity to compare two approaches to a 15 hour field experience presented itself for study. One group of five preservice teachers was assigned to schools to "observe" technology in action. A second group of five students taught side by side with university faculty in a two week, technology integration demonstration project. After examining the reflections of both groups, Norton and Sprague (2002-2003) concluded that although the study was preliminary and exploratory, "the contrast between the reflections of those who participated in the field experience and those who participated in the [demonstration] project calls into question the efficacy of more traditional field experiences" (p.94).

"We teach the way we were taught" goes an old adage that holds much truth. Observing teaching that fits the model of how we were taught has little consequence on rethinking the teaching/learning process. So, why not teach teachers the way we want them to teach. Believing that the best type of modeling is that personally experienced, the second guiding design strategy that informs the ITS program is the urgency to teach our graduate students as we want them to teach. We model the integration of technology during class meetings and in between. For instance, activities are designed to engage teacher-learners with telecommunication tools (e. g. email, discussion boards, synchronous chat) between face to face sessions. Used to support their own learning, teacher-learners come to see how these tools and learning goals are afforded by a variety of telecommunication tools (Warrick, Connors, & Norton, 2004; Warrick & Norton, 2002). Face to face meetings use a variety of tools to scaffold meaning making from readings, to structure reflections on how designed strategies have informed group activity, to engage teacher-learners with content lessons "as if" they were K-12 learners, and to generally shape the look and feel of face to face meetings. We have taken the adage "we teach the way we were taught" and reformulated it to be "we teach the way we want them to teach." ITS teacher-learners experience design; they learn in a technology-rich educational environment. They do not study *about* the tools; they learn about teaching and learning *with* the tools.

We are confident in the power of this design strategy as ITSers repeatedly report the importance of the notion of learning by experiencing. In 2009, we redesigned a five week video module as part of the ITS curriculum using five design principles for using video: video production is a positive use of time; video production is an instructional strategy not an object of study; video production is a tool for teaching content; video production ought to be related to an authentic problem to establish purpose and audience; and video production must be guided by an explicit design process. One year later as part of their practicum experiences, teacher-learners designed and taught video-using instructional units. They wrote reflections about their units as part of design-based research projects. Over a three year period, we collected these reflections and analyzed them for evidence of the five design principles for using video (Norton & Hathaway, 2010a).

There was ample evidence in teacher-learners' written reflections that the five video design principles modeled in our use of video were readily evident in their discussions of their practice. While teacher-learners' reflections focused on the dynamic between their actions and their students' learning, a third dynamic emerged when analyzing their reflections. When teacher-learners wrote about the importance of an authentic problem to establish purpose and audience, they might have added "just as we experienced when challenged in class to create an essay to convince the public to endorse video games." When teacher-learners wrote about the power of the treatment and storyboard for student planning, they might have added "just like we did in our class." When teachers talked about the ways in which student content knowledge took shape and form during video planning, they might have added "just as my understanding of educational games and the codes and conventions of video solidified when we produced our video essay." When teachers talked about the ways in which they modeled critical analysis as preparation for video production, they might have added "just as we did when we watched and watched and analyzed and analyzed the essay example."

Although teacher-learners did not explicitly link their own learning experiences with their teaching and their students' learning, they might well have for the goals associated with their graduate learning experience were clearly evident in their reflections on their own practice. Video production was discussed as an instructional strategy not as an object to be studied. Clear evidence of connections with content and the power of an authentic problem to anchor that content were present throughout their reflections. Time was recognized as a challenge but not seen as a barrier to the use of video production. Teacher-learners structured their practice using the video design process and often reflected on its importance. In fact, their teacher education experiences were not only evident in their reflections but served as a third voice alongside their voices and the voices of their students. They were teaching as they had been taught.

Developing a Designer's Identity

There is some controversy and a great deal of discussion these days about the role of the classroom teacher. Some say, in a rather pejorative way, that the role of teachers has traditionally been that of a "sage on the stage" and seek a different identity for teachers. Yet, how are students to develop expertise if there is no expert present? How are we to know if students' constructions are viable and rigorous if there is no sage in the classroom? Deep content understanding is a prerequisite to good teaching. Others would describe the role of a teacher as a "director." And, while some might disparage such a role, someone must lead the organizing, planning, and directing functions. Various alternative descriptors of the educator's role include: a teacher is a facilitator; a teacher is a coach; a teacher is a cognitive mentor. These descriptors of an educator's role reflect the no-

tion that students not the teacher are the locus of the learning act and suggests that as learners what students need is a "guide on the side" - a provocateur and support system.

Within the search for an appropriate conception of teacher identity, there is another more fundamental but rarely discussed role. That is, the teacher as designer. The teacher as a designer recognizes the centrality of planning, structuring, provisioning, and orchestrating learning. While the role of designer may be the least observed or recognized teacher role, the intellectual analysis of content filtered through an understanding of learning and learners and the subsequent construction of learning opportunities for students underpins all robust and worthwhile learning opportunities. Teachers are and ought to come to see themselves as designers. Supporting teachers to conceptualize their identity as a designer is a central strategy guiding ITS program decisions.

ITS graduates are encouraged to try on and experiment with a designer's identity. Readings, presentations, research, and activities are not completed to be remembered; they are mined for the design principles and processes they suggest to a teacher designer. Program faculty may lead a model lesson but not as an example of possible practice but as a shared experience for deriving and discussing design principles. Teacher-learners are often asked to analyze a shared group lesson for the ways in which it reflects a design principle. Conversely, when teacher-learners are asked to create a technology-rich lesson for their own context, they are asked to write about how that lesson is informed by and reflects design principles and processes. A database using lesson is not only described as objectives, standards, sequences, and materials needed. Rather, it is described for the ways in which it uses the SSCC principle – how it engages learners in becoming good users of information by asking them to search (S), sort (S), create (C), and communicate (C) about information. The lesson is further discussed to examine how it is informed by the ACTS principle – how it incorporates an authentic problem (A), a clear outcome (C), analysis and scaffolding of thinking skills (T), and development of only those software skills necessary for learning success (S).

Beginning in their first semester and proceeding throughout the program, ITSers keep a Designer's Blog. These blogs serve as a personal journal of reflections about design – what it means to be a designer, what challenges a designer faces, ways they used a particular design principle or process successfully, how one of their designs might have failed, and the like. Teacher-learners comment on each others' blogs, lending support, proposing ideas, validating positive accomplishments, empathizing with challenges, and sharing ideas that might clarify and expand understanding and use of design principles. They use these blogs and the comments and ideas from fellow ITSers to construct reflections for their end of semester portfolios.

ITSers will tell you they earn graduate degrees but, more importantly, they will tell you they fill their "bag" with dozens of design principles and processes to be used and reused, shared with colleagues, and discussed articulately with parents and administrators. They shed their "teacher's" identity and develop a "designer's" identity. They experience technology-rich teacher education that embraces the notion of teachers as designers and builds activities, readings, tools, and assignments that promote design as the central educating act. They experience technology-rich teacher education that empowers them with design principles and processes for planning, structuring, provisioning, and orchestrating learning opportunities for their students. They experience technology-rich teacher education that does not promote teaching and learning as a "technical" act of sequencing but as a "creative" act of designing and are, thus, empowered to recognize themselves as designers and to act as designers act.

A Designer's Best Friend

One of the most important tools of the designer is design-based research - an emerging paradigm for the study of learning in context through design that includes strategies and tools that help create and extend knowledge about developing and sustaining learning environments. In design-based research, learning is "engineered" and systematically studied in context. Design experimentation is concerned with the full, interacting system of learning to include tasks or problems, kinds of discourse, norms of participation, tools and related materials, and the means by which teachers orchestrate relations among these elements. "Design experiments therefore constitute a means of addressing the complexity that is a hallmark of educational settings" (Cobb, Confrey, diSessa, Lehrer, & Schauble, 2003, p. 9). Design-based research has as its goals not the "right" answer but the ability to improve educational practice. Its promise is to provide opportunities to explore possibilities for creating novel learning and teaching environments, to develop contextualize theories of learning and teaching, to construct cumulative design knowledge, and to increase the human capacity for innovation (The Design-Based Research Collective, 2003).

A central principle of good design research is that it should focus on development and research that takes place through continuous cycles of design, enactment, analysis, and redesign (Cobb, 2001; Collins, 1992). Design studies involve a pronounced emphasis on the narrative report of the complex interactions and feedback cycles that can significantly blur the roles of researchers, teachers, curriculum developers, instructional designers, and assessment experts (Kelly & Lesh, 2000). Bannan-Ritland (2003) argued that a program of research is a design event. That is, a well crafted single study is "part of an entire scope of work from original idea to diffusion of results" (p. 21). Thus, design researchers do not think in terms of a study defined by a clear beginning and end but as an agenda centered on a clear question. The design researcher engages in a series of design events – each crafted to illustrate and assess specific and intentional design features or theories. Pursuing an iterative process of design and assessment, the design researcher, over time, is able to derive design principles and processes that lead to theories about how to achieve desired learning outcomes.

Design-based research has been our most important ally on the journey to creating technology-rich teacher education. Each time we attempt a new design we also construct a design-based research project to inform the next design. We have shared some of those projects in preceding sections. For instance, when we first integrated Web 2.0 tools with the ITS curriculum, we collected both anecdotal and survey data to inform our practice. As reported earlier (Norton & Hathaway, 2008a), results of that data allowed us to confirm the power of teaching the importance of focusing on these tools' affordances by using them as part of the cohort's study of leadership and advocacy. As ITSers used these tools to support their own learning, they were able to take their understanding of the tools' affordances and design learning opportunities for K-12 learners. As we wrestled with the ways in which we could counter ITSers temptations to dismiss video production as a possible strategy in their classrooms, we designed an approach to teaching video production created to counter their concerns (Norton & Hathaway, 2010a). As we looked at their reflections on their use of video production in their own practice, we were able to observe how our video design principles shaped their designs. Perhaps our most sustained and iterative practice of design-based research has been to study the ways in which online learning might inform technology-rich teacher education. We have summarized that journey in Norton and Hathaway (2009) and learned through various research projects that a blended approach works with ITSers most appreciating collaborative projects (Warrick & Norton, 2002), that no matter

how online learning is designed careful attention to the role of the group, the skill of the instructor, and the manner that self-regulation is scaffolded emerge as the central design concerns (Norton & Hathaway, 2008b), that building community is not a necessary prerequisite to productive online learning (Norton & Hathaway, 2008c), and that public conversations with peers and private conversations with an expert have different impacts (Norton & Hathaway, 2010b). Design-based research has and continues to empower us with the knowledge we need to be effective designers of technology-rich teacher education.

As we have come to understand the power of design-based research, we have introduced it to ITSers. Originally, ITSers completed the standard research course associated with graduate study. Next, they were instructed in how to use teacher action research as a guide to assess and reflect on their teaching. We now scaffold not only their emerging identity as a designer but their emerging identity as a design researcher. ITSers begin thinking about their designs by blogging. In their fourth semester, they systematically design lessons and examine the impact of those lessons using a design-based research framework. They draw conclusions about design principles that work and that need to be modified as well as how those design principles might inform future practice. They repeat the process in their final semester. This time they research the design of larger chunks of instruction, the unit. Just as design ought to drive technology-rich education, design-based research ought to drive design.

LESSONS FOR THE DESIGN OF TECHNOLOGY-RICH TEACHER EDUCATION

Given our experiences and research teaching teachers to create technology-rich learning environments for their students, what do we have to offer to those who seek to create technology-rich teacher education? Below are our suggestions:

- Technology-rich teacher education happens not in curriculum or program development meetings but through continuous attention to design.
- Teacher educators must come to understand that technology-rich teacher education is a process not a course, a collection of courses, or even a program. Designing technology-rich teacher education using a cohort structure promotes the ability to move beyond courses and, instead, supports the construction of shared knowledge and dispositions.
- Technology-rich teacher education is not about technology, mastering the intricacies of operations, or a technology integration example. It is about learning to think deeply about the intersection of learning goal and the potential and constraints offered by a range of tools. It is about understanding the affordances that technology offers.
- Teacher educators must have as their central core a designer's identity and seek to promote a similar identity for prospective teachers. Technology-rich education depends on realistically assessing the requirements of educational practice, the structure of the educational system, and the complexities of culture. It depends on understanding the characteristics, developmental processes, and motivations of today's learner. It depends on clearly understanding the standards and curriculum guidelines that define learning goals. Most importantly, it depends on bringing these strands of influence together through the design of learning opportunities.
- Time is not well spent seeking to either find or create models of effective or innovative technology integration. Leadership in technology-rich teacher education is not about

teaching others to replicate or critique current practice in the field. Leadership in technology-rich teacher education must serve as a model of what technology-rich education ought to be. It must "practice what it preaches." It must *be* the model.
- Understanding what works in technology-rich teacher education does not come primarily from research that follows program graduates into the field or examines graduates in longitudinal ways. It derives from design-based research that addresses the complexity of educational settings and has as its goals not the *right* answer but the ability to improve educational practice.

We have come to understand that there is no substantive difference between innovative technology-rich teacher education and innovative technology-rich K-12 learning. Neither is naturally occurring; both are the result of design. Learning rarely happens in isolation. It is almost always enriched by social interactions and the ways in which those around us support, challenge, refine, and push our thoughts and ideas whether we are teacher educators or classroom teachers. Technology serves design that enhances teaching and learning goals not as an object to be studied but as a cluster of potentials and constraints strategically matched with the systematic attainment of learning goals. Technology's place in technology-rich teacher education and technology-rich K-12 classrooms is at the intersection of goal and tool – its power to serve as an affordance. Learning is the result of the interplay between *what* we learn and *how* we learn it. Thus, the way we learn shapes how we understand and how we use what we learn. This is true regardless of educational setting. Teacher educators ought to see themselves as designers; classroom teachers are designers too. Both teacher educators and classroom teachers create robust learning opportunities for students when they use design principles and processes to guide the ways in which they create, try, reflect, recreate, retry, and reflect again in a continuous process. This continuous process of design is best judged by both teacher educators and classroom teachers not as an outcome at journey's end but as an ongoing design-based research project that points to directions we must take and the ways in which we must travel.

REFERENCES

Bannan-Ritland, B. (2003). The role of design in research: The integrative learning design framework. *Educational Researcher*, *32*(1), 21–24. doi:10.3102/0013189X032001021

Brush, T., & Appelman, R. (2003). Transforming the pre-service teacher education technology curriculum at Indiana University: An integrative approach. In C. Crawford, et al. (Eds.), *Proceedings of Society for Information Technology and Teacher Education International Conference 2003* (pp. 1613-1619). Chesapeake, VA: AACE.

Cenzon, C. G. (2009). *Examining the role of various factors and experiences in technology integration: A description of a professional model* (Doctoral dissertation). Retrieved from ProQuest Dissertations and Theses, (AAT 3336176).

Cobb, P. (2001). Supporting the improvement of learning and teaching in social and institutional context. In Carver, S. M., & Klahr, D. (Eds.), *Cognition and instruction: Twenty-five years of progress* (pp. 455–478). Mahwah, NJ: Erlbaum.

Cobb, P., Confrey, J., diSessa, A., Lehrer, R., & Schauble, R. (2003). Design experiments in educational research. *Educational Researcher*, *32*(1), 9–13. doi:10.3102/0013189X032001009

Collins, A. (1992). Toward a design science of education. In Scanlon, E., & O'Shea, T. (Eds.), *New directions in educational technology* (pp. 15–22). New York, NY: Springer-Verlag.

Gaver, W. W. (1991). Technology affordances. In S. P. Scott, G. M. Olson, & J. S. Olson (Eds.), *Proceedings of CHI '91* (pp. 79-84). New Orleans, LA: ACM Press.

Gibson, J. J. (1986). *The ecological approach to visual perceptions*. Hillsdale, NJ: Erlbaum.

Guzdial, M., Rick, J., & Kehoe, C. (2001). Beyond adoption to invention: Teacher-created collaborative activities in higher education. *Journal of the Learning Sciences*, *10*(3), 265–279. doi:10.1207/S15327809JLS1003_2

Hammond, M. (2009). What is an affordance and can it help us understand the use of ICT in education? *Education and Information Technologies*, *15*(3), 205–217. doi:10.1007/s10639-009-9106-z

Heraclitus. (n.d.). *BrainyQuote.com*. Retrieved from http://www.brainyquote.com/quotes/quotes/h/heraclitus107157.html

Kay, R. H. (2006). Evaluating strategies used to incorporate technology into preservice education: A review of the literature. *Journal of Research on Technology in Education*, *38*(4), 383–408.

Kelly, A. E., & Lesh, R. A. (Eds.). (2000). *Handbook of research design in mathematics and science education*. Mahwah, NJ: Erlbaum.

Mims, C., Polly, D., Shepherd, C., & Inan, F. (2006). Examining PT3 projects designed to improve preservice education. *TechTrends*, *50*(3), 17–24. doi:10.1007/s11528-006-7599-5

Norton, P. (1994). Integrating technology in schools: a cohort process for graduate level inquiry. *Journal of Information Technology for Teacher Education*, *3*(2), 163–174. doi:10.1080/0962029940030204

Norton, P. (1995). Integrating technology: Using telecommunications to augment graduate teacher education. *Journal of Technology and Teacher Education*, *3*(1), 3–12.

Norton, P., & Farrell, N. (2001). When attitudes change, do changes in practice follow? In J. Price, et al. (Eds.), *Proceedings of Society for Information Technology & Teacher Education International Conference 2001* (pp. 959-964). Chesapeake, VA: AACE.

Norton, P., & Hathaway, D. (2008a). On its way to K-12 classrooms: Web 2.0 goes to graduate school. *Computers in the Schools*, 25(3-4), 163–180. doi:10.1080/07380560802368116

Norton, P., & Hathaway, D. (2008b). Exploring two online learning environments: A classroom of one or many? *Journal of Technology on Research in Technology Education*, 40(4), 475–495.

Norton, P., & Hathaway, D. (2008c). Reflections on the notion of community in online learning. In K. McFerrin, et al. (Eds.), *Proceedings of Society for Information Technology & Teacher Education International Conference 2008* (pp. 3097-3104). Chesapeake, VA: AACE.

Norton, P., & Hathaway, D. (2009). Exploring online learning through design and design-based research. In Maddux, C. (Ed.), *Research Highlights in Technology and Teacher Education 2009* (pp. 239–246). Chesapeake, VA: AACE.

Norton, P., & Hathaway, D. (2010a). Video production as an instructional strategy: Content learning and teacher practice. *Contemporary Issues in Technology & Teacher Education*, 10(1). Retrieved from http://www.citejournal.org/vol10/iss1/currentpractice/article2.cfm.

Norton, P., & Hathaway, D. (2010b). Online conversations with peers and with an expert mentor. In Maddux, C., Gibson, D., & Dodge, B. (Eds.), *Research Highlights in Technology and Teacher Education 2010* (pp. 239–246). Chesapeake, VA: AACE.

Norton, P., & Schell, G. (2001). How much is enough? Comparing certificate and degree teacher education options. In J. Price, et al. (Eds.), *Proceedings of Society for Information Technology & Teacher Education International Conference 2001* (pp. 965-970). Chesapeake, VA: AACE.

Norton, P., & Sprague, D. (1996). Changing teachers - Teachers changing schools: Assessing a graduate program in technology. *Journal of Information Technology and Teacher Education*, 5(1/2), 93–105.

Norton, P., & Sprague, D. (1999). Timber Lane tales: Problem-centered learning and technology integration. In J. Price, et al. (Eds.), *Proceedings of Society for Information Technology & Teacher Education International Conference 1999* (pp. 89-94). Chesapeake, VA: AACE.

Norton, P., & Sprague, D. (2002-2003). Timber Lane technology tales: A design experiment in alternative field experiences for preservice candidates. *Journal of Computing in Teacher Education*, 19(2), 40–46.

Nussbaum, B. (2005, January 3). Getting schooled in innovation [Electronic version]. *Business Week Online*. Retrieved from http://www.businessweek.com/bwdaily/dnflash/jan2005/nf2005013_8303.htm

Ottenbreit-Leftwich, A., Glazewski, K., & Newby, T. (2010). Preservice technology integration course revision: A conceptual guide. [Chesapeake, VA: AACE.]. *Journal of Technology and Teacher Education*, 18(1), 5–33.

Pellegrino, J., Goldman, S., Bertenthal, M., & Lawless, K. (2007). Teacher education and technology: Initial results from the "what works and why" project. *Yearbook of the National Society for the Study of Education*, 106(2), 52–86. doi:10.1111/j.1744-7984.2007.00115.x

Preece, J., Rogers, Y., & Sharp, H. (2002). *Interaction design*. New York, NY: Wiley.

Sprague, D., & Norton, P. (1999). Studying technology as a cohort: Teachers' reflections on the process. In J. Price, et al. (Eds.), *Proceedings of Society for Information Technology & Teacher Education International Conference 1999* (pp. 722-727). Chesapeake, VA: AACE.

The Design-Based Research Collective. (2003). Design-based research: An emerging paradigm for educational inquiry. *Educational Researcher, 32*(1), 5–8. doi:10.3102/0013189X032001005

U.S. Congress. (2001). *No Child Left Behind Act of 2001* (PL 107-110). Title II: Teacher Quality Enhancement. Retrieved from http://www.ed.gov/legislation/ESEA02/pg121.html

Warrick, W., Connors, S., & Norton, P. (2004). E-mail, discussion boards, and synchronous chat: Comparing three modes of online collaboration. In R. Ferdig, et al. (Eds.), *Proceedings of Society for Information Technology & Teacher Education International Conference 2004* (pp. 2732-2738). Chesapeake, VA: AACE.

Warrick, W., & Norton, P. (2002). Graduate instruction combining online, on-site, and face-to-face: A study. In D. Willis, et al. (Eds.), *Proceedings of Society for Information Technology & Teacher Education International Conference 2002* (pp. 881-885). Chesapeake, VA: AACE.

Chapter 3
Meeting the Needs of Exceptional Students:
The Importance of Technology in Teaching and Implementing Universal Design for Learning Principles

Timothy J. Frey
Kansas State University, USA

E. Ann Knackendoffel
Kansas State University, USA

ABSTRACT

Today's K-12 classrooms are learning environments that present teachers with the challenge of meeting the diverse needs of learners. Utilizing technology and the principles of Universal Design for Learning (UDL) can help teachers to meet the exceptional needs of learners in a variety of areas. This chapter presents ideas and strategies to utilize technology to facilitate the implementation of UDL principles (using multiple means of representation, engagement, and expression in the design of instruction) in teacher education and K-12 classrooms. Each principle of UDL is described, and examples of technology that can support implementation of the principle are shared. The chapter concludes with considerations for teacher education programs including providing modeling of UDL instruction and designing instruction with UDL in mind.

INTRODUCTION

Classrooms today are more diverse than any other time in history in terms of race, ethnicity, language, and ability. Teachers at all levels need to recognize and respond to academic diversity

DOI: 10.4018/978-1-4666-0014-0.ch003

in ways that allow all students to benefit from the content being taught. Some educators, who are not well versed in Universal Design for Learning (UDL) principles, falsely believe this means watering down the curriculum. This is simply not true. Educators must move beyond the mistaken belief that high standards means there is only one way to complete an academic task. Instruction can be designed to enable learners of all abilities and backgrounds to access, engage, and succeed in mastering core academic tasks.

Powerful emerging technologies are providing new and exciting avenues for teachers to support the learning needs of today's diverse classrooms (Cardinali & Gordon, 2002). Future teachers need a clear understanding of these technologies and their benefits for K-12 students (Marino, Sameshima, & Beecher, 2009; Bausch & Hasselbring, 2004). Teacher educators need to model the use of technology to support student learning and provide opportunities for preservice teachers to practice using UDL principles. This chapter focuses on how technology can be used to support learners with diverse learning needs, both within teacher education programs and in K-12 settings. The first section provides an overview of the need for UDL and the background of the UDL concept. Next, examples of technologies that can be used to support each of three key principles of UDL are provided. The chapter concludes with our recommendations for teacher educators on implementing UDL in their programs and providing future teachers with the expertise and experiences needed to use technology to meet the needs of their future K-12 exceptional learners.

THE PROBLEM: ONE SIZE DOES NOT FIT ALL

The achievement gap in schools is well documented. In Figure 1 below, the diagonal line illustrates the expected level of achievement of students where students gain one year of academic achievement for each year they are in school. The dotted line illustrates the pattern of achievement for many under-achieving students. Rather than offering multiple pathways to help students learn, the "one size fits all" printed textbooks and other traditional resources that typically comprise the general curriculum often serve as barriers to many students in classrooms today (Rose & Meyer,

2002). This pattern of underachievement results in students falling further and further behind.

The area between the dotted line of performance by low achievers and the diagonal line of expected grade level is known as the "achievement gap." The graphic reveals the cumulative effect of students' underachievement. Chronic academic underachievement is a significant educational problem. In fact, concern about chronic underachievement is one of the core tenets of the federal education reform law known as No Child Left Behind (NCLB), as illustrated in the law's emphasis on measuring adequate yearly progress (Edyburn, 2006a). NCLB mandates increased expectations for all students, including those with disabilities, "to access, participate in, and progress in the general curriculum" (Pisha & Stahl, 2005, p. 70). According to Edyburn (2006b), the lessons one can take away from the achievement gap phenomenon are very clear:

- Current teaching practices are not effective for some groups of students.
- Continuing to operate in the same manner, doing what educators have always done will perpetuate rather than eliminate the gap.
- Repeated failure over time creates an achievement gap that is so entrenched that it becomes exceedingly difficult to close.

What is the solution? How long do teachers allow students to fail before providing them with appropriate support tools? If teachers wait too long, students give up and quit trying. They begin to believe they cannot learn or be successful at a task. They become firmly entrenched in the self-fulfilling prophecy that they are "failures". Unfortunately, rather than addressing the issues behind the poor performance of some students, educators often search for reasons to explain poor performance, thus becoming sidetracked, and failing to intervene with appropriate supports. Again, one-size-fits all instruction clearly is not working.

Figure 1. Achievement gap (Edyburn, 2006a used by permission)

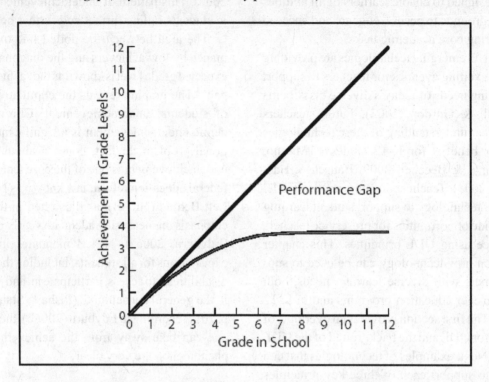

Sadly, if you walked into many classrooms today, the learning activities you'd likely observe, would not look much different than what you might have seen 20, 30, 40 or even 50 years ago. Now think about what has happened in those same years outside of schools. Technology has had a tremendous impact on life and has fundamentally changed how many everyday tasks are completed—bills are paid online and Internet banking is commonplace, if your car needs repair, mechanics use engine diagnostic systems, food purchasing, preparation and cooking options are very different (soup in a box, instant pasta entrées prepared in the microwave) and so on. Still, the mainstay in most classrooms today for learning about a subject is the printed textbook. One might compare this to the many choices we have to view a movie—cable or satellite television, on-demand, renting a DVD at the neighborhood movie rental store, having it delivered to our physical home mailbox, or to a virtual mailbox on our TV or media home-storage unit. One can record from TV for later playback at a time of our choosing with DVR technology, watch it on a computer or other personal media device, or even watch the movie the old fashioned way, at the movie theater. With all of these options for watching a movie for pleasure, one might ask, why are the options so limited in schools where much of learning about a topic being taught is reduced to reading a textbook? (Edyburn, 2006a)

Recent educational innovations, such as differentiated instruction and universal design for learning, offer insights into proactively planning instruction that recognizes the academic diversity in today's general education classrooms. Recognizing the need for both physical and cognitive access to learning provides a rationale and template for exploring existing technologies that could come to bear which would fundamentally alter the way specific school-related tasks can be accessed, manipulated, and completed in much the same transformational way that technology has impacted other areas of daily life.

THE CONCEPT OF UNIVERSAL DESIGN FOR LEARNING

The concept of Universal Design for Learning has become a point of emphasis as a means to improve the performance of students with disabilities in general education settings (Hitchcock & Stahl, 2004; Pisha & Coyne, 2001). UDL provides options to make curriculum and instruction more accessible to students with differing abilities, learning styles, and backgrounds (Rose & Meyer, 2002). UDL principles encourage educators to design their instruction to provide more students greater access to the curriculum (Pisha & Coyne, 2001) and utilize alternative instructional methods to "remove the barriers to student learning" inherent in the typical elementary and secondary classrooms (Kortering, McClannon, & Braziel, 2008, p. 353).

Universal Design emerged from the field of architectural design in the 1970s by Ron Mace (Center for Universal Design, 1997) when federal legislation required universal access to buildings and other structures for individuals with disabilities. As a result, architects began to design accessibility into buildings during their initial design stage rather than retrofitting existing structures. The idea behind universal design is to design products and environments to be usable by all people, to the greatest extent possible, without the need for adaptation or specialized design. The intent of universal design is to simplify life for everyone by making products, communications, and the environment more usable by as many people as possible at little or no extra cost. Universal design benefits people of all ages and abilities. Using this same principle, UDL is now applied in instructional planning to consider and eliminate barriers that students may encounter to learning. Like universal design features in architecture, once in place, one realizes a broader slice of the public is able to benefit from these features beyond the original intended audience. For example, curb cuts originally intended for those in wheelchairs benefit many others with baby strollers, luggage on wheels, bicycles, etc. Likewise, even something as design specific as closed captioning, originally designed exclusively for the hearing impaired, is now commonly used in noisy public areas or to supplement the voices on TV or movie programming for many people who would not put themselves in the category of significantly hearing impaired.

As students with disabilities are more and more visible in general education classrooms, educators need to move beyond retrofitting or adding accommodations and modifications after the fact as we plan our instruction and instead, think about and purposefully plan lessons in such a way that the broadest spectrum of students are considered in the initial stages of our planning, allowing for multiple pathways for them to learn. Strategic uses of instructional technology provide unique opportunities for teachers to design instruction with UDL principles in mind and proactively plan for student needs by utilizing technology to embed multiple means of representation, engagement, and expression into their instruction. Educators utilizing UDL principles intentionally plan instruction that is inclusive. UDL instructional design is not intended to make learning "easier" for students, but rather to make learning *possible* (NCD, 2001). Specifically, a UDL approach to instruction emphasizes proactive consideration of the broad spectrum of student accessibility and learning needs. These needs have begun to be addressed by scholars committed to providing education access to education both at the K-12 and postsecondary levels (Castellani & Warger, 2010).

Briefly, the three principles of universal design for learning are: (a) provide multiple means or representation, giving learners various ways to acquire information and knowledge (i.e., content); (b) utilize multiple means of engagement, tapping into learners' interests, challenging them appropriately, and motivating them to learn; and (c) allow opportunities for the use of multiple means of expression, providing learners with alternatives for demonstrating what they know (Rose & Meyer, 2002). In the remainder of the chapter, we describe each of the three principles of Universal Design for Learning, emphasizing strategies that can be implemented in both teacher education and K-12 classrooms. Each section also provides specific example technology applications that can be utilized to facilitate the implementation of UDL principles to support students with diverse learning needs (e.g. English language learners, students with learning disabilities, intellectual disabilities, autism spectrum disorders, emotional/behavioral disorders, visual impairments, hearing impairments, traumatic brain injury, and speech/language impairments) and how those examples can be used to teach UDL principles to pre-service teachers as part of a technology-rich teacher education program.

MULTIPLE MEANS OF REPRESENTING CONTENT

The first guiding principle of UDL is to ensure that multiple means are utilized to represent content. Delivering content is often perceived to be one of the most important teacher instructional roles. Teachers and educators provide resources and information to students to provide background knowledge, build frameworks for discussion and application activities, and encourage in-depth understanding of topics in a given curriculum. In the Universal Design framework, content is interpreted as the information or knowledge the educator or teacher expects to deliver to the student. Technology-rich teacher education programs and K-12 educators can utilize technology to make content more accessible to students with diverse learning needs by using multiple strategies to represent course content. Application of this UDL

principle in teacher education programs typically focuses on three areas: text-based content, web and multimedia content, and lecture and notes content.

Text-Based Information

A traditional example of providing content is a course textbook. Textbooks are a long-established and often essential part of delivering information to students. A typical textbook contains information and examples that provide foundational knowledge of the course content. Despite their extensive usage in education, textbooks often prove difficult to access for students with a variety of disabilities. For example, students with learning disabilities may struggle to process the text and make meaning from the words (Siegel, 2003). Students with visual impairments may have difficulty seeing the words and images on the pages, while other students may face physical challenges in turning pages and transporting the often-heavy texts.

The use of electronic format e-books or digital versions textbooks provides meaningful accommodation options for meetings the needs of many students. E-books provide students with a variety of options including the ability to readily enlarge text and images, change font, adapt color schemes, and even convert text to Braille. For students with learning disabilities, e-books combined with text-to-speech readers provide students a second way to access the information in the textbook. Students who listen and follow along with text significantly improve reading comprehension and speed (Wexler, Vaughn, Edmonds, & Reutebuch, 2008). Providing the textbook in an e-format allows all students the flexibility to use either audio or text to access the information.

Text readers are available in a variety of formats and levels of support. Basic text-to-speech tools are not commonly included in the accessibility features of both Windows and Mac operating systems as well as common word processing programs. Additional tools like ReadPlease and

Natural Readers are available from websites and provide substantial text-to-speech support to meet a variety of student needs (Table 1 provides a list of each product/resource mentioned as well as a URL which directs the reader to a product website.) Reading educational content continues to be a key learning activity in classrooms and providing multiple formats and supports for reading helps make text more accessible to students who struggle with reading.

Web and Media Information

A second common source for presenting content information is the use of web and multimedia presentations. Using videos and other supplementary multimedia to present content information is a good way to get information to students who are more visual learners. However, using video is not enough, educators must also ensure that video and multimedia content is accessible to all students. For students with hearing impairments or even minor hearing losses, providing captions, annotations, or full text transcripts are important accommodations. The National Center for Accessible Media Guidelines for captioning also apply to multimedia and web-based presentations (Freed & Rothberg, 2006). It is important that educators take advantage of all aspects of tools for creating multimedia presentations like Glogster and include embedded captions for visual images and adding transcripts of audio content in their presentation. Website images and links should be fully readable when accessing the site with a screen reader. Educators can check the "readability" of their web-based presentations using tools like the Web Accessibility Inspector and WAVE. Universally designed websites include alternative text tags for screen readers that are detailed and complete descriptions of an image, figure, or diagram on the web page. This allows students with visual impairments to have access to the information conveyed by the images.

Notes/Lecture

Another aspect of classroom content presentations is facilitating student note-taking. Taking notes in the classroom presents difficulties for many students. For some students taking notes is a struggle because of the often quick pace required to keep up with the teacher as she or he talks. In this case, a number of technologies are available to allow students to "take notes" using a supported media other than handwriting. Students can work with educators to utilize speech-to-text software such as Dragon Dictation. Educators can wear a microphone so that their lecture is audio recorded or recorded using speech-to-text providing a written transcript of their lecture or an audio file that student can access and playback at a speed they can keep pace with. Similarly, smart pens like those developed by Livescribe can be used to help students organize, track, and review notes from classes. Such tools provide simple and unobtrusive means for students to get extra support in order to follow along with lecture notes.

MULTIPLE MEANS OF ENGAGEMENT

The second UDL principle focuses on the use of multiple instructional strategies to engage students in learning activities. Engagement includes the facilitation of multiple pathways for students to process, manipulate, and reflect on concepts and applications from course content (Pintrich, 2000). In order for students to remain engaged in learning activities they must also remain motivated and committed to the task (Blumenfeld, Kempler, and Krajcik, 2006). Students need an appropriate balance of challenge and support. Vygotsky (1978) described the ideal balance as the point where the goal is just beyond reach but achievable with effort. He calls this the Zone of Proximal Development. Such engaged learning environments can be facilitated at all levels by

Table 1. Example UDL tools

Text-to-Speech	ReadPlease http://www.readplease.com/ Natural Readers http://www.naturalreaders.com/
Speech-to-Text	Yakitome http://www.yakitome.com Vozme http://vozme.com/ Dragon Dictation http://nuance.com/for-individuals/by-solution/accessibility/index.htm
Captioning Tools	Universal subtitles http://universalsubtitles.org/ National Center for Accessible Media http://ncam.wgbh.org/webaccess/tools/index.html
Classroom Audio Amplification	Lightspeed http://www.lightspeed-tek.com/redcat.aspx
Collaboration tools	Voicethread http://voicethread.com Ning http://www.ning.com Wikispaces http://www.wikispaces.com
Note-Taking tools	Ghotit http://www.ghotit.com Smart Pen http://www.livescribe.com/en-us/smartpen/
Text editing tools	SOLO http://www.donjohnston.com/products/solo/
Creative Output	Glogster http://edu.glogster.com Museum Box http://museumbox.e2bn.org
Organization	LiveBinders http://livebinders.com
Web-Accessibility	Web Accessibility Inspector http://www.fujitsu.com/global/accessibility/assistance/wi/ WAVE http://wave.webaim.org/

providing students multiple pathways to participate in learning. Educators at in both K-12 and postsecondary settings can provide opportunities for students to engage in the content including: using online interactive learning modules, facilitating asynchronous online discussions, and supporting field experiences.

Online Interactive Learning Modules

We define online interactive learning modules (OILM) as instructional content delivered via an online portal that provides stand-alone options

for user learning, engagement in content, and assessment. OILMs related to teacher education content are often developed by research and technical assistance centers at universities. Others are developed by private professional development companies, university faculty and graduates students, or textbook publishers. Regardless of their source, OILMs can provide an option for engaging learners. Often modules are available at little or no cost for educators to use to supplement current instructional resources. OILMs can be particularly beneficial to educators teaching online courses who lack the time or expertise to develop their own accessible online content activities.

One example of an OILM is the module developed by the IRIS Center (n.d.) at Vanderbilt University called *Universal Design for Learning: Creating a Learning Environment that Challenges and Engages All Students*. The IRIS website indicates that the module "examines the three principles of Universal Design for Learning (UDL) and discusses how to apply these principles to the four curricular components (i.e., goals, instructional materials, instructional methods, and assessments"). Each of the OILMs created at the IRIS Center is based on sound instructional design theoretical framework such as the How People Learn (HPL) (National Research Council, 1999), and uses problem-based approach to engage students in the content. Embedded in the modules are audio and video files, documents and case studies, and opportunities for self-reflection and evaluation of learning. All IRIS Center modules also adhere to UDL guidelines for websites mentioned previously including providing captions for images and transcripts for audio/video content. OILM formats provide learners with choices that allow them to tailor the module to their needs by selecting to view a video, listen to an audio file, skipping multimedia and reading a transcript, or bypassing an activity completely. Learners are also free to work through activities at their own pace, adjusting for their processing needs and allowing multiple reviews of content. The flexibility built in to OILMs designed with UDL principles in mind provides opportunities for students engage with content in multiple ways.

Facilitating Asynchronous Discussions

Facilitating discussions of important issues and concepts is an often-utilized instructional approach for engaging learners in content in teacher education and K-12 courses. Discussions can take on a variety of formats that include large group conversations, small group interactions, debates, and Socratic circles. The goal of discussion is often to allow students to share their ideas and engage peers and their educators in dialogue about the issue or topic. However, discussion-based activities can be challenging for many students. For example, students with speech and language disorders can struggle to articulate ideas verbally, students with hearing impairments many have difficulty hearing others' contributions to the discussion, and students with emotional/behavioral difficulties may feel uncomfortable sharing in large group setting. Today's technologies can be utilized to help meet students' needs and facilitate discussions.

One technology that is becoming more frequently utilized is classroom audio amplification systems. Classroom audio systems typically consist of one or two audio speaker and a series of wireless microphones. The educator wears the primary microphone and additional microphones are provided to discussion participants as needed. The systems allow all the students in the classroom to hear the educator clearly. Early research in K-12 classrooms suggests that use of a system increases on-task behavior and reduces problem behaviors for all students. Amplification systems allow students to hear teacher directions and prompts more consistently and students are more likely to actively participate in class (DiSarno, Schowalter, & Grassa, 2002). These systems can be either portable, moving from classroom to classroom, or be stationary and built in to a high-tech classroom setting.

A second technology-based option to support student discussions is the use of online asynchronous message boards to facilitate discussion. Asynchronous discussion activities have several advantages for students. Asynchronous discussions allow participants a longer timeframe to process information and respond to a question or prompt from an educator. Discussion formats also often allow for every student to participate in the discussion. Classroom time schedules often do not allow enough time for every student to contribute his or her thoughts about the discussion topic. In addition, the written asynchronous format allows students who may be uncomfortable speaking out loud in front of their peers or even those students who are unable to speak to be active participants and engage in classroom discussion activities (Barnett-Queen, Blair, & Merrick, 2005).

Technology to Support Field Experiences

Providing and supervising field experiences for preservice and inservice teachers is an important aspect of nearly all teacher education programs. Field experiences allow teacher educators to provide opportunities to participating teacher candidates to practice skills and apply concepts from their courses. Traditionally, field experiences are supervised by cooperating K-12 school personnel and teacher education program faculty. Faculty supervisors typically visit the field placement classroom and conduct observations and evaluations of teaching practices.

Today's technologies are providing teacher educators with new options for supervising field experiences and encouraging candidates to reflect on their teaching practices. In particular, digital video conferencing technologies are allowing teacher education faculty to support students in field experiences in new ways. Teacher educators have begun utilizing live video conferencing to allow observation and supervision of students from a distance. Faculty can view live classroom video from any location without having to travel to multiple school sites. Videos can also be archived and viewed later by the supervisor and the teacher. Having instant access or video "replays" of instruction that can be viewed from a distance promotes self-reflection, which can lead to improved teaching practices (Alger & Kopcha, 2009).

Establishing networks of teachers in online learning communities has also proven to be a powerful support tool for teachers in field expe-

riences. Learning communities provide opportunities for teachers to share experiences, lesson ideas, encouragement, and learning strategies (Frey, 2008). Learning communities often use peer mentoring to provide support to teachers as they engage in field experiences (Knapczyk, Hew, Frey, & Wall-Marencik, 2005). Some teacher education programs have also added a digital video component to online learning communities allowing peers and faculty to see their classroom setting and share about strategies to support K-12 students in their classrooms.

MULTIPLE MEANS OF EXPRESSION

The third and final UDL principle focuses on the multitude of ways students can express what they know and have learned. In general, utilizing multiple means of expression includes flexible options in output and performance for students to demonstrate their understanding of the material in some fashion consistent with their ability. The idea behind this last UDL principle of multiple means of expression is not to see how many bells and whistles you can incorporate into your assessment of learning, but rather to focus on the desired learning outcomes. Wiggins and McTighe (2005) referred to this as backwards design where the teacher identifies the desired results, determines what would serve as acceptable evidence, and plans learning experiences and instruction that lead students to the targeted outcomes of the learning process. These outcomes will include the "big ideas" or overarching concepts or understandings that you want all students to leave the course with. Once these outcomes are determined, one can then plan multiple evaluation options that allow students to demonstrate their understanding through any number of assessment tools. Technology-rich K-12 schools and teacher education programs can provide opportunities for students to demonstrate their learning of content including: using tiered assignments and innovative non-traditional expression tools.

Tiered Assignments

Tiered assignments can be operationalized in a number of different ways. According to Tomlinson (1995), tiered assignments are used by teachers within a heterogeneous classroom in order to meet the diverse needs of the students within the class. Teachers implement varied levels of activities to ensure that students explore ideas at a level that builds on their prior knowledge and prompts continued growth. Student groups are able to use varied approaches to explore essential ideas. Tiered assignments are parallel tasks at varied levels of complexity, depth, and abstractness with various degrees of scaffolding, support, or direction. Students work on different levels of activities, all with the same essential understanding or goal in mind. Tiered assignments accommodate mainly for differences in student readiness and performance levels and allow students to work toward a goal or objective at a level that builds on their prior knowledge and encourages continued growth.

When teachers want to know what students have learned, many still rely on traditional paper and pencil test or assign a written paper for students to demonstrate their knowledge on a topic of study. Some educators pride themselves on the fact that they go beyond these conventional methods and provide a variety of ways for students to demonstrate their learning across the semester or course, but few educators allow the flexibility within a given assessment or assignment so students can choose the option that works best for them. This might be done by providing three varied options for completing an assignment or end-of-unit evaluation that would either account for student ability levels and/or preferences. In some K-12 classrooms, teachers might even offer nine choices in a visual tic-tac-toe format and

ask students to choose three of the nine options to demonstrate their learning across a unit of study.

Technology can play a prominent role as educators work to develop tiered assignment options for their courses. For example, in a secondary or post-secondary setting, teachers might allow students the option of responding to an online question stem by word processing their response using personalized text-editing tools that best meet their needs, ranging from simple built-in universal spell checkers to more elaborate software programs (e.g. SOLO by Don Johnston) that provide a variety of levels of support based on student needs. SOLO includes supports leaner needs such as word prediction, read aloud support to hear the text as they write and even outlining or other graphic organizers to help organize their thoughts. Similar to using the support of a dolly to move heavy objects, text-editing tools enable students to express their thoughts more clearly. Other students may benefit from recording their response to the question using speech-to-text technology. It is easy to understand how students who struggle with writing due to any number of reasons such as a learning disability in written language, a physical impairment that limits their motor skills and speed in accessing a keyboard would clearly benefit from being able to give their response orally. Even more advanced students who want to improve their oral communication skills might also benefit by having this option, as it provides them an opportunity for additional practice. Similarly, students who are learning English might find it easier to express their knowledge orally.

If the goal of a given assignment is to determine if students understand the concept being taught, it does not matter if they show that in writing or by some other means of expression. Often times, students who have limited writing skills are prevented from expressing their full understanding of the topic. Flip the task around and consider when teachers call for only oral and/or public responses. Some students are reluctant to share their knowledge orally in front of the class. If asked a question during class, the teacher might think they do not know the answer because of their poor quality response when, in fact, it may be that they are simply timid, have limited oral expression skills, or may not want to appear brighter than their peers by giving you the high level response they are capable to giving. By offering a variety of options for students to demonstrate what they know about a topic, it allows some students to show what they have learned in possibly the only way they can and it might encourage others to try alternative methods they might not have otherwise explored.

Innovative and Non-Traditional Expression Tools

There are a number of online tools that can help students express their knowledge in non-traditional and creative ways. Consider Glogster EDU, a tool mentioned earlier in the section on presenting web-based content. This is a student and classroom-friendly (ad-free) version of the popular site for making multimedia posters. "Glogs" can incorporate text, graphics, images, links, audio, video, and more. Glogster offers a useful tool for documenting big projects because digital content can go deep and be organized in layers in these online posters. It lends itself to students working in teams and the site includes a showcase of student work.

Another useful tool that can be used to allow students to demonstrate their understanding is Museum Box. This website enables student to display their understanding of history, art, or a controversial current topic by selecting a few key artifacts and explaining their importance. This innovative online tool was inspired by abolitionist Thomas Clarkson, who carried a box of props to support his anti-slavery speeches. Museum Box is a good fit for projects that require students to make arguments and defend their choices. In a teacher education environment, future teachers could use this tool to defend continued use

of charter schools, inclusion, or even UDL in K-12 settings.

LiveBinders are a good choice if students are working on complicated projects either alone or with others and need to stay organized. It allows users to create virtual three-ring binders and organize digital documents in one place. Students and teachers alike can share information they have gathered with others in much the same way that one might gather and store artifacts in a three-ring binder except that LiveBinders is more flexible in its ability to store, update, and share digital information. Students might create a single LiveBinder to present one project, or they can combine several projects into a digital portfolio. Faculty in a teacher education program might use this tool to collect and share websites, journal articles, PowerPoint presentations, online video clips, and other artifacts with future teachers about a particular topic being covered in a course.

Podcasts or Blogs are another way for students to express their learning in a different way. Students might pair together to research a topic, condense the information into the most important big ideas, plan how to present it in an engaging way and then create a podcast to be shared with other students or a larger audience. Similarly, students could be encouraged to start a Blog to share their learning across the span of semester or year.

It is important to keep in mind that these should include authentic "real-life" forms of demonstrating understanding (Wiggins & McTighe, 2005). These real-life applications are just as important at the post-secondary level as they are in K-12 classrooms, maybe even more so. In particular, young adults preparing to become teachers often identify more closely to the role of student than they do to the role of teacher while they are in their teacher education-preparing program. Their experiences need to help them transition into wearing the shoes of educator rather than those of the student.

RECOMMEDATIONS FOR UDL IN TEACHER EDUCATION

The future of teacher education includes preparing teachers for diverse classrooms and student populations with diverse learning needs. Technology can play an important role and be a valuable tool for K-12 teachers as they seek to facilitate learning and meet the learning needs of their students. Technology tools can provide teachers with flexibility and strategies to implement UDL principles, making the content more accessible to students with exceptional learning needs and enhancing instruction for all the students in their classrooms. We believe teacher educators can support these goals by modeling UDL practices that utilize technology in their preparation programs, developing and preparing teachers to use instructional planning strategies that emphasize UDL principles, and conducting research on the impact of UDL on teacher candidates and their K-12 students.

UDL Modeling in Teacher Education Programs

It is a common truism in teacher education that "teachers are most likely to teach their students in ways they were taught." It is therefore imperative that teacher educators model effective practices in their courses including the use of technology to implement UDL principles. We believe preservice teachers who experience the impact that UDL can have on their own learning, are much more likely to use those same UDL instructional practices in their future classrooms. Teacher educators can model UDL even during routine teaching or when using traditional lecture methods. For example, when using a PowerPoint presentation, the educator has several options for providing students with supports for note taking. One of the most common options used by educators is to publish the slides for students to download or to print them and distribute as a handout with or

without room for additional notes (3 slide per-page handout option). Providing guided notes provides a more engaging option (Konrad, Joseph & Itoi, 2011). An easy way to create guided notes is to go into the outline view and copy and paste the text from the slides into a word processing document. Then make a copy for the student version and go through and delete a few key words and replace with blank, underlined spaces for the students to write in the missing text. One can also go into the original slides and underline or highlight the text that is missing on the handout so students can easily locate it on the slide. By doing this, even the competent, successful learners in the class discover that they can more easily focus on what is being said and still be engaged in the lecture. Learners leave the presentation knowing that they have the key content in their notes and see how, even though they may not have any significant learning issues, they found this made their learning easier. The cognitive understanding to realizing how this would not only make learning easier for many students but it might just make learning possible for students who otherwise might not be able to both take notes and process the oral information as it is being presented simultaneously. Providing instruction for preservice teachers in effective design and implementation of lessons that integrate technology and explicitly reflect UDL principles provides important modeling of a valuable skill set necessary for today's inclusive classrooms (CAST, 2010).

UDL Included in Lesson Design and Planning

Universal Design's history in the field of architecture and design is a constant reminder that the principles of UDL are intended to be a proactive design process, not a retroactive revision process. Teacher education programs must reexamine their lesson planning models and incorporate a proactive approach to meeting students' needs. Too often lesson planning templates simply include a space at the end of the lesson for "adaptations" or "accommodations" for students with special needs. Those areas are still important, but teachers need to work to anticipate student needs and proactively design their instruction in ways that make it accessible to as many learners as possible. Regardless of how much preferred lesson planning formats may vary across content areas and age groupings, teacher educators should seek ways to embed opportunities for teachers to identify the UDL aspects of their lesson design. Providing options for preservice teachers to reflect and provide rationales for their instructional plans is also important. Teacher educators need to ensure (a) that students understand it is their responsibility to meet the needs of all the learners in their classroom and (b) that they have the tools and strategies to meet those learner needs.

Conduct Research on Impact of UDL on Student Outcomes

Teacher educators must also accept the challenge of conducting research on the impact of UDL principles in the classroom. Researchers are beginning to examine the effects of UDL instructional models on K-12 students with and without identified needs. In order to examine outcomes of technology-related UDL approaches, teacher educators must collaborate with K-12 teachers to gather and analyze data classrooms and schools that have begun implementing instructional strategies designed to impact learners.

Early research is promising and research related to the use UDL principles to plan and deliver instruction has yielded improved results for K-12 student learning. Examples of effective implementation of UDL appear in multiple subject areas and with various populations of students with exceptionalities including science (Kurtis, Matthews, & Smallwood, 2009; Dymond, Renzaglia, Rosenstein, Chun, Banks, Niswander, & Gilson, 2006), math (Kortering, et al., 2008), and language arts (Michael & Trezek, 2006). Research has also

bolstered the belief that UDL principles also have potential to improve instructional outcomes for typical students (CAST, 1998; Kortering, et al., 2008; Kurtis, et al., 2009).

These findings are promising and suggest that using UDL principles to guide classroom instruction can make a meaningful difference in today's and future classrooms. However, many questions are left unanswered. We reiterate important calls for more research to evaluate the merit and effectiveness of UDL in both higher education and K-12 settings (McGuire, Scott, & Shaw, 2006). More research on UDL is needed to further evaluate the impact and effectiveness of various strategies. Teacher education researchers should look to conduct research that clearly provides evidence of specific UDL-focused strategies on teacher candidates and their K-12 students.

FINAL THOUGHTS

In light of the new technologies now available to teachers and students, what keeps education moving forward in the same way as other areas of daily life have changed as a result of technology? Unfortunately, it might largely boil down to the fact that education places a premium on knowledge that is contained in one's head. Performance that is completed without the aid of external devices and resources is prized over performance that is dependent on tools or resources. Knowledge is of two types: the kind you know and the kind you know how to find. Researchers in assistive technology outcomes have termed this form of bias "naked independence," as it exults the performance of able-bodied individuals and devalues the performance of others who must rely on external devices or tools (Edyburn, 2006a). That would be comparable to telling a person who wears eyeglasses that they must remove them when reading a textbook or taking a test.

Thanks to a few forward thinking educators, there are examples of where assistive technologies have been utilized to reduce the achievement gap for exceptional students and students with diverse learning needs. It is not a matter of watering down the curriculum, but rather making it more accessible and adaptable. Tomlinson (1999) uses the term "equalizer" to discuss the concept of control that could be used to alter the level of support a student receives in a UDL environment. Just like a volume control slider or a dimmer switch allows us to adjust the volume or brightness of the light, we can extend this metaphor to the educational environment. In her vision of differentiated instruction, Tomlinson envisions any number of equalizers that could be developed to control the level of challenge and support a student needs throughout the learning process. One example might be in the area of how knowledge or content is represented. The equalizer slider could move from abstract, down to concrete. Other equalizers might include simple to complex, less to greater independence, or slower to faster pace of study. For example, a text reader might be an available option for a student who reads below grade placement. For some students, it might be used to simply reinforce aurally what they read or to help with certain words or sections of the text, but, with others, it could be used in place of reading the text independently.

Researchers, teachers and students consistently report that implementation of UDL principles can enhance student learning and increase engagement in the learning process (CAST, 2010; Kortering, et al., 2008). Instruction designed with UDL principles in mind engages students at multiple ability levels and, much like Tomlinson's (1999) concept of differentiating instruction, seeks to meet the diverse learning needs of students. Preparing teachers to meet the needs of their future students is critical for the future of public education. Teacher education programs should continue to implement curriculum and emphasize instructional strategies that utilize technology in the implementation of UDL principles, providing access to educational resources for all students.

REFERENCES

Alger, C., & Kopcha, T. J. (2009). eSupervision: A technology framework for the 21st century field experience in teacher education. *Issues in Teacher Education, 18*(2), 31–46.

Barnett-Queen, T., Blair, R., & Merrick, M. (2005). Student perspectives of online discussions: Strengths and weaknesses. *Journal of Technology in Human Services, 23*, 229–244. .doi:10.1300/J017v23n03_05

Bausch, M. E., & Hasselbring, T. S. (2004). Assistive technology: Are the necessary skills and knowledge being developed at the pre-service and inservice levels? *Teacher Education and Special Education, 27*(2), 97–104. doi:10.1177/088840640402700202

Blanton, L. P., Griffin, C. C., Winn, J. A., & Pugach, M. C. (Eds.). (1997). *Teacher education in transition*. Denver, CO: Love.

Blumenfeld, P. C., Kempler, T. M., & Krajcik, J. S. (2006). Motivation and cognitive engagement in learning engagement. In Sawyer, R. K. (Ed.), *The Cambridge handbook of the learning sciences* (pp. 475–488). New York, NY: Cambridge University Press.

Cardinali, R., & Gordon, Z. (2002). Technology: Making things easier for all of us – For the disabled making things possible. *Equal Opportunities International, 21*(1), 65–79. doi:10.1108/02610150210787064

CAST (Center for Applied Special Technology). (1998). *What is universal design for learning?* Wakefied, MA: Author. Retrieved from http://www.cast.org/research/udl/index.html

CAST (Center for Applied Special Technology). (2010). *Technologies supporting curriculum access for students with disabilities*. Retrieved from http://www.cast.org/publications/ncac/ncac_techsupport.html

Castellani, J., & Warger, C. (Eds.). (2010). *Accessibility in action: Universal design for learning in postsecondary settings*. TAM Monograph Series.

Center for Universal Design. (1997). *Environments and products for all people*. Raleigh, NC: North Carolina State University, Center for Universal Design.

Davern, L. (1999). Parents' perspectives on personnel attitudes and characteristics in inclusive school settings: Implications for teacher preparations programs. *Teacher Education and Special Education, 22*, 165–182. doi:10.1177/088840649902200304

DiSarno, N., Schowalter, M., & Grassa, P. (2002). Classroom amplification to enhance student performance. *Teaching Exceptional Children, 34*(6), 20–26.

Dymond, S. K., Renzaglia, A., Rosenstein, A., Chun, E. J., Banks, R. A., Niswander, V., & Gilson, C. L. (2006). Using a participatory action research approach to create a universally designed inclusive high school science course: A case study. *Research and Practice for Persons with Severe Disabilities, 31*, 293–308.

Edyburn, D. L. (2006a). Assistive technology and mild disabilities. *Special Education Technology Practice, 8*(4), 18–28.

Edyburn, D. L. (2006b). Failure is not an option. *Learning and Leading with Technology, 34*(1), 20–23.

Fisher, D., Frey, N., & Thousand, J. (2003). What do special educators need to know and be prepared to do for inclusive schooling to work? *Teacher Education and Special Education, 26*(1), 42–50. doi:10.1177/088840640302600105

Freed, G., & Rothberg, M. (2006). *Accessible digital media guidelines*. Retrieved from the http://ncam.wgbh.org/invent_build/web_multimedia/accessible-digital-media-guide

Frey, T. J. (2008). Determining the impact of online practicum facilitation for in-service teachers. *Journal of Technology and Teacher Education, 16*, 181–210.

Hitchcock, C., & Stahl, S. (2004). Assistive technology, universal design, universal design for learning: Improved learning outcomes. *Journal of Special Education Technology, 18*, 45–52.

Hunt, P., & Goetz, L. (1997). Research on inclusive education programs, practices, and outcomes for students with severe disabilities. *The Journal of Special Education, 31*(1), 3–31. doi:10.1177/002246699703100102

Knapczyk, D. R., Hew, K., Frey, T. J., & Wall-Marencik, W. (2005). Evaluation of online mentoring of practicum experiences for limited licensed teachers. *Teacher Education and Special Education, 28*(4), 207–220. .doi:10.1177/088840640502800407

Konrad, M., Joseph, L. M., & Itoi, M. (2011). Using guided notes to enhance instruction for all students. *Intervention in School and Clinic, 46*(3), 131–140. .doi:10.1177/1053451210378163

Kortering, L. J., McClannon, T. W., & Braziel, P. M. (2008). Universal design for learning: A look at what algebra and biology students with and without high incidence conditions are saying. *Remedial and Special Education, 29*, 352–363. .doi:10.1177/0741932507314020

Kurtis, S. A., Matthews, C. E., & Smallwood, T. (2009). (Dis)solving the differences: A physical science lesson using universal design. *Intervention in School and Clinic, 44*, 151–159. doi:10.1177/1053451208326051

Lesar, S., Benner, S. M., Habel, J., & Coleman, L. (1997). Preparing general education teachers for inclusive settings: A constructivist teacher education program. *Teacher Education and Special Education, 20*, 204–220. doi:10.1177/088840649702000303

Marino, M. T., Sameshima, P., & Beecher, C. C. (2009). Enhancing TPACK with assistive technology: Promoting inclusive practices in preservice teacher education. *Contemporary Issues in Technology & Teacher Education, 9*(2). Retrieved from http://www.citejournal.org/vol9/iss2/general/article1.cfm.

Mcguire, J. M., Scott, S. S., & Shaw, S. F. (2006). Universal design and its applications in educational environments. *Remedial and Special Education, 27,* 166–175. doi:10.1177/07419325060270030501

Michael, M. G., & Trezek, B. J. (2006). Universal design and multiple literacies: Creating access and ownership for students with disabilities. *Theory into Practice, 45,* 311–318. doi:10.1207/s15430421tip4504_4

National Council on Disability. (May 31, 2001). *Federal policy barriers to assistive technology.* A report by the National Council. Washington, DC. Retrieved from http://ned.gov.newroom/publications/assistivetechnology/html

National Research Council. (1999). *How people learn: Bridging research and practice* (M. S. Donovan, J. D. Bransford, & J. W. Pellegrino, Eds.). Committee on Learning Research and Educational Practice. Commission on Behavioral and Social Sciences and Education. Washington, DC: National Academy Press.

Office of Special Education Programs. (2006). *26th annual report to Congress on the implementation of the Individual with Disabilities Act, 2004* (Vols. 1, 2). Washington, DC: U.S. Department of Education.

Pintrich, P. R. (2000). Multiple goals, multiple pathways: The role of goal orientation in learning and achievement. *Journal of Educational Psychology, 92*(3), 544–555 .doi:10.1037/0022-0663.92.3.544

Pisha, B., & Coyne, P. (2001). Smart from the start: The promise of universal design for learning. *Remedial and Special Education, 22,* 197–205. doi:10.1177/074193250102200402

Pisha, B., & Stahl, S. (2005). The promise of new learning environments for students with disabilities. *Intervention in School and Clinic, 41,* 67–75. doi:10.1177/10534512050410020601

Rose, D., & Meyer, A. (2000). Universal design for learning. *Journal of Special Education Technology, 15*(1), 67–70.

Rose, D., & Meyer, A. (2002). *Teaching every student in the digital age.* Alexandria, VA: ASCD.

Siegel, L. S. (2003). Basic cognitive processes and reading disabilities. In Swanson, H. L., Harris, K. R., & Graham, S. (Eds.), *Handbook of learning disabilities* (pp. 158–181). New York, NY: Guiliford Press.

The IRIS Center for Preparing Enhancements. (n.d.). *Universal design for learning: Creating a learning environment that challenges and engages all students.* Retrieved from http://iris.peabody.vanderbilt.edu/udl/chalcycle.htm

Tomlinson, C. A. (1995). *How to differentiate instruction in mixed ability classrooms.* Alexandria, VA: ASCD.

Tomlinson, C. A. (1999). *The differentiated classroom: Responding to the needs of all learners.* Alexandria, VA: ASCD.

Van Learhoven, T. R., Munk, D. D., Lynch, K., Bosma, J., & Rouse, J. (2007). A model for preparing special and general education preservice teachers for inclusive education. *Journal of Teacher Education, 58,* 440–455. doi:10.1177/0022487107306803

Vygotsky, L. S. (1978). Interaction between learning and development. In Cole, M., John-Steiner, V., Scribner, S., & Souberman, E. (Eds.), *Mind in society: The development of higher psychological processes.* Cambridge, MA: Harvard University Press.

Wexler, J., Waughn, S., Edmonds, M., & Reutebuch, C. K. (2008). A synthesis of fluency interventions for secondary struggling readers. *Reading and Writing, 21*, 317–347. doi:10.1007/s11145-007-9085-7

Wiggins, G. P., & McTighe, J. (2005). *Understanding by design*. Alexandria, VA: Association for Supervision & Curriculum Development.

KEY TERMS AND DEFINITIONS

Achievement Gap: Generally we would expect students to gain one year of academic achievement for each year they are in school but for many under-achieving students they tend to fall further and further behind the longer they are in school. The achievement gap widens as a factor of time.

Backward Design: An approach to designing instruction with the end in mind. This approach, while seemingly logical, is called backward because many teachers begin their unit design with the means—textbooks, favorite lessons or activities— rather than deriving those from the end—the targeted results such as content standards or understandings. The backward design approach starts with the desired results and then identifies the evidence necessary to determine if the desired results have been achieved.

Guided Notes: Teacher-prepared hand-outs that outline or map lectures, but leave blank spaces for key concepts, facts, definitions, etc.

As the Lecture Progresses: the learner then fills in the spaces with content. Guided notes help lessen the cognitive load of simultaneously listening to the lecture, processing the information and recording notes. Guided notes also make note taking easier or even possible for students who struggle with written language or have motor limitations that might impede on their physical ability to write.

Naked Independence: Naked independence is the idea that knowledge contained in one's head and performance that is completed without the aid of external devices and resources is prized over performance that is dependent on tools or resources. Researchers in assistive technology outcomes have coined this form of bias as "naked independence," as it exults the performance of able-bodied individuals and devalues the performance of others who must rely on external devices or tools.

Online Interactive Learning Modules (OILM): Instructional content delivered via an online portal that provides stand-alone options for user learning, engagement in content, and assessment. OILMs related to teacher education content are often developed by research and technical assistance centers at universities. Still others might be developed by private professional development companies, university faculty and graduates students, or textbook publishers.

Tiered Assignments: Tiered assignments are used to meet the diverse needs of the students within heterogeneous classes. Tiered assignments are parallel tasks at varied levels of complexity, depth and abstractness with various degrees of scaffolding, support, or direction. Students work on different levels of activities, all with the same essential understanding or goal in mind. Tiered assignments accommodate mainly for differences in student readiness and performance levels and allow students to work toward a goal or objective at a level that builds on their prior knowledge and encourages continued growth.

Universal Design for Learning (UDL): A framework for guiding educational practice that: (A) provides flexibility in the ways information is presented, in the ways students respond or demonstrate knowledge and skills, and in the ways students are engaged; and (B) proactively reduces barriers in instruction, provides appropriate accommodations, supports, and challenges, and maintains high achievement expectations for all students, including students with disabilities and students who are limited English proficient.

Chapter 4
Guiding Framework and Principles for Technology Integration:
What Are the Key Questions?

Minchi C. Kim
Purdue University, USA

ABSTRACT

Promoting student utilization of technology has been a challenging and persistent theme in education for the past twenty years. Many teachers find it difficult to interpret and transform their daily routines to incorporate new pedagogies to promote such skills. Given the emergence of new technologies including social network, Web 2.0, simulations and games, and pedagogical frameworks to support learning and teaching with technologies, teachers are expected to use technology not only as an assistive tool to accomplish certain objectives, but also as a well-coordinated stage where students can learn more meaningfully and authentically. The purpose of this chapter is to discuss definitions, frameworks, and examples of technology integration and to elaborate on four key principles of technology integration: authenticity, collaboration, inquiry, and scaffolding.

WHAT IS TECHNOLOGY INTEGRATION?

Promoting student utilization of technology has been a challenging and persistent theme in education for the past twenty years. The National Educational Technology Standards for Students (NETS-S) emphasize the need to prepare students to be able to "learn effectively and live productively in an increasingly digital world" (International Society for Technology in Education, 2008). They describe six areas where students can benefit from utilizing technologies: (1) creativity and innovation; (2) communication and collaboration; (3) research and information fluency; (4) critical thinking, problem solving, and decision making;

DOI: 10.4018/978-1-4666-0014-0.ch004

(5) digital citizenship; and (6) technology operations and concepts.

Many teachers find it difficult, however, to interpret and transform their daily routines to incorporate new pedagogies to promote such skills.. Given the emergence of new technologies, including social networking sites, Web 2.0, simulations and games, and pedagogical frameworks to support learning and teaching with technologies, teachers are expected to use technology not only as an assistive tool to accomplish certain objectives, but also as a well-coordinated stage where students can learn more meaningfully and authentically (Ertmer, 1999; Salomon & Perkins, 1996). It is unclear what support teachers need and what principles teachers need to use in designing and fostering such stages (learning environments) using various technologies. The purpose of this paper is to discuss definitions, frameworks, and examples of technology integration and to elaborate on four key principles of technology integration: authenticity, collaboration, inquiry, and scaffolding.

CONCEPTUALIZATION OF TECHNOLOGY INTEGRATION

Definitions and foci of technology integration vary widely. According to the National Center for Educational Statistics (NCES, 2003), technology integration is defined as "the incorporation of technology resources and technology-based practices into the daily routines, work, and management of schools" (p. 75). This definition underscores the importance of everyday uses of technologies in schools for instruction and administration (NCES, 2003); yet, it does not adequately explain the complexity, dynamics, and questions involved in technology integration, such as how this integration can be accomplished and what learning and teaching activities constitute successful technology integration.

Hew and Brush (2007) define technology integration as "the use of computing devices such as desktop computers, laptops, handheld computers, software, or Internet in K-12 schools for instructional purposes" (p. 225). This definition highlights the goal of technology integration in classroom environments. More precisely, Roblyer and Doering (2010) define integrating educational technology as "the process of determining which electronic tools and which methods for implementing them are the most appropriate responses to given classroom situations and problems" (p. 8). This definition underscores both the use of technology tools and the methods involved in determining optimal instructional practices using them.

Hughes' (2005) classification delineates the three different variations in the pedagogy for technology integration: replacement, amplification, and transformation. Technology may be used to replace existing teaching practices and learning processes as a different medium with the same established goals. Technology may be utilized to amplify what teachers and students have been doing by making the process more effective and efficient (Cuban, 1988). Technology may also transform learning and teaching tasks and routines in a way that incorporates new pedagogies and technological affordances to foster student problem solving.

PROMISES AND PROBLEMS

A vast amount of research has investigated the learning outcomes and processes involved in technology integration in the classroom. Studies have demonstrated the positive impact of technology on students' academic performance when the use of technology is parallel to curriculum objectives and standardized tests (Bain & Ross, 2000). Some researchers have found that technology may enhance student long-term understanding of curriculum (Lehrer, 1993). Research also indicates that the positive influence of technology use may be greater when students work in pairs (Kulik, 2003) or groups (Scardamalia & Bereiter, 1996) for collaborative knowledge building. Technology can also enhance student critical thinking and problem-solving skills by providing an authentic problem context and just-in-time feedback (White & Frederiksen, 1998).

Several challenges have been documented in the design, facilitation, and sustenance of technology-infused curricula. The challenges exist at various levels: (a) personal (teachers' knowledge, skills, experience, attitudes, vision, and beliefs); (b) technological (affordances and constraints of technology tools); (c) pedagogical (learning and teaching tactics to support technology integration); (d) contextual (classroom settings and school environments); and (e) institutional (resources, teacher education, standardized assessments, and national- and state-level standards). Hew & Brush (2007) provide a comprehensive review of the barriers to technology integration and categorize them into the following six areas:

- Resources (lack of technology, lack of access to technology, lack of time, lack of technical support)
- Knowledge and skills (lack of technology skills, lack of technology-supported-pedagogy skills, lack of technology-related-classroom management skills)
- Institution (leadership, time-tabling structure, lack of technology integration plan)
- Attitudes and beliefs
- Assessment
- Subject culture (pp. 233—234)

Expanding on Brickner's (1995) classification of first- and second-order barriers for technology integration, Ertmer (1999) note that second-order barriers, such as teachers' beliefs through web-based resources, are less apparent, more fundamental, and harder to eliminate. Alternatively, first-order barriers, such as resources, time, and support, are extrinsic and relatively easy to adjust.

The second-order barriers may accumulate when new technologies are introduced to teach students higher-order, twenty-first century standards. One way to address this challenge may be to have a clear, meaningful vision of higher levels of technology integration; for instance, students may use technology to make virtual observations of natural phenomena, collect evidence through web-based resources, and formulate their own hypotheses and proposals.

WHAT FRAMEWORKS GUIDE TECHNOLOGY INTEGRATION?

Kim, Hannafin, and Lynn (2007) developed a pedagogical framework for teaching and learning with technology. The framework consists of three levels: macro context (systemic reform, the standards), teacher community (teacher education programs, professional development), and micro context (classroom settings supported by interactions among teachers, students, and tools). In the ideal framework, the innermost frame (classroom) is embedded in a teacher community that is supported by the outermost frame (macro context, systemic reform, the standards). The nested characteristics of the framework imply that effective and meaningful integration of technologies should be supported not only by teachers, but also by teacher education programs that are closely aligned with the national, state, and school district reform initiatives.

When teacher education programs do not support teachers' use of technologies or the programs are not aligned with classroom conditions and broader initiatives, technology integration may remain at the replacement or amplification level (Cuban, Kirkpatrick, & Peck, 2001; Hughes, 2005). Figure 2 illustrates the current state of technology integration, mirroring these potential discrepancies. The next section describes four principles that may be used to guide the transformation of daily teaching routines using technologies and

Figure 1. A pedagogical framework for teaching and learning with inquiry tools: Ideal framework (Kim, Hannafin, & Bryan, 2007)

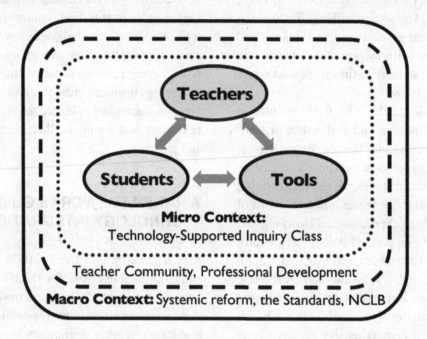

bridge the gap between the ideal framework and the state-of-practice framework.

How Can Teachers Integrate Technology?: Four Principles of Technology Integration

Kim & Freemyer (2011) proposed four principles of technology integration to illustrate how science teachers can effectively utilize technologies in classroom settings. The principles were derived from a pedagogical framework to guide teaching and learning with inquiry tools (Kim, Hannafin, & Bryan, 2007) with a goal of bridging the gap between the ideal framework (Figure 1) and the current state of practice (Figure 2):

- Principle 1: Authenticity—Revolve Around Authentic Real-World Situations
- Principle 2: Inquiry--Facilitate Development of Inquiry Skills

- Principle 3: Scaffolding—Utilize Scaffolding to Maximize Effectiveness
- Principle 4: Collaboration—Abound with Collaboration (Kim & Freemyer, 2011)

Figure 3 represents examples of teaching and learning practice that are aligned with each principle at the macro context, teacher community, and micro context levels. This chapter discusses each principle, providing definitions, key aspects, examples, and implications for teacher education programs.

Authenticity

The term "authenticity" has been widely used among educators, although its concept is still ambiguous to most practitioners. Shaffer and Resnick (2009) describe four types of authentic learning::

- Learning that is personally meaningful for the learner

Figure 2. A pedagogical framework for teaching and learning with inquiry tools: State of practice framework (Kim, Hannafin, & Bryan, 2007)

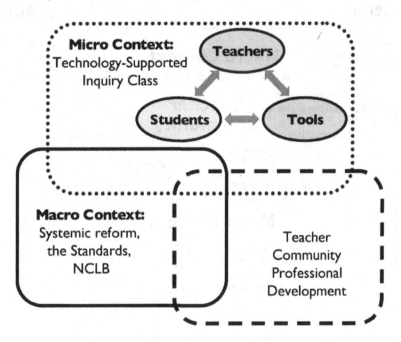

- Learning that relates to the real-world outside of school
- Learning that provides an opportunity to think in the modes of a particular discipline, and
- Learning where the means of assessment reflect the learning process (p. 195).

The principle of authenticity for technology integration refers to the use of technology to increase the authenticity of student learning experiences, fostering a dynamic interaction between learners, tasks, and the learning environment. Students can engage in personally meaningful, real-world problems that require complex, ill-defined, and multiple ways of solving. While students solve the problems, authenticity can be found "not in the learner, the task, or the environment, but in the dynamic interactions among these various components" (Barab, Squire, & Dueber, 2000, p. 38). Students may also have ample opportunities to reflect upon their learning process through

formative assessment imbedded in the learning environment (Means, 2006).

The national standards for mathematics and science underscore the authentic aspect of student learning. The National Science Education Standards (National Research Council, 1996) suggest that students need to learn in a way scientists actually carry out their scientific research through authentic scientific inquiry. The National Council of Teachers of Mathematics (NCTM) suggests that students should explore problems situated in authentic settings to enhance their understanding of data analysis:

A natural link exists between data analysis in statistics and algebra. Students' understanding of graphs and functions can both enhance and be enhanced by tackling problems that involve data analysis and statistics in authentic situations (NCTM, 2009, p. 5).

Figure 3. Four principles of technology integration (Kim & Freemyer, 2011)

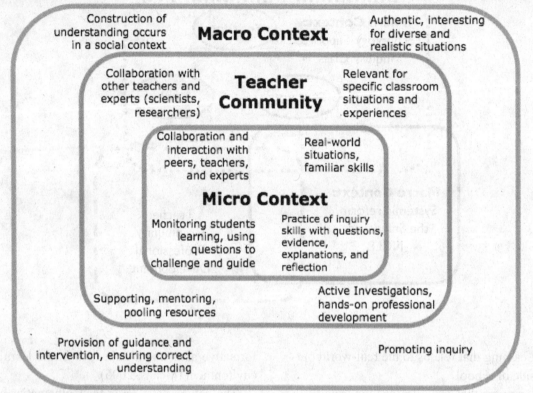

The central advantage of this approach, grounded in situated cognition (Brown, Collins, & Duguid, 1989; Lave & Wenger, 1991), is to immerse students in an environment that is similar to the real world so that students can relate their learning context to everyday experience. Technology serves as a tool to provide and facilitate such environments. For instance, students can use an interactive videodisc to understand and solve a real-life math problem. Through this approach, called anchored instruction, students use stories found on the videodisc as anchors to find clues and problem-solving paths (Bransford et al., 1990). Then, how can teachers design an authentic learning environment for classroom teaching? What

are the critical concerns? These two issues are discussed in more detail.

First, teachers need to actually experience learning through authentic learning activities. To many teachers, the concept of authenticity is still new somewhat nebulous. Teacher education programs may incorporate learning activities that mirror teachers everyday experience using the following guidelines (Reeves, Herrington, & Oliver, 2002):

- *Authentic activities have real world relevance.*
- *Authentic activities are ill-defined, requiring students to define the tasks and subtasks needed to complete the activity.*

- *Authentic activities comprise complex tasks to be investigated by students over a sustained period of time.*
- *Authentic activities provide the opportunity for students to examine the task from different perspectives, using a variety of resources.*
- *Authentic activities provide the opportunity to collaborate.*
- *Authentic activities provide the opportunity to reflect.*
- *Authentic activities can be integrated and applied across different subject areas and lead beyond domain specific outcomes.*
- *Authentic activities are seamlessly integrated with assessment.*
- *Authentic activities create polished products valuable in their own right rather than as preparation for something else.*
- *Authentic activities allow competing solutions and diversity of outcome* (pp. 564).

Second, the issue of how to align authentic learning activities to existing assessments (such as standardized tests with multiple-choice items) remains challenging and critical to many teachers and teacher educators. In contrast to traditional assessment that emphasizes the summative aspect of evaluation, authentic assessment focuses on the formative, developmental nature of learning and evaluating. According to the National Science Education Standards (National Research Council, 1996), authentic assessment activities "require students to apply scientific knowledge and reasoning to situations similar to those they will encounter in the world outside the classroom, as well as to situations that approximate how scientists do their work" (p. 78).

Teacher communities and professional development programs can design and incorporate new ways of linking assessment items to student ways of learning; so that students can learn which taking tests through contextualized questions and process-oriented feedback. Teachers may also use other forms of assessment portfolio, exhibition, performance tasks, self-evaluation, and electronic journals (Ertmer, 1999).

Inquiry

Dewey (1938) viewed inquiry as a logical process of transforming an "indeterminate situation" that is perceived as problematic into "one that is so determinate in its constituent distinctions and relations" (pp. 104-105). He also characterized inquiry as a problem-solving process, "a progressive determination of a problem and its possible solution" (p. 110) that involves myriad skills such as observation, prediction, examination, and reasoning. Similarly, in science classrooms, scientific inquiry refers to a scientific way of investigating natural phenomena that requires multifaceted activities including making observations, generating hypotheses, collecting and analyzing data, making a prediction, drawing a conclusion, and communicating the results with others (National Research Council, 1996). Scientific inquiry is considered to be an essential way to help students become scientifically literate (American Association for the Advancement of Science, 1993; National Research Council, 1996).

In contrast to traditional teacher-centered instruction, this inquiry approach is rooted in constructivism, which asserts that learning occurs when students build their own understanding in meaningful ways, such as through engaging in hands-on activities, reflecting, and learning by doing. In such learning environments, teachers serve as facilitators of student learning rather than simply providers of knowledge. In a year-long study involving the observation of a science teacher, Crawford (2000) identified ten roles that are required for teachers to successfully facilitate inquiry classrooms: motivator, diagnostician, guide, innovator, experimenter, researcher, modeler, mentor, collaborator, and learner. As illustrated in Figure 4, Crawford concluded that teachers' levels of involvement in student learning

Figure 4. Level of teacher involvement in different instructional modes (Crawford, 2000)

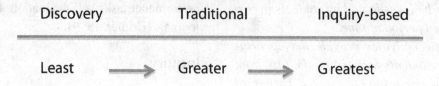

are greater in inquiry classrooms than in discovery or traditional classes because facilitation of inquiry learning necessitates clear understanding of student progress, needs, and learning contexts.

Dewey also recognized the teachers role as facilitator, guide, and partner in student learning helping students construct their own meaning of new knowledge (1897):

The teacher is not in the school to impose certain ideas or to form certain habits in the child, but is there as a member of the community to select the influences which shall affect the child and to assist him in properly responding to these influences (pp. 9).

The underlying premises of inquiry learning, necessary support, and new roles for teachers should be introduced in teacher education programs. It is also imperative that teacher educators be capable of utilizing technologies to assist students in engaging inquiry and teachers in facilitating the process in multiple ways. For example, technology can provide a learning context and structure that students need to conduct inquiry. In the WISE (Web-based Inquiry Science Learning Environments) projects, developed by the University of California-Berkeley, students utilize a scaffolded inquiry process to identify, investigate, and solve scientific problems; reflect on their inquiry process by writing journals; and share the results with peers and teachers (Linn, 2006). Teachers should not only learn how to perform

inquiry, but also how to facilitate it. WISE also supports teacher communities where teachers can learn inquiry and inquiry teaching by reviewing examples of science research and teaching.

Scaffolding

A scaffold refers to any "assistance from a more knowledgeable person that helps learners to do a learning task beyond their capability" (Kim & Hannafin, 2011, p. 407). Scaffolding has been studied in various domains (literacy, science, mathematics) and has been found to foster student problem solving and critical thinking. When integrated into technology-enhanced learning environments in various forms, such as prompts, models, and visualizations, scaffolding can be effective and powerful in supporting student sense-making (Quintana et al., 2004), task problematization (Reiser, 2004), visualization and representations of knowledge (Linn, Clark, & Slotta, 2003), and construction of arguments and explanations (Aleven & Koedinger, 2002). Technologies can also provide an environment where highly calibrated, interactive scaffolds enable students to successfully solve problems and attain specific competencies.

Research has identified four types and goals of scaffolds (Kim & Hannafin, 2007): (a) conceptual scaffolds to guide student understanding of content (e.g., What is the relationship between these two variables in this mathematical model?); (b) metacognitive scaffolds to help students monitor their thinking and learning (e.g., What relevant experience do I have to apply this computational model to everyday life?); (c) procedural scaffolds to assist students in determining steps and activities necessary for inquiry, modeling, and problem solving (e.g., How can I find evidence for complex systems in the model?); and (d) strategic scaffolds to identify alternate ways of investing and understanding models (e.g., What would other engineers have done to generate an energy saving plan in this city?).

What are the implications of research on scaffolding for teachers and teacher educators? Two issues are pertinent to teacher education programs. First, teacher education programs including pre-service teacher education, teacher induction, and professional development programs for in-service teachers need to integrate the emergent, synergistic, and holistic views on scaffolding student learning in classroom environments. Traditionally, teachers were taught to implement technologies without much transformation of pedagogies and deliberation of dynamic interactions among diverse factors that influence student learning in the classroom. Teachers and technologies scaffolded student activities by providing structures and guidance in an explicit and linear manner.

However, promoting student problem solving in a classroom environment is an extremely complex exercise because it requires a careful coordination of multiple sources of support in response to student needs and progress, teacher knowledge, skills, and beliefs, technological affordances and other available resources and time. Tabak (2004) introduced the concept of synergistic scaffolds to denote the interactive nature of scaffolds:

For example, scaffolds that constrain students to vary-one-variable-at-a-time do not guarantee that students understand the utility of this method or that they are able to integrate it with the explanatory demands of the discipline. Yet, if these types of scaffolds are augmented with additional supports, particularly the flexible, dynamic, or just-in-time

support of the teacher so that the teacher and software work in concert, it increases the likelihood that these supports will be understood and effectively used (p. 320).

Second, teacher education programs need to provide concrete models of scaffolding that are situated in specific learning tasks and problems. Scaffolding can be more powerful and effective when it is tied into learning contexts and tasks. In each domain of learning and teaching, more examples are needed to clearly show what constitutes good teaching and scaffolding when technologies are being used.

Collaboration

The concept of collaboration has been accepted as being a constructive way of learning and building knowledge. Collaborative learning emphasizes students acting together, whereas cooperative learning implies partners splitting the tasks and individually working on sub-tasks (Dillenbourg, 1999). When students collaborate, they act as members of a group and learn how to present, negotiate, and justify ideas (National Research Council, 1996). Students can engage in knowledge-building activities through collaboration (Scardamalia & Bereiter, 2006). Students may develop higher-order thinking skills when working collaboratively in groups to solve problems with computers (Brush, 1997). Student's motivation may be enhanced through collaboration (Blumenfeld, Kempler, & Krajcik, 2006).

Various types of technology-enhanced learning environments have been developed to promote student collaboration. For instance, Knowledge Forum, the next generation of CSILE (Computer-Supported Intentional Learning to Knowledge-Building Environments), is an online, community-oriented environment where users can visualize an organization of certain concepts through concept maps, pictures, and diagrams and make contributions to change the hierarchy and its contents (Scardamalia & Bereiter, 2006). The design of this environment was based upon the following beliefs about knowledge-building as a learning practice:

- Knowledge advancement as a community rather than individual achievement
- Knowledge advancement as idea improvement rather than as progress toward true or warranted belief
- Knowledge *of* in contrast to knowledge *about*
- Discourse as collaborative problem solving rather than as argumentation (pp. 98)

However, teacher education programs and support are rarely rooted in a theoretical and pragmatic understanding about how teachers learn and grow. Moreover, there has been a disjunction between teacher preparation programs provided at the university level and professional development at the school districts and state levels. Feiman-Nemser (2001) delineated three phases of teaching profession from professional lifelong- learning continuum: preservice teachers' preparation, new teachers' induction into teaching, and inservice teachers' lifelong learning through their profession. One way to address the aforementioned gap is to promote collaboration and mentoring among pre-service teachers, new teachers, and experienced teachers. For instance, the Learning to Teach with Technology Studio (LTTS) project (http://ltts.indiana.edu/) allows teachers to take self-paced modules and receive individual feedback from experienced teachers (mentors).

Teacher education programs can also incorporate emergent technologies such as social networking sites and Web 2.0 to facilitate interaction between teachers. Blogs have been found effective for teachers to share their teaching practices. Luehmann (2008) studied one urban middle school science teacher, Ms. Frizzle and her exceptional blog as a professional community.

Ms. Frizzle used her blog to "tell stories of herself and her classroom, reflect on her practice, work through dilemmas, solicit feedback, and display competence, among other things" (Luehmann, 2008, p. 287), as well as to interact with five different groups of people: mentees (new teachers to whom Ms. Frizzle provided mentoring through the blog), "real" people (her colleagues and friends), experienced professionals (teachers with more experience that Ms. Frizzle seeks help), issue people (people whose resources and blogs are referenced in Ms. Frizzle's blog), and the unknowns (people that read her blog without leaving comments). It is important to note that the mentees (new teachers) were the most actively participating in the blogs to find examples and answers to the issues with which they were tackling. Clearly, teachers need more support for mentoring and coaching as they continue a teaching profession as a lifelong learner.

CONCLUSION

This chapter examined technology integration, from a synergistic standpoint, to incorporate the dynamic nature of multiple interactions among students, teachers, technology tools, teacher education programs, teacher communities, and the national standards. The four principles of authenticity, inquiry, scaffolding, and collaboration stress the importance of aligning various levels of technology-enhanced curricular design, enactment, and support. More research is warranted to further investigate the interactions and coordination between and within the three levels of micro context, teacher community, and macro context..

REFERENCES

American Association for the Advancement of Science. (1993). *Benchmarks for science literacy*. New York, NY: Oxford University Press.

Bain, A., & Ross, K. (2000). School reengineering and SAT-1 performance: A case study. *International Journal of Educational Reform, 9*(2), 148–153.

Barab, S. A., Squire, K. D., & Dueber, W. (2000). A co-evolutionary model for supporting the emergence of authenticity. *Educational Technology Research and Development, 48*(2), 37–62. doi:10.1007/BF02313400

Blumenfeld, P. C., Kempler, T. M., & Krajcik, J. S. (2006). Motivation and cognitive engagement in learning environments. In Sawyer, K. (Ed.), *The Cambridge handbook of the learning sciences* (pp. 475–488). New York, NY: Cambridge University Press.

Brush, T. A. (1997). The effects on student achievement and attitudes when using integrated learning systems with cooperative pairs. *Educational Technology Research and Development, 45*(1), 51–64. doi:10.1007/BF02299612

Cuban, L., Kirkpatrick, H., & Peck, C. (2001). High access and low use of technologies in high school classrooms. *American Educational Research Journal, 38*(4), 813–834. doi:10.3102/00028312038004813

Dewey, J. (1897). My pedagogic creed. *School Journal, 54*, 77–80.

Dewey, J. (1991). *Logic: The theory of inquiry*. Carbondale, IL: Southern Illinois University Press.

Dillenbourg, P. (1999). What do you mean by collaborative learning? In Dillenbourg, P. (Ed.), *Collaborative-learning: Cognitive and computational approaches* (pp. 1–19). Oxford, UK: Elsevier.

Feiman-Nemser, S. (2001). From preparation to practice: Designing a continuum to strengthen and sustain teaching. *Teachers College Record, 103*(6), 1013–1055. doi:10.1111/0161-4681.00141

Hughes, J. (2005). The role of teacher knowledge and learning experiences in forming technology-integrated pedagogy. *Journal of Technology and Teacher Education, 13*(2), 277–302.

Kim, M. C., & Freemyer, S. (2011). Technology integration in science classrooms: Framework, principles, and examples. *Educational Technology, 51*(1), 25–29.

Kim, M. C., & Hannafin, M. J. (2007). Foundations and practice for Web-enhanced science inquiry: Grounded design perspectives. In Luppicini, R. (Ed.), *Online learning communities: A volume in perspectives in instructional technology and distance education* (pp. 53–72). Greenwich, CT: Information Age Publishing.

Kim, M. C., & Hannafin, M. J. (2011). Scaffolding problem solving in technology-enhanced learning environments (TELEs): Bridging research and theory with practice. Computers & Education, 56(2), 403-417.

Kim, M. C., Hannafin, M. J., & Bryan, L. A. (2007). Technology-enhanced inquiry tools in science education: An emerging pedagogical framework for classroom practice. *Science Education, 91*(6), 1010–1030. doi:10.1002/sce.20219

Kulik, J. (2003). *Effects of using instructional technology in elementary and secondary schools: What controlled evaluation studies say*. Arlington, VA: SRI International. Retrieved February, 2011 from http://www.sri.com/policy/csted/reports/sandt/it/Kulik_ITinK-12_Main_Report.pdf

Lehrer, R. (1993). Authors of knowledge: Patterns of hypermedia design. In Lajoie, S. P., & Derry, S. J. (Eds.), *Computers as cognitive tools*. Hillsdale, NJ: Lawrence Erlbaum.

Linn, M. C. (2006). The knowledge integration perspective on learning and instruction. In Sawyer, R. K. (Ed.), *The Cambridge handbook of the learning sciences* (pp. 243–264). New York, NY: Cambridge University Press.

Luehmann, A. L. (2008). Using blogging in support of teacher professional identity development: A case-study. *Journal of the Learning Sciences, 17*(3), 287–337. doi:10.1080/10508400802192706

National Research Council. (1996). *National science education standards: Observe, interact, change, learn.* Washington, DC: National Academy Press.

Reeves, T. C., Herrington, J., & Oliver, R. (2002). Authentic activities and online learning. In Goody, A., Herrington, J., & Northcote, M. (Eds.), *Quality conversations: Research and development in higher education* (*Vol. 25*, pp. 562–567). Jamison, Australia: HERDSA.

Scardamalia, M., & Bereiter, C. (1996). Computer support for knowledge-building communities. In Kotchmann, T. (Ed.), *CSCL: Theory and practice of an emerging paradigm.* Mahwah, NJ: Lawrence Erlbaum Associates.

Scardamalia, M., & Bereiter, C. (2006). Knowledge building: Theory, pedagogy, and technology. In Sawyer, K. (Ed.), *Cambridge handbook of the learning sciences* (pp. 97–118). New York, NY: Cambridge University Press.

Shaffer, D. W., & Resnick, M. (1999). Thick authenticity: New media and authentic learning. *Journal of Interactive Learning Research, 10*(2), 195–215.

Tabak, I. (2004). Synergy: A complement to emerging patterns of distributed scaffolding. *Journal of the Learning Sciences, 13*(3), 305–335. doi:10.1207/s15327809jls1303_3

The National Council of Teachers of Mathematics. (2009). *Guiding principles for mathematics curriculum and assessment.* Retrieved February, 2011 from http://www.nctm.org/standards/content.aspx?id=23273

White, B. Y., & Frederiksen, J. R. (1998). Inquiry, modeling, and metacognition: Making science accessible to all students. *Cognition and Instruction, 16*(1), 3–188. doi:10.1207/s1532690xci1601_2

Section 2
Integration of Web 2.0 Tools into Teacher Education Programs

Chapter 5
A Framework for Developing Pre-Service Teachers' Web 2.0 Learning Design Capabilities

Matt Bower
Macquarie University, Australia

ABSTRACT

This chapter presents and evaluates a Web 2.0 Learning Design Framework that can be used to develop pre-service teachers' learning design capabilities. The framework integrates the TPACK model of educational practice, Anderson and Krathwohl's Taxonomy of learning, teaching and assessing, and different types of constructive and negotiated pedagogies, with a range of contemporary Web 2.0 based learning technologies. Pre-service teachers in a second year learning technology subject felt that the framework helped them to better understand the relationship between technology, pedagogy, and content, as well as create more effective learning designs for their students. Examples of student learning designs are used to illustrate the way that pre-service teachers applied the framework. Students' reflective responses to the framework are also used to explain how the Web 2.0 Learning Design Framework can be more effectively used to develop pre-service teachers' Web 2.0 learning design capabilities.

INTRODUCTION

21st Century Skills as an Imperative for Students and Teachers

A growing number of business leaders, politicians, and educators agree that students will need '21st Century skills' to be successful in our world of tomorrow (AACTE & P21, 2010; ISTE, P21, & SEDTA, 2008; Rotherham & Willingham, 2009). Twenty-First Century Skills include problem solving, communication, collaboration, information and media literacy, critical thinking, and creativity (Lambert & Gong, 2010).

A perceived discord between the future skills required of students and the current practices of many teachers has led to governmental calls for a revolutionary change of University-based teacher preparations programs (Duncan, 2010). Teacher education programs have been criticized for no

DOI: 10.4018/978-1-4666-0014-0.ch005

longer providing prospective teachers with the skills for teaching students to survive in today's workplace (UNESCO, 2008). U.S. Department of Commerce statistics show that education is the least technology-intensive field among fifty-five U.S. industry sectors (ISTE, et al., 2008).

A vision of 21st century knowledge and skills for all students requires that educators are supported to master competencies that ensure positive learning outcomes for students, including the ability to appropriately integrate technologies to support learning and teaching (AACTE & P21, 2010). In order for students to develop 21st Century skills it is critical that our teachers possess these skills themselves (Rotherham & Willingham, 2009). Teacher education programs should provide technology-rich experiences throughout all aspects of the curriculum (UNESCO, 2008). While it is assumed by some that pre-service teachers who have recently graduated from school will automatically possess technology capabilities, research has shown that their knowledge of contemporary technologies is often limited to surface understandings and in many cases does not extend to how technology can and should be used for learning and teaching purposes (Lei, 2009).

Web 2.0 as a Potential Driver of Educational Reform

Part of modernizing the pre-service teacher education curriculum involves preparing teachers to effectively utilize Web 2.0 tools in the classroom (Albion, 2008). In the past the education profession has struggled to integrate technology into learning and teaching, generally having a narrow conception of how technology can be used (ISTE, et al., 2008). Web 2.0 technologies are a new range of open online technologies that support collaboration and sharing of content through sophisticated yet easy to use interfaces (Alexander, 2006). Web 2.0 platforms enable user-initiated publishing of information, social networking to take place, and online communities to be formed

around specific content (Rosen & Nelson, 2008). In education, Web 2.0 technologies provide the potential for seamless transfer of information, collaborative as well as individualized learning, and active participation by all members of a class (Richardson, 2006).

Requiring teachers to consider pedagogy in the context of new and emerging technologies provides a significant driver of change in educational systems (Attwell, 2007). Rosen & Nelson (2008) present a vision of 'Education 2.0' where digital tools "transform teaching and learning by having learners, as well as teachers, participate in knowledge creation and interactively build distributed communities, or networks, of learning" (p. 221). A central challenge for teacher educators is how to integrate Web 2.0 into the pre-service teacher curriculum in ways that enable teachers of the future to successfully leverage such technologies in their classes (Voithofer, 2007). Effectively utilization of Web 2.0 technologies requires an seismic epistemological shift – a transformation in our understanding of how people come to know (Eijkman, 2010). Without adequate frameworks to support their thinking and practice, beginning teachers often struggle to make more than superficial use of online technologies (Moore & Chae, 2007).

There have been some examples of education courses that require students to design using a range of Web 2.0 technologies (Lambert & Gong, 2010; Oliver, 2007). As well, He and Hartley (2010) have provided a range of online tools that can support Web 2.0 use by teachers. When attempting to integrate technology into the classroom, pre-service teachers often focus too heavily on the mechanics of learning new technologies at the expense of their strategic pedagogical thinking (Marra, 2004). Yet none of these approaches to embedding Web 2.0 in education courses provide an overarching framework to help students conceptualize Web 2.0 technologies and cope with the massive and ever-evolving nature of the field.

One frame of reference for considering the integration of technology into learning and teaching is the field of Learning Design. The term 'learning design' has been defined as "the process of designing effective learning experiences [by using] a wide set of knowledge, skills and competencies, including: learning theory and its applications, course design principles and procedures, use of media, [and] use of different technologies" (MacLean & Scott, 2007). Several general frameworks have been developed to support learning design (Barker, 2008; Brown & Voltz, 2005; Conole, Dyke, Oliver, & Seale, 2004; Diego, et al., 2008; Donald, Blake, Girault, Datt, & Ramsay, 2009; Tsoi, Goh, & Chia, 2005) but none of these have attempted to conceptualize the wide range of technologies at teachers' disposal and none have been specifically designed for Web 2.0.

This chapter reports on pre-service teachers' perceptions of an integrated framework for conceptualizing and performing Web 2.0 learning design. The framework is based upon the TPACK model of educational practice (Mishra & Koehler, 2006), Anderson and Krathwohl's (2001) Taxonomy of Learning, Teaching and Assessing as well as different types of negotiated and productive pedagogies. The Web 2.0 Learning Design Framework has been presented in earlier work (Bower, Hedberg, & Kuswara, 2010), and is summarized below for completeness.

THE WEB 2.0 LEARNING DESIGN FRAMEWORK

The Web 2.0 Learning Design Framework is based upon Mishra & Koehlers' (2006) Technological Pedagogical and Content Knowledge (TPACK) model of teacher professional practice. The TPACK model highlights the need for teachers to possess Technological Knowledge, Pedagogical Knowledge and Content Knowledge when designing and implementing learning experiences, and proposes that effective integration of technology

into the curriculum requires a synergistic understanding of the relationship between all three components (Koehler & Mishra, 2009). This is represented diagrammatically in Figure 1.

A range of work has been undertaken to investigate how to develop teachers' TPACK knowledge (for instance Chai, Koh, & Tsai, 2010), and the preparedness of pre-service teachers for this endeavor (Jamieson-Proctor, Finger, & Albion, 2010). Instruments and approaches have also been developed to measure TPACK of educators (Groth, Spickler, Bergner, & Bardzell, 2009; Schmidt, et al., 2009). For further discussions of epistemological and methodological issues relating to the used and development of TPACK, see Angeli & Valanides (2009).

The three dimensions of the TPACK model are represented in the Web 2.0 Learning Design Frameworkas follows:

- the **content** is the discipline knowledge and thinking that the learning design will address
- the **pedagogies** are the types of learning approaches that the task attempts to engage (according to their intended level of narrative and construction), and
- the **technologies** are the Web 2.0 tools at the teachers' disposal.

The models used to conceptualize these dimensions are explained below.

Content and their Tasks

Anderson and Krathwohl's (2001) Taxonomy of Learning, Teaching and Assessing provides a general framework for conceptualizing the sort of content that learning designs may address. It incorporates two dimensions; a Knowledge dimension and Cognitive Process dimension. The Knowledge dimension of Anderson and Krathwohl's (2001) Taxonomy relate to the sorts

Figure 1. The TPACK model of educational practice

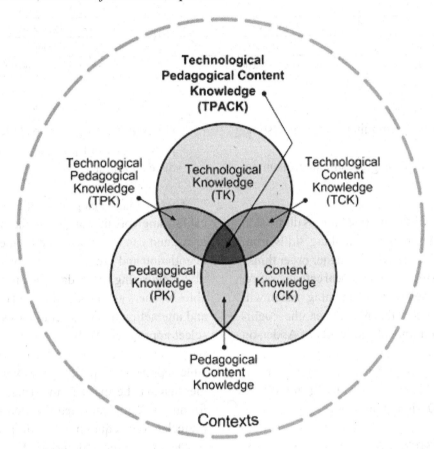

of subject matter content being addressed, either (Anderson & Krathwohl, 2001, pp. 27-29):

1. *Factual knowledge* – discrete pieces of elementary information underpinning a learning domain
2. *Conceptual knowledge* – interrelated items of information, including schemas, categorization hierarchies, and explanations
3. *Procedural knowledge* – the skills to perform processes, to execute heuristics and to know the criteria for their appropriate application
4. *Metacognitive knowledge* – awareness of one's own cognition and how it can be improved.

Whereas the knowledge types provide a means of describing the sort of information that is the focus of learning in a particular discipline area, the Cognitive Process dimension of Anderson and Krathwohl's (2001) model relates to the type of thinking engendered. The levels include (Anderson & Krathwohl, 2001, pp. 67-68):

1. *Remembering* – recognising, recalling, identifying, retrieving
2. *Understanding* – interpreting, summarising, inferring, explaining
3. *Applying* – implementing, carrying out, using, executing
4. *Analysing* – organising, deconstructing, attributing, structuring

Table 1. Pedagogies categorised according to their degree of negotiation and production

	Non-Negotiated	**Negotiated**
No product	Transmissive	Dialogic
Product	Constructionist	Co-constructionist

5. *Evaluating* – critiquing, judging, testing, checking
6. *Creating* – designing, constructing, planning, producing.

The levels of the Cognitive Process dimension represents a continuum of thinking skills from lower order thinking skills to higher order thinking skills, and offers a hierarchical categorization of the type of thinking that a learning design will attempt to engage. Taken together, the cognitive process and knowledge levels of Anderson & Krathwohls' (2001) Taxonomy provide an interdisciplinary array for defining the focus of learning tasks being designed using in the Web 2.0 Learning Design Framework.

Online Pedagogies

For the purposes of conceptualizing the types of pedagogies that may be applied using Web 2.0 technologies, four different possibilities were identified for the Web 2.0 Learning Design Framework:

- **Transmissive** – transmission-based information delivery approaches, where a stream of information is broadcast to learners
- **Dialogic** – centred on discourse between participants, and often involving exemplars followed by periods of activity and feedback
- **Constructionist** – where learning occurs by developing a product

- **Co-constructive** – groups of learners complete a series of goal-related tasks to produce an artefact.

These pedagogies provide a generally applicable framework that can be used across discipline areas, and can be categorized by their degree of negotiation and production as shown in Table 1.

Categorizing the pedagogies in this way enables teachers to consider the level of production and interaction that they require of students, and select appropriate Web 2.0 tools accordingly. It is acknowledged that this is but one of many possible approaches to defining the range of pedagogies that may be applied – the critical point is that for any pedagogical categorization that is used, the technology requirements of the pedagogy help teachers select the appropriate Web 2.0 tools.

Web 2.0 Technologies

The range of Web 2.0 technologies at educators' disposal is ever-expanding and practically impossible to categorize. While not claiming to be exhaustive, Table 2 below attempts to provide a summary of types of Web 2.0 technologies currently available and the potential they afford for representing content and facilitating collaboration.

Distinguishing characteristics of these tools are the modalities of representation (text, image, audio, video) that they incorporate and the degree of synchronicity they enable. More detailed descriptions of the categories of Web 2.0 tools and their instances can be found in Bower et al (2010).

Table 2. Types of Web 2.0 tools and example instances

Type	Description	Examples
Social Bookmarking	Site that allows users to save and share bookmarked websites online	http://delicious.com http://diigo.com
Wikis	Website that authorized can edit using a standard web-browser	http://pbworks.com http://wikispaces.com
Shared document creation	Tool that allows groups to collaboratively author a document (such as MS Word) through a browser	http://docs.google.com http://makebook.com.au
Blogs	A website that organizes the posts of individuals or groups in chronological order	http://edublogs.org http://wordpress.com
Microblogging	A synchronous tool that allows instant upload and sharing short pieces of information	http://twitter.com http://plurk.com
Presentation tools	Web based tools that enable composition and sharing of presentations through a web-browser	http://prezi.com http://authorstream.com
Image creation and editing	Browser-based tools for image creation and editing, in some cases collaborative using whiteboards	http://www.pixlr.com/editor http://www.scribblar.com
Podcasting sites	Sites that enable the upload and sharing of audio recordings that can be played through a browser	http://voicethread.com http://voxopop.com
Video editing and sharing	Sites that enable video editing (sometimes collaborative) and dissemination	http://jaycut.com http://www.shwup.com
Screen recording	Tools that allow users to record (and often share) computing operations and instructions	http://screenr.com http://jingproject.com
Mindmapping	Browser-based mindmapping tools, often facilitating collaborative representation	http://mind42.com http://mindmeister.com
Digital storytelling	Sites that enable users to create and share stories (often animated) online	http://xtranormal.com http://goanimate.com

Applying the Web 2.0 Learning Design Framework

The Web 2.0 Learning Design Framework encourages teachers pre-identify the type of content being addressed and pedagogical approach that will be applied so that they may select appropriate Web 2.0 tools for their learning designs. The type of content being examined will often influence the modality of representation (for instance video for an Understanding-Procedural Knowledge task) and the type of pedagogy may influence the degree of collaboration required by the Web 2.0 tools. Examples learning designs that utilize Web 2.0 technologies are presented Table 3.

Anderson and Krathwohl's (2001) Taxonomy has been used to organize the different types of knowledge and cognitive processes that can be addressed using Web 2.0 tools. Abbreviations have been used to indicate whether the nature of the learning design is more transmissive (T), dialogic (D), constructionist (C) or co-constructive (CC).

Critically for teachers, Table 3 demonstrates how different Web 2.0 technologies are selected to match the type of content being addressed and the pedagogies being applied, based on the affordances of the tools. For instance, microblogging supports sharing of factual knowledge, wikis are suitable for conceptual knowledge, desktop sharing enables the exchange of procedural knowledge, and blogs and mindmaps facilitate representation of metacognitive knowledge. Some Web 2.0 tools are designed more for creation by single users and thus may be more appropriate for constructive pedagogies (such as creating an illustration

Table 3. A framework of Web 2.0 learning designs (Bower et al, 2010)

Knowledge Dimension	Cognitive Process Dimension					
	Remember	**Understand**	**Apply**	**Analyze**	**Evaluate**	**Create**
Factual Knowledge	**Microblogging** – document and share new items of factual knowledge with a group as they come to hand (D).	**Social bookmarking** – bookmark with facts relevant to a certain topic (D). **Podcasting** – provide definitions of terms on an audio discussion board (D).	**Image creation** – construct an image that represents or describes an item of knowledge (C).	**Wikis** – analyze the definitions provided by peers and provide them with constructive comments on how to improve (D).	**Social bookmarking** – post comments evaluating the quality of factual information saved to the group social bookmarking site (D). **Blogs** – evaluate the factual quality of information on peer blogs and post constructive feedback (D).	**Image creation** – use a collaborative whiteboarding tool to create new definitions for an area of innovation being considered (CC).
Conceptual Knowledge	**Wikis** – identify the main concepts relevant to the topic on the wiki (C). **Image creation** – draw an image to represent a concept or set of concepts (C). **Podcasting** – listen to a podcast of a lecture and attempt to recall the main concepts (T).	**Blogs** – explain the concepts and issues of a topic as they arise (C). **Presentation tools** – represent and present the knowledge and relationships of a conceptual domain (C). **Wikis** – explain a set of concepts on a wiki (C). **Mindmaps** – draw a mindmap representation of a concept or domain (C).	**Digital storytelling** – create a story that exemplifies/applies a concept (C). **Video** – create a video that applies the concepts you have learnt to a concrete situation (C).	**Wikis** – construct/adjust a knowledge network so that it appropriately interrelates concepts (C). **Podcasts** – collaboratively analyze an image or artifact using Voicethread (D).	**Wiki** – evaluate the quality of peer conceptual explanations and make alterations/suggestions as appropriate (CC). **Blog** – evaluate the conceptual quality of peers based on their blog postings and provide them with constructive feedback (CC).	**Shared document creation** – collaboratively construct a report/campaign that addresses the key issues of a topic of study (CC). **Mindmaps** – demonstrate a new conceptual understanding or innovation using a mindmap (C).
Procedural Knowledge	**Video** – watch a video of a process and recall the key stages (T). **Podcasting** – create a podcast describing a process that has been observed (C).	**Podcasting** – describe to your peers on Voxopop about the best way to perform a process and then provide constructive feedback to one another (D). **Digital storytelling** – observe an online storyboard and be able to explain the reasons for the processes' sequence of stages (T).	**Blogs** – create a portfolio explaining stages of a products development (C). **Desktop recording** – create a desktop recording that demonstrates how to perform an IT process (C). **Video** – create a video that demonstrates the application of a kinaesthetic process (C).	**Video** – analyze the way in which peers/self performs a process by posting comments on the video page (D).	**Blogs** – evaluate the production process that peers have described and post constructive feedback (D). **Desktop recording** – evaluate the efficiency of peer/self IT process (C). **Video** – evaluate performance of a kinaesthetic process and provide constructive feedback (D).	**Image creation** – draw a flowchart to explain a new process (C).

Table 3. continued on following page

Table 3. continued

Knowledge Dimension	Cognitive Process Dimension					
	Remember	**Understand**	**Apply**	**Analyze**	**Evaluate**	**Create**
Metacognitive Knowledge	**Mindmaps** – describe own cognition using a mindmap (C).	**Mindmaps** – explain own thinking based on theories of thinking using a mindmap (C).	**Blogs** – explain how own approaches to learning changes as the subject progresses and as a result of reflecting on learning own processes (C).	**Blogs** – analyze own learning processes throughout a unit of study (C).	**Blogs** – evaluate the degree to which own learning processes improve as a result of self-reflection (C).	**Mindmaps** – suggest more efficient ways of thinking as a mindmap (C).

of how rain clouds form using the Pixlr editor at http://www.pixlr.com/editor). Other Web 2.0 tools are designed to support conversation and thus are suitable for dialogic pedagogies (for instance debating the quality of an advertising campaign using the Voicethread tool available at http://voicethread.com).

It should also be noted that Table 3 comprises propositional tasks rather than an empirical collection, and many other alternatives could have been included. While the brief and general descriptions provided in Table 3 cannot demonstrate the full potential of each learning design, they provide teachers with catalysts for designing Web 2.0-based learning tasks. The framework also offers a catalyst for discussion and analysis in pre-service teacher education classes.

EVALUATING THE USE OF THE FRAMEWORK WITH PRE-SERVICE TEACHERS

Method

In the first Semester of 2010 students studying the subject Information and Communication Technologies and Education at Macquarie University were encouraged to review an early version of the Web 2.0 Learning Design Framework (Bower, Hedberg, & Kuswara, 2009) as part of their Week 8 coursework. This was one of several prescribed readings in the subject. As part of the assessment for the subject students were required to design and develop a short topic of work in Moodle Learning Management System. Students were provided a one-hour in-class guided tutorial session on how to use the tools and features of Moodle, after which time they were encouraged to draw upon their peers and the online documentation to learn more about the Moodle system. The Moodle course design task was completed in groups of two or three students in order to develop their collaborative curriculum design capabilities and allow students to learn from one another. As well as drawing upon the tools embedded in Moodle, students were also encouraged to integrate other tools if it supported accomplishment of the learning outcomes identified for their topic of work. To support this embedding of external tools and the learning design process generally, students were referred to the Web 2.0 Learning Design Framework.

The assignment itself was due at the beginning of Week 12, after which the pre-service teachers were asked to complete some reflective questions relating to the utility of the Web 2.0 Learning Design Framework for supported their ability to conceptualize and create Web 2.0 Learning Designs. The questions were:

1. What are the advantages of the Web 2.0 Learning design framework? In what ways is it helpful?

2. What are the disadvantages of the Web 2.0 Learning design framework? In what ways could it be made more helpful?

3. The Web 2.0 Learning design framework helped me to understand how technology, pedagogy and content were interrelated (seven item Likert scale from strongly agree to strongly disagree).

4. The Web 2.0 Learning Design Framework helped me to complete my learning design tasks (seven item Likert scale from strongly agree to strongly disagree).

Fifty-five out of the 102 students enrolled in the unit provided responses to the reflective questions. These fifty-five students were drawn from four out of the six non-streamed tutorial classes, and thus provided a reasonably representative sample of the cohort. Advantages and disadvantages of the framework were categorized and tallied in order to provide an indication of relative frequencies. Each distinct reason provided by a respondent was included in the tallying process, meaning that one person's response to a question could increase the frequency of several different categories. Representative and pertinent student comments were noted in order to provide primary-source illumination of the key issues. Responses to the two categorical questions were analyzed using two-tailed Z-tests, where the seven items of each Likert scale were assigned an integer value from zero ('strongly disagree') to six ('strongly agree'). It should be noted that while caution should be exercised whenever analyzing categorical data in this way, these type of descriptive to quantitative transformation of Likert scales is commonplace.

As well as this, the learning designs of students were subjectively analyzed in order to gauge the quality of the learning designs that students created. These are described in the section below to provide an illustration of how the Web 2.0 Learning Design Framework was applied.

Students' Learning Designs

Of the thirty-eight learning designs submitted by the groups of students, all incorporated some form of Web 2.0 technologies identified in the Web 2.0 learning design framework. Many of these were available as native tools in the Moodle Learning Management System (for instance, wikis and blogs). However over half of the groups (20) included collaborative and creative tools that were not part of the Moodle Learning Management System, often in synergistic and constructive ways. An illustration of this is shown in Example 1.

Example 1

The Japanese Culture module was designed for third and fourth grade students to simultaneously learn about Japanese culture at the same time as developing their technological capabilities. A screenshot of the module homepage is shown in Figure 2. The students first complete a chat to elicit what they already know about Japan and Japanese society. They are provided with instructions on how to locate Japan on a map using Google maps and compare it to Australia. Students then read some information about a day in the life of a Japanese child, and are asked to leave their reflections on a Voicethread board. After this students are asked to research a Japanese hobby and are asked to post information about it on a class blog. The class is then divided into groups to research the history of the Samurai during different time periods. All students find online resources about the Samurai and share them using the class Diigo site. Based on the resources students then create a Glogster poster explaining the different eras of the Samurai. Students are also required to research one of Japan's latest and greatest technologies, and in pairs create a Prezi presentation about the technology that they deliver to the rest of the class. The final task involves the whole class contributing to a wiki in order to summarize what has been learnt in the topic.

Figure 2. Pre-service teacher designed course on Japanese culture

Throughout the module students are referred to several websites and videos to enrich their understanding. Scaffolding is provided in the form of explaining how to best complete the tasks and instructions and links describing how to use the various Web 2.0 technologies.

All thirty-eight of the groups embedded images into their learning designs, and in some instances their students were required to create images using tools such as Pixlr as part of the learning process. Thirty-six out of the thirty-eight learning designs used video for instructive or illustrative purposes. On some occasions, pre-service teachers integrated video creation tasks into their learning designs. An illustration of this is shown in Example 2.

Example 2

The Once Upon A Time module is designed to develop Year Seven students' understanding of the 'fairytale' genre and enable them to create engaging fairytales using technology. A screenshot of this group's module is shown in Figure 3. The module begins by students sharing different versions of the 'Snow White' fairytale using Diigo and comparing and contrasting the different forms. Students then divide into groups and brainstorm ideas for a modern day fairytale on the class wiki. The second lesson involves a discussion of narrative structure, and guides student groups through an online brainstorming activity to map out key

Figure 3. Pre-service teacher designed course on fairytale construction

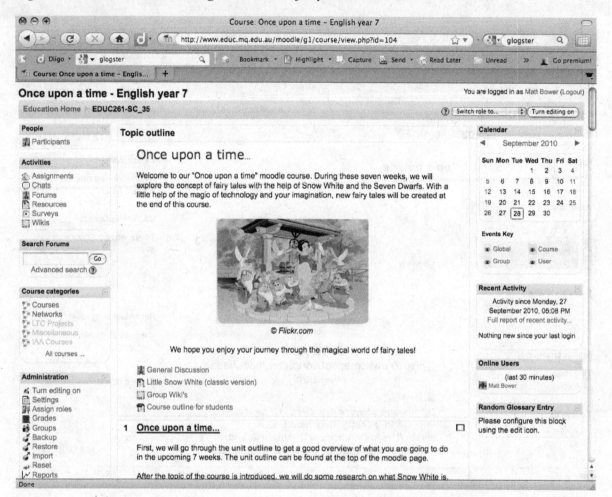

features of their fairytale. Students then use an online comic-strip tool (Comic Life) to create an initial storyboard of their fairytale. In the third lesson students are provided with two fairytale texts and consider ways in which meaning is conveyed using perspective and language. Students' critical reflections about the techniques used in each of the texts are posted on Twitter as a way for the class to synchronously sharing many ideas at once. Students are led through an instructional sequence that deconstructs the composition of fairytale characters, and consider the role of a moral in a fairytale through group-chat discussions.

Based on these foundational tasks students are then required to construct a short video of a modern-day fairytale. They are provided with clear directions and online resources explaining how to use the video technology as well as techniques for filming successful videos. The final session is a 'popcorn' lesson that involves the class having a movie screening celebrating each of the groups' fairytales.

Several of the thirty-eight groups included learning objects, online games, or Google applications (such as Google Sketchup or Google Maps) to add elements of interactivity into their learning designs.

Figure 4. Pre-service teachers' perceptions of the advantages of the Web 2.0 learning design framework

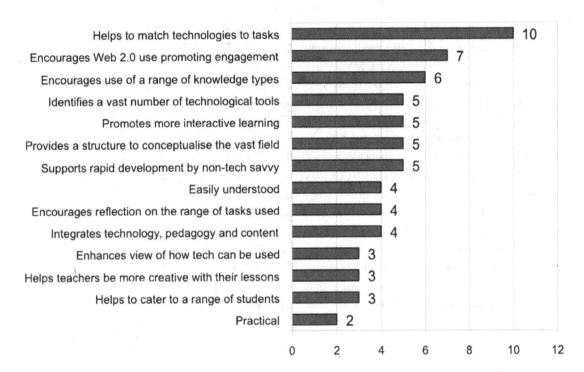

Student Perceptions of the Learning Web 2.0 Design Framework

Advantages

Students identified a range of ways in which the Web 2.0 Learning Design Framework supported their understanding and learning design capabilities. A summary of responses with a frequency of two or greater is provided in Figure 4. The most common advantages of the framework were that it provided support in matching technologies to tasks and that it promoted more engaged student learning by encouraging the use of Web 2.0 technologies. Several students emphasized the way in which the framework helped to organize and simplify a vast amount information to expedite the learning design process:

[The framework] formalises and gives some structure to the huge amount of information and it's different methods of delivery that are available to the modern student and modern teacher. With the Web 2.0 framework we can start to better program lessons that incorporate the different technologies. The result should be an easier and more effective achievement of student outcomes when using Web 2.0

The web 2.0 learning framework helps a teacher to translate the normal curriculum into a technology-rich lesson. By selecting what type of knowledge you want to teach (content) and to what extent you want them to learn (cognitive process) you can then check this framework to look up possible web 2.0 technologies and a possible way of teaching it.

Figure 5. Pre-service teachers' perceptions of the disadvantages of the Web 2.0 learning design framework

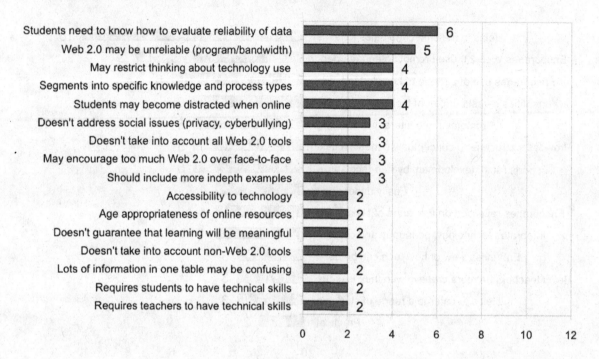

What are the disadvantages of the Web 2.0 Learning design framework? In what ways could it be made more helpful?

Student responses indicated that the framework supported the development of an integrated understanding of the role of technology:

It shows the ways that technology can interact with pedagogy and content, so that technology is integrated into learning, and not treated separately.

Students also explained how the framework helped them to create Web 2.0 learning designs, particularly in relation to providing tasks that incorporated a range of knowledge levels and learning processes.

[The framework] assisted in the development of the program of lessons we developed for the Moodle. By the end of the unit of work we had developed lessons which required students to work more in the higher-order thinking knowl-

edge dimensions, such as evaluative and creative [thinking]. By structuring our lesson development in that way our aim was to build upon factual and conceptual knowledge.

Three students identified the way in which the framework encouraged students to be creative, moving beyond traditional lesson types to use more dynamic and interactive Web 2.0 approaches. Other advantages of the framework not reported in Figure 4 included that it provided a framework for analysis of new technologies, could be used to create lessons about technology, was a contemporary framework and encouraged reflection during the design process.

Disadvantages

Students identified less disadvantages of the model than advantages (63 as opposed to 70), and were in less agreement about what the disadvantages were. Critically, most of the disadvantages that pre-service teachers identified related to learning and teaching using Web 2.0 technologies as opposed to disadvantages of the framework itself. A summary of responses with a frequency of two or greater is provided in Figure 5.

The most commonly identified disadvantages of the framework related to reliability; the unreliable nature of online content and the potentially unreliable nature of Web 2.0 technology itself. Neither of these issues related to the framework, but rather are points for teachers to consider when utilizing Web 2.0 learning designs with their students. The two most common criticisms of the framework itself included 'May restrict thinking about technology use' and 'Segments into knowledge and process types'. These are both important considerations for teacher educators to address when introducing the framework – the intention of the framework is to provide structure for thinking about content, pedagogy and technology and that there are many different design possibilities that may simultaneously attend to a range of thinking levels. Three students also felt that the fact that the framework did not take into account more technologies (Web 2.0 and non-Web 2.0) was a limitation, but at the same time two students felt that there was too much information being presented already. A helpful suggestion from students was to include more examples in the framework, which could be included at the time the framework was introduced.

While several of the disadvantages of teaching using Web 2.0 that students did not relate to the Web 2.0 Learning Design Framework itself, they did provide a useful checklist of considerations for teaching using Web 2.0 in the classroom, including:

1. Students need to know how to evaluate the reliability of data
2. Teachers need to be prepared for unreliable Web 2.0 access
3. Strategies may need to be applied to avoid students becoming distracted by online content
4. Social issues need to be considered (privacy, cyberbullying etc)
5. Web 2.0 learning designs should be used in moderation so as not to replace face-to-face contact
6. Accessibility to technology should be considered (especially if students are to access from home)
7. Content should be appropriate for the target audience
8. Using Web 2.0 tools does not guarantee meaningful learning (this depends on the task)
9. The technological capabilities of students needs to be taken into account
10. Teachers need to have adequate technological skills to facilitate the lesson.

Some individual students raised other pertinent general considerations, including the need to consider copyright, authentication, and assessment issues (if being used for that purpose). One student pointed out that the particular student cohort needed to be considered, and anther identified the disciplinarity as an important issue. Several students qualified the disadvantages of the model, identifying how in some cases the model needed to be limited in order to be useful: "it is obviously not an exhaustive list of the technologies available, but it does provide a good means of categorising them".

Utility

Forty-four out of the fifty-five students who completed the reflective questionnaire felt that the Web 2.0 Learning Design Framework helped

Figure 6. Extent to which pre-service teachers perceived that the Web 2.0 learning design framework helped to complete their learning design tasks

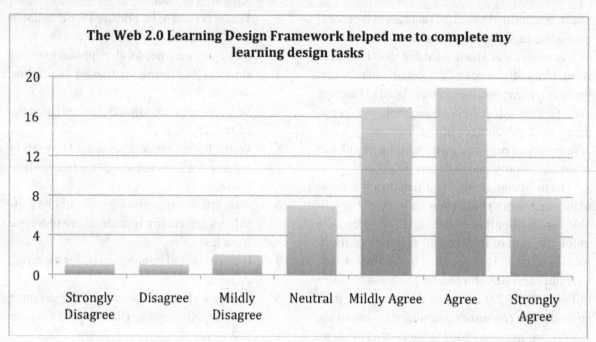

them to complete their learning design tasks (see Figure 6).

Although this result indicates a significantly better than neutral response (Z = 7.70, p<0.001), it does include eight students who provided neutral or disagreeing responses. These students may have decided not to use the framework to complete their learning design task.

Fifty-one out of the fifty-five students who responded to the reflective questionnaire agreed that the Web 2.0 Learning Design Framework helped them to understand how technology, pedagogy and content was interrelated (see Figure 7). This was a statistically significant effect (Z = 12.66, p<0.001), with only four students not agreeing that the framework helped them to develop an interconnected conceptualisation of Web 2.0 learning design.

DISCUSSION

The Web 2.0 Learning Design framework provided pre-service teachers with a structure for organizing and thinking about Web 2.0 learning design concepts. By incorporating a range of content types and pedagogies within the framework, pre-service teachers were encouraged to include a variety of creative and socially-interactive learning experiences in their Web 2.0 enabled lessons. Engaging education students with the Web 2.0 Learning Design Framework encourages them to broach the interconnected nature of content, pedagogy and technology.

Pre-service teachers were able to recognize the conceptual and practical support that the Web 2.0 Learning Design Framework provided, both assisting them to understand the relationships between content, pedagogy and technologies, as well as create learning designs for their students. The main ways in which the framework was useful to them was by helping them to match

Figure 7. Extent to which pre-service teachers perceived that the Web 2.0 learning design framework helped them understand the interrelationship between technology, pedagogy and content

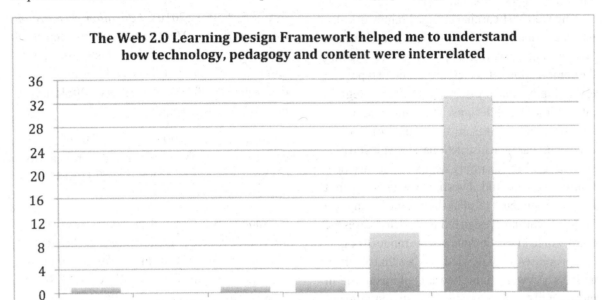

technologies to tasks and create more engaging learning experiences for students. They also appreciated the way the framework enabled them to conceptualize a vast amount of information in order to expedite their learning design processes. Students also identified important considerations for teacher educators when using the framework with pre-service teachers, including the need to explain how the framework is a tool for thinking rather than a constraining prescription, to discuss ancillary Web 2.0 issues such as copyright and authentication and assessment, and the utility of providing case study examples.

The concrete learning design task applied in this study required the pre-service teachers to actualize their Web 2.0 learning design capabilities and allowed the teacher to gauge the extent of their learning. Compelling students to embed emerging technologies into their learning designs not only meant that they considered how Web 2.0 could be utilized in their teaching area, by

using the Web 2.0 tools students developed the technological capabilities to operate the tools. It is intended that through this process of application (rather than just identification or understanding) pre-service will be more likely to integrate Web 2.0 technologies when they commence gainful employment. Several pre-service teachers reported how they had already incorporated some of the technologies into their practicum lessons.

The framework includes higher order thinking skills (analysis, evaluation, creation) as well as dialogic and constructive pedagogies. In this way the framework directly attends to the call for more 21st Century learning in today's classroom. As well as providing teachers with a practical and concrete guide for creating Web 2.0 learning designs, it also acted as a tool to promote reflection on learning and teaching generally. In this way the framework supports the notion of technology as driver for educational reform (Attwell, 2007) and Web 2.0 as a medium for the epistemological shift of teachers (Eijkman, 2010).

The Web 2.0 Learning Design Framework also provides a means of analyzing teachers' learning designs. Future work could include investigating the combinations of pedagogies, content types and technologies that pre-service teachers integrate into their learning designs. The framework could also be used to measure the impact of various teacher preparation instructional strategies on pre-service teachers' learning designs. For instance, future studies could investigate whether or not requiring students to plan their topics using the Web 2.0 Learning Design Framework increases the quality of learning designs and the range of cognitive processes and knowledge types that teachers address. As well, future work could examine in more detail the reasons why some students did not find the framework beneficial and how it may be adjusted to better meet their needs.

CONCLUSION

The dynamic and rapidly evolving nature of the Web 2.0 landscape presents a range of challenges to teachers, but also opportunities. The Web 2.0 Learning Design Framework presented in this paper acted as a catalyst for pre-service teachers to reflect on the interrelationship between technology, pedagogy, content, and learning. Utilizing the framework enabled pre-service teachers to select and embed a range of Web 2.0 technologies into their learning designs in a way that attended to the constructive and collaborative needs of their students. This responds to calls by government and industry bodies (such as Duncan, 2010; ISTE, et al., 2008; UNESCO, 2008) to incorporate more contemporary 21st Century approaches to learning and interaction within teacher education programs.

REFERENCES

AACTE, & P21 (2010). *Education preparation - A vision for the 21st Century (draft)*. Retrieved from http://aacte.org/email_blast/president_e-letter/files/02-16-2010/Educator%20Preparation%20and%2021st%20Century%20Skills%20DRAFT%20021510.pdf

Albion, P. R. (2008). Web 2.0 in teacher education: Two imperatives for action. *Computers in the Schools, 25*(3), 181–198. doi:10.1080/07380560802368173

Alexander, B. (2006). *Web 2.0 - A new wave of innovation for teaching and learning?* Retrieved 22nd February, 2011, from http://www.educause.edu/EDUCAUSE+Review/EDUCAUSEReviewMagazineVolume41/Web20ANewWaveofInnovationforTe/158042

Anderson, L., & Krathwohl, D. (2001). *A taxonomy for learning, teaching and assessing: A revision of Bloom's taxonomy of educational objectives*. New York, NY: Longman.

Angeli, C., & Valanides, N. (2009). Epistemological and methodological issues for the conceptualization, development, and assessment of ict-tpck: advances in technological pedagogical content knowledge (TPCK). *Computers & Education, 52*(1), 154–168. doi:10.1016/j.compedu.2008.07.006

Attwell, G. (2007). *Web 2.0 and the changing ways we are using computers for learning: What are the implications for pedagogy and curriculum?* Retrieved 28 September, 2010, from http://www.elearningeuropa.info/directory/index.php?page=doc&doc id=9756&doclng=6

Barker, P. (2008). Re-evaluating a model of learning design. *Innovations in Education and Teaching International, 45*(2), 127–141. doi:10.1080/14703290801950294

Bower, M., Hedberg, J., & Kuswara, A. (2009). Conceptualising Web 2.0 enabled learning designs. In *Australasian Society for Computers in Learning in Tertiary Education (ASCILITE)*, Aukland, (pp. 1153-1162).

Bower, M., Hedberg, J., & Kuswara, A. (2010). A framework for Web 2.0 learning design. *Educational Media International, 47*(3), 177–198. doi:10.1080/09523987.2010.518811

Brown, A. R., & Voltz, B. D. (2005). Elements of effective e-learning design. *International Review of Research in Open and Distance Learning, 6*(1).

Chai, C. S., Koh, J. H. L., & Tsai, C.-C. (2010). Facilitating preservice teachers' development of technological, pedagogical, and content knowledge (TPACK). *Journal of Educational Technology & Society, 13*(4), 63–73.

Conole, G., Dyke, M., Oliver, M., & Scalc, J. (2004). Mapping pedagogy and tools for effective learning design. *Computers & Education, 43*(1-2), 17–33. doi:10.1016/j.compedu.2003.12.018

Diego, J. P. S., Laurillard, D., Boyle, T., Bradley, C., Ljubojevic, D., & Neumann, T. (2008). Towards a user-oriented analytical approach to learning design. *ALT-J. Research in Learning Technology, 16*(1), 15–29. doi:10.1080/09687760701850174

Donald, C., Blake, A., Girault, I., Datt, A., & Ramsay, E. (2009). Approaches to learning design: Past the head and the hands to the HEART of the matter. *Distance Education, 30*(2), 179–199. doi:10.1080/01587910903023181

Duncan, A. (2010). Teacher preparation: Reforming the uncertain profession. *Education Digest, 75*(5), 13–22.

Eijkman, H. (2010). Dancing with ostmodernity: Web 2.0+ as a new epistemic learning space. In Lee, M. J. W., & McLoughlin, C. (Eds.), *Web 2.0-based e-learning* (pp. 343–364). Hershey, PA: IGI Global. doi:10.4018/978-1-60566-294-7.ch018

Groth, R., Spickler, D., Bergner, J., & Bardzell, M. (2009). A qualitative approach to assessing technological pedagogical content knowledge. *Contemporary Issues in Technology & Teacher Education, 9*(4), 392–411.

He, W., & Hartley, K. (2010). A supporting framework of online technology resources for lesson planning. *Journal of Educational Multimedia and Hypermedia, 19*(1), 23–37.

ISTE, P21, & SEDTA. (2008). *Maximizing the impact: The pivotal role of technology in a 21st century education system.*

Jamieson-Proctor, R., Finger, G., & Albion, P. (2010). Auditing the TK and TPACK confidence of pre-service teachers: Are they ready for the profession? *Australian Educational Computing Journal, 25*(1), 8–17.

Koehler, M. J., & Mishra, P. (2009). What is technological pedagogical content knowledge? *Contemporary Issues in Technology & Teacher Education, 9*(1), 60–70.

Lambert, J., & Gong, Y. (2010). 21st century paradigms for pre-service teacher technology preparation. *Computers in the Schools, 27*(1), 54–70. doi:10.1080/07380560903536272

Lei, J. (2009). Digital natives as preservice teachers: What technology preparation is needed? *Journal of Computing in Teacher Education, 25*(3), 87–97.

MacLean, P., & Scott, B. (2007). Learning design: Requirements, practice and prospects. *Campus-Wide Information Systems, 24*(3), 187–198. doi:10.1108/10650740710762220

Marra, R. M. (2004). An online course to help teachers use technology to enhance learning: Successes and limitations. *Journal of Technology and Teacher Education, 12*(3), 411–430.

Mishra, P., & Koehler, M. J. (2006). Technological pedagogical content knowledge: A framework for teacher knowledge. *Teachers College Record, 108*(6), 1017–1054. doi:10.1111/j.1467-9620.2006.00684.x

Moore, J. A., & Chae, B. (2007). Beginning teachers' use of online resources and communities. *Technology, Pedagogy and Education, 16*(2), 215–224. doi:10.1080/14759390701406844

Oliver, K. (2007). Leveraging Web 2.0 in the redesign of a graduate-level technology integration course. *TechTrends, 51*(5), 55–61. doi:10.1007/s11528-007-0071-3

Richardson, W. (2006). *Blogs, wikis, podcasts, and other powerful web tools for classrooms*. Thousand Oaks, CA.

Rosen, D., & Nelson, C. (2008). Web 2.0: A new generation of learners and education. *Computers in the Schools, 25*(3), 211–225. doi:10.1080/07380560802370997

Rotherham, A. J., & Willingham, D. (2009). 21st century skills - The challenges ahead. *Educational Leadership, 67*(1), 16–21.

Schmidt, D. A., Baran, E., Thompson, A. D., Mishra, P., Koehler, M. J., & Shin, T. S. (2009). Technological pedagogical content knowledge (TPACK): The development and validation of an assessment instrument for preservice teachers. *Journal of Research on Technology in Education, 42*(2), 123–149.

Tsoi, M. F., Goh, N. K., & Chia, L. S. (2005). Multimedia learning design pedagogy: A hybrid learning model. *US-China Education Review, 2*(9), 59–62.

UNESCO. (2008). *ICT competency standards for teachers – Policy framework*. Retrieved from http://cst.unesco-ci.org/sites/projects/cst/The%20Standards/ICT-CST-Policy%20Framework.pdf

Voithofer, R. (2007). *Web 2.0: What is it and how can it apply to teaching and teacher preparation?* Paper presented at the American Educational Research Association Conference, April 9-13, Chicago, IL.

KEY TERMS AND DEFINITIONS

21st Century Skills: Contemporary skills required for students (and teachers) to be successful today and in the future, including problem solving, communication, collaboration, information and media literacy, critical thinking, and creativity.

Affordances: The features or attributes of a tool that determine how it can be used.

Blog: A website that organizes the posts of individuals or groups in chronological order.

Microblogging: Using a synchronous tool that allows instant upload and sharing short pieces of information (for instance, Twitter).

Podcast: An uploaded audio recording that others can play through a web-browser.

Social Bookmarking: Use of an online system designed for online storage and sharing of bookmarked websites.

Taxonomy of Learning, Teaching and Assessing: A framework created by Anderson & Krathwohl (2001) that categorizes learning by the knowledge level (factual, procedural, conceptual, and metacognitive) as well as the cognitive process (remembering, understanding, applying, analyzing, evaluating, and creating).

TPACK: Technology, Pedagogy and Content Knowledge.

Web 2.0 Learning Design Framework: A framework to support the conceptualization and use of Web 2.0 tools in learning and teaching (presented in this paper).

Web 2.0 Technologies: A range of new and open online technologies that support collaboration and sharing of content through sophisticated yet easy to use interfaces.

Wiki: A dynamic website that authorized users can edit using a standard web-browser.

Chapter 6
Web 2.0 Visualization Tools to Stimulate Generative Learning

Jennifer Banas
Northeastern Illinois University, USA

Carol A. Brown
East Carolina University, USA

ABSTRACT

Twenty-first century learners' learning experiences require vastly different instructional opportunities than the generation before. These electronically bred learners have become "wired" to learn best from and to prefer instructional activities that allow them to manipulate their learning environment. With this understanding, educators should respond with instructional practices that not only support learners' fundamental and preferred learning behaviors but also provide environments that foster creative and critical thinking experiences. New Web 2.0 educational technologies can help educators to deliver rich instruction that is relevant, appropriate, and that affords a "playground" in which generative learning can take place. This chapter introduces readers to a category of interactive technology instruments called visualization tools and how these tools can be used to stimulate generative learning. Examples are provided and criticisms of text visualization tools are also carefully considered. Readers are challenged to explore new uses for and the impact of visualization tools.

INTRODUCTION

Twenty-first century learners have increasingly become a generation whose learning experiences require and afford vastly different instructional opportunities than the generation before. Not only

do today's learners prefer to engage in learning activities that allows them to manipulate their learning environment, but they have also become "wired" to do so. With this understanding of 21st century learners, educators should respond with instructional practices that not only support learners' fundamental and preferred learning behaviors. According to Considine, Horton, and Mormon

DOI: 10.4018/978-1-4666-0014-0.ch006

(2009), "today's teenagers bring to school a rich and different set of literacy practices and background that is often unacknowledged or underused by educators" (p. 471). Rather than viewing digital media as a distractor in the education system, it should be embraced as an opportunity. New Web 2.0 educational technologies abound that can help educators to deliver rich instruction that is relevant, appropriate, and that afford a "playground" in which generative learning can take place.

While new Web 2.0 technologies surface every day, this chapter introduces readers specifically to a category of interactive technology instruments called visualization tools. Visualization can be defined as the conversion of information to a symbolic representation of a particular idea, concept, or data object. According to Burley (2010) visualization tools are used to organize, integrate, and display a large amount of information into a more easily understood format. These representations often reveal patterns, relationships, and concepts with potential for new understandings and deeper comprehension of reading materials.

The chapter begins with an introduction to current visualization tools and an overview of generative learning theory. Next a discussion about how text visualization tools can stimulate generative learning will be shared. Criticisms of text visualization tools are also carefully considered and presented for the readers' review and evaluation. The authors' experiences with text visualization tools in their own instruction are provided as supportive examples. The chapter concludes with an exploration of other uses for text visualization tools and makes a case for integrating text visualization tools into teacher education programs.

WEB 2.0 VISUALIZATION TOOLS

Visualization tools are interactive in design, thus information becomes more accessible and allows users to explore text in a way not afforded by traditional reading and processing of text alone. Uploading or pasting text into one of these visualization tools lets users create images that point to possible relationships, main ideas, and key terms. These images can facilitate the process of content analysis and quite possibly expand reader comprehension. Early proponents reported successful use of visualization retrieval tools to present bibliographic displays generated from huge amounts of digital information (Koshman, 2005; Rorvig & Lunin, 1999; Shneiderman, (1998). According to Wise et al. (1995) data sources become manageable and information retrieval efficient through organized graphic displays. Zhang refers to these visualizations as metaphors. Mental images can be formed and conceptual ideas more easily recognized, communicated, understood, and remembered (Zhang, 2008). Knowing that people recall 10% of what they read when tested three days after exposure compared to 65% if a picture or visual element is added (Medina, 2008), visualization tools may even support long term recall of information read.

While a number of visualization tools exist on the web, this chapter will highlight those on the Many Eyes web site (manyeyes.alphaworks.ibm. com). This particular web site was selected due to its comprehensive selection of visualization tools made available to users. Also discussed is the web site Wordle (www.wordle.net). .

Many Eyes was developed by researchers from the Visual Communications Lab, a subgroup of IBM's Collaborative User Experience research team, as a means to help people collectively understand data. Because visualizations created are published on the web site for public viewing and solicit comments, Many Eyes transforms information into a participatory, social experience. Many Eyes offers several interactive technology instruments to transform both textual and numerical data. What follows is a brief description of four tools: Word Clouds, Phrase Net, Tag Clouds, and Word Trees.

Figure 1. Visualization using Phrase Net

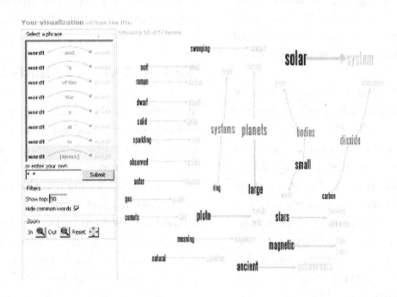

Word Clouds is one of the most basic of the visualization tools. Word clouds generate word clusters from provided text, giving greater prominence to words that appear more frequently in the source text. See bibliography for a current list of websites with word cloud generators.

Phrase Net diagrams show relationships between different words used in a text. It uses a simple form of pattern matching to provide multiple views of concepts contained in a book, article, speech, poem, etc. Much like a word cloud, words that appear most often in a text also appear more predominantly in the webbed output produced by the Phrase Net tool. Phrase Net also allows the users to restrict or expand the number of words appearing in the visualization, thus giving the user control over the complexity of the image produced. In addition to this feature, an arrow appears between words conjoined most often in the text. The larger the font size of a particular word and the greater the bandwidth of the connection between words indicates the strength of the relationship between a given pair of terms.

Figure 1 shows a Phrase Net image generated from a science article about the solar system. The user will specify a particular pattern such as the terms *earth* or *planets*. Phrase Net will create a network diagram of the words it found as matches. The terms *earth/planets* will be connected if they occurred in the same phrase. When viewing the output from the visualization, the user can compare differences in font size, color, and size of connectors to determine frequency and relationship of the terms. The size of a word is proportional to the number of times it occurred in a match.

Note in the figure above the term "dioxide" is connected to terms "atmosphere" and "carbon". Bold lines indicate a strong connection between terms "solar" → "system"; and "magnetic" → "field(s)". The thicker the line, the more often those two words appear together side by side in the text. The connection between the words "solar" and "system" might not be that surprising given the commonality of this pairing, but if one were analyzing a literary text, associations between different concepts might be uncovered. Then, by looking at the thickness of the line, the reader could compare the strength of the connections. Drawing attention to strong and weak connections between ideas enhances the reader's conceptual understanding of complex reading material (Chun & Plass, 1997).

Tag Clouds have a variety of features and enable the user to see how frequently words appear in a given text. The user might also visualize output based on the relationships between a column of words and a column of numbers. Like a World Cloud, words that appear most often in a text are given greater prominence than others in a Tag Clouds. Unlike a Word Cloud, images produced by a Tag Cloud permits mouse-over of specific terms yielding a brief selection of the text in which that word appears in a passage of text. Tag Clouds also allow the user to search for and highlight words within the cloud. Another unique feature is the ability to compare two different bodies of text. For example, one could compare the number of times President Barack Obama used the word "hope" at the Democratic National Convention (14 times) to the number of times at his Pre-Inauguration Address (6 times).

Word Trees are a visual search tool that allows the user to see, by way of branches, all the different ways a selected word is used in a given text. Consider this application: the word "like" can be used as a noun, verb, adverb, adjective, preposition, particle, conjunction, hedge, or a quotation. A speech instructor could have his/her students create a word to tree to map (and then later label) all of the occurrences of the word "like" in a transcribed interview. These word trees can even be further divided to identify common sub-phrases. Like Phrase Net, users can zoom in on and highlight text.

Each of these visualization tools offers users an opportunity to view text in a uniquely different way, affording educators a powerful a tool to help their learners deepen existing or generate new understandings about the text or information they read. These tools can also help to support the principles encompassed within generative learning

theory. An overview of generative learning theory can help to better illuminate this relationship.

GENERATIVE LEARNING THEORY

Wittrock's (1992) model of generative learning and teaching focuses on the cognitive processes employed to generate meaning and understanding from instruction. Studied primarily in the context of reading, the premise is that the mind is a builder, not just a processer (Wittrock, 1985, Grabowski, 1996). It seeks to make relevant connections and consequential plans of action based on perceived realities. These connections are made by way of comparing existing conceptions with new information. Instead of focusing on the structural properties of knowledge, generative learning focuses on the following four areas: a) learning processes such as attention, b) motivational processes such as relevancy, self-efficacy, and expectations, c) metacognitive processes, and d) knowledge generation processes including analogies, metaphors, and summaries (Wittrock, 1985, 1992).

Generative Activities

Generative learning activities allow learners to mentally "play with" information to create a personal understanding of the subject to be learned. There are two types of generative learning activities: (1) activities that generate the development of organizational relationships amongst the parts or components of a larger whole, and (2) activities that generate integrated relationships between what the learner sees, hears, or reads and existing comprehensions. Examples of each type are given next.

Activities that generate the development of organizational relationships amongst the parts or components of a larger whole might include the provision or development of titles, headings, objectives, summaries, graphs, tables, and main ideas. For example, a freshman level biology teacher who is introducing her students to the plant kingdoms might have students consider how form and function play into the classifications. A 7th grade language arts teacher might teach his students about nouns, verbs, adjectives, adverbs, and prepositions by breaking down a complete paragraph and categorizing the parts of speech into a pre-labeled table.

Activities that generate integrated relationships between what the learner sees, hears, or reads and existing comprehensions can include demonstrations, metaphors, analogies, examples, pictures, applications, interpretations, paraphrases, inferences. Elaborating on the plant classification example, a freshman biology teacher might ask her students to borrow from plant forms and functions to construct a green living environment. The high school math teacher who is teaching geometry might introduce basic concepts with the context of the architectural blueprint for their school.

The idea behind these types of activities is to move transitory knowledge residing in short-term memory into a place where is can recalled on a long-term basis to construct new understandings and plans of action (Foote, 2009). In K-12 settings, such activities have proven to be successful in with making connections and predicting themes within expository text (Foote, 2009; Oliver, 2009; Wittrock, 1985). These types of activities are also on par with the concept of infusion-based teaching practices. Infusion, a concept introduced in the 1980's, refers to classroom instruction that blends the teaching of thinking skills with content (Shulman, 1986, 1987). Teaching thinking skills in a content-based course not only improves thinking, but also fosters a deeper understanding of the subject matter therein (Swartz, Costa, Beyer, Reagan, and Kallick, 2008). It is this deeper level of thinking that both supports and propagates generative learning.

HOW VISUALIZATION TOOLS SUPPORT GENERATIVE LEARNING

Wittrock (1985) wrote of ancient Roman and Greek teaching practices which promoted student generated images to improve memory. Learners would create a vivid interactive image between a first and second point to be remembered. Subsequent events were events were added in and remembered by way of their association with the others. The point of such an activity was that learners were making connections between ideas, while also constructing their own meanings from teaching.

Word Clouds, Phrase Nets, Tag Clouds, and Word Trees, and other Web 2.0 visualization tools provide learners with a similar opportunity. More specifically, visualization tools allow users to manipulate information to interpret concepts, make inferences, and generate predictions as they explore the symbolic structure of a text. According to Linnenbrink and Pintrich (2003), learners who try to paraphrase, summarize, or organize materials by way of concept maps, outlines, and other similar visual organizers, they often display deeper, more conceptual learning. This is in contrast to learners using surface processing strategies like memorization and rehearsal, which is less likely to lead to deep learning (Weinstein & Mayer, 1986). As they become engaged more deeply with the material by way of building connections, they are more likely to better understand it. This is on par with the aforementioned infusion-based instruction. In *Thinking-Based Learning,* Swartz, Costa, Beyer, Reagan, and Kallick (2008) share "thinking" words collected from state educational standards. Many of these infusion-based thinking words, including "analyze, classify, compare, conclude, connect, contrast, generalize, hypothesize, identify, interpret, judge, predict, and summarize" can all be taught in conjunction with text visualizations.

In addition to supporting deeper understanding by perceiving connections, visualization tools also can be used as a simple, but powerful tool to improve reader comprehension. Word Clouds,

Tag Clouds, and Phrase Nets enlarge words that appear most often; many of these words point to key terms. O'Donnell, Weber and McLaughlin (2003) found that students obtained higher reading comprehension scores when they previewed materials and discussed keywords prior to reading. Foote (2009) and Oliver (2009) found that concept maps, pictographs, and word clouds can be used for making connections and predicting themes within expository text. This means that text visualization tool images could help students to prepare to read a selected text. From a perseverance standpoint, visualization tools might also help to capture struggling reader's attention and motivate them to stay on task. These assumptions are worthy of further research

In higher education, Google visualization tools (Hook & Borner, 2005), Wordle (Viegas, Wattenberg, & Feinberg, 2009), and Many Eyes tools have been used to foster deeper learner of course material (Eisenberg, 2008). The authors of this chapter, too, experienced success with text visualization tools in their own classrooms to help graduate and undergraduate students understand complex ideas and abstract concepts in course readings, to generate additional and deeper understandings about a film that they had watched, and to glean ideas from students on how visualization tools could be used in K-12 classrooms. These case study examples are described next.

Case Study Group #1

The first group involved graduate students in a master's level program for instructional technology. Visualization tools were used to analyze the contents of a job description for school technology specialists. Understanding the requirements for positions as technology specialists would ensure interns are well prepared for future jobs. Following the readings, students generated visualizations using Wordle tools. In small group discussion forums, students analyzed the keywords included in the visualization, predicting

what might be the main functions for the position of technology facilitator in a K-12 school. After the online discussions were concluded, students submitted proposals for internship experiences at their local schools. After writing the first draft of the internship proposal and posting these to the online discussion forum, students participated in a second discussion forum to compare interpretations of job functions for technology facilitators. Students then submitted a final proposal to the course instructor for evaluation.

A qualitative analysis of the proposals was used to identify key ideas about what students considered important for the internship experience. The quality of the proposals was also examined for (1) objectives aligned with national standards and state department expectations; (2) projects and activities leading to achievement of objectives; (3) valid methods for evaluating outcomes from the internship projects. The analysis showed a clear and consistent alignment with national standards for these positions in K-12 schools. Students' proposals from previous semesters did not reveal the same depth of understanding evident in this group who used visualization tools to analyze future job descriptions. These students were able to identify main functions associated with job of the technology facilitator in a K12 school. Key words predominate in the Wordle images prompted interns to plan around terms such as "teacher support", "instruction"; and "collaboration." These were then used as prompts for negotiating projects for the semester internship experiences (Brown & Banas, 2010).

Case Study #2

A second case study group involved pre-service teachers who received instruction in use of Phrase Net tools to visualize main concepts and relationships in an assigned reading. Students (pre-service teachers) in a traditional face-to-face health education methods class were given the task of reading a selected chapter from an online book

Table 1. Mean Reading Comprehension Scores Pertaining to Connections Before and After Visualization Tool Use

	N	Mean	SD	SE
Before tool use	14	2.571	.852	.228
After tool use	14	3.000	.785	.210

on the topic of learning and cognition. Reading comprehension assessment questions prompted students to identify main themes and relationships between concepts. They also were prompted to make connections between what they had read and personal and/or professional experiences. For each response, students rated their confidence in their responses on a 3-point Likert scale. Following this task, students received a follow up assignment directing them to generate a visualization of the chapter using Phrase Net, a tool available through Many Eyes. After viewing the image generated by Phrase Net, students were prompted to re-respond to the same reading comprehension assessment questions previously answered and to re-rate their confidence in the response.

Students' reading comprehensions responses were rated on a scale of 0 to 4 with 4 being the highest score possible. T Test analyses were used to compare assessment for the following: (1) understanding main ideas; (2) comprehension of relationships between main ideas in the readings; (3) ability to make connections between main ideas and personal learning experiences, and (4) self-reported confidence levels in understanding and comprehension for the readings. Differences in reading comprehension assessment scores related to main ideas before and after use of

Phrase Net were marginally significant (p < .04, 2-tailed). There also were no significant differences identified between before and after reading comprehension assessment questions pertaining to connections with personal experiences. However, T Test comparison showed a significant difference in reading comprehension assessment scores of students' ability to see relationships between ideas when using the Phrase Net tool (p < .000, 2 - tailed). Note in Tables 1 and 2 differences in T scores (T = 11.3; p < .000, 2 - tailed) for before use of Phrase Net compared to T scores (T = 14.3, p < .000, 2 tailed) for after use of Phrase Net.

Students' confidence levels in identifying relationships among ideas also appear to be impacted through the use of Phrase Net visualization tool. In Table 3, differences in pre and post self-reported confidence levels are significant (p < .000, 2-tailed).

Students' comments following the use of Phrase Net seem to support the positive effect of the visualization tools used to help students understand relationships between major terms appearing in assigned reading. One student commented:

To visually see the connections of how strongly two concepts are linked to one another made me view

Table 2. Comparison of Reading Comprehension Scores Pertaining to Connections Before and After Visualization Tool Use

	t	df	P	MD	Confidence Interval	
					lower	upper
Before tool use	11.298	13	.000*	2.571	2.080	3.063
After tool use	14.309	13	.000*	3.000	2.547	3.453

Table 3. Sample Instructional Activities Using Word Cloud and Tag Clouds

Skill	Instructional method	Outcome	Assessment
Identify main idea	View word cloud selected text, compare key words; write one sentence with main idea.	Students make connection between font size and number of occurrences in the narrative; discussion on meaning of prominent words.	Teacher observation; enhance concept of "Big Idea"
Critical thinking	Individually generate a list of terms associated with educational theme; groups generate a 2nd list of terms; independently generate word cloud from assigned reading on the theme; compare independent and group lists.	Critical thinking required to compare and contrast word lists; accurate analysis of assigned reading; self-assessment associated with reflections on personal word clouds representative of themes in the reading	Comparison of word clouds representative of themes and main ideas within the reading; knowledge and understanding of vocabulary in the reading.
Expressive Writing	Assign writing describing oneself; paste into word cloud software; compare characteristics with others in class; identify repeated words; reflect on self-image and best attributes	Creative writing; good use of adjectives and adverbs; positive reinforcement for all students; identify the purpose of "sparkle words" for narrative writing.	Teacher assessment of writing style, use of vocabulary and positive dialog during whole class discussions.

this article in a different light. Previously, I selected main subjects points that were not as important or had fewer connections compared to the ones that I have selected after using PN. It reinforced the main issues that were being discussed in the article, rather than focusing on mini subjects that ewer not he key points. For example, PN greatly reinforced the strong connection between synapse over production and loss, which is an imperative method in how information is translated into learned concepts.

While some of these additional connections could be attributed to re-reading the chapter, the increase in self-reported confidence that they reported could possibly lead to a motivated interest in learning more about the topic (Brown & Banas, 2010).

Case Study #3

A third case study group was a group of undergraduate students taking a course entitled Current Health Concepts. In this course, students explored a variety of current health topics including environmental health. To launch this topic, the instructor showed the film Inconvenient Truth, the film produced by former Vice-President Al Gore to elucidate climate change and to uncover that state of our global environment. At the end of the film, students were prompted to respond to the following questions:

1. So far, what have you learned from watching this film that you didn't know before? What proof was offered? Explain.
2. So far, what has been one of the most shocking facts that you learned. What was shocking to you about it?
3. So far, what have you learned that you think many others did not know about? Why do you think it is less known?

After submitting their responses at the next class meeting, the instructor demonstrated how to use the Wordle visualization tool. Next, she provided the students with the typed transcript for the film and requested that students create a word cloud with it. Then, students were prompted to respond to the following question:

What does seeing the transcript from the film in this format make you think in regards to global warming that you didn't think about when you watched the film? What stands out more to you now?

An analysis of responses frequently revealed comments like "Seeing this image made a couple of words jump out that I had not really thought about before." Another student commented that it didn't make her think of new ideas, but rather that it re-affirmed her existing ones. Comments like these indicate that the word cloud help to unveil ideas that the student might have otherwise missed.

A final point worth mentioning is how visualization tools help students to self-initiate the generative learning process. One student from Case Study #3, after viewing the word cloud image for the Inconvenient Truth transcript commented how word clouds could help him to write a paper. He explained, "I often find that the hardest part to writing a paper is deciding how to start it. By seeing all of the major concepts laid out are a giant brainstorm." Word trees and tag clouds could help to elucidate otherwise undetected relationships and ideas that might further support the kind of thinking (analyze, classify, compare, etc.) to which Swartz et al. (2008) refer and lead to more thoughtful, meaningful writing experiences. Other ideas are shared in Case Study #4.

Case Study #4

In a fourth setting, a group of pre-service teacher education students partook in a discussion board activity in which they practiced using Wordle and made suggestions as to how visualization tools could be used in a K-12 setting.

These four case studies help to illustrate the benefits of using visualization tools in instruction (Brown & Banas, 2010). In the next section, suggested means to instruct learners in the use of visualization tools are shared.

INSTRUCTING LEARNERS IN THE USE OF VISUALIZATION TOOLS

Due to the potentially abstract nature of visualization tools as a learning tool, direct instruction from educators can help to ensure that students learn how to maximize their use. Direct instruction is instruction that has (a) clear and explicit learning goals, (b) focuses on a specific task, (c) states explicitly the steps in the task, (d) employs structured learning activities, (e) provides opportunities for practice, and (f) provides continual monitoring on progress with feedback (Swartz et al., 2008, p. 60). Because visualization tools are indeed a "tool," not the end result, learners not only need to know *how* to use them, but *when* to use them and *why*. Below are some practical considerations to heed when introducing learners to a new visualization tool:

1. Preview and review with learners the selected visualization tool(s) being taught
2. Have learners use the visualization tool(s) several times
3. Engage learners in reflecting on and verbalizing how they used the visualization tool(s)
4. Ask learners to share with other learners the steps they completed to use the visualization and provide each other with feedback
5. Have learners summarize and critique how they applied the visualization tool and what they learned about its use.

Once students have mastered a selected visualization tool by way of explanation, modeling, and practice with feedback, they need to be guided in the development of their understanding of and value for its use. Discussion and reflection are important components of this process.

Simply showing students how to drop text into the PhraseNet visualization creator, demonstrating how to zoom in and out of phrases in a Word Tree image, or making pretty Wordle images with lyrics from students favorite rock songs are not without practical or esthetic significance; but these tasks alone will not help students to transfer their skills to new contexts and situations in a way supports the type of generative learning required to create new knowledge and understandings. To help learners successfully transfer skills to new contexts and situations, Swartz et al. (2008, p. 65) offer some helpful suggestions: (a) continue to require learners to use the step-by-step procedures they initially learned so that those steps become habit; (b) use the same language and methods of application employed during the initial instruction; and (c) scaffold and cue students to apply their skills until they demonstrate the ability to use them on their own. In doing so, and in the context of visualization tools, the hope is to manifest skillful and appropriate application of visualization tools to self-identified other contexts.

CRITCISMS OF TEXT VISUALIZATION TOOLS

Critics of text visualizations might decry their use in that that the relationships between words shown in PhraseNet or the words enlarged in Wordle do not always point to "true" relationships or key concepts. And they are right! Phrase Net, Tag Clouds, Wordle, or other text visualizations tools are not a perfect science. They are based on frequencies and as researchers know just because an event happens more than others doesn't make it right. In the classroom, teachers should caution their students to review critically the visualizations. Going back to Swartz et al's (2008) "thinking" words (analyze, classify, compare, conclude, connect, contrast, generalize, hypothesize, identify, interpret, judge, predict, and summarize), teachers could use the images produced by text visualization tools to spark a discussion, to generate alternative perspectives, to test hypotheses, to solicit supported opinions, to compare and contrast "truths" and "fallacies," or many other critical-thinking based tasks. These

activities would support the kind of thinking associated with generative learning.

OTHER APPLICATIONS AND FUTURE RESEARCH

In addition to supporting generative learning, text visualization tools afford other applications. These applications include, but are not limited to, English Language Learner instruction, visual literacy instruction, and a research tool. This section briefly highlights and makes research suggestions for each of these uses.

ELL Instruction

Key word identification prior to reading text was cited earlier (O'Donnell, Weber, & McLauglin, 2003) as a means to improve reading comprehension. Fagan (2003) and DeCourcy and Birch (1993) found that English Language Learners (ELL's) particularly benefit from such an exercise. By identifying and learning the meaning of key words prior to reading a text, ELL's can better glide through reading without getting caught up on unfamiliar words. This chapter's authors would contend this also holds true for all learners. A teacher education candidate from Case Study #3 commented, "I think this [Wordle] is a wonderful tool to utilize with students in order to increase their vocabulary knowledge and to alert them to words they have seen before but did not recognize or to words that may have more than one meaning depending on the context. The English language has many words that take on more than one meaning and this is a great exercise to expose students to different meanings." Additional research into how visualization tools as a key word identifier improves reading comprehension for ELL learners and supports ELL instructors in their teaching is warranted.

Visual Literacy

According to Sibbet (2008), "visual intelligence is a key to navigating an information economy rich with multimedia" (p. 118). Visual metaphors, including pictures, charts, and graphs are often used to present both simple and complex ideas. The ability to interpret these metaphors is a learned skill. Research conducted by Ziemkiewicz and Kosara (2009) indicates that preconceived metaphors for data and other individual differences play an important role in the interpretation of such images. These findings indicate that not only must students be taught how to interpret and de-code visual metaphors, but also that their instructors must uncover and be cognizant of pre-existing student interpretations. Visualizations tools can provide a useful tool to establish an instructional playground for visual metaphor deconstruction. For example, a Word Trees can be a useful tool to help educators teach students about interpreting visual hierarchies. Phrase Nets could be used to teach about the strength of related terms. Additional research into the transferability of using visualization tools to improve visual literacy skills would further support these ideas.

A Qualitative Research Analysis Tool

Word Clouds, Tag Clouds, Phrase Nets, and Word Trees can offer researchers a unique tool to analyze text-based data. For example, Word Clouds were used by Banas (2010) to categorize qualitative data about teacher's use of technology in the classroom. In this study, students end of the course reflections were compiled and dropped into the Wordle data box. Words that appeared most often in the reflections, as shown via enlarged text in the Wordle image, helped to identify predominant words used in responses. These words helped to generate coded themes for further data analysis. In the case of this study, those codes related to barriers and supporters for technology integration in the classroom. Another research-based application of visualization tools could include meta-analytical investigation and interpretation of literature. For example, a researcher seeking to uncover language patterns in written works about socio-cultural events might find Phrase Net or Word Trees to be useful research tools. Tag Clouds could help researchers zoom in on the part of the text in which the predominant words appear.

A support for ELL instruction, a playground for visual literacy deconstruction, and a research tool are only a few of the opportunities afforded by text visualization tools. Additional research into and application of these tools can substantiate and maximize their use.

CONCLUSION

Today's learners require different instructional experiences than learners just a few decades early. They must have the opportunity to make connections between existing knowledge and new information in order to create new knowledge. The outcome is reconceptualizations and elaborations that support a deeper understanding. Practice, feedback, discussion, reflection, and opportunities for real-world application are activities that can help to support such outcomes. Text visualization tools can help to support this process.

In this chapter, the authors introduced and explored means by which text visualization tools include Phrase Net, Tag Clouds, Word Clouds, and Word Trees can support generative learning and elicit improved reader comprehension. Additionally, they uncovered how text visualization tools can support ELL and visual literacy instruction, and function as a research tool. Consequently, text visualization tools are a technology worthwhile introducing into pre-service teacher education and into practicing teachers' continuing education. Further research into how text visualization tools can support instruction and students' continued use of them will uncover practical applications still unknown. What will those be?

REFERENCES

Brown, C. A., & Banas, J. (2010, November). Open source visualization tools to enhance reading comprehension. In M. Simonson (Ed.), *33rd Annual Proceedings: Selected Research and Development Papers at the Annual Convention of the Association for Educational Communications and Technology*. North Miami Beach, FL: Nova Southeastern University. Retrieved from http://www.aect.org/pdf/proceedings10/2010I/10_07.pdf

Burley, D. (2010). Information visualization as a knowledge integration tool. *Journal of Knowledge Management Practice*, *11*(4). Retrieved from http://www.tlainc.com/articl240.htm.

Chun, D. M., & Plass, J. L. (1997). Research on text comprehension with multimedia. *Language Learning & Technology*, *1*(1), 60–81.

Considine, D., Horton, J., & Moorman, G. (2009). Teaching and reading the millennial generation through media literacy. *Journal of Adolescent & Adult Literacy*, *52*(6), 471–481. doi:10.1598/JAAL.52.6.2

de Courcy, M., & Birch, G. (1993). *Reading and writing strategies used in a Japanese immersion program*. ERIC database.

Eisenberg, A. (2008, August 31). Lines and bubbles and bars, oh my! New ways to sift data. *New York Times*. Retrieved from http://www.nytimes.com

Fagan, B. (2003). Scaffolds to help ELL readers. *Voices from the Middle*, *11*(1), 38–42.

Foote, C. (2009, July). It's a mad mad Wordle. *School Library Journal*, *55*(7), 32–34.

Grabowski, J. (1996). Writing and speaking: Common grounds and differences. Towards a regulation theory of written language production. In Levy, M., & Ransdell, S. (Eds.), *The science of writing (pp. 73–91)*. Hillsdale, NJ: Erlbaum.

Hook, P. A., & Borner, K. (2005). Educational knowledge domain visualizations: Tools to navigate, understand, and internalize the structure of scholarly knowledge and expertise. In Spink, A., & Cole, C. (Eds.), *New directions in cognitive information retrieval* (pp. 187–208). Netherlands: Springer. doi:10.1007/1-4020-4014-8_10

Koshman, S. (2005). Testing user interaction with a prototype visualization-based information retrieval system. *Journal of the American Society for Information Science and Technology*, *56*(8), 824–833. doi:10.1002/asi.20175

Linnenbrink, E. A., & Pintrich, P. R. (2003). The role of self-efficacy beliefs in student engagement and learning in the classroom. *Reading & Writing Quarterly*, *19*, 119–137. doi:10.1080/10573560308223

McCormick, B., DeFanti, T., & Brown, M. (1987, November). Visualization in scientific computing. *Computer Graphics*, *21*(6), 681–684.

McGuinness, C. (1993). Teaching thinking: New signs for theories of cognition. *Educational Psychology*, *13*(3 & 4), 395–316.

Medina, J. (2008). *Brain rules: 12 principles for surviving and thriving at work, home, and school*. Seattle, WA: Pear Press.

O'Donnell, P., Weber, K. P., & McLaughlin, T. F. (2003). Improving correct and error rate and reading comprehension using key words and previewing: A case report with a language minority student. *Education & Treatment of Children*, *26*, 237–254.

Oliver, K. (2009). An investigation of concept mapping to improve the reading comprehension of science texts. *Journal of Science Education and Technology*, *18*(5), 402–414. doi:10.1007/s10956-009-9157-3

Rorvig, M., & Lunin, L. F. (1999). Introduction and overview: Visualization, retrieval, and knowledge. *Journal of the American Society for Information Science American Society for Information Science, 50*(9), 790–793. doi:10.1002/(SICI)1097-4571(1999)50:9<790::AID-ASI7>3.0.CO;2-C

Shneiderman, B. (1998). *Designing the user interface: Strategies for effective human-computer interaction* (3rd ed.). Menlo Park, CA: Addison Wesley.

Shulman, L. S. (1986). Those who understand: Knowledge growth in teaching. *Educational Researcher, 15*(2), 4–14.

Shulman, L. S. (1987). Knowledge and teaching: Foundations of the new reform. *Harvard Educational Review, 57*(1), 1–22.

Sibbet, D. (2008). Visual intelligence: Using the deep patterns of visual language to build cognitive skills. *Theory into Practice, 47*(2), 118–127. doi:10.1080/00405840801992306

Swartz, R., & Costa, A. Beyer, B., Kallick, B., & Reagan, R. (2008). *Thinking based learning.* Norwood, MA: Christopher Gordon.

Viegas, F. B., Wattenberg, M., & Feinberg, J. (2009). Participatory visualization with Wordle. *IEEE Transactions on Visualization and Computer Graphics, 15*(6), 1137–1144. doi:10.1109/TVCG.2009.171

Weinstein, C. E., & Mayer, R. E. (1986). The teaching of learning strategies. In Wittrock, M. (Ed.), *Handbook of research on teaching* (pp. 315–327). New York, NY: Macmillan.

Wise, J. A., Thomas, J. J., Pennock, K., Lantrip, D., Pottier, M., Schur, A., & Crow, V. (1995) Visualizing the non-visual: Spatial analysis and interaction with information from text documents. *INFOVIS Proceedings of the 1995 IEEE Symposium on Information Visualization,* Atlanta, Georgia.

Wittrock, M. (1985). Teaching learner generative strategies for enhancing reading comprehension. *Theory into Practice, 24*(2), 123. doi:10.1080/00405848509543158

Wittrock, M. C. (1992). Generative learning processes of the brain. *Educational Psychologist, 27*(4), 531–541. doi:10.1207/s15326985ep2704_8

Zhang, J. (2008). The implication of metaphors in information visualization. *Visualization for Information Retrieval, 23,* 215–237. doi:10.1007/978-3-540-75148-9_10

Ziemkiewicz, C., & Kosara, R. (2009). Preconceptions and individual differences in understanding visual metaphors. *Computer Graphics Forum, 28*(3), 911–918. doi:10.1111/j.1467-8659.2009.01442.x

KEY TERMS AND DEFINITIONS

Cognitive Mapping: A thinking process that makes associations using spatial knowledge. In order to travel through space, one must know how points are connected to make sense of the journey. Ideas, concepts, and numbers are joined through logical connections based on relationship.

Computers in Schools: As defined by the U.S. General Services Administration (Computersforlearning.gov) - making modern computer technology an integral part of every classroom; providing teachers with the professional development they need to use new technologies effectively; connecting classrooms to the National Information Infrastructure; and encouraging the creation of excellent educational software.

Generative Learning: A theoretical base for a type of constructivist learning experience. New ideas are generated as a person makes mental connections between and across ideas, concepts, images, and emotions.

Health Education: The profession used to educate people in characteristics of good health, prevention of illness, and promotion of life-long enjoyment of wellness. It begins with prenatal care and extends to positive attitudes associated with aging.

Interactive Tools: Most often associated with social networking, software designed to permit users to enter text, images, video and audio are considered interactive. Users publish, as well as read and view, the work of other interactive users. Interactivity is a hallmark of Web 2.0.

Reading Comprehension: A complex multi-faceted process that begins with identifying and defining words to make meaning of a passage of text. The reader must also be able to analyze text to see relationships and purpose for the message. Reading becomes meaningful when comprehension includes a personal connection with a story or factual presentation of information.

Tag: A bit of information used as an Internet bookmark. Most tags are hyperlinked to other tags with the same information. The process is used to display bits of information, usually one word, in font size and color as dictated by coding in an html file.

Visual Metaphors: An image or graph used to represent an implied comparison between two unlike things. A point of association between ideas is presented through imagery. Love is a rose. The thorn on the rose is a point of association with the pain often associated with unrequited love.

Visualization: The process of converting text based information into metaphors or a word picture. A wide range of tools can be used to transform alphanumerical data into an image or graph.

Web 2.0: A version of the Internet that promotes interactive use of webpages. It differs from traditional static pages. Web 2.0 permits the user to contribute to the knowledge published to the Web. Readers are also authors through the use of blogs, wikis, and podcasting.

Word Clouds: Also known as *tag cloud* is a digital text box with words tagged with most prominent words displayed with larger font size. Word clouds can be text-based with numerical values assigned and/or as graphical image with colors and font styles assigned through calculation of most prominent tags.

Chapter 7
Supporting Teacher Development through Social Networking

Oliver Dreon
Millersville University, USA

Nanette Marcum-Dietrich
Millersville University, USA

ABSTRACT

Over the last decade, social networking has emerged as a new way for groups to communicate and collaborate online. Especially popular with "digital natives" who have grown up with technology infused in all facets of their daily lives, social networking is changing the way people interact and altering traditional views of community and participation. Recent educational reform movements have advocated for teacher educators to embrace learning communities as a way to prepare and support new teachers. Considering the current student population in schools of education and their affinity for digital communication, social networking can be used to foster online learning communities where preservice teachers' development can be supported. This chapter examines social networking and outlines recent research related to its use in the support of teacher education. The chapter concludes with design considerations for teacher educators who wish to develop social networks to foster their own online learning communities.

INTRODUCTION

Quality teacher preparation programs understand that both teaching and learning are social processes that require vibrant communities in order to thrive (see, for example, Cochran-Smith & Lytle, 1999; Grossman et al., 2001). The definition of "community," however, has evolved in the digital age. It is not uncommon for close friends to communicate daily on social networks such as Facebook, while only meeting infrequently in person. And it is now more common for business colleagues to network via online spaces such as LinkedIn than on the golf course. For today's students, develop-

DOI: 10.4018/978-1-4666-0014-0.ch007

ing a vibrant community of learners is enhanced by the use of social networking where students can collaborate about course content, create and share ideas, and manage group projects. Teachers in K-16 environments are increasingly exploring ways to use online social networking tools to extend learning beyond the classroom walls and to cultivate a sense of community in their students. In order to prepare teachers for teaching and learning in the digital age, schools of education also need to harness the power of social networking to complement classroom instruction and to create supportive online learning communities.

In this chapter, we discuss social networking and its prevalence as both a communication and instructional tool in 21st Century teacher education classrooms. We then examine the present state of teacher education programs and explore recent challenges to achieving the institutional vision of fostering the development of professionals who are life-long learners committed to fostering student learning using the best tools and techniques available. After defining social networking and the goals of teacher preparation, we attempt to re-envision teacher preparation as a space that builds communities of learners who continue to grow and support each other well into their professional careers with the help of social networks. Throughout the chapter, we reference contemporary research that demonstrates how social networking can be used in teacher education to foster learning communities that support teachers' growth professionally. Lastly, we conclude the chapter by outlining design considerations for teacher educators who want to include social networking as a means of supporting teacher development.

BACKGROUND

What is Social Networking?

Traditionally, the term "networking" has been used to describe massive webs of wires and machines that are connected to form some larger system of interaction. But the term has also been used in other ways. For instance, "networking" can also be used to describe a social gathering such as a cocktail party where people attend in order to casually meet other professionals in hopes of making important business connections. Social networking can be viewed as cross between these traditional images. Built upon a system of computers and Internet hubs, social networks allow users to communicate and interact in a virtual cocktail party. Users of social networking sites employ digital media (photos, videos, etc) to build online profiles that represent their personal or professional identities. This network affords them the opportunity to connect with friends and colleagues, form online relationships and have conversations with others across geographical divides. Where once the primary form of communication online was email, social networks have changed how people interact online. Whether for business or pleasure, users of social networks can instantaneously chat, post "status updates," maintain web logs (blogs), and identify their current location through GPS coordinates on their smart phones. With these multiple forms of communication, social networks have made the Internet a much more interactive space.

To understand the influence of social networking sites, consider the following statistics: Facebook, the most popular social networking site worldwide, has surpassed Google as the site where online users spend the most time (Schroeder, 2010). Eighty six percent of 18- to 29-year-olds say they use social-networking sites and the fastest growing demographic for social networking sites are older adults where 47 percent of internet users from 50-64 said they use social media, as did

26 percent of those 65 and older (Gross, 2010). Facebook is available in 70 different languages, creating a space that transcends national borders and language barriers. Facebook announced in 2010 that it had passed 500 million active users (Facebook, 2010) and on any given day, 50% of those active users log into their Facebook accounts. With millions of people logging in each day and actively participating in the network to some degree, if Facebook were its own country, it would be the third most populous nation in the world (US Census Bureau, 2010). Professional social networks are also experiencing unprecedented growth. Created in 2003, LinkedIn is the largest social network for professionals. LinkedIn membership includes executives form all Fortune 500 companies. With over 80 million members in over 200 countries on all 7 continents, LinkedIn has radically changed how professionals connect (LinkedIn, 2010).

The rapid growth of social networking sites is testament to society's desire to feel connected both personally and professionally. But just because an activity is popular and desirable, does not mean it is necessarily appropriate for educational purposes. An important litmus test for any new instructional tool or strategy is simply to ask, "will it enhance teaching and learning?" If the answer is yes, than it is necessary to examine how the tool or strategy can be implemented into the learning process to maximize its potential benefits and minimize its weaknesses. At the onset of incorporating social networks into an educational setting, it is critical to examine the purpose for utilizing social networking processes, the population that will be using the social networking tool, how social networking aligns with theories of learning and development, and the expected outcome from using social networking. These considerations can help to guide the process of inclusion of social networking features into classroom settings, especially in teacher education programs where supporting a beginning teacher's development

is integral to their future success (Luehmann & Tinelli, 2008; Saka et al., 2009).

21ST CENTURY LEARNERS

It is not a stretch to claim that students today are fundamentally different than students of past generations. Having grown up bathed in "bytes" of information, 21st century learners are accustomed to being constantly connected to peers and family and having knowledge instantly available. Often referred to as digital natives, today's students have the unusual distinction of being more knowledgeable of current tools and more skillful in their use than most educated adults (Trilling & Fadel, 2009). Technology shapes their daily life as a means to share and create new knowledge; the knowledge needed to make sense of and navigate new situations. Having transitioned as a nation from the industrial age to the knowledge age, students are challenged to not only read and receive knowledge but to transform and create new knowledge. In the 21st century, knowledge and ideas drive the economy and are the main source of economic growth. "Knowledge Age knowledge is defined—and valued—not for what it *is*, but for what it can *do*. It is produced, not by individual experts, but by 'collectivising intelligence' – that is, groups of people with complementary expertise who collaborate for specific purposes" (New Zealand Council for Educational Research, 2010). Using the concept of a collective intelligence, we harness the power of social networking to support the development of our preservice teachers through a community sharing of ideas and knowledge.

Online communication can create a deeply connected culture. While some may argue that digital communication is superficial and lacks the intimacy of face-to-face contact, few can deny technology's ability to facilitate communication. Recently in our university class, we posed the following question to the undergraduates, "Has technology (the Internet, mobile phones) increased your ability to stay connected with your parents?" Many of the students responded that the technology has made them less connected with their parents. We then asked them, "How many of you communicate with your parents at least once a week?" With this question, students seemed shocked. "Once a week?" they wondered. Most of the students said they called, emailed, or texted their parents at least once a day. This exchange highlights the instant communication expectations of digital natives but also suggests that they desire more intimacy in their communication. When designing a social network to support preservice teacher development, it is important to design the site in a manner that not only enables communication but also cultivates ideas and focuses participants on goal of developing as a professional through a community of sharing. A productive social network is not a site for idle chatter but rather a place for collective growth.

LEARNING AS A SOCIAL PROCESS

People rarely work or learn in isolation. Individuals communicate and participate in various communities that utilize unique language patterns, tools and objects (Gee, 2005; Vygotsky, 1978). From a situated and social constructivist perspective, learning is not individualistic in nature. Learning is an active, social process that occurs through participation in communities (Brown, Collins & Duguid, 1989; Lave & Wenger, 1991). Viewed in this light, knowledge is not static information stored in an individual's head, but exists in and is distributed amongst the actions of the community (Brown et al., 1993; Gee, 2003). As an individual learns in this community, she develops new roles of participation within the group. This participation not only transforms the entire community but also transforms the individual in the process, shaping her identity through her involvement with the group. This constant interplay between the individual and the community captures how

learning occurs for single participants and how groups evolve from their participation.

In the digital age, the traditional view of community is evolving as a result of converging technological and social factors. One technological factor is the influx of Web 2.0 applications that allow users to easily generate online content. More of the work we do is moving online through the use of web based applications like Google Documents, wikis and blogs. With increased Internet speed and web design that promotes user participation, the Internet has evolved from being an information-rich environment where people are merely passive gathers of information into a platform for social interaction and collaboration. This evolution in how we use the Internet has changed not only how we work but also how we define relationships and how we interact in groups that exist primarily in virtual space. Communities that exist online are no longer bound geographically or temporally. Whether these groups participate and communicate through MySpace, Facebook, Twitter or some other social network, interaction can occur in authentic ways, creating a support structure that might be virtual in its delivery but no less real in its effect. For instance, an online community of people suffering from myeloproliferative disorders (MPD) started as an email conversation between one MPD patient and his doctor (Wenger et al., 2009). Over the last fifteen years, the conversation has grown to a worldwide learning community of over 2500 people, allowing practitioners, families and patients to share stories, tips and research as well as offer support for one another.

FOSTERING LEARNING COMMUNITIES THROUGH SOCIAL NETWORKING

Current understandings of teacher development are informed by theories of learning in a community. In their overview of how teachers learn and develop, Hammerness et al (2005) suggest a framework of teacher learning where new teachers learn to teach through participation in a larger learning community. By participating in a larger learning community, the authors argue, new teachers begin to reflect on their work and develop a vision of their teaching and the tools, understandings, practices and dispositions that enable them to successfully teach (Cochran-Smith & Lytle, 1999; Schon, 1996). Engaging in learning communities need not be reserved for practicing teachers, rather this pedagogical structure can be an effective vehicle for the training of pre-service teachers. Ultimately the goal of any teacher education program is to prepare new teachers of the highest quality by providing learning experiences that help them acquire the knowledge, skills and dispositions to be successful in their future classrooms. By constructing a learning community around the practice of teaching and learning, teacher educators can provide affective and instructional support for preservice teachers as they navigate these learning experiences and begin to forge their identities as future teachers (Bianchini & Brenner, 2010).

Considering the emergence of online tools for interaction and communication, teacher educators need to thoughtfully examine traditional views of community and consider how social networking can be used to foster teacher development. Examining the framework presented by Hammerness et al (2005), social networking applications offer features that can support the development of online learning communities where preservice teachers can reflect on their practice and be supported as they develop the tools and dispositions of the profession. For example, Luehmann (2008) examined the role that blogging played on a teacher's identity development. Unlike private journals, blogs are public conversations where writer and reader engage in topics together. While blogging is often considered to be a solitary reflective activity, Luehmann examined the larger blogging community and its influence on the teacher/blogger. Luehm-

ann found that this online environment offered powerful opportunities for teachers to reflect on their practice and wrestle with their professional identities. In another study, Luehmann and Tinelli (2008) formed an online community of science teachers who were using reform-based practices in their classrooms. Utilizing individual blogs to form a larger social network of participants, Luehmann and Tinelli found that the community engaged in conversations that the researchers identified as "cognitive, affective or social work." Besides providing words of encouragement and support, the community also discussed pedagogical issues and instructional implications of their practices. Because the social network was intentionally designed to support a targeted pedagogical practice, participation and conversation in the network was purposeful. The social network gave participants the opportunity to engage in discourse about their teaching and receive "collaborative interpretation, encouragement and advice." These examples demonstrate how social networking can be used to foster learning communities. While these learning communities are distributed geographically and mediated through technological means, they still can have an impact on individual teachers and the group as a whole.

In our work with preservice teachers during their final year of university preparation we used social networking as a way to create and manage small learning communities (Dreon & Marcum-Dietrich, 2010). The social network used to manage the learning communities was intentionally designed to support our preservice teachers during their field experiences and was targeted to focus them on the connections between the theory they were studying in their formal university courses and their practicum work in secondary classrooms. In observing the preservice teachers' interactions in the social network, we found that our preservice teachers utilize social networking in much the same way as Luehmann and Tinelli report. In the social network, the community uploaded videos of teaching demonstrations, contributed photos of themselves and participated in individual blogs and group discussions. Across these different networking avenues, we found that community engaged in "cognitive work" where they discussed pedagogical issues, "affective work" where group members shared emotions and "social work" where community members shared materials and supported one another socially (Luehmann & Tinelli, 2008).

In observing the preservice teachers' online interactions, it is evident that the online community support provided by the social network is distinctly different than face-to-face interactions and results in a new layer of community exchange and support. This distinction is evident in an examination of the nature of the conversations between the members of our social network. Consider this exchange between Daniel and Melissa, two student teachers who were completing their field placements in the same secondary school building. Melissa and Daniel teach with their cooperating teachers in adjoining classrooms and have multiple face-to-face interactions throughout the school day. On one particular day, Daniel was wrestling with classroom discipline issues with one of his classes and chose to use the blog to share his experiences with the community:

"The basic classes have taken a turn for the worse. (my cooperating teacher) and I have been stricter in discipline and our class expectations, but they have struck back with more disrespect and general immaturity that at times is maddening. For instance, today one of my students was sitting in the back of the room "listening" to (my cooperating teacher) introduce the simple instructions that took 6 times longer than it needed to because of CONSTANT talking. Anyway, I went to collect the student's IPOD that he was less than creative about hiding. I asked him to give it to me, and he said "no." I was literally dumb-founded. I told him to give it to me, but he just stared at me and said "you can't get me to do anything." - Daniel (February 23, 2010 at 7:34 PM)

In response to Daniel's post, Melissa writes:

"That is awful about 6th period!! Kids can be absolutely cruel sometimes! And why didn't you tell me about this after school today?!?!?! See you tomorrow!" - Melissa (February 23, 2010 at 8:33 PM)

Even though Daniel and Melissa taught in neighboring classrooms, Daniel chose to use the social network to share his experiences with the community rather than talk about it face-to-face with Melissa after school. Posting less than an hour after Daniel's self-described "rant," Melissa was able to provide support through online communication avenues brokered through the community's social network.

DEVELOPING A SOCIAL NETWORK

Even when it exists in a social network, the development of a learning community hinges on participants' ability to engage with other members of the group (Wenger, 1998). Engagement within a community, Wenger (1998) writes, requires "the ability to take part in meaningful activities and interactions, in the production of sharable artifacts, in community-building conversations, and in the negotiation of new situations" (p 184). In his book on communities of practice, Wenger (1998) outlines four dimensions of design that can help designers confront the fundamental "issues of meaning, time, space and power" inherent in communities. (p 231) While presented as different dimensions, the constructs complement one another and offer a lens to view the larger community and its design and management. These dimensions include:

Participation and reification: In developing a community, designers must consider the balance between participation and the reified products of that participation. In social networks, this balance is infused in such decisions as who is able to participate in the community, what communication features are built into the network and what objects (video, images, etc) are shared by community members.

The designed and the emergent: Developers of learning communities must weigh how much of the participation of the community is prescribed by designers and how much of it emerges from the community itself. This duality influences the social norms of the membership and how the community views the space.

The local and the global: In Wenger's view, learning is distributed across the individual and the community, involving those who organize learning and those who realize it. Viewing communities from this perspective can influence how instructors see their roles and how they participate in a learning community.

Identification and negotiability: Design has the power to influence the identification and negotiation of meaning and responsibility in a community. In a social network, design can foster participation and engagement in multiple ways. An instructor developing a social network for use with a group of beginning teachers can restrict negotiability by disallowing certain features and communication avenues or share the meaning-making power with group members by allowing more open forms of communication and participation.

Developing a social network to support beginning teachers requires teacher educators to thoughtfully weigh these different dimensions of design. They are not simply philosophical concepts or aesthetic choices. The dimensions afford different modes of participation, cultivate different avenues of communication and interaction and foster different perceptions of the online space. These dimensions are embedded into a host of practical design decisions that must be considered as a learning community is developed and revisited continually during the life of the network.

Open vs. closed membership: At the onset of developing a social network for preservice teachers, a teacher educator must decide who will be able to participate in the online community. Defining the membership will ultimately define the purpose, the use, the social norms, and ultimately the outcome of the community. Questions to consider include: will mentor teachers be a part of a network of preservice teachers, will members be able to invite other people to join, or will membership be open to anyone? When considering the inclusion of different stakeholders into any social network, the network designer must consider their primary objective for fostering the online community. If the network exists only to provide an online social space for individuals to communicate and interact, the membership can be more open. If however, as in our situation, the network is designed to support the learning and development of the community, the membership must be thoughtfully constructed to allow user participation in an environment where they can safely wrestle with their views of teaching, reflect on their classroom experiences, and be motivated to effective action.

In developing a social network with the preservice teachers in our secondary science Professional Development School, we decided to only include preservice teachers and university faculty in our online community. This decision to limit membership was intentional in order to create a learning community which acted as a reflective space to support the preservice teachers during their field placement. By excluding the cooperating teachers from involvement in the social network, we hoped the community would provide preservice teachers opportunities to reflect on their experiences in a open and unguarded manner without worrying about their cooperating teacher's reactions. In crafting the membership in this manner, cooperating teachers were aware of existence of the social network and how the preservice teachers would be using the space. Most cooperating teachers agreed that the preservice teachers would be better supported in a community of peers where they could participate without the cooperating teacher's involvement and perceived oversight.

Single vs. multiple forms of participation: An effective social network is more than a place to congregate online, as a learning community it must be constructed to afford opportunities for members to participate and to reify their participation. This participation can come in a variety of ways. In Luehmann and Tinelli's work, the community participated in a blog space where each member wrote reflections and commented on other member's work. Members' participation was reified in the blogs and comments in which they contributed. Other communities, however, may choose to use other means of participation, communication, and reflection. Besides blogs, social networks allow members to upload audio and video files, share documents and instantaneously chat with one another. These additional features extend the modes of participation for members and allow members to choose what degree they feel comfortable participating in the space.

In our online community of preservice teachers, members use multiple forms of participation to interact with their peers and negotiate the meaning of their experiences. Some of these features are designed into the space and others have emerged from the members themselves. For instance, members use the online space to reflect in blogs and to post videos of their teaching lessons. This participation is a result of our design. We added those features and asked the members to participate. Other features, however, have emerged from the members themselves and their desire to extend their interaction and participation. For instance, members began posting times for face-to-face meetings and social outings using the online network as a means of organizing offline activities. Some members also added photos of themselves, their classrooms, and their professional activities to an online photo album that one of the members started in the network. The photo album emerged from one members' desire to make the space more personal and to represent the activities of

the community. Sharing the design power with the members of the community fosters a sense of ownership of the online space and provides a foundation on which support can be built.

Free response vs. assigned posts: Teacher educators who develop social networks for their preservice teachers can take a variety of approaches on managing the online space. For instance, prompts can be assigned where community members must participate on a scheduled basis. This approach, however, can alter how members view the social network. Participants may begin to see the space as another academic assignment to complete. Providing no guidance, however, may undermine the objectives of the social network and may cultivate the belief that any participation (or non-participation) from members is acceptable.

When developing our social network, we wrestled with this design consideration and ultimately decided to take a reductive approach. In order to model the type of communication our network was designed to foster, we supplied the reflective prompts at the start of the school year. At the start, students were required to both post a response to the prompt and to comment on the posts of a prescribed number of peer responses. The goal of this structure was to establish a community of personal reflection and peer support. These beginning "prescribed" prompts helped to establish the online community as a reflective and purposeful space for the preservice teachers' development. The prompts encouraged participants to wrestle with their beliefs and their views of self. As the semester progressed, we began giving more open-ended prompts until students, without prompting, began to initiate their own prompts. At this stage, preservice teachers had assumed control of the space and used it to reflect on topics of their choosing. This scaffolded approach allowed preservice teachers to first develop an understanding of their participation and reflection within the social network and the opportunity to assume freedom in their continued participation in the space. This method was an attempt to create a balance between the "designed" and the "emergent" and to foster a sense of ownership of the space and participation amongst the preservice teachers in the community.

Defined vs. developed social norms: Participation in any community is governed by social norms and practices that are unique to that group. For example, how a teacher acts, dresses and communicates in a school setting is guided by the social norms of the school district in which she works. Those norms and practices can be explicitly defined in a contract or be implicitly understood as acceptable practices of the profession that have developed over a period of time. Participation in another group, however, may involve different norms and practices. For instance, if a teacher is a member of a community of marathon runners, her participation in that group would be governed by different norms for communication and dress compared to her workplace expectations.

Participation in a social network is also governed by social norms and practices. On Facebook, users can "tag" or "poke" their friends. On Twitter, participants can use a series of textual characters ($@, \#, RT$) to communicate additional information to their "followers." These online conventions must be understood and followed in order for people to fully participate in the space in acceptable manners. Whenever an individual's participation is not acceptable according to the social norms, however, other members of the network can ostracize her. People can be "unfriended" on Facebook or lose "followers" on Twitter based on their online participation. The real challenge is when the social norms for an online community collide with the social norms of the offline world. This can be especially problematic for preservice teachers who are accustomed to adhering to the norms of Facebook but now must reassess their online actions to align with the expectations of behavior of the teaching profession (Shapira, 2008).

Looking at the social network we developed with our preservice science teachers, we considered whether to allow the social norms of our online community to emerge on their own or to design the social norms at the start of the semester. Our struggle not only related to Wenger's design aspects of emergent vs. designed elements but also to the population we are supporting with the space. Working with preservice teachers, we are conscious of the types of norms and practices that are acceptable in their professional lives offline. We wanted the online space to reflect the acceptable behaviors in members' current field placements and also in their future classrooms. While we did not want to fully prescribe the norms of interaction within the space, we also wanted to foster a safe, professional environment for members to participate. Instead of providing a laundry list of do's and don'ts, however, we offered a guiding vision for the space to be used as a means for professional collaboration, reflection and support. By explicitly stating this guiding vision, we help to define acceptable behaviors of participation within the online community and also allow avenues of participation to emerge from the group.

Instructor vs. mentor role: How an instructor participates in an online community may affect the participation of the group. For instance, if an instructor views the reflections and participation of members as items to assess and grade, the climate of the online space will be governed by that view. If, however, an instructor chooses to take on a mentoring role, the space and the participation will reflect this. Returning to Wenger's design aspects, the local can have an effect on the global and each individual has the power to affect the entire group. As teacher educators who are developing social networks for use with preservice teachers, it is critical to remember that our participation can affect the group's paricipation as well.

Examining our roles in the social network we use with our preservice teachers, we try to maintain mentor roles that help support the members' development as teachers. While we ask members to share videos of their teaching and post reflections, these products are not assessed or graded.

Instead, we provide supportive comments and ask questions to help the members thoughtfully consider their practices.

FUTURE RESEARCH DIRECTIONS

In this chapter we describe how we harness the power of social networking to support the development of our preservice teachers through a community sharing of ideas and knowledge during their university studies. But in our initial attempt to re-envision teacher preparation as a space that builds communities of learners who continue to grow and support each other well into their professional careers with the help of social networks, we have yet to see whether the professional learning communities established as part of our teacher education program will be sustained as our graduates transition into the teaching profession. With a goal of creating sustained professional learning communities, more research needs to be conducted into the methods and strategies for encouraging graduates to remain active within the social networks formed during their pre-service teacher preparation programs. Questions of whether continued involvement should be allowed to sustain itself organically through the informal use of non-institutional social networks such as Facebook or whether schools of education should take a more active role in sustaining graduate involvement via the creation of alumni social networks that retain the professional learning community focus on reflection and innovation of teaching and learning are unanswered. A primary goal of most schools of education is to encourage graduates to be life-long learners, understanding how social networking can be used as a vehicle for sustained professional development needs to be explored.

CONCLUSION

Today's preservice teachers are digital natives who have grown up essentially online, using digital spaces as their area for communication, reflections, and expression. Schools of Education can capitalize on preservice teachers' comfort in digital spaces to support their development by creating online learning communities that foster reflective practice and professional growth. When used appropriately, social networking's digital tools such as blogs, wikis, video uploading, and chat can extend thoughtful personal reflection and community support beyond traditional course work and classroom walls. In order to maximize the potential of social networking to support of preservice teachers' development, the social network must be designed and structured in a manner that encourages participation, cultivates the sharing of ideas, and encourages reflection on professional practice. By considering the different design aspects outlined here, teacher educators can create social networks that do more than allow social interaction between individuals. The space can grow into an online learning community where preservice teachers can develop their teaching and the tools, understandings, practices and dispositions that enable them to successfully teach.

REFERENCES

Bianchini, J., & Brenner, M. E. (2010). The role of induction in learning to teach toward equity: A study of beginning science and mathematics teachers. *Science Education, 94,* 164–195.

Brown, A. L., Ash, D., Rutherford, M., Nakagawa, K., Gordon, A., & Campione, J. C. (1993). Distributed expertise in the classroom. In Salomon, G. (Ed.), *Distributed cognitions: Psychological and educational considerations.* New York, NY: Cambridge University Press.

Brown, J. S., Collins, A., & Duguid, P. (1989). Situated cognition and the culture of learning. *Educational Researcher, 18*(1), 32–42.

Cochran-Smith, M., & Lytle, S. L. (1999). Relationships of knowledge and practice: Teacher learning in communities. *Review of Research in Education, 24,* 249–305.

Dreon, O., & Marcum-Dietrich, N. (2010). *The Ning is the thing: Supporting interns through social networking.* Paper presented at the Professional Development Schools National Conference, Orlando, FL.

Facebook. (2010). *Statistics.* Retrieved September 28, 2010, from http://www.facebook.com/facebook?v=app_10531514314#!/press/info.php?statistics

Gee, J. P. (2003). *What video games have to teach us about learning and literacy.* New York, NY: Palgrave Macmillan.

Gee, J. P. (2005). *An introduction to discourse analysis.* New York, NY: Routledge.

Gross, D. (2010). Report: Older users flocking to Facebook, Twitter. *CNN Tech.* Retrieved August 27, 2010, from http://www.cnn.com/2010/TECH/social.media/08/27/older.users.social.networks/index.html

Grossman, P., Wineburg, S., & Woolworth, S. (2001). Toward a theory of teacher community. *Teachers College Record, 103,* 942–1012. doi:10.1111/0161-4681.00140

Hammerness, K., Darling-Hammond, L., Bransford, J., Berliner, D., Cochran-Smith, M., & McDonald, M. (2005). How teachers learn and develop. In Darling-Hammond, L., & Bransford, J. (Eds.), *Preparing teachers for a changing world: What teachers should learn and be able to do.* San Francisco, CA: Jossey-Bass.

Lave, J., & Wenger, E. (1991). *Situated learning: Legitimate peripheral participation.* New York, NY: Cambridge University Press.

Luehmann, A. (2008). Using blogging in support of teacher professional identity development: A case study. *Journal of the Learning Sciences, 17,* 287–337. doi:10.1080/10508400802192706

Luehmann, A., & Tinelli, L. (2008). Teacher professional identity development with social networking technologies: Learning reform through blogging. *Educational Media International, 45*(4), 323–333. doi:10.1080/09523980802573263

New Zealand Council for Educational Research. (2010). *The knowledge age.* Retrieved September 27, 2010, from http://www.shiftingthinking.org/?page_id=58

Saka, Y., Southerland, S., & Brooks, J. (2009). Becoming a member of a school community while working toward science education reform: Teacher induction from a cultural historical activity theory (CHAT) perspective. *Science Education, 93,* 996–1025. doi:10.1002/sce.20342

Schon, D. A. (1996). *Educating the reflective practitioner: Toward a new design for teaching and learning in the professions.* San Francisco, CA: Jossey-Bass, Inc.

Schroeder, S. (2010). Web users now on Facebook longer than Google. *CNN Tech.* Retrieved September 10, 2010, from http://www.cnn.com/2010/TECH/social.media/09/10/facebook.google.time/

Shapira, I. (2008). When young teachers go wild on the web. *Tech Policy.* Retrieved August 28, 2010, from http://www.washingtonpost.com/wp-dyn/content/article/2008/04/27/AR2008042702213.html

Trilling, B., & Fadel, C. (2009). *21st century skills: Learning for life in our times.* San Francisco, CA: Jossey-Bass.

US Census Bureau. (2010). *International database*. Retrieved September 2, 2010, from http://www.census.gov/cgi-bin/broker

Vygotsky, L. S. (1978). *Mind in society: The development of higher psychological processes*. Cambridge, MA: Harvard University Press.

Wenger, E. (1998). *Communities of practice: Learning, meaning, and identity*. New York, NY: Cambridge University Press.

Wenger, E., White, N., & Smith, J. D. (2009). *Digital habitats: Stewarding technology for communities*. Portland, OR: CPsquare.

ADDITIONAL READING

Albion, P. (2008). Web 2.0 in teacher education: Two imperatives for action. *Computers in the Schools*, *25*(3/4), 181–198. doi:10.1080/07380560802368173

Bennett, S., Maton, K., & Kervin, L. (2008). The "digital natives" debate: A crtical review of the evidence. *British Journal of Educational Technology*, *39*(5), 775–786. doi:10.1111/j.1467-8535.2007.00793.x

Brady, K., Holcomb, L., & Smith, B. (2010). The use of alternative social networking sites in higher educational settings: A case study of the e-learning benefits of Ning in education. *Journal of Interactive Online Learning*, *9*(2), 151–170.

Cotten, S. R. (2008). Students' technology use and the impacts on well-being. *New Directions for Student Services*, (124): 55–70. doi:10.1002/ss.295

Dawson, S. (2010). 'Seeing' the learning community: An exploration of the development of a resource for monitoring online student networking. *British Journal of Educational Technology*, *41*(5), 736–752. doi:10.1111/j.1467-8535.2009.00970.x

Foulger, T., Ewbank, A., Kay, A., Popp, S., & Carter, H. (2009). Moral spaces in MySpace: Preservice teachers' perspectives about ethical issues in social networking. *Journal of Research on Technology in Education*, *42*(1), 1–28.

Fox, A., & Wilson, E. (2009). 'Support our networking and help us belong!': Listening to beginning secondary school science teachers. *Teachers and Teaching*, *15*(6), 701–718. doi:10.1080/13540600903357025

Gee, J. P. (2003). *What video games have to teach us about learning and literacy*. New York: Palgrave Macmillan.

Gunawardena, C., Hermans, M., Sanchez, D., Richmond, C., Bohley, M., & Tuttle, R. (2009). A theoretical framework for building online communities of practice with social networking tools. *Educational Media International*, *46*(1), 3–16. doi:10.1080/09523980802588626

Heiberger, G., & Harper, R. (2008). Have you Facebooked Astin lately? Using technology to increase student involvement. *New Directions for Student Services*, (124): 19–35. doi:10.1002/ss.293

Junco, R., & Cole-Avent, G. A. (2008). An introduction to technologies commonly used by college students. *New Directions for Student Services*, (124): 3–17. doi:10.1002/ss.292

Kist, W. (2008). "I gave up MySpace for Lent": New teachers and social networking sites. *Journal of Adolescent & Adult Literacy*, *52*(3), 245–247. doi:10.1598/JAAL.52.3.7

Lei, J. (2009). Digital natives as preservice teachers: What technology preparation is needed? *Journal of Computing in Teacher Education*, *25*(3), 87–97.

Luehmann, A., & Tinelli, L. (2008). Teacher professional identity development with social networking technologies: learning reform through blogging. *Educational Media International*, *45*(4), 323–333. doi:10.1080/09523980802573263

Makinster, J., Barab, S., Harwood, W., & Andersen, H. (2006). The effect of social context on the reflective practice of preservice science teachers: Incorporating a web-supported community of teachers. *Journal of Technology and Teacher Education*, *14*(3), 543–579.

Nackerud, S., & Scaletta, K. (2008). Blogging in the academy. *New Directions for Student Services*, (124): 71–87. doi:10.1002/ss.296

Roblyer, M., McDaniel, M., Webb, M., Herman, J., & Witty, J. (2010). Findings on Facebook in higher education: A comparison of college faculty and student uses and perceptions of social networking sites. *The Internet and Higher Education*, *13*(3), 134–140. doi:10.1016/j.iheduc.2010.03.002

Timm, D. M., & Duven, C. J. (2008). Privacy and social networking sites. *New Directions for Student Services*, (124): 89–101. doi:10.1002/ss.297

Trilling, B., & Fadel, C. (2009). *21st Century Skills: Learning for Life in Our Times*. San Francisco: Jossey-Bass.

Wenger, E. (1998). *Communities of practice: Learning, meaning, and identity*. New York, NY: Cambridge University Press.

Wenger, E., White, N., & Smith, J. D. (2009). *Digital habitats: Stewarding technology for communities*. Portland, OR: CPsquare.

KEY TERMS AND DEFINITIONS

Blogs: Online web journals which allow users to reflect on experiences and receive feedback from readers.

Digital Native: A person who has grown up with technology infused in all facets of their daily lives. Often used synonymously with 21st Century Learners.

Learning Communities: A group of people who share common values and beliefs and who are actively engaged in learning together from one another.

Participation: Active involvement in a community, whether online or face-to-face. In an online community, participation can include contributing to discussions, reflecting in blogs, etc.

Preservice Teacher: Individuals who are enrolled in a teacher education program but are not yet certified to teach.

Reification: The tangible products that result from a user's participation in a community.

Social Networking: An online communication system that allows users to interact and collaborate with other people and form online communities.

Web 2.0 Technology: Web applications that facilitate interaction, collaboration, information sharing and user-centered design. Popluar examples include blogs, wikis and social networks.

Chapter 8
Learning to Teach in Web 2.0

Mark Gura
Fordham University, USA

ABSTRACT

This chapter presents and analyzes an instructional practice developed in an Instructional Technology course required of Education students at Fordham University. The practice was employed to ensure a high level of engagement by assigning students the hands-on development of Web-based, instructional resources suitable for use with their own public school classes. The author describes the transformative quality of the assignment and discusses how it strongly supported students in forming a mental image of Instructional Technology as a viable, desirable dimension of their teaching practice. Discussed in detail are the attitudes and understandings about Instructional Technology of the students, the Web 2.0 tools and content items they selected for use in their projects, the ways they applied them to the instructional resources they developed, and how those satisfied their needs as teachers. The implications of the practice and how it evolved are presented in the broad context of how all those involved in teacher preparation programs may understand and apply them.

INTRODUCTION

In teaching a required Educational Technology course at Fordham University, my understanding of how the use of technology is perceived by new teachers has been both informed and changed radically. My efforts to provide my students with something of genuine value that they could carry into their new teaching practices led me to see the traditional approach often taken in such courses, that of surveying the field of Educational Technology, as providing little of worth for them. Instead, I developed a term-long project that many students indicated resonated as a high point in their teacher preparation and continue to draw on now that they have entered the field. I feel this approach has some important implications for the design of teacher preparation courses intended to

DOI: 10.4018/978-1-4666-0014-0.ch008

support and encourage teachers to make technology a vital part of their teaching practice.

In the following, I describe the project in detail and discuss why it was successful with my students. The intention is to analyze my experience with an eye toward identifying the universal needs of teachers, the factors that made the practice I developed flexible and broadly applicable to these needs, and the specific ways my students responded to the practice as well as the instructional resources they produced as a result. I include descriptions of the Web 2.0 resources and digital content items selected by my students, and the ways they apply them in their projects. Also, I present insights into how these directly address classic instructional issues within the context of today's typical schools and classrooms.

Background: Putting Practice in Context

In 1997 I was promoted from my citywide technology staff developer position with the New York City Department of Education to the post of Director of the Office of Instructional Technology, a citywide, central office position. The school system had just made its first, massive purchase of computers, installing a cluster of them in practically every middle school classroom in the city. Providing professional development and curricular support for the many thousands of teachers involved became my job, one I would hold for 7 years before retiring and taking up new challenges, including teaching Education courses.

Getting those first teachers to use the new computers in their classrooms proved to be a challenge for me and the many people I worked with. The pattern that emerged was one of older teachers, people to whom technology seemed foreign and off putting, resisting its use and favoring paper-driven teaching with which they were comfortable (Gura & Percy, 2006).

New teachers must be exposed to ways of teaching with technology during formal teacher preparation programs (Russel, Bebell, O'Dwyer, & O'Conner, 2003). However, I was dealing with teachers who had received their teacher education before the advent of technology placement in classrooms. In the years since this first experience, though, much has changed. The field of EdTech has matured (Pierson, 2005), with countless books, articles, conferences, online repositories of lessons and implementation guides, and other resources available to teachers. Teachers, too, have changed; the older ones eventually relenting and adopting technology under pressure of supervisors, parents, and students – at least to a degree. Newer teachers are generally familiar and comfortable with working with technology (Russel, et al., 2003). I expected to find a high degree of acceptance of the concept that technology has great potential for instruction by the new crop of teachers that has entered the field, young people who've come of age with computers, video games, and the Internet as part of the landscape of their everyday lives.

I was deeply surprised, therefore, as it became clear when initially interacting with my Fordham classes, that this group of younger students was quite resistant to the idea that technology had any real significance for their new jobs as classroom teachers.

The Challenge

Unlike the first groups of teachers I worked with, for whom technology was a mystery, these new teachers were very comfortable with computers and the web. However, they simply couldn't see how this fit in to the big picture of what their supervisors would expect of them or of what they personally hoped to do in their classrooms. Perhaps this was not so surprising. After all, as they shared with me, a great deal of what they'd encountered over the course of their own education took place in print-centric classes. Teachers need to conceptualize how the use of various computer programs facilitates teaching and learning. This can more easily be done if they actually see students using technology that has been integrated into a curriculum (Bitner & Bitner, 2002). My students hadn't personally experienced much technology use in their own education or witnessed colleagues use much technology with their classes.

The Fordham School of Education's Conceptual Framework specifically states that its "Programs are committed to developing candidates' knowledge and skill in the use of technology to improve student learning." Further, it "(1) Values the variety of technological resources for enhancing an individual's learning, (2) Views growth in technological expertise as integral for professional practice." Still, the course I taught was exclusively devoted to this aspect of teaching and fostered intense and unique focus on it. In probing my students' beliefs and understandings as we began to delve into this experience intended to intensely examine the role of technology in teaching and learning, my students became more aware of their own positions on it and verbalized them enthusiastically as we jointly set the stage for the course that we would share.

I've taught this course several times over several semesters and this pattern has held throughout. These were conscientious students, though, and they complied with the requirements of my course admirably. We plowed through readings, both from our textbook and online sources – sampled YouTube videos, podcasts, and other digital media items – tried WebQuests – took advantage of rich online resources like Read Write Think, and had professional conversations sharing our reflections on the variety and quality of practices and resources we'd reviewed and tried.

Having taught for 18 years before becoming involved in professional development, I was adept at reading the reactions to, and the level of engagement precipitated by, curriculum and teaching. I had experience with a very considerable number of learners, both youth and adult. My assessment, therefore, of the course I was requested to refine and deliver, was that this would be an effective, although uninspiring experience for both my

students and myself. The course would get these students informed about the subject of EdTech, but likely wouldn't move them to adopt much of what they learned. Until, that is, a shift I made in instructional approach precipitated a transformation in affect and engagement.

The initial design of my course was simple and typical. The face-to-face classes, as well as the away-from-class reading, research, and reflection assignments created to support them, represented a survey of the broad field of Ed Tech, its philosophy, practices, commonly used resources and their applications, and the like. I expected my students to do the readings, participate in the reflective discussions about them in class, turn in a traditional essay-style assignment for each, and then do an extended bit of research as a term report. This, they would present in class to me and their classmates toward the end of the semester.

Description of Students

My students, by the way, were largely teaching fellows, slightly older than average new teachers. Many of them had experiences like the Peace Corps or other exchange experiences of a year or more behind them. A few were pursuing a second career, or returning to the work force. All this made them a little more experienced. The projects they developed for my class were designed for a hypothetical class they conceived based on recent experience in actual classrooms as part of the program they were enrolled in.

In New York City there is no standard technology deployment model in the schools. On the contrary, with the exception of a few centrally networked resources, the amount and types of instructional technology available in a school is very much the product of how that school has evolved on its own over the years. What's available is there by virtue of the unique knowledge and inclinations of the various staff members who worked in or passed through the school. There is no set comprehensive methodology or mandated set of methods, practices, approaches or resources. This, I took as a good background against which to teach the course, as my exchanges with my students would center on the big bullet issues in a teacher's life, the 'what should we do in the classroom?' and 'how should we best do it?' questions, not simply learning some of the 'how to?' for a program or resource already in place with approaches to such issues already conceived by others.

A New Approach and Context

After a couple of initial sessions in which I observed my students learning about classroom technology, I followed my instincts and shifted the focus to an active, learning by doing approach; learning by doing being a basic tenet of adult learning (McKenzie, 2001). This, I accomplished through changing the final project/term assignment and making it much more the central focus for ongoing class activities. These ongoing 3 hour sessions were re-contextualized as preparing the students for the extended project. They were to select items covered in class for deeper investigation as they fit general ideas on for size, determining how these would be used in their own teaching practice and in the community of learners to which they belonged. I also set time aside for some group technology resource demonstrations. In these, simple procedures and how-to techniques in using Web 2.0 resources for application to the specific instructional purposes we'd been discussing, were covered. As we also had a lab available, I devoted a portion of class time for small group exploration and collaboration on blog, media sharing, and other Web 2.0 resources.

The specific final project assignment I tasked these students with contained a serendipitous element. In traditional fashion, I asked my students to develop a multisession instructional unit that engaged their own students in Project Based Learning. In this, I expected them to use technology in a variety of simple ways: to support them in presenting the learning project they would design to their students, to support their students in doing the project, as well as provide a means for their students to create the product or performance they would present at project completion. My students were to produce a mock sample of what their own students might produce, both as proof of concept for the viability of their instructional unit, and as a teaching aid to help explain to their students what was expected of them. This assignment, to my pleasant surprise, was accepted readily and enthusiastically by my students who seemed highly engaged, if not completely intrigued, right off the bat.

One further dimension of the project helped transform the class experience from mere credit bearing, worthwhile effort to an activity they found inspiring and motivating. They were to produce 2 finished items to present to me and their classmates at finish: 1) a standard lesson/unit plan and 2) a "digital hand off" a way of presenting their project to their students without directly presenting it themselves – a way that the students could present it to themselves, or a substitute teacher or a colleague could present it in their stead.

To carry this a little further, the assignment would replicate the communications revolution (Cairncross, 1997) underway in the real world; their work would be crafted to be accessible across the traditional barriers of distance and time, as part of the vast evolving library of instructional content on the World Wide Web. I assigned my students to upload their finished project to the web, using either a blog or simple website resource (like Google Sites). Constituent elements might be uploaded to document sharing websites like scribd.com, slide presentation sharing resources like slideshare.com, videos to resources like TeacherTube or SchoolTube or YouTube, and audio to resources like DivShare or OurMedia – all to be linked to, or embedded in, their online presentation to the students.

Meaningful Learning

In our initial, text-driven discussions held during the first session or two of our course, the students and I discussed alternatives to test driven and test validated instruction. We were looking for ways to teach for meaningful learning. In order for meaningful learning to occur, the task that students pursue should engage active, constructive, intentional, authentic, and cooperative activities (Jonassen, Howland, Marra, and Crismond, 2008). A broad category of practice that became a focus for our approach to meaningful learning was Project Based Learning (PBL), one that has a special relationship to Educational Technology.

Our focus would be PBL supported and enabled by a variety of Web 2.0 applications. Project-based learning allows students to practice higher-order thinking and use knowledge (Higher-Order Thinking Skills, 2010). This assignment would give my class an opportunity to produce a resource for their own students that would foster the learning of Higher Order Thinking Skills.

Technology is often listed as an enabler of PBL (D' Orio, 2010). More to the point though, PBL is a progressive approach to instruction in which educators have long expressed interest, looking for ways to implement it since before classroom technology was commonly available. While PBL is emblematic of aspects of progressive education like authentic learning, collaborative student work, the production of learning artifacts, portfolio assessment, and the like, it has had disappointing sparse actual adoption. This is true because it presents a significant change from traditionally organized instruction, and related to that, represents more effort on the part of the instructor in terms of planning and a degree of risk taking as it requires a loosening of teacher control over student behavior, Overall, it has been considered logistically more difficult to implement. That is, until recently when technology has been applied to PBL, facilitating greatly many of its facets, including those which have represented some of the greatest disincentives for teachers in the past.

In our discussions, my students revealed not only a knowledge of PBL, but that they had already assimilated the attitude held by a great many with whom they now shared the teaching profession, that PBL is a goal, something to aspire to, but not something to be taken terribly seriously as it was unrealistic for today's teachers in today's schools to be held responsible for implementing it.

Consequently, one of the great attractions to the technology I was showing these students and to the project I had assigned them was that it clearly made Project Based Learning infinitely more do-able than they had believed before. This was liberating enough for them to become enthusiastic about the approach, and once they engaged in the assignment I had given them, the creation of a project based unit of study, they became very satisfied with the product of their own tech-fueled creativity.

Which aspects of the technology accounted for this? For one thing my students could create a website as a presentation platform, so that they didn't have to personally relate the particulars of the project they created for their students. The students or another adult acting on their behalf as a media facilitator (in the case of very young students) could activate and navigate through the websites at their own pace and as often as they liked to get the gist of the assignment and see examples of how they might handle it.

The projects my students created for use with a class of their own were somewhat open ended; taking advantage of the way technology, in turn, could encourage their own students to make an inquiry individualized to their own interests and levels.

Finally, through the use of technology, their students could produce a product or performance that could be saved, archived, and shared over great distances or broadly to large, real audiences, just the sort Web 2.0 content creation, self publishing, and dissemination that make today's world so exciting. I believe that this explains much of the core of what's compelling and valuable in the project.

From Implementer to Creator

As my students shared with me, they found the assignment to be especially engaging because it called on them to use skills they rarely got to use in their work as teachers and because it gave them a platform from which they could express themselves within the context of teaching. Part of this response from the students clearly had to do with an opportunity to be creative. Among other ways the technology functioned in the project, was as a palette of colors with which they could paint a picture; in this case an instructional experience.

One point of the discussion among us centered on how today's teachers often feel their role has become that of implementer, implementer of priorities, curriculum, and methods developed by others. While my students could see, at least theoretically, how adding technology to the equation might make these more relevant for their digital native students, they couldn't see how it would make the things they were called on to implement more relevant for them. At least not before doing our term project.

On reflecting, I realized that a good measure of what was related to me is the need for teachers to have a voice. On one level, technology, at least the way the assignment I gave them encouraged them to use it, allowed them to interpret and communicate the things they were required to teach, but in their own voice. Doing this, they found satisfying and inspiring as it allowed them to satisfy their need to improve and perfect what they were presenting to their students, as well as how they presented it, in an ongoing fashion. This added a creative dimension to what otherwise might be an inert and inflexible curriculum and teaching methodology. Furthermore, we were using the technology, among other ways, as a publishing platform. This allowed them to capture and archive what they had created. And, it enabled them to

disseminate it to colleagues and others globally. In a very real sense my technology-supported project had transformed the job of teaching to the act of creation, something that resonated greatly with my students.

For my part, as the instructor, someone keenly sensitive to the reactions of what I presented, I'll add that the energy and enthusiasm level for my classes, at least when our schedule called for me to present material relating to the project described, and the students to work on and develop their 'solutions', was palpable.

A further refinement of the assignment that added still more to the all important context of the project was my creation of a virtual project gallery, actually a section of the website I set up for the class. I had assigned my students to establish a blog or website of their own as a vehicle with which to "publish" their individual project. Instead of their turning in their work in traditional, hard copy printout, I directed them to send me simply the URL of their project's online presence. In this "gallery" on my own class site, I simply listed the students' projects and gave a link for each. Once clicked, this would take the viewer to the student's work. I titled this gallery "Teaching in Web 2.0."

I made it clear to the students that they were free to take their work down from the web as soon as the class had reviewed one another's projects and I had graded them at the conclusion of the course. I take it as an indication of their pride and pleasure in their projects that now, over 2 years after the first group did this assignment for me, hardly a single student has "unpublished" his work. In fact, a few students have voluntarily chosen to build upon and add to their projects, indicating how thoroughly they have integrated it into their teaching practice.

On perusing the virtual gallery's list of titles of my students' projects, one encounters names like "Choose Your Own Adventure", "What is Urban Farming?", "How can I help?" and "Who am I?" These clearly convey the interests of these young teachers and their understanding that common, required portions of curriculum and standards can be presented through the lenses of themes that they personally have high interest in and feel enrich their own lives.

In projects Like "Bloggin with Ms. Shockly (to learn about the Great Depression)" my student presents a project of her design to her own students. This she accomplishes by embedding a YouTube video of herself giving a rehearsed, and idealized live performance of the project presentation. In doing this, she was afforded a somewhat unique opportunity for urban teachers who must subordinate their desire to be center stage in order to deal with the broad spectrum of distractions and compromises that come with the territory of teaching in today's schools, learning environments that are very much less than ideal in many cases.

Not surprisingly, many of my students gravitated to the production or appropriation of items in YouTube, and similar, education-centric video sharing sites like SchoolTube and TeacherTube, as powerful, enabling instructional resources. The use of video has advantages over graphic and textual media. E.g.: portrayal of concepts involving motion, the alteration of space and time, the observation of dangerous processes in a safe environment, dramatization of historical and complex event; demonstration of sequential processes the viewer can pause and review (Remenyi, 2007).

A good example is another student's project titled "Understanding the Background of The Scarlet Letter." In this, via a YouTube video embedded in her project blog, she taps the services of an accomplished scholar/presenter as a teaching assistant. By using the very simple technique I modeled in class of copying a video's YouTube "Embed Code" and pasting it in her blog post's HTML editing mode, this student skillfully appropriated the work of a 'personality' who remains ready and poised to deliver a performance in support of her lesson whenever and as often as she and her students feel the need to play it.

Much is mentioned these days about the need for, and powerful effect of, differentiation in student assignments. In this sense, it is small wonder that my students responded so favorably to the assignment I had given them. They found the Web 2.0 resources we were working to be highly empowering in self differentiating the assignment and coming up with a solution that very much captured and expressed their personal interests and preferences while adhering perfectly well to the required curriculum.

In some of the blog titles themselves we can be see how my students rose to the opportunity of personal expression with names that communicate their young teacher idealism. Even though the general environment in which teaching currently takes place is not always nurturing of it, this need endures. My students saw my term project as a way to focus on this aspect of their teaching experience. One good example is "There are no mistakes in Ms. G's class." Another is "Making Teaching Relevant", with "Teaching Perfection" and "Strive and Thrive – The Upward Spiral" more of my students' project titles that illustrate this. Even my, at first doubtful, student who registered for her blog by requesting the URL "antibloggerblogger. blogspot.com" revealed in her subsequent work how she was won over to the infectious, positive spirit of the assignment by titling her project "I Like School" in the blog's header.

Technology as an Integrator

Technology is a vehicle by which numerous important, but seemingly disparate, items may be effectively integrated into the curriculum. Part of the restrictive nature of the now dying, pre-technology era paradigm of education is the "Either/Or" nature of instruction. In this understanding it is held that either we have time, energy, and resources to teach basic, core curriculum skills OR we have them to teach other important, but generally less highly prioritized subjects like The Arts. Technology, in many ways, helps us move beyond this restrictive understanding. It provides a platform with which many highly valued dimensions of intellectual activity can be easily integrated. In this sense, my students understood how their desire to bring a wide variety of arts-related learning into the teaching of basic skills, for which they were held responsible, could be accomplished through the use of technology. The projects my students created are liberally peppered with arts elements: performances, visual works, and literature. They also call on, and guide students through, the appreciation for and understanding of works of art as well as the creation of poems, posters, collages, and other original works. All of this is done at the service of core curriculum teaching and learning and accomplished through the productivity and integrative capabilities of the Web 2.0 technologies employed by my students.

Technology to Generate the Resources Needed for Teaching and Learning

Technology offers ways for teachers to structure and manage their teaching that have great advantages. The development of digital technologies has largely been conceived and directed at fostering and supporting productivity. Using technology, teachers who otherwise would likely not be able to, can move into the creation of instructional resources (leveraging WEB 2.0's content creation and publishing dimensions). They can research and locate materials, adapt them for specific classroom needs, can tweak and mix and match them, and can use them as the basis on which the produce original items. In other words, the project I created for my students showed them how to generate the teaching and learning resources they needed.

The "How-To"

To my surprise, while almost all of the new teachers I worked with, middle aged second career fellows included, were familiar with common Web 2.0 technologies, very, very few of them had actually ever created a blog or website personally, other than perhaps to dabble briefly, and certainly never considered the creation of one to support their teaching.

Once the class launched into the project, what ensued was round after round of experimentation, with students trying things out on their own, sometimes coming back to class to ask how to do things or for an assist with a troubling or confusing bit of blog use or site construction. It is important to point out here that the resources my students used for this assignment are described by their providers as "easy to use" and "user friendly" and, in fact, my students did find them to be just that. I'll also point out that all of what we used was free, requiring nothing to be purchased, as well. The following is a brief rundown of the resources that proved to be popular in my class. These represent but a small segment of the body of free, Web 2.0 tools on the web, though.

- Google Sites and Blogger resources: My students were given a choice of producing their final project as either a blog or a website with these. Their ease of use, stability, and general trustworthiness supported my students tremendously in creating sophisticated projects. Of note, I discussed student security in using web-based resources as part of the class and as an extension, showed my students how to remove the "Nav Bar" of a Blogger blog so that their young students would not be lured into distracting or inappropriate sites from the instructional blog.
- Voki: This talking head avatar, which is easy to program to speak on one's behalf, absolutely captivated my students. A very large percentage of them embedded a Voki greeter into their blog or site.
- Comic Strip Maker: One of many "comic book engines" on the web that make the creation of professional looking, sophis-

ticated comic strips easy. This was used not only by my students to present ideas to their classes, but as a tool for their students to use in doing their projects.

- Survey Monkey: Data collection is a core approach in much upper elementary through high school curriculum. Including a powerful tool to help accomplish this is one of the things a number of my students opted to include in their project.
- DocStock and Scribd: The ability to upload a simple word processed document to the web, publish it on a site, and then link to or embed a 'viewer ' of that document in their site or blog, my students found fascinating, liberating, and highly useful. Their products using these also illustrated how quickly my students caught on that finished web resources for instruction are not generally single items, but collections of digital items integrated together to produce functional, clear experiences for an audience of students.
- SlideShare and Animoto: Similar to DocStock and Scribd, but intended for slideshow type presentations, these free media sharing resources were put to good use by my students. A similar item, but with a particular personality, is Hallmark's Smilebox resource that several of my students discovered and used.
- Photo Story 3: A free download, this resource from Microsoft allows users to craft presentations that combine photos, recorded sound, music, etc. to produce a polished whole.
- Video Sharing Resources: YouTube, SchoolTube, TeacherTube and others were a favorite media type for my students to integrate into their work.
- Screen Capture Tools: Whether using the screen capture function that comes with the Windows or MAC operating system, or one of the free or for purchase downloads,

the ability to capture what is created or located on the screen of a computer and save it as a jpg (or other format) file, is a bit of functionality that made a great deal of this type of tech-based creation possible for my students.

Adapting Technology as an Inducement to Adopting Technology

My student's project titled "Mr. Ski's ESL Blog" presents content through YouTube and other video sharing sites from museums about marine mammals. To support the students in reflecting on and understanding their learning task, for which this content is provided, my student, Mr. Ski, produced a KWL chart (what I Know, what I Want to know, and what I want to Learn) as a digital file, uploaded it to the online document sharing resource Scribd.com, and then embedded the player of this within the blog he created to present the project to his students. This is a good example of how the members of my class responded to the challenge I set for them by taking traditional methods they firmly believed in, in this case the use of KWL, and adapting them for digital use. My students' blogs or sites functioned as a platform from which to organize and present these digitally re-established resources to their own students. In my mind, this is a perfect example of how technology need not supplant what teachers do traditionally for them to make good use of it; one of the primary reasons, I feel, that the earlier generation of teachers resisted adopting technology so vehemently. The task and approach I presented my students with leaves the situation much more flexible, empowering each teacher to honor traditional practices as they adapt them, which in turn proved to be a method of encouraging them to adopt technology. Other students used this approach, similarly, to create neat rubrics that they embedded in their blog.

Of the many tools and good-to-go resources I presented to my students as 'possibles' that they might elect to use as they crafted their projects, none was more enthusiastically adopted than VOKI, a simple form of talking avatar. My students' VOKIs greet visitors to their project sites, acting as gateway hosts. In a warm, amusing, and friendly voice these avatars quickly establish a relationship between their project and the young students they've designed them to present to. In many ways this is emblematic of the humanizing effect the technology resources they selected had on their projects they created for their term assignments. This dimension was not expected, but as soon as my students saw the ease of doing this and the potential it had for establishing and maintaining a tone for their teaching they found very desirable, they were convinced that it was an element that would add a great deal to their work.

The Google Blogger blog resource that most of my students opted to use as the platform on which to construct and present their units, itself is emblematic of a dimension of the technology they identified as having value. Simple and template driven as it may be, the options for color, type face and size, placement of elements, as well as the broad assortment of widget carried content and resources it would permit them to present to their students, all added to the understanding that this is an approach that would draw out their individualism, put a best foot forward face on it, and have it work for them as it satisfied the demands of their challenging new professions.

Most interestingly, once my students became comfortable with the Web 2.0 tools I set before them, they were soon tweaking and cross breeding them to fit their needs, making them still more useful within the context of our class assignment. And clearly they did this too, to amuse themselves through their own creativity. A good example is "blobertblogkey", an admittedly nonsense name one of my students titled his instructional blog. In the introduction to his project, my student created a slide show out of numerous still graphics he had produced using tools and techniques my course presented. These he gave captions as he strung them together in proper order to make his lead point for the unit he was presenting. Next, he created audio narration for his slide show. Once this was done he uploaded the piece to YouTube. This complex process, one that he said he enjoyed going through, he concluded by embedding the YouTube video in his blog where his students would see it.

Michelle, another of my students, presented Shel Silverstein's poem The Giving Tree with her project. Embedding a YouTube video that presents a 1973 animated film actually narrated by Mr. Silverstein, who is now deceased, turned out to be easy and effective. She followed this up with the following statement in her project blog:

Yesterday we watched an animated version of The Giving Tree by Shel Silverstein. We learned that trees can give us a lot of things! Think back and I will show you pictures from the book to help you remember, what things did the tree give to the boy/man? Let's make a class list of all the things the tree gave to the boy/man.

Now, let's see what else we can get from trees. Let's look at these websites below to find out more products that come from trees:

http://www.idahoforests.org/wood_you.htm

http://owic.oregonstate.edu/teachers. php#common

Your Task:

Once you have finished exploring I want you to go back to the section that says I'm reading! (with the little dragon) and look through the stories. I would like you to create your very own comic. If you would like you can use this fun comic creator website to help you: http://www.makebeliefscomix. com/.

This project is another good example of how the blog platform serves as a canvas in which a variety of digital resources, here we see how embedded videos – links to instructional resources – and an online comic book engine, are integrated to provide the students with a continuum of digital content and resources. These are made to fit very well together at the service of a traditional sort of lesson. In presenting them to students, poems are truly meant to be read aloud and not just read silently (Hamilton, 2009). My student had fluidly matched resources that present the reading of a poem and then provide a way to powerfully foster and capture her student reaction to it. Her comfort and creativity in and mixing these resources in a logical sequence, I feel, demonstrated quick learning as a result of high engagement and personalization of the task I had assigned.

This approach to using embedded videos enabled a number of my students to make wonderful leaps in locating and adapting resources for instruction. For instance, one student appropriated a YouTube video of the comic actor Steve Martin's hilarious performance as Inspector Clouseau in the remake of the film The Pink Panther. In this video Mr. Martin is being coached by an English pronunciation specialist who is walking him through the exercise of saying "I would like to buy a hamburger." Obviously uploaded to YouTube as one of the vast assortment of entertainment oriented snippets posted there, it proved to be a perfect choice for the ESL pronunciation lesson my student included in her project.

Presenting Projects

The blog or website format chosen by my students for their projects proved to be remarkably practical, flexible, and advantageous in a number of unexpected ways. It is typical of the sort of 3 credit graduate level course I was guiding my students through for students to do a term project. Further, a classic dimension of scheduling such classes is to devote a session or two for students to deliver their projects to their class peers. Not only does this procedure offer an important impetus

and focus for doing the project, but it affords the students the opportunities to benefit from seeing and reflecting on related or alternate solutions to the common task on which they all worked. By absorbing the work of peers, offering suggestions and responses back and forth, and reflecting on these as they make comparisons to their individual thinking and work, the students benefit from the social learning aspects of the project and the learning community that evolved during the course of the class. The blog format supported this directly and in the process modeled dimensions of class management that hit home for the students as they planned how they would take advantage of such technology applications in their own work as teachers.

The presentation of projects is not only usually a somewhat anxiety producing experience for the students, but presents scheduling and management issues for the instructor. Devoting enough time to do justice to project presentation can be challenging, as can be student absences. In fact the temporal nature of the experience is a major detractor to its value. Once the presentations are completed their value is gone. Using a blog or simple website as a platform to produce, present, and preserve projects gives great flexibility. Students may learn from one another's efforts during their formal presentation or they can share their work with one another informally simply by looking at one another's online work when convenience dictates. This, too, offers collaborative dimensions as students may comment and suggest things based on online viewing across distances and in non-synchronous time flow.

Modeling an Approach to the Use of Teacher-Created Instructional Resources

In our early conversations, many of my students shared their doubts about the value of technology in the classroom. In probing this I found this was based on a mental picture of instructional technology use that was uninformed and that prejudiced them from taking the subject to heart. As with most learning, learning to use technology in teaching is influenced by predispositions that the learner brings to the learning opportunity (Laffey & Musser, 1998). A great many of my students shared their understanding that because they didn't have access to technology in a one-to-one, computer to student ratio, either by a scheduled visit to a computer lab or access to a rolling cart of laptops, therefore, by definition, they didn't have technology available and couldn't be expected to make it part of their teaching. This complaint was voiced nearly from the very beginning of the class and I simply allowed the students to share their views without arguing for the first couple of sessions.

Throughout that time, my teaching modeled a different definition of technology. I used only a single computer that threw a large projected image on a screen in the front of the room via an LCD projector. We would have our conversations as usual, but from time to time I would make a point illustrated with a website, or show the students a video, or perhaps play a podcast or type some notes using a word processor that would appear on the screen. This, the students accepted easily and readily and soon I began to shy away from working the technology myself, calling the students to the presentation station to conduct a Google search or navigate a website or perhaps build a PowerPoint presentation in front of the class. When stuck for knowhow or ideas as they worked through these chores, the student at the computer would receive supportive help from the students seated around the room who, while their hands were not on the technology, were deeply involved in the content and learning process it established in our classroom. They were thoroughly invested in the positive outcome of technology use for our learning and amusement during the class. There were times that 2 or 3 students together would take control of the computer presentation station, one interacting with peers around the room verbally

as an idea or process collaboratively formed throughout the group and the other working the keyboard and mouse.

At a certain point in session 2 or 3 I gently made my point, which was acknowledged by the class, that while we had been using only a single computer, our lessons had been very much supported and directed by the presence of technology. Not only did this EdTech "ah ha" bring home the point that one-to-one computer deployments were not the sole legitimate way of using technology in the classroom, but my students could see that they are not necessarily the best, either. In this way, we had a great opening for a reconsideration of what instructional technology is and how it fits in with what teachers do. The point resonated strongly, also, because a single computer and an LCD projector were things that are available in schools even when class sets of computers are not.

Most importantly, the things I would present to the class over the duration of the course, for the sake of convenience and of having a well organized permanent archive of them, were things that I had put in my own class blog. By launching the blog at the beginning of a class, I had my notes, my instructional materials, my records of what had been done and shown in classes before, and more at my keyboard fingertips. This practical approach to classroom and instructional management resonated and paved the way for acceptance of the online project my students were to do for me that semester as a valuable, innovative step forward in their own teaching practice.

Implications and Recommendations

My teaching this course took place against a background in which virtually all standards documents governing preK-12 Education in the US insist that technology be integrated thoroughly into the learning experiences given students. As a measure of this, by 2008 44 states had technology standards for teachers (Reed, 2008). Furthermore, for some time now, teacher education programs have been under fire for inadequately preparing educators for the demands of technology-rich learning environment found in PK–12 schools (Lamb, 2003). Consequently, there has been a shift in the perception of the need for technology to be an important part of teacher preparation and the inclusion of some sort of technology class is now becoming more and more common. Such a course may dutifully explain technology to young teachers, but if it doesn't result in their seeing a practical way to personally integrate what's learned into their own teaching practice, it will probably foster the conclusion that technology for instruction is perhaps interesting, but not something to seriously consider doing in their own classrooms. My students, while required to take the course, didn't initially share enthusiasm for it with the policy makers whose work ultimately resulted in the course's creation. It was the experience of the practice I describe here that fostered that enthusiasm.

In the current climate of schools, one often described with the term the "culture of accountability", it is largely a given that teachers will follow directives. The notion of "teacher buy-in" that was a major concern in the previous era is not often discussed. Still, those in the field of teacher preparation will understand that many of our students are entering a profession in which they may practice for a lifetime. Compliance is not a dimension of the experience that may be sufficient, let along desirable, to carry involvement over several decades. Providing young teachers with approaches by which they may stay engaged and enthused with their work, as well as take their own place in carrying the profession's work further, will likely pay dividends in this field – one in which dissatisfaction and attrition are high and costly. This is one sense in which I see significant implications for the serendipitous development of this term project and course I refined at Fordham. The project my classes took on taps technology to individualize and personalize their work as teachers, and in numerous ways empower and

engage them as they satisfy personal needs while very competently demonstrating best teaching practices to serve their students.

It is effective to guide students in the use of technology to create instructional resources as part of their Education learning, not to simply study *about* the use of technology with the expectation that they'll come to the ways and rationale for using it personally later on. The project I assigned my students is hands-on; in it, they use technology to produce resources that may be implemented with their own real-world students. One of the important inferences to be had from the Web 2.0 revolution, is how the technology empowers 'everyman' to move beyond even more effective and intelligent consumption of content, and transforms him to competent creator of content. The project I assigned my students may be seen as an Education application of this broader phenomenon.

CONCLUSION

As stated previously, practically all of my students have kept their term projects up and running online, some of them more than 2 years old at this point in time. Others have communicated to me how they continue to use the project in their actual, current teaching assignments and others how they have updated them and continue to do so. In the greater scheme of what instructors of Education courses can hope to produce in terms of actual impact, I don't think I would aspire to anything greater.

Since developing this practice at Fordham, I have begun to teach similar courses at other teacher preparation institutions. Furthermore, I have met other faculty who assign projects that share a few of the dimensions of mine. The work becomes richer the more student projects are online for their peers to reflect on and benefit from. This mirrors the general effect and value of the web and ultimately establishes a richer environment in which today's Education students may be prepared to take their place in the evolving 21st Century classroom.

REFERENCES

Bitner, J., & Bitner, N. (2002). Integrating technology into the classroom: Eight keys to success. *Journal of Technology and Teacher Education, 10*, 1.

Cairncross, F. (1997). *The death of distance: How the communications revolution is changing our lives.* Boston, MA: Harvard Business School Press.

D'Orio, W. (2010, October 2). The power of project learning. [Editorial]. *Scholastic Administrator*, 1-2.

Gura, M., & Percy, B. (2005). *Recapturing technology for education - Keeping tomorrow in today's classrooms.* Lanham, MD: Scarecrow Education.

Hamilton, B. (2009, August 30). Poetry goes 2.0. *Library Media Connection*, 26–29.

Higher-Order Thinking Skills. (2010). Retrieved September 25, 2010, from http://www97.intel.com/pk/projectdesign/thinkingskills/higherthinking/

Jonassen, D., Howland, J., Marra, R. M., & Crismond, D. (2008). *Meaningful learning with technology.* Upper Saddle River, NJ: Pearson.

Laffey, J., & Musser, D. (1998). Attitudes of preservice teachers about using technology in teaching. *Journal of Technology and Teacher Education, 6*, 223–242.

Lamb, A. (2003). Workshops that work! Building an effective, technology-rich faculty development program [Electronic version]. *Journal of Computing in Teacher Education, 21*, 77–83.

McKenzie, J. (2001). How teachers learn technology best [Editorial]. *From Now On. The Teachers Technology Journal, 10*, 6.

Pierson, M. (2005). Technology in the classroom: Thinking beyond machines. In Hughes, L. W. (Ed.), *Current issues in school leadership* (pp. 245–264). Mahwah, NJ: Lawrence Erlebaum Associates.

Reed, A. (2008). Most states have technology standards for teachers. *edweek.org, 1*, 1.

Remenyi, D. (2007). *Proceedings of the 6th European Conference on e-Learning.* London, UK: Academic Conferences Ltd.

Russel, M., Bebell, D., O'Dwyer, L., & O'Conner, K. (2003). Examining teacher technology use: Implications for pre-service and in-service teacher preparation. *Journal of Teacher Education, 54*, 2971–310. doi:10.1177/0022487103255985

Chapter 9
Supplementing the Learning Management System:
Using Web 2.0 for Collaboration, Communication, and Productivity in the Preparation of School Technology Leaders

Stephanie A. Jones
Georgia Southern University, USA

Lucilia Green
Georgia Southern University, USA

Charles B. Hodges
Georgia Southern University, USA

Kathryn Kennedy
Georgia Southern University, USA

Elizabeth Downs
Georgia Southern University, USA

Judi Repman
Georgia Southern University, USA

Kenneth F. Clark
Georgia Southern University, USA

ABSTRACT

This chapter describes how and why Web 2.0 tools are being used in a completely online M.Ed. program in Instructional Technology. Examples of specific tools and their implementation are provided along with the theoretical or pragmatic bases for their use. McGee and Diaz's (2007) categories for Web 2.0 tools, documentative, communicative, generative, interactive, and collaborative, are used to structure the examples. A description of the evolution of the M.Ed. program and reasons for supplementing learning management systems with Web 2.0 tools establishes the context of the discussion.

DOI: 10.4018/978-1-4666-0014-0.ch009

INTRODUCTION

Online education continues to redefine higher education, impacting colleges and universities worldwide. According to the Sloan Report, "the 17 percent growth rate for online enrollments far exceeds the 1.2 percent growth of the overall higher education student population" (Allen & Seaman, 2010, p. 1). This growth has occurred at Georgia Southern University, a doctoral research university with an enrollment of 20,000 students. The Instructional Technology (ITEC) program in the College of Education was one of the first programs at the university to offer courses in an online format, beginning the migration during the 1990s and becoming fully online by 2007. The ITEC program offers two tracks: one leading to K-12 library media certification and the second designed for students desiring a technology coordinator position in a K-12, business, or industry setting.

The ITEC faculty are committed to providing teachers, school librarians, instructional supervisors, and postsecondary personnel the skills and competence necessary to select and use technology in all its forms and to nurturing the leadership skills they need to succeed. Program faculty have a history of seeking creative ways to use technologies for instruction to meet that goal. This chapter will use case studies to illustrate how the program has used Web 2.0 tools to enhance the learning environment to prepare 21st century technology leaders.

BACKGROUND

The program's use of distance learning technologies dates to 1992, when the Georgia Statewide Academic & Medical System (GSAMS) network was established. The Instructional Technology program adopted GSAMS to simultaneously offer courses to multiple sites. In 1998, faculty began utilizing the Blackboard course management system to provide resources such as handouts and lecture notes to students. Eventually Blackboard was used for creating hybrid courses with online course meetings taking the place of some face-to-face classes.

In 2007, the Georgia Board of Regents announced a new initiative; University System of Georgia (USG) programs throughout the state would compete for inclusion in a state supported "online franchise" called Georgia OnMyLINE (GOML). GOML provides students with a single portal that identifies online program and degree options, specifies program and admission requirements, and lists available courses. The ITEC program at Georgia Southern was selected as the GOML Instructional Technology franchise. As a result, the program grew from 65 students with three faculty members in 2008 to a 2010 enrollment of over 280 students and seven full-time, tenure-track faculty.

The Office of Information and Instructional Technology (OIIT) at the USG is responsible for maintaining an Integrated Learning Environment to serve the administrative and instructional needs of the USG clients. Georgia supports one common learning management system (LMS) throughout the state. Known as GeorgiaVIEW, the system currently utilizes WebCT VISTA (GeorgiaVIEW, 2010). All online ITEC courses are delivered using GeorgiaVIEW.

TERMINOLOGY USED

Watson and Watson (2007) observed that the non-standardization of terminology such as content management system (CMS), learning management system (LMS), and various other names and acronyms for e-learning systems is confusing. Learning Management System and Course Management System have become interchangeable. Moodle is self-described as a "Course Management System (CMS), also known as a Learning Management System (LMS) or a

Virtual Learning Environment (VLE)" (Moodle. org, 2010). Blackboard now avoids any of these terms in their promotional literature and refers to its product as a "*platform* [emphasis added] for delivering learning content, engaging learners, and measuring their performance" (Blackboard Inc., 2010).

In this chapter, the authors will refer to a learning management system (LMS) as a system which instructors use to "provide their students with learning materials and activities while tracking participation and progress through data systems and assessments" (Falvo & Johnson, 2007, p. 40). The label Web 2.0 will be used as Oliver (2007) describes it: "an umbrella term for many individual tools that have been created with web collaboration, sharing, and/or new information creation in mind" (p. 55).

OVERVIEW: LMS LIMITATIONS

Many college campuses rely on their LMS for the delivery of instruction in online and hybrid courses, as well as for nonacademic uses such as document sharing, committee work, and student organizations (Ingerman, Yang, & the 2010 EDUCAUSE Current Issues Committee, 2010). Stability and reliability of LMSs are essential elements for administrative functions, but by their very nature they also "slow the integration of new functionality" (Severance, Hanss, & Hardin, 2010, p. 246). When students and faculty compare an LMS to the menu of ever-emerging Web 2.0 tools and social networking services, "the LMS may be perceived as inflexible and 'cookie-cutter' in its method of organizing instruction" (Ingerman, et al., 2010, "Issue #8," para. 4). Key problems for teaching and learning using an LMS include:

- The instructor retains nearly all of the control of the learning experience (Martindale & Dowdy, 2010; Mott, 2010).

- The learning environment is restricted to the traditional semester timeframe and then only to students enrolled in the course (Mott, 2010).
- LMSs are "focused on administrative support (e.g. grading, attendance) rather than … creative and collaborative learning activities" (Repman, Zinskie, & Downs, 2010, pp. 46-47).

One result of this growing dissatisfaction is a move toward faculty supplementing the institutional LMS with Web 2.0 tools (Craig, 2007; Mott, 2010; Repman, et al., 2010). By moving out of the LMS and onto the Internet with Web 2.0 tools, students can have control over their learning experience; artifacts from learning can exist indefinitely beyond the end of a formal class; and the focus can move from administrative functions to "collaborative, authentic opportunities for students to engage in meaningful experiences related to the curriculum" (Nelson, Christopher, & Mims, 2009, p. 85).

The ITEC faculty began using wikis in 2005 as a way to build resource libraries for students. Since that time Web 2.0 tools have become an integral part of every course. Additionally, the electronic portfolio, the summative assessment for the students, is created and hosted using Web 2.0 tools. The next section presents case studies documenting how the ITEC faculty enhance their mandated LMS with Web 2.0 tools.

INTRODUCTION TO THE CASES

Case based reasoning, reasoning by remembering, describes how human beings search their memories for experiences that guide them in creating solutions to encountered obstacles (Kolodner, 1993; Schank, 1999). Exploring case studies on technology integration helps to deepen understanding of the relationships between pedagogy and technology by increasing awareness of realistic obstacles, strengths and weaknesses of technology integration, as well as technology usefulness (Kim & Hannafin, 2008; Pierson, 2001).

McGee and Diaz (2007) organize Web 2.0 tools into categories dependent not on tool characteristics but on how the tools are used. The categories identified are documentative, communicative, generative, interactive, and collaborative. The following case studies are organized by the *primary* instructional goal that determined the choice of the selected tools.

Overview: Documentative Uses

The World Wide Web makes a tremendous number of resources available on nearly every topic. Even though the instructor selects high quality, relevant resources, there is still uncertainty about the usefulness of those resources to the learners. Most instructional design models include a feedback loop to clarify this uncertainty. LMS products typically provide assessment or survey tools to collect feedback. Data is traditionally collected at the conclusion of instruction and is then used to improve instruction for the next wave of learners. The information is segregated by course section and kept from others who might benefit. Two cases demonstrate the use of real-time feedback to collect and document student feedback on course materials, with this feedback directly embedded in the current instructional process.

Documentative Case Study
1: Online Polling

In a graduate-level course involving digital video editing, the instructor reviewed and selected three potentially useful resources to share with students. Polldaddy (http://polldaddy.com) was used to create a poll asking learners to indicate the resource that was most useful for their video production work. The poll was embedded using standard HTML tags directly within the content created in the LMS so that it was presented di-

rectly at the point of use of the resource. The poll allowed learners to view the live results as they were selecting a resource or voting on a resource they had utilized.

The choice to collect feedback outside of the LMS had several benefits. One poll could be embedded in multiple sections of the same course. If the instructor were using tools available through the LMS only, the creation of multiple polls would be required. Learners were able see feedback from all members of the course without section limitations. The poll can continue to exist across multiple semesters so that the feedback on resources aggregates over time, as long as the instructor offers those resources to learners.

Documentative Case Study
2: Online Survey

Professional association standards for the program focus on helping students understand 21st century skills and the needs of 21st century learners. By design, the program provides students with opportunities to interact and reflect on content in a variety of formats. One objective required students to develop a reflective statement about the changing nature of learning in the 21st century. During week one of the activity, 11 relevant videos were selected by the instructor and organized into a playlist using Mag.ma (http://mag.ma/). During that week students watched and reflected on each of the videos. Then students used SurveyMonkey (http://www.surveymonkey.com) to vote for the video they wanted to discuss with the rest of the class. During the second week, the instructor used VoiceThread (http://voicethread.com/) to upload the winning video and pose questions for reflection. Students spent the next week adding their own threads in response to the video. Instead of watching one video, students watched an entire set of related videos and made a decision about which video would promote discussion. This resulted in a high level of interactivity with content across the two weeks of the activity. In addition,

Table 1. Expert content available online

Individual	Content	Format	URL
Howard Gardner	Multiple Intelligences	Video	http://www.edutopia.org/multiple-intelligences-howard-gardner-video
Allison Rossett	Discussion of performance support tools	Audio	http://www.xyleme.com/podcasts/archives/5
Multiple	Discussion of design-based research	Video	http://projects.coe.uga.edu/dbr/expertinterview.htm
Michael Wesch	How we will learn in the future	Video	http://vimeo.com/11183976

through Survey Monkey, VoiceThread and student use of Doppelme (http://doppelme.com/) to create avatars for VoiceThread student accounts, learners were exposed to several new technologies.

Live user feedback, as described in these two case studies, is something that Internet users now consider commonplace. Consumer opinion sites and integrated customer reviews are an established feature of the Internet landscape. Educators can use online polling services to leverage a consumer attitude and create a more participatory learning environment while collecting and documenting valuable formative feedback.

Overview: Communicative Uses

Several strategies exist for communicating information to students in engaging ways (Hodges, 2004). Online audio and video options allow for this variety in presentation format in courses, which are often predominantly text-based. You-Tube (http://www.youtube.com) and similar tools provide the ability to bring motivating guest lecturers into their courses without having to coordinate those visits with guests. Table 1 provides examples of experts available online.

Communicative Case Study 1: Online Video Lecture

In this case, students in an online instructional design course were asked to view *Learning Styles*

Don't Exist (Willingham, 2008) while studying learner analysis. After viewing the video, students shared their reactions. While the learners' opinions were valued, they were required to support their statements with information beyond personal experiences. By bringing the expert into the class, students were able to see and hear a primary source, Willingham, and engage in a lively debate about the ideas in the video – arguably more so than if the course instructor had simply provided his own opinion. That is, the third party was more readily criticized than the course instructor.

This particular video reinforces motivation not only through a varied delivery format but also by what Keller (1987) describes as incongruity or conflict since the video presents information that contradicts the learners' prior experience. Requiring students to support their statements encouraged them to seek out multiple perspectives. The video was embedded directly into the HTML content of the course within the LMS, so students did not have to leave the learning environment to view the video.

Communicative Case Study 2: Online Audio Podcasts

Audio podcasts have been found to be motivating instructional components (Bolliger, Supanakorn & Boggs, 2010). This case uses podcasting to expose future school librarians to the struggles and thought process of teachers who attempt technology integration. The goal was to help learners flesh out their roles as instructional partners by identifying the challenges classroom teachers face when using technology in instruction and discerning how they might better address these needs during future partnerships.

Researchers recommend that learners observe practicing teachers integrate technology in the classroom, whether in the field or vicariously through electronic mediums (Kim & Hannafin, 2008). For this learning module, students selected two programs from a series of podcasts on classroom technology integration. Each podcast consisted of an interview with a practicing teacher who discussed a successful and an unsuccessful experience with integrating technology into two lessons. Students then posted a short description of the interviews and discussed how a school librarian might have collaborated with that teacher to improve the integration experience.

In addition to the benefits students derived from listening to actual teachers describe their own experiences, learners were able to develop concrete strategies and resource lists to address their chosen cases. Students described specific ideas for collaboration and shared the resource lists they would have used when planning with the teacher. The American Association of Colleges for Teacher Education and the National Council for Accreditation of Teacher Education both address the importance of this type of work sampling to help educators reflect on their pedagogical beliefs (Schalock & Myton, 2002).

Overview: Generative Uses

Generative strategies for learning (Wittrock, 1989) are promoted by Lohr (2008) to "help learners think about information more deeply and learn it more thoroughly" (p. 111). Concept mapping is a generative strategy where terms, concepts, or ideas are visually arranged using shapes and lines or arrows to represent relationships between terms (Oliver & Raubenheimer, 2007a). Concept

maps can be used for collaborative critiquing, decision-making, planning, problem solving (Oliver & Raubenheimer, 2007b), organizing and representing knowledge, accessing prior knowledge, and exploring new ideas (Cennamo, Ross & Ertmer, 2010).

Generative Case Study: Concept Mapping

Concept mapping has been implemented in at least two courses. Instructional design students use tools such as Gliffy (http://www.gliffy.com) or Bubbl.us (http://bubble.us) to develop task analysis diagrams. The online tools allow students to maintain their task analysis diagram as a living document that is easily edited and which evolves during the design process. These tools afford geographically-dispersed students the ability to collaborate on their instructional design projects.

In the Administration of Technology Resources course, students create concept maps of their initial perceptions of course content using online concept mapping tools. Those initial perceptions are shared and discussed. Since concept mapping tools have large workspaces, in terms of height and width, students can arrange ideas without the restrictions imposed by tools that limit users to a standard 8.5 x 11.5 page size. As the course progresses, students revisit their initial perceptions and compare them with subsequent concept maps created while exposed to learning experiences in the course.

The concept mapping strategies described here demonstrate how technology can be used to help achieve technology standards for creativity, communication, and collaboration like those detailed in the *National Educational Technology Standards for Students* (International Society for Technology in Education, 2007). Program students, most of whom work or plan to work in educational settings, will have models to adapt for their own students.

Overview: Interactive Uses

When serving an interactive purpose, Web 2.0 tools encourage people to "exchange information, ideas, resources and materials" that they review and collect over time (McGee & Diaz, 2007, p. 32). Collecting and organizing these resources can be done using technologies such as PBworks (http://pbworks.com) or Ning (e.g., http://teacherlibrarian.ning.com/). In contrast to LMS file managers, students can access Web 2.0 collections outside of their courses and after graduation. These resources are easily shared during collaborative teaching, teacher trainings, job interviews, and in electronic portfolios.

The ITEC program must demonstrate how students meet relevant Specialized Professional Association standards and learning outcomes as part of the College's accreditation. The ITEC program follows standards from the American Association of School Librarians and the Association for Educational Communications and Technology. These standards intersect on the topic of lifelong learning, which includes both skills and dispositions. State content standards stress the importance of preparing students for the ever-changing world of the 21st century. The program addresses this area by requiring students to establish a personal learning network (PLN). Another approach is the requirement for students to create video-based instructional tutorials.

Interactive Case Study 1: Personal Learning Networks

The concept of a PLN is not new. As it is introduced, instructors remind students that their colleagues, the literature they read, and the conferences and workshops they attend are all part of their PLN. Students generally have some knowledge of the vast amount of professionally-relevant information that is available through blogs and Twitter, but they lack an understanding of how to "capture and tame" (Warlick, 2009, p. 13) that informa-

tion. This gap in knowledge is easily filled by using Web 2.0 tools to build a PLN. Setting up a PLN has become an introductory week activity in several program classes.

David Warlick (2009) notes that while everyone's PLN should be unique, many PLNs include common elements and a similar structure. Since use of a PLN is a program expectation, the students tend to include similar elements and resources in their own PLNs. Using tools like NetVibes (http://netvibes.com) or PageFlakes (http://www.pageflakes.com), students organize RSS feeds and widgets into a current and usable single location. Students refer to information from their PLNs during class activities and link their PLN in their electronic portfolio, the capstone project for the program. Although some learners find the idea of a PLN conceptually challenging, across the program they come to see its value for current awareness, collaboration, and conversation.

Interactive Case Study 2: Screencasting

In Applications of Instructional Technology, students create screencasts, video captures of computer monitors which record activities, including mouse movements, clicks, and audio commentary to further explain the demonstrated activity (Peterson, 2007). The screencast tutorial is designed to show a user how to work with a web or software-based computer application and uses a web-based screencasting tool such as ScreenCast-O-Matic (http://www.screencast-o-matic.com/), Jing (http://www.techsmith.com/jing/), or Screenr (http://screenr.com/).

Requiring Web 2.0 technologies for production and hosting of this video-based instructional tutorial is two-fold: authentication and practicality. Students' perceptions of the project as an authentic endeavor depend on the project's proximity to tools used by practicing professionals (Erstad, 2002). Students in the program have access to screencast examples in their respective fields, such as the state-wide library database, Galileo (http://www. usg.edu/galileo/help/searching/tutorials.phtml).

Web 2.0 tools allow students to produce screencast products that resemble professional screencasts without the financial burden of purchasing software. Practicality is also addressed because students do not have to struggle with file size limitations. Many projects in an instructional technology program are large and difficult to send through email, attach to a post, or upload to an LMS. Hosting the project online circumvents this issue. Assuming the tool remains operational, projects remain accessible to the students beyond graduation.

Overview: Collaborative Uses

Perhaps one of the most popular characteristics of Web 2.0 technologies is their applicability to social learning. Student artifacts created with Web 2.0 tools, ranging from publishing opinions to video production, are easily shared with as large an audience as the instructor and the student desires (Grant & Branch, 2005). These artifacts can then be used to inform and motivate their creators to incorporate responses those artifacts elicit so that learning becomes a social endeavor (Ackermann, 2009). The following three cases describe how the ITEC program promotes social learning and collaboration.

Collaborative Case Study 1: Student Introductions

In online courses, building community is essential in helping to minimize students' feelings of transactional distance (Moore, 2007). With Web 2.0 tools, students can now create unique personal introductions. Instead of text introductions on the discussion board, students upload videos, pictures, voice, and share links to what is meaningful in their lives. Marc Prensky (2010) maintains that this information is invaluable to instructors who want to encourage collaborative student learning:

"Knowing that you know and really care about their [students] interests – and not just what you are teaching them – will often motivate them to do things they might otherwise not" (p. 55).

In most courses students create their introductions using tools such as YouTube (http://www. youtube.com), Glogster (http://www.glogster. com/), VoiceThread (http://www.voicethread. com) or Animoto (http://www.animoto.com). In many instances, the shared information leads to lasting connections between the students, overcoming geographic barriers. Some students share pictures of their pets, while other students share family photos and talk about the importance of family in their daily lives. Students connect on a professional level by sharing teaching stories. These exchanges enhance discussions since the majority of the students in the program are currently teachers or school librarians.

The tools mentioned in this case are different in their own way and continuously offer more capabilities. One student's Glogster introduction highlighted her professional interests. Her glog included a picture of herself in her classroom, a short information bite about her teaching career, a video of what her life is like as a teacher, and a list of websites that she frequents to help her stay organized and up-to-date.

Collaborative Case Study 2: Online Maps

Selection and Development of Instructional Technologies is a production-intensive course. Among the course requirements, students produce an original instructional video. This project includes identifying a project plan, creating a storyboard, writing a script, and acquiring the necessary production equipment, actors and shooting location. Before the course was offered online, students came to the University for face-to-face meetings, and video groups of students were created based on geographical proximity. Once the program moved online, the geographic boundaries expanded far beyond reasonable driving distances. From time to time, students connected through class email accounts, attempting to locate someone who lived within a drivable distance. Inevitably, most students elected to do the video project independently. A group setting for a digital video project provides emotional support and modeling through the process of collaboration (Hakkarainen, 2009). Groups can engage in genuine team efforts to produce complex digital products. Consequently, the course instructors wanted to encourage group formations for the project.

During the 2009-2010 academic year, four sections of the course were offered, with a total of 100 students taught by two different instructors. The LMS prevented students from accessing each other's course introductions to locate others in their region and even prevented students from communicating with friends and colleagues in other sections. As a solution, a Google Map (http://maps.google.com/) was created with as few security barriers as possible. Anyone who accessed the map could also edit its contents. The map was embedded into the homepage of each of the course sections. Students placed a pushpin on their school location with their name and email address, providing an opportunity for students across course sections to collaborate.

Collaborative Case Study 3: Blogging

As part of a learning module on censored and banned books, students select and read current books from a banned book list provided by the instructor. Afterwards, students discuss the book on an Intellectual Freedom in the 21st Century blog hosted on Blogger (http://www.blogger.com). The choice to promote collaborative conversations is well supported by research, which has continually defined learning as a social process (Bruner, 1996; Lave & Wenger, 1991; Vygotsky, 1978). Blogs hosted in Blogger allow immediate authorship access through email accounts that many students already have. Usernames may not

reflect who students really are, making it difficult to know who is posting what comment. This quirk is overcome by requiring students to sign posts with a first or last name, or by requesting that students enter their usernames on a spreadsheet created in Google Sites and linked within the LMS.

The discussions on this blog tend to be livelier than on the LMS discussion boards for several reasons. First, students across all sections participate in the same blog, expanding the pool of ideas and providing students with the opportunity to exchange views with a larger constituency. In past semesters, the blog has also been opened to students taking similar courses in other universities, further broadening the conversation. This external audience increases student motivation and investment in the topic (Schofield & Davidson, 2002). Second, the blog structure records posts and comments in the order they occur, encouraging all students to read through larger discussion blocks. Studies consistently promote web publishing to promote reflection as well as helping students more readily identify the purpose of their instructional activities (Snyder, Lippincott, & Bower, 1998; Spitz, 1996). Third, all instructors have the ability to create blog content using other Web 2.0 tools. In one instance, an instructor created a Glog, which housed links to other resources. The Glog was then linked on a post in the Intellectual Freedom blog. Students responded well to this modeling of technology use as evidenced in their choice to use Glogster for a separate group assignment.

INTRODUCTION: AUTHENTIC ASSESSMENT

In a professional preparation program the alignment between student assessment and on-the-job practice is critical (Jones, 2010). This alignment includes several components: domain knowledge, a commitment to reflective practice in terms of skills and dispositions, and the ability to articulate and modify an approach to using knowledge and theory in practice (Jones, 2010). The program's e-portfolio system, which has evolved over the past decade, incorporates these components and has become an important learning experience in itself.

Implementing Electronic Portfolios

An electronic portfolio (or e-portfolio) is "a digitized collection of artifacts, resources, and accomplishments that represent an individual, group, community, organization, or institution" (Lorenzo & Ittelson, 2005, p. 2). The strategies used within the program have evolved to address new understandings of teaching and learning, changing standards, changing students, and the availability of new technologies.

In the program's earliest efforts students used PowerPoint to create a collection of artifacts and reflections that demonstrated mastery of professional association standards (AASL or AECT standards as adopted by NCATE, http://www.ncate.org/public/programStandards.asp?ch=4). Students came to campus on a Saturday to present their portfolios to their fellow students and program faculty. While this approach marked a significant upgrade in terms of demonstration of authentic mastery of program content, the cookie-cutter formula did not allow for much creativity. Given the 100% online format, it was no longer practical or desirable to require students to come to campus. The use of PowerPoint was also seen as limiting the abilities of the students to demonstrate the range of practice necessary for their ultimate performance on the job.

By 2005, capstone presentations were made using the two-way audio/video tools provided within the LMS. Students were reluctant to give up the security of using a familiar tool like PowerPoint, so beginning in 2007, use of Web 2.0 tools (such as a wiki or free web hosting site) for portfolios was required. Synchronous presentations of the portfolios to program faculty and other students continued using the audio-video system embedded in the LMS.

Steps in Portfolio Development

Students need time to select portfolio artifacts, craft thoughtful reflections based on those artifacts, identify appropriate tools to organize and present the artifacts and reflections, and to design an attractive and engaging e-portfolio. Every required course syllabus states that all students will be expected to create an e-portfolio during their capstone practicum course. Students are encouraged to maintain copies of artifacts for possible inclusion in their e-portfolios. Students are provided with a link to examples of recent e-portfolios. Access to these examples aligns with the program's philosophy about sharing knowledge and serves as a catalyst for students to begin thinking about how they can take their own work to the next level. For example, during 2008-2009 faculty and students expressed dissatisfaction with the use of an attachment model for artifacts. The use of attachments requires additional steps (such as opening the artifact), which occasionally results in software compatibility issues. In 2009-2010, the use of tools like SlideShare (www.slideshare.net/) and Scribd (www.scribd.com/) was encouraged. In the 2010-2011 academic year, students began to construct their portfolios as an activity in one of the program's required courses.

The faculty value the freedom and creativity the use of Web 2.0 tools allows for the students, in addition to the lack of cost for the use of these tools (Lorenzo & Ittelson, 2005). Since the students are completing an online ITEC program, this approach allows them to further develop their skills in the use of these tools and to professionally showcase their skills. Many students use e-portfolios as part of their job search (Barrett, 2000). Additionally, using Web 2.0 tools throughout the program makes the artifacts more accessible because they are not walled off in the LMS. Review of sample portfolios is a powerful reflective activity for students. This approach comes with the standard Web 2.0 drawbacks in terms of changes in the tools, as well as security and privacy concerns. Not requiring a standardized procedure may also make assessment of the portfolio more labor intensive for faculty members, although the emphasis on clear navigation and organization has minimized that effect.

Assessment of Electronic Portfolios

Research has found that portfolios are a valid approach to assessment of knowledge and skills, particularly in terms of authentic performance (Jones, 2010; Pecheone, Pigg, Chung & Souviney 2005; Tucker, Stronge, Gareis & Beers 2003). The program uses a set of key assessments that students are required to include in their portfolios. Inclusion of these key assessments guarantees that students address all of the major standards. Students choose to select other artifacts from classes or from their practicum experience that further demonstrate how they meet the standards. Students are required to include a personal philosophy statement that becomes a meta-reflection of their overall experience in the program. The rubric used to assess student portfolio presentations focuses on the quality of reflections that accompany the artifacts, the creative use of technology, and on the ability of the students to synchronously present their portfolios. The program's model incorporates Jones' (2010) recommendations for effective e-portfolios.

OVERVIEW: BENEFITS AND CHALLENGES OF WEB 2.0 TOOL USE

The ITEC faculty at Georgia Southern University use Web 2.0 tools to enable students to be participants in the creation and dissemination of information on their own time and on their own terms. Faculty view themselves as facilitators, sharing many sources of information beyond the instructor and the textbook (Sherry, 1995). As the case studies have highlighted, Web 2.0 tools allow for more meaningful learning, enabling students to be more active, cooperative, constructive, inten-

tional, and authentic (Jonassen, Howland, Marra, & Crismond, 2007). Students reflect on their learning, actively sharing these learning experiences with others through wikis and blogs. Learning with Web 2.0 tools is intentional. Program faculty urge students to explore their interests as they progress through various courses. Thus, student learning is authentic as well because the topics the students choose have personal meaning for them outside of school (Prensky, 2010).

Benefits for Students

Web 2.0 tools give the students the ability to stay connected with their content and their profession outside of school. By using RSS aggregators (Bloglines, Google Reader) and PLNs (Sclater, 2008; Sigala, 2007), students are able to stay current on issues, events, and professional development opportunities. Since there is no longer a single source of information – the instructor – everyone can participate in knowledge creation (Birdsall, 2007). Faculty use Web 2.0 tools to individualize students' learning experiences by connecting them to information that broadens their perspectives of issues in various professions.

Instead of offering courses structured as independent studies, where students only interact with content in a static textbook, students work with a wide range of content from many sources and share their evolving understanding with Web 2.0 tools. Integrating new technologies into coursework allows student educators to develop the technological fluency essential to preparing them for embracing innovations in technology and integrating them into their own teaching practice (Gibson, 2009). Teaching in this way models to students how they can use Web 2.0 tools to help build personal learning environments for their own future students (Carlson & Gooden, 1999).

The ITEC students use a variety of Web 2.0 tools such as wikis, blogs, Google Docs, and Google Sites to communicate with each other regarding peer review of assignments (Solomon

& Schrum, 2007). The peer review process gives students greater perspective and more feedback than what a teacher can solely provide. It also builds on students' communication, writing, and editing skills (Topping, 2003). Via tools like Twitter, FaceBook, podcasts, vodcasts, and Voice-Thread, the students communicate with other professionals, thus building an educational network (Hargadon, 2010) for professional development and information exchange. Because Web 2.0 tools mitigate geographic barriers, students are able to network with people who are involved in similar work anywhere in the world.

Web 2.0 tools such as YouTube, Skype, Elluminate, Wimba, or GoogleTalk, give students an opportunity to hear from experts and also share their own expertise with others while learning how to use these tools for purposes of their own jobs. These tools provide for more flexibility in learning because students and those who are teaching them, whether it be experts or the professors, do not have to be in the same place at the same time. This promotes true anywhere, anytime learning (Johnson, Smith, Levine, & Haywood, 2010).

Benefits for Faculty

Faculty members ensure that the program remains current by participating in Webinars, viewing professional vodcasts, and listening to educational podcasts. Informally, the use of Twitter, Facebook, and other social networking tools helps the program to maintain a professional network with faculty at other schools that house similar offerings. These strategies keep the program fresh and expose the students to what is new in teaching and learning through dynamic technologies.

Using Web 2.0 tools has enabled the ITEC faculty to collaboratively create and share content for scholarship and teaching. Because the faculty all collaborate in teaching the courses, it is essential that they have the ability to share content, resources, and strategies with one another via Web 2.0 tools. Course wikis are constantly updated with new resources for use by both students and faculty. Faculty members share and create documents using Google Docs.

Challenges for Students and Faculty

While Web 2.0 tools provide many benefits, they also bring some challenges, including issues surrounding privacy and security. Instructors must be aware of what course content should or should not be publicly shared on the Internet. Many free tools contain advertisements or user-created content that may not be appropriate in an educational setting. Consideration must also be given to the available privacy settings of the tools as students may not want their work to be publicly available.

Web 2.0 tools are typically free and managed by an open source development team; subsequently, there is no school-sponsored technical support. If users encounter technical difficulties, they have to seek help from the tool developers' network, which may become time-consuming and frustrating. Faculty must provide a back-up plan if and when these tools do not work. Beyond technical issues are concerns about the learning curve involved when it comes to adopting a new Web 2.0 tool. Some tools, such as Wordle (www.wordle.net), can be learned quickly, while other tools, such as Diigo (www.diigo.com), may need longer orientation periods. Each person brings different skill sets, so part of the course may have to be dedicated to learning how to use these tools.

Web 2.0 tools are constantly evolving; they may be in continual development, in a Beta or trial period, or may simply disappear, raising concerns over the preservation of content (Anderson, 2007). This is a potential difficulty considering that the students use these tools over a period of two or more years to create their electronic portfolios. K-12 schools do not always have access to these tools because of school-level or district-level Internet filters. These barriers prevent student educators from applying their coursework into their professional work, thereby minimizing authenticity.

While some students and faculty will effectively use the Web 2.0 tools that are good for organizational purposes, such as RSS aggregators, some may still suffer from information overload. Some students may not yet understand how to differentiate between reliable information and misinformation. Educating both faculty and students on fair use guidelines and copyright concerns is essential to ethical Web 2.0 usage.

Finally, incorporating Web 2.0 tools can be a time investment for instructors because of the necessity to not only learn the new application, but more importantly, to incorporate it into the curriculum in meaningful ways and design its uses so that it meets the learning needs of students. Ultimately, the goal for instructional design with Web 2.0 should be rich user experiences (O'Reilly, 2007).

CONCLUSION

Despite the challenges discussed in this chapter, the Instructional Technology faculty at Georgia Southern University believe the integration of Web 2.0 tools into the program addresses the limitations of the GeorgiaView LMS and provides students with an enriching, creative learning experience. Through the use of Web 2.0 tools, the program has created a learning environment with these advantages:

- Student have more control of their learning experience;
- The learning environment is no longer restricted to the traditional semester timeframe and can be opened to the public; and
- The LMS retains its functionality for administrative support while the infusion of Web 2.0 tools enables creative and collaborative learning activities.

There is no doubt that technology skills are vital in this present society (Johnson, et al., 2010). For the ITEC students, who will serve as the technology leaders of the future, they are essential. Through the use of Web 2.0 tools to promote collaboration, communication, and productivity, Georgia Southern University instructional technology students will be well equipped with the technology skills they need for success.

REFERENCES

Ackermann, E. (2009). *Piaget's constructivism, Papert's constructionism: What's the difference? Future of Learning Group*. MIT Media Laboratory.

Allen, I. E., & Seaman, J. (2010). *Learning on demand: Online education in the United States, 2009*. The Sloan Consortium. Retrieved from http://sloanconsortium.org/publications/survey/pdf/learningondemand.pdf

Anderson, P. (2007). *What is Web 2.0? Ideas, technologies and implications for education*. Joint Information Systems Committee Technology & Standards Watch. Retrieved from http://citeseerx.ist.psu.edu/viewdoc/download?doi=10.1.1.108.9995&rep=rep1&type=pdf

Barrett, H. (2000). Electronic teaching portfolios: Multimedia skills + portfolio development = Powerful professional development. In *Proceedings of Society for Information Technology & Teacher Education International Conference 2000* (p. 7). Chesapeake, VA: AACE.

Birdsall, W. F. (2007). Web 2.0 as a social movement. *Webology, 4*(2).

Blackboard Inc. (2010). *Engaging learners, for engaging learning: Introducing Blackboardlearn*[+] *Release 9.1*. Retrieved from http://www.blackboard.com/Teaching-Learning/Learn-Platform.aspx

Bolliger, D. U., Supanakor, S., & Boggs, C. (2010). Impact of podcasting on student motivation in the online learning environment. *Computers & Education, 55*(2), 714–722. doi:10.1016/j.compedu.2010.03.004

Bruner, J. (1996). *Culture of education.* Cambridge, MA: Harvard University Press.

Carlson, R. D., & Gooden, J. S. (1999). Mentoring pre-service teachers for technology skills acquisition. In J. Price, et al. (Eds.), *Proceedings of Society for Information Technology & Teacher Education International Conference 1999* (pp. 1313-1318). Chesapeake, VA: AACE.

Cennamo, K. S., Ross, J. D., & Ertmer, P. A. (2010). *Technology integration for meaningful classroom use: A standards-based approach.* Belmont, CA: Wadsworth, Cengage Learning.

Craig, E. M. (2007). Changing paradigms: Managed learning environments and Web 2.0. *Campus-Wide Information Systems, 24*(3), 152–161. doi:10.1108/10650740710762185

Erstad, O. (2002). Norwegian students using digital artifacts in project-based learning. *Journal of Computer Assisted Learning, 18*, 427–437. doi:10.1046/j.0266-4909.2002.00254.x

Falvo, D. A., & Johnson, B. F. (2007). The use of learning management systems in the United States. *TechTrends, 51*(2), 40–45. doi:10.1007/s11528-007-0025-9

Georgia, V. I. E. W. (2010). *University system of Georgia: GeorgiaVIEW.* Retrieved from http://www.usg.edu/gaview/

Georgia Statewide Academic & Medical System (GSAMS) receives business & industry partnership award at IDLCON Distance Learning Conference in Washington, D.C. (1995, March 24). *Business Wire.* Retrieved from http://www.highbeam.com/doc/1G1-16705164.html

Gibson, S. (2009). *Are our preservice teachers prepared to teach in a digital age?* Paper presented at the World Conference on E-Learning in Corporate, Government, Healthcare, and Higher Education (E-LEARN) 2009, Vancouver, Canada.

Grant, M., & Branch, R. (2005). Project-based learning in a middle school: Tracing abilities through artifacts of learning. *Journal of Research on Technology in Education, 38*(1), 65–98.

Hakkarainen, P. (2009). Designing and implementing a PBL course on educational digital video production: Lessons learned from design-based research. *Educational Technology Research and Development, 57*, 211–228. doi:10.1007/s11423-007-9039-4

Hargadon, S. (2010). Educational networking: The role of Web 2.0 in education. *MultiMedia & Internet @Schools.* Retrieved from http://www.mmischools.com/Articles/Editorial/Features/Educational-Networking-The-Role-of-Web-2.0-in-Education-5bAvailable-Full-Text2c-Free5d-61342.aspx

Hodges, C. B. (2004). Designing to motivate: Motivational techniques to incorporate in e-learning experiences. *Journal of Interactive Online Learning, 2*(3).

Ingerman, B. L., Yang, C., & the 2010 EDUCAUSE Current Issues Committee. (2010, May/June). Top ten IT issues 2010. *EDUCAUSE Review, 45*(3). Retrieved from http://www.educause.edu/EDUCAUSE%20Review/EDUCAUSEReviewMagazineVolume45/TopTenITIssues2010/205503

International Society for Technology in Education. (2007). *National educational technology standards and performance indicators for students.* Retrieved from http://www.iste.org/Content/NavigationMenu/NETS/ForStudents/2007Standards/NETS_for_Students_2007_Standards.pdf

Johnson, L., Smith, R., Levine, A., & Haywood, K. (2010). *The 2010 horizon report: K-12 edition*. Austin, TX: The New Media Consortium.

Jonassen, D. H., Howland, J., Marra, R. M., & Crismond, D. P. (2007). *Meaningful learning with technology*. Upper Saddle River, NJ: Prentice Hall.

Jones, E. (2010). A professional practice portfolio for quality learning. *Higher Education Quarterly, 64*(3), 292–312. doi:10.1111/j.1468-2273.2010.00458.x

Keller, J. M. (1987). Development and use of the ARCS model of instructional design. *Journal of Instructional Development, 10*(3), 2–10. doi:10.1007/BF02905780

Kim, H., & Hannafin, M. (2008). Grounded design of web-enhanced case-based activity. *Educational Technology Research and Development, 56*(2), 161–179. doi:10.1007/s11423-006-9010-9

Kolodner, J. (1993). *Case-based reasoning*. San Mateo, CA: Morgan Kaufmann Publishers, Inc.

Lave, J., & Wenger, E. (1991). *Situated learning: Legitimate peripheral participation*. New York, NY: Cambridge University Press.

Lohr, L. L. (2008). *Creating graphics for learning and performance: Lessons in visual literacy* (2nd ed.). Upper Saddle River, NJ: Pearson.

Lorenzo, G., & Ittelson, J. G. (2005). *An overview of e-portfolios*. ELI Paper 1: 2005, EDUCAUSE Learning Initiative. Retrieved from http://net.educause.edu/ir/library/pdf/ELI3001.pdf

Martindale, T., & Dowdy, M. (2010). Personal learning environments. In Veletsianos, G. (Ed.), *Emerging technologies in distance education* (pp. 177–193). Edmonton, Canada: Athabasca University Press.

McGee, P., & Diaz, V. (2007). Wikis and podcasts and blogs, oh my!: What is a faculty member supposed to do? *EDUCAUSE Review, 42*(5), 28–41.

Moodle.org. (2010). *Moodle.org: Open-source community-based tools for learning*. Retrieved September 18, 2010, from http://moodle.org/

Moore, M. G. (2007). The theory of transactional distance. In Moore, M. G. (Ed.), *The handbook of distance education* (2nd ed.). Mahwah, NJ: Lawrence Erlbaum Associates.

Mott, J. (2010). Envisioning the post-LMS era: The open learning network. *EDUCASE Quarterly, 33*(1). Retrieved from http://www.educause.edu/EDUCAUSE+Quarterly/EDUCAUSEQuarterlyMagazineVolum/EnvisioningthePostLMSEraTheOpe/199389

Nelson, J., Christopher, A., & Mims, C. (2009). TPACK and Web 2.0: Transformation of teaching and learning. *TechTrends, 53*(5), 80–85. doi:10.1007/s11528-009-0329-z

O'Reilly, T. (2007). What is Web 2.0: Design patterns and business models for the next generation of software. *Communications & Strategies, 1*, 17.

Oliver, K. (2007). Leveraging Web 2.0 in the redesign of a graduate-level technology integration course. *TechTrends, 51*(5), 55–61. doi:10.1007/s11528-007-0071-3

Oliver, K., & Raubenheimer, C. D. (2007a, June). Strategies for online concept mapping part 1. *Online Cl@ssroom. Ideas for Effective Instruction, 1*, 7–8.

Oliver, K., & Raubenheimer, C. D. (2007b, July). Strategies for online concept mapping part 2. *Online Cl@ssroom. Ideas for Effective Instruction, 1*, 3.

Pecheone, R. L., Pigg, M. J., Chung, R. R., & Souviney, R. J. (2005). Performance assessment and electronic portfolios: Their effect on teacher learning and education. *Clearing House (Menasha, Wis.), 78*(4), 164–176. doi:10.3200/TCHS.78.4.164-176

Peterson, E. (2007). Incorporating screencasts in online teaching. *International Review of Research in Open and Distance Learning, 8*(3), 1–4.

Pierson, M. (2001). Technology integration practice as a function of pedagogical expertise. *Journal of Research on Computing in Education, 33*(4), 413–430.

Prensky, M. (2010). *Teaching digital natives: Partnering for real learning.* Thousand Oaks, CA: Corwin.

Repman, J., Zinskie, C., & Downs, E. (2010). Fulfilling the promise: Addressing institutional factors that impede the implementation of e-learning 2.0. In Yang, H. H., & Yuen, S. C.-Y. (Eds.), *Collective intelligence and e-learning 2.0: Implications of Web-based communities and networking* (pp. 44–60). New York, NY: Information Science Reference.

Schalock, H. D., & Myton, D. (2002). Connecting teaching and learning: An introduction to teacher work sample methodology. In Girod, G. (Ed.), *Connecting teaching and learning: A handbook for teacher educators on teacher work sample methodology.* Washington, DC: AACTE.

Schank, R. C. (1999). *Dynamic memory revisited.* New York, NY: Cambridge University Press. doi:10.1017/CBO9780511527920

Schofield, J. W., & Davidson, A. L. (2002). *Bringing the internet to school: Lessons from an urban district.* San Francisco, CA: Jossey-Bass.

Sclater, N. (2008). *(2008 June 24). Web 2.0, personal learning environments, and the future of learning management systems. EDUCAUSE* (p. 13). Center for Applied Research Bulletin.

Severance, C., Hanss, T., & Hardin, J. (2010). IMS learning tools interoperability: Enabling a mash-up approach to teaching and learning tools. *Technology, Instruction. Cognition & Learning, 7*(3-4), 245–262.

Sherry, L. (1995). Issues in distance learning. [Charlottesville, VA: AACE.]. *International Journal of Educational Telecommunications, 1*(4), 337–365.

Sigala, M. (2007). Integrating Web 2.0 in e-learning environments: A socio-technical approach. *International Journal of Knowledge and Learning, 3*(6), 628–648. doi:10.1504/IJKL.2007.016837

Snyder, J., Lippincott, A., & Bower, D. (1998). The inherent tensions in the multiple uses of portfolios in teacher education. *Teacher Education Quarterly, 25*(1), 45–60.

Solomon, G., & Schrum, L. (2007). *Web 2.0: New tools, new schools.* Washington, DC: International Society for Technology in Education.

Spitz, B. (1996). Imagine the possibilities: Exploring the Internet with middle school students. In Valauskas, E. J., & Ertel, M. (Eds.), *The Internet for teachers and school library media specialists: Today's applications tomorrow's prospects* (pp. 181–191). New York, NY: Neal-Schuman.

Topping, K. (2003). Self and peer assessment in school and university: Reliability, validity and utility. *Innovation and Change in Professional Education, 1*, 55–87. doi:10.1007/0-306-48125-1_4

Tucker, P. D., Stronge, J. H., Gareis, C. R., & Beers, C. S. (2003). The efficacy of portfolios for teacher evaluation and professional development: Do they make a difference? *Educational Administration Quarterly, 39*(5), 572–602. doi:10.1177/0013161X03257304

Vygotsky, L. S. (1978). *Mind in society: The development of higher psychological processes.* Cambridge, MA: Harvard University Press.

Warlick, D. (2009). Grow your personal learning network. *Learning & Leading with Technology.* Retrieved from http://istelearning.org/wp-content/uploads/2010/04/Grow-Your-PLN.pdf

Watson, W. R., & Watson, S. L. (2007). An argument for clarity: What are learning management systems, what are they not, and what should they become? *TechTrends*, *51*(2), 28–34. doi:10.1007/s11528-007-0023-y

Willingham, D. T. (Producer). (2008, September 8, 2010). *Learning styles don't exist*. Retrieved from http://www.youtube.com/watch?v=sIv9rz2NTUk

Wittrock, M. C. (1989). Generative processes of comprehension. *Educational Psychologist*, *24*(4), 345–376. doi:10.1207/s15326985ep2404_2

Chapter 10
Grappling with Change:
Web 2.0 and Teacher Educators

Janice W. Butler
University of Texas at Brownsville, USA

ABSTRACT

Technology is not a panacea for educational reform, but the use of technology in the classroom can enable teachers to engage today's students in learning content. While some believed that new, young teachers would bring technology to the PK-12 classroom, this clearly has not happened. Since teacher educators generally do not model technology integration and instead use primarily teacher-centered instruction, many new teachers do not know how to integrate technology, particularly Web 2.0 technologies, into instruction. To encourage teacher educators to learn about these easy-to-use technologies, this chapter examines wikis as a low-threshold Web 2.0 tool. This chapter will discuss the power of using these technology tools.

INTRODUCTION

Mrs. Rosales was eager to begin her first year of teaching. Newly graduated, she had many ideas about integrating technology into her sixth grade science class. During new teacher inservice, Rosales found out that her classroom would have four computers and Internet connectivity available every day. Her professors had modeled multiple ways to use technology with only one to four computers in a classroom and she wanted to try out the online scavenger hunt she had saved from her methods class. Armed with her lists of students in each team, she was ready for the first day of class. Looking at the faces of the students, she said, "Hello students; my name is Mrs. Rosales. We are going to have fun learning from each other and experts in the field of science for the rest of the year. Let's begin.. ."

DOI: 10.4018/978-1-4666-0014-0.ch010

A dilemma facing many teacher educators today is how to effectively teach the content based on current laws and the whims of school boards or legislators. Simultaneously, these same teacher educators are expected to integrate technology-rich, student-centered, problem-based learning into their classes. Most school districts expect new teachers to know how to use technology in teaching. However, typically little has changed in many college classrooms. Professors, who did not grow up in the digital era, continue to use primarily teacher-centered direct instruction. Thus, new teachers frequently enter the classroom uncertain how to teach any differently than what they experienced in the college classroom – *teacher-centered, direct instruction*. In order to inculcate technology usage into the preservice and inservice teachers' repertory of instructional methodologies, they must experience technology being used effectively in a variety of ways, especially in the high-stakes test environment in which most teachers are working (Ertmer & Ottenbreit-Leftwich, 2010).

In hopes of graduating highly qualified and technology literate teachers, universities expect college faculty to incorporate technology into all courses. Thus, teacher education faculty members feel pressured to become technology savvy quickly so they can model effective use of technology within each course. With the demands of teaching, research, community service, and committee work, the challenge for faculty is finding time to learn new technologies, and then learn how to integrate them into their coursework. Web 2.0 applications offer a solution for quickly learning new technologies that can be modeled to pre-service teachers. These technologies are easy-to-use and can be integrated into the teacher preparation course without requiring major changes in curriculum or projects. In addition, the Web 2.0 technologies provide faculty with productivity tools that can make their research and collaboration easier to accomplish.

Indeed, Web 2.0 technologies offer a hope for changing the paradigm of teacher-centered instruction still prevalent in the classroom. While the process of change is difficult and sometimes painful, this chapter will focus on simple, but highly effective Web 2.0 tools that faculty can learn quickly and incorporate in the classroom immediately. A discussion of low-threshold technologies will be included with an emphasis on wikis and their power to change the classroom environment. Links to resources used in PK-12 as well as higher education will also be provided.

LACK OF TECHNOLOGY IN TEACHER EDUCATION PROGRAMS

Mrs. Rosales was having a rough year, typical for first-year teachers. School requirements and paperwork that she had never seen before kept her busy. Even though she stayed late after school every day, Mrs. Rosales wondered if she would ever catch up. Just as she was most overwhelmed, her assistant principal, Ms. Poteet, visited her classroom for a walk-through evaluation. The students were working in tandem with a class in China to better understand cultures in different countries. Her students, excited about talking to students in China, were noisy as they shared information. To her relief, Ms. Poteet was extremely pleased to see students adding content to group wikis that housed all their research on the Chinese culture. After Ms. Poteet left, Mrs. Rosales smiled. She was glad that she had completed so many similar activities in her teacher education program and was well-prepared to integrate a variety of technology tools into her lessons. Working with Web 2.0 technologies was the easy part of her job.

Educational reform is of significant concern to Americans and as research suggests, U.S. students continue to lag behind in math and science (Gray, Thomas, & Lewis, 2010). In the documentary movie *Waiting for Superman* (2010), Geoffrey Canada, President and CEO of the Harlem Children's Zone summed up the consensus of many stakeholders in our educational system when he stated, "Either the kids are getting stupider every year or something is wrong in the educational system" (Chilicott & Guggenheim, 2010). Indeed, across the world, sweeping changes due to technological advances have changed the fabric of our lives, in conducting business, holding meetings and conferences, collaborating with peers, detecting and curing diseases, discovering new universes, visiting virtual worlds, buying and selling, reading books, and playing with others. While essentially all facets of our world have been changed by technology, the typical PK-12 classroom shows little evidence of these changes. As Dr. Ron Paige, former U. S. Secretary of Education stated, "Education is the only business still debating the usefulness of technology" (U.S. Department of Education 2004, 10). Yet, despite massive investments in computers and networks, the school room of today remains largely the same as a school room in the 1900's. If the responsibility for adequately preparing young people for the challenges they will face in this new era rests with the schools of today (Okojie & Olinzock, 2006), then the responsibility for adequately preparing teachers for the challenges they will face in the classroom rests with the teacher education programs of today.

Many hoped that technology usage in education would increase when young teachers, who have grown up with computers and other technology, entered the profession. However, Bebell, Russell, and O'Dwyer (2004) found that the overall frequency with which teachers use technology does not vary significantly between new and veteran teachers, young or old. Teachers who have been in the profession for more than eleven years report approximately the same technology usage as novice teachers. Upon looking at specific characteristics, newer teachers report they use technology less frequently for delivery and for student use in class

than do their more experienced colleagues, but more frequently to prepare for class. According to data collected from teachers in 2008-2009, this paradigm has not changed. For example, 35% of teachers with three or fewer years of experience used database management software "sometimes or often" as compared to 50% of the teachers with 20 or more years of experience who used database management software "sometimes or often." Software for desktop publishing was used sometimes or often by 46% of those teachers with three or fewer years of experience as compared to 58% by teachers who had 20 or more years of experience. In addition, the more years of experience a teacher had, the more likely they were to use technology for classroom preparation (Gray et al., 2010). These data suggest that teacher education programs have not yet been successful in preparing teachers to use technology tools as a catalyst for learning. Once pre-service teachers do enter the classroom, technology is viewed as a personal productivity tool but does not seem to significantly impact student learning or change the direct-instruction paradigm.

Teacher usage of technology has not yet been translated into student usage of technology as it is used for higher order processes in the "real" world: for communication, collaboration, innovation, and problem-solving. Instead, a substantial majority of students in elementary and secondary schools use technology sometimes or often primarily for fundamental drill and skill activities (69%), word processing (61%), and conducting basic research (66%). A much smaller portion of students are using technology to communicate (31%), contribute to blogs or wikis (9%) or collaborate on social networking sites (7%) (Gray et al., 2010). Teachers are generally not using Web 2.0 technologies to tap into the potential for learning at the highest level of Bloom's Digital Taxonomy (Churches, 2009).

Because of the rapid proliferation of computers and other technology in schools, many teachers feel ill-prepared to use computers in their instruction or to encourage their students to use these tools. Often, they are not aware "of the teaching and learning pedagogies that computers and the Internet are able to support" (Judge, Puckett, & Cabuk, 2004, 393). The integration of technology into the "ongoing educational process, can play a significant role in creating educational environments that reflect the way people interact with the real world, sharing representational and computational task burdens" (Norton & Wiburg, 2004, 34). Therefore, it is important that teachers become familiar with the technologies that can provide students with access to a vast world beyond the classroom.

USING TECHNOLOGY IN TEACHER EDUCATION PROGRAMS

Mrs. Rosales walked into the faculty meeting tired from a long day at work, but excited to see the guest speaker that afternoon. The principal had invited Kristi McNabb to share information on using Web 2.0 tools in the classroom. McNabb had been Mrs. Rosales' professor at the university and she knew how interesting this afternoon session would be. Coach Moreles, who had been unwilling to use technology in his classroom, raised his hand to ask why he even needed to use technology since he had been successfully teaching the same way for 25 years. McNabb just smiled. She knew that the coach of the rival football team had been using Web 2.0 technologies to improve learning outcomes for students and had not lost any players to failing grades in two years. "Let me see if I can change your mind a bit," McNabb said, smiling.

Teaching the Teachers to use Technologies

Gardner (2004) said, "Current formal education still prepares students primarily for the world of the past, rather than for possible worlds of the future" (p. 17). Technology offers the potential for reforming current educational practices – but only when it is used by the students in the classroom. Research studies suggest that pre-service teachers will be much more likely to integrate technology into their curriculum if they see technology integration modeled by their teacher education instructors (Kim, Jain, Westoff, & Rezabek, 2008; Krueger, Hansen, & Smaldino, 2000; Persichitte, Caffarella, Tharptitle, 1999). A systemic infusion of technology in *every* course engenders understanding that using technology in teaching is important. Thus, teacher preparation programs need to ensure that technology integration becomes an expectation in each education course as pre-service teachers experience technology integration within all content areas.

If ubiquitous usage and modeling of technology in teacher preparation programs is the most effective method of ensuring that teachers are prepared to integrate technology in the PK-12 classroom, then college instructors must *themselves* become skilled in technology usage and integration. Ertmer (2005) advocates training teachers to use relatively simple technology tools as an effective method of initiating the adoption process. Gilbert (2006) suggests that while college faculty can be resistant to increasing their already demanding workload by learning to integrate technology, they are more willing to do so when introduced to low-threshold technologies.

In 2002, Gilbert coined the term *low-threshold applications* to describe technology applications that are highly accessible because they are easy to learn, free or inexpensive, reliable, and have observable positive outcomes when used in the classroom. These applications address the need for increasing technology integration in the classroom while addressing the challenges involved in paying for software, training and maintenance. Since low-threshold applications are easy to learn and require faculty to reconceive only a small portion of their identity, roles, and workload, faculty often welcome opportunities to contribute to the overall change process – within reasonable limits (Gilbert, 2006).

The characteristics that define applications as low-threshold also address problems in time, support and costs that are barriers to technology usage commonly expressed by teachers (Brzycki & Dudt, 2005). Many emerging Web 2.0 applications can be identified as low-threshold because they are often free, easy to learn, do not require major changes to the curriculum in order to use them in the classroom, and can have a strong impact on student learning. Teacher educators can incorporate these technologies in their courses, quickly modeling a classroom environment which is more appealing to students today.

Web 2.0 Applications as Low-Threshold Technologies

A precise definition of Web 2.0 is a bit difficult to nail down, but includes a wide array of web-based applications which allow users to collaboratively build content and communicate with others across the world. Sometimes called the participatory Web, sharing and collaborating are inherent in Web 2.0 applications as the users themselves build content. One only has to look at commercial sites, such as the International Movie Database to see an example of the participatory web. Consumer reviews of movies, comments and discussion carry at least as much and sometimes more weight than professional movie reviewers such as Roger Ebert. Travelocity is another example of the participatory Web, where the 5-smiley face consumer rating system for hotels has become more important than the 5-star rating from the hotel industry. All ages have become comfortable sharing their interests and expertise with others in the world on everything from antiques to zoos. Yet, in school, students are often relegated to learning in isolation and sharing expertise with their teacher alone.

A plethora of applications are available for classroom use. These Web 2.0 applications can be used for student-centered, project-based, au-thentic, and collaborative activities – strategies that typically immerse the learner in the content. Some of the more common Web 2.0 applications are blogs, wikis and social networking applications such as FaceBook and MySpace. However, thousands of Web 2.0 applications are available, many geared toward education. Web 2.0 tools offer students the opportunity to communicate with others who share similar interests but different geographic locations, ages, grade levels and even "walks in life." Students can find themselves talking, via Web 2.0, to the designers of their favorite game and giving them advice on improving the fight sequences or story line. Second graders can talk to astronauts and middle school students can blog with archaeologists in Egypt. Students are already using these applications when they are out of school. These same students are increasingly entering the classroom expecting much more than a static textbook can provide.

EMBRACING WIKIS IN THE CLASSROOM

Mrs. Rosales wondered why the other teachers did not use technology in their classes. She saw a lot of equipment in the rooms, but most of it was just gathering dust. When her mentor came in for her weekly meeting, Mrs. Rosales decided to talk to her about it. "They don't know how to use technology and are afraid they will look dumb if they make mistakes," her mentor replied. Mrs. Rosales could certainly sympathize with that feeling, but volunteered to show the rest of the department how to set up a wiki for student use. At first, the others in the department were skeptical about the tools and did not believe they would increase learning. However, when they saw Mrs. Rosales' examples of her wikis, they were impressed with the caliber of student writing and collaboration. The rest of her department decided to use wikis the next semester and Mrs. Rosales volunteered to teach them how to use this low-threshold tool.

With the variety of tools available, how can faculty find time to learn how to use them much less to incorporate them into the classroom? The most expeditious and least stressful solution would be for each member of the education faculty to select one powerful and correspondingly easy-to-learn Web 2.0 tool and integrate it into the coursework for at least one year. Faculty can minimize time to learn by selecting one tool and use it in the classroom until they are comfortable and eventually integrate a few more Web 2.0 tools into the curriculum. In the best possible world, with all education faculty members modeling the effective integration of one or two tools, preservice teachers would have a wide array of skills and the knowledge necessary for integrating technology upon graduation.

One of the most powerful low-threshold applications available for novice technology users is the wiki. Wikis meet the specifications for being low-threshold in that they are free (or very inexpensive) for educators and students, easy to learn, have a user-friendly interface that is non-intimidating and will not require major changes in teaching or learning. Wikis are reliable and consistent. They can be counted on to work each time the students create, revise, and share content. Students who post to wikis often produce higher quality work since the product will be viewed by the world. The following sections will give you an overview of wikis, examples of wikis in use, and suggestions on making wiki instruction effective. With wikis alone incorporated into a course, teacher educators can go far in preparing their preservice teachers to effectively integrate technology in the classroom.

Wikipedia – The Most "Notorious" Wiki

Most have heard of and many have used the controversial Wikipedia. Wikipedia began in 2001 and currently contains almost 3.5 million articles. Hailed as the free encyclopedia that anyone can edit, open access can sometimes result in information being intentionally entered incorrectly. However, many articles are written by those who have a passion for the topic and want to share that passion with others. Those passionate writers serve as a good buffer to eliminate erroneous information that is added intentionally or inadvertently. Many articles have been written by students as an alternative to a research paper and improved upon by students in successive classes and, more importantly, by the global community. Wikipedia has strict requirements for establishing the topic and creating an article so should a teacher educator want to delve into something less structured, an excellent Web 2.0 option would be open source or commercial wikis.

Other Wiki Options and Features

Wikipedia is only one example of wiki, albeit a very large one. A wiki is, quite simply, a webpage that can be created, viewed and modified by anyone who has Internet access, permission to edit the wiki and a browser. "Wiki" comes from the Hawaiian word *wiki*, which means quick. Wikis are indeed quick to create, quick to populate and quick to become a preferred method of collaboration among students and teachers. They permit students to collaborate and communicate asynchronously and allow educators to look "behind the scenes" and identify who did what in the project. Wikis also allow contributors to incorporate pictures, sounds, movies, surveys and presentations to create a rich, mixed media experience. The rapidly expanding variety of Google apps, which can do many things from creating virtual pets to embedding a discussion board forum, add more options for wikis.

For faculty who are technology novices, three commercial products, PBworks, Wikispaces, and Wetpaint are easy to learn and used frequently in education. Both PBworks and Wikispaces offer advertisement free, no cost subscriptions to educators and students. They strongly support the educational community with resources and features geared to the education arena. The wiki interface looks like any word processor on the market today. Thus, higher education faculty and preservice teachers can comfortably create and revise content in a very short period of time as they recognize the icons in the WYSIWYG (what you see is what you get) interface. In addition, the content for these wikis resides on the company server, so institutions do not need extra staff to manage and maintain the wiki. Since wikis grow and evolve over time, a variety of pedagogical strategies can be used such as active learning, cooperative or collaborative learning, trial and error learning, group discussion, and focus group discussion.

Probably the easiest way to understand the potential of wikis would be to visit a few educational wikis provided at the end of the chapter. In addition to being eye-catching, easy-to-use and media rich, wikis have the following additional features that make them quite powerful for educators:

- Since many people can join and edit wikis, they becomes powerful as a vehicles for group projects. Students no longer need to live in the same geographic location to collaborate on projects.
- Contributors have the ability to retrieve data that may have been inadvertently erased by another student (or faculty just learning to use wikis). Thus, students can use trial and error in learning to use the wiki and know that they will not "break" anything.
- Teachers can look at the history to determine who did what in the project thus eliminating the common, "He isn't doing his share," comments that frequently arise in group projects.
- Wikis can be accessed from any browser so students and instructors can view or add content via mobile phone or other mobile device.

- Embedding media, photographs, student-made movies, YouTube videos, audio files, surveys, calendars, games, Glogster projects, and the thousands of Google apps available for free is easy.

In the College Classroom

In the college classroom, wikis can be used in as many different ways as an instructor teacher can imagine. Wikis are effective for both undergraduate as well as graduate students. Once teacher educators embrace the concept of wikis, they find it conducive to individual or group research activities and group projects with peers. Some brief examples of wikis in the college classroom are included below.

Wiki Activities in Teacher Education Classes

In a teacher education course on school law, the instructor developed a scenario in which the school board president, a special education teacher, a principal, a student and a parent were battling over modifications for the visually-impaired student. Using a wiki as the interface, each student took a different role in the case and spent the semester arguing for their side. Not only did they have to see the incident through the eyes of someone who has stakes in the outcome, they also had to research the laws that supported the case. As the semester progressed, the students became quite passionate about their position and spent time poring over what the others had included in the wiki. Students were able to post movies supporting their position as well as other evidence to win the case. The caliber of student understanding in this project far exceeded the typical research paper that was assigned in the past. Because students are able to read what others write, view all pages and revise as they continue on the project, the wiki is a highly effective platform for collaborative learning.

To continue wiki involvement for students, a course page can be built to house all student projects, calendars, and course communication. One educational psychology professor selected the wiki as her technology tool and quickly moved all of her course online except for grades. The wiki was easy for students to learn, engaging, interactive and dynamic, unlike the course management system. Once students became comfortable using the wiki, they participated in content development, added a page for FAQs about the course, shared links to resources and provided assistance to other students in the course. Another faculty member now adds all content for the course into a wiki and links it to the previous semesters so that the content remains available to the public. This encourages students to put forth their best work since they know that others will see it. The instructor also believes that the stakes have been raised for *all* work, as students see the caliber of work completed by others and want to emulate or improve it. Students continue to access the wiki and make changes, even after graduating. Still another professor assigns students to use a wiki to develop Reusable Learning Objects (*RLOs*) on critical topics in the course or program. Creating a separate wiki for each project or for each student simplifies management and accessibility of projects for the instructor. A topical page can be created to house all the links relevant to the topic for current as well as past and future classes. In this way, knowledge can be shared and access to information continues long after the semester is over.

Additional Wiki Ideas

Perhaps one of the most significant uses for a wiki is the development of large collaborative projects with either the entire class, groups within the classes, or the world. For example, one instructor developed a special topics course for emerging technologies, a frequently requested course. Knowing that individually she could only cover a few technologies in the short summer session, the instructor decided to have the students develop their own manual or textbook on Web 2.0 technologies. Each student in the class selected a different application and spent the first month learning about the technology as well as how to use it. Throughout the semester, students developed their own chapter about the Web 2.0 technology following a template provided by the instructor. As students began to work through their chapters, they made important decisions about the format of the book. For example, after several discussions, the students decided that the book was professional and was going to be seen by others and thus needed to be consistent with formatting such features as font size, font face, and titles in chapters. Anyone deviating from the agreed upon standard was expected to go back and comply with requirements agreed upon by the class. Students were rewarded by their hard work as they saw that others across the Internet were using the wiki book to learn about the different Web 2.0 topics. Those who participated in the class still use the book as a resource and send others who are interested in information on emerging technologies to the resource.

Steve Hargadon, blogger and computer entrepreneur understands that blogging has potential as an educational tool. In an interesting twist, he created a wiki for teachers to collaborate on the power of the blog for the classroom. Volunteers began contributing almost immediately by adding such topics as blogging basics, how to get started, case studies, testimonials, and resources. Because it is a wiki, it remains a work in progress that others can add content to and revise. If a resource is missing, Carvin (2006) explains, "all you have to do is click the edit button and add it yourself. You don't have to go through a bureaucratic process to submit the information - you just do it" (¶ 10). His wiki remains, as of this printing, a valuable resource for bloggers.

Another educator, Richard Webb, created a wiki to demonstrate the use of Google Earth in

Irish education. Videos, tutorials, and a variety of attachments make this an extremely interactive site, even without becoming a writer on the wiki. The link to the wiki can be found at the end of this chapter. The Sugar River Valley Health Occupations Students of America (HOSA) chapter created a wiki to provide information on local health related events, as well as sections for upcoming HOSA events, state rallies and competitions, homework assignments, and announcements. Some interesting photos of simulated hospital experiences complete with fake blood show the involvement of the students in the organization. Katy, TX ISD uses PBworks for a variety of tasks. Students can collaborate on projects whenever, wherever as long as they have a computer and Internet access. Students post projects some of which includes student generated movies, book reviews, and other projects. Students are reported to be more engaged and enthusiastic about their learning since the district began using wikis in the classroom (PBworks, n.d.). Additional links to educational wikis from PK-12 and higher education can be found at the end of this chapter.

Science and Wiki in the Classroom

Teacher educators can learn a great deal about preservice teachers' interactions with students by requiring them to create class wikis for student-teaching. Those wikis can include lessons, movies, links to important online resources, as well as student comments and interactions within the wiki itself. When preservice teachers are required to maintain a wiki in the class, they have a better understanding of how the wiki can be used in the PK-12 classroom once they graduate and begin teaching. Science topics profit from the wiki structure because the scientific method is a series of steps that may require the scientist to back up and repeat or modify steps through an iterative process before reaching final conclusions. The wiki can serve as the laboratory journal in which all students write about the topic and reflect on

what changes need to be made as they share information or make suggestions. One graduate science professor became sold on his students using wikis when he discovered that he could better understand the teacher's knowledge of science and the scientific process upon reviewing the comments they made to their students. Whether for undergraduate or graduate students in science education courses, the wiki can make a powerful tool for assessment.

Wikis and Parents/e-Portfolios

School districts are increasingly using tools such as wikis to maintain contact with parents. Because wikis have the option to be public or private, parents can be given access to the course pages while the public is blocked from viewing anything with student information. By having classroom wikis, parents are able to become more involved in their children's education. After work, and at home, parents can view assignments, participate in asynchronous meetings when they are unable to attend the Parent Meetings at night, contact the teacher, view the work of their children, and check on upcoming events. In addition to class wikis, each student can create their own wiki and use it for an e-Portfolio that will house all their work from PK-adulthood. Beginning in kindergarten, students can scan their drawings and upload the digitized version into the wiki, add their recorded voices, and include all projects that they want to showcase each year. Parents will be able to view this e-Portfolio to see what students are doing each year. It is also an invaluable record for all the student has accomplished throughout their schooling. If students are using wikis for an e-Portfolio, they need to be taught about Internet safety and warned to remove any personal information that could identify them to online predators. While it is unfortunate that educators face those challenges, teaching online safety is paramount when using *any* online tool.

Incorporating Other Web 2.0 Tools into the Wiki

Wikis are a great initial entry point for technology integration. Not only are they easy to learn, but they also encourage additional technology usage. For research, students can create a survey using Google Docs and then embed the survey into their wiki and analyze the data gathered. Digital stories are also great way to incorporate technology into reading, language arts, social studies, and essentially any content area. Those stories can be uploaded into the wiki – yet another technology mastered. A calendar can be embedded into a wiki, so students can learn to manage their time and projects using online technology tools. Preservice and inservice teachers can embed content-rich videos from YouTube, TeacherTube or SchoolTube into the wiki, providing annotations about the key points in the videos. A slideshow of photos about an important concept saved on Flickr can be embedded into the wiki and students can generate a VoiceThread or Glogster and embed it into the wiki. While it seems like a cliché, wikis are indeed only limited by the creativity of teacher educators and students who are using them. Since abundant, easy to follow tutorials are provided for all wikis that cater to educators, instructors as well as students can quickly learn the basics or know where to go to find out how to use a feature. Beyond the basics, Net-Gen students quickly discover all that can be done with wikis and begin generating wiki content immediately.

Caveats – Permissions

Some commercial Learning Management Systems (LMS) have attempted to incorporate wikis into the tools. This provides seamless access to wiki projects for preservice and inservice teachers. However, teacher educators should consider several points when deciding whether to use a commercial, albeit free for educators, wiki or one interfaced with the LMS that houses their course content. Some questions to answer before deciding which is more appropriate include:

- Is the wiki project intended to be accessible by the public? If the intent is to encourage outside participation, then a commercial project might be better. Making wiki access dependent upon enrollment in the course defeats the power of wikis to engage with the larger global population.
- What age are the wiki builders? If students are adults, then the relative safety is not as much of a concern as it is for minors. In either type of wiki, care should be taken to ensure the student identity remains anonymous.
- Is money available for wiki purchase? With tight budgets the rule, *free* wikis allow anyone to create and maintain one. If teacher educators, preservice teachers and inservice teachers have to learn one wiki for class projects and another for use in the PK-12 classroom, they may find learning yet another technology more trouble than beneficial.
- Do students need/want access to the wiki after completing the course? If the wiki is to be used just for one project and will not be amended in the future, then a LMS wiki could be used. If teachers and students want to continue using it after the course is completed, then a commercial one would be more appropriate.

Another issue for teacher educators is the requirement for privacy for college as well as PK-12 students. Since many people will see the content in the wiki, a disclaimer can ensure that students understand the content will be available publicly. Including a disclaimer such as the one below and requiring students to sign and return it will ensure that they understand their products are available for everyone to view and that they have an option to submit their work for teacher's eyes only.

I have read the following statements in the syllabus under **Student Web Publishing and Publicly Accessible Course Projects**.

I understand *that all my projects for this class will be posted in either the course wiki or my professional wiki or both. The course wiki is available to the world for viewing. This allows me to better understand the power of collaborating with others across the world. Other students in the program benefit by viewing examples of what other students have contributed in the past.*

However, **IF I DO NOT WANT OTHERS TO HAVE ACCESS TO OR TO SEE MY WORK,** *I may block access to my projects by creating my personal wiki and only allowing my instructors access to the wiki. I may choose public access to my projects on an individual basis. Thus, if I want my Web 2.0 projects accessible to the public, but not other projects, I can do so.*

Importantly, **my grades or comments that the instructor may have for me on my projects WILL NOT be accessible to anyone except me through the gradebook** *component of course.*

Making my work private or public will not negatively impact my grade(s) in the course in any way.

In some cases permission on who can open, close or control a wiki has led to problems (see Appendix A).

CONCLUSION

In addition to state and federal legislative mandates to integrate technology into curriculum, recent empirical evidence points to technology as an effective tool to increase academic achievement and higher order thinking in the classroom (Branigan, 2002; Foltos, 2000; Norman, 2000; Wenglinsky, 2005) But, change is a painful process and most teachers resist the incorporation of new ideas into their teaching for a variety of reasons. Sanchez (as quoted in Collis & Moonen, 2008) cites several reasons for resistance to technology usage. Some include absence of pedagogical models for using technology, lack of confidence in personal technology skills, uncertainty about the "staying power" of new technologies, and the persistent belief that innovations cause more work for the instructor. These beliefs are couched in the model for teacher-centered direct instruction that is all too prevalent in education courses and the PK-12 classrooms today. However, the ease of learning to use Web 2.0 low-threshold technologies can overcome the afore-mentioned resistance to using technology in teaching.

In addition to using technology, teacher educators need to model student-centered learning and technology integration to prepare the teachers to do the same in their classrooms. While teacher educators will find the wiki easy to learn and use, the most significant point to remember is that technology *must* get into the hands of the preservice and inservice teachers so they will understand how to integrate it into their content. Once teachers see technology integration modeled in a variety of educational situations, they are more likely to understand how technology can be incorporated into student-centered instruction.

More than 100 years ago, John Dewey (1933) looked critically upon the educational system in the United States. Unfortunately, his suggestions did not foster educational reform. Instead, the educational system a century ago looks much like it does today. Dewey favored learning through experience, learning by engagement in meaningful activities, and learning in collaboration with others. Papert (1998) surmises Dewey's suggestions did not result in reform for two reasons. In Dewey's day, children only had access to information provided by the teacher and had little ability to challenge the teacher or find information themselves. They were not privy to the abundance of information resources that students can access today. However, unlike any generation before, children today have access to information and they can demand that school is more meaningful to them. But, Papert thinks a more important reason for Dewey's failure at reform is the lack of technological infrastructure that was not available until recently. The technological infrastructure and access to information and experts alike now allows students to virtually travel the world as they communicate and collaborate to solve world problems with others across the globe. Students now collaborate in learning and question what they hear in the classroom. As Papert predicted, when students gained the power they have today, they would be the ones to insist on educational reform. Have we reached that day?

Mrs. Rosales was glad the year was over. While her students looked forward to the summer break, they were also excited about going to the next grade and learning even more. Most of the students had email and traded addresses so they could continue their wiki from home. When her students told her good-bye, she knew that were ready for the next grade and for the new world they would enter in the fall. Her students told her that they never had so much fun learning. She closed the door with a sigh. "I only hope that their teacher next year will use technology to encourage engagement and make learning fun," she thought. "I probably don't have to worry, though," she thought. "It is likely that the students won't ever stand for just using a textbook in class."

REFERENCES

Bebell, D., Russell, M., & O'Dwyer, L. (2004). Measuring teachers' technology uses: Why multiple-measures are more revealing. *Journal of Research on Technology in Education, 37*(1), 45–63.

Branigan, C. (2002, May). Study: Missouri's ed-tech program pays off. Students' test scores higher than average. *eSchool News.* Retrieved September 30, 2006, from http://www.eschoolnews.com/news/ showstory.cfm?ArticleID=3673

Brzycki, D., & Dudt, K. (2005). Overcoming barriers to technology use in teacher preparation programs. *Journal of Technology and Teacher Education, 13*(4), 619–642.

Carvin, A. (2010). *Using a wiki to promote educational blogging.* Retrieved September 12, 2010 from http://www.pbs.org/teachers/learning.now

Chilicott, L. (Producer), & Guggenheim, D. (Director). (2010). *Waiting for Superman* [Motion picture]. United States: Paramount Vantage and Participant Media.

Churches, A. (2009). *Bloom's digital taxonomy: It's not about the tools, it's using the tools to facilitate learning.* Retrieved September 20, 2010, from http://edorigami.wikispaces.com/file/view/bloom%27s+Digital+taxonomy+v3.01.pdf

Collis, B., & Moonen, J. (2008). Web 2.0 tools and processes in higher education: Quality perspectives. *Educational Media International, 45*(2), 93–106. doi:10.1080/09523980802107179

Dewey, J. (1933). *How we think: A restatement of the relation of reflective thinking to the educative process.* New York, NY: Heath.

Ertmer, P. A. (2005). Teacher pedagogical beliefs: The final frontier in our quest for technology integration? *Educational Technology Research and Development, 53*(4), 25–39. doi:10.1007/BF02504683

Ertmer, P. A., & Ottenbreit-Leftwich, A. T. (2010). Teacher technology change: How knowledge, beliefs, and culture intersect. *Journal of Research on Technology in Education, 42,* 255–284.

Foltos, L. (2002). *Technology and academic achievement.* Retrieved September 6, 2010, from http://www.newhorizons.org/strategies/ foltos. htm

Gardner, H. (2007). *Five minds for the future.* Boston, MA: Harvard Business School Publishing.

Gilbert, S. (2002). *The beauty of low threshold applications.* Retrieved September 1, 2010, from http://www.tltgroup.org/gilbert/Columns/ BeautyLTAs2-2-2002.htm

Gilbert, S. (2006). *TLT/Collaborative change: Low threshold applications (LTAs).* Retrieved August 24, 2010, from http://www.tltgroup.org/ resources/rltas.html

Gray, L., Thomas, N., & Lewis, L. (2010). *Teachers' use of educational technology in U.S. public schools: 2009 (NCES 2010-040).* Washington, DC: National Center for Education Statistics, Institute of Education Sciences, U.S. Department of Education.

Judge, S., Puckett, K., & Cabuk, B. (2004). Digital equity: New findings from the early childhood longitudinal study. *Journal of Research on Technology in Education, 36*(4), 383–396.

Kim, K., Jain, S., Westhoff, G., & Rezabek, L. (2008). A quantitative exploration of preservice teachers' intent to use computer-based technology. *Journal of Instructional Psychology, 35*(3), 275–287.

Krueger, K., Hansen, L., & Smaldino, S. (2000). Preservice teacher technology competencies. *Tech-Trends, 44*(3), 47–50. doi:10.1007/BF02778227

Norman, M. (2000). The human side of school technology. *Education Digest, 65*(2), 45–52.

Norton, P., & Wiburg, K. M. (2004). *Teaching with technology: Designing opportunities to learn.* Toronto, Canada: Thomson Wadsworth.

Okojie, M. C., & Olinzock, A. (2006). Developing a positive mind-set toward the use of technology for classroom instruction. *International Journal of Instructional Media, 33*(1), 33–41.

Papert, S. (1998). *Child power: Keys to the new learning of the digital century.* Speech delivered at the eleventh Colin Cherry Memorial Lecture on Communication on June 2, 1998 at the Imperial College in London.

Persichitte, K., Caffarella, E. P., & Tharptitle, D. D. (1999). Technology integration in teacher preparation: A qualitative research study. *Journal of Technology and Teacher Education, 7*(3), 219–233.

U.S. Department of Education, Office of Educational Technology. (2004). *Toward a new golden age in American education: How the internet, the law and today's students are revolutionizing expectations.* Washington, DC: U.S. Government Printing Office.

Wenglinsky, H. (2005). *Using technology wisely: The keys to success in schools.* New York, NY: Teachers College Press.

ADDITIONAL READING

Brooks, J. G., & Brooks, M. G. (2001). *In search of understanding: The case for constructivist classrooms.* Upper Saddle River, NJ: Prentice-Hall, Inc.

Cifuentes, L., Sharp, A., Bulu, S., Benz, M., & Stough, L. (2010). Developing a Web 2.0-based system with user-authored content for community use and teacher education. *Educational Technology Research and Development, 58*(4), 377–398. doi:10.1007/s11423-009-9141-x

Drexler, W., Baralt, A., & Dawson, K. (2008). The Teach Web 2.0 Consortium: A tool to promote educational social networking and Web 2.0 use among educators. *Educational Media International, 45*(4), 271–283. doi:10.1080/09523980802571499

Graham, C. R., Tripp, T., & Wentworth, N. (2009). Assessing and improving technology integration skills for preservice teachers using the teacher work sample. *Journal of Educational Computing Research, 41*(1), 39–62. doi:10.2190/EC.41.1.b

Lim, W-Y., So, H-J., & an, S-C. (2010). eLearning *2.0* and new literacies: Are social practices lagging behind? *Interactive Learning Environments, 18*(3), 203-218.

McPherson, S., Wang, S. K., Hsu, H. Y., & Tsuei, M. (2007). New literacies instruction in teacher education. *TechTrends: Linking Research & Practice to Improve Learning, 5*(51), 24–31.

Moursund, D. (1999). *Will new teachers be prepared to teach in a digital age? A national survey of information technology in teacher education. Milken Exchange on Education Technology.* A publication of the Milken Family Foundation. Retrieved September 1, 2010 from http://www.mff.org/publications/publications.taf?page=154

Norton, P., & Hathaway, D. (2008). On its way to K-12 classrooms, Web 2.0 goes to graduate school. *Computers in the Schools, 25*(3/4), 163–180. doi:10.1080/07380560802368116

Rhoades, E. B., Friedel, C. R., & Morgan, A. C. (2009). Can Web 2.0 improve our collaboration? *Techniques: Connecting Education & Careers, 83*(9), 24–27.

Tapscott, D., & Williams, A. D. (2008). *Wikinomics: How mass collaboration changes everything.* New York, NY: Penguin Group, Inc.

Toledo, C. (2005). A five-stage model of computer technology integration into teacher education curriculum. *Contemporary Issues in Technology and Teacher Education, 5*(2). Retrieved September 20, 2010 from http://www.citejournal.org/vol5/iss2/currentpractice/article2.cfm.

University of Delaware. (2008). *Wikis in higher education: An exploratory report about the value of wikis in higher education, from a faculty perspective.* Retrieved August 31, 2010 from http://www.udel.edu/sakai/training/printable/wiki/Wikis_in_Higher_Education_UD.pdf.

Wikis in education and other tools for collaborative writing (n.d.). Retrieved September 16, 2010 from http://tep.uoregon.edu/shared/blogswiki-spodcasts/WikisBiblio.pdf

KEY TERMS AND DEFINITIONS

Blog: A portmanteau of *web log*, blogs are online journals that are posted in reverse chronological order, so the most recent thought is reflected first. Blogs can be made private to ensure students are safe. For more information, google: *blogs in education, K-12 blogs, blogmeister student blogs.*

Digital Storytelling: An emerging art form allowing individuals to tell a story using photos, video, narration, motion and transitions. Stories can be embedded in a wiki and can be a narrative of a personal event or an educational tool. Free for everyone. For more information, google: *digital stories, digital storytelling, stories, Photo Story 3.*

Glogster: A glog is a collaborative multimedia environment in which students create an interactive thematic poster with audio, text narration, YouTube-type movies, photographs, drawings, music, and more. Free for educators. For more information, google: *Glogster, glogs, glogs in education.*

Google Apps: Google offers a variety of web-based applications that are stored online and can be edited by more than one person at the same time simultaneously. These applications are browser-based and have free or professional accounts that include word processors, spreadsheets, multimedia presentations, and databases. Also, Google offers thousands of Gadgets that can be embedded in a wiki. For more information, google: *Google Apps, Google Apps for Educators, Google Gadgets.*

VoiceThread: A browser based application allowing users to create a collaborative, multimedia slide show. Others can comment via voice, text, audio file, or video. Slides can be annotated; video can be paused and annotated as well. VoiceThreads can be embedded into wikis. For more information, google: *VoiceThread.*

Wikis: A web-based application that allows anyone to quickly create a web page that is interactive and can be edited by multiple individuals. Wikis have a WYSIWYG (what you see is what you get) interface that enables users to build attractive web pages. Free for educators. For more information, google: *wikis, wikis in education, PBworks, Wikispaces, Wetpaint, WikiPedia.*

APPENDIX A

A Final Critical Suggestion for Wiki and Groups

Several semesters ago, a graduate professor was using wikis for class projects. In the past, all had gone smoothly with these projects and having students create their own wiki improved their understanding of wiki usage. However, one summer, he received a frantic phone call from one of his students asking that she be removed from the team. After meeting with two other female students, he found out that a male in the group was engaging in behavior that aggressive and demeaning during group synchronous meetings. In addition, if they did not come to meetings, he would call continually and harass them. After observing this behavior in the synchronous meetings the group conducted, the professor realized that this went beyond the typical *not getting along with each other* which can happen as groups learn how to work together. Of concern to the professor was the information on the group wiki that could have been used to stalk the female students or make life very unpleasant. Since the professor did not create the wiki, he could not delete it either. Luckily, when the group was disbanded, the aggressive behavior was transferred to the professor. Now, that professor recommends that group wikis always be created by the instructor and students only be given writer access so they cannot delete pages or delete the wiki. At the same time, the professor has full control to close a wiki, if needed.

Wikis Worth a Look

http://supportblogging.com/Educational+Blogging – This 2006 Edublog Award Nominee is used to support blogging with contributions from educators who use blogging.

http://www.googleearthireland.com - Google Earth Ireland uses Ireland to teach geography in an interactive wiki.

http://mrsibrahim.wikispaces.com/ - Mrs. Ibrahim's wiki shows how effective wikis can be, even for second grade students.

http://toolsforsearch.wikispaces.com/ - Contains lists of great Web 2.0 tools.

http://6thgrade-07.pbworks.com/ - Sixth grade wiki from Peru helps remedial students learning English as a foreign language.

http://digitalartstechacademy.wikispaces.com/DATA+Wiki+Home - Beautiful wiki from the Digital Arts Technology Academy is worth looking at for the slide show alone.

http://teachandlearn.sydneyinstitute.wikispaces.net/ - Australian wiki contains outstanding information about using media for teaching and learning and includes embedded media.

http://butleratutb.pbworks.com - Author's "work in progess" wiki is used as the portal for all courses. The ability to look back at students work in prior semesters is helpful to current students.

http://educationalwikis.wikispaces.com/Examples+of+educational+wikis - Contains links for hundreds of educational wikis for all grade levels.

http://www.wikimatrix.org/ - Wiki matrix allows you to compare features of different wikis.

Section 3
Integration of Technology into Teacher Education Courses

Chapter 11

The Importance of Using Subject-Specific Technology Uses to Teach TPACK:
A Case Study

Anne T. Ottenbreit-Leftwich
Indiana University, USA

ABSTRACT

The objective of this chapter is to describe a case study of an educational technology course that uses subject-specific contexts to address preservice teachers' development of TPACK. Many have indicated that in order for technology knowledge to be transferred to the classroom, teachers need to find the knowledge being taught relevant to their future classrooms. This course uses various workouts and cases to develop preservice teachers' technology abilities within the context of their future classrooms. Through these activities, preservice teachers showed improvement in technology knowledge (TK), technological pedagogical knowledge (TPK), and technological pedagogical and content knowledge (TPACK). Recommendations are made to other teacher educators on how to apply such principles within their own educational technology courses.

INTRODUCTION

Experts and policymakers advocate technology integration as an essential tool in K-12 education. Research studies conducted in the United States have indicated that although schools are currently equipped with adequate technological resources, teachers are still not utilizing those resources in their classrooms (CDW-G, 2010; Project Tomorrow, 2008). This could be due, in part, to a lack of relevant teacher training with regards to technology (Kleiner, Thomas, & Lewis, 2007). To encourage teacher education students to transfer knowledge gained during technology

DOI: 10.4018/978-1-4666-0014-0.ch011

experiences to their future classrooms, teacher education programs may need to improve on the instructional design of those technology experiences (Ottenbreit-Leftwich, Glazewski, & Newby, 2010).

Many have indicated that in order for technology knowledge to be transferred to the classroom, teachers need to find the knowledge being taught relevant to their future classrooms (Ertmer, 2005; Ertmer & Ottenbreit-Leftwich, 2010). Teachers adopt technology based on their own value beliefs (Ottenbreit-Leftwich, Glazewski, Newby, & Ertmer, 2010). Value beliefs with regards to technology are based on "whether or not teachers think technology can help them achieve the instructional goals they perceive to be most important. Whether a new pedagogical approach or tool is presented, teachers make value judgments about whether that approach or tool is relevant to their goals. The more valuable they judge an approach or tool to be, the more likely they are to use it" (Ottenbreit-Leftwich, Glazewski, Newby, & Ertmer, 2010, p. 1322).

Logically, teachers consider valuable uses of technology to align with things they can use in their classroom. Research has shown that when teachers learn how to use technology within their specific content areas and/or grade levels, they report being able to more readily transfer that knowledge to their own classrooms (Hughes, 2005; Snoeyink & Ertmer, 2001/2002). Often times, technology uses are taught outside of the context of the subject area (Ottenbreit-Leftwich, Brush, et al., 2010). For example, one teacher education program has preservice teachers enroll in technology workshops (e.g., Endnote, Microsoft Word), but does not discuss how to use this technology in the classroom (Ottenbreit-Leftwich et al). When learning experiences are focused solely on the technology itself, with no specific connections to grade or content learning goals, teachers are unlikely to incorporate technology into their practices (Hughes, 2005; Niess, 2005). Successful professional development programs

that have facilitated teacher acquisition of technology integration knowledge, such as Learning By Design (Koehler, Mishra, & Yahya, 2007), have introduced technology integration within situated contexts. This could be due to that face that "the more content-specific the example, the more likely the teacher will see value and learn it" (Hughes, p. 295). Therefore, educational technology experiences in teacher education programs should place heavy emphasis on learning content-specific uses of technology that can be transferred to future classroom experiences.

Teachers are reluctant to adopt technology that does not align with their subject's sub-culture (Hennessey, Ruthven, & Brindley, 2005; Ertmer & Ottenbreit-Leftwich, in press). In a review of literature on effective professional development for teachers, Hew and Brush (2007) found similar results that technology skills and experiences need to be introduced within an educational context, and should be consistent with specific and authentic needs and problems teachers faced in their professional contexts. In order to create effective teacher training where teachers will transfer technology knowledge to their future classrooms, teacher education programs need to help preservice teachers understand how to use technology in relevant was for their different subject areas and grade levels (Zhao, 2003). The objective of this chapter is to describe a case study of an educational technology course that uses subject-specific contexts to address preservice teachers' development of TPACK.

BACKGROUND: TECHNOLOGICAL PEDAGOGICAL AND CONTENT KNOWLEDGE

National organizations have begun to place more emphasis the integration of technology within the curriculum as opposed to a separate subject (Thomas & Knezek, 2008). The most recent National Educational Technology Standards advocate K-12 student technology use that will facilitate learning and help prepare students for their futures; "students will be expected to apply the basics in authentic, integrated ways to solve problems, complete projects, and creatively extend their abilities" (ISTE, 2008). In other words, students should be able to use technology to learn in various subject areas. Even subject-specific standards (e.g., National Research Council, 1996; National Council of Teachers of Mathematics, 2000) include statements of the importance of technology within their content specific curriculum (Niess, 2005).

The focus on subject-specific uses of technology aligns well with one recent conceptual framework representing teacher knowledge with regards to technology integration: technological pedagogical and content knowledge (TPACK) (Cox & Graham, 2009; Koehler & Mishra, 2008). TPACK is based on Schulman's work regarding Pedagogical Content Knowledge (PCK) (Shulman, 1986). PCK refers to a teacher's knowledge of how the best methods for teaching particular subject areas: "ways of representing and formulating the subject that make it comprehensible to others" (Schulman, 1987, p. 9). Technological Pedagogical and Content Knowledge (TPACK) adds the requirement of understanding technology integration within the classroom and teaching practices to the PCK model (see Figure 1). The TPACK framework illustrates a relationship between the pedagogy within a subject area (PK), the subject domain, culture (CK) and the technology (TK) (John & Sutherland, 2005). TPACK represents quality teaching because teachers must understand the relationships between all three constructs (technology, pedagogy, and content) to develop the appropriate teaching and learning materials (Koehler et al., 2007).

The difficulty in developing TPACK with preservice teachers is the lack of knowledge (or variance of knowledge) in all areas (pedagogical, content, and technical knowledge). In the educational technology course described in this chapter, the majority of preservice teachers are freshman. This means they are typically novice in both pedagogical and content knowledge as they have not taken any teacher education courses nor subject-specific courses necessary for content. Preservice teachers will eventually develop PK and PCK through other teacher education courses, and CK and TCK through content courses. Therefore, the educational technology course is responsible for developing TK, TPK, and TPACK (Cox & Graham, 2009). Technology knowledge (TK) refers to basic technology knowledge and skills, as well as being able to apply these skills (Koehler & Mishra, 2008). Technological pedagogical knowledge (TPK) refers to the "understanding of how teaching and learning changes when particular technologies are used. This includes knowing the pedagogical affordances and constraints of a range of technological tools as they relate to disciplinary and developmentally appropriate pedagogical designs and strategies" (Koehler & Mishra, p. 17). Technological pedagogical and content knowledge (TPACK) enables teachers to know when and how to use technology to teach subject-specific concepts (AACTE, 2008).

Teachers are more likely to adopt and use technology when they find them to be valuable and subject-specific (Ertmer & Ottenbreit-Leftwich, 2010; Schrum, Thompson, Maddux, Sprague, Bull, & Bell, 2007). Teacher education programs should consequently design subject-specific technology experiences for preservice teachers in order to increase the likelihood of transfer into future classrooms. The course discuss in this chapter placed heavy importance on tying technology uses to preservice teachers' the subject areas/grade levels they would teach in the future, using the TPACK framework to illustrate how teacher knowledge should be approached with regards to technology integration. Through this lens, educational technology courses should facilitate preservice teachers development of TK, TPK, and TPACK through relevant subject-specific context uses of technology for their future classrooms.

Figure 1. TPACK model

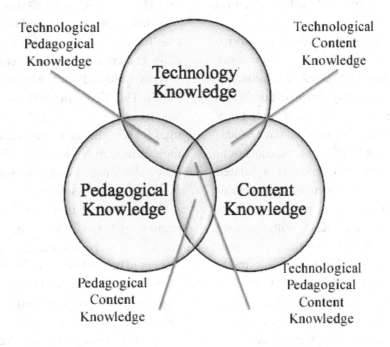

EDUCATIONAL TECHNOLOGY COURSE CASE STUDY

Course Background and Overview

This chapter discusses how one teacher education program has developed preservice teachers' TK, TPK, and TPACK related to the subject areas/grade levels they would teach in the future. The only required educational technology experience in this teacher education program was a stand-alone, 3-credit hour course. This course was a pre-requisite requirement for being accepted into the teacher education program; admittance into the teacher education program depends on successful completion of the course. Approximately 400 preservice teachers registered for the course during the Spring 2010 semester. The course was divided into 15 sections; each section contained 28 preservice teachers. The 15 sections all met in a computer lab with access to a wide range of software (e.g., Microsoft Office, Open Office, KidPix, Kidspiration, Inspiration, Inspiredata,

Google Earth, Geometer SketchPad, Kurzweil, etc.). Each lab also had access to a teacher computer and projector. There was a separate computer lab called the Technology Teaching Lab (TTL); this lab was open daily with support staff and was designated to help education majors with technology. The TTL also contained education-specific equipment available for check-out (e.g., science probes and sensors, LeapPads, FlyPens, etc.). The resources and support available added to the broader context and potential for addressing the needs associated with various subject-areas and grade levels.

Because this course was a pre-requisite to admittance into the teacher education program, this impacted the entry-level skills and knowledge of the preservice teachers (e.g., PK, CK). This is typically the first education course completed in by preservice teachers. Therefore, prior teacher knowledge was based primarily on their experiences as K-12 students. This was problematic because most students were unaware of how to design instruction and had not developed a teachers' persona. More than half of the students were in the first year of their teacher education programs (Figure 2).

As the course was required for all preservice teachers, there was a wide variety of majors (early education, elementary education, secondary math education, secondary science education, secondary language arts education, secondary social studies education, foreign language education, physical/health education, music education, art education, and many other education-related fields)(see Figure 3). There were no separate sections for the various majors; all preservice teachers registered for the same course. With this wide range, aligning technology uses with subject-areas was overwhelming as all subject-areas (e.g., math, social studies) and grade levels (preK to 12th grade) needed to be covered (see Figure 3).

The entire course was based on open educational resources (free and available sources). The entire course was viewable online; all presentations, podcasts, videos, tools, and articles used were embedded in the course website. Each semester, the instructors updated the course curriculum to reflect the ever-updating field of educational technology: http://www.indiana.edu/~educw200.

The course was chronologically divided into three units: Why Technology, Technology for Teaching and Learning, and Teaching as a Profession in a Digital World. In the first unit (Why Technology), they were provided with a rationale for why technology is important to 21st century teaching and learning. This aligns with the notion of value beliefs (Ottenbreit-Leftwich, Newby, et al., 2010). Preservice teachers need to be convinced of the value of technology in education. Therefore, the curriculum included inspiring YouTube videos (such as Shift Happens) to encourage them to think about why technology should be used in K-12. Particular importance was placed on the pedagogical aspects of technology use based on the National Educational Technology Standards for Teachers published by the International Society for Technology in Education (ISTE 2008). Specifically, the main focus was that technology should only be used in the classroom when it is an effective, efficient, or an enhancement to a particular teaching or learning activity (adapted from Merrill's 3 e's; Merrill, 2008). This first unit ended with the preservice teachers reflecting on why technology should be used for teaching and learning. During this time, they were required to build a digital storytelling movie detailing how they would use technology in their future classrooms.

In the second unit, the focus was on what technology to use for teaching and learning. Each week, they were introduced to technology tools that could be used for specific tasks (productivity, content exploration, production, communication, and data collection/analysis). At the end of this unit, preservice teachers made authentic decisions on what technology to use. Preservice teachers were provided with cases relevant to their majors. They analyzed the case using a scaffolded template and created the artifacts they proposed to create. The second unit demonstrated how they could use subject-specific technology tools for their future classrooms. Each week, the curriculum required them to review and apply different hardware and software within the subject-specific context of their future classrooms.

In the third unit, the curriculum focused on issues associated with using technology in the classroom. These issues included assistive technology, plagiarism, cyber-bullying, sexting, digital footprints, and the digital divide. At the end of this unit, preservice teachers completed a Teacher Website showcasing how they would use technology in the classroom and address these issues.

Throughout the course, there were four main assignments: Weekly Review and Application of Different Software/Hardware (Class Prep Activities, In-Class Workouts), Digital Storytelling Movie, Cases (Case Analysis, Case Artifacts), and Teacher Website. Depending on their majors, they

Figure 2. Year in teacher education program

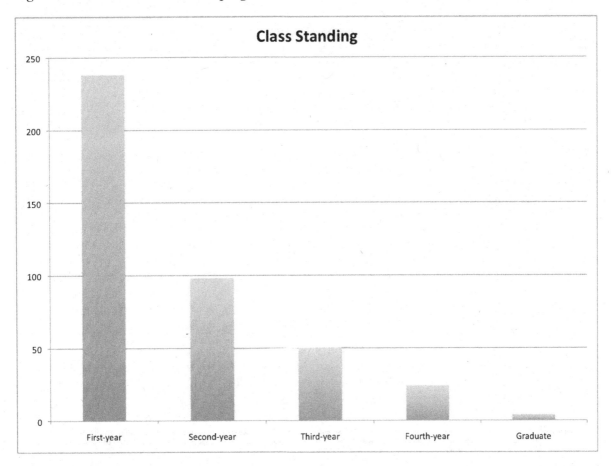

learned about how technology can be applied in subject-specific ways to their future classrooms.

Weekly Review and Application of Different Software/Hardware

Each week, preservice teachers were introduced to new technology tools and examples of how to use these tools in their future classrooms. Depending on the major of preservice teachers, the application of a specific technology tool during that week varied. For example, week eight focused on technology tools for communication tasks. Elementary majors chose to investigate ePals or PikiWiki, while secondary foreign language majors investigated Skype or LiveMocha. Before coming to class, preservice teachers completed

Class Prep Activities. Class Prep Activities were comprised of specific podcasts, articles, or Web 2.0 tools related to that week's topic. Preservice teachers were required to answer corresponding questions on a Google Form, reflecting on how they would use this type of tool in their future classrooms. During the class, lectures, discussions, videos, and hands-on workshops helped preservice teachers consider subject-specific uses for these tools.

Each week, preservice teachers also completed an In-Class Workout where they used one of the technology tools introduced that week to produce a deliverable that they can use in their future classrooms. There were 15 In-Class Workouts: (1) digital natives description, (2) webquest (e.g., Yola, Weebly), (3) teacher website skeleton, (4)

Figure 3. Majors in teacher education program

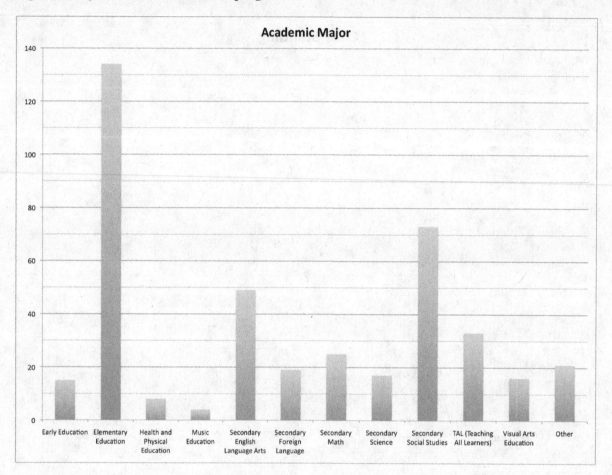

list resources for students, (5) concept map student example (e.g., Webspiration, Kidspiration), (6) screenshot and description of a content exploration tool (e.g., LeapPad, Geogebra), (7) student production example (e.g., Prezi, KidPix), (8) wikipage of a communication tool (e.g., Skype, Edmodo, Learning Connection), (9) data collection and analysis station activity (e.g., GoMotion, Inspiredata), (10) formative assessment (e.g., Google Forms, iRubric), (11) digital identify reflection (12) screenshot and description of how to teach online, (13) cyberbullying presentations for parents, (14) screenshot and description of assistive technologies, (15) final paper reflection on the course. Each of these workouts were adjusted to each preservice teacher's major. For example,

in week two, preservice teachers made webquests based on an Indiana state standard in the subject-areas/grade levels they plan on teaching. Through these workouts, preservice teachers developed a wide range of TK, TPK, and TPACK that all aligned within their own subject-specific contexts.

Digital Storytelling Movie

In the first unit, preservice teachers created a digital storytelling movie detailing how they will use technology in their future classrooms. Initially, preservice teachers were provided with information and examples on how digital storytelling could be used for educational purposes. Preservice teachers were exposed to a universal tips on how to facilitate digital storytelling in their own future classrooms (peer review of scripts, storyboards), thus developing general technological pedagogical knowledge (TPK). This assignment also required the development of technological knowledge (TK); preservice teachers used MovieMaker, iMovie, or Adobe Premiere to create a short movie. In the digital story movie, preservice teachers were asked to reflect on how technology could be used in their future classrooms, making sure they incorporated subject-specific examples. By discussing specific examples, preservice teachers demonstrated their technological pedagogical and content knowledge (TPACK).

Case Analysis and Case Artifacts

The preservice teachers were required to complete three cases. The cases were created by inservice teachers; they described an instructional situation that they believed could benefit from technology. For example, one secondary history teacher described that her high school students needed constantly updated resources for a current events class. Preservice teachers completed a Case Analysis using a scaffolded template. The template provided structured guidelines for students to follow, in order to help them make strong technology integration decisions. As they were at the beginning of their teacher education program, the Case Analysis template helped them consider different technologies and scaffolded development of their TPK and TPACK. They were required to list potential options, select the best option, and explain the rationale for why it is the best option. For example, in the secondary history example above, preservice teachers could have provided a range of RSS feeds, websites, twitter accounts, or blogs as technology options for constantly keeping high school students updated on current events.

After considering the additional restrictions embedded in the case (availability of resources in the school, time restrictions, student disabilities, etc.), each preservice teacher selected one of the options and explained why that option was the best choice. After receiving feedback from the instructor, each preservice teacher created the Case Artifacts they selected in the Case Analysis (see Figure 4). As the cases were ill-structured problems, the Case Artifacts varied for each preservice teacher. By constructing the Case Artifacts, preservice teachers developed a wide range of TK and TPK within their own subject-area contexts. They received feedback on how to use technology, as well as how to structure technology artifacts to promote student learning. The case assignments began in the middle of the course, during unit two. Over the last six weeks of the course, preservice teachers completed one case analysis or artifact each week (e.g., Case Analysis #1 in week six, Case Artifact #1 in week seven).

Teacher Website

The final assignment was the Teacher Website (Figure 5). The Teacher Website shell was created in the first unit; preservice teachers added to the website each week. The Teacher Website contained all the assignments completed during the course including the weekly assignments and cases (e.g., teacher presentations, newsletters, calendars, student examples, resources, reflections). In the NETS-T section, preservice teachers described how they met the national teacher standards and reflected on their development, using the weekly assignments and cases as evidentiary support. The Teacher Website was developed over the 15 weeks of the course; it was the final product to holistically assess preservice teachers' TK, TPK, and TPACK.

The Teacher Website enabled preservice teachers to develop TK from building the website. Preservice teachers used Google Sites to embed Google Docs, YouTube videos, pdf documents, images, and a wide range of Web 2.0 tools. In addition, preservice teachers were provided with general tips on how to design their websites to facilitate student learning (TPK). The Teacher

Figure 4. Case analysis and artifact example

Website was bounded in the meaningful contexts of their future classrooms in order to increase the likelihood that they would transfer this TK and TPK to their future classrooms.

Evaluation and Discussion

At the beginning and at the end of the semester, pre-service teachers were asked to rate their technology skills and knowledge of NETS-T standards by completing an online questionnaire. The purpose of this pre- and posttest was to investigate the impact the course had on the preservice teachers' technology skills as well as their abilities to meet NETS-T standards. The questionnaire included 72 questions addressing general technology skills and five NETS-T standards and was administered online through Profiler Pro (a free survey tool with image capabilities). The pretest was administered in the second week of classes and the posttest in the final week. Preservice teachers responded to each item using a 5-point Likert scale (1-strongly disagree, 2-disagree, 3-neutral, 4-agree, 5-strongly

agree) to self-assess their technology skills and knowledge of NETS-T.

To evaluate the impact the course, paired-samples t-tests were conducted to compare each area on the pre- and posttests of the questionnaire. Results showed a significant difference in all areas; significant differences were found in preservice teachers' technology skills and knowledge about NETS-T standards. While all areas showed significant increases, technology skills showed the largest improvement. The measurement used a Likert-scale to have preservice teachers self-assess their technology skills and knowledge of NETS-T on a scale of one to five, one meaning they felt weak and five meaning they felt strong. If preservice teachers rated their abilities as high, the pink color expand further. Figure 6 illustrates the differences in the self-rated abilities of the approximately 400 preservice teachers at the beginning and the end of the semester.

Similarly to Learning By Design (Koehler & Mishra, 2005), preservice teachers in this course developed TK, TPK, and TPACK in the context

Figure 5. Teacher website example

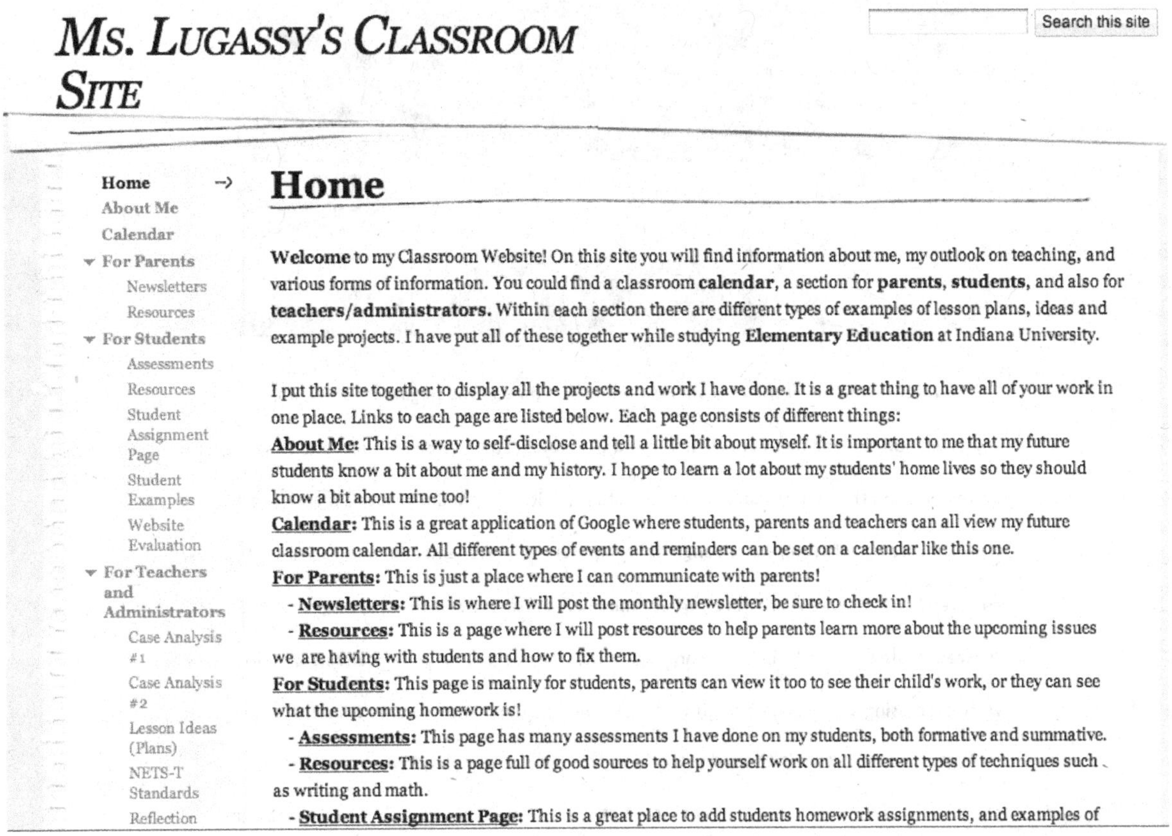

Ms. Lugassy's Classroom Site

Home

Home → **Home**
About Me
Calendar
▼ For Parents
    Newsletters
    Resources
▼ For Students
    Assessments
    Resources
    Student Assignment Page
    Student Examples
    Website Evaluation
▼ For Teachers and Administrators
    Case Analysis #1
    Case Analysis #2
    Lesson Ideas (Plans)
    NETS-T Standards
    Reflection

Welcome to my Classroom Website! On this site you will find information about me, my outlook on teaching, and various forms of information. You could find a classroom **calendar**, a section for **parents**, **students**, and also for **teachers/administrators**. Within each section there are different types of examples of lesson plans, ideas and example projects. I have put all of these together while studying **Elementary Education** at Indiana University.

I put this site together to display all the projects and work I have done. It is a great thing to have all of your work in one place. Links to each page are listed below. Each page consists of different things:

About Me: This is a way to self-disclose and tell a little bit about myself. It is important to me that my future students know a bit about me and my history. I hope to learn a lot about my students' home lives so they should know a bit about mine too!

Calendar: This is a great application of Google where students, parents and teachers can all view my future classroom calendar. All different types of events and reminders can be set on a calendar like this one.

For Parents: This is just a place where I can communicate with parents!
  - **Newsletters:** This is where I will post the monthly newsletter, be sure to check in!
  - **Resources:** This is a page where I will post resources to help parents learn more about the upcoming issues we are having with students and how to fix them.

For Students: This page is mainly for students, parents can view it too to see their child's work, or they can see what the upcoming homework is!
  - **Assessments:** This page has many assessments I have done on my students, both formative and summative.
  - **Resources:** This is a page full of good sources to help yourself work on all different types of techniques such as writing and math.
  - **Student Assignment Page:** This is a great place to add students homework assignments, and examples of

of creating specific products they could use in their classrooms. Each week, preservice teachers encountered new technology tools through hands-on workshops and tutorials. During class, preservice teachers were provided with generic pedagogical tips on technology use (TPK) and then created their own deliverables specific to their subject-areas/grade levels. For example, during the Production Tools week, preservice teachers were introduced to a wide range of TK (e.g., Prezi, Google Presentations, PowerPoint, SlideShare). The curriculum covered how to use technology to organize presentations (TPK) and preservice teachers created a presentation (In-Class Work-outs) directly related to their subject-areas/grade levels (TPACK). Each of these knowledge areas were evaluated.

Through the Weekly Review and Application of Different Hardware/Software, Digital Storytelling Movie, Case Artifacts, and Teacher Website preservice teachers developed their TK. The questionnaire specifically asked them to self-rate their abilities regarding technology hardware and software on a scale from one to five (five meaning they strongly agreed with the statement). One sample item for this section was "I am highly skilled at using podcasting software (e.g., iTunes, Podcaster)." There was a significant difference in the pretest score for technology skills (M = 3.05, SD = .55) and the posttest score for technology skills (M = 4.11, SD = .45), t(270)= -33.66, p < .05. These results suggest that the course had an effect on student learning regarding technology skills. Specifically, the results indicate that when

Figure 6. Profiler Pro: Preservice teachers' self-reported technology skills

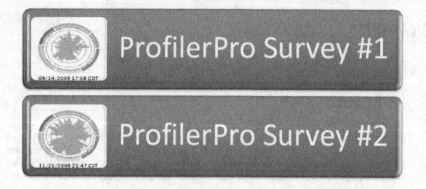

After taking the ProfilerPro survey for the first time at the beginning of this fall

semester, I discovered that I knew little about technology, the various options and usages that

it provides, and the opportunities I could create using it. I only had a vague familiarity with basic

word processing software, search engines, computer etiquette, and communication tools. I now

have retaken the same ProfilerPro survey, and my results have drastically changed. This survey

showed my new strengths in the technological field. I once had no understanding of complex

word processing, database, podcasting, movie editing, audio, image, spreadsheet, blogging, and

as Photoshop (as shown in the red section) and remain unclear about what constitutes

formative and summative assessments (as shown in the green section), but by looking at my

results and seeing the progressive trends displayed, I believe it will not be long until I master

such skills as I have since taking my first survey.

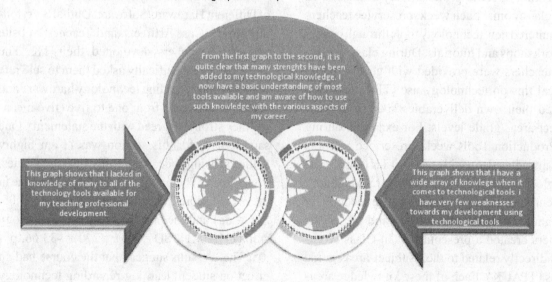

students complete the course, the students' technology skills increase.

Their development of technology knowledge was also evident in the course evaluation reports; they were surprised by the amount of technologies that could be used for teaching and learning. When asked to report the most valuable aspect of the course, almost 50 percent of preservice teachers mentioned the wide range of tools they were shown for teaching and learning: "Learning all the different technology option available [was the most valuable]," "the step-by-step explanations of different programs were most valuable because now I am comfortable using those programs on my own," "It was a good opportunity for me to learn more technological resources that have been able to help me with a lot of other things as well," and "I like that we were actually able to work hands on with the computer along with the teacher. It really helped to learn what we were doing." One preservice teacher specifically mentioned they would transfer these skills into their future classroom: "The aspects of the course that were most valuable were that we learned and used so many new tools and resources. I learned so many new things that I will most certainly use in my future classroom." Perhaps they were able to see the connection because the technology tools were introduced within the relevant subject-specific context of their future classrooms.

Other stakeholders and researchers have indicated that preservice teachers are more technologically savvy and require less education on using technology (U.S. Department of Education, 2000; Gao, Wong, Choy, & Wu, 2010; Project Tomorrow, 2008). However, in 2003, one study (Russell, Bebell, O'Dwyer, & O'Connor) found that "the skills teachers have developed—whether through their own experiences, professional development, or preservice training—may be leading to substantial use of technology outside of the classroom but have had smaller effects on instructional uses in the classroom" (p. 302). In other words, most of these new "tech-savvy"

teachers are proficient in using technology for personal purposes, but this does not necessarily transfer to the classroom (Andersson, 2006; Russell et al., 2003; Wright & Wilson, 2005). Many lack the knowledge of how to use technology to improve teaching and learning. They also seem to lack technical knowledge of Web 2.0 tools and educational specific technology tools (e.g., science probes, KidPix).

Technological pedagogical knowledge (TPK) means be able to understand "the pedagogical affordances and constraints of a range of technological tools as they relate to disciplinary and developmentally appropriate pedagogical designs and strategies" (Koehler & Mishra, 2008, p. 17). The Case Analysis assignment provided preservice teachers with scaffold to build TPK. In this assignment, preservice teachers listed a wide range of technology options, but eventually decided on one option. They considered the various affordances of the particular technology and described why it was the most appropriate decision. On average, preservice teachers earned 40/45 points for their case analyses. This may indicate they have started to develop TPK after finishing the course.

TPK was well-represented by the NETS-T #2: Design and develop digital-age learning experiences and assessments. This section evaluated preservice teachers' abilities to design and develop technology-based learning activities. They rated themselves on a scale of one to five (five meaning they strongly agreed with the statement). One sample item for this section was "I know how to customize and personalize learning activities to address students' diverse learning styles, working strategies, and abilities using digital tools." There was a significant difference in the pretest score for NETS-T#2 (M = 3.25, SD = .56) and the posttest score for NETS-T#2 (M = 4.14, SD = .47), t(270)= -23.55, p < .05. These results indicate that when preservice teachers completed the course, they increased their TPK to "design, develop, and evaluate authentic learning experiences and assessment incorporating contemporary tools and resources to maximize content learning in context and to develop the knowledge, skills, and attitudes identified in the NETS-S" (ISTE, p. 1, 2008).

Technological pedagogical and content knowledge (TPACK) enables teachers to know when and how to use technology to teach subject-specific concepts (AACTE, 2008). TPACK building activities were targeted throughout the course, asking preservice teachers to think about how they could use each technology introduced within their future classrooms. TPACK seemed to align with the NETS-T #1: Facilitate and inspire student learning and creativity. This section focused on their abilities to facilitate student learning through the use of technology. They rated themselves on a scale of one to five (five meaning they strongly agreed with the statement). Sample items for this section were "I can design technology-based learning activities" and "I can create visual representations of concept development and problem solving using digital tools." There was a significant difference in the pretest score for NETS-T#1 (M = 3.17, SD = .65) and the posttest score for NETS-T#1 (M = 4.26, SD = .43), t(270)= -27.87, p < .05. These results suggest that when students complete the course, the students' increase their knowledge "of the subject matter, teaching and learning, and technology to facilitate experiences that advance [their future] student learning, creativity, and innovation" (ISTE, p. 1, 2008).

CONCLUSION AND FUTURE RESEARCH

Perhaps one of the greatest difficulties associated with developing TPACK within educational technology courses is the variance. The preservice teachers enrolled in these courses come from a wide range of majors (e.g., secondary math, elementary education) that require different examples and software. This can be overwhelming for teacher educators. However, in order for

teachers to transfer the technology knowledge gained during their teacher education programs, it is important to introduce technology within a relevant subject-specific context (Koehler et al., 2007), one that may directly be transferred to their future classrooms. One of the preservice teachers in this study explained that the subject-specific uses of technology helped them developed technical knowledge: "I liked that for each type of technology that was discussed, we were able to try out different examples to get a better feel of how it could be incorporated into the classroom." Several studies have also indicated that teachers are more likely to use technology if they can see the alignment with their own specific subject area (Hughes, 2005). If they perceived no value tied directly to their content area, they were less likely to use the technology (Ertmer & Ottenbreit-Leftwich, 2010; Hughes, 2005; Niess, 2005).

In order to develop TPACK in teacher education programs, preservice teachers should be shown technology uses that are relevant for different subject areas and grade levels. It may be difficult for teacher educators to access examples in this wide range, but unless it is done, the knowledge may not transfer to future classrooms. For example, the wide range of workouts each week in this course were adjusted to address every subject area and grade level. For example, when asked to create a concept map (4), different state standards were specified for the various majors. Preservice teachers that worked with early elementary used Kidspiration to complete a basic concept map regarding their family unit, while secondary biology majors used Inspiration to construct a dichotomous key. This approach requires more preparation for teacher educators, but seems to result in a more meaningful learning experience for preservice teachers – one that may be more likely to transfer to their future classrooms.

To decrease the workload on teacher educators, a shared resource should be developed that provides a wide range of examples on how technology is used for all subject areas and grade levels.

Some have attempted this (Krueger, Bobac, & Smaldino, 2004; Roblyer & Doering, 2010), but technology becomes quickly outdated and needs to be constantly updated. Perhaps the educational technology community could collaborate to create one central location for links to the wide range of examples. Another possibility could be collaboration through personal learning network

In addition, each subject-specific area has best educational practices to consider. One of the concepts not explicitly covered in this example course is technological content knowledge. Koehler and Mishra (2008) indicate that "TCK is the most neglected aspect of the various intersections in the TPCK framework" (p. 16). Perhaps teacher educators responsible for educational technology courses should update themselves on best practices in all subject areas in order to recommend TPACK that aligns with best practices in all areas.

REFERENCES

AACTE Committee on Innovation and Technology (Ed.). (2008). *Handbook of technological pedagogical content knowledge (TPCK) for educators*. New York, NY: Routledge.

Andersson, S. B. (2006). Newly qualified teachers' learning related to their use of information and communication technology: A Swedish perspective. *British Journal of Educational Technology*, *37*(5), 665–682. doi:10.1111/j.1467-8535.2006.00563.x

Beck, R. J., King, A., & Marshall, S. K. (2002). Effects of video case construction on preservice teachers' observations of teaching. *Journal of Experimental Education*, *70*(4), 345–355. doi:10.1080/00220970209599512

Bennett, C. (1991). The teacher as decision maker program: An alternative for career-change preservice teachers. *Journal of Teacher Education*, *42*(2), 119–130. doi:10.1177/002248719104200205

Betrus, A. K., & Molenda, M. (2002). Historical evolution of instructional technology in teacher education programs. *TechTrends*, *46*(5), 18–21, 33. doi:10.1007/BF02818303

Britten, J., Mullen, L., & Stuve, M. (2003). Initial reflections: The benefits of using a continuous portfolio development in preservice teacher education. *Teacher Educator*, *39*(2), 79–94. doi:10.1080/08878730309555332

Brush, T. (1998). Teaching pre-service teachers to use technology in the classroom. *Journal of Technology and Teacher Education*, *6*(4), 243–258.

CDW-G. (2010). *The 2010 CDW-G 21st century classroom report: Preparing students for the future or the past?* Retrieved March 28, 2010, from http://newsroom.cdwg.com/features/

Cox, S., & Graham, C. (2009). Diagramming TPACK in practice: Using an elaborated model of the TPACK framework to analyze and depict teacher knowledge. *TechTrends*, *53*(5), 60–69. doi:10.1007/s11528-009-0327-1

Ertmer, P., & Ottenbreit-Leftwich, A. (2010). Teacher technology change: How knowledge, confidence, beliefs, and culture intersect. *Journal of Research on Technology in Education*, *42*(3), 255–284.

Ertmer, P. A. (2005). Teacher pedagogical beliefs: The final frontier in our quest for technology integration? *Educational Technology Research and Development*, *53*(4), 25. doi:10.1007/BF02504683

Gao, P., Wong, A., Choy, D., & Wu, J. (2010). Developing leadership potential for technology integration: Perspectives of three beginning teachers. *Australasian Journal of Educational Technology*, *26*(5), 643–658.

Hennessy, S., Ruthven, K., & Brindley, S. (2005). Teacher perspectives on integrating ICT into subject teaching: Commitment, constraints, caution, and change. *Journal of Curriculum Studies, 37,* 155–192. doi:10.1080/0022027032000276961

Hew, K., & Brush, T. (2007). Integrating technology into K-12 teaching and learning: Current knowledge gaps and recommendations for future research. *Educational Technology Research and Development, 55*(3), 223–252. doi:10.1007/s11423-006-9022-5

Hsu, S. (2004). Using case discussion on the web to develop student teacher problem solving skills. *Teaching and Teacher Education, 20,* 681–692. doi:10.1016/j.tate.2004.07.001

Hughes, J. (2005). The role of teacher knowledge and learning experiences in forming technology-integrated pedagogy. *Journal of Technology and Teacher Education, 13,* 277–302.

International Society for Technology in Education (ISTE). (2008). *NETS for teachers.* Retrieved on April 23, 2010, from http://www.iste.org/Content/NavigationMenu/NETS/ForTeachers/2008Standards/NETS_for_Teachers_2008.htm

Kay, R. H. (2006). Evaluating strategies used to incorporate technology into preservice education: A review of the literature. *Journal of Research on Technology in Education, 38*(4), 383–408.

Kim, H., & Hannafin, M. (2009). Web-enhanced case-based activity in teacher education: A case study. *Instructional Science, 37,* 151–170. doi:10.1007/s11251-007-9040-7

Kleiner, B., Thomas, N., & Lewis, L. (2007). *Educational technology in teacher education programs for initial licensure (NCES 2008-040).* Washington, DC: National Center for Education Statistics, Institute of Education Sciences, U.S. Department of Education.

Koehler, M., Mishra, P., & Yahya, K. (2007). Tracing the development of teacher knowledge in a design seminar: Integrating content, pedagogy and technology. *Computers & Education, 49*(3), 740–762. doi:10.1016/j.compedu.2005.11.012

Koehler, M. J., & Mishra, P. (2008). Introducing TPACK. In American Association of Colleges for Teacher Education Committee on Innovation and Technology (Eds.), *Handbook of technological pedagogical content knowledge (TPACK) for educators* (pp. 3-29). New York, NY: Routledge.

Krueger, K., Bobac, M., & Smaldino, S. (2004). InTime impact report: What was InTime's effectiveness and impact on faculty and preservice teachers? *Journal of Technology and Teacher Education, 12*(2), 185–210.

Lasley, T. J., & Matczynski, T. J. (1995). Reflective teaching. In Ornstein, A. C. (Ed.), *Teaching: Theory into practice* (pp. 307–321).

Lin, Q. (2008). Preservice teachers' learning experiences of constructing e-portfolios online. *The Internet and Higher Education, 11*(3-4), 194–200. doi:10.1016/j.iheduc.2008.07.002

Merrill, M. D. (2008). Reflections on a four decade search for effective, efficient and engaging instruction. In Allen, M. W. (Ed.), *Michael Allen's 2008 e-learning annual* (*Vol. 1,* pp. 141–167). Wiley Pfeiffer.

Mims, C., Polly, D., Shepherd, C., & Inan, F. (2006). Examining PT3 projects designed to improve preservice education. *TechTrends, 50*(3), 17–24. doi:10.1007/s11528-006-7599-5

National Council of Teachers of Mathematics. (2000). *Principles and standards for school mathematics.* Reston, VA: NCTM.

National Research Council. (1996). *National science education standards.* Washington, DC: National Academy Press.

Niederhauser, D., & Lindstrom, D. (2006). Addressing the NETS for students through constructivist technology use in K-12 classrooms. *Journal of Educational Computing Research, 34*(1), 91–128. doi:10.2190/E0X3-9CH0-EE2B-PLXG

Niess, M. L. (2005). Preparing teachers to teach science and mathematics with technology: Developing a technology pedagogical content knowledge. *Teaching and Teacher Education, 21*(5), 509–523. doi:10.1016/j.tate.2005.03.006

Ohlund, B., & Yu, C. (2009). *Threats to validity of research design.* Retrieved on April 23, 2010, from http://www.creative-wisdom.com/teaching/WBI/threat.shtml

Ottenbreit-Leftwich, A., Glazewski, K., & Newby, T. (2010). Preservice technology integration course revision: A conceptual guide. *Journal of Technology and Teacher Education, 8*(1), 5–33.

Ottenbreit-Leftwich, A., Glazewski, K., Newby, T., & Ertmer, P. (2010). Teacher value beliefs associated with using technology: Addressing professional and student needs. *Computers & Education, 55*(3), 1321–1335. doi:10.1016/j.compedu.2010.06.002

Pellegrino, J., Goldman, S., Bertenthal, M., & Lawless, K. (2007). Teacher education and technology: Initial results from the "what works and why" project. *Yearbook of the National Society for the Study of Education, 106*(2), 52–86. doi:10.1111/j.1744-7984.2007.00115.x

Polly, D., Mims, C., Shepard, C., & Inan, F. (2010). Evidence of impact: Transforming teacher education with preparing tomorrow's teachers to teach with technology (PT3) grants. *Teaching and Teacher Education, 26*, 863–870. doi:10.1016/j.tate.2009.10.024

Project Tomorrow. (2008). *21st century learners deserve a 21st century education: Selected national findings of the Speak up 2007 survey.* Retrieved March 28, 2009, from http://www.tomorrow.org/speakup/speakup_congress_2007.html

Roblyer, M., & Doering, A. (2010). *Integrating educational technology into teaching* (5th ed.). Boston, MA: Pearson Education.

Rosaen, C., & Bird, T. (2005). Providing authentic contexts for learning information technology in teacher preparation. *Journal of Technology and Teacher Education, 13*(2), 211–231.

Sadler, D. R. (1989). Formative assessment and the design of instructional systems. *Instructional Science, 18*(2), 119–144. doi:10.1007/BF00117714

Schrum, L., Thompson, A., Maddux, C., Sprague, D., Bull, G., & Bell, L. (2007). Editorial: Research on the effectiveness of technology in schools: The roles of pedagogy and content. *Contemporary Issues in Technology & Teacher Education, 7*(1), 456–460.

Shulman, L. S. (1986). Those who understand: Knowledge growth in teaching. *Educational Researcher, 15*(2), 4–14.

Weston, C., McAlpine, L., & Bordonaro, T. (1995). A model for understanding formative evaluation in instructional design. *Educational Technology Research and Development, 43*(3), 29–48. doi:10.1007/BF02300454

Wright, V. H., & Wilson, E. K. (2005). From preservice to inservice teaching: A study of technology integration. *Journal of Computing in Teacher Education, 22*(2), 49–55.

Zhao, Y. (2003). Introduction: What teachers need to know about technology? Framing the question. In Zhao, Y. (Ed.), *What should teachers know about technology: Perspectives and practices.* Greenwich, CT: Information Age Publishing.

ADDITIONAL READING

Bai, H., & Ertmer, P. A. (2008). Teacher educators' beliefs and technology uses as predictors of preservice teachers' beliefs and technology attitudes. *Journal of Technology and Teacher Education, 16*(1), 93–112.

Ertmer, P. A., Ottenbreit-Leftwich, A., & York, C. S. (2006-2007). Exemplary technology-using teachers: Perceptions of factors influencing success. *Journal of Computing in Teacher Education, 23*(2), 55–61.

Hennessy, S., Ruthven, K., & Brindley, S. (2005). Teacher perspectives on integrating ICT into subject teaching: Commitment, constraints, caution, and change. *Journal of Curriculum Studies, 37,* 155–192. doi:10.1080/0022027032000276961

Hermans, R., Tondeur, J., van Braak, J., & Valcke, M. (2008). The impact of primary school teachers' educational beliefs on the classroom use of computers. *Computers & Education, 51,* 1499–1509. doi:10.1016/j.compedu.2008.02.001

Hew, K. F., & Brush, T. (2007). Integrating technology into K-12 teaching and learning: Current knowledge gaps and recommendations for future research. *Educational Technology Research and Development, 55,* 223–252. doi:10.1007/s11423-006-9022-5

Mills, S. C., & Tincher, R. C. (2003). Be the technology: A developmental model for evaluating technology integration in classrooms. *Journal of Research on Technology in Education, 35,* 382–401.

Park, S. H., & Ertmer, P. A. (2008). Impact of problem-based learning (PBL) on teachers' beliefs regarding technology use. *Journal of Research on Technology in Education, 40*(2), 247–267.

Somekh, B. (2008). Factors affecting teachers' pedagogical adoption of ICT. In Voogt, J., & Knezek, G. (Eds.), *International handbook of information technology in primary and secondary education* (pp. 449–460). New York: Springer. doi:10.1007/978-0-387-73315-9_27

Straub, E. (2009). Understanding technology adoption: Theory and future directions for informal learning. *Review of Educational Research, 79,* 625–649. doi:10.3102/0034654308325896

Subramaniam, K. (2007). Teachers' mindsets and the integration of computer technology. *British Journal of Educational Technology, 38,* 1056–1071. doi:10.1111/j.1467-8535.2006.00693.x

Swain, C. (2006). Preservice teachers' self-assessment using technology: Determining what is worthwhile and looking for changes in daily teaching and learning practices. *Journal of Technology and Teacher Education, 14,* 29–59.

KEY TERMS AND DEFINITIONS

Case Analysis: A scaffolded template used to guide preservice teachers on how to make strong technology integration decisions based on authentic cases.

Case Artifacts: Preservice teachers create authentic technology artifacts to address the analysis.

Class Prep Activities: Completed before coming to class – typically podcasts, articles, or Web 2.0 explorations related to the week's topic.

Digital Storytelling Movie: A short movie created by preservice teachers on how they will use technology in their future classrooms.

In-Class Workout: Preservice teachers complete hands-on technology activities during class applied directly to subject-specific areas.

Teacher Website: This website contains all assignments from the course. Preservice teachers also describe how they met the national teacher standards and reflected on their development.

Technology Knowledge (TK): Basic technology knowledge and skills, as well as being able to apply these skills.

Technological Pedagogical and Content Knowledge (TPACK): Enables teachers to know when and how to use technology to teach subject-specific concepts.

Technological Pedagogical Knowledge (TPK): Understanding of how teaching and learning changes when particular technologies are used. This includes knowing the pedagogical affordances and constraints of a range of technological tools as they relate to disciplinary and developmentally appropriate pedagogical designs and strategies.

Chapter 12
The Iron Grip of Productivity Software within Teacher Education

Joan E. Hughes
The University of Texas at Austin, USA

Gloria Gonzales-Dholakia
The University of Texas at Austin, USA

Yu-Chi Wen
The University of Texas at Austin, USA

Hyo-Jin Yoon
The University of Texas at Austin, USA

ABSTRACT

This chapter discusses several challenges and recommendations in obtaining the desired outcome from technology-rich teacher education programs, including a novice teacher prepared to make decisions supporting students' subject-area learning with technology. The authors shape the discussion using select findings from two studies of preservice teachers enrolled in a technology-rich teacher education program at a U.S. university. The authors discuss the importance of the modeling relationship between instructors' and preservice teachers' experiences with digital technologies and describe productivity software's enduring grip as the most used digital technology among preservice teachers during teacher education – even in technology-rich teacher education programs. The authors argue that teacher education's overemphasis on productivity tools is not adequately preparing new teachers for the knowledge society in which teachers live, work, and educate. The authors argue that educational change, such as shifts toward technology-rich teaching and learning, will only be successful with a concerted change effort in both teacher education programs and PK-12 institutions.

DOI: 10.4018/978-1-4666-0014-0.ch012

INTRODUCTION

One of the aims of creating technology-rich teacher education programs is an underlying assumption that digital information and communication technologies can be harnessed for educational gains. Both the enrolled teacher education student, also referred to as a preservice teacher, as well as those preservice teachers' future students – the PK-12 students who will be pupils of the novice teachers graduating from teacher education programs – can accomplish such educational gains with digital technologies. Digital technology has a positive effect on learning (Bransford, Brown, & Cocking, 2000), yet preservice teachers and practicing teachers do not innately know how to harness technology's affordances for meaningful learning and instruction in the classroom. Teachers will make gatekeeper decisions regarding technology (Zhao, Pugh, Sheldon, & Byers, 2002), which necessitates teacher education programs to consider their stances and approaches to preparing teachers to integrate technology in classroom learning.

Teacher education programs must consider the vision or definition of technology integration within which they operate. We conceptualize 'technology integration' as the use of digital information communication technologies by teachers and/or students supporting constructivist and socio-constructivist instruction and learning (Cole & Griffin, 1980; Greeno, 1989; Greeno, Collins, & Resnick, 1996; Vygotsky, 1978) of subject area content (e.g., math, science, social sciences, languages, etc.). Optimal learning is a social practice that involves individual or group participation in activities that make use of contextually- and culturally-relevant (i.e., global, community, cultural, and individual) artifacts across time and spaces (Bransford, Brown, & Cocking, 2000). Thus, our conceptualization of 'technology integration' is one in which digital technologies are harnessed in support of optimal learning activities, as described by Bransford and colleagues. Such technology-supported learning

and instruction involves students and teachers working together with digital tools that, as much as possible, mimic authentic tools and activities within the subject areas. Students use these tools to explore, conjecture, analyze, test, and discover concepts and topics within subject areas. Apprenticeship into a profession serves as a metaphor in which learners of science, for example, would use tools most closely matching authentic tools of actual scientists. Scientists might be using digital microscopes or field-based data collection tools like mobile probes for assessing temperature, pH, or motion. Journalists use word processors, blogs, web pages, and books. Historians access primary source materials that may include multiple types of media. These examples provide glimpses of a range of 'authentic digital tools' that professionals use. From our definition of technology integration, we argue that PK-12 learners should be using these authentic digital tools for their own learning of subjects. Our definition of 'technology integration' does not imply that schools or teachers use the most recent technologies available; instead, it assumes teachers make decisions to use digital tools when they carry authenticity for the field and support in students' learning of subject matter. Certainly, there are other uses for technology, such as for administrative tasks like grading and attendance or for remediation or test preparation through technological tutoring systems. While these uses may yield positive impact on measures related to their goals, they do not fit within our definition of optimal learning or technology integration.

Teachers are the gatekeepers of technology (Zhao et al., 2002), and thus the importance of preservice teacher education programs rises to the fore. It is in the teacher education programs that preservice teachers gain experiences that most closely match what they will do and become as professional teachers. Their experiences impact the development of attitudes, beliefs, and knowledge that guide instructional decision-making.

In this chapter, we will explore relationships between how technologies are employed by faculty within the preservice teacher education program and the extent to which preservice teachers harness digital technologies in university classrooms and in PK-12 student teaching experiences. We discuss what we see as an enduring, iron grip on productivity software within preservice preparation programs that exists even within a technology-rich teacher education program. There is a history of data showing faculty instructors' and preservice teachers' predominant use of productivity software, such as word processing and presentation software (e.g., Graham, Tripp, Wentworth, 2009; Gronseth et al., 2010). Our data from a technology-rich teacher education program reveals this same trend. Thus, we refer to it as enduring and having an iron grip because even in a teacher education program with ample digital access to a range of tools, we still see productivity tool use as most prevalent. In the chapter, we discuss the implications of such an enduring focus on the preparation of teachers to integrate technology and the impact it may have on technology integration practices within PK-12 schools. We describe two key issues: (a) what and how much instructors and students use digital technology impacts each other; and (b) teacher education with digital technologies must move beyond productivity tools to include subject-specific and Web 2.0 tools. Finally, we suggest teacher education must take a lead role - in concert with PK-12 schools - to support the meaningful use of technology to support subject-matter learning by students.

BACKGROUND

The process of preparing a teacher to make technology integration decisions for learning and instruction is not simple (Doering, Hughes, & Huffman, 2003; Hughes, 2004; 2005). Instead, the process is complex combination of variables and contexts interacting across time. Of particular importance are: the nature of the preservice teacher education program, the innate and developing characteristics of the novice teachers, and the context of a particular school and district that a novice teacher enters as a professional.

Teacher Education Programs

Teacher education programs operate in various formats, with more or less focus on technology integration. Historically, technologies (such as, radio, filmstrips, overhead projectors, and more recently, computer-based technologies and handheld digital tools) have been incorporated into preparation programs in a single, 3-credit course. In the past, 70 to 80% of teacher education programs reported using a single-course design to educate preservice teachers about technology, media, and/or instructional design (Betrus & Molenda, 2002; Hargrave & Hsu, 2000). Yet, the single course approach has been critiqued in the literature for its lack of content-specificity and effectiveness in preparing teachers to integrate technology in their future classrooms (Bitner & Bitner, 2002; Doering et al., 2003; Kay, 2006; Lipscomb & Doppen, 2004/2005).

Identifying best practices in preservice technology teacher education lacks a solid empirical base, though the field has identified a range of strategies that are implemented. The U.S. Department of Education's Preparing Tomorrow's Teachers to Use Technology (PT3) initiative inspired reform of many teacher education programs to better prepare new teachers to integrate with technology. Thompson (2005), however, acknowledges the dearth of empirical research that emerged from these funded initiatives. Yet, Polly, Mims, Shepherd & Inan (2010) conducted a document analysis of PT3 reports and determined that PT3 programs utilized three common approaches: mentoring university faculty, promoting growth in knowledge of how technology works with content and pedagogy (Mishra & Koehler, 2006), and designing curricula materials of K-12 units for teacher education coursework.

In a review of teacher education programs, Kay (2006) determined ten main strategies used to teach about technology integration in preservice teacher education, including: a single technology course; mini-workshops; integrating technology in all courses; modeling how to use technology; using multimedia; collaboration among preservice teachers, mentor teachers and faculty; practicing technology in the field; focusing on education faculty; focusing on mentor teachers; and improving access to software, hardware, and/or support. Kay discovered 30% of the programs use only one approach (such as a single course), 28% use two approaches (such as 'collaboration' and 'mentor teachers'), and 40% use three or more approaches (such as 'integration of technology' across the program with 'faculty training' and 'absence of a single technology course'). Fifty-seven percent used two or fewer strategies to teach technology. This review provides descriptions of strategies, but Kay indicates the reviewed articles lacked methodological rigor, so the field still does not have evidence of which strategies might be better than others, due to a lack of longitudinal studies and sharing of data (Kay, 2006; Polly et al., 2010; Thompson, 2005). Using examples in the literature (e.g., Beyerbach, Walsh & Vannatta, 2001; Gillingham & Topper, 1999; Howland & Wedman, 2004; Johnson-Gentile, Lonberger, Parana & West, 2000; Pierson & McNeil, 2000; Seels, Campbell & Talsma, 2003; Strudler, Archambault, Bendixen, Anderson & Weiss, 2003; Thompson, Schmidt & Davis, 2003; Wright, Wilson, Gordon & Stallworth, 2002), Kay provides a guiding model with three critical components: a) access to technology resources and support throughout university courses and field placements; b) regardless of the strategy used, modeling and opportunities to create genuine teaching activities; c) most important, collaboration between preservice teachers, professors, and mentor teachers.

Overall, research indicates teacher education programs use a combination of strategies to teach technology skills and develop knowledge, which can be time-consuming and expensive (Strudler & Wetzel, 1999; Strudler & Wetzel, 2005). Most important, the technology integration approaches a teacher education program adopts will impact the preservice students' experiences, which, in turn, impact their developing attitudes and beliefs. The field needs to continue better understandings of these connections.

Teacher Characteristics

Preservice teachers are apprenticed into the profession (Brown, Collins & Duguid, 1989) through the preparation programs in which they enroll. Situated learning and cognition (Lave, 1991; Putnam & Borko, 2000) in teacher education is accomplished through combining classroom-based instruction at the university with field-based experiences, such as classroom observations, tutoring children, and student teaching. In a technology-rich teacher education program, the preservice learning context situates the use of technology throughout these experiences, such as with the use of various strategies that Kay (2006) describes. By situating learning in technology-rich physical and social contexts, preservice teachers may develop or strengthen their experiences and knowledge of how digital technologies inform pedagogy and curriculum. Preservice teachers develop knowledge and attitudes that begin to set the tone for their future teaching. Teacher characteristics such as high digital self-efficacy (Cassidy & Eachus, 2002; Chen, 2010), positive attitudes towards learning technologies in education (Anderson & Maninger, 2007; Brinkerhoff, 2006) and more 'constructivist' pedagogy (Ertmer & Ottenbreit-Leftwich, 2010; Ravitz, Becker, & Wong, 2000; Overbay, Patterson, Vasu, & Grable, 2010; Sang, Valcke, van Braak, & Tondeur, 2010) position teachers to more likely consider the use of technologies for instruction and learning with children.

As teachers experience the use of digital technologies within their coursework and field experiences, they also develop knowledge that helps them understand technology's role in education. A body of work conceptualizes such knowledge as interactions among content knowledge, pedagogical knowledge, and technological knowledge (e.g., Angeli & Valanides, 2009; Hughes, 2000; 2005; Margerum-Leys & Marx, 2002; Mishra & Koehler, 2006; Mouza & Wong, 2009), referred to as TPCK or TPACK. Research on preservice teachers' TPACK reveal less deep or less integrated knowledge which may impact their design of technology-supported content-area learning (e.g., Ozgun-Koca, Meagher, & Edwards, 2010).

These beliefs, attitudes, and knowledge can be informed through technology-rich teacher education settings. Graduates of teacher education programs, however they are designed, will draw on this personal knowledge and experience with technology to plan how to use technology as a novice teacher (Carter, 1990).

PK-12 School Context

As preservice teachers graduate and earn a position as a novice teacher, they take with them their knowledge, attitudes, beliefs, and experiences cultivated during their preparation but are faced with working in one particular PK-12 context: their school (Hammerness, Darling-Hammond, & Bransford, 2005). A school context has conditions that may impact teachers' technology integration efforts. Zhao et al. (2002) described how interactions among the innovator (teacher), the innovation (technology) and the context (school) impact a teacher's success with integrating technology. The teacher's technological proficiency, pedagogical approaches, and social awareness impact how s/he perceives opportunities to use and receive support for technology. The innovation, or potential technology, is more likely adopted by the teacher if it does not disrupt the school culture, requires few resources, and closely matches the teacher's pedagogical practices. Finally, the context, including human infrastructure, technological infrastructure

and social support, is important. Teachers need access to technology infrastructure, consisting of digital devices and software, which match their instructional needs. Teachers need social support of their integration endeavors, such as support from peers, staff, and parents. Teachers also need systematic human infrastructure, such as supportive school administration, knowledgeable technology integration specialists, and flexible technical staff.

Thus, as we attempt to prepare preservice teachers to become novice teachers who can make informed, thoughtful decisions regarding technology integration in classrooms, (Hughes, 2004; 2005) we must consider the ways in which we cultivate learning about technology integration within our teacher education programs. These approaches are the experiences preservice teachers will use to develop attitudes, knowledge, and behaviors regarding technology integration. Then, as novice teachers, they will access their knowledge and attitudes in decision-making.

Our chapter uses data from a research program that examines teacher preparation in a laptop-infused teacher education program in the United States. In the last decade, this teacher preparation program initiated a laptop requirement for all teacher-education students for use throughout their academic preparation and field experiences. In relation to the ten different approaches of integrating technology into preservice teacher education that Kay (2006) describes, this university program included the following four strategies: (a) "integrated" – technology woven into all courses with no dedicated technology course, (b) "education faculty" – a focus on developing education faculty's technology attitude, ability, and use, (c) "workshop" – short seminars offered for both faculty and students on particular technological topics of interest, and (d) "access" – provide infrastructural support and access to technology, especially through the requirement that all preservice teachers purchase a laptop. In Kay's (2006) study, 57% of the programs reviewed used two or fewer of the approaches. This university combined four of the approaches - a rarer example in practice and in the research literature.

We establish our chapter's discussion using selected data findings from two, multi-year data sets. The first data set ($n = 802$) includes survey data collected from student teachers (i.e., preservice teachers in their last semester of the program) across seven semesters between 2004-2007. The survey was administered anonymously at the end of the semester and asked about preservice teachers' and their instructors' use of a range of digital applications at the university, in PK-12 contexts, and for personal use. The second data set includes survey data from student teachers across three semesters in 2008-2009 ($n=93$). This confidential survey was also administered at the end of the student teaching semester and sought preservice teachers' frequency of use, focus of use (educational vs. personal), and skill level across a range of digital technology activities grouped within the following categories: Communication, Web, Productivity, and Creativity tools. Preservice teachers also reported their perceptions of their instructors' frequency of use, and fielded a range of questions (closed and open-ended) about their attitudes toward learning technologies in education and future use of technologies as teachers. The students responded to all questions by considering their university coursework and field experiences in the preceding year. The question guiding our research program is: To what degree are graduates of the laptop-infused teacher preparation program prepared to integrate technology in their future classrooms? For this chapter, we use selected results from our larger research to highlight three key issues for technology-rich teacher education:

- the importance of the modeling relationship between instructors' and preservice teachers' experiences with digital technologies;
- productivity software's enduring grip as the most used digital technologies among preservice teachers during teacher education;

- a shift toward technology-rich teaching and learning will only be successful with a concerted change effort in both teacher education programs *and* PK-12 institutions.

KEY ISSUES FOR TECHNOLOGY-RICH TEACHER EDUCATION

Relationships between Instructor and Preservice Teacher Digital Technology use

In Kay's (2006) review of approaches of integrating technology into different teacher education programs, four of the ten strategies involve the education faculty: 'workshops' on technological topics for faculty; 'modeling'; 'education faculty' – developing faculty's technological capabilities and attitudes; and 'integrated' – technology woven into the courses by faculty. Faculty are core to this process because if faculty do not "buy into" the use of technology in education, it is highly unlikely that preservice candidates will develop a positive attitude toward the use of technology. Preservice teachers will have reduced opportunities to observe educational uses of technology. When faculty model how technology can be used in the classroom, the teacher candidates will develop a range of "possibilities" that may increase the transfer of their knowledge and skill into their future classroom when they will be called upon to make instructional decisions regarding the use of technology.

Duran, Fossum and Luera (2007) pointed out three elements contributing to the comprehensive preparation of technology-proficient educators including core course work, effective faculty modeling of instructional technology, and technology-enriched field experiences. An effective use of educational technology by the preservice teachers most strongly depends on observing proficient mentor teachers who modeled technology-enriched instruction (Brown & Warschauer, 2006; Dexter & Riedel, 2003). When comparing three training environments, including practicum, student teaching, and the university, in the acquisition of preservice teachers technological skills, Fleming, Motamedi and May (2007) found that observing university instructors use was most related to preservice teachers' perception of their computer skills. They explained the reason was the fact that preservice teachers were exposed to university instruction over a greater period of time than practicum and student teaching experiences.

Indeed, we found significant and strong relationships between what technologies instructors and preservice teachers used in university classrooms. We explored the possible relationship between instructor and preservice teachers' use of laptops in the classroom using our data from 2004-2007 using a Pearson's chi-square test. For this specific analysis, we collapsed the four categories of use for these variables into two: "low" or use in less than 50% of classes and "high" or use in more than 50% of classes. There was a significant association between instructors' use of laptops and whether or not preservice teachers used laptops in the university class ($\chi2 = 207.245$, $df = 1$, $p < .001$). Cramer's statistic is $.512$ ($p < .001$), indicating a large, statistically-significant relationship. Based on the odds ratio, the odds of high laptop use by preservice teachers was 13.45 times higher if their instructors also had high laptop use in class. These statistical tests show associations, not causation. Thus, it also could be interpreted that if preservice teachers had high use of laptops, the odds their instructors would have high use was 13.45 times higher, but we feel that direction of association is unlikely since the faculty design the coursework and class activities. Therefore, in a technology-rich teacher education program such as this, if instructors do not use their own laptops it is unlikely the students will use theirs, which reduces chances for meaningful contemplation of digital media for educative purposes.

We also found statistically significant, strong associations between instructor use of media to

that of preservice teachers' use in the university classroom in the 2004-2007 data set. For example, a significant association between instructor and preservice teachers' use of web browser was found ($\chi2 = 189.21$, $df = 1$, $p < .001$, $n = 803$). Cramer's statistic was $.485$ ($p < .001$), indicating a large, statistically-significant relationship. Based on the odds ratio, the odds of web browser use by preservice teachers was 17.1 times higher if their instructors also used a web browser in class. Other significant association was found in the use of search engine ($\chi2 = 162.073$, $df = 1$, $p < .001$, $n = 802$, Cramer's V= $.45$) and computer-based presentation, such as PowerPoint, ($\chi2 = 156.81$, $df = 1$, $p < .001$, $n = 803$, Cramer's V= $.44$) with the odds ratio being larger than 10. It could be interpreted the odds of preservice teachers using search engine and presentation tools is at least 10 times higher if instructors use search engine and presentation tools in their classes. We saw strong relationships between the use of technologies by instructors and the use of the same technology by their preservice teachers in the classroom with technology. These statistically high associations were drawn from the technologies used most by students including presentations, the web browser, word processing, and search engines (see Table ,1). Our data indicated the opportunity of seeing instructors modeling use of technology statistically will increase the odds that preservice teachers use the modeled technology in their teacher education courses. Our data support the value of modeling (e.g., Brown & Warschauer, 2006; Dexter & Riedel, 2003; Fleming, Motamedi & May, 2007). Yet, we feel it is important that instructors realize the strength and powerful impact of their use/non-use on what the preservice teachers do with technology. Even in the laptop-rich setting of our research, there are faculty and preservice teachers who reported low use, which removed opportunities for preservice teachers to consider how technologies play a role in learning and instruction. Furthermore, faculty should consider the specific technologies they choose to use because,

Table 1. Percentage of preservice teachers reporting digital technology use by media tool in university classes and PK-12 Schools, 2004-2007

Media Tool	University Classrooms (%)			PK-12 Schools (%)		
	High	Med	Low	High	Med	Low
Word processing	90.2				70.0	
Web Browser	87.4				64.3	
E-mail	84.8				42.9	
Presentation	82.8				54.2	
Search Engine	81.8				64.3	
Digital Movies	66.3					31.2
Digital Photo		61.7		46.0		
Online course management		64.3				10.8
Student electronic submission		60.3				13.2
Online Forum		56.3				7.3
Concept mapping		41.3				32.5
Web Page Creation		38.9				8.7
Spreadsheet		38.7				22.4
Instant Messaging		36.6				5.0
Graphic Application			29.6			19.9
Digital Audio Record/Edit			29.1			16.5
Electronic portfolio			28.1			7.4
Multimedia Development tool			17.3			9.7
Computer games			8.9			14.7
Database			8.7			4.8
Content area software			8.0			9.2
Desktop publishing			6.2			4.1
Statistical Package			6.2			2.8

with use, the odds of use by preservice teachers increase. In other words, choosing to not use an important media tool will lessen the chances of it being used by preservice teachers during coursework, but more important, in field experiences and eventually in their own teaching.

Conceptually, we argue that such technology experiences in the preparation program coursework impact preservice teachers' experiences in PK-12 settings, such as when they do field observations or student teach. In our data, we found there were associations, albeit less strong, between preservice teachers' use of technology in the classroom with preservice teachers' use of the same technology in the PK-12 educational setting.

To understand the extent to which our preservice teachers transferred their knowledge and skills from the teacher education coursework to a PK-12 classroom setting, we explored the possible relationship of the preservice teachers' use of technology between university classes and PK-12 school classes. Again, using our data from 2004-2007, we found preservice teachers' use of word processing in the university classes showed significant association with their use of word processing in the PK-12 school classes ($\chi2$

= 155.864, $df = 1$, $p < .001$, $n = 803$). Cramer's statistic is .44 ($p < .001$), indicating a strong association. Based on the odds ratio, the odds of preservice teachers using word processing in the PK-12 school classes were 33.78 times if the student teachers used word processing in the university class. In addition to word processing, the use of a web browser ($\chi2 = 138.0$, $df = 1$, $p < .001$, Cramer's $V = .415$) and a search engine ($\chi2 = 153.141$, $df = 1$, $p < .001$, Cramer's $V = .437$) in the university classes were also highly associated with the use in PK-12 school classes. The odds of preservice teachers' use of web browser and search engine in the PK-12 school classes were 18.88 and 11.56 times, respectively, if the preservice teachers used them in the university classes. While acknowledging these strong associations and odds of use among these high use applications (see Table 1), there is still much room for growth in instructors' use of a variety of other technologies and strengthening the relationship between classroom and field experience.

In many cases, a challenge to transfer technology practices learned in the university classroom to the PK-12 education setting is infrastructural resources at the PK-12 site. Our more recent data (2008-2009) asked whether preservice teachers had access to learning technology resources. They reported strong agreement on having access to learning technology resources for both course activities/projects in the university setting ($M = 3.37$, $SD = .506$, $n = 93$) and for field-based experiences ($M = 3.17$, $SD = .689$, $n = 92$) (1-Strongly disagree, 4-Strongly agree). At least with the preservice teachers in our research, they felt able to access some university-owned technology resources for use in their field experiences. Yet, preservice teachers would likely use these resources for instructor-centric uses because there were no classroom sets of technologies for check-out at the university.

While many studies have shown the need for the university faculty to upgrade their technological expertise, to model technology infusion into curricula, and to provide a comfortable learning environment for technology application, a mismatch between faculty members' desires to integrate technology and their technology skills can occur (Waddoups, Wentworth & Earle, 2004). Moreover, some preservice teachers have reported that they observe little or no faculty modeling of technology integration (Brown & Warschauer, 2006). Such a lack of modeling can decrease preservice teachers' confidence in using technology for teaching. Without effective models of technology integration, preservice teachers tend not to transfer technological skills to their future classroom instruction (Brown & Warschauer, 2006; Kay, 2006). Most important, our data show the strength of impact when instructors *do* use technologies in their instruction. The next key issue is the dearth of high-use technologies used by faculty and their preservice teachers and the over-emphasis on digital productivity tools.

The Imperative to Move beyond Digital Productivity

High Use Digital Technologies

Digital activities within preservice teacher education, even in technology-rich programs, appear skewed toward digital productivity. Productivity tools, conveniently offered through office suites such as Microsoft Office, include word processing, spreadsheets, presentation tools, databases, and communication tools (e.g., web / email access). Although these products were designed for the business arena, education has widely adopted them.

The preservice teachers from 2004-2007 reported high use (see Table 1) of word processing, web browser, email, presentation, search engine, and digital movies within their university classes. With the exception of digital movies, all these technologies are productivity tools. Preservice teachers have high use of digital movies because they are required to create a case reflection that involves capturing and annotating video they collect while student teaching. These preservice teachers reported *no* high use of *any* technologies when they worked within PK-12 settings.

The preservice teachers from 2008-2009 reported high use of course management software (e.g., BlackBoard) word processing, presentation software, spreadsheet, digital video, reading discussion boards, and use of the university library website for predominantly educational purposes (see Table 2). They also reported reading and sending email as a high use for both educational and personal purposes. Productivity activities remains entrenched with use of presentation software, word processing, spreadsheet, and course management, while digital video continues to be used for their teaching reflection projects. Preservice teachers in 2008-2009 reported high use of discussion boards, which are hosted via university learning management software, as compared with student teachers in 2004-2007 who reported medium use. There is evidence of reading and writing on blogs as emergent during Fall 2009 as students reported mixed (educational and personal) use of this activity, as compared with more personal use of blogs in Fall 2008 and Spring 2009.

Digital concept mapping was reported used by preservice teachers in 2008-2009 at a medium level for educational purposes. Another emergent digital media is reading and writing wikis, which were reported used at a medium and low level for mixed and educational purposes, respectively. Other emergent technologies of note used at a low level for mixed purposes were social bookmarking, online productivity tools (such as Zoho or GoogleApps), digital audio, and podcasts.

Subject-Specific Digital Technologies

It is also essential for preservice teachers to learn how to make technology integration more subject-specific. A study conducted in the U.K. compared the use of ICT (information and communication technology) in different subjects (Haydn & Barton,

2007) found that preservice teachers felt a need to see examples of science department staff using information ICT in their teaching. They felt that having an ICT model was one of the key factors influencing progression in the ability to use ICT in subject teaching. We explored the degree to which student teachers in our data sets had exposure to subject-specific technologies.

Our data indicate an increasing focus on content area or subject-specific technologies in preservice teacher education. The preservice teachers in 2004-2007 reported low use of content area software across both the university class and PK-12 settings. Across 2004-2007, between 0%-15.2% of preservice teachers reported using subject-specific technologies in class compared to 4%-13% of students in PK-12 settings. We explored the possible relationship between instructor and preservice teachers' use of subject-specific software using a Pearson's chi-square test. For this specific analysis, we collapsed the four categories of use for these variables into two: "low" or use in less than 50% of classes and "high" or use in more than 50% of classes. There was a significant association between instructors' use of subject-specific software and whether or not student teachers used subject-specific software in their university class ($\chi2 = 381.685$, df = 1, $p < .001$). Cramer's statistic is .692 ($p < .001$), indicating a very large, statistically-significant relationship. Based on the odds ratio, the odds of use of subject-specific software by student teachers was 98 times higher if their instructors also had used subject-specific software. Again, these statistical tests show associations, not causation.

Our 2008-2009 data indicate between 48.5% and 77.8% (average of 61.3% across the three semesters) of preservice teachers reported moderate use of subject-specific technologies. When we asked preservice teachers from 2008-2009 an open-ended question regarding their "most valuable learning technology that you cannot imagine teaching without that you or your students will use in the future, if available," respondents

Table 2. Percentage of preservice teachers reporting digital technology use and focus of use by media tool, 2008-2009

Media Tool	Preservice Teachers' Use (%)								
	Fall 08			Spring 09			Fall 09		
	High*	Med	Low	High	Med	Low	High	Med	Low
Course Management System	84.8[a]			95.3[a]			100[a]		
Word Processing	78.6[a]			84.9[a]			90.0[b]		
Presentation software	78.6[a]			84.9[a]			85.0[a]		
Read email	78.6[b]			90.6[b]			95.0[b]		
Send email	78.6[b]			90.6[b]			95.0[b]		
Spreadsheet	69.0[b]			73.6[a]			85.0[a]		
Read discussion board	69.0[a]			75.5[b]			80.0[b]		
Digital video	66.7[a]			77.4[a]			80.0[a]		
Text-based instant messaging	69.0[c]			73.6[c]			90.0[c]		
Text message via phone	78.6[c]			84.9[c]			90.0[c]		
Access music	78.6[c]			84.9[c]			85.0[b]		
Social networking sites	76.2[c]			81.1[c]			90.0[c]		
Digital pictures	73.8[c]			75.5[c]			80.0[c]		
E-portfolio	72.7[a]				54.8[a]			50.0[a]	
Download music	71.4[c]			83.0[c]			75.0[c]		
Digital photo galleries	69.0[c]			67.9[c]				55.0[c]	
Use the library website		54.8[a]		67.9[a]			75.0[a]		
Post on discussion board		54.8[b]			60.4[b]		60.0[a]		
Concept maps		52.4[a]		49.1[a]					25.0[a]
Read blog		52.4[c]		73.6[c]			85.0[b]		
Subject-specific software		48.5[a]			64.3[a]		77.8[a]		
Read Wiki		45.2[b]			60.4[b]			65.0[b]	
Write/Comment on Blogs		40.5[c]			50.9[c]		70.0[b]		
Accessing online music or video			31.0[c]		52.8[c]			60.0[c]	
Use the web from a phone			31.0[c]		35.8[c]			40.0[c]	
Online productivity suite			26.2[b]			9.4[b]			0.0
Making webpages			21.4[c]		39.6[a]				10.0[a]
Email listserv			23.8[b]		41.5[b]				10.0[c]
Desktop publishing			21.4[b]			7.5[a]			10.0[b]
Digital audio			19.0[c]			26.4[b]			25.0[b]
Social bookmarking			14.3[b]			15.1[b]			25.0[b]

Table 2. continued on following page

Table 2. continued

Media Tool	Preservice Teachers' Use (%)								
	Fall 08			Spring 09			Fall 09		
	High*	Med	Low	High	Med	Low	High	Med	Low
Online multiuser computer games			14.3 [c]			3.8 [c]			10.0 [c]
Write/edit Wiki			7.1 [c]			13.2 [a]			10.0 [a]
Podcasts			2.4 [c]			0.0			5.0 [b]
Online virtual worlds			2.4 [c]			0.0			0.0
Webcasts			0.0			0.0			0.0

*Notes: L = mean use reported 0-33%; M = mean use reported 34-66%; H = mean use reported 67-100%. [a] = Focus of use reported to be educational; [b] = Focus of use reported to be both educational and personal; [c] = Focus of use reported to be personal.

mentioned, on average two digital technologies. Across the items, there was a prevalence of productivity software, such as PowerPoint and Word, as well as general hardware, such as computers, projectors, and document cameras (e.g., Elmo). The few content-specific learning technologies mentioned include: Word and iMovie (related to English Language Arts writing process activities and publishing), math/reading games, digital audio creation (for fine arts/music), and theater performance videos on YouTube (for fine arts/theater). Overall, we see a slightly upward trend in the use of subject-specific software but agree with Haydon and Barton (2007) of the importance of modeling with subject-specific software.

Web 2.0 Technologies

The apparent popularity of productivity tools overshadows subject-specific applications and affordances of Web 2.0 technology for subject-specific learning. "Web 2.0" refers to the shift from a read-only web to a read-write web in which web users assume a more interactive role through communication, collaboration, creation, publication, and identity-play (Greenhow, Robelia, & Hughes, 2009a; 2009b; Jenkins, 2006). Web users have transitioned from consuming what others post on web pages to consuming, creating, and reacting to information through social affiliations in communities of interest. When learners use

Web 2.0 in these ways, their learning processes closely match that which sociocultural theorists describe as important - especially the emphasis on learning with people, materials, and tools built by society (Dede, 2008; Greenhow & Robelia, 2009; Greenhow, Robelia, & Hughes, 2009a). This sociocultural perspective accords well with our definition of technology integration and our ultimate goal of getting the digital technologies into the hands of the students for subject-specific learning opportunities.

When novice teachers assume their first professional teaching positions after graduation, they will face youth steeped in Web 2.0 digital technologies and attitudes - experiences that are often banned to youth from 8:00 AM to 4:00 PM while in formal school contexts. Today, youths' multitasking with digital technologies accounts for nearly 11 hours of their day (Rideout, Foehr, & Roberts, 2010). Rideout et al. (2010) also reveal that Black and Hispanic youth spend more time with media (about 13 hours) than White youth (about 8.5 hours), including more time on computers (1:49, 1:24, and 1:17 hours/min, respectively). Some youth have experience sharing content, remixing data and information and reposting, and blogging online - affordances of Web 2.0 technologies (Lenhart, Purcell, Smith, & Zickuhr, 2010). Watkins (2009) argues youths' media use is intensifying the social interaction among friends. Yet, little to none of this occurs in formal school settings. Data from our preservice teacher respondents in 2004-2007 and 2008-2009 reflect a low, but emergent use of Web 2.0 tools such as blogs, podcasts, wiki, and social bookmarking (see Table 1 and 2). We feel this is a positive trend toward better preparation of teachers to integrate technology into their future PK-12 teaching, but we feel a necessity for more emphasis and progress.

While students of different ethnicities possess growing digital technology prowess outside of school, youth are not necessarily using digital technologies for worthwhile educational purposes within school contexts. The teachers are the key to making prudent choices about the use of technology by learners. Preparation is key to technology integration for meaningful learning. While our recent preservice teachers from 2008-2009 "agree" ($M = 2.97$, $n = 87$) that learning technologies used in their courses adequately prepared them for teaching (scale: strongly disagree (1) to strongly agree (4)), this still leaves room for growth. Furthermore, the over-attention on productivity software does not provide preservice teachers the breadth of digital technology experience to support the many decisions concerning the use of digital information and communication technologies they will face in their new classrooms.

Making Changes in Teacher Education and PK-12 Settings

A key process to transforming our current educational system to reflect the desires and needs of a knowledge society (Collins & Halverson, 2009) is educational change (Fullan, 1993, 2007). We argue for fundamental and simultaneous change in both teacher education programs and the PK-12 school settings.

In the last decade, numerous policies and reforms have been enacted to address the necessary and beneficial usage of digital technologies in the PK-12 and teacher education settings. Many of these new state and national education initiatives and standards place importance on the use of tech-

nology to enhance learning by allowing genuine, collaborative, technology-rich learning spaces. The National Educational Technology Standards for Teachers (NETS-T) (International, 2008) and the 2010 National Educational Technology Plan (NETP) (Office of Educational, 2010) provide guidance and vision for technology integration efforts. The technology integration described in these documents reflect much more than simple skill acquisition. These initiatives mandate rich technology integration, providing students with opportunities to construct culturally-relevant knowledge within a digital information age and knowledge society (Collins & Halverson, 2009; Office of Educational Technology: U.S. Department of Education, 2010).

If teacher education institutions commit to enacting practices that align with the technology vision and goals of these aforementioned documents or to the vision with which we opened our chapter, a paradigm shift must occur. Actions to support growth in knowledge and practices of technology integration by preservice teachers must shift from teacher-centered, generic technology activities (such as PowerPoint or word processing) to student-centered, subject-specific media activities that involve an array of digital tools with different affordances for supporting PK-12 content area learning through collaborative, hands-on learning.

This vision of 'technology integration' we suggest may be a shift for both teachers educators as well as preservice teachers. Teacher education programs are a vital component in driving this shift in vision. To support a socio-constructivist, technology-rich, learning environment, teacher education programs must develop complementary technology practices and philosophies among preservice teachers before they enter the classroom as novice teachers. Yet, most teacher education programs have not yet provided preservice teachers with either effective models of technology use or sufficient examples of meaningful technology integration (Brown, 2003; Smerden et al., 2000;

Thompson, 2005). Within the past two decades, various models of technology integration have been practiced in teacher education programs, such as the single-course approach, subject-specific cohort single course approach, integrated across all courses, modeling, and others (Dexter, 1997; Dexter, Doering & Riedel, 2006; Kay, 2006; Shin et al., 2009). Even the technology-rich teacher education program highlighted in this chapter "combined" four of the ten approaches of integrating technology into preservice education outlined by Kay (2006), but our research data revealed a predominance of generic productivity technology use supporting teacher-centric pedagogy and minimal, but growing, subject-specific technology integration. While there was a presence of technology throughout the teacher education program, the focus remained on teacher-facilitated use of productivity technologies.

To create effective technology-rich teacher education programs, universities must create a sustainable set of resources that will be available in perpetuity. Establishing a "technology-rich" teacher education program to only falter in a few years after initial funding wanes will not achieve the kind of meaningful educational change Fullan (2007) describes involving change in beliefs, materials, and instructional practices. The data we shared in this chapter illustrate the importance of the university faculty instructor in this process. There must be ongoing buy-in, professional development, and resources provided for faculty. It is through the faculty's shifts in instruction and modeling of subject-specific technology use that evidence of change among the preservice teachers will appear. Once preservice teachers' knowledge, attitudes, and beliefs shift, we will see instructional practices change in PK-12 settings, such as in student teaching or when novice teachers assume responsibility of their own classroom.

When preservice teachers possess a depth of knowledge and experience in subject-specific technology as they graduate into novice teachers, they will possess an important key to help shift expectations and practice within PK-12 schools. This depth of knowledge will only be beneficial to students if the PK-12 setting has the available resources and capabilities. Without the technologies necessary for authentic subject-specific teaching and learning, novice teachers' attempts to integrate technology will be futile unless they take on leadership efforts to make change in their own schools. We are concerned that many of these teachers will become frustrated with antiquated PK-12 resources and either abandon meaningful technology-supported teaching, or, worse, abandon teaching as a profession altogether.

We believe educational change for technology-rich, subject-specific learning must occur through collaborative efforts of teacher education programs and PK-12 schools so that both work towards enacting a similar vision of technology integration. One such collaboration could involve a university teacher education program locating, as much as possible, "university-based coursework" within PK-12 schools. In these schools, the university would establish mini-learning technology centers that provide access to an array of technologies. This relationship would allow both the teacher education program and the PK-12 school an opportunity to learn and evolve within consideration of the other. PK-12 schools would be exposed to the latest research and best practices in technology integration. University technological resources, such as laptops, software, GPS devices, would be available for whole classroom learning activities. Equally beneficial, teacher education programs could more accurately understand the challenges to meaningful, subject-area technology integration within formal school settings. These collaborations would provide learning and advancement for the teacher education program faculty/staff and the PK-12 faculty/staff with both groups sharing, offering solutions, and making change. Such change would not occur rapidly (Fullan, 2007), but by working together, change could occur over time. Both the student teachers and existing PK-12 teachers would be granted a meaningful experience enabling them to be teacher leaders. This invaluable experience could then be transferred to other PK-12 school settings.

While we hope such collaborations improve both teacher education and PK-12 education, in the short-term we face PK-12 contexts that have few resources, little vision, and unimaginative technology use. We also face high technology schools where teachers use technology to support teacher-centered instruction (Peck, Cuban, & Kirkpatrick, 2002). Regardless of the current technology initiatives and availability of technological resources, teachers ultimately decide when and how to use technology in their classroom (Ertmer, 2005). Thus, teacher education must focus on developing the most reflective graduates who, as novice teachers, will make thoughtful decisions with their technology integration knowledge and experience. These graduates should be inspired to work in a technology-rich PK-12 setting or assume a teacher leadership role in a technology-poor or visionless PK-12 setting in order to disrupt the status quo, inspire reflection and growth among teacher peers, and encourage expansion of subject-specific digital media activities. Real change will only be successful with a concerted change effort in both institutions: teacher education and the PK-12 schools.

FUTURE RESEARCH DIRECTIONS

We are very supportive of establishing technology-rich teacher education programs because we believe they are one way to instigate educational change within the field of education. However, we cannot assume that providing resources, requiring technology, and even preparing faculty in teaching education will prompt and perpetuate the development of novice teachers with the capacity to enact meaningful technology integration in their new educational settings. As Fullan (2007) indicates, real educational change requires a change in beliefs, educational materials, and instructional practices.

The most important direction for future research is to examine these change processes (beliefs, materials, and practices) from a longitudinal perspective. We must institute disciplined research processes to examine technology-rich teacher education programs across time (longitudinally). Many programs become technology-rich through a grant process or private donor without sustained support to continue year to year. In addition, Fullan (2007) warns that educational change takes time – usually three to five years to see noticeable change. We cannot expect to see substantial shifts within one to two years. Therefore, it is necessary to examine how beliefs, materials, and practices change over time. Important research questions for consideration include:

- How/do the influx of resources sustain over time?
- What are teacher education faculty's attitudes and beliefs toward technology integration?
- How do teacher education faculty use/model digital technologies in the teacher education program?
- What instructional approaches develop what kinds of knowledge about technology integration among preservice teachers, over time?
- How do preservice teachers use their knowledge and experience of technology integration in practice when they graduate and become novice teachers?
- How does the PK-12 context support / bar novice teachers' (recent graduates') technology integration efforts?
- To what degree are novice teachers (graduates of technology-rich preservice programs) inspiring change in PK-12 education settings?

By pursuing these research questions, we may be more equipped to establish best practices and a research-based knowledge base in technology-rich teacher education – an unusual accomplishment heretofore (Thompson, 2005).

CONCLUSION

"The technology is here, but we have not yet learned how to employ it to our full advantage." (President Nixon, 1970, Address to Congress on educational reform)

For decades, our educational system has struggled to meet the demands of our changing society and the needs of the current students. President Nixon's challenge appears timeless, as most perceive our current educational system in need of change to accommodate society's transformations. Our society has shifted from an information society to flat, open, and knowledge society (Bonk, 2009; Darling-Hammond, 2010; Friedman, 2007). This shift necessitates change across all facets of society, including education. Work in our current society is often facilitated through modern technologies. These workplaces value creativity, collaboration, inquiry and problem-solving. Yet, while education is the primary location individuals seek preparation for the workforce and continued education, it lags in change efforts.

To promote change, we need more technology-rich teacher education programs to provide models and mentorship. Yet, our data indicate that establishing a technology-rich program is not necessarily a sufficient condition to develop the beliefs, attitudes, and behaviors within preservice teachers to support meaningful technology-decision-making as novice teachers. Our data, as well as others, show the importance of faculty modeling. We need to shift from the pedagogically-generic productivity software (i.e., it can be used similarly across all subject areas) to an increase in teacher education faculty modeling of subject-specific technology use within university coursework. Alone, our data indicate with faculty use of subject-specific technology, the odds are 100 times more likely that preservice teachers will use subject-specific technology.

To shift away from generic productivity toward subject-specific technologies, teacher educators must adopt the knowledge, dispositions, and practices associated with subject-specific technology integration. Successfully integrating technology into a teacher education program includes at a minimum rethinking the curriculum and methods of instruction; providing mentoring and support for associated faculty members; and developing collaborative relationships between and among faculty, students, school districts, and beyond (Waddoups et al., 2004).

In regards to collaboration, the colleges of education and other institutions preparing future teachers should play an ongoing role in the professional growth of their graduates by partnering with PK-12 schools and organizations to provide engaging and relevant learning experiences throughout the entire course of their careers. In consideration of modeling, teacher educators should establish relationships with other education and subject-specific faculty and PK-12 school districts.

Teacher education cannot change independently from PK-12 educational settings. We must work in concerted effort. If we optimize preparation of teachers but prepare them for a rare technology-rich setting, we are no farther ahead. If we focus on optimizing PK-12 educational settings but certify novice teachers who are unprepared for technology-rich settings, we are no farther ahead. We must work in a connected fashion to establish technology-rich teacher education programs focused on subject-specific technology tools. Simultaneously, we must also advise, collaborate with, and prepare PK-12 educational sites to support technology-rich, subject-specific teaching and learning. Collaborative endeavors could include situating university courses in PK-12 sites co-taught by university and PK-12 teachers, or teaching inservice and preservice teachers together to maximize exchange and development of pedagogical, technological, and content expertise (Brown & Warschauer, 2006; Duran, Fossum, & Luera (2007). Ultimately, though, our technology-rich teacher education programs must prepare the preservice teacher to become the novice teacher who is an educational leader. This teacher-leader is ready to make informed decisions regarding technology integration and poised to effect change in any school s/he encounters.

REFERENCES

Anderson, S. E., & Maninger, R. M. (2007). Preservice teachers' abilities, beliefs, and intentions regarding technology integration. *Journal of Educational Computing Research, 37*(2), 151–172. doi:10.2190/H1M8-562W-18J1-634P

Angeli, C., & Valanides, N. (2009). Epistemological and methodological issues for the conceptualization, development, and assessment of ICT-TPCK: Advances in technological pedagogical content knowledge (TPCK). *Computers & Education, 52*(1), 154–168. doi:10.1016/j.compedu.2008.07.006

Betrus, A. K., & Molenda, M. (2002). Historical evolution of instructional technology in teacher education programs. *TechTrends, 46*(5), 18–21, 33. doi:10.1007/BF02818303

Beyerbach, B., Walsh, C., & Vannatta, R. A. (2001). From teaching technology to using technology to enhance student learning: Preservice teachers' changing perceptions of technology infusion. *Journal of Technology and Teacher Education, 9*(1), 105–127.

Bitner, N., & Bitner, J. (2002). Integrating technology into the classroom: Eight keys to success. *Journal of Technology and Teacher Education, 10*(1), 95–101.

Bonk, C. J. (2009). *The world is open: How Web technology is revolutionizing education.* San Francisco, CA: Jossey-Bass.

Bransford, J. D., Brown, A. L., & Cocking, R. R. (Eds.). (2000). *How people learn: Brain, mind, experience, and school.* Washington, DC: National Academy Press.

Brinkerhoff, J. (2006). Effects of a long-duration, professional development academy on technology skills, computer self-efficacy, and technology integration beliefs and practices. *Journal of Research on Technology in Education, 39*(1), 22–43.

Brown, D., & Warschauer, M. (2006). From the university to the elementary classroom: Students' experiences in learning to integrate technology in instruction. *Journal of Technology and Teacher Education, 14*(3), 599–621.

Brown, J. S., Collins, A., & Duguid, P. (1989). Situated cognition and the culture of learning. *Educational Researcher, 18*(1), 32–42.

Brown, S. (2003). *The effects of technology on effective teaching and student learning: A design paradigm for teacher professional development.* Retrieved from http://www.waukeganschools.org/TechPlan/ResearchFindings.pdf

Carter, K. (1990). Teachers' knowledge and learning to teach. In Houston, W. R., Huberman, M., & Sikula, J. (Eds.), *Handbook of research on teacher education* (pp. 291–310). New York, NY: MacMillan.

Cassidy, S., & Eachus, P. (2002). Developing the computer user self-efficacy (CUSE) scale: Investigating the relationship between computer self-efficacy, gender, and experience with computers. *Journal of Educational Computing Research, 26*(2), 133–153. doi:10.2190/JGJR-0KVL-HRF7-GCNV

Chen, R. (2010). Investigating models for preservice teachers' use of technology to support student-centered learning. *Computers & Education, 55*(1), 32–42. doi:10.1016/j.compedu.2009.11.015

Cole, M., & Griffin, P. (1980). Cultural amplifiers reconsidered. In Olson, D. (Ed.), *Social foundations of language and thought*. New York, NY: W.W. Norton.

Collins, A., & Halverson, R. (2009). *Rethinking education in the age of technology: The digital revolution and schooling in America*. New York, NY: Teachers College Press.

Cuban, L. (2001). *Oversold and underused: Computers in the classroom*. Cambridge, MA: Harvard University Press.

Darling-Hammond, L. (2010). *The flat world and education: How America's commitment to equity will determine our future*. New York, NY: Teachers College Press.

Dede, C. (2008, May/June). A seismic shift in epistemology. *EDUCAUSE Review*, (pp. 80–81). Retrieved March 4, 2009, from http://net.educause.edu/ir/library/pdf/ERM0837.pdf

Dexter, S. (1997). *Taxonomies and myths: A case study of technology planning and implementation*. Paper presented at SITE 97: The Eighth International Conference of the Society for Information Technology and Teacher Education, Orlando, Florida.

Dexter, S., Doering, A. H., & Riedel, E. S. (2006). Content area specific technology integration: A model for educating teachers. *Journal of Technology and Teacher Education, 14*(2), 325–345.

Dexter, S., & Riedel, E. (2003). Why improving preservice teacher educational technology preparation must go beyond the college's walls. *Journal of Teacher Education, 54*(4), 334–346. doi:10.1177/0022487103255319

Doering, A., Hughes, J. E., & Huffman, D. (2003). Preservice teachers: Are we thinking with technology? *Journal of Research on Technology in Education, 35*(3), 342–361.

Duran, M., Fossum, P. R., & Luera, G. R. (2006). Technology and pedagogical renewal: Conceptualizing technology integration into teacher preparation. *Computers in the Schools, 23*(3/4), 31–54.

Ertmer, P. A. (2005). Teacher pedagogical beliefs: The final frontier in our quest for technology integration? *Educational Technology Research and Development, 53*(4), 25–39. doi:10.1007/BF02504683

Ertmer, P. A., & Ottenbreit-Leftwich, A. T. (2010). Teacher technology change: How knowledge, confidence, beliefs, and culture intersect. *Journal of Research on Technology in Education, 42*(3), 255–284.

Fleming, L., Motamedi, V., & May, L. (2007). Predicting preservice teacher competence in computer technology: Modeling and application in training environments. *Journal of Technology and Teacher Education, 15*(2), 207–231.

Friedman, T. (2007). The world is flat: A brief history of the twenty-first century: *Vol. 1. Further expanded*. New York, NY: Picador.

Fullan, M. (1993). *Change forces: Probing the depths of educational reform*. London, UK: Falmer Press.

Fullan, M. (2007). *The new meaning of educational change* (4th ed.). New York, NY: Teachers College.

Gillingham, M. G., & Topper, A. (1999). Technology in teacher preparation: Preparing teachers for the future. *Journal of Technology and Teacher Education, 7*(4), 303–321.

Graham, C. R., Tripp, T., & Wentworth, N. (2009). Assessing and improving technology integration skills for preservice teachers using the teacher work sample. *Journal of Educational Computing Research, 41*(1), 39–62. doi:10.2190/EC.41.1.b

Greenhow, C., & Robelia, B. (2009). Old communication, new literacies. Social network sites as social learning resources. *Journal of Computer-Mediated Communication, 14*(4), 1130–1161. doi:10.1111/j.1083-6101.2009.01484.x

Greenhow, C., Robelia, B., & Hughes, J. E. (2009a). Learning, teaching, and scholarship in a digital age: Web 2.0 and classroom research: What path should we take now? *Educational Researcher, 38*(4), 246–259. doi:10.3102/0013189X09336671

Greenhow, C., Robelia, B., & Hughes, J. E. (2009b). Research on learning and teaching with Web 2.0: Bridging conversations. *Educational Researcher, 38*(4), 280–283. doi:10.3102/0013189X09336675

Greeno, J. (1989). The situativity of knowing, learning, and research. *The American Psychologist, 53*(1), 5–26. doi:10.1037/0003-066X.53.1.5

Greeno, J. G., Collins, A., & Resnick, L. B. (1996). Cognition and learning. In Berliner, D., & Calfee, R. (Eds.), *Handbook of educational psychology.* New York, NY: MacMillan.

Gronseth, S., Brush, T., Ottenbreit-Leftwich, A., Strycker, J., Abaci, S., & Easterling, W. (2010). Equipping the next generation of teachers: Technology preparation and practice. *Journal of Digital Learning in Teacher Education, 27*(1), 30–36.

Hammerness, K., Darling-Hammond, L., & Bransford, J. (2005). How teachers learn and develop. In Darling-Hammond, L., & Bransford, J. (Eds.), *Preparing teachers for a changing world* (pp. 358–389). San Francisco, CA: Jossey-Bass.

Hargrave, C. P., & Hsu, Y. (2000). Survey of instructional technology courses for preservice teachers. *Journal of Technology and Teacher Education, 8*(4), 303–314.

Haydn, T. A., & Barton, R. (2007). Common needs and different agendas: How trainee teachers make progress in their ability to use ICT in subject teaching. Some lessons from the UK. *Computers & Education, 49*(4), 1018–1036. doi:10.1016/j.compedu.2005.12.006

Howland, J., & Wedman, J. (2004). A process model for faculty development: Individualizing technology learning. *Journal of Technology and Teacher Education, 12*(2), 239–263.

Hughes, J. E. (2000). *Teaching English with technology: Exploring teacher learning and practice.* Unpublished doctoral dissertation, Michigan State University, East Lansing, MI.

Hughes, J. E. (2004). Technology learning principles for preservice and in-service teacher education [Electronic Version]. *Contemporary Issues on Technology in Education, 4.* Retrieved from http://www.citejournal.org/vol4/iss3/general/article2.cfm

Hughes, J. E. (2005). The role of teacher knowledge and learning experiences in forming technology-integrated pedagogy. *Journal of Technology and Teacher Education, 13*(2), 277–302.

International Society for Technology in Education (ISTE). (2008). *National educational technology standards (NETS) and performance indicators for teachers.* Eugene, OR: Author. Retrieved October, 27, 2009, from http://www.iste.org/AM/Template.cfm?Section=NETS

Jenkins, H. (2006). *Confronting the challenges of participatory culture: Media education for the 21st Century.* Chicago, IL: MacArthur Foundation.

Johnson-Gentile, K., Lonberger, R., Parana, J., & West, A. (2000). Preparing preservice teachers for the technological classroom: A school-college partnership. *Journal of Technology and Teacher Education, 8*(2), 97–109.

Kay, R. H. (2006). Evaluating strategies used to incorporate technology into preservice education: A review of the literature. *Journal of Research on Technology in Education, 38*(4), 383–408.

Lave, J., & Wenger, E. (1991). *Situated learning: Legitimate peripheral participation.* Cambridge, MA: Cambridge University Press.

Lenhart, A., Purcell, K., Smith, A., & Zickuhr, K. (2010). *Social media & mobile internet use among teens and young adults* [Electronic Version]. Retrieved June 6, 2010, from http://pewinternet.org/Reports/2010/Social Media and Young Adults.aspx

Lipscomb, G. B., & Doppen, F. H. (2004/2005). Climbing the stairs: Pre-service social studies teachers' perceptions of technology integration. *The International Journal of Social Education, 9*(2), 70–87.

Margerum-Leys, J., & Marx, R. W. (2002). Teacher knowledge of educational technology: A case study of student/mentor teacher pairs. *Journal of Educational Computing Research, 26*(4), 427–462. doi:10.2190/JXBR-2G0G-1E4T-7T4M

Mishra, P., & Koehler, M. J. (2006). Technological pedagogical content knowledge: A framework for teacher knowledge. *Teachers College Record, 108*(6), 1017–1054. doi:10.1111/j.1467-9620.2006.00684.x

Mouza, C., & Wong, W. (2009). Student classroom practice: Case development for professional learning in technology integration. *Journal of Technology and Teacher Education, 17*(2), 175–202.

Nixon, R. (1970). *Special message to the Congress on education reform.* Retrieved from http://www.presidency.ucsb.edu/ws/index.php?pid=2895

Office of Educational Technology. U.S. Department of Education (2010). *Transforming American education: Learning powered by technology. National Educational Technology Plan.* Retrieved on September 16, 2010 from www.ed.gov/technology.netp-2010

Overbay, A., Patterson, A. S., Vasu, E. S., & Grable, L. L. (2010). Constructivism and technology use: Findings from the IMPACTing Leadership project. *Educational Media International, 47*(2), 103–120. doi:10.1080/09523987.2010.492675

Ozgun-Koca, S. A., Meagher, M., & Edwards, M. T. (2010). Preservice teachers' emerging TPACK in a technology-rich methods class. *Mathematics Educator, 19*(2), 10–20.

Peck, C., Cuban, L., & Kirkpatrick, H. (2002). Techno-promoter dreams, student realities. *Phi Delta Kappan, 83*(6), 472–480. Retrieved from http://www.pdkintl.org/kappan/k0202pec.htm.

Pierson, M. E., & McNeil, S. (2000). Preservice technology integration through collaborative action communities. *Contemporary Issues in Technology & Teacher Education, 1*(1), 189–199.

Polly, D., Mims, C., Shepherd, C. E., & Inan, F. (2010). Evidence of impact: Transforming teacher education with preparing tomorrow's teachers to teach with technology (PT3) grants. *Teaching and Teacher Education, 26*(4), 863–870. doi:10.1016/j.tate.2009.10.024

Putnam, R. T., & Borko, H. (2000). What do new views of knowledge and thinking have to say about research on teacher learning? *Educational Researcher, 29*(1), 4–15.

Ravitz, J. L., Becker, H. J., & Wong, Y.-T. (2000). *Constructivist compatible beliefs and practices among U.S. teachers* (Teaching, Learning & Computing Report 4.) Irvine, CA: Center for Research on Information Technology and Organizations, University of California. Retrieved from http://www.crito.uci.edu/TLC/findings/report4/

Rideout, V., Foehr, U. G., & Roberts, D. F. (2010). *Generation M2: Media in the lives of 8- to 18-year-olds*. Menlo Park, CA: Kaiser Family Foundation.

Sang, G., Valcke, M., van Braak, J., & Tondeur, J. (2010). Student teachers' thinking processes and ICT integration: Predictors of prospective teaching behaviors with educational technology. *Computers & Education, 54*(1), 103–112. doi:10.1016/j.compedu.2009.07.010

Seels, B., Campbell, S., & Talsma, V. (2003). Supporting excellence in technology through communities of learning. *Educational Technology Research and Development, 51*(1), 91–104. doi:10.1007/BF02504520

Shin, T., Koehler, M., Mishra, P., Schmidt, D., Baran, E., & Thompson, A. (2009). *Changing technological pedagogical content knowledge (TPACK) through course experiences.* Paper presented at the Society for Information Technology & Teacher Education International Conference 2009, Charleston, SC, USA.

Smerden, B., Cronen, S., Lanahan, L., Andersen, J., Iannotti, N., & Angeles, J. (2000). *Teachers' tools for the 21st Century: A report on teachers' use of technology*. Retrieved from http://nces.ed.gov/pubs2000/2000102A.pdf

Strudler, N., Archambault, L., Bendixen, L., Anderson, D., & Weiss, R. (2003). Project THREAD: Technology helping restructure educational access and delivery. *Educational Technology Research and Development, 51*(1), 39–54. Retrieved from http://coe.nevada.edu/nstrudler/ETRD03.pdf. doi:10.1007/BF02504517

Strudler, N., & Wetzel, K. (2005). The diffusion of electronic portfolios in teacher education: Issues of initiation and implementation. *Journal of Research on Technology in Education, 37*(4), 411–433.

Strudler, N., & Wetzel, L. (1999). Lessons from exemplary colleges of education: Factors affecting technology integration in preservice programs. *Educational Technology Research and Development, 47*(4), 63–81. doi:10.1007/BF02299598

Thompson, A. D. (2005). Scientifically based research: Establishing a research agenda for the technology in teacher education community. *Journal of Research on Technology in Education, 37*(4), 331–337.

Thompson, A. D., Schmidt, D. A., & Davis, N. E. (2003). Technology collaboratives for simultaneous renewal in teacher education. *Educational Technology Research and Development, 51*(1), 73–89. doi:10.1007/BF02504519

Vygotsky, L. S. (1978). *Mind in society: The development of higher psychological processes*. Cambridge, MA: Harvard University Press.

Waddoups, G. L., Wentworth, N., & Earle, R. (2004). Principles of technology integration and curriculum development: A faculty design team approach. *Computers in the Schools, 21*, 15–23. doi:10.1300/J025v21n01_02

Watkins, S. C. (2009). *The young and the digital: What the migration to social network sites, games, and anytime, anywhere media means for our future*. Boston, MA: Beacon.

Wright, V. H. (2005). Bridging and closing technology gaps. In Vrasidas, C., & Glass, G. V. (Eds.), *Preparing teachers to teach with technology* (pp. 359–367). Greenwich, CT: Information Age Publishing.

Wright, V. H., Wilson, E. K., Gordon, W., & Stallworth, J. B. (2002). Master technology teacher: A partnership between preservice and inservice teachers and teacher educators. *Contemporary Issues in Technology & Teacher Education, 2*(3), 353–362.

Zhao, Y., Pugh, K., Sheldon, S., & Byers, J. L. (2002). Conditions for classroom technology innovations. *Teachers College Record, 104*(3), 485–515. doi:10.1111/1467-9620.00170

KEY TERMS AND DEFINITIONS

PK-12 School: Schools that may include grade levels from preschool and kindergarten through twelfth grade.

Preservice Teacher: A university student, often undergraduate, enrolled in a teacher certification program that consists most often of university coursework, field experiences (observations), and student teaching. Upon graduation and successful passing of any state-level exams, the preservice teacher becomes certified to teach in a particular grade level and/or content area.

Productivity Software: Tools used to create and produce documents, presentations, databases, charts and graphs. Microsoft Office is a dominant productivity software suite.

Student Teaching: A length of time, often several months, when a preservice teacher assumes sole responsibility for teaching a class of PK-12 students.

Technology Integration: The use of digital information communication technologies by teachers and/or students supporting constructivist and socio-constructivist instruction and learning of subject area content (e.g., math, science, social sciences, languages, etc.). Such technology-supported learning and instruction involves students and teachers working together with digital tools that, as much as possible, mimic authentic tools and activities within the subject areas.

TPCK/TPACK: "Technological Pedagogical Content Knowledge (TPACK) attempts to capture some of the essential qualities of knowledge required by teachers for technology integration in their teaching, while addressing the complex, multifaceted and situated nature of teacher knowledge. At the heart of the TPACK framework, is the complex interplay of three primary forms of knowledge: Content (CK), Pedagogy (PK), and Technology (TK)." (http://tpack.org)

Web 2.0: A term characterizing the transition of the web from predominantly "read only" to a "read-and-write" web. Web 2.0 provides a technological platform for the development of a range of applications that afford participatory, collaborative, and distributed practices across users, media, time, and space.

Chapter 13
Using Student Choice to Promote Technology Integration:
The Buffet Model

Marshall G. Jones
Winthrop University, USA

Lisa Harris
Winthrop University, USA

ABSTRACT

This chapter describes the results of a curriculum redesign of a course in technology integration in an initial licensure undergraduate program. By looking at the diversity of interests and skills as a strength of students, rather than a problem with the class, the authors have been able to develop a class structure that increases student achievement and interest. The purpose of this chapter is to describe a course model that better accommodates the diversity of majors and technology experiences available to students. While all students are held accountable to the same course objectives, multiple options are provided for learners to choose a path to meet those objectives. Rather than requiring all students to participate in the same activities, students are allowed to select activities and content related to their individual content areas and skill levels. Allowing students choices helps alleviate problems in delivering content to students with different majors and background knowledge.

INTRODUCTION

It is common for teacher education programs to require an introductory educational technology course. Like many schools, our College of Education has seen the focus of this class shift over the

DOI: 10.4018/978-1-4666-0014-0.ch013

years. Historically these courses served as a place for students to learn how to use the computer. We thought of these as computer literacy courses, and assignments focused on demonstrating mastery of applications and various tools (Fewell & Gibbs, 2003). As more and more students come to these classes with significant technical skill and experience in using technology for personal use, the focus of these courses has changed. We think of them now as classes in technology integration, and we turn our focus from teaching pre-service teachers how to do things with technology to how to use technology to impact learning (Roblyer & Doering, 2010; Grabe & Grabe, 2007; and Newby, Stepich, Lehman, Russell, Ottenbreit-Leftwich, 2011). As such, the content of these courses has moved from technical skills to issues in technology integration, such as determining the affordance (Norman, 1988) or relative advantage (Roblyer, 2003) of a technology, instructional planning, learner engagement, project-based learning (Harris, 2010), learning theory, instructional strategies and assessment.

Students enrolled in these courses come to us with wildly varying interests, experiences, and curricular foci. For example, a typical class will have a mix of majors from elementary and early childhood education, to physical education, to music education, to math education and everything in between. The problem we face is one of relevance. For example, it seems obvious that what works well in a secondary social studies class may not work well in a middle school music class. However, student expectations in these classes are for examples of what to do in *their* classes. This is not, in our opinion, an unreasonable expectation. But if you add this expectation to the vast range of technology proficiencies that our students bring to the class, you can see how difficult it is to keep everybody focused on the ultimate goal of learning to integrate technology into *their* future classes. The question for us has become: How can we teach the course content while still making the examples relevant to everyone?

We have examined these issues and concerns for a number of years. We have worked with faculty in methods courses to figure out how we can help bridge the gap between our class and the clinical experiences in a vast array of content areas. We have found that we can drive student achievement by focusing on a student's individual strengths and interests and that the

interest of the individual student can be a tool to bridge this gap. By looking at the diversity of interests and skills as a strength of our students, rather than a problem with the class, we have been able to develop a class structure that increases student achievement and interest. The purpose of this chapter is to describe a course model that better accommodates the diversity of majors and technology experiences available to students. We are using the Buffet model (Twigg, 2002) to help develop strategies that allow for choice.

THE BUFFET MODEL

The buffet model is one model of course redesign studied by the National Center for Academic Transformation. The focus of the Center is to "provide leadership in using information technology to redesign learning environments to produce better learning outcomes for students at a reduced cost to the institution" (National Center for Academic Transformation, 2005, para 1). While our focus was not cost reduction, we thought that several aspects of the Buffet model would solve the problems discussed above. Specific concepts from the buffet model we used to redesign the introductory educational technology course include:

- Offering students multiple options to reach the same learning outcomes;
- Providing multiple ways for students to work with the content such as lectures, individual discovery opportunities, team/group discovery opportunities, and individual and group projects;
- Using face-to-face meeting time to explain the buffet structure, the course content, and the various ways that students might choose to learn the material;
- Offering course content organized in modules;
- Dividing tasks among faculty to eliminate duplication of effort and capitalize on fac-

ulty strengths and interests to develop and offer particular learning opportunities on the buffet.

(National Center for Academic Transformation, 2005)

The underlying principle of the buffet model is the idea of student choice. Students are allowed to choose different pathways to meet the same learning goals (Twigg, 2002). Rather than requiring all students to participate in the same activities, students are allowed to select activities and content related to their individual content areas and skill levels. Allowing students choices helps alleviate problems in delivering content to students with different majors and background knowledge. The goals of using the buffet model in an educational technology course are varied. In our chapter we will describe how the model can provide for:

1. increasing student engagement through self-pacing and project choice;
2. generalization to future methods courses and classroom practice;
3. opportunities to explore general education and content specific technologies;
4. variance in technology proficiencies among students.

Course Redesign with the Buffet Model

In order to talk about how the course design is different, we should probably talk about how the initial course was organized. As early as 2001, the course contained many of the components of a skills based class. Over the years the course moved away from mastery of skills to a class focused more on projects and collaboration. Based on the work of Roblyer (2003) and Ertmer and Newby (1993), we began to implement the course on more of a continuum from some basic skills, to a more fully developed project-based type of

experience. In this class, all students used the same technologies, but focused the use of those technologies on their content area. Individual projects were done on technologies such as website creation, designing graphic organizers, and image editing, but group projects were completed using technologies such as digital video and claymation. We had great success with this model for a period of time. But we struggled with the amount of class time it took to do some of these group projects, and we struggled with the fact that some content areas found the application of projects such as claymation a stretch to match to their content areas.

In 2006, we hit upon the idea of no longer doing lectures in the class. Based on the work of Wiley (2000) we began to work with reusable learning objects. Reusable Learning Objects are known by the acronym RoLO, and can be defined as "any digital resource that can be reused to support learning" (Wiley, 2000). A RoLO can be any type of digital document, such as a PDF file, an audio file, such as a Pod-cast, a video file, such as a Vod-cast, or a PowerPoint presentation to name but a few digital file types and formats. A good example of a database full of RoLOs would be MERLOT (Multimedia Educational Resource for Learning and Online Teaching), available at http://www.merlot.org/. As stated by Educause Learning Initiative (2005), these technologies "provide educators one more way to meet today's students where they live – on the Internet and on audio players" (p. 2). First, learning becomes mobile. Students can access content while exercising, driving, or doing laundry. Second, knowledge and expertise continue past the classroom doors. Students are able to listen to lectures or review materials before coming to class thus leaving more time to engage in discussion, project development, debate, etc. They can have materials on hand at home when they are working on completing a class assignment and revisit challenging content. Finally, Pod-casting and VOD-casting engage the learner of the 21st century. These learners, also known as "digital natives" or "millenials" not

Figure 1. Screen shot of Web page for learning objects

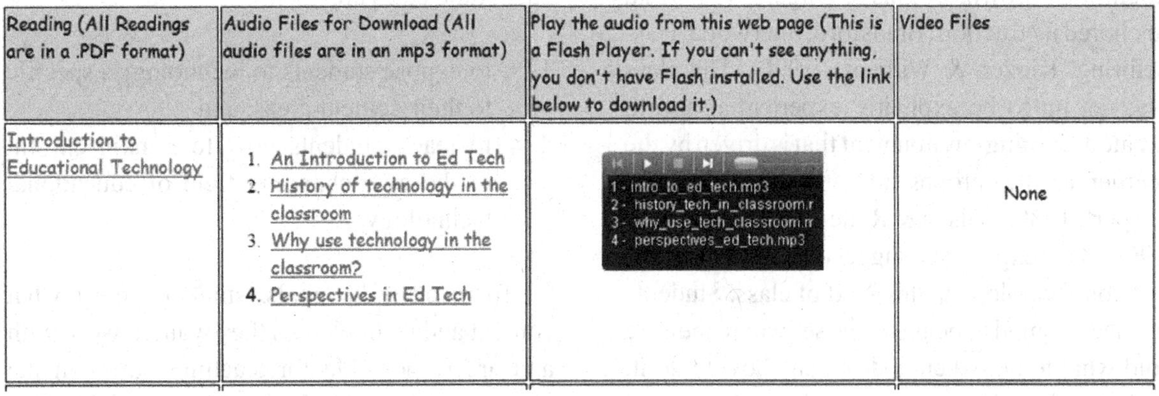

Reading (All Readings are in a .PDF format)	Audio Files for Download (All audio files are in an .mp3 format)	Play the audio from this web page (This is a Flash Player. If you can't see anything, you don't have Flash installed. Use the link below to download it.)	Video Files
Introduction to Educational Technology	1. An Introduction to Ed Tech 2. History of technology in the classroom 3. Why use technology in the classroom? 4. Perspectives in Ed Tech	1 - intro_to_ed_tech.mp3 2 - history_tech_in_classroom.r 3 - why_use_tech_classroom.rr 4 - perspectives_ed_tech.mp3	None

only have grown up experiencing technology as a seamless thread of their lives, but expect and see the value of its use in learning environments (Jones, Harmon, & O'Grady-Jones, 2005).

When developing RoLOs, we determined what content applied to everyone, divided it up between the two faculty members who teach the class, and created podcast lectures about each topic. Each topic was broken up into smaller components and podcasts were created for each component. Podcasts range from four to six minutes each. For example, the set of lectures on Learning Theory includes the following five podcasts: Introduction to Learning Theory, Behaviorism, Cognitivism, Constructivism, and The Continuum of Learning Theory. The idea was to create objects that are relevant to the class, while being granular and general enough to be useful in other classes as well. We posted all podcasts on the course website. Students are responsible for the readings and the lectures before coming to class. This allows for more time to work with content and less time spent in the presentation of didactic information. These podcasts are available online at http://coe.winthrop.edu/educ275/ROLO_2010. Figure 1 shows the webpage where students access the RoLOs.

This innovation proved to be key in the evolution of our move to a choice model for two reasons.

First, because we were able to standardize the presentation of didactic course content across several sections, it opened up an opportunity for more in class work. This work consists largely of applying the information covered in the learning objects. Faculty guide students in applying the information through assignments requiring the use of specific technologies rather than telling them what they can do. For example, students create graphic organizers, podcasts, digital videos, and interactive white board lessons, and manipulate digital images. These assignments model appropriate technology integration strategies, and require students to work with the course content to create meaning. Second, putting the onus of not only reading, but listening to the lectures before coming to class on the students, created an expectation of some individual work and the expectation for applying knowledge instead of simply consuming it. By the time we read of the Buffet model (Twigg, 2002), we had put into place many of the pieces we would need to redesign the class based on a model of choice.

The design of the course is, of course, influenced by the Buffet model (Twigg, 2002). This model drives much of the way our class runs. However, a number of historical antecedents are represented in the course design as well. The course itself is aligned tacitly with the ideas of

195

constructivist learning (Jonassen, 1999), situated cognition (Brown, Collins & Duguid, 1989) and anchored instruction (Bransford, Sherwood, Hasselbring, Kinzer, & Williams, 1990). The class was set up to be explicitly experiential and to create a learning environment that is driven by the learner, an idea proposed by numerous theorists (Papert, 1980; Wilson & Ryder, 1996; Greening, 1998). Our experience suggests that students are not comfortable with this kind of class. Students are accustomed to being in classes where they are told what to do, when to do it, and how to do it. To be told, suddenly, that they have the control is not seen as a positive. They want and require some structure. Given how much is riding on their grades in these classes, such as scholarships and admission to the teacher education program, we understand this concern.

To help manage the concern, we employ a pedagogical shift approach as suggested by Jones and Harmon (2009). We begin class from a positivist perspective with instructor delivered content early in the semester, albeit through the use of reusable learning objects, and move carefully to a more constructivist perspective with student-generated content and instructor guidance later in the semester. For example, the goals for the first part of the course are to:

1. expose students to the content (e.g., learning theory, Universal Design for Learning, National (NETS) and State (Curriculum) Standards, Participatory Active Learning and assessment),
2. expose students to technology tools such as digital video and digital audio, that go beyond those traditionally taught, and
3. model appropriate technology integration strategies.

These activities and technology requirements are initiated by the instructor. All students study the same content and complete the same technol-

ogy integrated activities. The goals for the second part of the class are:

1. to expose students to technologies specific to their content areas, and
2. to teach students how to remain current in the ever changing field of educational technology.

To reach these goals, students select what content and technologies they want to work with and are responsible for teaching others in the class about the technologies they work with. This shift allows the students to gain confidence in the class and master the fundamental knowledge and skills they need to succeed later on, while still affording them the benefits usually conferred by a student-centered learning environment, i.e. greater motivation and enhanced transfer (Land & Hannafin, 2001). This is particularly important since motivation has been found to be a key component for success in learning (Kawachi, 2003).

Description of Redesign Process

The Buffet model was used to address two National Educational Technology Standards for Teachers (NETS-T) in depth: Design and Develop Digital-Age Learning Experiences (NETS-T 2) and Assessments, and Engage in Professional Growth and Leadership (NETS-T 5). Because students came to us with varying teacher education majors and skill levels, it made sense to us to allow student choice for this part of the course. We felt that we had delivered the foundational content related to educational technology and modeled technology integration activities specific to that content. Now it was time for our students to work with their own content standards to develop technology integration activities. We also knew that we ourselves did not know how to use every piece of technology our students would come across in their discipline. We felt that this was an appropriate time to admit this to our students and have them take responsibility for their own growth in the field of educational technology and to get comfortable with the fact that they may not always be the expert in a technology.

Three key elements were created to support the model of choice we used: 1) the Technology Selection Guide, 2) Faculty Delivered Professional Development Workshops, and 3) Student Created Professional Development Workshops.

The Technology Selection Guide

The Technology Selection Guide is a web-based list of hardware, software, and Web 2.0 applications from which students select new technologies to learn. The list is organized by National Educational Technology Standards for Students (NETS-S). Each entry includes the name of the software or hardware, a brief description of its purpose and capabilities, and a link to a website to get additional information about the selection. This list is dynamic in that we add to it and delete from it as needed. Figure 2 shows the Technology Selection Guide entries for two of the many technologies in the guide to choose from.

We also worked with content area faculty to locate discipline specific hardware and software for every content area that we work with in our classes. Examples include digital microscopes, midi keyboards, GPS, heart rate monitors, assistive technology, and drawing tablets to name a few. The Technology Selection Guide is available at http://coe.winthrop.edu/educ275/assign_tech_select_guide2.htm.

Students are required to choose three pieces of hardware or software to explore. Students work in and out of class to explore technologies new to them, create a product using the new technology, and develop a technology integrated activity related to their content area standards. Selections range in difficulty from a simple PowerPoint presentation to a digital video. This range allows students to advance their knowledge regardless of their beginning skill level. We remind students

that the goal is not cool technology; the goal is meaningful representations of human learning. As such, we focus less on technical proficiency and more on discipline specific content.

Students can learn the technology individually or in small groups and, again, this was a decision made by the student. We wanted students to explore the various ways teachers stay current in their field and this sometimes means investigating a topic with peers. Whether students work individually or in groups, each student is required to keep a running list, what we refer to as the *Technology Integration Log,* of every technology they work with and to create a product with the new piece of software or hardware. The entire *Technology Integration Log* is turned in at the end of the semester for a grade. However, students turn the log in for formative assessment by instructors at different stages. We have found it critical to provide informative feedback on student reflections early in the process. In the *Technology Integration Log* students are required to provide:

- The name of the technology.
- A state curriculum standard it could help support.
- A NETS-S it could help support.
- An example of a student use of the technology to demonstrate learning.
- An example of a teacher use of the technology.
- A sample of a product created and a reflection on working with the technology.

The *Technology Integration Log* is turned in for a grade, but students also keep a copy for themselves. They are told that this list should be used to help them remember things they did in this class that they can do when they are designing lesson plans in methods courses and working with students during their internships. This is an important bridge between their university course work and their work with students during field experience and internship. Figure 3

Figure 2. Image of Web page for the technology selection guide

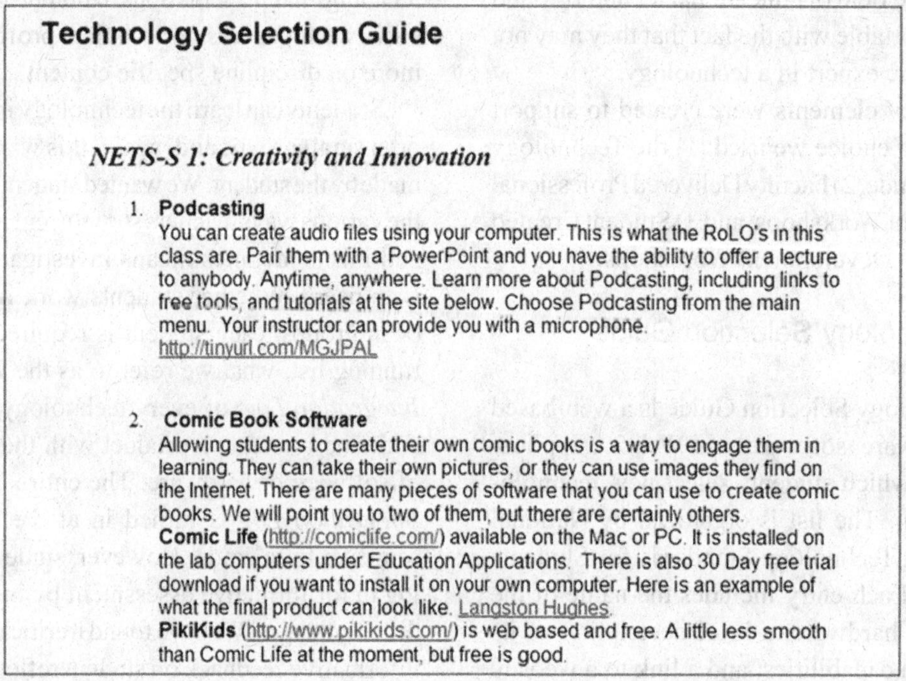

Technology Selection Guide

NETS-S 1: Creativity and Innovation

1. **Podcasting**
   You can create audio files using your computer. This is what the RoLO's in this class are. Pair them with a PowerPoint and you have the ability to offer a lecture to anybody. Anytime, anywhere. Learn more about Podcasting, including links to free tools, and tutorials at the site below. Choose Podcasting from the main menu. Your instructor can provide you with a microphone.
   http://tinyurl.com/MGJPAL

2. **Comic Book Software**
   Allowing students to create their own comic books is a way to engage them in learning. They can take their own pictures, or they can use images they find on the Internet. There are many pieces of software that you can use to create comic books. We will point you to two of them, but there are certainly others.
   Comic Life (http://comiclife.com/) available on the Mac or PC. It is installed on the lab computers under Education Applications. There is also 30 Day free trial download if you want to install it on your own computer. Here is an example of what the final product can look like. Langston Hughes.
   PikiKids (http://www.pikikids.com/) is web based and free. A little less smooth than Comic Life at the moment, but free is good.

---

shows the *Technology Integration Log* entry for digital cameras.

Faculty Delivered Professional Development Workshops

Students are given class time to work on their technology selections, but not all classes are devoted to those activities. During the final third of the semester when students are working on their technology selections, faculty members are also delivering Professional Development Workshops (PDW). Each faculty member conducts six PDW's as part of the regular class schedule. Students are required to attend four workshops but are allowed to select the four that interest them the most. Modeled after the same type of workshops often offered at schools and conferences, these workshops are intended to show pre-service teachers one of the most common methods of staying current in the use of educational technology. Faculty conduct Professional Development Workshops on topics such as using technology to support English language learners, visual literacy, digital storytelling, assistive technology, and overviews of particular technologies. These workshops also serve as a model for the final course requirement, a Student Created Professional Development Workshop.

Student Created Professional Development Workshops

The final area of student choice in the course is a student created professional development workshop based on the Innovations Mini-teach model (Foulger, Williams, & Wetzel, 2008). In this project, students work in curriculum related teams to create a professional development workshop based on a topic of their choice. They then conduct the workshop during class time. Students are required to attend all Student Created Professional Development Workshops. Workshop requirements

Figure 3. Technology integration log

Technology	Primary user	Description of Use/Activity and Standards Met	Why is this a good use of technology?	Reflection on use or creating your product. Attach your product to this document or paste the URL.
Digital Camera (this is an example, do not delete)	Teacher	Activity: The teacher will take photos as the students tour Historic Brattonsville. SC Content Standard: Social Studies Standard 3-3: The student will demonstrate an understanding of the American Revolution and South Carolina's role in the development of the new American nation. Teacher Technology Standard: NETS-T 3 Note: Include one SC Content Standard and one NETS-T	These images will help students remember more about what they learned during the fieldtrip to Brattonsville. Also, if some students couldn't attend the fieldtrip, they could look at the pictures and get a better idea of what the rest of the class saw. (Multiple means of representation.)	I can see multiple ways that my students and I can use a digital camera in my future classroom. Some ideas I have include .... I didn't have any trouble using the digital camera for this project; however, I think it will be important to stress to my students that they need to be careful with the cameras and always wear the neck strap!
Digital Camera (this is an example, do not delete)	Student (the students are using the technology to learn)	SC Content Standard: Science 2-2.5 Illustrate the various life cycles of animals (including birth and the stages of development). Student Technology Standard: NETS-S 1 Activity: Raise butterflies in the classroom. The students can take pictures of the butterfly throughout its lifecycle and put the pictures in order in a presentation when the butterflies hatch. The pictures can also be displayed on a screen so that everyone can see what the teacher is talking about. Note: Include one SC Content Standard and one NETS-S	Students will be able to see one life-cycle in nature as it actually occurs. The pictures can be used to provide visual cues when reviewing the process at the end. Students can sequence actual pictures rather than less detailed drawings. (Dale's Cone of Experience)	

include an overview of the technology, a handout that includes links to resources to help learn the technology and technology integration strategies, and hands-on instruction in how to use the technology (Foulger, Williams, & Wetzel, 2008). These are to be more than presentations about a topic. Professional Development Workshop teams are required to design a hands-on activity for the workshop participants. In this way, the teams gain experience not only in teaching, but in teaching technology skills in a lab setting. Workshop teams are required to trouble-shoot and answer individual questions as their classmates work with the technology. This provides for some interesting teachable moments. For example, one group learned the importance of "walking the room" to assist in trouble shooting problems. Initially, everyone stood by the presentation computer to talk about the technology. But when many of their peers began to have problems with their lesson, they quickly learned that having the whole team up at the front of the class huddled around the podium was not an effective teaching strategy. In subsequent group presentations, students demonstrated better management skills simply by watching what worked and did not work in other presentations. We had no groups huddling around the presentation computer after that.

Bridging the Gap between Educational Technology Courses, Methods Courses, and Clinical Experiences

We feel that the buffet model increases a student's ability to apply what they learned in the educational technology course to methods courses and eventually to the classroom. Earlier we mentioned that the *Technology Integration Log* is seen as a bridge between our class and the internship. It is also a valuable tool to help prepare students for methods classes. Students are asked to think actively about how specific technologies may be used in their future classrooms and to assess the relative advantage or affordance of a technology quickly. We encourage students to revisit the Technology Integration Log in methods courses and incorporate those technology activities that are already tied to curriculum standards in lesson plans. We have also talked with methods faculty to make them aware of this assignment so that they can remind the students of the planning they have already started. We also hope that because students have practiced teaching technology skills, they will feel more comfortable teaching technology integrated lessons during their clinical experiences.

MANAGING AND IMPLEMENTING CHOICE

The use of reusable learning objects in our class means that students are responsible for getting some of the content outside of class that would traditionally be offered in class. Selling the students on the idea that they have to listen to a lecture before class is not easy. Early use of the podcasts showed student resistance to the idea. One course evaluation comment summed it up pretty well: "Why should I have to listen to a lecture outside of class and still come to class?" The comment suggests that there is a prevailing attitude about what a class is about: teachers tell us what we need to know. On the face of it, it is hard to find fault with this idea. It is true that we are institutionally authorized to impart knowledge, if you will. However, as the use of reusable learning objects began to grow on campus, and as we built an institutional expectation for their use, we saw less of this attitude. Additionally, as students began to see that we were spending less time talking, and more time applying, they saw the utility of the podcasts as well.

We saw the use of the learning objects as instrumental in implementing the model of choice. If students did much of the gathering of information outside of class, it made it possible for us to make some classes optional. Attending four of six professional development workshops is an example of this. We also found it necessary to take a more liberal attitude on attendance while still maintaining the integrity of our contact hours. For example, if a physical education student wanted to work with biomechanics software not available in our building, we had to learn to say it was fine not to be in class. Because we were putting students in charge of their learning and their time, we had to accept that learning could be happening even if we were not present.

To help us manage this, we put clear guidelines in place as to our expectation for their attendance and work in and out of class. For example, students are responsible for a professional development workshop attendance sheet. It needs to be signed by the faculty member on the day of the workshop and turned in at the end of class. Students need to submit regular individual progress reports and group progress reports. Students evaluate each group member based on attendance, participation, and the value of the individual's contributions. And finally, as discussed above, each student is required to keep a log of every technology they worked with. The Technology Integration Log serves as the running record of everything they do. So if a student chooses to liberate a day or two, but still manages to get everything done in the log, we are largely OK with that. While the amount of record keeping we had to do increased, we offset the time by doing the lectures beforehand through the use of the learning objects. Students are not only responsible for managing the process, but for documenting their work as well.

In some cases, students do not use their time well, or they do not document it appropriately. We heard anecdotal evidence that a student may have not shown up simply because they didn't have to. This is hard to hear sometimes, but we had to learn to let go of the smaller details on order to allow for greater choice. But support for the program by students was generally positive. Some students commented on course evaluations that they learned that they needed to manage their time better. Some students did not like keeping track of their PDW attendance card, but understood the larger lesson of keeping up with records. But as one student remarked on an evaluation: "I felt like I was treated like an adult, and I liked that."

Recommendations for Implementation

Use of the buffet model in our class has proven to be largely effective. Student assessment data and student evaluations would support this claim. There are other classes that we teach that may not support the amount of choice provided in this class, and it goes without saying, possibly, that we don't recommend universal application of the buffet model to every course, or even every technology integration course. We recommend that you consider carefully the following set of issues before moving forward. These curricular and technical needs associated with the buffet model can help in deciding if you should implement such a model, and then how to proceed.

1. *Determine what needs are not being met in your current class.*

All classes are in a constant state of revision. Hopefully. We recommend that you talk to others teaching the same class, or people teaching at other institutions. What are they doing that you are not? As you look at your syllabus and course schedule, what are topics that you would like to see covered that are not covered? But consider not only content, but experiences as well. We found that it was important to begin treating our students like adults, as it were, by having them keep track of their own attendance, evaluate their peers, manage their learning, and make choices about how and where to spend their time. We did this by looking to our institution's conceptual framework and national standards, such as the NETS.

2. *Determine what course content everyone needs to learn.*

Carefully review the official syllabus, taking care to attend to the course objectives. Be brutal about what is required versus what is optional. We found that some of our favorite activities simply did not rise to the level of required. Claymation is an example of this. It is a great tactile activity that can encompass many curricular standards. However, it is time consuming and not particularly useful in PE or Music classes. We still offer support for claymation, but it is now a part of student choice. Looking candidly at core, foundational content that is supported by your curriculum, what is required, and what may be a good option for some, but not for everyone.

3. *Determine optional course content.*

Optional content is not optional because it is unimportant. The optional content becomes key for student learning. The options are the bridges between our core, foundational curriculum and how it is applied to a particular discipline. For example, Wolfram Alpha (http://www.wolframalpha.com/) may be a Google-like curiosity to an English teacher, but a Social Studies teacher will see the power it has to provide demographic data nearly immediately. Similarly, the Wii Fit may look like a distraction to a Math teacher, but PE teachers see immediately how it can help students move and be fit. When considering options, talk to as many people as you can. Read widely; focus broadly.

4. *Determine how each set of content will be delivered, i.e. face-to-face, on-line modules, podcasts, etc.*

You have many options as to how to present course content. YouTube channels, iTunesU, WebCT/Blackboard, and simple posting to a webpage are but a few of your options. We recommend that you consider the nature and character of the university as a way to determine how you best proceed. Keep in mind that the Buffet model is about choice. So you will need to develop those choices, which means create the podcasts, videos and other materials that you will require. We did not read about the Buffet model and implement it immediately. For us, the process was evolutionary. We experimented with project based learning, reusable learning objects, and active learning long before we implemented this model.

5. *Develop thorough directions and procedures for the optional course content and activities.*

Write it down. Read it again. Have other people read it. Be specific. Be prepared to answer questions. Be flexible. Be understanding. These are but a few of our recommendations for you here. Keep in mind that there is an institutional culture where you teach. Your students understand it currently. If you change it, you should be clear on what that means. We have learned that we needed to be clear about the smallest details early on. Now, however, students have heard from others what

to expect. Having changed our culture a bit, we find ourselves explaining it less.

6. *Develop a record keeping strategy so that you know which students participated in what activities.*

This is vital for fairness and assigning grades. Be prepared for an increase in record keeping. We recommend automating as much of this as possible. Simple check sheets, translated into spreadsheets, worked for us as a management strategy. We also recommend putting the responsibility on students to keep up with this information as well. We see most of our students as sophomores, which means in two years they will have to keep track of information on every student in their classes. If we scaffold them in record keeping early we may be doing them a great favor later on.

CONCLUSION

Providing students with more choices through The Buffet model enabled us to meet the diverse needs of our students. In a class that serves all majors, students made it clear to us that something needed to change. Providing students with choices in what content they studied and in what technologies they learned helped make the course more meaningful for the students. Because they were allowed to select content and technologies specific to their disciplines, students were able to develop technology integrated activities that they can expand on in methods courses and student teaching. In addition, they also learn the skills necessary to explore and stay current in the ever changing world of technology. Through the Technology Selection Guide, attending Professional Development Workshops, and conducting Student Created Professional Development Workshops themselves, students broaden their knowledge of technology in the classroom and develop personal strategies to help them stay current in technology for teaching and learning in their area.

REFERENCES

Bransford, J. D., Sherwood, R. D., Hasselbring, T. S., Kinzer, C. K., & Williams, S. M. (Eds.). (1990). *Anchored instruction: Why we need it and how technology can help*. Hillsdale, NJ: Lawrence Erlbaum.

Brown, J. S., Collins, A., & Duguid, P. (1989). Situated cognition and the culture of learning. *Educational Researcher*, *18*(1), 32–42.

Ertmer, P. A., & Newby, T. J. (1993). Behaviorism, cognitivism, constructivism: Comparing critical features from an instructional design perspective. *Performance Improvement Quarterly*, *6*(4), 50–70. doi:10.1111/j.1937-8327.1993.tb00605.x

Fewell, P. J., & Gibbs, W. J. (2003). *Microsoft Office for teachers*. Upper Saddle River, NJ: Merrill Prentice Hall.

Foulger, T., Williams, M. K., & Wetzel, K. (2008). *Innovative technologies, small groups, and a wiki: A 21st century preservice experience founded on collaboration*. Proceedings from NECC 2008. San Antonio, TX: ISTE.

Foulger, T., Williams, M. K., & Wetzel, K. (2008). We innovate: The role of collaboration in exploring new technologies. *International Journal of Teaching and Learning in Higher Education*, *20*(1), 28–38.

Grabe, M., & Grabe, C. (2007). *Integrating technology for meaningful learning* (5th ed.). New York, NY: Houghton Mifflin Company.

Harris, L. (2010). Project based learning. In Evers, R. B., & Spencer, S. (Eds.), *Planning effective instruction for students with learning and behavior problems*. Columbus, OH: Merrill / Pearson Publishers.

International Society for Technology in Education. (2007). *National educational technology standards for students*. Eugene, OR: Author.

International Society for Technology in Education. (2008). *National educational technology standards for teachers* (2nd ed.). Eugene, OR: Author.

Jonassen, D. H. (1999). Designing constructivist learning environments. In Reigeluth, C. M. (Ed.), *Instructional design theories and models: Their current state of the art* (2nd ed.). Mahwah, NJ: Lawrence Erlbaum Associates.

Jonassen, D. H. (1999). *Computers as mindtools for schools: Engaging critical thinking* (2nd ed.). Upper Saddle River, NJ: Merrill Prentice-Hall, Inc.

Jones, M. G., & Harmon, S. W. (2009). Instructional strategies for teaching in synchronous online learning environments (SOLE). In Yang, H., & Yuen, S. (Eds.), *Collective intelligence and e-learning 2.0: Implications of Web-based communities and networking* (pp. 78–93). Hershey, PA: IGI Global. doi:10.4018/978-1-60566-729-4.ch005

Jones, M. G., Harmon, S. W., & O'Grady-Jones, M. K. (2005). Developing the digital mind: Challenges and solutions in teaching and learning. *Teacher Education Journal of South Carolina*, *2004-2005*, 17–24.

Kawachi, P. (2003). Initiating intrinsic motivation in online education: Review of the current state of the art. *Interactive Learning Environments*, *11*(1), 59–82. doi:10.1076/ilee.11.1.59.13685

Land, S., & Hannafin, M. (2001). Student-centered Learning Environments. In Jonassen, D., & Land, S. (Eds.), *Theoretical foundations of learning environments* (pp. 1–23). Mahwah, NJ: Lawrence Erlbaum Associates.

National Center for Academic Transformation. (2005). *The Buffet model.* Saratoga Springs, NY: Author. Retrieved from http://www.thencat.org/PlanRes/R2R_Model_Buffet.htm

National Center for Academic Transformation. (2005). *Who we are.* Saratoga Springs, NY: Author. Retrieved from http://www.thencat.org/whoweare.html

Newby, T. J., Stepich, D. A., Lehman, J. D., Russell, J. D., & Ottenbreit-Leftwich, A. (2011). *Educational technology for teaching and learning* (4th ed.). Boston, MA: Pearson.

Norman, D. (1988). *The design of everyday things.* New York, NY: Doubleday.

O'Neill, L. M. (2001). Universal design for learning: Making education accessible to all learners. *Syllabus, April,* 31-32.

Papert, S. (1980). *Mindstorms: Children, computers, and powerful ideas.* Basic Books.

Roblyer, M. D., & Doering, A. H. (2010). *Integrating educational technology into teaching* (5th ed.). Boston, MA: Allyn & Bacon.

Roblyer, M. K. (2003). *Integrating educational technology into teaching* (3rd ed.). Upper Saddle River, NJ: Merrill Prentice-Hall, Inc.

Twigg, C. (2002). Improving learning and reducing costs: new models for online learning. *EDUCAUSE, 38*(5), 28-38. http://net.educause.edu/ir/library/pdf/erm0352.pdf

Wiley, D. A. (2000). Connecting learning objects to instructional design theory: A definition, a metaphor, and a taxonomy. In D. A. Wiley (Ed.), *The instructional use of learning objects: Online version.* Retrieved January 23, 2006, from the http://reusability.org/read/chapters/wiley.doc

Chapter 14
Rethinking Technology in Teacher Education Programs:
Creating Content–Centric Learning Environments

Jeanne Samuel
Louisiana State University, USA

Janice Hinson
University of North Carolina at Charlotte, USA

ABSTRACT

This chapter is organized around shifting paradigms of information literacy, instructional literacy, and technology literacy. Information literacy focuses on the questions of what knowledge management is. Instructional literacy advocates the promotion of new teaching methods rather than new technology. Technology literacy should be rise from grounded contexts rather than be considered a skill. The chapter explores the impact of these shifts on the role of teacher, student, and content to promote knowledge creation (learning). The authors seek to identify the most effective ways to present instruction. Finally, the chapter discusses technology literacy as the merging the two constructs—teaching and using technology.

INTRODUCTION

Many years ago one of the authors of this manuscript attended a conference at which the speaker provided an excellent example of learning by osmosis, which refers to gradual and often process of assimilation (Roberts, 2008). The presenter sang or whistled some theme songs from TV programs from the 1960's and 70's. Many of us had immediate recall and shouted out the name of the shows – Andy Griffith, Green Acres, Petticoat Junction, and the Adams Family. He asked us who taught us the names of the songs. We answered no one taught us – we just knew them. We were

DOI: 10.4018/978-1-4666-0014-0.ch014

unaware that we had been learning. Learning with technology should be that transparent – students should learn by osmosis. In the classroom, the learning experience should be the focus, not the technology. Therefore, instruction should start with what do teachers want the students to learn, and then they should decide how technology can be used to support the learning activity. This chapter focuses on rethinking technology training in teacher education programs to enable teacher candidates to integrate technology into instruction in more meaningful ways.

To date, teacher education coursework focuses on ways to use technology in classrooms and often addresses ways to use specific tools, such as blogs, wikis, etc. As a result, candidates learn how to use specific technology tools and apply them in certain contexts. However, they often lack the ability to look beyond specific assignments to use technology as a learning tool, not the focal point of the lesson. Instead of worrying about adding technology to lesson plans, candidates should be thinking about the best possible ways to meet curricular objectives with technology. Therefore, rather than thinking about how to use technology in lessons, we propose a return to the roots of computer-supported collaboration. In this chapter, the term social will be purposefully used instead of Web 2.0 to return focus from product to purpose because the center of attention is not on what we use to get there, but what is needed to arrive. This chapter is organized around the shifting paradigms of information literacy, instructional literacy, and technology literacy. Throughout the chapter, we explore the impact of these shifts on the role of teacher, student, and content to promote knowledge creation (learning). Information literacy focuses on managing knowledge. Instructional literacy is moving toward the promotion of new teaching methods rather than new technology. Technology literacy is rising from grounded contexts. As a result, technology literacy is the merging the two constructs -- teaching and using technology to effectively present instruction.

During the mid-1990's, the push for technology literacy emphasized putting technology in classrooms. Technology literacy was conceived as a stand-alone construct – synonymous with computer literacy or tools. This description of technology literacy is demonstrated within *President Clinton's Call to Action for American Education in the 21st Century* (U.S. Department of Education, Archived Information, 1997). Throughout the 1990's and early 2000's, distinct literacies emerged by definition and practice. Literacy expansion included information literacy, digital literacy, new literacy, computer literacy, media literacy, as well as other emerging literacies (Holum & Gahala, 2001).

In this chapter we propose reducing multiple literacies to one by looking at technology as a structure grounded in the contexts of learning and teaching. This change is the reduction of three distinct education competencies into two integrated competencies. We present technology literacy within the context of information literacy and pedagogical (instructional) literacy.

In the first section, we will discuss the paradigm shifts occurring in education within the context of pedagogy. In other words, what is the impact of these shifts on the role of teacher, student, and content to promote knowledge creation – learning? Lee and Lan (2007, p. 48) note that from the initial static or read-only web (Web 1.0) to the read-write, collaborative, and social web (Web 2.0), there has been a shift from personal-focus to community-focus. Knowledge management shifted from a focus on individual intelligence to communal or collective intelligence (Nikolov, 2007, p. 2). Similarly, in education, the pedagogical dialogue moved from teacher-centric to learner-centric. Now, a new paradigm is emerging in response to current and emerging technology enhancements – a shift from learner-centric to content-centric. Content-centric is not about the final product, but instead, focuses on the generation of content. This is a shift from the content product-consumption model to the content-user-producer model (Bruns,

Cobcroft, Smith, and Towers, 2007). In other words, the shift is from knowledge management as knowledge repository to knowledge management as knowledge generation (Lee & Lan, p. 51). In that context, content is not about merely storing and accessing content individually (Bloom levels 1-3), but about synthesizing and sharing content as well as creating new content as a community (Bloom levels 4-6). Lee and Lan call this collaborative intelligence (p.49) and it is defined as the measure of the "collaborative ability of an entity or a group" (p. 53). This integrates information literacy with pedagogical or instructional literacy. In this context, technology literacy is about facilitating knowledge generation rather than knowledge organization and delivery.

In the second section, we will discuss instructional literacy. Of course, the focus of all teacher education programs is instructional literacy, or how to become an effective teacher. However, in many teacher education programs, there are two separate constructs in place – learning to teach, and learning to use technology. In this section, we will review seminal best practices. What are the most effective ways to present instruction regardless of technology? This does not imply that technology is not important. Technology *is* important. But, in order to design courses to promote technology literacy we must re-define the concept. Shifting the definition of technology literacy to a "when" rather than a "what" changes technology literacy from technology-based skills to enabling the implementation of pedagogical techniques only now possible through the use of technology. Technology literacy is about *when* to select technology The point is, technology literacy is no longer about becoming skillful with a tool and looking for a way to implement it in the classroom. It is about becoming familiar with the available tools and selecting the technology most appropriate for lesson goals and objectives.

In section three, we will discuss technology literacy in grounded contexts by merging the two constructs—teaching and using technology. We

look at technology selection and use through the lens of the established best practices in Section Two and include specific examples from K-12 Classrooms. For example, virtual, anonymous voting is facilitated by the use of student response systems (clickers) rather than students raising hands. Not only does the technology permit anonymity or confidentiality, but it can collect data for later item analysis and report generation. Technology lets teachers spend time developing critical thinking in the learners rather than managing content and classroom administration. For example, creating multiple test versions, passing out tests, collecting tests, and grading tests. In addition, technology permits accurate, real-time evaluation and assessment leading to just-in-time learning. Students no longer have to wait days or weeks for feedback.

Over the past 20 years, the emphasis in technology education has been on using technology as tools out-of-the-box. As a result, teacher educators have not spent a lot of time reflecting on technology transparency during the instructional design process. We've been breezing along without a firm grip on how to merge technology and instruction. In this chapter, we intend to present thoughtful dialogue and well-constructed examples for moving this paradigm forward to improve the abilities of teacher candidates to impact learning in PK-12 settings.

CHANGING PARADIGMS

The definition of knowledge, in the context of education, is shifting from the end result, or a product, to a life-long process known as knowledge building. According to Hmelo-Silver and Barrows (2008, p. 48), "Knowledge building involves increasing the collective knowledge of a group through social discourse. For knowledge building to occur in the classroom, the teacher needs to create opportunities for constructive discourse in order to support student learning and collective knowledge building." When knowledge is the

Table 1. Instruction paradigms

Teacher-Centric	Learner-Centric	Content-Centric/ Mutually-Generated
Knowledge about		Knowledge of
Teacher as sage on stage	Teacher as facilitator who guides learners to discover content	Teacher as coach who guides learners to develop life-long learning skills
Learner as empty vessel	Learner as co-educator/learner; explorer	Learners as developers; builders; inventors; critics
Content (Knowledge) as product; regurgitation process	Content (Knowledge) as product (emphasis shift from facts to critical thinking); reflection process	Content (Knowledge) as process; dynamic; non-ending; improvement; creation process
Learning is a passive process regulated by teacher; the goal is to acquire "x" amount of content	Learning is an active process regulated by the learner; the goal is to acquire "x" amount often at "y" level of content	Learning becomes an acquisition of content to fulfill another goal, often personal

end result, it is often fact-based and performance evaluation is comparing what we currently know to what the student states or demonstrates. When education is viewed as a life-long process, there is no end. The measure is how well the learner evaluates and uses current knowledge to cultivate new ideas at best and to deepen their knowledge reservoir at minimum. The shift is expressed as moving *from knowledge as personal* to *knowledge as communal* (Lee & Lan, 2007; Scardamalia & Bereiter, 2006). The focus shifts from learner-centric to content-centric. In the context of knowledge, Bruns, Cobcroft, Smith, and Towers (2007) describe the shift as one from consumption to producer. Simply stated this shifts knowledge from the context of *about* something to context *of* something (Scardamalia & Bereiter, 2006). The Table 1 outlines the shifting paradigms.

K-12 STUDENTS' REALITIES

On the Project Tomorrow 2009 Survey, K-12 students (n= 299,677) were asked about the how they would like to use technology for instruction (Project Tomorrow, 2010). Their answers were categorized into three areas. First, students want to use social networking tools to collaborate and create personal learning just as they do outside of school through blogs, wikis, and social networking sites. Second, students want un-tethered learning experiences – meaning that they want to use mobile devices such as cell phones and MP3 players to create instructional experiences that are not confined to locale, on site knowledge and skills, or resources. Finally, students want digitally-rich learning experiences that drive learning productivity. These digitally rich environments would make better use of resources such as real-time data, simulations, game-based environments, and animations to help students develop higher order thinking skills (p. 12).

Actual Use

On the Speak Up Survey (Project Tomorrow, 2008), almost 300,000 K-12 students reported that they used technology in school for writing assignments (74%); conducting online research (72%); checking assignments or grades online (58%); creating slideshows, videos, WebPages for schoolwork (57%); or using e-mail or instant message (IM) with classmates about assignments (44%) (p. 5). Reasons for the disconnect between how kids want to use technology and how they are actually using technology in schools can be found in the survey results teacher candidates reported (Project Tomorrow, 2010, p. 13). The results indicated that

- 53% of student teachers are taught to use office applications such as word processor, spreadsheet, or database;
- 44% are taught how to create multimedia presentations;
- 40% are integrating some early social (2.0) technology such as video, audio, and digital images in their course lessons;
- Only 28% are taught how to create these resources (p. 13).

When looking across results, it seems that classroom teachers are implementing the strategies they learned in their methods courses without considering alternative ways to integrate technology into instruction. In other words, they're teaching as they were taught. Means (2010) confirms this. She wrote:

As the lives of students and teachers outside of school have evolved to include more and more use of technology, the situation presents a paradox. Despite decades of national, state and local promotion of educational uses of technology, classroom practice in most schools has changed little from the middle of the mid-20th century (p. 285).

The importance individuals attach to technology use is one factor affecting change (Ertmer & Ottenbreit-Leftwich, 2010). According to Ertmer and Ottenbreit-Leftwich, individual change is affected by personal beliefs, content knowledge, pedagogical knowledge, and access to resources and materials (p. 2). Considering the heavy emphasis on student outcomes, Means (2010) found that teachers are most interested in integrating technology into their teaching practices when they are convinced that it will have an impact on student learning outcomes. If teachers don't think technology will provide a significant payoff, they are less willing to use it.

School climate is another factor that influences change. If new teachers are place in schools where technology use is not valued, then they tend to minimize use. Ertmer and Ottenbreit-Leftwich (2010) developed an extensive review of the literature on technology change. In their synthesis, they wrote, "…experienced teachers who don't see the value of integrating technology into their classrooms can negatively impact the use of instructional technologies newer teachers" (p. 9). As a result, new teachers who want to use technology may curtail use due to the climate. Rather than moving forward with innovative and challenging lessons that use pocket-ready technology, K-12 students are being held back by teachers who adapt to the status quo.

Moving the Content-Centric Paradigm Forward

As teacher educators, how do we break this cycle? One approach is to rethink how students gain knowledge. Scardamalia and Bereiter (2006), for example, suggest viewing knowledge building as an educational approach rather than the result of education. Their model emphasizes acceptance of theories and models generated by students as "tools enabling further growth" (p. 5). This approach they say, considers core elements of knowledge building – knowledge innovation and knowledge creation (p. 3). The shift from students as learners to students who are "members of a knowledge building community" is supported by six themes (Scardamalia & Bereiter, p. 3):

1. Knowledge advancement as a community rather than individual achievement;
2. Knowledge advancement as idea improvement rather than as progress toward true or warranted belief;
3. Knowledge of in contrast to knowledge about;
4. Discourse as collaborative problem solving rather than as argumentation;

5.   Constructive use of authoritative information;
6.   Understanding as an emergent.

These themes can be distilled to several axioms. One is that knowledge is emergent understanding leading to idea improvement and culminating from collaborative problem-solving. In other words, knowledge acquisition is no longer individual or finite or the result of competition.

According to Ertmer and Ottenbreit-Leftwich (2010), modeling and practice are two of the most powerful ways to enable teacher candidates to develop effective technology-based instructional practices. Therefore, teacher education programs should foster instruction that enables candidates to observe faculty modeling effective technology practices – especially in methods courses. Candidates also need to see effective uses of technology in the field as demonstrated by their supervising teachers during their student teaching experiences. Additionally, teacher candidates need to engage in opportunities to practice what they have learned in real situations. We can start this change by reassessing the messages that we, as teacher educators, send to candidates pertaining to technology use and by engaging them in integrated learning opportunities via social media.

MERGING TECHNOLOGY LITERACY AND LEARNING METHODS

Schooling, even in this electronic age, is still compartmentalized. Students learn science, social studies, math, and reading during designated blocks of time. The same is true for teacher education methods courses and unfortunately this compartmentalizes technology use. To provide K-12 students with opportunities to engage in the types of learning experiences they prioritized on the Project Tomorrow Surveys (2008; 2010), including more sophisticated uses of mobile technologies, teacher educators must develop ways to extend technology across curricula that provide

both models and practice for teacher candidates. While teacher candidates may be digital natives and bring to the discussion different perspectives and experiences, experienced teachers are needed to guide the new teachers in effectively integrating new technologies.

Prensky (2001) says that kids today operate at "twitch speed." Literally, from their parents' laps to college, today's kids are the first generation to grow up surrounded by computers, videogames, iPods, iphones, BlackBerrys, and digital cameras, MySpace, YouTube, etc. Quick access to information is just part of their everyday lives. As they noted in the Speak Up Surveys, twitch speed kids want to use the tools of their generation to learn and do more. So, how do we prepare teachers to provide quality education experiences for 21st Century twitch speed kids? One solution is blended learning. Although the term "blended learning" has been over used, the concept is still in its infancy and more needs to be done to help teacher candidates blend technology into instruction. Blended learning usually refers to technology use in K-12 classrooms and is offered here as prerequisite for everyone graduating from teacher education programs now. Furthermore, the technology use must be integrated or blended into the curriculum.

Blended Learning

Blended learning is a mix of traditional face-to-face instruction that is supported by online learning activities. What this usually means is that K-12 teachers maintain a Web presence that they use to post instructional materials, e-discussions, Web-based resources, assignments, etc. Often, these Web presences are part of course management system, such as BlackBoard (http://www.blackboard.com/us/index.Bb) or open source systems such as Moodle (http://moodle.org/), however; some are using a growing set of free standing Web-based resources such as blogs, glogs, and wikis to promote interactive e-learning experiences for students. The purpose is to extend instruction beyond face-to-face class time through virtual discussion and collaborative e-learning activities. There are three application phases of blended instruction: basic, interactive, and communal. In the following sections, we describe one teacher's progression through all three of these phases to illustrate the types of classroom activities that are possible at each phase.

Basic Applications

In this section, we introduce you to Ms. Miller, a fourth-grade teacher in Illinois. Ms. Miller holds an undergraduate degree in sociology and was a stay-at-home mom until her two children graduated from high school. She then entered a Graduate Teaching Certificate Program and became certified to teach Grades K-6. She is in her fourth year of teaching and is comfortable integrating Web-based resources such as Web sites and videos into instruction. In social studies, her students were using the Internet to research the Lakota Indians and using the information to create a native village, which was under construction in the middle of the classroom. Ms. Miller's students had developed basic information literacy skills, and they were comfortable finding information, evaluating it, and applying it to new situations. For this assignment, Ms. Miller's actions represented very basic blended learning applications. She had posted some Web-based information, but students were engaged in "read only" uses of the Web. Recently, however, Ms. Miller had started using a learning management system to post homework and house Web-resources. However, it was the action of one of her students, named James, that caused her to leap to the second level of blended learning, interactive applications.

Interactive Applications

While researching the Lakota Indians online, James found a picture of an American Indian village with the caption: *Hostile Indian Village of*

the Lakota Sioux Indians (http://www.old-picture.com/old-west/Village-Indian-Lakota.htm). The picture, however, depicted a very calm village scene with people going about their daily activities. The picture was taken in 1891, and the caption was provided by the photographer. Bothered by the apparent bias, James showed the picture to Ms. Miller, who posted the picture in the class discussion section of their course management system. She then invited her students to express their opinions about the caption and reasons that might have led the photographer to title it that way. A discussion such as this one could take place face-to-face, however, an electronic discussion enables students to think about their responses before posting, keep a running record of their thoughts, and expand the discussion by posting, and discussing other digital pictures related to the topic.

Communal Applications

Ms. Miller's students realize they were learning a lot about the history of the Lakota people and decided to use the Internet to search for information about modern-day Lakota people. It didn't take them long to learn that not only are the Lakota people alive and well, but in December, 2007, they withdrew from all treaties with the United States and are trying to become a sovereign nation! Ms. Miller contacted a fourth-grade teacher at school a school in South Dakota with a large Lakota student population, and the two classrooms began to communicate. Using Skype, the first effort involved having the South Dakota students critique the model of the Lakota village created by Ms. Miller's students. In the second project, students from both classes participated in cooperative learning teams to study issues related to becoming a sovereign nation. Their research questions included:

- What are the advantages and disadvantages to becoming an independent nation?

- How will the Lakota nation support itself?
- What types of community infrastructures are necessary for becoming an independent nation?
- How will sovereignty affect schools?

The students used wikis and blogs to share information and to participate in live discussions with tribal leaders. Each group then created videos representing what they learned, possible solutions to critical problems, and the impact sovereignty might have on children. These interactions – and the opportunity to extend knowledge beyond locally-housed resources, were invaluable to all 4th grade students participating in this project.

SOCIAL WEB (2.0) TOOLS AND BLENDED LEARNING

Currently, Web users are moving between Static Web (1.0) and Social Web (2.0) seamlessly and unconsciously. Mash-ups are a good example. People use them all time, but often they may be unaware that they are. An example of a mash-up is the combination of two or more applications on a single site. Suppose that you're going to Montreal on vacation and want to use the subway to get around. An interactive subway map (http://www. stm.info/English/metro/a-index.htm) allows users to click on subway stations and access information about nearby attractions, intersections, scheduled stops, etc. Teachers, such as Jerome Berg (Boss & Krauss, 2007) use mash ups to create interactive learning experiences for their students. For example, students reading *The Slave Dancer* by Paula Fox use Google Earth to follow the trail of Jesse, a thirteen year old boy from New Orleans, who is kidnapped and forced to play his fife on a slave ship (http://www.googlelittrips.com). Following route paths in Google Earth, students "fly" to scenes in the story and access embedded files that contain audio or video clips, photographs, or other resources such as story questions or vocabulary exercises (Boss & Krauss). Berg has created a Web site, googlelittrips.com, where teachers can download or post lit trips, chat about assessment procedures, or get directions for creating "route paths" in Google Earth. These examples provide easy ways for educators to provide relevant blended learning experiences to "twitch-speed" students.

TECHNICAL LITERACY: LINKING LEARNING TO INSTRUCTIONAL PARADIGMS

Earlier in this chapter, we described three instructional paradigms: Teacher-Centric, Student-Centric, and Content-Centric/Mutually-Generated. Currently, all three of these paradigms are being used. In the Teacher-Centric paradigm, instructors, especially in large lecture-style classrooms, instructors are using clickers (Student Response Systems) and online polling to engage students. For example, a biology professor gauges students' content knowledge by displaying multiple choice questions to his 600 member class. After students have selected their answers using their clickers, the results are tallied and displayed in graph form. If the results indicate that a nearly equal number of students have chosen two different answers, say C and D, the professors then tells his students that they have one minute to convince someone that their answer is correct. He then takes a second vote. If the correct answer doesn't get a high percentage of votes, the professor knows that the students do not understand the material, and he reviews the concept. If most of the students get the answer right on the second vote, he moves on to new material. This example demonstrates how technology can be used to increase student interactivity, assess student knowledge, and adjust the instructional pace to increase learning in teacher-centered environments.

In the Student-Centric Learning Paradigm, learning is more collaborative, and students work in groups on projects and assignments. Consequently, teachers who are comfortable technology-users themselves are using Web-resources to create more innovative and participatory learning experiences for students. For example, fourth grade students from Turkey, Mexico, and the United States recently participated in a project to promote awareness of different cultures and learn more about life in these countries. The students attended schools that were members of the International Baccalaureate Organization Primary Years Program (IBOPYP). All of the students were fluent in English, so language barriers were not a problem.

Mr. Robinson, the 4th grade teacher in United States, created a Blackboard site for the project and developed activities that were integrated into classroom instruction at all three schools. Initially, he posted discussion prompts that encouraged students to share information about favorite hobbies, their schools, and the current events they were discussing in their classrooms. The students posted pictures of themselves, and shared links to favorite Web sites and videos, and discussed things that were interesting and relevant to preteens.

Once teachers begin to use interactive e-learning resources in classrooms, such as discussion boards, wikis, or blogs, instruction becomes less teacher-centered. Additionally, the use of learning management systems, such as BlackBoard, or social networking tools, such as blogs and wikis, provide students with opportunities to participate in communal learning spaces. These spaces provide platforms or forums that promote participatory cultures, as described by Jenkins, Clinton, Purushotma, Robison, and Weigel (2006, p. 7). According to them, communal learning spaces provide users with:

1. Low barriers to artistic expression and civic engagement;
2. Strong support for creating and sharing one's creations with others;
3. Some type of information mentorship whereby what is known by the most experienced is passed on to novices;
4. Belief that contributions member's contributions matter; and
5. Social connections to one another

In the Content-Centric/Mutually-Generated Instructional Paradigm, teachers and students share instructional decision making which contributes to the creation of communal learning spaces. Julie Ramsay's 5th grade students in Alabama, provides us with a good example. Ramsay and her students are working on collaborative projects with other 5th grade students 1,500 miles away in Arizona. For one project, all of the students read *Bud not Buddy* by Christopher Paul Curtis. *Bud not Buddy* is a fictional story about a boy who lived in an orphanage during Great Depression. In groups, students developed "create your own adventure" e-stories using primary sources (including relatives), news reels from United Streaming and books about the Great Depression. Students in Alabama wrote the adventure stories and the Arizona students created PowerPoint presentations of them using hyperlinks to select adventure options. Students used instant messaging to edit their work in real time.

Francisco Nieto, a Spanish teacher, presents us with another example of ways to promote student engagement in classrooms. He has increased student interaction in online discussions through the use of a software product called DyKnow (www.dyknow.com), a commercial software program that supports collaborative note taking, chats, polling, whiteboard capabilities, and video conferencing. Students engage in brainstorming and free-flow idea sharing by writing their answers using tablet PCs rather than typing them. This allows students to engage in free-flow of ideas online without physically typing their answers in Spanish, which Nieto finds is a lot faster for his students. DyKnow also allows students and teachers to save and archive their notes. This means that the handwritten examples and on-the-fly learning experiences are captured and can be reviewed at a later time. This type of software product can have a huge impact in formula-laden courses such as chemistry, statistics, or advanced math. It also allows teachers/professor to incorporate video conferencing, and as a result, Mr. Nieto was able to access his class Web site to teach and interact with his students in real time while visiting relatives in Spain. Even though there was a substitute teacher in the room, learning continued as if Mr. Nieto was there himself.

Mathew Joseph, a newly minted elementary principal in Massachusetts, provides us with yet another example. He wanted to improve home-school communications while enticing his teachers and students to engaging in more interactive technology uses. He approached his third grade teachers with an idea.

They gasped. "You want the kids to do what?"

"Podcast the daily announcements," he replied.

Each week, a different classroom is responsible for broadcasting the morning announcements, which consist of birthdays, vocabulary words, and interesting facts of the day. The student announcer speaks into two microphones simultaneously. One broadcasts to the school and the other records the announcements as audio files. Using a Macintosh laptop and GarageBand software, the 3rd grade tech team edits and uploads the files to the school's Apple iWeb site. Matthew Joseph then links the file to the school's Web site, where they are archived for one year.

During the past year, the school's Web site has registered 43,263 hits. Who's listening? Parents, school board members, relatives in other states, community leaders, newspaper reporters, anyone who's interested in the news at Hill-Roberts Elementary School. Joseph explained that the podcasts are having a tremendous effect on school-community relations, "This has opened the doors to families. School is everywhere." Parents are listening to the pod casts at work and downloading their children's podcasts to share at family gatherings. As a result, they are more informed about the curriculum and school news. Joseph has noticed that parental attendance at school functions is up almost 20%.

The examples presented in this section demonstrate how interactive technology uses are being integrated into teacher-centered, student-centered and mutually-generated learning paradigms. They also demonstrated how technology is quietly changing the culture of schools. Mathew Joseph summed it up by saying, "Technology has moved from awe-inspiring to just something we do." In all of these examples, students are building upon existing knowledge to develop new knowledge as members of participatory learning cultures.

CREATING PARTICIPATORY CULTURES

Initially, information literacy referred to the skills students need to locate, evaluate, and use information. In general, information literacy skills focused on (1) defining the task, (2) locating, extracting and synthesizing the information, and then (3) evaluating the product or process (Eisenberg & Berkowitz, 1990; James-Maxie, 2007). Advance uses of the Internet are creating a need for more sophisticated skills. These skills address students' abilities to:

- Select the right tools for the task and use them efficiently (Distributed Cognition)
- Pool knowledge, compare notes, and develop collaborative projects/products/solutions (Collective Intelligence)
- Follow the flow of stories and information across multiple modalities (Transmedia Navigation)
- Access diverse opinions, discern, respect, and represent multiple perspectives (Negotiation) (Jenkins, et al., p. 4).

The three examples presented earlier as part of the Content-Centric/Mutually-Generated Instructional Paradigm provide us with ways that students are developing these skills. For example, by collaborating with peers in another state, Ramsay's students are engaging in distributive cognition by experimenting with and deciding on which tools can most effectively communicate their message/product. They are also using transmedia navigational skills to make critical decisions about the most effective ways to collaborate and publish their work. Their development of cognitive intelligence and negotiation skills include sharing expertise and engaging in group problem solving in social networking contexts, which also requires them to respect the efforts and opinions of others.

Francisco Nieto and Mathew Joseph are modeling core literacy skills so that their students and faculty can become more aware of and adept at using them. Nieto, for example, is engaging students in distributive cognition by using various types of media tools to present instruction face-to-face or online. As a result, his students are learning not only Spanish, but how to use these tools to communicate more effectively. The same is true of Joseph. Through the use of podcasting, students as young as 3rd grade are beginning to develop distributed cognition and collective intelligence skills by learning to produce, edit, and publish digital media. As technology leaders, what must we do to prepare our teacher education students to spiral into fast-paced participatory learning environments or be at the forefront of creating these learning environments in their schools? The easiest way is to develop blended-learning communities as standard protocols in teacher education programs, and then expand from there.

CONCLUSION: NEXT STEPS

What do 21st Century learners look like? According to Kukulska-Hulme (2010, p. 6) these learners are analytical, and engaged. They can think independently, are equipped with research skills, and are motivated to learn. They are co-

creators and producers of knowledge who can communicate across language and cultural barriers. So, how do we prepare teacher candidates to teach these students? It begins by rethinking how we prepare teacher candidates. However, educational change usually happens very slowly, so we shouldn't expect drastic changes anytime soon. However, there are some adjustments that can be made easily. For example, to provide teacher education students with more modeling and practice, professors at UNC Charlotte have restructured the undergraduate K-6 teacher education program to highlight curriculum integration. It is common practice for teacher education programs to group coursework together in blocks that includes courses such as Math I, Reading I, and Science; Math II, Reading II, Language Arts and Social Studies. Until recently, these courses, much like the elementary school subjects, are taught as individual subjects with little integration. However, to foster curriculum integration, program leaders began planning together and have inserted a two-week clinical experience into the semester. During that time, teacher candidates teach integrated lesson plans they've developed. This framework has been designed to break the mold of compartmentalized instruction, promote curriculum integration, and extend technology across content areas. Admittedly, these changes are small steps, but they reflect an effort to move beyond traditional pedagogy and practices.

Eventually, the digital natives will outnumber the digital immigrants in teacher education programs and in K-12 classrooms. Until that happens, current teacher educators must be sensitive to changing paradigms and their manifestation in schools and adapt teacher preparation programs accordingly. This is necessary to if we are going to meet the educational needs of twitch speed kids who are adjusting their epistemologies daily.

REFERENCES

Boss, S., & Krauss, J. (2007). The power of the mashup. Learning &. *Leading with Technology, 34*(1), 12–17.

Bruns, A., Cobcroft, R., Smith, J., & Towers, S. (2007). Mobile learning technologies and the move towards user-led education. *Mobile Media 2007 Conference Proceedings*, Sydney, Australia.

Cochrane, T. (2006). Learning with wireless mobile devices and social software. *Proceedings of the 23rd Annual ASCILITE Conference: Who's Learning? Whose Technology?* (pp. 143-146). Sydney, Australia. Retrieved from http://www. ascilite.org.au/conferences/sydney06/proceeding/ pdf_papers/p50.pdf

Eisenberg, M. B., & Berkowitz, R. E. (1990). *Information problem-solving: The big six skills approach to library & information skills instruction*. Norwood, NJ: Ablex.

Ertmer, P. A., & Ottenbreit-Leftwich, A. T. (2010). Teacher technology change: How knowledge, confidence, beliefs, and culture intersect. *Journal of Research on Technology in Education, 42*(3), 255–284.

Hmelo-Silver, C. E., & Barrow, H. S. (2008). Facilitating collaborative knowledge building. *Cognition and Instruction, 26*, 48–94. doi:10.1080/07370000701798495

Holum, A., & Gahala, J. (2001). *Critical issue: Using technology to enhance literacy instruction*. North Central Regional Educational Laboratory. Retrieved from http://www.ncrel.org/sdrs/areas/ issues/content/cntareas/reading/li300.htm

James-Maxie, D. (2007). Information literacy skills in elementary schools: A review of the literature. *Journal of Instruction Delivery Systems, 21*(1), 23–26.

Jenkins, H., Clinton, K., Purushotma, R., Robison, A. J., & Weigel, M. (2006). *Confronting the challenges of participatory culture: Media education for the 21st Century*. John D. and Catherine T. MacArthur Foundation Web site. Retrieved from http://www.macfound.org/site/apps/nlnet/ content2.aspx?c=lkLXJ8MQKrH&b=1135955 &ct=2946895

Kukulska-Hulme, A. (2010). Learning cultures on the move: Where are we heading? *Journal of Educational Technology & Society, 13*(4), 4–14.

Lee, M. R., & Lan, Y. (2007). From Web 2.0 to conversational knowledge management: Towards collaborative intelligence. *Journal of Entrepreneurship Research, 2*(2), 47–62.

Means, B. (2010). Technology and education change: Focus on student learning. *Journal of Research on Technology in Education, 42*(3), 285–307.

Nikolov, R. (2007). Towards Web 2.0 schools: Rethinking the teachers professional development. In D. Benzie, & M. Iding (Eds.), *Proceedings of IFIP-Conference on Informatics, Mathematics and ICT: A golden triangle*. Boston, MA. Retrieved from http://dspace.ou.nl/bitstream/1820/1064/1/ Nikolov-R-paper-IMICT07.pdf

Prensky, M. (2001). Digital natives, digital immigrants. *On the Horizon, 9*(5). NCB University Press. Retrieved from http://pre2005.flexible-learning.net.au/projects/resources/Digital_Natives_Digital_Immigrants.pdf

Project Tomorrow. (2008). *21st Century students deserve a 21st century education*. Speak Up 2007 for students, teachers, parents & school leaders: Selected national findings - April 8, 2008. Retrieved from http://www.tomorrow.org/docs/national%20 findings%20speak%20up%202007.pdf

Project Tomorrow. (2010). *Unleashing the future: Educators "Speak up" about the use of emerging technologies for learning.* Retrieved from http://www.tomorrow.org/speakup/pdfs/SU09UnleashingTheFuture.pdf

Roberts, T. (2008). What's going on in Room 13? *Art Education, 19*(6), 19–24.

Scardamalia, M., & Bereiter, C. (2006). Knowledge building: Theory, pedagogy, and technology. In K. Sawyer (Ed.), *Cambridge handbook of the learning sciences* (pp. 97-118). New York, NY: Cambridge University Press. Retrieved from http://www.ikit.org/fulltext/2006_KBTheory.pdf

U. S. Department of Education. (1997). *President Clinton's call to action for American education in the 21st Century: Technological literacy.* Retrieved from http://www2.ed.gov/updates/PresEDPlan/part11.html

Chapter 15
EDM310:
A Case Study

John Hadley Strange
University of South Alabama, USA

ABSTRACT

This case study of EDM310 at the University of South Alabama covers the transition of the class from a group of face to face courses, which covered Microsoft Office, to face to face classes of 20 students taught by different teachers, which emphasized, to varying degrees, the use of Web 2.0 tools, blogging, commenting on blogs; then to a set of face to face courses all delivering instruction using Web 2.0 tools, blogs, and commenting on blogs. Finally the chapter discusses a course of 170 students taught by one faculty member with assistance from graduate and undergraduate students' course almost entirely on the Internet and in an open lab conducted by undergraduate assistants. A detailed description is provided, showing how projects are used as a central learning tool; how blogging and comments on blogs play a critical role in the course; how students react to these new instructional approaches. The case study also contains specific suggestions on how to organize such a course, and how it was implemented at the University of South Alabama with great success.

INTRODUCTION

Throughout this book you have been reading about the key issues that surround the creation of technology-rich education programs. In this chapter I take you to a discussion of the development and implementation of such a course at the University of South Alabama.

EDM310 is the only course offered by the College of Education to teach aspiring students the uses of technology in educational programs. When the course was added to the curriculum some 10 years ago, it offered instruction in basic computer use, word processing, presentation, spreadsheets

DOI: 10.4018/978-1-4666-0014-0.ch015

and databases. The proficient use of Microsoft Office was its primary objective.

Revisions to EDM310 began in 2007. More and more students were arriving from high school with the ability to use the Microsoft Office tools. Older students, often seeking recertification, needed a course that taught the basic skills necessary to operate a computer, as well as Microsoft Office. The differing needs of the students, as well as the emergence of Web 2.0 tools, led to EDM310 becoming a course for those already familiar with the use of computers and basic office tools. Students needing those skills and that knowledge were counseled to other courses in the University and nearby community colleges or commercial entities.

By 2008 students were blogging, using Skype, watching YouTube and other videos, making use of iTunes U, and mastering the transfer of the Office suite of tools to Google Docs. By the fall semester of 2009 EDM310 had become a face to face class covering new communication technologies and web 2.0 tools and approaches. It was taught by one professor and two Ph. D. graduate students under the general supervision of the faculty member. In the spring semester of 2010 efforts were begun to change EDM310 from a face to face course to what the University of South Alabama calls a *blended course*. A blended course can be any course that involves at least 20% but no more than 60% face to face instruction. In the summer of 2010 the first trial of EDM310 as a blended course took place. In the fall semester of 2010 the blended version of EDM310 was completely implemented as a single course of 170 students taught by one full time professor with the assistance of two Ph.D. graduate assistants and three undergraduate lab assistants. In the spring 2011 term the two graduate assistants were replaced with 1 ½ undergraduate assistants who had taken EDM310.

DISCLOSURE

EDM310 as it is currently offered at the University of South Alabama is largely my product. I initiated the efforts to change EDM310 beginning in 2007 continuing through its full implementation in the fall 2010 semester. I am primarily responsible for its objectives, design and content. I have been the lead instructor for EDM310 since the spring 2008 term. Although I reported frequently to the chair of my department on what I was doing with the course, I received no mandates, instructions, guidance or objections to what I was undertaking. I have received considerable help and ideas from many people including William Chamberlain, Dorothy Burt, Joe McClung, Jarod Lamshed, Alec Couros, G. Tashbin, Steve Sullivan, Anthony Capps, Jamie Lynn Miller and many EDM310 students. They deserve a great deal of credit for the successes of EDM310. I thank them for their help. Ultimately, however, I am responsible for the successes and failures of EDM310. I have a great deal of ownership in EDM310 as well as pride in how it has been implemented. So be cautious when you read what I have to say about EDM310. It is my baby and parents are often prejudiced when their children are discussed.

I share with you this case study because I am firmly convinced that the teachers of the future must be able to combine great instruction with the use of very powerful tools. It is my hope that this telling of the story of EDM310 will help others develop and implement their own courses that attempt to attain some or all the objectives that I seek. This is not like a "patent medicine chest where one can come and get a pill of wisdom to be swallowed like an aspirin" (Murrow, 1951) that will solve the problem of how to design and implement such a course. Rather, the EDM310 story can serve as a guidepost. Yes, it reveals much of what *I* believe about education, schools, technology, and learners. This is *my* story. This is what I believe. The intent of telling it is to help you create *your* story, to express in action *what you believe.*

MY BELIEFS

I do not believe in "burp back education." Facts learned are forgotten in almost exactly the same amount of time that it takes to learn them *unless* they are used.

I believe that we learn all things experientially. You cannot learn to ride a bicycle without (a) practice in actually riding the bicycle and (b) falling off. You cannot learn to read unless you read. You cannot learn to make movies unless you make movies. You cannot learn to think unless you think. You cannot learn to use technology unless you (a) use the technology and practice it regularly and (b) make mistakes (many them). Consequently, I believe project based education is most appropriate for EDM310.

I believe all members of the education profession must be learners. Educators must be *eager* learners. If we are not excited about learning ourselves, we are in the wrong profession.

I believe in connectivism. By this I mean that I believe we learn best in networks, preferably worldwide networks. Although I have assigned Wendy Drexler's video *The Networked Student* (Drexler, 2008) every semester since June 2009, I didn't really realize how accurately and completely she describes what I mean by connectivism. Watch the video!

I believe that we need teachers that do these things: demonstrate how to build personal learning networks, provide guidance in the practice of learning, demonstrate proper communication skills using the most advanced communication technologies, encourage questions, teach how to find experts and to ask respectfully for help, show a student how to evaluate a resource and organize information, provide evaluation of the student as a part of the student's own self evaluation, and produce life long independent learners. We should

probably rename teachers. I haven't come up with a good name yet. Let me know if you do!

I believe that questions are more important than answers. I am unhappy when a student tells me "Dr. Strange, I'm sorry but I have a question." We should never be sorry that we have a question. We need to always have questions and we should always be searching for answers to those questions (if answers exist).

I believe in outcome based education in which we clearly set forth what we want a student to know, be able to do and have experienced.

I believe that we will soon have "all information in all places at all times" (Godfrey, 1979, p.1) and that all learners (in other words all of us) must have the best technologies possible to access and process that information. I would note that my use of "information" includes text, audio, video and graphical information.

I believe that there is and continues to be great resistance to the changes currently taking place as a result of new technologies being increasingly intrusive on the old teaching procedures, organizations and personnel. David Godfrey (1979) wrote "...there will be no greater cries of protest [to the mechanization of education] than those that come ... from manual labourers of the educational field. Teachers will at last understand the plight of the handweaver." (p. 9) A considerable number of my students every semester fall into this category, as do many of the teachers that I know.

I believe that as an educator I should reduce the cost to my students as much as possible. I do not use textbooks. If I did I would seek the least expensive ones. And I would use them if students had to buy them. In EDM310 I assign no work that involves the expenditure of money. EDM310 is free except for three things: a personal computer, access to high speed Internet, and a web camera attached to their computer or available for use. All software and programs and software I have the students use in EDM310 are free.

I believe that we should be as green as possible in our teaching. EDM310 requires no paper in or out on the part of either the students or the staff. All materials are available in electronic form and all assignments must be submitted in electronic form. Many students prefer to print some or all of the instructional manuals and assignment materials. They may do so but I discourage it as much as possible.

I believe that we should learn in public and that the work we do for a class should be available to the public as part of our "intellectual trail."

EDM310 OBJECTIVES

In order to understand EDM310 you should be aware of the objectives for the course. Here are the objectives as I listed them in the Fall 2010 EDM310 Syllabus. They are quite likely to be slightly different by the time you read this chapter. There is always something new that I have encountered and learned that results in revisions to these objectives.

The objectives of EDM310

1. To start you on your way to becoming a tech literate educator.
2. To spark in you, or further encourage you in, a desire to learn rather than a desire to get a degree.
3. To understand the role that technology is playing and will play in society, especially in the educational systems of which you are a part.
4. To comprehend the rapid changes in methods of communication and to be able to plan for the ensuing changes in the way learning takes place.
5. To increase your proficiency in using cloud based tools, including word processor, database, spreadsheet, presentation and other communication tools.
6. To communicate effectively and regularly with others throughout the world using all multimedia components that are part of our communications systems today: sounds, digital still pictures, digital motion pictures, text, and graphics.
7. To develop and regularly post to a blog, using Google Blogger, and to understand and be able to write the HTML tags necessary to create links, display an image, comply with basic accessibility standards and to provide citations for source materials using title tag modifiers or other appropriate tools.
8. To have the understanding and confidence to use both common computer platforms - Macintosh and Windows - and to see their inherent similarities.
9. To be able to find and use information, in all multimedia forms, "from the cloud", i.e. the World Wide Web.
10. To use modern information gathering tools such as Delicious, Diigo, Twitter and RSS Feeds.
11. To develop and use a personal learning network composed of individuals throughout the United States and the world.
12. To understand the use of social networks in contemporary society, and to be able to use those tools where appropriate to advance teaching and learning.
13. To create and use podcasts, videocasts and other media products.
14. To collaborate effectively with your peers (fellow classmates).
15. To collaborate effectively with others in world wide learning communities.
16. To continue your learning as a lifelong learner and to become and stay a "tech literate teacher."
17. To apply the skills and knowledge necessary to leave an intellectual trail which you will be proud to have Googled.
18. To learn to be and act like a professional educator.
19. To engage effectively in self directed learning.
20. To manage your time effectively.

21. To value project learning more than burp back learning

COURSE ORGANIZATION AND COMMUNICATION

EDM310 meets as four individual classes of 40 students each in weeks 1, 2, 9 and 15, the last week of classes. In Weeks 1 and 2 I introduce the staff (two graduate assistants and three undergraduate lab assistants who have taken EDM 310) and I reiterate information about how EDM310 is different from other classes the students have taken. This same discussion is made available to students through the class blog in a video which very few students watch before the class starts. Students are shown how to access the Class Blog, the Instruction Manual, the Google Voice Help line and the EDM310 Help email. Each student establishes a Gmail account (if not established as requested in a series of emails sent to the student's university address prior to the start of class). Students also ask lots of questions, create their blogs, establish groups for collaborative activities, and have a picture taken for use in their blogs if desired. The pictures are also used by the staff to learn the names of the students.

Week 9 is used for presentations of SMART Technology projects as well as provide a mid term "correction" opportunity. Week 15 is for final wrap up activities and the submission of Foliotek (electronic portfolios required by the College of Education) materials.

During weeks 3-8 and 10-14, students work independently following the EDM310 Instruction Manual and materials linked to it. Students must also consult the EDM310 Class Blog regularly since the Class Blog is the primary method I use to communicate with the students and where I add additional material and assignments in text, audio and video.

The Syllabus and the Instruction Manual contain all of the specific initial assignments as well as instructions on how to accomplish the assignments or links to other sources of information useful in completing the assignments and projects. To fully understand the process, visit the EDM310 Class Blog at http://edm310.blogspot.com, read the Syllabus and the Instruction Manual, and peruse the posts made to the blog over the course of a semester. Links to the latest Syllabus and Instruction Manual are found in the right column of the EDM310 Class Blog. Use the Archive links to navigate quickly to earlier portions of the EDM310 Class Blog.

Projects

During a 15 week semester I assign students sixteen projects which are described in the Instruction Manual. These assignments are supplemented by additional assignments that are added because of the availability of important new material or to support other aspects of the course. In the fall 2010 term there were 13 individual products and 3 collaborative projects. Two additional blog assignments have been added to the weekly blog assignments through the sixth week of class in the fall 2010 semester as I write this. At least two more will be added later in the term.

Personal Class Blog

The project that takes the most time for students is their personal Class Blog. This blog hosts all of the work done by a student. Each week during the semester a student has to read, watch or listen to from one to four assignments and post a summary on their blog of what they learned from the assignment. The assignments are designed to raise questions about technology and learning, how schools use (or don't use) technology, how teachers are using technology in their classes, and to provide examples of student work (at all grade levels). The list changes every semester. You can consult my current list of blog assignments (found in the Instruction Manual) to sample them. Another excellent list is maintained by Alex Couros (2009, December 3) who teaches similar courses at the University of Regina. I also get a large number of suggestions, many of which I use, from EDM310 students and by monitoring my Twitter flow (@ drjohnhadley). Most blog posts must include text, links, and images (with appropriate HTML code). I encourage students to not only write with text but to also use audio, video or a combination of these communication methods. I try to model these in the EDM310 Class Blog.

In addition to providing space in which students write (with or without multimedia) about assigned topics, their blogs are also the public repositories of all of their work. Ever project they complete is embedded in their class blog or made available with a link on their blog. This is how all student work is made public. I undertake many efforts to increase the likelihood that EDM310 students will have a large audience who react to their writings, media comments and projects. A considerable number of the teachers they interact with do read and comment on their work. In addition, every student post is commented upon by at least one member of the instructional staff every week. I read and comment on every student's blog at least every three weeks (about 60 students a week). Every student comments each week on a class-mate's blog. This is the C4C project described in more detail below.

In creating and maintaining their blog, students practice writing and other communication skills. They also master certain ancillary skills such as using a limited amount of HTML code, recording and posting audio and video and reflecting on the work of others in a supportive but critical way. The staff provides a model. Instructional materials are provided which support the model used by the staff. The students quickly learn how to comment in a similar way. In addition, students begin to realize that they are leaving an "intellectual trail" (Capps, 2009, September 16) and that everything they do and write can and will be Googled (Strange, 2009, September 23).

Comments for Classmates, Kids and Teachers

Other projects which are critical to the success of EDM310 are assignments to read and leave comments on the blogs of three other audiences: classmates, kids and teachers. I label these **C4C, C4K and C4T**. I would like to add a fourth group to this list: teachers in training. So far I have not found a sufficient number to add them.

Each week every student is assigned (C4C) to read and comment on a fellow classmate's blog post for the previous week. In addition, they are assigned (C4K) to comment on a kid's blog every week and a teacher's blog (C4T) every two weeks. The kids' blogs are selected from a large list of K-12 students who blog regularly. I have compiled this list from many sources. I will continue to add to the list and by the time this book is published I would not be surprised if the list contains at least a thousand links. Since my list changes weekly, a link to it would be useless. You will be able to find it when you read this chapter by consulting the EDM310 Blog. In addition, William Chamberlain who teaches at the Noel Elementary School in Noel, Missouri maintains a dynamic list of kids' blogs (http://comments4kids.blogspot.com) that is linked to Twitter. Teachers throughout the world also connect with other teachers and provide lists of their students' blogs for which they are seeking comments. I make use of this list as well.

William Chamberlain, Carey Pohanka and Derek Smith started C4K in 2009 on Twitter in an attempt to expand the number of people commenting on kids' blogs. I already had my students in EDM310 reading the blogs of teachers and kids as well as creating and using blogs of their own. But I had never encouraged, or even suggested the use of comments, until one of my students left a comment on At The Teacher's Desk (http://attheteachersdesk.blogspot.com), a blog to which Mr. Chamberlain is a major contributor. As a result of that comment Mr. Chamberlain contacted me, urged me to have my students participate in commenting on kids' blogs, and also got me to use Twitter which is now my most important source of professional development. I am now convinced that commenting on other peoples' blogs is as important, or perhaps more important, than posting on a blog of your own.

I have written about the importance of commenting on blogs in several places. In *Kaia and Room 10 - Why Blogs and Commenting on Blogs Are So Important* (Strange, 2009, November 5) I take you on a journey through the story of the EDM310 students and their interactions with a three year old in Qatar named Kaia, a room full of third graders, Room 10, at the Pt. England School in Auckland, New Zealand and the sixth graders in Mr. Chamberlain's class in Noel, Missouri. Links allow you to read, see and hear the experiences of all parties involved in this exchange. Only by reliving that journey can you fully appreciate the importance of these interactions and the learning that resulted from them. I will attempt to summarize the major impacts that blogging and commenting had on all concerned.

First, the blogs allowed my aspiring teachers access into two different learning environments, a classroom and a family learning event, as participant observers.

Second, my students got out of Alabama, at least virtually. I happen to think that is a good thing for Alabama residents to do that from time to time! The world is very different from Alabama.

Third, my students provided a real audience for the kids which they greatly appreciated as we know from many interactions with my students.

Fourth, my students made lasting friendships with several of the teachers involved in the odyssey.

Fifth, my students were introduced to Skype and its power to connect learners and teachers anywhere for free.

Sixth, out of necessity, one of my students decided to make a movie, for Kaia, a task I had not yet added to EDM310. This encouraged me

to expand the communication tools I had students use to include movies.

Seventh, my movie making student, who took that on without my knowledge, later thanked me for allowing her the freedom to learn by doing what she felt was necessary in this instance. That got me to thinking about the freedom to explore that I was providing my students. I had never considered freedom as a necessary component of EDM310. I just assumed my students knew they possessed it. Later discussions revealed that was not the case in most other courses they were taking. So I have emphasized it even more since these events took place.

I make the assignment to my students to comment on kids' blogs around the world because I want to:

1. Encourage comments on blogs they visit
2. Get them to see what kids can do with blogs (kids - not students in a college class!)
3. Get them to see real classes that use technology - and to understand its role in the curriculum
4. Let them identify teachers who could be helpful to them when they start teaching
5. Get them out of a classroom into the world
6. Use the technologies themselves

The list above is just a summary of bullet points. It does not let you see, feel and hear the excitement that you can get if you follow the path of links in the original post I wrote. It is that excitement about learning that drove home to me the importance of blogging and commenting on blogs. As a result, I have expanded the commenting effort to include regular comments on classmates' blogs and comments on blogs of exemplary teachers throughout the world. I consider this virtual field experience to be a vital part of preparing teachers to teach in a world that is being revolutionized by the rapid spread of technology. The experiences in these field placements offer a far greater exposure to the best uses of technology in learning and provide for interactions with a far more diverse student and teacher population than will be accomplished in traditional placements in Mobile and Baldwin counties in Alabama.

Personal Learning Network

I had written the header for this section and was about to begin my comments on why I think it is critical for my students to develop a Personal Learning Network. Then I noticed in my Twitter stream a tweet from @wmchamberlain. He was recommending a new TED talk by Professor Sugata Mitra (Mitra, 2010). I watched. In this short video Professor Mitra describes his experiments with children in schools where teachers do not want to go. He demonstrates that motivated children, working with computers and internet access, teach themselves quite successfully without any teachers around. The necessary ingredient is a desire to learn.

Before I watched Professor Mitra's video, I was about to write that I considered the development of a Personal Learning Environment, or a Personal Learning Network, as a key component of the Projects that I will absolutely retain in future versions of EDM310. My approach has been to encourage my students to form links with other students, teachers and guides in a Personal Learning Network or a Personal Learning Environment. One example I use is assigned as a blog post assignment. It is the description by a seventh grade student of Wendy Drexler of her Personal Learning Environment and how she constructed it (Unnamed, 2009).

Now I am not so sure that a PLN is the only choice we have. Perhaps there are other ways to get learners connected in a common learning effort without consciously creating a personalized network as I seek to inculcate in my students. In concluding his TED talk, Professor Mitra (2010) suggests that he has found in his experiments a self organising (he uses English English) system that he defines as a system where "the structure appears without explicit intervention from outside the system." (16:13) He goes on to contend that a self-organising system also always displays "emergence" which is the "appearance of a property not previously observed as a functional characteristic of the system." In other words things happen that were not planned. He believes he will be able to prove that "education can be a self-organising system, where learning is an emergent phenomenon" within five years.

If Professor Mitra is correct, we can provide the organizational structure where motivated children can and will successfully teach themselves without teachers. His vision calls for daily, personal interaction by the students with other students in a setting where computers and access to the Internet are provided as well as some questions that are to be addressed and/or problems that are to be solved. Personal Learning Networks are related to Professor Mitra's vision. They may be adequate substitutes where interpersonal face to face communication is impossible. Or perhaps they are important, maybe even necessary components of the process. I am not sure. Nevertheless, I intend to keep using them. Professor Mitra's findings so far reinforce my belief that the education profession is changing so rapidly that we may be training students for "teaching" positions that will soon disappear. Not just because students can teach themselves but for other reason as well which will be discussed later in this chapter.

Other Projects

Students are required to do a variety of other projects. These projects, unlike those discussed above, are projects that are designed to provide a way of learning to use important tools currently available for use in the classroom. They are quite likely to change as new tools and new software appear. To be included in my assignments they must be free, must work on both PCs and Macs (or have an equivalent alternative) and must be useful for a range of age levels. In Fall 2010 the list of tools that must be used to undertake and complete the projects includes Google and its many advanced and specialized search tools; WolframAlpha; Google Earth; Aviary, Picasa or iPhoto; Wordle; Google Docs (all parts); TimeToast; Skype; Twitter; Delicious; Audacity and Vocaroo; YouTube; Glogster; webcams, Flip cameras or other video cameras; iMovie or Camedia for movie editing; and a Smart Board or a Prometheus Board and its associated software. The products produced through the use of these tools include podcasts; videocasts; movies; various instructional materials; interviews; Google Earth Lit Tours; Skype interviews; multimedia products attempting to emulate the multimedia writing techniques encouraged by Dr. Richard Miller (Miller, 2009a) (Miller, 2009b); GPS scavenger hunts; and many other projects proposed by the students themselves. Next spring this list will likely be different. By the time you read this chapter it *will* be different.

DISCUSSION

Student Problems

Honest Self Reflection

I insist that students periodically review their own work and progress in the class and report on it to me. I could easily abandon grades if the University would allow it.

Many students do not like the fact that I do not report on their progress through grades. They have had little or no experience in developing skills of self-reflection and find it quite difficult. Good students tend to underestimate their performance and abilities. Poor students almost always overestimate their accomplishments. Poor students, initially, reported false information about the quantity and timeliness of their work. This was evident in the mid term self reflection questionnaire that I gave students in the Spring 2010 semester. The dichotomy between the data

generated automatically by Google and the responses of many students resulted in my posting a lengthy blog post emphasizing that self-reflection was to be an *honest* self-reflection (Strange, 2010, March 22). This generated considerable debate among the students. I was accused of not helping students, of "throwing them under the bus" and of creating a situation in which they might bring harm to themselves as a result of my criticism of dishonest responses (Strange, 2010, April 26). I then realized that many students did not understand that I had data on when they had submitted their work as well as the quantity of their work. I was not asking them to report what assignments they had completed and when they had done those assignments so that I would know. I knew already. Rather I wanted them to acknowledge their strengths and weaknesses to themselves. I now incorporate both of the cited posts as part of the assignments in the first week of class.

Difficulty in Transitioning to Learning from Memorizing

Students taking EDM310, for the most part, have no significant difficulties in using the technologies that are emphasized in the class. They are generally well skilled in using computers, cell phones, texting tools, basic search engines. They enter less skilled in using digital recording devices (audio or video) but they rapidly learn the use of these tools with little or no instruction. They are generally unaware of many of the specific tools and software programs used in EDM310 and they are generally more familiar with PCs than Macs, but neither of these poses any significant impediments to making use of the EDM310 tools. This is not surprising given the significant use of the "new" technologies by students in their late teens or early twenties.

For some students, however, the technologies themselves present a significant learning hurdle. These tend to be older students, especially those in their mid thirties and older, who dropped out of school some years ago and are just returning or students who have an undergraduate degree but who must take this course to maintain their certification or re-certification. This is especially true if these older students have little experience in the use of computers and bring a "fear" of technology to class with them. Despite the warnings that we give emphasizing that EDM310 is not for students with minimal computer skills, a considerable number in that category still start the class either because they don't believe or didn't read the warnings in the Syllabus. They overestimate their skills because they are unaware that the modern use of computers extends beyond email and word processing. They think they will try it anyway since they need to complete the course immediately for monetary or employment purposes. These neophytes either drop out or succeed in the course because they are unusually persistent and dedicated in mastering new skills on their own, are helped by the lab assistants and, quite often, receive considerable tutoring and assistance from their school age children.

Students taking EDM310 often have difficulty in moving from a curriculum which has stressed the memorization of factual information to a class which is entirely project based. EDM310 provides guidance for the acquisition of the tools necessary to solve problems but does not provide an explicit set of step by step instructions to follow. The student is provided with a problem to solve or a project to complete. The road to the solution of the problem or to the completion of the project is to be discovered and determined by the student. For students who have been well trained to memorize and then burp-back answers this can be difficult. In the spring term of 2010 one student told me: "Dr. Strange, this course really bothers me. I just want you to teach me so I don't have to learn." Memorizing and burping back in a short period of time is much less difficult than the discovery learning process for a significant number of EDM310 students.

Organize and Use Time

Another problem for EDM310 students is that many of them cannot, or do not know how to, manage their time. In previous courses I have been lenient in setting and enforcing deadlines. In the early versions of EDM310 I started with that approach. It did not work. Now I set very explicit deadlines and insist they be met. My operating mottos have become: "You are preparing to be a professional. Act like one."; "You must set aside 9 hours per week for EDM310. Mark it off in your daily planner or on your digital calendar."; "Consider EDM310 your job for 9 hours a week. To keep your job, be on time with your work." Despite these efforts and warnings, about 20% of the work so far this term has been submitted late. Last semester the late submissions were similar.

I collect a considerable amount of data when students enter EDM310. In the summer of 2010 I theorized that the busiest students, those who worked many hours a week, those who had several children, or those who were taking more than the standard load of classes, or a combination of all of these, would be the students submitting their work late. When I analyzed the data I had collected I found I was wrong. The busiest students were always on time. "Late" students were those who lived on campus, did not work, and were taking no more than a standard number of classes. I have not compiled these data for this semester yet. It will be interesting to see if the "busy" students are again the on time students. My guess now is that will be the case. They *have* to organize their lives!

Collaborative Learning

The collaborative assignments have posed no unusual issues.

Technological Literacy

EDM310 students enter EDM310 thinking that they are "technologically literate." To a certain extent they are correct. They know how to use their computers and cell phones, over half of which are smart phones. They know how to Google and use Facebook. Many have used Skype to contact friends or relatives. They all have heard of smart boards but only a very few have used them. None, or at least almost none, have any knowledge of blogs, TED, iTunes U, web based audio and video tools, web 2.0 tools, podcasts, videocasts, Google Docs, Google Squared, Wolfram Alpha or other advanced search engines. Nor do they enter into EDM310 with an understanding of how close we are to having all information available in all places at all times. Nor are they familiar with the free, powerful tools that allow these data to be accessed, compared, combined and analyzed. Most enter thinking that using technology for instructional purposes means only using computers for word processing and powerpoints and using smart boards in some classrooms. And they are certain that it is unnecessary for good teachers to know about or use technology as a teaching tool. In fact, many of the students do not think of educational technologies as tools but rather as a subject matter, like history or literature.

I use blog post assignments to acquaint EDM310 students with the current advanced uses of technology, new tools such as iPads, iPod Touches, Flip cameras, cell phones and approaches to teaching such as blogging and commenting on blogs and connectivist approaches to instruction.

By the end of the semester most students admit that even though they believed they were technologically literate when they entered EDM310, they were not.

Undergraduate Assistants and the EDM310 Lab

There have been a number of university undergraduate classes, covering practically every discipline, that has been "redesigned." Redesigned courses use new approaches to course organization and also use advanced information technologies. The goal is to serve more students at a higher level of instructional quality and at a reduced cost. The principal catalyst for this movement has been the National Center for Academic Transformation (NCAT) (http://www.thencat.org). NCAT's research has demonstrated that a key element in the success of redesigned courses can be attributed to the involvement of undergraduate students in the instructional process. This is also true with EDM310. Undergraduate lab assistants were first introduced in the summer trial version of EDM310. In the spring 2011 term we are operating a staffed lab every day from 9:00 am to 6:30 pm (8:30 on Wed) and 1:00 pm to 6:00 pm Saturdays and Sundays. The labs are staffed by undergraduates who have taken EDM310 within the past three semesters. The labs are the most important part of EDM310. It is here that students feel free to ask questions because, I believe, they are asking their peers instead of the professor.

Staff Assignments

What tasks do the members of the instructional staff do since the instruction and accompanying materials have been in large part completed before the class starts?

We answer a lot of questions. This is accomplished in the lab and through the other ways we are in touch with the students. Undergraduates carry the responsibility for most of the work in the lab. They work a total of 90 hours a week in the lab. I am in the lab six to eight hours a week during a normal week, more when major projects are due. Every week I receive blog comments or other messages thanking me for the "amazing, helpful and patient staff" provided by Anthony, Jamie Lynn, Stephen, Allie and Amberly and reminding me how fortunate it is to have them as part of the EDM310 learning community.

We also answer questions and provide assistance by email, phone calls and text messages.

We comment on student blogs. Generally I leave comments on about 50-60 of the student blogs each week. Each full time undergraduate (20 hours a week) comments on 18-20 and the half time undergraduate assigned is assigned 10 blogs on which to leave comments. It takes between 5 and 15 minutes per student post to leave a useful comment. A major part of my time is devoted to this aspect of the course.

Staying in Touch with the Students

In a course which meets face to face only four weeks during a semester, how do we stay in touch with the students?

A stated goal of EDM310 is to respond to all requests for assistance from students within 24 hours of the receipt of a request for help. Our goal is to respond within 6 hours except between the hours of 11 pm and 6 am. We have met our goal of a 6 hour response without exception so far this semester. Most requests for help have been responded to within an hour during normal days. On Sundays, when there are more requests for help because most deadlines for submission of work is Sunday midnight, responses are a bit slower.

We use several different methods for staying in touch with students. These include the lab, Gmail, Google Voice, telephones, text messages, Skype and Twitter. We will add Google Chat and may add a Facebook page next semester.

The EDM310 Class Blog is used to communicate information, new assignments, changes to assignments, new tools and other information to all of the students at one time. Unfortunately (for them) our evidence indicates that not all of the students read the Class Blog regularly even though we insist that there be a RSS feed of the EDM310 Class Blog on their personal blog.

Labs

I have discussed the importance of the labs elsewhere, including the importance of the undergraduate assistants. The labs are open 59 1/2 hours a week. Students are encouraged to bring their own portable computers since the University computers have been reduced through attrition and age. The course was developed (over a two and a half year period) using my personal equipment. I also have purchased, and given to the University two 20.5" iMacs; one 15" MacBook Pro; one Shure USB omni-directional microphone; two Flip cameras; two ink jet printers and the ink for them. I have supplied two of my undergraduate assistants with iPhones (and pay all associated fees) and one undergraduate an iPod Touch 4.0. I retain ownership of the iPhones and the iPod Touch. The College purchased five new PCs, three iMacs, and six Flip cameras for the EDM310 Lab. The lab inherited fourteen 4-5 year old PCs a laser printer. In addition, I use my own iPhone 4 and my home 27" iMac to do all my class development and class work.

Email

I have established several Gmail accounts. All members of the staff access these Gmail accounts. The primary account is EDM310Help. Students are asked to send all requests for help to this Gmail account. We also provide our personal Gmail addresses and many students use them as well, especially when they wish to communicate with a specific member of the instructional staff. Gmail accounts are also used for project submissions and to monitor comments left on all student blogs and the EDM310 Class Blog. Other Gmail accounts used in EDM310 reveal their purpose in their names: EDM310presentations; EDM310forms; EDM310checklists; EDM310podcasts. We are collecting data on the use of email. These data will be analyzed at the end of the semester.

Help Phone

I established a Google Voice account that enables us to provide a single EDM310 Help telephone number for students to use. Calls are sent to the cell phones of all staff members simultaneously. In the event that no one answers, a voicemail can be left and Google sends a text message with a transcription of the message to all of the cell phones of the staff. We also provide the personal cell phone numbers of the cell phones of all staff members. In addition, we provide the landline number of the secretarial staff supporting the Department of Professional Studies in which EDM310 is located.

Text Messaging

One of the favorite ways students communicate with the staff is through text messages. These are routed to our cell phones or the Google Voice number that puts the text on all phones linked to that number.

Other

We also monitor individual Skype accounts and individual Twitter accounts. We also have a unified EDM310 Skype account and a unified Twitter account. We also use Google Chat as a contact method.

Alumni

During the Spring 2010 term Jacki Gorski began an EDM310 Alumni Blog (http://edm310alumniblog.blogspot.com). This blog continues to have posts added regularly by EDM310 alumni. Alumni frequently leave comments on current student blogs and visit the lab to either work with current students or just to visit. I have never had a class, nor have I heard of others, in which class alumni continued to participate. Needless to say, I am very pleased.

Where EDM310 Visitors Live

Students in EDM310 regularly comment on kid and teacher blogs throughout the world. As of February 7, 2011 the class blog for the redesigned EDM310 has been visited a total of 25,574 times. Of those visits 1,460 have been from 111 countries

other than the United States. The international connections provide exposure to different types of schools, different cultures and different approaches to teaching. I consider these international connections to be a major contribution to the education of students in EDM310.

Irony of Writing for Print

I am writing this chapter in September 2010. It is expected to be published in late 2011. I do not know when you are reading it. One thing is certain. EDM310 will have changed and teaching in a technologically rich environment will have changed.

What changes will have taken place other than the normal modifications that all courses undergo? What new influences and tools will have emerged within a year? My crystal ball is not as clear as it should be, but I think I can safely say that more electronic books will be available; the iSchool first proposed by Travis Allen (2009) when he was 17 and in high school will have been implemented in several schools; face to face video conversations will be common; tablet computers such as iPads will be ubiquitous on many high school and college campuses; battles will be being waged by some to keep these "distractions" (including cell phones) from being allowed in classrooms; and many teachers will be increasingly nervous that they are being left out of the technological revolution and can no longer effectively combat or ban the use of personal technologies by students. Prices will be lower; the tools will be more powerful; the students will own the tools and use them with permission or not; and debates will rage as to whether and how to use technology as part of the educational process. And schools will be moving closer to extinction unless they are embracing change more rapidly than I think is likely.

And there is another irony as well. I am writing this chapter without embedded links to other materials of all types: text, audio, video. This is the *old* method of communicating ideas and information. It is on its way out. Why is it still being used? Because universities reward their faculty for publishing in old formats but only rarely, if at all, for using the new communication tools. You should be able to read this book and this chapter shortly after it is written. There should be links to other materials throughout. How ironic to be writing about a world which you could be participating in right now but are not!

CONCLUDING THOUGHTS

I have said what I want to say. Here are the things I think are most important:

Technology is merely a tool. Use it wisely. Also think about the teaching. No burp-back education. Projects please. Use Self-reflection instead of grades as much as possible. No lectures. No banning of tools, just direct their use.

The times they are a changing. You must change with it. And so must the courses you teach.

Be a guide, a facilitator.

Questions are more important that the answers.

You won't know a lot and that will happen very often. That provides a learning opportunity. Adopt our motto: *I don't know. Let's find out.* And remember that *Let's* is plural.

Response time to questions or requests for help must be very short. Try the 6 hour goal. It can work.

Don't settle for domestic connections. Search out the international ones as well.

Blog. And perhaps more importantly, comment on blogs.

Add a lab with undergraduate students in charge. Use the lab as an opportunity for all to learn in a true learning community.

Embrace change. Direct it. You cannot stop it.

Learn from your students. There are often experts when you are not. Don't forget that teachers must be learners also. And learning should never end.

Write with multimedia. This chapter is pure text. It should have links, videos, and audio embedded in it. It may be the last purely text book in old fashioned print form you ever see again.

Have fun. It helps!

REFERENCES

Allen, T. (2009, April 26). *The iSchool initiative* [Video]. Retrieved from http://www.youtube.com/watch?v=68KgAcx_9jU

Alloul, A. (2010, September 28). *Comment on blog post: Great.* Retrieved from http://strangethoughtsbyjohn.blogspot.com/2010/09/great.html

Capps, A. (2009, September 16). *How to make your own podcast.* Retrieved from http://cappsaedm310fall2009.blogspot.com/2009/09/how-to-make-your-own-podcast.html

Couros, A. (2009, May 21). *90+ videos for tech. & media literacy.* Retrieved from http://educationaltechnology.ca/couros/1480

Couros, A. (2009, December 3). 90+ *videos for tech. & media literacy.* Retrieved from http://couros.wikispaces.com/TechAndMediaLiteracyVids

Drexler, W. (2008). *The networked student* [Video]. Retrieved from http://www.youtube.com/watch?v=XwM4ieFOotA&feature=player_embedded#!

Edublog. (2011, February 5). *Student blogging challenge.* Retrieved from http://studentchallenge.edublogs.org/

Godfrey, D. (1979). Introduction. In Godfrey, D., & Parkhill, D. (Eds.), *Gutenberg two: The new electronics and social change.* Toronto, Canada: Press Porcépic.

Miller, R. (2009a). *How we dream, part 1* [Video]. Retrieved from http://www.youtube.com/watch?v=PHvoBPjhsBA&feature=player_embedded

Miller, R. (2009b). *How we dream, part 2* [Video]. Retrieved from http://www.youtube.com/watch?v=6KsEQnOkTZ0&feature=player_embedded

Mitra, S. (2010). *Sugata Mitra: The child-driven education* [Video] Retrieved from http://www.ted.com/talks/sugata_mitra_the_child_driven_education.html?awesm=on.ted.com_8YCW&utm_campaign=sugata_mitra_the_child_driven_education&utm_medium=on.ted.com-twitter&utm_source=direct-on.ted.com&utm_content=ted.com-talkpage

Murrow, E. (1951). *Introduction: This I believe* [radio broadcast]. Audio and written transcript: Specific quotation at 3:31-3:38. Retrieved from http://thisibelieve.org/essay/16844/

Strange, J. (2009, September 23). *You are creating your intellectual trail – And it can and will be Googled.* Retrieved from http://edm310fall2009.blogspot.com/2009/09/required-reading-anthony-capps-m6-post.html

Strange, J. (2009, November 5). *Kaia and room 10 – Why blogs and commenting on blogs are so important.* Retrieved from http://edm310fall2009.blogspot.com/2009/11/kaia-reads-book-and-her-father-skypes.html

Strange, J. (2010, March 22). *Honest reflection is required.* Retrieved from http://edm310.blogspot.com/2010/03/honest-reflection-is-required-new.html

Strange, J. (2010, April 26). *ZZZ and the honest reflection post – Response to comments.* Retrieved from http://strangethoughtsbyjohn.blogspot.com/2010/04/zzz-and-honest-reflection-post-response.html

Unnamed. (2009). *Welcome to my PLE.* Retrieved from http://www.ted.com/talks/sugata_mitra_the_child_driven_education.html?awesm=on.ted.com_8YCW&utm_campaign=sugata_mitra_the_child_driven_education&utm_medium=on.ted.com-twitter&utm_source=direct-on.ted.com&utm_content=ted.com-talkpage

Chapter 16
Modeling Online Teaching and Learning to Pre- and In-Service Teachers through the use of the Web 2.0 Social Networking Tool NING

Kelly L. Unger
Wayne State University, USA

Monica W. Tracey
Wayne State University, USA

ABSTRACT

The rise of the Internet and Web 2.0 tools for "anytime, anywhere" learning is impacting K-12 and teacher education programs. Many teacher education (TED) faculty and professional development (PD) providers are now encouraged or required at a minimum to incorporate an online learning component into courses. Not only are they teaching the required course content to pre- and in-service teachers in an online environment, but are also modeling the use of that environment to teachers who will ultimately be required to design, develop, and provide online instruction to their future students. The purpose of this chapter is to discuss: (1) transitioning instruction from face-to-face to an online learning environment, (2) examples of learning activities to implement with the Web 2.0 social networking tool NING, and (3) implications the NING has for those instructing pre- and in-service teachers.

TRANSITIONING TO ONLINE INSTRUCTION

Why the Need for a Transition?

The National Educational Technology Plan for 2010, released by The United States Department of Education's Office of Educational Technology, centers many of its goals on preparing future leaders for engagement in a global economy through incorporating the Internet in daily educational tasks (U.S. Department of Education, 2010). A central focus of the plan is aimed at creating online learning environments that support collaboration among students and teachers. The plan claims to guide the U.S. in achieving two main goals by

DOI: 10.4018/978-1-4666-0014-0.ch016

2020: (1) raise the proportion of the U.S. population that holds a 2 or 4-year degree from 39% to 60%, and (2) ensure that all high school graduates, regardless of race or income, are ready to succeed in college and careers (U.S. Department of Education, 2010). The New Media Consortium's Horizon Project, which was established to identify emerging technologies potentially altering education around the globe, also report online learning and social networking as factors that will impact teaching and learning between 2010-2015 (Johnson, Smith, Levine, & Haywood, 2010). For any student to succeed in college today it is imperative that K-12 students are prepared to attend classes in an online environment. Allen and Seaman (2008) estimated approximately 4 million college students were enrolled in at least one online course during the fall 2007 term. As information becomes more readily available learners will continue to desire anytime, anywhere instruction and universities need to be prepared to meet those needs and desires of online learning.

K-12 schools throughout the U.S. are taking the necessary steps to ensure students are prepared for online learning in higher education. Picciano and Seaman (2009) estimated over 1,000,000 K-12 students were engaged in online learning, during 2007-2008, and 75% of school administrators report having at least one or more students enrolled in a fully online or blended course. Some states, with Michigan leading the way in 2006, incorporated an online learning graduation requirement. Michigan students can meet the requirement in one of three ways: (1) complete an entire online course, (2) complete, at a minimum, twenty hours of an online learning experience in an existing course, or (3) participate in an online course or learning experience that is incorporated into each course of the required curriculum (Michigan Department of Education, 2006). To require students to participate in online learning, teachers need to be prepared to provide online instruction. The International Society for Technology in Education (ISTE), an association focused on improving teaching and learning by advancing the effective use of technology in PK-12 and teacher education programs, developed National Education Technology Standards (NETS) for students, teachers, and administrators. The NETS for teachers (NETS-T) encourage teachers to model and apply the NETS for students (NETS-S) in their instructional practice. The NETS-T advise that all teachers: (1) facilitate and inspire student learning and creativity in both face-to-face and virtual environments, (2) design and develop digital-age learning experiences and assessments, (3) model digital-age work and learning of an innovative professional in a global and digital society, (4) promote and model digital citizenship and responsibility, and (5) engage in professional growth and leadership through promoting and demonstrating the use of digital tools (ISTE, 2010).

While standards from ISTE are an excellent guide for educators, states, teacher education (TED) programs, and K-12 administrators need to make online learning a priority in today's educational system. Watson, Gemin, Ryan and Wicks (2009), in their annual review of state-level policy and practice of K-12 online learning, noted all but fifteen states have a state virtual school or state-led online initiative. Michigan, in 2008, proposed two standards to be added to the Entry-Level Standards for Michigan teachers, which impacts all teachers:

Successfully complete and reflect upon collaborative online learning experiences;

Demonstrate an understanding of and the ability to create an online learning experience and demonstrate continued growth in technology operations and concepts, including strategies for teaching and learning in an online environment (Michigan State Board of Education, 2008, p.3.).

These additional standards also impacted the State's Educational Technology endorsement, which recognizes the accomplishments of educators who gain expertise in Information Age knowledge and skills, by requiring recipients to achieve proficiency levels in three additional standards related to online technology experiences and skills, and course design and delivery (Michigan State Board of Education, 2008). While these initiatives seem to be taking steps to support online learning in educational practice, research shows teachers are still not prepared to instruct in the online environment. Barbour and Unger (2009), in their study on in-service teachers' perceptions of online learning in Michigan, a state with a virtual school, found that teachers perceived online learning to be unsuccessful because of the lack of information provided to teachers, students, parents, and administrators about the possibilities and benefits of online learning, and the lack of support for this method of instruction from administration. Rice, Dawley, Gasell, and Florez (2008) in their study of online teachers, found 62% of respondents (n=584) reported receiving no training prior to teaching online. Research shows that while good communication and classroom organization skills are important for any successful instructor (Easton, 2003; Roblyer & McKenzie, 2000) others claim there are additional qualities necessary for successful online instruction. Cyrs (1997) through synthesis of a variety of studies concluded that distance instructors must be competent in the following:

1. Course planning and organization
2. Verbal and nonverbal presentation skills
3. Collaborative teamwork
4. Questioning strategies
5. Subject matter expertise
6. Involving students and coordinating their activities at field sites
7. Basic learning theories
8. Knowledge of the distance learning field
9. Design of study guides correlated with the technology
10. Graphic design and visual thinking

Additionally, Easton (2003) noted that a successful online instructor must also consider "new paradigms for thinking about time and space for teaching" (p. 101). To combat these obstacles, and prepare teachers with the instructional competencies for teaching online, states need to provide ways to inform all stakeholders of the urgency to provide online instruction, and establish efficient and effective ways to provide pre- and in-service teachers with the knowledge and skills necessary to teach in this environment. Teacher education programs and professional development providers must take the lead in this initiative.

How Did We Transition?

The Educational Technology plan includes five goals addressing learning, assessment, teaching, infrastructure, and productivity (U.S. Department of Education, 2010), with a central focus of online and virtual learning, and encourages schools to embrace this form of educational change. Teachers can no longer teach with tradition teaching tools. These goals directly affect the direction, performance, and organization and planning of TED and professional development (PD) programs throughout the U.S. These specialists and professionals need to be prepared and equipped to effectively instruct the pre- and in-service teachers in their programs how to teach in an online environment using the current and emerging technologies, while simultaneously teaching them appropriate online instructional strategies and activities. The plan stresses:

Just as technology is at the core of virtually every aspect of our daily lives and work, we must leverage it to provide engaging and powerful learning experiences, content, and resources and assessments that measure student achievement in more complete, authentic, and meaningful ways (U.S. Department of Education, 2010, p. v).

The questions then are: How do we leverage the current technology in educational environments? Which technologies do we use to provide the most engaging and authentic learning experiences? How do we prepare teachers to teach in and online environment with the latest technology tools?

One model created to prepare pre-service teachers for online instruction is the Teacher Education Goes Into Virtual Schooling (TEGIVS) model. A consortium of TED programs, led by Iowa State University, created the model that provides examples of effective online instruction in K-12 settings "so that pre-service teachers may study the whole educational process and develop their own reflective practice" (Davis & Roblyer, 2005, p. 402). The initial findings from the program suggest that the TEGIVS model can "influence future educators' thinking about teaching and learning in the 21st century" (Davis, et al., 2007). Wayne State University implemented the TEGIVS materials into a graduate level course of in-service teachers and administrators, titled *Internet in the K-12 Classroom,* and also found the materials to be effective in providing educators experience with K-12 online learning (Barbour & Unger, 2009).

A CASE: ONE PROFESSOR'S TRANSITION TO ONLINE TEACHING

The following is a vignette of a research study. A professor at an urban Midwest university, who teaches in a graduate instructional technology program in the college of education, knew that it would not be long until the mandates from the college would impact her face-to-face teaching. Like so many other professors, she was already using the university's learning management system (LMS), Blackboard, for posting articles and support materials that accompanied class lectures, but she had never instructed or facilitated class in an online environment. Before preparing her course schedules and syllabi for the fall 2009 semester, she looked at various online teaching

methods. There were numerous options for her to consider. To help her choose the optimum method she developed a list of questions:

Will all instruction for the course be delivered in the online environment?
Which technology tools will I use for instructing in the online environment?
Which instructional strategies and activities can I implement in the online environment?

Answering these questions assisted in preparing the syllabi and constructing a schedule for the course. It also provided a starting point for designing the instructional activities.

Will all Instruction for the Course be Delivered in the Online Environment?

As a novice to online instruction, the professor knew she was not ready to teach entirely in the online environment. The method she thought would be most beneficial to her and her students was blended instruction. Blended instruction has many different names, including, hybrid, distributed, distance, or flexible instruction (Mason & Rennie, 2008). Oliver & Trigwell (2005) considered the term, blended instruction, to be ill-defined. They describe the three most commonly used definitions to include:

the integrated combination of traditional learning with web-based online approaches (drawing on the work of Harrison);
the combination of media and tools employed in an e-learning environment; and
the combination of a number of pedagogic approaches, irrespective of learning technology use (drawing on the work of Driscoll) (as cited in Oliver & Trigwell, 2005, p. 17).

In this case, blended is referenced as a style of teaching where the class sometimes meets face-to-face, and other times meets in an online environment. The blended approach is often beneficial to both the professor and students because it allows them to ease into online teaching and learning. The face-to-face meetings at the beginning of the semester allow others to meet and interact in a learning environment that is familiar to them. Conducting class online just a few weeks out of the semester allows the professor to practice using the features of the LMS. It also provides an avenue for shifting the time and space paradigm competency discussed by Easton (2003). This professor blended five online classes into each of the two fifteen week courses that met once a week for 3.5 hours. She scheduled the online weeks to fall approximately every third week; i.e. the classes met face-to-face for the first two weeks of class, then met online. They reconvened face-to-face for weeks four and five, and then online.

Which Technology Tools Will I use for Instructing in the Online Environment?

The university where the professor teaches uses the LMS, Blackboard Version 9.0, and prefers their professors use this for delivering and facilitating online instruction. Blackboard provides an online location where professors can post documents, such as Power Point files that accompany lectures, assignment documents in Word, PDF's of reading materials and a variety of other course materials. There is a discussion board and email feature that can be used for interaction between students and professor. Blackboard is a technology tool that she had previous experience using, and assumed her students did as well. Her experiences, however, was with posting and retrieving documents and sending emails on the system; she had never used any of the other features, including the discussion board.

When teaching in an online environment, whether fully or blended, the teacher needs to be easily accessible to the students to meet the need of traditional office hours. For example, if a professor teaches in the face-to-face environment they are required to have office hours during each week, so students can schedule appointments to meet and discuss the course, or any other issues. During the online weeks, the professor needed to make sure she was available during the set office hours, so she scheduled to be available virtually. The university LMS system supported Wimba Version 6, where the professor could log into a course Blackboard site and interact through chat or sound with students to conduct virtual office hours.

Which Instructional Strategies and Activities can I Implement in the Online Environment?

When deciding which online instructional strategies and activities to implement, the professor needed to make an initial decision: would activities be synchronous (students and instructor meet online at a designated time) or asynchronous (students work independently online during a time that works best for them)? Thinking of her student population, those with full-time jobs during the day, most with families, and graduate students who need to be able to construct thoughtful and detailed responses to the course materials, asynchronous appeared to be the best approach for the courses. She chose online discussions; the most commonly used instructional practice in higher education online courses (Mason & Rennie, 2008). During the online instructional weeks, the professor decided she would post two discussion prompts on the discussion board in Blackboard, which centered on the readings for that week. Students were required to respond in detail to both prompts. Students were also required to respond to two other students' postings. This activity would allow the students to reflect on the reading materials and compose a scholarly response. It also provided an avenue for dialogue about the content between the students and the professor. The professor set a time frame for completing the responses: seven days for responding to the two prompts and the responses to two of their classmates' postings. She felt this would allow the students enough time to read and digest the readings, develop an in-depth response, and compose thoughtful responses to their classmates. This structure would also provide her sufficient time to develop a quality response to each of their postings.

Implementation of Blended Instruction

The professor began the blended approach to instruction by meeting with her students for the first two weeks of the semester face-to-face in the classroom. The third week of class was held online. Students responded to the two discussion prompts she developed and posted in Blackboard, and to two other students' postings. The professor had an extremely difficult time reading the responses because of the design of the Blackboard discussion board; it only allowed her to read one student posting at a time. She thought that if she was having a difficult time reading and responding to all of the posts that the students may be experiencing the same frustration. The virtual office hours for the online week were also a huge disappointment for the professor; no one signed into Wimba to discuss the readings or pose any questions. She gathered feedback from the students during the next face-to-face class, which exposed their frustration. Students explained similar feelings of the difficulty in reading and following the posts in Blackboard; the environment was not cohesive to support a clear understanding of the different posts. Coupling her frustration with that of the students, the professor decided to alter the next online class requirement. For the next online week, students had ten days to respond to the postings, instead of seven, and were only required to respond to one other student instead of two. Again the professor posted two discussion prompts related to the week's readings. Again, no

students showed in Wimba for the virtual office hours. While she did not know the students feelings about the new requirements for the online postings, she did know that this process was not only time consuming, but was also not engaging. She found the discussion board in Blackboard's standard links flat and not cohesive. During the face-to-face class following the second online week, through student feedback, it became apparent that the timeframe and amount of postings required of the student was not the impacting factor of frustration; it was the technology tool, Blackboard. At this point it was imperative for the professor to change the frustrating external factor, the LMS, Blackboard, in order to prevent reduction in learner motivation (Keller, 2009) throughout the rest of the course. The instructor knew her students were not only learning with an LMS system for this class, but as educators would most likely teach using some type of LMS system in the future. Soliciting their recommendations as knowledgeable professionals was essential to maintain their engagement and improve this process, so she asked for student suggestions on which technology tool they would like to use for the remaining online learning weeks. One student suggested the social networking tool NING[i]. The students and professor agreed to give it a try.

SOCIAL NETWORKING TOOL NING

Why the NING?

Along with LMS' like Blackboard, other technology tools for facilitating online instruction are Web 2.0 tools. These tools, such as blogs, wikis, social bookmarking, and social networking sites are used by people in all aspects of society for communicating and collaborating on information that is of interest to them. People without computer programming experience can contribute their thoughts, ideas, and feelings directly to the World

Wide Web, where others can read and comment on their posted material.

Studies conducted between 2005 and 2008 demonstrate that 90% of adolescents between the ages of 12 and 17 were the largest and fastest growing group of users of the Internet and that most go online daily or several times a day, mostly from home (as cited in Greenhow, Robelia, & Hughes, 2009). Students, roughly 55%, are using Web 2.0 tools that provide an opportunity to contribute and share content with friends on the Internet on a regular basis, some devoting 9hrs per week to social networking (as cited in Greenhow, Robelia, & Hughes, 2009). While students are using and mastering these tools outside of education (U.S. Department of Education, 2004), teachers have not yet shifted their teaching to incorporate these new forms of communication (Levin, Arafeh, Lenhart, & Rainie, 2002; Sewlyn, 2006). The U.S. Department of Education (2004) claims that, "Today's students, of almost any age, are far ahead of their teachers in computer literacy" (p. 10). Students believe that integrating Web 2.0 tools into education would increase their engagement and preparedness (as cited in Greenhow, Robelia, & Hughes, 2009). The National Council of Teachers for English (NCTE) recommends that teachers, "explore technologies students are using outside of class and finding ways to incorporate them into teaching" (National Council of Teachers of English, n.d.). This is a key issue regarding the importance of incorporating Web 2.0 tools into the classroom. Students are learning how to use these tools on their own without any guidance or direction as teachers are not teaching students how to use these tools appropriately.

How?

In the example described in this chapter, the professor and students decided to use the Web 2.0 social networking tool NING to facilitate the remaining four online weeks of the blended course. The first step for the professor was to create a NING Network. To do so, she had to visit the NING website (http://www.ning.com/), and follow the steps for creating a network. She created two networks; one for each course she was teaching that semester. When creating the network, she had to decide whether or not to make the network public or private. When a NING network is public, anyone can search for that NING network and join it as a member; if it is private, the creator of it must approve the request for a person to join and become a member. This professor wanted her networks to be private. She felt that this protected her intellectual property of the course material, and also kept students' responses from being exposed to the world. Once the networks were created, she emailed the students the network site address. Students were then required to visit the site, create an account, and request to become a member of the site. The professor received email notifications that someone wanted to join the network, and she accepted the requests in order for the students to become members of the site. If someone requested to join the network that is not a student, the creator of the NING network, in this case the professor had the option to deny membership to the network. As the creator of the NING network sites, the professor had the ability to choose what features she wanted to use. She reflected on the needs to the students and the course materials and created the "home page" of each site to include a discussion forum, latest activities, events, chat, photos, videos, groups and blogs (Figure 1). The NING structure allowed this novice technology professor to simply click and drag each feature to the place on the homepage she wanted each to be displayed. At the end, she simply clicked OK, and the NING was set-up and launched.

The NING is a social networking tool similar to other social networking sites like Facebook and Myspace. Student members had their own profiles that they created during their account set up (Figure 2). Usually, a profile contains a picture of the member, and some general information

Figure 1. Main (Home) page: Shows latest activity, event announcements, discussion board, blogs, and chat

about them including: gender, location and birthday. They can also upload personal pictures and videos, and can change the background of their profile. Customizing their profiles provided each student member the opportunity to express their personality, and gave them a sense of ownership of their page. The professor was immediately impressed with the NING. She had never used a social networking site before, and instantly began using the features that were available: she uploaded a picture, changed the layout of her page to a design that appealed to her, and created a welcome message to the students.

Instructional Activities on the NING

Discussion Forum

After all students created accounts and the professor accepted the students as members, it was time to start using the tool for online educational activities. The professor did not change the online discussion format; she created two initial discussion prompts in the discussion forum features, and the students were to respond to each discussion and one other student's postings (Figure 3). The NING's discussion forum is similar to the discussion board in Blackboard, but after using the NING for the third online class, the professor and the students found it much easier to use than Blackboard.

The major benefit was in the ease of reading the responses. For example, when students responded to one of the discussion questions, all of their responses were visible on one page. In Blackboard, users could only view one student posting at a time. This tool allowed for a better visual linkage and cohesiveness of the postings, which enabled the discussion to flow similar to a conversation. Another added benefit of the discus-

Figure 2. Profile page: Each member personalizes their own space with pictures, information, and background template

sion forum in the NING compared with Blackboard was that each posting was accompanied by the student profile picture (Figure 4). This provided members a way to associate the posting with the picture of who was communicating the thought, which added more personalization and uniqueness to the post.

Latest Activities

On the main page of the NING is a column called "Latest Activities." This column is constantly updated on the most recent postings and activities that have occurred. Every time a user signed in they could view the latest activities column to see who had been posting different items and when the item was posted. This allowed students to be instantly updated on course communications and activities.

Events

NING has an Events feature where the professor posted dates and times when assignments were due. This feature was also used by members to post other events that may have been of interest to the class, such as, a presentation on or off campus related to the subject of the course, a social event happening in the community, or a meeting for an organization that may relate to the students' field of study. The Events feature provided another opportunity to build a community among the members and increase interaction.

Email

Emailing members is another feature available to NING members. Individual or group emails can be exchanged to other members on the network. The NING mass email feature was similar to Blackboard, but the professor found the ease of

Figure 3. Discussion forum: Location for students to respond to instructor's questions and place for sharing other information

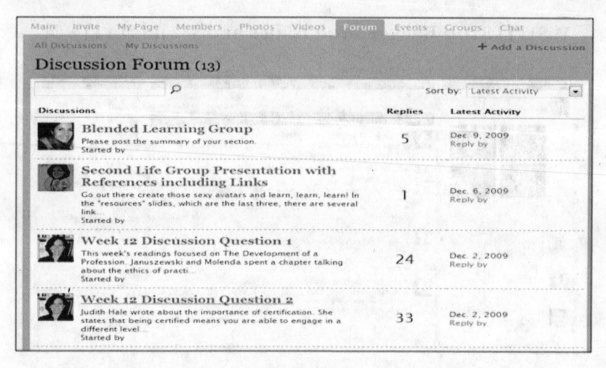

sending a mass email in the NING along with visual elements of the email quite different. The professor began using email to touch base with her students throughout the course, sending motivating messages and updates on important issues occurring in the community aligning with the course content. The messages were colorful, easy to send and read. Students also used it to email other students, or the professor, a specific question that they did not feel comfortable enough asking on the main page of the network for everyone to view.

Chat

Instead of having to sign into another system, like Wimba, NING provides a chat area for synchronous chatting (Figure 5). When a member is signed into the network, their picture appears on the chat feature, and is accompanied by a little

dot. When the dot is green, it means the person is there and available to chat. If the dot is yellow, the person is signed into the network, but has not been active for some time, so they may not be there to chat. The professor used the chat feature for office hours. During the online weeks she would sign into the NING and be available to chat synchronously with students. Another advantage of this feature is that students could log into the network and if another student was available they could instantly chat and ask a question if they needed assistance or wanted to discuss, in real-time, the weekly readings.

Photos

Not only can members post profile and personal photos of themselves, they can post any photos. Students in this case started taking pictures of

Figure 4. All responses include pictures to help familiarize the readers who is posting, increase interaction and deeper understanding of each person's post; helps personalize the response

the face-to-face activities and posting them on the NING (Figure 6). The posted photos could be used for studying for exams, and also be used as reference points when completing the online discussions (Figure 7). Through the posting of the face-to-face class activities online, the students were truly blending both learning environments and contributing to the value of the course content.

Videos

The content area for this case was instructional technology. The professor incorporated another Web 2.0 activity into one of the online weeks. The students were to attend to the assigned readings, just as previous weeks, but this time instead of simply posting a response to the discussion questions, students had to search YouTube, TeacherTube, or another online video source, for a video that applied one of the learning theories that was covered in the assigned weekly readings. Students then needed to post, or embed, the video on the

NING, and provide a description of the learning theory being demonstrated in the video. After all of the videos were posted, the professor used an application on the NING to create a poll for the all of the students. Students were then required to vote for the video which best applied the learning theory discussed. This activity was beneficial in a few ways. It created an activity to use more Web 2.0 tools. It also showed students that they could also post videos to the NING. Using the poll feature was a way to ensure that the students had watched the other student videos.

Groups

One of the professor's blended courses had a group project to complete. The NING provided a way for group members to collaborate on their group projects from a distance. Groups can be created inside the network by any member, and can also be set to private (Figures 8 and 9). For example, one group was doing a presentation on

Figure 5. Chat: Used for instant student and instructor communication. Instructor used this for office hours

Second Life, so they created a group on the network called Second Life. They only people that had access to it were the members of that group. Some groups found it beneficial to include the professor in the group in case they needed some direction or advice for their project, while other groups decided not to include her. The groups feature provided a personalized and private space for sharing documents and ideas about the group project while saving the trip to campus and trying to find a meeting time that works best for busy professionals.

Blogs

Another Web 2.0 tool feature integrated into the NING network is blogs. Blogs, short for web logs, are similar to a personal diary or journal, and was one of the first Web 2.0 tools. Each member has their own blog attached to their page, and can post anything on it. Maybe they came across a certain article or book and wanted to write a synopsis of the writing on their blog to share with others.

The Overall Experience of the NING

In this case, the NING proved to be a more conducive environment, over Blackboard, for the professor and the students, due to its visual appeal, ease in use, and increased ability to interact and communicate. An additional benefit of using the NING was the opportunity for the professor to model the use of a Web 2.0 social networking tool for future instructional designers and educators.

Figure 6. Photos: Students took pictures of class activities and posted them on the NING for review for exams and discussion posts

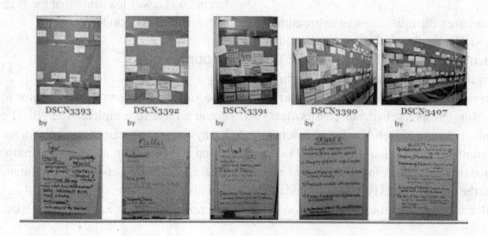

Figure 7. The photos of class activities were a benefit for when students were working during the online weeks

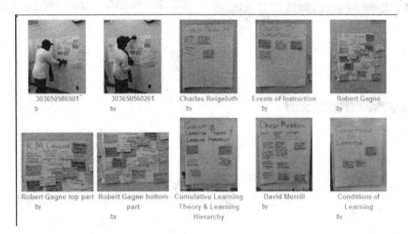

IMPLICATIONS FOR TEACHER EDUCATION AND PROFESSIONAL DEVELOPMENT PROGRAMS

The case study described throughout this chapter demonstrates the importance of the ongoing interaction between professors and students when blending face-to-face and online instruction. Communication assists in student engagement, altering the learning process based on student need, and provides the opportunity for the students to add their own input and create value for the course.

Mandates and Incentives for TED Faculty and PD Providers to use These Tools for Instruction

Using the Web 2.0 social networking tool NING for teaching pre- and in-service teachers in TED and PD programs meets the NCTE's recommendation by providing and modeling the use of a Web 2.0 tool for instructional activities, and equips the teachers with a tool that students find engaging outside of the classroom and can use for their future educational purposes.

Social networking tools are free, or fairly cheap to use, and students are familiar with the layout

Figure 8. Groups: NING allows groups to create their own space and provide access to specific members

Figure 9. Groups: Students used the group feature to collaborate on group projects

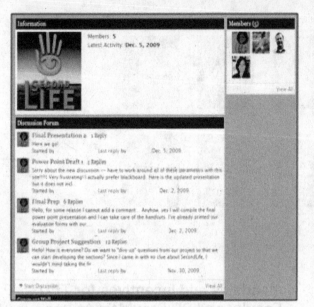 

and structure of these tools, often because they are personally using other similar social network tools for personal use. This reduces the amount of time needed to educate students on how to use the tool. Additional specific benefits include:

- Educators can invite authors, politicians, artists, and other professionals and experts to join the NING and interact with the students
- The instructor has control over membership, she doesn't need permission to add an external person to class as with closed learning management systems such as Blackboard
- Web 2.0 tools are emerging technologies and educators need to be able to adapt to the new technologies and be equipped with the skills and ability to adjust and adapt them into instruction to meet student needs
- Use of these tools assists in explaining and modeling online/virtual schooling roles: facilitator, designer, and instructor

It is imperative for educators, in both K-12 and higher education to integrate the use of these tools into their instruction. In order for pre- and in-service teachers to be ready to utilize Web 2.0 tools for instructional purposes, TED faculty and PD providers need to model the appropriate use of these tools, and provide effective and efficient training on integrating the tools into curricular activities. This case illustrates a professor who modeled the benefits of engaging student feedback, accepted the challenge of learning a new tool and as a result improved student communication and learning.

It is the job of educators to properly educate students on the skills needed to effectively use Web 2.0 tools. These tools are being used in higher education, so K-12 students need to be instructed on them now. In order for K-12 students to learn how to utilize these tools in an educational and productive way, and not just for socializing with friends and relatives, pre- and in-service teachers need to be trained on the technical skills of using the tools. Beyond the technical skills, teachers also need to be trained on "why" using these technologies in their instruction is important to the current and future success of their students. TED programs and PD providers must also teach teachers how to integrate Web 2.0 tools with their classroom curriculum. In order for students to be successful in a globalized economy and educational system, they will need to learn how to leverage these tools for their benefit. They will need highly developed skills to effectively use these tools for communication and collaboration.

Learning and teaching in an online environment requires high levels of responsibility and self management. Teachers must remember that it is their duty to provide timely feedback to student postings and questions that are received electronically. It is their duty to communicate assignment timelines, instructions, requirements, and expectations appropriately. Educators, especially those involved in TED programs and PD must stick to following these items in order to appropriately model online instructional behaviors to their students. K-12 teachers must witness and participate in sound online instructional practice in order to benefit their students. Students use these tools in their personal life, but it is the responsibility of the teachers to design appropriate learning strategies and activities that will increase their digital responsibility, self-management, and online behaviors.

REFERENCES

Allen, I. E., & Seaman, J. (2008). *Staying the course: Online education in the United States, 2008*. The Sloan Consortium. Retrieved from http://sloanconsortium.org/sites/default/files/staying_the_course-2.pdf

Barbour, M. K., & Unger, K. (2009). Challenging teachers' preconceptions, misconceptions, and concerns of virtual schooling. In I. Gibson, et al. (Eds.), *Proceedings of the Annual Conference of the Society for Information Technology and Teacher Education* (pp. 785-790). Norfolk, VA: AACE.

Blackboard. (n.d.). *Blackboard, version 9.0 service pack 5* [Web-based course system]. Washington, DC: Blackboard Inc.

Cyrs, T. E. (1997). Competence in teaching at a distance. *New Directions for Teaching and Learning*, (71): 15–18. doi:10.1002/tl.7102

Davis, N., Roblyer, M. D., Ferdig, R., Schoeny, Z., Ellis, R., Demiraslan, Y., & Compton, L. K. L. (2007). Creating real tools & curriculum to prepare virtual teachers. In R. Carlsen et al. (Eds.), *Proceedings of Society for Information Technology & Teacher Education International Conference 2007* (pp. 281-285). Chesapeake, VA: AACE.

Davis, N. E., & Roblyer, M. D. (2005). Preparing teachers for the "schools that technology built": Evaluation of a program to train teachers for virtual schooling. *Journal of Research on Technology in Education, 37*(4), 399–409.

Easton, S. (2003). Clarifying the instructor's role in online distance learning. *Communication Education, 52*(2), 87–105. doi:10.1080/03634520302470

Greenhow, C., Robelia, B., & Hughes, J. E. (2009). Learning, teaching, and scholarship in a digital age: Web 2.0 and classroom research: What path should we take now? *Educational Researcher, 38*(4), 246–259. doi:10.3102/0013189X09336671

International Society for Technology in Education. (2010). *The ISTE national educational technology standards (NETS-T) and Performance Indicators for Teachers*. Retrieved from http://www.iste.org/Content/NavigationMenu/NETS/ForTeachers/2008Standards/NETS_T_Standards_Final.pdf

Johnson, L., Smith, R., Levine, A., & Haywood, K. (2010). *2010 horizon report: K-12 edition.* Austin, TX: The New Media Consortium.

Keller, J. M. (2009). *Motivational design for learning and performance: The ARCS model approach.* New York, NY: Springer.

Levin, D., Arafeh, S., Lenhart, A., & Rainie, L. (2002). *The digital disconnect: The widening gap between Internet-savvy students and their schools.* Washington, DC: Pew Internet and American Life Project.

Mason, R., & Rennie, F. (2008). *E-learning and social networking handbook: Resources for higher education.* New York, NY: Routledge.

Michigan Department of Education. (2006). *Michigan merit curriculum guidelines: Online learning.* Lansing, MI: Author. Retrieved from http://www.michigan.gov/documents/mde/Online10.06_final_175750_7.pdf

Michigan State Board of Education. (2008). *Standards for the preparation of teachers in educational technology: NP endorsement.* Retrieved from http://webcache.googleusercontent.com/search?q=cache:sW_hO6R1eQQJ:www.michigan.gov/documents/mde/EducTech_NP_SBEApprvl.5-13-08.A_236954_7.doc+Standards+for+the+Preparation+of+Teachers+in+Educational+Technology+(NP+Endorsement)&cd=2&hl=en&ct=clnk&gl=us&client=firefox-a

Oliver, M., & Trigwell, K. (2005). Can blended learning be redeemed? *E-learning, 2*(1), 17–26.

Picciano, A. G., & Seaman, J. (2009). *K-12 online learning: A survey of U.S. school district administrators.* The Sloan Foundation. Retrieved from http://sloanconsortium.org/publications/survey/pdf/k-12_online_learning_2008.pdf

Sewlyn, N. (2006). Exploring the digital disconnect between net-savvy students and their schools. *Learning, Media and Technology, 31*(1), 5–17. doi:10.1080/17439880500515416

U.S. Department of Education. (2004). *National educational technology plan. Toward a new golden age in American education: How the internet, the law and today's students are revolutionizing expectations.* Washington, DC: U.S. Department of Education. Retrieved from http://www2.ed.gov/about/offices/list/os/technology/plan/2004/plan.pdf

U.S. Department of Education. (2010). *National educational technology plan. Transforming American education: Learning powered by technology.* Washington, DC: U.S. Department of Education. Retrieved from http://www.ed.gov/sites/default/files/NETP-2010-final-report.pdf

Watson, J. F., Gemin, B., Ryan, J., & Wicks, M. (2009). *Keeping pace with K–12 online learning: A review of state-level policy and practice.* Naperville, IL: Learning Point Associates. Retrieved from http://www.kpk12.com/downloads/KeepingPace09-fullreport.pdf

Wimba. (n.d.). *Wimba, version 6* [Online Conferencing Software]. New York, NY: Wimba, Inc.

ADDITIONAL READING

Crane, B. E. (2009). *Using Web 2.0 tools in the K-12 classroom.* New York: Neal-Schuman Publishers, Inc.

Duncan, H. E., & Barnett, J. (2009). Learning to teach online: What works for pre-service teachers. *Journal of Educational Computing Research, 40*(3), 357–376. doi:10.2190/EC.40.3.f

Hadley, J. (2010, April 8). How Ning social networks can improve university classes. Retrieved from http://lava7.com/2010/04/how-ning-social-networks-can-improve-university-classes/

Junco, R., & Timm, D. M. (Eds.). (2008). *Using emerging technologies to enhance student engagement*. San Francisco: Jossey-Bass.

Karabulut, A., Lindstrom, D., Braet, D., & Niederhauser, D. S. (2009). Student level of commitment and engagement with Ning as a learning management system. In I. Gibson et al. (Eds.), *Proceedings of Society for Information Technology & Teacher Education International Conference 2009* (pp. 2564-2569). Chesapeake, VA: AACE.

Martinez Aleman, A. M., & Wartman, K. L. (2009). *Online social networking on campus: Understanding what matters in student culture*. New York: Routledge.

Rice, K., & Dawley, L. (2009). The status of professional development for K-12 online teachers: Insights and implications. *Journal of Technology and Teacher Education, 17*(4), 523–545.

Vrasidas, C., & Glass, G. V. (Eds.). (2005). *Preparing teachers to teach with technology*. USA: Information Age Publishing, Inc.

KEY TERMS AND DEFINITIONS

Blended Instruction: Style of teaching where the class sometimes meets face-to-face, and other times meets in an online environment.

Online Learning: Style of learning where the student receives instruction in a different place than the instructor through the Internet. If instructor and student are engaging simultaneously at the same time it is referred to as synchronous. If the student is engaging in the instruction at a different time than the instructor it is referred to as asynchronous.

Professional Development: Organized instruction aimed at increasing the knowledge and skills of educators.

Social Networking Tools: Customizable personal spaces online where people with a common interest can share ideas and communicate on various topics.

Web 2.0 Tools: Web 2.0 tools are Internet-based tools that allow everyday users of the Web to interact with others by creating and sharing thoughts and ideas directly on the web without having any computer programming experience.

ENDNOTE

[i] It should be noted that at the time the professor created these NINGs for these two courses, it was a free service. Starting in July 2009 NING began charging a fee to create a NING network. Currently there are three different plans ranging in price from $2.95 per month to $49.95 per month. Each of the plans have different features available; the more you pay, the more features you and the members of your NING network will have access to. At the time of this writing, educators in both the K-12 and higher education arenas are can apply for a grant to have their NING network paid for by an educational software company. The grant will only cover the $2.95 plan which does not provide access to all of the features.

Chapter 17
ePortfolio Integration in Teacher Education Programs:
Does Context Matter from a Student Perspective?

Albert D. Ritzhaupt
University of Florida, USA

Michele A. Parker
University of North Carolina Wilmington, USA

Abdou Ndoye
Qatar University, Qatar

ABSTRACT

Though ePortfolios have grown in acceptance by teacher education programs across the United States, there still remain many questions regarding whether the tools are meeting student and teacher education program needs. This chapter will address this concern by first describing ePortfolios within teacher education. Next, the chapter will present a stakeholder interaction model and identify the individuals involved in an ePortfolio system. Then, a series of integration questions will be highlighted from a teacher education perspective. Two teacher education programs' ePortfolio initiatives are evaluated using the Electronic Portfolio Student Perspective Instrument (EPSPI) (Ritzhaupt, Singh, Seyferth, & Dedrick, 2008) in relation to several integration characteristics. Finally, recommendations to teacher education programs are made.

INTRODUCTION

ePortfolios have moved to the forefront of teacher preparation programs across the United States. Wheeler (2003) defines an ePortfolio as "a collection of purposefully-organized artifacts that support backward and forward reflection to augment and assess growth over time" (Wheeler, 2003, p. 2). There are several possible explanations for the widespread adoption. One explanation is the widespread acceptance of constructivism whereby preservice teachers learn to use tools for learning and are guided by self-discovery (Meeus,

DOI: 10.4018/978-1-4666-0014-0.ch017

Questier, & Derks, 2006; Strudler & Wetzel, 2005a). A second explanation is the ease of accessibility and use of information and communication technology (Meeus, Questier, & Derks, 2006). And yet a third explanation is the organizational uses of ePortfolios which emphasize documenting preservice teachers ability to meet curricular standards for assessment and accountability (e.g., accreditation) (Ritzhaupt et. al., 2008; Ritzhaupt, Ndoye & Parker, 2010).

EPORTFOLIOS IN TEACHER EDUCATION

How do we describe an ePortfolio in a teacher education program? This question is one that cannot be completely answered at this time as ePortfolios are still in their early years of integration into teacher education programs (Strudler & Wetzel, 2005). What we do know, however, is that ePortfolios have key purposes for pre-service teachers, the primary stakeholders, and other stakeholders. ePortfolios can serve as learning systems for personal and professional development, employment portfolios, and as tools for their organizational uses (Hartnell-Young & Morriss, 1999; Ritzhaupt et. al., 2008). While the structure and nature of ePortfolios vary depending on its purpose, the different expectations of stakeholders (e.g., field-experience coordinators, department chairs, students, hiring officials and other school administrators) pose an indefinite challenge. The reality of ePortfolios fulfilling multiple functions is questionable because there are times when one function may conflict with another.

From a pre-service and in-service teacher perspective, ePortfolios serve in three ways - known as the three "R's" (Acker, 2005; Lorenzo & Ittelson, 2005): representation, reflection and revision. Representation, the first "R", refers to the use of ePortfolios as a means of documenting student products and skills acquired over time. The second "R", reflection, emphasizes how self-critique and

feedback from other stakeholders can enrich the learning experience. And finally, revision, which is the third "R", is when the pre-service /or in-service teacher takes the step to improve his/her products or skills using the feedback or critiques received from other stakeholders. In this manner, ePortfolios serve as a learning system.

ePortfolios can also serve as an employment portfolio. In a survey conducted by Temple, Allan, and Temple (2003), results indicated that students and career professionals both agreed that the ePortfolio was an effective way to address key selection criteria questions. Additionally, employers responding to the survey revealed experiencing a missing link between candidates' statements of what they can do and their abilities to actually do it, and that the ePortfolio can fill that void by showing evidences of teacher candidates' competencies through artifacts, video and other digital means. Thus, ePortfolios also provide an employment capacity, if properly designed to reach the hiring officials (e.g., principals).

Finally, ePortfolios also serve organizational uses, which can be plentiful. Literature illustrates a number of organizational purposes, including meeting requirements from accrediting boards (Siemens, 2005; Strudler & Wetzel, 2005); meeting states' approved technology standards (Curts, Yanes, & McWright, 2003); formative and summative evaluation of a teacher education program (Barrett & Knezek, 2003); and aiding in the tenure, promotion and review process (Ritzhaupt & Singh, 2006). The organizational uses refer to things that directly benefit the teacher education program as oppose to the primary user - the pre-service teacher.

STAKEHOLDER INTERACTION MODEL

Since ePortfolios are both instructional and informational tools that can be used for a variety of purposes, their audience is diverse. University

Figure 1. Stakeholder interaction model

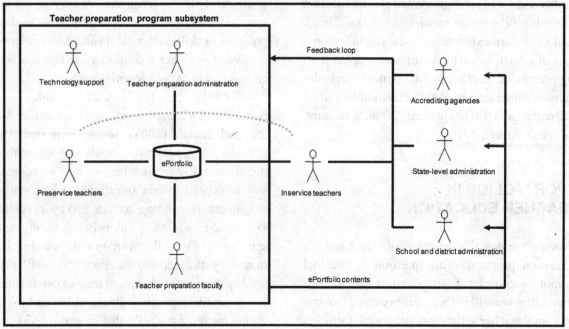

faculty, university support staff, university administration, school and school district administrators, accrediting agencies, and state-level administration are among those who have vested interest in ePortfolios (Campbell, Cignetti, Melenyzer, Nettles, & Wyman, 2007; Johnson & Rose, 1997; Ritzhaupt et. al., 2008). The various stakeholders are presented in the stakeholder interaction model in Figure 1.

Pre-service teachers create ePortfolios as part of their program of study. Some teacher education programs require students to contribute to their ePortfolios from the beginning of their programs. By adding artifacts over time, students are encouraged to reflect on their learning and coursework by documenting their development. In other instances, students compose their ePortfolio as an exit requirement during their student-teaching internship. Regardless of type of implementation, students use ePortfolios to organize and reflect on artifacts such as lesson plans and classroom management techniques (Strudler & Wetzel,

2005). Within the teacher preparation program subsystem, faculty members evaluate ePortfolios to determine whether or not students or programs are meeting teaching standards and to identify where improvements are necessary (Strudler & Wetzler, 2005). ePortfolios can help with program evaluation, which may lead to new courses, revised syllabi, or policy changes.

Technology support staff within the university support both the faculty and students in creating and using their ePortfolios. The technology support staff represent instructional technologists, instructional designers, information technology specialists and many more titles all of which contribute to the integration of ePortfolios within a teacher education program. Meanwhile, teacher preparation administration (e.g., field-experience coordinators, advisors, department chairs, and deans) use ePortfolios to track student's academic progress. When an ePortfolio is composed early, it can be used to introduce the candidate to the cooperating teacher and administrators during field experiences and student teaching and may help identify focal areas during these experiences (Campbell, Cignetti, Melenyzer, Nettles, & Wyman, 2007).

During their search for employment, pre-service teachers often use their ePortfolios as marketing tools by providing a website URL that hosts the material or providing a DVD or CD (Strawhecker, Messersmith, & Balcom, 2007) to principals, teachers, superintendents or school board members (Strudler & Wetzel, 2005; Campbell et. al., 2007). K-12 administrators may request ePortfolios in the application process or interview stage because they show evidences not easily displayed through other means (e.g., video of teaching) (Strawhecker, Messersmith, & Balcom, 2007). Outside of the teacher education subsystem, pre-service teachers become in-service teachers upon gainful employment. Upon employment, supervisory staff may require in-service teachers to maintain an ePortfolio to chart their professional development. ePortfolios may also be used to make tenure and promotion decisions (Campbell et. al., 2007).

Accrediting agencies use ePortfolios to document student's knowledge, critical thinking, problem solving (Arter & Spandel, 1992) and 21st century skills (Campbell et. al., 2007; Barrett & Knezek, 2003; NETS for Teachers, 2008). Accrediting agencies view the ePortfolios and assessments connected to those ePortfolios as part of their comprehensive program accreditation. ePortfolio systems, like Chalk & Wire or TaskStream, provide comprehensive reporting utilities to facilitate this process. Used in this way, Schools and Colleges of Education use ePortfolios for formative and summative assessment (Barrett & Knezek, 2003). Data from ePortfolios can help state-level administration (e.g., State Boards of Education) assess the degree to which they are meeting their objectives. For instance, in certain states, ePortfolios are used for licensing purposes (Campbell et. al., 2007).

EPORTFOLIO INTEGRATION CONCERNS

ePortfolios used in a student-centered manner can serve three purposes: as learning systems for personal and professional development, employment portfolios, and as tools for organizational uses (Hartnell-Young & Morriss, 1999; Ritzhaupt et. al., 2008). The main challenge for teacher education programs is fulfilling these functionalities with the same ePortfolio. This will keep it appealing to all stakeholders so that benefits of the ePortfolio can be clearly communicated and highlighted for all partners (Strudler & Wetzel, 2008). Below are examples of general questions that teacher education may need to wrestle with in their efforts to fulfill the multiple functionalities of the ePortfolio.

What is the Purpose of Using the ePortfolio?

Teacher education programs have to grapple with choosing and clarifying the type and purpose of ePortfolio that will be used. ePortfolio can be used to store evidences or as a reflection and learning tool throughout a teacher candidate's program of study. As indicated by Hicks, Russo, Autrey, Gardner, Kabodian, and Edington (2007), the purpose of the ePortfolio will impact stakeholders' attitude and whether or not they will support and sustain it. In some cases the purpose of ePortfolio can be seen only as an add-on to a course, or as part of an external assessment initiative. As such, stakeholders (students and faculty members) may view it as an isolated event, a standalone product, which is disconnected from the program as a whole. The ePortfolio can, however, in other cases be conceived as a learning tool that helps students think critically about their learning, reflect on the work products, and provide faculty members with a means to assess their educational practices through the examination of their students' growth.

ePortfolio can clearly serve several purposes, but unfortunately, the purpose of ePortfolios in teacher education programs seem to be focusing more on treating it like an exit requirement to measure standards (Strudler & Wetzel, 2005). Instead, it could be a very appropriate tool for rich and sustained learning and growth for the students and an effective tool for hiring officials to judge a candidate's competencies. Wilhelm et. al. (2006) suggests that using the same ePortfolio system for student-centered purposes and for satisfying organizational uses such as program evaluation and accreditation is problematic. However, if the data are managed appropriately, assessment evidence can be extracted from student archival databases to create an electronic assessment system. Ideally, the electronic tool chosen supports both student and organizational purposes and does not influence the processes of depositing student work, reflection and feedback.

How to Assess Student Artifacts

Regardless of the purpose of the ePortfolio, there needs to be a streamlined and agreed upon set of criteria by which student artifacts and other ePortfolios content will be assessed and judged. Therefore, teacher education programs need to address early on questions related to what those criteria will be. What constitutes an acceptable artifact? Do we need to have designated artifact or do we let students choose their own artifacts? Is it a course level or a program level? Who will be responsible for checking and making sure content is appropriate? Is it going to be one faculty member or a pool of faculty members and if so how do we guarantee inter rater reliability? How frequently do we assess the ePortfolio? Are we looking at ePortfolio content for each course of the program or how do we select the courses that need to provide evidences of student learning and reflection and growth? All these questions need to be addressed in order to produce an assessment system that will provide stakeholders with reliable

and valid information they can use to address their ePortfolio interests.

How to Guarantee Technological Access

This question is at the heart of any ePortfolio initiative in teacher education. First, teacher education programs will have to select or develop a tool to support the ePortfolio initiative. Some of the challenges teacher education programs face in the integration of ePortfolio is to make sure students have enough technical support, and whether or not there is a system robust enough to facilitate student access at anytime and also to back up information to prevent data loss. Answers to these questions may also lead to the decision whether to use an open source or a commercial platform for ePortfolios. Strudler and Wetzel (2005) found that 24/7 access, ongoing support and data management capabilities as some of the main concerns teacher education programs face in integrating an ePortfolio. Another access point is whether or not cooperating teachers will have access to student intern's ePortfolios, which can facilitate discussions and be used to target experiential learning.

How to Aggregate and Disaggregate Data at the Different Levels

While individual programs and courses will be using an ePortfolio system to capture information, teacher education as a unit will also need to look a trends and information at an aggregated level. Therefore, a major concern for teacher education is the ability of an ePortfolio system to allow data mining at different levels (courses, program, and school wide). ePortfolio systems such as Taskstream (Taskstream, 2010) and Chalk & Wire (Chalk & Wire, 2010) provide the ability to aggregate at different levels of the organization. This capability will be mostly appealing to school wide committees and accrediting agencies. As Strudler and Wetzel (2005) point out, teacher

Table 1. Integration characteristics

Integration Characteristic	University One	University Two
Time of integration	Program-wide	Capstone course
Student artifact choice	Faculty selected	Student selected
Tool selection	Chalk & Wire	Taskstream
Duration of program	Two years	15-weeks
Authority	Faculty per course	Faculty supervisor
Level of support	Help desk	Tech support
Standards	Aligned to state	Aligned to INTASC and state
Accreditation	NCATE	NCATE

education programs can align course artifacts with standards from National Council for Accreditation of Teacher Education (NCATE) or Interstate New Teacher Assessment and Support Consortium (INTASC), for example, in order to aggregate their data at the unit level.

The questions raised above represent a sample of questions and concerns that teacher education programs will encounter in their efforts to integrate ePortfolios. These and other eventual questions will depend on the school/college of interest and the ultimate purpose of the ePortfolio. These questions and concerns are in no way the only ones to be dealt with, but they provide an initial set of considerations that must be addressed to successfully institutionalize an ePortfolio program.

TWO EPORTFOLIO INTEGRATION CONTEXTS

The ways in which ePortfolios are integrated into the curriculum are likely key factors in how they will be perceived by the students creating them. In this chapter, two universities involved with integrating ePortfolios into their teacher education programs were examined. There are eight criteria that are used to evaluate how two ePortfolio programs were integrated into teacher preparation programs. These criteria include time of integration, student artifact choice, tool

selection, duration of program, authority, level of support, standards, and accreditation. Table 1 shows the various criteria and relevant status for each of the universities involved. The purpose of the study was to examine ePortfolio use in two different contexts. The research question is: Do students' perceptions of "learning", "assessment", and "visibility" differ in each university context?

At university one, the ePortfolio initiative is integrated program-wide. That is, students starting in their junior year were required to submit artifacts to their ePortfolios from their various education courses. In contrast, at university two, the implementation was in a capstone course during students' field experiences in their final semester. Students were required to create their ePortfolios while simultaneously student teaching.

In terms of student choice of artifacts, at university one, faculty selected the various artifacts that students would submit to their ePortfolios. On the other hand, at university two, students were provided the flexibility in selecting the various artifacts they would include in their ePortfolios. Both institutions required that the artifacts be aligned with state standards and both institutions were seeking accreditation from the NCATE. At university one, the Chalk & Wire (Chalk & Wire, 2010) application was employed while at university two, TaskStream (Taskstream, 2010) was employed. Both applications provide students with a suite of tools to construct their ePortfolios; and reporting facilities.

METHOD

Participants

Four hundred twenty-eight participants from two public universities in the southeastern United States participated in this study. Two hundred twenty four participated from university one, and 204 participants from university two. Approximately 90% of the participants were female, which is typical for a teacher education program. Approximately 87% of the participants were pursuing a bachelor's degree, 12% a master's degree, and 1% were classified as non-degree seeking students. Of the ethnicity of the participants, 79% were classified as Caucasian/White, 6% were Hispanic/Latino, 4% were African American, and the remaining classified as Other. Participants had been using the ePortfolio system for an average of 10.79 (*SD*=4.48) months when responding to the survey.

Instrument

The instrument employed in this research is titled the *Electronic Portfolio Student Perspective Instrument* (EPSPI), which has been validated in previous studies (Ritzhaupt et. al., 2008; Ritzhaupt, Ndoye, & Parker, 2010). The EPSPI validly measures three internally consistent constructs from a student perspective: learning, assessment, and visibility. The learning factor refers to how a student perceives their ePortfolios as a viable tool to learning. The learning factor had a high degree of internal consistency reliability at α = .97. The assessment factor refers to how a student perceives their ePortfolio as a device to represent their learning and demonstrate their abilities. The assessment factor had a high degree of internal consistency reliability at α = .96. The visibility

factor involves students' perspectives of how various stakeholders viewing their ePortfolio makes them feel. The visibility factor also had a high degree of internal consistency reliability at α = .95.

Procedures

At both institutions, the instrument was made accessible in a web-based format. The researchers made arrangements to send a hyperlink to the instrument in an email encouraging student participants to respond to the survey. The data was collected during the Spring of 2006, Fall of 2008 and Spring of 2009 semesters. In each semester, the survey was available for a three-week period, and during this time, three emails were sent. Student participants were informed that the purpose of the research was to: (1) monitor the progress of the ePortfolio initiative, and (2) aid in the development integration of ePortfolios in teacher preparation programs. Participants were also informed that participation was voluntary and that their responses would be anonymous.

Data Analysis

Quantitative analyses of the data included descriptive analysis, internal consistency reliability analysis, and independent t-tests. T-tests were conducted to examine the differences across the context criteria. All quantitative analyses were conducted using SPSS© version 16. An alpha of .05 was used for all statistical tests.

RESULTS

The data results from the two universities are reported in the following sections, organized by construct. Subscale means and standard deviations are provided.

Table 2. Learning factor items by university

Items	University One		University Two	
	M	SD	M	SD
I would use an ePortfolio to help me develop my skills (e.g., word processing).	1.79	0.92	3.38	1.06
I would use an ePortfolio as a way to monitor my skills as they develop over time.	2.06	1.1	3.56	1.02
I would use an ePortfolio to help me develop my knowledge (e.g., European History).	1.77	0.91	3.12	1.10
I would use an ePortfolio as a way to monitor my knowledge as it develops over time.	2.16	1.19	3.53	1.01
I think viewing my peers' ePortfolios would be a valuable learning experience.	2.90	1.29	3.75	0.97
I would use an ePortfolio to guide my skill development.	2.12	1.06	3.51	0.96
I use my ePortfolio to learn from my mistakes.	1.90	0.95	3.35	1.00
I plan to continue to enhance my ePortfolio for life-long learning.	1.78	0.95	3.12	1.08
I would use an ePortfolio to guide my knowledge development.	2.01	1.03	3.42	1.02

Learning

Table 2 shows the mean and standard deviation for each item in the learning subscale. The subscale mean at university one is $M = 1.94$ ($SD = 0.84$) while the subscale mean for university two was $M = 3.37$ ($SD = 0.90$). There was a significant difference detected between university one and university two on the learning subscale at $t(419) = 16.88$, $p < .01$. Pre-service teachers within university two had overall higher perception of their ePortfolio as a viable tool for learning. University two required students to create their ePortfolio as part of a capstone experience as oppose to implementing within their entire program of study. The duration of the implementation in university two was 15-weeks as oppose to the two years within university one. It is possible that the type of implementation as well as the flexibility left for students to choose their own artifacts impacted student perceptions of learning here. However, future research will have to investigate the cause and effects between these items.

Assessment

Table 3 shows the mean and standard deviation for each item in the assessment subscale. The subscale mean at university one is $M = 2.50$ ($SD = 1.06$) while the subscale mean for university two was $M = 3.75$ ($SD = 0.87$). There was a significant difference detected between university one and university two on the assessment subscale at $t(411) = 13.15$, $p < .01$. Again, university two had overall higher perception, but this time in the use of an ePortfolio as an assessment tool. In the implementation at university one, faculty members in each course assessed student ePortfolios as they progressed through their academic program. In contrast, at university two, students were assigned a faculty member during a 15-week period to assess their ePortfolios contents. It appears that the latter model resulted in higher student perceptions.

Visibility

Table 4 shows the mean and standard deviation for each item in the assessment subscale. The subscale

Table 3. Assessment factor items by university

Items	University One		University Two	
	M	SD	M	SD
I feel that an ePortfolio is a better way for faculty to assess my knowledge than a multiple choice test.	3.02	1.35	4.00	0.92
I feel comfortable if an ePortfolio is used as part of a capstone course in my program of study (eg., It is required that you develop an ePortfolio for your internship).	2.18	1.21	3.71	0.99
I would be comfortable with an ePortfolio used as an assessment tool by faculty for an assignment in a course.	2.54	1.28	3.71	1.01
I feel comfortable with an ePortfolio used as an assessment tool by faculty for part of my grade in a course.	2.49	1.26	3.67	1.06
I use the faculty comments about my ePortfolio as constructive criticism.	1.95	1.23	3.63	1.07
I would be comfortable with an ePortfolio used as a graduation requirement to my program of study (e.g., It is required that you develop an ePortfolio to complete your program of study).	2.72	1.34	3.84	0.99
I feel that an ePortfolio is a better way for faculty to assess my knowledge than an essay test.	2.54	1.22	3.67	0.95
I am comfortable with an ePortfolio used as an assessment tool by faculty in other courses.	2.54	1.22	3.72	0.98

mean at university one is $M = 2.65$ ($SD = 0.96$) while the subscale mean for university two was $M = 3.68$ ($SD = 0.76$). There was a significant difference detected between university one and university two on the assessment subscale at $t(398) = 12.05$, $p < .01$. As in the previous measures, university two had higher overall perceptions of their ePortfolio being used as tool for visibility. At university one, the Chalk & Wire ePortfolio application was used. At university two, the TaskStream ePortfolio application was used. Both ePortfolio applications provide the pre-service teachers with the ability to share their ePortfolio either as a URL or CD/DVD. Both applications also have reporting utilities for the teacher education program administration. At university two, students were allowed to select their own artifacts, while at university one, the faculty selected the artifacts. This may also be a contributing factor to the differences in perception, but more future research is necessary to determine whether student choice of artifacts is a major factor.

DISCUSSSION

Interpretation of the Findings

So, what can be concluded from the analysis of two different contexts of an ePortfolio integration initiative? These results provide compelling evidence that the way in which ePortfolios are integrated into the curriculum will significantly influence the ways in which primary users (pre-service teachers) perceive ePortfolios. Although the integration characteristics and context could not be isolated to determine cause and effect, the results suggest that the university two implementation was more positively received by the pre-service teachers that were involved in the initiative. We, unfortunately, cannot pinpoint the factors that led to this perceived gap by pre-service teachers, but can elaborate on the integration initiative by further discussing how it was adopted by the teacher education program.

In relation to the aforementioned factors, the findings revealed statistically significant differences between the universities, which have varying

Table 4. Visibility factor items by university

Items	University One		University Two	
	M	SD	M	SD
I am comfortable with an accrediting agency looking at my ePortfolio for accreditation of the school I attend (Accrediting agencies are external organizations that ensure that education provided by institutions of higher education meets acceptable levels of quality).	3.11	1.24	3.78	0.99
I would feel comfortable with an accreditation agency examining faculty evaluations of my ePortfolio work.	3.06	1.24	3.77	0.98
I would be comfortable with faculty evaluations of my work posted to my ePortfolio as long as only I could view them.	2.51	1.27	3.68	1.05
I would feel comfortable with my teachers showing my ePortfolio to other teachers.	2.33	1.18	3.56	1.07
I would use an ePortfolio to showcase my work to my family.	2.93	1.24	3.97	0.81
I would use an ePortfolio to showcase my work to my friends.	2.36	1.23	3.52	1.07
I would feel comfortable with my teachers showing my ePortfolio to potential employers.	2.39	1.2	3.49	1.1
I would use an ePortfolio as a snapshot of my knowledge and skills to show potential employers.	3.14	1.19	3.90	0.80
I think my ePortfolio would be beneficial to me getting a job.	2.78	1.20	3.68	0.95
I would feel comfortable if an employer requested to see my ePortfolio to aid in the hiring process.	2.26	1.21	3.53	1.12
I would use an ePortfolio as an electronic résumé to show potential employers.	2.24	1.19	3.42	1.14
If I were an employer, I would use an applicant's ePortfolio, if available, to aid in the hiring process.	2.61	1.26	3.82	0.89

integration characteristics. University two had a higher mean than university one for each factor under investigation. At university two, ePortfolios were implemented in a capstone course during students' field experiences in their final semester. Students were required to create their ePortfolios while student teaching. At university two, students were provided the flexibility in selecting the various artifacts they would include in their ePortfolios. In contrast, at university one, the ePortfolio initiative is integrated program-wide. That is, students starting in their junior year were required to submit artifacts to their ePortfolios from their various education courses. In terms of student choice of artifacts, at university one, faculty selected the various artifacts that students would submit to their ePortfolios.

Pre-service teachers at university two are required to create their work samples and to showcase their work during their internship. Pre-service teachers are advised to follow a standard format for their ePortfolios by using Taskstream templates (a web-based software for organizing artifacts that can be aligned with national or state standards). The ePortfolio is also intended to be a valuable medium for showcasing competencies, skills, and dispositions to potential employers. The ePortfolio, upon completion, should provide evidence of preservice teacher competencies with respect to state teaching standards. In particular, preservice teachers have the opportunity to use their ePortfolios to demonstrate competencies in areas like lesson plan writing, developing survey template and assessment tools, addressing needs of diverse learners, and several more. The development of these activities are intended for pre-service teachers to focus on learning, professional development and growth.

The ePortfolio artifacts include a description of the setting, which includes class, school, community, and other relevant demographic information. The artifacts generally include a unit of study or lesson plan with corresponding state and national standards. Pre-service teachers may include unit goals and lesson outcomes, long range goals in the cognitive, affective and/or psychomotor domains. In addition, the condition, the behavior, and the criteria by which performance will be measured are indicated. Pre-service teachers are also encouraged to answer the following reflective questions, such as, what did you learn about teaching, learning, and yourself? Using TaskStream, the pre-service teachers communicate with their university supervisor about their ePortfolio artifacts and receive timely feedback.

While students at university two may have perceived the ePortfolio initiative more favorable than university one, this does not mean that the 15-week experience is the best approach. In fact, a recent qualitative study involving 244 students at university two revealed that while the ePortfolio experience was beneficial (students recognized their growth, appreciated being able to store their artifacts, and became familiar with teaching standards), a majority of them indicated wanting more time to work on their ePortfolio and their desire to increase its scope within the school of education, rather than having to compose their ePortfolio as an exit requirement (Parker, Ndoye, & Ritzhaupt, under review). Although students do not want more work, they recognize that a longer ePortfolio implementation period, with the appropriate guidance and support, might enhance their experience. These students' perceptions prompt us to think about which set of conditions best supports their academic and professional needs. Another consideration is whether or not leadership and governance issues at the respective schools (Strudler & Wetzel, 2005) influenced the context

in which ePortfolios were implemented and hence students' perceptions.

Key Points

This chapter has provided conceptual tools for teacher education programs seeking to integrate ePortfolios into their respective programs. In this section, we will summarize some of the key points made and further discuss ePortfolio integration. As previously noted, ePortfolios can serve as learning systems for personal and professional development, employment portfolios, and as tools for their organizational uses. The challenge for teacher education programs is to implement ePortfolios that simultaneously meet the requirements for all of these purposes. As noted by Ritzhaupt et. al. (2008), ePortfolios are intended to be a student-centered learning device; however, as the popularity of ePortfolios has increased, teacher education programs are recognizing that an ePortfolio system can benefit students as well as their organization. The goal of an ePortfolio initiative should be to maximize student benefits while still meeting organizational needs.

This chapter has presented a stakeholder interaction model to illustrate the many stakeholders of an ePortfolio system (see Figure 1). The stakeholders include pre-service teachers, teacher education faculty and administration, technology support staff within a teacher education subsystem, and in-service teachers, accrediting agencies, state and school district administration. A point that was not previously emphasized is the feedback loop that serves as input for the teacher education subsystem. This feedback loop represents the perspectives, insights, reflections, and evaluation of the ePortfolio system by external stakeholders. This information is invaluable to a successful ePortfolio program. In creating an ePortfolio system, teacher education programs must ensure that the proper channels are in place for this feedback loop to fully benefit from the initiative.

The chapter has also outlined a series of questions and concerns that should be addressed to successfully implement an ePortfolio system within a teacher education program. The first concern is to clearly define the purpose of an ePortfolio system within the teacher education program. The purpose of an ePortfolio is key to its implementation. After, questions about the types of artifacts, how they will be assessed, how frequently they will be assessed, who they will be assessed by, whether system will be implemented at a course or program level, and how the artifacts will be connected to state and accrediting agency standards must be addressed. Addressing these concerns are necessary to implement and institutionalize a valid and reliable, program-wide ePortfolio system with a teacher education program. Also important is the tool that is selected or developed and how it will be supported within the teacher education program. Aggregation of the data within the ePortfolio system to meet reporting requirements is a final consideration and must be considered early in the initiative.

While a lot of attention is being placed on ePortfolios in the literature, none of the research studies, to our knowledge, attempts to measure pre-service teacher attitudes toward ePortfolios based on the context of their integration. This research shows that the way in which ePortfolios are integrated into the fabric of our educational enterprise will influence pre-service teacher attitudes towards the initiative. This has implications for how pre-service and in-service teachers use the ePortfolio in relation to the three "R's": to represent their work, as well as reflect on and revise (Acker, 2005; Lorenzo & Ittelson, 2005) their instructional practices to improve K-12 student learning. There is a need for longitudinal research on pre-service teachers' and faculty perceptions of the use of ePortfolios in teacher education, in different integration contexts or programs (if the requirements differ within a department/school, or college of education) and whether this process ultimately enhances classroom instruction and pu-

pil achievement. Another study may examine the likelihood that pre-service teachers who completed ePortfolios use them as in-service teachers and how they use them. At a minimum, this study should encourage more research on this important issue.

RECOMMENDATIONS

Here are some recommendations that can be followed to encourage successful ePortfolio integration in any context. We suggest that teacher education administration (e.g., deans, department chairs) answer the questions that have been raised within this chapter.

1. What is the purpose of the ePortfolio system within the teacher education program?
2. When will students start contributing artifacts to their ePortfolios (e.g., program-wide, capstone course, etc.)?
3. What is the streamlined and agreed upon set of criteria by which student artifacts and other ePortfolios content will be assessed and judged?
4. What constitutes an acceptable artifact? Do we need to have designated artifact or do we let students choose their own artifacts? Is it a course level or a program level?
5. Will the artifacts be connected to state, national, or international standards?
6. Who will be responsible for checking and making sure content is appropriate? Is it going to be one faculty member or a pool of faculty members and if so how do we guarantee inter rater reliability?
7. How frequently do we assess ePortfolio?
8. How often will students be able to revise their artifacts? And will the revised artifacts be re-assessed?
9. How do we guarantee technological access?
10. How do we support students and faculty in creating and maintaining their ePortfolio?

11. When do we start implementation? Will it be from the beginning? Or as a capstone experience?

Though the answer to these question will definitely help choose the most appropriate approach to ePortfolio integration in a given context, we are also aware that some of the answering these questions can be an evolving process as answers may evolve or be revisited based on experience. As such, teacher education programs will definitely benefit from all stakeholders in their efforts to provide answers to the questions above. A major recommendation will be to find ways to implement a participatory approach that would provide mechanisms and venues for all stakeholders to be involved in the planning and management process of the ePortfolio integration initiative (Wetzel & Strudler, 2005).

While the answer to the questions above will help increase chances of successful integration of ePortfolio, it is also recommended that teacher education programs clearly articulate roles and responsibilities of the different stakeholders and partners in this initiative. This is important especially in terms of time commitment for faculty. Reviewing and assessing student ePortfolios will definitely have an impact on faculty work load. How will we compensate for that? Similarly, students may view this integration in a more positive way if their roles and responsibilities are clarified from the beginning. If students see the ePortfolio initiative as meaningful, they are more likely to engage in the ePortfolio task, regardless of when it is implemented during their program of study. If students are uploading and reflecting on their artifacts and using the feedback they receive from faculty and peers to improve their work, there will be evidence of personal and professional development that can be used for other purposes (accreditation, assessment, employment, program evaluation). With this, the ePortfolio system is more likely to meet the needs of all of its stakeholders.

Teacher education administration should consider issues such as storage space, security, linking and grouping, reflection, publishing and portability of the ePortfolio, which Barrett and Knezek (2003) outline in their paper on ePortfolio assessment and accountability. Networking with other ePortfolio system-level users and learning variations in ePortfolios use (e.g., Strudler & Wetzel, 2005; Jafari & Kaufman, 2006;) may also prove helpful. Ultimately, using ePortfolios in a student-centered manner can help meet student and organization needs.

REFERENCES

Acker, S. (2005). *Technology-enabled teaching/eLearning dialogue: Overcoming obstacles to authentic ePortfolio assessment*. Retrieved June 25, 2005, from http://www.campus-technology.com/news_article.asp?id=10788&typeid=155.

Barrett, H., & Knezek, D. (2003). *e-Portfolios: Issues in assessment, accountability and pre-service teacher preparation*. Retrieved from http://www.electronicportfolios.com/portfolios/AERA2003.pdf

Campbell, D. M., Cignetti, P. B., Melenyzer, B. J., Nettles, D. H., & Wyman, R. M. Jr. (2007). *How to develop a professional portfolio: A manual for teachers. NETS for Teachers 2008. International Society for Technology in Education*. Boston, MA: Pearson.

Chalk & Wire. (2010). *Product overview*. Retrieved from http://chalkandwire.com/index.php/product/overview

Curts, J., Yanes, J., & McWright, B. (2003). Assessment of preservice teachers' Web-based electronic portfolio. *Education Technology for Teacher Preparation and Certification,* (pp. 92-98). Retrieved July 25, 2006, from http://www.nesinc.com/PDFs/2003_11Curts.pdf

Hartnell-Young, E., & Morriss, M. (1999). *Digital professional portfolios for change.* Arlington Heights, IL: Skylight Professional Development.

Hicks, T., Russo, A., Autrey, T., Gardner, R., Kabodian, A., & Edington, C. (2007). Rethinking the purposes and processes for designing digital portfolios. *Journal of Adolescent & Adult Literacy, 50*(6), 450–458. doi:10.1598/JAAL.50.6.3

Jafari, A., & Kaufman, C. (2006). *Handbook of research on ePortfolios.* Hershey, PA: Idea Group. doi:10.4018/978-1-59140-890-1

Lorenzo, G., & Ittelson, J. (2005). *An overview of ePortfolios.* The Educause Learning Initiative. Retrieved November 15, 2005, from http://www.educause.edu/ir/library/pdf/ELI3001.pdf.

Meeus, W., Questier, F., & Derks, T. (2006). Open-source eportfolio: Development and implementation of an institution-wide electronic platform for students. *Educational Media International, 43*(2), 133–145. doi:10.1080/09523980600641148

Parker, M. A., Ndoye, A., & Ritzhaupt, A. D. (Manuscript submitted for publication). Qualitative analysis of ePortfolios in teacher education: Implications for successful integration. *Journal of Digital Learning in Teacher Education.*

Ritzhaupt, A., Ndoye, A., & Parker, M. (2010). Validation of the electronic portfolio student perspective instrument (EPSPI): Conditions under a different integration initiative. *Journal of Digital Learning in Teacher Education, 26*(3), 111–119.

Ritzhaupt, A. D., Ndoye, A., & Parker, M. (2010). Validation of the electronic portfolio student perspective instrument (EPSPI): Conditions under a different integration initiative. *Journal of Digital Learning in Teacher Education, 26*(3), 111–119.

Ritzhaupt, A. D., & Singh, O. (March, 2006). Student perspectives of ePortfolios in computing education. *Proceedings of the Association of Computing Machinery Southeast Conference,* Melbourne, FL, (pp. 152 - 157).

Ritzhaupt, A. D., Singh, O., Seyferth, T., & Dedrick, R. (2008). Development of the electronic portfolio student perspective instrument: An ePortfolio integration initiative. *Journal of Computing in Higher Education, 19*(2), 47–71. doi:10.1007/BF03033426

Shulman, L. (1998). Teacher portfolios: A theoretical activity. In Lyons, N. (Ed.), *With portfolio in hand* (pp. 23–37). New York, NY: Teachers College Press.

Siemens, G. (2004). *eLearnSpace: Everything elearning.* ePortfolios. Retrieved June 27, 2005, from http://www.elearnspace.org/Articles/eportfolios.htm.

Strawhecker, J., Messersmith, K., & Balcom, A. (2007). The role of electronic portfolios in the hiring of K–12 teachers. *Journal of Computing in Teacher Education, 24*(2), 65–71.

Strudler, N., & Wetzel, K. (2005). The diffusion of electronic portfolios in teacher education: Issues of initiation and implementation. *Journal of Research on Technology in Education, 37*(4), 411–433.

Strudler, N., & Wetzel, K. (2008). Costs and benefits of electronic portfolios in teacher education: Faculty perspectives. *Journal of Computing in Teacher Education, 24*(4), 135–142.

Taskstream. (2010). *Products and services.* Retrieved from http://www.taskstream.com/pub/ProductsAndServices.asp

Temple, V., Allan, G., & Temple, B. (2003). *Employers' and students' perceptions of electronic employment portfolios.* Retrieved from http://www.aare.au/03pap/tem03523.pdf

Wetzel, K., & Strudler, N. (2005). The diffusion of electronic portfolios in teacher education: Next steps and recommendations from accomplished users. *Journal of Research on Technology in Education, 38*(2), 231–243.

Wetzel, K., & Strudler, N. (2006). Costs and benefits of electronic portfolios in teacher education: Student voices. *Journal of Computing in Teacher Education, 22*(3), 69–78.

Wheeler, B. C. (2003). *EPortfolio project: Open source eportfolio release*. Andrew W. Mellon Foundation, Version 2.0, Retrieved from http://juicy.mellon.org/RIT/MellonOSProjects/%20ePortfolio/Portfolio_Proposal_Public.doc.

Wilhelm, L., Puckett, K., Beisser, S., Wishart, W., Merideth, E., & Sivakumaran, T. (2006). Lessons learned from the implementation of electronic portfolios at three universities. *TechTrends: Linking Research & Practice to Improve Learning, 50*(4), 62–82.

Wolf, K., & Dietz, M. (1998). Teaching portfolios: Purposes and possibilities. *Teacher Education Quarterly, 25*(1), 9–22.

KEY TERMS AND DEFINITIONS

ePortfolio: A collection of purposefully-organized artifacts that support backward and forward reflection to augment and assess growth over time.

Section 4
Technology Integration across the Content Areas

Chapter 18

Multiliteracies:
Moving from Theory to Practice in Teacher Education Courses

D. Bruce Taylor
University of North Carolina at Charlotte, USA

ABSTRACT

In this chapter, the author explains how a theory of Multiliteracies helped to shape the development of a graduate course which, in turn, initiated changes in an undergraduate content-area literacy course in a teacher education program. Both courses are described, and ways in which digital technologies changed the way the instructor and students collaborated, worked and learned are discussed. Service learning aspects of these courses are explored with examples of how pre- and inservice teachers engaged with K-12 students and teachers in the community. Implications for teacher education faculty and students are presented as well as the need to implement Multiliterate pedagogies across the K-12 spectrum.

INTRODUCTION

Technology has always played an integral role in literacy and literacy education. The tools of literacy from clay tablets to paper and pencil are technologies that have enabled humans to be literate. However, over the past few decades, the rapid growth of computers and other Information Com-

munication Technologies (ICTs) have expanded our notions of text and literacy. *Multiliteracies*, a term coined by the New London Group (1996), captures this shifting notion of literacy to include the "multiplicity of communications channels and increasing cultural and linguistic diversity in the world today call for a much broader view of literacy than portrayed by traditional language-based approaches" (p. 60). In short, these scholars looked beyond the limitations of traditional notions of

DOI: 10.4018/978-1-4666-0014-0.ch018

literacy to include social and cultural changes in society and the emergence of new technologies that enable students to negotiate "the evolving language of work, power, and community, and fostering the critical engagement necessary for them to design their social futures and achieve success through fulfilling employment" (p. 60). These ideas have been echoed by organizations including the International Reading Association (IRA) and the National Council of Teachers of English (NCTE). The NCTE's policy statement on 21st Century literacies states:

As society and technology change, so does literacy. Because technology has increased the intensity and complexity of literate environments, the twenty-first century demands that a literate person possess a wide range of abilities and competencies, many literacies. These literacies—from reading online newspapers to participating in virtual classrooms—are multiple, dynamic, and malleable. As in the past, they are inextricably linked with particular histories, life possibilities and social trajectories of individuals and groups (National Council of Teachers of English, 2010).

While the scholarship of literacy has in many ways attempted to keep up with the rapid changes of an increasingly "flat world" (Friedman, 2007), schools and other educational institutions including teacher education programs have not (Collins & Halverson, 2009). States have attempted to enact policies to help bridge this gap between literate technologies used beyond the school and those used in classrooms. For example, The North Carolina State Board of Education established *A Strategic Plan for Reading Literacy* in April 2007 which states:

Reading is the fundamental skill needed for success in life, especially in the 21st century. While students must be at proficiency or above in basic literacy (reading, writing, listening, speaking, using conventional or technology-based media),

these skills are no longer sufficient for college- and work-ready high school graduates. As the world continues to change rapidly, schools must evolve to meet future needs. In many cases, this means we are trying to refine and structure an educational system for a future that many people cannot visualize. (p. 1)

The North Carolina *Strategic Plan for Reading Literacy* calls for teachers and schools to prepare students to be globally competitive 21st Century citizens and professionals able to provide leadership for innovation using 21st Century technologies. The State Board of Education places teacher preparation and professional development at the top of its list of factors that influence literacy instruction and student growth. However, the need to advance the teaching and learning using 21st Century technologies is not limited to P-12 educational institutions. Colleges and university instructors have been slow to adopt Web 2.0 technologies especially at the individual course level (Ajjan & Hartshorne, 2008; Maloney, 2007).

In this chapter, I describe *r/evolutions*, a term I invoke to capture the varied and often increasing pace of change in my own teaching of undergraduate and graduate literacy teacher education courses that have developed over the past three years in response to ICTs and other technologies[1]. These changes include replacing Web 1.0 technologies (printed copies of word processed documents and static websites, for example) with interactive Web 2.0 tools (wikis, blogs, and shared document spaces) to foster and enable collaboration on assignments.

However, these changes in the use of technology did not remain within the university classroom walls. Service learning clinical assignments required teacher education students to implement literacy instruction using digital technologies with elementary, middle, and high school students. University students developed theme based projects with K-12 students which included the creation of websites, digital video projects and other digital technologies.

The primary focus of this chapter is on the integration of technology into teaching and learning in these university courses (r/evolutions), but I include the role that service learning played in creating authentic uses for those technologies. I have chosen to organize this chapter chronologically focusing first on the graduate-level Multiliteracies course I developed and then describing a content-area literacy course I often teach that is offered to students seeking their initial teaching license[2]. I do this because it was in the Multiliteracies course I first explored the use of Web 2.0 tools, some of which I later brought into use in the face-to-face and online sections of the content-area literacy courses. Before describing those courses and how technologies shaped teaching and learning, I provide a review of the related literature and a brief description of my experience with technology up to the point I began more fully integrating it into my teaching.

A BRIEF REVIEW OF THE LITERATURE

Multiliteracies: An Expanding View of Literacy and Text

The term Multiliteracies arose in the mid-1990s by a group of scholars meeting in New London Connecticut. They published their ideas in a seminal piece in the *Harvard Educational Review* (New London Group, 1996). Since that time educators and scholars across different fields of study have explored what it means to be multiliterate (Cope & Kalantzis, 2000; Gee, 2003; Luke & Elkins, 1998; Rush, 2002) and to chart "new literacies" that have emerged as a result of new information communication technologies (Lankshear & Knobel, 2003; Leu, 2002; O'Brien & Bauer, 2005). In what Luke and Elkins (1998) dub "New Times," literacy is viewed as multi-modal processes that

include the reading of print-based and electronic texts, use of visual, spatial, gestural, and aural representations. The ideas behind the term Multiliteracies provide an expanded and expanding notion of text and what it means to be literate. In short, the concept of Multiliteracies has pushed what it means to be literate in today's world from a long-held tradition that focuses on reading and writing of print-based material such as books to a broader definition of literacy that encompasses a multitude of texts including but not limited to web pages, e-readers, social networking sites, video, audio and performance texts.

The changes in thinking about literacy are seen by some as a radical shift away from long-held traditions of what it means to read and write and have given rise to new literacy communities not imagined two decades ago (Bruce, 2002). *Millennials* is one of several names given to those growing up in these times characterized by rapidly changing social, technological and economic environments (Gee, 2002). A mark of this change in terms of economics for the Millennial generation is the move from the Industrial Age to the Knowledge Age which Trilling and Fadel (2009) place in 1991 when, for the first time, knowledge-based expenditures like computers, servers, software and phones exceeded industrial expenditures (for example, engines and machines for agriculture, mining, transportation, manufacturing and energy production). Recognizing that tensions arise for teachers and students with such rapid changes in ICTs, Collins and Halverson see this shift as a "digital revolution" that schools must embrace (2009).

The Role of Technology in Teaching and Learning

In spite of the rapid advancement of technology over the past two to three decades, schools have been slow to respond (Cuban, 2001). The K-12 education establishment has long been resistant to adopting new technologies (Cuban, 1986; Collins

& Halverson, 2009) and new teaching methods (Evans, 1996; Tyack & Cuban, 1995). Besides institutional resistance, there are other barriers to implementing technology into teaching and learning including issues around cost and access. Nationally, the ratio of students to computers is around five to one, but in urban schools it is a 9:1 ratio (Collins & Halverson, 2009). In 2005, 89% of all households owned a personal computer, and 81% of all households had Internet access, but only 68% percent of households with income less than $25,000 had computers (Carroll, et al., 2005). Yet, some advocates argue that computers cannot be effective until there is a one-to-one correspondence between computers and users in schools (Norris & Soloway, 2003).

Arguments for the use of technology in education include its widespread use in the workplace and impact on the global economy (Friedman, 2006). Others point to the multiple social uses of technology within and beyond schools and offices (Leander & Boldt, 2008). Collins and Halverson (2009) present research suggesting that technology offers learners greater customization in meeting their own learning needs, greater control of the process, and more interaction including more immediate feedback (Gee, 2003). A review of research commissioned by Cisco Systems (2006) concludes that while the research is still emergent, "technology does provide a small, but significant, increase in learning" (p. 15).

Although much research needs to be conducted, teachers and students continue to find ways to integrate technology into teaching and learning. Teachers at the elementary level (Barone & Wrights, 2008; Labbo, 2005; Zawilinski, 2009; Zucker, & Invernizzi, 2008), middle grades (Oakley & Jay, 2008), and high school level (Huffaker, 2005; Krucli, 2004; Wolfson, 2008) have developed numerous applications of technology for teaching and learning. These span the gamut from more traditional Web 1.0 applications (Krucli, 2004) to Web 2.0 applications such as blogging (Zawlinski, 2009). Teachers have found ways to use technology to help students with the writing process (Davis & McGrail, 2009; Morgan & Smith, 2008) as well as teaching specific reading skills (Marcaruso & Walker, 2008), and higher-order thinking skills (Zawlinski, 2009).

Service Learning

Service learning is a form of pedagogy that links learning to community service. The Learn & Serve America Clearinghouse on its website defines service learning as a "teaching and learning strategy that integrates meaningful community service with instruction and reflection to enrich the learning experience, teach civic responsibility, and strengthen communities" (Learn & Serve America, 2010). Research has shown that service learning opportunities provide a variety of positive impacts on preservice teacher education candidates such as: increased academic learning, understanding of students and communities; development of capacities needed to provide equitable, caring instruction; knowledge of the teaching profession and development of professional skills; understanding and acceptance of diversity; and knowledge and skills needed to implement service learning (Anderson, 2008). For these reasons and others, many have advocated for service learning to be integrated into teacher education (Callahan & Root, 2003).

Service learning has been shown to be relevant for teachers across all content areas (Kirtman, 2008; Meaney, Griffin, & Bohler, 2009) and has positive learning outcomes for college students in teacher education programs (Freeman & Swick, 2003; Strage, 2000 & 2004; Wade & Anderson, 1996) as well as K-12 learners (Billig, 2000; Billig & Klute, 2003; Center for Information and Research on Civic Learning and Engagement, 2007; Conrad & Hedin, 1991; Conrad & Hedin, 1982). For preservice teacher education students, participation in service learning often leads to the affirmation of teaching as a career choice and the ability to self-reflect (McClam et al., 2008; Miller et al., 2007).

Service learning by its nature is collaborative including partnerships between university faculty and students and with community organizations and schools with whom they work. Faculty must demonstrate a commitment and value for the service learning experience, as well as provide opportunities for teacher education candidates to reflect (Billig, 2000; Potthoff et al., 2000) and share in decision-making (Hart & King, 2007). Benefits for preservice teachers rise when university instructors are directly involved with the service learning experience (Potthoff et al., 2000). The inclusion of service learning in the Multiliteracies and the content area literacy courses provided opportunities for authentic teaching and learning with technologies that involved the teacher education students as well as K-12 students.

BRINGING CONTEMPORARY TECHNOLOGIES INTO MY TEACHING

Background

My starting point in developing courses that attempt to meaningfully integrate technology into teaching and learning began with my own evolutionary use of technology personally and professionally. I provide a brief overview of my use of digital and web-based technologies that relate to my later use of technology in my teaching.

While I have owned and used personal computers for over 25 years, about a decade ago my use of computers changed, and I went from primarily being a consumer of digital content to beginning to produce content. Up to this point, I had most often used computer-based applications such as word processing programs and CD ROM applications and basic web and communication applications (web browsers and email programs). After moving to another part of the country, I began building simple websites as a way to share family photos and updates with friends and family members.

During my graduate studies I created a website in fulfillment of an assignment in a research course. The course focused on ethnography and my website recounted the stories of family members who lived during and fought in World War II. I began integrating my use of technology into my teaching. I asked students in an adolescent literature course I taught to submit to me annotated bibliography entries of young adult books they were reading, and I posted them on a website that my students could access.

Six years ago, when I began my current position, like many faculty members in my college, I was provided the server space to build my own faculty webpage. I began creating web pages for each course I taught. I uploaded copies of my syllabus and assignment handouts. Eventually I added examples of student work as models to guide future students in my courses. Since content-area literacy courses are a staple in my teaching, I created a resource page with teaching strategies, handouts, and links to useful websites and professional organizations. I also began studying more deeply the literature on digital literacies and Multiliteracies as well as the role of technology in teaching and learning.

In late 2006, our program, which offers a Masters of Education in Reading as well as a doctorate in literacy education, decided that we needed to offer a course focused on the role of technology in literacy. As one of the proponents for this course, I agreed to develop a syllabus and ideas for assignments and during the Summer 2007 I taught the first section of what became the Multiliteracies course. That summer I also taught my first fully online course, a section of the content-area literacy course. These experiences began shaping my thinking about the role of teaching and learning in other courses I taught. Below I share what seemed first evolutionary and then revolutionary—or, *r/evolutionary*—changes I experienced in my teaching. I focus on two courses: the graduate Multiliteracies course and the content area literacy course available to undergraduate and graduate certificate students seeking their initial teaching license.

The Multiliteracies Course

My thinking for this course began in 2006 with the proposal that our graduate reading program develop a course that consider the role of technology in literacy education. Scholarship in the field of literacy and literacy education over the past two to three decades has centered around an expanded notion of text (New London Group, 1996) moving from traditional notions of print as text to include visual, performance, and digital media, to name a few, as text. Moreover, the work of scholars such as James Paul Gee, Alan Luke and others has similarly expanded our understanding of literacy. Our college already had educational technology courses and programs, so I knew that this course should not duplicate the technology applications courses offered to our students. I was familiar with the work of the New London Group (1996) and other scholarship (Alvermann, 2002; Lankshear & Knobel, 2003; Leu, 2002). I was also aware of a policy document soon to be voted on by the North Carolina State Board of Education[3] (2007) that calls for North Carolina educators across grade levels and subject areas to support students' "basic" literacy skills, which it defines as reading, writing, listening, speaking, using conventional or technology-based media and pushes for greater competence in digital literacies. My thinking coalesced around both the scholarship of Multiliteracies and how educators might implement that in their classrooms and schools.

I felt that the theoretical foundation laid out by the New London Group and others was vital to developing an understanding of the concepts around Multiliteracies but that there also had to be a pedagogic focus of how to enact that in the classroom. Most of our master's students who would take this course are classroom teachers seeking to enhance their own teaching and/or move into reading coach or literacy facilitator positions in schools, so a focus on application seemed important.

I framed the course around two questions: 1) what is a theory of multiliteracies? and 2) what are possible pedagogies of multiliteracies? I made a practical decision regarding the kinds of literacies we would explore in this course. While the theory of Multiliteracies acknowledges "multiplicity of communications channels" and textual forms from traditional print-based forms to digital and performance texts, for example, I felt my students would benefit by focusing on more recent technological and digital texts rather than traditional print-based texts and literacies. Moreover, this move acknowledged key tenets of the North Carolina *Strategic Plan for Reading Literacy* to embrace digital literacies and bring them into K-12 classrooms. At this point I was able to flesh out my plans. In the course, students read and discuss issues around globalization and how technologies have served to "flatten" the world (Friedman, 2006) and how that has impacted education. Students read the New London Group article (1996) and other texts that delve into the theoretical aspects of Multiliteracies before considering pedagogic implications.

Based on my experience teaching other courses in our M.Ed. in Reading program, I knew my students would bring varying levels of comfort and experience with technology. I knew that a course of this nature would best be served if it allowed for exploration and risk-taking. Additionally, I knew that technology is dialogic (Bakhtin, 1981) in nature, often emergent, and that the notion of "expertise" is ephemeral at best. In short, I was certain that I would learn from and with my students as we explored the theory and practice of Multiliteracies. I tried to capture these tensions in the overview section of my syllabus:

It is the purpose of this course to develop a pedagogy of Multiliteracies, to propel literacy education into the present and future by creating literacy learners who are fluent in current and emerging information technologies. We will do so by immersing ourselves in new literacies. As such this course will always be a fluid and dynamic learning environment—an emerging work in progress. I ask students that they be willing to take risks, take on new roles, immerse themselves in new texts, contexts and modes of learning (Author, 2010a).

As I tried to move from my concepts about the course to the nuts and bolts of implementation, I found three concepts best captured my thinking: praxis, pedagogy and service. Praxis refers to the intersection of theory and practice, or put another way, to the implementation of theory into practice. I needed to create an assignment and activities in the course that helped students link the theory of Multiliteracies to their practice as educators. Since I felt that Multiliteracies would be unfamiliar territory for many of my students, it made sense to me to help them capture their learning of both theory and practice in a kind of portfolio. With this in mind, I began to conceive of a digital portfolio, a web-based home for my students to inventory, ponder, and share their ideas regarding both the theory and practice of Multiliteracies. What emerged was the Multiliteracies Digital Portfolio, which took the form of a wiki, a digital home for their theoretical understandings, reviews of scholarship, and thoughts on pedagogic tools. This portfolio took on the name and identity of the Multiliteracies Wiki (http://multiliteraciesatuncc. pbworks.com/). Figure 1 provides a view of the front page of the Multiliteracies Wiki as of the writing of this chapter.

During class I introduced some of the applications or tools we explored but also invited my students to research others or share some they were using in their classrooms or schools. I referred my students to web sites such as Go2Web2.0 (http://www.go2web20.net/) to explore Web 2.0 applications for teaching and learning. Together we explored shared document sites (Google Documents and Adobe Buzzword, for example),

wikis, blogs, social networks such as Facebook, online social worlds (SecondLife), and many other applications. Many of these found their way into the Multiliteracies Wiki.

As can be seen in Figure 1, my students and I developed categories to organize different aspects of the applications and tools we found. We wrestled with this but found the following categories useful:

- *Researching* is a way of analyzing, investigating, and collecting information in order to gain knowledge, find the resolution of a problem, or to gain a greater understanding of a phenomenon. Some of these tools include search engines, research and informational websites, and YouTube and TeacherTube.
- *Communicating* tools are those that allow teachers and students to connect and communicate with others outside the classroom (Skype, E-Pal, teacher and student email tools, for example).
- *Collaborating* tools are those that aid in the ability to collaborate with other people through a single document, presentation, etc. with people that live and/or work in different locations. These include wikis, podcasts, shared document spaces like Google Documents, and video spaces such as YouTube.
- *Exploring* applications allow teachers and students to look beyond the classroom to explore new places and ideas. We included tools such as Google Earth and Google Maps, WebQuests, and SecondLife and Teen SecondLife.
- *Creating* connotes authoring, and, in the context of digital literacies, authoring digital texts. Tools in this category include those for creating and editing photos such as Picasa and Photoshop, audio including Garage Band and Audacity, videos including MovieMaker, iMovie, and Jing.

Figure 1. The Multiliteracies Wiki

As can be seen above, these are not discrete but overlapping categories but served our purposes for making sense of the kinds of technologies that might come under the umbrella of Multiliteracies. Figure 2 provides a view of the section of the Multiliteracies Wiki dealing with tools for Collaboration.

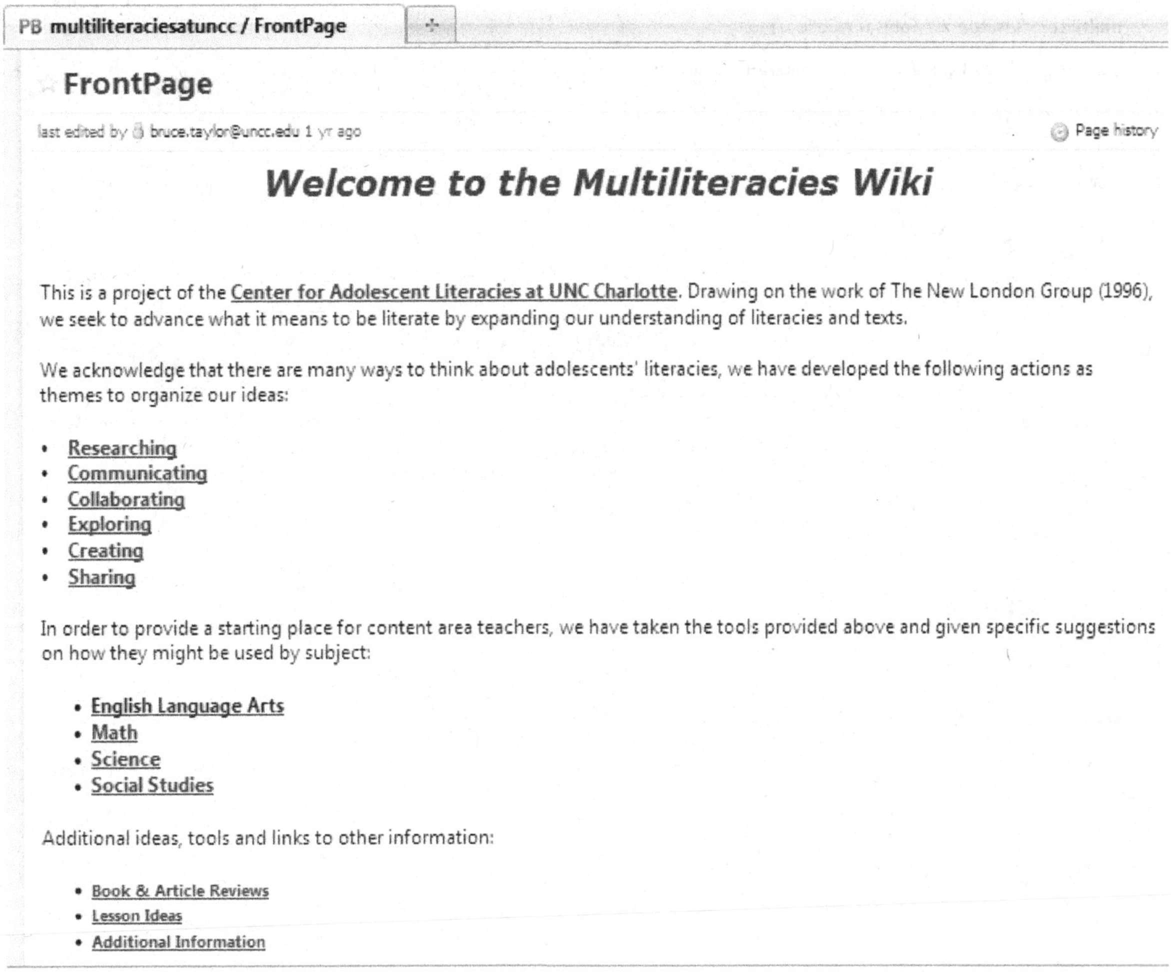

- *Sharing* tools, like those for communicating to some degree, are those that allow creators of content to share it with others. As we describe in the Multiliteracies Wiki, "We create and edit texts so that others may read, view, discuss, analyze and enjoy them." We include in this category, tools that enable the creation of Web content (HTML editors), wikis, blogs but also, Web 2.0 tools such as the many photo sharing websites, the timeline site Dipity (www.dipity.com) and digital storytelling sites.

Pedagogy is the study of teaching or the practice of teaching. While the Multiliteracies Digital Portfolio provided a place to explore the intersection of theory and practice, I felt my students needed to think about how they would enact Multiliteracies in their own classrooms. To this end, I developed the Multiliteracies Instructional

Figure 2. The collaboration section of The Multiliteracies Wiki

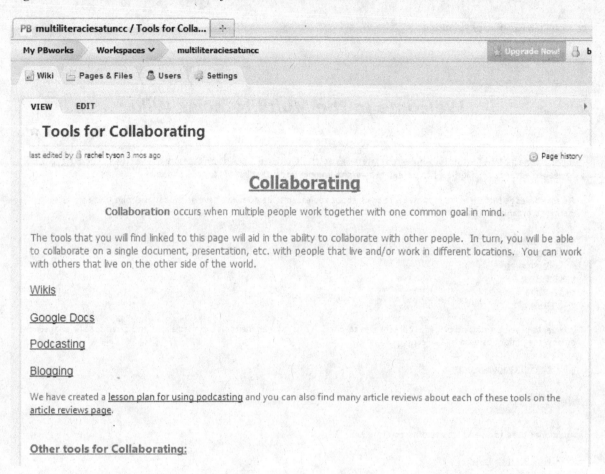

Project, an assignment for my students to work individually or in small groups to devise an instructional project to be taught at some level of the K-12 spectrum, preferably with their own students in mind. Although I did not prescribe a specific format other than these had to be shared in a digital, web-based format, most took the shape of lesson plans or how-to's for teachers to use in their classrooms. Figure 3 is an example of one such lesson/how-to on podcasting created by students in the Multiliteracies course.

Lessons and how-to's for the Multiliteracies Instructional Project covered topics including podcasting, WebQuests, digital storytelling, blogs as a tool to support high school seniors working on required exit projects, creating digital book reports using iMovie or MovieMaker, communicating with students abroad using ePals, exploring ancient Rome using Google Earth, exploring and writing poetry in VoiceThread and MovieMaker, and more. Some of these instructional ideas found their way into our culminating project for the Multiliteracies course, the Instructional Service Project.

Finally, I felt and continue to believe that there is no greater teacher than practice, so I thought about how my students might develop a Multiliteracies lesson or activity and work with K-12 students to enact that. I had already embraced service learning, a form of experiential learning linking service with learning goals, as a form of pedagogy with enormous potential pre- and

Figure 3. A Multiliteracies instructional project example on blogging

Podcasting Lesson Plan

last edited by 🔲 bruce.taylor@uncc.edu 0 mins ago   🔾 Page history

Proof-Revising With Podcasting

Grade Level: 3-12
I. **Objectives**: This lesson integrates the use of technology with a complex thinking and learning task that goes beyond editing for surface errors and engages students in rereading, listening, thinking, and relating to the reader.

II. **Rationale**: Students often lack an understanding of how their writing comes across to the readers and have difficulty turning their writing into clear, well-organized, and engaging stories for their readers.

III. **Introductory Activity**: Allow the students time to participate in an authentic writing assignment through the use of blogging, simple word processing, or paper and pencil. The prompt may be open or suggested by the teacher based on a currrent classroom theme.

IV. **Procedures**:
  1. Introduce Audacity/Garage Band and explain/model the tools used for the program.
  2. Allow time for the students to explore the program and experiment with the tools. Teacher shows examples of completed podcasts and class discusses the strengths/weaknesses of each one.
  3. Younger students- teacher records the podcast of the student writing exactly as it is written
     Older students- students record their peers writing exactly as it is written
  4. Reader provides feedback either on the student's blog or at the end of the podcast.

inservice teachers. From this I developed the Instructional Service Project, an assignment I describe this way on my syllabus:

Service, social justice and civic engagement are necessary ideals in a post-industrial, globally connected world. To accept that we are multiliterate is to accept that we are literate for a reason that must have meaning in our own lives. In this course, students will share their talents with K-12 learners and/or their teachers by collaborating on a service project that incorporates literacy with issues that matter to the K-12 learners, their teachers, families and community. Both groups of students—UNC Charlotte and K-12 learners/ teachers—will employ diverse texts and technolo-
gies to make a difference their lives, community and world (Author, 2010b).

In practice, the Instructional Service Project has taken two forms. Most often, this project has paired my graduate students with K-12 students in a summer program to implement a project that incorporates recent technologies around a theme or topic identified by the K-12 students and the summer program personnel. At times when we could not work with a summer youth program, my students developed and hosted a multi-day workshop for K-12 teachers to deliver professional development around the topic of Multiliteracies. I share here a brief glimpse of my students' work through the Instructional Service Learning Projects.

Graduate students in the Multiliteracies course most often have worked with students in the Children's Defense Fund's (CDF) Freedom School© programs sponsored in Charlotte, N.C. by Freedom School Partners, Inc., a non-profit organization serving at-risk students and families living in poverty in Charlotte. The Freedom Schools curriculum has been develop by the CDF and includes a primary emphasis on reading and literacy using culturally relevant books. The CDF also identifies other themes or topics for their Freedom School students or Scholars, as they are known in the program, to explore. Students in the Multiliteracies course worked with Freedom School students on two of these themes during the Summers of 2008 and 2009. In 2008, the Freedom School staff asked us to work with Scholars on the CDF topic spelled out in the organization's Cradle to Prison Pipeline© Campaign which seeks to counteract the numbers of Black, Latino and other youth growing up in poverty who are at risk of imprisonment during their lifetime. We agreed to work with this topic and after meeting with Freedom School staff, my graduate students developed a WebQuest (Dodge, 1995), a structured web learning activity, to explore this with the Scholars. We worked with the Freedom School Scholars for a week at one Charlotte site and began with the WebQuest on our first day. The Scholars documented their learning through the WebQuest using PowerPoint which we viewed together on the second day. Our focus then moved from problem to solution. My students in the Multiliteracies course brainstormed with the Freedom School Scholars to come up with ways to deal with this complex problem. We agreed to create Public Service Announcements (PSAs) using Microsoft MovieMaker with the idea of uploading them to YouTube where they could be shared with others. We split into teams of Scholars working with pairs of my students to identify themes like developing neighborhood watch groups, conflict resolutions and setting goals including that of going to college. We planned our work with the Freedom School Scholars early in

the week writing scripts and rehearsing. During the middle of the week the Scholars shot video using digital cameras and finally edited each PSA using MovieMaker. On the last day, we viewed these videos together and gave each Scholar a DVD with a copy of all the PSAs.

In the Summer 2009, the Freedom School staff, noting the high-level of enthusiasm and engagement during the previous year, asked us to take a similar approach but to address a different topic of concern raised by the CDF, that of healthy living. Again we developed a WebQuest activity and worked with Freedom School Scholars to create digital video, but rather than creating PSAs, the Scholars decided to create a news format-type program with segments focusing on nutrition, exercise, and cooking. What emerged was a morning TV news/variety show along the lines of *The Today Show* or *Good Morning America*. The video opened with a small group of "hosts" introducing segments written, taped, and edited by the Scholars. Again, the video took a week to research and produce, and we shared a DVD copy with each Scholar.

It has not always been possible for students in the Multiliteracies course to work with Freedom School Scholars or other children in summer programs. I taught a section of the course early in the summer of 2009 when the school year was just ending and few summer programs, including the Freedom Schools in Charlotte, had not yet begun. As part of another course I teach, our graduate students had hosted a 3-hour professional development program for teachers in three districts near our university. The program was offered free of charge and hosted at a local school and more than 125 teachers attended. Feedback from that event and discussions with teachers and other school district personnel had made us aware of the increasing need for professional development opportunities. The tightening economy and decline in state and local budgets had caused many districts to cut deeply into their professional development funds. With this in mind my students agreed to develop and host a weeklong professional development program on the topic of Multiliteracies.

In June 2009, my students hosted the *Going Digital! Teaching & Learning through Technology Seminar* for 27 teachers. We met at a local elementary school, and, as the flyer we created to promote the free workshop described, my students addressed topics including:

- **Creating blogs, wikis and podcasts** using free and readily available technologies
- **Fostering collaboration among students** using shared document spaces such as Google Documents and Buzzword
- **Using multiple applications to guide student research and foster engagement** with web-based learning activities
- **Engaging students in digital video and photography** projects
- **Introducing teachers to useful websites** for use across subject areas and grade levels

The program was conducted across five half-day blocks of time in an interactive format with a mixture of presentations by my students and application by the participants using wired laptops and a computer lab in the school. Response to the workshop was positive with 71% of the participants rating it as "Excellent" and 29% as "Satisfactory." All participants indicated that they learned technologies they could apply to their teaching.

To date, the Multiliteracies course has been offered as an elective in our graduate reading program, but in the Spring 2010 was approved by our university as a permanent offering and as a result of revising our M.Ed. in Reading program, has been adopted as a required course. My experiences with the Multiliteracies course began to shape my thinking about other courses I teach. In the next section, I share some of the changes I made to the content-area literacy courses I teach.

The Content-Area Literacy Course

The content-area literacy course has been a staple in my teaching since coming to UNC Charlotte. All students seeking initial licensure as middle and secondary teachers are required to take the course, so several sections are offered each semester and in the summer. The students represent a diverse range of teaching areas including science, mathematics, English language arts, social studies, second language instruction, fine arts, and performance arts to name several. Other students in special education take it as an option to meet program requirements. The focus of the class is on integrating literacy support for diverse students across subject areas. Key topics in the class include reading comprehension, vocabulary learning, writing to learn across subjects, motivation and engagement, and diversifying text selections.

My thinking on the class has changed over time and, as a result, assignments have evolved. However, over the past three years or so I have found three key assignments to be beneficial to students in the class. There is an emphasis in the class on developing teaching strategies to help students with comprehension and vocabulary learning, for example, so I developed an assignment requiring students to compile strategies useful to teaching and learning in their subject area. I call this assignment the Literacy Toolkit and have had students work in small groups by teaching area (math teachers, science teachers, etc.) to develop these toolkits of teaching ideas. They also identify and evaluate texts that are useful for students to use in their subject area and websites that are helpful. Typically, students compiled their toolkits in a Word document and submitted a printed copy to me which I evaluated and graded using a rubric. Key facets of the toolkit include:

1. Literacy Learning Tools: comprehension, vocabulary, and writing and inquiry tools
2. Text Selection Tools: an annotated bibliography with 20 or more texts on topics useful

for middle and secondary students in the group's subject area.

3. Technology Tools: an annotated list of a minimum of 10 websites useful for teaching in the group's subject area.

Because I wanted students to apply some of these strategies to their teaching, I also developed a unit plan assignment, the Literacy Integration Unit, in which students develop a concept for a unit and focus on how they would apply strategies to support student learning. Students work individually or in small groups to, as my assignment description says:

Create a teachable unit for use in their classrooms. Unlike other units you may have done for other classes, this unit looks less at detailed daily lesson plans but rather at key texts, assignments, goals, and assessment for a unit. The focus of this unit will be on unit-level planning with support for literacy and learning (Author, 2009).

Like the toolkit assignment, the Literacy Integration Unit was produced in a word processing document by students and submitted to me in a printed format which I assessed and graded using a rubric.

Since the other assignments had students identify learning strategies and implement them into a teaching unit, it seemed logical to have students work with a middle or secondary student using some of the strategies they were identifying as useful in their subject area. The clinical assignment developed over time but requires students to work with a middle or high school student tutoring 10 to 12 hours over the semester in their subject area. Students are required to develop lesson plans, conduct informal assessment, and document their work and student progress in a written narrative. Like other assignments this was typically turned into me as a printed document at two points in the semester. This was the state of the content-area

literacy course until I began to explore ways to integrate other technologies.

As I have mentioned, two events shaped my thinking about the face-to-face classes I teach, especially the content-area literacy course, which is a staple of my course load. First, my work in developing and implementing the Multiliteracies course required me to immerse myself deeply in Web 2.0 tools and other technologies used in teaching and learning. The other event is that I was asked to teach an online section of the content-literacy course at the same time I was developing the Multiliteracies course. In short, my initial experience with teaching online was overwhelming. I applied what I knew about teaching the course face-to-face in an asynchronous online format and found myself immersed in discussion threads that by the end of the course had over a thousand responses. I also found myself responding to student questions in dozens of emails. I also spent numerous hours writing responses to student work, the assignments described above, which were submitted to me as Word documents. It seemed far more demanding than face-to-face sections of the class I had taught.

I turned to professional development offered by our university and the SLOAN Consortium to learn more about online teaching, and I began to reflect on what I was learning in the Multiliteracies course. In my online courses, I added a weekly synchronous class meeting using Centra and Wimba, online learning environments supported by our university. In both my online and face-to-face sections, I began using online collaborative programs like Adobe Buzzword and Google Documents for the unit plan assignment and wikis for the toolkit assignment. I experimented with blogs as a way for students to record their experiences about the clinical tutoring. What I found was that the online collaborative tools facilitated group communication and collaboration far beyond what I had seen when students were using word processing documents. Figure 4 is an example of a

Figure 4. The Wiki toolkit, an example

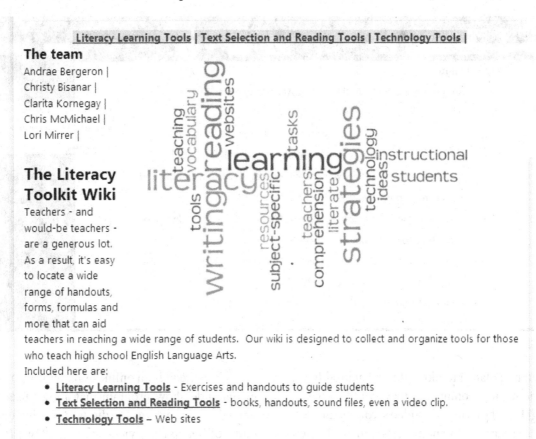

toolkit created by a group of English language arts students using PBWorks (www.pbworks.com).

The online collaboration tools also improved assignment logistics. Additions and changes in assignment documents were not lost as versions were emailed among group members. Also, because I had students include me as a member of their groups in the wikis and online document spaces, I had a window into students' work throughout the process. I could provide feedback on a more systematic basis through the development of the unit or toolkit. Figure 5 is a screenshot of a Literacy Integration Unit created in Buzzword which includes my feedback using the comment feature in the program. Word processing programs like Microsoft Word also allow for typed feedback using a comment feature but since I had access

to the group's unit throughout its creation, I was able to provide feedback and answer questions throughout the process.

I found other Web 2.0 tools helpful to me and my students. In my online sections, students used Jing (www.jingproject.com), a free screen capture program, to create overviews of their units to share with the class. This allowed us to provide instructor and peer feedback prior to turning in the final product. I also used Jing in my evaluation of the unit plans and wikis. In addition to my typed comments in their wikis and unit plans, I recorded one or two 5-minute video overviews of my thoughts using Jing, which I uploaded to Screencast.com (server space for video recordings provided by TechSmith, the creators of Jing). I sent the assignment creators a link to my video

Figure 5. The integrated literacy unit plan, an example

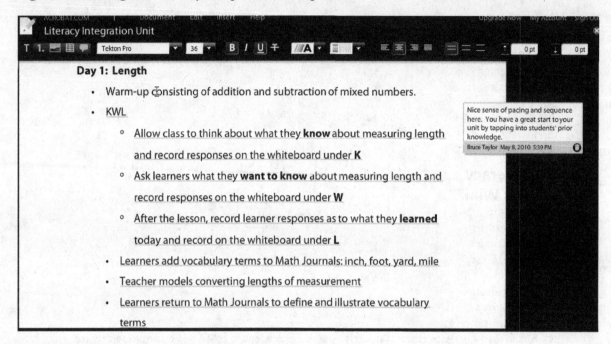

of their unit plan or toolkit wiki so that in addition to reading my comments, they could hear my thoughts as they viewed a video scrolling through their assignment. In another assignment I often use in the course, students write an autobiography of their development as readers and writers. I find it useful for them to reflect on their own literacy histories. Typically, this has been in the form of a short essay but during the time I began using online tools in the content area literacy course, I created digital options for this assignment. I mention two here: Dipity (www.dipity.com) and VoiceThread (www.voicethread.com). Dipity is a free, online timelining program that allows users to create their own timelines. For my assignment, students could upload digital photographs, texts and documents that helped describe their growth as readers and writers. Students wrote captions to go with these images, and other students and I could write comments with their online document. Figure 6 is an example of a timeline I created to share with my students.

VoiceThread is an online collaborative multimedia slide show program that allows users to upload a wide variety of digital texts include a range of image files, video formats, PowerPoint slides, word processing texts and Adobe PDF files to name some. These can be stitched together and the author can write captions and record an audio narrative so that the finished product is a visual text with audio that views like a short video. As with Dipity, other students and I could write comments but could also record audio or video feedback.

The changes to the content area literacy course were challenging for some of my students especially those less familiar with Web 2.0 technologies. The transition was easier for others. I argue that the benefits far outweighed the challenges in that these technologies fostered greater collaboration, improved communication, and allowed me to provide more substantial feedback throughout the process. Moreover, I feel that by using digital technologies I was modeling and better preparing my students to use them in their own classrooms.

Figure 6. Example of a literacy autobiography created in Dipity

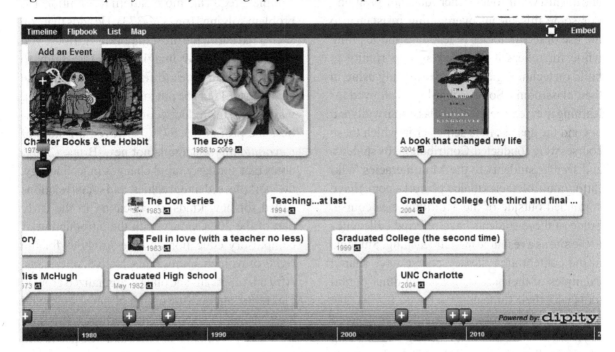

For me, the changes were transformative especially in teaching the online sections of the course. My experience as an instructor moved from that of being overwhelmed to feeling in control of a course that seemed to me to provide significant benefit to my students. While I acknowledge that the experience of teaching and learning in an online course differs from that of a face-to-face course, I now believe that both can be effective learning experiences for students and instructors.

TEACHING AND LEARNING IN A MULTILITERATE ENVIRONMENT: IMPLICATIONS AND CONCLUSIONS

The changes I describe in this chapter to integrate technology into teaching and learning in two courses did not begin with great forethought on my part. There was not a long period of planning on my part leading up to the changes. Change began with discussions about the need to update our graduate reading program with a course focusing on digital

and Multiliteracies. This process coincided with my introduction—and initial frustration—with online teaching. The changes in these courses took place in a relatively brief span of time, a few semesters, and felt revolutionary to me. As I look back on my teaching career, this seems in contrast to most changes I have experienced which have seemed more sequential or evolutionary. Nor do I claim that the changes I navigated are an example of "best practice," a template for others to use. On the contrary, I view my efforts as an attempt at managing chaos. To borrow a metaphor, the train was leaving the station, and I jumped on for the ride.

I have provided an account of the technologies students and I used to do the work of teaching and learning in these courses, citing changes to course assignments and digital tools we used to complete them, and highlighting ICTs we adopted to foster communication. I argue that these changes provided stronger experiences to preservice and inservice teachers to meaningfully integrate technology in their educational practice and not just within our teacher education program. For some this meant overcoming resistance to the use of technologies in teaching and learning while for others it provided an opportunity to build on technologies they were already using in their classrooms. Some technologies allowed for learning to extend beyond our classroom walls and beyond the space of the semester in which these courses were conducted. Contributions by students and former students to the Multiliteracies Wiki (http://multiliteraciesatuncc.pbworks.com/) have continued outside of the Multiliteracies course. Some of these students have referred colleagues to the site as a resource in their teaching. Students in the content-area literacy course have shared examples of their use of wikis and other digital tools with their students.

I believe learning is socially constructed (Vygotsky, 1997) and that teaching and learning exist in a dialogic relationship (Bakhtin, 1981). That is, they are part of an ongoing process in which each informs the other. The act of teaching is necessarily an ongoing act of learning, and learning informs our work in teaching. The move to incorporate digital and Web 2.0 tools into my teaching enhanced dialogue among my students and allowed me to enter conversations about key learning experiences more often. Our work together in university classrooms, in online meeting spaces, and through the use of Web 2.0 tools, allowed us to scaffold our collective learning. Then, through service learning with middle and secondary students, Freedom School Scholars and in professional development with inservice teachers, we, in turn, led others to explore how these tools can be used in K-12 classrooms to further their learning.

The need to raise Multiliterate students into Multiliterate citizens extends beyond the walls of the modern classroom into our economic, political and social lives (Gee, 2002). It is vital to participating in our democracy. As Thomas Freidman (2006) states, "As we push the frontiers of human knowledge, work at every level becomes more complex, requiring more pattern recognition and problem solving" (pp. 372-373). He adds that "on such a flat earth, the most important attribute you can have is creative imagination—the ability to be first on your block to figure out how all these enabling tools can be put together in new exciting ways to create products, communities, opportunities, and profits" (p. 571). However, this kind of *r/evolutionary* change is not new. Bruce (2002) notes that similarly rapid changes in technology, the workplace, demographics, and social relations called for new kinds of education in the early part of the 20th Century with the introduction of compulsory education and the struggles for the rights of women, immigrants, Native Americans, African Americans and other marginalized groups.

I return again to the notion of *r/evolutions* and how change in teaching and learning seem both slow and incremental at times and fast-paced and revolutionary other times. Change works that way—for the most part it happens at a reasonable rate but occasionally something spurs the need for rapid growth, adaptation and the need to climb a steeper learning curve. Changes in technologies continue to advance and as they do, so does our need to be literate in multiple ways. In an ever flattening world, if we do not make changes in how we teach and learn, we risk having schools that prepare students for a world that no longer exits. Some would argue we are at or beyond that point. Regardless, I side with those who would argue it is time to engage in some revolutionary change.

NOTE

Correspondence concerning this chapter can be sent to Dr. Bruce Taylor, Department of Reading & Elementary Education, University of North Carolina at Charlotte, 9201 University City Blvd., Charlotte, NC 28223, 704-687-8707 (phone), 704-687-3749 (fax). Address email to bruce.taylor@uncc.edu.

REFERENCES

Ajjan, H., & Hartshorne, R. (2008). Investigating faculty decisions to adopt Web 2.0 technologies: Theory and empirical tests. *The Internet and Higher Education, 11*(2), 71–80. doi:10.1016/j.iheduc.2008.05.002

Alvermann, D. (Ed.). (2002). *Adolescents and literacies in a digital world.* New York, NY: Peter Lang.

Anderson, J. B. (2008, January). *An overview of the research on service-learning in preservice teacher education.* A paper presented at the Student Coalition for Action in Literacy Education (SCALE): Learning to Teach, Learning to Serve Conference. Chapel Hill, NC.

Bakhtin, M. M. (1981). *The dialogic imagination.* Austin, TX: The University of Texas Press.

Barone, D., & Wrights, T. (2008). Literacy instruction with digital and media technologies. *The Reading Teacher, 62,* 292–302. doi:10.1598/RT.62.4.2

Billig, S. H. (2000). Research on K-12 school-based service learning: The evidence builds. *Phi Delta Kappan, 81,* 658–664.

Billig, S. H., & Klute, M. M. (2003). *The impact of service-learning on MEAP: A large-scale study of Michigan Learn and Serve grantees.* Presentation at National Service-Learning Conference, Minneapolis, MN.

Bruce, B. C. (2002). Diversity and critical social engagement: How changing technologies enable new modes of literacy in changing circumstances. In Alvermann, D. (Ed.), *Adolescents and literacies in a digital world* (pp. 1–18). New York, NY: Peter Lang.

Callahan, J., & Root, S. (2003). The diffusion of academic service-learning in teacher education: A case study approach. In S. H. Billig & J. Eyler (Eds.), *Advances in service-learning research: Vol. 3. Deconstructing service-learning: Research exploring context, participation, and impacts* (pp. 77–101). Greenwich, CT: Information Age.

Carroll, A. E., Rivara, F. P., Ebel, B., Zimmerman, F. J., & Christakis, D. A. (2005). Household computer and internet access: The digital divide in a pediatric clinic population. *AMIA Annual Symposium Proceedings,* (pp. 111-115). Retrieved on September 22, 2010 from http://www.ncbi.nlm.nih.gov/pmc/articles/PMC1560660/

Center for Information and Research on Civic Learning and Engagement. (2007). *Classrooms produce positive civic outcomes for students: Results from a longitudinal study of Chicago public school students.* College Park, MD: CIRCLE.

Cisco Systems. (2006). *Technology in schools: What the research says.* Retrieved from http://www.cisco.com/web/strategy/docs/education/TechnologyinSchoolsReport.pdf.

Collins, A., & Halverson, R. (2009). *Rethinking education in the age of technology: The digital revolution and schooling in America.* New York, NY: Teachers College Press.

Conrad, D., & Hedin, D. (1982). The impact of experiential education on adolescent development. *Child and Youth Services, 4*(3/4), 57–76. doi:10.1300/J024v04n03_08

Conrad, D., & Hedin, D. (1991). School-based community service: What we know from research and theory. *Phi Delta Kappan, 72*(10), 743–749.

Cope, B., & Kalantzis, M. (2000). *Multiliteracies: Literacy learning and the design of social futures.* New York, NY: Routledge.

Cuban, L. (1986). *Teachers and machines.* New York, NY: Teachers College Press.

Cuban, L. (2001). *Oversold and underused: Computers in the classroom.* Cambridge, MA: Harvard University Press.

Davis, A., & McGrail, E. (2009). Proof-revising with podcasting: Keeping readers in mind as students listen to and rethink their writing. *The Reading Teacher, 62*(6), 522–529. doi:10.1598/RT.62.6.6

Dodge, B. (1995). WebQuests: A technique for internet-based learning. *Distance Education, 1*(2), 10–13.

Evans, R. (1996). *The human side of school change: Reform, resistance, and the real-life problems of innovation.* San Francisco, CA: Jossey-Bass Publishers.

Freeman, N. K., & Swick, K. J. (2003). Preservice interns implement service learning: Helping young children reach out to their community. *Early Childhood Education Journal, 31*(2), 107–112. doi:10.1023/B:ECEJ.0000005309.44716.06

Friedman, T. L. (2006). *The world is flat [Updated and Expanded]: A brief history of the twenty-first century.* New York, NY: Farrar, Straus and Giroux.

Gee, J. P. (2002). Millennials and bobos. *Blue's Clues* and *Sesame Street*: A story for our times. In Alvermann, D. (Ed.), *Adolescents and literacies in a digital world* (pp. 51–67). New York, NY: Peter Lang.

Gee, J. P. (2003). *What video games have to teach us about literacy and learning.* New York, NY: Palgrave MacMillan Press.

Hart, S. M., & King, J. R. (2007). Service learning and literacy tutoring: Academic impact on preservice teachers. *Teaching and Teacher Education, 23*(4), 323–338. doi:10.1016/j.tate.2006.12.004

Huffaker, D. (2005). The educated blogger: Using weblogs to promote literacy in the classroom. *AACE Journal, 13*(2), 91–98.

Kirtman, L. (2008, March). Preservice teachers and mathematics: The impact of service-learning on teacher preparation. *School Science and Mathematics, 108*(3), 94–102. doi:10.1111/j.1949-8594.2008.tb17812.x

Krucli, T. E. (2004). Making assessment matter: Using the computer to create interactive feedback. *English Journal, 94*, 47–52. doi:10.2307/4128847

Labbo, L. (2005). From morning message to digital morning message: Moving from the tried and true to the new. *The Reading Teacher, 58*(8), 782–785. doi:10.1598/RT.58.8.9

Lankshear, C., & Knobel, M. (2003). *New literacies: Changing knowledge and classroom teaching.* Philadelphia, PA: Open University Press.

Leander, K., & Boldt, G. (2008). *New literacies in old literacy skins.* Paper presented at the Annual Meeting of the American Educational Research Association, New York.

Learn & Serve America. (2010). *What is service learning?* Retrieved September 28, 2010 from http://www.servicelearning.org/what_is_service-learning/service-learning_is

Leu, D. J. Jr. (2002). The new literacies: Research on reading instruction with the Internet and other digital technologies. In Samuels, J., & Farstrup, A. E. (Eds.), *What research has to say about reading instruction* (pp. 310–336). Newark, DE: International Reading Association.

Luke, A., & Elkins, J. (1998). Reinventing literacy in "New Times". *Journal of Adolescent & Adult Literacy, 42*(1), 4–7.

Maloney, E. (2007). What can Web 2.0 teach us about learning? *The Chronicle of Higher Education, 25*(18), B26.

Marcaruso, P., & Walker, A. (2008). The efficacy of computer-assited instruction for advancing literacy skills in kindegraten children. *Reading Psychology*, *29*(3), 266–287. doi:10.1080/02702710801982019

McClam, T., Diambra, J., Burton, B., Fuss, A., & Fudge, D. (2008). An analysis of a service learning project: Students' expectations, concerns, and reflections. *Journal of Experiential Education*, *30*(3), 236–249. doi:10.5193/JEE.30.3.236

Meaney, K., Griffin, K., & Bohler, H. (2009). Service-learning: A venue for enhancing preservice educators' knowledge base for teaching. *International Journal for the Scholarship of Teaching and Learning*, *3*(2), 1–17.

Miller, K., Dunlap, C., & Gonzalez, A. (2007). The impact of a freshman-year service-learning experience on the achievement of standards articulated for teacher candidates. *School Community Journal*, *17*(2), 111–121.

Morgan, B., & Smith, R. (2008). A Wiki for classroom writing. *The Reading Teacher*, *62*(1), 80–82. doi:10.1598/RT.62.1.10

National Council of Teachers of English. (2010). *The NCTE definition of 21st century literacies*. Retrieved from http://www.ncte.org/positions/statements/21stcentdefinition

New London Group. (1996). A pedagogy of multiliteracies: Designing social futures. *Harvard Educational Review*, *66*, 60–92.

Norris, C., & Soloway, E. (2003). The viable alternative: Handhelds. *School Administrator*, *60*(4), 26–28.

North Carolina State Board of Education, Department of Public Instruction. (1997). *A strategic plan for reading literacy*. Retrieved from http://www.ncpublicschools.org/docs/curriculum/languagearts/elementary/strategicplanforreadingliteracy.pdf

O'Brien, D. G., & Bauer, E. (2005). New literacies and the institution of old learning. *Reading Research Quarterly*, *40*, 120–131. doi:10.1598/RRQ.40.1.7

Oakley, G., & Jay, J. (2008). Making time for reading factors that influence the success of multimedia reading in the home. *The Reading Teacher*, *62*(3), 246–255. doi:10.1598/RT.62.3.6

Potthoff, D. E., Dinsmore, J. A., Stirtz, G., Walsh, T., Ziebarth, J., & Eifler, K. (2000). Preparing for democracy and diversity: The impact of community-based field experiences on preservice teachers' knowledge, skills, and attitudes. *Action in Teacher Education*, *22*(1), 79–92.

Rush, L. S. (2002). Taking a broad view of literacy: Lessons from the Appalachian Trail community. *Reading-Online*. Retrieved April 22, 2004 from http://www.readingonline.org/newliteracies/lit

Strage, A. (2000). Service learning: Enhancing student outcomes in a college level lecture course. *Michigan Journal of Community Service Learning*, *7*, 5–13.

Strage, A. (2004). Long term academic benefits of service learning: Where and when do they manifest themselves? *College Student Journal*, *38*(2), 257-262. ERIC Database (EJ704958).

Taylor, R. B. (2009). *Literacy integration unit assignment handout for READ 3255*. University of North Carolina at Charlotte, Department of Reading & Elementary Education.

Taylor, R. B. (2010a). *Syllabus for READ 6265*. University of North Carolina at Charlotte, Department of Reading & Elementary Education.

Taylor, R. B. (2010b). *Instructional service project assignment handout for READ 6265*. University of North Carolina at Charlotte, Department of Reading & Elementary Education.

Trilling, B., & Fadel, C. (2009). *21st century skills: Learning for life in our times*. San Francisco, CA: Jossey-Bass.

Tyack, D., & Cuban, L. (1995). *Tinkering toward utopia: A century of public school reform*. Cambridge, MA: Harvard University Press.

Vygotsky, L. S. (1978). *Mind in society: The development of higher psychological processes*. Cambridge, MA: Harvard University Press.

Wade, R. C., & Anderson, J. B. (1996). Community service learning: A strategy for preparing human service-oriented teachers. *Teacher Education Quarterly, 23*. Retrieved June 13, 2008, from www.teqjournal.org/backvols/1996/23

Wolfson, G. (2008). Using audio books to meet the needs of adolescent readers. *American Secondary Education, 36*(2), 105–114.

Zawilinski, L. (2009). HOT blogging: A framework for blogging to promote higher order thinking. *The Reading Teacher, 62*, 650–660. doi:10.1598/RT.62.8.3

Zucker, T. A., & Invernizzi, M. (2008). My e-sorts and digital extensions of word study. *The Reading Teacher, 61*, 654–658. doi:10.1598/RT.61.8.7

ADDITIONAL READING

Alvermann, D. E., Hinchman, K. A., Moore, D. W., Phelps, S. F., & Waff, D. R. (2006). *Reconceptualization the literacies in adolescents' lives* (2nd ed.). Mahwah, NJ: Erlbaum.

Anstey, M., & Bull, G. (2006). *Teaching and learning multiliteracies: Changing times, changing literacies*. Newark, DE: International Reading Association.

Black, R. W. (2006). Language, culture, and identity in online fanfiction. *E-learning, 3*(2), 170–184. doi:10.2304/elea.2006.3.2.170

Bonk, C. J. (2009). *The world is open: How web technology is revolutionizing education*. San Francisco, CA: Jossey-Bass.

Chandler-Olcott, K., & Mahar, D. (2003). Tech-savviness meets multiliteracies: An exploration of adolescent girls' technology-mediated literacy practices. *Reading Research Quarterly, 38*, 356–385. doi:10.1598/RRQ.38.3.3

Hendron, J. G. (2008). *RSS for educators: Blogs, newsfeeds, podcasts, and wikis for the classroom*. Washington, D.C.: International Society for Technology in Education.

Karchmer, R. A., Mallette, M. H., Kara-Soteriou, J., & Leu, D. J. (Eds.). (2005). *Innovative approaches to literacy education: Using the internet to support new literacies*. Newark, DE: International Reading Association.

Lankshear, C., & Knobel, M. (2006). *New literacies: Everyday practices and classroom learning* (2nd ed.). Berkshire, UK: McGraw-Hill/Open University Press.

Lankshear, C., & Knobel, M. (2007). Sampling the "new" in new literacies. In Knobel, M., & Lankshear, C. (Eds.), *A new literacies sampler* (pp. 1–24). New York: Peter Lang.

Solomon, G., & Schrum, L. (2007). *Web 2.0: New tools, new schools*. Washington, D.C.: International Society for Technology in Education.

KEY TERMS AND DEFINITIONS

Blog: A contraction of the term "web log"; a blog is a website maintained by an individual and may include regular posts, pictures and other media, RSS feeds, and commentary from guests or visitors to the blog. Popular blogging tools include WordPress, EduBlogs, Blogger, and LiveJournal.

Information Communication Technologies (ICTs): Computer-based technologies that facilitate communication. These include radio, television, cellular phones, computer and network hardware and software, and satellite systems. Computer applications including Skype, email, chat, and texting would forms computer software applications that are ICTs.

Multiliteracies: A term coined by the New London Group in 1996 to describe the rapidly evolving forms of literacy beyond traditional print-based forms used to communicate within diverse cultural and social settings.

Service Learning: On its website, the Learn & Serve America Clearinghouse defines service learning as a "teaching and learning strategy that integrates meaningful community service with instruction and reflection to enrich the learning experience, teach civic responsibility, and strengthen communities." Service learning is a form of pedagogy that combines learning outcomes with community service and reflection on the part of the learner.

Web 2.0: A term coined by Dale Dougherty of O'Reilly Media to capture changes in the Internet and web-based technologies that allow for my dynamic use of the web. Instead of passively consuming text on the web, users use tools such as blogs, wikis, comments, RSS feeds, and social networking sites (to name just a few) to read, write, and edit to the web.

Web 1.0: A retrofit term that arose after the term Web 2.0 came into popular usage. The primary concept the term Web 1.0 attempts to capture is the static nature of some web content and applications. Web pages that can only be read most often fall into this category. Some applications such as word processing programs and spreadsheets that are computer specific (i.e., the software exists on each computer on which it is used) are sometimes considered to be Web 1.0 applications.

Wiki: A web-based application that allows multiple users to create and edit content, which can include text, hypertext, audio, video, and more. Popular wiki tools and applications include Wikipedia, PBWorks, and WetPaint.

ENDNOTES

[1] The term *technology* means the use of tools, techniques, knowledge or craft to accomplish a goal. Under this broad definition, a pencil or pen, clothing, or stick used to reach something would be technologies. For my purposes in the chapter, I use the term technology/technologies to invoke more recently developed digital tools used in teaching and learning. I include computers, ICTs, and Web 1.0 and Web 2.0 tools, for example.

[2] In our teacher education programs, undergraduate students in our middle and secondary education programs take a 3000-level content-area literacy course while the graduate certificate students, who already have a bachelors degree, take a 5000-level content-area literacy course. Both courses are similar in content and structure.

[3] The report, *A Strategic Plan for Reading Literacy,* was approved by the North Carolina State Board of Education in April 2007.

Chapter 19
Weebly, Wikis, and Digital Storytelling:
The Potential of Web 2.0 Tools in Writing Classrooms

Brian Kissel
University of North Carolina at Charlotte, USA

ABSTRACT

In this chapter, the author explores three questions: 1. How is the practice of writing in K-12 classrooms influenced by this era of new technologies? 2. How can online technologies be brought into the classroom so students can understand that they read and write everyday in digital forms? 3. In what ways can teachers create technology-rich experiences to support 21st century writers? To answer these questions the author briefly examines the theoretical foundation of the process model for writing and how online technologies have impacted this model in classrooms. Next, the author describes three Web 2.0 tools that are available to teachers to use in their classrooms during writing: digital portfolios, wikis, and digital storytelling. The author explains how he uses these tools within his own college classroom. Finally, the author provides a rationale for why teachers should consider using these within their own K-12 classrooms so that digital technologies become a natural part of students' writing experiences.

INTRODUCTION

In my undergraduate Language Arts course, I begin the semester with a simple exercise. I ask students to think back to the past week and make a list of the various types of writing they composed, their

DOI: 10.4018/978-1-4666-0014-0.ch019

purposes for composing them, and their intended audiences. Drawing from personal, school, and work lives, students consider the types of writing they crafted. They have ten minutes to complete this exercise, but they usually finish in two. Typical responses are included in Table 1.

This past semester, when I asked students about their responses, one student explained, "I don't

Table 1. Types of writing

Type of Writing	Purpose	Audience
Notes in class	To remember	Self
Term papers	To get a good grade	Professor
Grocery List	To remember	Self
Order slips for work	To communicate with the cook	Cooking staff
Notes in planner	To organize, remember	Self

write because I don't really have time to write anything other than stuff for school. At work I write orders. At home I write lists of things I have to do. And at school I write papers for classes, but besides those things, I don't write much else." When students don't view themselves as writers, they don't see the types of writing they do every day in different forms.

I then asked the class to consider what they do online as readers and writers. Encouraged to expand on their charts, students began to identify the various ways they wrote within their online worlds. They considered what it meant to be 21st century writers, composing in an era where technology is ever-present, and using mediums such as smart phones and computers as platforms for their messages. With this lens, students broadened their lists to include the following in Table 2.

Initially, students didn't see themselves as writers; they never considered their texts, tweets, and status updates as actual pieces of writing. When students considered the digital ways they composed, they began to see the different types of writing they created, the varied purposes for creating it, and diverse audiences who consume it. They realized that, indeed, they did write and they did so daily and hourly. In fact, they identified themselves as voracious consumers and producers of literacy.

Even though students started to accept the uses of these technologies in their own lives, they still viewed these literacies as somehow divorced from what they considered *real* forms of writing; the forms most accepted in school settings. And they certainly didn't consider the possibility of incorporating these types of writings into their own classrooms as future elementary school teachers.

This chapter is presented as a how-to and a what-if for teachers and teacher-educators interested in incorporating digital portfolios, wikis, and digital stories into their classrooms. It is meant to show how the digital forms of writing might be expanded into both college and K-12 classrooms. The purpose of this chapter is to start asking, and answering, the following three questions: 1.) How is the practice of writing in K-12 classrooms

Table 2. Types of writing, including digital writings

Type of Writing	Purpose	Audience
Facebook (Status updates)	To connect with friends/to communicate	Friends
Blogs	To respond to others' comments	Self, blogosphere
Texts	To communicate/inform	Friends, family
Email	To communicate, inform, connect, respond	Friends, family, co-workers, professors, classmates
Instant Messaging	To communicate	Friends
Twitter	To communicate, inform, entertain	Friends, Twitterverse

influenced by this era of new technologies? 2.) In what ways can we bring online technologies into the classroom so students can understand that they read and write everyday in digital forms? 3.) In what ways can teachers create technology-rich experiences to support 21st century writers?

To begin answering these questions I will briefly examine the theoretical foundation of writing processes and reflect on how online technologies have impacted what writers do to process texts in this digital age. Following a brief explanation of my instructional stance, I describe three Web 2.0 tools available to teachers to use in their classrooms during writing: digital portfolios, wikis, and digital storytelling. I explain how I use these technologies in my own college classroom, and then consider the promise and pratfalls these tools present for K-12 teachers. This chapter ends with a plea for teachers to consider bringing these technologies forward into their classroom so students can experience the relevance of these technologies within their writerly lives.

BACKGROUND

For the past 30 years, theoretical models of the processes writers use to compose texts describe a combination of the following: planning, drafting, revising, editing, and publishing (Calkins, 1994; Fletcher & Portalupi, 2000; Graves, 1983). Or, as Donald Murray (2004) more succinctly states, writers collect, plan, and develop.

On paper, this process looks rather concrete. Concept maps or outlines show pathways during planning; quick, messy orthographic forms show the fervor of drafting; chunks of added or deleted text reveal the complicated cycle of revising; circled misspellings and strike-throughs mark the intricate nature of editing. And, after writers proceed through these individualized processes their work goes public—consumed by a pre-determined audience.

The advent of new technologies, specifically online technologies, redefines what happens when writers compose. Backspace replaces the eraser, highlighting chunks of text to cut and paste marks revision, and spelling/grammar checks aid editing. The entire notion of a recursive process for writing is challenged by what writers currently do when composing online (Yancy, 2009). Now, writers often compose using a two-step process; they write a fast draft, then publish immediately to an instant audience. In this way writers use social networking sites such as Facebook and MySpace, along with instant messaging and blogging, to revolutionize the way we process online texts.

Writing, and our students' engagement in the process, is evolving because new technologies require students to write in far different ways than in previous centuries. For example, in a typical 20th century classroom where students wrote memoirs, students might spend a day or two planning their memoirs, another several days drafting, and a few more days revising. They probably received editing suggestions from peers or the teacher before they were ready to be rewritten and polished for publication. Audiences for their work included the teacher, and certainly the child's family. The book might find a prominent place on the book shelf of their home or classroom, or the parents might place the book away in a storage container where it would remain in the attic until nostalgia brings the book back out.

Compare this with a 21st century memoir, the Web log or *blog*. On a blog students might also write short memoirs about their lives, but they may do so in a matter of hours, rather than days. Writers might type their musings or anecdotes quickly, re-read their work to revise, use a spell and grammar checker to do a quick edit, then click *publish* where an audience has instant access. Just as quickly as the author drafted, the audience may likewise offer a hasty response. But, the writing is ever-present, available to all viewers instantly with a click of the mouse.

Within the past 10 years, the ways we envision, compose, and publish our memoirs are dramatically different. Our language, and use of it, has evolved. Our students certainly know it, but there are still many in our schools who have failed to acknowledge this evolution, or resist the change this evolution might bring to writing classrooms. Consequently, students in classrooms where technology is not embraced may become members of technology gap—positioning them in a disadvantage from more experienced technological peers. The closing of this gap compels us to consider incorporating more Web 2.0 technologies into our classrooms.

Complicating this evolution is the preparation of teachers charged with bringing these new technologies into their classrooms (Alvermann, 2004). The constant changes in technology require equally constant changes in the ways we teach literacy within our classrooms (Kinzer, 2010). As Kinzer (2010) notes, "The tools available for teachers and students and the skills necessary to use those tools have profound implications for how we define literacy and the reading and writing curriculum" (p. 51). For teachers unprepared to teach using such technologies, there are classrooms of students who face another year disconnected at school from the possibilities these technologies may bring into their lives.

Engaging students in online technologies is a critical need to develop a literate citizenry (Leu, Kinzer, Coiro, & Cammack, 2004). To prepare literate students in the 21st century, students must have access to, and experience with, online technologies. And, because they need these experiences, teachers must bring such technologies into their classrooms so students have practical, hands-on opportunities to interact with the Digital Age. It is not enough for us to casually sprinkle the classroom with digital possibilities. We must immerse students in these Web 2.0 tools so they see the real purposes these tools might bring to their writerly lives.

In the next section we focus on what teachers can do to bring these technologies into their classrooms. By helping teachers see these technological possibilities, students find opportunities to connect their home literacies, the ones done on computers and cell phones, with school expectations.

TECHNOLOGY IN THE CLASSROOM

I teach my courses using an experiential-based teaching stance. That is, I believe teachers must become writers themselves in order to effectively teach writing to their students. Likewise, I believe teachers must be technology-users themselves so they can see the possibilities of using such technology within their own classrooms. To prepare teachers to teach writing in the 21st century, I incorporate three different Web 2.0 tools into my Language Arts course. These tools include digital writing portfolios, wikis, and digital storytelling movies. In the following section, I provide a description of each technology, explain how I incorporate them into my Language Arts classroom, and examine the possibilities and challenges of incorporating these technologies within K-12 classrooms.

DIGITAL PORTFOLIOS

In the fields of architecture and the arts, professionals create portfolios to show the breadth and depth of their work: what they've learned, what they've accomplished, and how they've grown from these experiences. For the past couple decades, in a response to one-shot tests that do little to measure the breadth and depth of their writing lives, teachers have incorporated portfolios in their classrooms to give students voice to defend their own learning (Sunstein, 1996; Johnston, 1997). To do so, students select pieces of writing that answer these questions: *Who are you as a writer? What have you learned as a writer in this classroom?*

These questions guide students' decision-making. They pour through all their writings—the finished and unfinished—to find documentation to support their assertions about themselves. They might, for example, choose a list they generated of various writing ideas to show how they gather topics for writing. Or, they may choose a sample of a revised draft—showing the many ways they added details, deleted unnecessary information, and restructured a piece. Or, they may choose to include a comic strip they created to show their experimentation with various genres. Or, they may choose various pieces that show them to be creative thinkers, reflectors, collaborators, and reading responders. Their choices are unlimited. And, because teachers empower students with these choices, the portfolios reveal unique, distinctive voices.

For many years, the use of paper-based writing portfolios has been a common form of assessment in the classroom. Students collect documents from their writer's notebooks or folders, make copies, encase them in sheet protectors, and write reflections to describe and analyze their decisions. These portfolios are typically collected by the teacher, assessed (graded in some cases), and shown to parents to chart progress—or lack thereof.

In recent years, teachers have taken portfolios into the digital age, increasing the possibilities of form, and expanding potential audiences (Hicks, et. al, 2008). They use websites that allow users to create spaces to multi-modally share their work with others. Weebly (www.weebly.com) is one such platform.

Weebly is a free, online website creator. It allows users to easily create websites via various templates. Writers use the simple "drag and drop" elements to create visually appealing widget-based pages to house their work. The appeal of Weebly is its simplicity; if writers want to add a photo gallery of work, they simply click on the photo gallery widget and drag the widget to its desired location on the website. When the writer clicks publish, the work saves and is viewable by other Internet users. Other elements (Figure 1) include paragraphs with titles, photos, videos, columns, photo galleries, files, audio players, videos, embedded documents, flash videos, maps, slideshows, and links to YouTube videos. In a matter of ten minutes, students can easily create their own Weebly website, register a domain name, design multiple pages, and upload files.

Digital Portfolios: The College Classroom

In keeping with the rich tradition of writing portfolios in K-12 classrooms, I ask my students in Language Arts to create their own portfolios. In one way, these portfolios serve as a housing station for the required coursework. However, I encourage students to think of these portfolios in more expansive ways—to push beyond the boundaries of course requirements to use these portfolios to show who they are as writers, learners, and future teachers. In response, students modify their websites in unique and distinctive ways, showing who they are and what they know through the content they upload to the pages.

The required work consists of four separate pages on their Weebly sites. Alone, they fulfill the requirements of the course. Combined, they give the viewer a sense of who the writer is and provides an overview of the writer's work. They include:

1. *A Home Page*. For this page, students create profiles to introduce themselves to the reader. Typically, they upload self-portraits and write personal background information. Many students post mini-biographies, offering the reader highlights about hometowns and past experiences. They also offer insight into why they chose teaching as a profession and a calling. The homepage introduces writers to the audience and sets the stage for viewing their work. It serves as an introduction.

2. *A Personal Piece Page: Multigenre Life Stories*. Students write a personal piece of writing in the form of a multigenre project. The writer

chooses a personal topic, determines the purpose for the writing, and indicates the intended audience. Many students write about influential people in their lives, meaningful events, or topics they know much about. Throughout the years, students have written about various topics: surviving cancer, giving children up for adoption, getting married, raising children, remembering those who have died, and honoring those who live—to name a few. The purpose of this writing is to provide students an opportunity to experience their own writing process while connecting to a powerful and meaningful subject from their lives. This project provides personal insight into what it is like to be a writer and helps pre-service teachers develop their knowledge about writing processes and writing pedagogy. In addition to the Multigenre Project, students write a reflection to accompany the finished product. This reflective piece requires writers to explain the process they used to create the product, examine what they have learned by engaging in this process, and explore how this knowledge impacts them as future writing teachers.

3. *Clinical Report:* The Language Arts class has a clinical component which requires students to spend 8-10 hours within an elementary classroom. Within this clinical assignment, students observe, interview, teach, and participate with the class during writing instruction. For their digital portfolios, students write about these experiences and post them to their website. Oftentimes, students will post photos, upload collected documents, incorporate videos, and embed interviews using several of the different Weebly elements. This results in a multi-modal, multigenre, multi-sensory experience for the viewer who experiences elements of the clinical experience through the students' eyes.

4. *Daybook Reflections:* The final page requires the writer to examine their daybooks (also known as Writer's Notebooks) to find pages that show what they have learned as writers in the class. This webpage is led by a guiding question: *What have you learned as a writer this semester?* Students

then pour through their daybooks to find exemplars. They scan or take photos of the page, upload it to their Weebly site, and write a reflection that answers the question (Figure 2).

Digital Portfolios: Possibilities and Pitfalls

In my classroom, students can add a widget to their digital portfolios to allow peers to comment on their work. In this way, students who create the digital portfolios position themselves in rhetorical situations—they reveal who they are by creating a version of themselves. Others will view, analyze, comment upon, and reference to formulate opinions (Yancy, 2004). This positioning serves as an avenue to document knowledge and growth. Writers think reflectively and critically about their learning and record this on a digital space. At the same time, peers in the classroom, or blogosphere, have opportunities to respond to this documentation, offering comments, making suggestions, asking questions, or finding ways they personally connect. This allows the writer of the digital portfolio to reach a wider audience—where response to writing is not limited to just the teacher's comments.

While this unlimited response offers promise for many digital portfolio writers, for others, this uncontrolled, sometimes unwelcomed intrusion into their learning processes may elicit unwanted comments from the public. This was the case when a group of high school teacher-researchers created digital portfolios with their students (Hicks, et. al., 2007). When their portfolios went public, and other teachers had access to view the work done by the writers, one teacher, rather than responding to the rich content created by the student, focused instead on a single spelling error, disappointing the teacher who was proud of the rich content the students created. When the writer's work goes public, as it does via digital portfolios, the responses from the public are not always the positive, critically responsible responses writers seek.

Our current digital landscape requires teachers to consider alternatives to the writing portfolios of the past. We have to consider whether or not the traditional portfolio—a portfolio created using paper, pens, and folders, and viewed by only one audience member, the teacher—achieves the same goals as digital portfolios. That is, do we want our students to only inform themselves and the teacher of what they know, or do we want them to go public with their knowledge so that, in their own way, the digital portfolio can be not only a learning tool, but also a teaching tool? This is a question that continues to undergird our instruction implementation decisions.

WIKIS

Wikis (Hawaiian term for "quick") are websites that allow multiple users to write collaboratively about a particular topic and link the information with other web pages. These linkages create interwoven webs—allowing readers to navigate through multiple pages to discover detailed information about various topics. Because this is a collaborative writing space, multiple users have authority to write, edit, and save information.

In 2001 Wikipedia, an online encyclopedia written by the general public, entered the public consciousness and catapulted the popularity of wikis as reference guides for learners. In ten short years, Wikipedia writers (around 13 million) have written over 3 million articles and created over 21 million pages. And, amongst these pages, users have edited content over 415 million times. Whereas, with blogs and social networks, writers draft and quickly publish, wiki writers must do so knowing that others will check their content to revise and edit where appropriate.

Recently, I co-authored a chapter in a book with a colleague. To write this chapter, we brainstormed an outline over the phone and divided the portions of the chapter between ourselves. We established a deadline for each piece, and, when we com-

pleted our respective pieces, emailed them back and forth to one another for feedback. Initially, this procedure worked; we downloaded, saved to the computer, revised and edited with tracked changes, saved again, attached our revisions to a new email, and sent. After our third time doing this, however, the procedure became cumbersome, confusing, and unmanageable. Our state of constant confusion wasted valuable writing time.

We heard about wikis from our colleagues and decided to write our chapter using this platform. Instead of writing on separate documents, we wrote using a shared document. To see the changes each person made, we wrote using different font colors. With my changes in blue and her changes in purple, we witnessed each other's revisioning and editing processes in action. And, conveniently, the hosted site was accessible from any computer with an Internet connection. So, I could make some revisions from my computer at work, then come home and make further revisions in my home office. She could do the same. The nature of the wiki allowed us to co-create in a way I've never collaborated with another writer before. We experienced, first-hand, how writers can use these tools to foster collaboration.

Wikis: The College Classroom

In my undergraduate Language Arts course, students use a Wetpaint wiki to construct, consolidate, and disseminate information about various genres of writing through an assignment titled: *Collaborative Writing—The Genre Study Wiki.* Inspired by Katie Wood Ray's book *Study Driven* (2006), students study various genres of writing using her instructional framework. This structure includes gathering representational texts of the genre, setting the stage for study, immersing with the texts by reading thoroughly, closely studying the texts by making lists of noticings and wonderings, and, finally, writing under the influence. The underlying concept is that poets learn to write one poem after they have opportunities to read and study many poems. Likewise, writers learn to write by reading, and studying genres, in-depth, provides the necessary background knowledge writers need to do so successively (Dean, 2008).

As students immerse in this intensive study, they record what they've learned on a class wiki (Figure 3). The class wiki allows students to determine the information they wish to convey to classmates. Most students choose to write a description and overview of the genre, create a comprehensive list of mentor texts teachers could use to teach this genre, examples of exemplary texts that represent the genre, lists of helpful websites (including author websites, YouTube videos, and lesson plan sites), and lists of authors who write within the genre.

The wiki allows students to write collaboratively with others. In groups they work independently to instruct readers about a particular genre. Collectively, they create a site full of resources for one another. In this way, writing becomes both a generative and collaborative act. Students produce content based on what they have learned. Then, they consume this content when they read the writing of others who inform them about unfamiliar genres. Further collaboration occurs when students find connections amongst their genres and link their pages together creating that interwoven web. For several successive years, students have maintained the wiki—constantly updating the information and adding new genres as they become known. And they bring this wiki into their K-12 classrooms as they look for resources to guide their genre studies with young children.

Wikis: Possibilities and Pitfalls

Wikis present possibilities for collaboration amongst writers in K-college classrooms. Rather than writing in isolation, writers write in consultation—using digital spaces to plan, draft, revise, edit, and publish—together. Whereas physical space can sometimes limit the possibility of collaboration, digital spaces eliminate the need for writers to sit side-by-side to write.

Teachers who teach K-12 students have found ways to harness the possibilities of this powerful tool within their classrooms. This is why wikis are quickly becoming popular Web 2.0 tools in writing classrooms. Wiki sites such as Wetpaint, PB Works, and Wikispaces allow teachers to easily create spaces for students to collaborate as writers. And as they collaborate, students merge social learning and literacy development, forming connective bonds as writers (Kissel, Hathaway, & Wood, 2010).

Working collaboratively on shared spaces does present challenges for writers. When a text is co-created, who makes the final revision decisions? Who decides the piece is ready for publication? Who decides the audiences for the writing? And, as multiple authors click edit to change the document, what if authors have conflicts about how to best compose the work? All these decisions must be shared, and sometimes this positioning causes conflicts amongst the authors. When multiple authors are *author*ities on a single piece of writing they might unwillingly trespass on another author's terrain. These questions arise whenever writers co-construct texts. But wikis bring these conflicts public through the open, digital space.

DIGITAL STORYTELLING

My son, Ben, was born two months early, along with his twin brother Charlie. Charlie, always active during my wife's pregnancy, decided he was ready to enter the world. His brother wanted a bit more time, but didn't get it. So, when they did arrive, Charlie had no problems, but his tiny brother struggled.

I wasn't quite prepared to see my son's tiny body covered in gauze and attached to tubes. It was never how I envisioned his birth, and it robbed my wife and me of a storybook delivery.

When we saw him laying helpless in an isolette, we tried to be strong, but often cried at his side.

I consider myself a writer before anything else, and, typically I use the medium as a way to understand my life, or, at the very least, try to make sense of it. It comes in handy during the more difficult times. But, in Ben's case my hand fell silent. No words could convey my worry. So, instead, I picked up a camera and told Ben's story through images. During the initial hours of his life, I snapped a photographs of his mother seeing him for the first time, reading him his first story, placing her hands on his chest, looking fondly into his little eyes, praying silently for his safe recovery, and crying quietly. To preserve this memory, I organized the photos in iMovie, added music, and told the story multi-modally (Figure 4). I then sent this video, via YouTube to friends and family so they could get a sense of our mood and experience (http://www.youtube.com/watch?v=J-B8WHTwnQs).

Not all writing is conveyed through written words. Sometimes, stories can be better conveyed through images, music, and spoken words. This is what happens when writers create digital stories through software like Microsoft Movie Maker or Apple iMovie. Audiences view the writer using multiple senses of sight, sound, and emotional feelings. Writers of digital stories combine various types of multimedia so readers can view the content on digital platforms. For 21st century writers, "the combination of powerful, yet affordable, technology hardware and software meshes perfectly with the needs of many of today's classrooms, where the focus is on providing students with the skills they need to thrive" (Robin, 2008, p. 222).

Digital Stories: The College Classroom

In my courses, students use digital storytelling to tell their own stories, using memoir to tell snippets about their lives. To do this, students record their voices using a podcast, combine their voices with images, and add music. For viewers, this creates a multi-modal experience. Viewers begin to understand the writer's experience because they are inundated with sensory details that provide a sense of mood and emotion.

Oftentimes, these digital stories are powerfully emotional. When one student in my class narrated a story about the childhood abuse he suffered from the hands of his father, the audience heard the anger in his spoken voice and wanted to enact revenge for damaging the sweet soul who often sat quietly in the back of our classroom. When another student constructed a visual timeline of her husband's experiences with her sons, the class grew devastated when, at the end of the movie, we discovered their father recently died. Sometimes our students have stories they *need* to tell. And, as audience members and peers, we *need* to hear these stories to develop deeper, richer understandings of our classmates as human beings.

To create these stories, students follow similar processes as they do when they write using paper and pens. That is, they make plans (usually in the form of storyboards) and find or create materials to tell their stories; draft by writing, then recording their voices; revise by making sure their meanings and voices are clear; edit to clarify any recording mistakes; and, finally, publish in ways to make their work viewable by others. Oftentimes, publication happens on Facebook or YouTube where friends, family, and other viewers may view their work and offer comments. In most cases, the comments give the writer validation, confirmation, and motivation to continue creating more stories.

Digital Stories: Possibilities and Pitfalls

Digital stories offer writers the promise of voice. This was the case for high school students in California who came from low-income, migrant homes (Nixon, 2009). Through digital storytelling, the students, often marginalized because of their socio-economic and cultural status, were given agency to tell their stories and offer their views of their social worlds. In most written contexts, these written voices are often considered deficient. In a multi-media context, their voices are bold, loud, and hard to ignore.

Those hesitant to bring digital stories into the classroom cite the time-consuming nature of the medium. Unlike other technologies explained within this chapter, digital stories take longer to construct. To do so, writers must collect materials, plan the story, take photographs or find some, write scripts, record voices, arrange images, browse music, and intricately edit the materials within the frames of the software in coordination with all the other materials. Not only does this require copious amounts of time, it requires the same amount of patience—for both students and teachers.

As with most things, writers get better with practice. Their hands-on experiences creating these stories reveal time-saving tricks, speeding the process along for future projects. And, it is often the positive reactions of viewers that persuade writers that this is a powerful medium to continue to pursue.

CONCLUSION

This digital age necessitates that K-12 classrooms welcome, within its walls, the promise of digital literacies into the language arts curriculum. When we weave this technology into the classroom, and offer it as a choice amongst the vast repertoire of choices available to students as writers, the possibilities become expansive.

We learned how three such Web 2.0 tools offer purpose for writers in classrooms. Digital portfolios allow writers to show their work to broad audiences, welcoming comments, suggestions, and questions while presenting writers opportunities to show others what they know. Wikis provide students opportunities to co-construct. Through this co-construction of texts, writers find common topics, common purposes, and common processes

to fulfill those agendas. Digital stories convince writers that not all stories must be print-based in order to be compelling. In fact, by combining words, voice, images, and music, writers can evoke emotions from viewers that are just as moving as a beautifully constructed written piece.

Sara Kajder (2008) states, "I firmly believe that valuing and seeing the ways in which kids are engaging with new technologies outside of school can teach us a great deal about possibilities in engaging them as readers and writers in our classrooms" (p. 213). Indeed, literacy learning stands at the intersection of two crossroads. In one direction, schools offer students opportunities to read and write in ways we have always read and written. Students hold picture books, chapter books, informational texts, and great literature in their hands and grasp pencils, pens, crayons, and markers in their fingers to construct texts on various writing surfaces. In the other direction, the one that points homeward, students have smart phones and computers that provide portals towards all sorts of digital possibilities. They have websites to browse and consume, blogs, wikis, and social networking sites to produce. This new generation of literacy learners are constructing what it means to be literate—and it's changing by the minute.

Our job as educators is to safely bring these literacy mediums together—to assimilate, instead of collide. And, in doing so, we must be careful not to privilege one over the other because they both hold value in our literate lives. Students bring their lives into literacy, whether it is by paper-and-pen or keyboard and screen. It's our obligation to allow both possibilities to unfold within our 21st century classrooms.

REFERENCES

Alvermann, D. (2004). *Adolescents and literacies in a digital world*. New York, NY: Peter Lang.

Calkins, L. (1994). *The art of teaching writing*. Portsmouth, NH: Heinemann.

Dean, D. (2008). *Genre theory: Teaching, writing, and being*. Urbana, IL: NCTE.

Fletcher, R., & Portalupi, J. (2001). *Writing workshop: The essential guide*. Portsmouth, NH: Heinemann.

Graves, D. (1983). *Writing: Teachers and students at work*. Portsmouth, NH: Heinemann.

Hicks, T., Russo, A., Autrey, T., Gardner, R., Kabodian, A., & Edington, C. (2007). Rethinking the purposes and processes for designing digital portfolios. *Journal of Adolescent & Adult Literacy, 50*(6), 450–458. doi:10.1598/JAAL.50.6.3

Johnston, P. (1997). *Knowing literacy: Constructive literacy assessment*. Portland, ME: Stenhouse.

Kajder, S. (2007). Unleashing potential with emerging technologies. In Beers, G. K., Probst, R., & Rief, L. (Eds.), *Adolescent literacy: Turning promise into practice* (pp. 213–229). Portsmouth, NH: Heinemann.

Kinzer, C. (2010). Considering literacy and policy in the context of digital environments. *Language Arts, 88*(1), 51–61.

Kissel, B., Hathaway, J., & Wood, K. (2010). Digital collaborative literacy: Using wikis to promote social learning and literacy development. *Middle School Journal, 41*(5), 58–63.

Leu, D. J., Kinzer, C. K., Coiro, J. L., & Cammack, D. W. (2004). Toward a theory of new literacies emerging from the Internet and other information and communication technologies. In Unrau, N. J., & Ruddell, R. B. (Eds.), *Theoretical models and processes of reading* (5th ed., pp. 1570–1613). Newark, DE: International Reading Association.

Murray, D. (2004). *A writer teaches writing*. Boston, MA: Heinle.

Nixon, A. (2009). Mediating social thought through digital storytelling. *Pedagogies: An International Journal, 4*, 63–76.

Ray, K. W. (2006). *Study driven: A framework for planning units of study in the writing workshop*. Portsmouth, NH: Heinemann.

Robin, B. (2008). Digital storytelling: A powerful technology tool for the 21st century classroom. *Theory into Practice, 47*, 220–228. doi:10.1080/00405840802153916

Sunstein, B. (1996). Assessing portfolio assessment: Three encounters of a close kind. *Voices from the Middle, 3*(4), 13–22.

Yancy, K. B. (2004). Postmodernism, palimpsest, and portfolios: Theoretical issues in the representation of student work. *College Composition and Communication, 55*, 738–761. doi:10.2307/4140669

Yancy, K. B. (2009). *Writing in the 21st Century*. Urbana, IL: National Council of Teachers of English.

Chapter 20
Educational Technology in Early Childhood Teacher Education:
Taking the Road Less Traveled

Sudha Swaminathan
Eastern Connecticut State University, USA

ABSTRACT

Educational technology usage in early childhood education stands at a fork in the road. One path embellishes existing curricula with technology. The other, the more difficult passing, holds promises of technological transformations to the curricula and assessment in ways that can facilitate and propel child development. To support teachers in this path, early childhood teacher education programs need to transform themselves. The purpose of this chapter is to outline how these changes may occur within the context of national standards and policies, pedagogy and beliefs, curricular transformations, impact on children, and special tools. The authors suggests re-conceptualizing the content and delivery of college courses to support and inspire teachers to take the road less traveled. Additionally teachers need ongoing and recurrent support for continued progress in their educational technology usage.

INTRODUCTION

It's been 15 years since I co-authored a review of research in which we proposed that early childhood education stood at the crossroads of development in terms of technological infu-

sion and transformation (Clements, Nastasi, & Swaminathan, 1995). There were still skeptics who worried about the impact of computers on young children, and a growing cadre of enthusiasts who saw great potential for transforming curriculum and teaching. At that time, the computer was almost the only major piece of technology available and was almost synonymous with technology.

DOI: 10.4018/978-1-4666-0014-0.ch020

Since then, the field has exploded in many ways. Shoving aside the computer and claiming more intense educational attention are newer and intuitively clever and child-friendly tools such as the digital camera, the hand-held digital microscope and the iPad. However, while several research studies and classroom action research projects have illuminated creative ways for educational technology to both propel and facilitate child development, teacher support and usage of these 'innovative tools' has remained hesitant, sporadic and spotty, at best (Wood, Specht, Willoughby, & Mueller, 2008).

Where do we go from here? In this chapter, I propose that educational technology in early childhood teacher education stands at a clear fork in the road: Taking the road well traveled leads to existing curriculum embellished with educational technology propagating current practices; or, taking the road less traveled could lead us to incredible content-rich and technology-rich curricular and pedagogical practices. What does the road less traveled look like within early childhood teacher education? Where do these rich educational practices exist (as indeed, they do)? What hardships await those who travel this path? And finally, where does this path lead us? I propose to address these metaphorical questions in my chapter, within the context of five major sub-topics: Standards and expectations, pedagogy and beliefs, curricular transformations, impact on children and use of special tools.

Educational Technology Standards for Early Childhood Education

It takes a while for most educational reform to pervade the field of education, but it takes even longer for technological interpretations to seep into Early Childhood Education, hitherto referred as ECE (Wartella & Nancy, 2000). To illustrate, we need only look at a few dates on the teacher education timeline. It was not until 2007 that the International Society for Technology in Education

(ISTE) started including preschool within their NETS*S standards for students (International Society for Technology in Education, 2007). The National Association for the Education of Young Children (NAEYC), the premier professional organization for ECE put forth a position statement on technology and young children (a well written, comprehensive document, by the way) in 1996, and this document (NAEYC, 1996) has remained the sole official document from NAEYC for close to 15 years even whilst technological tools for the young child in the commercial world erupted into a mushroom cloud of talking, moving and sometimes sensing toys. It is anticipated that NAEYC will finally have an updated position statement in mid-2011.

Even acknowledging the gradual pace of the educational change, what are the expectations and guidance afforded by these documents for navigating the roads less traveled in ECE?

First and foremost, by relegating technology operations and concepts as the sixth and final NETS*S standard, we receive the clear message that no longer can operation of technology tools be taught in isolation. The learning of technical skills becomes subsumed within the execution of the first four curricular integrated standards of creativity, communication, research and critical thinking. This is an acknowledgment of a developmental change in the thinking and learning styles of the newest generation of young school children. It is an acknowledgement that as adults we need to shift our own thinking from *how do I do this* to *what can I do with this*. I discuss and detail with examples the particular impact of these ideals in later sections. To provide a single example here, within ECE, this shift consists of moving the computer center from its one fixed location all year round to rotating it to the art, the writing, or the science center, and offering it as just another integral tool available for the children to use in creative or research endeavors. Learning theories (Resnick, 1985) have expounded on the value of changing the time of day and place of study as a simple way to refresh our brain and to keep our understanding more active. So too, in the young child's classroom, shifting and integrating technology within other physical locations can initiate creative thinking. But, just as college students resist sitting anywhere other than the same chair/desk week after week, for an entire semester, so too do ECE teachers resist moving their computers. It remains a road not as often traveled.

A second implication of these new standards, especially within the NETS*T, is the expectation that teachers will facilitate, inspire, design, develop and model—not teach. Within ECE, this is not easy to implement. The more autonomy we give to children, the harder we have to work (Papert, 1993). Here is an example to illustrate the point: Some ECE teachers of an older generation are not very tech-savvy. During professional development, it is far easier for me as teacher educator to grab the mouse off a struggling teacher's palms and reset a dead program than to sit impatiently still (but with a sincere demeanor of support) while he slowly figures it out. And yet, I find that only when I grit my teeth and sit on my hands, does the teacher learn to navigate his own way through the reset issues. More critically, he also knows enough now to show or talk others through similar issues, and most importantly, is not worried when it happens again. This is a road that is difficult to travel for all teacher educators, to facilitate and not to instruct (Swaminathan, Barbuto, Trawick-Smith, & Wright, 2004; Wood, et al., 2008).

The third implication from these standards is the integrated nature of learning for children, for teachers and for teacher educators. While not a new concept by any means, an explicit awareness of this dramatic and systemic interconnection between content, pedagogy and technology affords stepping stones of assistance. Recently, this has been crystallized into a theoretical framework, TPCK or technological pedagogical content knowledge (Mishra & Koehler, 2006). Once again, I offer a single example here. Similar to the authors of this seminal theory, we have used digital movie

making as a self-monitoring tool with ECE teacher candidates (Swaminathan, 2000). Our pre-service teachers routinely video-tape their teaching, and edit it, using our state teacher certification expectations as an analytical framework. What used to be a simple essay on their teaching prowess is now an actively constructed and self-created digital video story (Technology) that scrutinizes their teaching strengths and weaknesses (Pedagogy) in the light of the domains of expectations for teachers (Content). The process of technical editing and captioning as per the domains has alerted both my teacher candidates and me to the dynamic interconnections and power afforded by the simple tool of video editing. This needs to become a road well traveled.

Pedagogy and Beliefs

Incredible as it may seem, even with these standards and expectations and the swift infusion of myriad multi-media and technological devices into the schools, the biggest hurdle to educational technology usage in early childhood teacher education comes from within. Many within ECE still question the value of educational technology (Cordes & Miller, 2000) and continue to raise questions about its worth, even in the light of growing research (Clements & Sarama, 2003a). The message from the skeptics touches a resonant chord in some teachers who have their own doubts about 'throwing machines at children.' Changing someone's belief system is an intricate task, as indicated by research in that field (Lin, 2008); however, what is more disturbing is that most college preparatory programs do not facilitate this critical process. Not many universities offer educational technology courses focused on the early years. A cursory survey of graduate courses reveals a pattern that is all too familiar: Technology is infused into Math and Science content courses, perhaps some writing courses, but very little effort in made to include technology for its best usage, i.e., critical thinking; and very, very few of these rare courses focus on ECE. It is not surprising therefore that graduates of ECE programs often feel inadequate, unsure and unprepared to think creatively with any piece of technology. Not armed with the knowledge and skills, it is no surprise that most new teachers choose the path well traveled, with little to no educational technology infusion.

In the wake of the 2008 NETS*T standards (International Society for Technology in Education, 2008), and the imminent NAEYC position statement on educational technology (2011), teacher education programs are being forced to explicitly acknowledge the need to include educational technology as an important content area topic within their ECE courses. This ideology is strongly supported by the teacher accreditation standards (National Council for Accreditation of Teacher Education, 2008) which require teacher preparation institutions to develop teacher candidates who can "integrate technology into instruction to enhance student learning" (p. 4).

What are the implications of these major standards and position statements for ECE teacher training and education? I outline two critical theoretical and paradigmatic changes: Re-structuring the college course and re-conceptualizing course requirements.

RESTRUCTURING THE COLLEGE COURSE

Most typical college courses involve 14 to 15 weeks of continuous and ongoing reading, discussion and projects. The completion of a course carries a deceptive aura of accomplishment and learning. Rarely are these one-shot efforts enough to transform someone's pedagogy or provide them with enough support to venture forth on their own. Research on professional development has proven time and time again that single workshops or even a single series of short courses do little to change a teacher's beliefs or practices (Chen & Chang, 2006; Medvin, Reed, & Behr, 2002; Swaminathan,

Barbuto, Trawick-Smith, et al., 2004). Multiple training sessions or workshops, across time, and with consistent support is needed to ensure that teachers successfully imbibe their lessons, understand it enough to try it once, and feel supported enough to continue to implement it, before finally being able to function independently.

What are some research-driven suggestions for re-structuring the college classroom and course content? I outline some of these ideas below.

One easy modification currently being implemented in some universities is to break a course into cyclical modules of on-campus learning, clinical placements and online seminars, each supporting the other. This will allow the teacher candidate (and also the in-service teacher) to revisit the same content at various times and in multiple formats, with each re-visit acting as prior knowledge and support to subsequent learning.

Using online learning environments as classroom space for discussion and collaboration is yet another instructional practice that is gaining strength (Shin & Lee, 2009). It is particularly popular amongst those with busy schedules who can log in at their convenience. It also saves them one leg of travel from work or clinical placement to the college campus for classes. However, any discussion of such virtual learning centers must constantly evaluate their effectiveness in reaching a population that may not be ready to be taught virtually. An interesting cultural comparison study of learning styles (Wang, 2007) used PDI—power distance index (Hofstede, 2001) as the theoretical framework. They found that some adult learners found the online discourses unsettling because one's written communications were available to all other students and because an unknown instructor is the authority evaluating every word they wrote. We might therefore need to balance the convenience afforded by the online learning environment by opting for a hybrid model of learning, with online sessions intermingled with face/face connections, video, and podcasts (Brown et al., 2009; Lee, Ginsburg, & Preston,

2009; Shin & Lee, 2009; Uzunboylu, 2007; Wang, 2007). The important question in any training program for ECE teachers is this: Can the road be traveled if it does not show up in one's learning map? Therefore the training method used has to connect to the teacher's learning style first before any critical change can be expected to happen.

Besides matching the teachers' learning style, college preparation programs must ensure that they address the 'whole teacher' (Chen & Chang, 2006). Taking a developmental approach to teacher training, these researchers recommend first assessing teacher's readiness skills on an individual basis, and then starting the training within their zones of proximal development. These authors also suggest isolating and working on teacher attitudes, skills, content knowledge and applications separately.

One such study (Lim, Lee, & Hung, 2008) traces the transformative journey of a teacher who underwent an individualistic and a holistic training, as suggested by Chen and Chang (2006). Interestingly, this teacher's journey was not just a personal voyage but was deeply influenced by systemic factors extending from the district level right down to her classroom; ironically the factors that facilitated her progress were at times a hindrance to her growth. It is important that teacher educators recognize the roles of these double-edged swords.

Another important attribute of successful training (Chen & Chang, 2006) is the location. Any professional development that occurs within the context of teachers' own work environments is more powerfully assimilated than any in alien college classroom environments. While difficult to enforce, in our own professional development (Swaminathan, Barbuto, Trawick-Smith, et al., 2004), we noticed that teachers showed the greatest growth and benefit when we traveled to their classrooms and worked on individual training sessions that were rooted in their own classroom curriculum. Only such continual and long term training efforts can effectively affect a teacher's pedagogy and most importantly, their beliefs.

Otherwise, it may well remain as the road once tried, but never again re-visited.

Another interesting model to consider is the ethical dialectical discourse (Newman & Findlay, 2008) within a community learning experience using multiple input devices operating on a single computer (either face/face or in remote locations). In this study, social construction of knowledge as a collective team was tangibly evident amongst all the participants leading to enhanced comfort and more integrative collaboration.

Besides the technical and cognitive aspects, college courses must also focus on the emotional and social collaborations of teams for they could help to alleviate teacher anxiety (Medvin, Reed et al. 2002). In this study, teachers reported anxiety over equipment damage with such trepidation negatively affecting their ability to work with the technologies creatively. Learning collaboratively and learning about collaboration qualitatively enhanced the teacher's abilities to work efficiently and to work with less angst.

Besides the college courses, clinical and student teaching placements should be re-structured as well. Typically, novice student teachers are placed in the classrooms of expert teachers so that the latter can supervise and mentor the former. Re-conceptualizing this model would mean acknowledging that the novice student teacher is likely more proficient in newer tools and therefore could well mentor her classroom teacher on aspects of educational technology. While such reverse learning does take place informally and to a slight extent (Bell & Fidishun, 2009) formalizing this process and acknowledging this valuable resource and explicitly making learning from my student teacher a requirement for all cooperating teachers could lead to professional development in the classroom.

Finally, and most critically, before any dramatic learning can be expected of the teacher candidate, an important change in the course structuring calls for college professors to re-organize their own pedagogical practice. Most college professors have research agendas that do not always include teacher education as the primary goal. This disparity of goals can translate into disparity of teaching. For instance, an early childhood Math educator may be well versed in the curricular goals, objectives of any number of math curriculum, instructional strategies for reaching diverse children, understand the trajectories of children's mathematical thinking and be able to evaluate their progress; but be not so well versed in the art of constructively facilitating the learning of this content knowledge in others. There is only a smattering of research on college teaching. Within ECE, faculty have to acknowledge the vast gap between teaching teachers and teaching children and learn to connect to adult learners in ways that are developmentally and culturally appropriate for them. For instance, the pool of ECE teacher candidates is usually equally distributed amongst young college students (digital natives) and non-traditional adult learners, most of whom are digital immigrants. The college professor must connect to both in terms of beliefs, content knowledge and technology skills, while at the same time, adjusting their own beliefs and abilities to teach.

RECONCEPTUALIZING COURSE REQUIREMENTS

The NETS*T (International Society for Technology in Education, 2008) outlines two firm expectations for all teachers: They must facilitate and inspire student learning and creativity and design and develop digital-age learning experiences and assessment. And yet, most college courses fail to achieve these themselves. Rarely has an ECE teacher education college course rested on mere exams or even papers. Classroom-based projects have long been a classic "final product" of most classrooms; but that is not enough. Course requirements should expect teacher candidates and in-service teachers to function as teachers/researchers or as advocates exploring and under-standing and documenting their own learning in ways that make sense to them.

Let's look at a few studies to get a glimpse of how this might look.

Consistently and repeatedly, collaborative wikis or community networks appear in literature as a strong learning tool in both college courses and professional development workshops. Just as data teams and curricular teams are expected to work together to develop learning experiences for an entire grade level, so too can we have group projects attesting to everyone's knowledge. We do need to ensure that these do not dwindle down to individual scores for individuals within the groups, but remain as group projects indicative of everyone's efforts. During a professional development study (Dreon & Dietrich, 2009), teachers almost accidentally started developing interactive wikis about assistive technology. Instead of everyone writing a paper on the same idea, the group developed a collective resource wiki that benefited everyone more than any sharing of their individual papers could have accomplished. This same idea is echoed by Parette (2009) who highlights the extended time his teachers spent in discussing and sharing ideas. At times, these ideas crystallized into "gradable" projects but perhaps, if we are to inspire students (NETS*T, Standard 1), then it should be okay to spend time just developing ideas. Sometimes, the germination of ideas and clever projects is by itself an inspiration to seek out and learn more, and will remain with the learner as personal confidence building memories, to be unleashed when faced with tangles in the road less traveled.

Too often, college courses depend on verbal-linguistic intelligence for students to demonstrate their understanding. In a radical change, Dreon and Dietrick (2009) suggests the use of videos from You tube to view demonstrations of products and practice; and I suggest that perhaps term papers could also utilize videos and pictures in a clever way to visually present what the student has gleamed. These visuals will translate to the ECE classroom much more easily than most verbal papers; and connecting visuals to theories and research ideas can be an enriching experience. An inspiring example and description is presented by Moran and Tegano (2005) wherein ECE teachers gradually shift from using photographs as a representational tool (documentation of children's work and actions) towards a more inquiry-oriented purposeful look at photographs of children as clues to interpreting one's own teaching and the classroom environment. ECE has too long rested on the phrase "hands-on" to describe the interactive nature of our children's learning; we need to add the dimensions of "eyes-on" (Dreon, 2009) and "minds-on" (Trawick-Smith, 2009).

A strong ECE teacher would loathe to give a coloring book and a box of crayons to young children and expect them to color inside the lines. She is more likely to give a blank sheet of paper, open the art supplies (including the PAINT tool on a nearby computer) and suggest a few interesting queries to trigger their imagination. So too can college courses or other training programs focus on the knowledge and skills and let the participants decide what and how they demonstrate their learning? It might actually prepare them better for the mind-set for taking the road less traveled if they have been already forced to do so in their college preparation classes.

CURRICULAR TRANSFORMATIONS

Any discussion about the effectiveness of an early childhood teacher education program must ultimately look within the ECE classroom itself: The roads of teacher education do end there. I would like to present views of what the road less traveled can lead to both ideally and realistically. For a conceptual framework and a guiding curricular structure, it is helpful to understand the key foci of NETS*S, the 2007 ISTE standards for students. Creativity, research, communication, collaboration and critical thinking lead the charge for curricular emphasis, while technology operations is rightfully relegated to a distant sixth and last goal. Once again, the emphasis is on constructive teaching infused with educational technology, as clearly mirrored in the ISTE student profiles for children from preschool to grade 4. This projects an image of children as active and vibrant creators and developers: They communicate their original ideas using multi-media, they conduct research using electronic resources and they evaluate information critically.

Inspiring as these images are and setting high expectations for the ECE classroom, it is also important that we look at actual classroom examples. Scrutinizing classroom practices of technology integration with LoTi, or Levels of Teaching innovation (Moersch, 2001), an all too familiar pattern does emerge. There is pervasive use of technology at the Level 1, Awareness and Level 2, Exploration phases as classrooms begin to integrate digital tools into their existing curricular, without necessarily changing it. A sad example of this would be the use (or mis-use) of the Interactive white board (IWB), probably the most significant addition to any classroom, in the recent few years. This interactive tool is not often used for all its potential and strength (Lisenbee, 2009; Morgan, 2010; Vincent, 2007). Too often, initial classroom usage reveals a didactic instructional stance wherein the IWB presents merely a hyperlinked array of facts and ideas that are atypically arranged in words and images with auditory connections (Vincent, 2007). What makes such lower level usage of the IWB (and other digital tools) more troubling is the overwhelming perception of innovation and cutting edge creativity that any use of digital technology mistakenly projects (Parette, Quesenberry, & Blum, 2010). It is therefore with extreme scrutiny and caution that I offer the following examples of curricular integration as samples of the road less traveled.

Offering scythes for successful navigation through the roads less traveled are the time established principles of good teaching. First, cross-curricular pedagogies will allow for content area learning across multiple curricular areas (Aston & Jackson, 2009); ECE has been doing this for years and needs to remember to continue to do so with technology infusion. Secondly, ECE has long advocated for developmentally appropriate practices in terms of curricular and assessment exercises (Bredekamp & Cople, 1997); now, this policy has to embrace technology as well, accommodating both for children's developmental thinking and innate interests (Rosen & Jaruszewicz, 2009). Third, no educational technology devise can function on its own. For children to use it creatively, teacher mediation and scaffolding is essential (Lau, Higgins, Gelfer, Hong, & Miller, 2005; Nir-Gal & Klein, 2004). Finally, as with any tool and as we have always done, we, as educators have to re-evaluate everything that has been declared effective by commercial manufacturers, making sure to consider the pedagogy, the content, the design interface and other culturally relevant aspects unique to ECE (Nikolopoulou, 2007).

Let us look at some examples of curricular work in ECE that reaches up to LoTi Level 5 or 6 integration. Some of these, such as the primary grade example (Graham, 2009) include a reflective teacher using her forte in children's literature to make the challenging leap into connecting with digital technology. Another (Buckleitner, 2003) offers a way to expand children's interests into science content- and process-oriented studies with multiple digital resources, including digital microscopes, webquests and the ever-useful open-ended Kidspiration. Similarly, within music education, multiple digital tools and online resources geared particularly for the primary grades (Kersten, 2006) offer teachers a multi-media toolkit for infusing a social, visual and collective forum for music appreciation and composition, hitherto not readily feasible with younger children. Examples such as these allow and encourage technology integration into student-led problem-solving and creative endeavors.

In choosing effective technology tools (whether it be software or other resources) for these endeavors, it is critical that we select materials that challenge children's thinking. One such is logo, the programming language for young children. Research on children's use of logo has established its efficacy in enhancing children's problem solving, geometric and measurement concepts (Clements & Meredith, 1993; Clements & Sarama, 2002, 2003b). Today, logo is available as a virtual manipulative, a stand-alone applet and even as an app. Even so, logo remains a road less traveled in ECE. This is mainly because of its deceptive simplicity and open-ended nature that makes even the drawing of a triangle a mind-boggling and frustrating exercise in angles, turns and lengths. And yet, children who navigate through logo successfully show remarkable growth in math content and process skills. Why then is logo not as prevalent as it needs to be? Could it be that we expect all technology to solve problems and to be simpler than regular paper and pencil tasks, and therefore balk at logo that appears to bring into conflict all our doubts and questions? To truly transform ECE curriculum, we need to embrace challenges afforded by logo and immerse our children in its problem solving.

For yet another inspiring example of Level 5-6 Loti educational technology integration in ECE, I refer to a collaborative project on butterflies engaged by multiple schools in diverse locations (McPherson, 2009). The project consciously used the UDL (Universal Design for Learning) principles to tap into the technology affordances of desktop, online and handheld digital devices. This is a powerful example of analytical research and multi-modal communication in the early and primary grades. Curricula, such as these, make the integration and use of technology seamless for children, as they begin to reach for it naturally to seek answers to their inquiries (Swaminathan & Rezai, 2010). During a study on bones and the human body, children used the internet and

Figure 1. Researching with Google images for models of X-Ray machines

Google naturally to seek out images and information, as needed.

In other classroom projects (Hertzog & Klein, 2005), teachers were able to use technology strategically to differentiate instruction and goals for both their challenged and challenging children, finding a way to merge diverse student needs within the same curricula. Similarly, other action research projects (Gimbert & Cristol, 2004) outline technological connections in multiple early childhood classrooms. Each project stemmed from children's individual interests and were supported by the teacher's guidance and encouragement to become a coherent, content-rich, and process-focused creative exercise. Similarly, in a Reggio model of child inspired activities and documentation (Hong & Trepanier-Street, 2004), teachers were able to utilize regular technology tools in powerful visual ways for children to engage in knowledge construction and for the teacher to differentiate instruction to include all

children. In most of these studies, the teachers received ongoing professional development from a teacher education program, thereby corroborating my earlier stance for pedagogical training that intermingles courses with clinical practice in a cyclical manner.

Connecting to families and the child's communities is an integral part of the early childhood curriculum, as acknowledged by Standard 2 of the NAEYC standards for teacher education programs. ECE teachers are known for reaching out to the families of their children and to include them both formally and informally in the planning and implementation of the curricula. The following two examples of creative technology usage by teacher educators offer us guidance for the road less traveled within family connections. In the first, video technology was used to convey information about the school, curricula and the children's development (Calabrese, 2006). Video allowed parents to see how they could be more connected to their children in ways beyond what a parent/teacher conference could have achieved. In the second study (Meadows, 2004), teachers bridged the families social/cultural background to the classroom environment by creating child and family portfolios with digital images, as well as virtual field trips into the child's neighborhood. These are simple, and yet invaluable curricular strategies for extending and connecting to the communities.

Ultimately, these creative examples of educational technology usage are 'innovative' because they transform the everyday practice by making everyone's time and efforts more effective and efficient. For such successful transformations of the classroom curricula to occur, teachers have to maintain a self-reflective framework (Snider & Hirschy, 2009) probing themselves continually about the value and effectiveness of their educational technology usage, every step of the way. The road less traveled does not always become easier to traverse, after multiple efforts; it needs continual attention, reflection and refining.

IMPACT ON CHILDREN

Accountability is the buzzword of the day, and educational technology does not escape its scrutiny either. Periodically research studies review the effects of educational technology usage on children's developmental growth, and outline critical factors such as age, home use, types of program, time and the critical nature of usage. (Kumtepe, 2006; Schmidt et al., 2009; Subrahmanyam, Greenfield, Kraut, & Gross, 2001). It is not my goal herein to study the impact of educational technology on children but to discuss creative and technology-rich ways to assess.

How can the ECE teacher education program encourage teachers to use educational technology to both document *and* evaluate children's learning and potential? Some assessment models (those embedded within established curricular programs)

propose a road well traveled: Checking children's progress based on completion of tasks and activity charts. The road less traveled includes the use of digital devices and other online assessment management systems to track children's progress through formative and summative digital means (Salend, 2009).

In a classroom action research, (Boardman, 2007) digital images were used to capture children's learning, and to engage them in reflective thinking about their development. This subscribes to a model of reflective revisiting of one's own actions and words, or Instant Video Revisiting (Forman, 1999, 2002). Our own research using this model with preschoolers and primary grade children within the areas of numerical thinking bore clear evidence that after only three weeks of video revisiting, individual children's counting, one-to-one correspondence skills, keeping track and reasoning abilities showed positive growth (Swaminathan & Gardner, 2008). Children re-viewed edited clips of their own numerical activities, and engaged in self-correcting and monitoring of their own earlier actions, which gradually seeped into their current actions and eventually into their numerical conceptualizations. Interestingly, such video-revisiting showed strong cross-over effects into other domains of development such as social and emotional areas with the children gaining an inner confidence about their overall abilities.

A separate benefit of using digital images for assessment is the authenticity and weight that it provides to evaluation reports whether it be to district offices or to individual parents. Preschool teachers were able to effectively use digital documentation of their inclusive classroom to advocate for the continuation of their program (Swaminathan et al., 2004). District officials could "see" how the children with and without special needs were supporting each other, could "hear" the speech of impaired children as they communicated with peers and could "watch" mobility-impaired children being seamlessly integrated

Figure 2. Revisiting an earlier work using digital video

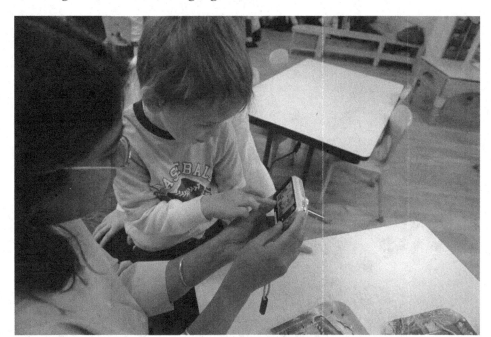

within learning centers. Boardman (2007) also speaks of the value of digital documentation to help parents understand how various actions play out in the classroom and to 'show' rather than merely 'tell' how their children are progressing. Earlier, we saw how being able to see educational concepts in action helped parents realize their value and to connect to aspects at home that they could work on (Calabrese, 2006).

For a few years now, we have been conducting professional development for early childhood teachers on digital portfolios embedded within a child-centered curriculum. Teachers purposely plan and conduct investigations with clear learning outcomes for specific children; capture children's thinking using multiple formats of digital documentation (voice, images and video); and evaluate these artifacts against national or state benchmarks to arrive at valuable understanding of a child's capability both as an individual and as a participant in the collective classroom community and the child's potential for growth and

development (Swaminathan, 2005; Swaminathan, Barbuto, Hines, et al., 2004).

Our more recent work (Swaminathan & Rezai, 2010) looked at the effects of participating in portfolio assessment itself on young children. Preschoolers in this study actively engaged in choosing artifacts for their portfolio and reflecting (with the teacher's scaffolding) on what the artifacts indicated about their own learning.

Preschoolers showed remarkable growth in their self-awareness, goal-setting and abilities to monitor their own progress, vastly aided in this mental process by the technical possibility of "flipping" through their portfolios to see documentation of their earlier 'less-finished' products.

Research such as the ones above is inviting and inspires one to step into the road less traveled enthusiastically. However, these studies also don't shy from alerting us about the various impediments that await any teacher venturing forth in this path, including time, commitment, effort, and finances (Boardman, 2007; Salend, 2009; Swaminathan, Barbuto, Hines, et al., 2004). And

Figure 3. Reviewing and selecting artifacts for their portfolio

yet teacher education programs in ECE have the responsibility to mentor teachers (both novices and veterans) to try this path. Not only does it allow diversification of assessment methods but it enables us to dig deeper and to understand child development better ourselves. And for the children themselves, participating in digital assessment methodologies as outlined here offers a road that is definitely less traveled in their school career: Being able to participate and engage in their own learning *and* assessment.

SPECIAL TOOLS OR ASSISTIVE TECHNOLOGIES

No discussion on ECE teacher education can exclude the mention of special tools for disabilities. Assistive technology is a separate field by itself and one that is burgeoning with special tools to serve the needs of young learners. (Tinker, 2001).

For complete integration and facilitation of these tools, it is imperative that assistive technology usage is intermingled with the pedagogical principles for adaptation and accommodation (Gruenberg & Miller, 2011). Assistive toolkits (Judge, Puckett, & Bell, 2006) can support development using multiple modes of visual, auditory and kinesthetic processing. However, it is important to acknowledge that while these tools can transform a child's social, emotional and cognitive interaction with his or her environment, they also concomitantly call for deep transformations in the teacher education programs. No longer can special education reside as a separate course taught by subject-specific faculty, but it needs to be infused within all teacher education programs. The child with special needs will utilize these tools presumably in all curricular areas and throughout the day.

Starting with desktop accessories and control panel options, all teachers need to know how to do simple and useful adaptations for the unique

Figure 4. Reflecting on portfolio entry with a teacher's help

needs of children, including slowing down the speed of the mouse, the keyboard, increasing font sizes and so on (Kimball, Cohen, Dimmick, & Mills, 2003-04). Regular teachers must be trained to know when a tool is needed, which one and how it should be utilized (Judge, et al., 2006). They should also concomitantly know how to employ assistive technology in ways that accommodate for and merge the child into the regular curriculum. For older primary children, handheld assistive tools can offer a way to self-monitor themselves (Gulchak, 2008) but teachers should learn to accommodate for this flexibility in their instructional planning. Ultimately, with the goal being to enhance children's functioning, it is important that as teachers, we focus on the effectiveness of the tool and not be beguiled by its technical aspects. Sometimes low-tech tools, used well are more effective than high-tech equipment (Gulchak, 2008; Hamm, Mistrett, & Ruffino,

2006), once again, sending an important message to teacher preparation programs.

What all this means is that the educational technology road will need to have byroads, from other programs, feeding into it that may or may not be also well traveled. Teacher education therefore needs to transform its content to accommodate the rich environment of special tools, assistive technology and special education.

CONCLUDING REMARKS

There is no doubt that we stand at a fork bifurcating the future of ECE teacher education. Educational technology offers many tools for those who can wield it in the road less traveled, with resource-fulness and creativity. For others, it presents a deceptively easy tool to continue walking the same path. Which path teachers take is to a great extent governed by the depth and versatility of their own teacher preparation programs. ECE teacher education programs need to re-conceptualize their professional preparation practices such that teachers will at least pause, consider the two paths and make the decision about the path best suited for them. Sometimes, this is the road well traveled, and sometimes they may return months later to try the road less traveled with additional support. As with any other path to progress, it takes multiple attempts, and time and support to walk down and to pave the road less traveled.

REFERENCES

Aston, S., & Jackson, D. (2009). Blurring the boundaries or muddying the waters? *Design and Technology Education*, *14*(1), 68–76.

Bell, V., & Fidishun, D. (2009). Learning from each other: Student teachers, cooperating teachers and technology. *International Journal of Instructional Media*, *36*(2), 195–205.

Boardman, M. (2007). "I know how much this child has learned. I have proof!": Employing digital technologies for documentation processes in kindergarten. *Australian Journal of Early Childhood*, *32*(3), 59–66.

Bredekamp, S., & Cople, C. (Eds.). (1997). *Developmentally appropriate practice in early childhood programs*. Washington, DC: National Association for the Education of Young Children.

Brown, A., Brown, C., Fine, B., Luterbach, K., Sugar, W., & Vinciguerra, D. C. (2009). Instructional uses of podcasting in online learning environments: A cooperative inquiry study. *Journal of Educational Technology Systems*, *37*(4), 351–371. doi:10.2190/ET.37.4.b

Buckleitner, W. (2003). Turning collections into curriculum--Technically speaking. *Scholastic Early Childhood Today*, *17*(6), 6–7.

Calabrese, N. M. (2006). Video technology: A vehicle for educators to enhance relationships with families. *Education*, *127*(1), 155–160.

Chen, J.-Q., & Chang, C. (2006). A comprehensive approach to technology training for early childhood teachers. *Early Education and Development*, *17*(3), 443–465. doi:10.1207/s15566935eed1703_6

Clements, D. H., & Meredith, J. S. (1993). Research on logo: Effects and efficacy. *Journal of Computing in Childhood Education*, *4*(4), 263–290.

Clements, D. H., Nastasi, B. K., & Swaminathan, S. (1995). Young children and computers: Crossroads and directions from research. *Young Children*, *48*(2), 56–64.

Clements, D. H., & Sarama, J. (2002). The role of technology in early childhood learning. *Teaching Children Mathematics*, *8*(6), 340–343.

Clements, D. H., & Sarama, J. (2003a). Strip mining for gold: Research and policy in educational technology-A response to "Fool's Gold". *Educational Technology Review*, *11*(1).

Clements, D. H., & Sarama, J. (2003b). Young children and technology: What does the research say? *Young Children*, *58*(6), 34–40.

Cordes, C., & Miller, E. (2000). *Fool's gold: A critical look at computers in childhood*. Retrieved November 15, 2010, from http://drupal6.alliance-forchildhood.org/fools_gold

Dreon, O. Jr, & Dietrich, N. I. (2009). Turning lemons into lemonade: Teaching assistive technology through Wikis and embedded video. *TechTrends: Linking Research and Practice to Improve Learning*, *53*(1), 78–80.

Forman, G. (1999). Instant video revisiting: The video camera as a "tool of the mind" for young children. *Early Childhood Research & Practice*, *1*(2), 1–8.

Forman, G. (2002). *Wondering with children: The goals, strategies, and theories of ordinary moments.* Paper presented at the Reggio Conference, Seoul, Korea.

Gimbert, B., & Cristol, D. (2004). Teaching curriculum with technology: Enhancing children's technological competence during early childhood. *Early Childhood Education Journal, 31*(3), 207–216. doi:10.1023/B:ECEJ.0000012315.64687.ee

Graham, L. (2009). It was a challenge but we did it! Digital worlds in a primary classroom. *Literacy, 43*(2), 107–114. doi:10.1111/j.1741-4369.2009.00520.x

Gruenberg, A. M., & Miller, R. (2011). *A practical guide to early childhood inclusion: Effective reflection.* Upper Saddle River, NJ: Pearson.

Gulchak, D. J. (2008). The special ways of handhelds. *District Administration, 44*(8), 22–23.

Hamm, E. M., Mistrett, S. G., & Ruffino, A. G. (2006). Play outcomes and satisfaction with toys and technology of young children with special needs. *Journal of Special Education Technology, 21*(1), 29–35.

Hertzog, N., & Klein, M. (2005). Beyond gaming: A technology explosion in early childhood classrooms. *Gifted Child Today, 28*(3), 24–31.

Hofstede, G. (2001). *Culture's consequences: Comparing values, behaviors, institutions, and organizations across nations* (II ed.). Thousand Oaks, CA: Sage.

Hong, S. B., & Trepanier-Street, M. (2004). Technology: A tool for knowledge construction in a Reggio Emilia inspired teacher education program. *Early Childhood Education Journal, 32*(2), 87–94. doi:10.1007/s10643-004-7971-z

International Society for Technology in Education. (2007). *National educational technology standards (NETS•S) and performance indicators for students.* Eugene, OR: ISTE.

International Society for Technology in Education. (2008). *National educational technology standards for teachers: Preparing teachers to use technology.* Eugene, OR: ISTE.

Judge, S., Puckett, K., & Bell, S. M. (2006). Closing the digital divide: Update from the early childhood longitudinal study. *The Journal of Educational Research, 100*(1), 52–60. doi:10.3200/JOER.100.1.52-60

Kersten, F. (2006). Inclusion of technology resources in early childhood music education. *General Music Today, 20*(1), 15–26. doi:10.1177/10483713060200010105

Kimball, W. H., Cohen, L. G., Dimmick, D., & Mills, R. (2003-04). No special equipment required. *Learning and Leading with Technology, 31*(4), 12–15.

Kumtepe, A. T. (2006). The effects of computers on kindergarten children's social skills. *Online Submission, 5.*

Lau, C., Higgins, K., Gelfer, J., Hong, E., & Miller, S. (2005). The effects of teacher facilitation on the social interactions of young children during computer activities. *Topics in Early Childhood Special Education, 25*(4), 208–217. doi:10.1177/02711214050250040201

Lee, J. S., Ginsburg, H. P., & Preston, M. D. (2009). Video interactions for teaching and learning (VITAL): Analyzing videos online to learn to teach early childhood mathematics. *Australian Journal of Early Childhood, 34*(2), 19–23.

Lim, W.-Y., Lee, Y.-J., & Hung, D. (2008). "A prophet never accepted by their own town": A teacher's learning trajectory when using technology. *Asia-Pacific Journal of Teacher Education, 36*(3), 215–227. doi:10.1080/13598660802232605

Lin, C.-Y. (2008). Preservice teachers' beliefs about using technology in the mathematics classroom. *Journal of Computers in Mathematics and Science Teaching, 27*(3), 341–360.

Lisenbee, P. (2009). Whiteboards and websites: Digital tools for the early childhood curriculum. *Young Children, 64*(6), 92–95.

McPherson, S. (2009). "A dance with the butterflies:" A metamorphosis of teaching and learning through technology. *Early Childhood Education Journal, 37*(3), 229–236. doi:10.1007/s10643-009-0338-8

Meadows, M. (2004). Using technology in early childhood environments to strengthen cultural connections. *Information Technology in Childhood Education Annual, 2004*(1).

Medvin, M. B., Reed, D. M., & Behr, D. S. (2002, June 26-29, 2002). *Computer training for preschool teachers: Impact on computer self-efficacy and anxiety.* Paper presented at the Head Start National Research Conference, Washington, DC.

Mishra, P., & Koehler, M. J. (2006). Technological pedgogical content knowledge: A framework for teacher knowledge. *Teachers College Record, 108*(6), 1017–1054. doi:10.1111/j.1467-9620.2006.00684.x

Moersch, C. (2001). Next steps: Using LoTi as a research tool. *Learning and Leading with Technology, 29*(3), 22–27.

Morgan, A. (2010). Interactive whiteboards, interactivity and play in the classroom with children aged three to seven years. *European Early Childhood Education Research Journal, 18*(1), 93–104. doi:10.1080/13502930903520082

NAEYC. (1996). Position statement on technology and young children--Ages three through eight. *Young Children, 51*(6), 11–16.

National Council for Accreditation of Teacher Education. (2008). *Professional standards for the accreditation of teacher preparation institutions.* Washington, DC: NCATE.

Newman, L., & Findlay, J. (2008). Communities of ethical practice: Using new technologies for ethical dialectical discourse. *Journal of Educational Technology & Society, 11*(4), 16–28.

Nikolopoulou, K. (2007). Early childhood educational software: Specific features and issues of localization. *Early Childhood Education Journal, 35*(2), 173–179. doi:10.1007/s10643-007-0168-5

Nir-Gal, O., & Klein, P. S. (2004). Computers for cognitive development in early childhood--The teacher's role in the computer learning environment. *Information Technology in Childhood Education Annual,* 97–119.

Papert, S. (1993). *The children's machine: Rethinking schools in the age of the computer.* New York, NY: Basic Books.

Parette, H. P., Quesenberry, A. C., & Blum, C. (2010). Missing the boat with technology usage in early childhood settings: A 21st century view of developmentally appropriate practice. *Early Childhood Education Journal, 37*(5), 335–343. doi:10.1007/s10643-009-0352-x

Resnick, L. B. (1985). Cognition and instruction: Recent theories of human competence. In Hammonds, B. L. (Ed.), *Psychology and learning (Vol. 4,* pp. 127–186). Washington, DC: American Psychological Association. doi:10.1037/10053-004

Rosen, D. B., & Jaruszewicz, C. (2009). Developmentally appropriate technology use and early childhood teacher education. *Journal of Early Childhood Teacher Education, 30*(2), 162–171. doi:10.1080/10901020902886511

Salend, S. J. (2009). Technology-based classroom assessments: Alternatives to testing. *Teaching Exceptional Children, 41*(6), 49–58.

Schmidt, D. A., Baran, E., Thompson, A. D., Mishra, P., Koehler, M. J., & Shin, T. S. (2009). Technological pedagogical content knowledge (TPACK): The development and validation of an assessment instrument for preservice teachers. *Journal of Research on Technology in Education, 42*(2), 123–149.

Shin, M., & Lee, Y.-J. (2009). Changing the landscape of teacher education via online teaching and learning. *Techniques: Connecting Education and Careers, 84*(1), 32–33.

Snider, S. L., & Hirschy, S. (2009). A self-reflection framework for technology use by classroom teachers of young learners. *He Kupu, 2*(1), 31–44.

Subrahmanyam, K., Greenfield, P., Kraut, R., & Gross, E. (2001). The impact of computer use on children's and adolescents' development. *Applied Developmental Psychology, 22*(1), 7–30. doi:10.1016/S0193-3973(00)00063-0

Swaminathan, S. (2000). Integrating technology within the curriculum: Teachers' challenges and teacher educator's insights. *Journal of Early Childhood Teacher Education, 21*(2), 289–294. doi:10.1080/0163638000210223

Swaminathan, S. (2005, March). *Facilitating mathematical and scientific reasoning and reflection in young childen through digital documentation.* Paper presented at the Keefe-Bruyette Symposium, West Hartford, CT.

Swaminathan, S., Barbuto, L. M., Hines, N., Piquette, K. B., Trawick-Smith, J., & Wright, J. L. (2004). *Digital portfolios: Powerful tools for documenting and evaluating student learning.* Paper presented at the National Educational Computing Conference, New Orleans, LA.

Swaminathan, S., Barbuto, L. M., Trawick-Smith, J., & Wright, J. L. (2004). *Technology training for preschool teachers: Study of the training model, pedagogical changes and student learning.* Paper presented at the Annual Meeting of the American Educational Research Association, San Diego, CA.

Swaminathan, S., & Gardner, P. (2008). *Digital video documentation as a reflective tool for enhancing children's mathematical and social understanding and reseasoning.* Paper presented at the National Institute for Early Childhood Professional Development, New Orleans, LA.

Swaminathan, S., & Rezai, N. (2010). *Documenting, reflecting, & teaching: Digital portfolios in the preschool classroom.* Paper presented at the International Society for Technology in Education, Denver, CO.

Tinker, R. (2001). Future technologies for special learners. *Journal of Special Education Technology, 16*(4).

Trawick-Smith, J. (2009). *Early child development: A multicultural perspective* (5th ed.). New York, NY: Prentice Hall.

Uzunboylu, H. (2007). Teacher attitudes toward online education following an online inservice program. *International Journal on E-Learning, 6*(2), 267–277.

Vincent, J. (2007). The interactive whiteboard in an early years classroom: A case study in the impact of a new technology on pedagogy. *Australian Educational Computing, 22*(1), 20–25.

Wang, M. (2007). Designing online courses that effectively engage learners from diverse cultural backgrounds. *British Journal of Educational Technology, 38*(2), 294–311. doi:10.1111/j.1467-8535.2006.00626.x

Wartella, E. A., & Nancy, J. (2000). Children and computers: New technology--old concerns. *Children and Computer Technology, 10*(2), 31–43.

Wood, E., Specht, J., Willoughby, T., & Mueller, J. (2008). Integrating computer technology in early childhood education environments: Issues raised by early childhood educators. *The Alberta Journal of Educational Research, 54*(2), 210–226.

Chapter 21
Re-Thinking Pre-Service Mathematics Teachers Preparation:
Developing Technological, Pedagogical, and Content Knowledge (TPACK)

Margaret L. Niess
Oregon State University, USA

ABSTRACT

Powerful and modern digital technologies have significantly impacted mathematics teaching – both what is to be learned and how it should be learned. Technology, pedagogy, and content knowledge (TPACK) is the knowledge that teachers rely on for teaching content with appropriate digital technologies. What preparation do mathematics teachers need in order to develop this knowledge needed for integrating appropriate digital technologies as teaching and learning tools? The challenges of understanding TPACK and identifying appropriate educational programs for pre-service mathematics teachers call for thoughtful attention toward the development of the knowledge, skills, and dispositions that support the dynamic nature embedded within the TPACK construct. The design of appropriate pre-service teacher learning trajectories for developing a rigorous TPACK emphasizes that both how and where they learn to teach mathematics are fundamental to what is learned about teaching and learning mathematics. Redesign ideas and models support re-thinking and re-designing pre-service mathematics teacher preparation programs.

INTRODUCTION

Mathematics as a body of knowledge evokes many different descriptions. Some view mathematics as a study of patterns while still others envision mathematics as an art. Some suggest that mathematics is the language of science. Others describe mathematics as a way of thinking that results in organizing, analyzing, and synthesizing data. Irrespective of the various descriptions, the mathematics discipline has been significantly impacted by the use of digital technologies with advanced computational, graphical, and symbolic

DOI: 10.4018/978-1-4666-0014-0.ch021

capabilities. These advanced capabilities have changed how mathematicians are able to think about and do mathematics. Has this change shifted how students today are learning mathematics? Are they using today's technologies for learning mathematical ideas? If students learn mathematics with the tools of the 20th century, will they be able to compete mathematically in the society and culture of the 21st century?

In 2000, the National Council for School Mathematics (NCTM) declared that *the existence, versatility, and power of technology make it possible and necessary to reexamine what mathematics students should learn as well as how they can best learn it* (NCTM, 2000, p. 25). Many digital technologies are promoted as useful tools for students learning mathematics: graphing calculators, applets or virtual manipulatives, spreadsheets, dynamic geometry tools, computer algebra systems and a host of Web 2.0 technologies. These digital technologies offer advanced capabilities for visual representations to engage students in dynamic explorations and communicating their understandings while learning mathematics. NCTM further reinforced this view through its Technology Principle: *Technology is essential in teaching and learning mathematics; it influences the mathematics that is taught and enhances students' learning* (2000, p. 24). The Association of Mathematics Teacher Educators (AMTE) expanded on this call for integrating appropriate technologies in mathematics programs through its Technology Position. *Mathematics teacher preparation programs must ensure that all mathematics teachers and teacher candidates have opportunities to acquire the knowledge and experiences needed to incorporate technology in the context of teaching and learning mathematics* (AMTE, 2006, p. 1).

Three key questions arise with the challenge of adequately preparing teachers for meeting the challenges and demands for teaching mathematics with appropriate 21st century digital technologies: What knowledge do teachers need to effectively teach mathematics with current and emerging digital technologies? What preparation adequately develops this knowledge for teaching mathematics? How should pre-service teachers' preparation programs be re-designed to describe appropriate learning trajectories for learning to teach mathematics in the 21st century? The purpose of this chapter is to respond to these questions within an emerging framework for teacher knowledge – technology, pedagogy, and content knowledge or TPACK (Niess, 2008b; Thompson & Mishra, 2007). Since the TPACK construct stems from a cognitive constructivist view of individual learning, the responses to the questions additionally attend to the importance of the social context and how the pre-service teachers' participation in that context impacts their personal understanding and learning. Thus, the responses to the questions emphasize the importance of *how* and *where* they learn mathematics and how to teach mathematics as being fundamental to *what* is learned about teaching and learning mathematics (Greeno, Collins, & Resnick, 1996).

KNOWLEDGE FOR TEACHING MATHEMATICS WITH TECHNOLOGY

While teacher preparation programs have been struggling with preparing teachers to teach mathematics in the 21st century, a new framework for thinking about the knowledge teachers need for teaching with technology has emerged. In recognition of a broader perspective with respect to the knowledge needed for teaching with appropriate digital technologies, numerous researchers have proposed thinking about the integration of technology, pedagogy, and content in much the same way that Shulman (1986, 1987) did in describing pedagogical content knowledge (PCK). Technological pedagogical content knowledge (TPCK) was envisioned as the interconnection and intersection of content, pedagogy (teaching and student learning), and technology (Margerum-Leys & Marx, 2002;

Mishra & Koehler, 2006; Niess, 2005; Pierson, 2001; Zhao, 2003). Over time the acronym was recast as TPACK, the total knowledge package needed for teaching that integrates technology, pedagogy, and content knowledge (Niess, 2008b; Thompson & Mishra, 2007).

TPACK is proposed as a dynamic knowledge construct in depicting the knowledge teachers rely on in designing and implementing curriculum and instruction to effectively guide students' thinking and learning with digital technologies in subjects such as mathematics. To focus the description and understanding for this TPACK construct, Niess (2005) adapted Grossman's (1989, 1990, 1991) four components of PCK to incorporate technology. These four components call for a broader perspective on the specialized teacher knowledge for teaching their subjects – a perspective that specifically characterizes the impact of modern and emerging digital technologies on teaching and learning in the 21st century. Expanding these four components with respect to teaching mathematics reveals a more in depth understanding of how the components help to frame a mathematics teacher's TPACK.

TPACK Component 1: Overarching Conception

The first component of TPACK indicates that teachers need to incorporate an overarching conception about the purposes for incorporating technology in teaching mathematics topics. This conception is what the teacher knows and believes about the nature of mathematics, what is important for students to learn, and how technology supports learning mathematics topics.

As an example of this overarching conception, the concept of a variable is fundamental to mathematics. Variables play key roles in solving problems using the language of mathematics. A variable might be conceived as a placeholder for an unknown found by solving the equation ($\square + 2 = 10$ or $x + 3 = 10$). It might represent a domain

of possible values in a particular situation ($x + 3 > 5$). It might even be used in functional representations to provide a general description of an idea that includes the idea of covariation, such as with the area of a rectangle ($A = LW$, where the area (A) of a rectangle is a function of its length (L) and width (W) (Lappan, 2000; NCTM, 2000).

How are these different ideas developed and how can digital technologies assist in the development of these differences? Calculators and spreadsheets offer capabilities for exploring and enhancing these different meanings. Teachers' knowledge, beliefs, and understandings about variables provide the basis for their decisions as to how these technologies might support students in learning about variables. This conception may hold that a rich understanding of variables is developed prior to any use of digital technologies, thus mimicking how teachers have learned these ideas, without using digital technologies. Alternatively, the overarching conception may hold that digital technologies hold promise in the process of developing a more comprehensive understanding of variables. Teachers may value experiences with dynamic spreadsheets as providing an environment for exploring variation. Figure 1 displays a dynamic spreadsheet where users can enter their specific data and explore the variation of the colors in candy packaging. The process of changing the values for the number of candies in the spreadsheet results in instantly updating the table and the accompanying pie and bar charts. Through this dynamic experience, the concept of variable is directed beyond the idea of variable as a placeholder for a specific value.

The foundation of teachers' knowledge, beliefs, and understandings about teaching mathematics with technology ultimately serves as the basis for their decisions about classroom instruction. Their overarching conception of the purposes for specific technologies ultimately directs their objectives, strategies, assignments, curriculum and textbook, and assessments of students' learning.

Figure 1. Exploration of variables in the candy colors

Skittles Data	Enter your data in the gray box and view how your particular package of Skittles varies from others					
Number of...						
	Red	Orange	Yellow	Green	Purple	Sum
Actual	15	20	23	21	16	95
Min	15					
Max	23					
Range	8					

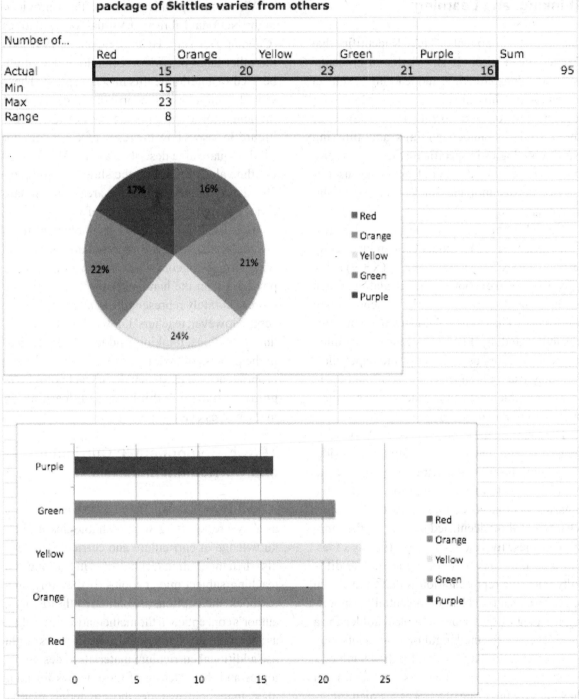

TPACK Component 2: Students' Understandings, Thinking, and Learning

The second component of TPACK identifies that teachers need a robust knowledge of students' understandings, thinking, and learning in subject matter topics with technology. In this component, teachers rely on and operate from knowledge about students' understandings and thinking with technologies in specific mathematics topics and have developed a belief about the usefulness of the technologies in learning particular mathematics topics.

Consider the topic of squaring binomial expressions such as $(x + 3)^2$. Students often incorrectly respond with $x^2 + 9$ (instead of $x^2 + 6x + 9$) using a distributive-like action for the calculation. When teaching about squaring binomials, teachers might use Algebra Tiles to help students overcome this misunderstanding. Figure 2 depicts a common template students use to cut out the paper tiles; then they use their paper versions of the tiles to consider problems involving ideas such as squaring a binomial expression.

For squaring the expression of $x + 3$, students create a square that is $x + 3$ length on each side. They combine the x tile with three unit tiles to frame each side of the square to represent the squaring action. Next, they need to determine what tiles fill the identified square. As they manipulate these tiles they find one x^2 tile, six x tiles, and nine unit tiles best fill the area. The difficulty with this representation is that the x tile in paper form is a fixed length, potentially supporting the idea of a variable as a placeholder for a specific value for the length of x. Students may even resort to finding a value for the length of x with a ruler (say that it measures 2 inches). Then they identify the value of $x + 3$ as 5 which is correct, if and only if the x tile measures 2 inches. After a period of time, they may even forget that their result depended upon that measurement.

Ultimately, they perceive a variable as a placeholder waiting for the actual value.

Virtual manipulatives, such as those provided in the National Library of Virtual Manipulatives (Cannon, Dorward, Heal, & Edwards, 1999), on the other hand provide a technology that might be used to ameliorate this misconception. These virtual manipulatives incorporate sliders to vary the length of x and thus the area of the x^2 tile. Figure 3a shows how the result of $x^2 + 9$ does not fill the square area described as $(x + 3)^2$. Changing the values for x with the slider (as in Figure 3b) visually confirms that the area of the square is not covered for all instances of x.

The graphical power of technological tools affords access to visual representations such as with virtual Algebra Tiles that are often more powerful than the handheld objects in that they more accurately represent the mathematical concepts. However, teachers' knowledge of students' understandings, thinking, and learning is critical in the process of making decisions about the appropriateness of particular digital technologies in guiding students' thinking and learning in mathematics classrooms.

TPACK Component 3: Curriculum and Curriculum Materials

A third TPACK component that teachers rely on as they are teaching with technologies is their knowledge of curriculum and curricular materials when integrating technologies in learning and teaching subject matter topics. If they rely on a textbook, their options are limited by the textbook author's conception of the mathematics curriculum as a sequence of chapters and topics. Others might use additional curriculum materials to design the topics and the ordering of those topics for their mathematic courses. Often those materials identify specific technologies to expand the sequences to provide students with opportunities to make connections among multiple topics.

Figure 2. Algebra tiles template

1	1	1	1	1	1	1
1	1	1	1	1	1	1
1	1	x		x		
1	1	x		$\cdot$x		
x	x	x^2		x^2		
x	x	x^2		x^2		

Geometer's Sketchpad (GSP) offers a virtual, visual environment in which students are able to make mathematical conjectures. Rather than telling students the sum of the angles of a triangle is 180 degrees, teachers might ask students to explore various triangles where they also identify the sum of the angles through GSP. Using the dynamic capabilities of GSP, students are able to manipulate the triangle showing that the sum of the angles appears to remain constant, regardless of the particular triangular shape. Figures 4a and 4b display how students might change the size, shape, and orientation of the triangle and observe that the sum of the angles remains at 180 degrees.

The next challenge is to **prove** that the sum of the angles of **any** triangle is 180 degrees. Figure 5 shows the construction of a line parallel to one side of a triangle. Measuring the angles through the vertex point B indicates that < CAB has the same measure as < DBA and that < BCA has the same measure as < CBE. Since the sum of the angles of a straight line is 180 degrees, < DBA + < CBE + < ABC = 180. Students use the dynamic features of GSP to change the size and orientation of the triangle to confirm that the sum is 180 degrees and that this value does not change.

However, it is the construction of the parallel line to the side AC of the triangle that provides the geometric proof of the conjecture (rather than simply using GSP features to shift the visual representation) where students rely on the theorem that states that alternate interior angles created by the transversal connecting parallel lines are congruent.

Taking advantage of the capabilities in GSP, teachers can rearrange the curriculum to have students make geometric conjectures that more naturally lead them to geometric proofs. It is the teachers' TPACK that supports and guides them in taking advantage of multiple technologies available for teaching specific topics. This knowledge impacts how they organize, scaffold, structure, and assess concept and processes in a technology-enhanced environment throughout the curriculum.

TPACK Component 4: Instructional Strategies and Representations

The fourth component of TPACK indicates teachers' knowledge, beliefs, and understandings of instructional strategies and representations for teaching and learning subject matter topics with technologies are essential in their implementations of technologies in teaching and learning. Teachers must adapt and incorporate mathematical representations with technologies in multiple ways to meet specific instructional goals and the needs of the diverse learners in their classes. The technology does not determine the specific instructional strategies to be incorporated when the technology is in the hands of students. This task belongs to the teacher.

The technology does not replace the teacher. The teacher must make decisions that impact the students' learning, thinking, and understanding. Should a previously prepared dynamic spreadsheet be provided to students for exploration without opportunities to develop these dynamic spreadsheets (as in Figure 1)? Would designing the

Figure 3. a and b. The slider varies the values for x in the virtual algebra tiles

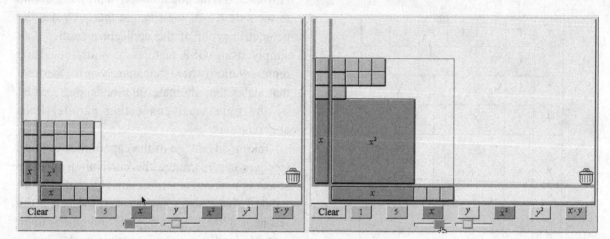

spreadsheet provide a more in-depth understanding of how the changes in the variables alter the graphical displays? When thinking about Algebra Tiles, teachers need to determine if students need experiences with the fixed length, hand-held tiles prior to experiences with the virtual manipulatives. When considering the use of GSP, teachers must determine what experiences with GSP are essential prior to engaging students in meaningful mathematical investigations. Is it better to have a mathematical task to guide the learning about the capabilities? Teachers might begin with the question of the sum of the angles of a triangle as the introduction to creating a triangle, labeling the vertices, and demonstrating the dynamic nature of shapes created in GSP. The challenge for students is to make a conjecture about the sum of the angles of the triangle; this challenge leads to explorations of the measurement capabilities. Once students understand the nature of making constructions in GSP (perpendicular and parallel), they might be ready to consider the challenge of identifying a proof for all triangles that the sum of the angles is 180 degrees.

When students are engaged in technology-enhanced experiences, teachers have unique opportunities to examine students' mathematical thinking and learning in the investigations. Engaging students in mathematical discourse is essential as they work with each of these representations. Students need to explain their current understandings of the ideas to reveal their developing mathematical conceptions. These experiences enrich the information that teachers are able to use in making instructional decisions about appropriate uses of technologies for learning mathematics.

PRE-SERVICE TEACHER DEVELOPMENT OF TPACK

The four TPACK components provide a framework for the preparation of mathematics teachers for the 21st century. This framework requires more than attention to the development of knowledge about potential digital technologies for teaching mathematics. The TPACK components emphasize the importance of a subject-specific teacher preparation focused on the intersection of content, pedagogy, and technology. Future teachers need to be challenged to reconsider their subject matter content and the impact of technology, such as virtual manipulatives, spreadsheets, and dynamic geometry software, on the development of mathematics itself. They must concurrently reconsider the mathematics content and what it means to teach and learn mathematics with these digital technologies. This recognition defies long-

Figure 4. a and b. Dynamic actions suggesting the sum of the angles of any triangle is 180 degrees regardless of shape

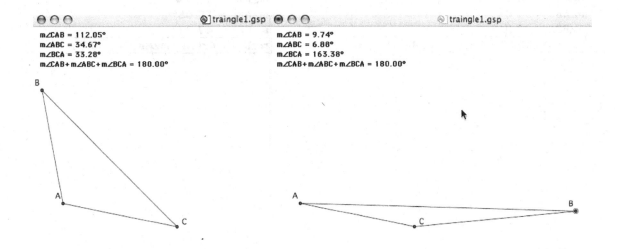

held assumptions that (1) in-depth knowledge of mathematics is sufficient for teaching mathematics with technologies and (2) developing PCK with no attention to teaching with technology is sufficient for learning to teach with technology.

Calculators – from limited four-function calculators to more powerful computer algebra systems (CAS) – have traditionally been challenged as tools that do the mathematics rather than engaging students in learning mathematics. Thus, mathematics teachers have limited use of these tools for learning mathematics. Currently, many future teachers (particularly elementary) have few, if any, experiences learning mathematics in kindergarten through grade 12 with digital technologies. They have limited experiences upon which to rely for developing an overarching conception about the purposes for incorporating these and emerging technologies for teaching mathematical topics. Pre-service teachers must be prepared to rethink, unlearn and relearn, change, revise, and adapt to teach in the 21st century filled with new, more powerful digital technologies. Shreiter and Ammon (1989) propose that atten-

tion to these challenges requires that pre-service teachers be engaged in a process of assimilation and accommodation toward the reconstruction of their personal experiences and understandings in learning mathematics. Given this perspective, developing TPACK is then viewed much as that of developing PCK as a constructive and iterative process where pre-service teachers must confront, reflect on, and carefully revise multiple experiences and events for teaching their content with appropriate technologies based on their existing knowledge, beliefs, and dispositions (Borko & Putnam, 1996; Niess et al., 2009).

TPACK is more than a set of multiple domains of knowledge and skills for teaching. TPACK is a way of thinking strategically within these multiple domains of knowledge. Relying on ideas from Shavelson, Ruiz-Primo, Li, and Ayala (2003), TPACK strategic thinking involves planning, organizing, critiquing, and abstracting for specific content, specific student needs, and specific classroom situations while concurrently considering the affordances and constraints of the digital technologies. Future teachers need experi-

Figure 5. Visual representations supporting the conjecture that the sum of the angles is 180 degrees

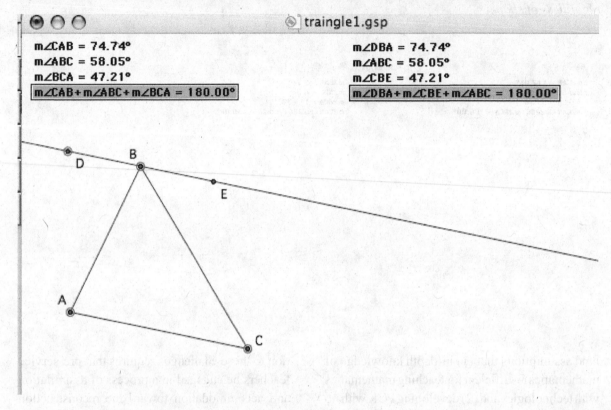

ences that engage them developing this strategic thinking for teaching mathematics.

Redesigning pre-service mathematics teacher education with respect to developing TPACK is a *wicked problem* (Rittel & Webber, 1973) because of the incompleteness in understanding the knowledge needed and how it is developed. The wickedness results from the complex inter-dependencies that require pre-service teachers to reconstruct their personal knowledge in a way that results in a dynamic equilibrium among content, pedagogy, and technology (Koehler & Mishra, 2008, p. 18). Teacher educators must recognize and prepare to build upon pre-service teachers' knowledge, skills, and dispositions with respect to the content, the pedagogy, and the technology that they bring to the programs.

Students in pre-service programs bring a broad diversity of technology expertise. Many pre-service students were born around the time of the emergence of the Internet and might be considered as *digital natives* (Prensky, 2001) since they have grown up with more natural access to modern digital technologies than prior genera-tions. Another group of pre-service students might also be considered as *digital immigrants* because they are hoping to enter a second profession after having worked in a different profession for about 10-20 years. These students often have had fewer experiences with modern digital technologies. However, few, if any of these pre-service students (both natives and immigrants), have experienced learning mathematics with digital technologies in the ways envisioned today. The challenge for the redesign of teacher education at the pre-service level is to design programs that provide experiences with digital technologies as well as with teaching and learning mathematics with these technologies.

Compounding this challenge, views about learning have undergone significant shifts. Situational and social learning perspectives have become increasingly recognized that *how* and *where* a person learns an idea is fundamental to *what* is learned (Greeno, Collins, & Resnick, 1996). These perspectives contend that learning must reflect multiple contexts and consider learners as well as the physical and social systems within which they participate (Putnam & Borko, 2000). While the TPACK construct presents primarily a *cognitive, constructivist* view of individual learning, the situational and social perspectives are directed toward the *social context and how* a person's participation in that context impacts personal understanding. As Cobb and Yackel (1996) suggest, these social and constructivist ideas are reflexive rather than in conflict with one another (Cobb & Bowers, 1999; Cobb, Stephan, McClain, & Gravemeijer, 2001; Gravemeijer & Cobb, 2006; McClain & Cobb, 2001).

The learning trajectories in the redesign of pre-service mathematics teacher education programs must consider the context within which they are developing TPACK. Elementary programs have limited mathematics coursework whereas secondary programs have many more mathematics courses that are also more advanced. Each of these contexts impacts the knowledge that pre-service teachers will develop and rely on when teaching mathematics since they are continuing to learn mathematics while they are learning to teach mathematics. These different contexts must reflect learning mathematics with appropriate technologies to support the development of TPACK. Faculty teaching content courses are focused on the mathematics content rather than the teaching of that content; however, they must consider appropriate tools for learning mathematics as part of their courses—where they incorporate appropriate digital technologies in learning the content.

In addition to the content course concerns, current research results and recommendations suggest additional considerations for learning trajectories for pre-service mathematics teacher development of the knowledge needed for teaching with technologies.

Pre-Service Technology Course

Since the early 1990s, pre-service teacher preparation programs have traditionally included a technology course as part of the academic program. This course has focused on learning about different technologies along with their affordances and constraints for use as educational technologies (such as, word processors, spreadsheets, databases, the Internet and designing web pages, and presentation software). However, over 20 years of such course content has not resulted in much evidence of pre-service teachers implementing these or other digital technologies in their teaching. More importantly, as noted by Earle (2002),

Integrating technology is not about technology – it is primarily about content and effective instructional practices. Technology involves the tools with which we deliver content and implement practices in better ways. Its focus must be on curriculum and learning. Integration is defined not by the amount or type of technology used, but by how and why it is used. (p. 8)

More recently, research by Mishra, Koehler, Shin, Wolf, and DeSchryver (2010) challenges teacher preparation programs to retain a technology course but reconsider its curriculum and instruction. They recommend that the course needs to consider the newer, digital technologies and must recognize that the majority of these technologies were not designed for educational uses. They propose that the technology-focused courses engage students in more than learning about the technology. They propose that the course focus on *learning by design* in ways that engage pre-service students with rich pedagogical, technological, and content problems, maintaining the interrelationships. They proposed a spiral approach for the course content that engages students in micro design, macro design, and reflection on the total package required in TPACK. This approach has potential for engaging pre-service students in multiple components of TPACK while they also learn about specific technologies.

For the micro design stage, pre-service students engage in exploration of the features of a specific technology. For example, pre-service teachers might be asked to explore the digital camera to learn about its capabilities within the framework of understanding a mathematical phenomenon observed in nature, such as fractals. With the slideshow feature of the camera software, they might present the photos in an interesting and informative manner where they focus on the mathematical content of fractals and providing displays of fractals in nature (e.g., Romanesco broccoli).

At the macro design stage, students use the technology (such as the digital camera) to conduct research where they present their results in a video format. A mathematics pre-service student might explore students' understandings of multiplication. In this project, the literature search examining students' views and misconceptions identifies a common children's misconception that multiplication on a number always increases that number. Through the research, the pre-service student finds explanations about children's development of this misconception. With this research, the pre-service student develops a protocol for interviewing children about their understanding of the impact of the operation of multiplication. During the interviews, the video captures what the students write on a paper and their audio commentary rather than their visual expressions.

The final stage in this macro design emphasizes a metacognitive, reflective view of the students' learning and using the technology as an educational tool. At this stage, the pre-service students are now asked to design a reflective video (to be submitted to YouTube) in an educationally informative manner discussing children's misconceptions

about multiplication and ways to reframe their understandings; appropriate interview clips provide supportive evidence of children's ideas about multiplication without revealing their identities. This reflective video incorporates a defense for how and why teachers might redesign their instruction to help children develop a more robust understanding of the operation of multiplication.

Throughout this macro design stage, the pre-service students investigate and experience the use of digital cameras and videos through an educational lens. The use of YouTube as the communication medium incorporates investigations and experiences in communicating mathematical ideas to a diverse audience and adds the education about protecting the anonymity of the individuals in videos displayed to a worldwide audience.

Throughout these design processes, pre-service teachers are engaged in learning about the technology within an educational context. With respect to the four TPACK components, they are engaged in investigating the capabilities of specific technologies within specific mathematics topics. They are challenged to investigate children's understandings and thinking. They are expected to focus their work within the mathematics curriculum and consider how instruction has potential for leading to misconceptions. Through this *learning by design* process, the emphasis is on interaction of content, pedagogy, and technology rather than simply a consideration of the features of a specific technology.

Pre-Service Methods Coursework Strategies

Typically in pre-service programs, students complete at least one mathematics methods course emphasizing teaching mathematics content for specific grade levels. Lee and Hollebrands (2008) created and tested teacher education materials to be used in such mathematics methods coursework. The focus of their work used an approach that integrally develops teachers' understandings of content, technology, and pedagogy to prepare them to teach data analysis and probability topics using specific technology tools. They developed videocases focused on enhancing the pre-service teachers' knowledge of students' thinking and understanding as they were learning about data analysis in technology-enhanced environments. The videocases illustrate ways the technology can be used to expedite mathematical process with the potential to change the way students and teachers think about mathematical ideas. In the process of engaging the pre-service teachers with the videos, they also provide situations to challenge the traditional mathematics curriculum and instruction based on the enhanced capabilities of the technology. In the process, they confront pre-service teachers' conceptions of integrating technology with specific mathematics topics in the development of a deeper understanding of the use of algebraic representations in regression analysis.

Pre-service teacher preparation programs are also expected to provide coursework in educational methods such as learning to design lessons and units of instruction for identified instructional objectives. Multiple methods courses highlight the development of teaching strategies and classroom management, learning theories and planning for instruction, and assessment of learning. As Putnam and Borko (2000) indicate that *how a person learns a particular set of knowledge and skills, and the situation in which a person learns, become a fundamental part of what is learned.* Thus, with a desire to develop a more robust teacher knowledge called TPACK, teacher educators must re-think these courses in ways that emphasize and provide important activities and learning experiences at the intersection of content, pedagogy, and technology with careful attention to the situations within which pre-service students are developing their strategic thinking instructional processes.

Angeli and Valanides (2009) identified a Technology Mapping (TM) model as a situative methodology for the development of TPACK in first and second year elementary teacher prepara-

tion coursework. Using a design-based research technique, they identified TM as *a methodology for guiding teacher thinking about the ill-defined problem of designing technology-enhanced learning... TM is predicated on the view that, while there is no one right way to deal with design problems, it is possible to guide teachers' thinking with an instructional design (ID) model that is deeply rooted and situated in their real practices* (p. 17). TM is promoted as a mechanism for teaching how to design technology-enhanced lessons where the pre-service teachers apply ideas from lectures and laboratories on instructional design processes. In the laboratory, they map software affordances with content representations and pedagogical uses. For example, they might indicate that hyperlinks in a particular software afford multi-model representations of specific content (auditory, textual, visual, and interactive representations); pedagogically, they might suggest: *Students can 'travel' to the Internet to read about something, to hear about something, to view a video, to explore different points of view, to run a model or simulation, or even to visit a virtual museum* (p. 47). At the end of the fifth and tenth weeks of the course, students designed technology-enhanced lessons for a topic of their choice. In the eighth week of the course, they participated in peer assessment of the first design tasks. Lessons were posted on Blackboard for evaluation by peers organized in groups of five using asynchronous communication. Students then prepared reflections and self-assessment papers about their individual performances on the design task. During the last week, the students as a group reflected on their design experiences, sharing the challenges they faced as they framed the lessons.

Through these activities, the students were engaged in strategic thinking around integrating technologies in lessons as they designed their lessons after completing the TM activities. When they worked in their peer assessment groups, the instructor directed their attention to researcher-identified TPACK criteria: (1) the identification of suitable topics to be taught with technology, (2) the identification of appropriate representations to transform content, (3) the identification of teaching strategies difficult to be implemented by traditional means, (4) the selection of appropriate tools and appropriate pedagogical uses of their affordances, and (5) the identification of appropriate integration strategies. These criteria were used to assess the students' TPACK performance on the two design tasks indicating that the outcomes of the course attended to all four of the TPACK components with specific attention to instructional strategies and representations. Moreover, the researchers added the importance of the situational value of the social exchanges during the peer assessments on the pre-service teachers' developing understandings and strategic thinking about integrating technology in the lessons.

While lectures provide opportunities to present general ideas about teaching and learning, they do not adequately provide key reasoning experiences required in developing TPACK strategic thinking processes. In my work, a collaborative study group strategy engaged pre-service teachers in pedagogical reasoning in the design of a unit of instruction (Niess, 2008). This reasoning process is essential in the development of the knowledge of when, where, and how to integrate knowledge mathematics content, teaching and student learning in mathematics, and technology applications for enhancing mathematics learning. The end result of *planning* is the enhancement of the reasoning process. Each study group identifies a mathematics unit topic for integrating appropriate technologies with a specific group of students (e.g., heterogeneous groups of students). Using a backward design approach (Wiggins & McTighe, 2006), the study groups begin with what they plan for students to do at the conclusion of the unit. What problems are the children expected to solve at the end of the unit? What skills will they demonstrate? How will they demonstrate their knowledge of the content? Such questions help the study group members clarify their ideas about the content while carefully considering dif-

ferent knowledge levels (declarative, procedural, schematic, strategic) that distinguish the student thinking required in the end-of-the-unit problems or expectations (Shavelson et al., 2003).

A wiki as shown in Figure 6 provides a dynamic collaborative space for members of a study group to present their ideas in the process of framing, organizing, and clarifying the thinking about the content they plan to include in the unit. As they select specific cells in the matrix, they are able to insert their ideas as well as review the posted ideas of others. After completing the *content* column, they discuss, debate, and propose specific pedagogical strategies (*teaching & student learning*) and appropriate *technologies* for the specific thinking levels desired.

This process results in the iterative evolution of their thinking about the unit. A more detailed description of the progress of one group's thinking about a unit for fourth grade students learning to make change for amounts tendered in particular transactions is available in the *Handbook of Technological Pedagogical Content Knowledge (TPCK) for Educators* in the pre-service chapter (Niess, 2008a). In this example, the study group identified multiple technologies and some instructional strategies that might be useful in the unit on making change. Through this process the pre-service teachers are engaged in the integration of content, pedagogy, and technology in a manner that simulates teacher exchange of ideas in the development of an instructional unit.

With the identification of the importance of TPACK, additional research-based strategies are needed for developing the knowledge pre-service teachers need for teaching mathematics with technologies for the methods coursework. The tension that exists in the development of ideas for pre-service programs is the importance of a focus on the intersection of content, pedagogy, and technology given that many teacher preparation programs are more generic than subject specific. However, developing specific pedagogical reasoning suggested by TPACK requires purposeful and supportive attention to the intersection that is more easily incorporated in subject-specific program coursework (Niess, 2001; Suharwoto & Niess, 2006).

Pre-Service Practicum Coursework

While technology and educational methods instruction are important, the pre-service teacher preparation program must explicitly incorporate experiences where the students are required to engage in the application of their learning to teach – in practicum experiences that directly require application of the intersection and interconnection of technology, pedagogy, and content. In other words, pre-service teachers must have experiences where they are mentored in teaching their content with appropriate technologies with specific grade-levels students. Such *student teaching* experiences are crucial for the development of the knowledge, skills, and dispositions described in the four TPACK components (Niess, 2001, 2005; Suharwoto, 2006).

Multiple challenges hamper the ability of teacher preparation programs when requiring pre-service teachers to complete student teaching that includes teaching mathematics with technology – access to technology, appropriate curriculum materials, and the availability of cooperating mentor teachers with an understanding and facility in teaching mathematics with appropriate technologies as they manage the classroom experiences. In response to this concern, Harrington (2008) documented a Technology Partnership Project that proved influential in pre-service teachers' development of TPACK while also meeting the challenge of appropriate cooperating mentor teachers. Teams of three pre-service teachers were matched with volunteer in-service middle school mathematics teachers. The composition of each team specifically recognized the mathematics teacher's PCK expertise and the pre-service teachers' technological expertise. The task for the team was to collaboratively design a sequence of

lessons that integrated an appropriate technology with a mathematics topic incorporating specific pedagogies. During the teaching phase, one team member taught the first lesson while the others observed. The team reflected and made revisions prior to the next lesson. By the conclusion of the instruction, all team members (including the middle school mathematics teacher) taught at least one lesson that integrated the technology as a learning tool. This experience facilitated the development of the pre-service teachers' TPACK thinking, including: (1) opportunities to advocate for their own ideas, their peers' ideas, and the in-service teacher's ideas while convincing others of the validity of those ideas, (2) opportunities to teach, building on their learning from those ideas, reflections, and revisions, and (3) a way to connect preconceptions about the way students learn with actual examples of student learning. This project provided pre-service teachers with essential teaching experiences in mathematics with appropriate technologies. Additionally, this project provided the cooperating mentor teachers with important learning and teaching experiences for integrating appropriate technologies in teaching mathematics extending their PCK to TPACK.

ASSESSING PRE-SERVICE TEACHER DEVELOPMENT OF TPACK

Developing pre-service teachers' TPACK assumes that TPACK is clearly defined and can be adequately assessed. Angeli and Valanides (2009) identified specific criteria to be used in assessing the work of the pre-service teachers in the Technology Mapping work from a TPACK perspective.

Niess, Lee, and Sadri (2007) proposed a similar developmental model using the lens of Roger's (1995) five developmental levels that technology innovators make when working with innovations: knowledge, persuasion, decision, implementation, and confirmation. Five TPACK levels were

Figure 6. Study group wiki for engaging in the pedagogical reasoning of unit design

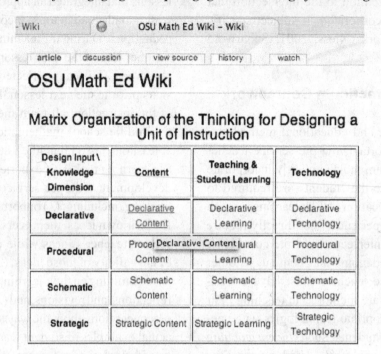

identified through extensive observations and data collection to describe in-service teachers' development when learning to integrate technologies such as spreadsheets in teaching and learning.

1. Recognizing: Teachers are able to use spreadsheets and recognize the alignment of spreadsheet capabilities with subject matter content, but are not yet integrating spreadsheets in teaching and learning in their content and at their grade level.

2. Accepting: Teachers form attitudes toward teaching and learning content topics at their specific grade levels with spreadsheets. They may try activities they have experienced with their students in the process of forming their attitudes toward acceptance.

3. Adapting: Teachers engage in activities leading to teaching and learning subject matter topics with spreadsheets. They adapt activities they have experienced for their students.

4. Exploring: Teachers actively integrate teaching and learning of content topics with spreadsheets where they rephrase and design activities to align with their curriculum.

5. Advancing: Teachers evaluate the results of the decision to integrate teaching and learning content with spreadsheets and willingly make changes in the curriculum to take advantage of the affordances of spreadsheets.

These levels provide a framework for assessing the impact of a technology-rich program on participants' knowledge and integration of technology in their own classrooms. Recognition of these levels of knowledge development calls for assessments that can validly and reliably identify teachers' growth and development of TPACK as their knowledge expands for teaching with multiple technologies.

Schmidt, Barn, Thompson, Koehler, Mishra, and Shin (2009) undertook the task of developing and validating an instrument to gather pre-service teachers' self-assessment of their TPACK and related knowledge domains (technology knowledge (TK), content knowledge (CK), pedagogical knowledge (PK), pedagogical content knowledge (PCK), technological content knowledge (TCK), technological pedagogical knowledge (TPK) and TPACK). The design of the instrument focused on the multiple content areas that pre-service teachers were preparing to teach (i.e., literacy, mathematics, science, social studies) where the items were framed around each of the separate content areas with respect to the individual knowledge domains. The resulting self-assessment survey was based on pre-service teachers' assessment of the specific statements judged to incorporate the related domains in TPACK.

Harris, Grandgenett and Hofer (2010) developed a valid and reliable rubric for assessing teaching artifacts such as lesson plans and have plans for developing an observation instrument for assessing teachers' TPACK while teaching. These efforts provide a beginning for assessing TPACK but future research must identify ways that teacher educators can measure the knowledge development of their participants in specific courses and programs if they are to be able to make adequate revisions for guiding the development of TPACK. With the emergence of the TPACK construct, the work in developing various assessment mechanisms will certainly impact the thinking about the meaning and recognition of TPACK.

A recent study explored the use of an electronic teaching portfolio (called a Scoop portfolio based on the work of Borko, Stecher, and Kuffner (2007)) for engaging teachers in assessing their own implementation of reform-based instructional practices that demanded the knowledge and skills envisioned in the construct of TPACK (Niess, 2010). The participants were asked to provide evidence of their progress in advancing their knowledge and skills with instructional strategies and representations as well as with curriculum and curriculum materials as a means of demonstrating their strategic planning, implementation, and critical analysis

in a K-8 mathematics class while integrating appropriate technologies as teaching and learning tools. The electronic portfolios documented their instruction teaching mathematics with technology over a series of lessons (4-5 hours). During this time, they gathered and analyzed videos of two lessons along with copies of student work. They also prepared extended reflections prior to the Scoop, after each lesson, and upon completion of the series of lessons. An important aspect of the process of teaching and gathering essential artifacts was that the participants were engaged as a community of learners where they helped each other in the description and analysis of the multiple artifacts. As they gathered the artifacts they discussed, debated, and challenged the usefulness of specific reform-based instructional strategies for engaging students in learning with technologies – e.g., questioning, challenging students to propose conjectures and hypotheses; engaging students in meaningful discussions about the content; engaging students in problem solving and inquiry tasks; dealing with hands-on activities working with multiple representations to develop clearer understandings of concepts; motivating student learning; and capitalizing on learners' prior knowledge.

While this study focused on in-service teachers, the process is one that might be useful in engaging pre-service teachers in investigating their teaching of mathematics with technology. Analysis of the data sources demonstrated ways pre-service teachers might gather valid and reliable artifacts to be used for judging their knowledge and understandings of the interplay among technology, pedagogy, and content.

IMPLICATIONS AND CHALLENGES IN RE-DESIGNING PROGRAMS FOR TPACK DEVELOPMENT

Recognition of the specialized knowledge required for teaching mathematics with appropriate technologies challenges many previously held assumptions. The assumption that teachers only need a solid mathematical knowledge has been recognized as erroneous. The recognition of the intersection of mathematical content knowledge with pedagogical knowledge as the specialized knowledge for teaching has not appeared to incorporate the knowledge for teaching mathematics with appropriate digital technologies. The assumption that knowledge about technologies is sufficient for teaching mathematics with technologies has also been shown to be erroneous.

TPACK has been identified and described as the highly complex and challenging knowledge that teachers need for teaching mathematics with appropriate digital technologies – as the interaction and integration of technological, pedagogical, and content knowledge. Simply adding a calculator tool to show students how to rapidly roll two dice a thousand times so they can propose that the most common sum is 7 is not the understanding embodied in TPACK. Rather, TPACK embodies the strategic thinking that involves planning, organizing, critiquing, and abstracting for specific mathematical ideas, specific student needs, and specific classroom situations while concurrently considering the affordances and constraints of the digital technologies.

The recognition and acceptance of TPACK as the knowledge teachers need for teaching requires teacher educators to rethink the design of preparation for teaching mathematics with technologies. While ideas and models for the redesign have been conceived and researched, many questions can be raised. Is the inclusion of additional practical experiences as in Harrington's (2008) technology partnership project an essential experience for pre-service teacher preparation? Is *learning by design* as promoted by Mishra et al. (2010) a strategy that results in TPACK development? What experiences are essential for guiding pre-service teachers through the TPACK developmental process as identified by Niess et al. (2006)?

Perhaps, the most important recognition when thinking about TPACK is that pre-service teachers must have opportunities to continue learning, unlearning and relearning about teaching mathematics with newer and more powerful technologies. Many of the technologies call for questioning the mathematics that students are expected to learn to be productive citizens in the 21st century. Few people argue with the calculator being used to find the square root of a number. Effective mathematics teaching focuses on understanding the concept of square root and identifying a reasonable estimate of the square root. Yet, many elementary and middle school mathematics teachers continue to resist allowing the use of the calculator as a mathematical learning tool. If the mathematics curriculum is focused on calculation rather than conceptual mental estimation then the calculator is not an appropriate learning tool. Alternatively, many mathematics teachers with a more robust TPACK encourage the use of calculators as mathematical learning tools rather than tools that do the mathematics. These teachers engage students in exploring mathematical ideas and estimating solutions prior to using calculators for verification.

Pre-service teachers must have directed experiences that engage them in strategic thinking with the technology, the mathematics, and the pedagogies; they must plan, organize, critique, and abstract the ideas for specific content, specific student needs, and specific classroom situations while concurrently considering the affordances and constraints of the digital technologies. This situation calls for serious reconsiderations of teacher preparation programs. The challenge for teacher educators is to re-design the programs with the recognition that *how*, *what*, and *where* pre-service teachers learn mathematics is as important in their TPACK education as *how*, *what* and *where* they learn about teaching and learning mathematics. As identified in AMTE's position statement, pre-service teachers need knowledge for integrating appropriate technologies in the teaching of K-12 mathematics, knowledge that is actualized through:

- *a deep, flexible, and connected conceptual understanding of K-12 mathematics that acknowledges the impact of technology on what content should be taught;*
- *a research-based understanding of how students learn mathematics and the impact technology can have on learning;*
- *a strong pedagogical knowledge-base related to the effective use of technology to improve mathematics teaching and learning; and*
- *appropriate experiences during their teacher preparation program in the use of a variety of technological tools to enhance their own learning of mathematics and the mathematical learning of others.* (AMTE, 2006, p. 1)

REFERENCES

Angeli, C. M., & Valanides, N. (2009, April). *Examining epistemological and methodological issues of the conceptualizations. Development and assessment of ICT-TPACJ: Advancing technological pedagogical content knowledge (TPCK) – Part I. Teachers.* Paper presented at the meeting of the American Educational Research Association (AERA) Annual Conference, San Diego, CA.

Association of Mathematics Teacher Educators (AMTE). (2006). *AMTE technology position statement: Preparing teacher to use technology to enhance the learning of mathematics.* Retrieved from http://www.amte.net/publications

Borko, H., & Putnam, T. (1996). Learning to teach. In Berliner, D. C., & Calfee, R. C. (Eds.), *Handbook of educational psychology* (pp. 673–708). New York, NY: Simon and Schuster Macmillan.

Borko, H., Stecher, B., & Kuffner, K. (2007). *Using artifacts to characterize reform-oriented instruction: The Scoop Notebook and rating guide.* (Technical Report 707). Los Angeles, CA: National Center for Research on Evaluation, Standards, and Student Testing. (ERIC Document Reproduction Service No. ED495853).

Cannon, L., Dorward, J., Heal, R., & Edwards, L. (1999). *National library of virtual manipulatives.* Utah State University. Retrieved from http://nlvm.usu.edu/en/nav/vlibrary.html

Cobb, P., & Bowers, J. (1999). Cognitive and situated learning perspectives in theory and practice. *Educational Researcher, 28*(2), 4–15.

Cobb, P., Stephan, M., McClain, K., & Gravemeijer, K. (2001). Participating in classroom mathematical practices. *Journal of the Learning Sciences, 10*(1&2), 113–163. doi:10.1207/S15327809JLS10-1-2_6

Cobb, P., & Yackel, E. (1996). Constructivist, emergent, and sociocultural perspectives in the context of developmental research. *Educational Psychologist, 31*(3/4), 175–190.

Earle, R. S. (2002). The integration of instructional technology into public education: Promises and challenges. *ET Magazine, 42*(1), 5–13.

Gravemeijer, K., & Cobb, P. (2006). Design research from a learning design perspective. In van den Akker, J., Gravemeijer, K., McKenney, S., & Nieveen, N. (Eds.), *Educational design research.* London, UK: Routledge.

Greeno, J. G., Collins, A., & Resnick, L. B. (1996). Cognition and learning. In D. C. Berliner & R. C, Calfee (Eds.), *Handbook of educational psychology.* New York, NY: Macmillan.

Grossman, P. L. (1989). A study in contrast: Sources of pedagogical content knowledge for secondary English. *Journal of Teacher Education, 40*(5), 24–31. doi:10.1177/002248718904000504

Grossman, P. L. (1990). *The making of a teacher: Teacher knowledge and teacher education*. New York, NY: Teachers College Press.

Grossman, P. L. (1991). Overcoming the apprenticeship of observation in teacher education coursework. *Teaching and Teacher Education, 7*, 245–257. doi:10.1016/0742-051X(91)90004-9

Harrington, R. A. (2008). *The development of pre-service teachers' technology specific pedagogy*. (Unpublished doctoral dissertation). Oregon State University, Corvallis, OR.

Harris, J. B., Grandgenett, N., & Hofer, M. (2010, March). *Testing a TPACK-based technology integration assessment rubric*. Paper presented at the Annual Meeting of the Society for Information Technology and Teacher Education (SITE), San Diego, CA.

Koehler, M. J., & Mishra, P. (2008). Introducing TPCK. In Silverman, N. (Ed.), *Handbook of technological pedagogical content knowledge (TPCK) for educators* (pp. 1–20). New York, NY: Routledge.

Lappan, G. (2000). The language of mathematics: The meaning and use of variable. *NCTM News Bulletin*. Retrieved from http://www.nctm.org/about/content.aspx?id=994

Lee, H., & Hollebrands, K. (2008). Preparing to teach mathematics with technology: An integrated approach to developing technological pedagogical content knowledge. *Contemporary Issues in Technology & Teacher Education, 8*(4). Retrieved from http://www.citejournal.org/vol8/iss4/mathematics/article1.cfm.

Margerum-Leys, J., & Marx, R. W. (2002). Teacher knowledge of educational technology: A study of student teacher/mentor teacher pairs. *Journal of Educational Computing Research, 26*(4), 427–462. doi:10.2190/JXBR-2G0G-1E4T-7T4M

McClain, K., & Cobb, P. (2001). Supporting students' ability to reason about data. *Educational Studies in Mathematics, 45*, 103–109. doi:10.1023/A:1013874514650

Mishra, P., & Koehler, M. J. (2006). Technological pedagogical content knowledge: A framework for integrating technology in teacher knowledge. *Teachers College Record, 108*(6), 1017–1054. doi:10.1111/j.1467-9620.2006.00684.x

Mishra, P., Koehler, M. J., Shin, T. S., Wolf, L. G., & DeSchryver, M. (2010). *Developing TPACK by design*. A part of the symposium titled Strategies for Teacher professional Development of TPACK presented at Society for Information Technology and Teacher Education Annual Conference in San Diego, CA.

National Council of Teachers of Mathematics. (2000). *Principles and standards for school mathematics*. Reston, VA: Author.

Niess, M. L. (2001). Research into practice: A model for integrating technology in preservice science and mathematics content-specific teacher preparation. *School Science and Mathematics, 101*(2), 102–109. doi:10.1111/j.1949-8594.2001.tb18011.x

Niess, M. L. (2005). Preparing teachers to teach science and mathematics with technology: Developing a technology pedagogical content knowledge. *Teaching and Teacher Education, 21*(5), 509–523. doi:10.1016/j.tate.2005.03.006

Niess, M. L. (2008a). Guiding preservice teachers in developing TPCK. In Silverman, N. (Ed.), *Handbook of technological pedagogical content knowledge (TPCK) for educators* (pp. 223–250). New York, NY: Routledge.

Niess, M. L. (2008b). Knowledge needed for teaching with technologies – Call it TPACK. *AMTE Connections*, Spring, 9-10.

Niess, M. L. (2010, May). *Using classroom artifacts to judge teacher knowledge of reform-based instructional practices that integrate technology in mathematics and science classrooms.* Paper presentation for American Educational Research Association (AERA) Annual Conference, Denver, CO.

Niess, M. L., Lee, K., & Sadri, P. (2007, April). *Dynamic spreadsheets as learning technology tools: Developing teachers' technology pedagogical content knowledge (TPCK)* Paper presentation for the American Education Research Association Annual Conference, Chicago, IL.

Niess, M. L., Ronau, R. N., Driskell, S. O., Kosheleva, O., Pugalee, D., & Weinhold, M. W. (2009). Technological pedagogical content knowledge (TPCK): Preparation of mathematics teachers for 21st century teaching and learning. In F. Arbaugh & P. M. Taylor (Eds.), *Inquiry into mathematics teacher education. Association of Mathematics Teacher Educators (AMTE) Monograph Series, 5,* 143-156. January 2009.

Pierson, M. E. (2001). Technology integration practices as function of pedagogical expertise. *Journal of Research on Computing in Education, 33*(4), 413–429.

Prensky, M. (2001). Digital natives, digital immigrants. *Horizon, 9*(5). doi:10.1108/10748120110424816

Putnam, R. T., & Borko, H. (2000). What do new views of knowledge and thinking have to say about research on teacher learning? *Educational Researcher, 29*(1), 4–15.

Rittel, H., & Webber, M. (1973). Dilemmas in a general theory of planning. *Policy Sciences, 4*(2), 155–169. doi:10.1007/BF01405730

Rogers, E. (1995). *Diffusion of innovations.* New York, NY: Simon and Schuster Inc.

Schmidt, D. A., Baran, E., Thompson, A. D., Koehler, M. J., Mishra, P., & Shin, T. S. (2009). *Technological pedagogical content knowledge (TPACK): The development and validation of an assessment instrument for preservice teachers.* Paper presented at the annual meeting of the American Educational Research Association (AERA), San Diego, CA.

Shavelson, R., Ruiz-Primo, A., Li, M., & Ayala, C. (2003). *Evaluating new approaches to assessing learning (CSE Report 604).* Los Angeles, CA: University of California National Center for Research on Evaluation.

Shreiter, B., & Ammon, P. (1989). *Teachers' thinking and their use of reading contracts.* Paper presented at the Annual Meeting of the American Educational Research Association, San Francisco, California.

Shulman, L. (1987). Knowledge and teaching: Foundations of the new reform. *Harvard Educational Review, 57*(1), 1–22.

Shulman, L. S. (1986). Those who understand: Knowledge growth in teaching. *Educational Researcher, 15,* 4–14.

Suharwoto, G. (2006). *Secondary mathematics preservice teachers' development of technology pedagogical content knowledge in subject-specific, technology-integrated teacher preparation program.* (Unpublished doctoral dissertation.) Oregon State University.

Suharwoto, G., & Niess, M. L. (2006, March). *How do subject specific teacher preparation programs that integrate technology throughout the courses support the development of mathematics preservice teachers' TPCK (Technology Pedagogical Content Knowledge)?* Paper presentation for the Society of Information Technology and Teacher Education (SITE) Annual Conference, Orlando, Florida.

Thompson, A. D., and Mishra, P. (2007). Breaking news: TPCK becomes TPACK! *Journal of Computing in Teacher Education, 24*, 38, 64.

Wiggins, G., & McTighe, J. (2006). *Understanding by design*. Upper Saddle River, NJ: Pearson Education, Inc.

Zhao, Y. (2003). *What teachers should know about technology: Perspectives and practices*. Greenwich, CT: Information Age Publishing.

Chapter 22
Technology Integration in Mathematics:
A Model for Integrating Technology through Content Development[1]

Chandra Hawley Orrill
University of Massachusetts Dartmouth, USA

Drew Polly
University of North Carolina at Charlotte, USA

ABSTRACT

This chapter describes Technology Integration in Mathematics (TIM), an iterative professional development model that focused on integrating technology into elementary school mathematics instruction. Grounded in the American Psychological Association's Learner-Centered Principles, the program provided teachers with ownership of their own learning and situated teachers' learning of technology in the context of learning mathematics. The authors provide design principles, a description of the project, examples, and challenges from their work.

INTRODUCTION

The Technology Integration in Mathematics (TIM) project was a technology integration-oriented professional development (PD) effort focused on elementary school mathematics. The project featured an iterative design approach that allowed us to revisit and refine our model of professional development through a series of one and two year projects in four school districts over the course of five years. TIM emerged out of the first author's interest in school change and a hypothesis that supporting elementary teachers' use of learner-centered, constructivist pedagogies could be accomplished through supporting the integration of technology in their teaching (e.g.,

DOI: 10.4018/978-1-4666-0014-0.ch022

Sandholtz, Ringstaff, & Dwyer, 1997; Roschelle, Pea, Hoadley, Gordin, & Means, 2001). Since teachers generally have not had the opportunity to develop a personally meaningful definition or model for teaching with technology and have had few opportunities to teach content in ways that integrate technology, they have not formed approaches and patterns to effectively integrate technology (Penuel et al., 2007; Schrum, 1999). Therefore, PD has the potential to substantially shape their initial interactions with technology to support content learning (Author, 1999; Lawless & Pellegrino, 2007). Based on the literature and our own experiences, we posited that if we could influence the ways teachers taught mathematics when they had access to computers and calculators and if teachers could see benefits in using those new pedagogies, then they would start using some of these pedagogies in other mathematics lessons—and, eventually, other subject areas.

The iterations of the TIM project, which embodied our theory of teacher change, focused on elementary mathematics. Specifically, we sought to support teachers in developing richer content knowledge as they developed pedagogical knowledge necessary for integrating technology into their classrooms. Numerous educational technology researchers have found that teachers' simultaneously develop technological, pedagogical and content knowledge (TPACK) while learning about technology integration (Polly, 2011; Mishra & Koehler, 2006; Niess, 2005).

Throughout the lifespan of the project, the TIM staff worked to build each teachers' dispositions toward technology and mathematical knowledge. This dedication to finding ways to meet the teachers' needs paid off as evidenced in teacher self-reports. On five of the six individual projects that comprised the TIM effort[2], at least 89% of the participating teachers reported the project being a positive experience with up to 100% of the teachers in one project noting that the project had taught them some "great new ways to teach mathematics; and up to 85% of teachers in another project agreeing that the project had "taught me a lot about using computers with my math students."

Over the course of the five-year lifespan of the TIM efforts, we had the opportunity to try a number of variations on this approach. However, specific aspects of the professional learning model either became central through our successive attempts to meet our goals or they proved from the beginning to be critical to the success of the professional development efforts. We present these aspects of the TIM approach as design principles and discuss them in detail following the introduction of our PD model. We will conclude the chapter with a discussion of the challenges we were unable to overcome in our own efforts.

The TIM Professional Development Model

The goal connecting all of the TIM projects was to promote the creation and implementation of learning opportunities for students that were consistent with the *Principles and Standards for School Mathematics* (NCTM, 2000). As pointed out in the *Standards'* Technology Principle (NCTM, 2000), technology can help connect skills and procedures to mathematical understandings and technology can limit the necessity of particular skills once critical to mathematical success. This opens up opportunities for teachers to engage students in working at higher cognitive levels and focusing on generalizing and problem solving in ways that were not feasible without modern classroom technologies. As a concrete example of the power of technology in the elementary mathematics classroom, a dynamic geometry package can be used by the teacher to construct two-dimensional shapes. Students can then be given opportunities to manipulate those shapes by resizing (dilating), rotating, flipping (reflecting), and moving (translating) them to see what stays the same about the shapes and what changes. This is an activity that cannot be replicated in the "real" world. In the real world, teachers are constrained, for example, to sets of shapes that may or may not support students in really understanding the attributes of a given shape because there are not enough ways for students to make and test conjectures about which attributes define a shape (e.g., the size of angles, the relationship of sides, the number of sides and angles, etc.).

While the Technology Principle includes a specific vision for the use of technology in the mathematics classroom, the NCTM Standards (2000) provide a clear vision for mathematics teaching and learning. Drawing from the Standards, we relied heavily on technology-rich experiences that allowed students to engage in open-ended tasks, to experience mathematics in ways that were impossible in a paper and pencil situation (e.g., through the use of animations and microworlds), and that supported other critical dispositions toward learning mathematics including exploring tasks, communicating about mathematics and developing the ability to make and test conjectures.

While aspects of the TIM project changed through our successive refinement efforts, our underlying PD model remained grounded in a desire to support standards-based learning. Our operationalized definition of standards-based teaching and learning was grounded in constructivism (e.g., Erbas, Ledford, Orrill, & Polly, 2004) and in the learner centered principles (McCombs & Whisler, 1997). We believe that people construct their understanding of mathematics (and everything else) through repeated encounters over time. To help learners better understand a concept, a teacher needs to be able to create a learning environment in which students will engage in meaningful experiences that challenge their naïve thinking so that they can develop more sophisticated and expert-like understandings (e.g., diSessa, 2006). That is, the teacher needs to find ways to grant authority to a student's initial ideas by recognizing them and using them as a baseline, then the teachers needs to engage the

student in conversations and experiences that will help the student modify his or her ideas in ways that are accountable to the conventions and values of the field of mathematics (Stein, Engle, Smith, & Hughes, 2006). Thus, in our vision of elementary mathematics, derived from the NCTM *Standards*, the teacher's job is to pose worthwhile tasks and ask students questions that require more than simply reporting actions to engage students in reflectively analyzing their own mathematics thinking, anticipate and capitalize on misconceptions by understanding what aspects of a lesson might lead to confusion and by listening to student reasoning to understand issues as they arise. The teacher also needs to facilitate discussions to unpack mathematics content and create learning situations that challenge emerging understandings that the students are developing. This is a drastic change from the traditional model of mathematics teaching that prevails in elementary classrooms. The traditional model, in contrast to our model, relies on the teacher providing the students with information about a new concept, then giving them a hands-on opportunity to practice that idea, typically using worksheets or other forms of problem sets. In the TIM model, students may spend an entire class period on a single task whereas in a typical classroom, students will work 15 or 20 problems. To further highlight differences between our vision of elementary mathematics teaching and learning and that found in typical elementary schools, we provide Table 1.

To support teachers' construction of ideas related to teaching mathematics with technology, we focused on three critical components: teachers' knowledge of mathematics, teachers' knowledge of technology to support mathematics, and teachers' confidence to teach mathematics with technology. Three critical aspects were employed in each of the TIM projects: posing meaningful tasks; engaging teachers with high-quality technologies; and supporting the design and teaching of technology-rich lessons during the school year. These three aspects formed a foundation for fundamen-

Table 1. Comparing elementary mathematics instruction in typical and TIM classrooms

	Typical Elementary Mathematics Classroom	**TIM Elementary Mathematics Classroom**
Role of the Teacher	Illustrate new ideas Provide examples of ideas Assess correctness Monitor activity	Present compelling, worthwhile mathematical task Support students in invoking existing understanding and skills to solve the task Ask questions about understanding
Characteristics of Problems/Tasks	Procedural – single correct answers, often featuring one particular procedure applied to several items Small – typically take only a few minutes to complete Focused on a single mathematical concept	Open – may have more than one right answer, may have more than one way to get the answer Big – may take an entire period to complete Connecting two or more mathematical ideas
Use of Manipulatives	Used to introduce the topic, then students are weaned from them as quickly as possible	Always available–teachers prompt students to think of more efficient approaches they might use
Role of Technology	Drill and practice Used to provide immediate feedback Used as a demonstration tool during instruction	Microworlds, dynamic tools, simulations & digital manipulatives Used to develop and test conjectures Used for pattern finding and generalization
Role of Collaboration	Use teams to compare answers or split up workload across team members	Use collaborative problem solving strategies (e.g., jigsaw) Use teams to compare strategies for solving problems

tally changing the ways in which mathematics was taught and technology was used at these schools, while attending to principles for effective professional development (e.g., Loucks-Horsley, Love, & Stiles, Mundry and Hewson, 2009; NPEAT, 2000).

Posing Meaningful Tasks

Tasks offer the opportunity for teachers to engage students in hands-on, minds-on mathematics using concrete tools or technology that have been shown to be effective in raising student performance (e.g., Milken Family Foundation, 2000). Meaningful tasks also provide opportunities to develop problem solving and higher-order thinking skills. For example, consider the mathematical opportunities embedded in the following task:

There are 10 legs in this group. There are 3 heads in this group.
There are 6 ears in this group. There are 10 fingers in this group.
There are 2 tails in this group. Who could be in this group?

(Economopoulos & Wright, 1998)

This task has a number of potential ways for finding an answer and multiple correct answers. A student might use a drawing program to create pictures of each animal they have in mind, labeling the legs, heads, ears, fingers, and tails. Another student might use a calculator and record answers on paper or create a table in a simple spreadsheet program with columns for each value and fill in a number of animals to find an appropriate combination. In their support for multiple approaches to a solution, tasks support students in developing their mathematical thinking through drawings, symbols, or computer-based representations – a powerful way of supporting mathematical thinking that is promoted by the Standards (NCTM, 2000).

Mathematical tasks embody the principles of learner-centered design, which are critical to the TIM model of technology-rich elementary mathematics learning. A task's effectiveness as a tool for promoting learning is dependent on both its design and its implementation (Stein, Smith, & Henningsen, & Silver, 2009). Thus, Table 2

Table 2. Characteristics of tasks in the TIM framework (adapted from Author, 2006-a)

Task	Characteristic	Learner-centered tasks	Learner-Centered Principles (APA Work Group, 1997)
Design	Realistic	Personally relevant to students' lives or otherwise meaningful and built upon prior experience or prior knowledge (van den Heuvel-Panhuizen, 2003).	The learning of complex subject matter is most effective when learners construct meaning from information and experience (Principle 1). The successful learner can link new information with existing knowledge in meaningful ways (Principle 3). An individual's motivation is influenced by their beliefs and interests (Principle 7), the learner's creativity and curiosity (Principle 8), and their background and experiences (Principles 10, 12 and 13).
	Open	Designed so that learners have ownership over the approaches taken in solving as well as some influence on how the products of the task are represented (Stein et al., 2009).	An individual's motivation is influenced by their beliefs and interests (Principle 7), the learner's creativity and curiosity (Principle 8), and their background and experiences (Principles 10, 12 and 13).
	Connection-promoting	Allow learners to refine their understanding and make connections between concepts or approaches used to complete the task (NCTM, 2000).	Higher order strategies for selecting and monitoring mental operations facilitate creative and critical thinking (Principle 5).
	Communication-focused	Provide opportunities to student to communicate understanding in a variety of ways so that the teacher can evaluate understanding (NCTM, 2000).	Setting appropriately high and challenging standards and assessing the learner as well as learning progress - including diagnostic, process, and outcome assessment - are integral parts of the learning process (Principle 14).
	Technology-rich	Enhanced through technology that allows students to gather information, explore concepts, collaborate with peers or represent knowledge (NCTM, 2000; Niess, 2005).	Learning is influenced by environmental factors, including culture, technology, and instructional practices (Principle 6).
Implementation	Facilitated	Facilitated by teachers or peers that model or scaffold student learning while still maintaining the rigor and high cognitive demand of tasks (Stein et al., 2009).	The successful learner, over time and with support, can create meaningful, coherent representations of knowledge (Principle 2).
	Collaborative	Students learn with each other and from each other (NCTM, 2000).	Social interactions, interpersonal relations, and communication with others all provide opportunities for learning (Principle 11).

highlights both the factors that define a good task as written and as delivered.

We found that teachers often lack experience designing and posing worthwhile tasks. We recognized that the teachers needed experience participating *as learners* in this form of mathematics (e.g., Cohen, 1990; Orrill, 2001). Thus, the TIM approach not only focused on the use of mathematical tasks in K-5 classrooms, but also grounded a substantial amount of the work done

with teachers in our professional development sessions in these tasks. For example, project staff modeled technology-rich teaching in ways that we expected teachers to employ in their own classroom (Hill, 2004; Loucks-Horsley et al., 2009). That effort then extended into designing lessons for participants' classrooms.

Access to and Practice with High Quality Technology

In our partner schools, we found two consistent, problematic trends. First, there was very limited access to computers and/or to software on those computers for our teachers. Second, the teachers had a very limited model of using technology to support mathematics learning – namely, they saw it as either a motivating tool (e.g., 'My students love to play on the computer, so I let them do that when they finish their work early.') or as a practice tool that provided immediate feedback on skill-building. For example, we worked with a number of teachers who primarily used the computers to engage their students in practicing their multiplication tables. In our observations, we noted that even in classrooms where teachers were pleased with their students' use of computers for practicing multiplication facts, the students were undermining the effort by choosing levels of the practice programs that were extremely easy and not challenging themselves at all. In addition to these two pervasive issues, some schools also had requirements for technology to be used in support of test preparation. In these schools, the district had selected a computer-based learning system to support students' learning, which acted as a replacement for the teacher as students answered an assortment of multiple choice items related to basic skills.

In our TIM vision of technology integration, we seek to capitalize on the potential of technology for mathematics teaching and learning by using technology to bring content to life and allow students to interact with mathematics in ways that are not possible in the real world. This is consistent with NCTM's (2000) position that developing students' conceptual understanding of mathematical and scientific ideas, lessons should encourage students "to explore, conjecture, and reason logically…" It is also consistent with NAEP results showing that by 8th grade the use of computer-based drill and practice and mathematics games led to lower achievement scores than using no technology at all; and that using computers for concept demonstration and simulations led to significantly higher scores (Braswell et al., 2001).

The effective use of technology depends on teachers knowing about mathematics software, applets, and resources as well as how to adapt and develop activities to support learning (CEO Forum, 1999; Gabriel & MacDonald, 1996). In TIM, we built from the assertion that hands-on use of technology in professional development increases the likelihood of its use in the classroom. Further, we hypothesized that for teachers to successfully adopt technology, they must be able to see it modeled, reflect on their own practices with it, and engage in retooling their existing classroom materials. "In this way the teacher is first the learner using the technology and therefore will model how she learned her way around, learning what resources are available, learning how to use those resources in conducting your activities productively and enjoyably" (National Research Council, 2002, p.138).

To this end, the TIM project provided two kinds of tools to the participating teachers as well as hands-on time with the tools. First, we used project funds to purchase specific software titles that we determined were appropriate to supporting mathematics learning. These included titles such as the simulation *Ice Cream Truck* from Sunburst Software, the problem-solving series *Math Mysteries* from Tom Snyder Productions, microworld software such as *Fraction Bars* from Transparent Media, skill-building software that also incorporated problem solving like *Ten Tricky Tiles* from Sunburst Software, logic-building games such as *Logical Journey of the Zoombinis* from TERC, and simple handheld calculators. Second, we created a website of hand-picked applets from across the Web that supported the goals of our project. These applets included many from the NCTM Illumination website (http://illuminations.nctm.org/), applets from the National Library of Virtual Manipulatives (http://nlvm.usu.

Figure 1. Data collection sheet developed by the TIM team for Ice Cream Truck

| Day of the week | | | Starting Amount: | | Time: | | Temperature: | | | | |

Before Selling								After Selling			
Item	Buying COST	# bought	YOUR COST	SELLING price	Maximum Possible GROSS	Maximum Possible NET		Number Sold 1st stop / 2nd stop		Actual GROSS	Actual NET
Ice cream cones											
Fruit Bars											
Shuttle Pops											
		Operating Costs (gas, towing)									
Totals											

Ending Amount:

edu/) as well as single applets from a variety of other websites. We made sure every applet listed was consistent with our vision for technology-enhanced mathematics and that each was freely available to teachers for use in their classroom. This alleviated teachers' stress over having to find appropriate tools or conduct website evaluations, thus allowing them to focus on the big idea: teaching mathematics in ways that capitalized on the affordances of technology.

In each of our workshops, we developed activities that engaged teachers as learners in using the library of tools available to them. To support the development of pedagogy, each session also included time for discussion about pedagogical moves that were critical. For example, when we worked with teachers using the Ice Cream Truck simulation, which is a game that allows students to run their own ice cream truck, we asked teachers to record their decisions on worksheets developed by a member of the TIM team. Then, when they had completed the activity, we not only debriefed the mathematics that was supported through the game and the benefits of using the game, but also discussed the benefits of having the students record their moves. By recording simple data such as the number of each kind of ice cream product purchased, the number sold, and the profit, users are able to develop a more refined strategy for

making decisions. Further, having a written record of the session allowed teachers to ask students reflective questions about their mathematical decision-making that would not be possible if the students did not record their answers. See Figure 1 and figure 2 for examples of the data students were asked to collect and the analysis of these data we proposed.

Providing Support in Using Technology and Designing Lessons for Technology throughout the School Year

Professional development standards (e.g., Hill, 2005; NPEAT, 2000) and research recommends that professional development be conducted in settings that are relevant to teachers and that it be conducted over a long period of time (Penuel et al., 2007; Polly & Hannafin, 2010). Consistent with these guidelines and consistent with our own observations that teachers are often nervous about using technology with their students, the TIM team was committed to providing as much support to the teachers as possible. To this end, we typically set up a particular schedule to be in the building and made sure the teachers knew we were there. During our "office hours" we would work with teachers to develop lesson plans, model teach or

Figure 2. Data collection and analysis sheet for Ice Cream Truck activity

Before Selling	After Selling
What day is it?	How many ice cream cones did you sell?
	How many fruit bars did you sell?
What temperature is it outside?	How many shuttle pops did you sell?
	How much money did you make?
What time of day is it?	
	Do you have more or less money at the
How much money did you spend buying Ice Cream?	end of the day than you did at the beginning?
How much money do you have?	What's the difference between yesterday's profit and today's profit?

Use this area for your work

co-teach with technology in their own classrooms. We quickly found that having a second adult in the classroom calmed a nervous teacher. In schools where there were eager teachers, we often seized the opportunity to work with these early adopters to simultaneously support their interests and to help them spread the word to their colleagues. We learned that teachers who are early adopters could help our efforts spread much more quickly than anything we did as external consultants. To this end, in some of our projects, TIM team members essentially partnered with a single teacher for a longer time – sometimes weeks or more – to co-plan and co-teach lessons. This was a model that was effective for raising the likelihood of the adoption lasting beyond the school year and it was a model that provided the TIM team with valuable real-world classroom experience.

VIGNETTES FROM THE CLASSROOMS

One of the best ways to demonstrate the power of technology supported mathematics learning at the heart of the TIM model is through examples we saw in our teachers' classrooms. Below, we offer two vignettes of lessons that demonstrate teachers taking steps toward the vision of technology integration we were promoting. Note that these teachers were taking big steps for themselves, yet these were first steps toward making dramatic shifts in the ways they approached mathematics instruction.

Representing Data Using an Internet-Based Graphing Tool

This vignette comes from the 4th grade classroom of a TIM-Participant in one of the highest-needs school districts involved in TIM during its five-year lifespan. Over 80% of the students in this large, urban district qualified for free or reduced lunch. In this lesson, students used a free internet-based graphing tool, Create a Graph (Figure 3; http://nces.ed.gov/nceskids/graphing/classic/) to generate graphs from data that they had collected from surveys. In lessons earlier that week, students had created a question of interest, asked their classmates the question to collect data, and then organized the data in a table. In this lesson, the teacher hoped to use the website as a tool to

Figure 3. Graph created from NCES Create a Graph

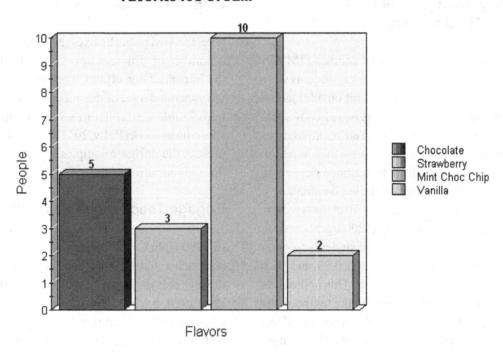

Favorite Ice Cream

Legend:
- Chocolate
- Strawberry
- Mint Choc Chip
- Vanilla

Y-axis: People
X-axis: Flavors

help students generate a graph. During TIM, we emphasized to teachers that technology can help create representations and allow students to focus on the mathematical concepts or generalizations rather than being burdened with the creation of a mathematical representation.

In this lesson, the technology was used to quickly make the various graphs, and the students were then able to focus their conversation on interpreting the graphs, answering questions about the data, and posing further questions based on the graphical representations. While the teacher had hoped to focus on the mathematics, she found that most of her time was spent trouble shooting with the website and helping some students figure out how to create their graphs. This was typical of TIM teachers during the early part of the year; they found themselves spending most of their technology time problem solving how to use technology with students than being able to focus

on mathematical ideas. Over time this became less problematic as the teachers become more proficient in introducing their students to the tools.

One of the critical mathematical issues that came up during the lesson was determining which type of graph was appropriate—line graphs, bar graphs, or pie charts. By using the graphing tool to quickly and easily generate bar graphs, pie graphs, and line graphs from their data, the students came to understand that bar graphs and pie graphs were the most appropriate, since they had separate representations for the data. The line graph, some reasoned, was not appropriate since the graph showed continuity rather than distinct representations. This was an important mathematical conclusion for the students that the technology facilitated. Were it not for the ease of moving between graph types, the students would have spent their time creating graphs rather than analyzing them. This is one of the fundamentally important aspects of technology for mathematics classrooms (NCTM, 2000).

Adding Decimals with Virtual Manipulatives

In the fifth grade classroom of another TIM participant in the same school district, students were in the middle of a two-week unit on adding and subtracting decimals. Students had already spent a few days working with concrete manipulatives to represent decimals, and the teacher hoped to use virtual manipulatives to continue deepening students' understanding of adding decimals.

The applet (Figure 4; http://www.harcourtschool.com/activity/elab2004/gr5/2.html) that the teacher chose allowed students to enter two decimals between 0.00 and 0.99 and then asked students to enter the sum. This applet was one that had been included with the textbook the school had adopted. The applet supported students through the offering of the "Rearrange" button that joined the shaded pieces to facilitate students' work. In this lesson, the teacher posed a variety of tasks; some were simple computation (e.g., $0.6 + 0.42$), while others were situated in real-life contexts (e.g., Steve has 0.58 liters of soda, and Tyrisha has 0.93 liters of soda. How much do they have total?) While these were not the most challenging tasks, they were at least a step closer to the types of technology-rich mathematical tasks that we wanted teachers to pose. In this case, the technology provided students with a representation of the numbers with which they were working. Because of the number of hundredth-sized pieces involved in these problems, drawing such representations would have been very time-consuming for the students to draw and moving the pieces around to see the sum would have been extremely difficult. The technology facilitated both of these tasks immediately, allowing students to focus on understanding base-10 numbers and to reason about addition rather than focusing on rote memorization and/or drawing pictures.

PRINCIPLES FOR THE DESIGN OF TECHNOLOGY-RICH PROFESSIONAL DEVELOPMENT FOR MATHEMATICS

Over the TIM project's five-year timeline, we tried a number of different approaches to maximize the impact of our efforts. Through those efforts, we generated a set of design principles that were transferable across iterations of the project and subsequent work (Polly, 2011). In this section, we present the design principles that have emerged through our efforts.

Engage Teachers as Learners

In 1990 Cohen and Ball mused "How can teachers teach a mathematics that they never learned, in ways that they never experienced?" (Cohen & Ball, 1990, p. 233). This is one of the underlying questions of the TIM project. Because we know that elementary teachers are notoriously weak in mathematics content (e.g., Ball, Lubienski, & Mewborn, 2001; Ma, 1999) and we know that most of today's practicing teachers had limited or no exposure to technology as students, the TIM team recognized that we were asking teachers to teach a mathematics they had not learned on two levels. First, we were promoting a conceptually-driven understanding of mathematics and second, we were recommending a technology-rich mathematics. Because of this issue, we created an environment that modeled the mathematics experiences we wanted students to have. To this end, every workshop engaged teachers in engaging with meaningful mathematics using technology. The activities we selected were focused on the mathematics that the teachers taught, but often modified to be at a higher level than most elementary textbooks promote. In this way, the teachers were engaged in authentic mathematics experiences as learners, they used the technology to support their own learning and understanding, and the workshop facilitators took on the role that

Figure 4. Screen capture from Harcourt eLab

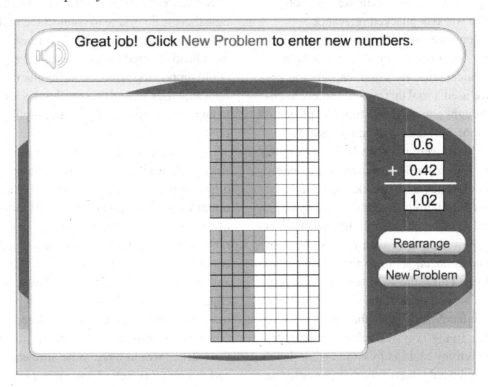

we would like teachers to take on: asking questions about mathematical thinking, highlighting multiple strategies being used, and helping the teachers connect their experiences in the workshop to both their understanding of mathematics, and to their lives outside of the workshops. To this end, there were certainly discussions of the uses of mathematics tasks and technology use from a pedagogical perspective, but they arose out of the experiences the teachers were having as mathematics learners.

This approach provided the teachers with opportunities to gain some level of comfort with the technology and with mathematical tasks, which, we hypothesized, should lead to higher levels of adoption. Further, by engaging with technology-enhanced mathematics as learners, the teachers had opportunities to experience the struggle of working on tasks and to experience the benefits of relying on their own mathematical reasoning as well as talking to others to solve problems (NCTM, 2000).

This meant that the teachers were experiencing a new mathematics—one that was not focused on solving sheets of problems in predetermined ways. Rather, it was a mathematics that relied on problem solving, application of prior knowledge to new situations, and more than one right answer.

Contextualized and Relevant

Every aspect of the professional development needs to be contextualized and relevant. This means that the teachers need to be able to readily understand how and when they can use both the mathematics and the technology tools in their own classrooms. Teachers commonly complained if they could not connect the activities of our workshops to their teaching. For example, if the mathematics we focused on was whole number arithmetic, the higher-grade teachers often felt the tools and lesson ideas were not appropriate for their students. Similarly, if the teachers felt they did not have adequate access to a particular technology, they felt the workshop lacked relevance.

We implemented three key ways to address this issue. First, we refrained from using tools (e.g., software, calculators, etc.) that teachers did not have. If we used a tool that was not freely available, we bought copies of that tool and placed it in their school. Second, our most successful effort focused on narrower grade bands. For example, separating K-2 from 3-5 teachers immediately raises the relevance of the workshop. Similarly, working with the non-mathematics teachers (e.g., physical education, music, or art teachers) is immediately more engaging than relying on them to make the connections from their field to the mathematics. Third, the TIM team made every effort to tie the activities of the workshops to the content standards for which the teachers were responsible. In this way, we helped the teachers see how an activity could address their grade-level standards and what kinds of modifications to the activity would improve the standards alignment.

Accessible Technologies that Support Standards-Based Mathematics

As mentioned elsewhere in this chapter, we found that many teachers' images of technology-enhanced mathematics were extremely narrow. Most teachers started our workshops having only used technology to reward good behavior or to provide students with drill and practice opportunities. While standards-based mathematics does acknowledge the role of motivation in student learning and the development of procedural fluency, those are two small roles for technology to play. The NCTM Standards highlight that technology fundamentally affects the mathematics that can be taught. Further, the Standards assert that technology should be used in ways that support students' decision making, reasoning, problem solving, and their reflection on their learning (NCTM, 2000). However, for teachers who have

only experienced drill and practice uses of technology, there is no bridge to connect technology use to the vision of the standards. To this end, the TIM team hand selected a suite of technology tools that could support the vision of the Standards. And, we built activities around those technologies in which to engage the teachers that really highlighted the power of the technology.

As one example, in a workshop for third to fifth grade teachers, we focused on the use of a digital version of tangrams (available at the National Virtual Manipulatives Library, http://nlvm. usu.edu). The advantages of using these digitally rather than using tangram pieces is that there are enough, the computer provides tangram puzzles automatically, and the teacher does not have to engage in set-up activities that often prohibit the use of manipulatives in classrooms because of the time it takes. In the case of tangrams, for example, the teacher would have to be sure each student had a complete set of tangram pieces, which might require her to have to dig through hundreds of pieces looking for the right ones because the pieces are easily mixed together when students use tangrams in class.

For the purposes of the workshop, we highlighted the role of tangrams for developing spatial reasoning as well as communication skills. To this end, we asked the teachers to do two different things. First, they had to work in pairs to complete tangram puzzles where one partner was the mouse user and the other had to communicate, using proper mathematical terms such a rotate (turn), reflect (flip), and translate (slide) to create a solved puzzle on the page. Then, we asked the teachers to create puzzles for their partner to solve. Once they had completed the puzzle, the partner tried to solve it and again, the teachers could only use proper mathematical terms to guide each other through the solution. In this way, the tangrams activity not only focused on developing mathematical vocabulary and spatial reasoning, but also on communicating and working together to solve compelling problems.

Intuitive Software

To maximize the likelihood that teachers would adopt technology, we selected those applets and programs that were the most intuitive to use. We learned that teachers did not want to spend a lot of time learning a lot of features; rather, they wanted easy solutions for their classrooms. While we recognize that this limits the technology choices and that it limits particular mathematics opportunities because it excludes robust tools like dynamic geometry software and all but the simplest uses of spreadsheets, the TIM team determined that this was a reasonable trade-off in working toward our goal of supporting our vision of mathematics. We believed that focusing on one or two more robust pieces of software would violate our other design principles because it would not be as readily accessible or as engaging because rather than developing mathematics understanding, the teachers would be focusing instead on understanding the computer program. To this end, we remained focused on user-friendly software that either embedded the instructions (e.g., *Logical Journey of the Zoombinis* where each challenge is explained as it is started) or applets that teachers could readily use because they simulated real-world manipulatives (e.g., GeoBoards applets that provide a geoboard and "rubber bands" that the user loops around the posts on the geoboard) or because they were intuitive. Further, we excluded applets and software that were difficult to figure out or that constrained mathematical exploration.

We supplemented our careful selection process with the creation of two kinds of job aids. First, TIM team members created short instruction booklets for some of the more complex software. These were created to be as friendly for the teachers' needs as possible. Second, the TIM team created half-page descriptions of each of the software and key applets they were recommending. Our goal was to provide teachers with an easy resource to use when selecting software

for their own classrooms. These resources were made available to the teachers.

Teachers Plan and Design

Because the ultimate goal of TIM was to impact the students' experiences in mathematics and because the most authentic activity for teachers to engage in is planning for student learning, focusing workshops and follow-up activities on classroom planning was an important element. This was accomplished a few different ways in TIM. First, debriefing discussions focused on the activities in the TIM workshops often included the teachers thinking about how an activity might be modified to be appropriate for their students. Second, we set up requirements for technology integration as part of satisfactory completion of the workshops. In order to receive credit for participation and their small stipends, the teachers had to implement at least two technology-rich lessons related to the professional development in their classroom. Third, our ongoing support was designed explicitly to help the teachers think about technology integration in their classrooms. A TIM team member worked with each teacher to develop a lesson and to implement that lesson if the teacher wanted help. This ongoing support element of the professional development required a TIM team member be at the school for regularly-scheduled times each week so that she or he became a part of the school. However, our experience showed that this element of the program was important both for getting teachers to use technology in their classrooms and in supporting their implementation of mathematically worthwhile lessons.

Mathematics-Centric Framework for Technology Integration

While the TIM team fundamentally believed that teachers should be able to use technology across the curriculum, we also recognized that our time with the teachers was rather limited. For example, we generally had between 35-50 hours of workshops during an entire school year. Because of this, we had to focus on those activities that would provide the most benefit to teachers meeting our goals of integrating technology into a mathematics course. However, in one TIM experience, we did attempt to incorporate a more broadly-defined technology integration model. We quickly realized that this created a tension in terms of how the time in the workshops was spent. Further, because they were novices at integrating technology at all, providing them with a generic model and promoting the use of mathematics activities created a dissonance for the teachers. They did not understanding how the technology integration model could help them with their teaching. Based on that experience, we created two different frameworks to support teachers in making good decisions about technology to use. The first framework capitalized on a focus on data-driven decision making that our partner school had adopted for the year. This model is shown in Figure 5. The second of these was simpler and attempted to focus the teacher on selecting software that would support teachers in solving specific problems of practice. This model is shown in Figure 6. Clearly, either of these two frameworks could be readily adapted to other content area, but we had more success when we helped teachers focus on mathematics instruction.

Glimpses of Other Classrooms

Finally, we found that one of the most effective, though less popular, design decisions we made was to include case studies of other teachers teaching standards-based mathematics. We drew these from a number of resources such as the *Developing Mathematical Ideas* professional development series (Schifter, Bastable, & Russell, 2002) and the Annenberg video series titled *Teaching Math* (http://learner.org). We also created some cases that specifically supported aspects of our work for which we did not have premade materials. There are not many published cases that highlight

technology-enhanced mathematics instruction, therefore, we used the cases to focus discussions on issues related to student thinking and learning and the ways in which a teacher can support a standards-based mathematics environment. By using these case studies, we were able to provide teachers with glimpses into other teachers' classrooms. They could read about or watch how other teachers worked with students engaged in solving worthwhile mathematical tasks. Our intention was to help teachers feel more confident about this approach to teaching mathematics. The one drawback to the cases was that teachers did not enjoy reading the written ones. We had to constantly consider the length of the cases before selecting them because in an afterschool workshop, when teachers are already tired from teaching all day, engaging in reading more than a couple of pages results in dissatisfaction and withdrawal.

CHALLENGES

Overall, the TIM project offered numerous insights into the design and implementation of professional development. Our evaluations, year after year, were strong with over 80% of each year's participating teachers reporting that participation in TIM had been a positive experience for them. Further, by our later implementations, we had over 95% of participating teachers agreeing on an end-of-year survey that TIM provided them with ideas for teaching mathematics and 85% agreeing that TIM succeeded in teaching them ways to use computers with their students. Given that these later groups included over 30 teachers each, we are pleased with this level of success.

In the spirit of our approach to successively refining TIM, however, we also note that there were challenges for which we never found acceptable solutions. We end the chapter with a discussion of these challenges because they are critical to the success of any professional development program.

Figure 5. Technology integration for mathematics framework that capitalizes on data-driven decision making (Wizard image Copyright © Tony Martin)

Data Driven Co-Planning for
Technology Integration

1. Identify the Problem you are trying to solve
   a. What are the learners' needs
   b. Use multiple sources: standardized test scores, classroom assignments, classroom tests, reflections, observations, student work, etc.
2. Decide what you want to do about it
   a. Reteach
   b. Change Teaching Plan
   c. Create/Find investigation
   d. Provide Additional Practice
   e. Other
3. Resources available
   a. Internet
   b. Software
   c. Books
   d. White board
   e. Floor space/physical space
   f. Other lesson plans
4. Create a Plan
   a. Focus on problem
   b. Develop activity(-ies) to address problem
      i. Initiating activity (launch)
      ii. Guided learning (explore)
      iii. Culminating Performance (look what I can do!)
      iv. Assessment (may be part of culminating or separate)
5. Implement lesson
6. Guided reflection on lesson and make refinements
   a. What went well? Why?
   b. What didn't go well? Why?
   c. What would you change for next time?
   d. What is the next step for these learners?

Individual Learners Construct Individual Meanings

Consistent with the learner-centered professional development design principles (NPEAT, 2000; Polly & Hannafin, 2010), we embraced the notion that each teacher would build from his or her current understanding of mathematics and technology. We saw our role, as professional developers, to be offering experiences that challenged pre-existing understandings and pushed teachers' knowledge deeper. However, we found that teachers attended to those aspects of the experience that were of interest to them at that moment. For example, we consider our tangrams lesson described above. One of our participants modified it for her classroom. She provided the students with multiple sets of tangrams cut from paper (technology access was an issue for her) and copies of puzzles to solve. This was problematic because the challenge of tangrams is in solving a puzzle using only one set of the shapes (See Figure 7 for an example). By providing students with multiple sets, the teacher had modified the task in ways that made it easier.

Figure 6. Technology integration in mathematics framework for technology integration focused on problems of teaching

Software Evaluation for Mathematics

What problem are you trying to address?

What is your goal for this lesson?

Which standard(s) are you planning to address?

Technology selected?

Brief Description of Plan (e.g., What will you do? What will student do?):

How will this plan address your problem? How will it help you meet your goal?

How does this software package/internet application support meeting the goal(s) you have set?

When asked why she had made this modification, the teacher indicated that having multiple sets would allow her students to make prettier puzzles. In other words, her learning from the workshop had been that (a) tangrams are worth doing and (b) they are engaging. However, she seemed to have missed the special elements of tangrams that made them challenging and she had totally removed the mathematics communication-oriented aspects of the tool.

Individual interest and interpretation among participants is a pervasive issue for anyone who designs learning experiences for others. We continued, over time, refining our approach to help teachers share our focus as much as possible, but they bring their understandings and interests to class and those inherently drive the lens through which the teachers filter their experiences (Orrill & The InterMath Team, 2006).

Shifting Foci

Beginning with our very first implementation of TIM, we were struck by the way teachers and administrators organized teacher development. In our experience, there was a strong tendency in the schools with which we worked to have a yearly focus (e.g., the year for literacy professional

Figure 7. (a) Picture of the 7 basic tangram pieces in a square and (b) creating a house puzzle

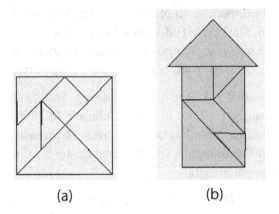

(a)   (b)

development). And, that focus changed each year in our partner schools. Therefore, while the teachers spent a lot of time on technology-integrated mathematics during an academic year only to completely change their focus the following year. This is problematic because it lacks the kind of continuity necessary for long-term change (e.g., NPEAT, 2000) and because we know it often takes two years for the impact of professional development to be felt in the classroom (Penuel et al., 2007). At the same time, however, the reality of K-5 education is that, in most schools, teachers have to be proficient in teaching all of the major content areas, therefore they need to grow in all areas. This creates an inherent systemic tension for both supporting teachers and making meaningful change in classroom practices (Hawley & Valli, 1999).

Technological Barriers

While there are certainly computers and Internet access in all of the schools with which we worked, the ways in which that technology was made accessible varied considerably. For example, in many of the schools in which we worked, there was one or more computer lab. This, theoretically, allowed the teacher to work on technology-integrated mathematics in a setting where all students could have access. However, we found at least three barriers to this. First, many of the labs were heavily scheduled with priority access being given to teachers who were going to use them to use district-purchased test preparation software or word processing activities. Technology-rich mathematics lessons had to be wedged into occasional slots in which these priority activities were not happening.

Second, many of the technology coordinators with whom we worked did not have systems set-up to make it easy for teachers to access the software and tools we provided for the schools. That is, they were reluctant to load software on the machines, they did not provide teachers with access to CDs with software on it that were necessary to use certain programs, or they simply did not provide anyone with information about how to access particular materials. We do not imply that the technology coordinators were trying to undermine our efforts, rather, our efforts were outside of the normal flow of the school and the technology coordinators lacks systems for working with us in ways that were productive for the teachers. As outside professional developers, we only rarely ran into problems with our workshops because these same technology folks were extremely helpful to us. After all, providing professional development did fit within the regular business of the school and there was a system in place for working with us.

Finally, technology glitches can undermine entire lessons. Internet settings and firewall software or incompatibilities with operating systems sometimes led to the tools simply failing to work properly for the teachers when they tried them with their students. Because the teachers were, generally, not sophisticated users of technology, one experience with technology glitches could undermine our efforts with the teacher for the rest of the school year. One limited, but effective, workaround for these problems was to have TIM team members teach model lessons in a teacher's classroom. We quickly learned that an otherwise-leary teacher could be changed to an adopter by watching as her students had a successful encounter with technology-supported tasks.

To address these technology issues, the TIM team worked very closely with the technology coordinators to try to overcome the issues. However, in some cases, there were not simple solutions and access to technology for mathematics remained a challenge for us throughout.

CONCLUSION

In conclusion, we offer the TIM professional development project as an example of effective professional development grounded in a theory of learning and refined through an iterative design cycle. We never shifted our core beliefs about what TIM should be accomplishing, but aspects of the project changed from one setting to the next both to meet the needs of each particular school setting and to address shortcomings we noted in previous implementations. We believe that our efforts were successful based on both the informal feedback we received from teachers and the increases in teacher satisfaction over time. From the various implementations, the TIM team continued to learn a lot about teaching mathematics with technology, about working with teachers to meet their needs, and about interacting with the systemic issues inherent in all elementary schools. From this work, we were able to identify seven design principles that seem to support success as well as three challenges for future efforts.

REFERENCES

Ball, D. L., Lubienski, S. T., & Mewborn, D. S. (2001). Research on teaching mathematics: The unsolved problem of teachers' mathematical knowledge. In Richardson, V. (Ed.), *Handbook of research on teaching* (4th ed., pp. 433–456). New York, NY: Macmillan.

Borko, H., & Putnam, R. T. (1995). Expanding a teacher's knowledge base: A cognitive psychological perspective on professional development. In T. R. Guskey, M (Ed.), *Professional development in education: New paradigms and practices* (pp. 35-65). New York, NY: Teachers College Press.

Braswell, J. S., Lutkus, A. D., Grigg, W. S., Santapau, S. L., Tay-Lim, B., & Johnson, M. (2001, August). *The nation's report card: Mathematics 2000.* Washington, DC: National Center for Educational Statistics.

Cohen, D. K., & Ball, D. L. (1990). Policy and practice. *Educational Evaluation and Policy Analysis, 12*(3), 233–239.

diSessa, A. A. (2006). A history of conceptual change research: Threads and fault lines. In Sawyer, R. K. (Ed.), *The Cambridge handbook of the learning sciences* (pp. 265–282). New York, NY: Cambridge University Press.

Economopoulos, K., & Wright, T. (1998). *How many pockets? How many teeth?* White Plains, NY: Dale Seymour Publications.

Erbas, A., Ledford, S., Orrill, C. H., & Polly, D. (2004). Engaging students through technology. Mathematics Teaching in the Middle School, 9, 300-305.

Forum, C. E. O. (1999). *Professional development: A link to better learning.* Washington, DC: Author.

Gabriel, M. A., & MacDonald, C. J. (1996). Preservice teacher education students and computers: How does intervention affect attitude? *Journal of Technology and Teacher Education, 4*(2).

Hawley, W. D., & Valli, L. (1999). The essentials of effective professional development. In Darling-Hammond, L., & Sykes, G. (Eds.), *Teaching as the learning profession: Handbook of policy and practice* (pp. 127–150). San Francisco, CA: Jossey-Bass.

Hill, H. C. (2004). Professional development standards and practices in elementary school mathematics. *The Elementary School Journal, 104*(3), 215–231. doi:10.1086/499750

Lawless, K. A., & Pellegrino, J. W. (2007). Professional development in integrating technology into teaching and learning: Knowns, unknowns, and ways to pursue better questions and answers. *Review of Educational Research, 77*(4), 575–614. doi:10.3102/0034654307309921

Lemke, C., & Sweeney, J. F. (Eds.). (1999). *Transforming learning through technology: Policy roadmaps for the nation's governors*. Washington, DC: National Governors' Association.

Loucks-Horsley, S., Love, N., Stiles, K. E., Mundry, S., & Hewson, P. W. (2009). *Designing professional development for teachers of science and mathematics* (3rd ed.). Thousand Oaks, CA: Corwin Press.

Ma, L. (1999). *Knowing and teaching elementary mathematics: Teachers understanding of fundamental mathematics in China and the United States*. Mahwah, NJ: Lawrence Erlbaum Associates.

McCombs, B. L., & Whisler, J. S. (1997). *The learner-centered classroom and school: Strategies for increasing student motivation and achievement* (1st ed.). San Francisco, CA: Jossey-Bass.

Millken Family Foundation. (2000). *How teaching matters: Bringing the classroom back into discussions of teacher quality*. Princeton, NJ: ETS. Retrieved from http://www.etc.org/research/pic

Mishra, P., & Koehler, M. J. (2006). Technological pedagogical content knowledge: A framework for teacher knowledge. *Teachers College Record, 108*(6), 1017–1054. doi:10.1111/j.1467-9620.2006.00684.x

National Commission on Mathematics and Science Teaching (NCMST). (2000). *Before it's too late: A report to the nation from The National Commission on Mathematics and Science Teaching for the 21st century*. Jessup, MD: Author.

National Council for Teachers of Mathematics. (2000). *Principles and standards for school mathematics*. Reston, VA: Author.

National Partnership for Excellence and Accountability in Teaching (NPEAT). (2000). *Revisioning professional development: What learner-centered professional development looks like*. Oxford, OH: Author. Retrieved September 10, 2003, from http://www.nsdc.org/library/policy/npeat213.pdf

National Research Council (NRC). (2002). *How people learn*. Washington, DC: National Academy Press.

Niess, M. L. (2005). Preparing teachers to teach science and mathematics with technology: Developing a technology pedagogical content knowledge. *Teaching and Teacher Education, 21*, 509–523. doi:10.1016/j.tate.2005.03.006

Orrill, C. H. (2001). Building learner-centered classrooms: A professional development framework for supporting critical thinking. Educational Technology Research and Development, 49(1), 15-34.

Orrill, C. H., & The InterMath Team (2006). What learner-centered professional development looks like: The pilot studies of the InterMath professional development project. The Mathematics Educator-Special Issue on InterMath Project, 16(1), 4-13.

Penuel, W., Fishman, B., Yamaguchi, R., & Gallagher, L. (2007). What makes professional development effective? Strategies that foster curriculum implementation. *American Educational Research Journal, 44*(4), 921–958. doi:10.3102/0002831207308221

Polly, D. (2006). Examining the influence of learner-centered professional development on elementary mathematics teachers' instructional practices, espoused practices and evidence of student learning. Unpublished Doctoral Dissertation: University of Georgia.

Polly, D. (2011). Developing teachers' technological, pedagogical, and content knowledge (TPACK) through mathematics professional development. International Journal for Technology in Mathematics Education, 18(2), 83-96.

Polly, D., & Hannafin, M. J. (2010). Reexamining technology's role in learner-centered professional development. Educational Technology Research and Development, 58(5), 557-571. doi:10.1007/s11423-009-9146-5

Renyi, J. (1996). *Teachers take charge of their learning: Transforming professional development for student success*. Washington, DC: National Foundation for the Improvement of Education.

Roschelle, J., Pea, R., Hoadley, C., Gordin, D., & Means, B. (2001). Changing how and what children learn in schools with computer-based technologies. *The Future of Children, 10*(2), 76–101. doi:10.2307/1602690

Sandholtz, J. H., Ringstaff, C., & Dwyer, D. C. (1997). *Teaching with technology: Creating student-centered classrooms*. New York, NY: Teachers College Press.

Schifter, D., Bastable, V., & Russell, S. J. (2002). *Developing mathematical ideas: Measuring space in one, two, and three dimensions*. Parsippany, NJ: Dale Seymour.

Schrum, L. (1999). Technology professional development for teachers. *Educational Technology Research and Development, 47*(4), 83–90. doi:10.1007/BF02299599

Stein, M. K., Engle, R. A., Smith, M. S., & Hughes, E. K. (2006). Orchestrating productive mathematical discussions: Five practices for helping teachers move beyond show and tell. *Mathematical Thinking and Learning, 10*, 313–340. doi:10.1080/10986060802229675

Stein, M. K., Smith, M. S., Henningsen, M., & Silver, E. A. (2009). *Implementing standards-based mathematics instruction. A casebook for professional development*. New York, NY: Teachers College Press.

van den Heuvel-Panhuizen, M. (2003). The didactical use of models in realistic mathematics education: An example from a longitudinal trajectory on percentage. *Educational Studies in Mathematics, 54*(1), 9–35. doi:10.1023/B:EDUC.0000005212.03219.dc

ENDNOTES

[1] The work reported here was supported by funding through Georgia's Eisenhower Higher Education Program and Georgia's Improving Teacher Quality Grants Program as well as funding from the school districts with which we worked. We express our gratitude to the teachers who helped us refine our thinking as well as to the faculty and graduate students who supported these efforts over the lifespan of the Technology Integration in Mathematics efforts.

[2] Satisfaction data were not collected on the 6th project.

Chapter 23
A Call for the use of Technology within Mathematics and Science Preservice Teacher Methods Courses

Darci J. Harland
Illinois State University, USA

Ydalisse Pérez
Illinois State University, USA

Cheri Toledo
Illinois State University, USA

ABSTRACT

Over the past several years, teacher preparation programs have used a variety of approaches to introduce their students to the integration of technology and pedagogy. However, once preservice teachers move into the classroom, many lack the confidence and ability to assimilate technology into their teaching. The purpose of this chapter is to provide teacher education faculty, specifically mathematics and science methods instructors, with a variety of approaches for integrating technology into their courses. Practical strategies are provided to assist faculty with effective uses of technology for delivering content and scaffolding student collaboration. Sample assignments are provided to assist faculty in encouraging their students (future teachers) to look beyond the textbook for teaching resources and learning assessments.

INTRODUCTION

This chapter introduces teacher education faculty, specifically mathematics and science methods instructors, to a variety of approaches for integrating technology into their courses. The first part of the chapter, based on a review of the literature, presents a background of the methods that teacher preparation programs have employed to equip their preservice teachers to integrate technology into their future teaching practices. The remainder of the chapter delineates strategies that mathematics and science methods instructors can utilize when

DOI: 10.4018/978-1-4666-0014-0.ch023

modeling technology use to their students. These methodologies have been categorized according to: integrating technology into content instruction, technology to encourage collaboration, and technology assignments and assessments. The last section provides a variety of projects for preservice teachers.

BACKGROUND

In addition to their current responsibilities, teachers are also expected to prepare students technologically for the workforce and professional life. For many years, the National Council of Teachers of Mathematics' *Principles and Standards for School Mathematics* (NCTM, 2000) and the National Research Council's *National Science Education Standards* (NSES, 1996) have expected science and mathematics teachers to integrate technology into their instruction. NCTM emphasizes that "technology is essential in teaching and learning mathematics" (p. 25), since technology is able to "furnish visual images of mathematical ideas, … facilitate organizing and analyzing data, … compute efficiently and accurately, … [and] support investigation … in every area of mathematics" (p. 24). Similarly, the NSES states, "the relationship between science and technology is so close that any presentation of science without developing an understanding of technology would portray an inaccurate picture of science" (p. 190). While these national standards highlight the importance of technology integration, preservice teachers' knowledge of technology integration comes from their own experiences.

Similarly, the National Council for Accreditation of Teacher Education (NCATE, 2008) requires teacher educators to "understand and demonstrate expertise in technology operation and concepts" (p. 52), and "assist teachers in identifying technology systems and resources to meet specific student learning needs" (p. 52). To meet these needs, teacher preparation programs have tried many ways to introduce preservice teachers to technology.

In the past decade, government funds have been available to help teacher preparation programs redesign their technology training to make positive changes on preservice teachers' technology attitudes and abilities. *Preparing Tomorrow's Teachers to use Technology (PT3)*, a grant program funded by the U.S. Department of Education, was created to increase technology integration in teacher education programs. Many of these programs focused on training teacher education faculty to model effective technology integration (Polly, Mims, Sheperd, & Inan, 2010). Some programs targeted technological pedagogical knowledge, while others emphasized the content knowledge associated with technological pedagogy. One program sought to increase faculty knowledge of digital tools and to reflect on the value of technology for teacher preparation, focusing on the pedagogical advantages of technologies such as WebCT, BlackBoard, Word, PowerPoint, and other specific software (Whittier & Lara, 2003).. Unfortunately, there is limited research about the effectiveness of these PT3 programs (Polly et al., 2010), which makes it challenging to determine which methods had the most impact on preservice teachers' ability to integrate technology.

Methods of Technology Training for Teachers

The assumption that preparing college faculty to effectively utilize technology results in preservice teacher technology use has not been strongly supported or rejected by the literature (Adamy & Boulmetis, 2006; O'Bannon, Matthew, & Thomas, 1998; Parker, 1996). However, the structure of teacher education programs continues to change in attempts to help make that connection occur. There are two main ways that technology training occurs: a stand-alone technology course or an integrated approach (Toledo, 2002; Diem, 1982). Some teacher education programs separate education technology into a course, taught by a technology expert, to teach preservice teachers about available technologies (Duran, Runvand, & Fossum, 2009). Much of the literature reveals that these courses are concerned with specific technological knowledge such as computer skills, spreadsheets, and multi-media presentations. These courses are usually designed to increase preservice teachers' digital literacy, assuming that this will help them teach using technology (Berlin & White, 2010; Dusick, 1998; Shelton & Jones, 1996; Hardy, 2003; Topp, Mortenson, & Grandgenett, 1996). This approach is problematic because it presupposes that preservice teachers will be able to combine their new technology skills with their new knowledge of pedagogy. The lack of classroom contextualization results in a disconnect for preservice teachers between technology practices and pedagogy (Shelton & Jones, 1996). As a result, graduates from these types of programs feel inadequate and unprepared to incorporate technology into their instruction (Hardy, 2010; OTA, 1995; Pope, Hare, & Howard, 2002).

The other type of approach integrates technology training throughout the coursework (Toledo, 2002; Diem, 1982). This type of technology training occurs in combination with another course, within multiple courses, or within an entire program. While Anderson's (2002) study determined that integrated technology training was the strongest predictor of success, this claim has not been substantiated by subsequent research. Instructors of courses that include department-required technology components may or may not have strong technology skills. If students do not learn technology skills in concert with the appropriate pedagogies, the likelihood that they will integrate technology into their future teaching may be low.

Framework for Studying Technology Integration

As the debate continued over what type of technology training best prepared novice teachers to embrace technology, Mishra and Koehler (2006) developed a theoretical framework, extending Shulman's (1986) PCK framework (pedagogical and content knowledge) to include technology, to better evaluate and discuss the basis of the issues of teachers' technology use. Technological, pedagogical, and content knowledge (TPCK) has been used as a theoretical model for designing and/or evaluating technology training programs, content courses, and methodology courses (Angeli & Valanides, 2009; Banas, 2010; Hardy, 2010; Kramarski & Michalsky, 2010; Niess, 2005). However, there are likely other variables to consider; for example, studies have shown that teachers' beliefs and attitudes toward the inclusion of technology in instruction influence teachers' practices (Chen, 2010; Ertmer, 2005, Ertmer & Ottenbreit-Leftwich; 2010; Guerrero, 2010; Niess, 2005, 2006), as well as how the availability of technology in public schools affects a teacher's technology use (Guerrero, 2010; Niess, 2005).

Instructors teaching mathematics and science methods courses within teacher preparation programs have a unique opportunity to help preservice teachers increase the overlap between technology, pedagogy, and content knowledge. It is in these methods courses that preservice teachers learn about the appropriate pedagogy for their content areas, starting off with a strong passion for their content area and ready to learn how to be effective teachers. While preservice teachers have preconceived ideas of what constitutes effective teaching, each is ready to develop concrete teaching skills that match their beliefs about teaching and learning. Methods teachers who create a technology-rich learning environment and require their students to practice technology integration are likely to positively impact future teacher's attitudes toward and likelihood of integrating technology in their future classrooms (Polly et al., 2010).

While integrating technology use across the teacher education curriculum seems to be the most effective approach, there is no guarantee that it will have the desired effect. Stand-alone technology courses may increase technological literacy, but inexperienced preservice teachers are unable to transfer those skills to their developing teaching practice (Duran et al., 2009). The integration of technology is a complicated task, and the approach to helping preservice teachers must be multifaceted. However, no matter what approaches are used, mathematics and science education faculty should be on the leading edge of technology integration, particularly in methods courses (Adamy & Boulmetis, 2006; O'Bannon et al., 1998; Parker, 1996). Methods instructors are in a prime position to support future teachers in their development of technology, pedagogy, and content knowledge by modeling technology use as a tool for content instruction, collaboration, and assessment. The next three sections will delineate these processes.

INTEGRATING TECHNOLOGY INTO CONTENT INSTRUCTION

Modeling technology as a method of instruction is one way that mathematics and science teacher educators can support preservice teachers as they learn about the connections between technology, content, and pedagogy (Adamy & Boulmetis, 2006; Ozgun-Koca, Meagher, & Todd, 2010). In fact, methods instructors should include digital technologies as a way to help students learn the content of the course (Davis & Falba, 2002; Guy & Li, 2002; OTA, 1995). This content includes teaching strategies, curriculum organization, laboratory skills and the application of differing philosophy to teaching and learning. It is the responsibility of methods instructors to teach preservice teachers how a twenty-first century

K-12 classroom should function, and approaches for developing the best learning environment in those classrooms.

There are essentially two ways in which technology intersects with learning: technology for learning and technology for learners. Technology for learning represents instructor-directed technologies, whereas technology for learners focuses on how K-12 students use the technology (Halverson & Smith, 2010). The next sections describe three teacher-centered suggestions and two student-centered suggestions for using technology as part of content instruction.

Implementing Teacher-Centered Technologies

Utilizing Course Management Systems

The most common technology use by education faculty is in the organization and delivery of content (Duran et al., 2009). While integrating technology should be more than just putting overhead lecture notes into an electronic presentation software program, that is often the starting point for many faculty members. Using some sort of class management program allows faculty to provide twenty-four hour access to electronic course documents such as lectures, assignments, and online resources.

Utilizing RSS Feeds

Faculty should use technology tools to stay current in content, pedagogy, and technology. Organizing online resources using an RSS (Real Simple Syndication) feed reader is another way that faculty can prepare to use technology as an instructional tool (Richardson, 2009). Essentially an RSS feed reader is an electronic mailbox that aggregates important news, articles, blogs, podcasts, wikis, search engine results, and other digital media. Common RSS readers include Google Reader, Yahoo Reader, and Netvibes. One can subscribe by searching within the reader or clicking on any RSS icon. Teacher educators should use readers to locate relevant and current digital media that relate to course content. However, instructors should not do this behind closed doors, but share how they use RSS feeds, modeling technology use for their students.

Utilizing Digital Media

RSS readers can also be used as a method of content delivery (Franklin & Van Harmelen, 2007; Martindale & Wiley, 2005). Digital media like blogs, online newspapers, or audio/video podcasts can be used to engage preservice teachers in specific educational topics. For example, students can listen to a podcast of a world-renowned teacher discussing a pedagogical issue, or of a scientist explaining how their research relates to high school science. Podcasts are easily accessible through iTunes or through a podcast search engine. For instance, "Lab Outloud," produced by two science teachers with support from the National Science Teachers Association (NSTA), highlights science topics supporting the integration of inquiry and popular science into the classroom. A mathematics teacher could have his students watch the TED video (http://www.ted.com/) of Dan Meyer on the lack of good problem-solving skills of today's high school student (Meyer, 2010). Utilizing digital media as a method to spark discussion, instead of reading traditional paper text (Abell, Bryan & Anderson, 1998), is a great way to model technology. It can help elicit preservice teachers' ideas about education and how these ideas will impact how they teach, while connecting them to resources for long-term professional development.

Implementing Student—Centered Technologies

Utilizing WebQuests

Allowing students to use technology to learn content can be an even more powerful approach to helping preservice teachers make connections between technology, pedagogy, and content. One widely used student-centered method of delivering content in methods courses is the WebQuest, an "inquiry-oriented lesson format in which most or all the information that learners work with comes from the web" (Dodge, 2010, para 3). WebQuests that model good pedagogy and effective use of technology for inquiry learning tend to focus on investigation, collaboration, multiple viewpoints, and role-playing. These types of WebQuests have been shown to increase higher-order thinking (Allen, 2007). WebQuest participants are prompted with a problem or issue to address. Usually WebQuests are collaborative projects in which each participant addresses a specific aspect of the topic using online resources. The project is broken down into a set of role-specific tasks that the instructor assigns to individual group members. Upon completion of their individual parts, groups work together to develop a final product.

While WebQuests have been most commonly used in primary and secondary classrooms (Gaskill, McNulty, & Brooks, 2006; Lipscomb, 2003), they have also been used in college-level science and mathematics content courses (Williams, 2007), as well as educational methods courses (Allen, 2007; Halat, 2008; Kundu & Bain, 2006; Smith, Draper, & Sabey, 2005). For example, in a college ecology course at San Diego State University, students worked collaboratively to argue about issues of global climate change and biodiversity in a mock town hall meeting (Williams, 2007). This project ensured that students would integrate information from the science disciplines to construct scientific arguments supported by appropriate evidence. In methods courses, the purpose of having students complete WebQuests is two-fold: (a) to model an effective constructivist learning activity and (b) to encourage students to work with their peers on strategies for engaging future students in technology-enhanced inquiry-based learning activities. In essence, the WebQuest is used as an instructional tool. (Smith et al., 2005).

Utilizing Content Specific Software and Webware

Because mathematics and science have strong analytical components, technology is well situated to support learning in these content areas. There are a growing number of quality software, hardware, and web-based tools available that preservice teachers should be made aware of, even if the instructors have not used them.

Mathematics-Specific Technologies

Like in other content areas, there is software and hardware designed for mathematics and science students. As a way to focus on pedagogy specific to the content area, methods instructors often highlight the ability of technology to help students learn by solving problems in ways not easily accomplished without technology. (Capobianco, 2007; Park & Ertmer, 2008; Schwartz, Lederman, & Crawford, 2004; Thompson, 2010)

For example, in a technology course geared to mathematics preservice teachers, Thompson (2011) invites them to objectively look at how math is commonly presented in textbooks. He then helps them become more aware of students' thought processes, misconceptions, and previous knowledge about mathematical topics. He introduces the software Geometer's Sketchpad as a way for high school students to create visualizations as they begin to connect mathematics concepts and properties and solve problems. As an assessment, students develop their own lesson plan that incorporates Geometer's Sketchpad. A similar software program available as a free download is

Geogebra. This software incorporates a computer algebra system (CAS) and a spreadsheet, making it possible to incorporate geometry, algebra, and calculus. Geogebra provides students with the opportunity to manipulate algebraic equations and compare how they change in different representations, including graphs, functions, and spreadsheets. Texas Instruments (TI) Nspire offers similar capabilities.

Smartboards, or interactive whiteboards, that use touch detection technology can help mathematics instructors at all levels to create visual representations and geometric figures quickly and precisely, leaving more time for the students to interact with the figures. This time can be best utilized by having students explain the concepts behind the process. Additionally, when technology is put into the hands of mathematics students, students can present multimedia, multimodal presentations; model information and communication technology (ICT) skills; and increase their mathematics interactivity by participating in hands-on activities (Smith, Higgins, Wall, & Miller, 2005).

Common technology tools found in secondary mathematics classrooms are graphing calculators—newer models include CAS capabilities. The graphing calculator is useful for understanding algebra, pre-calculus, and calculus. Use of the calculator can reduce the time it takes to determine Cartesian coordinates, leaving more time for problem-solving activities, construction of concepts, and therefore, a deeper understanding of mathematical concepts. (Harshkamp, Suhre, & Van Streun, 2000; Monk, 2003). It also can be used to focus students' attention in the understanding a real life situation represented in a graph and find ways to connect mathematics to the real world. Graphing calculators manipulate mathematical expressions into their simplest symbolic form. As a result, students often have a difficult time reconciling the expression given with the expression they expected. They do not see these as equivalent expressions since they do not always possess the skill of symbolic manipulation (Ball, Pierce, & Stacey, 2003; Drijvers, 2003). Therefore, instructors should use some precautions when using CAS tools—focusing on reflection of equivalence of expressions rather than only computation (Kieran & Saldanha, 2005).

For example, when a student inputs $\sqrt{8 + \sqrt{5} - \sqrt{6 - 2\sqrt{5}}}$ into CAS, the output is $\sqrt{8 + \sqrt{5} - \sqrt{6 - 2\sqrt{5}}} = 3$. The student may not realize that $6 - 2\sqrt{5} = (\sqrt{5} - 1)^2$ and that most of the terms cancel out. CAS should be used to prompt justification and draw reasoning from students as to why CAS gave the answer. In some algebraic equations, CAS has the option to provide multiple equivalent expressions, or just one. For example the following expression $2\sqrt{x} - 7x^2 = x + 2\sqrt{x}$ CAS can produce (1) $\sqrt{x}(7x^{3/2} - 2) = (\sqrt{x} + 2)\sqrt{x}$ and (2) $-7x^2 - x = 0$. In the first, CAS factors the equation; in the second, CAS eliminates the like terms. The teacher can prompt students for these types of explanations and determinations as to why the equations are equivalent. In other words, using CAS pushes students to focus on the concepts and processes, rather than final answers.

Spreadsheets are readily available resources that mathematics teachers should use to pose and solve problems with their students. NCTM (2000) expects K-12 students to use spreadsheets for these processes as well as for examining data and investigating patterns (p. 207). Spreadsheets could be used in recursive problems, analysis of data, and in the beginning of the development of the concept of functions in secondary schools. Additionally, in the preparation of elementary teachers, spreadsheets have been modeled as a way for teachers' to provide open-ended problem solving experiences for their students (Abramovich & Cho 2006).

Free online resources like WolframAlpha (http://www.wolframalpha.com), which helps students investigate connections of mathematical concepts, are also available. *The On-Line Encyclopedia of Integers Sequences* (OEIS™) (http://www.research.att.com/~njas/sequences/) supports students as they seek to find formulas for sequences and patterns. Additionally, specially designed java applets can be useful to generate examples and data, to show students the steps of an example, to display proofs by pictures, and to generate challenging mathematical puzzles. These virtual manipulatives are interactive, web-based, and computer-mediated visual representations of dynamic objects. The National Library of Virtual Manipulatives (http://nlvm.usu.edu/en/nav/vlibrary.html) contains a large collection of applets than can be used throughout K-12 to create effective instruction.

Science-Specific Technologies

In science teaching, technologies like probes that display information on scientific calculators or separate technology systems like Vernier (http://www.vernier.com), Spark (http://www.pasco.com/products/sparkscience/), or Fourier (http://www.its-about-time.com/htmls/tech/fourier.html) are handheld computers that can be taken outside for field studies, enabling students to collect and analyze data. These handheld technologies can also be used to assess student work during labs and to manage cooperative learning (Scribner-MacLean, Nikonchuk, Kaplo, & Wall, 2006).

Free online activities appropriate for high school classrooms are constantly being developed. One example is GENIQUEST, (http://geniquest.concord.org/nsta) which helps students learn Mendelian genetics as well as Quantitative Trait Loci (QTL) analysis (Southworth, Mokros, Dorsey, & Smith, 2010). Another is The Mind Project (http://www.mind.ilstu.edu), which provides several different online virtual labs where students role-play researchers, scientists, or doctors in order to learn cutting edge science. The Jason Project, from National Geographic (http://www.jason.org/

Table 1. Assessment of online resources assignment

Your Tasks are to (1) identify, (2) critique, and then (3) share how to implement an educational online simulation or game that could be used to help teach students a difficult concept.

Identify

Search online to find an educational interactive simulation or game. This could be a role-playing game that takes an hour to play, or a java applet that animates a difficult concept. Just be sure that it has educational value for a specific content related topic.

Critique

Write a critique of the online simulation or game. Allow the following questions to guide your critique.

    1. How clear were the rules and goals?

    2. How compelling or engaging was the experience? Did you choose to continue on to the next level or stage when given the opportunity?

    3. Did the graphic quality help or hinder the experience?

    4. How often did you receive feedback on your progress? Was the feedback helpful in learning the concept?

    5. How accurately is the concept being taught? Does the game address misconceptions or difficult aspects of the concept?

    6. What is the purpose of the game? Does it introduce a new topic or provide practice and review of a concept already learned?

Implementation Tips

Describe context for this activity. What topic within a specific course would this fit? How would you prepare students to complete the activity? Would you prefer that students work individually or in groups? And most importantly, how would you tie in the activity to content they would be learning at the time. Include a list of discussion questions you might use the day after students complete the activity.

---

public/whatis/games.aspx), has a large collection of digital labs and games that accompanying curriculum for use in the classroom. When searching for quality online activities, instructors should ensure that the activity does more than just reinforce the science content students have already learned. The power of technology experiences should allow students to make choices, to be immersed in a scientific role or environment, and to collect and interpret data (even if it is simulated). Otherwise, the experience is uni-dimensional and most likely focused on reading and reporting on the content, having no more value than what students get from reading a print-based text.

Because the collection of online activities is always changing, preservice teachers in methods courses need to practice their web literacy skills. They must know how to locate, critique, and implement virtual simulations and games (Ray & Coulter, 2010). Therefore, the following activity would be a valuable assignment to give to preservice teachers. See Table 1.

TECHNOLOGY TO ENCOURAGE COLLABORATION

While preservice teachers may use digital interactions with their friends and family, they often have negative attitudes toward digital collaboration among students in the classroom (Adamy & Boulmetis, 2006; Burnett, 2009; Shoffner, 2009). Because preservice teachers' experiences with technology tools are so basic, they are uncomfortable with the idea of using basic (let alone more advanced technologies) with students in the classroom (Koc & Bakir, 2010). Although they may socially interact with others online or via mobile devices, they are unaware of the power of collaboration for learning. Therefore, if more preservice method instructors model collaboration among their students, these future teachers may be more likely to utilizing technology with their future students (Carlson & Gooden, 1999; Fleming, Motamedi, & May, 2007)

Collaborative technology tools include weblogs (blogs), wikis, social bookmarking, online photo galleries, and audio/video-casting (Richardson, 2009). At the heart of each of these tools is the ability to share something online, whether that is text, image, voice, or video. Shared items are uploaded with the purpose of soliciting comments, feedback, and possibly edits from others. Instructors can require online tool use for collaborative projects within the course. Students frequently will not take the time to use an online tool, even if they know of its potential value, unless required to do so. By making the use of such tools mandatory within a methods course, instructors can provide opportunities for future teachers to gain the technology skills and comfort necessary to incorporate those same tools in their future classrooms. This may also help in expanding their views of technology's role in problem-solving and student-centered learning. The next section will provide more detail on introducing these technologies into methods courses.

Before describing specific ways to encourage collaboration, there is a pedagogical concept that needs to be addressed. Preservice teachers who are involved in a competitive environment, where peers are not encouraged to share ideas or construct products as teams, often need assistance when participating in a collaborative environment (Wheeler, Yeomans, & Wheeler, 2008). Both competitive and collaborative learning "leverage[s] social interaction…to resolve learning difficulties and motivate participation in the system" (Halverson & Smith, 2010; p. 52). In addition, working collaboratively online may not come intuitively for all students. Class time should be spent learning how collaborative technologies work and also how to participate appropriately on collaborative activities. Individuals within a group should contribute their own ideas and also edit the ideas of others with the goal of developing a single product that is better than any one individual could have produced. Participants in the collaborative environment often need encouragement to edit one another's ideas. Instructors must help students understand the need to be invested in the idea that the product will evolve, that it can always be made better, and that transparent collaboration is a valuable process (Richardson, 2009). When first assigning collaborative work, it is important to state clear individual and group expectations.

Table 2 lists a set of behaviors that students should agree to. Instructors can have students read and sign a group agreement that contains some or all of these expectations.

Student-Generated Resources

A powerful method for encouraging collaboration among preservice teachers is to have them identify online resources they will use as teachers. For example, preservice science teachers can compile resources of current events to supplement textbook content. Preservice mathematics teachers can construct a list of applets for teaching difficult concepts. Instead of having each student individually submit an annotated list of websites in a word processing document, divide students into groups of four or five and have them collectively develop lists. These "lists" can be compiled in Google Doc, a wiki, posted to a blog, or shared through social bookmarking sites like Diigo (http://www.diigo.com). The goal in such an assignment is to teach students how to collaboratively construct a product in the online environment. Group members who become invested in compiling the list will easily learn the value and power of collaboration. Note that while learning collaboration tools is important, the real benefit occurs as preservice teachers see the value in the pedagogy and become more likely to start seeing the benefits of appropriately using educational technologies to meet the needs of their own future classrooms.

Student-Generated Products

While university instructors may use wikis as course management systems (Schroeder, 2009), the power of this read-write web tool lies in the feature that allows multiple users to edit the same content. Once students are registered and signed in, they can create, edit, and revise the content and material. In a methods courses, wikis are quite effective for coordinating groups of preservice teachers as they co-write lesson plans (He &

Table 2. Tips for online collaboration

Directions: Read the following individual and group expectations and discuss with your group members. Then have each member sign at the bottom.
- Individual responsibilities
    - Respect one other and their rights to express their views
    - Debate issues rather than argue personal beliefs
    - Assign roles that take advantage of each member's skills or help members develop new skills (instructor assistance needed)
    - Divide work equally, but no need for everyone to work on each task
    - Help one another understand concepts and processes
    - Be open to compromise
    - Carry out their roles within the group
    - Listen to input from each group member
    - Be involved in the discussions
    - Be collaborative, help and ask for help when needed
    - Share information and resources
- Group dynamics
    - Decide on a method of communication and then communicate regularly
    - Set deadlines and meet them
    - Designate only one person to contact the instructor (but cc all members of the group)
    - Use individual and cultural differences as a away to empower group dynamics
    - Recognize and appreciate the contribution of each group member
- Provide feedback
    - When editing a group member's work do so respectfully, if large changes need to be made consider contacting them first
    - Ask for clarification for what you do not understand
    - Provide descriptive rather than evaluative or judgmental comments
    - Phrase suggestions in the positive voice

Signatures:

_____

Adapted from Rankin (2001) and Azer (2004)

Hartley, 2010). Instructors are easily able to view the process of lesson development, rather than just the final product. Clicking on the "History" tab on a wiki page shows each saved version, the author of each edit, and a date stamp for each edit. The added and deleted materials are highlighted in different colors, thus speeding up the collaboration process. The "Discussion" tab allows users to talk to one another about the content they are constructing. After a student makes an edit, she may leave a post explaining the changes and ask for others to add more content in certain areas. Instructors can also chime in by providing feedback on the wiki page or by posting to the wiki discussion. Most of the features available on wiki sites are also available in Google Docs, another great tool for collaborative lesson planning. Google Docs allows multiple users to edit the same page simultaneously, while wikis are only editable by one person at a time. When groups are working simultaneously it is helpful to have one person act as the scribe, ensuring that all the compiled information is saved.

Educational Networking

Sites that scaffold educational networking (Davis, 2008) enable educators to set up classroom portals that differ from standard classroom management systems. College students are more apt to be comfortable in these environments because they function much like social networking sites; e.g., Facebook and MySpace. Online spaces such as Grouply (http://www.grouply.com/) or Grou.ps (http://grou.ps/) are intuitively organized with discussions, blogging capabilities, and document posting and sharing features; all of which are important for instructors who are trying to model the use of these technologies for future teachers.

TECHNOLOGY ASSIGNMENTS AND ASSESSMENTS

Using technology to support content delivery and encourage collaboration dovetails nicely with the use of technology in the assessment process. In addition to modeling appropriate technology use, it is important that teacher educators provide models of sound assessment. Some of the most difficult types of assessment are those associated with collaborative work. As mentioned earlier, many of the online tools lend themselves to formative and summative assessment. Lindsay and Davis (2010) creators of the Flat Classroom Project—an award winning global project for high school students—have developed an excellent structure for assessing student work in collaborative projects. Their construct provides assessment parameters for several categories: *Digital Stories, Engagement, Reflection, and Evaluation*, and a *Wiki Grading Rubric* (http://flatclassroomproject.wikispaces. com/Rubrics). Instructors can use these types of assessment tools to grade student work, as well as encourage their students to emulate these models as they create assessment components for their technology projects.

The following sections are focused on teacher-centered and student-centered methods for using technology for assessment. Both are important to model for future teachers.

Using Technology to go Paperless

Assessments previously turned in on paper, can be submitted electronically. Students can upload or email documents to the instructor and then receive feedback electronically. Most instructors like the option of writing notes in the margins of papers and correcting mistakes. Electronically, this can be done effectively by using the "track-changes" feature in word processing programs. When the instructor turns on track–changes, any changes are highlighted in a different color. Comments can be communicated by highlighting the text and clicking on the "insert a comment" button; the comment will appear in a colored bubble near the text. Instructors resave the document and send it to the student when complete. When implementing electronic feedback assessment, it is best to require that students have their name (or other personal identifier) as part of the file name, identifying the author without having to opening each document.

If instructors are interested in the final product as well as the process of an assignment, students can post their work in Google Docs and then link them in the online class management system weeks before the assignment is due. This previewing allows students to see one another's ongoing work and encourages a collaborative classroom environment.

Lesson Planning

Lesson planning geared specifically for mathematics and science teachers is a critical component of any methods course. Another way to add a technology-based assignment/assessment into a course is to have students write lessons that integrate technology. It is best if they can actually teach the lesson with students so that they can reflect on the experience and determine its effectiveness (Krueger, Boboc, Smaldinom, Cocrnish, & Callahan, 2004). Table 3 provides an example of how a lesson assignment might be presented to preservice teachers.

Another way to add a technology-based assessment into a course is to have students take a lesson they have taught, or a lesson they have observed (if they have not had the experience of teaching yet), and rewrite it to include inquiry and some form of technology.

Student-Generated Multimedia

Assignments that previously were turned in on paper can be improved by encouraging students to use multimedia (Willett, 2009). Multimedia

Table 3. Technology integrated lesson plan assignment

Your task is come up with a topic for a lesson plan that could be taught using three different technologies. Carefully consider the advantages and disadvantages of each technology and be prepared to address instructional techniques for each.

Within this paper please address the following:

  • Provide a context for the lesson. What would have been taught in the days leading up to this lesson, and what will be taught after?
  • For each technology:
      o Explain how to use this particular technology to teach the concept.
      o Describe the concepts that are demonstrated effectively using this technology.
      o Describe the concepts are not demonstrated effectively using this technology.
      o Explain what misconceptions students might have while learning the concept using this technology.
      o Describe what you could do as the teacher to address the weaknesses and misconceptions that students might face learning the concept this way.
      o Describe how you would assess students learning of the topic using this technology.
Example:
Content: Algebra
Topic: Functions
Possible technologies that could be used: Geometer's Sketchpad, Excel spreadsheets and java applets, graphing calculator, Geogebra, WolframAlpha, or National Library of Virtual Manipulatives

includes the integration of text, graphics, animation, sound, and/or video. It is likely that in a science methods course students will design, or rewrite an inquiry-based, hands-on lesson that they must teach, either to actual classroom students, or to college peers. Since writing lab reports is commonly associated with science (Porter et al., 2010; Robertson & Lankford, 2010), the assignment could be extended to include an example multimedia report that a science student would create after completing the lab. Preservice teachers may choose to create a digital video to highlight critical methods performing the lab, use digital photographs to show experiment results, and then add text in conjunction with audio and video to emphasize methods and to explain the analysis. The entire project could be placed in a PowerPoint, blog, or wiki. This may necessitate that students learn a video editing software, such as Photo Story, iMovie, or Movie Maker, but there are hundreds of tutorials available on the web. Table 4 shows a sample assignment description for introducing a similar project to preservice science students.

Another version of this assignment would require preservice teachers to create a lab safety video or podcast to support students in a specific skill they need to complete a lab experiment. Videos can be posted to the class wiki or blog and also be made available on YouTube, TeacherTube, or GoogleVideo for other teachers and students to access.

Similarly, mathematics methods instructors can assign a multimedia project, having preservice teachers create a digital portrait of a mathematics student they worked with during field observations or one-on-one tutoring. Similar to Kerin's (2009) digital portrait of a literacy student, the preservice mathematics teacher could design a project showing his ability to assess student learning and resulting instruction modification. The video might include photographs of sample math problems completed by the student, or an audio/video recording of a student describing their thought processes as they solve a mathematical problem. The preservice teacher would then explain how the student's mathematical reasoning skills could be addressed instructionally.

Lessons that could not Exist without Global Access

With technology comes global access to scientific and mathematical data. Without much effort, teachers can reach outside their own classrooms, allowing their students to manipulate actual data collected by scientists or coordinate a unit with

Table 4. Multimedia science lab report

Your task is to create a multimedia version of a student lab write up for a laboratory experiment you might assign students. This multimedia lab report will be a visual representation of the lab experience. The project should include text, graphics/photographs, audio (music & voice), and video.
Concepts that must be addressed:
 • Purpose: Hypothesis or research questions that was tested
 • Materials used
 • Procedures
 • How data were collected
 • How data were analyzed
 • The results of the lab: Explaining graphical and/or photographic data
 • Final conclusions based on the data collected
 • Additional questions raised
 • Confidence that the question asked was tested appropriately (Describe limitations that my weaken the ability to claim confident conclusions)
 • New questions raised by the experiment
 • Real world applications of this lab
Here are ideas on where you might include photographs and/or video:
 • Experimental set up
 • How measurements were taken
 • Important steps of the methods
 • Close up shots of the results, taking care to label the experimental groups and control groups for easy comparison
Resources for tools to help you construct the multimedia lab (There are many tutorials for these programs available online.)
 • Video Editing Software: Photo Story, iMovie, Movie Maker

teachers around the globe. Their students can collect data that will be added to a national database, allowing other students around the world to compare experimental results. One example is the study of coral reefs using remote sensing technology (Palandro, Thoms, Kusek, Muller-Karger, & Greely, 2005). Purdue University's MultiSpec software is available for free (https://engineering.purdue.edu/~biehl/MultiSpec/), and detailed directions for students are available on the ORBITaL website (http://education.imars.usf.edu/coral_classification.doc). Completing the activity is the method by which students learn about coral reefs, environmental impacts on the reefs, and how technology is used to monitor changes. Another set of free online data is Science Pipes (http://sciencepipes.org). This website contains biodiversity data that allow students to combine sets of data to determine correlations. Using the data, students conduct guided and open inquiry investigations analyzing the data to get their answers (Wilson, Trautmann, MaKinster, & Barker, 2010).

In addition to gathering data from the Web, students can collect data and enter it national and international databases. For example the North American Reporting Center for Amphibian Malformations (NARCAM) allows contributions regarding amphibian malformations from not only scientists, but also from informed students. Local universities are also a good resource for this type of collaboration (Marx, Honeycutt, Clayton, & Moreno, 2006). For example, chemistry students in Montana collected and analyzed air samples for the University of Montana (Adams et al., 2008). These broader scientific activities help students to see the connection between the environment and public health, and more importantly, that scientific data are important and valuable.

Even if national or international data are not used, two teachers in different parts of the world can have their students complete the same activity or experiment, and then pool the data together for analysis. Student motivation often increases when they know that others will be using their data. The communication between the two groups can be done via a wiki with occasional Voice Over Internet Protocol (VOIP)—like Skype—conver-

Table 5. Global access to data assignment

Your Task is to create a unit plan that includes web access. The project could include accessing or contributing to global data, and/or it could include designing a project that would allow your future students to virtually collaborate with individuals around the world to solve a problem.

Examples of data available online are:

• Road Statistics: provides historical and real time traffic and travel time reports for Chicago and Milwaukee. (http://www.gcmtravel-stats.com/opsreport.aspx)

• National Oceanic and Atmospheric Administration (NOAA) National Weather Service (http://www.noaa.gov/wx.html)

• Goddard Institute for Space Studies (NASA): technical data on different climate variables (http://data.giss.nasa.gov/gistemp/)

• Earthscope: interactive map of seismographic data (http://www.earthscope.org/)

• Center for Disease Control and Prevention (CDC): health related data (http://wonder.cdc.gov/)

• Data.gov: cross referenced data from multiple agencies (http://www.data.gov/)

• U.S. Environmental Protection Agency (EPA) (http://www.epa.gov/)

• U.S. Geological Survey (USGS): reports data like stream flow, wildfire, and volcano activity (http://www.usgs.gov/)

Tips:

• Get ideas from existing collaborative projects (http://flatclassrooms.ning.com).

• Research whether local universities or businesses have ongoing projects in which high school or middle school students could be involved.

• Determine if you, or your students, will identify the problem to be solved.

• Establish which technologies will help in the collection, organization, and analysis of the data. Also determine which technologies could be used to support the collaboration process. Here's a listing of 100 tools to use for collaboration, http://ozgekaraoglu.edublogs.org/tag/100-collaboration-tools/

What to turn in:

1. A URL link to an online space you have created for this project. It could be a wiki, blog, educational network, or any other appropriate space. Include the requirements below somewhere in this space.

2. A table that provides an overview of the unit plan (10-15 days). Include the following for each day: the topic of instruction/discussion, the tasks students will be working on, and any assignments that they will complete as homework.

3. A narrative describing:

    a. Context for the unit. Describe what course this lesson would be implemented in, the age/grade level of targeted students, and what students have previously learned that will help them succeed.

    b. Resources you would need to complete this unit plan. Include technology resources as well as human resources. What community and online networking would help you implement the project? How you would go about making those connections?

    c. A plan for both formative and summative assessment. How will you monitor and assess group work? How will you gauge whether or not students are learning while completing the project? What sort of product will students create as a culmination of the activity?

    d. Reflection: What parts during the development of this unit were exciting? Difficult? Do you feel it is a valuable experience for students? Why or why not? Do you intend to implement this unit in the future? Why or why not?

sations to make the connection between students even stronger.

Another assignment that methods instructors could give their preservice teachers would be searching for lesson or unit ideas that would allow their future students to reach outside the walls of their own classroom and learn to use or collect data that are important to the scientific community as a whole. The assignment shown in Table 5 could be a theoretical unit plan in which they describe the resources they would need, the networking they would have to do, and the technologies, skills, and tools they and their students would employ.

CONCLUSION

Ensuring that future generations of teachers are both capable and confident to integrate technology into their teaching pedagogy is a complicated task. Many factors influence the likelihood that a teacher will use technology (Ertmer, 2005; Ertmer & Ottenbreit-Leftwich, 2010; Sockman & Sharma, 2007), however, learning technology skills in pedagogically appropriate ways is a critical component (Ozgun-Koca et al., 2010). Having university mathematics and science methods instructors model appropriate technology use is arguably the best way to ensure that preservice teachers are able to combine their technology skills, teaching pedagogy, and content knowledge.

As indicated throughout this chapter, relying on instructors to model technology use is not enough. We cannot assume that students will be able to make the connections between what they experience in class and what they could do in their future classrooms. Teacher educators must carve out time to discuss the relationship between content, pedagogy, and technology as it relates to what students have seen modeled. Preservice teachers often struggle with seeing themselves as teachers—they are consumed by their role as students—so they must be reminded to look at what goes on in their classes through the lens of a teacher. And who better to provide the scaffolding that enables them to make the important connections between pedagogy and technology then their mathematics or science methods instructors? Making these connections "will not be accomplished through isolated technology experiences or without ongoing discussion, modeling, and evaluation" (Bowman, 2000; para. 1).

Therefore, reflection is a key component that personalizes the technology modeling. Preservice teachers can be asked to explain why certain technologies were, or were not, effective or reflect on how they could use similar technologies for instruction in their future classrooms. Without discussions such as these, preservice teachers are likely to miss the connections that methods teachers are trying to model. They must be encouraged to reflect on the intricate relationship between technology, pedagogy, and content knowledge. Instructors must work hard at making invisible processes more visible—state the obvious and take advantage of teachable moments as they occur. If mathematics and science methods faculty integrate technology into their content delivery, encourage online collaboration, encourage technology-rich assignments, and engage preservice teachers in dialog about these processes, future teachers will be excited about the prospect of the appropriate application of educational technologies in their future classrooms.

REFERENCES

Abell, S. K., Bryan, L. A., & Anderson, M. A. (1998). Investigating preservice elementary science teacher reflective thinking using integrated media case-based instruction in elementary science teacher preparation. *Science Education*, *82*(4), 491–509. doi:10.1002/(SICI)1098-237X(199807)82:4<491::AID-SCE5>3.0.CO;2-6

Abramovich, S., & Cho, E. K. (2006). Technology as a medium for elementary preteachers' problem-posing experience in mathematics. *Journal of Computers in Mathematics and Science Teaching*, *25*, 309–323.

Adams, E., Smith, G., Ward, T. J., Vaneck, D., Marra, N., & Jones, D. (2008). Air toxins under the big sky: A real-world investigation to engage high school science students. *Journal of Chemical Education*, *85*(2), 4. doi:10.1021/ed085p221

Adamy, P., & Boulmetis, J. (2006). The impact of modeling technology integration on pre-service teachers' technology confidence. *Journal of Computing in Higher Education*, *17*(2), 100–120. doi:10.1007/BF03032700

Allen, J. (2007). The quest for deeper learning: an investigation into the impact of a knowledge-pooling WebQuest in primary initial teacher training. *British Journal of Educational Technology*, *38*(6), 1102–1112. doi:10.1111/j.1467-8535.2007.00697.x

Angeli, C., & Valanides, N. (2009). Epistemological and methodological issues for the conceptualization, development, and assessment of ICT-TPCK: Advances in technological pedagogical content knowledge (TPCK). *Computers & Education*, *52*, 154–168. doi:10.1016/j.compedu.2008.07.006

Azer, S. A. (2004). Becoming a student in a PBL course: Twelve tips for successful group discussion. *Medical Teacher*, *26*(1), 12–15. doi:10.1080/0142159032000156533

Ball, L., Pierce, R., & Stacey, K. (2003). *Recognizing equivalent algebraic expressions: An important component of algebraic expectation for working with CAS*. Paper presented at the 27th International Group for the Psychology of Mathematics Education Conference Held Jointly with the 25th PME-NA Conference (Honolulu, HI, Jul 13-18, 2003).

Banas, J. R. (2010). Teachers' attitudes toward technology: Considerations for designing preservice and practicing teacher instruction. *Community & Junior College Libraries*, *16*(2), 14. doi:10.1080/02763911003707552

Berlin, D. F., & White, A. L. (2010). Preservice mathematics and science teachers in an integrated teacher preparation programs for grades 7-12: A 3-year study of attitudes and perceptions related to integration. *International Journal of Science and Mathematics Education*, *8*(1), 97–115. doi:10.1007/s10763-009-9164-0

Bowman, C. A. (2000). Infusing technology-based instructional frameworks in the methods courses: A response to Pope and Golub. *Contemporary Issues in Technology & Teacher Education*, *1*(1).

Burnett, C. (2009). Personal digital literacies versus classroom literacies: Investigating preservice teachers' digital lives in and beyond the classroom. In Carrington, V., & Robinson, M. (Eds.), *Digital literacies: Social learning and classroom practices* (pp. 115–129). Thousand Oaks, CA: Sage Publications.

Capobianco, B. M. (2007). A self-study of the role of technology in promoting reflection and inquiry-based science teaching. *Journal of Science Teacher Education*, *18*(2), 217–295. doi:10.1007/s10972-007-9041-z

Carlson, R. D., & Gooden, J. S. (1999). Are teacher preparation programs modeling technology use for pre-service teachers? *ERS Spectrum*, *17*(3), 11–15.

Chen, R.-J. (2010). Investigating models for preservice teachers' use of technology to support student-centered learning. *Computers & Education*, *55*, 32–42. doi:10.1016/j.compedu.2009.11.015

Davis, K. S., & Falba, C. J. (2002). Integrating technology in elementary preservice teacher education: orchestrating scientific inquiry in meaningful ways. *Journal of Science Teacher Education*, *13*(4), 303–329. doi:10.1023/A:1022535516780

Davis, V. (2008, January 17). *It is about educational networking NOT social networking* [Web log comment]. Retrieved from http://coolcatteacher.blogspot.com/2008/01/it-is-about-educational-networking-not.html

Diem, R. A. (1982). *The role of technology in teacher education: Preparation for the twenty-first century classroom*. Paper presented at the Annual Meeting of the American Association of Colleges for Teacher Education.

Dodge, B. (2010). *WebQuest.org*. Retrieved Sep 22, 2010, from http://webquest.org

Drijvers, P. H. M. (2003). *Learning algebra in a computer algebra environment* (doctoral dissertation). Utrecht, The Netherlands: Freudenthal Institute.

Duran, M., Runvand, S., & Fossum, P. R. (2009). Preparing science teachers to teach with technology: Exploring a K-16 networked learning community approach. *Turkish Online Journal of Distance Education, 8*(4), 21–42.

Dusick, D. M. (1998). What social cognitive factors influence faculty members' use of computers for teaching? A literature review. *Journal of Research on Computing in Education, 31*(2), 123–137.

Ertmer, P. A. (2005). Teacher pedagogical beliefs: The final frontier in our quest for technology integration. *Educational Technology Research and Development, 53*(4), 25–39. doi:10.1007/BF02504683

Ertmer, P. A., & Ottenbreit-Leftwich, A. T. (2010). Teacher technology change: How knowledge, confidence, beliefs, and culture intersect. *International Society for Technology in Education, 42*(3), 255–284.

Fleming, L., Motamedi, V., & May, L. (2007). Predicting preservice teacher competence in computer technology: Modeling and application in training environments. *Journal of Technology and Teacher Education, 15*(2), 207–231.

Franklin, T., & Van Harmelen, M. (2007). *Web 2.0 for content for learning and teaching in higher education*. Bristol, UK: JISC. Retrieved September 23, 2010, from http://ie-repository.jisc.ac.uk/148/1/web2-content-learning-and-teaching.pdf

Gaskill, M., McNulty, A., & Brooks, D. W. (2006). Learning from WebQuests. *Journal of Science Education and Technology, 15*(2), 133–136. doi:10.1007/s10956-006-9005-7

Guerrero, S. (2010). Technological pedagogical content knowledge in the mathematics classroom. *Journal of Digital Learning in Education, 26*(4), 132–139.

Guy, M. D., & Li, Q. (2002). *Integrating technology into an elementary mathematics methods course: Assessing the impact on pre-service teachers perception to use and teach with technology*. New Orleans, LA: Paper presented at The Annual Meeting of the American Educational Research Association annual meeting.

Halat, E. (2008). The effects of designing Webquests on the motivation of pre-service elementary school teachers. *International Journal of Mathematical Education in Science and Technology, 39*(6), 793–802. doi:10.1080/00207390802054466

Halverson, R., & Smith, A. (2010). How new technologies have (and have not) changed teaching and learning in schools. *Journal of Computing in Teacher Education, 26*(2), 6.

Hardy, M. (2003). *It should have been stressed in all education classes: Preparing preservice teachers to teach with technology*. Paper presented at the Annual Meeting of the American Educational Research Association, Chicago, IL, April, 21-25, 2003. (ERIC Document Reproduction Service ED 478 379).

Hardy, M. (2010). Enhancing preservice mathematics teachers' TPCK. *Journal of Computers in Mathematics and Science Teaching, 29*(1), 73–86.

Harskamp, E. G., Suhre, C. J. M., & Van Streun, A. (2000). The graphics calculator and students' solution strategies. *Mathematics Education Research Journal, 12*(1), 37–52. doi:10.1007/BF03217073

He, W., & Hartley, K. (2010). A supporting framework of online technology resources for lesson planning. *Journal of Educational Multimedia and Hypermedia, 19*(1), 23–37.

Kerin, R. (2009). Digital portraits: Teacher education and multiliteracies pedagogy. In Carrington, V., & Robinson, M. (Eds.), *Digital literacies: Social learning and classroom practices*. Thousand Oaks, CA: Sage Publications.

Kieran, C., & Saldanha, L. (2005). Computer algebra systems (CAS) as a tool for coaxing the emergence of reasoning about equivalence of algebraic expressions. In H. L. Chick & J. L. Vincent (Eds.), *Proceedings of the 29th Conference of the International Group for the Psychology of Mathematics Education*, (vol. 3, pp. 193-200). Melbourne, Australia: PME.

Koc, M., & Bakir, N. (2010). A needs assessment survey to investigate pre-service teachers' knowledge, experiences and perceptions about preparation to using educational technologies. *Turkish Online Journal of Distance Education*, *9*(1), 13–22.

Kramarski, B., & Michalsky, T. (2010). Preparing preservice teachers for self-regulated learning in the context of technological pedagogical content knowledge. *Learning and Instruction*, *20*(5), 14. doi:10.1016/j.learninstruc.2009.05.003

Krueger, K., Boboc, M., Smaldinom, S., Cocrnish, Y., & Callahan, W. (2004). InTime impact report: What was InTime's effectiveness and impact on faculty and preservice teachers? *Journal of Technology and Teacher Education*, *12*(2), 185–210.

Kundu, R., & Bain, C. (2006). WebQuests: Utilizing technology in a constructivist manner to facilitate meaningful preservice learning. *Art Education*, *59*(2).

Lindsay, J., & Davis, V. (2010). *Rubric assessment*. Flat Classroom Project. Retrieved September 30, 2010, from http://flatclassroomproject.wikispaces.com/Rubrics

Lipscomb, G. (2003). "I guess it was pretty fun": Using WebQuests in the middle school classroom. *Clearing House (Menasha, Wis.)*, *76*(3), 152–155. doi:10.1080/00098650309601993

Martindale, T., & Wiley, D. A. (2005). Using weblogs in scholarship and teaching. *TechTrends*, *49*(2), 55–61. doi:10.1007/BF02773972

Marx, J. G., Honeycutt, K. A., Clayton, S. R., & Moreno, N. P. (2006). The Elizabeth Towns incident: An inquiry-based approach to learning anatomy developed through high school-university collaboration. *The American Biology Teacher*, *68*(3), 7. doi:10.1662/0002-7685(2006)68[140:TETIAI]2.0.CO;2

Meyer, D. (2005). *Math class needs a makeover*. TED: Ideas worth spreading. Retrieved September 21, 2010 from http://www.ted.com/talks/dan_meyer_math_curriculum_makeover.html

Mishra, P., & Koehler, M. J. (2006). Technological pedagogical content knowledge: A framework for teacher knowledge. *Teachers College Record*, *108*(6), 1017–1054. doi:10.1111/j.1467-9620.2006.00684.x

Monk, S. (2003). Representation in school mathematics: learning to graph and graphing to learn. In Kilpatrick, J., Martin, W. G., & Schifter, D. (Eds.), *A research companion to principles and standards for school mathematics* (pp. 250–262). Reston, VA: NCTM.

National Council for Accreditation of Teacher Education (NCATE). (Feb 2008). *Professional standards for the accreditation of teacher preparation institutions*. Washington, DC: NCATE.

National Council of Teachers of Mathematics (NTCM). (2000). *Principles and standards for school mathematics*. Reston, VA: NCTM.

National Research Council. (1996). *National science education standards*. Washington, DC: National Academy Press.

Niess, M. L. (2005). Preparing teachers to teach science and mathematics with technology: Developing a technology pedagogical content knowledge. *Teaching and Teacher Education*, *21*, 15. doi:10.1016/j.tate.2005.03.006

Niess, M. L. (2006). Guest editorial: Preparing teachers to teach mathematics with technology. *Contemporary Issues in Technology & Teacher Education*, *6*(2), 195–203.

O'Bannon, B., Matthew, K. I., & Thomas, L. (1998). Faculty development: Key to the integration of technology in teacher preparation. *Journal of Computing in Teacher Education*, *14*(4), 7–11.

Ozgun-Koca, S. A., Meagher, M., & Todd, M. (2010). Preservice teachers' emerging TPACK in a technology-rich methods class. *Mathematics Educator*, *19*(2), 10–20.

Palandro, D., Thoms, K., Kusek, K., Muller-Karger, F., & Greely, T. (2005). Satellite remote sensing of coral reefs: By learning about coral reefs, students gain an understanding of ecosystems and how cutting-edge technology can be used to study ecological change. *Science Teacher (Normal, Ill.)*, *72*(6), 51–55.

Park, S. H., & Ertmer, P. A. (2008). Examining barriers in technology-enhanced problem-based learning; Using performance support systems approach. *British Journal of Educational Technology*, *39*(4), 12. doi:10.1111/j.1467-8535.2008.00858.x

Parker, D. R. (1996). *Integrating faculty use of technology in teaching and teacher education*. Paper presented at the Annual Meeting of the Mid-South Educational Research Association.

Polly, D., Mims, C., Sheperd, C., & Inan, F. (2010). Evidence of impact: Transforming teacher education with preparing tomorrow's teachers to teach with technology (PT3) grants. *Teaching and Teacher Education: An International Journal of Research and Studies*, *26*(4), 863–870. doi:10.1016/j.tate.2009.10.024

Pope, M., Hare, D., & Howard, E. (2002). Technology integration: Closing the gap between what preservice teachers are taught to do and what they can do. *Journal of Technology and Teacher Education*, *10*(2), 191–203.

Porter, R., Buarienti, K., Brydon, B., Robb, J., Royston, A., & Painter, H. (2010). Writing better lab reports. *Science Teacher (Normal, Ill.)*, *77*(1), 6.

Rankin, E. (2001). *The work of writing: Insights and strategies for academics and professionals*. San Francisco, CA: Jossey-Bass.

Ray, B., & Coulter, G. A. (2010). Perceptions of the value of digital mini-games: Implications for middle school classrooms. *Journal of Digital Learning in Teacher Education*, *26*(3), 92–100.

Richardson, W. (2009). *Blogs, wikis, podcasts, and other powerful web tools for classrooms*. Thousand Oaks, CA: Corwin Press.

Robertson, C., & Lankford, D. (2010). Laboratory notebooks in the science classroom. *Science Teacher (Normal, Ill.)*, *77*(1), 5.

Schroeder, B. (2009). Within the wiki; Best practices for educators. *AACE Journal*, *17*(3), 181–197.

Schwartz, R. S., Lederman, N. G., & Crawford, B. A. (2004). Developing views of nature of science in an authentic context: An explicit approach to bridging the gap between nature of science and scientific inquiry. *Science Education*, *88*(4), 36. doi:10.1002/sce.10128

Scribner-MacLean, M., Nikonchuk, A., Kaplo, P., & Wall, M. (2006). In sync with science teaching. *Science Teacher (Normal, Ill.)*, *73*(7), 26–29.

Shelton, M., & Jones, M. (1996). Staff development that works! A tale of four T's. *NASSP Bulletin*, *80*(582), 99–105. doi:10.1177/019263659608058214

Shoffner, M. (2009). Personal attitudes and technology: Implications for preservice teacher reflective practice. *Teacher Education Quarterly, 36*(2), 143–161.

Shulman, L. S. (1986). Those who understand: Knowledge growth in teaching. *Educational Research, 15*(4), 4–14.

Smith, H. J., Higgins, S., Wall, K., & Miller, J. (2005). Interactive whiteboards: Boon or bandwagon? A critical review of the literature. *Journal of Computer Assisted Learning, 21*, 91–101. doi:10.1111/j.1365-2729.2005.00117.x

Smith, L. K., Draper, R. J., & Sabey, B. L. (2005). The promise of technology to confront dilemmas in teacher education: The use of WebQuests in problem-based methods courses. *Journal of Computing in Higher Education, 21*(4), 99–108.

Sockman, B. R., & Sharma, P. (2007). Struggling toward a transformative model of instruction: It's not so easy! *Teaching and Teacher Education, 24*(4), 13.

Southworth, M., Mokros, J., Dorsey, C., & Smith, R. (2010). The case for cyberlearning: Genomics (and dragons!) in the high school biology classroom. *Science Teacher (Normal, Ill.), 77*(7), 28–33.

Thompson, K. (2011). *University high school: Thompson's math homepage.* Retrieved from http://www.uhigh.ilstu.edu/math/thompson/thompsonbio.htm

Toledo, C. (2002). *Computer technology infusion: Three case studies of California university teacher education programs.* Unpublished Dissertation, United States International University, San Diego, CA.

Topp, N. W., Mortenson, R., & Grandgenett, N. (1995). Goal: Technology-using teachers- Key: Technology-using education faculty. In Willis, J., Robin, B., & Willis, D. (Eds.), *Technology and Teacher Education Annual 1995* (pp. 840–843). Charlottesville, VA: Association for the Advancement of Computing in Education.

U.S. Congress, Office of Technology Assessment. (1995). *Teachers and technology: Making the connections. OTA-HER 616.* Washington, DC: U.S. Government Printing Office.

Wheeler, S., Yeomans, P., & Wheeler, D. (2008). The good, the bad, and the wiki: Evaluating student-generated content for collaborative learning. *British Journal of Educational Technology, 39*(6), 987–995. doi:10.1111/j.1467-8535.2007.00799.x

Whittier, D., & Lara, S. (2003). Preparing tomorrow's teachers to use technology (PT3) at Boston University through faculty development. *Estudios Sobre Educación, 5*, 47–60.

Willett, R. (2009). Young people's video productions as new sites of learning. In Carrington, V., & Robinson, M. (Eds.), *Digital literacies: Social learning and classroom practices* (pp. 13–26). Thousand Oaks, CA: SAGE Publications.

Williams, K. S. (2007). *Using WebQuests to improve understanding of ecology.* Paper presented at the ESA/SER Joint Meeting, San Jose, CA.

Wilson, C., Trautmann, R., Ma, N. M., Kinster, J. G., & Barker, B. J. (2010). Science pipes: A world of data at your fingertips. *Science Teacher (Normal, Ill.), 77*(7), 34–39.

KEY TERMS AND DEFINITIONS

Assessment: Both the process of evaluating student work and the activity that demonstrates student learning.

Collaboration: Working together to come to consensus; not to be confused with cooperative learning where students divide a task into parts and complete each independently. Collaborative work requires students to work as a team, compromise, negotiate, and adjust individual viewpoints for the common good.

Educational Networking: A term coined by Vicki Davis (2008) to de-emphasize the play element reflected in the term social networking. Although educational networking sites have many of the same functionalities—like file sharing, discussion forums, multimedia sharing, profiles, and connections—the emphasis is on building learning communities that provide a foundation for lifelong learning.

Multimedia: A product that represents information using a variety of communication tools; e.g., text, graphics, audio, video, virtual reality, etc.

Multimodal: Human interaction with information that requires more than one communication mode; e.g., speaking, typing, texting, listening, manipulating a game controller, etc.

TPCK: A theoretical framework developed by Mishra and Koehler (2006) to evaluate and discuss the basis of the issues of teachers' technology use. Based on Shulman's (1986) PCK framework (pedagogical, content, knowledge), adding a technology component to give the structure three domains: technological (T), pedagogical (P), and content (C) knowledge (K).

Chapter 24
A Practical Guide for Integrating Technology into Social Studies Instruction

John H. Curry
Morehead State University, USA

David L. Buckner
Brigham Young University – Hawaii, USA

ABSTRACT

This chapter provides a resource to practitioners not only about what types of technologies can be integrated into Social Studies instruction, but also provides resources by Social Studies content area (U.S. History, World History, Government, Civics, Economics, Geography, Anthropology, Sociology, and Psychology). The intended audience is the Social Studies teacher who wants ideas on how to improve their instructional delivery and learning environment through the integration of technology. Differing levels of technology integration are defined. Major types of technologies covered in the chapter include audio, video, simulations, and interactive whiteboards. Implications include the opportunities for Social Studies educators to provide students content in more readily understandable ways and in richer learning environments.

INTRODUCTION

"In the twenty-first century, participatory media education and civic education are inextricable" (Rheingold, 2008).

DOI: 10.4018/978-1-4666-0014-0.ch024

Technology is as old as the first crude tool invented by prehistoric humans, but today's technology forms the basis for some of our most difficult social choices. Modern life as we know it would be impossible without technology and the science that supports it. But technology brings with it many questions: Is new technology always better than that which it will replace? What can we learn from the past about how new technologies result in broader social change, some of which is unanticipated? How can we cope with the ever-increasing pace of change, perhaps even with the feeling that technology has gotten out of control? How can we manage technology so that the greatest number of people benefit from it? How can we preserve our fundamental values and beliefs in a world that is rapidly becoming one technology-linked village? This theme appears in units or courses dealing with history, geography, economics, and civics and government. It draws upon several scholarly fields from the natural and physical sciences, social sciences, and the humanities for specific examples of issues and the knowledge base for considering responses to the societal issues related to science and technology.

Young children can learn how technologies form systems and how their daily lives are intertwined with a host of technologies. They can study how basic technologies such as ships, automobiles, and airplanes have evolved and how we have employed technology such as air conditioning, dams, and irrigation to modify our physical environment. From history (their own and others'), they can construct examples of how technologies such as the wheel, the stirrup, and the transistor radio altered the course of history. By the middle grades, students can begin to explore the complex relationships among technology, human values, and behavior. They will find that science and technology bring changes that surprise us and even challenge our beliefs, as in the case of discoveries and their applications related to our universe, the genetic basis of life, atomic physics, and others. As they move from the middle grades to high school, students will need to think more deeply about how we can manage technology so that we control it rather than the other way around. There should be opportunities to confront such issues as the consequences of using robots to produce goods, the protection of privacy in the age of computers and electronic surveillance, and the opportunities and challenges of genetic

engineering, test-tube life, and medical technology with all their implications for longevity and quality of life and religious beliefs.

BACKGROUND

In the past, the use of technology in the social studies classroom has been minimal at best (Becker, 1986). Pre-service technology instruction for potential social studies teachers has primarily focused on the information taught in early technology courseswork, with little or no additional instruction or modeling being provided. In addition, if and when supplemental instruction is provided, it is often provided by a methodology professor who is focusing his/her attention on preparing students to take certification examinations, or who generally has little knowledge or understanding of the use of technology beyond the use of chalk or a periodic PowerPoint presentation. Research has found that there has been doubt that the integration of technology will improve Social Studies education in any significant way (Martorella, 1997; Pahl, 1996; Shaver, 1999; White, 1997). Conversely, research has been done as well on how to rectify this in Social Studies methods classes. Specifically, Mason et.al. challenged Social Studies methods teachers with the following guidelines to integrating technology to prepare teachers:

1. Extend learning beyond what could be done without technology.
2. Introduce technology in context.
3. Include opportunities for students to study relationships among science, technology, and society.
4. Foster the development of skills, knowledge, and participation as good citizens in a democratic society.
5. *Contribute to the research and evaluation of social studies and technology.* (Mason, Berson, Diem, Hicks, Lee, & Dralle, 2000)

In addition, the National Council for Social Studies (NCSS) released a position statement on media literacy reaffirming the need for a re-thinking of Social Studies education. The NCSS affirms:

The 21st century world is media saturated, technologically dependent, and globally connected. We live in a multimedia age where the majority of information people receive comes less often from print sources and more typically from highly constructed visual images, complex sound arrangements, and multiple media formats. The multimedia age requires new skills for accessing, analyzing, evaluating, creating, and distributing messages within a digital, global, and democratic society. The acquisition and application of critical analysis and media production skills are part of what constitutes media literacy. The Internet and the everyday use of social networking technologies, together with the expansive growth of corporate entertainment media and the integration of popular culture, also require us as social studies educators to link participatory media literacy with civic education.

. . . what is considered acceptable text to include multiple ways people read, write, view, and create information and messages. This more inclusive notion of "legitimate texts" includes popular culture, advertising, photographs, maps, text (SMS) messages, movies, video games, Internet, all sorts of hand-held devices and information communication technologies (ICTs) as well as print. Along with analysis, media literacy involves production as students learn to create messages with different media and technology. Students should be presenting their research and learning through interactive multimedia presentations, as Internet blogs, videos, podcasts, etc. (National Council for the Social Studies, 2009)

This renewed focus by the NCSS and more readily available resources will hopefully facili-

tate a change in how pre-service Social Studies teachers are taught to integrate technology in their methods classes.

Levels of Integration

Not all integration of technology into teaching is equal in purpose or effectiveness, nor is there one specific formula on how to integrate technology that applies to all instructional situations. It is the responsibility of each individual instructor to make an informed decision about not only *how* they are going to integrate technology into their teaching, but also *why* they are doing so. Simply using "technology for technology' sake", or in other words, using technolgy just because you can isn't a good enough reason. The integration of technology into instruction should enhance the instructional experience, be invisible in the instructional process, and not detract from the proposed learning.

There are many different bodies of research that deliniate levels of technology integration such as LoTi (Moersch, 1995) and Type I/Type II applications (Maddox, 1984). There has also been specific levels of integration defined for Social Studies instruction (Bolick, Berson, & Coutts, 2003). However, the authors prefer defining two different approaches or levels of integration of technology into instruction. In the first approach, the teacher-centered approach, the teacher uses technology for professional development. Conversely, the second approache of integration is student-centered. In addition, the second approach breakes down into two levels: in the first, the teacher creates resources for student use in the classroom, and in the second level, the students create resources for use in the classroom.

Teacher-Centered Approach: Teacher Uses Technology for Professional Development

Technology resources provide rich opportunities for professional development. Teachers can find stay current in their content area, stay connected with collegues or professional organizations, or to acquire new skill sets. With the ubiquity of the World Wide Web and the plethora of information seemingly available on any subject, every teacher should be able to personally integrate technology at this level. The real question isn't *if* teachers should do it, but instead why wouldn't they?

Learner-Centered Approaches, Level One: Teacher Creates Technology Resources for use in the Classroom

As the approach of integration moves from a teacher-centered to student-centered, the first, and most natural, level of integration is one in which the instructor creates or integrates technology resources to enhance the learning experience of the student. This can be done by creating something as simple as a PowerPoint to create a lecture or as complex as creating and producing podcasts or videos for use outside of class. Providing these diverse resources also takes into account the different learning preferences of students and gives multiple entry points to the content.

Learner-Centered Approaches, Level Two: Students Create Technology Resources for use in the Classroom

The second level of learner-centered integration isn't necessarily as natural to the teacher as the first, but it does provide the opportunity for very rich learning experiences for the students. In this level, it is the students, *not the teacher*, who create the technology resources for integration in the classroom. Having the students create their own technology resources not only immerses them in

the content, but by creating resources that others will also view, students become accountable for the qualitiy of their work to their peers in addition to the teacher.

TYPES OF TECHNOLOGY TO INTEGRATE

There are numerous technologies that can be integrated into teaching, and this chapter in no way could cover them all. With that in mind, the authors decided on the obvious inclusion of audio and video resources, and included one technology type (simulations) that especially lends itself to the field of Social Studies, and another technology type (interactive white boards) that is currently being implemented more widely. The list of resources is in no way meant to be comprehensive, but it does represent some readily accessible resources that could be easily integrated into a Social Studies classroom.

Audio

Audio has long been used in classrooms as a way to engage students and to give them experiences beyond the teacher lecturing. Integrating audio in the classroom can be more than just listening to historical speeches. Instructors and students alike can create podcasts on any topic and not only share them with the others in the classroom, but they can also be shared with a worldwide audience. The following lists give some ideas of differing types of audio recordings that can be used both inside and outside the classroom.

Podcasts

Podcasts are locally downloadable audio broadcasts. The term, podcast, actually comes from the joining of the terms "**P**layable **O**n **D**emand" and "broadcast". Podcasts give the listener the opportunity to automatically download new "episodes" of a selected podcast and listen to them when they have the time to do so. The portable nature of these recordings, along with the prevalence of portable music players make podcasts an especially interesting way to integrate technology in the classroom.

Selected Podcasts for the Social Studies classroom (in addition to these, there are numerous others listed in the iTunes podcast directory):

- Education Podcast Network (http://epnweb.org/index.php?openpod=11#14)
- This is a repository of podcasts on any number of subjects. It is important to realize that anyone can submit their podcast feed here, and the content is not varified or monitored. You may also encounter a podcast that hasn't been updated recently.
- Speaking of History (http://speakingofhistory.blogspot.com)
- An excellent collection of history podcasts created by Mr. Eric Langhorst, an 8th grade history teacher in Liberty, Missouri. The site is often updated and has a variety of resources.
- The History Faculty (http://www.thehistoryfaculty.com)
- This collection of podcasts is collected and maintained by a group of university-based historians and faculty members. There is a broad selection of podcasts over not only general history, but also based on the history of different countries.
- The 60-second Civics Podcast (http://www.civiced.org/index.php?page=60_second_civics_podcast)
- This is a daily podcast aimed at quick lessons on the Nation's government, Constitution, and history. It is produced by the Center for Civic Education.
- The White House Podcasts (http://www.whitehouse.gov/podcast)
- An official collection of not only the weekly addresses of the President of the United

States, but also addresses of the First Lady and White House press briefings.

- Historical Podcasts (http://sites.google.com/site/historicalpodcasts/)
- A collection of history podcasts put together, as the site states, "for no other reason than we like history podcasts." It contains a number of podcasts about historical figures rather than events.
- Colonial Williamsburg Past & Present (http://www.history.org/media/podcasts.cfm)
- This website is continually updated not only with podcasts about colonial life, but it also features electronic field trips and other video and multimedia resources.
- Stuff You Missed in History Class (http://history.howstuffworks.com/stuff-you-missed-in-history-class-podcast.htm)
- A quirky collection of podcasts on history in pop culture. They track down everything from historical references in TV shows to the top 10 executions during the reign of Henry VIII.

Historical Recordings

One of the great opportunities afforded by today's technologies to teachers is the opportunity to use so many primary resources. Historical recordings in the classroom are just one example of how, by integrating technology, a teacher can make the learning experience richer for students.

- Historical recordings available for the Social Studies classroom:
  ○ Library of Congress American Memory Project Audio Collections (http://memory.loc.gov/ammem/browse/ListSome.php?format=Sound+Recording)
  ○ A directory listing of all the different audio collections in the Library of Congress American Memory project.

- ○ Great Speeches in History (http://epnweb.org/index.php?request_id=2099&openpod=11#anchor11)
- ○ This collection is ''devoted to great thinkers, statesman, and other public orators.''
- ○ American Rhetoric (http://www.americanrhetoric.com/speechbank.htm)
- ○ This online speech bank contains everything from induction speeches to the Rock 'n Roll Hall of Fame to the greatest political speeches of the modern era.
- ○ History and Politics Outloud (http://www.hpol.org/)
- ○ This collection is from Michigan State University and is part of the "Historical Voices" funded by the National Endowment for the Humanities.
- ○ History Channel Speech Archive (http://www.history.com/static/sitemap/audio/1.html)
- ○ The title says it all! A comprehensive list of audio recordings maintained on the History Channel's website.
- ○ The American Presidency Project (http://www.presidency.ucsb.edu/media.php)
- ○ Not only does this contain a vast collection of audio pertaining to the Presidency of the United States, but it is also a comprehensive website on the subject. It contains over 88,000 documents on the Presidency.

Video

Much like audio, video can also add a richness to instruction in a Social Studies classroom. Instead of simply reading about Ronald Reagan's speech at the Berlin Wall, students can watch it. And much like podcasts, students and instructors have the opportunity to create vodcasts, or video podcasts.

Vodcasts

A vodcast is simply a ''video podcast.'' They are simple to create, and with the advent of today's portable video players and smart phones, have become almost as prevalent as their audio counterparts. To find vodcasts, one need simply to go to the iTunes store and search the podcast directory for the desired subject. Many podcast subcriptions contain both audio and video episodes. One example of a vodcast is found on the Colonial Williamsburg website (http://www.history.org/media/videoPlayer/index.cfm?cat=vodcast).

Historical Video

We are fortunate to live in an era when so much of what happens is recorded. And while we don't have video of Lincoln giving the Gettysburg Address, we do have access to many other great moments in history. Showing these primary source videos in class not only can be used to put students ''in the moment'' and illustrate a point, but could also be used to gain attention at the beginning of a lesson.

- • Historical video available for use in the Social Studies classroom:
- • Library of Congress American Memory Project Video Collections (http://memory.loc.gov/ammem/browse/ListSome.php?format=Motion+Picture)
- • A directory listing of all the different video collections in the Library of Congress American Memory project.
- • History Channel Video Archive (http://www.history.com/static/sitemap/videos/a-1.html)
- • A comprehensive list of video recordings maintained on the History Channel's website.

- The March of Time (http://www.thoughte-quity.com/video/home/mot.do)
- An extensive repository of historical newsreel and television documentary content.
- Encyclomedia History Videos (http://www.encyclomedia.com/history.html)
- A vast collection of historical videos including everything from early commercials to news reports and silent movies.
- EASE History (http://www.easehistory.org/index2.html)
- A collection of historical video that examines U.S. history through the lens of presidential campaign ads.
- United States Holocaust Memorial Museum (http://www.ushmm.org/research/collections/filmvideo/)
- This collection contains over 1,000 hours of video footage dealing with the Holocaust and related topics in European history.

Simulations

Simulations are an extremely powerful instructional strategy. Their power comes from the ability to allow the participant to practice without penalty. While used widely to do things like train pilots, astronauts, and law enforcement officials, they can be just as powerful in a Social Studies classroom. Many students have benefitted from participating in activities such as a mock Congress. In addition to classroom-based simulations, there are some computer-based simulations that can be integrated into the classroom.

Real Lives

Real Lives (http://www.educationalsimulations.com/) is an extremely robust simulation that allows the user to take upon themself the persona of a person born somewhere in the world. Using data from sources like the World Health Organization, the user is ''born'' into a new life and must make all the decisions, socially, politically, economically, as

well as personally, that this ''life'' would have had to make. According to their website, Real Lives® ''is a unique, interactive life simulation game that enables you to live one of billions of lives in any country in the world. Through statistically accurate events, Real Lives® brings to life different cultures, human geography, political systems, economic opportunities, personal decisions, health issues, family issues, schooling, jobs, religions, geography, war, peace, and more!''

Oregon Trail

Many remember fondly the fun had as the wagon train moved westward. Oregon Trail (http://www.broderbund.com/p-56-oregon-trail-5th-edition-pc.aspx) is the original computer-based simulation about the movement of the pioneers across the plains. As with other simulations, the user makes all the decisions for their persona, and must suffer the consequences of those decisions. Whether hunting buffalo, turning over the wagon as it crosses the creek, or dying of dysentery, this game is a crowd pleaser. If a teacher really wants to, a search will yield the opportunity to buy some of the sequels to this game such as: The Amazon Trail or Westward Ho!

You are there: Western Civilization/World History Simulations

This free collection of primarily text-based simulations (http://www.wadsworth.com/history_d/special_features/ext/westciv_sims/) gives the learner the opportunity to explore everything from Ancient Greece to the Middle Ages to WWII and Postimperialism. Included in the website are instructor manuals for each specific simulation that include not only explanations and details about the simulation, but also give key concepts and have quizzes.

Interactive White Boards

Interactive white boards, whether they be a SmartBoard (http://www.smarttech.com/), Promethian (http://www.prometheanworld.com/) or some other brand, are perhaps the technology most rapidly being adopted in classrooms today. More than simply a projected computer screen, interactive white boards give users the opportunity to interact directly with content literally with the touch of a finger. Whether the activity is designed for one board or the other, the ideas remain the same and can be implemented in the classroom.

- Interactive White Board resources available for use in the Social Studies classroom:
  - The Simply Curious Wiki (http://simplycurious.wikispaces.com/whiteboard) Dr. Susan Stansberry of Oklahoma State University has a comprehensive website that includes ideas for integrating interactive white boards for all different age groups.
  - The Smart Lesson Exchange (http://exchange.smarttech.com/index.html#tab=0)
  - This searchable lesson plan repository is full of activities for all age groups and content areas. Smart Notebook files accompanying the activites are available for a free download.
  - Engaging Learners the SmartBoard Way (http://eduscapes.com/sessions/smartboard/)
  - An excellent, comprehensive resource that not only teaches someone how to use a SmartBoard, but also how to manipulate existing activities found on the Internet.
  - Interactive Internet Resources (http://www1.center.k12.mo.us/edtech/resources/SBsites.htm)

  - The Center School District's website of interactive websites and activities by content area.
  - Lee's Summit Technology Integration: Smart Board (http://its.leesummit.k12.mo.us/smartboard.htm)
  - A repository of SmartBoard resources including everything from interactive websites that can be displayed and used on the SmartBoard to places to download pre-made activities.

AREA-SPECIFIC RESOURCES AND IDEAS

As a curricular area, Social Studies breaks down to nine separate sub-content areas: U.S. History, World History, Government, Civics, Geography, Economics, Anthropology, Sociology, and Psychology. Each of these areas has numerous different opportunities for integrating technology, of which a few are highlighted in the following sections.

General Social Studies

- The National Council for Social Studies (http://www.socialstudies.org/)
- As the official website of the NCSS, this page is full of resources including everything from information on professional organizations, conferences and publications to grant information and national standards.
- International Center for Education Statistics (http://nces.ed.gov/)
- Maintained by the U.S. Department of Education Institute of Education Sciences, this website contains data from national surveys, fast facts, annual reports, and school district demographic information. It also includes a Kids Zone that includes the

opportunity graph information, participate in surveys or make statistical comparisons.

- The Discovery Channel (http://dsc.discovery.com/)
- A rich repository of not just information on what programs are airing on the channel, but it also has video and news archives in areas like history and archaeology, as well as educational games.
- Teachers Helping Teachers Social Studies Resources (http://www.pacificnet.net/~mandel/SocialStudies.html)
- This website contains ideas and resources for all content areas. While the ideas are not all computer technology-based, they can easily be adapted for use with tools like interactive white boards.
- The Library of Congress (http://www.loc.gov)
- Our Nation's repository of everything from audio to video and beyond. It also includes links to current exhibits, resources for children and families, educators, librarians and researchers.
- Teaching Today's Integrating Technology into Social Studies Ideas (http://www.glencoe.com/sec/teachingtoday/subject/integrating_tech_ss.phtml)
- This website has quick and easy ideas on how to integrate technology into the Social Studies classroom. It includes quick lesson plan ideas.
- The Nation's Report Card (www.nationsreportcard.gov)
- This is the official website of the results from the National Assessment' of Educational Progress. It has information for not only educators and students, but also parents and policymakers. It also breaks down the statistics by content area.
- National Geographic (http://www.nationalgeographic.com)
- This site is everything you would expect from National Geographic. A sensory-rich environment that is overflowing with resources ready to be integrated into any classroom's curriculum. There are photos, videos, educational games and so much more.

U.S. History

- The American memory Project at the Library of Congress (http://memory.loc.gov/ammem/index.html)
- A repository of everything from audio to video and beyond. It also includes maps, and information on everything from culture, religion and dialects. Educators will also find an extensive Teacher's Resource page.
- The History Channel (http://www.History.com)
- Much like any other network's website, the History Channel website has information on current and upcoming programming. However, beyond that there are extensive audio and video archives that can be easily integrated into any Social Studies curriculum.
- The Congressional Record (http://www.gpoaccess.gov/crecord/)
- The official record of the Congress of the United States. It is published daily when Congress is in section.
- The Animated Atlas (http://AnimatedAtlas.com)
- The Animated Atlas illustrates large chapters of American history quickly using animated maps. It is very simple and easy to use.
- The Journal of American History podcast (http://www.journalofamericanhistory.org/podcast/)
- This podcast includes interviews with authors discussing the topics of their work published in the Journal of American History.

World History

- Learn Out Loud World History Podcasts (http://www.learnoutloud.com/Podcast-Directory/History/World-History)
- A directory of podcasts dealing with World History. Included are topics such as European civilization, world religions and authors from organizations like the BBC and PBS.
- World War II History (http://wwarii.com/blog/)
- A growing archive of information on World War II. It includes image galleries, timelines, and podcasts as well as pages on historical figures.

Government

- The White House (http://www.whitehouse.gov)
- The official website of the White House and the President of the United States. It includes history of the office and house as well as audio, video and image archives.
- The Supreme Court (http://www.supremecourt.gov)
- The official website of the Supreme Court of the United States. Comprised mainly of information on the day-to-day business of the Court, it also has some information on the history of the Court, its rulings, and its justices.
- The House of Representatives (http://www.house.gov)
- The official webiste of the U.S. House of Representatives. It contains all pertinent information about the House and its members, but it also has a ''Kids in the House'' page that includes activities and Teacher resources.
- The United States Senate (http://www.senate.gov)
- The official website of the United States Senate. This website is primarily for the business of the Senate. It does have some information on the history of the Senate and its votes, but no teacher resource page exists.
- American Bar Association (http://www.abanet.org/)
- The official website of the American Bar Association. The information here about attorneys and legal matters would make a great contribution to any government class.

Civics

- First Amendment Center (http://www.first-amendmentcenter.org/)
- Maintained out of the First Amendment Center at Vanderbilt University, this web site is a comprehensive repository of everything dealing with the First Amendment: stories in the news, commentary and analyses by experts, and other related materials.
- The Bill of Rights Institute (http://www.billofrightsinstitute.org/)
- An excellent site with everything anyone would ever need to know about the Bill of Rights. Included in the website are both teacher and student pages as well as other games and activites.
- C.I.R.C.L.E. (http://www.civicyouth.org/)
- The official website of the Center for Information & Research on Civic Learning and Engagement. This website is full of facts, figures and statistics, but it also breaks down research topics into things like K12 Civics Education and Concepts of Citizenship.
- The James Madison Foundation (http://www.jamesmadison.com)
- The purpose of the James Madison foundation is to improve teaching about the United States Constitution in secondary schools. Included in the website are les-

son plans and other resources created by current James Madison Constitutional Scholars.

- Civitas (http://www.civnet.org/index.php)
- This website is the home of an online community of civics educators, scholars, policymakers, and the like. It has image and video repositories as well as information on grants.
- We the People Program (http://www.wethepeople.gov/)
- This website is dedicated to the strengthening the teaching, study and understanding of American History and culture. Not only is there information on grants, but there is also access to the Picturing America project.
- Legal and Constitutional Studies Podcast (http://itunes.apple.com/us/podcast/legal-constitutional-studies/id306177744)
- This podcast is produced by the American Enterprise Institute for Public Policy Research and examines the legal and constitutional aspects of current policies.

Geography

- Library of Congress American Memory Project Map Collection (http://memory.loc.gov/ammem/browse/ListSome.php?format=Map)
- This website provides access to the map collections in the Library of Congress. Included are such things as Civil War maps, maps of the Louisiana Purchase, maps of the National Parks, and early railroad maps.
- A View from the Top (http://www.dirjournal.com/articles/view-from-top/)
- This website has images of the views from some of the world's tallest skyscrapers.
- Google Earth (http://www.google.com/earth/index.html)

- When you integrate Google Earth into your curriculum, you have the whole world in your hands—literally!
- National Council for Geographic Education (http://www.ncge.org/i4a/pages/index.cfm?pageid=1)
- Not only is this the official website for the council, but it also includes lesson plan ideas, geography club activity ideas, and information on the National Geography Challenge.
- The Animated Atlas (http://AnimatedAtlas.com)
- The Animated Atlas illustrates large chapters of American history quickly using animated maps that include geographic features. It is very simple and easy to use.

Economics

- National Council for Economic Ecuation (http://www.councilforeconed.org/)
- While this is the official website of the NCEE, it also includes over 1,200 lesson plan ideas as well as an online personal finance game.
- Economic Policy Studies podcast (http://itunes.apple.com/us/podcast/economic-policy-studies-at/id306177739)
- Created by the American Enterprise Institute, this podcast discusses the functioning of free economies. Related topics include things like monetary policy, tax and fiscal policy, and financial services.

Anthropology

- Social and Cultural Studies podcast (http://itunes.apple.com/us/podcast/social-cultural-studies-at/id306177724)
- Another podcast reated by the American Enterprise Institute, this podcast discusses topics such as religion, education, social welfare, and other cultural issues.

- Oxford University Anthropology podcast (http://itunes.apple.com/WebObjects/MZStore.woa/wa/viewPodcast?id=381703011)
- This podcast is presented as part of Oxford University's iTunes U offerings. Covering a wide array of topics, it features recordings from the School of Anthropology and Museum Ethnography.

Sociology

- Sociology podcast (http://deimos3.apple.com/WebObjects/Core.woa/Browse/cornell-public.1638119144.01638119149)
- Available as part of Cornell University's iTunes U offerings, this podcast addresses questions about how the social world is organized and how it is changing.
- Introduction to Sociology podcast (http://deimos3.apple.com/WebObjects/Core.woa/Browse/southwest.tn.edu.1794722957.01794722959)
- This podcast was created as a part of Southwest Tennessee Community College's iTunes U offerings. It serves as an excellent introduction to the field of Sociology as a whole, its concepts, methods, theories, and theorists.

Psychology

- Psychology in Everyday Life: The Psych Files (http://itunes.apple.com/WebObjects/MZStore.woa/wa/viewPodcast?id=215516451)
- This is a collection of both podcasts and vodcasts exploring how the concepts covered in psychology apply in everyday life.
- Great Ideas in Psychology Podcast (http://deimos3.apple.com/WebObjects/Core.woa/Browse/missouristate.edu.1860240119.01860240122)

- Created as a part of Missouri State University's iTunes U offerings, this podcast discusses the greatest ideas that have come from the field of Psychology. Sample topics include Sigmund Freud, Motivation, Multiple Intelligences and Personality.

INTEGRATION EXAMPLES

While these resources may be beneficial, they of themselves don't necessarily provide ideas on how to integrate them into Social Studies instruction. The following are examples of how select teachers have taken some of these resources and used them to create new integrated instructional experiences in their classrooms.

SMART Boards, Digital Cameras, and Being There. . .

Mr. Joseph is a 5th grade teacher. He had been looking for a way to inspire his students to think about what it must have been like to actually be a participant in history. He gave his students an assignment requiring them to use digital cameras and PowerPoint© to produce presentations having historical or geographical themes. As part of the assignment, students would use the Interactive Smart Boards to make visual presentations of their work, as well as use as an Internet resource. Here are some of the results.

One group of students took digital pictures of themselves, and then using photo editing software, digitally inserted themselves into pictures of the Boston Tea Party. The students wrote stories about their adventures when, dressed as Indians, they dumped English tea into Boston Harbor. They detailed the events with pictures of themselves in Indian clothing and, of course, arrows with bubble statements of "that's me" showing themselves as characters in the Tea Party.

Another group used the same concepts, but placed themselves as characters in both the signing of the Declaration of Independence and the writing of the Constitution.

A third group placed themselves at Yorktown, and the surrender of British forces under Lord Cornwallis. They displayed several artworks showing Cornwallis and themselves as onlookers in the audience. Their essays told of Cornwallis shame at his defeat, and even indicated that he couldn't believe colonials had defeated him.

The fourth group took a different approach and placed themselves as mountain climbers scaling K2 and climbing mountains in Antarctica. Their essays told about the hard work involved in the climb, and how cold they were. One of the students inserted his own picture over the face of one of the climbers placing a red flag on the top of K2.

While the activity was relatively simple in nature, the use of technology has enabled students to view the world, and its history, in a much different perspective than was possible even 5-10 years ago. Students are more comfortable using technology, and having the ability to manipulate existing materials enabled each of them to better understand significant events and wondrous places that they could only dream of a short while ago.

How Exactly does one Interview George Washington?

Ms. Ball is a first year History teacher. During her group's planning meeting she begins to think about the upcoming assignment for the students to write a biographical paper about an influential American in history. While she understands the necessity of learning to research and write, she wants to do something to make the assignment more exciting and meaningful. She decides to have the students still research an influential American in history, but instead of having them write a biographical paper, the students work in groups of two to write a scripted interview with that historical figure. The students then recorded a podcast acting out the scripts they wrote.

One group researched George Washington. In their podcast not only did they interview him about the Revolutionary War and being the first President of the United States, but they also asked him about his wooden dentures and whether or not the story about chopping down the Cherry tree was true.

Another group chose to create their podcast over Brigham Young. In their "interview," they had Brigham recount what it was like to lead a group of pioneers across the plains and the hardships they endured.

Interested in the Civil Rights movement of the 1960s, another group chose to research Rosa Parks. They enjoyed discussing what it was like the day Rosa refused to give up her seat on the bus. She was able to recount to the students what it was like to live in a time and place where segregation was the norm.

The interesting thing about what Ms. Ball did is that she really didn't change the nature of the assignment at all. Students were still researching and writing, but instead of the lesson ending there, Ms. Ball used technology to take what the students one step further and allow them to further personalize their learning and create an artifact that could be shared with others. When the assignment was over and all podcasts had been turned in, Ms. Ball posts them on her classroom blog and takes a little time the next few days to play part of each podcast to her classes. Her students were excited about getting to share their work and asked if they could create another podcast in the future.

"I Don't Even Know where Guatemala is. . ."

Mrs. Jensen was concerned that her 8th grade Social Studies students weren't grasping the differences between countries not only culturally, but also socially and economically. After some research, she comes across the Real Lives® simulation software. She installs the program on her classroom computer and decides to have her students simulate three different lives and write an essay comparing and contrasting the lives.

Students had a wide range of responses, but the most were amazed at how realistic the simulation seemed. In their essays, they said things like, "It really opened my eyes to what it could be like for people living in other countries," or "It showed me that the world is not simply our country, but includes all kinds of people in all kinds of places." Students quickly became invested in the simulated lives and quickly felt attached to the person. Students generally began their papers referring to the simulated lives as just that, simulations, but as they began to discuss their experiences, they shifted tone and began to refer to the lives in the first person: "I was a farmer," or "I wasn't allowed to go to school."

Unlike many teachers might, Mrs. Jensen didn't see Real Lives® as a video game. Instead, she recognized the power the simulation could have in her students' educational experience. She saw the opportunity to have the students experience life in another culture in a safe way and had them synthesize that experience through writing.

CONCLUSION

One of the challenges to implementing technology into teaching is that it changes so rapidly. Once a teacher becomes familiar with a particular software it seems to be ready for an update or a different software altogether. Some teachers don't have access to up-to-date softwares or Internet connections in their classrooms. Others don't have any sort of technology support or incentives for integrating technology or designing innovative lessons. However, Social Studies as a field, by nature of the diverse topics that fall under its umbrella, especially lends itself to a wide array of technologies to enhance the learning process. From primary resources like historical audio and video that provide learners the opportunity to experience moments in history almost as if in

"real time" to simulations that allow learners to experience different cultures, climates, peoples and politics, the opportunities both use existing resources and create new resources abound. Instructors and students alike have the opportunity to be both consumers and creators of content and participate in a global conversation about what they are learning and doing.

Beyond Social Studies as a field, any instructor who wants to improve the effectiveness of their instruction should consider the integration of appropriate technologies into the classroom. Lack of skill in using differing technologies can be overcome with some training, but it *can* be overcome. The same goes for a lack of knowledge about what technologies and resources are available. With a little time and research, an almost endless lesson ideas and resources as well as tools to integrate are available at the click of a mouse. And while no technology integrated into a classroom is a guarantee of better performance, it can provide a richer learning environment and multiple entry points for the students into the classroom content.

REFERENCES

Becker, H. (1986). *Instructional use of school computers: Reports from the 1985 national survey* (pp. 1-3).

Bolick, C., Berson, M., & Coutts, C. (2003). Technology applications in social studies teacher education: A survey of social studies methods faculty. *Contemporary Issues in Technology & Teacher Education, 3*(3), 1–9.

Maddox, C. (1984). Educational microcomputing: The need for research. *Computers in the Schools, 1*(1), 35–41. doi:10.1300/J025v01n01_04

Martorella, P. (1997). Technology and social studies or: Which way to the sleeping giant? *Theory and Research in Social Education, 25*(4), 511–514.

Mason, C., Berson, M., Diem, R., Hicks, D., Lee, J., & Dralle, T. (2000). Guidelines for using technology to prepare social studies teachers. *Contemporary Issues in Technology & Teacher Education*, *1*(1), 1–14.

Moersch, C. (1995, November). Levels of technology implementation (LoTi): A framework for measuring classroom technology use. *Learning and Leading with Technology*, *23*(3), 40–42.

National Council for the Social Studies. (February 2009 r.). *NCSS position statement on media literacy*. Retrieved January 21, 2011, from http://www.socialstudies.org/positions/medialiteracy

Pahl, R. (1996). Tech talk-for social studies teachers. *Social Studies*, *87*(4), 186–187. doi:10.1080/00377996.1996.9958437

Rheingold, H. (2008). 'Using participatory media and public voice to encourage civic engagement. In B W. L. Bennett (Ed.), *Civic life online: Learning how digital media can engage youth*, (pp. 97-118). John D. And Catherine T. MacArther Foundation Series on Digital Media and Learning. Cambridge, MA: MIT Press.

Shaver, J. (1999). Electronic technology and the future of Social Studies in elementary and secondary schools. *Journal of Education*, *181*(3), 13–41.

White, C. (1997). Citizen participation and the Internet: Prospects for civic deliberation in the information age. *Social Studies*, *88*(1), 23–28. doi:10.1080/00377999709603741

Chapter 25

Pre–Service Teachers' Perspectives on Learning to Teach Social Studies in a Technology–Rich Pedagogy Course

Susan Gibson
University of Alberta, Canada

ABSTRACT

Preparing new teachers for teaching with technology is a multi-faceted process. The study reported in this chapter examined the impact that immersion in two technology-enriched, pre-service social studies pedagogy courses had on the way beginning teachers approached technology use in their teaching of social studies. The study took place over two years and tracked education students through their social studies pedagogy course experiences and their practice teaching as part of their teacher preparation program then into their first year of teaching. The findings identified that the pre-service pedagogy courses did assist in increasing the education students' understanding of a variety of ways to approach the use of various technology tools as well as their willingness to use them in their teaching. However, the results also point to the importance of pre-service teachers' developing a positive attitude and a willingness to take risks with technology; of all instructors being prepared to infuse technology use in their classes in ways that fit with what is current in the schools; and of schools and mentor teachers encouraging, supporting, and modeling best practice with technology.

INTRODUCTION

A common assumption amongst educators is that the current generation of new teachers is more technologically savvy and therefore more inclined to infuse technology into their teaching. However,

a recent 2010 study of teachers' use of technology in the classroom surveyed more than 1,000 teachers and administrators and found that newer teachers were not necessarily using technology more often than experienced teachers and that most felt their pre-service program did not sufficiently prepare them for using technology or for teaching 21st century skills (Grunwald Associates, 2010).

DOI: 10.4018/978-1-4666-0014-0.ch025

Technology in schools is becoming more readily available as is the expectation by school district personnel and ministry officials that teachers are using it both to support their teaching and enhance their students' learning. These expectations are reflected in the information and communication technology (ICT) outcomes found in school curricula. Accordingly, our new teachers need to feel better prepared for this reality upon completion of their formal teacher preparation experiences.

Customarily most teacher education programs have attempted to develop pre-service teachers' technology skills through a mandatory stand-alone technology course focused on learning how to use various computer-based programs. However what we do know from the research is that to best prepare our beginning teachers for technology infusion, we must build educational experiences throughout the entire teacher education program, including the student teaching (Brush & Saye, 2009; Grove, Strudler & Odell, 2004; Lambert, Gong & Cuper, 2008). While a stand-alone technology course can assist with the development of technological skills, effectively integrating new technology into educational practice is not just a matter of learning how to use a particular technology. In addition to exposure and practice with these tools, pre-service teachers need to develop deeper understandings about how a technology rich environment can help to develop and deepen children's subject-specific knowledge (Angeli, 2004; Bai & Ertmer, 2008; Beaudin & Hadden, 2005; Belland, 2009; Brown & Warschauer, 2006; Brush & Saye, 2009; Dexter, Doering & Riedel, 2006; Magliaro & Ezeife, 2007). According to Wiske, Franz, and Breit (2005), pre-service technology education should be a "process of reflecting on how to teach and how students can learn most effectively in today's world" (p. 3). Thus pre-service teachers need to be encouraged to think about where the use of digital technologies fits into their philosophy of teaching, especially their beliefs about the nature of students and learning (Windschitl & Sahl, 2002). These opportunities to examine why, when and how to use technology are best infused while pre-service teachers are developing subject specific knowledge structures and thinking about pedagogy (Brush & Saye, 2009; Dexter & Riedel, 2003). Additionally, if Internet-based technologies are to be used to enhance 21st century skills such as problem solving, collaborating and higher level thinking, then pre-service teachers need to see these uses modeled (Brown & Warschauer, 2006; Fleming, Motamedi & May, 2007). In addition to modeling, pre-service teachers need opportunities to practice their emerging technology knowledge and skills in authentic ways in order to become more familiar with their use and to see their potential for enhancing students' learning (Jacobsen, Clifford & Friesen, 2002). This direct exposure to and practice with technology can also help them to develop self-efficacy and increase comfort with technology use (Cassidy & Eachus, 2002; Magliaro & Ezeife, 2007; Wang, Ertmer & Newby, 2004).

Subject specific pedagogy courses are a natural fit for examining the potential of various technologies for supporting and enhancing teaching and learning. The literature in the area of strategies for blending social studies pedagogy and technology is quite extensive (Bates, 2008; Brush & Saye, 2009; Doering, et al., 2009; Garcia & Rose, 2007; Hammond & Manfra, 2009; Lee, 2008; Swan & Hofer, 2006); however, much of it is focused solely on examining the technological knowledge and skill developed during the course experiences and on secondary education. More needs to be known about how helpful these courses are in preparing beginning teachers for technology use in their future classrooms, especially for elementary classroom teachers.

This chapter describes a study that examined the impact of immersion in two technology-enriched, pre-service elementary social studies pedagogy courses on the way beginning teachers approached technology use in their teaching of social studies. The study findings add to the discussion about the affects of technology-infused social studies pedagogy courses on pre-service teachers' actual classroom practice by examining the experiences of a cohort of elementary student teachers throughout their social studies pedagogy courses and in their practicum in schools, then into their first year of classroom teaching.

BACKGROUND

Pre-service teachers in the Faculty of Education at our large Canadian university are required to take one introductory technology course. All elementary education majors are also required to take an introductory social studies pedagogy course and then may take the second advanced social studies pedagogy course as an option. Over the last few years our social studies instructors have been attempting to embed the use of a variety of technologies within the two subject-specific social studies pedagogy courses in order to supplement our education students' technology experiences. Decisions about what technology experiences would be most effective for preparing our pre-service teachers to infuse technology into their teaching of social studies were made based on informal conversations with practicing teachers, on the ICT outcomes infused throughout the prescribed provincial curriculum [see http://education.alberta.ca/teachers/program/ict/programs/division/div1.aspx] and on a review of the research literature.

The provincial social studies curriculum is framed by a constructivist view of teaching and learning in which children are to be actively engaged in knowledge construction [see http://education.alberta.ca/teachers/program/social-studies/programs.aspx]. Teo, Chai, Hung and Lee (2008) argue that pre-service teachers need exposure to such student-centred pedagogy and "should be guided to become well-versed with the principles of the constructivist use of technology and be acquainted with the impact of such practices on the learning outcomes in the

classroom" (p. 170). Therefore, in the introductory social studies pedagogy course, technology is used to expand education students' knowledge and understanding of constructivism as well as developing their understanding of key social studies concepts such as citizenship, identity and diversity. Examples of technology-supported best practices using online video clips of master teachers working with elementary students help education students to identify and clarify how and why to use constructivist pedagogy. This approach to knowledge transfer develops cognitive flexibility as education students look at teaching and learning concepts and instructional issues from authentic settings and from multiple perspectives (Brown, Collins & Duguid, 1989), which are key features of a constructivist learning environment (Fosnot, 2005). Teacher tools such as rubric generators, lesson plan databases, and repositories of primary sources for teaching history are also investigated and evaluated in terms of their fit with the mandated curriculum and their suitability for supporting a constructivist learning environment. Student assignments introduce technology-supported modes of representing learning, of supporting metacognitive thought, and of deepening understanding of abstract concepts, as well as introducing the idea of technology as a mindtool (Jonassen, 2005). These assignments make use of internet-based tools such as weblogs, digital mapping, podcasts, and VoiceThreads. A class Wiki serves as the hub of the class by providing a space to host course content as well as a collaborative environment for education students to construct their knowledge and reflect on their learning.

In the advanced social studies pedagogy course, the focus shifts to modeling and developing education students' understanding of inquiry-based teaching and learning, which is the backbone of the provincial social studies curriculum. Constructivist strategies are used to reinforce the integration of online teaching tools and to create a culture of inquiry and collaborative learning (Belland, 2009; Jacobsen et al., 2002). Using internet-based tools such as Wordle, Inspiration and Glogster, education students are encouraged to represent their social studies subject matter knowledge and to share their understandings with others in the class. One assignment requires them to critically examine online sources and find multiple perspectives on a specific controversial issue drawn from the social studies curriculum then to prepare a digital scrapbook (using Zoho Notebook, Glogster. or Mixbook) to demonstrate how to use these online tools to study the issue with children. As well, two-way audio and video technology is used to bring the realities of classroom teaching into the course. At several points throughout the course, education students are connected synchronously to practicing teachers and children in elementary classrooms while social studies is being taught to demonstrate both inquiry and collaborative learning in action. One such lessons shows Grade One children using a SMARTBoard to demonstrate their understanding of the services in their community. These videoconferencing sessions allow education students to share a common observation of skilled teachers, which can then be discussed in class, as well as the opportunity to see how such a technology can be used in the elementary classroom to promote collaboration and communication (Basham, Lowrey, & Jones, 2006; Lehman & Richardson, 2007). As a final assignment, students in the class design an online, grade-specific telecollaborative project for teaching some aspect of the social studies curriculum.

INVESTIGATING THE PRE-SERVICE TEACHERS' TECHNOLOGY EXPERIENCES

Research Study: Methodology

A formal study of the influence of the technology initiatives in the two social studies pedagogy courses on pre-service teachers' teaching of social studies with technology-in-practice was begun in the fall of 2008. The research questions were: What is the nature and extent of pre-service teachers' technological knowledge and skill for teaching social studies subject matter both prior to and following their pedagogy courses, and, What influence does immersion in technology-enriched pedagogy courses have on the way pre-service teachers approach technology use in their practice teaching and in their first year of teaching?

A mixed methods design including both surveys and interviews was used. The study spanned two years and had three phases. Phases One and Two took place in 2008/2009 and Phase Three occurred over the 2009/2010 school year. The first phase of the study from September to December 2008, examined pre-service teachers' experiences with technology infusion while immersed in the two social studies pedagogy courses. The focus of this phase was on the impact of the technology infused social studies pedagogy courses on the pre-service teachers' evolving understandings about and comfort with technology use. A pre- and post-course online survey that examined the nature and extent of their technological knowledge and skill for teaching social studies subject matter both prior to and following their courses was completed anonymously by 100 course participants. Twelve volunteers were also interviewed by a research assistant about their perspectives on why, when and how to most effectively infuse technology in their teaching of social studies and on their feelings of preparedness to use those technologies in their teaching. The interviews provided greater depth and allowed for further exploration of items raised on the questionnaires (Creswell, 2003).

The second phase of the study took place over the winter 2009 term. The purpose of this second phase was to determine the impact that modeling various technologies in the social studies pedagogy courses had on the pre-service teachers' willingness to and interest in using those tools during practicum. Six of the original 12 pre-service teachers interviewed in the fall agreed to participate in this phase. Two were male and four were female.

As a part of the project, participants were provided with a laptop and a data projector to use in their classrooms during the nine week practicum. They were interviewed prior to and following the completion of the practicum. The research team also visited them once at their practicum schools to discuss their use of the technology in their teaching.

The final phase during the 2009/2010 school year tracked the technology use of three of these same participants as beginning teachers throughout their first year of teaching. The purpose of this phase was to ascertain the long-term effects of their experiences with technology integration during their pedagogy courses and student teaching. One teacher was teaching Kindergarten, one was teaching Grade Four and the third had a Grade 5/6 split class. Each teacher was interviewed at four points over the school year. During these interviews, the teachers shared their technology backgrounds, behaviours, successes and challenges, strategies, and motivators for using technology.

Simple descriptive statistics were used to analyze the questionnaire results (Trochim & Donnelly, 2007). Transcripts were analyzed with a constant comparison method. The initial set of transcripts (from Phase One) was read and segments of information (phrases, sentences and paragraphs) were marked that pertained to pre-service teachers' technology skill development and use. These segments were then labeled with codes (e.g. tools to support learning). Codes were clustered and examined for redundancy and overlap. Codes then were collapsed into categories, which were used to identify patterns and themes. These emerging themes were used to sort the data collected during all of the subsequent interviews, while also keeping an eye out for any new themes as well as irregularities (Creswell & Clark, 2007).

Research Study: Findings and Implications

Phase One

The questionnaires and interviews from Phase One identified that, for the most part, by the end of the social studies pedagogy course the pre-service teachers were feeling prepared and ready to use technology in their teaching (88% up from 44%). 97% agreed that they could think of lots of ways to use computers in teaching social studies after the courses (up from 83%). More were familiar with wikis and blogs (90% up from 28%), digital mapping and storytelling tools (74% up from 12%), audio and visual recording tools like podcasts and VoiceThread (72% up from 18%), and videoconferencing (58% up from 26%). 93% felt more comfortable with how to find quality educational web sites (up from 68%) and more saw the value in using the Internet as a news source (96% up from 83%). However, more also felt that the use of computers in their teaching would be time consuming after the course exposure (53% up from 43%) and half continued to feel nervous about using technology in teaching.

The midpoint interviews shed some further light on these findings. The pre-service teachers were able to articulate the benefits of using technology in their teaching, including enhancing children's interest in their learning, engaging children in inquiry and exploration, allowing for increased interaction in the classroom both between the teacher and the students and student-to-student, and incorporating multiple perspectives on issues through easy access to a wealth of information in a variety of formats. They were also able to identify a range of tools that would allow them to accomplish these things. However, they also talked about a number of concerns they had regarding the use of technology in their teaching. These concerns included: having to deal with technology glitches; classroom management issues; ensuring the safety of children in an online environment; having access to equipment in the schools; having a supportive mentor teacher; and, needing to learn more tools.

One additional concern raised by a few of the interviewees was a perceived lack of preparedness to teach social studies due to time "lost" while focusing on technology. Several of the pre-service teachers felt that the social studies pedagogy courses addressed technology integration in the place of social studies content. Here are some of their comments:

I do not feel prepared to teach social studies. Technology is fine, but there is a time and a place for it. I need to find out more about teaching social studies.

I do not want to spend [class] time learning about this one website or telecollaborative approaches. Tell me about it, and maybe I'll figure it out on my own, but I am here to learn about other elements of teaching social studies.

However another had this to say:

I have never been so exposed to so much technology [as in this social studies course], which is great... The assignments are great, because if you do not have the technology in the classroom, it is still something you can do without the technology, but if you do have it, it will enrich their [the children's] learning.

In summary, the social studies pedagogy courses appeared to have provided the pre-service teachers with both knowledge of and skill with a number of technological tools to for supporting their teaching of social studies, however, many continued to lack confidence in their ability to actually use these tools in their teaching during their upcoming student teaching experience in the schools.

Phase Two

Analysis of the information provided in the three interviews with the six participants during their student teaching term points to the following results. In the initial interview before the student teaching round began, five of the six student teachers talked about feeling prepared and ready to use the laptop and data projectors provided through the study in diverse ways as they began their practice teaching. One was still feeling quite reticent about technology use.

All six of the schools where the students did their practice teaching were in smaller and, in several cases, rural school districts. All of their schools had limited access to technology and none of their classrooms had wireless access to the Internet. The only computer available in each classroom was on the teacher's desk. School labs were available in each case but scheduling was limited, Internet access was slow, and many labs were outdated.

All of the mentor teachers were making limited to no use of computers in their teaching. As noted by one of the participants,

My experience of going into the classroom is that nothing seems to be touched. We go into the computer lab, and nothing is really utilized the way I think students need to learn technology... The teachers were petrified of the SMARTBoard. They were scared to use them. The school had two SMARTBoards and they never even touched it. So I saw the technology, but was not in reach of it.

While none of the mentor teachers refused to let the student teachers use technology in their teaching, they also did not encourage its use nor make suggestions for further use beyond what the student teachers wanted to try.

The student teachers mainly used the laptop and data projector provided to plan lessons and units, to create a class wiki, to show the children pictures captured from the web, to provide the children with access to websites related to topics under study, to play online games, to show videos, and for graphing, poster design and digital mapping activities.

All of the student teachers were able to see a number of benefits for the children's learning arising from the use of the laptop and data projector in their teaching including: the children's increased excitement and interest in what was being taught; the ability to make the children's learning more concrete; the ability to extend and relate learning to the children's worlds; the ability to increase the children's feeling of controlling their own learning; the ability to meet the needs of visual learners; and, the opportunity for increased communications between the teacher and the children and between the home and the school.

The student teachers also encountered challenges as they attempted to try out a variety of technologies in their teaching. One that they didn't anticipate was the level of school district restrictions on access to the web, to email and to connecting their personal laptops to the school network. They found that they often had to spend time at home at night caching sites and video clips that they wanted to use in their lessons. Other challenges included: inaccessible and/or slow Internet access in the classrooms and in the children's rural homes; classroom management issues, particularly in a lab setting; outdated applications, computers and data projectors in schools; the children's deficient computer skills; computer lab booking issues; and, the lack of technical support in the schools. Many of these concerns had correctly been identified in the survey and interview responses in Phase One.

The student teachers talked about being on their own when glitches occurred so they had to learn to "think on their feet" and try to develop strategies for addressing some of the technical challenges they encountered. They came to understand that to integrate technology successfully in their lessons required careful preparation and planning especially "always having a back up plan."

I learned that sometimes when you have a spectacular lesson nothing works and you have to pull the lesson out of thin air and do it without technology.

They were surprised by the amount of time outside of classroom teaching that it took to prepare to use the technology. Despite the fact that the student teachers encountered many challenges with their attempts to integrate technology during their student teaching, for the most part, they kept a positive attitude.

Additional benefits from this project were felt by the school communities in which the pre-service teachers completed their student teaching both in terms of the children's learning and of the mentor teachers' learning about a variety of technologies.

The other teachers at my mentor school had never heard of any of these tools - the wiki, Wordle, they were all new to them. I am enjoying being able to share them with other teachers.

One student teacher shared his knowledge of wikis with his mentor teacher and was pleased to hear that the mentor teacher intended to continue to work with the class wiki after the practicum was finished.

In sum, even though the schools were not using many of the digital tools that student teachers were exposed to in their social studies pedagogy courses, all but one of the student teachers still felt that it was beneficial to have had the experience with the technologies that they did in their social studies pedagogy courses prior to their student teaching and they were pleased that they got to try out some of what they had learned about. The student teacher who was reticent about technology use at the beginning of the practicum did not change his mind.

Phase Three

Data collected in the interviews with the three beginning teachers, all of whom were female, showed that the positive attitude toward technology integration and the ability to trouble shoot and problem solve developed during their student teaching carried over into their first year of teaching where they continued to investigating the use of a variety of tools. Two of the three displayed more confidence in their ability to 'figure things out' but all three continued to grow in their abilities to work with the technology over the school year. They all demonstrated flexibility and adaptability to changing circumstances, and a willingness to take risks. Their motivation for incorporating technology into their teaching was based on a number of factors including: having a supportive learning environment in their school; having opportunities to watch other teachers model technology use; having access to ongoing professional development related to technology use; administrative support; collaborative and helpful colleagues; and, having access to the latest technology including high speed Internet and up-to-date hardware. The Grade Four teacher was lucky enough to have a SMARTBoard in her classroom, which she used on a daily basis, whereas the other two teachers had to rely on computer labs and the one computer and data projector available in their classroom.

The prime motivation to use technology in their teaching for these first year teachers was the positive learning response they got from their students whenever they were engaged in computer enhanced activities. All three beginning teachers stated unequivocally that effective use of technology is a powerful tool to engage students in their learning. Although they all used Powerpoint presentations and video downloads to 'hook' the students, to play class games such as jeopardy, and to present information, these teachers found the most effective student learning occurred during curricular-related online process-based and product-based tasks, such as engaging in inquiry and problem solving activities. All three thought that the best learning experiences occurred when the children used the computers collaboratively.

At times, the teachers found that their technical skills were lacking. The upper elementary teachers relied on their students to assist during computer lab time or when the technology was balky, but all the teachers readily admitted to the class when they did not know something. In doing so, they felt they modeled how to be a learner to their students and as a result, built collaborative learning communities within their classrooms. When the kindergarten class used the school's computer lab, the teacher arranged for a Grade Three class to help her students log on to the computers. She felt that this arrangement benefitted both classes.

Well they're pretty little, aren't they? And meanwhile the Grade Threes are getting a lot out of this, right? They're increasing their understanding too. How to do simple things that I don't think they knew before. Volume control on the computer. Restarting it if something's going on or refreshing pages.

All three of the teachers talked about having limited exposure to technology training in their pre-service education. Experience with SMARTBoards was one area in particular that all three mentioned was missing in their teacher education program, especially given their increasing prominence in the schools. Perhaps, as one participant indicated,

It has a lot to do with the fact that there isn't a lot of technology in our university classrooms. How many of the university classrooms have SMART-Boards? It's probably getting more, now that I'm gone. But since we [teachers] are expected to know how to use them and work with them on a daily basis it would be nice to have had that modeled to me before I came here [her school].

Two of these teachers only saw the use of technology modeled in their social studies pedagogy classes, while one also experienced it in her art pedagogy class. All three felt that they would have been even better prepared for their classrooms if they had been exposed to technology in all their pedagogy courses. One suggested that,

[We] should learn how to use technology in other courses, not just social studies. Using it in math, and health and science. But it can't be a Power-point presentation or making a Jeopardy game. Because we all know how to do that.

While all three had also taken the required stand-alone technology course as well, two mentioned that it was of little use to them since it focused on computer operations rather than teaching and learning with technology. They contended that it wasn't enough just to learn about how to use technology to support teaching in their pre-service education; they also would have liked to have more emphasis on learning how to help the children use it to enhance their learning. As one participant stated,

I think it would have been nice to have at least had some training on how to teach kids how to use a search engine or training on how to teach kids how to use certain tools. ...I know how to use most applications and I can figure my way out. If I find something I don't get, I can kind of figure it out, but that's different from using it as a teaching tool. Me being able to know how to use it is very different from me showing someone else how to use it.

Equally critical to their willingness to try the various technologies out in their teaching was having had hands-on experience through technology-based projects in their pre-service courses and having ongoing access to the online resources used in those courses (e.g., through a course wiki, blog, webpage). One teacher recommended,

Use it lots. Use it more than you think you need to because it's through that modeling that we learn how to use that technology. And as we see instructors show us how to use technology we can be more confident to use it ourselves. And if we understand a program really well, we're going to use it in our classrooms. But if we've only just glanced at it or if we haven't even seen it at all and we've just been given a website, that's nice and all, but we'll be more likely to use things that we've actually manipulated ourselves.

Decisions about what technologies to model in pre-service pedagogy courses should be based on what is currently being used in schools. As one teacher stated,

Basically, if professors know what teachers are expected to use in the classroom they should be teaching us how to use that, whether it be a SMARTBoard or a laptop or a video conferencing system. If we are expected to use them as teachers we should be trained on that in university.

Of equal importance to the three beginning teachers was the need to have exposure to strategies for dealing with technology glitches in order to help pre-service teachers develop the skills to deal with technology malfunctions on their own. They felt that knowing how to resolve issues is a key component to fostering teachers who are willing to take risks with technology integration in their classroom. They also all talked about the importance of having a "can do" attitude toward the use of technology and not being too hung up on having all the answers.

To recap, the three beginning teachers entered their classrooms with varying levels of confidence in their ability to use technology in their teaching but with a strong willingness to give it a try. They were able to incorporate technology in a variety of ways to support their teaching and enhance their students' learning over their first year of teaching. In addition to the exposure they received to the various tools in their social studies courses, they also created a supportive school environment and easy access to current technology for their success. All strongly recommended increased exposure to technology in their teacher education program.

DISCUSSION AND FUTURE RESEARCH DIRECTIONS

Our literature review identified two gaps in the existing research; one being a lack of longitudinal studies of pre-service and beginning teachers' technology use and the second being a need for further study of beginning elementary teachers' experiences learning to teach with technology. Accordingly, this research study set out to answer two questions. The first was, what is the nature and extent of our pre-service teachers' technological knowledge and skill for teaching social studies subject matter both prior to and following their pedagogy courses? Our findings showed that our pre-service teachers came into their social studies courses with limited prior exposure to technology tools for teaching and learning, and varied technological knowledge and skill. For the most part, they claimed that their technological knowledge and skill regarding tools for teaching and learning social studies subject matter was more extensive following the two pedagogy courses. They were able to envision a variety of ways to approach the use of technology in their teaching of social studies and to articulate what they saw as benefits for the children's learning arising from its use. However, one concern that arose which is of particular interest to us as social studies educators was the education students' belief that there was an overemphasis on technology in our social studies courses. Some of the interviewees perceived that the social studies pedagogy courses addressed technology integration in the place of social studies content, rather than seeing that the various technologies were being introduced as tools for helping children to learn the important

skills of social studies including researching, thinking critically and creatively, problem solving, and collaborating with others. This issue raises a number of potential questions for further research. Why is subject area knowledge perceived by pre-service teachers to be separate from knowledge of technology when the technology is used to deepen their understanding of that subject area knowledge? What is the best way to make the use of technology in our education courses seamless?

A second concern arising from our findings was the overall lack of confidence of our education students in dealing with technology-related issues. Despite the regular infusion of technology experiences that modeled a variety of tools for supporting social studies teaching and learning and frequent hands on experience working with the tools, at the end of our courses half of our education students continued to feel nervous about using technology in their teaching, particularly when it came to dealing with technology glitches. It became apparent over the duration of the study that one of the primary players in a pre-service teacher's technology education is the education student him/herself. We repeatedly heard and observed the difference that a positive attitude and a willingness to experiment had on the success of the pre-service and practicing teachers' use of technology. How do we help to instill this positive attitude toward technology in our education students? How do we help pre-service teachers to embrace uncertainty and "think on their feet" when it comes to technology use as a part of our teacher education program? Should a combination of a stand alone course focused on how the computer works and what to do when it breaks down be combined with the pedagogy courses focused on learning about tools to enhance teaching and learning or should each course deal with problem solving and trouble shooting? If the latter, do we risk loosing even more of focus on the subject area content knowledge? Future research might be directed at examining the places in pre-service teacher education programs where the focus is on developing these problem solving skills and what these experiences should look like to better prepare our education students for the realities of technology use in the classroom.

A third disquiet that arose was the lack of exposure to technologies in other teacher education course work. Indeed the participants recommended that all education professors model both the infusion of technology in their own teaching and emphasize how technology can be used most effectively to enhance children's learning. Often instructors give lack of access to technological resources (i.e. SMARTBoards) at their institution as a reason for not making more frequent use of technology in their courses. However, professors can model flexibility and adaptability for education students by using basic technology such as their own laptop (loaded with SMARTBoard applications) and data projectors in their classes. As well, it is important that instructors go beyond basic Powerpoint presentations to modeling best practice with technology as a tool for supporting interactive, engaged learning. Advice about what technologies to include in pre-service courses should be sought from practicing teachers so that what is being modeled in teacher preparation programs fits with what is being used in the schools. Providing education students with continuous access to online curricular-related resources even after courses are completed is equally as important and can be accomplished through the use of open access wikis websites and blogs. Additionally, education students could be encouraged to bring a netbook or laptop to class with the same applications being used in class to more effectively engage in collaborative learning activities. Future research could examine the longitudinal benefits of such extensive technology experience on beginning teachers' technology use.

Our second research question was: what influence does immersion in technology-enriched pedagogy courses have on the way pre-service teachers approach technology use in their practice teaching and in their first year of teaching? The students in our study were able to put some of what they learned in their social studies courses into practice during their practicum and in their first year of teaching. In addition, they demonstrated an increased willingness to use those tools during their practice teaching and as beginning teachers. However, several concerns expressed by the participants were troublesome for the researchers.

One major concern was the level of exposure to technology being provided for student teachers during their practice teaching experiences. The findings of the study point to the importance of school-based experience with technology while teachers are in training. While access to technology is becoming more widespread in many schools overall, some still lack basic technology in the classroom beyond a computer on the teacher's desk. Consequently, many teachers are not integrating technology use into their teaching. Even in cases where the technology is available there are teachers who are still reluctant to use it. It is very difficult to get pre-service teachers to buy into the value of technology infusion into their teaching if they don't see it reflected in what is happening in the classroom with children. The importance of the role of the mentor teacher cannot be over emphasized as research shows that the use of technology by the cooperating teachers positively impacts the pre-service teachers' perceptions of technology integration (Doering, Hughes, & Huffman, 2003; Strudler & Wetzel, 1999, Wang, Ertmer, & Newby, 2004). How do we ensure that our student teachers, especially those who are keen to try out new technologies, are placed in practicum settings where they receive the encouragement and support needed to develop their confidence in using technology in their teaching? How can we help mentor teachers and schools to recognize the importance of providing support and assistance for our pre-service teachers in their efforts at integrating technology into their teaching during their student teaching experiences?

A final concern raised by this study is the tendency of many school administrators and school districts to block access to valuable online learning tools. Our student teachers struggled with issues related to lack of high speed Internet access in their classrooms as well as restricted access to excellent teaching websites that they worked with in their social studies pedagogy courses. Computers and technology learning outcomes have been a part of schooling for a significant number of years now. Given the lengthy history of computer usage in schools, we were quite discouraged about the decision that many school districts seem to be making to significantly limit access to the Internet. This was both a detriment to the children in terms of doing research as well as to the student teachers who were unable to try out many of the social studies-related online tools examined and projects designed during their university classes. While it is understood that the main reason for such restrictions on access is to protect the safety of the children, future research needs to examine alternatives to blocking Internet access.

CONCLUSION

Preparing pre-service teachers for the realities of teaching with technology is a multi-faceted process that involves many partners including pre-service instructors, mentor teachers, school administrators and district personnel, and the pre-service teachers themselves. First and foremost, pre-service teachers need to move beyond a fear of the technology in order to develop a positive attitude about the benefits afforded for children's learning. Despite the fact that this generation of new teachers is known as 'digital natives' (Prensky, 2001), we cannot assume that they are knowledgeable about or comfortable with using technology to support and enhance teaching and learning.

Regular exposure to a variety of technologies in all courses throughout our teacher preparation programs is one way to build education students'

confidence with technology for learning and change their perspectives on the use of emerging learning technologies. Consequently, all pre-service teacher education course instructors need to see themselves as partners in the technology education of our pre-service teachers. Decisions about what tools to model in pre-service courses need to be made in conjunction with the schools so that what is modeled in our classes is also seen in school classrooms. Where technology is not easily accessible (i.e. SMARTBoards in the university classroom), instructors need to model flexibility and adaptability. Instructors also need to model trouble shooting and problem solving skills in order to help foster new teachers who are willing to take risks with technology integration in their own classrooms.

The schools and mentor teachers also need to see themselves as important partners in preparing beginning teachers for technology use. Schools need to be places where technology use is prevalent and effective in supporting children's learning. Cooperating teachers need to be technology mentors. As well, school administrators and districts need to revisit policies on blocking access to technology and they need to provide access to at least basic technology in every classroom rather than rely on computer labs. All in all schools and teacher preparation institutions need to work together to ensure that all of these pieces of the technology preparation puzzle fit together as one united effort if we hope to encourage our future teachers to go out to schools as beginning teachers and make effective and frequent use of technology to support and enhance teaching and learning.

REFERENCES

Alberta Education. (2005). *Social studies kindergarten to grade 12 program of studies*. Edmonton, Canada: Author. Retrieved November 18, 2010, from http://education.alberta.ca/teachers/program/socialstudies/programs.aspx

Angeli, C. (2004). The effects of case-based learning on early childhood pre-service teachers' beliefs about the pedagogical use of ICT. *Journal of Educational Media, 29,* 139–151. doi:10.1080/1358165042000253302

Bai, H., & Ertmer, P. (2008). Teacher educators' beliefs and technology uses as predictors of pre-service teachers' beliefs and technology attitudes. *Journal of Technology and Teacher Education, 16*(1), 93–113.

Basham, J. D., Lowrey, K. A., & Jones, M. L. (2006). Making use of the net: Internet based videoconferencing and online conferencing tools in teacher preparation. In Crawford, C., Willis, D. A., Carlsen, R., Gibson, I., McFerrin, K., Price, J., & Weber, R. (Eds.), *Association for the Advancement of Computing in Education Handbook* (pp. 1440–1444). Chesapeake, VA: AACE.

Beaudin, L., & Hadden, C. (2005). Technology and pedagogy: Building techno-pedagogical skills in pre-service teachers. *Innovate, 2*(2). Retrieved Nov. 10, 2010 from http://www.innovateonline.info/index.php?view=article&id=36

Belland, B. (2009). Using the theory of habitus to move beyond the study of barriers to technology integration. *Computers & Education, 52,* 353–364. doi:10.1016/j.compedu.2008.09.004

Brown, D., & Warschauer, M. (2006). From the university to the elementary classroom: Students' experiences in learning to integrate technology in instruction. *Journal of Technology and Teacher Education, 14*(3), 599–621.

Brown, J., Collins, A., & Duguid, P. (1989). Situated cognition and the culture of learning. *Educational Researcher, 18,* 32–42.

Brush, T., & Saye, J. W. (2009). Strategies for preparing preservice social studies teachers to integrate technology effectively: Models and practices. *Contemporary Issues in Technology & Teacher Education, 9*(1), 46–59.

Cassidy, S., & Eachus, P. (2002). Developing the computer user self-efficacy (CUSE) scale: Investigating the relationship between computer self-efficacy, gender and experience with computers. *Journal of Educational Computing Research, 26*(2), 133–153. doi:10.2190/JGJR-0KVL-HRF7-GCNV

Creswell, J. (2003). *Research design: Qualitative, quantitative, and mixed method approaches.* Thousand Oaks, CA: Sage Publications.

Creswell, J., & Clark, V. (2007). *Designing and conducting mixed methods research.* Thousand Oaks, CA: Sage Publications.

Dexter, S., Doering, A., & Riedel, E. (2006). Content area specific technology integration: A model for educating teachers. *Journal of Technology and Teacher Education, 14*(2), 325–345.

Dexter, S., & Riedel, E. (2003). Why improving pre-service teacher educational technology preparation must go beyond the college's walls. *Journal of Teacher Education, 54,* 334–346. doi:10.1177/0022487103255319

Doering, A., Hughes, J., & Huffman, D. (2003). Pre-service teachers: Are we thinking with technology? *Journal of Research on Technology in Education, 35*(3), 342–361.

Fleming, L., Motamedi, V., & May, L. (2007). Predicting preservice teacher competence in computer technology: Modeling and application in training environments. *Journal of Technology and Teacher Education, 15*(2), 207–232.

Fosnot, C. (Ed.). (2005). *Constructivism: Theory, perspectives and practice.* New York, NY: Teachers College Press.

Grove, K., Strudler, N., & Odell, S. (2004). Mentoring toward technology use: cooperating teacher practice in supporting student teachers. *Journal of Research on Technology in Education, 37*(1), 85–109.

Grunwald Associates. (2010). *Educators, technology and 21st century skills: Dispelling five myths*. Retrieved October 10, 2010, from http://www.waldenu.edu/Documents/Degree-Programs/Full_Report_-_Dispelling_Five_Myths.pdf

Jacobsen, M., Clifford, P., & Friesen, S. (2002). Preparing teachers for technology integration: Creating a culture of inquiry in the context of use. *Contemporary Issues in Technology & Teacher Education, 2*(3), 363–388.

Jonassen, D. (2005). *Modeling with technology: Mindtools for conceptual change* (3rd ed.). Upper Saddle River, NJ: Prentice Hall.

Lambert, J., Gong, Y., & Cuper, P. (2008). Technology, transfer, and teaching: The impact of a single technology course on preservice teachers' computer attitudes and ability. *Journal of Technology and Teacher Education, 16*(4), 385–410.

Lehman, J. D., & Richardson, J. (2007). *Linking teacher preparation programs with K-12 schools via videoconferencing: Benefits and limitations*. Paper presented at American Educational Research association Annual Conference. Retrieved September 7, 2010, from http://p3t3.education.purdue.edu/AERA2007_Videoconf_Paper.pdf

Magliaro, J., & Ezeife, A. (2007). Pre-service teachers' preparedness to integrate computer technology into the curriculum. *Canadian Journal of Learning and Technology, 33*(3), 95.

Prensky, M. (2001). Digital natives, digital immigrants. *On the Horizon, 9*(5). Retrieved June 10, 2005 from http://www.marcprensky.com/writing/Prensky%20-%20Digital%20Natives,%20Digital%20Immigrants%20-%20Part1.pdf

Teo, T., Chai, C., Hung, D., & Lee, C. (2008). Beliefs about teaching and uses of technology among pre-service teachers. *Asia-Pacific Journal of Teacher Education, 36*(2), 163–174. doi:10.1080/13598660801971641

Trochim, W., & Donnelly, J. (2007). *The research methods knowledge base* (3rd ed.). Mason, OH: Atom Dog Publishing.

Wang, L., Ertmer, P., & Newby, T. (2004). Increasing pre-service teachers' self-efficacy beliefs for technology integration. *Journal of Research on Technology in Education, 36*(3), 231–250.

Windschitl, M., & Sahl, K. (2002). Tracing teachers' use of technology in a laptop computer school: The interplay of teacher beliefs, social dynamics, and institutional culture. *American Educational Research Journal, 39*(1), 165–205. doi:10.3102/00028312039001165

Wiske, M., Franz, K., & Breit, L. (2005). *Teaching for understanding with technology*. San Francisco, CA: Jossey Bass.

ADDITIONAL READING

Cyrus, J. (2008). *Pre-service teachers' perceptions for integrating technology in content areas*. Saarbrücken, Germany: VDM Verlag.

Doering, A., Scharber, C., Miller, C., & Veletsianos, G. (2009). GeoThentic: Designing and assessing with technology, pedagogy, and content knowledge. *Contemporary Issues in Technology and Teacher Education, 9*(3). Retrieved Oct. 9, 2010 from http://www.citejournal.org/vol9/iss3/socialstudies/article1.cfm

Gibson, S., & Kelland, J. (2009). Connecting preservice teachers with children using blogs. *Journal of Technology and Teacher Education, 17*(3), 299–314.

Hammond, T. C., & Manfra, M. M. (2009). Giving, prompting, making: Aligning technology and pedagogy within TPACK for social studies instruction. *Contemporary Issues in Technology and Teacher Education* [Online serial], *9*(2). Retrieved Oct. 2, 2010 from http://www.citejournal.org/vol9/iss2/socialstudies/article1.cfm

Hixon, E., & So, H. (2009). Technology's role in field experiences for preservice teacher training. *Journal of Educational Technology & Society*, *12*(4), 294–304.

Irving, K. (2009). Preservice science teachers' use of educational technology in student teaching. *Journal of Computers in Mathematics and Science Teaching*, *28*(1), 45–70.

Kesten, A. (2007). *Computer technology and social studies: Perceptions of preservice teachers.* Saarbrücken, Germany: VDM Verlag.

Lee, J. (2008). Toward democracy. Social studies and TPCK. The AACTE Committee on Innovation and Technology (Ed.) *Handbook of technological pedagogical content knowledge for educators* (pp. 129 – 144). New York: Routledge.

Lemke, C., Coughlin, E., Garcia, L., Reifsneider, D., & Baas, J. (2009). *Leadership for Web 2.0 in education: Promise and reality.* Culver City, CA: Metri Group.

Shoffner, M. (2009). Personal attitudes and technology: Implications for preservice teacher reflective practice. *Teacher Education Quarterly*, *36*(2), 143–162.

Thiean, G. Y. (2008). Using technology as a tool for learning and developing 21st century citizenship skills: An examination of the NETS and technology use by preservice teachers with their K-12 students. *Contemporary Issues in Technology and Teacher Education, 8*(4). Retrieved Oct. 8, 2010 from http://www.citejournal.org/vol8/iss4/socialstudies/article1.cfm

Wang, L. (2009). *Preservice teachers' self-efficacy for technology integration.* Saarbrücken, Germany: VDM Verlag.

Williams, M., Foulger, T., & Wetzel, K. (2009). Preparing preservice teachers for 21sat century classrooms: Transforming attitudes and behaviors about innovative technology. *Journal of Technology and Teacher Education, 17*(3), 393–418.

Wright, V., & Wilson, E. (2009). Using technology in the social studies classroom: The journey of two teachers. *Journal of Social Studies Research, 33*(2), 133–157.

KEY TERMS AND DEFINITIONS

Education Student/ Pre-Service Teacher/ Student Teacher: All referring to students at various stages of their teacher training.

Pedagogy Course: Course focused specifically on one subject taught in schools, aimed at developing understanding of the important content of that subject and how best to develop children's understanding of that content.

Pre-Service Instructor: All individuals teaching pre-service teacher preparation courses.

Pre-Service Teacher Education: In this case refers to a four year teacher preparation program consisting of course work and two practice teaching placements totally 14 weeks.

Risk Taker: A teacher who is willing to experiment with technology.

Self-Efficacy: Pre-service teacher's belief about and confidence in their ability in to infuse technology in their teaching.

Social Studies: A subject taught in schools focused on developing learners understanding of the roles and responsibilities of citizenship.

Technology Infusion: Threading of technology use throughout one's teaching and in the experiences of learners.

Chapter 26

Knock Down the Walls, Open the Doors:
How Hybrid Classrooms can Improve Education

Kristen G. Taggart
University of Delaware, USA

ABSTRACT

Hybrid classrooms, or blended instruction, blend the traditional face-to-face instruction model with newer technologies of online learning. 21st Century students crave a more interactive learning environment, but unfortunately, today's teachers largely lack exposure to Web 2.0 technologies and technological expertise to offer such learning tools to their students. Therefore, teacher preparation programs, state departments of education, and local education authorities must improve the technical skills of teachers. Once teachers have 21st Century skills, they will be prepared to offer a more dynamic learning environment to students, including hybrid learning environments. This chapter will explore the possibility and effectiveness of utilizing hybrid-learning environments at the high school level. This will be accomplished through review of the literature, an evaluation of the educational objectives met through the implementation of hybrid learning, addressing the obstacles to implementation, and suggesting methods of improvement for teacher preparation programs, state departments of education, and local education authorities to improve the technical skills of teachers.

INTRODUCTION

Hybrid courses blend the traditional face-to-face instruction model with newer technologies of online learning (also known as blended instruction). The purpose of this chapter is to explore the possibility and effectiveness of utilizing hybrid-learning environments at the high school level. The potential use of such courses reaches the entire spectrum of high school students – those who are in need of credit recovery to graduate, those who are in the Talented and Gifted Program and seek acceleration; students with special needs who require remediation; and students who are

DOI: 10.4018/978-1-4666-0014-0.ch026

not able to attend the traditional classroom, for either medical or disciplinary reasons. Hassell & Terrell (2004) and Picciano & Seaman (2009) identify a number of benefits of online learning environments, including online assessment possibilities, employment skills, preparation for college learning environments, and financial benefits to schools. As technology continues to evolve, and more technologies make their way into the classroom, it is critical that we continue to evaluate the role and effectiveness of technology's place in the classroom.

At present, there is no standardized assessment for student's technology abilities. However, this will not be the case for long, as the National Assessment of Educational Progress (NAEP) is currently developing test items for the NAEP Technology and Engineering Literacy Assessment, to be administered in 2014. This assessment will draw heavily from the six technology standards identified by the International Society for Technology in Education (ISTE) for students in 2007; Creativity and innovation; Communication and collaboration;, Research and information fluency; Critical thinking, problem solving, and decision making; Digital citizenship; and Technology operations and concepts. Each of these has performance indicators to measure a student's fluency within each domain. As will be discussed in detail later, hybrid courses will help students meet these standards, thereby being better prepared to perform at a higher level on the 2014 NAEP Technology and Engineering Literacy Assessment.

A second goal is that hybrid environments allow students and teachers to become more familiar with online working environments. As the economy continues to expand to a global workforce, colleagues find themselves in the physical presence of each other less and less. ZDNET predicts that by 2016, 63 million American workers, 43% of the U.S. workforce, will telecommute (Schadler, 2009). Considering this change in the technology, many of our students will use their laptop as their office at some point during their career, requiring

educators to develop the skills of collaboration and professional online communication among our students. Hybrid classrooms allow students to develop skills of digital citizenship that will become increasingly important to them as they leave the k-12 learning environment.

Further, those students who chose to continue their education are likely to take at least one online or hybrid course in their post-secondary career. According to the 2010 Sloan Survey of Online Learning, student enrollment in online higher education courses increased by almost one million, with over three million students taking at least one online course during the Fall 2009 semester (Allen & Seaman, 2010). Considering this, it is in the students' best interest to have some exposure to an online learning environment prior to entering their post-secondary education.

Finally, schools may wish to increase the number of online and hybrid courses to reduce their overhead costs. Hybrid or online classes may allow a teacher to have a part-time schedule, releasing the district from higher salary rates and benefit packages. Further, courses with smaller enrollments, such as AP and upper level foreign language courses, can be taught by a teacher who is not on staff, and perhaps not even in the same region as the students. One teacher can then specialize in this course, and teach the same content in several districts, states, or even countries.

However, prior to implementation of such programs, educators must be exposed to emerging Web 2.0 technologies that will allow them to deliver the same high quality instruction online as their students receive in a traditional classroom. As such, it is critical to evaluate not only the practicality and effectiveness of such learning environments, but also the skills of today's teachers to implement a hybrid-learning environment. After a review of the literature and an examination of the obstacles to implementation, suggestions are provided to teacher preparation programs, state departments of education, and local school authorities to improve the technological prowess of today's teachers.

LITERATURE REVIEW

According to the Distance Education and Training Council (DETC), approximately eight million Americans are enrolled in distance learning courses, with enrollment increasing by approximately 25% each year (2007-08). Most of these learners have historically been adult learners engaged in enriching their professional credentials; however, as technology becomes more common, online learning is beginning to proliferate in the K-12 classroom as well. Picciano and Seaman (2009) report that in 2007-08 the number of k-12 students enrolled in online courses was approximately 1,030,000, a 47% increase from 2005-06. Distance education allows high school students to take courses not offered in their own buildings, especially AP courses and other electives. However, according to a meta-analysis conducted by the US Department of Education, "A systematic search of the research literature from 1994 through 2006 found no experimental or controlled quasi-experimental studies comparing the learning effects of online versus face-to-face instruction for K–12 students that provide sufficient data to compute an effect size" (Means, Toyama, Murphy, Bakia & Jones, 2009). Considering the limited research conducted in regards to distance learning for K-12 students, further research is needed in this area.

Before implementing a change to the curriculum, all educators, school administrators, and state officials must measure the impact such change will have on the goals of education. All educators, regardless of the grade level and content area, share common goals. "These enduring goals include creating a learning environment in which the student is comfortable yet intellectually challenged, providing current and relevant subject content in a professional manner, fostering the concept of life-long learning and leading by set-

ting examples of high standard" (Black, 2002). As society matures into the 21st Century, the concept of a "21st Century Student" has taken hold. The Partnership for 21st Century Skills identifies the key elements of a 21st Century student, including life and career skills, learning and innovation skills, information, media, and technology skills, and core subjects. Students today have instant access to information, not only when they sit in front of a computer, but on their mobile devices. The 21st century student must have a command of the core academic content, but they must also be able to master the expanding digital world. Secondary schools are still experimenting with these technologies as they seek to find a balance between absolute prohibition of mobile devices and the appropriate and effective use of personal technologies in the classroom. While school districts seek to maintain classroom management by limiting distractions from technologies, such as MP3 players and cell phones, today's student is seeking a reformed learning environment, one that embraces the technology they have grown up knowing, not shunning it. According to the Speak Up 2009 National Findings, the technology students most actively desire are: (1) social-based learning to increase collaboration between their classroom peers as well as the greater academic community, (2) un-tethered learning to increase the geographical reach of their educational experiences, and (3) digitally-rich learning environments to allow them to gain not only content knowledge, but marketable technological skills.

As educators, we must embrace the changing world, and with that the changing nature of education, including the rapid and ever-evolving nature of technology. Within the last decade, teachers and school administrators have come to recognize and embrace the improved efficiency of managerial tasks utilizing technology. Included with this are: online grade books, which have allowed frequent and instantaneous feedback regarding student achievement to the students and their parents; file sharing to allow small groups to collaborate on tasks; and classroom web pages to allow greater access "into" the classroom. This can be seen by comparing the use of technology for instruction to the use of technology for managerial tasks in the Technology in Teacher Preparation Survey (Taggart, 2010). When looking at technology for instructional purposes, most respondents indicated that they rarely used the technologies surveyed or did not have access to the technology (the exception being the ELMO projector, which has replaced the overhead projector in many classrooms). Conversely, most teachers responded that they used technology for managerial tasks, e-mail, attendance, and grade books, daily, with the exception of document sharing tools, such as Google Docs. Such success in regards to teacher and administrative productivity should serve as encouragement to those "digital immigrants" (Prensky, 2009) who are fearful of letting the technologies of the 21st Century into their classroom. Might it be possible that with improved technological training, teachers may be able to utilize technology to make their lessons more effective?

EDUCATIONAL OBJECTIVES

One technology that teachers and administrators might explore implementing in their classrooms is hybrid-learning environments. Through the blend of the traditional learning environment and an online environment, students will be able to achieve all three desired technology goals identified in the Speak Up 2009 findings: (1) social-based learning to increase collaboration between their classroom peers as well as the greater academic community, (2) un-tethered learning to increase the geographical reach of their educational experiences, and (3) digitally-rich learning environments to allow them to gain not only content knowledge, but marketable technological skills. In addition to these three, a fourth benefit is that teachers can also increase the amount of assessments, both formative and summative students are exposed to, in an effort to improve student achievement on standardized assessments.

1. Increased content driven interaction with peers

The 21st Century student spends a significant amount of time engaged in computer based activities, whether it be on the cell phone, social networking, or gaming. Should the education system be able to evolve (McDougall, 2006) to incorporate such technologies, it is possible that students will be more engaged with the content. Using a hybrid environment as a platform for learning, it is hopeful that students will "see" each other online in the "classroom" and engage each other utilizing the chat room or e-mail functions available. With these tools, students can ask for and provide assistance to their peers. This objective should be the least daunting, for both the teacher and the students, as 43 percent of American high school students communicate with their friends through online social networking sites (Speak Up, 2009). The pervasiveness of sites such as Facebook and MySpace will allow many students to have "expertise" in such environments already. Educators and other students with less experience in online social environments can utilize the knowledge of these students to improve their own understanding of the functionality of online interactions. The same report also indicated that 24 percent of high school students used technology to tutor other students, and 26 percent of students received assistance from others via social networking sites (Speak Up, 2009). As such, activities are already occurring, it seems only natural that teachers should encourage this dialogue among students, but also monitor the interactions in an online classroom setting.

2. Increased geographic reach of the classroom

While hybrid learning environments demand face-to-face time between the students and instructor(s), the fact that some of the learning is done online allows students to learn from experts located throughout the world. Further, students who are engaged in several extracurricular activities, who have afterschool jobs, or who have family obligations, often find the burden of reading a textbook too great. These students will often find themselves falling behind in the course content, regardless of their previous academic success or intellectual abilities. One method to mitigate this is to allow students to listen or to watch podcasts covering specific content from an expert in another state or country. Approximately ten percent of high school students listen to podcasts as a resource for schoolwork (Speak Up 2009). A driving force within this area, especially for the Advanced Placement student, is iTunesU. iTunesU can serve as a clearinghouse for legitimate expertise in a field of study. Here, students can download lectures from universities and colleges throughout the United States, as well as a few select K-12 broadcasts. Using the iTunesU Power Search, students can enter a topic as simple as "religion" and an array of selections is provided. However, this can be a bit intimidating to the student as well. Instead, the K-12 teacher might provide a list of suggested podcasts to the students to enhance the course content. This might also allow parents to learn along with their student, allowing parents to feel empowered to assist their child with their course work or just engage the child in dialogue of the content.

3. Increased technological skills, as set forth by NETS

Of the six ISTE National Education Technology Standards for Students, a hybrid course will seek to improve student skills in four areas; Communication and collaboration; Research and information fluency; Digital citizenship; and Technology Operations and Concepts.

a. Communication and Collaboration

Hybrid classrooms encourage students to develop their communication skills online as well as in person. This will require students to understand the appropriateness of certain "text-speak" acronyms, such as "LOL", versus professional online interactions with their instructor, their peers, and other experts the students might interact with online. It appears that since technology is so pervasive in society, technology driven communication appears less formal to our students, as that is their most common means of communication, especially via texting and chatting online. Considering this, it is critical for educators to teach the students appropriate written communication via technologies. We need to model for students how to compose a letter using e-mail, how a letter is different from a memo, and when it is appropriate to use abbreviations with professional colleagues. While technology is constantly evolving, it is unlikely that as a society we will return to hand written letters to communicate for business correspondence.

b. Research and Information Fluency

It is often assumed by educators that the "Millennials" (Oblinger, 2003) are well versed in technology. While a "Millennial" may have greater technology based skills, in so far as navigating the internet or trouble shooting basic technology headaches, such students do not possess any greater analytical skills in evaluating text than previous generations. Maintaining a hybrid-learning environment might encourage the teacher to create more research based assessments due to the release of the constraint of the school day schedule. In turn, this will expose students to various levels of credibility on the internet. As such, as the student evolves into a more eloquent researcher, he will be better equipped to do a more scholarly search for information, as well as evaluate internet sites for credibility and bias. Teachers must model for their students such skills and place parameters on web sources for research. With such open access to information as the internet provides, it is not only unrealistic to expect our students to stay away from web sites for information, but it ignores an opportunity to discuss with students the validity of data.

c.   Digital Citizenship

Creating good citizens has long been a goal of education. As technology evolves, citizenship has expanded to include digital citizenship, which Ribble, Bailey, & Ross (2004) define as, "the norms of behavior with regard to technology use." Recognizing the simplistic nature of this definition, the authors identified nine areas of digital citizenship: etiquette, communication, education, access, commerce, responsibility, rights, safety, and self-protection (Ribble, et al., 2004). While each is an important component, within the educational arena, administrators and teachers should focus their efforts on all but one of these components - commerce. In utilizing a hybrid-learning environment, teachers can educate their students not only in the course content, but also in how to be a good digital citizen.

d.   Technology Operations and Concepts

By immersing students in a hybrid-learning environment, they will be able to interact with their peers and instructor in such a fashion that will allow the student to develop skills that otherwise would have gone untrained, if the issue were not forced. To balance that, teachers must be sure that the student is assessed on his understanding of the course content, not his technological prowess. Too often, students impress teachers with ostentatious power points and video presentations, which lack content. Educators must be diligent in providing rubrics to measure the content as well as technological skills. This concept is reinforced by the Partnership for 21st Century Skills: The MILE

Guide (2009). According to this organization, one of the leading proponents for developing the skill set of the 21st Century Student, "Core academic subject mastery is a fundamental component of any 21st century skills implementation; core academic subjects are presented along with 21st century themes, learning and innovation skills, information, media, and technology skills, and life and career skills." While the course content will continue to be the focus of the hybrid course, the technology skills gained by both the teacher and the students should not be overlooked.

4.   Increased preparation for standardized assessments

Due to recent legislation, many schools and teachers must improve student achievement on standardized assessments or face restructuring. Limits of the academic calendar and the breadth of content that must be covered often force teachers to create one unit assessment for all students. Such assessments cannot differentiate to the needs of the individual student. As such, some students find these assessments quite easy while others struggle with basic concepts from the unit of study. If a teacher has a highly diversified group of students, he can create two or three forms of the same unit assessment, each of which measures the grade level expectations of the students, but also allows for remediation and acceleration questions for the appropriate students. Using an online quiz function, the instructor can offer more out of class quizzes on smaller concepts or use it as a remediation tool when a significant group of students did not understand a concept as deeply as needed. Further, the online classroom can be used to link to other practice tests and content so students may see the same content assessed in different methods. Such tools are currently available and offered almost universally by textbook publishers. In fact, sixty percent of high school students currently want to use their digital textbook for the quiz and assessment function to improve their own content knowledge and level of academic achievement (Speak Up, 2009).

OBSTACLES TO IMPLEMENTATION OF HYBRID CLASSROOMS

As is the case with all initiatives, there are obstacles to overcome. One of the more researched obstacles is the digital divide that may exist between some students. Regardless of how far we have progressed as a society, there are still many students from low socioeconomic backgrounds who do not have reliable access to computer-based technologies. Glaser (2007) identifies several "digital divides", between rural and urban, poor and rich, African-American and white, old and young, disabled and able, and developing nations and underdeveloped nations (Glaser, 2007). Similar to other gaps in education, such as the achievement gap, minorities are less likely to have reliable and consistent access to computers and internet technologies (Dickard & Schneider, 2002). However, accessibility to technology while at school is more balanced between low socioeconomic and high socioeconomic schools (Warschauer, Knobel, & Stone, 2004).

The second hurdle to overcome is getting both the instructor and the students familiar with the online learning environment. Depending on the technology skills of the instructor, this task can appear to be insurmountable. It is therefore suggested that if a school is looking to implement online or hybrid classes, that it first utilize teachers with a higher degree of technical fluency and have an implementation plan for the remaining courses that spans several academic years. This will allow some students to gain exposure in the hybrid environment, allow tech savvy teachers to work through issues, and measure the effectiveness of the program for the students.

Additionally, since there will not always be a teacher looking over the students' shoulder to ensure work is getting done and assessments are completed, it is suggested that schools begin working with a smaller group of students who are motivated to engage in hybrid learning environments. After exposure to the student body of the learning platform, the school can then begin to implement the hybrid classroom to the student body at large. This can be accomplished through a variety of means, such as an introduction or tutorial meeting in a computer lab with the students (and possible the parents as well), allowing time within the course for students to explore the online classroom without risk, and assigning more basic tasks at the onset of the course. Fortunately, this hurdle is one that is overcome rather easily, as the fluency of the teacher and students will increase with the natural progression of time.

A third obstacle to successful implementation is specific to the online component of the course. Since students will complete more assignments at home in the online learning setting, the instructor will not be physically present while students are completing such assignments. As pointed out by Albert Moore, a Mississippi student who participated in an online Japanese course, "There is no teacher to hang over our shoulders, so we have to supply our own motivation and desire to succeed in the class. .. [at the same time, this experience] provided me not only with classes I would otherwise not be able to take, but an opportunity to work with some of the most advanced technology of today, which is a learning experience within itself" (Moore, 1989). Considering this, schools must be aware that hybrid-learning environments are not appropriate for all learners, and that neither the teacher nor the students are forced to enroll in a hybrid learning environment. Instead, such environments should target students who are intrinsically motivated to complete the course of study offered. By no means does this limit the student enrollment of hybrid courses to the more academically successful students. High school students who may be behind in credits may also find the hybrid-learning environment beneficial to catching up to their peers. Hybrid learning should be looked at as one more tool available to teachers to reach and teach as many students as effectively and efficiently as possible. However, as many teachers, school administrators, and state officials are realizing, technology is not a magic bullet to cure the ails of education.

PREPARING 21ST CENTURY TEACHERS

It is clear from the research, most notably the Speak Up 2009 report, which surveyed 299,677 K-12 students, that the 21st Century student is ready for a technology based classroom, however, it appears that the teachers of the early 21st Century lack some key skills to implement a hybrid classroom. Cyrs (1997) noted that while the skills teachers attain in the classroom also transfer to an online environment, there are additional skills necessary. Ragan (2009) identified six critical competencies for teaching online: Teaching and learning; Technology Aptitude; Classroom Administration/ Management; Faculty Workload Management; Building Community; and Attitude / Philosophy. While teacher preparation programs are working on addressing such needs, the educational community also needs to address the teachers with 20th Century skills at the state, district, and building levels.

In a two month survey, which collected responses from 184 teachers, with over 80% of the respondents teaching for five years or more, it appears that teachers are not unwilling to implement technology in the classroom, but are either uninformed regarding the technologies available to them or about how to effectively use technology in the classroom (Taggart, 2010). This survey examined the exposure teachers had to technology based courses in their teacher preparation programs, their current usage of technology in the classroom, and the technologies teachers wish to learn more about. Utilizing both the Speak Up Survey (2009) and the Technology in Teacher Preparation Survey (Taggart, 2010), the following suggestions are made in an effort to improve the use and effectiveness of educational technology to increase student achievement.

Suggestions for Teacher Preparation Programs

From the survey mentioned above (Taggart, 2010), 48% of teachers were not required to take technology based courses in order to secure their teaching credentials. Fortunately, many schools are now aware of the deficit of technological skills their graduates possess. In order to become more marketable after graduation, teacher accreditation programs must increase the use of technology as a model for their students, as well as offer a program of study focusing on Education Technology. One example that schools can look to is the University of Delaware and the Minor in Educational Technology offered within the School of Education starting in fall 2010. While not unique, the University of Delaware has made great strides over the past several years to increase the course offerings in Educational Technology. Previously such offerings were limited to the Master's and Doctoral programs. The limited courses available to undergraduates, and the increasing demand of local markets to have teachers with technology skills, led the University toward offering a variety of courses. Courses such as "eLearning", "Multimedia Literacy" and "Technology and Cognition" are certain to increase the use of technology in the K-12 classrooms when these undergraduates move from the pre-service to the in-service world of education.

In addition to offering the courses in Educational Technology, the University strongly encourages the use of hybrid courses through the Sakai platform. Sakai is an open-source platform, distributed under the Educational Community License, used in over 200 universities, colleges, and schools. The platform was developed by universities to improve the communication and learning tools of the staff and can be personalized to reflect the needs and the culture of the institution (Sakai Project, 2010). At current, all courses offered at the University of Delaware are able to utilize Sakai for hybrid and distance learning environments. Sakai includes, but is not limited to, functions for online classroom chats, online quizzes and tests, grade books, RSS feeds, podcasts, and course schedule. As a part-time instructor at the University, it appears that students now have an expectation that instructors will use Sakai. Many of my students have shared their frustration when a faculty member does not use Sakai, as it is a central location for the students to see their grades, assignments, and academic calendar. All of these functions are helpful in the secondary environment as well. As the pre-service teachers are increasingly exposed to hybrid learning environments, I anticipate they will be better prepared and more willing to utilize this technology in their future classrooms for their own students.

A third suggestion for teacher preparation programs that will help model another use of technology to help reach and teach students is the use of iTunesU. This newest addition to the iTunes family of applications allows universities, colleges, and K-12 schools to upload course content, such as lectures, labs, films, and tours, both in audio and video format. At current, iTunesU is most widely used by universities, but other organizations, such as the Museum of Modern Art, PBS, and the New York Library also utilize the application to distribute academic content. With over 600 universities uploading content to iTunesU, many publically accessible, access to knowledge continues to evolve and grow. By increasing the utilization of this product at the postsecondary level, education students enrolled in courses using iTunesU will become more familiar with the application and hopefully be more at ease using similar technologies in their own future classrooms. Additionally, if teachers upload their classroom content, parents will be better equipped to assist their children at home with academic assignments, improving the relationships between schools and home.

Suggestions for State Departments of Education

With increasing emphasis on student assessment achievement, it is critical for states to find ways to improve the use of technology in the classroom, both to benefit the teacher as well as increase student understanding of the course content. Given the current financial crisis many states find themselves in, it is often difficult purchase emerging technologies to the extent needed to implement hybrid learning. However, an examination of the recent Race to the Top (RTT) winners illustrates how most of the winners of the second round of RTT states had some form of online learning involved in their application (Quillen, 2010). This is evidence that many in the policy world of education see the benefit of online and blended education for both students and teachers.

One suggestion is that states increase the use of online learning environments, as distance learning platforms as well as a place to hold hybrid course content. States can explore several options, including Sakai, Moodle, and Blackboard Academic Suite. Both Sakai and Moodle are open-source platforms, while Blackboard Academic Suite requires a subscription. Each platform is widely used throughout the world in various educational settings. Sakai is used by over 350 organizations throughout the world (Sakai Project). There are over 50,000 registered Moodle sites in over 200 countries. Over one million teachers are users in Moodle and enrollment in Moodle classrooms exceeds 18 million (Moodle, 2010). Blackboard is used by k-12 institutions, colleges and universities, and corporations throughout the world.

Regardless of the platform selected, and only one should be utilized in the state, the State Department of Education must support and maintain the technical personnel needed to begin the initiative of increasing online and hybrid courses. By having one universal system in place throughout the state, all stakeholders, state officials, school administrators, teachers, students and their parents will experience increased familiarity with the platform. At the University of Delaware, as familiarity of Sakai among the student body and faculty increased, the utilization of Sakai has also increased. During the fall 2008 semester, the University hosted two online learning platforms, Sakai and WebCT. During that semester, 571 courses utilized WebCT and 597 courses utilized Sakai. In fall 2009, only 21 courses utilized WebCT and 978 courses utilized Sakai (University of Delaware, Fall Course Sites, 2009). By the spring 2010 semester, 1226 courses were utilizing the Sakai platform, representing 40% of course sections offered (Plourde, 2010). This data allows school administrators and teachers to see how increasing awareness of the technology available and the increased familiarity with the learning platform will increase implementation over time. This is best witnessed through the Florida Virtual School (FVS).

Implemented in 1997 as, "the country's first, state-wide Internet-based public high school," (Florida Virtual School) the FVS serves K-12 students both in Florida and throughout the world, although the majority of courses are for students in grades 6-12. Today, the FVS offers courses in all four core academic areas, the arts, technology education, drivers' education, foreign languages, and 15 AP courses to students. One major goal of the FVS is to improve accessibility to an enriched curriculum to students in rural and high poverty schools. It is strongly suggested that states model their own program after the Florida model, although it is unrealistic to expect all states to have such intricate web-based learning platforms available in the next several years. However, it is reasonable to expect full implementation within the next decade.

A second suggestion is that states increase the professional development opportunities for teachers in regards to technology. Considering the pervasiveness of technology in our society, it is critical that our teachers receive consistent and effective training in educational technologies. According to the Technology in Teacher Preparation Survey (Taggart, 2010) more than half of the teachers surveyed crave professional development in the areas of webpage development and effectively using interactive whiteboards. Further, 48% want training in creating and implementing internet based lesson activities. In the same survey, a large percentage of respondents stated that they did not have access to open-source and freely accessible technologies. For instance, 61% of respondents stated that they did not have access to an online classroom environment, such as Moodle or Blackboard. It is my contention that due to the availability of open-source software these teachers are not prevented from accessing such technology, but instead are not aware of the options present to them. Similar results were found with online blogs / chat rooms, where 51% of respondents claimed to not have access to this technology. Clearly, with the abundance of free blogging sites, it is more likely that these teachers are unaware of educationally sound blogging site, such as Edublog and Wikispaces, or are uncomfortable implementing this technology as a classroom activity. Offering workshops in these areas is also cost-effective. Rarely, will a state be without an expert in one of these areas that can facilitate a series of workshops. Additionally, the professional development workshop can be recorded and distributed via iTunesU to reach a wider audience and a diminished cost. New Jersey currently has five school districts using iTunesU to distribute course content to students and professional development materials to teachers. Other states are encouraged to follow in the steps of New Jersey and begin uploading professional development content to iTunesU.

As teacher preparation programs are improving their own programs to allow more tech savvy educators to enter the workforce in the future, it is up to the states to provide training to the teachers in the classroom today. Our 21st Century students crave more interactive technologies to improve their education experience. Sadly, most teachers in the 21st Century classrooms have only 20th Century technology skills.

Suggestions for District and Building Administrators

According to the Speak Up 2009 Survey, 60% of parents identified a school website or portal as their top choice for driving student achievement. As such, it is reasonable to expect district and building level administrators place a focus on increasing online communication to all stakeholders - parents, students, and the community. It is hard to imagine a district or building not having a web site at this point, however, the effectiveness of the site as a communication tool can be called to question. A cursory examination of school district and building web sites shows an inconsistency between the layouts of the sites. That reduces the ease of navigation for parents, as they move from the district site to each building's site. An immediate and relatively easy suggestion to district and building administrators is to develop a common website template for all district sites. In addition, each teacher, content area, or grade level, should be strongly encouraged to create and maintain a web site reflecting the culture of the school and timely information pertinent to their specific students. With the increasing availability of user-friendly web design tools, such as Google Sites, EduBlogs, Class Jump, and Educator Pages, it is realistic to expect teachers to maintain timely information available for parents and students online. Hosting a hybrid classroom will go beyond the basic web site content, allowing parents and guardians to see what is going on in their student's classrooms. Parents will be able to access lesson materials, such as power points, podcasts, and class assignments, and also be able to see upcoming assessments, have links to help them review course materials with their students at home, and

contact the teacher if they are concerned regarding their child's progress.

Finally, district and building administrators need to encourage teachers to experiment with technology in the classroom. This requires administrators not to penalize teachers in observations when technical difficulties are experienced. It also requires that effective professional development and exposure to various technologies be provided. Most notably, the administrative team must encourage the use of the state-sponsored hybrid classroom environment. Students are eager for the opportunity to interact online with their peers beyond social networking sites. In fact, 47% of middle school students and 40% of high school students identified "discussing how to solve a problem with my classmates" and "helping other students with their math problems" would be most beneficial to them in math class (Speak Up, 2009). Allowing students the opportunity to discuss their content outside the normal school day will improve their ability to practice content skills at home with their peers.

CONCLUSION

The trend of technology in the classroom illustrates tremendous growth. Today's teachers frequently use technology to improve their professional effectiveness for office tasks, such as communicating via e-mail and online grade reporting and calculating. This would not have been true a decade ago. Further, more advanced technologies, such as online document collaboration tools such as Google Docs, and classroom web sites are gaining momentum. Only 7% of respondents to the Technology in Teacher Preparation Survey (Taggart, 2010) responded that they had no access to document sharing platforms, while the 49% of respondents stated they used this technology "rarely", 44% use such features weekly or daily. Considering that Google Docs was only made available in February 2007 to Google Apps users

(Google Docs), the rapid adoption of this tool is evident that as teachers and administrators become more comfortable with using the technology, online collaboration will continue to grow at an expeditious pace.

As the digital immigrants enter retirement age, and the digital natives (Prensky, 2009) constitute the bulk of the workforce, I anticipate the use of technology in the classroom will continue to increase. Today's teacher candidates take a greater number of education technology courses as undergraduates. Further, their own experiences in their high school and undergraduate studies with interactive education software, web-based lessons, and hybrid classrooms will make it more likely that the rate of technology use in the classroom will increase sharply in the coming years.

REFERENCES

Allen, I. E., & Seaman, J. (2010). *Class differences: Online education in the United States.* Sloan Consortium. Retrieved from http://sloanconsortium. org/sites/default/files/class_differences.pdf

Black, G. (2002). A comparison of traditional, online, and hybrid methods of course delivery. *Journal of Business Administration Online, 1*(1).

Blackboard Academic Suite. (n.d.). Retrieved from http://www.blackboard.com/

Cyrs, T. (1997). Competence in teaching at a distance. *Teaching and Learning, 1997*(71), 15–18.

Dickard, N., & Schneider, D. (2005). *The digital divide: Where we are today.* The George Lucas Foundation. Retrieved from http://www.edutopia. org/php/print.php?id=Art_995&template=printa rticle.php

Distance Education and Training Council. (2007-08). *Is distance education for you?* Distance Education and Training Council. Retrieved from http://www.detc.org/downloads/publications/Is%20Distance%20Education%20for%20 You%207-08.pdf

Docs, G. (n.d.). In *Wikipedia, The Free Encyclopedia.* Retrieved from http://en.wikipedia.org/w/index.php?title=Google_Docs&oldid=382349371

Education Report, 13(2). Retrieved from http://blogs.ubc.ca/distanceteaching/files/2009/11/How-Would-You-Rank-the-Critical- Competencies-for-Teaching-Online.pdf

Florida Virtual School. (2010). *About us.* Retrieved from http://flvs.net/areas/aboutus/Pages/default.aspx

Glaser, M. (2007). *Your guide to the digital divide.* PBS. Retrieved from http://www.pbs.org/mediashift/2007/01/your-guide-to-the-digital-divide017.html

Guide, M. I. L. E. Milestones for Improving Learning and Education. (2001). *Partnership for 21st Century Skills.* Retrieved from http://www.p21.org/documents/MILE_Guide_091101.pdf

Hassel, B. C., & Terrell, M. G. (2004). *How can virtual schools be a part of meeting the choice provisions of the No Child Left Behind Act?* U.S. Department of Education Secretary's no Child Left Behind Leadership Summit, Increasing Options Through E-learning. Retrieved from http://www2.ed.gov/about/offices/list/os/technology/plan/2004/site/documents/Hassel-Terrell-VirtualSchools.pdf

ITunes. (2010). *iTunes U.* Retrieved from http://www.apple.com/education/itunes-u/

LoTi Connection. (2009). *About the LoTi digital age survey.* Retrieved from http://loticonnection.com/lotitake.html

McDougall, S. (2006). *One tablet or two? Opportunities for change in educational provision in the next 20 years*. Future Lab Publications. Retrieved from http://www.futurelab.org.uk/resources/documents/discussion_papers/One_tablet_or_two.pdf

Means, B., Toyama, Y., Murphy, R., Bakia, M., & Jones, K. (2009) *Evaluation of evidence-based practices in online learning: A meta-analysis and review of online learning studies*. US Department of Education. Retrieved from http://www.ed.gov/rschstat/eval/tech/evidence-based-practices/finalreport.pdf

Moodle. (2011). *Statistics*. Retrieved from http://moodle.org/stats/

Moore, A. (1989). Testimony before the Senate Subcommittee on Education, Arts, Humanities of the Committee of Labor and Human Resources, field hearing, Jackson, MI. April 27, 1989, in U.S. Congress, Office of Technology Assessment, *Linking for Learning: A New' Course for Education, OTA-SET-430* (Washington, DC: U.S. Government Printing Office, November, 1989). Retrieved from http://www.princeton.edu/~ota/disk1/1989/8921/8921.PDF

National Assessment of Educational Progress Technology and Engineering Literacy Assessment. (n.d.). Retrieved from http://www.edgateway.net/cs/naepsci/print/docs/470

National Education Technology Standards for Students. (2007). *International Society for Technology in Education*. Retrieved from http://www.iste.org/Libraries/PDFs/NETS_for_Student_2007_EN.sflb.ashx

Oblinger, D. (2003). Boomers, gen-xers, and millennials: Understanding the new students. *EDUCAUSE Review, 38*(4), 37–47.

Partnership for 21st Century Skills. (n.d.). *Home page*. Retrieved from http://www.p21.org/index.php?option=com_content&task=view&id=254&Itemid=120

Picciano, A. G., & Seaman, J. (2009). K-12 online learning: A 2008 follow-up of the survey of US school district administrators. Sloan Consortium. Retrieved from http://sloanconsortium.org/publications/survey/pdf/k-12_online_learning_2008.pdf

Plourde, M. (2010). *Sakai @ UD progress report*. University of Delaware. Retrieved from http://www.slideshare.net/mathplourde/2232010-sakaiud-progress-report?from=ss_embed

Prensky, M. (2009). H. sapiens digital: From digital immigrants and digital natives to digital wisdom. *Innovate, 5*(3).

Project Tomorrow. (2009). *Speak up 2009: Creating our future: Students speak up about their vision for 21st century learning*. Retrieved from http://www.tomorrow.org/speakup/pdfs/SU09NationalFindingsStudents&Parents.pdf

Quillen, I. (2010). Analysis notes virtual ed. priorities in RTT winners. *Education Week, 30*(3).

Ragan, L. (2009). *How would you rank the critical competencies for teaching online?* Distance.

Ribble, M. S., Bailey, G. D., & Ross, T. W. (2004). Digital citizenship: Addressing appropriate technology behavior. *Learning and Leading with Technology, 32*(1), 6–12.

Sakai Project. (n.d.). Retrieved from http://sakaiproject.org/

Taggart, K. G. (20100. *Technology in teacher preparation survey*. Retrieved from https://sites.google.com/site/technologyteachersurvey/home

University of Delaware. (2009). *Fall course sites in a learning management system at UD*. Retrieved from http://www.udel.edu/udlms/images/10-08-2009-UD-SakaiFallCourses.jpg

University of Delaware. (2010). *Minor in educational technology*. Retrieved from http://www.udel.edu/education/ed-tech-minor.html

Warschauer, M., Knobel, M., & Stone, L. A. (2004). Technology and equity in schooling: Deconstructing the digital divide. *Educational Policy*, *18*(4), 562–588. doi:10.1177/0895904804266469

Watson, J., Murin, A., Vashaw, L., Gemin, B., & Rapp, C. (2010). *Keeping pace with k-12 online learning: An annual review of policy and practice.* Retrieved from http://www.flvs.net/areas/aboutus/Documents/Research/KeepingPaceK12_2010.pdf

ADDITIONAL READING

2010A Few Degrees of Uncertainty Regarding Online Learning. Distance Education Report, 14(23), 6, 8. Retrieved from Education Full Text database on January 18, 2011.

Beldarrain, Y. (2006). Distance education trends: Integrating new technologies to foster student interaction and collaboration. *Distance Education*, *27*(2), 139–153. doi:10.1080/01587910600789498

Bethel, E. C., & Bernard, R. M. (2010). Developments and trends in synthesizing diverse forms of evidence: beyond comparisons between distance education and classroom instruction. *Distance Education*, *31*(3), 231–256. doi:10.1080/01587919.2010.513950

Hilton, III, & John, L., Graham, Charles, Rich, Peter and Wiley, David. (2010). Using online technologies to extend a classroom to learners at a distance. *Distance Education*, *31*(1), 77–92. doi:10.1080/01587911003725030

Muir, M., Knezek, G., & Christensen, R. (2004). The power of one to one: Early findings from the Maine learning technology initiative. *Learning and Leading with Technology*, *32*(3), 6–11.

No Significant Difference Phenomenon. [Online]: http://www.nosignificantdifference.org/

Obringer, S. J., & Coffey, K. (2007). Cell phones in American high schools: A National Survey. *The Journal of Technology Studies*. 41-47. [Online]: http://www.akademik.unsri.ac.id/download/journal/files/scholar/obringer.pdf

Oliver, K., Osborne, J., & Brady, K. (2009). 'What are secondary students' expectations for teachers in virtual school environments?'. *Distance Education*, *30*(1), 23–45. doi:10.1080/01587910902845923

Picciano, A. G., & Seaman, J. (2010). Class connections: high school reform and the role of online learning. Babson Survey Research Group. [Online]: http://www3.babson.edu/ESHIP/research-publications/upload/Class_connections.pdf

Traxler, J. (2010). Distance education and mobile learning: Catching up, taking stock. *Distance Education*, *31*(2), 129–138. doi:10.1080/01587919.2010.503362

U.S. Congress. Office of Technology Assessment, *Linking for Learning: A New' Course for Education, OTA-SET-430* (Washington, DC: U.S. Government Printing Office, November, 1989). [Online]: http://www.princeton.edu/~ota/disk1/1989/8921/8921.PDF

U.S. Congress. Office of Technology Assessment, *Education and Technology: Future Visions,* OTA-BP-EHR-169 (Washington, DC: U.S. Government Printing Office, September 1995). [Online]: http://www.princeton.edu/~ota/disk1/1995/9522/9522.PDF

Watson, J., Murin, A., Vashaw, L., Gemin, B., & Rapp, C. (2010). Keeping Pace with K-12 online Learning: An Annual Review of Policy and Practice. [Online]: http://www.flvs.net/areas/aboutus/Documents/Research/KeepingPaceK12_2010.pdf

Chapter 27
Infusing Technology into a Physical Education Teacher Education Program

Joanne Leight
Slippery Rock University, USA

Randall Nichols
Slippery Rock University, USA

ABSTRACT

Technology is changing the way Physical Education is taught. From heart rate monitors and pedometers to podcasting, exergaming, and desktop applications, tomorrow's teachers need to know how to infuse technology into their teaching. The use of technology in Physical Education can increase both student learning and teacher productivity. Courses in a comprehensive PETE (Physical Education Teacher Education) program can be divided into the following categories: Fitness related courses, Activity courses, Assessment courses, and Methods courses (including field experiences and student teaching). A strong PETE program will infuse technology into the course work in all four categories, in addition to a stand-alone technology course that introduces the various forms of technology that will be used in their future Physical Education classroom. This chapter will describe how to prepare future physical educators to utilize the myriad of technological options available in the field.

INTRODUCTION

The fusion of technology and physical education can seem to be counterproductive, however, implementing technology in physical education can be an asset and beneficial to the goals of physical education (Bennett, 2006). There is an increasing demand for technology savvy physical education teachers, individuals who are equipped with skills to not only instruct using technology, but equipped to use data to change the design of physical education curriculum to meet the demands of lifestyle illnesses that begin in childhood (Edginton & Kirkpatrick, 2007). Leading

DOI: 10.4018/978-1-4666-0014-0.ch027

the future teachers of physical education into the 21st Century requires new, dynamic and innovative approaches by Physical Education Teacher Education (PETE) programs; these approaches should utilize technology as a way of motivating and inspiring students as well as promoting self directed learning experiences. University programs need to provide experiences and skills that will prepare future teachers to create learning environments that use a holistic approach to educating youth at home and in the community (Edginton & Kirkpatrick, 2007). Using technology resources in a physical education environment can be exciting and stimulating for teachers and their students (Nye, 2008). This chapter includes methods and examples of embedding technology within a PETE program and methods for developing technology savvy physical education teachers for the future.

BACKGROUND

The world of education has changed dramatically in the last few decades. Research over the past twenty years in the field of education has indicated that computer technology can impact teaching and learning in a positive manner at all levels of education (Brayley, 1999; Hokanson & Hopper, 2000; LeMaster, Williams, & Knop, 1998; Reeves and Reeves, 1997; Wilkinson, Hiller & Harrison, 1998). When teachers become more competent with the technology, then teacher effectiveness is increased, and this results in greater student learning (Zemelman, Daniels, & Hyde, 1998). In a study conducted by Woods, Karp, Hui and Perlman, teachers reported that technology can enhance student learning because it facilitates individual development, aids the visual learner, and is useful for assessment purposes. This same study found that teachers indicated a high level of perceived competency with many forms of technology, but there were differences based on years of experience, teaching level and gender

(2008). In 1994 only 20% of public schools teachers felt competent to integrate technology into their teaching. Nine years later that number soared to 99%, as indicated by the National Center for Education Statistics (NCES) (USDOE and NCES, 2005). This confidence covered areas such as using a computer, email and the Internet. This self-assurance dipped when asked about technologies such as presentation software (35%) and video cameras (18%) (USDOE & NCES, 2005). Additionally, physical education teachers reported low competency levels for website creation, heart rate monitors, body composition analyzers and PDA's (Woods et al, 2008). "Before educators can successfully integrate technology into the learning environment, they must first be proficient it its use" (USDOE & NCES, 2005, p. 1). It was determined that teachers who had fewer years of experience were more inclined to use technology than their more experienced colleagues (Dorman, 2001; Lam, 2000). This is not surprising since younger teachers have been exposed to technology throughout their lifetime and are not afraid to learn and implement this knowledge into their classrooms.

Early Technology in Physical Education

Many physical educators can remember a time when technology was non-existence. A gymnasium, athletic equipment and a whistle were the only teaching tools these educators had to do their job. Technology is definitely changing the way physical education is taught. The first use of technology in the field of physical education was in the 1970's and 1980's when college professors used computers to analyze fitness scores. The students would be tested, the data would be inputted into a computer, and then a report would be printed (Mohnsen, 2004). Physical educators are still collecting fitness scores, but the equipment has become much more sophisticated, the criteria for the data is different, and the results can be sent electronically and viewed by both parents and students (Dillon, 2008).

With the exception of these early fitness reports, the discipline of physical education has been slow to join the technological revolution (Sharpe and Hawkins, 1998). This could be explained with the findings of Liang, Walls, Hicks, Clayton, and Yang (2006). These researchers discovered that physical educators did not feel they were skilled nor confident users of instructional technology in their professional careers. It's only within the last decade or so that the use of technology to improve school-based physical education received any attention. In the past, technology was often thought of as software and computers, or more recently the Internet and World Wide Web. According to Mohnsen (2010), "Technology is anything that helps students improve their physical performance, social interaction, or cognitive understanding of physical education concepts (p. 7)." Despite the unique subject matter (i.e. movement) in physical education, technology can aid instructors in both the psychomotor and cognitive domains as well (Castelli & Fiorentino, 2004; Forbus & Mills, 1997).

Technology Integration in Physical Education

Recent literature has an abundance of suggestions on how to integrate technology into physical education (Castelli, 2001; Mohnsen, 2010). The use of technology in physical education has been effectively used in the classroom with computer-assisted instruction and various assessment techniques (Mohnson, 1995; Monsma, 2003; Silverman, 1997), and also through exchanging resources and information available on the Internet (Elliot & Manross, 1996). Using technology in physical education can increase both student learning and teacher productivity. Whether it is for preparation, instruction or assessment, technology can play a vital role in the development of future physical education teachers, and so it is important

to prepare potential physical educators to utilize the myriad of technological options available in the field. From digital video to podcasting to exergaming, tomorrow's teachers need to know how to infuse technology into their teaching.

Although there are many ways that technology can be incorporated into a physical education setting, it is still not a widely used medium. A challenge of using technology in a PETE program is having PETE faculty use the technology effectively as a teaching tool, while also teaching students how to incorporate technology into their own future classrooms (Schell, 2004). In higher education, many students are more advanced than their professors with regard to technology, and so technology is not used and modeled in teacher preparation classes (Silverman, 1997). If the instructor does not feel comfortable using technology, and is unaware of the potential of this medium, then it does not matter what kinds of technological advances have occurred in the world; it still will not be used. Faculty may also not utilize technology because they are unaware of what is available to them and their students. In public schools there are time limitations to learn and implement the technology, and money to purchase the necessary software and electronic devices.

Castelli and Fiorentino (2004) discovered that preservice physical education teachers have mixed feelings regarding technology use in the gymnasium. Some embrace the integration of technology due to their own positive experience with technology. Others, however, believe that there is no place for technology in teaching because it promotes physical inactivity. Technology has certainly led to more and more inactivity in society in general (video games, television), but research shows that technology can definitely aid in activity levels if used correctly. Physical educators need to encourage programs based more on physical and active participation instead of sedentary, technology-related games. "That is the way to inspire continued play, both virtually and in real life. If technology's mission is to make it easier to accomplish tasks, we should use the latest available technology to encourage children to be more active and healthier on a regular basis (Fiorentino & Gibbone, 2005, p. 16)."

When teaching undergraduate PETE majors, focusing merely on the various types of technology used in Physical Education is not be enough. Rather, being able to teach students how to integrate this technology into their lessons is of paramount importance. This chapter will describe how one university is integrating technology across the program in our courses, and in the preservice teaching experiences.

CATEGORY OF COURSES

What makes a physical education program different than many other programs across campus is the variety of the courses that are required for PETE majors. These four required courses must be completed before graduation and can be placed in four different categories: Fitness related course(s), Activity related course(s), Assessment related course(s) and Methods or Field related course(s), including student teaching. The following sections will discuss how technology can be infused into these various categories/courses. A final section will discuss a stand-alone technology course for PETE majors, and what technology can be included in such a course.

Activity Courses

Physical education is unique simply because of the physical nature of the subject matter. It is the only subject that deals with the entire student: cognitive, affective and psychomotor. PETE students are required to take a number of physical activity courses so they are proficient in skill development and instruction. These courses can variety by name, but most include some type of sports skills and strategy. Some programs include traditional team sports (basketball, soccer, volleyball, softball, football, field hockey, etc.), others have traditional individual sports (tennis, badminton, archery, bowling, etc.), and still others have combined many of these classes into similar courses and taught skills and strategies across subjects (territory games, striking/fielding games, lifetime leisure games, net/wall games). In addition to the activities mentioned, there may be fundamental courses required such as aquatics, educational gymnastics, dance, and movement education. Technology can be infused in a number of these courses.

Video

Due to the physical nature of the discipline, an invaluable tool in a PETE program is the use of video. This can include the old fashion VHS tapes or newer DVDs to illustrate and demonstrate the correct skill, technique or strategy for numerous activities (e.g. give and go in soccer or basketball, correct follow through in softball throw or volleyball serve). When a clip is played, the students have a visual representation of what is to be performed. This is a perfect teaching cue for visual learners. With the many resources available, students can now film themselves performing a skill and view it instantly for feedback. With digital video it can be uploaded to a computer and edited or stored for future use.

Biomechanical Analysis Software

With biomechanical analysis software (e.g. Dartfish) students are now able to analyze their own performance. Students can be filmed performing a skill in an activity class, download the video to a computer, and use software such as Dartfish, to analyze skills such as a serve in badminton, tennis or volleyball and determine angle of contact, acceleration, velocity, and follow through (to name just a few). The potential for student learning is great, especially since the student is the performer and the evaluator of their own activity. This biomechanical analysis is not limited to just gymnasium or outdoor activities. With the use of underwater video cameras students can also analyze their swimming strokes and flip turns. Whether biomechanical software is included in the assessment, or just viewing immediately after performing, filming students involved in various activities still remains one of the strongest teaching tools in physical education.

Pedometers and Heart Rate Monitors

Other tools that could be used in an activity course would be pedometers and heart rate monitors. Although discussed extensively in the fitness courses section, these devices can be worn and utilized as a teaching tool in various activity courses. Pedometers can provide an indication of how many steps were taken when performing certain sports or activities. An appropriate teaching tool would be to compare the number of steps taken for each activity. Occasionally, when engrossed in an activity, students are not aware of the number of steps that are taken when participating fully. Heart rate monitors are a great tool to use for assessing if the students are within their target heart rate zone when participating in a class activity. The heart rate monitors can be worn each day and the students can assess which activities elevated their heart rate and which did not. They can also determine if they need to put forth more or less effort, depending on what their heart rate may be for each activity. These can be an excellent teaching tool to use when combining fitness into activity courses.

Fitness Education Courses

With the recent emphasis on health-related fitness and obesity in our society many PETE programs have increased their requirements for their students and often have one or two classes that are related to health related fitness. Fitness courses are an easy way for PETE majors to learn how to implement some content specific technology such as heart rate monitor, pedometers and GPS units into their lessons.

Heart Rate Monitors

Heart rate monitors have become increasingly more common within school physical education programs, (1) to supplement the physical education fitness curriculum, (2) to motivate students to achieve higher intensity levels, and (3) to assess student progress in reaching higher intensity levels (Nichols, Davis, McCord, Schmidt & Slezak, 2009). It is important for PETE students to be aware of several different methods for using heart rate monitors to motivate and assess exercise intensity during physical education classes.

The role of physical educators' teaching has changed from one of teaching the guidelines and assessment of physical activity within physical education classes only to one of teaching students to be physically active outside of the physical education classes. Heart rate monitors help specifically to assess whether students in physical education classes have exercised in the appropriate heart rate zones in order to achieve a training effect for cardiovascular endurance, one of the components of health-related fitness (Nichols, et al., 2009). Depending on the grade level of the students taught, there may be specific advantages/disadvantages involved with using heart rate monitors.

PETE students should be made aware of the advantages of heart rate monitor use along with any disadvantages associated with the use of heart-rate monitors. Among many advantages, heart rate monitors allows a student to choose an aerobic activity (swim, run, walk, basketball, racquetball), and as long as there is a predetermined amount of time in the target heart rate zone, the activity session can be considered a success (Nichols, et al., 2009). Another advantage is the trust that students develop in the accuracy of palpating their own heart rates. Giving students more responsibility for their own learning increases their motivation to exercise. In addition, teachers are able to measure the effort of students more readily and easily with heart rate monitors in order to hold students accountable for their own learning. This accountability is also valuable for program assessment and documenting program quality (Nichols, et al., 2009).

The main disadvantage of heart rate monitors in physical education is the cost. The cost issue can be overcome by purchasing just a few monitors, and to use those monitors to help demonstrate their worth to administrators and parents (Nichols, et al., 2009). PETE students can be taught that, in an effort to advocate for their programs, they should invite the school's principal to do an observation during one of those lessons. If a physical education teacher can demonstrate that a budget request will be spent on something that truly helps students, the chance of getting the requested equipment increases dramatically. In addition, grant writing is another strategy that can be employed to help offset the lack of budget. Another funding option that PETE students should be made aware of is that of grant opportunities for obtaining physical education equipment and resources are at an all-time high (e.g., Physical Education for Progress, NASPE, Flag house, Sport time, Polar, and state education department grants), and the assistance necessary for writing these types of grants is more readily available than ever (Nichols, et al., 2009). Another disadvantage to heart rate monitor use is that, at first, there may be difficulties with the logistics of putting the monitors on, recalling data, and getting a signal. However, those drawbacks will be temporary after continued use, and they are far outweighed by the benefits of using heart rate monitors to assess intensity of exercise.

Pedometers, Accelerometers and Activity Monitors

Technology tools which assess activity levels but are less invasive and cost less to purchase compared to heart-rate monitors have become extremely popular within many PE programs and therefore should be a strong component of PETE program curriculum. Today's teachers work in an era of accountability and emphasis on physical activity (Beighle, Pangrazi & Vincent, 2001). Pedometers and activity monitors are small electronic devices that fasten to one's waistband or wrist and either count the number of steps taken or the amount of time that the individual has been physically active. Although pedometers do not measure intensity levels of physical activity these devices have been found to be reliable tool for measuring step counts and physical activity levels for both adults and youth (Bassett, 1996). Pedometers have many advantages to being a part of a PETE program. Pedometers are low in cost, easy to distribute and activate for PE class and provide meaningful instantaneous feedback to students. PETE students can become familiar with using pedometers when teaching micro lessons and incorporating an emphasis on physical activity along with skill acquisition by using step counts as the indicator for physical activity levels during a lesson. Upon reflection of the lesson, and step counts, PETE students can learn to make modifications for increasing physical activity levels within the lesson. Additionally, PETE students can learn to use the pedometer/activity monitor as an advocacy tool by signing out pedometers to family members so that they can then track their own physical activity patterns in a normal workday and encourage these individuals to find ways to increase their own physical activity levels. Pedometers and Accelerometers have been in use at varying levels of education and public use for quite some time, however, something relatively new to the market are activity monitors. Activity monitors like the *Fitbit, Fitbug* and Polars' *Activity Monitor* provide the same benefits of a pedometer but can also be used to track levels of physical activity within the moderate to vigorous paradigm which gives the PETE student along with the school aged youth more specific data on the physical activity level during the PE lesson.

Global Positioning Systems (GPS)

In order to locate a specific position on Earth, GPS receivers use data received from a network of satellites orbiting the earth, called the Navigation Satellite Timing and Ranging Global Positioning System (McNamara, 2004). GPS devices have enabled individuals to create games and activities that can enhance physical activity. The most popular use has become simply tracking distance and pace for people walking, running or cycling. PETE students can use this type of data to motivate students during running or walking units. Another very popular physical activity involving the use of GPS receivers is *geocaching*. Geocaching is a unique opportunity to combine a love of the outdoors, technology and physical activity and involves finding secret hidden treasures (pre placed by teacher) using GPS and some simple clues (Schlatter, 2005). PETE students can create a variety of obstacles and challenges using the Geocaching theme. Related to the geocaching theme is the adventure race concept which also uses the GPS receivers along with heart-rate monitors to challenges students to complete an adventure type activity in a predetermined order in different spots on the campus, all while being within their target-heart rate (Dejager, 2008).

Exergaming

Exergaming is a type of video game that is creating a revolution in physical education (Hicks, 2010). Exergaming combines physical activity and video gaming to create an enjoyable appealing way for students to be physically active (Hicks, 2010). Recent research has shown that youth can reach the recommended levels of intensity desired in typical physical activity sessions by engaging in exergaming activities (Siegel & Haddock, 2009). Exergaming is a technology that PETE students can use to help motivate students who are not motivated to participate in typical physical education activities. One concern that PETE programs should be aware of is that exergaming activities should not be a standalone lesson and that a cognitive objective should be linked to the exergaming session, i.e. target-heart rate, interval training, etc.

Health-Related Fitness Assessment Software

Fitness assessment software is a type of technology that PETE students can learn to use to provide meaningful feedback to students following fitness testing. Software packages like Fitness gram, Fit Stats and Tri-Fitt allow PE teachers to enter data from a variety of different fitness assessments and give the students feedback on their current fitness levels based on either criterion referenced standards or norm referenced standards. Following the return of this data to students, PETE students should learn how to help the students interpret their results and use this information to set goals and link what they are learning in PE to their own individual fitness goals.

Assessment / Measurement Courses

Assessment or measurement and evaluation courses are an ideal place to infuse technology in a PETE program. Technology can allow students to assess the completion of their objectives from lesson plans and provide feedback to students within the class.

Heart-Rate Monitors

Heart rate monitors (HRM) can become a meaningful assessment tool for students and teachers. They provide the opportunity to objectively assess students in many different ways: time-on-task, exercise intensity, and meeting personal fitness goals. Students feel empowered when they have used a heart rate monitor to assess their own performance. In addition to allowing students to exercise in a safe manner, each student can download the results of his/her activity providing quick and accurate documentation of his/her level of exertion during the physical education class (Nichols et al., 2009). Through this downloaded data, students are able to recognize and analyze the training effect that aerobic exercise has on their hearts over time. For example, they will see graphic representations of their heart's improved efficiency demonstrated through its ability to move more blood with fewer beats (lower resting heart rate), the body's ability to do more work while the heart beats at the same intensity, and the heart's ability to recover faster following exercise (Nichols et al., 2009). This workout data can be easily collected at any grade level to create a student portfolio in order to showcase how students have progressed during their time spent in physical education. PETE students can use HRM's to assess physical activity intensity of any lesson that involves movement and physical activity.

Part of the instruction involved with using heart rate monitors is to also have students palpate their own heart rate and compare it to heart rate monitor readings over a period of time. This will develop students' accuracy and confidence in palpating their own heart rate and assessing their own physical activity intensity levels. It also provides a perfect teachable moment at the end of each class to show students that, regardless of their ability level, they all met their individual goals for the day and got a great workout (Nichols et al., 2009).

In a time when test scores, standards based teaching, assessment, and documentation of student learning are paramount in education, PETE students should understand that the use of heart rate monitors gives the physical educator the ability to give documented feedback to students, parents, administrators and community members about the level of physical activity within the school's physical education program. It also gives physi-

cal educators a means to teach interdisciplinary subjects through physical activity, as well as the means to promote the use of technology in teaching and learning (Nichols et al., 2009). Students are able to receive instant feedback on their activity during lessons by downloading data and printing reports to send to parents. Students are also able to keep individual recording logs based on data from their heart rate monitors. This same data can be used to help promote quality physical education program goals within the community.

Pedometers and Activity Monitors

Because of the cost of heart rate monitors, many physical educators choose to use less-expensive pedometers to assess step counts or activity monitors to assess physical activity in terms of moderate to vigorous physical activity (MVPA). While pedometers are valid instruments for assessing step counts and activity monitors for assessing MVPA, there is no intensity levels assessment with pedometers, as there are with the target heart rate zones associated with heart rate monitors. PETE student can use pedometers to teach and assess the difference between physical activity and exercise; additionally PETE students should be aware that it is very easy for the students to "cheat" with pedometers. Almost every single child in elementary and high school shakes their pedometer just to see the numbers change.

Health-Related Fitness Assessment Software

As mentioned earlier in the chapter, software packages like Fitness gram, Fit Stats and Tri-Fitt allow PE teachers to enter data from a variety of different fitness assessments and give the students formative feedback on their current fitness levels based on either criterion referenced standards or norm referenced standards.

Field / Methods Courses & Student Teaching

All PETE programs have courses that teach basic pedagogy and most include a teaching component to those classes. Whether teaching peers or children in the schools, this is an invaluable aspect of a PETE program. The final capstone course for all PETE majors is student teaching, which is a semester long assignment in the public schools.

The use of technology in field/methods courses and student teaching can vary due to the technology available at each teaching site. Some school districts are blessed with a large budget (or grants) and have a great deal of technology, and other settings may be financially strapped and have very little technology available in the gymnasium. Some teaching sites have heart rate monitors, pedometers, fitness centers with cardio machines, exergaming equipment and more. Due to the infusing of technology across the PETE program, students assigned to these sites should have the knowledge and resources to use the available technology. A strong PETE program will empower the students to embrace this technology and utilize it in their teaching.

Video

One area of technology that is very valuable in field/methods courses and student teaching is the use of videotaping. The use of videotaping has been mentioned often in this chapter, and this is another example of its use. PETE students can be filmed while teaching their lessons in the school setting. The PETE student, university faculty member, and the cooperating teacher can then view this video and each can provide feedback. The student can chart a number of teaching variables such as: time on task, amount of feedback, type of feedback, transition time, and inappropriate mannerisms (to name a few). This digital video can be uploaded and saved on the computer. It can be edited into small video montages for use in an electronic portfolio or end of semester presentation. There is great value in viewing oneself when teaching. With the development of smaller video cameras (flip video, smart phone video cameras) it has become very easy to incorporate this form of technology into the classroom.

Software Applications

A final use of technology for these courses would be utilizing the various software applications for completion of course assignments, such as lesson plans, unit plans, task sheets, bulletin boards and rubrics, to name just a few examples. Utilizing word processing, desktop publishing and presentation software, students can create dynamic resources for use in their classes or for end of the semester presentations. They can create interactive games with PowerPoint.

Internet

There exists a wealth of information available online for student to utilize as a resource to supplement their lesson planning. The use of the Internet for lesson ideas, research information, or to communicate with professionals in the field through listservs or discussion boards is definitely a positive use of technology in field/methods and student teaching courses in a PETE program.

Technology Course for Physical Education Teacher Education

An invaluable course in any PETE program is a stand-alone technology course just for Physical Education majors. This course can provide the opportunity to introduce PETE majors to all of the various forms and types of technology available for use in the discipline. An instructional technology course available to all education majors does not meet the specific demands of a physical education environment. The technology used in the gymnasium is very different than the technology used in a traditional classroom setting. PETE students should get technology infused across the PETE program, but a stand-alone technology course permits the students more hands on opportunity to learn the technology, and how it is used in the classroom/gymnasium. Then, when introduced in other PETE courses, they already know the basics of using the technology and are now able to implement it more fully into the course activity.

When teaching undergraduate PETE majors, focusing merely on the various types of technology used in Physical Education is not be enough. Rather, being able to teach students how to integrate this technology into their lessons is of paramount importance. This section will focus on the various forms of technology taught in a Technology for PETE course, an explanation of each type, and examples of uses in the classroom.

Word Processing (e.g., Microsoft Word)

Most people are familiar with basic word processing software. There are so many things that can be done with this software. Being able to add diagrams or movement patterns into lesson plans or insert a picture of a correctly executed athletic skill on a task sheet are some of the ways PETE students can use the different functions of word processing software. It can also be used for rule sheets, evaluations, worksheets, task cards, rubrics, curriculum guides, homework assignments and letters to parents. Students can also use this software to create an electronic portfolio, which is a wonderful way to showcase progress over time and can also be used as an assessment tool to meet a number of different standards.

Desktop Publisher (e.g., Microsoft Publisher)

This is a comprehensive program for creating a wide variety of professional-looking desktop publications. Numerous templates and wizards are provided to create a variety of publications such as flyers, award certificates, newsletters, brochures and calendars, just to name a few. In no time at all students can create a newsletter to parents informing them of special events, a certificate for a "good work award," a flyer promoting field day, or a calendar to send home for daily fitness activities.

Presentation Software (e.g., Microsoft PowerPoint)

There is a fairly new method for utilizing this software in a classroom that may be of interest to some health and physical educators. *Interactive PowerPoint*, as the name implies, provides an opportunity for the student to interact with the software based on how the teacher creates the presentation. With this method, the slides are linked together (hyperlinked) like a website and are run in a non-sequential order, unlike a regular PowerPoint presentation that goes in sequence as the slides are created. A good example of utilizing *Interactive PowerPoint* would be setting up a multiple choice quiz similar to the popular game show *Who Wants to be a Millionaire* for the students to navigate. It is especially useful if there is only one computer available in the gymnasium. It could be used as a separate station during class, for an injured student unable to participate, for remediation for struggling students, or as a review for a quiz or test. *Interactive PowerPoint* can also be set up as a *Jeopardy* game board and students could compete as teams to answer the questions correctly. Teachers utilizing PowerPoint can also use the animation function to provide a visual aid to illustrate movement patterns in the gymnasium or field of play. Demonstrating a give and go, the breakdown of a defensive scheme, or simply how to get a class to move into groups can be illustrated with PowerPoint with the click of a mouse.

Spreadsheet (e.g., Microsoft Excel)

This program can be used for organizing grades, taking attendance, keeping track of your budget and/or equipment, or using as a rubric for assessment. Spreadsheets, like the previous applications, can be downloaded to a handheld device to aid in record keeping during class time such as taking attendance or scoring with a rubric.

Web Design (e.g., Microsoft FrontPage, Dreamweaver)

Many web design applications make creating a web page as easy as creating a number of word processing documents and linking them together. Construction of the website takes many hours, but understanding the basic format and learning to use most web design software can be learned very quickly. There is no better way to promote the positive things physical educators are doing in the classroom than to have an updated, innovative, and informative website for their program.

Digital Video Editing (e.g., Microsoft Movie Maker, iMovie)

Digital video plays a huge part in the discipline of physical education since movement is essential to what is done in PE. Digital video editing software makes the editing process very easy to do. PETE students can learn how to take videos of students performing a skill or task and edit them to create teaching tools for future classes. Options for digital video projects could have students demonstrating mastery of a skill, progression from the beginning of a unit/school year to the end, or create a video of various fitness components. Another alternative for teachers would be to create a digital video of their program and share it with parents at open house, highlighting all of the great and innovative things that are being done in the classroom/gymnasium. This is an especially valuable tool when advocating for ones' program. One of the best

things that can be done for the discipline of physical education is being pro-active in promoting all of the positive things that are being performed in the gymnasium and classroom.

Electronic Portfolio (E-folio)

PETE students can use a word processing program (e.g., Microsoft Word) to complete an E-folio by learning how to save documents as Web (html) pages, and linking the web documents together. Students can link artifacts together in an electronic portfolio format, navigating like a website. Included in a PETE student's e-folio is basic information such as resume, clearances, certifications, letters of recommendation and courses completed. Students also include reflections and numerous artifacts (e.g. lesson plans, unit plans, observations, rubrics, etc.) that are linked to the various National and State Standards. Students can also include a video introduction and video clips of teaching episodes during field experience and student teaching.

Newsgroups and Discussion Boards

An excellent online option for professionals in physical education is participation in professional newsgroups and discussion boards. Newsgroups are, "forums on almost any topic imaginable. They are essentially bulletin boards where people can read and post messages about topics of their choice (Mohnsen, 2006)." Whenever a subscriber posts a message to a newsgroup, it appears on the discussion board immediately and anyone can read the postings and respond if they wish. Interested users can subscribe to a discussion board (e.g., NASPE Forum and NASPE Talk) provided by the National Association for Sport and Physical Education (NASPE) for physical education professionals and PETE students from around the world. NASPE is the national organization that provides program review for colleges and university PETE programs and also standards for beginning Physical Education teachers. The discussion boards of NASPE Talk and NASPE Forum are both an ongoing dialogue among health and physical educators from around the world. This is a great option for those physical educators who may be isolated and need a sense of community (as there is often only one physical educator per building in some districts), for those who need advice or input, or just a place to post relevant and interesting information pertaining to any topic imaginable. Participating in a discussion board can be a wonderful learning experience for PETE students as they can contribute to the professional dialogue by asking questions and providing comments.

Personal Digital Assistant (Pocket PC, Palm, ITouch, Smart Phones)

Personal digital assistants (PDA) have great potential in Physical Education, as the classroom can be the gymnasium, pool area, or playing field. Physical educators can use handheld devices such as personal digital assistants to collect and store student information, including medical history and emergency contact numbers. There are a number of different software options that are available for both the pocket PC and the Palm device. The most common type is fitness software that is utilized is in conjunction with heart rate monitors. Students can sync their heart rate information to the handheld device and this information can be downloaded to a laptop or desktop computer. Student reports can be generated and printed for each individual student. PDA's may soon be phased out with the development of smart phones (e.g. iPhone, Blackberry, Droid). Smart phones (phones with a data plan) are becoming more multi functional, and with the addition of many of the applications that are now available, may become the handheld device of preference in the gymnasium. Not only can the teacher store valuable student information (health records, emergency numbers), but they can also have access to video clips to show students

who many need a visual cue, a camera to take pictures of class activities, an MP3 player to play music during a warm up activity, and of course a working phone if a call needs to be made to the office or the nurse. Smart phones have become invaluable in the physical education environment.

Heart Rate Monitors and Aerobic Devices (Cardio Respiratory Machines)

These useful devices have definitely aided the fitness movement in physical education. The PETE students are introduced to these devices in the technology course, but they are used extensively in fitness related courses and were discussed previously.

Web 2.0 Activities

There exists many resources available on the Internet for use in the physical education program. Web 2.0 tools permit the user to interact and collaborate in an online environment. These resources can supplement what is being taught in the classroom and can also provide a forum for a dialogue that may not be possible in the gymnasium. Tools such as podcasting, blogs and wikis can be taught very easily in a technology course for PETE majors.

Podcasting

Students use the free software available on the Internet (e.g. Audacity) to create a podcast of a health or physical education topic of their choice, or a topic determined by the teacher (creating an anticipatory set for a second grade class on locomotor skills or introducing ball handling skills to sixth graders). The podcast can be brief (4-5 minutes in length) and is uploaded to the class course management site. There are options available to upload to sites on the Internet if privacy is not an issue.

Blogging

A blog is a great online medium to connect with others on a daily basis. A blog is basically just a web log, or online journal. It is easier to update than a website and it permits interaction as readers can post comments or questions. PETE students can create a blog using one of the many free on-line blog creators (e.g. blogger, wordpress), and requirements may be to blog on three different days during the week. Students can also respond to many of their classmates' blogs on a weekly basis. The topic options can be limited to technology, health, physical education or left open for the students' creativity. This is an exciting medium in which to create a dialogue and work on writing and communication skills among PETE majors.

Wiki

A wiki is an online collaboration tool. There are a number of free wiki creation sites on the Internet (e.g. pbworks). Students can work in pairs or groups to create a wiki based on a health or physical education topic. In combining Web 2.0 activities, students can be required to collaborate on a script for their podcast and use a wiki as the forum for creating that script. What a wiki provides is an online site for students to interact and collaborate asynchronous. This eliminates the need for the students to be in the same room or even online at the same time. It is also more effective than countless email exchanges that fill inboxes and require attachments with every new editing change. A wiki can be set so the instructor has access to every student wiki and can receive emails when the wiki has been updated, can check and see which student made which changes, and also see the entire editing process simply by logging onto the wiki site.

Other Technology Options

With the Internet expanding and changing daily, there will always be new resources available to explore in a technology course. Social Networking (Facebook, Linked in) is a tool that has met both praise and criticism for use in the classroom. Google has produced so many applications available in cloud computing that it is changing the way teachers collaborate, research and communicate (Google docs, buzz, scholar, calendar, Gmail, chrome, etc). Skype has permitted educators to bring experts into the classroom from around the world, simply with a computer and a webcam. Video games are not just for couch potatoes any longer. The explosion of exergaming (e.g. Wii, Dance, Dance Revolution) has changed the activity levels of children and it is being used in our gymnasiums to help combat obesity. The Apple iPad has tremendous potential for use in the physical education environment. These are just a few of the newest advancements in technology that can be utilized in our programs. Technology is always changing, and so will a technology course for PETE majors.

CONCLUSION

There are a few challenges to infusing technology into any academic program. These challenges include, keeping up to date with ever changing software and hardware. Many times technology devises and software are purchased with grant money but when the technology becomes dated new monies must be found to upgrade. Licensures, some software require site licenses, which are renewed yearly and can become a challenge to fund year after year. Finally unique to physical education is the issue of cleanliness. When using heart-rate monitors it is imperative that antibacterial cleaning solutions are used on all devices before other students use that same device, This can become a challenge. As the discipline of physical education moves forward and looks for new and creative ways to help create generations of movers, infusing technology in developmentally appropriate manners is one way to reach students who in past cases have been turned off by traditional physical education methods and activities. It is also important to point out that as technology changes so must the delivery of it within physical education. The challenges are endless but so are the possibilities.

REFERENCES

Bassett, D., Ainsworth, B., Leggett, S., Hunter, D., & Duncan, G. (1996). Accuracy of five electronic pedometers for measuring distance walked. *Medicine and Science in Sports and Exercise, 28,* 1071–1077. doi:10.1097/00005768-199608000-00019

Beighle, A., Pangrazi, R., & Vincent, S. (2001). Pedometers, physical activity and accountability. *Journal of Physical Education, Recreation & Dance, 72*(9), 16–19.

Bennett-Walker, S. (2006). *Technology use among physical education teachers in Georgia public schools.* Ph.D. dissertation, The University of Southern Mississippi, United States -- Mississippi. Retrieved September 27, 2010, from Dissertations & Theses: A&I.(Publication No. AAT 3257001).

Brayley, R. E. (1999). Using technology to enhance the recreation education classroom. *Journal of Physical Education, Recreation & Dance, 70*(9), 23–26.

Castelli, D. (2001). Using inquiry to create tech-savvy teachers. *The Chronicle of Kinesiology and Physical Education in Higher Education, 17*(1), 8-9. 13.

Castelli, D. M., & Fiorentino, L. (2004). The effects of different instruction on preservice teacher perceived ability and comfort with technology in physical education. *Research Quarterly for Exercise and Sport, 75*(1), 63.

DeJager, D., & Himberg, C. (2008). *Adventure racing activities for fun and fitness.* Champaign, IL: Human Kinetics.

Dillon, N. (2008). PhysTech: Schools are turning to technology to improve student health and wellness. *The American School Board Journal, 195*(3), 33–35.

Dorman, S. M. (2001). Are teachers using computers for instruction? *The Journal of School Health, 71,* 83–84. doi:10.1111/j.1746-1561.2001.tb06500.x

Edginton, C., & Kirkpatrick, P. (2007). Teaching with technology: Leading physical education into the 21st century. *Sports International, 2*(4), 138–144.

Elliot, E., & Manross, M. (1996). Physical educators and the internet: Part II: The World Wide Web. *Teaching Elementary Physical Education, 7*(5), 12–15.

Fiorentino, L. H., & Gibbone, A. (2005). Using the virtual gym for practice and drills. *Teaching Elementary Physical Education, 16*(5), 14–16.

Forbus, W. R., & Mills, B. D. (1997). The future of technology in physical education. *Journal of Interdisciplinary Research in Physical Education, 2*(2).

Hicks, L., & Higgins, J. (2010). Exergaming: Syncing physical activity and learning. *Strategies: A Journal for Physical and Sport Educators, 42*(1), 18-21.

Hokanson, B., & Hopper, S. (2000). Computers as cognitive media: Examining the potential of computers in education. *Computers in Human Behavior, 16*(5), 537–552. doi:10.1016/S0747-5632(00)00016-9

Holligan, S. (2001). Issues: Should K-12 physical educators make more use of technology in their classes? *Journal of Physical Education, Recreation & Dance, 72*(2), 12–15.

Lam, Y. (2000). Technophilia vs. technophobia: A preliminary look at why second-language teachers do or do not use technology in their classrooms. *Canadian Modern Language Review, 56,* 390–420. doi:10.3138/cmlr.56.3.389

LeMaster, K., Williams, E., & Knop, N. (1998). Technology Implementation: Let's do it! *Journal of Physical Education, Recreation & Dance, 69*(9), 12–16.

Liang, G., Walls, R., Hicks, V., Clayton, L., & Yang, L. (2006). Will tomorrow's physical educators be prepared to teach in the digital age? *Contemporary Issues in Technology & Teacher Education, 6*(1), 143–156.

McNamara, J. (2004). *Geocaching for dummies: A reference for the rest of us.* Hoboken, NJ: Wiley.

Mohnsen, B. (2004). *Using technology in physical education* (4th ed.). Cerritos, CA: Bonnie's Fitware.

Mohnsen, B. (2006). *Using technology in physical education* (5th ed.). Cerritos, CA: Bonnie's Fitware.

Mohnsen, B. (2010). *Using technology in physical education* (7th ed.). Cerritos, CA: Bonnie's Fitware.

Mohnsen, B. S. (1995). *Using technology in physical education*. Champaign, IL: Human Kinetics.

Monsma, E. V. (2003). Using handheld technology for observational assessment in middle school physical education. *Teaching Elementary Physical Education, 14*(4), 35–37.

Nichols, R., Davis, K., McCord, T., Schmidt, D., & Slezak, A. (2009). The use of heart-rate monitors in physical education. *Strategies: A Journal for Physical and Sport Educators, 22*(6), 19-23.

Nye, S. B. (2008). Teaching with technology resources in physical education. *VAHPERD Journal, 29*(4).

Reeves, T. C., & Reeves, P. M. (1997). Effective dimensions of interactive learning on the World Wide Web. In Khan, B. H. (Ed.), *Web-based instruction* (pp. 59–66). Englewood Cliffs, NJ: Educational Technology Publications.

Schell, L. (2004). Teaching learning styles with technology. *Journal of Physical Education, Recreation & Dance, 75*(1), 14–18.

Schlatter, B., & Hurd, A. (2005). Geocaching: The 21st century hide and seek. *Journal of Physical Education, Recreation & Dance, 76*(7), 28–32.

Sharpe, T., & Hawkins, A. (1998). Technology and the information age: A cautionary tale for higher education. *Quest, 50*(1), 19–32.

Siegel, S., Haddock, B., & Wilken, L. (2009). Active video games (exergaming) and energy expenditure in college students. *International Journal of Exercise Science, 2*(3), 165–174.

Silverman, S. (1997). Technology and physical education: Present, possibilities, and potential problems. *Quest, 49,* 306–314.

U.S. Department of Education (USDOE) & National Center for Education Statistics. (NCES). (2005). *Computer technology in the public school classroom: Teacher perspectives.* Washington, DC: NCES.

Wilkinson, C., Hiller, R. F., & Harrison, J. M. (1998). Technology tips: Improving computer literacy of preservice teachers. *Journal of Physical Education, Recreation & Dance, 69*(5), 10–13, 16.

Woods, M. L., Karp, G. G., Hui, M., & Perlman, D. (2008). Physical educators' technology competencies and usage. *Physical Educator, 65*(2), 82–99.

Zemelman, S., Daniels, H., & Hyde, A. (1998). *Best practice: New standards for teaching and learning in America's schools.* Portsmouth, NH: Heinemann.

Section 5
Technology–Rich Clinical and Student Teaching Experiences

Chapter 28

Attempting to Bridge Theory to Practice:
Preparing for Moving Day with Tele–Observation in Social Studies Methods

Amy J. Good
University of North Carolina at Charlotte, USA

Drew Polly
University of North Carolina at Charlotte, USA

ABSTRACT

Preparing teacher candidates to move from the methods course to K-12 classrooms is not an easy task. Educational methods instructors desire to provide a common experience with exemplars of powerful instruction for their teacher candidates. This project builds on previous research related to tele-observation by presenting an observation scheme while capturing a "live case" of social studies instruction prior to the practicum experience with the help of videoconference capabilities. The research questions guiding this study include: (a) In what way (s) could videoconference be part of the process of bridging theory to practice? (b) In what way (s) will teacher candidates pack up the concepts from the methods course and take them to their own practicum experience? Data sources include a three part tele-observation survey and the context of the live case is shared. Teacher candidates report teaching strategies and management strategies they will use in the classroom following the tele-observation experience.

INTRODUCTION

Think about your first moving day. Anyone who has ever moved knows it can be a stressful day. There is confusion as to where things go; some boxes can be labeled, some are not, some boxes are strong and sturdy, while some fall apart and end up in the trash. Some things are left behind on moving day and some things are given away. Most people have had a stressful moving day while others have a stress free time where a moving company moved everything for them. Regardless, they will still have to decide where certain things will be placed in their new home. In a sense, new

DOI: 10.4018/978-1-4666-0014-0.ch028

teachers and preservice teachers are in a constant moving day, because they are always trying to "pack and unpack" the content of their methods classes, so that one day, they can move into their own classroom. What do they do with what they see in the practicums and what they learn in all of their methods courses, assigned readings, and interactions with other professionals? Ultimately, teacher candidates should be able to transfer their knowledge from what Snow (2005) calls declarative knowledge to reflective knowledge with their methods instructors facilitating the move.

Methods professors want to help bridge theory to practice for the teacher candidates and want to make "moving day" from methods courses to classroom instruction a smooth transition (O'Connor, Good, & Greene, 2006). This is difficult to do in any content area, especially social studies methods. First, it is difficult to find social studies taught in the elementary classroom since it is not a tested subject in some states (Rock, Heafner, Oldendorf, Passe, O'Connor, Good, & Byrd, 2006). It is difficult for teacher candidates to connect university learning to classroom practice when they are not seeing the subject taught in the classroom (Schrum, 1999). The purpose of this study is to build on previous tele-observation projects in social studies methods classes and to examine two research questions: a) In what way (s) could videoconference be part of the process of bridging theory to practice? And b) In what way (s) will teacher candidates pack up the methods course and take it with them to their own practicum experience?

BACKGROUND

A review of the literature reveals various projects where methods instructors in various subject areas try to bridge theory to practice with various techniques; including the use of closed circuit television, case studies, digital video, videocases, videotaped lesson samples, and interactive videoconference experiences have been used in practice

(Bjerstedt, 1967; Bronack, Kilbane, Herbert, & McNergney, 1999; Harris, 1999; Hoy & Merkley, 1989; Mason, 2001; and Karran, Berson & Mason, 2001) Institutions of higher education have used videoconferencing as a central tool for linking theory to practice and collaboration for undergraduate teachers in social studies methods (Bell & Unger, 2003; Good, O'Connor, & Greene, 2005; Kent, 2007; Vannatta & Reinhart, 1999; Venn, Moore & Gunter, 2001).

The focus of student teaching and other field experiences should be on placing candidates in exemplary classrooms with exemplary teachers (Backes & Backes, 1999), where observation of instruction matches closely to what is learned in the methods course. Observation is only part of the field experience. Teacher candidates need experience actually teaching. You can't learn to play a sport only by *watching* a game; however, observing the techniques of an Olympic athlete may help. Unfortunately, observing best practices in the classroom is not always as easy as buying a ticket to a game or turning on ESPN. In social studies, it is possible the classroom teacher will not welcome a social studies methods field placement because of the marginalization of the subject. Field experiences can provide a connection between theory and practice. Yet, Bednar, Ryan, and Sweeder (1994) point out that even when clinical teachers mentor teacher candidates, they often do so without meaningful communication with the institution of higher education sponsoring the teacher candidate. Progressively, teacher educators are turning to technology and technologically mediated assistance to address the limitations of traditional observation experiences.

Videoconferencing

There is importance in "being there" to learn, but when being there is intrusive or may impact student's behavior it is better to find another way. Videoconference allows you to "be there" through non- intrusive technology connection (Goldman,

Pea, Barron, & Derry, 2007). Videoconferencing capabilities have been used successfully in business for training and meetings for years. The education profession is realizing benefits for this technologically mediated method mainly for the broad idea of distance education. The term videoconferencing is defined by Laurillard (1993) as a "one to many medium making it a sensible way to provide access for many sites to a remote academic expert." (p. 166). It is synchronous, as in the system is used at the same time by all participants. While many can see the benefits of video conferencing for distance learning, it has potential for other forms of support of student learning, is not quite so obvious. Recent studies seem to focus on the practical advantages (saving gasoline and saving time) that the medium has rather than focusing on the quality of teaching and learning. There are disagreements as to the best way to utilize video conferencing- for lecture, for interaction, and now we add the possibility for field experience.

"Live Case"

Teacher educators strive to give a common experience to their teacher candidates. Taped video classroom scenarios and videocases are used to give common experiences. These range in professional quality and price. They have motivated preservice teachers but they can be costly. This project presents a *"Live Case"* based on reflection, sociocultural experience, and videoconference capabilities. Student teaching and field experiences in teacher education programs are examples of situating learning within the realm of professional experience. Often, case method is used as an alternative for field observation (Shulman, 1992; Sudzina, 1999). This research project presents "live cases" of the university course instructors teaching elementary social studies in real time.

A cohesive "lab" is created in the live case-anchored in the campus environment in order to create a situated learning environment, where methods instructors attempt to model the practicum experience for a social studies methods class. The researchers who are methods instructors are involved in the delivery of lecture related to the curriculum area studied, as well as the teaching demonstration, attempting to bridge the theory to practice. The live case includes a facilitator who helps the teacher candidates in noting both teacher and student behaviors and may explain certain classroom occurrences, with a muted microphone. In other words, this methods instructor is a faclitator who helps the teacher candidates with "labeling the boxes" (helping them take good notes) for moving day.

Tele-Observation Requires Reflective Practice

Teachers are generally prepared with a repertoire of teaching skills they bring from their methods courses but many are unable to adapt and apply what they know (Hyun and Marshall, 1996). The ability to reflect on the methods class and on the practicum class requires reflection *in*-action and *on*-action (Lee, 2007) and part of this critical reflection could lead to applying theory based strategies during the practicum and beyond. Whitaker (1995) states how reflective and beneficial tele-education can be- it forces a teacher to rethink and fine tune methodology, through whatever medium may be practiced. The transfer of this reflection to actual practice in the teacher candidates' own practicum is a goal of any methods instructor. Kagan (1992) has told us that teaching remains ".. . rooted in personality and experience and that learning to teach requires a journey into the deepest recesses of one's self-awareness, where failures, fears, and hopes are hidden" (p. 137). Time for reflection and thinking through these dilemmas affords the opportunity for the student to articulate their reasoning and helps them develop consciously informed actions (Valli, 1992). This project attempts to describe if in the reflective process, the teacher candidate will decide to use the theory based instruction observed in their own practicum.

Field experiences for teacher candidates can serve as catalysts for the development of new insights and instructional techniques (Darling-Hammond, 1998, Nichols & Sorg, 1998). The benefits of past tele-observation experiences included the teacher candidates reported that they learned social studies content (when it is not a content class), teacher candidates learned social studies classroom pedagogy, teacher candidates observed social studies teaching, and the teacher candidates learned some management techniques (Author, 2006). Now that these items were reported, what will they take with them to the practicum experience and their own class.

The 2007 Tele-Observation Project

Throughout the semester, teacher candidates had listened to their professor lecture about how important theory-based instruction would be for them later, in their own classroom and practicum that semester. The Social Studies Alive Program Sampler (Bower, 2006) was used as a supplemental text for the methods course. Teacher candidates read about several teaching and management strategies linked with social studies instruction. The lessons were demonstrated in the methods course, but the methods instructor wanted the teacher candidates to see the methods instructor 'practicing what she preaches', in action with children- in real time, not rehearsed, not on video, and NOT where the teacher candidates had to act like they were ten year old children. Also, the professor wanted to model the practicum experience for her 24 teacher candidates, who were in the third year of their program, preparing for their year long internship.

A teacher in a rural community 45 miles from the campus, graciously opened her fifth grade classroom doors to a tele-observational experience in her classroom. She allowed a university methods professor, to bring videoconference equipment into her room, so the professor could model the

practicum experience for teacher candidates at the university. There is a need for teachers in this rural area and past collaborations have inspired teacher candidates to consider employment with this rural community. The school where this teacher was employed is within a school district already involved in a larger collaborative TeleEducation Project between the district and the university. All proper IRB and permission was acquired. The thirty children had parent permission to participate.

Modeling the Practicum Experience

One methods instructor, within the team of three methods instructors began communication with the clinical teacher, similar to a teacher candidate, planning what lessons to teach. The professor was assigned the content and standards to be "covered" with the students. Similar to the practicum, there was one brief meeting where the professor met the clinical teacher and her class. The lesson was planned and the professor returned to the school the next week, ready to teach. The lesson was taught while teacher candidates watched through the help of videoconference equipment in their college classroom. This provided a non-rehearsed "live case". The professor was able to walk in the shoes of the teacher candidates and model the practicum while attempting to bridge theory to practice. The fifth grade students were able to participate in an adapted Social Studies Alive lesson on the American Revolution (Bower, 2006).

Teacher Candidate Side in the University Classroom

The teacher candidates came to class as usual, were provided the lesson plan ahead of time, and also given Part I of the Survey to complete during the tele-observation. The other methods instructors served as the facilitator in the university classroom. They monitored the technology, delivered the survey, and made notes of any observations. The instructor was able to field any questions the methods class had about the lesson plan, instruction, and management. The teacher candidates observed the lesson on a large screen with audio and visual. There were limited technical difficulties. The teacher candidates were able to see and hear the entire lesson, while interacting with their classmates and a methods course professor. They were able to do this with the microphone muted on the university side. The intention was for this side to be recorded but there were technical difficulties so the only data from this side are the three part reflective survey responses, including notes taken by the teacher candidates in Part I and two surveys completed following the tele-observation live case.

On the Elementary Side in the 5th Grade Classroom

Because the larger Tele-Education Project is supported by the university a technology expert traveled to the elementary school with the methods instructor. The methods instructor could focus on the instruction and slip into the role of a teacher candidate preparing for practicum. The methods instructor taught her lesson on the American Revolution. The 5th Grade students were aware of the Polycom equipment but were not distracted by the camera. The monitor was turned around so the university classroom would not be seen. The adapted lesson plan is provided in Appendix D.

Project Summary and Equipment Needs

The professors provided their preservice students with an unedited observation experience that allowed preservice teachers to view real "on the spot" management decisions, instructional decisions, and behavioral decisions. Preservice teachers had a chance to view social studies lessons before they entered their field experience. The teacher candidates completed one survey during and two short surveys after the tele-observation. Following the tele-observation, the teacher candidates planned and taught their six lessons for their methods practicum unit requirement. The methods instructor supervised and observed the practicum experience, looking for evidence teacher candidates actually used strategies they planned to do on the survey. The methods instructor looked for evidence the teacher candidates actually "took" the specific strategies "with them" when they moved to the practicum the following week.

Equipment needs for videoconferencing are surprisingly affordable, with a school's entire setup costing less than $2,500- $3,000. For videoconferencing and telecollaborative teaching experiences, both university sites or the university site and the public school partner site need an Internet Protocol (IP) address, microphones, H.323 video conferencing equipment (i.e., Tandberg, Polycom), software, a way of displaying video (i.e., a television monitor or Liquid Crystal Display (LCD) projector), a speaker system, and transmission lines. The videoconference units are portable and need only electrical power, a high-speed Internet connection of 384 kilobits per second, microphones, and a television monitor for displaying the video and playing the audio. Once purchased, this equipment can be used in multiple classrooms, or classes can reserve space in a room dedicated to hosting videoconferences.

METHOD

A three part instrument was designed to collect data for this project, including a four item Tele-observation Guide, a six item Teaching Strategies Survey, and a four item Overall Reflective Survey. The open-ended guides were developed from the assigned readings, lectures, and supplemental text for the methods course, *Social Studies Alive*, by Bert Bower. The researcher can be thought of as an "instrument" as well, observing the teacher candidates in the practicum, taking notes, and offering feedback and constructive advice.

Part I: Tele-Observation Guide

The Tele-observation Guide includes four items related to *general* instruction and management. The guide is open-ended with items directly related to readings and lectures in class, including theory-based instruction, standards-based content, preview assignment, and overall management. The teacher candidates were asked to complete this during the tele-observation experience. The instrument provided space for notes, thoughts, and questions related to the readings and the lesson being observed. Part I served as a protocol and thinking space for discussion with the methods professor who was facilitating on the university side of the videoconference. The purpose of Part I is to provide a guide for what to be observing, notes for Part II and III, and it also served as an open discussion guide.

Part II: Tele-Observation Strategies Survey

The Tele-observation Strategies Survey includes items related to *specific* teaching strategies discussed in the social studies methods class. These include the following teaching strategies: visual discovery, social studies skill-builders, experiential exercises, writing for understanding, response groups, and problem solving group work. Bower (2006) defines visual discovery as students viewing, touching, and interpreting images. He continues with skill builders as focused worksheets, providing clear evidence the objective is met, and experiential exercises as memorable activities to focus the learners. When students are involved in writing for understanding, writing is purposeful, response groups allow students the opportunity to grapple with issues. Bower (2006) continues to explain that problem- solving group work is the use of collaborative groups where students cooperate to solve a common problem or answer a question.

The survey asks the teacher candidates to respond to evidence of these strategies in the lesson observed and also items refer to whether the teacher candidate is planning to incorporate the strategies in their practicum. This survey was completed following the tele-observation experience, outside of class. By completing the survey outside of class, there was more time for reflection and the teacher candidates were not constantly writing and potentially missing the instruction during the tele-observation experience.

Part III: Overall Reflective Survey

The Overall Reflective Survey provides the teacher candidate space for notes, thoughts, and questions related to whether or not the teacher candidate learned anything from this experience, whether they plan on "taking the strategy with them" into their own practicum experience. The items on the survey relate to social studies content, management strategies, and specifically, what will they do with the information and how can it help them in the classroom.

Part IV: Observations of Practicum Following the Tele-observation Experience

The observations of practicum include anecdotal notes, and specific feedback and advice. The teacher candidates were observed teaching in their assigned practicum classroom following the tele-observation experience. In general, during the teacher candidate's lesson, the methods instructor takes anecdotal notes, and meets with the teacher candidate after the lesson to discuss. The observations are seen as colleague to colleague and are constructive and supportive in nature.

This study follows a combination of theories in the data analysis. Qualitative responses were analyzed using a combination of content analysis (Silverman, 1999) and the constant comparative method (Glaser & Straus, 1967) to determine

Table 1. Possible teaching strategies viewed and potential use

Theory-Based Teaching Strategy	Yes, I plan to use	Possibly, I will use	Not planning or N/A	*Actually observed in practicum*
Visual Discovery	66%	25%	8%	50%
Social Studies Skillbuilders	54%	25%	21%	29%
Experiential Exercise	58%	33%	8%	42%
Writing for Understanding	62%	13%	25%	42%
Response Groups	46%	29%	21%	25%
Problem Solving Groupwork	71%	17%	13%	13%

patterns or themes in the data. The responses were organized and reported in tables. Then the responses were read and re-read for common themes and evidence that the teacher candidates did in fact use the theory based instruction methods in their practicum classrooms. The tables allowed for an organized clear comparison, after they were reviewed and summarized.

FINDINGS

Findings reported include evidence from the surveys and observations given to the 24 teacher candidates in the ELEM 4550/4551- social studies methods class. The findings from the survey are presented in two tables while data from—are shared in sample direct quotes.

Following the tele-observation experience, the teacher candidates were asked on Part II of the survey if they would use various theory based instruction strategies in their practicum. The teacher candidates' responses are shown in Table 1. The last column represents the percentage of the teacher candidates who were observed actually using the strategy in their practicum. Note the difference between the first column and the last. The teacher candidates planned on using the strategies but most would not use the strategies once they entered the practicum the following week. For example, the majority of the teacher candidates (71%) planned to do group work but

only a small number of teacher candidates (13%) actually did use group work in their practicum, shown in Table 1.

When asked if the teacher candidate would "take anything with them to the practicum", the following items were reported in Table 2.

The following is a discussion of three summary statements based on the recurring themes the teacher candidates reported would help them in their practicums and future classrooms. The themes were repeatedly noted in the survey responses and the observations. The four summary statements regarding the ways in which teacher candidates "pack up the methods" and take it with them to the practicum, provide evidence there is some preparation for "Moving Day".

1. Teacher candidates plan on using management strategies that were observed in the tele-observation and act immediately. One teacher candidate responded:

"Once I saw (the teacher) give the students paper 'rations' as a behavior management technique linked with instruction, I created my own system for next week on my notes page"

"I don't know about using experiential exercises because our practicum teacher would probably say the children couldn't handle it. From the first

Table 2. Overall reflection on the tele-observation

What will you take with you?	What will help you in your future classroom?	Did you learn content?
50% responded Management Strategies	63% responded Management linked with Instruction	71% reported they had learned social studies content
21% responded Active participation is important	20% responded Active and relevant instruction	16% reported it was a review of content
17% responded Artifacts and visuals must be shared	13% responded Positive Atmosphere will help	8% reported they did not learn anything new

meeting, I do not think our teacher uses much active movement"

If the teacher candidate reads about the strategy and sees the strategy work with children, they may try it. But ultimately, if the clinical teacher does not believe in the strategy or is not familiar, the teacher candidate will not try it in the practicum. For example, almost all of the teacher candidates (71%) planned on using group work but only a small number (13%) actually did use group work, following the tele-observation experience. This does not necessarily mean teacher candidates will NOT use the strategy on their own in their own classroom, but it could mean they are discouraged, in spite of the methods learned in class. Considering the social studies content and methods blend well with collaborative and interactive grouping strategies, this concerns the methods professors, that the teacher candidates will not teach the children collaboration, interaction, and cooperation.

3. Teaching strategies and management strategies observed during the tele-observation experience will be tried in the practicum even if the strategy does not fit the content or context of the lesson. An excerpt from the practicum observation feedback for a teacher candidate, written by the methods instructor:

"I am glad you are trying a management strategy that could potentially link with the instructional goal. However, giving the students soldier rations and calling them soldiers during a geography lesson may be confusing. Please try having them assume the role of "geographer" and perhaps they can be handed passports to hold on to as they travel the globe..."

Even though the focus of the tele-observation experience was on an adapted Social Studies Alive lesson (Bower, 2006) and teaching strategies observed within the lesson, the teacher candidate responses related to the management strategies learned. Overwhelmingly, management strategies were mentioned in all data sources as the overall tool the teacher candidates planned to try out in the practicum. It seems that prior to the practicum, teacher candidates are most concerned with managing the learning environment and student behavior.

DISCUSSION

The teacher candidates have provided evidence they took some of the strategies and theory based instruction with them to the practicum. There were lessons including visual discovery, some response groups, and experiential exercises. The management linked to instruction was attempted and other strategies the teacher candidates planned to take from the tele-observation experience were actually used in the practicum in some manner; including visual discovery with technology integrated, and successful use of reading and writing techniques. Visual discovery through artifacts, artifact boxes, posters, overheads, PowerPoints, and primary sources was the most common strategy used with 50% of the teacher candidates trying this, some using the exact visuals as were shown in the tele-observation. Visual discovery seems to be "well packed" where the use of group work does not seem to be something we can surely see in these teacher candidates classrooms of the future. The next step of attempting to bridge theory to practice is to look for evidence of these strategies in their classroom of the future in the years to come.

University instructors will continue to search for best practices in social studies methods courses using interactive video-conferencing. At this particular university, technology integration is supported with technology personnel, funding, and equipment. The researchers will certainly continue to take advantage of this technical support infrastructure and advocate for innovative ways to observe social studies lessons in regular public school classrooms to enhance their methods courses. Plans are being developed to increase elementary school participation in various urban locations to augment the diversity included in the experience.

The professors have shown videotapes in earlier courses and discovered that videos can quickly become obsolete if not kept current with the latest best practices. Furthermore, videotapes have several downfalls when compared to live, uninterrupted teaching. First, there is the possibility that a videotaped lesson is scripted and staged, instead of being a live case, as was used in this study.

IMPLICATIONS FOR FUTURE RESEARCH

Following this study, what can be implied for teacher education is the need to constantly evaluate existing methods for helping teacher candidates transition from candidate to teacher in to their own classroom. The use of videoconference, in this study, proved to be less distracting than other methods of modeling, the technology was easily integrated into the course. Since the teacher candidates did not have to be concerned with sitting in the back of another teacher's classroom, they could be comfortable in their own college classroom being guided by a methods instructor.

Video becomes a mirror for those who are videotaped to reconsider their actions (Goldman, Pea, Barron, & Derry, 2007). In the near future, the plan is to incorporate voice over recordings of what the teacher and methods professor were thinking before, during, and after the lesson. The next steps include reporting the professor's perspective and sharing through voice over recordings the reflection in action and after action of the tele-observation experience. This will involve a transcribed voice over recording from the teacher, the professor, and a principal's reflective perspective as well. The principal's voice over will be the thoughts he or she might have during a routine 'walk through' of the classroom. Next steps include following identified students from the class as they begin their teaching career to observe for evidence of theory-based instruction and a potential smooth, stress-free, "moving day" from theory to practice.

CONCLUSION

The use of videoconference in teacher education has the potential to remove barriers of time and space, allowing teacher candidates to connect with best practice, while not disrupting the classroom. The chapter began with a comparison of teacher candidates learning teaching methods to a "moving day", where attempts are made to create an atmosphere where the teacher candidate will "pack" and "label" the theories learned in class to "take" to his or her practice of the future. On moving day, we may have many people help us, ultimately, we must organize ourselves, but we can hire professionals to get us there or ask friends to help. In this analogy, teacher educators are the hired professionals who need to take their assisting in the "moving" process seriously. If things are not transferred properly, it is a bad move.

REFERENCES

Backes, C., & Backes, L. (1999). Making the best of a learning experience. *Techniques, 74*(5), 23–24.

Bednar, M. R., Ryan, F. J., & Sweeder, J. J. (1994). Voices from the field: Teachers' responses to student teaching orientation videos. *Journal of Technology and Teacher Education, 2*(3), 293–303.

Bell, J. K., & Unger, L. C. (2003). Videoconferencing takes Cape Elizabeth Middle School on a distance learning adventure. *T.H.E. Journal, 31*, 51.

Bjerstedt, A. (1967). *Tele-observation- Closed circuit television and video-recording in teacher training.* ERIC Document Available # ED017178

Bower, B. (2006). *Social studies alive: Engaging diverse learners in the elementary classroom.* Palo Alto, CA: Teachers' Curriculum Institute.

Bronack, S., Kilbane, C., Herbert, J., & Mc-Nergney, R. (1999). Inservice and preservice teachers' perceptions of a Web-based, case-based learning environment. *Journal of Information Technology for Teacher Education, 8*(3), 305–320. doi:10.1080/14759399900200066

Darling-Hammond, L. (1998). Teachers and teaching: Testing policy hypotheses from a national commission report. *Educational Researcher, 27*(1), 5–15.

Glasser, B. G., & Strauss, A. L. (1967). *The discovery of grounded theory: Strategies for qualitative research.* New York, NY: Aldine.

Goldman, R., Pea, R., Barron, B., & Derry, S. (2007). *Video research in the learning sciences.* Mahwah, NJ: Lawarence Erlbaum Associates.

Good, A. J. O'Connor, K. A., Greene, H. C., & Luce, E. (2005). Collaborating across the miles: Telecollaboration in a social studies methods course. *Contemporary Issues in Technology & Teacher Education, 5*(3/4).

Harris, J. (1999). First steps in telecollaboration. *Learning and Leading with Technology, 27*(3), 54–57.

Hoy, M., & Merkley, D. (1989). *Teachers on television: Observing teachers and students in diverse classroom settings through the technology of television.* Ames, IA: Iowa State University.

Hyun, E., & Marshall, J. (1996). Inquiry-oriented reflective supervision for developmentally appropriate practice. *Journal of Curriculum and Supervision, 11*(2), 127–144.

Karran, S., Berson, M., & Mason, C. (2001). Harnessing Internet2: Enhancing social science education through tele-collaborative teaching and learning. *Social Education, 65*(3), 151–153.

Kent, A. (2007). Powerful preparation of preservice teachers using interactive videoconferencing. *Journal of Literacy and Technology, 8*(2), 41–59.

Laurillard, D. (1993). *Rethinking university teaching: a framework for the effective use of educational technology.* London, UK: Routledge.

Lee, J. (2008). *Visualizing elementary social studies methods.* Hoboken, NJ: Wiley and Sons.

Mason, C. (2001). Collaborative social studies teacher education across remote locations: Student experiences and perceptions. *The International Journal of Social Education, 15*(2), 46–61.

O'Connor, K., Good, A., & Greene, H.C. (2006). Lead by example: The impact of tele-observation on social studies methods courses. *Social Studies Research and Practice, 1*(2).

Rock, T., Heafner, T., Oldendorf, S., Passe, J., O'Connor, K., Good, A., & Byrd, S. (2006). One state closer to a national crisis: A report on elementary social studies in North Carolina schools. *Theory and Research in Social Education, 34*(4), 455–483.

Shulman, L. S. (1992). Toward a pedagogy of cases. In *Case methods in teacher education* (pp. 1–30). New York, NY: Teachers College Press.

Silverman, D. (1993). *Interpreting qualitative data: Methods for analyzing talk, text, and interaction*. London, UK: Sage.

Snow, C. (2005). *Knowledge to support the teaching of reading: Preparing teachers for a changing world*. San Francisco, CA: Jossey-Bass.

Sudzina, M. R. (1999). *Case study applications for teacher education: Cases of teaching and learning in the content areas*. Needham Heights, MA: Allyn & Bacon.

Valli, L. (1992). *Reflective teacher education: Cases and critiques*. Albany, NY: State University of New York Press.

Venn, M., & Moore, R., L., & Gunter, P. L. (2001). Using audio/video conferencing to observe field based practices of rural teachers. *Rural Educator, 22*(2), 24–27.

KEY TERMS AND DEFINITIONS

Live Case: A videoconference experience where methods instructors attempt to model the practicum experience for a social studies methods class. A case study in videoconference format.

Methods Course: A college course where models of teaching, theories, and strategies are taught specific to an area of content such as social studies.

Practicum Experience: Any practical teaching experience the teacher candidate can have while still studying to be a teacher. This experience is usually linked to a methods course.

Teacher Candidate: One who is studying to become a teacher, a student-teacher.

Teaching Strategy: A systematic plan of action to be used in the classroom, based on teaching theory.

Tele-Observation: A classroom observation that can take place without regard for distance by using videoconference capabilities.

Videoconference: A teleconference conducted using television equipment and the Internet.

Chapter 29
Implementing the Remote Observation of Graduate Interns:
Best Practices and Lessons Learned

Teresa M. Petty
University of North Carolina at Charlotte, USA

Richard Hartshorne
University of Central Florida, USA

Tina L. Heafner
University of North Carolina at Charlotte, USA

ABSTRACT

In this chapter, unexpected challenges, "lessons learned," as well as the best practices that have resulted during the implementation of a program involving the remote observation of graduate interns are addressed. More specifically, best practices and lessons learned related to a series of logistical, pedagogical, and technological issues encountered during both the pilot and full implementation of the ROGI process are presented. Logistical best-practices and lessons-learned address gaining school- and district-level approval to conduct remote observations; communication, verification, and documentation of the remote observations; gaining university supervisor and student intern buy-in; and e-documentation involved in the ROGI process. Pedagogical best-practices and lessons-learned attend to conducting face-to-face seminars and post-conferences remotely and camera movement during the observation. Finally, technological best-practices and lessons-learned focus on hardware and software selection and support for university supervisors and graduate interns.

DOI: 10.4018/978-1-4666-0014-0.ch029

INTRODUCTION

Rationale for ROGI: Teacher Shortages

Each year North Carolina's public schools seek to hire over 10,000 teachers just to staff existing classrooms. With increased yearly demands for teachers, attention shifts to teacher education programs. Yet, these programs fall short in addressing the needs of North Carolina's public schools by annually producing approximately 4,000 licensed teachers (Stancill, 2006). The North Carolina University system general administration, has noted this impending crisis and has challenged teacher education programs in the UNC system to "produce quicker and better solutions to the state's public school teacher shortage" (pg. 5). Administrative expectations call for the examination of existing programs for a critical analysis of student needs to determine if there are more creative and efficient methods. According to U.S. Department of Education, Office of Innovation and Improvement (2004), schools cannot simply rely on traditional teacher preparation programs to meet the growing demands of highly qualified teachers in every classroom. Instead, teacher preparation programs need to develop new routes to teacher certification that provide greater access to more teacher candidates.

According to Fulton, Glenn and Valdez (2004), the best teacher preparation programs need to constantly analyze, reflect on and renew their programs to make certain "they are responsive to changing expectations for teachers and to make sure the programs take advantage of the opportunities offered by ever more powerful technologies for teaching and learning" (pg. 3). Graduates of teacher preparation programs need to be exposed to these technologies and equipped with the knowledge and skills that will allow them to provide effective technology integration for their future students. Technology can certainly enhance student learning; however, this only occurs when teachers use technology effectively to support instruction. This underscores the importance for institutes of higher education to model appropriate and effective uses of technology within a teacher preparation program.

Impending changes within teacher education, whether motivated by national or state educational mandates, teacher shortages, shifting teacher education candidate needs, growth of second career professionals seeking employment, or tighter operating budgets, have encouraged teacher education programs to seek alternative methods for teacher preparation programs that promote growth while considering budget constraints. These changes come at a time when emerging technologies are being explored as pedagogical tools for new learning pathways.

Although many education programs have investigated or implemented online coursework and teacher preparation experiences (Sharpe et. al., 2003; Kent, 2007; Good et. al., 2005), challenges of conducting clinical experiences and teaching observations in a virtual setting still pose a barrier limiting the scope of online licensure opportunities. Addressing these issues require new approaches to current practices, course offerings, and program structures, which must be done through the careful and thoughtful examination of existing programs.

Teacher Education Programs Respond

In response to the teacher shortage in North Carolina, the Department of Middle, Secondary, and K-12 Education created the Graduate Certificate program for teacher licensure. This program allows teacher candidates with bachelors' degrees the opportunity to achieve teacher licensure in a timely manner. The Graduate Certificate program was initially placed online so that lateral entry classroom teachers could take courses conveniently and obtain licensure. Lateral entry teachers are teachers in their first three years of teaching who have a bachelor's degree and have not yet obtained teacher licensure.

Initially, due to the graduate internship experience, this online Graduate Certificate program was limited to lateral entry teachers. This internship consists of the student teaching experience for students in the Graduate Certificate program, while also requiring supervision of the Graduate Intern's teaching. In considering program expansion in an effort to address teacher shortages, the first thought was to limit the online program only to graduate interns who were lateral entry teachers. This tackled potential issues with the supervision component, as lateral entry teachers are formally observed by both their mentor teachers and school administration and, thus, would not need to be observed by a University Supervisor. This worked for a few years, however, as the College of Education was called upon by the state of North Carolina to assist in producing more teachers for this increasing teacher shortage faced by the state, alternative methods of teacher certification needed to be explored.

The decision was made to expand the online Graduate Certificate program to non-teaching graduate teacher education candidates and open the program to anyone in the state. While there were minimal issues associated with students from across the state completing coursework online, there were a number potential problems associated with supervising these individuals in their graduate internships. So, the department began exploring methods of offering a graduate internship (and the associated supervisory component) in a 100% online venue.

ROGI: A CREATIVE TECHNOLOGY SOLUTION

In an attempt to address the challenge of offering a fully online graduate internship experience, the *Remote Observation of Graduate Interns* (*ROGI*) was developed. The purpose of *ROGI* was to transcend traditional geographical boundaries required for face-to-face classroom observations through the application of technology as a means to expand access to teacher licensure programs and to increase teacher recruitment and enrollment.

What is ROGI?

The *Remote Observation of Graduate Interns* is a non-traditional method of observing graduate interns as they enter the final course of their programs in pursuit of teacher licensure (Petty & Heafner, 2009a). *ROGI* allows for a 100% online graduate internship semester and also for a technology mediated performance-based assessment and reflection of teaching that utilizes a multimedia conferencing platform to facilitate the observation aspect of the graduate internship and to communicate with graduate interns remotely (Petty & Heafner, 2009b).

It is important to consider that there are many different aspects of the graduate internship semester. First, if licensure candidates are not currently employed as teachers or cannot use their own classroom, graduate interns are placed with a cooperating teacher. Throughout the graduate internship semester, candidates are observed teaching at least three times by university supervisors. Following each of these observations, interns have a post-observation debriefing with their supervisor. Additionally, interns are required to attend a monthly seminar throughout the entirety of the graduate internship. Lastly, there are a number of additional assignments that graduate interns are required to complete and submit throughout the semester. These include submission of lesson plans, reflective journals, and others. It was important to program designers that these requirements remain consistent for graduate interns participating in *ROGI*.

Figure 1. Example of Centra screen during an observation

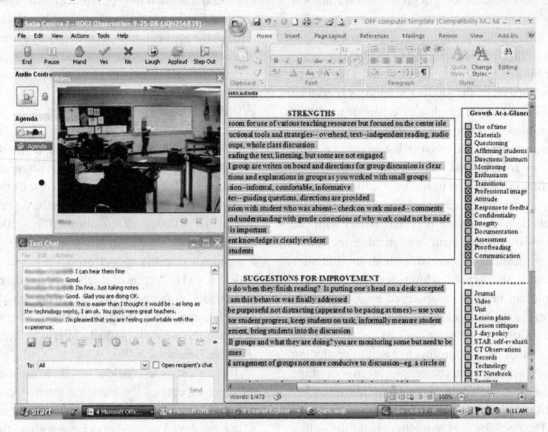

The Remote Observation Experience

Concurrent with traditional face-to-face internship experience, interns participating in the *ROGI* experience are observed three times during the internship semester. During the pilot phases of *ROGI*, the observation component was facilitated using the following equipment:

- Centra (a state of the art multimedia conferencing platform)
- A laptop computer with Internet access
- A net streaming camera
- Tripod
- Wireless microphone and headset

First, the laptop computer was networked with each school and then connected with the Internet-streaming camera. Additionally, the wireless microphone was connected to the laptop and was worn by the graduate intern throughout both the observation of teaching and the post-observation debriefing sessions. The University Supervisor wore a headset and both the University Supervisor and the graduate intern logged onto Centra (see Figure 1) to begin the observation process. Thus, the University Supervisor was able to see the graduate intern teaching his/her class in real-time from his/her office.

The Post-Observation Debriefing Experience

As previously mentioned, following each observation of teaching, a post conference debriefing occurred. This involved both the university supervisor and the graduate intern. Whenever possible, the intern remained in the classroom

Figure 2. Example of Centra screen during a post conference

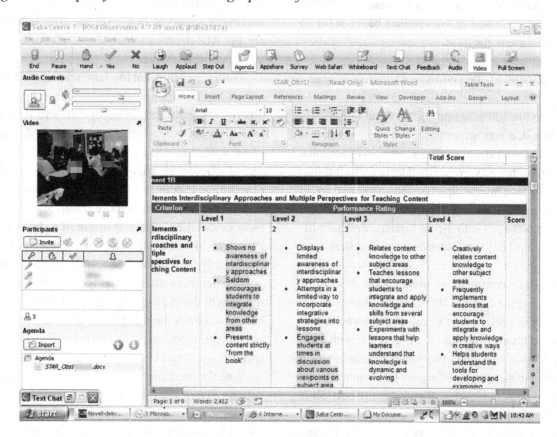

for the post-observation debriefing conference. When this occurred, the equipment setup used for the observation did not change. When the intern had to move to a different location to conference after the observation, he/she logged onto Centra from a different computer that had Internet access, while both the intern and the university supervisor wore a headset. During the post-observation debriefing conference, the university supervisor shared the completed observation instruments (see Figure 2) with the intern and explained the various ratings received, along with supportive comments made by the university supervisor. The intern then had time to ask questions about his/her teaching experience.

The Online Seminar Experience

The online seminar sessions were conducted monthly for the duration of the semester-long internship. During the remote seminars, both the university supervisors and the graduate interns logged onto Centra to participate. To facilitate the online seminars, a computer with Internet connection and headset were needed by all participants. University supervisors not proficient in using Centra received training. For the online seminar, the university supervisor might upload presentations and/or other documents to utilize during the seminar, prior to the actual meeting. Additionally, the text chat feature could be used among interns or between the supervisor and a specific intern. The text chat could also be either public or private, so that an intern could ask a more individualized question or make a comment, without everyone in the seminar being privy to the comment/question.

Electronic Paperwork

Due to the 100% online delivery and facilitation of *ROGI*, it was important that all paperwork associated with the graduate internship experience be submitted electronically. During a traditional face-to-face internship experience, interns would develop and maintain paper-based portfolios, which were put into 3-ring binders, and submitted as hard copies. Supervisors would then read through the portfolios when they would visit schools to complete an observation or conference. To maintain the 100% online characteristic of *ROGI*, participants developed a website that housed their portfolios (see Figure 3), with each portfolio containing the same documentation present in those of their face-to-face counterparts. Supervisors could view the electronic portfolios at any time, simply by accessing a specific web address, provided by the graduate intern. Interns were also required to submit their lesson plans and any lesson resources electronically prior to each observation, so that the university supervisor could provide any necessary feedback prior to an observation. The university supervisor also participated in the electronic exchange of paperwork, as he/she was required to send feedback electronically, to complete evaluation instruments electronically, and to communicate with the intern electronically.

PROGRAM ANALYSIS AND LESSONS LEARNED

The pilot semester of *ROGI* involved four graduate interns, each of which were located in four different schools, two middle schools and two high schools, across two school districts. One intern's future licensure area was social studies,

one was mathematics, and two were science. The university supervisors during the pilot semester are the ROGI project creators, researchers, and authors of this chapter.

Throughout the pilot implementation of *ROGI*, numerous unanticipated challenges related to a series of logistical, pedagogical, and technological issues were encountered. Logistical issues were related to topics such as gaining school- and district-level approval to conduct remote observations; communication, verification, and documentation of the remote observations; and e-documentation involved in the *ROGI* process. Pedagogical issues focused on topics such as conducting traditional face-to-face seminars and post-conferences remotely; and camera placement/movement during the observation. Finally, technological issues included hardware and software equipment selection issues; and providing training and support for all involved in the *ROGI* process.

With the implementation of creative strategies, such as *ROGI*, unanticipated challenges are sure to emerge and often limit the potential to broaden outreach programs. With unanticipated challenges and issues, however, come "lessons learned." These lessons are shared from the perspective of the project participants with specific attention devoted to the experiences of the authors of this chapter. From this point forward, we will share our lessons learned in hopes of helping other users of online learning in teacher education. The lessons we learned have eventually have come to increase our programmatic outreach and benefit our online teacher licensure program.

Logistical Issues: School vs. District Level Approval

During the implementation of the *Remote Observation of Graduate Interns*, we encountered several logistical issues that made the implementation of *ROGI* challenging. First, it was essential to gain school-level approval. It was critical that school-level administration understand the

Figure 3. Example of an intern's electronic teaching portfolio

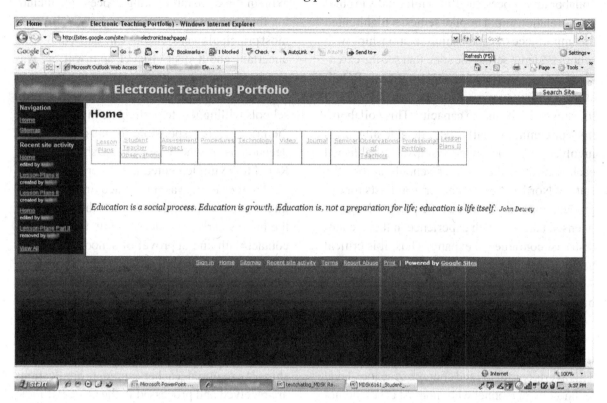

process of *ROGI*, how it worked, and potential problems that could arise. It was also important for the principal to "buy in" to the idea about an innovative approach to the observation experience. Due to hectic schedules and limited knowledge of *ROGI*, making initial contact with principals proved problematic for *ROGI*. Additionally, late changes in school administration in one of our four targeted schools emerged as a potential major area of concern for the implementation of *ROGI* in future semesters. In one instance, there was a change in a school principal one day before *ROGI* was to be implemented, forcing us to try to convince this new principal to allow us to try *ROGI* in his school. In this instance, the new principal did not allow our project in his school, forcing us at the last minute to select another intern to participate in this piloting of *ROGI*.

Second, to fully implement *ROGI*, access to school networks was essential. However, obtain-

ing this access, at times, proved challenging. As we began setup in the schools, we worked with the technology facilitators at the schools who felt the project needed district-level approval. Because of this additional level of permission, we were forced to backtrack and secure approval with each of the two districts before proceeding with full implementation. One school system was initially reluctant, but decided after much dialogue to continue with *ROGI* because of its innovative nature.

Lessons Learned

As a result of these logistical issues, we learned some important lessons that would benefit us in future semesters. Research (Rice, 2002) indicates that it is important to sustain strong university-school district partnerships that begin as voluntary with a shared vision, analyze and reflect on the collaborative process, and meet informally to build on the relationship. The pilot semester highlighted the importance of establishing relationships with school systems across the state that see the extensive mutual benefits of a program such as ROGI, and are willing to work with graduate interns and the university in such a capacity. This collaboration (or common goal) is beneficial to all parties involved and, as new relationships are established each semester, the pool of schools across the state of North Carolina that serve as hosts for our graduate interns, as well as the potential pool of licensed teachers with experience in their school districts, continues to expand. Thus, it is critical to strengthen these partnerships each semester, as well as develop new partnerships, in an effort to broaden the outreach of ROGI.

We also learned that developing district partnerships early allows for the addressing of logistical issues prior to forging school partnerships. This averts confusion and concern of school-level technology personnel who, in most cases, do not have authority over individual school networks, as network security is typically a responsibility of the school district. With the collective goal of ROGI articulated and supported at the district level, training could be provided at the district level, and disseminated to individual schools within existing communication and administrative structures. Having someone at the district level that is familiar with ROGI and how it works is extremely beneficial, as it allows them to be able to assist with any problems or concerns that may arise throughout the district with any schools allowing interns to use this method of observation.

Logistical Issues: Communication, Verification, and Documentation

Other logistical concerns related to communication, verification and documentation. First, communication with principals was very time-consuming. Initially, we visited every school to communicate project goals to principals and to explain the decision-making process for including their school as a participant in ROGI. While most principals were receptive initially, they were uncertain about district-level approval, as was previously mentioned. It is worth noting that even with district-level approval, this does not ensure a schools willingness to participate in ROGI, since the principal is responsible for making the final decision as to whether or not he/she will allow ROGI to be implemented in his/her school.

Another issue was that of acquiring graduate interns. It was important to gain the consent of the interns early, in order to allow for the initial contact with and approval of schools; however, problems can, and did, arise. Several steps were required to obtain graduate interns to participate in the initial phase of ROGI. A list of potential participants was obtained by the Office of Field Experiences, the office responsible for placing students in individual schools for their internships. As required teacher candidate applications are received and processed in the Office of Field Experiences a few months prior to the actual internship, the list of potential participants often changes shortly before the beginning of any given semester. Thus, it is important to have a plan for moving graduate interns from one school to the next. For instance, in the initial implementation of ROGI, the list of potential applicants changed just days prior to the beginning of the semester. Consequently, graduate interns were then moved from one school to the next. While several graduate interns were able to get jobs as lateral entry teachers, this affected schools by bringing new participants into the ROGI program. These last minute changes made it difficult to be proactive in setting up the ROGI experience, and are something that will be addressed in subsequent implementations of ROGI.

As with any course or internship experience, it was also important to clearly communicate expectations of ROGI to the participating graduate interns. This proved challenging because most of the required university documentation and support materials were developed with the traditional face-to-face observation experience in mind. This resulted in most documentation and support materials needing to be updated to online versions to make their use easier for the university supervisor and the graduate intern. It was also important to get "buy in" from all potential participants, including interns. When we met with the potential participants, they were provided with a detailed overview of the project, and subsequently determined whether or not they wished to participate. For those who chose to participate, there was a detailed explanation regarding all of the differences between the traditional face-to-face observation method and ROGI, a list of participant expectations, and how they could make their experience with ROGI a pleasant and effective graduate internship semester.

Lastly, documentation proved quite challenging with ROGI. Due to the 100% online delivery and implementation of ROGI, all paperwork had to be in an electronic format, as well as be submitted electronically to appropriate individuals (University Supervisors, licensing offices, Office of Field Experiences, etc.). For example, the graduate intern submitted all course activities electronically and developed a website rather than a traditional intern three-ring binder portfolio previously discussed. The university supervisor ensured that he/she was familiar with completing the observation ratings and forms prior to the first observation so that he/she could offer thorough and effective feedback in the appropriate electronic manner. In a traditional face-to-face observation the intern has his/her lesson plan, resources, portfolio, etc. are available for the supervisor on the day of the observation. In contrast, for the remote observation these materials were sent prior to the observation so that the supervisor could organize the materials in preparation for the observation. This required both the intern and the supervisor to plan ahead accordingly.

Lessons Learned

Using top-down strategies in forging relationships and project support at the district-level was a critical lesson learned. First, it is necessary to obtain contracts from the school systems that document their commitment to ROGI. It is also important to note that it is not necessary to visit every school to talk with the principal, as in many instances, a phone call was sufficient to complete all tasks associated with gaining initial approval and discussing "next steps" for implementing ROGI. As one of the benefits of ROGI is its 100% online nature, and as *ROGI* grows, it would certainly be counter-productive to drive to all schools utilizing this innovative instructional process.

As mentioned previously, it is important to determine, as early as possible, the graduate interns participating in ROGI, as it is critical to secure the necessary relationships and approvals with the school systems involved. Thus, if a graduate intern's placement changed, it would typically be changed to a school located in the same school system. So, if a relationship has already been established, accommodating such changes would not be as difficult as if these changes arose at the last minute without established relationships and approvals.

It is also important to clarify expectations of graduate interns up front, and this can be accomplished remotely. The ROGI experience will be much more effective and efficient if expectations are clear to everyone involved as early as possible in the process.

Logistical Issues: e-Documentation

E-Documentation was a challenge during the implementation of ROGI as the graduate intern experience has relied on paper-based documentation with various color coding features in the past. However, this traditional way of doing business was not feasible or appropriate for the online environment. As a first step, it was essential to convert all of the teaching evaluation instruments from paper-based to electronic. These included observation forms, evaluation forms, and school system verification forms that were all multiple color-coded carbon copies required for licensure.

In addition to these evaluation instruments were resources for both the graduate intern and the Cooperating Teacher/Mentor. These included an internship handbook for the cooperating teacher, as well as other supporting materials, all of which existed only in paper-based form. During the implementation, it was difficult and cumbersome to gain electronic access or permission to create electronic versions to all needed documentation; as a result, some paperwork had to be mailed or delivered to the school. This seemed to be at odds with the ROGI process which called for a 100% online experience. While we have made strides in developing online evaluation forms, a few obstacles still exist.

Lessons Learned

A great deal was learned about e-Documentation during the initial implementation of ROGI. First, electronic methods of documentation needed to be established. It was learned that this could be done through the college's current assessment software. The importance of eSignatures as a tool for submitting documents that required various signatures (for licensure or approval) emerged. The validity of eSignatures as a tool to replace pen-based signatures eliminated the need to mail, fax or deliver numerous documents. Extending e-Documentation also eased the collection and reporting of teacher candidate data necessary for future accreditation purposes.

Pedagogical Issues: Face to Face Seminars and Post-Conferencing

Graduate interns are required to attend monthly seminar sessions during the internship semester. Typically, interns come to campus to participate.

However, in order to support a truly 100% online internship, monthly seminars would need to be conducted in an online environment. During the pilot semester, remote seminars were conducted using Centra as a multimedia conferencing tool. Benbunan-Fich and Hilz (2003) determined that online courses improve when professors structure them to support the growth of a learning community by using collaborative learning methods and being available to interact with students. To conduct remote seminars, university supervisors had to transfer their curriculum materials from a format suitable for a face-to-face seminar to a format appropriate for an online seminar, a very time consuming process. The university supervisor also had to develop expertise in teaching synchronous online seminar sessions, which required some training for the supervisors, as this concept was foreign to most university supervisors. Additionally, in conducting the online seminar sessions, there were concerns of privacy in sharing materials. Thus, course enrollment was set up in order to limit the use of many technology resources. Because of this setup, the course management system supported by the university was not an option in facilitating seminars. Additionally, problems with hardware, such as lack of headsets, and technical issues, limited participation.

Immediately following the observation by the university supervisor, interns were expected to participate in a post-conference debriefing. In a traditional setting, the intern and university supervisor either conferenced in the classroom or moved to another setting while another teacher supervised the students in the classroom. In a remote setting, the equipment was located in the room where the intern is teaching. If the intern had planning time or lunch immediately following the observation, the conferencing could take place in the classroom. However, if the classroom was still occupied by students, the equipment had to be moved to a different location where the Internet was accessible. This typically eliminated the use of video during the conferences as the camera software had to be installed on the computer that housed the camera. If moving the equipment was not an option, another time had to be scheduled for the post-conference debriefing. This increased the amount of time between the teaching experience and the receipt of feedback from the university supervisor, which was problematic.

Lessons Learned

Through this experience, we learned that requiring students to purchase headsets would be beneficial for all participants in the ROGI process. Additionally, the creation of electronic versions of all evaluation instruments, seminar materials, course assignments, student handbooks, resources for cooperating teachers, and documents for schools is critical. While time consuming, and initially costly, these documents will be necessary for a 100% online graduate internship.

Lastly, post-conferences can be completed via alternative technologies. If it is not feasible to move equipment or if a post-conference needs to be scheduled at a time outside of the school day, this can be done via phone or VOIP (Skype). It is useful to e-mail evaluation instruments prior to this meeting, so that interns can view the documents during the discussion with the university supervisor.

Technological Issues: Hardware and Software Selection

During the implementation of ROGI, various video methods were used. We experimented with both asynchronous and synchronous methods of observation in which these video methods varied. During an asynchronous observation, the camera was placed in a part of the classroom that was out of the way of students and was attached to a tripod. This presented several limitations. The fixed scope of the camera allowed a limited view of the classroom so that an observer could only see where the camera was pointed. The sound was very

limited during this type of observation because we were relying on the camera to capture sound. The interns were asked to upload the video to a secure server following the observation so that the observer could view the teaching demonstration in a timely fashion. This resulted in many frustrations. The computer may or may not have capabilities to upload the video. The software used to do this had a very steep learning curve which resulted in a very frustrated intern. In most instances, the video had to be mailed which caused a delay in observation and in the intern receiving feedback from the observer.

During synchronous observations, the camera was again placed on a tripod in the classroom out of the way of students. The lighting of the room and the camera placement affected what the observer was able to see. We found it beneficial to test the lighting and camera placement before the actual observation took place. We also had a camera operator in the room that could span the camera when needed so that the observer could get a more accurate view of what was occurring in the classroom. This camera operator could be a cooperating teacher or mentor teacher that could text with the university supervisor providing updates on the intern's progress and/or needs.

While Centra proved to be a good tool to use in the synchronous observations, it did present limitations. The sound was limited, resulting in university supervisors not being able to hear well when the students/interns were at a distance from the camera. Lastly, the viewing window in Centra was very small (see Figure 1) and inhibited the quantity of the classroom that could be seen.

Lessons Learned

As a result of initially piloting both an asynchronous and synchronous observation method, it was determined that the synchronous method of observation was a more effective method to use when observing graduate interns (Petty, Heafner, & Hartshorne, 2009). A very important lesson emerged from this comparison: the observer needs to control what is viewed during the observation process. To do this, in the synchronous observations, the text chat feature in Centra could be utilized so that when the observer wanted to see a particular student or particular part of the classroom, he/she could text the camera operator and ask him/her to move the camera. For this to be effective, training would be needed for the camera operator so that he/she could learn all of the nuances of the camera used and the Centra environment.

It is also important to explore alternative technological tools (i.e. camera, software, hardware) in order to make the ROGI experience as close to the face-to-face observation as possible. For example, we discovered that a wireless microphone improved sound quality even beyond the capabilities of face-to-face observations. The voice of the teacher could be heard much better and exchanges between teacher/student and among students could also be heard. Thus, a wireless microphone was required for future implementations of ROGI. Also, we are continually re-evaluating software and hardware tools in order to modify to ROGI process in order to make it more effective and efficient, as well as comparable to the face-to-face observation process.

ROGI: Current

This pilot study of ROGI offered many lessons learned that have helped us to create a more efficient and effective ROGI experience. As a result of this study, we (the project directors) took the lessons learned and acted on them to shape ROGI into a more attractive, feasible option to observing graduate interns located remotely from the university. After five semesters of its use, the process now currently used is much different than the process originally implemented in 2008. From the initial appointment of interns to the equipment used in schools, ROGI has become much more streamlined, efficient, and cost-effective. The

logistical, pedagogical and technological issues we faced during the implementation of ROGI have lessened through the careful examination of the process.

Technological Issues

Because technical issues have a significant impact on both logistical and pedagogical issues, they are continually revisited. For example, during the six semesters of *ROGI*, we have tried numerous technologies, and will continue to experiment with new and innovative technologies, as *ROGI* is a continuously evolving process.

Next, the observation experience and seminar have changed in how they are facilitated. According to Walizer, Jacobs, and Danner-Kuhn (2007), the challenges of candidate observations in remote field experience locations, can be overcome by using web cameras and videoconferencing software. To participate in ROGI, the graduate intern is now responsible for purchasing a wireless headset and a webcam. The University supplies access to the videoconferencing software. The webcam is connected to a classroom computer or school laptop that has Internet access. If the graduate intern does not have access to a computer, he/she can check one out through the university to use during the observation. The technological requirements for the university supervisor includes only a headset, since access to a university computer with Internet is guaranteed. The expense to the university during the pilot phase of ROGI was approximately $2500 per set of equipment. In 2010, it costs approximately $100 for the university supervisor's headset which is used for multiple interns across multiple semesters.

The use of the wireless headset by the intern during observations provides clear audible sound quality whereas, during the implementation, difficulties hearing the interns and students were experienced. University supervisors are now able to hear the intern, regardless of where he/she is located in relation to the camera. Additionally, supervisors are able to hear conversations with students that might not be able to be heard if the observers were sitting in the room for a traditional face-to-face observation. For example, small group discussions can be heard when the graduate intern is talking with a group. Currently, the technology being used is very different than what was used during the initial implementation, resulting in not only a much less costly process, but also a much more pedagogically effective and logistically streamlined experience for all participants. Thus, the continual re-evaluation of the technological tools and processes involved in the ROGI process have been critical to its successful implementation and continued growth.

Logistical Issues

ROGI is now a formal part of the university online teacher education program. Students entering the online program know that if they are located at least 50 miles from the university, they will be observed remotely during their Graduate Internship. This allows program coordinators to know who will be participating in ROGI during any given semester and to prepare accordingly. This also allows for early contact with school systems ahead of time, perhaps even as soon as students enter the online program. This affords detailed explanations of the remote observation process, as well as informs the school systems that they have someone in their county who is a student in our program and who will need to be observed remotely. This has proved tremendously beneficial and has resulted in significant reductions in site visits and phone calls. After the relationship has been established with the school system, the principal is contacted with a detailed description of ROGI, and asked permission for the graduate intern to be observed using this process. This has decreased the amount of time to spent trying to contact principals by telephone or making visits to the schools to talk with the principals face-to-face.

Currently, the paperwork that is used for observations has been placed online and has become part of our College's data collection system. This has alleviated frustrations associated with paperwork completion. The completion and submission process is very streamlined and all documentation is located in a single location, making it easy for the university supervisor to complete all needed documentation and for the graduate intern to view feedback and submit assignments to the supervisor. As with re-evaluation of technological issues, logistical issues continue to emerge and are assessed on a semester-to-semester basis. Continually re-examining logistical processes and being proactive in the evaluation of potential issues has resulted in limited logistical problems throughout the existence of ROGI, particularly after the initial logistical issues were resolved.

Pedagogical Issues

A number of pedagogical benefits have emerged from the ROGI process. First, it is clear that, when necessary, it is much easier to have multiple observers in an online observation, compared to a face-to-face observation. This can be extremely beneficial when a struggling intern is encountered, and another observer can offer suggestions for intervention with the intern. Additionally, when requested, the principal at the school can join the observation. This could be an excellent recruitment tool when principals are looking for new teachers, not to mention the possibilities for school use in other capacities.

One pedagogical issue that continues to be a concern is the viewing of the entire classroom, when observing remotely. Too address this, when we prepare the cooperating teachers or mentor teachers to participate in the remote observation process, they are taught to access the text chat feature in Centra during the observation. The university supervisor can then text the cooperating teacher or mentor during the observation when the camera needs to be moved so that different students or a different section of the classroom needs to be viewed. The text chat feature can also be used for the cooperating teacher and supervisor to communicate during the observation. If, for example, the cooperating teacher has seen that the intern lacks in questioning skills, then he/she can make the supervisor aware of this and the supervisor can look for this during the observation. Again, pedagogical issues are continually re-visited on a semester to semester basis, in an effort to continually improve the *ROGI* process.

SOLUTIONS AND RECOMMENDATIONS

For institutions of higher education looking for creative approaches to teacher candidate observations and seeking to model appropriate and effective uses of technology in teacher preparation programs, ROGI is certainly a viable option. We offer suggestions for making the implementation of ROGI seamless in other licensing programs. We offer the recommendations that prior to ROGI implementation, future institutions should develop a manual and supporting website. We have found this to be an important form of communication and thus currently have a supporting website that offers important information for ROGI participants. This website contains graduate intern materials including videos of intern information sessions and an electronic manual that includes setup and troubleshooting information on all technology used in the ROGI process. The website also hosts faculty support materials which include observation evaluation documents and an electronic manual with directions on technology use and troubleshooting. The implementation of this website has been very beneficial to both interns and supervisors in supporting ROGI.

Another suggestion to assist in making the implementation of ROGI successful is the offering of training sessions for all those involved. The institution implementing ROGI should prepare hardware and software training sessions for all stakeholders. District-level technology specialists should be trained on the installation and use of the hardware and on the use of the videoconferencing software. The district-level technology specialists can then help the school level technology specialists with the setup at individual schools. The interns and supervisors also need training on how to use the videoconferencing software to effectively carry out the observation experience. Equipping those involved in ROGI with the knowledge and skills necessary for a successful experience will make the implementation of ROGI flourish. Establishing partnerships with various stakeholders in the process is very important and essential to success (Rice, 2002). ROGI partnerships need to be created at the district-level first beginning with the superintendent's office and then the instructional technology department. Relationships with individual schools can then be formed. As ROGI grows and become more widely used, more school districts can be added to the cadre. It would be sensible to establish apparent guidelines and policies for participation and a clear protocol for communication, support, and collaboration.

We offer these recommendations from our experiences and lessons learned across six semesters. Preparedness and Communication are central to implementing an innovative approach to traditional processes. ROGI offers an alternative method to the traditional face to face graduate internship (student teaching experience) through creative applications and technology integration. Seminars, observations, post-conference debriefings, and sharing of documentation are all made possible through the use of webcams, wireless headsets or microphones, and videoconferencing software allowing for a 100% online internship experience. Through implementation and many "lessons learned," ROGI has emerged as creative, efficient, and cost-effective solution to the needed expansion of our teacher preparation program. It has possibilities to redefine teaching observations in other institutions as well.

REFERENCES

Benbunan-Fich, R., & Hilz, S. R. (2003). Mediators of the effectiveness of online courses. *IEEE Transactions on Professional Communication, 46*(4), 298–312. doi:10.1109/TPC.2003.819639

Fulton, K., Glenn, A. D., & Valdez, G. (2004). *Teacher education and technology planning guide.* Naperville, IL: Learning Point Associates.

Good, A. J., O'Connor, K. A., Greene, H. C., & Luce, E. F. (2005). Collaborating across the miles: Telecollaboration in a social studies methods course. *Contemporary Issues in Technology & Teacher Education, 5*(3/4), 300–317.

Kent, A. (2007). Powerful preparation of preservice teachers using interactive video conferencing. *Journal of Literacy and Technology, 8*(2), 42–58.

Petty, T., & Heafner, T. (2009a). The remote observation of graduate interns: The missing piece of the puzzle. In G. Siemens & C. Fulford (Eds.), *Proceedings of World Conference on Educational Multimedia, Hypermedia and Telecommunications 2009* (pp. 4293-4297). Chesapeake, VA: AACE.

Petty, T., & Heafner, T. (2009b). What is ROGI? *Journal of Technology Integration in the Classroom, 1*(1), 21–27.

Petty, T., Heafner, T., & Hartshorne, R. (2009, March). Examining a pilot program for the remote observation of graduate interns. In R. Weber, K. McFerrin, R. Carlsen, & D. A. Willis, (Eds.), *2009 Society for Information Technology and Teacher Education Annual: Proceedings of SITE 2009* (pp. 2658-2660). Norfolk, VA: Association for the Advancement of Computing in Education (AACE).

Rice, E. H. (2002). The collaboration process in professional development schools: Results of a meta-ethnography, 1990-1998. *Journal of Teacher Education, 53*(1), 55–67. doi:10.1177/0022487102053001006

Sharpe, L., Hu, C., Crawford, L., Saravanan, G., Khine, M. S., Moo, S. N., & Wong, A. (2003). Enhancing multipoint desktop video conferencing (MDVC) with lesson video clips: Recent developments in pre-service teaching practice in Singapore. *Teaching and Teacher Education, 19*(3), 529–541. doi:10.1016/S0742-051X(03)00050-7

Stancill, J. (2006, February 20). Tough task set for teacher training. *The Raleigh News & Observer,* A1.

United States Department of Education, Office of Innovation and Improvement. (2004). *Innovations in education: Alternative routes to teacher certification.* Washington, D.C.

Walizer, B. R., Jacobs, S. L., & Danner-Kuhn, C. L. (2007). The effectiveness of face-to-face vs. Web camera candidate observation evaluations. *Academic Leadership, 5*(3), 1–9.

ADDITIONAL READING

Arbaugh, J. B., & Benbunan-Fich, R. (2005). Contextual factors that influence ALN effectiveness. In Hiltz, S. R., & Goldman, R. (Eds.), *Learning together online: Research on asynchronous learning networks* (pp. 123–144). Mahwah, NJ: Lawrence Erlbaum.

Benbunan-Fich, R., Hiltz, R., & Harasim, L. (2005). The online interaction learning model: An integrated theoretical framework for learning networks. In Hiltz, S. R., & Goldman, R. (Eds.), *Learning together online: Research on asynchronous learning networks* (pp. 19–37). Mahwah, NJ: Lawrence Erlbaum.

Bolick, C., Berson, M., Coutts, C., & Heinecke, W. (2003). Technology applications in social studies teacher education: A survey of social studies methods faculty. *Contemporary Issues in Technology & Teacher Education, 3*(3). Retrieved from http://www.citejournal.org/vol3/iss3/social-studies/article1.cfm.

Briggs, L. J. (Ed.). (1977). *Instructional design: Principles and applications*. Englewood Cliffs, NJ: Educational Technology.

Collias, K., Pajak, E., & Rigden, D. (2000). *One cannot teach what one does not know: Training teachers in the United States who know their subjects and know how to teach their subjects*. Retrieved from http://curie.umd.umich.edu/TeacherPrep/120.pdf

Constantine, J., Player, D., Silva, T., Hallgren, K., Grider, M., & Deke, J. (2009). *An evaluation of teachers trained through different routes to certification, Final report* (NCEE 2009-4043). Washington, DC: National Center for Education Evaluation and Regional Assistance, Institute of Education Sciences, U.S. Department of Education. Retrieved from http://ies.ed.gov/ncee/pubs/20094043/pdf/20094043.pdf

Cooper, J., & Bull, G. (1997). Technology and teacher education: Past practice and recommended directions. *Action in Teacher Education, 19*(2), 97–106.

Darling-Hammond, Chung, L. R., & Frelow, F. (2002). Variation in teacher preparation: How well do different pathways prepare teachers to teach? *Journal of Teacher Education, 53(*4), 286–302.

Darling-Hammond, L. (2000). Teacher quality and student achievement: A review of state policy evidence. *Education Policy Analysis Archives, 8*(1), 1–44.

Dawson, K., & Mason, C. (2000). Collaborative dialogue: A web-based, multimedia case study shared among geographically disparate social studies educators. In White, C. (Ed.), *Social studies* (pp. 2003–2005). Norfolk, VA: Society for Information Technology and Teacher Education.

Duncan, A. (2009). *Teacher preparation: Reforming the uncertain profession*. Address at Teachers College, New York, October 22.

Garrett, J., & Dudt, K. (1998). Using video conferencing to supervise student teachers. In *SITE 98: Society for Information Technology & Teacher Education International Conference Proceedings* (pp. 1084-1088) Washington, DC.

Gentry, C. G. (1995). Educational technology: A question of meaning. In Anglin, G. J. (Ed.), *Instructional technology: Past, present, and future* (pp. 1–10). Englewood, CO: Libraries Unlimited, Inc.

Good, A. J., O'Connor, K. A., Greene, H. C., & Luce, E. F. (2005). Collaborating across the miles: Telecollaboration in a social studies methods course. *Contemporary Issues in Technology & Teacher Education, 5*(3/4), 300–317.

Harris, J. (1999). First steps in telecollaboration. *Learning and Leading with Technology, 27*(3), 54–57.

Harris, J. (2001). Teachers as telecollaborative project designers: A curriculum-based approach. *Contemporary Issues in Technology & Teacher Education, 1*(3), 429–442.

Heafner, T., & Petty, T. (2010, April). *Evaluating modes of observations: A comparative study of face to face and synchronous learning*. Paper presented at the American Educational Research Association Annual Meeting, Denver, Colorado.

Knight, S., Pedersen, S., & Peters, W. (2004). Connecting the university with a professional development school: Pre-service Teachers' attitudes toward the use of compressed video. *Journal of Technology and Teacher Education, 12*(1), 139–154.

Kurtts, S., Hibbard, K., & Levin, B. (2005). Collaborative online problem solving with preservice general, education and special education teachers. *Journal of Technology and Teacher Education, 13*(3), 397–414.

Lehman, J. D., & Richardson, J. (2007). Linking teacher preparation program with k-12 schools via video conferencing: Benefits and limitations. Paper presented at the AERA. Retrieved from http://p3t3.education.purdue.edu/ AERA2007_Videoconf_Paper.pdf

Mason, C., Berson, M., Diem, R., Hicks, D., Lee, J., & Dralle, T. (2000). Guidelines for using technology to prepare social studies teachers. *Contemporary Issues in Technology & Teacher Education, 1*(1). Retrieved from http://www.cite-journal.org/vol1/iss1/currentissues/socialstudies/article1.htm.

McLaughlin, M. W. (2006). *Building school-based learning communities: Professional strategies to improve student achievement*. New York: Teachers College Press.

Northwest Educational Technology Consortium. (2005). *Overview of technology integration in schools*. Retrieved from http://www.netc.org/images/pdf/tech.integration.pdf

Partnership for 21st Century Skills. (2009). *Framework for 21st century learning*. Retrieved from http://www.21stcenturyskills.org/documents/framework_flyer_updated_jan_09_final-1.pdf

Petty, T., & Heafner, T. (2009). *I feel everything was successful about ROGI, even the glitches. Proceedings of Society for Information Technology in Teacher Education 09*. Charleston, SC: Association for the Advancement of Computing in Education.

Schulken, M. (2008, September 25). The end of brick and mortar era. *Charlotte Observer.* Retrieved from http://www.charlotteobserver.com/2008/09/25/212524/the-end-of-the-bricks-and-mortar.html

U.S. Department of Education. 2002. *The condition of education 2002*. Washington, DC: National Center for Education Statistics. Retrieved from http://nces.ed.gov/pubs2002/2002025.pdf

KEY TERMS AND DEFINITIONS

Asynchronous Distance Learning: A technology-mediated instructional method in which learners interact with the teaching and learning environment at both differing times and physical locations. Typical pedagogical activities associated with asynchronous distance learning include discussion forums, recorded lectures, and assessments.

Centra: A web-based multimedia conferencing software application that is used to facilitate synchronous distance learning meetings. Features supported by Centra include video-conferencing, whiteboard sharing, audio and text chat, file sharing, and other communicative tools (i.e. applause, yes/no, polling, archiving).

Internship: The internship requires a preservice teacher working with a collaborating inservice teacher in a "real world" classroom environment, and typically involves the preservice teacher gradually assuming more instructional responsibilities over the course of a semester, ultimately taking on all of the instructional responsibilities for the final portions of the internship semester. The main evaluation of candidate effectiveness and preparation is a series of four teaching observations conducted by a university supervisor. In addition to the observations of student teaching, the internship involves a preservice teacher participation in a monthly seminar meeting and post-observation debriefings, as well as satisfactory completion of a culminating instructional unit development project.

Online Learning: A technology-mediated instructional methodology in which learners are interacting with the instructional setting while in different physical locations.

Remote Observation: During the student internship (student teaching experience), the main evaluation of candidate effectiveness and preparation is a series of four teaching observations conducted by a university supervisor. The remote observation is a technology-facilitated process in which the university supervisor and the student teacher are in different physical locations. The remote observation is facilitated using a webcam, laptop/computer, a wireless microphone, and video-conferencing software in the teaching classroom and for the observer.

Student Teaching: Often used interchangeably with "internship," student teaching is one component of a preservice teacher internship. Student teaching involves a preservice teacher working with a collaborating inservice teacher in a "real world" classroom environment, and typically involves the preservice teacher gradu-

ally assuming more instructional responsibilities over the course of a semester. Student teachers are observed a varying number of times a semester (usually 3-5) by a university supervisor.

Synchronous Distance Learning: A technology-mediated instructional method in which learners interact with the teaching and learning environment at different locations, but at the same time. Typical pedagogical activities associated with synchronous distance learning include video-conferencing, chats, or small group meetings.

Chapter 30
Anchoring a Social Studies Teaching and Learning Experience with Digital Video:
The Impact of a Collaborative Recursive Model for Teacher Education

Ann C. Cunningham
Wake Forest University, USA

Adam M. Friedman
Wake Forest University, USA

ABSTRACT

This chapter presents a technology integration model designed to help teacher candidates recognize the value of collaboration, inquiry-based instruction, and the use of technology to capture and sustain student engagement. Faculty from three courses collaborated to scaffold an instructional experience that included a field-based collaborative teaching component for early stage elementary teacher candidates. Using a Collaborative Recursive Model (CRM), which involved faculty teaching social studies methodology, instructional design, and a field experience course, candidates worked in teams to design a lesson that incorporated a digital video anchor created specifically to engage elementary students in the lesson. In addition to the technology-enhanced teaching experience, candidates learned how to create their own digital video resources. This experience was designed to help candidates recognize the value of collaboration, student engagement, and technology as a tool to support multi-modal learning. Results from teacher candidate reflections indicated that the CRM was an effective method for promoting candidates' appreciation of collaboration as well as supporting the development of content and pedagogical knowledge.

DOI: 10.4018/978-1-4666-0014-0.ch030

INTRODUCTION

While teacher preparation programs continue to grapple with issues of technology access, effective technology-enhanced instruction, meaningful technology integration in field experiences and candidate assessment, standards associated with technology-enhanced pedagogy for PK12 students (21st Century Skills, 2008; National Educational Technology Standards for Students, 2007) move the bar higher for teacher educators and serve as guidelines, as well as reminders, that teachers are responsible for ensuring all students are not just facile with technology tools but are capable of discerning and using appropriate tools to complete a variety of tasks. Driven by a national concern for global economic competitiveness, the tasks 21st century students must be able to perform involve far more interaction with each other and with resources beyond the walls of the school. Expectations for PK12 student performance create an urgency for adjusting instructional methods to ensure all students are developing a solid base of content knowledge while simultaneously becoming facile with a skill set preparing them for full participation in a technology driven workforce demanding adaptability, flexibility, innovation, and problem-solving.

The rumble of bricks and mortar as education institutions morph to address 21st century anytime/anyplace asynchronous instruction is just the beginning of a profound period of change for higher education. The impact of a generation of digital natives and modern technology tools on instructional delivery in PK12 classrooms are now engendering profound changes in what teacher educators deliver. All 21st century teachers need to introduce, model, and develop attitudes and skills associated with a workplace that is asynchronous, international, and reliant on workers who are innovative, creative, collaborative and adaptive. While there will invariably be a variety of responses to this phenomenon, for teacher preparation there is only one acceptable and immediate response.

This chapter outlines one teacher preparation program's model to teach, support, and facilitate the development of candidates within the content domain of elementary social studies who value collaboration, facilitate inquiry instruction, and integrate technology in meaningful and relevant ways.

Theoretical Framework

The instructional model employed by the teacher education faculty capitalizes on social learning theory (Bandura, 1977; Vygotsky, 1978), primarily the concepts of modeling, scaffolding, and apprenticeship. Until all teacher candidates enter professional education programs with prior personal experience with non-traditional instruction, a need will exist for immersion in learning experiences that foster the development of instructional practices that promote collaboration, inquiry, and the use of technology as a seamless tool for information gathering, analysis, and product creation.

The cognitive base for the instructional model developed by the teacher candidates is built on the events of instruction (Gagne & Briggs, 1979) with attention to engagement, and Universal Design for Learning (Rose & Meyer, 2002). The best instructional design can be unsuccessful in the classroom unless the designer carefully structures repeated and various instances of engagement within the design, especially for younger or distractible learners.

Although lesson plan formats, style, and the degree to which students should be actively involved with their learning may differ among curriculum theorists, one generally agreed upon practice is the notion of gaining the attention of learners at the onset of any instructional sequence (Dick, Carey, & Carey, 2005; Gagné & Briggs, 1979; Hunter, 1984). Beal, Bolick, and Martorella (2009) note that instruction "should begin with some brief initiatory activity that arouses curiosity, puzzles the students, or somehow focuses attention on what is to be learned" (p. 109). It is clear that gaining learners' attention is paramount in the teaching and learning process; however, there are many ways in which this may take place. Examples include asking students to list what they know about a particular topic, read a passage, analyze an image, or watch a brief video.

While gaining the attention of the learner is a traditional component of instructional design, computer hardware and software has become increasingly present in the K-12 environment (van Hover, Berson, Bolick, & Swan, 2006), and numerous researchers (Braun & Risinger, 1999; Hicks & Ewing, 2003, VanFossen & Shiveley, 2000) lauded its potential for instruction and engagement, particularly in social studies. It has been well documented that computer hardware and software offer students opportunities to engage in learning experiences that would not be feasible with traditional instruction (Berson, 2004; Milson & LaComb, 2001; Rose & Meyer, 2002).

Technology use has been supported by the National Council for the Social Studies; in its position statement of how it should be used, the organization noted that there is a "need to consider the role of technology in students' daily lives and its implication for classroom practice" (National Council for the Social Studies, 2006, online). The use of technology in instruction has been advocated by state boards of education, exemplified by the North Carolina Professional Teaching Standards Commission (2006), which stated that teachers should "know when and how to use technology to maximize student learning" (p. 4). The potential for technology to impact instruction is great; however, it should not be used for its own sake. As Mason, Berson, Diem, Hicks, Lee, and Dralle (2000) pointed out, it should be integrated into social studies content and be used in a manner that allows students or teachers to engage in an activity that they otherwise would not be able to.

Anchored Instruction

Anchored instruction is a pedagogical strategy that places content learning within an authentic situation which promotes problem-solving while helping engage learners and address diverse learner needs (Brown, Collins, Duguid, 1989; Cognition and Technology Group at Vanderbilt, 1990, 1997). The anchor connects the content to a real, or imagined, meaningful problem solving context that inherently engages students in the learning experience. Often incorporating video, the goal of anchored instruction is to engage students in a scenario that requires them to absorb and reflect on the context in order to solve problems and/or identify solutions. Regardless of the context, anchors should possess four characteristics: capture the imagination, be perceived as important by learners, legitimize the disciplinary content they integrate, and accommodate a variety of learning approaches (Barab & Landa, 1997). Adding digital video to an anchor elevates student engagement and addresses diverse learner needs by providing multi-modal representation of content and permitting multiple playback options on command.

Technology and Teacher Education

The challenge for teacher educators often lies in the provision of opportunities for their teacher candidates to practice technology integration in the field, especially early field experiences (Kelley, Wetzel, Padget, Williams, & Odom, 2003). As hard as it might be to orchestrate technology-enhanced instructional experiences for teacher candidates, particularly in early field experiences, professional organizations have been calling for this since the turn of the century. The International Society for Technology in Education (ISTE) outlines performance profiles for the preparation of technologically proficient future teachers in the first version of the National Educational Technology Standards for Teachers (ISTE, 2000). The professional preparation performance profile expects teacher candidates to "design and teach technology-enriched learning activities that connect content standards with student technology standards and meet the diverse needs of students (II, III, IV, VI)" (p.16). As early as 2000, professional organizations committed to the development of technology-proficient teachers called for field-based technology-enhanced instructional opportunities for teacher candidates using materials they design on their own.

Implementation

At Wake Forest University, all elementary teacher candidates participate in what is commonly referred to as the 'junior block' of education coursework during the first semester after formal admission to the elementary education program. During this semester, candidates are enrolled in an instructional design course concurrently with social studies methods, science methods, reading methods, and a field experience course which provides a venue for practicing technology-enhanced pedagogical skills. The deliberate alignment of technology-enhanced instructional design, content-specific methods and a field experience fosters collaboration among the faculty responsible for the courses, resulting in rich opportunities to develop the technology-enhanced instructional strategies and experiences of the elementary teacher candidates while reinforcing the relationship between content and technology methods.

The instructional model described in this chapter evolved from the collaboration between faculty teaching the Instructional Design, Assessment, and Technology and the Teaching Elementary Social Studies courses who devised a technology-enhanced instructional design project focusing on teaching social studies content. With the inclusion of the clinical faculty member responsible for the field experience course, the Collaborative Recursive Model (CRM) developed resulting in an instructional design project that evolved into a powerful teaching experience for the teacher

candidates. Within the framework of the CRM, elementary teacher candidates worked in triads to develop the technology-enhanced instructional unit, developing digital video anchors as requirements for the instructional design course and integrating them into their lesson plans in their social studies methods course. The field experience enhanced the authentic task dimension associated with the instructional design and social studies course assignment as well as reinforced the apprenticeship of the teacher candidates with an experienced local classroom teacher. Under the guidance of the classroom teacher, candidates identified specific social studies content from the state pacing guide and created a project or problem-based lesson that included a digital video anchor designed to engage the group of learners in that specific classroom. The teacher candidate collaborative groups taught their lessons at the end of the semester to allow candidates sufficient time to develop the lesson to align with the elementary classroom curriculum. The coordination of the unit topics with the local teachers and the planning for the teacher candidates' lesson at the end of the semester was handled by the clinical faculty member teaching the field experience course.

The showcase lesson incorporating the digital video anchor was taught in a collaborative group to provide peer support for this challenging first teaching experience. Teaching the lesson at the end of the semester gave groups the maximum amount of time to design their lesson materials, create the video anchor, rehearse the lesson in front of their classmates, and get feedback from peers and faculty. Scaffolding occurred at a variety of levels, and opportunities to modify and improve the lesson were provided throughout the semester. The recursive nature of the scaffolding and the collaborative nature of the candidates as well as full collaboration among faculty and students are hallmarks of this model.

Two weeks prior to teaching their lesson in a school, candidates were assessed on several different levels. The video anchor was initially evaluated in the instructional design course by faculty and the peer cohort. Using the rubric provided with the assignment, the faculty gave feedback on content, potential for engagement, and ingenuity with video-editing techniques. The peer review came in the form of short responses in the "3 plusses and a wish" format; each person anonymously commented on three positive features of the video anchor and provided at least one statement about how the video anchor could be improved.

This feedback from faculty and peers was subsequently used by the candidates to revise their videos prior to the second evaluation. The second evaluation occurred in the social studies methods course when the candidates simulated teaching their lesson in an elementary classroom. In this instance, each group of candidates submitted a fully detailed lesson plan and collaborated to teach an abbreviated version of their lesson. They showed their video anchor, conducted questioning, and guided the post-viewing activity within the context of a real classroom teaching event while the other teacher candidates assumed the role of elementary students experiencing the lesson. Oral feedback was provided at the end of each teaching demonstration from faculty and from other teacher candidates. Faculty also met with each group and de-briefed the lesson, including the video anchor. At this point, the candidates could again modify their instruction and video anchor, as necessary. This process provided multiple opportunities and experiences with the technology, content, and methodology with the intent of improving candidates' ability to execute the lesson in the field. This approach fostered collaboration among and between faculty and teacher candidates while establishing a professional learning community for the purpose of promoting best instructional practice through repeated instances of rehearsal and feedback.

The final evaluation occurred when the candidates taught in the elementary classroom. During this event, faculty, cooperating teacher(s), and members of the elementary cohort observed the teaching episode, with attention to the interaction between the teaching group and the interaction between the teaching group and the elementary students. Faculty and non-teaching candidates documented general feedback during their observations with a focus on strategies the teaching group used to engage the students. All teacher candidates received written non-graded evaluations and feedback, and the teaching experiences were de-briefed in the social studies methods course. Informal feedback was provided by the cohort during the de-briefing and from the cooperating teacher while at the school. Employing low-stakes evaluation at the end of this challenging experience and after the professional learning community is thoroughly established increases the quality and effectiveness of the feedback and evaluation. These are critical skills for all teachers, and especially important for novice teachers. The faculty responsible for designing and implementing the collaborative recursive model noticed that candidates' skills of professional reflection were sharpened and their ability to give and receive constructive feedback developed significantly through the semester the model was implemented. As the integration of the CRM occurred during the first of three semesters as a cohort, and the semester prior to student teaching, faculty agreed that the model was an excellent opportunity to develop valuable collaborative relationships as well as professional habits and dispositions during the early stages of teacher candidacy. This led to further exploration of the impact of the model.

Teacher Candidate Perceptions of Digital Video as a Sound Instructional Tool and Value of Collaborative Recursive Instructional Model

Since written reflections are a common practice as well as a natural strategy for candidates to express their thoughts about teaching and learning experiences, the reflections submitted within a week of the collaborative teaching episodes in the field were analyzed using the constant-comparison method to identify patterns within the responses (Glaser & Strauss, 1985).

The three faculty read each of the 20 reflections noting significant references to the teaching and learning experience, then met to discuss their findings. Using grounded theory as described by Strauss and Corbin (1998) to review the reflections, the instructors "allow[ed] the theory to emerge from the data" (p. 12). Three categories emerged from the twenty reflections analyzed: impact of the CRM, instructional design and teaching strategies, and the value of DV anchor as a sound instructional tool. Faculty also noted that these main categories could be broken into sub-categories to provide more specific data from the candidate reflections. Table 1 provides descriptions of each category and subcategory.

Impact of the Collaborative Recursive Model

- *Model* – This category includes statements in the candidate reflections that relate to the value of the design, feedback, and recursive nature of the implementation model.
- *Collaboration* – This category includes statements in the candidate reflections that relate to the value of working in collaborative teams.

Instructional Design and Teaching Strategies

- *Instructional Methods to be Modified or Retained* – This category includes any statement in the candidate reflections that describes instructional or management strategies that the candidate feels were successful or would be modified in future instruction.
- *Instructional Methods Addressing Diverse Learner Needs* – This category includes

any statement in the candidate reflections that describe an instructional strategy that supports the needs of diverse learners.

Digital Video

- *Impact of Digital Video Anchor on Student Engagement* – This category includes statements that describe the candidate's perception of the students' reactions to the video anchor.
- *Digital Video as a Sound Instructional Tool* – This category includes any statement in the candidates' reflections that indicates their recognition of the use of digital video as an instructional tool that supports effective practice.

Table 1 also presents the number of responses for each category, and sub-categories, as determined by the faculty. The challenge of separating comments related to the teaching methods and the impact of the DV anchor on diverse learners were resolved by focusing on how candidates described the impact or value of the anchor. It should be noted that responses regarding teaching strategies supporting the needs of diverse learners are not counted in the category of "Instructional methods to be Modified or Retained", and responses regarding the impact of DV as an instructional tool are not counted in the category "Impact of the DV Anchor on Student Engagement". Although decisions about category placement of comments required a great deal of discussion, the fact that faculty had to engage in this discussion indicates that the digital video anchor was perceived as a powerful instructional tool that engaged students while also addressing diverse learner needs.

Analysis

Responses about the impact of the collaborative recursive model (CRM) totaled 75 with 19 com-

Table 1. Frequency of references in reflections by category and by lesson

Lesson All groups had 3 individual reflections except K with only 2	Impact of Collaborative Recursive Model		Instructional Design and Teaching Strategies		Value of DV anchor for instruction and engagement	
	Collaboration	Model	To be modified or retained	Diverse learner needs	Impact of DV on student engagement	DV as a sound instructional tool
K	0	4	12	0	2	0
1	5	5	15	1	6	5
2	1	11	12	1	5	0
2b	2	9	13	1	5	1
3	3	8	11	8	3	1
4	3	10	22	0	5	2
5	5	9	12	2	3	0
TOTAL All categories	19	56	97	13	29	9
TOTAL Major categories	75		110		38	

ments specifically related to the collaboration of the team members and 56 related to the CRM. The majority of the comments about the collaboration were positive and they addressed collaboration that occurred in the planning, revision, and implementation stages of the model. The overwhelming majority of the comments about the CRM were associated with the total experience. These comments were all positive and expressed satisfaction about this teaching opportunity.

The 97 responses about instructional methods to be retained or modified during the teaching episode did not include any specific references to the use of digital video. These comments focused specifically on instruction or management during the teaching of the lesson in the elementary classroom. Thirteen of those comments referred specifically to how the methods employed during instruction reinforced the learning experience for students with language or cognitive differences. There were 110 comments, the most of all three major categories, relating to instructional methods.

Thirty-eight comments focused specifically on the use of the digital video anchor during the teaching episode or more general references to the potential of digital video in the elementary classroom. Twenty-nine comments expressed satisfaction about the impact of the DV anchor on student engagement. Every candidate made at least one comment about how the DV anchor engaged the elementary students and some candidates made two or three references to student engagement related to the DV anchor.

Selected comments about each of the categories represented in the teacher candidate reflections are presented below.

Collaboration

I've also learned the benefits of working cooperatively. Too often individuals do not trust their group's potential enough to see the potential, and I even suffered from that a bit this semester but we came together and taught a really wonderful lesson.

We spend lots of hours brainstorming for this lesson, and I feel really lucky that all three of use were so dedicated to improving our lesson. We worked well together, and I felt extremely supported the whole time. Each of us had our own ideas to share and we built off each other.

It was nice to be able to teach in a group this first time because we could add anything that another group member forgot, we had three brains to answer students' questions with, and we had three imaginations and intelligences to pull from in creating this lesson. I know that it will be a lot different when I get into the classroom by myself, but this was still great practice with planning, creating, and executing a lesson.

Model

The biggest thing I learned from this lesson is that I can teach fifth grade. I was extremely worried about the content from the beginning, but I learned that if you spend the time becoming familiar with the material then it will show in your instruction. Every little detail is important. A good structured lesson will capture the attention of any class.

Having done the lesson in [the university] class already, I had complete confidence in my ability to repeat the lesson. The best part about doing the lesson in advance was that when it came time to do the lesson in the elementary school, I completely forgot about the observers and that I was being critiqued.

Having the opportunity to teach lessons in the classroom has truly given me confidence in my teaching abilities. In social studies, my group gave our fifth grade lesson on political parties. Our original mini-lesson that we gave to our peers essentially did not accomplish the learning objectives or goals that we had hoped. So, after a lot of constructive criticism, we decided that it would be best to start over. After reworking a new lesson plan, and creating a new video, our

group turned in a lesson, that I personally was not confident in or comfortable teaching, into a very engaging and fun fifth grade social studies lesson.

Instructional Methods to be Modified or Retained

Modified

Slowing down when it comes to instructions pays off because you will then be able to focus on the content of student performance, rather than how they are following instructions. Allow time for students to ask questions about these instructions and allow yourself time to clarify their questions.

It's always better to go slower than you think you might need to. Even though slowing down might seem like it takes so much time, student understanding and performance increases, so taking the extra time is worth it!

Retained

I learned that you need to double-check all technology before you teach the lesson as well as have some back-up activities prepared just in case something goes wrong.

Students respond greatly to how the teacher acts, so by being excited and animated, we were able to get the class to be excited and animated. It created a great learning environment and the students all were happy to be learning.

Relevance of Developmentally Appropriate Instructional Design and Methods

I especially feel like I learned a lot about adapting lesson to meet individual needs, and how to create an environment in which the students really felt comfortable and were able to learn and take risks while feeling secure and successful.

I feel like we provided a supportive environment to ensure that the students could succeed. The struggling students worked alongside the others and could not be recognized by those who watched the lesson. I was extremely surprised and excited at the participation of a BED (behavioral and emotional disorder) student and several other challenging students. In the ideal lesson, all students participate regardless of level or circumstances.

Impact of Digital Video Anchor on Student Engagement

During the lesson, the students were really engaged by the video and had even pulled us aside to tell us that they hoped that principal never came to their school! We prompted them with the video to write the principal a persuasive letter to try to convince him that having democratic principles in his school would help students learn better. They seemed very eager to write these letters to "Dr. Strictmyer" and wrote down very creative thoughts about how democracy should be present in the school.

As the video was playing, I looked around the room, and *every* student was completely focused and paying attention. It was fun to watch them glance back and forth at the teachers to see if we were really the characters they were watching in the video.

The students really seemed to love the video anchor. They seemed to really pay attention during the video, and our entire lesson was based on the scenarios presented in the video. The students were engage in thinking about the video, and they were really hooked and interested in the lesson from that point on. I think that students generally respond well to video, and this was a great example of using video to set up a whole lesson.

Impact of Digital Video as an Instructional Tool

I really feel like a strong technology background will set your students apart from the average elementary-schooler, so if I was going to teach this lesson again I would definitely keep the activities that involved technology.

The rest of the lesson's activities supported the foundation begun with the anchor and it was evident that the students were learning and synthesizing the new information. They were able to apply their new knowledge in a variety of situations which lets us know that we achieved our objectives.

I would love to use this lesson in the future, and I would do most of it exactly the same (if I am lucky enough to have the same technological resources!).

The video anchor and other types of technology are great ways to break the boring stereotypes of social studies, and I am eager to employ these methods in my classroom.

CONCLUSION

Faculty observations of the elementary students, as well as teacher candidate self-reports in their post-experience reflections support the value of a digital video anchor to deeply engage students in a social studies lesson. Descriptions of the teaching experience reported in the candidate reflections reveal that the digital video anchor helped sustain engagement in the lesson until the end, although it is likely that the extensive preparation and enthusiasm of the candidates contributed greatly to the sustained level of student engagement.

It was clear that the CRM was viewed by teacher candidates as an overwhelmingly positive experience. Teacher candidates clearly valued this method and expressed gratitude for the opportunity to be able to engage in this intensive, integrated and focused teaching and learning experience. The breadth of their learning about instructional methods was substantial, and their ability to express their understanding of the value of instructional design to support the needs of diverse learners was quite impressive for candidates who have not yet entered their student teaching internship.

The development of the digital video anchor within the structure of the CRM supports the development of technology, pedagogy, and content knowledge in way that is authentic and meaningful to the teacher candidates, and subsequently, the elementary students. As instructors, it was clear that the candidates worked hard to develop meaningful social studies materials and teaching strategies for their lessons in the field, and their collaborations were genuine and productive. The reflections reveal that the candidates were both pleased and comfortable with their technology integration, but their enthusiasm was focused on their ability to become better teachers by improving their pedagogical content knowledge, which is the type of technology integration that Harris, Mishra, and Koehler (2009) advocate.

Implications for Practice

The goal of both the CRM and 21st century teacher education is to produce teachers who know how to seamlessly integrate technology into instruction in ways that support their content goals while engaging students in authentic, real-world, and meaningful tasks. Additionally, 21st century teachers must also develop their content and pedagogical expertise to support the needs of diverse learners and the development of higher order skills. As Web 2.0 tools become more prominent and accessible in PK-12 schools, opportunities for integrating video into instruction increase. However, it is imperative that teacher candidates understand the challenges and benefits of Web 2.0 video integration, and those lessons are best taught within the context of an authentic teaching experience under the auspices of an expert teacher and/or instructional design media specialist. There are many challenges associated with Web-based video delivery in PK-12 schools. Many schools do not have the infrastructure to support for on-demand, full-class, streaming video due to lack of necessary bandwidth or inadequate hardware. Further, Internet filters oftentimes block student access

to Web 2.0 sites. Good educational resources are available on several educational Websites, but are also available on YouTube, which is typically blocked by most schools. Teachers who want to use good educational resources from blocked sites then grapple with copyright infringement and violation of school and/or district policies.

Teacher and student created resources can be uploaded to educational sites like TeacherTube and NextVista for sharing with the educational community. As sites like these develop and video capture/editing tools become more ubiquitous, opportunities to scaffold student (and teacher) creativity and innovation with digital video and on-demand classroom access to video creations from around the world will be more realistic. The need for preparing teachers to use digital tools effectively and appropriately will still be a vital part of pre-service instruction because when powerful tools, like digital video, become the least notable portion of a lesson reflection it can be assumed that teachers are comfortable with the use of such a valuable and effective instructional tool. Being able to design effective engagement tools with digital video and knowing how to integrate them appropriately into one's instructional design is a critical first step toward development as a 21st century teacher.

The implications for pre-service teacher education are clear. Sustained collaborative efforts among teacher education faculty can create deep and resonant learning experiences for pre-service candidates that broaden their skills, but more importantly, broaden their understanding of meaningful instruction that incorporates technology as a tool to facilitate pedagogy, support content, and scaffold student knowledge development.

This model is also useful for pre-service secondary education teachers as well as for in-service professional development with teachers at all grade levels. The key is to have an authentic instructional goal for each collaborative group to work toward, plenty of time for feedback and revision, and faculty with expertise in content, pedagogy, and technology applications to scaffold the process. In a higher education setting, course alignment is also a very important part of the success of this model. Aligning pedagogical experiences with field experiences is critical to developing the authentic task, and the ability to develop a product, use it, and witness the results in a real classroom. Experienced teachers may be more comfortable trying an innovative method with a group of students they do not know well, but it is helpful for the pre-service candidates to know the students and be more comfortable interacting and responding to familiar faces and behaviors, especially since their classroom management experiences are limited and their skills are emerging.

This model may also prove effective as a professional development method for promoting the development of technology, pedagogy, and content development with in-service teachers. In service teachers unfamiliar with digital video technologies or anxious about technology integration have the advantage of familiarity with their students in addition to refined instructional and classroom management techniques. For them, the experience might focus more on the mastery of digital video tools to scaffold and promote student engagement, critical thinking, problem-solving, and creativity. In-service teachers might find the collaborative experience a more supportive strategy for mastering digital video editing which could lead to increased integration of technology to support student creativity and collaboration in the classroom. This may work across semesters if field placements remain stable for pre-service teachers. For in-service teachers, the CRM could be easily used within a professional learning community. This could occur in one school or in multiple schools with teachers and media specialists. Not only could the video anchor creation be a team-building activity for teachers, it could be an opportunity to develop new skills and integration ideas that could then be applied to

instructional strategies that support 21st Century skill development.

The CRM, combining instruction and scaffolding from methods, technology, and field experience faculty, has the potential to shape instructional design choices for future teachers and could be modified for use as professional development. This model has been designed to reinforce the principle that solid instructional design relies on feedback, revision, and reflection as well as reinforce the disposition of teacher collaboration. These are all habits and practices identified with master teachers, and are worthwhile for teachers of all ages. While the goals identified for pre-service teachers might be different from those identified for in-service teachers, the fundamental principles are important for all teachers.

REFERENCES

Bandura, A. (1977). *Social learning theory*. Upper Saddle River, NJ: Prentice-Hall, Inc.

Barab, S. A., & Landa, A. (1997). Designing effective interdisciplinary anchors. *Educational Leadership, 54*(6), 52–55.

Beal, C., Bolick, C. M., & Martorella, P. H. (2009). *Teaching social studies in middle and secondary schools*. Boston, MA: Allyn & Bacon.

Braun, J., & Risinger, F. (1999). *Surfing social studies*. Washington, DC: National Council for the Social Studies.

Brown, J. S., Collins, A., & Duguid, P. (1989). Situated cognition and the culture of learning. *Educational Researcher, 18*(1), 32–42.

Cognition and Technology Group at Vanderbilt. (1990). Anchored instruction and its relationship to situated cognition. *Educational Researcher, 19*(6), 2–10.

Cognition and Technology Group at Vanderbilt. (1997). *The Jasper project: Lessons in curriculum, instruction, assessment, and professional development*. Hillsdale, NJ: Erlbaum.

Contemporary Issues in Technology and Teacher Education (CITE). (2008). *CITE Journal, 8*(3). Retrieved on October 10, 2008 from http://citejournal.org/vol8/iss3/maintoc.cfm?content=about

Dick, W., Carey, L., & Carey, J. O. (2005). *The systematic design of instruction* (6th ed.). Boston, MA: Allyn and Bacon.

Gagné, R. M., & Briggs, L. (1979). *Principles of instructional design*. New York, NY: Holt, Rinehart, & Winston.

Harris, J., Mishra, P., & Koehler, M. (2009). Teachers' technological pedagogical content knowledge and learning activity types: Curriculum-based technology integration reframed. *Journal of Research on Technology in Education, 41*(4), 393–416.

Hicks, D., & Ewing, E. (2003). Bringing the world into the classroom with online global newspapers. *Social Education, 67*(3), 134–139.

Hunter, M. (1984). Knowing, teaching, and supervising. In Hosford, P. (Ed.), *Using what we know about teaching*. Alexandria, VA: Association for Supervision and Curriculum Development.

International Society for Technology in Education. (2000). *NETS for teachers 2000*. Retrieved on October 15, 2008, from http://www.iste.org/Content/NavigationMenu/NETS/ForTeachers/2000Standards/NETS_for_Teachers_2000.htm

Kelley, M., Wetzel, K., Padget, H., Williams, M. K., & Odom, M. (2003). Early childhood teacher preparation and technology integration: The Arizona State University West experience. *Contemporary Issues in Technology & Teacher Education, 3*(1). Retrieved from http://www.citejournal.org/vol3/iss1/general/article5.cfm.

Mason, C., Berson, M., Diem, R., Hicks, D., Lee, J., & Dralle, T. (2000). Guidelines for using technology to prepare social studies teachers. *Contemporary Issues in Technology and Teacher Education, 1*(1). Retrieved July 13, 2006, from http://www.citejournal.org/vol1/iss1/currentissues/socialstudies/article1.htm

Milson, A. J., & LaComb, S. (2001). World-class sounds: Music, social studies, and the Internet. *Social Studies and the Young Learner, 13*(4), 1–2.

Mishra, P., & Koehler, M. J. (2006). Technological pedagogical content knowledge: A new framework for teacher knowledge. *Teachers College Record, 108*(6), 1017–1054. doi:10.1111/j.1467-9620.2006.00684.x

National Council for the Social Studies. (2006). *Technology position statement and guidelines*. Retrieved on August 10, 2009, from http://www.socialstudies.org/positions/technology

North Carolina Professional Teaching Standards Commission. (2006). *North Carolina professional teaching standards*. Retrieved on October 10, 2008, from http://ncptsc.org/Final%20Standards%20Document.pdf.

Rose, D. H., & Meyer, A. (2002). *Teaching every student in the digital age*. Virginia: Association for Supervision and Curriculum Development.

Strauss, A., & Corbin, J. (1998). *Basics of qualitative research: Techniques and procedures for developing grounded theory*. Thousand Oaks, CA: SAGE Publications, Inc.

van Hover, S. D., Berson, M. J., Bolick, C. M., & Swan, K. O. (2006). Implications of ubiquitous computing for the social studies curriculum (Republished). *Contemporary Issues in Technology & Teacher Education, 6*(2). Retrieved from http://www.citejournal.org/vol6/iss2/socialstudies/article3.cfm.

VanFossen, P. J., & Shiveley, J. M. (2000). Using the Internet to create primary source teaching packets. *Social Studies, 91*(6), 244–252. doi:10.1080/00377990009602473

Vygotsky, L. S. (1978). *Mind in society: The development of higher psychological functions*. Cambridge, MA: Harvard University Press.

KEY TERMS AND DEFINITIONS

Anchored Instruction: A pedagogical strategy that places content learning within an authentic situation which promotes problem-solving while helping engage learners and address diverse learner needs.

Collaboration: Working jointly with others on an intellectual endeavor.

Digital Video: Digital video is a type of video recording system that works by using a digital rather than an analog video signal.

Engagement: Holding the attention of; engrossing.

Instructional Design: The systematic process of translating principles of learning and instruction into plans for instructional materials and activities.

Social Learning Theory: Focuses on learning that occurs within a social context.

Universal Design for Learning: The design of instructional materials that makes learning goals achievable by students with cognitive, emotional, or physical challenges.

Chapter 31
Application of Computer, Digital, and Telecommunications Technologies to the Clinical Preparation of Teachers

Adriana L. Medina
University of North Carolina at Charlotte, USA

Maryann Tatum Tobin
Nova Southeastern University, USA

Paola Pilonieta
University of North Carolina at Charlotte, USA

Lina Lopez Chiappone
Nova Southeastern University, USA

William E. Blanton
University of Miami, USA

ABSTRACT

Computer-mediated communication (CMC) is becoming common place in the preparation of teachers. This chapter will focus on the application of CMC and will provide insight on how technology can be used in P-12 classrooms and potentially impact student learning. The purpose of the chapter is to: (a) describe the development, implementation, outcomes, and sustainability of a pre-service teacher (PST) supervision model arranged around digital technology and telecommunications, providing supervision and support for PSTs engaged in a student teaching internship, and (b) to discuss how the technology utilized may later be utilized by participating PSTs in their future classrooms (specifically videoconferencing, instant messaging, video sharing, and the critical analysis and reflection of current practices). The authors created a virtual-geographical third space in the form of a Teaching Lab that was mediated with a multimedia platform and designed around the principle of Cultural-Historical Activity Theory (CHAT). The authors also provided opportunities for PSTs to interact within that space for reflection and the sharing of best practices.

DOI: 10.4018/978-1-4666-0014-0.ch031

INTRODUCTION

Over the past several decades, information technologies have had an enormous impact in America's business sector; however, P-12 education has experienced only limited and isolated effects thus far, which stands in stark contrast with research on the ever-increasing interaction students today have with technology outside of the classroom (Cuban, 1986, 2001; President's Committee of Advisors on Science and Technology, 2000; Stephens & Ballast, 2010; U.S. Department of Education [U.S. DOE], 2010). It is reported that 87% of adolescents, age 12-17, engage in some kind of electronic communication through the use of personal technologies (Lenhart et. al, 2008; 2005). In contrast, inside the classroom, there is a ratio of one computer for every 4.2 students (Coley, Cradler, & Engel, 2000). While there are many reasons for this, an underlying one is that the field of education has grown without a solid foundation or clear goals as to how to best use emerging technologies, with tech proponents often ill-informed and blindly jumping on the tech bandwagon (Healy, 1999; Wachira & Keengwe, 2011) The National Education Technology Plan 2010 (NETP), states that there is a need for infrastructure and innovation in the education system and a need to lessen the technological gap (U.S. DOE, 2010).

One method of increasing and improving the use of technology in P-12 education is through the use of technology in teacher preparation programs. In fact, one of the goals of the NETP is to provide pre-service teachers (PSTs) and inservice teachers with "professional learning experiences powered by technology" (U.S. DOE, 2010, p. 16). Integrating technology into a teacher preparation program and having PSTs experience it firsthand can lead to the transfer of these technologies to PSTs' future classroom practices. This new wave of classroom teachers will be able to apply computer-mediated communication (CMC) with students at a distance, as near as down the hallway, or greater distances, about topics which students are studying.

One challenge to teacher preparation is to reconsider the emphasis it places on externally imposed standards, curriculum and assessment, and the emphasis that should be placed on creating structures that span the theory-practice divide designing innovative learning activities that support the gradual transition of PSTs from other-regulated prospective to self-regulated beginning teachers (See Figure 1). The challenge lies in developing these structures.

Gutierrez, Rymes, and Larson (1995) propose the development of a metaphorical "dialogical space" where PSTs bring their voices together to critique their experiences, challenge the voice of the "master" teacher, and reduce the pressure to appropriate local classroom teaching practices and identities. Similarly, Jahreie and Ottesen (2010) suggest a geographical third space where PSTs make their ideas, interpretations, reflections, failures, and successes available to supportive peers and faculty, explore and solve problems, and deal with the tensions created by the interactions between the collaborating institutions. We integrated these two notions and created a virtual-geographical third space in the form of a Teaching Lab that was mediated with a multimedia platform. A structure of this kind can be centrally located on campus, it can be face-to-face meetings in participating schools, or it can be a virtual space.

Theoretical Framework

The design of our Teaching Lab was informed by Cultural-Historical Activity Theory (CHAT) developed by Vygotsky (1962, 1978) and his colleagues, Leontiev (1978, 1981) and Luria (1932, 1966, 1979). CHAT's premise is that consciousness is the product of tool-mediated cultural activity (Cole, 1998). Four key principles derived from CHAT guided the design of our Teaching Lab:

Figure 1. Zone of proximal professional development (ZPD) and acquisition of practice

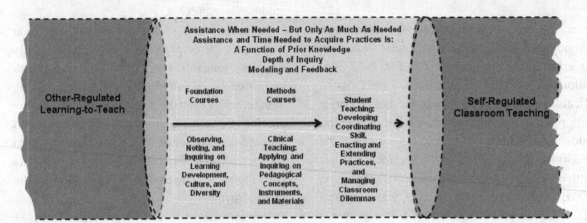

Learning Activities

1. Thinking processes, meaning, understanding, and self-regulation are located in social interactions and appropriated by participants (Vygotsky, 1978).

2. Human activity is mediated with instrumental and psychological tools. Instrumental tools, such as scissors, shovels, hammers, and saws, mediate activity aimed outward to transform material objects such as a piece of granite into a statue and social objects such as PSTs into classroom teachers. Psychological tools, such as language, plans, music notations, and pedagogical concepts are directed inward toward the individual and outward toward others (Vygotsky, 1978). The effects of psychological tools on individuals are transformations of thinking processes and self-regulation. External effects include the coordination of others and the collaborative production of public meaning, knowledge, and understanding.

3. The insertion of instrumental and psychological tools into activity fundamentally changes the structure of the activity and has a direct effect on the physical and cognitive processes of participants (Vygotsky, 1978, 1981).

4. Pedagogical and everyday concepts are similar to Vygotsky's (1978) idea of scientific and spontaneous concepts and follow similar paths of development. For example, pedagogical concepts such as top-down and bottom-up reading processes, monitoring comprehension, and remediation, are elements of a systemically organized body of knowledge that are acquired through formal instruction. They become more meaningful as they move "downward" and are used to mediate classroom instruction. In contrast, everyday concepts are encountered in the concrete events of practices in which they are typically used. For example, the meaning of phenomena such as call-outs, homework, block scheduling, and "word barking" develops as they move upward and are integrated into existing knowledge systems as the phenomena is encountered in the school context.

The above principles provide a framework for thinking about how to arrange a virtual-geographical third space to mediate learning experiences for PSTs as they take on-campus courses that are

Figure 2. Virtual teaching lab

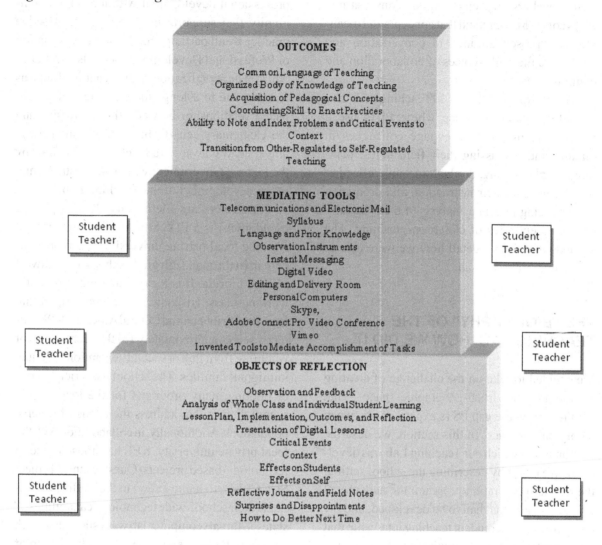

accompanied with field experiences and perform student teaching (See Figure 2).

The implication is that the social arrangements of activity mediated with a multimedia platform can have a positive impact on teacher preparation. CHAT proposes that learning and development are the outcomes of participation in goal-oriented practical activity on the social plane that prompts the qualitative and hierarchical reorganization of the psychological plane, a move that is semiotically and tool-mediated in social interactions. A central component of CHAT is that during activity, language and tool use are intertwined and change the thinking processes of the users. This conception of human cognitive development offers insights into the relations between the continued development of critical thinking and problem-solving, education processes, and implications for the appropriation and application of technology. A group of PSTs can move from the position of associating knowledge with master teachers to a position of associating knowledge and understanding with the distribution of knowledge among colleagues, faculty, and classroom teachers. By engaging in conversation, PSTs come to understand that concepts and meaning get "passed around" in conversation and appreciate the multi-voices of collaboration and communication.

Central to our idea of a Teaching Lab is a virtual-geographical space where PSTs use a multimedia platform to engage colleagues in reading and discussing their field notes; planning, implementing, evaluating, and reflecting on outcomes of their instruction; and producing and engaging in group analysis of their digitally presented episodes of classroom teaching. The sections that follow detail how we were able to create this Teaching Lab.

THE "BIOGRAPHY" OF THE TEACHING LAB: HOW WE DID IT

We decided to take-on the challenge of creating a structure – a virtual-geographic space – that would narrow the gap PSTs experience between theory and practice. In this section, we describe the context in which our Teaching Lab was developed. We begin by describing the school setting, the teacher preparation program, the new model for supervision that had to be developed, and the components of the student teaching internship that were created in order to implement the Teaching Lab model. It should be noted that the PSTs who participated in our Teaching Lab were all student teachers in the final semester of a teacher education program in elementary education.

Kingfisher Park Elementary: A Professional Development School

The implementation of the Teaching Lab took place at a Professional Development School (PDS). The PDS concept is based on the notion that a school-university partnership furthers the education profession by its commitment to the preparation of future educators through ongoing professional development within a school community that supports innovative and reflective practice by all participants (National Association of Professional Development Schools [NAPDS], 2007). The actualization of the Teaching Lab was feasible due to a long standing and well established relationship between the university and the elementary school. In addition, this private university was awarded a Teacher Quality Grant by the Federal Government which was instrumental in the development of the Teaching Lab.

Kingfisher Park Elementary (KPE) (this is a pseudonym) is a PDS working in collaboration with the local private university. It is a pre-kindergarten through fifth grade school in northwest Miami, Florida. It is located in a predominantly working-class, Hispanic community originating from the Caribbean and Central America. KPE currently serves approximately 1300 students, most of whom are from first or second generation Hispanic immigrant families. The school has a rich history of piloting many programs for the local public school district that address the needs of diverse populations. Additionally, in collaboration with the local private university, KPE has housed several technology-based projects (Quest Atlantis, Project SUCCEED, to name a few) in their efforts to upgrade their school-wide technology capabilities. A state-of-the-art computer lab was established with help from the university, and through the help of a supportive administration, each teacher is given opportunities for professional development in tech-based activities. KPE's diverse population, their commitment to incorporating new technologies whenever possible, and their trend of piloting innovative programs, made it a prime candidate for piloting our Teaching Lab.

School of Education

The local private university's School of Education, located in South Florida, offered a Bachelor of Science in Education. Students in the B.S.Ed. program graduated with eligibility for K-6 certification, as well as an ESOL endorsement, through the Florida Department of Education. Field experiences are assigned throughout the program, with 6-9 of those credits earned during the student teaching internship. Field experience placements take place across a wide variety of public schools; however, student teaching placements exist only at the university's eight PDS's, including KPE.

Teacher Preparation Program

The university's teacher preparation program centered its efforts on supporting the development of PSTs to equip them for the challenges of urban classrooms in high-need areas. Specifically, it was the intent of the university's PDS team to bridge the gap between theory and practice – taking textbook concepts and actuating them in real-world settings. The pre-professional training and on-going professional development activities at the PDS were guided by the objectives of the funding grant. The purposes of our Teaching Lab were aligned with two of the grant objectives (Project SUCCEED, n.d.):

- Ensure that prospective teachers are well prepared for the realities of the classroom.
- Prepare prospective teachers to use technology as a tool for integrative teaching and learning.

To this end, the university team developed a new supervisory model to provide support during the student teaching internship before completion of the teacher education program.

Supervision Model

Aside from the student teacher, a traditional model of supervision for student teaching has two "players" – a university supervisor and the cooperating teacher. In order to implement the Teaching Lab, a new supervision model had to be created. This model consisted of many players (See Figure 3) interacting together.

The College of Education assigned one of its faculty members to be the professor-in-residence (PIR) and function as a liaison between the university and the PDS. The PIR coordinated the model of supervision, supervised the student teachers, conducted observations, and met regularly with cooperating teachers and the administration. KPE had on average 8-10 student teachers a semester and upwards of 30 students doing field experience classroom observations. The semester we first implemented the Teaching Lab, there were 15 student teachers at the school.

The PIR also coordinated the on-site seminar that paralleled the student teaching internship and tailored it to the PSTs' needs. This course was facilitated by the PIR and the graduate assistants. The PIR, graduate assistants, and the cooperating teachers all supervised the student teachers. In addition, due to the fact that some student teachers had additional areas of concentration, a university supervisor also played a part in the model and he performed observations of the student teachers as well.

The university supervisory team had many years of combined experience working with PSTs in a PDS setting. All supervisors also had recent K-12 teaching experience, which was well received by the PSTs who expressed feeling a certain comfort level with the team when sharing classroom successes as well as shortcomings. The supervisory team together with the PSTs demonstrated an interesting continuum of grounded practitioner – at one end, a seasoned and respected PIR as the head of the supervisory team, complemented by classroom teachers-turned-doctoral students and veteran cooperating teachers, and PSTs at the other end.

Figure 3. Supervision model

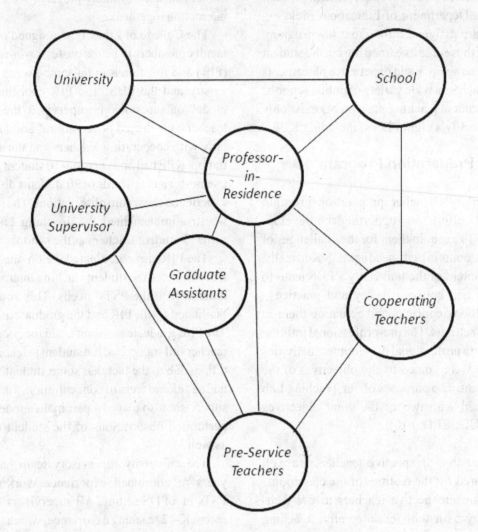

Using Technology in the Student Teaching Internship

A key to successful teacher education programs is the student teaching internship. It allows for the PST to put into practice what he or she has learned during the program under the guidance of an experienced professional. Though an invaluable experience, it can be challenging for colleges of education to provide proper supervision of the PST and to act as a link-between. The challenge emerges when there are large numbers of PSTs who need supervision and not enough supervi-

sors, or when PSTs are spread over such a large distance that periodic observations are unwieldy.

During the course of the 16-week student teaching internship, PSTs were in contact with the university team in various ways: at meetings held at the PDS, online in synchronous chat rooms, and through the use of asynchronous email.

In the traditional supervisory model, the student teaching seminar would have been held as a weekly class at the PDS or the university during the 16-week student teaching internship and attended by PSTs and the university team. Often, due to conflicting schedules and last-minute changes in school-based activities and related duties or even risky weather events, the supervisory team and/or the PSTs would have difficulty meeting this weekly commitment. In the alternate model of supervision, the university team devised a meeting schedule that used different formats. Some meetings were still held face-to-face, such as the initial meet and greet and others at key points during the student teaching internship. However, other interactions between the PSTs and the supervisory team occurred through the use of computer mediated communication (CMC) technologies. CMC can be categorized as asynchronous (that is email, blogs, and podcasts) or synchronous (that is text messages, voice chats or audio conferences, chat rooms, and video conferences). Both types of CMCs were utilized in this model.

The use of email and chat room discussions allowed for weekly meetings to occur regularly and undisturbed. It also afforded participants the luxury of receiving almost immediate feedback following classroom observations and other PST training experiences. In particular, PSTs scheduled "debriefing" sessions with their assigned supervision team member in order to discuss and receive feedback on lessons they taught as part of formal classroom evaluations.

In a traditional supervisory model, debriefing sessions often lose the effects of immediacy because PSTs are occupied with classroom responsibilities and are unable to meet with the university supervisor immediately following the observed lesson; or, if the lesson is evaluated by the classroom teacher, without the supervisor present, the feedback loop is even further complicated and meaningful feedback is replaced by a perfunctory review of checklists and other paperwork, with little substance for the PST to parlay into improvements of future lessons. With the use of CMC, the feedback loop was executed in a more opportune manner. If the university supervisor could not meet with the student teacher immediately, the student teacher did not have to wait until the supervisor's next visit. A chat using instant messaging took

place after school or in the evening of that same day, allowing for timely feedback.

In our Teaching Lab, the PSTs exhibited some hesitation at the onset of the student teaching internship when the computer mediated supervisory model was first described. Already experiencing trepidation with regard to their culminating student teaching internship, the newness of the seminar delivery modalities further raised angst among the PSTs, some of whom were resentful that PSTs in other PDSs were using the traditional supervisory model and thus avoided the added stress of incorporating technology. As the student teaching internship progressed, PSTs gradually reached a watershed moment in which they stopped dwelling on the differences between this supervisory model and what they had previously experienced in other university courses. PSTs embraced the new communication modalities they were using and recognized the powerful impact they had on their professional growth. Mezirow (1978) explains that stress is an important component of learning. As part of transformation learning theory, Mezirow contends that a "disorienting dilemma" spurs the growth of adult learning as it is transformed over time into a meaningful experience (de Leon & Pena, 2010). The PSTs, as well as the university supervision team, clearly experienced a disorienting dilemma as we adjusted to the use of new communication technologies during the student teaching internship. However, after some initial challenges, PSTs and supervisors felt comfortable operating in this new paradigm of supervision and learned to integrate the use of the communication technologies with near-seamless aplomb.

Student Teaching Requirements

There were four requirements for the student teaching internship. First, PSTs were to be observed a total of seven times. Three of those seven observations were to be video recorded. Second, PSTs needed to complete a reflection on the outcomes of the video recorded lessons. Third, PSTs needed to share and discuss a 5-10 minute clip from one of their video recorded lessons. Fourth, PSTs were expected to engage in a weekly reflective digital journal.

Observations and Reflections on Outcomes

During the semester, PSTs were asked to engage in an instant message chat room format to debrief and reflect upon the seven formal observations of classroom teaching conducted by the cooperating teacher and the supervisory team, three of which were video recorded. In an ideal situation, video-conference technology would be used to facilitate distance observations in real-time. However, in lieu of videoconferencing, as was the case with this pilot program, lessons can be recorded via video or DVD. Direct-to-DVD camcorders were used by the PSTs to record their teaching. This allowed for the ATs to view their teaching soon after taping was complete, which they were asked to do as part of their "Reflection on Outcomes" assignment (See Figure 4).

Team members scheduled appointments with the PSTs to meet online soon after but within a couple of days following a formal observation. During the chat room session, PSTs were asked to consider what was successful about the lesson they taught, how they engaged students, and how students were able to experience success. They were also asked to identify areas for growth. The same procedure was used with the videotaped lessons.

Critical to the transition from live to digital observations was the establishment of a uni-formed observation instrument, in this case, the Tri-Perspective Ethnographic Observation (3-PEO) Instrument (Medina, manuscript in preparation; See Figure 5). The 3-PEO Instrument divides notetaking, a description of what is being observed, into two columns, What I Heard and What I Saw. The third column, What I Thought, is used for notemaking, the observer's thinking

and interpretation of what is observed. During an observation, the observer attempts to capture as much of the talk and action as is feasible by writing it down in the first two columns. As the action is taking place, the observer is also record-ing his/her thoughts, questions, and comments in the third column. The notemaking become the basis for the post-observation conference and the notetaking serves as evidence.

Video Clip Sharing and Digital Reflective Journal

Another requirement was for each PST to share a video excerpt (5-10 minutes) of her teaching during one of the face-to-face meetings so they, their peers, and the supervisory team could discuss it and offer feedback. This group-enabled reflec-tion initially made the PSTs self conscious, but gradually they realized how many experiences were common to the whole group, helping to build a community of practice that supported transformational learning, a collateral benefit of the process, which had not been anticipated.

Weekly emails between the PSTs and their assigned supervisor were structured as digital re-flective journals. Over time, these entries evolved from weekly play-by-play recaps of classroom activities, to long-winded manifestos on all that is wrong in the world of education, to introspective and contemplative recollections of how the PST experienced successes, overcame challenges, and learned to balance the two in ways that presented learning experiences not only for students, but also provided the opportunity for transformational self-learning experiences. The road to shaping these reflective practitioners was not without a few bumps. Ongoing and regular communica-tion, prompt responses, and a patient ear helped steer the process. The university supervision team closely followed the PSTs' commentaries, offered personalized oral and written feedback, and keenly identified issues in which the teachers needed guidance or direction.

Figure 4. Reflection on outcomes

Reflection on Outcomes of the Video Taped Observations

Directions: Using the Lesson Plan Model, develop a lesson plan, video tape yourself, watch the video, and answer the questions below. You may want to attach your answers to another sheet.

- Develop a lesson plan
    - What was the purpose of your lesson?
    - What was the content (subject matter or skill) of your lesson?
    - What influenced your decision to teach this content?
    - What grouping organization did you use and why?
    - What activities did you plan and what influenced your choices?
    - What materials did you use?
    - What alternatives did you plan to use if the lesson did not progress as planned?
    - Did you consider anything about what your students knew while planning? Please elaborate.
- Implement the lesson and videotape yourself teaching the lesson
- View the lesson as soon as possible after taping the lesson. Ideally, you should view the tape the same day.
- Reflections on the Lesson
    - Select three critical segments from your video on which to focus. The segments should be related to your lesson plan. Record the time points of these segments on your reflection.
    - Using the critical segments, view the tape again and focus on the following questions:
        - What were you thinking during this incident and why? For example, why are you asking those questions, using that worksheet, explaining that skill?
        - What were you noticing about the students? For example, what makes you think that students might have difficulty with the meaning of those words, completing that exercise/worksheet, answering those questions, or why did you call on that student?
        - How are you going to use the information you obtained from the student responses and other behavior?
        - Did you consider any of the alternative activities you had planned during this part of the lesson? Did any student response or behavior make you act differently than you had planned?
- Think about your lesson in general
    - What caused you to decide to change your activities?
    - If drill and skill lessons were involved in this lesson, discuss why.
- Meet with your designated team member and discuss the results of the observation of your lesson
- Write a reflection that reveals your thinking about the questions in III and IV and the results of your team member's observation.
    - Write a reflection that reveals your general thinking about the overall success of this lesson.

Successes

There has been much evidence to support technology and multimedia as a means for providing flexible and effective tools for training PSTs (Dexter & Riedel, 2003; Doering, Hughes, & Huffman, 2003). The primary success of this observational process stemmed largely from flexibility - on the part of both the PSTs and their clinical supervisors, and indeed the flexibility of the technological tools themselves, as they aided in facilitating the PST's reflection after each lesson. Additionally, instantaneous self-reflection, which occurred as the PSTs viewed their recorded lessons, coupled with the pursuant IM chats with their supervisor, provided for several rich developmental experiences on the part of the teachers. A recurring theme in the post-program surveys completed by the PSTs was that the importance of reflecting on a lesson was to determine "what went well, what I could change, what was my objective, and was that objective accomplished." Because of the video recorded lessons, immediate viewing and self-reflection, and the follow-up IM chats, all parties were able to comment on the success of the lesson as a whole while the information and events were still fresh.

A second success of this system is the ability to isolate critical moments within the lesson and reflect on them. Having a recording allowed the PSTs and supervisors the opportunity to view key moments together during discussion and to share those moments with the other PSTs to encourage development. The act of sharing with their peers helped established a common language of teaching that was reflected in the post-surveys. Whereas

Figure 5. Tri-perspective ethnographic observation (3-PEO) instrument

What I Heard	What I Saw	What I Thought

their pre-surveys lacked specific terminology, the post-surveys yielded terms like "research-based strategies," "moments of learning," "meeting the needs of all learners," and "accomplishing objectives." These language tools were developed during seminar sessions as the PSTs engaged in the sharing of the critical moments of their lessons. A video recorded lesson artifact provides for this, as the video recorded lesson can be paused, rewound, and repeated for more detailed analysis and critique. Our conclusions support previous research by Rich and Hannafin (2008b) who found that video analysis is a valuable tool to "access, understand, and affect student teacher thinking and action in context" (pp 87-88).

A third success, as evidenced through PST's reflection on their own video analysis, is the ability to index recurring problems, as those problems can be issues that arise for the PST or problems specific to singular students. Trends and themes develop over the course of the 16-week internship and beginning teachers who continually have the same difficulties are provided with a record to evaluate. Similarly, if a student of theirs is having a specific issue, there is evidence that the PST can observe, reflect, and focus on in a procedural and timely fashion. As they learn the rhythm of teaching, it is often difficult to problem-solve on the spot, but a taped record allows them to consult research, class notes, professors, or others to determine the specific solution for any number of classroom issues that may arise. Video analysis promotes collaboration among educators (Rich & Hannafin, 2008a).

This leads to the outcome of having a record of the transition from other-regulated to self-regulated teaching. For several reasons, this venue of analysis is beneficial for studying the progress PSTs make towards independence during their student teaching internship. Noting their abilities to identify and understand student needs, coordinate their knowledge and resources to solve problems and set goals for learners, and to self-regulate their own abilities to class manage and effectively plan all play a part in while a visual record, accompanied by observation forms and notes, provide rich data for PST training and evaluation.

Current classroom atmospheres have begun to embrace a more multimodal approach to teaching in the form of providing multiple platforms for student discovery and expression (Heath & Street, 2008). These platforms are dynamic and incorporate not just the printed page, art, music and the use of computers, but other multimedia such as moving graphics, texts, sounds, and animation. If we aim to educate teachers to successfully motivate students to become proactive learners, as well as developing their creativity and processing skills, then we must start at the PST training level, by embracing a multimodal system that allows for reflection and analysis across several genres of media.

Lessons Learned

Because the availability of personal technology (smart phones, e-book readers, MP3 players, etc.) has grown exponentially in the last decade, a phenomenon is occurring. The current students who populate our school systems are "digital natives", who have facility with the modern digital technologies as a result of having grown up with them. Teachers, however, and even many PSTs are still "digital immigrants," who have learned to use technology later in their lives and are still assimilating them into their world (Prensky, 2005). It will be another decade before the digital natives are classroom teachers themselves, and although many PSTs might be tech-savvy, many of their supervisors may not be. Cooperating teachers, PSTs, and professors must navigate the distance between their own technological knowledge and skill and the technological fluency of current elementary and secondary students. It is important, therefore, to fully assess the technological knowledge of all parties participating in a digitally-based observation system before implementation.

Videoconferencing tools, such as Vimeo, Skype, and Adobe Connect are prevalent, but not all PSTs or university supervisors may be at ease using those programs, and frustration with the technology can cause general malaise about the observation process. It goes without saying that accessibility is also vital and that whatever software and equipment is used must be in working order.

In cases where DVD recording is used, it is also critical to familiarize the PSTs with the basic camera and tripod functions, as they may be filming themselves often, and camera malfunctions can be another layer of stress added to an already apprehensive PST about to test the waters with a new lesson. In general, due in part to their digital native-ness, most students will be unaffected by the presence of a camera in the classroom, especially if prepped by the teacher to ignore it. Further, research has shown that people become accustomed to the camera surprisingly quickly, especially if there is no one running it, and the presence of the camera is soon forgotten (Jordan & Henderson, 1995). After a few sessions, the camera becomes a normal part of the classroom.

Given the noise-level of a classroom, especially one where the students are engaged in discussion, good audio is essential to a well-recorded lesson. A stationary, unmanned camera will not have the flourish of a professionally edited film. However, quality audio can make up for the lack of pans or student close-ups. Since the goal is often to monitor the development of language as a tool (used by both the PST and the students) proper microphone placement should be taken into consideration. Ideally, lavalier (lapel) microphones should be worn by the PST to best enhance his/her own voice during direct instruction and small group/one-on-one work. A good lavalier will pick up all sound within a 6-8 foot radius. The onboard camera microphone will pick up the overall classroom sound, so a camera with the ability to split sound tracks is preferable. This will allow a skilled editor to eliminate the background noise of the classroom and allow specific instances picked up by the lavalier to be heard. If only one track is available, the teacher's microphone is all that is needed. If the laboratory classroom engages in a lot of group-work, investing in table microphones or hanging microphones, split between several channels, would be a great enhancement, if there is knowledgeable staff to maintain and install them. It is important, though, to keep in mind that even the most basic video recording is of benefit. The level of technology will vary, but the outcomes remain consistent.

An unanticipated challenge encountered was the lack of technological proficiency of the PSTs. While age-wise the PSTs were "digital natives," those who have grown up with fairly advanced technology and quick internet access ever-present in their lives (Prensky, 2005), they lacked the digital skills necessary for using video conferencing technologies (relatively new in education at the time the Teaching Lab was first implemented) and the direct-to-DVD camcorders themselves. In this case, transfer of the video recorded lessons to DVD, quality video and audio recording, and clip editing were done by a doctoral student with a Master of Fine Arts degree in Motion Pictures. However, we foresee that as "home movie" software (iMovie, Windows Movie Maker, etc.) and video sharing sites, such as YouTube, increase in popularity, amateur moviemaking will become, if it has not already, a more innate and common skill found in undergraduates. PSTs will enter their undergraduate programs with a set of already learned skills for recording and sharing their own videos (Bayne & Ross, 2007; Bennett & Maton, 2010). This base knowledge will help tremendously with implementing the technological observation components of the Teaching Lab. Flip video cameras, digital still cameras with video capability, and even smart phones can create digital recordings of lessons taught and those recorded lessons can be downloaded directly into any computer and immediately shared via TeacherTube, Facebook, email applications, and the like. It has become,

now, a question of how to use these burgeoning technologies to their fullest potential.

It is likely that in the future PSTs will enter teacher education programs with more technological proficiency. However, as the tools that can be used in teacher education evolve, it might still be necessary to educate technological savvy PSTs in the specific technological observation tools that will be used during student teaching. This education ideally should not occur during student teaching since the workload during student teaching increases and the burden of using a technology one is not familiar with might not encourage continued use of the tool beyond the teacher education program. Therefore, early exposure to the technology in teacher education courses prior to the student teaching internship might be beneficial to lessen the learning curve (Rich & Hannafin, 2008a). Additionally, an even larger goal for early exposure to video observation technology is to educate student teachers on how to analyze their teaching practices "based on observations and evidence of their own teaching" (Rich & Hannafin, 2008a) for when they are in-service teachers and no longer have a cooperating teacher and a teacher education professor to identify theories or frameworks that guide pedagogy.

CONCLUSION

For many of the university students, the experiences at KPE were among their first in addressing the needs of diverse learners from different linguistic, socioeconomic, and cultural backgrounds. The urban setting, the immigrant nature of the surrounding neighborhood, and a student population with diverse learning needs brought to life what it is like to teach "in the real world" with a student population that closely mirrors predictions for U.S. demographics in the coming years (Ovando, Combs, & Collier, 2011). Further, research indicates that reflective experiences working with diverse populations are necessary to the formation of culturally responsive teachers (Lenski, Crumpler, Stallworth, & Crawford, 2005). Working together with master teachers, the university team, and a supportive school administration, PSTs gained a wealth of experience from this special school setting that well prepared them for future careers.

The practical result of our Teaching Lab is a multimedia environment that mediates the geographical space between the college classroom, and practice. It allowed for PSTs' gradual development from other-regulated teaching to self-regulated teaching. In our work, we did not look for early compliance to standards and the like. We looked for change over time, through participation in both clinical practice and an activity system that mediated interactions among PSTs, cooperating teachers, and university supervisors. We understood that PSTs' use of conceptual and instrumental knowledge to mediate the formulation and writing of field notes, planning, implementing, evaluating, and reflecting on outcomes, producing, presenting, and engaging in group analysis of the digitally presented lessons, and engaging in group discussions improved over time.

Classroom Uses of CMCs

There are other uses for this technology aside from PST supervision. Teachers can use video-conferencing and instant messaging with their students. CMCs can be utilized to reach students who are homebound or hospital bound due to health issues, illnesses, or accidents. Also, for parents who travel and take their children with them, the CMCs can also be used so that students can continue to attend their classes, interact with their peers in a classroom setting, and keep up with their education.

Also within the scope of education, this available technology can be used to invite others into the classroom. For example, interviews can be conducted with an author via Skype, and interactions with students across the globe can be conducted through blogs. There are many ways to use this technology to maintain connections with students as well as to branch out and connect with others in our community and world (for example, http://www.iearn.org/).

Educators impact the future. As technology evolves and as we learn to apply it in innovative ways, we will better adapt these technologies to meet our needs in teacher education. In the meantime, technology exists and solutions are possible. We need to utilize CMC technology in our teacher education programs as a means of working with PSTs so that the use of these CMCs will transfer to their future classrooms.

RELATED RESOURCES

Below are some resources that can be used to further think about how to conduct distance observations and meetings and to learn more about this process.

Instant Messaging and Video Conferencing Web-Based Software

There are several free downloadable programs that can be used to communicate and collaborate via instant messages or video conferencing. When we conducted this study, we used AOL Instant Messaging to debrief with PSTs after a live observation or after watching a recorded video of their lesson. Although the quality of the audio and video may be an issue, these applications could also be used to observe a PST via video conferencing. The PST can wear a wireless headset with microphone to better capture the PST's voice over ambient noise. Below are some examples of popular programs:

- AOL Instant Messenger
- MSN Messenger
- Skype
- iChat
- Google Talk
- WebEx

Options for Video Observations

In the absence of videoconferencing capabilities, Skype accessibility, or other compressed video technologies, this process of distance observations can be completed through DVD or videotaping, as was the case with the Teaching Lab. Digital lessons can be instantaneously burned or uploaded for email to directing professors and supervisors remotely located. Real-time observation can be done through the use of Skype, Vimeo, Adobe Connect, or other teleconferencing programs. During both live and digital observations, consistency is maintained through the observation instrument.

Video Sharing Websites

Although the software mentioned above could be used to stream live video so a supervisor could observe a lesson as it takes place, the quality of the video may be an issue. Another option is for the PST to video record the lesson and then post it on a website so the supervisor can access it. Below is a list of websites that can be used to share videos privately.

- YouTube – though YouTube is known as a website where you can share videos publicly, you can also share your videos with selected viewers. Uploaded videos are limited to 15 minutes.
- TeacherTube – similar to YouTube, TeacherTube is specifically geared towards educators as a means of sharing teacher-made and student-made videos. TeacherTube also includes blogs, print materials, and photos. Unlike YouTube, TeacherTube is not blocked by most content filtering systems in place at P-12 schools.
- One True Media (www.onetruemedia.com) - this is another website where you can create, edit, and share videos. They

have a free version or a paid membership. The paid membership allows for increased storage space.

Literature

As educational technology practices increase so does the research available for learning about and assessing the purpose and effectiveness of different practices. Below are some texts on the topic.

Allen, M., Bourhis, J., Burrell, N., & Mabry, E. (2002). Comparing student satisfaction with distance education to traditional classrooms in higher education: A meta-analysis. *American Journal of Distance Education, 16*(2), 83-97. doi:10.1207/S15389286AJDE1602_3

- This article is a meta-analysis that summarizes the research on distance education. They conclude that students' satisfaction level does not decrease with distance education when compared to face-to-face methods of instruction.

Karabulut, A. & Correia, A. (2008). Skype, Elluminate, Adobe Connect, Ivisit: A comparison of web-based video conferencing systems for learning and teaching. In K. McFerrin et al. (Eds.), *Proceedings of Society for Information Technology & Teacher Education International Conference 2008* (pp. 481-484). Chesapeake, VA: AACE. • The article provides a comparison of four web-based video conferencing systems listing strengths and weaknesses of each so that teachers can select the best program based on their needs.

Rich, P. J., & Hannafin, M. (2009). Video annotation tools: Technologies to scaffold, structure, and transform teacher reflection. *Journal of Teacher Education, 60*(1), 52-67. doi: 10.1177/0022487108328486

- This article compared a variety of video annotation tools and described their application as it pertains to teacher reflection and practices. The tools are compared and contrasted based on how they connect evidence, incorporate analytical frameworks, allow the sharing of videos among peers, mentors, professors, and supervisors, and the technical effort needed to learn and use them.

Richardson, W. (2009). *Blogs, wikis, podcasts, and other powerful web tools for classrooms (2nd ed.)*. Thousand Oaks, CA: Corwin Press.

- This book shows teachers how to use a variety of web 2.0 tools in their classrooms, including videos and screencasting.

Smyth, R. (2005), Broadband videoconferencing as a tool for learner-centred distance learning in higher education. *British Journal of Educational Technology, 36*, 805–820. doi: 10.1111/j.1467-8535.2005.00499.x

- This article discusses how broadband videoconferencing can be used to facilitate student engagement and support collaboration.

Samsonov, P., Daspit, T., Mayers, E. & Briggs, C. (2009). Blogging, YouTube and Skype: New Ideas for Teachers. In I. Gibson et al. (Eds.), *Proceedings of Society for Information Technology & Teacher Education International Conference 2009* (pp. 2667-2669). Chesapeake, VA: AACE

- The article discusses how K-12 teachers can use blogs, YouTube videos, and Skype in their classrooms. The article also discusses how Skype can be used for providing instruction for home-bound children.

Websites

There are many websites available for learning about and utilizing educational technology. Below we offer a few. http://www.dummies.com/how-to/content/using-skype-at-school.html

This websites provides various examples of how teachers can use Skype in their schools. http://www.pbs.org/wgbh/pages/frontline/digitalnation/learning/literacy/friending-boo-radley.html

This video is a case study of a teacher who incorporated social networking into her unit on Harper Lee's "To Kill a Mockingbird."

http://www.google.com/events/digitalage/

"Breakthough Learning in the Digital Age" was a forum hosted by Google, Inc. in 2009 which brought together scholars, administrators, and business leaders to discuss new paradigms for learning with technology.

http://www.edutopia.org

"Edutopia" provides resources, strategies, and discussion forum for educators who want to incorporate video sharing sites, video conferencing, and other new technologies into their classrooms.

http://www.ncte.org/positions/statements/multimodalliteracies

The National Council for Teachers of English's position statement on multimodal literacy.

REFERENCES

Bayne, S., & Ross, J. (2007). The digital native and digital immigrant: A dangerous opposition. Presented at the *Annual Conference of the Society for Research into Higher Education.* www.malts.ed.ac.uk/staff/sian/natives_final.pdf

Bennett, S., & Maton, K. (2010). Beyond the digital natives debate: Towards a more nuanced understanding of students' technology experiences. *Journal of Computer Assisted Learning, 26*, 321–331. doi:10.1111/j.1365-2729.2010.00360.x

Cole, M. (1998). *Cultural psychology: A once and future discipline*. Cambridge, MA: Harvard University Press.

Coley, R. J., Cradler, J., & Engel, P. K. (2000). *Computers and the classroom: The status of technology in U.S. schools*. Princeton, NJ: Policy Information Center, Educational Testing Service.

Cuban, L. (1986). *Teachers and machines: The classroom use of technology since 1920*. New York, NY: Teachers College Press.

de Leon, L., & Pena, C. (2010). Transformational learning in multimedia: Tracking the comfort levels of PSTs engaged in a disorienting dilemma. *International Journal of Instructional Media*, *37*(2), 141–149.

Dexter, S., & Riedel, E. (2003). Why improving PST educational technology preparation must go beyond the college's walls. *Journal of Teacher Education*, *54*, 334–346. doi:10.1177/0022487103255319

Doering, A., Hughes, J., & Huffman, D. (2003). Preservice teachers: Are we thinking with technology? *Journal of Research on Technology in Education*, *35*(3), 342–361.

Gutierrez, K., Rymes, B., & Larson, J. (1995). Script, counterscript, and underlife in the classroom - Brown, James versus Brown v. Board of Education. *Harvard Educational Review*, *65*, 445–471.

Healy, J. M. (1999). *Failure to connect: How computers affect our children's minds – for better or worse*. New York: Simon & Schuster.

Heath, S. B., & Street, B. (2008). *On ethnography: Approaches to language and literacy research*. New York, NY: Teachers College Press.

Jahreie, C. F., & Ottesen, E. (2010). Construction of boundaries in teaher education: Analyzing PSTs' accounts. *Mind, Culture, and Activity*, *17*, 212–234. doi:10.1080/10749030903314195

Jordan, B., & Henderson, A. (1995). Interaction analysis: Foundations and practice. *Journal of the Learning Sciences*, *4*, 39–103. doi:10.1207/s15327809jls0401_2

Jordan, B., & Henderson, A. (1995). Interaction analysis: Foundations and practice. *Journal of the Learning Sciences*, *4*(1), 39–103. doi:10.1207/s15327809jls0401_2

Lehnart, A., Arafeh, S., Smith, A., & Macgill, A. R. (2008). *Writing, technology, and teens*. Washington, DC: Pew Internet and American Life Project.

Lehnart, A., Madden, M., & Hitlin, P. (2005). *Youth are leading the transition to a fully wired and mobile nation*. Washington, DC: Pew Internet and American Life Project.

Lenski, S. D., Crumpler, T. P., Stallworth, C., & Crawford, K. M. (2005). Preparing culturally responsive PSTs. *Teacher Education Quarterly*, *32*(2), 85–100.

Leont'ev, A. N. (1978). *Activity, consciousness, and personality*. Englewood Cliffs, NJ: Prentice Hall.

Leont'ev, A. N. (1981). *Problems of the development of the mind*. Moscow, Russia: Progress Publishers.

Luria, A. R. (1932). *The nature of human conflicts*. New York, NY: Liveright.

Luria, A. R. (1966). *Higher cortical functions in man*. New York, NY: Basic Books.

Luria, A. R. (1979). *The making of mind*. Cambridge, MA: Harvard University Press.

Medina, A. L. (in press.). *Tri-perspective form for clinical observations*. Manuscript in preparation.

Mezirow, J. (1978). *Education for perspective transformation*. New York, NY: Teacher's College, Columbia University.

National Association of Professional Development Schools. (2007). *What it means to be a professional development school*. Columbia, SC: Author.

National Writing Project. (2010). *National Commission on Writing*. Retrieved on January 30, 2011, from http://www.nwp.org/cs/public/print/resource/2432

National Writing Project. (2010). *Because digital writing matters: Improving student writing in online and multimedia environments*. San Francisco: Jossey-Bass.

Ovando, C., Combs, M. C., & Collier, V. P. (2011). *Bilingual and ESL classrooms: Teaching in multicultural contexts* (5th ed.). New York, NY: McGraw-Hill.

Prensky, M. (2005). Listen to the natives. *Educational Leadership, 63*, 8–13.

President's Committee of Advisors on Science and Technology. (2000). Report to the president on the use of technology to strengthen K-12 education in the United States. In Jossey-Bass Inc. (Eds.), *The Jossey-Bass reader on technology and learning*, (pp. 3-19). San Francisco, CA: Jossey-Bass Inc., Publishers.

Project, S. U. C. C. E. E. D. (n.d.). *Project SUCCEED*. Retrieved from http://www.education.miami.edu/succeed/

Rich, P., & Hannafin, M. (2008a). Capturing and assessing evidence of student teacher inquiry: A case study. *Teaching and Teacher Education, 24*, 1426–1440. .doi:10.1016/j.tate.2007.11.016

Rich, P. J., & Hannafin, M. J. (2008b). Decisions and reasons: Examining preservice teacher decision-making through video self-analysis. *Journal of Computing in Higher Education, 20*(1), 62–94. doi:10.1007/BF03033432

Stephens, L. C., & Ballast, K. H. (2010). *Using technology to improve adolescent writing: Digital make-overs for writing lessons*. Boston, MA: Pearson.

U.S. Department of Education Office of Educational Technology. (2010). *Transforming American education: Learning powered by technology*. Washington, D.C. Retrieved from http://www.ed.gov/technology/netp-2010

Vygotsky, L. S. (1962). *Thought and language*. Cambridge, MA: MIT Press. doi:10.1037/11193-000

Vygotsky, L. S. (1978). *Mind in society: The development of higher psychological processes*. Cambridge, MA: Harvard University Press.

Vygotsky, L. S. (1981). The development of higher forms of attention in childhood. In Wertsch, J. V. (Ed.), *The concept of activity in Soviet psychology* (pp. 189–240). Armonk, NY: Sharpe. doi:10.2753/RPO1061-0405180167

Wachira, P., & Keengwe, J. (2011). Technology integration barriers: Urban school mathematics teachers perspectives. *Journal of Science Education and Technology, 20*(1), 17–25. doi:10.1007/s10956-010-9230-y

KEY TERMS AND DEFINITIONS

Computer Mediated Communication (CMC): Communication using digital tools, including e-mail, network communication, instant messaging, text messaging, hypertext, distance learning, Internet forums, USENET newsgroups, bulletin boards, online shopping, distribution lists and videoconferencing. CMC can be categorized as asynchronous (that is, email, blogs, and podcasts) or synchronous (that is, text messages, voice chats or audio conferences, chat rooms, and video conferences).

Cultural-Historical Activity Theory (CHAT): A psychological theory put forth by Vygotsky and colleagues Leontiev and Luria that explained consciousness as the product of tool-mediated cultural activity. The insertion of instrumental and psychological tools into human activity fundamentally changes the structure of the activity and has a direct effect on the physical and cognitive processes of participants.

Dialogical Space: A metaphorical place where pre-service teachers can come together to share classroom experiences, challenge prevailing opinions and practices, and help mold their teacher identities through a process of dialogue regarding key issues (Gutierrez, Rymes, & Larson, 1995).

Digital Immigrants: Those not born into the digital world but who have adopted the new technologies at some point later in life, thus lacking fluent digital language (Prensky, 2005).

Digital Natives: Today's students who are the first to grow up surrounded by and using computers, videogames, digital music players, video cameras, cell phones, and other tools of the digital age. They are "native speakers" of the digital language (Prensky, 2005).

Professional Development Schools: A school-university partnership that furthers the education profession by its commitment to the preparation of future educators through ongoing professional development in collaboration with a local university and within a P-12 school community that supports innovative and reflective practice by all participants.

Teaching Lab: a space, either virtual or geographic, used as an academic laboratory focusing on exploring and solving problems in classrooms. The framework is based on the notion that growth in teaching emerges as the gap between theory and practice begins to diminish through dialogue, analysis, and reflection on teaching practices and classroom environments. Novice and veteran educators collaborate in teaching labs and learn from each other as they interpret critical moments in classrooms and reflect on best practices for real-world teaching.

Tools: In the Vygotskyian sense, human activity is mediated with instrumental and psychological tools. The effects of psychological tools on individuals are transformations of thinking processes and self-regulation.

Chapter 32
Training Teachers for a Virtual School System:
A Call to Action

Michael K. Barbour
Wayne State University, USA

ABSTRACT

Online learning at the K-12 level is growing exponentially. Students learning in supplemental virtual schools and full-time cyber schools, using a variety of delivery models that include and sometimes combine independent, asynchronous, and synchronous instruction, in almost every state in the US. In some instances the knowledge, skills, and abilities required by teachers in this technology-mediated environment is consistent with what they learned about face-to-face teaching in their teacher education programs, while in many instances, the two are quite different. Presently the lack of empirical research into effective K-12 online teaching limits teacher education programs. However, teacher education programs still need to better prepare pre-service and in-service teachers to design, deliver, and support students engaged virtual schooling.

INTRODUCTION

In the opening to her chapter on education and how the next generation of students should learn, Greenfield (2003) asks "What should we be teaching the next generation to equip them for citizen-

ship in the mid 21st century and beyond?" (p. 148). The North American Council for Online Learning (NACOL – later the International Association for K-12 Online Learning) and the Partnership for 21st Century Skills (2006) believed that "virtual schools provide access to online, collaborative and self-paced learning environments – settings that can facilitate 21st century skills" (p. 2). They

DOI: 10.4018/978-1-4666-0014-0.ch032

later described twenty-first century learning as including skills such as creativity, problem solving, communication and analytical thinking. If these are some of the skills valued in the new economy and the environment provided by virtual schools is consistent with the kind of work setting our students will have to compete and excel in, one approach to re-organizing K-12 schools is through the use of virtual schooling.

However, according to Friedman (2006), students are "shaped in large measure by school systems that have had, from the dawn of the industrial age, a main purpose to produce employees for boxed positions in corporate [organizational] charts" (p. 304). Moreover, we have been preparing our teachers for the same kind of school system. In this chapter, I describe the current state of K-12 online learning in the United States. Then I discuss the nature of teaching in a K-12 online learning environment. Next, I describe how teaching in an online environment differs from traditional face-to-face teaching. Then, I examine the existing literature on teacher education and professional development related to virtual schooling, with an emphasis on the limited research into K-12 online teaching, and how the paucity of published, empirical research hinders the ability of teacher education programs to develop effective training. Finally, I describe the small number of teacher education initiatives that have begun to address the issue of preparing pre-service and in-service teachers to design, deliver and support virtual schooling.

THE STATE OF K-12 ONLINE LEARNING

The use of distance education in the K-12 environment stemming from a need to provide equal educational opportunities to rural areas is common throughout North America (Haughey & Muirhead, 1999). The use of distance education at the K-12 level has been in place since the beginning of the twentieth century, beginning with a correspon-

dence model at the Calvert School of Baltimore in 1906 (Moore & Kearsley, 1996). Over the past 100 years, the model of distance education has evolved from these initial correspondence models to educational radio to instructional television to audiographics (Clark, 2007). In the past two decades, web-based or online delivery has become the dominant form of K-12 distance education delivery – with these online learning programs being organized into formal virtual or cyber schools, at least in North America (Barbour, 2009).

Clark (2000) defined a virtual school as "a state approved and/or regionally accredited school that offers secondary credit courses through distance learning methods that include Internet-based delivery" (p. i). While others distinguished between a virtual school (i.e., an entity where students took all of their courses from) and virtual schooling (where students take one or more courses through an online learning program) (Barker, Wendel and Richmond,1999); Clark (2001) has become the more accepted definition in the literature. In the United States, the first school to begin using K-12 online learning was the private Laurel Springs School in California around 1991. This was followed by the Utah eSchool in 1994-95, along with the Florida Virtual School and Virtual High School Global Consortium in 1996-97. In 2000-01 the for profit company K12, Inc. introduced the first full-time cyber school (Watson et al., 2009).

At the turn of the millennia, Clark (2001) estimated that there were between 40,000 and 50,000 virtual school enrolments. A decade later, Watson, Murin, Vashaw, Gemin and Rapp (2010) indicated that there were over 1,500,000 K-12 students enrolled in online courses in 48 states, and the District of Columbia. In 2006 Michigan became the first state in the US to require that all students complete an online learning experience in order to graduate from high school (a move that has been followed by other states). For example, the State of Florida requires that all school districts provide virtual schooling opportunities for any student who requests it, while New Mexico requires that students complete an Advanced Placement, an advanced or honors course, a dual-credit course offered in cooperation with an institution of higher education or a distance learning course in order to graduate. Some have even gone so far to predict that the majority of K-12 education will be delivered using online learning by the year 2020 (Christensen, Horn & Johnson, 2008).

MODELS OF K-12 ONLINE LEARNING

There are many different delivery models used by K-12 online learning programs. Kaseman and Kaseman (2000) described them as ranging from traditional correspondence courses with student interaction being limited to readings and written responses, while others allowed students to interact with their teacher and classmates through a variety of asynchronous and synchronous communication tools. However, three primary models of delivery have emerged for virtual schools: independent, asynchronous, and synchronous (or a combination of two or more of these methods). The term virtual school began to be used to describe supplemental programs where the student is enrolled in a traditional brick-and-mortar or physical school and enrolls in one or more online courses to supplement their in-school courses, while the term cyber schooling began to refer to full-time programs when a student is not enrolled in a brick-and-mortar school at all but completes all of their courses online. For the purposes of this chapter, I will use the term virtual school to include all forms of K-12 online learning.

Independent Model of Delivery

As Kaseman and Kaseman indicated one model of delivery, the independent one, is similar to a student in a traditional correspondence course. Greenway and Vanourek (2006) described the delivery model as:

In a "typical" day, a student might take mostly core courses with some electives and log on to the computer for an hour or two, clicking through interactive lessons with text, audio or video clips, Flash animation, and links to related sites; completing an online math quiz; e-mailing the teacher; and "chatting" with classmates online. Students complete the majority of their work offline in many of these online schools, for example, reading assignments, drafting an essay, conducting an experiment with school-supplied materials, and studying for an exam.. ...A parent or other responsible adult is asked to supervise—and sometimes to assist with instruction and motivation, all under the direction of a licensed teacher.

In this delivery model, the student is essentially teaching themselves or being taught by a parent, with only minimum involvement from a teacher and the virtual school simply providing the materials used by the student.

Asynchronous Model of Delivery

The asynchronous model of delivery is the most common. For example, Friend and Johnston (2005) described how students interact with an online curriculum that engages them in real-world applications, challenging them with content, and providing them with choice in the resources that they use and how they demonstrate their understanding of the content. When a student feels they have mastered the content, they turn "in assignments, and the teacher gives written feedback in the electronic course room or phones to discuss ways the student [sic] can improve performance" (p. 109). Zucker and Kozma (2003) described the asynchronous model as one where a student would use the online content and their textbook to work through the material and complete the written work – which would be submitted to the teacher for written feedback delivered to the student through the course management system. Along with the tools provided by the course management system, many K-12 online teachers utilize a variety of Web 2.0 tools (e.g., blogging, wikis, social networking, etc.) in their asynchronous instruction. In this model the role of the teacher is more active, guiding the students through their course content.

Many online teachers experience difficulty teaching in this asynchronous environment. For example, Barbour (2007) found that in one virtual school teachers assigned time to work on assignments and other "seat work" to students during their scheduled asynchronous class time. Barbour compared the nature of this work to the kind of "busy work" classroom teachers often assign students to complete at the end of a lesson to practice the skills or knowledge presented in the lesson, or simply to occupy the time remaining in the class. Surrey and Ely (2007) described how people are likely to adopt innovations that are consistent with their current beliefs and practices. For many teachers, the asynchronous instructional tools are foreign to their traditional teaching habits, and they are unable to utilize them in effective ways beyond the kind of asynchronous work they would assign students in a traditional classroom environment.

Synchronous Model of Delivery

Some virtual schools also offer synchronous classes during the school day, although this model of delivery is utilized by only a small number of virtual schools. Murphy and Coffin (2003) described a synchronous learning environment as a "virtual classroom, [where students] have access to DM [direct messaging] and hand raising. Access to other tools, such as the microphone or the WB [whiteboard], must be assigned by the teacher" (p. 236). Using these tools, the teacher can lead a traditional lecture, using slides on the whiteboard to guide their thoughts or as notes for the student. Nippard and Murphy (2007) described many of the forms of interaction that might occur. Teachers can facilitate both audio and text-based discussions. The audio discussion can allow one

person to speak at a time or multiple people, and the text messaging provides the opportunity for multiple individuals to participate in private or public discussions. These virtual classrooms also allow the teacher to have students to in groups in a variety of breakout rooms created by the teacher. Finally, the teacher can also allow the students to control various instructor functions to present material within the classroom.

Again, Barbour (2007) found that most of the actual instruction provided to students in that one virtual school occurred during the synchronous classes. The teachers' reliance on synchronous methods of instruction was consistent with the premise stated earlier by Surrey and Ely (2007). These teachers were drawn to the synchronous environment because the virtual classroom allowed them to teach in a way that they were familiar with (e.g., lecturing to students with the use of a whiteboard or other visual aids, students raising their hands to ask questions, speaking one at a time, etc.). The majority of synchronous instruction in virtual schooling occurs in Canadian programs, where education is controlled at the provincial level and provincial governments can expect accommodation as a condition of participation. As education is locally controlled in the United States, this kind of demand is not an effective tool. For example, if the Michigan Virtual School wished to have full-class synchronous sessions they would need as many of the 549 public schools districts that were participating in the Michigan Virtual School to agree upon a common schedule, start time, class period, lengths, etc.. This is why synchronous instruction in virtual schools in the United States are often limited to individual sessions or are outside of the school day.

A NEW MODEL OF TEACHING AND LEARNING

As evidenced by all three of these different models of virtual schooling, many of the teaching and learning interactions that are taking place in the virtual school environment are consistent with what one would find in a traditional brick-and-mortar classroom – only these interactions are being mediated by technology (e.g., having students read material in a textbook and then respond to written questions, a teacher giving a lecture that is accompanied by overheads or a PowerPoint to students who can take notes and ask questions, etc.). These current models notwithstanding, some continue to argue that virtual schools have the ability to provide K-12 students with "the knowledge and skills they need in typical 21st century communities and workplaces" (Partnership for 21st Century Skills, 2002, p. 3). These proponents believe there is potential for K-12 online learning to equip students to work in a "fully networked computing environment as more important than a desk.... [where] they cannot be supervised in the traditional sense. Rather they must be given the environment and tools to create and succeed" (Tapscott, 1998, p. 10). With the ability to learn in that environment preparing them with the information and communication skills, along with the interpersonal and self-direction skills that will be needed for the twenty-first century.

Like many aspects of K-12 education, there are examples of K-12 online learning that are breaking the mold and providing students with these twenty-first century skills. For example, since 2005 the Michigan Virtual School has offered courses that introduce students to the Chinese language and culture. This course is taught by a native-speaking Chinese teacher, with a background in second language acquisition (NACOL & the Partnership for 21st Century Skills, 2006). With the growing importance of Asia in the global economy, this kind of opportunity for secondary school students has the potential to provide them with the global awareness and second-language skills that will be critical to their futures.

Another example is the any time, any place, any pace delivery model used by the Florida Virtual School. Under this system, students have the option to complete their online courses in more or less time than would be provided by a traditional brick-and-mortar school. The ability to customize how they take the course to fit their individual needs – in terms of when, where and how long they take to complete the necessary work to master the course content (Friend & Johnston, 2005). This provides students the opportunity to develop self-directed learning skills that they will be required to have as lifelong learners in the workplace. However, the ability to provide these skills does not necessarily mean that virtual schools are providing these skills at present. There is ample evidence examining online learning in higher education that has found online learning to not only not have lived up to the potential of online learning proponents, but also to have limited most faculty members' ability within the teaching and learning process (Herrington, Reeves & Oliver, 2005; Reeves; 2003, 2005). While virtual schools may allow for the development of the skills and knowledge needed for the twenty-first century, it certainly does not guarantee it. The question then becomes whether teacher education programs ready to prepare teachers to support these technology-mediated twenty-first century experiences to their students.

TEACHING ONLINE IN A K-12 ENVIRONMENT

Smith, Clark, & Blomeyer (2005) believed that only 1 percent of the K-12 teachers in the United States have been trained to teach online. Wood (2005) indicated that there was a "persistent opinion that people who have never taught in this medium [i.e., online] can jump in and teach a class," quoting Robert Blomeyer of the North Central Regional Education Laboratory, who continued "a good classroom teacher is not necessarily a good online teacher" (p. 36). In this section I describe some of the characteristics related to teaching in an online environment, and how those characteristics are unique to the virtual school environment.

Characteristics of Teaching Online

Some of the skills necessary for teaching in an online environment are consistent with those provided by traditional teacher education programs, but there are other necessary skills that are largely absent (Davis & Roblyer, 2005). Roblyer and McKenzie (2000) stated that many of the factors that make a successful online teacher, such as good communication and classroom organization skills, were similar to those for any successful teacher. However, Davis, Roblyer, Charania, Ferdig Harms, Compton and Cho (2007) discovered "effective virtual teachers have qualities and skills that often set them apart from traditional teachers" (p. 28). Teaching in an online environment also requires a paradigm shift in how teachers perceive time and space, manage instructional activities and assessments, and engage students (Easton, 2003).

Morris (2002) described teachers who teach in technology-mediated environments, such as those provided by virtual schools, should have a high level of technology skills, be familiar with the curriculum, possess strong communication and organizational skills, and are excited about this new method of delivery. Lowes (2005) indicated that online teachers are required to use different strategies when determining "how to reach and evaluate, students when you cannot interact with them face-to-face on a daily basis" (p. 12). Since the skills to teach in an online environment cannot be assumed to transfer automatically from skills in teaching a face-to-face classroom, most online instructors are left unprepared to deal with the demands placed upon them because they do not understand the unique communication and pedagogical demands of teaching in an online environment (Davis et al., 2007).

Unfortunately, Harms, Niederhauser, Davis, Roblyer and Gilbert (2006) described the literature on effective teaching in virtual school environ-

ments as "often supported only by anecdotal evidence" (p. 4). Like other aspects of virtual schooling, there is little actual research into what specific factors or characteristics are different between teaching online and teaching in a face-to-face environment – only some acknowledgement that teaching in the two environments are different. One of the exceptions to this lack of research is Elizabeth Murphy and her colleagues, who have also examined a variety of aspects related to teaching in a virtual school environment. For example, these individuals have studied teachers' perceptions of learner centeredness in the online classroom (e.g., sage on the stage vs. guide on the side) (Murphy & Rodríguez-Manzanares, 2009a, 2009b), motivating students in the online environment (Murphy & Rodríguez-Manzanares, 2009c), and effective strategies for both asynchronous and synchronous instruction (Murphy, Rodríguez-Manzanares & Barbour, in press). However, Murphy and her colleagues focused their research on either a single virtual school or on the beliefs of teachers without verification of those beliefs. Murphy and another group of her colleagues also investigated the use of synchronous virtual classroom tools in the second-language courses (Murphy, 2010; Murphy & Coffin, 2003) or how online teachers project social presence – or a sense of community and belonging in the online classroom – in the synchronous virtual classroom environment (Nippard & Murphy, 2007). Unfortunately these studies were focused upon a single virtual school that used a high percentage of synchronous instruction – making it quite unique among virtual schools in North America, the majority of whom use a primarily asynchronous instructional model.

Similarly, DiPietro, Ferdig, Black and Preston (2008) outlined 37 best practices in asynchronous online teaching. However, these best practices were based upon interviews with teachers at a single virtual school selected by the virtual school itself. Additionally, these teachers' beliefs about their best practices were not validated through observation of the teaching or student performance. Further, DiPietro (2010) described five beliefs virtual school teachers had about effective instructional practices. Once again, these beliefs were based upon interviews with a purposeful sample of virtual school teachers and an examination of a sample of their online course content. There were no observations to determine if the virtual school teachers enacted their stated beliefs. There were also data collected from students to verify if the beliefs about effective instructional practices translated into better student performance or to examine whether students were aware of or found these beliefs to be effective. I highlight the methodological limitations of the work published by DiPietro and her colleagues, along with Murphy and her colleagues, not to imply that these individuals are poor researchers or that their results should be called into question. I do highlight these methodological weaknesses to illustrate that these findings are not generalizable beyond the settings where the research was conducted or are simply based upon the opinions of virtual school teachers. Simply put, the limited amount of research literature into teaching K-12 students in an online environment is still very much in its infancy.

Finally, in addition to the limited amount of research into teaching in an online environment, the main practitioner organization representing K-12 online learning organizations have further mudded the waters. In 2008, the International Association for K-12 Online Learning (iNACOL) conducted a review of published standards of K-12 teaching online that resulted in the release of the National Standards for Quality Online Teaching (see NACOL, 2008). Once again, it was unfortunate that these standards were essentially those that had been originally published by the Southern Regional Educational Board (SREB), with some additions related to twenty-first century learning skills (largely due to iNACOL's involvement in the Partnership for 21st Century Skills). Beyond the SREB standards, iNACOL also reviewed standards from the National Education Association's Guide to Teaching Online Courses, the Ohio Department of Education's Ohio Standards for the Teaching Profession, and the Electronic Classroom of Tomorrow's (ECOTs) Teacher Evaluation Rubric. With the exception of ECOT's rubric, none of the standards were based upon published research – and neither the SREB's nor iNACOL's standards have been verified as valid and/or reliable (although Ferdig, Cavanaugh DiPietro, Black & Dawson [2000] did attempt to map existing literature, not research, to the iNACOL teaching standards). Regardless, while standards exist, they provide little systematic guidance for teaching online.

Teaching Online and Teacher Professional Development

As very few virtual school teachers receive training to teach online from their teacher education programs, the vast majority of teacher preparation has been accomplished through teacher professional development. Since the inception of virtual schooling, practitioners and evaluators have believed in order to fully appreciate the challenges that students face that teachers need to have the same kinds of experiences as their students when it comes to learning in an online environment (Zucker & Kozma, 2003). Many virtual schools require their teachers to complete online training and professional development prior to teaching online. For example, the Virtual High School Global Consortium requires all prospective teachers to complete an online course in online pedagogy and all potential course developers to complete an online course in online course design (Pape, Adams & Ribeiro, 2005). Recently, they have expanded their offerings to five separate courses ranging from simply technology integration for classroom-based teachers to online pedagogy to the use of Web 2.0 tools (see http://www.govhs.org/Pages/ProfDev-Home). They have even a partnership with Plymouth State University, Framingham State College and Northwest Nazarene University to allow participants to receive graduate credits for completion of these courses, and a Certificate in Online Teaching and Learning if participants complete all five courses. The Illinois Virtual High School and Michigan Virtual School both offer similar six to eight-week web-based courses in online course design and online pedagogy to its teachers (see Barbour et al., 2010; Davis, 2003 respectively). Many other virtual schools in the United States offer their own teacher training in face-to-face or online formats.

These online courses usually focus on using the course management system and other tools, designing online curricular activities, and how to teach in an independent online environment (Watson, 2007). In addition to experiencing the same online environment that their students will have to use, "research into teaching has consistently shown that teachers teach the way they were taught" (Davis & Rose, 2007, p. 7). This concern was consistent with the finding of Barbour (2007), who indicated that virtual school teachers were able to use the synchronous virtual classroom efficiently because it allowed them to teach in a way that was familiar to them. He also found that these same teachers did not have effective asynchronous teaching strategies because it was foreign to them, and they often reverted to simply assigning students' seatwork or time to work on assignments. Without the experience of being taught in an online environment, these future online teachers have only a face-to-face paradigm to bring with them into the online classroom.

In fact, Rice and Dawley (2007) found that less than 40% of all online teachers in the United States reported to receiving professional development before they began teaching online. This indicates a need for teacher education programs to begin to address pre-service and in-service teachers' ability to teach in environments that are completely mediated by technology. Aronson and Timms (2003) also indicated that K-12 student success in online learning required support from both the online teacher and the local school-based teacher.

Recent studies have found supplemental virtual school programs placed a significant demand upon school-based teachers and administrators (Barbour & Mulcahy, 2004; Hannum, Irvin, Lei & Farmer, 2008; Mulcahy, Dibbon & Norberg, 2008; Roblyer, Freeman, Stabler & Schneidmiller, 2007). So while some virtual schools provide some training to their own teachers, in most instances no such training is provided to the school-based personnel. There is clearly a need for teacher education programs to equip all teachers with initial training in teaching and learning in online K-12 environments.

TEACHER TRAINING AND NEW MODELS OF TEACHER EDUCATION

Teacher education programs need to develop courses and complete programs that focus upon teaching and learning in a K-12 online learning environment (Davis & Rose, 2007). At present, there has only been one systematic initiative within teacher education to prepare teachers for the virtual school environment.

A Comprehensive Approach to Teacher Education and Virtual Schooling

Clark and Else (2003) indentified technology training as one of the key issues related to growing the virtual school movement. The continuing evolution of technology from the traditional static content that teachers could place online for their students to access to the read-write web (often referred to as Web 2.0) where teachers and students generate the online content together creates unique needs for teachers. Online teachers must be able to use these technologies, along with being able to instruct their own students on how to use them and have some limited knowledge of troubleshooting these technologies. Beyond a greater knowledge of and facilitation of technology, Kearsley and Blomeyer (2004) indicated that pre-service and in-service teachers also needed to be able to complete the following tasks in a technology-mediated environment timely and meaningful feedback; create learning activities that engaged students, keep students interested and motivated, get students to interact with each other, and encourage students to be critical and reflective.

At present, there are two resources at Iowa State University (ISU) that may provide a model, and even curricular materials, that teacher education programs can adopt to address Kearsley's and Blomeyer's five online teaching tasks: Good Practice to Inform Iowa Learning Online and Teacher Education Goes Into Virtual Schooling (TEGIVS). The Good Practice to Inform Iowa Learning Online (see http://projects.educ.iastate. edu/~vhs/) was a project by funded by Roy J. Carver Charitable Trust, where Iowa State University (ISU) partnered with Iowa Public Television, Iowa Department of Education, the University of Virginia, and Ottumwa Community Schools, and Wartburg College. The purpose of the project was to create "ten case studies of good practice and supported the development of three exemplary courses by pioneers in Iowa who [would] lead good practice and mentor others" (Davis, Niederhauser, Compton, Lindstrom and Schoeny, 2005, p. 342). The case studies, which have a decided focus upon courses from the science curriculum, provided users with a detailed rationale as for why the course was being offered in an online learning format, description of the course, and discussion of the online tools being used in that course. Each case study also included syllabi for each of the courses and a selection of course materials, activities and assessments as examples.

As a follow-up to these case studies, ISU secured funding from the U.S. Department of Education's Fund for the Improvement of Post Secondary Education (FIPSE) and partnered with the Universities of Florida and Virginia, Graceland University and Iowa Learning Online to cre-

ate TEGIVS (see http://ctlt.iastate.edu/~tegivs/ TEGIVS/homepage.html). The purpose of TE-GIVS was "to build on that work [i.e., the Good Practice to Inform Iowa Learning Online project] to incorporate virtual schooling into pre-service teacher education" (Davis et al., 2005, p. 342). The TEGIVS project would to introduce and orient new and current teachers to three roles in the virtual school environment:

Virtual School Site Facilitator: Mentoring & Advocating
Local mentor and advocate for students(s)
Proctors & records grades, etc.
Virtual School Teacher: Pedagogy & Class Management
Presents activities, manages pacing, rigor, etc.
Interacts with students and their facilitators
Undertakes assessment, grading, etc.
Virtual School Designer: Course Development
Design instructional materials
Works in team with teachers and a virtual school to construct the online course, etc. (Davis, 2007)

While the project had three objectives, this introduction and orientation was addressed by the creation of "instructional materials that [were] designed to illustrate and provide experiences with virtual schooling concepts and issues" (Davis et al., 2007, p. 29). These materials included five web-based scenarios – one for early childhood/ elementary, one for elementary/middle school, and three for secondary school – that focused on different virtual schooling issues and featured a variety of different tools (see http://ctlt.iastate. edu/~tegivs/TEGIVS/VSLab/all%20scenarios. html).

Each of these scenarios reflected four aspects of virtual schooling: pedagogy, technology, assessment and management (Davis, Demiraslan & Wortmann, 2007). The scenarios had different approaches to online learning, such as didactic inquiry, problem-based learning, and other teaching strategies. They also showcased on synchronous and asynchronous software used in the virtual school environment, and individual tools including discussion boards, chat room, e-mail, and the whiteboard to name a few. The scenarios provided examples of how assessment is conducted in virtual school environments, such as reflections, proctored exams, performance-based tests and quizzes, and other authentic assessments. Finally, the scenarios outlined a variety of management issues, including communications between teacher and students, motivation for challenges, teaching technology from a distance, and encouragement to complete activities in independent environments.

However, simply exposing current and future educators to these aspects of virtual schooling does not necessarily prepare them for any of the three roles that they may tasked with during their teaching career. As Davis and Rose (2007) cautioned, "simply viewing any online course cannot provide a rigorous experience. Quality teacher preparation requires careful selection of field experience and student teaching in the students' content areas and grade levels" (p. 11). In this regard, the TEGIVS project was designed to incorporate the instructional materials in technology integration and/ or teaching methodology course, and to provide a teaching seminar course (see http://ctlt.iastate. edu/~tegivs/CI280A/introduction.html for the course materials), a six hour field experience component (see http://ctlt.iastate.edu/~tegivs/TE-GIVS/curriculum.html for the course materials), and eventually a teaching practicum (see TEGIVS Newsletter 2 for a description of this sequence).

Virtual Student Teaching

While the TEGIVS program is the most extensive initiative in teacher education to address virtual schooling – with both with specific courses and a student teaching experience, there are other teacher education programs that have created virtual school specific courses or provide student teaching opportunities. For example, the Florida Virtual School (FLVS) has partnerships with the University of Central Florida and the University of South Florida to provide virtual school student teaching opportunities to pre-service teacher education students. The partnership with the University of Central was the first one that FLVS established in 2007-08, with a small pilot project that involved six students in three core courses.

Students at the University of Central Florida complete the student teaching experience over a two-semester period. During the first semester, which is often the first semester of the students' senior year, students complete two 7-week student teaching internships. These students have the opportunity to complete both 7-week student teaching internships in a physical or brick-and-mortar environment or students have the option to complete one 7-week student teaching internship in a brick-and-mortar environment and one 7-week student teaching internship in a virtual school environment. During the second semester, students complete a full 14-week internship. Students have the option to complete this 14-week student teaching internship in either a brick-and-mortar or a virtual school environment. It should be noted that students do not have to complete either of their 7-week internships in a virtual school environment during that first semester in order to be eligible for the virtual school internship in this second semester.

While the University of Central of Florida partnership began with a half dozen students, during the 2009-10 school year that had grown to include 17 student teachers. The partnership that the FLVS have with the University of South Florida is quite similar. It began in 2008-09 and had served 45 student teachers in its first two years of operation. FLVS is currently exploring other student teaching partnerships with universities inside and outside of the State of Florida.

Online Teaching Certificates and Endorsement Programs

In addition to the virtual school student teaching experience, another area where teacher education programs have become active is in the provision of Graduate Certificates in Online Teaching. Several universities have created programs that utilize three to five Master's-level courses to form a graduate level certificate in online teaching. Most of these programs are generalized in nature, which is to say the online teaching is not specifically focused on the K-12 environment. However, some universities have created specific K-12 focused programs or K-12 focused options within a more generalized program.

The graduate certificates offered at Arizona State University, Boise State University, the University of Florida, and Wayne State University are good examples of certificates that have K-12 focused options within a more generalized program. These programs have a sequence of courses that students would complete if they were interested in teaching a virtual school environment, and a different set of courses that students would complete if they were interested in online teaching in a higher education or corporate environment. Boise State University and the University of Florida have three course certificates, while Arizona State University and Wayne State University have four course certificates plus an online teaching practicum. Almost all of the programs require students to complete a course in the foundations or theories of distance education, a course in online course design, and a course in the facilitation of online learning.

In addition to these general programs with a K-12 track or option, there are also several graduate certificate programs that are specifically focused on K-12 virtual schooling. The two programs that have this specific focus are both based in Georgia, which is also the first state in the United States that has a specific endorsement to teacher certification for online teaching. At present, Georgia State University and Valdosta State University both offer programs that allow in-service teachers to gain the online teaching endorsement to their existing teacher certification. The Georgia State University program is a four-course certificate that includes courses in integrating technology into school-based environment, evaluation and assessment for online learning, the Internet for educators, and e-learning environments. The Valdosta State University is a three-course certificate that includes courses in course management systems for e-learning, resources and strategies for e-learning, and design and delivery of instruction for e-learning. Some states have integrated online teaching standards into other curricular areas, such as Michigan where half of the educational technology teaching endorsement standards are focused on the design, delivery and support of online learning. Finally, other states (such as Arizona and Idaho) are also in the process of considering and/or implementing online teaching endorsement programs for teacher certification.

Challenges for Teacher Education Program

Probably the biggest obstacle faced by teacher education programs when it comes to the introduction of courses and experiences to support pre-service and in-service teachers in being able to design, delivery and support virtual schooling experiences is the general lack of available models on which to design such courses and experiences. While not a complete list, the models presented above do represent a fairly comprehensive listing of the teacher education initiatives related to virtual schooling. This means that even if teacher education programs are willing and have few institutional obstacles to providing the necessary training for their students to be prepared for virtual schooling, in most instances they have to invent – an not re-invent – the wheel because K-12 online learning is often quite contextual to the jurisdiction where it occurs.

Beyond the general lack of models, another challenge that teacher education programs must overcome is the lack of systematic research into online teaching and learning at the K-12 level. Beyond the limited amount of research into the online teaching of K-12 students described earlier, there is a general paucity of research into virtual schooling and K-12 online learning in general (Rice, 2006). For example, in their review of the literature, Cavanaugh, Barbour and Clark (2009) found the literature on virtual schooling was largely limited to practitioner reports and issues surrounding the policies governing or the technology utilized. Unfortunately, the federally funded TEGIVS initiative that coupled the developed of a model and supporting curricular materials for the introduction of virtual schooling into a teacher education program, along with systematic research of its implementation has been a rare instance.

Within the Canadian context, Memorial University of Newfoundland has led a consortium of K-12 and post-secondary organization to create the Killick Centre for E-Learning Research (see http://www.mun.ca/killick/home/). Funded through the Social Sciences and Humanities Council of Canada's College-University Research Alliance program, the Killick Centre fosters research, training and new knowledge in the area of online learning – with a focus on the K-12 environment. Specific research studies have focused on effective online teaching, the impact of online learning on students when they enter post-secondary environments, effective management and leadership models for schools and districts, and the use of online learning to provide opportunities to students in rural and remote communities, along with aboriginal students. Beyond the TEGIVS and Killick Centre initiatives, there has been little systematic examination of how to prepare teachers to be able to design, delivery and support virtual school learning opportunities.

A CONCLUDING CALL TO ACTION

I began this chapter by echoing Greenfield (2003) query, "What should we be teaching the next generation to equip them for citizenship in the mid 21st century and beyond?" (p. 148). Almost daily there are reminders that today's economy is changing from an Industrial Age economy to a Digital Age economy. Educational reformers, many of whom are included in this book, call for increase use of technology in K-12 schools to allow students to transition from being consumers of media to creators of media. However, to date neither schools nor teacher education programs have changed to keep pace with the external pressures. Yet, research continuously points to the fact that teachers do not possess the necessary technical skills to keep up with their students in these technology-mediated environments (Duncan, 2005; Magliaro & Ezeife, 2007). Additionally, many new teachers still have limited knowledge of effective strategies for integrating technology into their classroom (Bauer, 2000; Hardy, 2003; Pellegrino & Altman, 1997), so even if they knew how to use the technology they would not know how to use it in pedagogically sound ways. Simply put, teacher education programs need to improve the depth and type of technology training provided to pre-service and in-service teachers.

Beyond providing teachers with the necessary technical skills, one of the five action items to address the training of teachers for these new realities provided by Davis and Rose (2007) was "that all regular universities and college integrate this new model of schoolings into their educational programs" (p. 14). The TEGIVS project included a Creative Commons Attribution-Non-Commercial-Share Alike 3.0 United States License, which would allow other institutions to use these curriculum materials provided that proper attribution was made, the materials were not being used for the purposes of making profit, and the materials (and any modifications thereof) continued to be shared under similar copyright restrictions. This allows any teacher education program to adopt and/or adapt these materials for use in their own programs. While the examples provided are based upon curriculum from the State of Iowa, the teacher roles highlighted, technologies showcased, pedagogy illustrated, and management issues discussed in this curriculum are common to most virtual schools throughout the United States.

While the models for integrating virtual schooling into teacher education may be limited, there are a variety of examples that currently exist; and even curricular materials that can be used. The missing link at this stage is the will to reform teacher education programs to prepare teachers to design, delivery and support virtual schooling. In her study of the potential for and ability of pre-tenured professors to reform teacher education programs, Cole (1999) was optimistic and characterized those who would mould and shape teacher education for the next generation as "highly competent, committed, and caring" (p. 294). However, she also cautioned that often these individuals are curtailed in their efforts at challenging the status quo as institutions "serve to perpetuate rather than challenge convention" (p. 294). I mention Cole's study because it is important to note that the majority of university faculty actively researching virtual schooling in the United States are pre-tenured faculty. The challenge will be to ensure that these teacher educators are able to overcome that status quo to enact changes to guarantee our future teachers do not whither.

Goodlad (1994) believed that innovation in K-12 schools needed to be matched with similar innovation in teacher education. Clearly innovation is occurring at the K-12 level with the increased use of virtual schooling. In order to this K-12 innovation to become widely accepted and adopted, teacher education programs must also innovate to prepare teachers who are ready for this and other changes.

REFERENCES

Aronson, J. Z., & Timms, M. J. (2003). *Net choices, net gains: Supplementing the high school curriculum with online courses*. San Francisco, CA: WestEd. Retrieved from www.wested.org/online_pubs/KN-03-02.pdf

Barbour, M. K. (2007). *What are they doing and how are they doing it? Rural student experiences in virtual schooling*. Unpublished Doctoral Dissertation. University of Georgia, Athens, GA.

Barbour, M. K. (2009). Today's student and virtual schooling: The reality, the challenges, the promise. *Journal of Distance Learning, 13*(1), 5–25.

Barbour, M. K., Kinsella, J., Wicks, M., & Toker, S. (2010). Continuum of change in a virtual world: Training and retaining instructors. *Journal of Technology and Teacher Education, 17*(4), 437–457.

Barbour, M. K., & Mulcahy, D. (2004). The role of mediating teachers in Newfoundland's new model of distance education. *The Morning Watch, 32*(1-2). Retrieved from http://www.mun.ca/educ/faculty/mwatch/fall4/barbourmulcahy.htm

Barker, K., Wendel, T., & Richmond, M. (1999). *Linking the literature: School effectiveness and virtual schools*. Vancouver, BC: FuturEd. Retrieved from http://www.futured.com/pdf/Virtual.pdf

Bauer, J. F. (2000, November). *A technology gender divide: Perceived skill and frustration levels among female preservice teachers*. A paper presentation at the Annual Meeting of the Mid-South Educational Research Association, Bowling Green, KY. (ERIC Document Reproduction Service No. ED447137). Retrieved from http://www.eric.ed.gov/ERICWebPortal/contentdelivery/servlet/ERICServlet?accno=ED447137

Cavanaugh, C., Barbour, M. K., & Clark, T. (2009). Research and practice in K-12 online learning: A review of literature. *International Review of Research in Open and Distance Learning, 10*(1). Retrieved from http://www.irrodl.org/index.php/irrodl/article/view/607.

Christensen, C. M., Horn, M. B., & Johnson, C. W. (2008). *Disrupting class: How disruptive innovation will change the way the world learns.* New York, NY: McGraw Hill.

Clark, T. (2000). *Virtual high schools: State of the states - A study of virtual high school planning and preparation in the United States.* Center for the Application of Information Technologies, Western Illinois University. Retrieved from http://www.imsa.edu/programs/ivhs/pdfs/stateofstates.pdf

Clark, T. (2001). *Virtual schools: Trends and issues - A study of virtual schools in the United States.* San Francisco, CA: Western Regional Educational Laboratories. Retrieved from http://www.wested.org/online_pubs/virtualschools.pdf

Clark, T. (2007). Virtual and distance education in North American schools. In Moore, M. G. (Ed.), *Handbook of distance education* (2nd ed.). Mahwah, NJ: Lawrence Erlbaum Associates, Inc.

Clark, T., & Else, D. (2003). Distance education, electronic networking and school policy. In Walling, D. R. (Ed.), *Virtual schooling: Issues in the development of e-learning policy* (pp. 31–45). Bloomington, IN: Phi Delta Kappa Educational Foundation.

Cole, A. L. (1999). Teacher educators and teacher education reform: Individual commitments, institutional realities. *Canadian Journal of Education, 24*(3), 281–295. Retrieved from http://www.csse.ca/CJE/Articles/FullText/CJE24-3/CJE24-3-Cole.pdf. doi:10.2307/1585876

Davis, N., Demiraslan, Y., & Wortmann, K. (2007, October). *Preparing to support online learning in K-12.* A presentation at the Iowa Educational Technology conference, Des Moines, IA. Retrieved from http://ctlt.iastate.edu/~tegivs/TEGIVS/publications/ITEC2007-presentations.pdf

Davis, N., Niederhauser, D., Compton, L., Lindstrom, D., & Schoeny, Z. (2005). Virtual schooling lab practice: Case studies for teacher preparation. *Proceedings of the International Conference of the Society for Information Technology and Teacher Education* (pp. 342-345). Norfolk, VA: Association for the Advancement of Computing in Education. Retrieved from http://ctlt.iastate.edu/~tegivs/TEGIVS/publications/conferenceproceedings2005.pdf

Davis, N., & Rose, R. (2007). *Research committee issues brief: Professional development for virtual schooling and online learning.* Vienna, VA: North American Council for Online Learning. Retrieved from http://www.nacol.org/docs/NACOL_PDforVSandOlnLrng.pdf

Davis, N. E. (2007, November). *Teacher education for virtual schools.* A presentation at Annual Virtual School Symposium, Louisville, KY. Retrieved from http://ctlt.iastate.edu/~tegivs/TEGIVS/publications/VS%20Symposium2007.pdf

Davis, N. E., & Roblyer, M. D. (2005). Preparing teachers for the "schools that technology built": Evaluation of a program to train teachers for virtual schooling. *Journal of Research on Technology in Education, 37*(4), 399–409.

Davis, N. E., Roblyer, M. D., Charania, A., Ferdig, R., Harms, C., Compton, L. K. L., & Cho, M. O. (2007). Illustrating the "virtual" in virtual schooling: Challenges and strategies for creating real tools to prepare virtual teachers. *The Internet and Higher Education, 10*(1), 27–39. Retrieved from http://ctlt.iastate.edu/~tegivs/TEGIVS/publications/JP2007%20davis&roblyer.pdf. doi:10.1016/j.iheduc.2006.11.001

Davis, N. M. (2003). Creating a learning community in the virtual classroom. In Walling, D. R. (Ed.), *Virtual schooling: Issues in the development of e-learning policy* (pp. 77–83). Bloomington, IN: Phi Delta Kappa Educational Foundation.

DiPietro, M. (2010). Virtual school pedagogy: The instructional practices of K-12 virtual school teachers. *Journal of Educational Computing Research, 42*(3), 327–354. doi:10.2190/EC.42.3.e

DiPietro, M., Ferdig, R. E., Black, E. W., & Preston, M. (2008). Best practices in teaching K-12 online: Lessons learned from Michigan Virtual School teachers. *Journal of Interactive Online Learning, 7*(1). Retrieved from http://www.ncolr.org/jiol/issues/getfile.cfm?volID=7&IssueID=22&ArticleID=113.

Duncan, H. (2005). On-line education for practicing professionals: A case study. *Canadian Journal of Education, 28*(4), 874–896. Retrieved from http://www.csse.ca/CJE/Articles/FullText/CJE28-4/CJE28-4-duncan.pdf. doi:10.2307/4126459

Easton, S. (2003). Clarifying the instructor's role in online distance learning. *Communication Education, 52*(2), 87–105. doi:10.1080/03634520302470

Ferdig, R. E., Cavanaugh, C., DiPietro, M., Black, E. W., & Dawson, K. (2010). Virtual schooling standards and best practices for teacher education. *Journal of Technology and Teacher Education, 17*(4), 479–503.

Friedman, T. L. (2006). *The world is flat: A brief history of the twenty-first century*. New York: Farrar, Straus and Giroux.

Friend, B., & Johnston, S. (2005). Florida Virtual School: A choice for all students. In Berge, Z. L., & Clark, T. (Eds.), *Virtual schools: Planning for success* (pp. 97–117). New York, NY: Teachers College Press.

Goodlad, J. (1994). *Educational renewal*. San Francisco, CA: Jossey-Bass Publishers.

Greenfield, S. (2003). *Tomorrow's people: How 21st-century technology is changing the way we think and feel*. London: Penguin Books Ltd.

Greenway, R., & Vanourek, G. (2006). The virtual revolution: Understanding online schools. *Education Next* (2). Retrieved from http://www.hoover.org/publications/ednext/3210506.html

Hannum, W. H., Irvin, M. J., Lei, P.-W., & Farmer, T. W. (2008). Effectiveness of using learner-centered principles on student retention in distance education courses in rural schools. *Distance Education, 29*, 211–229. doi:10.1080/01587910802395763

Hardy, M. D. (2003). *"It should have been stressed in all education classes": Preparing pre-service teachers to teach with technology*. Searcy, AR: Harding University. ERIC Document Reproduction Service No. ED478379. Retrieved from http://www.eric.ed.gov/ERICWebPortal/contentdelivery/servlet/ERICServlet?accno=ED478379

Harms, C. M., Niederhauser, D. S., Davis, N. E., Roblyer, M. D., & Gilbert, S. B. (2006). Educating educators for virtual schooling: Communicating roles and responsibilities. *The Electronic Journal of Communication, 16*(1-2). Retrieved from http://ctlt.iastate.edu/~tegivs/TEGIVS/publications/JP2007%20harms&niederhauser.pdf

Haughey, M., & Muirhead, W. (1999). *On-line learning: Best practices for Alberta school jurisdictions*. Edmonton, AB: Government of Alberta. Retrieved from http://www.phrd.ab.ca/technology/best_practices/on-line-learning.pdf

Herrington, J., Reeves, T. C., & Oliver, R. (2005). Online learning as information delivery: Digital myopia. *Journal of Interactive Learning Research, 16*(4), 353–367.

International Society for Technology in Education. (2008). *National educational technology standards for teachers.* Washington, DC: Author. Retrieved from http://www.iste.org/Content/NavigationMenu/NETS/ForTeachers/NETS_for_Teachers.htm

Kaseman, L., & Kaseman, S. (2000). How will virtual schools effect homeschooling? *Home Education Magazine* (November-December), 16-19. Retrieved from http://homeedmag.com/HEM/176/ndtch.html

Kearsley, G., & Blomeyer, R. (2004). Preparing K-12 teachers to teach online. *Educational Technology, 44*(1), 49–52. Retrieved from http://home.sprynet.com/~gkearsley/TeachingOnline.htm.

Lowes, S. (2005, June). *Online teaching and classroom change: The impact of virtual high school on its teachers and their school.* A paper presented at the meeting of the North Central Regional Educational Laboratory, Chicago, IL. Retrieved from http://www.ilt.columbia.edu/publications/lowes_final.pdf

Magliaro, J., & Ezeife, A. N. (2007). Preservice teachers' preparedness to integrate computer technology into the curriculum. *Canadian Journal of Learning and Technology, 33*(3), 95–111. Retrieved from http://www.cjlt.ca/content/vol33.3/Magliaro.html.

Moore, M. G., & Kearsley, G. (1996). The theoretical basis for distance education. In *Distance education: A systems view* (pp. 197–212). Belmont, CA: Wadsworth.

Morris, S. (2002). *Teaching and learning online: A step-by-step guide for designing an online K-12 school program.* Lanham, MD: Scarecrow Press Inc.

Mulcahy, D. M., Dibbon, D., & Norberg, C. (2008). *An investigation into the nature of education in a rural and remote region of Newfoundland and Labrador: The Straits.* St. John's, NL: The Harris Centre, Memorial University of Newfoundland.

Murphy, E. (2010). Online synchronous communication in the second-language classroom. *Canadian Journal of Learning and Technology., 35*(3). Retrieved from http://www.cjlt.ca/index.php/cjlt/article/view/539.

Murphy, E., & Coffin, G. (2003). Synchronous communication in a Web-based senior high school course: Maximizing affordances and minimizing constraints of the tool. *American Journal of Distance Education, 17*(4), 235–246. doi:10.1207/s15389286ajde1704_4

Murphy, E., & Rodríguez-Manzanares, M. (2009a). Learner-centredness in high-school distance learning: Teachers' perspectives and research-validated principles. *Australasian Journal of Educational Technology, 25*(5), 597-610. Retrieved from http://www.ascilite.org.au/ajet/ajet25/murphy.html

Murphy, E., & Rodríguez-Manzanares, M. (2009b). Sage without a stage: A cultural historical activity theory perspective on e-teaching in web-based, high-school classrooms. *International Review of Research in Open and Distance Learning, 10*(3). Retrieved from http://www.irrodl.org/index.php/irrodl/article/view/579/1300.

Murphy, E., & Rodríguez-Manzanares, M. (2009c). Teachers' perspectives on motivation in high-school distance education. *Journal of Distance Education, 23*(3), 1–24. Retrieved from http://www.jofde.ca/index.php/jde/article/view/602.

Murphy, E., Rodríguez-Manzanares, M., & Barbour, M. K. (2011). Asynchronous and synchronous teaching and learning in high-school distance education. *British Journal of Educational Technology, 42*(4). doi:10.1111/j.1467-8535.2010.01112.x

Nippard, E., & Murphy, E. (2007). Social presence in the web-based synchronous secondary classroom. *Canadian Journal of Learning and Technology, 33*(1). Retrieved from http://www.cjlt.ca/content/vol33.1/nippard.html.

North American Council for Online Learning. (2008). *National standards for quality online teaching.* Vienna, VA: Author. Retrieved from http://www.nacol.org/nationalstandards/NACOL%20Standards%20Quality%20Online%20Teaching.pdf

North American Council for Online Learning & Partnership for 21st Century Skills. (2006). *Virtual schools and 21st century skills.* Vienna, VA: Author. Retrieved 2008 from http://www.nacol.org/docs/NACOL_21CenturySkills.pdf

Pape, L., Adams, R., & Ribeiro, C. (2005). The virtual high school: Collaboration and online professional development. In Berge, Z. L., & Clark, T. (Eds.), *Virtual schools: Planning for success* (pp. 118–132). New York, NY: Teachers College Press.

Partnership for 21st Century Skills. (2002). *Learning for the 21st century: A report and mile guide for 21st century skills.* Washington, DC: Author.

Pellegrino, J. W., & Altman, J. E. (1997). Information technology and teacher preparation: Some critical issues and illustrative solutions. *Peabody Journal of Education, 72*(10), 89–121. doi:10.1207/s15327930pje7201_5

Reeves, T. C. (2003). Storm clouds on the digital education horizon. *Journal of Computing in Higher Education, 15*(1), 3–26. doi:10.1007/BF02940850

Reeves, T. C. (2005). No significant differences revisited: A historical perspective on the research informing contemporary online learning. In Kearsley, G. (Ed.), *Online learning: Personal reflections on the transformation of education* (pp. 299–308). Englewood Cliffs, NJ: Educational Technology Publications.

Rice, K., & Dawley, L. (2007). *Going virtual! The status of professional development for K-12 online teachers.* Boise, ID: Boise State University. Retrieved from http://edtech.boisestate.edu/goingvirtual/goingvirtual1.pdf

Rice, K. L. (2006). A comprehensive look at distance education in the K-12 context. *Journal of Research on Technology in Education, 38*(4), 425–448.

Roblyer, M. D., Freeman, J., Stabler, M., & Schneidmiller, J. (2007). *External evaluation of the Alabama ACCESS initiative: Phase 3 report.* Eugene, OR: International Society for Technology in Education. Retrieved from http://accessdl.state.al.us/2006Evaluation.pdf

Roblyer, M. D., & McKenzie, B. (2000). Distant but not out-of-touch: What makes an effective distance learning instructor? *Learning and Leading with Technology, 27*(6), 50–53.

Smith, R., Clark, T., & Blomeyer, R. L. (2005). *A synthesis of new research on K-12 online learning.* Naperville, IL: Learning Point Associates. Retrieved from http://www.ncrel.org/tech/synthesis/synthesis.pdf

Surrey, D. W., & Ely, D. P. (2007). Adoption, diffusion, implementation, and institutionalization of instructional innovations. In Reiser, R. A., & Dempsey, J. V. (Eds.), *Trends and issues in instructional design and technology* (2nd ed., pp. 104–122). Upper Saddle River, NJ: Pearson Education, Inc.

Tapscott, D. (1998). *Growing up digital: The rise of the net generation*. New York, NY: McGraw-Hill Companies.

Watson, J. (2007). *A national primer on K-12 online learning*. Vienna, VA: North American Council for Online Learning. Retrieved from http://www.nacol.org/docs/national_report.pdf

Watson, J. F., Gemin, B., Ryan, J., & Wicks, M. (2009). *Keeping pace with K–12 online learning: A review of state-level policy and practice*. Naperville, IL: Learning Point Associates. Retrieved from http://www.kpk12.com/downloads/KeepingPace09-fullreport.pdf

Watson, J. F., Murin, A., Vashaw, L., Gemin, B., & Rapp, C. (2010). *Keeping pace with K–12 online learning: An annual review of policy and practice*. Naperville, IL: Learning Point Associates. Retrieved from http://www.kpk12.com/wp-content/uploads/KeepingPaceK12_2010.pdf

Wood, C. (2005). Highschool.com: The virtual classroom redefines education. *Edutopia, 1*(4), 31-44. Retrieved from http://www.edutopia.org/high-school-dot-com

Zucker, A., & Kozma, R. (2003). *The virtual high school: Teaching generation V*. New York, NY: Teachers College Press.

ADDITIONAL READING

Barbour, M. K., & Reeves, T. C. (2009). The reality of virtual schools: A review of the literature. *Computers & Education, 52*(2), 402–416. doi:10.1016/j.compedu.2008.09.009

Berge, Z. L., & Clark, T. (2005). *Virtual schools: Planning for success*. New York, NY: Teachers College Press.

Cavanaugh, C. (2001). The effectiveness of interactive distance education technologies in K-12 learning: A meta-analysis. *International Journal of Educational Telecommunications, 7*(1), 73–88.

Cavanaugh, C. (2007). Effectiveness of K-12 online learning. In Moore, M. G. (Ed.), *Handbook of Distance Education* (2nd ed., pp. 157–168). Mahwah, NJ: Lawrence Erlbaum Associates, Inc.

Cavanaugh, C., & Blomeyer, R. (2007). *What works in K-12 online learning*. Eugene, OR: International Society for Technology in Education.

Cavanaugh, C., Gillan, K. J., Kromrey, J., Hess, M., & Blomeyer, R. (2004). *The effects of distance education on K–12 student outcomes: A meta-analysis*. Naperville, IL: Learning Point Associates. Retrieved July 4, 2005, from http://www.ncrel.org/tech/distance/k12distance.pdf

Clark, T. (2003). Virtual and distance education in American schools. In M. G. Moore (Ed.), *Handbook of distance education>* (pp. 673-699-168). Mahwah, NJ: Lawrence Erlbaum Associates, Inc.

KEY TERMS AND DEFINITIONS

Asynchronous: Not in real time. For example, a discussion forum is an asynchronous technology where one student posts a message and at a later time another student can read and respond to that message. A non-technical example would be like a community bulletin board where one person posts a for sale poster and at a later time another person may walk by and see that sign.

Cyber School: A full-time K-12 online learning program where students do not attend a traditional or brick-and-mortar school.

K-12 Online Learning: A generic term to encompass all forms of distance education at the K-12 level delivered over the Internet. This includes full-time cyber schooling and supplemental virtual schooling.

Synchronous: In real time. For example, a telephone conversation occurs in real time or is said to be synchronous.

Virtual School: A supplemental K-12 online learning program where students attend a traditional or brick-and-mortar school, but may also be enrolled in one or more online courses.

Section 6
Supporting Faculty in Technology–Rich Teacher Education Programs

Chapter 33
Ways to Mentor Methods' Faculty Integration of Technologies in their Courses

Tom Jackson
Aurora University, USA

ABSTRACT

This chapter reveals the significant and authentic challenges that methods faculty face as they step into a zone of uncertainty when integrating computer technology into lessons, classroom teaching, and student learning. While faculty may perceive that current instructional strategies are successful as measured by classroom scores, a look into the student perceptions of classroom practices, students' preferences for learning efficiently using technology demonstrates how they are undernourished and dissatisfied with current instructional strategies. The lack of modeling of technology use in higher education is a problem as new teachers leave the academic venue and venture into the classrooms of today. Energetic K-12 students prefer to use familiar technology tools to probe for dynamic knowledge and stimulate personal learning. Pedagogy, at all levels, must "open-up" and encourage students to seek enriched information and answers to questions for which "clarification and improvement" is the best answer. In this chapter, several themes are explored including challenges faced by faculty, significance of non-integrated technology, pathways to implementation, overcoming wait-long-enough attitudes, effective mentoring-coaching models for success, and conditions to begin a successful technology integration process.

INTRODUCTION

It must fill a need, be flexible and non-complex to learn. Baule (2007) reminds us, "if it is more complicated that a light switch it will not be as successful" (p. 16).

DOI: 10.4018/978-1-4666-0014-0.ch033

Making practice visible exposes strengths and challenges. Improving classroom craft for professors in Colleges of Education is similar to playing a clarinet with virtuosity, demonstrating a dance with finesse, or playing a ball game with expertise, but for some professors, improvement of teaching craft is more risky. When playing in a ballgame, encouragement is offered by supportive friends, family, and fans as these community members vicariously experience increased levels of achievement. Newer, unrehearsed skills are practiced multiple times in the presence of coaching and mentoring before being implemented into real-world situations. Developing professional learning of the classroom craft, however, is most authentically assessed with others present, always with students and many times with administrators, and can result in personal efficacy evaluations recorded as either pass or fail. A sense of reduced confidence may permeate professors who have mastered the craft of lecturing. Professors who use elaborate verbal models to explain content to students with a high degree of success, as compared to using technology where the student-audience possesses the skill and practiced knowledge, will likely feel less confident. It is a dilemma that faculty might like to ignore, but can't, as new students with new learning preferences have arrived in the classroom. Prensky (2001) identifies the changes in students as dramatic, and names the new breed of learner "digital native". Prensky describes them as, "students [who] have changed radically. Today's students are no longer the people our educational system was designed to teach." (p. 1).

Prensky delineates the differences and he attributes changed attitudes toward learning models to the tools digital natives encountered as they developed:

A really big discontinuity has taken place… today's students have spent their entire lives surrounded by and using computers, videogames, digital music players, video cams, cell phones, and all the other toys and tools of the digital age. Today's average college grads have spent less than 5,000 hours of their lives reading, but over 10,000 hours playing video games (p. 1).

He concludes the following about today's students. "students *think and process information fundamentally differently* from their predecessors." (p. 1)

The digital native student acquires knowledge using visual models and engages in opportunities to encode learning and receive feedback in a socially constructive manner. The professor wonders how to transfer abstract lecture content into meaningful concepts using technology. Transparency at times like this, leads to feelings of uncertainty and reduced self-efficacy and hostile interaction with the technology, the uninvited visitor. Faculty who see themselves as accomplished at delivering content using traditional means are being pushed outside of their comfort zone.

While effective practice reminds faculty that growth comes through both reflection and risk-taking, reality and pride in previous accomplishments maintain a firm grip on the risks that will be attempted. Trust in a collaborative culture and authentic mentoring-coaching is required, and a willing attitude to follow the trailblazer's marks which carve-out the path for methods faculty to integrate technology into their courses will be necessary. Uncertainty, isolation, and resistance are the sign posts that indicate that effective coaching-mentoring is necessary to move into the technology zone.

This chapter delves into themes that examine the ongoing challenges of integrated technology, including understanding the need for pedagogical status-quo, why mentors-coaches and students are needed to fully engage higher education professors in teaching with, and effective use of technology.

CLARIFYING INTEGRATION ISSUES

Issues One and Two: Professorial Beliefs, and the Need for Support in a New Culture

Gladwell (2002) explains the tipping point as the point at which an idea or product reaches the necessary critical mass to become epidemic. In his words, "It's the moment on the graph when the line starts to shoot straight upwards". Why hasn't use of classroom technology reached the "tipping point" in higher education classrooms? Exploration of that question as well as previous models for embracing change, and a suggestion for future professional development integrating technology is explored first.

Faculty members need a reason to change their practice. Evaluation of teaching practice indicates most professors feel existing methods are more than adequate to deliver content. This belief is held when improved teaching is seen as "an act of telling, rather than an act of transformation" (Edgerton, 1992). When status quo culture prevails faculty will ask "why change"?

Change in beliefs, first and second order barriers (Ertmer, 1999), is what professors believe they are being encouraged to wrestle with when integrated technology arrives at the classroom threshold. Ertmer describes overcoming technology barriers as having two facets, extrinsic, i.e. not having hardware or computer skills, and intrinsic, a modification of pedagogical beliefs. To amend the intrinsic beliefs means the professor is willing to, and can amend what is held as meaningful, trusted, and comfortable. Developing new beliefs in this sacred territory is not an easy task.

If faculty were to acknowledge the idea that technology could develop deeper learning on the part of education students, a long and bumpy ride toward integration of technology into higher education classrooms would still be expected. For example, several other hurdles exist including underdeveloped technology skill, evaluation criteria of faculty teaching performance, self-perception of reduced teaching efficiency and proficiency, and a status quo culture.

While faculty may be willing to accept minor changes, major change, i.e. that required to integrate technology into daily practice, may be strongly resisted. From a faculty perspective, uneasiness with adopting a new way to do professorial business is logical. To help understand the professors' concern with integrated technology Massy and Wilger (1998) explained the differences in three levels of technology use and what is required of the implementer. The first is technology used as a "personal productivity aid". In this scenario technology such as a word processing program is used to create assignments. The second level introduces "enrichment add-ins", while a third level calls for a "paradigm shift" (p. 50). Faculty members recognize opportunity for improved teacher process student comprehension, a level one use, and may use a video depicting content, a level two concept, but will likely feel that a paradigm shift, where students actually produce a video to demonstrate a teaching strategy is ineffective, time consuming, and beyond their understanding and pedagogical skills.

Another factor to consider is the emphasis on research achievement as compared to classroom teaching. The discrepancy is revealed through faculty evaluations and promotions to higher ranks. "Departments pay little attention to the teaching and learning process; research is carefully evaluated, but teaching and learning are seldom audited effectively" (Massy & Wilger, p. 53).

Change is a difficult pill to swallow, especially for faculty who "have their practice down". Many educators who are highly regarded teachers still entertain the notion that there is "a wait long enough and it will go away" implementation period. Fear of failure may be the most significant barrier that higher education professors face when introducing technology enhanced lessons. Friel, Britten, Compton, Peak, Schoch, and VanTyle, (2009) formulate that faculty fear or display an aversion to using new methods in their courses. "The pace of technology adoption by university faculty is often slow. Slow or no faculty technology adoption may result from fear of failure, disinterest, or aversion to change" (p. 300). Hall and Hord (2006) warn against trying to escape change: "[People] still hope that change will avoid us personally and professionally. When confronted with change there is a natural tendency to focus on how to defend ourselves from it instead of how to use and succeed with it" (p. 3).

It is not just organizations that change. It is necessary for the organization members to accept, practice, and become comfortable with new ideas. In the case of schools, the primary implementers must accept and use the innovation. This is difficult because faculty are wary of stepping into the realm of uncertainty where they may be judged as less proficient. Fullan (2001) describes the dilemma as "the implementation dip" (p. 40). The implementation dip is the place where teachers meet the unknown and untried classroom strategy in front of observers. Fullan writes:

The implementation dip is literally a dip in performance confidence as one encounters an innovation that requires new skills and new understandings. All innovations call on people to question and in some respects to change their beliefs. What happens when you find yourself needing new skill and not being proficient when you are used to knowing what you are doing? This kind of experience is classic change material. People feel anxious, fearful, confused, overwhelmed, deskilled, cautious, and if they have moral purpose deeply disturbed (2001, p. 40).

For many faculty using classroom technology is like entering the unknown, especially while being evaluated on classroom performance. Students' comments on classroom outcomes weigh heavily in faculty assessment. Faltering while using this tool may lead to reduced classroom efficiency and ultimately reduced self-efficacy. When faculty feel less proficient as a result of an innovative idea, it isn't long before traditional skills creep back into the classroom landscape. Eisner helps promote understanding this phenomena as he writes, "It is difficult to be pedagogically graceful when you are lost in unfamiliar territory. Teachers are often reluctant to release teaching repertoires that provide an important sense of security for them" (1992, p. 2).

Status-Quo values of the higher education culture pose another faculty consideration. If the framing organizing needs repair, it is a good bet that teaching and classroom innovation and "risks" will not be forthcoming. Trubowitz (2005) emphasizes why personal concerns are valid as cultural norms may prevent faculty from taking risks.

Another obstacle to establishing a culture for learning is the inevitability of resistance to new ideas. The teaching profession draws people who are hard workers, who are committed to service, and who place a high value on stability. Attempts to alter customary work patterns will encounter resistance. The desire for the security of the status quo will serve to reinforce customary modes of behavior and to block out ideas that are different. The challenge for those trying to create a new school culture is to empathize with the reluctance to change and, at the same time, to support those ready to explore new approaches to education (Trubowitz, 2005, p. 175-176).

Given these strong influences, faculty need to know the answer to the "so what is better with technology, why should I embrace use, and how will I be supported with classroom technology" questions.

Failures to use technology in methods classes are undervaluing and misleading education candidates. The teacher candidates are entering student teaching and encountering students who are digital natives. Teacher education candidates are aware of this. In a 2010 survey conducted by the college of education at Walden University more than 1,000 U.S. educators including 783 teachers, 53% of the respondents, *disagreed* with the statement, "My initial teacher preparation program taught me how to effectively incorporate technology in the classroom" (Grunwald, 2010, p.6).

Who is at fault? What is at fault? As the teacher of teachers, should methods faculty be expected to be part of the cutting-edge, pushing and pulling technology into their classes?

In response to professorial beliefs about effective classroom learning as well as the concern about advancement and tenure, a reframing of the teaching and learning model at institutions of higher education needs to be undertaken. The revised frame needs to address the concern of faculty who are challenged when teaching with a new tool, especially one that students use with fluency. To engage in this transformation the professor must become the student, and collaborate to learn to use the tool for teaching and learning purposes.

Success comes with acknowledgement that proficiency in technology utilization develops over time.

Conditions one and two leading to integration success emphasize:

1. Professors are the students and need time and encouragement for attempting technology integration
2. Administrators who visibly support engaging in technology attempts.

Issue Three: Living the Vision, Students' Learning is at Stake

Updated vision and administrator support is part of the re-constructed frame. One element that drives a shift toward integrated technology is a belief that using technology will improve student learning. This vision, embraced by many K-12 districts, needs to include a clear picture of the higher education students, and be advocated for if not led by professors who are supported in efforts and hold the belief that technology tools do stimulate student motivation and enrich learning opportunities.

Higher education students want to use technology in knowledge acquisition and expression of what they have learned. Higher education students recognize the benefits to their learning process as well as application of knowledge. A student reporting on the use of multiple learning strategies in a teacher education class wrote:

I felt that the hands on activities were most helpful in gaining an understanding of the course objectives. For me, actual application of topics helped me gain a full understanding of the material. For example, creating a video was a fun way to explain the instruction methods (Jackson, 2010).

To achieve higher recognition of the benefits of student technology use, both as student and as teacher, faculty technology use needs to be the norm in classrooms. There are several results of non-use in the college of education classroom.

The first result in techno-less classrooms is that students have not had opportunities to use technology as a learning tool. Students may understand how to use the technology to create a technology project, but what they have not achieved is the connection between the design of content and technology supported access to content.

Second, in techno-less classrooms students have not experienced how technology might be integrated into a learning environment. Larson (2009) believes that when we fail to provide a model for preservice teachers to embrace, the students lack understanding of how to integrate technology in their classrooms.

Third, in techno-less classes students are not given the opportunity to learn from successes and failures of individual and collegial experience when experimenting with technology as classroom teachers.

These outcomes are significant for higher education students who are about to take on the role of classroom teacher. Polly, Mims, Shepherd and Inan uncovered the significance of non-practice with technology prior to becoming a teacher, "without experience in methods courses… to witness firsthand how technology can be effectively integrated into K-12 schools, pre-service teachers are left with technology skills, but little idea about how to implement them into their own classrooms" (2010, p. 2). In a related publication (2006) these authors note, "teachers must not only learn to use technology, but also how to integrate technology into their teaching" (P. 19).

It is very likely that a new graduate, first year teacher, will avoid integrating a method they have not been able to test prior to the moment the students and administration evaluate teaching effectiveness. At best new innovations may receive a cursory overview, and if they seem interesting, innovations will be modified or only partially implemented to the faculty member's comfort.

It is likely the novice teacher will use the methods they have been taught with, and with which they feel confident.

Condition three for successful technology integration deals with relevant faculty development opportunities.

3. Encourage faculty members to observe student outcomes in meaningful classroom activities that feature technology use. Allow for faculty construction of how technology use may increase student engagement as well as observing that they are not alone in this learning process.

Issue Four: Getting on Board with Implementation Models, if There's a Trail, Explore it

Effective, fully integrated technology takes time to reach. Persichitte, Caffarella, and Ferguson-Pabst (2003) indicate that a settling period of reaching effective use of new programs requires approximately seven years. Fortunately, reform is not unique to education, and educators will find success by following trailblazers who took risks and invested time, hard work, and capital resources; a trail has been created in the wilderness leading to development of the technology-integrated classroom.

Numerous ways have been described to navigate change in education (Ertmer, 1999; Gladwell, 2002; Hall & Hord, 1987; Kopcha, 2010; Rogers, 2003; Rosenfeld & Martinez-Pons, 2005;

Schlechty, 1993). Hall and Hord (1987) in an influential study of educational change proposed the concerns based adoption model (CBAM). The CBAM framework explained that when experiencing change, participants' questions flow in a sequential manner from self-concerned: How will the change affect me, to task-oriented questions, how is the reform enacted? Following the path of the CBAM model requires that self- and task concerns are resolved before the impact of the reform or innovation can be focused on.

While in the self-concern stage individuals may find new processes and procedures frightening. The CBAM model encourages progress through "stages of concern" beginning with personal readiness, i.e. addressing the self-impact questions when they are asked. Because it takes time to develop trust and understanding, embracing the proposed reform can be long and clumsy, but experiencing the stages is necessary to smooth out the rough edges of the procedures. Evans (1996) states the following: "Organizational change—not just in schools, but in institutions of all kinds—is riddled with paradox. We study it in greater depth, but we practice it with continuing clumsiness" (p. 4). Generous allowance for time is essential as faculty become comfortable with a new way to deliver content.

As in the case in many professions, teachers would like to implement and be-done-with-it. However, sustaining change requires revisiting the outcomes to determine if desired results are prevailing and leading to previously determined results, or if revision to the initial implementation is necessary to achieve strategic results. CBAM incorporates several stages and includes a final reflective stage as teachers understand the learning possibilities and begin to enrich the new reform procedure. Hall and Hord provide for this eventuality by recognizing the need for revisiting. With CBAM full integration comes through continued reflection on the goals of the reform.

A second point is that change requires patience; experience indicates the need to step through phases until proficiency and self-efficacy are re-achieved. This is especially true when using technology in the classroom. While few teachers will be leaders and move the timeline forward, many others may appear to be more resistant. However, are they resistant or well-intentioned cautious "laggards" (Rogers, 2003)? A laggard as used here does not indicate a diminished purpose. Rather the laggard questions results and helps to fine tune and define the process and push for positive results.

Successful integration of a new technology requires a variety of people to make contributions. (Schlechty, 1993) reveals that "trailblazers" are the earliest faculty engagers in new innovations. These innovative types are willing to venture out without support to see what can be done with new innovation. "Trailblazers" are followed by "pioneers", and "early settlers", those who engage after the initial landscape has been marked out.

Other authors have described these phases of willingness to engage in new products or innovations using other terms that have similar themes and descriptions.

Gladwell writes about three influential personas in getting new innovations to the point at which they reach critical mass and become commonly accepted. According to Gladwell "Connectors" possess a gift for bringing the world together. They make friends and acquaintances easily and generally have large social networks in which they roam. Connectors then in the faculty setting could be described as those who uncover an idea and share it with others. While their influence is powerful, they do not possess the necessary detail to spell out exactly how it works. For that purpose Gladwell identifies the "Mavens", the information specialists; they are "people we rely upon to connect us with new information". "Salesmen", the third type are persuaders, with powerful negotiation skills. They tend to have an indefinable trait that goes beyond what they say, which makes others want to agree with them.

What is consistent throughout these and other models is that teachers who hold different perceptions of technology utility in classrooms exist. There are issues to be resolved, and reform may be seen as unsavory as people are required to learn unfamiliar ways of doing familiar processes.

Condition four involves administrator commitment and being prepared to risk.

4. One thing that may be learned from these models is each of these requires ongoing assistance, which may be, and usually is, of undetermined length. When budget items are scrutinized, it is frightening for an administrator to consider a blank check approach for professional development. Because it is difficult to pinpoint a specific result, the effort and associated costs, support for integrated technology may become trapped by "paralysis" analysis.

Issue Five: Generating Faculty Enthusiasm to Engage, Overcoming Wait Long Enough Attitudes

Since integrated technology remains underdeveloped or abandoned in many higher education classrooms, it is reasonable to ask what was missing or ineffective in these models. These models resulted in innovation that made it to the classroom, but once introduced the challenge was complete, and attention was turned toward other challenges.

In reality, the innovation may have been modified significantly to fit the teacher's preference and need, or it may not have been used at all. As Gladwell would explain, the tipping point for the innovation's benefits has not been reached, and the challenge of improving student learning opportunities continues. A successful plan needs to be dynamic, reflective, and persevere as it continues to serve the needs of the classroom community.

When a new innovation reaches the classroom, teachers need a variety of implementation strategies. "Staying power" requires guidance from scaffolding coaches who collaborate with the faculty member right in-their-classroom-environment.

In higher education classrooms, faculty need to be encouraged to accept that they will become the learners of technology skills, while they continue to be the facilitators of content knowledge. It is a new role where they are the student. Many professors question if it is okay for students to know more than they do. And, they wonder if/how students in university educational programs can assist faculty in using educational technology (Sandholtz, Ringstaff, & Dwyer, 1997; Ying-Chen L Milbrath, 2000)? Faculty are correct in recognizing that adding technology to simulate learning is more than just technologizing lessons.

Schaffhausen (2009) reports on the belief of Glenn Bull, the co-director of the Curry School of Education Center for Technology and Teacher Education at the University of Virginia. Bull indicates that integrating technology is complex because it is more than learning technology tools; it includes putting on a mindset that includes a clear understanding and connection between content, pedagogy, and instructional strategies. Bull states that integrated technology requires proficiency in three areas of classroom management.

Technological pedagogical content knowledge (TPACK), says that you have to know three things to use technology well. You first have to know the content. It's going to be hard to teach calculus if you don't know calculus yourself. You also need to know the pedagogy associated with that content--the instructional strategies that will be effective. Finally, you need to know the innovation or technology that you're going to then use (p. 3.)

In order to engage in technology challenges faculty members need evidence of positive use. Senge (1999) identifies an important, activating concept. Openness to revision of teaching philosophy must exist as faculty consider changing from a teacher-centered pedagogical belief to a more progressive student-focused, student-active hands-on approach. This is necessary as technology-using educators see the integration process as a "constructivist endeavor that involves collaboration, reflection, and negotiation within the content of authentic tasks" (Ludwig & Taymans, 2005, p. 2-3). For professors to change pedagogically to a student-centered process, an evolving process is to be expected as it significantly modifies how the professor experiences classroom "control". In the technology environment students actively develop their knowledge. This calls for a "student-centered constructivist educational practice, and active student learning needs to be the norm".

In the case of the technology integrated classroom, faculty would likely be more motivated to attempt integration if they observed positive learning gain. For example, when faculty witnessed students collaboratively constructing knowledge, and gaining knowledge through peer demonstration, connections between improvements in student learning and technology use could be drawn.

Several studies indicate that improved student accomplishment and longer more in-depth results are experienced by students who are engaged in using technology as a learning tool. Barnett (2003) reported the following results for students, who used computers as an enriching content media:

On statewide tests, students who learned from computers showed consistently higher gains. The researchers were able to determine that 11% of the gain was due to the use of technology. Students did better when the computers were integrated into the classroom, and the benefits and advantages of computer use extended through high school, where students took more advanced courses, had better grades, and were more likely to graduate than those who did not use computers (Barnett, 2003, p. 3).

In the Apple's Classrooms of Tomorrow (ACOT) study of computer use and its effects Sandholtz, Ringstaff, and Dwyer (1997) reported that, "Students routinely used higher-order thinking skills far beyond what was expected. .. they demonstrated an enhanced ability to collaborate with peers, and increased initiative" (p. 4). Sandholtz et al. also reported that "the use of technology coupled with teachers having time for reflection led, over time, to substantial changes in teachers' beliefs about teaching and learning".

Jackson (2008) reported that student accomplishments and understanding of assignment components increased when learning opportunities were enriched through computer integration, and this led to engaged teachers as well. Teachers included in this 2008 study indicated that, "computers engaged students longer and with greater attention. With student focus maintained for longer periods of time, deeper engagement and understanding of the learning content was possible" (p. 117).

In higher education classrooms using constructivist learning with technology to enrich student learning resulted in similar outcomes. Using an on-line anonymous survey Jackson (2010) solicited input from twenty-four pre-service teacher candidates on what they perceived as the most relevant learning in a course they had completed, and what they suggested as areas of improvement in future courses. Overwhelmingly the students reported keeping the technology component alive while reducing the lectures. One student commented, "[creating] the video [of a teaching strategy] was one of the most valuable learning resources in my opinion. Not only was it a lot of fun to do but it taught you how to step out of your comfort zone while reiterating educational material". Another student commented:

I would suggest that more technology instruction be incorporated. I really enjoyed being introduced to new classroom technology. .. it is such a large part of life both in and out of the classroom. Plus, student motivation, as demonstrated by our class, is easily increased through the integration of technology.

From the students' comments it was clear that including the technology component revealed an important lesson, that students demonstrated more content learning when technology was used.

Woodbridge (2008) explains that teachers who perceived technology as a tool to help themselves and their students work more productively defined technology integration as "putting the technology to work for you." "The computer is like an employee it has to earn its pay. I put it to work," explained a computer applications college professor. An elementary school computer teacher said, "Learning technology skills and content at the same time encourages fascination and student curiosity. Technology can expand or extend a teacher's time after the teacher gets over the hump of learning it" (p. 6).

To realize the integrated technology advantage, professors need encouragement, additional support, and a method to implement and use technology without an unrecoverable loss of self-efficacy. Faculty also need to internally build a connection between interactive student learning preferences, and how courses are taught. While moving through stages of development, which could be perceived as unattractive, faculty can be coached into making process changes as they remain in a familiar content domain and are assisted in learning a new way to deliver familiar content.

Condition five for successful technology integration involves staying connected with successful tech colleagues and recognition of improved outcomes.

5. Recognizing and rewarding the benefits of collegial coaching that leads to changing the belief from "I cannot" to "it is possible in my classroom with my students."

CONSTRUCTING THE FRAMEWORK, COLLABORATIVE, CONSTRUCTIVE LEARNING CLIMATES FOR FACULTY

To achieve a collaborative classroom framework, a re-imaged culture, one that rewards technology use in the classroom context, is desired. Trust in a collegial community becomes the precept.

Although the entire educational community may desire to improve student learning, they may not be prepared to support the changes necessary to re-culture the university. According to Ludwig and Taymans (2005) changing the culture to integrate technology "cannot occur without staff development" (p. 359). Shanker (1990) writes about new roles in re-cultured schools. "Recultured schools are founded on a different set of premises. ... [they] require teachers to know how to examine their practices" (p. 93). "Staff development is also different regarding the nature, source, and locus of learning". While the half-day professional workshop may provide interesting ideas to consider, it is likely that only the trailblazers will implement these ideas successfully. Shanker states,

The locus for staff development is in the [classroom]. ... it means that the school is structured so that staff development is ongoing, continuous, and an integral part of the school's mission. Faculty time is legitimately spent in the improvement of practice (p. 93).

Community recognition that change is needed is important, but even more vital is an understanding that adjustment to beliefs must occur. Openness to new thought must be real and not just rhetoric. Such change requires a modification of values and skills. The skills are put into play as a result of staff development that shapes the idea that adding technology is utilizing and enriching current knowledge about teaching rather than replacing beliefs. Ludwig and Taymans, in reporting in the results of the Teach Technology Leaders (TTL) PT3 project at George Williams

University, indicate this importance during the development process. "Training must account for higher education faculty's need for developing technology skills, but more important, it must be aimed at how technology can become part of their teaching repertoire" (p. 359). These authors underscore that technology is an instructional tool and not the curriculum for university courses. They observe technologies in the classroom as:

Successful professional development clearly keeps technology in the role of a tool and focuses on how technology integration improves the teaching-learning process with the curriculum driving the technology, rather than technology dictating the curriculum (p. 359).

Understanding the purpose is one key element of developing a technology integrated classroom. Other important elements include faculty having voice in the process, recognizing adequate preparation time and assistance for professional development (Jackson, 2008). It comes down to well-planned and executed professional development. Without that resistance to an unfamiliar approach is high.

A teacher in the Jackson study (2008) states it this way,

The training was horrendous. It was like the school assumed that we all knew how to do it. And, we were just fledglings, we didn't know it. I didn't learn anything. Every teacher that I know had to learn it from another teacher. I didn't know what I was doing, and I didn't know who to ask for help. The people around me are trying to figure it out, and I finally just gave up. I said I can't do this (p. 153).

The keys for implementation include providing well planned, differentiated, initial training, as well as ongoing support, and encouragement. Faculty members need to know they are sustaining effort at "the right things" and require support with appropriate interventions that expedite the learning process. To accomplish this, a quality professional development process must be utilized and reflected upon.

Signs of Progress

Prensky (2006) visions the world in the 21st century as characterized by a life much different in 2100 than today. But, he questions whether the classroom will make the changes necessary to keep up with the world outside the classroom, "When we will get to it? We all know that life will be much different in 2100. Will school? (Prensky, 2006, p.1).

How will progress in school technology be recognized and how will it be implemented successfully? In addition to a more general integrated use with less wasted classroom time for starting up and shutting down computers, students will be utilized as co-teachers and consultants. As self-regulated learners, faculty and students will partner to create authentic learning to achieve in-depth learning goals.

Powerful partnerships can occur when college students are given the opportunity to teach their teachers. By facilitating student mentor-faculty pairs, new relationships are established, new skills are acquired and modeled, coursework is reinforced by practical experience, and student knowledge is tapped and utilized (Lathem, Parker, Morris, Deyo, & Agne, 2002).

Additionally, colleagues who have traveled the integration path will need to be available to encourage others and scaffold as more professors attempt to use technology. Reaching the tipping point, inviting "settlers and stay at homes" into the technology-rich classroom will only be achieved when attention is given to the proficiency curve. The comfort of knowing that a peer has walked in these shoes is the validation that additional professors will be able to master this new task.

Attempts at pushing faculty members who are ill prepared to implement technology could cause faculty to go underground and return to traditional modes of instruction. What else can be done, so that methods faculty will remain engaged in the process?

Keeping talented faculty and encouraging them to engage in integrated technology requires scaffolded help to use technology and positive recognition of faculty for using classroom technologies. Two ways to vision success include, keeping the goal of using technology forefront, and mastering the integration of technology. Frequent reminders that technology use strengthens teaching and learning opportunities and yields improved student learning outcomes is important to hear. And, remembering that the focus of any integration program is not to teach technology applications by themselves. The successful integration plan is determined from a needs assessment approach followed by an implementation plan that demonstrates, guides, applies, and reflects on the learning outcomes that are strengthened through the use of technology.

Faculty will need to be taught and provided guided practice with applications as well as understanding how and when technology can be implemented to improve teaching and classroom learning. This will require skill development, time, persistence and encouragement. Joyce and Showers explain that you cannot expect people to engage in unpracticed learning easily, but that practice, practice, practice is necessary.

The benefits of practice are well known to educators. ... Yet, many trainees try a new skill or practice only once or else never try it at all. In learning a new skill, pushing oneself through the awkward first trials is essential. In initial trials (when performance is awkward and effectiveness appears to decrease rather than increase) driving through or persistence seems to differentiate successful from unsuccessful learners (p. 79-80).

Adding new ideas or tools into a tool belt will cause some discomfort and efficient teaching of content as compared to the traditional, familiar processes may slow down. It takes time to develop new practice. Faculty may assume that because they have seen something demonstrated they will be able to accomplish it readily. Joyce and Showers, say no. "Teachers tend to underestimate the cognitive aspects of implementation. .. they have assumed they only have to see something to use it skillfully and appropriately" (p. 80). In all likelihood, implementation just won't happen on its own. Even basic things like changing an LCD projector output from the Elmo to the computer desktop can challenge the technology novice. Frustration with using the new tool, because it isn't as easy as the old one, leads to uneasiness, and lack of persistence leads to a sounding of the retreat bugle. A more able technology mentor will be required to facilitate this technology skill growth. "Mentoring has the potential to better meet the needs of the teachers learning to use technology. . ." (Kopcha, 2008, p. 177).

WHAT TO KNOW/DO TO ENGAGE PROFESSORS IN INTEGRATED TECHNOLOGY

Mentors or coaches will be needed to survive the period of awkwardness. Staff development is necessary, and specifically the "benefits of peers in the implementation of innovations" (Joyce & Showers, p. 82). According to Joyce and Showers several contributions are revealed through coaching. A significant finding is that coached teachers practiced new strategies more frequently and as a result developed greater skill in using them.

A successful staff development model which includes a technology integration mentor would provide for achievement of class goals, and possess knowledge of available technology that advances opportunities for student learning. The technology mentor must be able to listen to and restate the user's needs and implement a technology answer that enriches the student learning. This is a tall order.

A collaborative approach is a way to accomplish this. Collaboration between an expert faculty member and non-technology faculty members would be ideal, but would require that the technology mentoring faculty member is willing to give up an inordinate amount of time to coach and observe and critique.

In universities and colleges where there is a focus on student learning of educational technology, collaboration could take place in another way.

A learning opportunity exists where college of education faculty and college of educational technology students could combine knowledge and skills. And where these situations do not exist allow the students to become the teachers. This approach would allow for demonstration, modeling, and most important, coaching in the classroom of the faculty member. Joyce and Showers (2002) report on the effectiveness of learning and self-efficacy "a dramatic increase in transfer of training occurs when coaching is added to initial training experience, comprised of explanation, demonstration and practice" (p. 77).

Where education technology is a focus this concept provides practical experience. Educational technology students upon graduation will seek employment in an educational venue, where they will be expected to suggest and demonstrate answers to "what do I do with technology in my classroom".

One vehicle to achieve these cooperative objectives is through engagement in a capstone course in which students would be afforded the opportunity to practice and engage in service learning to the university community. This constructivist learning model provides an authentic test bed for the graduating students as they work in a context where their skills and knowledge are called upon in an applied venue to assist with real questions and situations. These "technology mentors" will be guided as they design and develop a plan to assist a faculty member by the capstone advisor. The advisor assures that the integration plan is authentic for the student, and meaningful to the faculty member through cooperative communication and setting design objectives with each faculty member and the student-mentor.

An example was the faculty mentor program at University of Vermont (UVM) during the year 2001. In this collaborative experience students reinforced their technology expertise by becoming the teacher, and developed a better understanding of the rational and materials chosen for class. The team approach in the example led to the belief that in some cases, "student mentors have been instrumental in advising faculty members in ways they might improve class" (Lathem et al., 2002, p. 3).

Students in the UVM arrangement were involved in authentic leadership and collaborative roles that prepared them to take on the role of technology coordinator and teacher advocate. In the UVM concept they engaged in assisting in the "creation of online course syllabi, development of new online courses, and improvement of courses that were already in place". In addition with mentor guidance faculty "learned new software, new presentation models were explored, and have begun to use technology in their courses".

Franklin, Turner, Kariuki, and Duran (2001) report on students from a College of Education who provided professional development support for elementary school teachers. "The mentoring relationship provided the professional development support needed to promote opportunities for modeling the curriculum integration of technology, redesigning lessons around technology-rich resources, and overcoming barriers to technology use" (p. 10)

Larson (2009) supports the use of students as mentor-coaches termed reverse mentoring. It "is most often used in situations where younger or more experienced technology users provide technology professional development for senior members of an organization who have limited or no experience with technology" (p. 2).

In a study of teachers who participated in the Tennessee EdTech Launch (TnETL) Lowther, Inan, Strahl, and Ross (2008) reported that teachers exited the program with more positive attitudes toward technology integration, and "significantly more confidence to complete computer tasks". TnETL teachers "had higher agreement that they knew how to meaningfully integrate technology into lessons, that their computer skills were adequate to conduct classes that have students using technology, and that integration of technology positively impacted student learning" (p. 23).

This program described how "full-time, on-site technology coaches are used to prepare teachers to create lessons that engaged students in critical thinking and use of computers as tools in order to increase learning". And, survey results "showed that teachers had significantly higher confidence to integrate technology and in using technology for learning".

The experiences cited here demonstrate that successful technology integration for higher education faculty must include a variety of supports and anticipatory planning. These supports include but are not limited to

1. Time and allowance for new learning must be included.
2. In-the-classroom-support provided by mentors, students, or colleagues who understand the goals for course learning yet are techno-savvy is required.
3. Encouragement and rewards for attempting to integrate classroom technology must be modeled by administrators who are standing in the gap as professors learn a new instructional strategy.
4. Recognition that improved student outcomes are achievable, and worthy of the required effort.
5. And acknowledgment that in some cases temporarily reduced professorial efficacy should be expected and prepared for.

CONCLUSION

Successful integration and use of technology will be increased in higher education classrooms when planned interventions for anticipated issues have been prepared, and expert assistance to negotiate unplanned issues is present. The recognition of these needs and commencement of these supports will signal that technology is valued as a teaching tool, and faculty who engage in use of these methods are respected and rewarded for the attempt. These supports are more than "nice to do" as barriers are, and predictably will be present as innovations are placed at the classroom threshold.

Continued expert support will be needed. Half-day workshops followed-up with a "how are you doing call" will not be enough to move the innovation into daily practice. Practice and time needs to be a part of the learning. Faculty will abandon technology quickly if they become discouraged when introducing it without support in the presence of their students. A requirement for an investment in ongoing and just-in-time support is present in order to sustain use through the challenging times, especially as "teaching" is evaluated based on technology use. Continued professional learning that is well-organized and allows for conversation about seamless integration of technology needs to be included, explored, and reflected on. Faculty need to experience positive effects with their students as a result of technology integration. An underlying belief that technology enriches the lesson content, and is not a replacement for rich content must be a part of the mentoring process.

Finally, while faculty need to know about and understand how to use technology, they need to know they are viewed, even rewarded for engaging in technology use. "Risk-taking" must be viewed as necessary. Time for, and growth in, pedagogical process is to be expected as faculty truly learn how to effectively teach with new tools.

These goals are lofty and take time, but they are achievable when a vision, culture, and supportive mentoring/coaching are in place.

REFERENCES

Barnett, H. (2003). *Investing n technology: The payoff in student learning. ED479843. ERIC Digest.* Syracuse, NY: ERIC Clearinghouse on Information and Technology.

Baule, S. (2007). The components of successful technologies. *Teacher Librarian, 34*(5), 16.

Edgerton, R. (1991-1992). On the road with Russell Edgerton: AAHE's on-going salon on teaching. *The National Teaching and Learning Forum, 1*, 1–6.

Eisner, E. (1992). Educational reform and the ecology of schooling. *Teachers College Record, 93*(4). Teachers College. Columbia University.

Ertmer, P.A. (1999). Addressing first- and second-order barriers to change: Strategies for technology integration. *Educational Technology, Research and Development, 47*(4), 47. (Document ID: 47696907).

Evans, R. (1996). *The human side of school change: Reform, resistance, and the real-life problems of innovations.* San Francisco, CA: Jossey-Bass.

Franklin, T., Turner, S., Kariuki, M., & Duran, M. (2001). Mentoring overcomes barriers to technology integration. *Journal of Computing in Teacher Education, 18*(1), 26–31.

Friel, T., Britten, J., Compton, B., Peak, A., Schoch, K., & VanTyle, W. (2009). Using pedagogical dialogue as a vehicle to encourage faculty technology use. *Computers & Education, 53*(2), 300–307. doi:10.1016/j.compedu.2009.02.002

Fullan, M. (2001). *Leading in a culture of change.* San Francisco, CA: Jossey-Bass.

Gladwell, M. (2002). *The tipping point: How little things can make big difference*. New York, NY: Time Warner Book Group.

Grunwald Associates LLC. (2010). *Educators, technology and 21st century skills: Dispelling five myths*. Retrieved from www.WaldenU.edu/fivemyths 08-10-2010

Hall, G., & Hord, S. (1987). *Change in schools: facilitating the process*. Albany, NY: State University of New York press.

Hall, G., & Hord, S. (2006). *Implementing change: Patterns, principles, and potholes*. Boston, MA: Allyn & Bacon.

Jackson, T. (2008). *Integrated computer technology in a Catholic elementary school: A study in the dynamics of change*. Ed.D. dissertation, Northern Illinois University, United States -- Illinois. Dissertations & Theses: The Humanities and Social Sciences Collection. (Publication No. AAT 3335047).

Jackson, T. (2010). *Unpublished MATC student feedback survey*. Aurora University EDU5205. Aurora, Il. Retrieved May 26, 2010, from http://www.tinyurl.com/studentthoughts

Joyce, B., & Showers, B. (2002). *Student achievement through staff development*. Alexandria, VA: ASCD.

Kariuki, M., Franklin, T., & Duran, M. (2001). A technology partnership: Lessons learned by mentors. *Journal of Technology and Teacher Education, 9*(3), 407–417.

Kopcha, T. (2008). *A systems-based approach to technology integration using mentoring and communities of practice*. Association for Educational Communications and Technology.

Larson, L. (2009). A descriptive study of mentoring and technology integration among teacher education faculty. *International Journal of Evidence Based Coaching and Mentoring, 7*(1).

Lathem, S., Parker, H., Morris, J., Deyo, A., & Agne, R. (2002). *Student as faculty mentors: Reversing the role of teacher and learner*. Retrieved from http://www.uvm.edu/pt3/exhibits/pdf/mentors.pdf

Lowther, D., & Inan, F., Strahl, & Ross, S. (2008). Does technology integration "work" when key barriers are removed? *Educational Media International, 45*(3), 195–213. doi:10.1080/09523980802284317

Ludwig, M., & Taymans, J. (2005). Teaming: Constructing high-quality faculty development in a PT3 project. *Journal of Technology and Teacher Education, 13*(3), 357–372.

Massy, W. F., & Wilger, A. K. (1998). Technology's contribution to higher education productivity. *New Directions for Higher Education, 103*, 49–59. doi:10.1002/he.10304

Mims, C., Polly, D., Shepherd, C. E., & Inan, F. (2006). Examining PT3 projects designed to improve preservice education. *TechTrends, 50*(3). doi:10.1007/s11528-006-7599-5

Persichiitte, K., Caffarella, E., & Fergusion-Pabst, D. (2003). A continuing journey toward technology infusion within teacher preparation. *TechTrends, 4*(3).

Polly, D., Mims, C., Shepherd, C. E., & Inai, F. (2010). Evidence of impact: Transforming teacher education with preparing tomorrow's teachers to teach with technology (PT3) grants. *Teaching and Teacher Education, 26*, 863–870. doi:10.1016/j.tate.2009.10.024

Prensky, M. (2001). Digital natives, digital immigrants. *On the Horizon, 9*(5). Retrieved on January 14, 2011, from http://www.marcprensky.com/writing/Prensky%20-%20Digital%20Natives,%20Digital%20Immigrants%20-%20Part1.pdf

Prensky, M. (2006). *Shaping teach for the classroom*. Retrieved January 14, 2011, from http://www.edutopia.org/adopt-and-adapt-shaping-tech-for-classroom

Rogers, E. M. (2003). *Diffusion of innovations.* New York, NY: Simon & Schuster, Inc.

Rosenfeld, B., & Martinez-Pons, M. (2005). Promoting classroom technology use. *Quarterly Review of Distance Education, 6*(2), 145–153.

Sandholtz, J., Ringstaff, C., & Dwyer, C. D. (1997). *Teaching with technology: Creating student-centered classrooms.* New York, NY: Teachers College Press.

Schaffhauser, D. (2009). Which came first--The technology or the pedagogy? *T.H.E. Journal, 36*(8), 27–32.

Schlechty, P. C. (1993). On the frontier of school reform with trailblazers, pioneers, and settlers. *Journal of Staff Development,* (Fall): 1993.

Senge, P. (1999). *The dance of change: The challenges of sustaining momentum in learning organizations.* New York, NY: Doubleday.

Shanker, A. (1990). Staff development and the restructured school. In Joyce, B. (Ed.), *Changing school culture through staff development* (pp. 91–103). Alexandria, VA: ASCD.

Trubowitz, S. (2005). Creating a culture for learning. *Educational Horizons, 83*(3), 171–176.

Woodbridge, J. (2008). Technology integration as a transforming teaching strategy. *Tech Learning.* Retrieved on May 24, 2010, from www.techlearning.com/article/2022

Ying-Chen, L., & Kinzie, M. B. (2000). Computer technology training for prospective teachers: Computer attitudes and perceived self-efficacy. *Journal of Technology and Teacher Education (JTATE), 8*(4). Charlottesville, VA: Association for the Advancement of Computing in Education (AACE). ISSN 1059-7069.

KEY TERMS AND DEFINITIONS:

Capstone Project: A course requirement that provides educational technology students authentic situations for analysis and/or problem solving. The capstone requires planning, generating solutions, and application of a strategy to resolve the problem(s).

Change: Circumstances that require a modified and sometimes new set of beliefs or objectives that facilitate the achievement of a vision.

Classroom-Integration: The frequent, daily, use of computer technology in a classroom in an ongoing fashion to enrich the learning opportunities and expression of student knowledge.

Coaching: Enrichment of a previously developed skill through encouragement, modeling, and transfer of existing knowledge. Social reconstruction of knowledge is in use as faculty members adapt existing beliefs as a result of coaching and modeling.

Professional Development: A preventative, proactive development model that is based on known and anticipated issues. Professional technology development would include several steps including, 1) consultation on how technology might be used to strengthen and enrich student opportunities, 2) Frequent demonstration and supportive modeling of the technology skill or use of software or hardware, 3) Practice with a mentor-coach present prior to classroom use, followed by in-classroom use with a mentor-coach available, 4) follow-up learning to assess classroom use and challenge the proficient user with additional technology integration.

Mentoring: When knowledge of a skill or how to apply a skill in a domain does not exist mentoring is used. Mentoring involves the teaching processes of analysis, synthesis, and implementation of an innovation, idea, concept, or tool.

Status Quo Culture: The embedded beliefs and supporting environment that frame the expectations, and accepted practices of an organization.

Chapter 34
Lessons Learned From the Implementation of a Technology–Focused Professional Learning Community

D. Bruce Taylor
University of North Carolina at Charlotte, USA

Richard Hartshorne
University of Central Florida, USA

Sam Eneman
University of North Carolina at Charlotte, USA

Patti Wilkins
University of North Carolina at Charlotte, USA

Drew Polly
University of North Carolina at Charlotte, USA

ABSTRACT

In this chapter, "lessons learned" and best practices that have resulted from the implementation of technology-focused professional learning community in a College of Education, as well as recommendations for future implementations are addressed. The Technology & Teaching Professional Learning Community, which was created by faculty in the College of Education at UNC Charlotte, provided professional development to faculty engaged in teaching hybrid and online courses. This was one of several professional development efforts at UNC Charlotte, but one, the authors suggest, that created a safe and effective space for scaffolding instructors less familiar with online learning technologies and tools.

DOI: 10.4018/978-1-4666-0014-0.ch034

INTRODUCTION

The emergence of new technologies, such as e-mail, learning management systems, and more recently Web 2.0 applications, into various aspects of everyday life has considerably impacted the design and delivery of instruction at the university-level. Issues such as the methods in which teaching and learning materials and content are accessed, the methods of delivery of instruction, and the role of the instructor and student in the classroom, have changed significantly in recent years (Barnett, Keating, Harwook, & Saam, 2004). For example, many Web 2.0 applications (blogs, wikis, etc.) facilitate students becoming more active in the learning environment; and accessing, creating, and sharing new information from sources beyond those in traditional classrooms (Maloney, 2007). These tools also provide numerous additional pedagogical benefits in that they support scaffolding and active learner participation; provide opportunities for student publication, feedback, and reflection, and the potential for development of a community of learners (Ferdig, 2007).

While students entering higher education are typically prepared to utilize these tools in both social and educational contexts (Oblinger & Oblinger, 2005; Prensky, 2001), university faculty have been slow to integrate these emerging technologies into their classroom instruction (Ajjan & Hartshorne, 2008; Maloney, 2007). Research has also shown that, while faculty feel that these tools have significant pedagogical value, they typically have limited knowledge of how to use these tools in instructional contexts (Ajjan & Hartshorne, 2008). Thus, if the pedagogical value of these emerging technologies is to be realized, it is critical to provide professional development opportunities for faculty that facilitate increasing exposure and comfort-level with these tools, as well as addresses issues related to utilizing these tools in instructional settings.

One method of providing such professional development opportunities is through a technology-based professional learning community (PLC). In this chapter, the authors will report the results of a year-long faculty-initiated technology-based PLC in the College of Education at the University of North Carolina at Charlotte. This discussion will include an overview of the impetus, origins, and focus of the PLC, vignettes from two varied participants in the PLC, as well as "lessons learned," best practices, and recommendations for Colleges of Education and teacher education programs considering PLCs as an alternative to traditional professional development opportunities for faculty.

REVIEW OF THE LITERATURE

Pedagogical Affordances of Emerging Technologies

While many tools that are utilized in higher education classrooms were not developed specifically for educational purposes, many of them possess many characteristics that support their use in instructional settings (Ferdig, 2007). First, technologies such as learning management systems, social software, and various Web 2.0 tools can support active and social learning environments (Boulos & Wheelert, 2007; Franklin & Van Harmelen, 2007; Sturm, M., Kennel, T., McBride, M., & Kelly, M., 2008). These environments are more student-driven and provide arenas for social and collaborative efforts, characteristics espoused by constructivists as critical to effective teaching and learning environments (Bruner, 1966; Ferdig, 2007; Vygotsky, 1978). Secondly, learning management systems and other emerging technologies provide opportunities for both local and global student publication. Past studies have cited increased motivation, more positive attitudes toward the content area, and increased student achievement among the numerous benefits of the publication of student work (Dixon & Black, 1996; Riley & Roberts, 2000; Schofield and Davidson,

2002). Associated pedagogical benefits promotion of self reflection, providing analysis of content from multiple perspectives, and providing a clear and more purposeful visualization of one's work (Simões & e Gouveia, 2008; Maloney, 2007). Third, emerging technologies provide authentic, social environments which allow students to receive feedback from their instructors as well as other students and external social networks. Also, by providing these social connections and opportunities for feedback, these emerging technologies provide opportunities to scaffold student (Brown & Ferrara, 1985; Vygotsky, 1978). This is done by not only providing increased and varied opportunities for student-teacher, student-student, and student-content interactions, but they also providing for increased interactions with other pedagogical agents.

Professional Learning Communities

Technology also has great potential to support the establishment of professional learning communities (PLCs) through the use of Web 2.0 collaborative technologies, such as wikis and Google Documents (Polly & Hannafin, 2010). Previous studies have found that educators have benefited from meeting to share technology-rich resources (Ravitz & Hoadley, 2005), collaboratively plan instruction (Strahan, 2003; Snow-Gerono, 2005), and examine artifacts of teaching, such as videotaped lessons and student work (So et al., 2009; van Es & Sherin, 2008).

Professional learning communities have been empirically linked to the successful enactment of effective instructional practices and gains on student learning outcomes (Marzano, 2003; Vescio, Ross, & Adams, 2006). Research on PLC's have found benefits in collaborations between university faculty and classroom teachers (Snow-Gerono, 2005), district leaders and classroom teachers (Strahan, 2003) and teacher-leaders and their colleagues (Mims, Polly, Shepherd, & Inan, 2006; Hord, 2004). In each of these cases, success

has hinged on educators being willing to take the initiative to establish and sustain partnerships (DuFour & Eaker, 1998; Schlager, Farooq, Fusco, Schank, & Dwyer, 2009).

Establishing PLCs in Teacher Education Programs

The U.S. Department of Education Preparing Tomorrow's Teachers to Teach with Technology (PT3) grants provided ample opportunities for Schools, Colleges, and Departments of Education (SCDEs) to establish collaborations and PLCs in Teacher Education programs (U.S. Department of Education, 2002). These PLCs included partnerships between College of Education faculty, Education and Arts and Science faculty, Education faculty and P-12 teachers and administrators, and Education faculty and Community College faculty (Mims, Polly, Shepherd, & Inan, 2006). Each of these funded collaborations used grant resources to purchase technological resources, provide professional development to multiple groups, and give faculty incentives to collaborate about how to infuse technology into their courses and programs (Duffield & Moore, 2006).

At one university, Education faculty, Arts & Science faculty and P-12 teachers collaborated to redesign K-12 and university curricula (Graham, Culatta, Pratt, & West, 2004; Waddoups, Wentworth, & Earle, 2004). The multi-year project began when participants explored various technologies that they were curious about. Eventually, project activities evolved into designing technology-rich activities which could be used in both P-12 classes and university courses. In another case, Education and Arts and Science faculty were supported through a series of workshops and individual mentoring (Howland & Wedman, 2004; Strudler, Archambault, Bendixen, Anderson, & Weiss, 2003). Faculty at one university reported that the opportunities to collaborate and share resources and experiences with one another was the major factor in their integration of technology into their courses (Strudler et al., 2003).

THE TECHNOLOGY AND TEACHING PROFESSIONAL LEARNING COMMUNITY

Impetus

The move toward online education at our institution, the University of North Carolina at Charlotte, began about a decade ago. The emergence of online courses proceeded slowly at first with two engineering baccalaureate programs in Fall 2000. Each program offered six courses during the academic year. After the university adopted WebCT as the campus learning management system (LMS) in Fall 2001, more baccalaureate completion programs, master degrees, graduate certificates, and teacher licensure programs were introduced—primarily in the College of Health and Human Services and the College of Education. Some were 100% asynchronous; some included a synchronous component delivered via Web conferencing software such as Centra and more recently Wimba. In Fall 2010, there were 21 online programs with almost 90 courses offered through the Distance Education Office and dozens of other online courses offered by various departments.

In April 2009, the authors of this chapter came together with others at our university to share our thoughts and ideas regarding the of technology in teaching and learning. Each of us, we learned, was at a different place regarding the use of technology in our teaching. Some had been teaching online courses for several years while others were just beginning that process. During this time, the university was piloting a transition from using the Blackboard Vista [to distinguish from the "classic" Blackboard system] online learning environment to Moodle, a move that formally took place in the Fall 2009. This transition elevated both enthusiasm for the new online learning environment (Moodle)

but also anxiety regarding the transition and expected learning curve for instructors. From this emerged a Technology & Teaching Professional Learning Community to address the challenges of meaningfully integrating technology into our online, face-to-face, and hybrid courses.

Origins

One of the authors, a faculty member in the College of Education, had taken some online courses from the SLOAN Consortium as well as workshops offered by our university's Center for Teaching & Learning (CTL), which assists faculty in promoting excellence in face-to-face and online learning environments. As the email below suggests it became apparent to him that others in college were on a similar learning curve:

I've taken some workshops offered by the Center for Teaching & Learning and through the SLOAN Consortium to help me improve the online course I teach and to make better use of technology in my face-to-face courses. It seems each time I go up the hill to one of these one or two other College of Education faculty or staff are there, too. This has me wondering if anyone would be interested in forming a professional learning community or simply a study group to discuss the tools and pedagogies around online and blended teaching. I was thinking we could meet once a month and perhaps set up a blog to discuss between meetings. This would be informal. Let me know if you are interested.

Response to the email was significant. Within 48 hours, 24 faculty and teaching staff had responded expressing interest, and soon thereafter, over 30 faculty and teaching staff asked to be included in this initiative.

At the first meeting in early May 2009, 17 faculty and staff met face-to-face to brainstorm ideas for how the group might serve the needs of course instructors. Following brief introductions, the meeting focused on three goals: 1) establishing a purpose for the group, 2) possible outcomes for the group, and 3) determining next steps. A Google document was set up during the meeting as an initial tool for collaboration and sharing, with several attendees contributing notes of the discussion to the document.

The Center for Teaching and Learning and its Role

One campus organization that was separate from the College of Education but which played a pivotal role in the successful implementation of the Technology & Teaching PLC was the University's Center for Teaching and Learning (CTL). The CTL assists the UNC Charlotte faculty by promoting teaching and learning excellence, supporting the integration of learning technologies, and encouraging scholarly teaching. CTL offers a variety of instructional technology and pedagogical workshops, individual consultations, departmental workshops and programs, Web resources, faculty brown bag sessions and roundtables, Summer Institutes and on-going faculty support of all instructional technologies supported by the University.

The Center led the effort to adopt Moodle as the new learning management system and continues to assist faculty in the transition from Blackboard Vista with workshops, an online "Teaching with Moodle" course and more just-in-time content. It also has partnered with Academic Affairs to grow support of large courses on campus. CTL has explored opportunities for maximizing Moodle and other supported tools for large course management, sponsored Institutes on large courses and coordinated a grant program for large course redevelopment.

Clickers (remote response systems) are a tool that can play an important role in teaching large courses. CTL has offered workshops and support for faculty who want to incorporate clickers in their teaching and learning. As clicker adoption grew, CTL organized a clicker professional learning community. This PLC met for two semesters, Spring and Fall 2008. Attendance was steady during the first semester but waned during the second primarily due to scheduling difficulties and the group was discontinued. Thus, their prior experience in PLC's was useful.

So, when the word went out about a College of Education professional learning community centered around instructional technologies, CTL instructional team members attended from the beginning. They did not take the lead but brought their expertise and interest in the pedgagocial uses of technology to the table as willing participants. CTL was committed to sharing best practices for putting good pedagogy before the technology and providing whatever support the PLC needed. CTL also supported the PLC by hosting the meetings through the University's web conferencing system. This made it possible for people to participate remotely if they could not come to campus. The sessions were recorded and made available for playback via the PLC wiki that was created.

Focus of the PLC

What emerged from the first meeting was a plan to establish a Technology & Teaching Professional Learning Community (PLC) that would meet for an hour to an hour and a half once a month. Each meeting would focus on a particular topic of interest to the group and would be facilitated by a member of the group with experience using the technology or pedagogy under discussion. The following were topics or areas of interest discussed in this first meeting, and used to guide subsequent meetings:

- creating active engaging activities for synchronous and asynchronous online learning environments (i.e. Blackboard Vista and Moodle—asynchronous; Centra and Wimba--synchronous),

- using discussion boards available in University-supported learning management systems and how those differ from external resources (blogs, wikis, etc.), as well as specific instructional activities supported more effectively through each of the various modes,
- alternative public and free instructional technologies and methods that could be included in the instructional approaches of PLC participants,
- examples of blogs, wikis, shared document spaces (Google docs and Buzzword) and other public sites,
- a more in-depth look at some of the less well known tools in Blackboard Vista (the University-supported learning management system at the time),
- an overview of Moodle (the newly adopted learning management system at the time) to help faculty transitioning from Blackboard Vista,
- faculty-driven discussion of "best practices" and "lessons learned" in online teaching and hybrid courses.

It was also agreed that a wiki would be established to aid with meeting schedules and logistics, but also as a place to share instructional uses of technology and examples of online and Web 2.0-based teaching ideas. The wiki (see Figure 1) was created using PBWorks (http://pbworks. com) and is located at: http://eteachatuncc.pb-works.com/. The wiki was quickly established, with a small group of PLC participants making early contributions, such as setting up a meeting schedule, providing "how-to" information on using various Web 2.0 tools, and linking to numerous external sites deemed useful to teaching. Figure 2 provides a screen shot of the files and folders used to organize the wiki.

Certain "hot topics" were named during the first meeting and noted in the PLC's Google Document. These included methods of engaging students and effective emerging and traditional technologies in online, hybrid, and face-to-face courses. Another major issue was how to "level the playing field" between those who were more experienced or less experienced with the use of both traditional and emerging technologies in teaching and learning. From this discussion, it was determined that a major focus of the Technology & Teaching PLC would be to provide participants with exposure to a series of emerging technologies, as well as supporting resources and personnel to assist with implementing the various technologies into their courses in meaningful and effective ways. The following online tools were identified as key technologies for the PLC to discuss in subsequent meetings: Moodle (the newly adopted learning management system), wikis, blogs, online shared document spaces, and social networks, social bookmarks, and other miscellaneous emerging technologies.

After the initial PLC meeting, future meetings began focusing on several of the previously mentioned topics. The next two PLC meetings focused on wikis and their use by instructors and students in a variety of courses (both content and delivery method). Faculty using wikis shared examples of student activities using wikis, such as the development of collaborative class portfolios. An area of distinction in the wiki discussion was the use of internal (integrated with University learning management systems) and external (non-University supported) wikis, and subsequent uses, benefits, and drawbacks of each. Some of these examples were posted in the PLC wiki. In the third meeting, the primary theme was "collaborative online document sites," with Google Documents and Adobe Buzzword as the primary tools discussed. A secondary tool addressed in the third meeting was the screen capture software, Jing (http://www.jingproject.com). Again, the focus of these discussions was to provide participants with exposure to these tools, as well as real-world examples of pedagogical implementations, and

Figure 1. Screen shot of the technology & teaching PLC Wiki

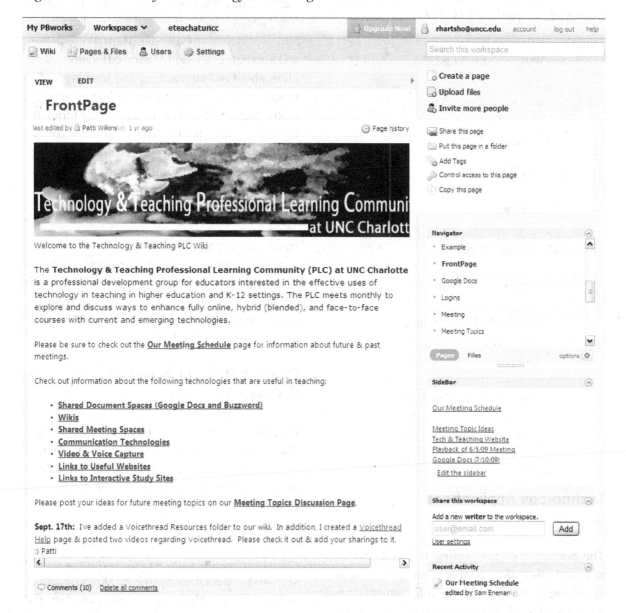

discussions of both real and perceived benefits and drawbacks of each.

The next two meetings, while still addressing the core focus of the PLC, took a bit of a shift in focus, but addressed an important technology-related issue that was facing the College of Education. One member of the PLC, who was involved in the College of Education's peer evaluation of teaching, asked the participants to provide input on an evaluation tool for online courses. Along with this topic, VoiceThread (http://voicethread.com), an online multimedia collaboration tool, was explored. It was clear at this point, that the PLC was quickly becoming a resource for tools, support personnel, and methods regarding the use of new University-supported instructional technologies, as well as tools that had been implemented in courses of PLC participants.

Figure 2. Organization of pages and files in the technology & teaching PLC Wiki

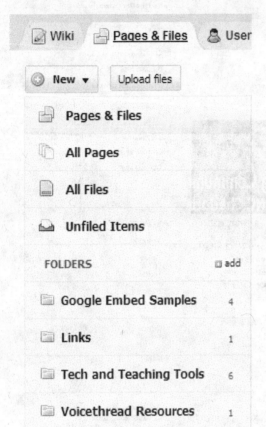

Technology Applications Discussed Via the Wiki

The primary tool for hosting resources, tools, and examples of uses of various instructional technologies of interest to the PLC members was the Technology & Teaching wiki developed as a support-site for the group. Numerous members of this group were given access to edit the wiki and provided materials related to a variety of teaching and learning tools. These included communication technologies such as Twitter, Facebook, blogs, and chatrooms; interactive sites such as Studiyo, Study Shack, and Brain Flips; shared domain spaces such as Google Apps and Buzzword; shared meeting spaces such as Skype, Illuminate, and Adobe Connect; video and voice capture tools

such as Audacity, Jing, Zamzar, VoiceThread and YouTube; various wikis, and Embedded Google Samples including Calendar, Maps, Presentation, and Survey tools. The PLC allowed faculty to share ideas about online teaching and learning and to introduce new pedagogic tools. As the vignettes below suggest, it also provided a useful forum for instructors who held differing attitudes toward online education and varying levels of experience integrating technology into teaching and learning.

Vignettes

Bruce and Brian, faculty members in the College of Education, were active members in the Technology & Teaching PLC. They share their thoughts about their journeys moving from the more traditional world of face-to-face teaching to that of the online classroom.

Bruce: A Recent Convert to Online Teaching

I began teaching online courses during the Summer 2007 when I was asked to teach an online section of our content-area literacy course, a staple of my face-to-face teaching since arriving at UNC Charlotte in 2004. With two summers of online teaching under my belt, I considered myself to be slightly more than a recent convert to online teaching. However, my experiences with these online sections were not wholly positive. I found teaching online to be overwhelming. Although familiar with the Internet, many Web 2.0 technologies, and a basic level of web design, I had not taught online courses before and found my early experiences frustrating. In short, in my early attempts at online teaching I tried to transfer what I knew from my face-to-face courses into the online environment. Everything I did was asynchronous. I posted a syllabus, assignments, and handouts. I emailed students and created threaded discussions. At some level the course worked, but I found myself buried in responses to numerous student emails, responses to threaded discussions, and evaluations of student projects, most of which were submitted as Word documents.

After two summers of feeling buried by the details of this course, I discussed my experiences about teaching online courses with a colleague, who suggested that I take some workshops offered by our Center for Teaching and Learning (CTL). I signed up for several one to two-hour workshops and a couple of online offerings by the SLOAN Consortium. This professional development was transformational. I learned about online synchronous tools such as Centra and (later) Wimba. I heard from other instructors about using collaborative tools such as Google Documents, Adobe Acrobat's Buzzword, and free wiki sites (PBWorks, for example).

What changed? I created online meetings that allowed me to meet with students to review assignments, teach minilessons, and answer questions. These greatly decreased emails from students with questions about assignments and course details. Online collaboration tools such as PBWorks, Buzzword, and Google Documents provided an avenue for students in online sections to collaborate in ways students in my face-to-face sections did. Screen capture programs such as Jing allowed me to provide more meaningful feedback and for students to provide the class with overviews of assignments or projects. In short, I moved from being a skeptic of online courses through a period of feeling overwhelmed by them to a point at which I viewed (and still view) online teaching as an effective and meaningful tool for teaching and learning.

Brian: A Skeptical Optimist of Online Teaching

I have a confession. When a colleague first suggested I consider creating an online course for a K-12 writing class, I hesitated. Okay. Resisted would be a more accurate word. It's not that I'm a technophobe. In fact, I'm quite comfortable with computers and I happily try new Web tools whenever possible. I just had a pedagogical problem with the notion.

I take a Vygotskian stance to learning; that is, I believe learning is a social act. And, in many ways, I believe computers take us away from the important face-to-face interactions that are reflective of the ones we have with our students in schools. It's like sending an email instead of engaging in a face-to-face conversation. The face-to-face interaction gives me contextual clues I don't get from email. A voice lets me hear sarcasm. Crossed arms allow me to see defensiveness. I have misinterpreted so many emails from others because the computer divorces me from these important body language signals.

I have another confession. Despite my worries about online courses, I taught one last summer. And, despite my greatest fears, the students offered feedback about the course that was incredibly positive. They loved the freedom it afforded. They enjoyed the ability to pause videos, take notes, and interact with peers through various online Moodle features. Perhaps the most encouraging thing I witnessed was the written dialogue that occurred during each class period. Students offered comments, questions, and connections to the course topic, and then responded to the comments, questions, and connections of their peers. The written dialogue was fascinating to read. It became obvious to me that students were engaged in the content, and the digital space gave them to freedom to voice their opinions in a format that didn't seem as intimidating when it is face-to-face.

I'm still not convinced an entirely online teacher education program benefits our students who will teach their students in entirely face-to-face contexts. I'm not sure they'll understand the power of face-to-face writing groups when they don't experience these online. I'm not convinced students will understand the nuances of writing conferences when they don't have the experience of sitting side-by-side with me, engaged in conversation. I'm still not sure they'll ever know how powerful a sharing session can be when the writer can't see the tears in the eyes of peers as they read their stories aloud to the class. But, as a teacher, and someone who understands the necessity of preparing students for the digital world, I'm going to try to find ways of replicating these experiences using digital technologies. And, I'll make one last confession that I'm not afraid to ask for advice or guidance to make this possible.

As Brian's final comment suggests, the Technology & Teaching PLC was a place both of these faculty members to share ideas, ask questions, and seek help in enhancing teaching and learning in the online environment. The vignettes also show that the PLC was not the only form of professional development that helped these faculty members with their efforts to improve their online courses; however, it was a form of professional development that created a discursive "space" to talk through their concerns about online teaching and learning.

REVISITING THE PLC EXPERIENCE: LESSONS LEARNED, BEST PRACTICES, AND RECOMMENDATIONS

The first year of the Technology & Teaching PLC brought together over 30 instructional faculty and staff from diverse departments within the College of Education and the Center for Teaching and Learning at UNC Charlotte with a united focus of exploring effective and efficient implementations of emerging technologies in face-to-face, hybrid, and online courses, in an effort to improve instructional practices, prepare

more technologically savvy future teachers, and to generally increase student achievement in teacher education programs, as well as other programs in the College of Education. Throughout the initial implementation of the Technology & Teaching PLC, numerous unanticipated challenges and issues were encountered. However, with such challenges come "lessons learned." In this section, we will address the lessons learned from the perspective of the authors of this chapter, PLC leaders, and major contributors to the PLC sessions. In addition to the "lessons learned," authors will share "best practices" that emerged from the implementation of the PLC, as well as recommendations for others considering the deployment of a technology-focused PLC.

Throughout the implementation of the PLC, a few unanticipated challenges and issues emerged. First, it seemed that a small group of individuals performed the majority of work associated with initial development and organization, as well as ongoing maintenance and continued implementation of the program. Thus, it is important to establish clear, participatory roles from all members in the PLC, as well as distributed workloads. This is important for a number of reasons. It helps to ensure faculty buy-in, which is critical to the ongoing success of the PLC, and also helps to ensure that the PLC serves the needs and motivations of all of the members, rather than just a select few. We see this flexibility as an important aspect of the PLC as a form of professional development that distinguishes it from other forms such as workshops or online courses such as those offered by the SLOAN Consortium.

As the PLC reached the end of its first year of implementation, participation from fringe members tended to wane and become more inconsistent. There were a number of potential reasons for this. First, a number of goals, while related to technology and teaching, were somewhat external to the original focus of the PLC. An example of this is the work the PLC did in helping revise the College of Education's online peer evaluation document. This was important work and the PLC was arguably well-suited to helping with this effort. However, it was outside the focus of the PLC. Second, other than the PLC wiki, there were no mechanisms for encouraging communication related to PLC-focus topics outside of the PLC meetings. Thus, the PLC tended to be more of a short-term, localized infusion of professional development. In examining these shortfalls, a number of recommendations have emerged. First, it is important to limit external goals of a PLC. While external goals can be a small component of a PLC, it is important to remain relatively focused on a centralized theme. In our experience, the inclusion of external goals resulted in detachment from fringe members. Next, it is critical to provide multiple mechanisms for facilitating communication among PLC members outside of the scheduled meetings. This could include sub-groups within the PLC, a social networking presence, or others. Also, due to limited technological proficiency of some of the PLC members, it might be useful to provide instruction on how to participate through various technological methods provided (wiki, etc.). Implementing these procedures would be useful in meeting one of the core goals of PLCs in that they foster continued active participation, are extended in duration, and are more global infusions of professional development.

While a number of challenges emerged, there were also a number of successes and "best practices" that were evident. First, the Technology & Teaching PLC served as an excellent repository of "help" resources for a variety of instructional technologies. While, as previously noted, contributors to the wiki were limited; the vast majority of PLC participants accessed the wiki. Whether for ideas related to using new technologies in their courses or "help" resources on specifics of how to use various tools, numerous participants cited increased implementation of emerging technologies into their courses as well as an increased awareness of various technological tools for teaching. The wiki also became a resource to faculty and

educators outside of the PLC. One reason for this was the organization of the wiki. PLC participants regularly commented on the usability and ease of finding information in the wiki. A final "best practice" was the use of multiple modes for conducting meetings. After the first meeting, which was conducted face-to-face, subsequent meetings allowed participants to participate remotely using either Centra or Wimba, the University-supported multimedia conferencing tool. In each meeting, a number of PLC members participated remotely for a variety of reasons. So, this flexibility in the mode of the delivery of the meeting was beneficial and allowed participants that were unable to come to campus (for one reason or another) the ability to actively participate in the PLC meetings. It also introduced several faculty to the multimedia conferencing tools. A final "best practice" or recommendation regarding the implementation of a technology-focused PLC is to have reasonable expectations upon inception. For a variety of reasons, the PLC discussed throughout this chapter did not continue after the first year. While this was initially viewed as somewhat disappointing, the authors subsequently thought this might be a strength of the PLC, as the appropriate and effective use of technology in teacher education programs and other programs in the College of Education has increased over the past year. Thus, the fact that the PLC did not "live" forever was not problematic, as the PLC participation was not "forced." Additionally, smaller groups of individuals within the College of Education have continued to meet informally and discuss issues related to the integration of technology into teaching and learning environments.

IMPLICATIONS AND CONCLUSIONS

The current body of literature has consistently cited a number of characteristics of effective technology-based professional development. Effective technology-based professional development opportunities are longer in duration, have clear and common goals regarding improved student outcomes, engage instructors in activities that are both meaningful and relevant to their everyday practice, provide access to emerging instructional technologies, facilitate modeling of technology use, foster cultures of technology integration, and promote collaborations and the development of community among participants (Porter et al., 2000; Sparks, 2000).

We conclude that the PLC model of professional development provided was an effective format in meeting the differing needs of faculty engaged in online teaching and learning. The PLC brought together skilled and frequent users of technology in teaching with the less skilled and neophytes. As research has shown, higher education faculty have been slow to adopt web-based technologies in teaching (Ajjan & Hartshorne, 2008). The PLC brought professional development physically and intellectually to our college providing access to a greater number of faculty than other forms of professional development such as workshops have done so in the past. Furthermore, by its very nature, the PLC focused on issues that mattered most to instructors such as learning about the array of online collaborative tools including wikis, shared document spaces like Google Documents and Adobe's Buzzword, and synchronous meeting spaces such as Wimba and Centra.

We acknowledge that the Technology & Teaching PLC existed for only a year, but in that year, it opened and sustained a professional conversation that had not previously existed in the college to any great degree. As Bruce's and Brian's vignettes show, many faculty face challenges in implementing online courses. The PLC was a tool that helped Bruce work through and share with others his experiences moving from face-to-face to online teaching—in particular, the sense of being overwhelmed. It allowed Brian to gain access to additional Web 2.0 tools to make his online courses more meaningful for he and his students.

The PLC also helped foster a culture of collaboration among faculty in the College of Education. Although the group no longer meets, members, including the authors of this chapter, have a greater awareness of the centers of expertise held by faculty in the college. More of us know the "go to people" when we have a question about technology and teaching. Moreover, it brought into the conversation staff from the Center for Teaching & Learning who shared their expertise to faculty who might otherwise not have attended one of the many workshops offered by CTL.

Finally, we know that technology is constantly evolving. New applications and tools emerge daily and our need to understand how to use them also increases. It is our sense that the Technology & Teaching PLC is currently on hiatus but that as the need for discussion around these topics arises, it is a group that can be easily reformed to meet that need.

NOTE

Correspondence concerning this paper can be sent to Dr. Bruce Taylor, Department of Reading and Elementary Education, University of North Carolina at Charlotte, 9201 University City Blvd., Charlotte, NC 28223, 704-687-8707 (phone), 704-687-3749 (fax). Address email to dbtaylor@uncc.edu.

REFERENCES

Ajjan, H., & Hartshorne, R. (2008). Investigating faculty decisions to adopt Web 2.0 technologies: Theory and empirical tests. *The Internet and Higher Education*, *11*(2), 71–80. doi:10.1016/j.iheduc.2008.05.002

Barnett, M., Keating, T., Harwook, W., & Saam, J. (2004). Using emerging technologies to help bridge the gap between university theory and classroom practice: Challenges and successes. *School Science and Mathematics, 102*(6), 299–314. doi:10.1111/j.1949-8594.2002.tb17887.x

Boulos, N. K., & Wheelert, S. (2007). The emerging Web 2.0 social software: An enabling suite of sociable technologies in health and health care education. *Health Information and Libraries Journal, 24*(1), 2–23. doi:10.1111/j.1471-1842.2007.00701.x

Brown, A. L., & Ferrara, R. A. (1985). Diagnosing zones of proximal development. In Wertsch, J. V. (Ed.), *Culture, communication, and cognition: Vygotskian perspectives* (pp. 273–305). New York, NY: Cambridge University Press.

Bruner, J. (1966). *Toward a theory of instruction.* Cambridge, MA: Harvard University Press.

Dixon, S., & Black, L. (1996). Vocal point: A collaborative, student run online newspaper. In Valauskas, E. J., & Ertel, M. (Eds.), *The Internet for teachers and school library media specialists: Today's applications tomorrow's prospects* (pp. 147–158). New York, NY: Neal-Schuman Publishers, Inc.

DuFour, R., & Eaker, R. (1998). *Professional learning communities at work: Best practices for enhancing student achievement. Bloomington, IN: National Educational Service and Alexandria.* VA: Association of Supervision and Curriculum Development.

Ferdig, R. (2007). Examining social software in teacher education. *Journal of Technology and Teacher Education, 15*(1), 5–10.

Franklin, T., & Van Harmelen, M. (2007). *Web 2.0 for content for learning and teaching in higher education.* London, UK: Joint Information Systems Committee.

Graham, C., Culatta, R., Pratt, M., & West, R. (2004). Redesigning the teacher education technology course to emphasize integration. *Computers in the Schools, 21,* 127–148. doi:10.1300/J025v21n01_10

Hord, S. M. (2004). *Learning together leading together: Changing schools through professional learning communities.* Oxford, OH: Teachers College Press.

Howland, J., & Wedman, J. (2004). A process model for faculty development: Individualized technology learning. *Journal of Technology and Teacher Education, 12*(2), 239–263.

Maloney, E. (2007). What Web 2.0 can teach us about learning? *The Chronicle of Higher Education, 25*(18), B26.

Marzano, R. J. (2003). *What works in schools: Translating research into action.* Alexandria, VA: Association for Supervision and Curriculum Development.

Oblinger, D., & Oblinger, J. (2005). Is it age or IT: First steps toward understanding the Net Generation. In D. Oblinger & J. Obligner (Eds.), *Educating the Net Generation,* Educause 2005. Retrieved from http://www.educause.edu/educatingthenetgen/

Polly, D., & Hannafin, M. J. (2010). Reexamining technology's role in learner-centered professional development. Educational Technology Research and Development, 58(5), 557-571. doi:10.1007/s11423-009-9146-5

Porter, A. C., Garet, M. S., Desimone, L., Yoon, K. S., & Birman, B. F. (2000). *Does professional development change teaching practice? Results from a three-year study.* (U.S. Department of Education Report No. 2000–04). Retrieved September 23, 2010, from http://www.ed.gov/rschstat/eval/teaching/epdp/report.pdf

Prensky, M. (2001). Digital natives, digital immigrants. *Horizon*, *9*(5), 1–6. doi:10.1108/10748120110424816

Ravitz, J., & Hoadley, C. (2005). Supporting change and scholarship through review of online resources in professional development settings. *British Journal of Educational Technology*, *36*(6), 957–974. doi:10.1111/j.1467-8535.2005.00567.x

Richardson, W. (2006). *Blogs, wikis, podcasts, and other powerful web tools for classrooms*. Thousand Oaks, CA: Corwin Press.

Riley, R. W., & Roberts, L. G. (2000, December). Putting a world-class education at the fingertips of all children: The national educational technology plan. *eLearning*. Washington, DC: U.S. Department of Education.

Schlager, M., Farooq, U., Fusco, J., Schank, P., & Dwyer, N. (2009). Analyzing online social networking in professional learning communities: Cyber networks require cyber-research tools. *Journal of Teacher Education*, *60*(1), 86–100. doi:10.1177/0022487108328487

Schofield, J. W., & Davidson, A. L. (2002). *Bringing the internet to school: Lessons from an urban district*. San Francisco, CA: Jolley-Bass.

Simões, L., & Gouveia, L. (2008). *Web 2.0 and higher education: Pedagogical implications*. Higher Education: New Challenges and Emerging Roles for Human and Social Development. 4th International Barcelona Conference on Higher Education Technical University of Catalonia (UPC).

Snow-Gerono, J. L. (2005). Professional development in a culture of inquiry: PDS teachers identify the benefits of professional learning communities. *Teaching and Teacher Education*, *21*(3), 241–256. doi:10.1016/j.tate.2004.06.008

So, H. J., Lossman, H., Lim, W., & Jacobson, M. J. (2009). Designing an online video based platform for teacher learning in Singapore. *Australasian Journal of Educational Technology*, *25*(3), 440–457.

Sparks, D. (2002). *Designing powerful professional development for teachers and principals*. Oxford, OH: National Staff Development Council.

Strahan, D. (2003). Promoting a collaborative professional culture in three elementary schools that have beaten the odds. *The Elementary School Journal*, *104*(2), 127–146. doi:10.1086/499746

Strudler, N., Archambault, L., Bendixen, L., Anderson, D., & Weiss, R. (2003). Project THREAD: Technology helping restructure educational access and delivery. *Educational Technology Research and Development*, *51*(3), 41–56. doi:10.1007/BF02504517

Sturm, M., Kennel, T., McBride, M., & Kelly, M. (2008). The pedagogical implications of Web 2.0. In Thomas, M. (Ed.), *Handbook of research on Web 2.0 and second language learning* (pp. 367–384). Hershey, PA: IGI Global. doi:10.4018/9781605661902.ch020

Taylor, J. (2008). Tapping online professional development through communities of practice: Examples from the NIFL discussion lists. *Adult Basic Education and Literacy Journal*, *2*(3), 182–196.

U.S. Department of Education. (2002). *Preparing tomorrow's teachers to use technology*. Retrieved October 5, 2010 from http://www.pt3.org/

Van Es, E. A., & Sherin, M. G. (2008). Learning to notice in the context of a video club. *Teaching and Teacher Education*, *24*(2), 244–276. doi:10.1016/j.tate.2006.11.005

Vescio, V., Ross, D., & Adams, A. (2006). *A review of research on professional learning communities: What do we know?* Retrieved February 16, 2008, from http://www.nsrfharmony.org/research.vescio_ross_adams.pdf

Vygotsky, L. S. (1978). *Mind in society: The development of higher psychological processes.* Cambridge, MA: Harvard University Press.

Waddoups, G. L., Wentworth, N., & Earle, R. (2004). Principles of technology integration and curriculum development: A faculty design team approach. *Computers in the Schools, 21,* 15–23. doi:10.1300/J025v21n01_02

ADDITIONAL READING

Adelman, N., Donnelly, M. B., Dove, T., Tiffany-Morales, J., Wayne, A., & Zucker, A. (2002). *The Integrated Studies of Educational Technology: Professional Development and Teachers' Use of Technology.* Arlington, VA: SRI International.

Ajjan, H., & Hartshorne, R. (2008). Investigating faculty decisions to adopt Web 2.0 technologies: Theory and empirical tests. *The Internet and Higher Education, 11*(2), 71–80. doi:10.1016/j.iheduc.2008.05.002

Barnett, M., Keating, T., Harwook, W., & Saam, J. (2004). Using emerging technologies to help bridge the gap between university theory and classroom practice: Challenges and successes. *School Science and Mathematics, 102*(6), 299–314. doi:10.1111/j.1949-8594.2002.tb17887.x

Baylor, A., & Ritchie, D. (2002). What factors facilitate teacher skill, teacher morale, and perceived student learning in technology-using classroom? *Computers & Education, 39*(1), 395–414. doi:10.1016/S0360-1315(02)00075-1

Carr, N. (2008). *The big switch: Rewiring the world, from Edison to Google.* New York: W.W. Norton.

Christensen, C., Johnson, C., & Horn, M. (2008). *Disrupting class: How disruptive innovation will change the way the world learns.* New York: McGraw Hill.

Collis, B., & Moonen, J. (2008). Web 2.0 tools and processes in higher education: Quality perspectives. *Educational Media International, 45*(2), 93–106. .doi:10.1080/09523980802107179

Dearstyne, B. W. (2007). Blogs, mashups, and wikis: Oh my! *Information Management Journal, 41*(4), 24–33.

Ferdig, R. (2007). Examining social software in teacher education. *Journal of Technology and Teacher Education, 15*(1), 5–10.

Franklin, T., & Van Harmelen, M. (2007). *Web 2.0 for content for learning and teaching in higher education.* London: Joint Information Systems Committee.

Friedman, T. L. (2005). *The world is flat.* New York: Farrar, Straus, & Giroux.

Klamma, R., Chatti, M. A., Duval, E., Hummel, H., Hvannberg, E. H., & Kravcik, M. (2007). Social software for lifelong learning. *Journal of Educational Technology & Society, 10*(3), 72–83.

Lawless, K. A., & Pellegrino, J. W. (2007). Professional development in integrating technology into teaching and learning: Knowns, unknowns, and ways to pursue better questions and answers. *Review of Educational Research, 77*(4), 575.614.

Lenhart, A., & Madden, M. (2007). *Social networking websites and teens: An overview* (pp. 1–10). Washington, DC: Pew Internet and American Life Project.

Maloney, E. (2007). What Web 2.0 can teach us about learning? *The Chronicle of Higher Education, 25*(18), B26.

Mims, C., Polly, D., Shepherd, C., & Inan, F. (2006). Examining PT3 projects designed to improve preservice education. Tech Trends, 50(3), 17-24.

Pence, II. E. (2007). Preparing for the real web generation. *Journal of Educational Technology Systems, 35*(3), 347–356. doi:10.2190/7116-G776-7P42-V110

Prensky, M. (2001). Digital natives, digital immigrants. *Horizon, 9*(5), 1–6. doi:10.1108/10748120110424816

Richardson, W. (2006). *Blogs, wikis, podcasts, and other powerful web tools for classrooms.* Thousand Oaks, CA: Corwin Press.

Rollett, H., Lux, M., Strohmaier, M., Gisela, D., & Tochtermann, K. (2007). The Web 2.0 way of learning with technologies. *International Journal of Learning Technology, 3*(1), 87–107. doi:10.1504/IJLT.2007.012368

Routman, R. (1991). *Invitations: Changing as teachers and learners K-12.* Toronto, Canada: Irwin Publishing.

KEY TERMS AND DEFINITIONS

Blackboard Vista: Blackboard Vista is an online teaching and learning platform typically used by educational institutions. A primary purpose of Blackboard Vista is to help educators create and support online learning environments, and can include such instructional strategies as class notes, discussion forums, assessment tools, audio streaming, and others.

Blog: A contraction of the term "web log"; a blog is a website maintained by an individual and may include regular posts, picture and other media, RSS feeds, and commentary from guests or visitors to the blog.

Digital Immigrants: Prensky (2001) defines "digital immigrants" as individuals "who were not born into the digital world but have, at some later point in our lives, become fascinated by and adopted many or most aspects of the new technology" (p. 1).

Digital Natives: Prensky (2001) defines "digital natives" as the first generation of students to "have spent their entire lives surrounded by and using computers, videogames, digital music players, video cams, cell phones, and all the other toys and tools of the digital age" (p. 1).

Moodle: Moodle, an acronym for Modular Object-Oriented Dynamic Learning Environment, is an open source course management system. A primary purpose of Moodle is to help educators create and support online learning environments, with a focus on constructivist learning principles.

Professional Learning Community (PLC): While "professional learning communities" have many variations; in the context of this chapter, a PLC is an professional development opportunity consisting of a collaborative forum in which colleagues within a particular work environment can address a specific topic(s) of interest.

Web 2.0: Also called the "read/write web", Web 2.0 is typically associated with interactive, interoperable, user-centered, collaborative applications on the World Wide Web. Examples of Web 2.0 applications include blogs, wikis, social networking sites, Internet telephony, social bookmarking sites, and others.

Wiki: A web-based application that allows multiple users to create and edit content, which can include text, hypertext, audio, video, and more.

Compilation of References

AACTE Committee on Innovation and Technology (Ed.). (2008). *Handbook of technological pedagogical content knowledge (TPCK) for educators*. New York, NY: Routledge.

AACTE, & P21 (2010). *Education preparation - A vision for the 21st Century (draft)*. Retrieved from http://aacte.org/email_blast/president_e-letter/files/02-16-2010/Educator%20Preparation%20and%2021st%20Century%20Skills%20DRAFT%20021510.pdf

Abell, S. K., Bryan, L. A., & Anderson, M. A. (1998). Investigating preservice elementary science teacher reflective thinking using integrated media case-based instruction in elementary science teacher preparation. *Science Education, 82*(4), 491–509. doi:10.1002/(SICI)1098-237X(199807)82:4<491::AID-SCE5>3.0.CO;2-6

Abramovich, S., & Cho, E. K. (2006). Technology as a medium for elementary preteachers' problem-posing experience in mathematics. *Journal of Computers in Mathematics and Science Teaching, 25*, 309–323.

Acker, S. (2005). *Technology-enabled teaching/eLearning dialogue: Overcoming obstacles to authentic ePortfolio assessment*. Retrieved June 25, 2005, from http://www.campus-technology.com/news_article.asp?id=10788&typeid=155.

Ackermann, E. (2009). *Piaget's constructivism, Papert's constructionism: What's the difference? Future of Learning Group*. MIT Media Laboratory.

Adams, E., Smith, G., Ward, T. J., Vaneck, D., Marra, N., & Jones, D. (2008). Air toxins under the big sky: A real-world investigation to engage high school science students. *Journal of Chemical Education, 85*(2), 4. doi:10.1021/ed085p221

Adamy, P., & Boulmetis, J. (2006). The impact of modeling technology integration on pre-service teachers' technology confidence. *Journal of Computing in Higher Education, 17*(2), 100–120. doi:10.1007/BF03032700

Ajjan, H., & Hartshorne, R. (2008). Investigating faculty decisions to adopt Web 2.0 technologies: Theory and empirical tests. *The Internet and Higher Education, 11*(2), 71–80. doi:10.1016/j.iheduc.2008.05.002

Alberta Education. (2005). *Social studies kindergarten to grade 12 program of studies*. Edmonton, Canada: Author. Retrieved November 18, 2010, from http://education.alberta.ca/teachers/program/socialstudies/programs.aspx

Albion, P. R. (2008). Web 2.0 in teacher education: Two imperatives for action. *Computers in the Schools, 25*(3), 181–198. doi:10.1080/07380560802368173

Alexander, B. (2006). *Web 2.0 - A new wave of innovation for teaching and learning?* Retrieved 22nd February, 2011, from http://www.educause.edu/EDUCAUSE+Review/EDUCAUSEReviewMagazineVolume41/Web20ANewWaveofInnovationforTe/158042

Alger, C., & Kopcha, T. J. (2009). eSupervision: A technology framework for the 21st century field experience in teacher education. *Issues in Teacher Education, 18*(2), 31–46.

Allen, I. E., & Seaman, J. (2008). *Staying the course: Online education in the United States, 2008*. The Sloan Consortium. Retrieved from http://sloanconsortium.org/sites/default/files/staying_the_course-2.pdf

Allen, I. E., & Seaman, J. (2010). *Class differences: Online education in the United States*. Sloan Consortium. Retrieved from http://sloanconsortium.org/sites/default/files/class_differences.pdf

Allen, I. E., & Seaman, J. (2010). *Learning on demand: Online education in the United States, 2009.* The Sloan Consortium. Retrieved from http://sloanconsortium.org/publications/survey/pdf/learningondemand.pdf

Allen, T. (2009, April 26). *The iSchool initiative* [Video]. Retrieved from http://www.youtube.com/watch?v=68KgAcx_9jU

Allen, J. (2007). The quest for deeper learning: an investigation into the impact of a knowledge-pooling WebQuest in primary initial teacher training. *British Journal of Educational Technology, 38*(6), 1102–1112. doi:10.1111/j.1467-8535.2007.00697.x

Alloul, A. (2010, September 28). *Comment on blog post: Great.* Retrieved from http://strangethoughtsbyjohn.blogspot.com/2010/09/great.html

Alvermann, D. (2004). *Adolescents and literacies in a digital world.* New York, NY: Peter Lang.

Alvermann, D. (Ed.). (2002). *Adolescents and literacies in a digital world.* New York, NY: Peter Lang.

American Association for the Advancement of Science. (1993). *Benchmarks for science literacy.* New York, NY: Oxford University Press.

American Association of Colleges of Teacher Education (Ed.). (2008). *The handbook of technological pedagogical content knowledge (TPCK) for educators.* Mahwah, NJ: Lawrence Erlbaum Associates.

Anderson, J. B. (2008, January). *An overview of the research on service-learning in preservice teacher education.* A paper presented at the Student Coalition for Action in Literacy Education (SCALE): Learning to Teach, Learning to Serve Conference. Chapel Hill, NC.

Anderson, P. (2007). *What is Web 2.0? Ideas, technologies and implications for education.* Joint Information Systems Committee Technology & Standards Watch. Retrieved from http://citeseerx.ist.psu.edu/viewdoc/download?doi=10.1.1.108.9995&rep=rep1&type=pdf

Anderson, L., & Krathwohl, D. (2001). *A taxonomy for learning, teaching and assessing: A revision of Bloom's taxonomy of educational objectives.* New York, NY: Longman.

Anderson, S. E., & Maninger, R. M. (2007). Preservice teachers' abilities, beliefs, and intentions regarding technology integration. *Journal of Educational Computing Research, 37*(2), 151–172. doi:10.2190/H1M8-562W-18J1-634P

Andersson, S. B. (2006). Newly qualified teachers' learning related to their use of information and communication technology: A Swedish perspective. *British Journal of Educational Technology, 37*(5), 665–682. doi:10.1111/j.1467-8535.2006.00563.x

Angeli, C. M., & Valanides, N. (2009, April). *Examining epistemological and methodological issues of the conceptualizations. Development and assessment of ICT-TPACJ: Advancing technological pedagogical content knowledge (TPCK) – Part I. Teachers.* Paper presented at the meeting of the American Educational Research Association (AERA) Annual Conference, San Diego, CA.

Angeli, C. (2004). The effects of case-based learning on early childhood pre-service teachers' beliefs about the pedagogical use of ICT. *Journal of Educational Media, 29*, 139–151. doi:10.1080/1358165042000253302

Angeli, C., & Valanides, N. (2009). Epistemological and methodological issues for the conceptualization, development, and assessment of ict-tpck: advances in technological pedagogical content knowledge (TPCK). *Computers & Education, 52*(1), 154–168. doi:10.1016/j.compedu.2008.07.006

Aronson, J. Z., & Timms, M. J. (2003). *Net choices, net gains: Supplementing the high school curriculum with online courses.* San Francisco, CA: WestEd. Retrieved from www.wested.org/online_pubs/KN-03-02.pdf

Association of Mathematics Teacher Educators (AMTE). (2006). *AMTE technology position statement: Preparing teacher to use technology to enhance the learning of mathematics.* Retrieved from http://www.amte.net/publications

Aston, S., & Jackson, D. (2009). Blurring the boundaries or muddying the waters? *Design and Technology Education, 14*(1), 68–76.

Attwell, G. (2007). *Web 2.0 and the changing ways we are using computers for learning: What are the implications for pedagogy and curriculum?* Retrieved 28 September, 2010, from http://www.elearningeuropa.info/directory/index.php?page=doc&doc id=9756&doclng=6

Azer, S. A. (2004). Becoming a student in a PBL course: Twelve tips for successful group discussion. *Medical Teacher*, *26*(1), 12–15. doi:10.1080/0142159032000156533

Backes, C., & Backes, L. (1999). Making the best of a learning experience. *Techniques*, *74*(5), 23–24.

Bai, H., & Ertmer, P. (2008). Teacher educators' beliefs and technology uses as predictors of preservice teachers' beliefs and technology attitudes. *Journal of Technology and Teacher Education*, *16*(1), 93–113.

Bain, A., & Ross, K. (2000). School reengineering and SAT-1 performance: A case study. *International Journal of Educational Reform*, *9*(2), 148–153.

Bakhtin, M. M. (1981). *The dialogic imagination*. Austin, TX: The University of Texas Press.

Ball, L., Pierce, R., & Stacey, K. (2003). *Recognizing equivalent algebraic expressions: An important component of algebraic expectation for working with CAS*. Paper presented at the 27th International Group for the Psychology of Mathematics Education Conference Held Jointly with the 25th PME-NA Conference (Honolulu, HI, Jul 13-18, 2003).

Ball, D. L., Lubienski, S. T., & Mewborn, D. S. (2001). Research on teaching mathematics: The unsolved problem of teachers' mathematical knowledge. In Richardson, V. (Ed.), *Handbook of research on teaching* (4th ed., pp. 433–456). New York, NY: Macmillan.

Banas, J. R. (2010). Teachers' attitudes toward technology: Considerations for designing preservice and practicing teacher instruction. *Community & Junior College Libraries*, *16*(2), 14. doi:10.1080/02763911003707552

Bandura, A. (1977). *Social learning theory*. Upper Saddle River, NJ: Prentice-Hall, Inc.

Bannan-Ritland, B. (2003). The role of design in research: The integrative learning design framework. *Educational Researcher*, *32*(1), 21–24. doi:10.3102/0013189X032001021

Barab, S. A., & Landa, A. (1997). Designing effective interdisciplinary anchors. *Educational Leadership*, *54*(6), 52–55.

Barab, S. A., Squire, K. D., & Dueber, W. (2000). A co-evolutionary model for supporting the emergence of authenticity. *Educational Technology Research and Development*, *48*(2), 37–62. doi:10.1007/BF02313400

Barbour, M. K. (2007). *What are they doing and how are they doing it? Rural student experiences in virtual schooling*. Unpublished Doctoral Dissertation. University of Georgia, Athens, GA.

Barbour, M. K., & Mulcahy, D. (2004). The role of mediating teachers in Newfoundland's new model of distance education. *The Morning Watch, 32*(1-2). Retrieved from http://www.mun.ca/educ/faculty/mwatch/fall4/barbour-mulcahy.htm

Barbour, M. K., & Unger, K. (2009). Challenging teachers' preconceptions, misconceptions, and concerns of virtual schooling. In I. Gibson, et al. (Eds.), *Proceedings of the Annual Conference of the Society for Information Technology and Teacher Education* (pp. 785-790). Norfolk, VA: AACE.

Barbour, M. K. (2009). Today's student and virtual schooling: The reality, the challenges, the promise. *Journal of Distance Learning*, *13*(1), 5–25.

Barbour, M. K., Kinsella, J., Wicks, M., & Toker, S. (2010). Continuum of change in a virtual world: Training and retaining instructors. *Journal of Technology and Teacher Education*, *17*(4), 437–457.

Barker, K., Wendel, T., & Richmond, M. (1999). *Linking the literature: School effectiveness and virtual schools*. Vancouver, BC: FuturEd. Retrieved from http://www.futured.com/pdf/Virtual.pdf

Barker, P. (2008). Re-evaluating a model of learning design. *Innovations in Education and Teaching International*, *45*(2), 127–141. doi:10.1080/14703290801950294

Barnett, H. (2003). *Investing n technology: The payoff in student learning. ED479843. ERIC Digest*. Syracuse, NY: ERIC Clearinghouse on Information and Technology.

Barnett, M., Keating, T., Harwook, W., & Saam, J. (2004). Using emerging technologies to help bridge the gap between university theory and classroom practice: Challenges and successes. *School Science and Mathematics*, *102*(6), 299–314. doi:10.1111/j.1949-8594.2002.tb17887.x

Barnett-Queen, T., Blair, R., & Merrick, M. (2005). Student perspectives of online discussions: Strengths and weaknesses. *Journal of Technology in Human Services*, *23*, 229–244. .doi:10.1300/J017v23n03_05

Barone, D., & Wrights, T. (2008). Literacy instruction with digital and media technologies. *The Reading Teacher, 62,* 292–302. doi:10.1598/RT.62.4.2

Barrett, H. (2000). Electronic teaching portfolios: Multimedia skills + portfolio development = Powerful professional development. In *Proceedings of Society for Information Technology & Teacher Education International Conference 2000* (p. 7). Chesapeake, VA: AACE.

Barrett, H., & Knezek, D. (2003). *e-Portfolios: Issues in assessment, accountability and preservice teacher preparation.* Retrieved from http://www.electronicportfolios.com/portfolios/AERA2003.pdf

Basham, J. D., Lowrey, K. A., & Jones, M. L. (2006). Making use of the net: Internet based videoconferencing and online conferencing tools in teacher preparation. In Crawford, C., Willis, D. A., Carlsen, R., Gibson, I., McFerrin, K., Price, J., & Weber, R. (Eds.), *Association for the Advancement of Computing in Education Handbook* (pp. 1440–1444). Chesapeake, VA: AACE.

Bassett, D., Ainsworth, B., Leggett, S., Hunter, D., & Duncan, G. (1996). Accuracy of five electronic pedometers for measuring distance walked. *Medicine and Science in Sports and Exercise, 28,* 1071–1077. doi:10.1097/00005768-199608000-00019

Bauer, J. F. (2000, November). *A technology gender divide: Perceived skill and frustration levels among female preservice teachers.* A paper presentation at the Annual Meeting of the Mid-South Educational Research Association, Bowling Green, KY. (ERIC Document Reproduction Service No. ED447137). Retrieved from http://www.eric.ed.gov/ERICWebPortal/contentdelivery/servlet/ERICServlet?accno=ED447137

Bauer, J., & Kenton, J. (2005). Toward technology integration in the schools: Why it isn't happening. *Journal of Technology and Teacher Education, 13*(4), 519–546.

Baule, S. (2007). The components of successful technologies. *Teacher Librarian, 34*(5), 16.

Bausch, M. E., & Hasselbring, T. S. (2004). Assistive technology: Are the necessary skills and knowledge being developed at the preservice and inservice levels? *Teacher Education and Special Education, 27*(2), 97–104. doi:10.1177/088840640402700202

Bayne, S., & Ross, J. (2007). The digital native and digital immigrant: A dangerous opposition. Presented at the *Annual Conference of the Society for Research into Higher Education.* www.malts.ed.ac.uk/staff/sian/natives_final.pdf

Beal, C., Bolick, C. M., & Martorella, P. H. (2009). *Teaching social studies in middle and secondary schools.* Boston, MA: Allyn & Bacon.

Beaudin, L., & Hadden, C. (2005). Technology and pedagogy: Building techno- pedagogical skills in pre-service teachers. *Innovate, 2*(2). Retrieved Nov. 10, 2010 from http://www.innovateonline.info/index.php?view=article&id=36

Bebell, D., Russell, M., & O'Dwyer, L. (2004). Measuring teachers' technology uses: Why multiple-measures are more revealing. *Journal of Research on Technology in Education, 37*(1), 45–63.

Becker, H. (1986). *Instructional use of school computers: Reports from the 1985 national survey* (pp. 1-3).

Beck, R. J., King, A., & Marshall, S. K. (2002). Effects of video case construction on preservice teachers' observations of teaching. *Journal of Experimental Education, 70*(4), 345–355. doi:10.1080/00220970209599512

Bednar, M. R., Ryan, F. J., & Sweeder, J. J. (1994). Voices from the field: Teachers' responses to student teaching orientation videos. *Journal of Technology and Teacher Education, 2*(3), 293–303.

Beighle, A., Pangrazi, R., & Vincent, S. (2001). Pedometers, physical activity and accountability. *Journal of Physical Education, Recreation & Dance, 72*(9), 16–19.

Belland, B. (2009). Using the theory of habitus to move beyond the study of barriers to technology integration. *Computers & Education, 52,* 353–364. doi:10.1016/j.compedu.2008.09.004

Bell, J. K., & Unger, L. C. (2003). Videoconferencing takes Cape Elizabeth Middle School on a distance learning adventure. *T.H.E. Journal, 31,* 51.

Bell, V., & Fidishun, D. (2009). Learning from each other: Student teachers, cooperating teachers and technology. *International Journal of Instructional Media, 36*(2), 195–205.

Benbunan-Fich, R., & Hilz, S. R. (2003). Mediators of the effectiveness of online courses. *IEEE Transactions on Professional Communication, 46*(4), 298–312. doi:10.1109/TPC.2003.819639

Bennett, C. (1991). The teacher as decision maker program: An alternative for career-change preservice teachers. *Journal of Teacher Education, 42*(2), 119–130. doi:10.1177/002248719104200205

Bennett, S., & Maton, K. (2010). Beyond the digital natives debate: Towards a more nuanced understanding of students' technology experiences. *Journal of Computer Assisted Learning, 26*, 321–331. doi:10.1111/j.1365-2729.2010.00360.x

Bennett-Walker, S. (2006). *Technology use among physical education teachers in Georgia public schools.* Ph.D. dissertation, The University of Southern Mississippi, United States -- Mississippi. Retrieved September 27, 2010, from Dissertations & Theses: A&I.(Publication No. AAT 3257001).

Berlin, D. F., & White, A. L. (2010). Preservice mathematics and science teachers in an integrated teacher preparation programs for grades 7-12: A 3-year study of attitudes and perceptions related to integration. *International Journal of Science and Mathematics Education, 8*(1), 97–115. doi:10.1007/s10763-009-9164-0

Betrus, A. K., & Molenda, M. (2002). Historical evolution of instructional technology in teacher education programs. *TechTrends, 46*(5), 18–21, 33. doi:10.1007/BF02818303

Beyerbach, B., Walsh, C., & Vannatta, R. A. (2001). From teaching technology to using technology to enhance student learning: Preservice teachers' changing perceptions of technology infusion. *Journal of Technology and Teacher Education, 9*(1), 105–127.

Bianchini, J., & Brenner, M. E. (2010). The role of induction in learning to teach toward equity: A study of beginning science and mathematics teachers. *Science Education, 94*, 164–195.

Billig, S. H., & Klute, M. M. (2003). *The impact of service-learning on MEAP: A large-scale study of Michigan Learn and Serve grantees*. Presentation at National Service-Learning Conference, Minneapolis, MN.

Billig, S. H. (2000). Research on K-12 school-based service learning: The evidence builds. *Phi Delta Kappan, 81*, 658–664.

Birdsall, W. F. (2007). Web 2.0 as a social movement. *Webology, 4*(2).

Bitner, J., & Bitner, N. (2002). Integrating technology into the classroom: Eight keys to success. *Journal of Technology and Teacher Education, 10*, 1.

Bjerstedt, A. (1967). *Tele-observation- Closed circuit television and video-recording in teacher training.* ERIC Document Available # ED017178

Blackboard Academic Suite. (n.d.). Retrieved from http://www.blackboard.com/

Blackboard Inc. (2010). *Engaging learners, for engaging learning: Introducing Blackboardlearn⁺ Release 9.1*. Retrieved from http://www.blackboard.com/Teaching-Learning/Learn-Platform.aspx

Blackboard. (n.d.). *Blackboard, version 9.0 service pack 5* [Web-based course system]. Washington, DC: Blackboard Inc.

Black, G. (2002). A comparison of traditional, online, and hybrid methods of course delivery. *Journal of Business Administration Online, 1*(1).

Blanton, L. P., Griffin, C. C., Winn, J. A., & Pugach, M. C. (Eds.). (1997). *Teacher education in transition*. Denver, CO: Love.

Blumenfeld, P. C., Kempler, T. M., & Krajcik, J. S. (2006). Motivation and cognitive engagement in learning engagement. In Sawyer, R. K. (Ed.), *The Cambridge handbook of the learning sciences* (pp. 475–488). New York, NY: Cambridge University Press.

Boardman, M. (2007). "I know how much this child has learned. I have proof!": Employing digital technologies for documentation processes in kindergarten. *Australian Journal of Early Childhood, 32*(3), 59–66.

Bolick, C., Berson, M., & Coutts, C. (2003). Technology applications in social studies teacher education: A survey of social studies methods faculty. *Contemporary Issues in Technology & Teacher Education, 3*(3), 1–9.

Bolliger, D. U., Supanakor, S., & Boggs, C. (2010). Impact of podcasting on student motivation in the online learning environment. *Computers & Education*, 55(2), 714–722. doi:10.1016/j.compedu.2010.03.004

Bonk, C. J. (2009). *The world is open: How Web technology is revolutionizing education*. San Francisco, CA: Jossey-Bass.

Borko, H., & Putnam, R. T. (1995). Expanding a teacher's knowledge base: A cognitive psychological perspective on professional development. In T. R. Guskey, M (Ed.), *Professional development in education: New paradigms and practices* (pp. 35-65). New York, NY: Teachers College Press.

Borko, H., Stecher, B., & Kuffner, K. (2007). *Using artifacts to characterize reform-oriented instruction: The Scoop Notebook and rating guide*. (Technical Report 707). Los Angeles, CA: National Center for Research on Evaluation, Standards, and Student Testing. (ERIC Document Reproduction Service No. ED495853).

Borko, H., & Putnam, T. (1996). Learning to teach. In Berliner, D. C., & Calfee, R. C. (Eds.), *Handbook of educational psychology* (pp. 673–708). New York, NY: Simon and Schuster Macmillan.

Boss, S., & Krauss, J. (2007). The power of the mashup. Learning &. *Leading with Technology*, 34(1), 12–17.

Boulos, N. K., & Wheelert, S. (2007). The emerging Web 2.0 social software: An enabling suite of sociable technologies in health and health care education. *Health Information and Libraries Journal*, 24(1), 2–23. doi:10.1111/j.1471-1842.2007.00701.x

Bower, M., Hedberg, J., & Kuswara, A. (2009). Conceptualising Web 2.0 enabled learning designs. In *Australasian Society for Computers in Learning in Tertiary Education (ASCILITE)*, Aukland, (pp. 1153-1162).

Bower, B. (2006). *Social studies alive: Engaging diverse learners in the elementary classroom*. Palo Alto, CA: Teachers' Curriculum Institute.

Bower, M., Hedberg, J., & Kuswara, A. (2010). A framework for Web 2.0 learning design. *Educational Media International*, 47(3), 177–198. doi:10.1080/09523987.2010.518811

Bowman, C. A. (2000). Infusing technology-based instructional frameworks in the methods courses: A response to Pope and Golub. *Contemporary Issues in Technology & Teacher Education*, 1(1).

Branigan, C. (2002, May). Study: Missouri's ed-tech program pays off. Students' test scores higher than average. *eSchool News*. Retrieved September 30, 2006, from http://www.eschoolnews.com/news/ showstory.cfm?ArticleID=3673

Bransford, J. D., Brown, A. L., & Cocking, R. R. (Eds.). (2000). *How people learn: Brain, mind, experience, and school*. Washington, DC: National Academy Press.

Bransford, J. D., Sherwood, R. D., Hasselbring, T. S., Kinzer, C. K., & Williams, S. M. (Eds.). (1990). *Anchored instruction: Why we need it and how technology can help*. Hillsdale, NJ: Lawrence Erlbaum.

Braswell, J. S., Lutkus, A. D., Grigg, W. S., Santapau, S. L., Tay-Lim, B., & Johnson, M. (2001, August). *The nation's report card: Mathematics 2000*. Washington, DC: National Center for Educational Statistics.

Braun, J., & Risinger, F. (1999). *Surfing social studies*. Washington, DC: National Council for the Social Studies.

Brayley, R. E. (1999). Using technology to enhance the recreation education classroom. *Journal of Physical Education, Recreation & Dance*, 70(9), 23–26.

Bredekamp, S., & Cople, C. (Eds.). (1997). *Developmentally appropriate practice in early childhood programs*. Washington, DC: National Association for the Education of Young Children.

Brinkerhoff, J. (2006). Effects of a long-duration, professional development academy on technology skills, computer self-efficacy, and technology integration beliefs and practices. *Journal of Research on Technology in Education*, 39(1), 22–43.

Britten, J., Mullen, L., & Stuve, M. (2003). Initial reflections: The benefits of using a continuous portfolio development in preservice teacher education. *Teacher Educator*, 39(2), 79–94. doi:10.1080/08878730309555332

Bronack, S., Kilbane, C., Herbert, J., & McNergney, R. (1999). Inservice and preservice teachers' perceptions of a Web-based, case-based learning environment. *Journal of Information Technology for Teacher Education*, 8(3), 305–320. doi:10.1080/14759399900200066

Brown, C. A., & Banas, J. (2010, November). Open source visualization tools to enhance reading comprehension. In M. Simonson (Ed.), *33rd Annual Proceedings: Selected Research and Development Papers at the Annual Convention of the Association for Educational Communications and Technology.* North Miami Beach, FL: Nova Southeastern University. Retrieved from http://www.aect.org/pdf/proceedings10/2010I/10_07.pdf

Brown, S. (2003). *The effects of technology on effective teaching and student learning: A design paradigm for teacher professional development.* Retrieved from http://www.waukeganschools.org/TechPlan/ResearchFindings.pdf

Brown, A. L., Ash, D., Rutherford, M., Nakagawa, K., Gordon, A., & Campione, J. C. (1993). Distributed expertise in the classroom. In Salomon, G. (Ed.), *Distributed cognitions: Psychological and educational considerations.* New York, NY: Cambridge University Press.

Brown, A. L., & Ferrara, R. A. (1985). Diagnosing zones of proximal development. In Wertsch, J. V. (Ed.), *Culture, communication, and cognition: Vygotskian perspectives* (pp. 273–305). New York, NY: Cambridge University Press.

Brown, A. R., & Voltz, B. D. (2005). Elements of effective e-learning design. *International Review of Research in Open and Distance Learning, 6*(1).

Brown, A., Brown, C., Fine, B., Luterbach, K., Sugar, W., & Vinciguerra, D. C. (2009). Instructional uses of podcasting in online learning environments: A cooperative inquiry study. *Journal of Educational Technology Systems, 37*(4), 351–371. doi:10.2190/ET.37.4.b

Brown, D., & Warschauer, M. (2006). From the university to the elementary classroom: Students' experiences in learning to integrate technology in instruction. *Journal of Technology and Teacher Education, 14*(3), 599–621.

Brown, J. S., Collins, A., & Duguid, P. (1989). Situated cognition and the culture of learning. *Educational Researcher, 18*(1), 32–42.

Bruce, B. C. (2002). Diversity and critical social engagement: How changing technologies enable new modes of literacy in changing circumstances. In Alvermann, D. (Ed.), *Adolescents and literacies in a digital world* (pp. 1–18). New York, NY: Peter Lang.

Bruner, J. (1966). *Toward a theory of instruction.* Cambridge, MA: Harvard University Press.

Bruner, J. (1996). *Culture of education.* Cambridge, MA: Harvard University Press.

Bruns, A., Cobcroft, R., Smith, J., & Towers, S. (2007). Mobile learning technologies and the move towards user-led education. *Mobile Media 2007 Conference Proceedings*, Sydney, Australia.

Brush, T., & Appelman, R. (2003). Transforming the pre-service teacher education technology curriculum at Indiana University: An integrative approach. In C. Crawford, et al. (Eds.), *Proceedings of Society for Information Technology and Teacher Education International Conference 2003* (pp. 1613-1619). Chesapeake, VA: AACE.

Brush, T. (1998). Teaching pre-service teachers to use technology in the classroom. *Journal of Technology and Teacher Education, 6*(4), 243–258.

Brush, T. A. (1997). The effects on student achievement and attitudes when using integrated learning systems with cooperative pairs. *Educational Technology Research and Development, 45*(1), 51–64. doi:10.1007/BF02299612

Brush, T., & Saye, J. W. (2009). Strategies for preparing preservice social studies teachers to integrate technology effectively: Models and practices. *Contemporary Issues in Technology & Teacher Education, 9*(1), 46–59.

Brzycki, D., & Dudt, K. (2005). Overcoming barriers to technology use in teacher preparation programs. *Journal of Technology and Teacher Education, 13*(4), 619–642.

Buckleitner, W. (2003). Turning collections into curriculum--Technically speaking. *Scholastic Early Childhood Today, 17*(6), 6–7.

Burley, D. (2010). Information visualization as a knowledge integration tool. *Journal of Knowledge Management Practice, 11*(4). Retrieved from http://www.tlainc.com/articl240.htm.

Burnett, C. (2009). Personal digital literacies versus classroom literacies: Investigating preservice teachers' digital lives in and beyond the classroom. In Carrington, V., & Robinson, M. (Eds.), *Digital literacies: Social learning and classroom practices* (pp. 115–129). Thousand Oaks, CA: Sage Publications.

Cairncross, F. (1997). *The death of distance: How the communications revolution is changing our lives.* Boston, MA: Harvard Business School Press.

Calabrese, N. M. (2006). Video technology: A vehicle for educators to enhance relationships with families. *Education, 127*(1), 155–160.

Calkins, L. (1994). *The art of teaching writing.* Portsmouth, NH: Heinemann.

Callahan, J., & Root, S. (2003). The diffusion of academic service-learning in teacher education: A case study approach. In S. H. Billig & J. Eyler (Eds.), *Advances in service-learning research: Vol. 3. Deconstructing service-learning: Research exploring context, participation, and impacts* (pp. 77–101). Greenwich, CT: Information Age.

Campbell, D. M., Cignetti, P. B., Melenyzer, B. J., Nettles, D. H., & Wyman, R. M. Jr. (2007). *How to develop a professional portfolio: A manual for teachers. NETS for Teachers 2008. International Society for Technology in Education.* Boston, MA: Pearson.

Cannon, L., Dorward, J., Heal, R., & Edwards, L. (1999). *National library of virtual manipulatives.* Utah State University. Retrieved from http://nlvm.usu.edu/en/nav/vlibrary.html

Capobianco, B. M. (2007). A self-study of the role of technology in promoting reflection and inquiry-based science teaching. *Journal of Science Teacher Education, 18*(2), 217–295. doi:10.1007/s10972-007-9041-z

Capps, A. (2009, September 16). *How to make your own podcast.* Retrieved from http://cappsaedm310fall2009.blogspot.com/2009/09/how-to-make-your-own-podcast.html

Cardinali, R., & Gordon, Z. (2002). Technology: Making things easier for all of us – For the disabled making things possible. *Equal Opportunities International, 21*(1), 65–79. doi:10.1108/02610150210787064

Carlson, R. D., & Gooden, J. S. (1999). Mentoring preservice teachers for technology skills acquisition. In J. Price, et al. (Eds.), *Proceedings of Society for Information Technology & Teacher Education International Conference 1999* (pp. 1313-1318). Chesapeake, VA: AACE.

Carlson, R. D., & Gooden, J. S. (1999). Are teacher preparation programs modeling technology use for pre-service teachers? *ERS Spectrum, 17*(3), 11–15.

Carroll, A. E., Rivara, F. P., Ebel, B., Zimmerman, F. J., & Christakis, D. A. (2005). Household computer and internet access: The digital divide in a pediatric clinic population. *AMIA Annual Symposium Proceedings,* (pp. 111-115). Retrieved on September 22, 2010 from http://www.ncbi.nlm.nih.gov/pmc/articles/PMC1560660/

Carter, K. (1990). Teachers' knowledge and learning to teach. In Houston, W. R., Huberman, M., & Sikula, J. (Eds.), *Handbook of research on teacher education* (pp. 291–310). New York, NY: MacMillan.

Carvin, A. (2010). *Using a wiki to promote educational blogging.* Retrieved September 12, 2010 from http://www.pbs.org/teachers/learning.now

Cassidy, S., & Eachus, P. (2002). Developing the computer user self-efficacy (CUSE) scale: Investigating the relationship between computer self-efficacy, gender and experience with computers. *Journal of Educational Computing Research, 26*(2), 133–153. doi:10.2190/JGJR-0KVL-HRF7-GCNV

CAST (Center for Applied Special Technology). (1998). *What is universal design for learning?* Wakefied, MA: Author. Retrieved from http://www.cast.org/research/udl/index.html

Castellani, J., & Warger, C. (Eds.). (2010). *Accessibility in action: Universal design for learning in postsecondary settings.* TAM Monograph Series.

Castelli, D. (2001). Using inquiry to create tech-savvy teachers. *The Chronicle of Kinesiology and Physical Education in Higher Education, 17*(1), 8-9. 13.

Castelli, D. M., & Fiorentino, L. (2004). The effects of different instruction on preservice teacher perceived ability and comfort with technology in physical education. *Research Quarterly for Exercise and Sport, 75*(1), 63.

Cavanaugh, C., Barbour, M. K., & Clark, T. (2009). Research and practice in K-12 online learning: A review of literature. *International Review of Research in Open and Distance Learning, 10*(1). Retrieved from http://www.irrodl.org/index.php/irrodl/article/view/607.

CDW-G. (2010). *The 2010 CDW-G 21st century classroom report: Preparing students for the future or the past?* Retrieved March 28, 2010, from http://newsroom.cdwg.com/features/

Cennamo, K. S., Ross, J. D., & Ertmer, P. A. (2010). *Technology integration for meaningful classroom use: A standards-based approach.* Belmont, CA: Wadsworth, Cengage Learning.

Center for Information and Research on Civic Learning and Engagement. (2007). *Classrooms produce positive civic outcomes for students: Results from a longitudinal study of Chicago public school students.* College Park, MD: CIRCLE.

Center for Universal Design. (1997). *Environments and products for all people.* Raleigh, NC: North Carolina State University, Center for Universal Design.

Cenzon, C. G. (2009). *Examining the role of various factors and experiences in technology integration: A description of a professional model* (Doctoral dissertation). Retrieved from ProQuest Dissertations and Theses, (AAT 3336176).

Chai, C. S., Koh, J. H. L., & Tsai, C.-C. (2010). Facilitating preservice teachers' development of technological, pedagogical, and content knowledge (TPACK). *Journal of Educational Technology & Society, 13*(4), 63–73.

Chalk & Wire. (2010). *Product overview.* Retrieved from http://chalkandwire.com/index.php/product/overview

Chen, J.-Q., & Chang, C. (2006). A comprehensive approach to technology training for early childhood teachers. *Early Education and Development, 17*(3), 443–465. doi:10.1207/s15566935eed1703_6

Chen, R.-J. (2010). Investigating models for preservice teachers' use of technology to support student-centered learning. *Computers & Education, 55*, 32–42. doi:10.1016/j.compedu.2009.11.015

Chilicott, L. (Producer), & Guggenheim, D. (Director). (2010). *Waiting for Superman* [Motion picture]. United States: Paramount Vantage and Participant Media.

Christensen, C. M., Horn, M. B., & Johnson, C. W. (2008). *Disrupting class: How disruptive innovation will change the way the world learns.* New York, NY: McGraw Hill.

Chun, D. M., & Plass, J. L. (1997). Research on text comprehension with multimedia. *Language Learning & Technology, 1*(1), 60–81.

Churches, A. (2009). *Bloom's digital taxonomy: It's not about the tools, it's using the tools to facilitate learning.* Retrieved September 20, 2010, from http://edorigami.wikispaces.com/file/view/bloom%27s+Digital+taxonomy+v3.01.pdf

Cisco Systems. (2006). *Technology in schools: What the research says.* Retrieved from http://www.cisco.com/web/strategy/docs/education/TechnologyinSchoolsReport.pdf.

Clark, T. (2000). *Virtual high schools: State of the states - A study of virtual high school planning and preparation in the United States.* Center for the Application of Information Technologies, Western Illinois University. Retrieved from http://www.imsa.edu/programs/ivhs/pdfs/stateofstates.pdf

Clark, T. (2001). *Virtual schools: Trends and issues - A study of virtual schools in the United States.* San Francisco, CA: Western Regional Educational Laboratories. Retrieved from http://www.wested.org/online_pubs/virtualschools.pdf

Clark, T. (2007). Virtual and distance education in North American schools. In Moore, M. G. (Ed.), *Handbook of distance education* (2nd ed.). Mahwah, NJ: Lawrence Erlbaum Associates, Inc.

Clark, T., & Else, D. (2003). Distance education, electronic networking and school policy. In Walling, D. R. (Ed.), *Virtual schooling: Issues in the development of e-learning policy* (pp. 31–45). Bloomington, IN: Phi Delta Kappa Educational Foundation.

Clements, D. H., & Meredith, J. S. (1993). Research on logo: Effects and efficacy. *Journal of Computing in Childhood Education, 4*(4), 263–290.

Clements, D. H., Nastasi, B. K., & Swaminathan, S. (1995). Young children and computers: Crossroads and directions from research. *Young Children, 48*(2), 56–64.

Clements, D. H., & Sarama, J. (2002). The role of technology in early childhood learning. *Teaching Children Mathematics, 8*(6), 340–343.

Clements, D. H., & Sarama, J. (2003a). Strip mining for gold: Research and policy in educational technology-A response to "Fool's Gold". *Educational Technology Review*, *11*(1).

Clements, D. H., & Sarama, J. (2003b). Young children and technology: What does the research say? *Young Children*, *58*(6), 34–40.

Cobb, P. (2001). Supporting the improvement of learning and teaching in social and institutional context. In Carver, S. M., & Klahr, D. (Eds.), *Cognition and instruction: Twenty-five years of progress* (pp. 455–478). Mahwah, NJ: Erlbaum.

Cobb, P., & Bowers, J. (1999). Cognitive and situated learning perspectives in theory and practice. *Educational Researcher*, *28*(2), 4–15.

Cobb, P., Confrey, J., diSessa, A., Lehrer, R., & Schauble, R. (2003). Design experiments in educational research. *Educational Researcher*, *32*(1), 9–13. doi:10.3102/0013189X032001009

Cobb, P., Stephan, M., McClain, K., & Gravemeijer, K. (2001). Participating in classroom mathematical practices. *Journal of the Learning Sciences*, *10*(1&2), 113–163. doi:10.1207/S15327809JLS10-1-2_6

Cobb, P., & Yackel, E. (1996). Constructivist, emergent, and sociocultural perspectives in the context of developmental research. *Educational Psychologist*, *31*(3/4), 175–190.

Cochrane, T. (2006). Learning with wireless mobile devices and social software. *Proceedings of the 23rd Annual ASCI-LITE Conference: Who's Learning? Whose Technology?* (pp. 143-146). Sydney, Australia. Retrieved from http://www.ascilite.org.au/conferences/sydney06/proceeding/pdf_papers/p50.pdf

Cochran-Smith, M., & Lytle, S. L. (1999). Relationships of knowledge and practice: Teacher learning in communities. *Review of Research in Education*, *24*, 249–305.

Cognition and Technology Group at Vanderbilt. (1990). Anchored instruction and its relationship to situated cognition. *Educational Researcher*, *19*(6), 2–10.

Cognition and Technology Group at Vanderbilt. (1997). *The Jasper project: Lessons in curriculum, instruction, assessment, and professional development*. Hillsdale, NJ: Erlbaum.

Cohen, D. K., & Ball, D. L. (1990). Policy and practice. *Educational Evaluation and Policy Analysis*, *12*(3), 233–239.

Cole, A. L. (1999). Teacher educators and teacher education reform: Individual commitments, institutional realities. *Canadian Journal of Education*, *24*(3), 281–295. Retrieved from http://www.csse.ca/CJE/Articles/FullText/CJE24-3/CJE24-3-Cole.pdf. doi:10.2307/1585876

Cole, M. (1998). *Cultural psychology: A once and future discipline*. Cambridge, MA: Harvard University Press.

Cole, M., & Griffin, P. (1980). Cultural amplifiers reconsidered. In Olson, D. (Ed.), *Social foundations of language and thought*. New York, NY: W.W. Norton.

Coley, R. J., Cradler, J., & Engel, P. K. (2000). *Computers and the classroom: The status of technology in U.S. schools*. Princeton, NJ: Policy Information Center, Educational Testing Service.

Collins, A. (1992). Toward a design science of education. In Scanlon, E., & O'Shea, T. (Eds.), *New directions in educational technology* (pp. 15–22). New York, NY: Springer-Verlag.

Collins, A., & Halverson, R. (2009). *Rethinking education in the age of technology: The digital revolution and schooling in America*. New York, NY: Teachers College Press.

Collis, B., & Moonen, J. (2008). Web 2.0 tools and processes in higher education: Quality perspectives. *Educational Media International*, *45*(2), 93–106. doi:10.1080/09523980802107179

Conole, G., Dyke, M., Oliver, M., & Seale, J. (2004). Mapping pedagogy and tools for effective learning design. *Computers & Education*, *43*(1-2), 17–33. doi:10.1016/j.compedu.2003.12.018

Conrad, D., & Hedin, D. (1982). The impact of experiential education on adolescent development. *Child and Youth Services*, *4*(3/4), 57–76. doi:10.1300/J024v04n03_08

Conrad, D., & Hedin, D. (1991). School-based community service: What we know from research and theory. *Phi Delta Kappan*, *72*(10), 743–749.

Considine, D., Horton, J., & Moorman, G. (2009). Teaching and reading the millennial generation through media literacy. *Journal of Adolescent & Adult Literacy*, *52*(6), 471–481. doi:10.1598/JAAL.52.6.2

Contemporary Issues in Technology and Teacher Education (CITE). (2008). *CITE Journal, 8*(3). Retrieved on October 10, 2008 from http://citejournal.org/vol8/iss3/maintoc.cfm?content=about

Cope, B., & Kalantzis, M. (2000). *Multiliteracies: Literacy learning and the design of social futures*. New York, NY: Routledge.

Cordes, C., & Miller, E. (2000). *Fool's gold: A critical look at computers in childhood*. Retrieved November 15, 2010, from http://drupal6.allianceforchildhood.org/fools_gold

Couros, A. (2009, December 3). *90+ videos for tech. & media literacy*. Retrieved from http://couros.wikispaces.com/TechAndMediaLiteracyVids

Couros, A. (2009, May 21). *90+ videos for tech. & media literacy*. Retrieved from http://educationaltechnology.ca/couros/1480

Cox, S., & Graham, C. (2009). Diagramming TPACK in practice: Using an elaborated model of the TPACK framework to analyze and depict teacher knowledge. *TechTrends, 53*(5), 60–69. doi:10.1007/s11528-009-0327-1

Craig, E. M. (2007). Changing paradigms: Managed learning environments and Web 2.0. *Campus-Wide Information Systems, 24*(3), 152–161. doi:10.1108/10650740710762185

Creswell, J. (2003). *Research design: Qualitative, quantitative, and mixed method approaches*. Thousand Oaks, CA: Sage Publications.

Creswell, J., & Clark, V. (2007). *Designing and conducting mixed methods research*. Thousand Oaks, CA: Sage Publications.

Cuban, L. (1986). *Teachers and machines*. New York, NY: Teachers College Press.

Cuban, L. (1986). *Teachers and machines: The classroom use of technology since 1920*. New York, NY: Teachers College Press.

Cuban, L. (2001). *Oversold and underused: Computers in the classroom*. Cambridge, MA: Harvard University Press.

Cuban, L., Kirkpatrick, H., & Peck, C. (2001). High access and low use of technologies in high school classrooms. *American Educational Research Journal, 38*(4), 813–834. doi:10.3102/00028312038004813

Cuban, L., Kirkpatrick, H., & Peck, C. (2001). High access and low use of technologies in high school classrooms: Explaining an apparent paradox. *American Educational Research Journal, 38*(4), 813–834. doi:10.3102/00028312038004813

Curts, J., Yanes, J., & McWright, B. (2003). Assessment of preservice teachers' Web-based electronic portfolio. *Education Technology for Teacher Preparation and Certification,* (pp. 92-98). Retrieved July 25, 2006, from http://www.nesinc.com/PDFs/2003_11Curts.pdf

Cyrs, T. (1997). Competence in teaching at a distance. *Teaching and Learning, 1997*(71), 15–18.

Cyrs, T. E. (1997). Competence in teaching at a distance. *New Directions for Teaching and Learning,* (71): 15–18. doi:10.1002/tl.7102

Darling-Hammond, L. (1998). Teachers and teaching: Testing policy hypotheses from a national commission report. *Educational Researcher, 27*(1), 5–15.

Darling-Hammond, L. (2010). *The flat world and education: How America's commitment to equity will determine our future*. New York, NY: Teachers College Press.

Davern, L. (1999). Parents' perspectives on personnel attitudes and characteristics in inclusive school settings: Implications for teacher preparations programs. *Teacher Education and Special Education, 22*, 165–182. doi:10.1177/088840649902200304

Davis, N. E. (2007, November). *Teacher education for virtual schools*. A presentation at Annual Virtual School Symposium, Louisville, KY. Retrieved from http://ctlt.iastate.edu/~tegivs/TEGIVS/publications/VS%20Symposium2007.pdf

Davis, N., & Rose, R. (2007). *Research committee issues brief: Professional development for virtual schooling and online learning*. Vienna, VA: North American Council for Online Learning. Retrieved from http://www.nacol.org/docs/NACOL_PDforVSandOlnLrng.pdf

Davis, N., Demiraslan, Y., & Wortmann, K. (2007, October). *Preparing to support online learning in K-12*. A presentation at the Iowa Educational Technology conference, Des Moines, IA. Retrieved from http://ctlt.iastate.edu/~tegivs/TEGIVS/publications/ITEC2007-presentations.pdf

Davis, N., Niederhauser, D., Compton, L., Lindstrom, D., & Schoeny, Z. (2005). Virtual schooling lab practice: Case studies for teacher preparation. *Proceedings of the International Conference of the Society for Information Technology and Teacher Education* (pp. 342-345). Norfolk, VA: Association for the Advancement of Computing in Education. Retrieved from http://ctlt.iastate.edu/~tegivs/TEGIVS/publications/conferenceproceedings2005.pdf

Davis, N., Roblyer, M. D., Ferdig, R., Schoeny, Z., Ellis, R., Demiraslan, Y., & Compton, L. K. L. (2007). Creating real tools & curriculum to prepare virtual teachers. In R. Carlsen et al. (Eds.), *Proceedings of Society for Information Technology & Teacher Education International Conference 2007* (pp. 281-285). Chesapeake, VA: AACE.

Davis, V. (2008, January 17). *It is about educational networking NOT social networking* [Web log comment]. Retrieved from http://coolcatteacher.blogspot.com/2008/01/it-is-about-educational-networking-not.html

Davis, A., & McGrail, E. (2009). Proof-revising with podcasting: Keeping readers in mind as students listen to and rethink their writing. *The Reading Teacher, 62*(6), 522–529. doi:10.1598/RT.62.6.6

Davis, K. S., & Falba, C. J. (2002). Integrating technology in elementary preservice teacher education: orchestrating scientific inquiry in meaningful ways. *Journal of Science Teacher Education, 13*(4), 303–329. doi:10.1023/A:1022535516780

Davis, N. E., & Roblyer, M. D. (2005). Preparing teachers for the "schools that technology built": Evaluation of a program to train teachers for virtual schooling. *Journal of Research on Technology in Education, 37*(4), 399–409.

Davis, N. E., Roblyer, M. D., Charania, A., Ferdig, R., Harms, C., Compton, L. K. L., & Cho, M. O. (2007). Illustrating the "virtual" in virtual schooling: Challenges and strategies for creating real tools to prepare virtual teachers. *The Internet and Higher Education, 10*(1), 27–39. Retrieved from http://ctlt.iastate.edu/~tegivs/TEGIVS/publications/JP2007%20davis&roblyer.pdf. doi:10.1016/j.iheduc.2006.11.001

Davis, N. M. (2003). Creating a learning community in the virtual classroom. In Walling, D. R. (Ed.), *Virtual schooling: Issues in the development of e-learning policy* (pp. 77–83). Bloomington, IN: Phi Delta Kappa Educational Foundation.

de Courcy, M., & Birch, G. (1993). *Reading and writing strategies used in a Japanese immersion program*. ERIC database.

de Leon, L., & Pena, C. (2010). Transformational learning in multimedia: Tracking the comfort levels of PSTs engaged in a disorienting dilemma. *International Journal of Instructional Media, 37*(2), 141–149.

Dean, D. (2008). *Genre theory: Teaching, writing, and being*. Urbana, IL: NCTE.

Dede, C. (2008, May/June). A seismic shift in epistemology. *EDUCAUSE Review*, (pp. 80–81). Retrieved March 4, 2009, from http://net.educause.edu/ir/library/pdf/ERM0837.pdf

DeJager, D., & Himberg, C. (2008). *Adventure racing activities for fun and fitness*. Champaign, IL: Human Kinetics.

Dewey, J. (1897). My pedagogic creed. *School Journal, 54*, 77–80.

Dewey, J. (1933). *How we think: A restatement of the relation of reflective thinking to the educative process*. New York, NY: Heath.

Dewey, J. (1991). *Logic: The theory of inquiry*. Carbondale, IL: Southern Illinois University Press.

Dexter, S. (1997). *Taxonomies and myths: A case study of technology planning and implementation*. Paper presented at SITE 97: The Eighth International Conference of the Society for Information Technology and Teacher Education, Orlando, Florida.

Dexter, S., Doering, A. H., & Riedel, E. S. (2006). Content area specific technology integration: A model for educating teachers. *Journal of Technology and Teacher Education, 14*(2), 325–345.

Dexter, S., Doering, A., & Riedel, E. (2006). Content area specific technology integration: A model for educating teachers. *Journal of Technology and Teacher Education, 14*(2), 325–345.

Dexter, S., & Riedel, E. (2003). Why improving preservice teacher educational technology preparation must go beyond the college's walls. *Journal of Teacher Education, 54*(4), 334–346. doi:10.1177/0022487103255319

Dickard, N., & Schneider, D. (2005). *The digital divide: Where we are today.* The George Lucas Foundation. Retrieved from http://www.edutopia.org/php/print.php?id=Art_995&template=printarticle.php

Dick, W., Carey, L., & Carey, J. O. (2005). *The systematic design of instruction* (6th ed.). Boston, MA: Allyn and Bacon.

Diego, J. P. S., Laurillard, D., Boyle, T., Bradley, C., Ljubojevic, D., & Neumann, T. (2008). Towards a user-oriented analytical approach to learning design. *ALT-J. Research in Learning Technology, 16*(1), 15–29. doi:10.1080/09687760701850174

Diem, R. A. (1982). *The role of technology in teacher education: Preparation for the twenty-first century classroom.* Paper presented at the Annual Meeting of the American Association of Colleges for Teacher Education.

Dillenbourg, P. (1999). What do you mean by collaborative learning? In Dillenbourg, P. (Ed.), *Collaborative-learning: Cognitive and computational approaches* (pp. 1–19). Oxford, UK: Elsevier.

Dillon, N. (2008). PhysTech: Schools are turning to technology to improve student health and wellness. *The American School Board Journal, 195*(3), 33–35.

DiPietro, M. (2010). Virtual school pedagogy: The instructional practices of K-12 virtual school teachers. *Journal of Educational Computing Research, 42*(3), 327–354. doi:10.2190/EC.42.3.e

DiPietro, M., Ferdig, R. E., Black, E. W., & Preston, M. (2008). Best practices in teaching K-12 online: Lessons learned from Michigan Virtual School teachers. *Journal of Interactive Online Learning, 7*(1). Retrieved from http://www.ncolr.org/jiol/issues/getfile.cfm?volID=7&IssueID=22&ArticleID=113.

DiSarno, N., Schowalter, M., & Grassa, P. (2002). Classroom amplification to enhance student performance. *Teaching Exceptional Children, 34*(6), 20–26.

diSessa, A. A. (2006). A history of conceptual change research: Threads and fault lines. In Sawyer, R. K. (Ed.), *The Cambridge handbook of the learning sciences* (pp. 265–282). New York, NY: Cambridge University Press.

Distance Education and Training Council. (2007-08). *Is distance education for you?* Distance Education and Training Council. Retrieved from http://www.detc.org/downloads/publications/Is%20Distance%20Education%20for%20You%207-08.pdf

Dixon, S., & Black, L. (1996). Vocal point: A collaborative, student run online newspaper. In Valauskas, E. J., & Ertel, M. (Eds.), *The Internet for teachers and school library media specialists: Today's applications tomorrow's prospects* (pp. 147–158). New York, NY: Neal-Schuman Publishers, Inc.

Docs, G. (n.d.). In *Wikipedia, The Free Encyclopedia.* Retrieved from http://en.wikipedia.org/w/index.php?title=Google_Docs&oldid=382349371

Dodge, B. (2010). *WebQuest.org.* Retrieved Sep 22, 2010, from http://webquest.org

Dodge, B. (1995). WebQuests: A technique for internet-based learning. *Distance Education, 1*(2), 10–13.

Doering, A., Hughes, J. E., & Huffman, D. (2003). Preservice teachers: Are we thinking with technology? *Journal of Research on Technology in Education, 35*(3), 342–361.

Donald, C., Blake, A., Girault, I., Datt, A., & Ramsay, E. (2009). Approaches to learning design: Past the head and the hands to the HEART of the matter. *Distance Education, 30*(2), 179–199. doi:10.1080/01587910903023181

D'Orio, W. (2010, October 2). The power of project learning. [Editorial]. *Scholastic Administrator,* 1-2.

Dorman, S. M. (2001). Are teachers using computers for instruction? *The Journal of School Health, 71,* 83–84. doi:10.1111/j.1746-1561.2001.tb06500.x

Dreon, O., & Marcum-Dietrich, N. (2010). *The Ning is the thing: Supporting interns through social networking.* Paper presented at the Professional Development Schools National Conference, Orlando, FL.

Dreon, O. Jr, & Dietrich, N. I. (2009). Turning lemons into lemonade: Teaching assistive technology through Wikis and embedded video. *TechTrends: Linking Research and Practice to Improve Learning, 53*(1), 78–80.

Drexler, W. (2008). *The networked student* [Video]. Retrieved from http://www.youtube.com/watch?v=XwM4ieFOotA&feature=player_embedded#!

Drijvers, P. H. M. (2003). *Learning algebra in a computer algebra environment* (doctoral dissertation). Utrecht, The Netherlands: Freudenthal Institute.

DuFour, R., & Eaker, R. (1998). *Professional learning communities at work: Best practices for enhancing student achievement. Bloomington, IN: National Educational Service and Alexandria.* VA: Association of Supervision and Curriculum Development.

Duncan, A. (2010). Teacher preparation: Reforming the uncertain profession. *Education Digest, 75*(5), 13–22.

Duncan, H. (2005). On-line education for practicing professionals: A case study. *Canadian Journal of Education, 28*(4), 874–896. Retrieved from http://www.csse.ca/CJE/Articles/FullText/CJE28-4/CJE28-4-duncan.pdf. doi:10.2307/4126459

Duran, M., Fossum, P. R., & Luera, G. R. (2006). Technology and pedagogical renewal: Conceptualizing technology integration into teacher preparation. *Computers in the Schools, 23*(3/4), 31–54.

Duran, M., Runvand, S., & Fossum, P. R. (2009). Preparing science teachers to teach with technology: Exploring a K-16 networked learning community approach. *Turkish Online Journal of Distance Education, 8*(4), 21–42.

Dusick, D. M. (1998). What social cognitive factors influence faculty members' use of computers for teaching? A literature review. *Journal of Research on Computing in Education, 31*(2), 123–137.

Dymond, S. K., Renzaglia, A., Rosenstein, A., Chun, E. J., Banks, R. A., Niswander, V., & Gilson, C. L. (2006). Using a participatory action research approach to create a universally designed inclusive high school science course: A case study. *Research and Practice for Persons with Severe Disabilities, 31*, 293–308.

Earle, R. S. (2002). The integration of instructional technology into public education: Promises and challenges. *ET Magazine, 42*(1), 5–13.

Easton, S. (2003). Clarifying the instructor's role in on-line distance learning. *Communication Education, 52*(2), 87–105. doi:10.1080/03634520302470

Economopoulos, K., & Wright, T. (1998). *How many pockets? How many teeth?* White Plains, NY: Dale Seymour Publications.

Edgerton, R. (1991-1992). On the road with Russell Edgerton: AAHE's on-going salon on teaching. *The National Teaching and Learning Forum, 1*, 1–6.

Edginton, C., & Kirkpatrick, P. (2007). Teaching with technology: Leading physical education into the 21st century. *Sports International, 2*(4), 138–144.

Edublog. (2011, February 5). *Student blogging challenge.* Retrieved from http://studentchallenge.edublogs.org/

Education Report, 13(2). Retrieved from http://blogs.ubc.ca/distanceteaching/files/2009/11/How-Would-You-Rank-the-Critical- Competencies-for-Teaching-Online.pdf

Edyburn, D. L. (2006a). Assistive technology and mild disabilities. *Special Education Technology Practice, 8*(4), 18–28.

Edyburn, D. L. (2006b). Failure is not an option. *Learning and Leading with Technology, 34*(1), 20–23.

Eijkman, H. (2010). Dancing with ostmodernity: Web 2.0+ as a new epistemic learning space. In Lee, M. J. W., & McLoughlin, C. (Eds.), *Web 2.0-based e-learning* (pp. 343–364). Hershey, PA: IGI Global. doi:10.4018/978-1-60566-294-7.ch018

Eisenberg, A. (2008, August 31). Lines and bubbles and bars, oh my! New ways to sift data. *New York Times.* Retrieved from http://www.nytimes.com

Eisenberg, M. B., & Berkowitz, R. E. (1990). *Information problem-solving: The big six skills approach to library & information skills instruction.* Norwood, NJ: Ablex.

Eisner, E. (1992). Educational reform and the ecology of schooling. *Teachers College Record, 93*(4). Teachers College. Columbia University.

Elliot, E., & Manross, M. (1996). Physical educators and the internet: Part II: The World Wide Web. *Teaching Elementary Physical Education, 7*(5), 12–15.

Erstad, O. (2002). Norwegian students using digital artifacts in project-based learning. *Journal of Computer Assisted Learning, 18*, 427–437. doi:10.1046/j.0266-4909.2002.00254.x

Ertmer, P. A. (1999). Addressing first- and second-order barriers to change: Strategies for technology integration. *Educational Technology, Research and Development, 47*(4), 47. (Document ID: 47696907).

Ertmer, P. A. (2005). Teacher pedagogical beliefs: The final frontier in our quest for technology integration. *Educational Technology Research and Development, 53*(4), 25–39. doi:10.1007/BF02504683

Ertmer, P. A., & Newby, T. J. (1993). Behaviorism, cognitivism, constructivism: Comparing critical features from an instructional design perspective. *Performance Improvement Quarterly, 6*(4), 50–70. doi:10.1111/j.1937-8327.1993.tb00605.x

Ertmer, P. A., & Ottenbreit-Leftwich, A. T. (2010). Teacher technology change: How knowledge, beliefs, and culture intersect. *Journal of Research on Technology in Education, 42*, 255–284.

Ertmer, P., & Ottenbreit-Leftwich, A. (2010). Teacher technology change: How knowledge, confidence, beliefs, and culture intersect. *Journal of Research on Technology in Education, 42*(3), 255–284.

Evans, R. (1996). *The human side of school change: Reform, resistance, and the real-life problems of innovation.* San Francisco, CA: Jossey-Bass Publishers.

Facebook. (2010). *Statistics.* Retrieved September 28, 2010, from http://www.facebook.com/facebook?v=app_10531514314#!/press/info.php?statistics

Fagan, B. (2003). Scaffolds to help ELL readers. *Voices from the Middle, 11*(1), 38–42.

Falvo, D. A., & Johnson, B. F. (2007). The use of learning management systems in the United States. *TechTrends, 51*(2), 40–45. doi:10.1007/s11528-007-0025-9

Feiman-Nemser, S. (2001). From preparation to practice: Designing a continuum to strengthen and sustain teaching. *Teachers College Record, 103*(6), 1013–1055. doi:10.1111/0161-4681.00141

Ferdig, R. (2007). Examining social software in teacher education. *Journal of Technology and Teacher Education, 15*(1), 5–10.

Ferdig, R. E., Cavanaugh, C., DiPietro, M., Black, E. W., & Dawson, K. (2010). Virtual schooling standards and best practices for teacher education. *Journal of Technology and Teacher Education, 17*(4), 479–503.

Fewell, P. J., & Gibbs, W. J. (2003). *Microsoft Office for teachers.* Upper Saddle River, NJ: Merrill Prentice Hall.

Fiorentino, L. H., & Gibbone, A. (2005). Using the virtual gym for practice and drills. *Teaching Elementary Physical Education, 16*(5), 14–16.

Fisher, D., Frey, N., & Thousand, J. (2003). What do special educators need to know and be prepared to do for inclusive schooling to work? *Teacher Education and Special Education, 26*(1), 42–50. doi:10.1177/088840640302600105

Fleming, L., Motamedi, V., & May, L. (2007). Predicting preservice teacher competence in computer technology: Modeling and application in training environments. *Journal of Technology and Teacher Education, 15*(2), 207–231.

Fletcher, R., & Portalupi, J. (2001). *Writing workshop: The essential guide.* Portsmouth, NH: Heinemann.

Florida Virtual School. (2010). *About us.* Retrieved from http://flvs.net/areas/aboutus/Pages/default.aspx

Foltos, L. (2002). *Technology and academic achievement.* Retrieved September 6, 2010, from http://www.newhorizons.org/strategies/ foltos.htm

Foote, C. (2009, July). It's a mad mad Wordle. *School Library Journal, 55*(7), 32–34.

Forbus, W. R., & Mills, B. D. (1997). The future of technology in physical education. *Journal of Interdisciplinary Research in Physical Education, 2*(2).

Forman, G. (2002). *Wondering with children: The goals, strategies, and theories of ordinary moments.* Paper presented at the Reggio Conference, Seoul, Korea.

Forman, G. (1999). Instant video revisiting: The video camera as a "tool of the mind" for young children. *Early Childhood Research & Practice, 1*(2), 1–8.

Forum, C. E. O. (1999). *Professional development: A link to better learning.* Washington, DC: Author.

Fosnot, C. (Ed.). (2005). *Constructivism: Theory, perspectives and practice.* New York, NY: Teachers College Press.

Foulger, T., Williams, M. K., & Wetzel, K. (2008). *Innovative technologies, small groups, and a wiki: A 21st century preservice experience founded on collaboration.* Proceedings from NECC 2008. San Antonio, TX: ISTE.

Foulger, T., Williams, M. K., & Wetzel, K. (2008). We innovate: The role of collaboration in exploring new technologies. *International Journal of Teaching and Learning in Higher Education, 20*(1), 28–38.

Franklin, T., & Van Harmelen, M. (2007). *Web 2.0 for content for learning and teaching in higher education.* Bristol, UK: JISC. Retrieved September 23, 2010, from http://ie-repository.jisc.ac.uk/148/1/web2-content-learning-and-teaching.pdf

Franklin, T., Turner, S., Kariuki, M., & Duran, M. (2001). Mentoring overcomes barriers to technology integration. *Journal of Computing in Teacher Education, 18*(1), 26–31.

Franklin, T., & Van Harmelen, M. (2007). *Web 2.0 for content for learning and teaching in higher education.* London, UK: Joint Information Systems Committee.

Freed, G., & Rothberg, M. (2006). *Accessible digital media guidelines.* Retrieved from the http://ncam.wgbh.org/invent_build/web_multimedia/accessible-digital-media-guide

Freeman, N. K., & Swick, K. J. (2003). Preservice interns implement service learning: Helping young children reach out to their community. *Early Childhood Education Journal, 31*(2), 107–112. doi:10.1023/B:ECEJ.0000005309.44716.06

Frey, T. J. (2008). Determining the impact of online practicum facilitation for in-service teachers. *Journal of Technology and Teacher Education, 16*, 181–210.

Friedman, T. L. (2006). *The world is flat [Updated and Expanded]: A brief history of the twenty-first century.* New York, NY: Farrar, Straus and Giroux.

Friedman, T. (2007). The world is flat: A brief history of the twenty-first century: *Vol. 1. Further expanded.* New York, NY: Picador.

Friedman, T. L. (2006). *The world is flat: A brief history of the twenty-first century.* New York: Farrar, Straus and Giroux.

Friel, T., Britten, J., Compton, B., Peak, A., Schoch, K., & VanTyle, W. (2009). Using pedagogical dialogue as a vehicle to encourage faculty technology use. *Computers & Education, 53*(2), 300–307. doi:10.1016/j.compedu.2009.02.002

Friend, B., & Johnston, S. (2005). Florida Virtual School: A choice for all students. In Berge, Z. L., & Clark, T. (Eds.), *Virtual schools: Planning for success* (pp. 97–117). New York, NY: Teachers College Press.

Fullan, M. (1993). *Change forces: Probing the depths of educational reform.* London, UK: Falmer Press.

Fullan, M. (2001). *Leading in a culture of change.* San Francisco, CA: Jossey-Bass.

Fullan, M. (2007). *The new meaning of educational change* (4th ed.). New York, NY: Teachers College.

Fulton, K., Glenn, A. D., & Valdez, G. (2004). *Teacher education and technology planning guide.* Naperville, IL: Learning Point Associates.

Gabriel, M. A., & MacDonald, C. J. (1996). Preservice teacher education students and computers: How does intervention affect attitude? *Journal of Technology and Teacher Education, 4*(2).

Gagné, R. M., & Briggs, L. (1979). *Principles of instructional design.* New York, NY: Holt, Rinehart, & Winston.

Gao, P., Wong, A., Choy, D., & Wu, J. (2010). Developing leadership potential for technology integration: Perspectives of three beginning teachers. *Australasian Journal of Educational Technology, 26*(5), 643–658.

Gardner, H. (2007). *Five minds for the future.* Boston, MA: Harvard Business School Publishing.

Gaskill, M., McNulty, A., & Brooks, D. W. (2006). Learning from WebQuests. *Journal of Science Education and Technology, 15*(2), 133–136. doi:10.1007/s10956-006-9005-7

Gaver, W. W. (1991). Technology affordances. In S. P. Scott, G. M. Olson, & J. S. Olson (Eds.), *Proceedings of CHI '91* (pp. 79-84). New Orleans, LA: ACM Press.

Gee, J. P. (2002). Millennials and bobos. *Blue's Clues* and *Sesame Street*: A story for our times. In Alvermann, D. (Ed.), *Adolescents and literacies in a digital world* (pp. 51–67). New York, NY: Peter Lang.

Gee, J. P. (2003). *What video games have to teach us about learning and literacy.* New York, NY: Palgrave Macmillan.

Georgia Statewide Academic & Medical System (GSAMS) receives business & industry partnership award at IDLCON Distance Learning Conference in Washington, D.C. (1995, March 24). *Business Wire*. Retrieved from http://www.highbeam.com/doc/1G1-16705164.html

Georgia, V. I. E. W. (2010). *University system of Georgia: GeorgiaVIEW*. Retrieved from http://www.usg.edu/gaview/

Gibson, S. (2009). *Are our preservice teachers prepared to teach in a digital age?* Paper presented at the World Conference on E-Learning in Corporate, Government, Healthcare, and Higher Education (E-LEARN) 2009, Vancouver, Canada.

Gibson, J. J. (1986). *The ecological approach to visual perceptions*. Hillsdale, NJ: Erlbaum.

Gilbert, S. (2002). *The beauty of low threshold applications*. Retrieved September 1, 2010, from http://www.tltgroup.org/gilbert/Columns/BeautyLTAs2-2-2002.htm

Gilbert, S. (2006). *TLT/Collaborative change: Low threshold applications (LTAs)*. Retrieved August 24, 2010, from http://www.tltgroup.org/resources/rltas.html

Gillingham, M. G., & Topper, A. (1999). Technology in teacher preparation: Preparing teachers for the future. *Journal of Technology and Teacher Education, 7*(4), 303–321.

Gimbert, B., & Cristol, D. (2004). Teaching curriculum with technology: Enhancing children's technological competence during early childhood. *Early Childhood Education Journal, 31*(3), 207–216. doi:10.1023/B:ECEJ.0000012315.64687.ee

Gladwell, M. (2002). *The tipping point: How little things can make big difference*. New York, NY: Time Warner Book Group.

Glaser, M. (2007). *Your guide to the digital divide*. PBS. Retrieved from http://www.pbs.org/mediashift/2007/01/your-guide-to-the-digital-divide017.html

Glasser, B. G., & Strauss, A. L. (1967). *The discovery of grounded theory: Strategies for qualitative research*. New York, NY: Aldine.

Godfrey, D. (1979). Introduction. In Godfrey, D., & Parkhill, D. (Eds.), *Gutenberg two: The new electronics and social change*. Toronto, Canada: Press Porcépic.

Goldman, R., Pea, R., Barron, B., & Derry, S. (2007). *Video research in the learning sciences*. Mahwah, NJ: Lawarence Erlbaum Associates.

Good, A. J. O'Connor, K. A., Greene, H. C., & Luce, E. (2005). Collaborating across the miles: Telecollaboration in a social studies methods course. *Contemporary Issues in Technology & Teacher Education, 5*(3/4).

Good, A. J., O'Connor, K. A., Greene, H. C., & Luce, E. F. (2005). Collaborating across the miles: Telecollaboration in a social studies methods course. *Contemporary Issues in Technology & Teacher Education, 5*(3/4), 300–317.

Goodlad, J. (1994). *Educational renewal*. San Francisco, CA: Jossey-Bass Publishers.

Grabe, M., & Grabe, C. (2007). *Integrating technology for meaningful learning* (5th ed.). New York, NY: Houghton Mifflin Company.

Grabowski, J. (1996). Writing and speaking: Common grounds and differences. Towards a regulation theory of written language production. In Levy, M., & Ransdell, S. (Eds.), *The science of writing (pp. 73–91)*. Hillsdale, NJ: Erlbaum.

Graham, C. R., Tripp, T., & Wentworth, N. (2009). Assessing and improving technology integration skills for preservice teachers using the teacher work sample. *Journal of Educational Computing Research, 41*(1), 39–62. doi:10.2190/EC.41.1.b

Graham, C., Culatta, R., Pratt, M., & West, R. (2004). Redesigning the teacher education technology course to emphasize integration. *Computers in the Schools, 21*, 127–148. doi:10.1300/J025v21n01_10

Graham, L. (2009). It was a challenge but we did it! Digital worlds in a primary classroom. *Literacy, 43*(2), 107–114. doi:10.1111/j.1741-4369.2009.00520.x

Grant, M., & Branch, R. (2005). Project-based learning in a middle school: Tracing abilities through artifacts of learning. *Journal of Research on Technology in Education, 38*(1), 65–98.

Gravemeijer, K., & Cobb, P. (2006). Design research from a learning design perspective. In van den Akker, J., Gravemeijer, K., McKenney, S., & Nieveen, N. (Eds.), *Educational design research*. London, UK: Routledge.

Graves, D. (1983). *Writing: Teachers and students at work*. Portsmouth, NH: Heinemann.

Gray, L., Thomas, N., & Lewis, L. (2010). *Teachers' use of educational technology in U.S. public schools: 2009 (NCES 2010-040)*. Washington, DC: National Center for Education Statistics, Institute of Education Sciences, U.S. Department of Education.

Greenfield, S. (2003). *Tomorrow's people: How 21st-century technology is changing the way we think and feel*. London: Penguin Books Ltd.

Greenhow, C., & Robelia, B. (2009). Old communication, new literacies. Social network sites as social learning resources. *Journal of Computer-Mediated Communication, 14*(4), 1130–1161. doi:10.1111/j.1083-6101.2009.01484.x

Greenhow, C., Robelia, B., & Hughes, J. E. (2009). Learning, teaching, and scholarship in a digital age: Web 2.0 and classroom research: What path should we take now? *Educational Researcher, 38*(4), 246–259. doi:10.3102/0013189X09336671

Greenhow, C., Robelia, B., & Hughes, J. E. (2009a). Learning, teaching, and scholarship in a digital age: Web 2.0 and classroom research: What path should we take now? *Educational Researcher, 38*(4), 246–259. doi:10.3102/0013189X09336671

Greenhow, C., Robelia, B., & Hughes, J. E. (2009b). Research on learning and teaching with Web 2.0: Bridging conversations. *Educational Researcher, 38*(4), 280–283. doi:10.3102/0013189X09336675

Greeno, J. G., Collins, A., & Resnick, L. B. (1996). Cognition and learning. In D. C. Berliner & R. C, Calfee (Eds.), *Handbook of educational psychology*. New York, NY: Macmillan.

Greeno, J. (1989). The situativity of knowing, learning, and research. *The American Psychologist, 53*(1), 5–26. doi:10.1037/0003-066X.53.1.5

Greeno, J. G., Collins, A., & Resnick, L. B. (1996). Cognition and learning. In Berliner, D., & Calfee, R. (Eds.), *Handbook of educational psychology*. New York, NY: MacMillan.

Greenway, R., & Vanourek, G. (2006). The virtual revolution: Understanding online schools. *Education Next* (2). Retrieved from http://www.hoover.org/publications/ednext/3210506.html

Gronseth, S., Brush, T., Ottenbreit-Leftwich, A., Strycker, J., Abaci, S., & Easterling, W. (2010). Equipping the next generation of teachers: Technology preparation and practice. *Journal of Digital Learning in Teacher Education, 27*(1), 30–36.

Gross, D. (2010). Report: Older users flocking to Facebook, Twitter. *CNN Tech*. Retrieved August 27, 2010, from http://www.cnn.com/2010/TECH/social.media/08/27/older.users.social.networks/index.html

Grossman, P. L. (1989). A study in contrast: Sources of pedagogical content knowledge for secondary English. *Journal of Teacher Education, 40*(5), 24–31. doi:10.1177/002248718904000504

Grossman, P. L. (1990). *The making of a teacher: Teacher knowledge and teacher education*. New York, NY: Teachers College Press.

Grossman, P. L. (1991). Overcoming the apprenticeship of observation in teacher education coursework. *Teaching and Teacher Education, 7*, 245–257. doi:10.1016/0742-051X(91)90004-9

Grossman, P., Wineburg, S., & Woolworth, S. (2001). Toward a theory of teacher community. *Teachers College Record, 103*, 942–1012. doi:10.1111/0161-4681.00140

Groth, R., Spickler, D., Bergner, J., & Bardzell, M. (2009). A qualitative approach to assessing technological pedagogical content knowledge. [CITE Journal]. *Contemporary Issues in Technology & Teacher Education, 9*(4), 392–411.

Grove, K., Strudler, N., & Odell, S. (2004). Mentoring toward technology use: cooperating teacher practice in supporting student teachers. *Journal of Research on Technology in Education, 37*(1), 85–109.

Gruenberg, A. M., & Miller, R. (2011). *A practical guide to early childhood inclusion: Effective reflection*. Upper Saddle River, NJ: Pearson.

Grunwald Associates LLC. (2010). *Educators, technology and 21st century skills: Dispelling five myths*. Retrieved from www.WaldenU.edu/fivemyths 08-10-2010

Grunwald Associates. (2010). *Educators, technology and 21st century skills: Dispelling five myths.* Retrieved October 10, 2010, from http://www.waldenu.edu/Documents/Degree-Programs/Full_Report_-_Dispelling_Five_Myths.pdf

Guerrero, S. (2010). Technological pedagogical content knowledge in the mathematics classroom. *Journal of Digital Learning in Education, 26*(4), 132–139.

Guide, M. I. L. E. Milestones for Improving Learning and Education. (2001). *Partnership for 21st Century Skills.* Retrieved from http://www.p21.org/documents/MILE_Guide_091101.pdf

Gulchak, D. J. (2008). The special ways of handhelds. *District Administration, 44*(8), 22–23.

Gura, M., & Percy, B. (2005). *Recapturing technology for education - Keeping tomorrow in today's classrooms.* Lanham, MD: Scarecrow Education.

Gutierrez, K., Rymes, B., & Larson, J. (1995). Script, counterscript, and underlife in the classroom - Brown, James versus Brown v. Board of Education. *Harvard Educational Review, 65*, 445–471.

Guy, M. D., & Li, Q. (2002). *Integrating technology into an elementary mathematics methods course: Assessing the impact on pre-service teachers perception to use and teach with technology.* New Orleans, LA: Paper presented at The Annual Meeting of the American Educational Research Association annual meeting.

Guzdial, M., Rick, J., & Kehoe, C. (2001). Beyond adoption to invention: Teacher-created collaborative activities in higher education. *Journal of the Learning Sciences, 10*(3), 265–279. doi:10.1207/S15327809JLS1003_2

Hakkarainen, P. (2009). Designing and implementing a PBL course on educational digital video production: Lessons learned from design-based research. *Educational Technology Research and Development, 57*, 211–228. doi:10.1007/s11423-007-9039-4

Halat, E. (2008). The effects of designing Webquests on the motivation of pre-service elementary school teachers. *International Journal of Mathematical Education in Science and Technology, 39*(6), 793–802. doi:10.1080/00207390802054466

Hall, G., & Hord, S. (1987). *Change in schools: facilitating the process.* Albany, NY: State University of New York press.

Hall, G., & Hord, S. (2006). *Implementing change: Patterns, principles, and potholes.* Boston, MA: Allyn & Bacon.

Halverson, R., & Smith, A. (2010). How new technologies have (and have not) changed teaching and learning in schools. *Journal of Computing in Teacher Education, 26*(2), 6.

Hamilton, B. (2009, August 30). Poetry goes 2.0. *Library Media Connection,* 26–29.

Hamm, E. M., Mistrett, S. G., & Ruffino, A. G. (2006). Play outcomes and satisfaction with toys and technology of young children with special needs. *Journal of Special Education Technology, 21*(1), 29–35.

Hammerness, K., Darling-Hammond, L., & Bransford, J. (2005). How teachers learn and develop. In Darling-Hammond, L., & Bransford, J. (Eds.), *Preparing teachers for a changing world* (pp. 358–389). San Francisco, CA: Jossey-Bass.

Hammerness, K., Darling-Hammond, L., Bransford, J., Berliner, D., Cochran-Smith, M., & McDonald, M. (2005). How teachers learn and develop. In Darling-Hammond, L., & Bransford, J. (Eds.), *Preparing teachers for a changing world: What teachers should learn and be able to do.* San Francisco, CA: Jossey-Bass.

Hammond, M. (2009). What is an affordance and can it help us understand the use of ICT in education? *Education and Information Technologies, 15*(3), 205–217. doi:10.1007/s10639-009-9106-z

Hannum, W. H., Irvin, M. J., Lei, P.-W., & Farmer, T. W. (2008). Effectiveness of using learner-centered principles on student retention in distance education courses in rural schools. *Distance Education, 29*, 211–229. doi:10.1080/01587910802395763

Hardy, M. (2003). *It should have been stressed in all education classes: Preparing preservice teachers to teach with technology.* Paper presented at the Annual Meeting of the American Educational Research Association, Chicago, IL, April, 21-25, 2003. (ERIC Document Reproduction Service ED 478 379).

Hardy, M. D. (2003). *"It should have been stressed in all education classes": Preparing pre-service teachers to teach with technology.* Searcy, AR: Harding University. ERIC Document Reproduction Service No. ED478379. Retrieved from http://www.eric.ed.gov/ERICWebPortal/contentdelivery/servlet/ERICServlet?accno=ED478379

Hardy, M. (2010). Enhancing preservice mathematics teachers' TPCK. *Journal of Computers in Mathematics and Science Teaching, 29*(1), 73–86.

Hargadon, S. (2010). Educational networking: The role of Web 2.0 in education. *MultiMedia & Internet @Schools.* Retrieved from http://www.mmischools.com/Articles/Editorial/Features/Educational-Networking-The-Role-of-Web-2.0-in-Education-5bAvailable-Full-Text2c-Free5d-61342.aspx

Hargrave, C. P., & Hsu, Y. (2000). Survey of instructional technology courses for preservice teachers. *Journal of Technology and Teacher Education, 8*(4), 303–314.

Harms, C. M., Niederhauser, D. S., Davis, N. E., Roblyer, M. D., & Gilbert, S. B. (2006). Educating educators for virtual schooling: Communicating roles and responsibilities. *The Electronic Journal of Communication, 16*(1-2). Retrieved from http://ctlt.iastate.edu/~tegivs/TEGIVS/publications/JP2007%20harms&niederhauser.pdf

Harrington, R. A. (2008). *The development of pre-service teachers' technology specific pedagogy.* (Unpublished doctoral dissertation). Oregon State University, Corvallis, OR.

Harris, J. B., Grandgenett, N., & Hofer, M. (2010, March). *Testing a TPACK-based technology integration assessment rubric.* Paper presented at the Annual Meeting of the Society for Information Technology and Teacher Education (SITE), San Diego, CA.

Harris, J. (1999). First steps in telecollaboration. *Learning and Leading with Technology, 27*(3), 54–57.

Harris, J., Mishra, P., & Koehler, M. (2009). Teachers' technological pedagogical content knowledge and learning activity types: Curriculum-based technology integration reframed. *Journal of Research on Technology in Education, 41*(4), 393–416.

Harris, J., Mishra, P., & Koehler, M. J. (2009). Teachers' technological pedagogical content knowledge and learning activity types: Curriculum-based technology integration reframed. *Journal of Research on Technology in Education, 41*(4).

Harris, L. (2010). Project based learning. In Evers, R. B., & Spencer, S. (Eds.), *Planning effective instruction for students with learning and behavior problems.* Columbus, OH: Merrill / Pearson Publishers.

Harskamp, E. G., Suhre, C. J. M., & Van Streun, A. (2000). The graphics calculator and students' solution strategies. *Mathematics Education Research Journal, 12*(1), 37–52. doi:10.1007/BF03217073

Hartnell-Young, E., & Morriss, M. (1999). *Digital professional portfolios for change.* Arlington Heights, IL: Skylight Professional Development.

Hart, S. M., & King, J. R. (2007). Service learning and literacy tutoring: Academic impact on preservice teachers. *Teaching and Teacher Education, 23*(4), 323–338. doi:10.1016/j.tate.2006.12.004

Hassel, B. C., & Terrell, M. G. (2004). *How can virtual schools be a part of meeting the choice provisions of the No Child Left Behind Act?* U.S. Department of Education Secretary's no Child Left Behind Leadership Summit, Increasing Options Through E-learning. Retrieved from http://www2.ed.gov/about/offices/list/os/technology/plan/2004/site/documents/Hassel-Terrell-VirtualSchools.pdf

Haughey, M., & Muirhead, W. (1999). *On-line learning: Best practices for Alberta school jurisdictions.* Edmonton, AB: Government of Alberta. Retrieved from http://www.phrd.ab.ca/technology/best_practices/on-line-learning.pdf

Hawley, W. D., & Valli, L. (1999). The essentials of effective professional development. In Darling-Hammond, L., & Sykes, G. (Eds.), *Teaching as the learning profession: Handbook of policy and practice* (pp. 127–150). San Francisco, CA: Jossey-Bass.

Haydn, T. A., & Barton, R. (2007). Common needs and different agendas: How trainee teachers make progress in their ability to use ICT in subject teaching. Some lessons from the UK. *Computers & Education, 49*(4), 1018–1036. doi:10.1016/j.compedu.2005.12.006

Healy, J. M. (1999). *Failure to connect: How computers affect our children's minds – for better or worse.* New York: Simon & Schuster.

Heath, S. B., & Street, B. (2008). *On ethnography: Approaches to language and literacy research.* New York, NY: Teachers College Press.

Hennessy, S., Ruthven, K., & Brindley, S. (2005). Teacher perspectives on integrating ICT into subject teaching: Commitment, constraints, caution, and change. *Journal of Curriculum Studies, 37,* 155–192. doi:10.1080/0022027032000276961

Heraclitus. (n.d.). *BrainyQuote.com.* Retrieved from http://www.brainyquote.com/quotes/quotes/h/heraclitus107157.html

Herrington, J., Reeves, T. C., & Oliver, R. (2005). Online learning as information delivery: Digital myopia. *Journal of Interactive Learning Research, 16*(4), 353–367.

Hertzog, N., & Klein, M. (2005). Beyond gaming: A technology explosion in early childhood classrooms. *Gifted Child Today, 28*(3), 24–31.

He, W., & Hartley, K. (2010). A supporting framework of online technology resources for lesson planning. *Journal of Educational Multimedia and Hypermedia, 19*(1), 23–37.

Hew, K. F., & Brush, T. (2007). Integrating technology in K-12 teaching and learning: Current knowledge gaps and recommendations for future research. *Educational Technology Research and Development, 55*(3), 223–252. doi:10.1007/s11423-006-9022-5

Hew, K., & Brush, T. (2007). Integrating technology into K-12 teaching and learning: Current knowledge gaps and recommendations for future research. *Educational Technology Research and Development, 55*(3), 223–252. doi:10.1007/s11423-006-9022-5

Hicks, L., & Higgins, J. (2010). Exergaming: Syncing physical activity and learning. *Strategies: A Journal for Physical and Sport Educators, 42*(1), 18-21.

Hicks, D., & Ewing, E. (2003). Bringing the world into the classroom with online global newspapers. *Social Education, 67*(3), 134–139.

Hicks, T., Russo, A., Autrey, T., Gardner, R., Kabodian, A., & Edington, C. (2007). Rethinking the purposes and processes for designing digital portfolios. *Journal of Adolescent & Adult Literacy, 50*(6), 450–458. doi:10.1598/JAAL.50.6.3

Higher-Order Thinking Skills. (2010). Retrieved September 25, 2010, from http://www97.intel.com/pk/projectdesign/thinkingskills/higherthinking/

Hill, H. C. (2004). Professional development standards and practices in elementary school mathematics. *The Elementary School Journal, 104*(3), 215–231. doi:10.1086/499750

Hitchcock, C., & Stahl, S. (2004). Assistive technology, universal design, universal design for learning: Improved learning outcomes. *Journal of Special Education Technology, 18,* 45–52.

Hmelo-Silver, C. E., & Barrow, H. S. (2008). Facilitating collaborative knowledge building. *Cognition and Instruction, 26,* 48–94. doi:10.1080/07370000701798495

Hodges, C. B. (2004). Designing to motivate: Motivational techniques to incorporate in e-learning experiences. *Journal of Interactive Online Learning, 2*(3).

Hofstede, G. (2001). *Culture's consequences: Comparing values, behaviors, institutions, and organizations across nations* (II ed.). Thousand Oaks, CA: Sage.

Hokanson, B., & Hopper, S. (2000). Computers as cognitive media: Examining the potential of computers in education. *Computers in Human Behavior, 16*(5), 537–552. doi:10.1016/S0747-5632(00)00016-9

Holligan, S. (2001). Issues: Should K-12 physical educators make more use of technology in their classes? *Journal of Physical Education, Recreation & Dance, 72*(2), 12–15.

Holum, A., & Gahala, J. (2001). *Critical issue: Using technology to enhance literacy instruction.* North Central Regional Educational Laboratory. Retrieved from http://www.ncrel.org/sdrs/areas/issues/content/cntareas/reading/li300.htm

Hong, S. B., & Trepanier-Street, M. (2004). Technology: A tool for knowledge construction in a Reggio Emilia inspired teacher education program. *Early Childhood Education Journal, 32*(2), 87–94. doi:10.1007/s10643-004-7971-z

Hook, P. A., & Borner, K. (2005). Educational knowledge domain visualizations: Tools to navigate, understand, and internalize the structure of scholarly knowledge and expertise. In Spink, A., & Cole, C. (Eds.), *New directions in cognitive information retrieval* (pp. 187–208). Netherlands: Springer. doi:10.1007/1-4020-4014-8_10

Hord, S. M. (2004). *Learning together leading together: Changing schools through professional learning communities*. Oxford, OH: Teachers College Press.

Howland, J., & Wedman, J. (2004). A process model for faculty development: Individualized technology learning. *Journal of Technology and Teacher Education, 12*(2), 239–263.

Hoy, M., & Merkley, D. (1989). *Teachers on television: Observing teachers and students in diverse classroom settings through the technology of television*. Ames, IA: Iowa State University.

Hsu, S. (2004). Using case discussion on the web to develop student teacher problem solving skills. *Teaching and Teacher Education, 20*, 681–692. doi:10.1016/j. tate.2004.07.001

Huffaker, D. (2005). The educated blogger: Using weblogs to promote literacy in the classroom. *AACE Journal, 13*(2), 91–98.

Hughes, J. E. (2000). *Teaching English with technology: Exploring teacher learning and practice*. Unpublished doctoral dissertation, Michigan State University, East Lansing, MI.

Hughes, J. E. (2004). Technology learning principles for preservice and in-service teacher education [Electronic Version]. *Contemporary Issues on Technology in Education, 4*. Retrieved from http://www.citejournal.org/vol4/iss3/general/article2.cfm

Hunter, M. (1984). Knowing, teaching, and supervising. In Hosford, P. (Ed.), *Using what we know about teaching*. Alexandria, VA: Association for Supervision and Curriculum Development.

Hunt, P., & Goetz, L. (1997). Research on inclusive education programs, practices, and outcomes for students with severe disabilities. *The Journal of Special Education, 31*(1), 3–31. doi:10.1177/002246699703100102

Hyun, E., & Marshall, J. (1996). Inquiry-oriented reflective supervision for developmentally appropriate practice. *Journal of Curriculum and Supervision, 11*(2), 127–144.

Ingerman, B. L., Yang, C., & the 2010 EDUCAUSE Current Issues Committee. (2010, May/June). Top ten IT issues 2010. *EDUCAUSE Review, 45*(3). Retrieved from http://www.educause.edu/EDUCAUSE%20Review/EDUCAUSEReviewMagazineVolume45/TopTenITIssues2010/205503

International Society for Technology in Education (ISTE). (2008). *National educational technology standards (NETS) and performance indicators for teachers*. Eugene, OR: Author. Retrieved October, 27, 2009, from http://www.iste.org/AM/Template.cfm?Section=NETS

International Society for Technology in Education (ISTE). (2008). *NETS for teachers*. Retrieved on April 23, 2010, from http://www.iste.org/Content/NavigationMenu/NETS/ ForTeachers/2008Standards/NETS_for_Teachers_2008.htm

International Society for Technology in Education. (2007). *National educational technology standards (NETS•S) and performance indicators for students*. Eugene, OR: ISTE.

International Society for Technology in Education. (2007). *National educational technology standards for students*. Eugene, OR: Author.

International Society for Technology in Education. (2010). *The ISTE national educational technology standards (NETS-T) and Performance Indicators for Teachers*. Retrieved from http://www.iste.org/Content/NavigationMenu/NETS/ForTeachers/2008Standards/NETS_T_Standards_Final.pdf

ISTE, P21, & SEDTA. (2008). *Maximizing the impact: The pivotal role of technology in a 21st century education system*.

ITunes. (2010). *iTunesU*. Retrieved from http://www.apple.com/education/itunes-u/

Jackson, T. (2008). *Integrated computer technology in a Catholic elementary school: A study in the dynamics of change*. Ed.D. dissertation, Northern Illinois University, United States -- Illinois. Dissertations & Theses: The Humanities and Social Sciences Collection. (Publication No. AAT 3335047).

Jackson, T. (2010). *Unpublished MATC student feedback survey*. Aurora University EDU5205. Aurora, Il. Retrieved May 26, 2010, from http://www.tinyurl.com/studentthoughts

Jacobsen, M., Clifford, P., & Friesen, S. (2002). Preparing teachers for technology integration: Creating a culture of inquiry in the context of use. *Contemporary Issues in Technology & Teacher Education, 2*(3), 363–388.

Jafari, A., & Kaufman, C. (2006). *Handbook of research on ePortfolios*. Hershey, PA: Idea Group. doi:10.4018/978-1-59140-890-1

Jahreie, C. F., & Ottesen, E. (2010). Construction of boundaries in teaher education: Analyzing PSTs' accounts. *Mind, Culture, and Activity, 17*, 212–234. doi:10.1080/10749030903314195

James-Maxie, D. (2007). Information literacy skills in elementary schools: A review of the literature. *Journal of Instruction Delivery Systems, 21*(1), 23–26.

Jamieson-Proctor, R., Finger, G., & Albion, P. (2010). Auditing the TK and TPACK confidence of pre-service teachers: Are they ready for the profession? [AEC]. *Australian Educational Computing Journal, 25*(1), 8–17.

Jenkins, H., Clinton, K., Purushotma, R., Robison, A. J., & Weigel, M. (2006). *Confronting the challenges of participatory culture: Media education for the 21st Century*. John D. and Catherine T. MacArthur Foundation Web site. Retrieved from http://www.macfound.org/site/apps/nlnet/content2.aspx?c=lkLXJ8MQKrH&b=1135955&ct=2946895

Jenkins, H. (2006). *Confronting the challenges of participatory culture: Media education for the 21st Century*. Chicago, IL: MacArthur Foundation.

Johnson-Gentile, K., Lonberger, R., Parana, J., & West, A. (2000). Preparing preservice teachers for the technological classroom: A school-college partnership. *Journal of Technology and Teacher Education, 8*(2), 97–109.

Johnson, L., Smith, R., Levine, A., & Haywood, K. (2010). *2010 horizon report: K-12 edition*. Austin, TX: The New Media Consortium.

Johnson, L., Smith, R., Levine, A., & Haywood, K. (2010). *The 2010 horizon report: K-12 edition*. Austin, TX: The New Media Consortium.

Johnston, P. (1997). *Knowing literacy: Constructive literacy assessment*. Portland, ME: Stenhouse.

Jonassen, D. (2005). *Modeling with technology: Mindtools for conceptual change* (3rd ed.). Upper Saddle River, NJ: Prentice Hall.

Jonassen, D. H. (1999). *Computers as mindtools for schools: Engaging critical thinking* (2nd ed.). Upper Saddle River, NJ: Merrill Prentice-Hall, Inc.

Jonassen, D. H. (1999). Designing constructivist learning environments. In Reigeluth, C. M. (Ed.), *Instructional design theories and models: Their current state of the art* (2nd ed.). Mahwah, NJ: Lawrence Erlbaum Associates.

Jonassen, D. H., Howland, J., Marra, R. M., & Crismond, D. P. (2007). *Meaningful learning with technology*. Upper Saddle River, NJ: Prentice Hall.

Jonassen, D., Howland, J., Marra, R. M., & Crismond, D. (2008). *Meaningful learning with technology*. Upper Saddle River, NJ: Pearson.

Jones, E. (2010). A professional practice portfolio for quality learning. *Higher Education Quarterly, 64*(3), 292–312. doi:10.1111/j.1468-2273.2010.00458.x

Jones, M. G., & Harmon, S. W. (2009). Instructional strategies for teaching in synchronous online learning environments (SOLE). In Yang, H., & Yuen, S. (Eds.), *Collective intelligence and e-learning 2.0: Implications of Web-based communities and networking* (pp. 78–93). Hershey, PA: IGI Global. doi:10.4018/978-1-60566-729-4.ch005

Jones, M. G., Harmon, S. W., & O'Grady-Jones, M. K. (2005). Developing the digital mind: Challenges and solutions in teaching and learning. *Teacher Education Journal of South Carolina, 2004-2005*, 17–24.

Jordan, B., & Henderson, A. (1995). Interaction analysis: Foundations and practice. *Journal of the Learning Sciences, 4*(1), 39–103. doi:10.1207/s15327809jls0401_2

Joyce, B., & Showers, B. (2002). *Student achievement through staff development*. Alexandria, VA: ASCD.

Judge, S., Puckett, K., & Bell, S. M. (2006). Closing the digital divide: Update from the early childhood longitudinal study. *The Journal of Educational Research, 100*(1), 52–60. doi:10.3200/JOER.100.1.52-60

Judge, S., Puckett, K., & Cabuk, B. (2004). Digital equity: New findings from the early childhood longitudinal study. *Journal of Research on Technology in Education*, *36*(4), 383–396.

Kajder, S. (2007). Unleashing potential with emerging technologies. In Beers, G. K., Probst, R., & Rief, L. (Eds.), *Adolescent literacy: Turning promise into practice* (pp. 213–229). Portsmouth, NH: Heinemann.

Kariuki, M., Franklin, T., & Duran, M. (2001). A technology partnership: Lessons learned by mentors. *Journal of Technology and Teacher Education*, *9*(3), 407–417.

Karran, S., Berson, M., & Mason, C. (2001). Harnessing Internet2: Enhancing social science education through tele-collaborative teaching and learning. *Social Education*, *65*(3), 151–153.

Kaseman, L., & Kaseman, S. (2000). How will virtual schools effect homeschooling? *Home Education Magazine* (November-December), 16-19. Retrieved from http://homeedmag.com/HEM/176/ndtch.html

Kawachi, P. (2003). Initiating intrinsic motivation in online education: Review of the current state of the art. *Interactive Learning Environments*, *11*(1), 59–82. doi:10.1076/ilee.11.1.59.13685

Kay, R. H. (2006). Evaluating strategies used to incorporate technology into preservice education: A review of the literature. *Journal of Research on Technology in Education*, *38*(4), 383–408.

Kearsley, G., & Blomeyer, R. (2004). Preparing K-12 teachers to teach online. *Educational Technology*, *44*(1), 49–52. Retrieved from http://home.sprynet.com/~gkearsley/TeachingOnline.htm.

Keengwe, J., Onchwari, G., & Wachira, P. (2008). Computer technology integration and student learning: Barriers and promise. *Journal of Science Education and Technology*, *17*(6), 560–565. doi:10.1007/s10956-008-9123-5

Keller, J. M. (1987). Development and use of the ARCS model of instructional design. *Journal of Instructional Development*, *10*(3), 2–10. doi:10.1007/BF02905780

Keller, J. M. (2009). *Motivational design for learning and performance: The ARCS model approach*. New York, NY: Springer.

Kelley, M., Wetzel, K., Padget, H., Williams, M. K., & Odom, M. (2003). Early childhood teacher preparation and technology integration: The Arizona State University West experience. *Contemporary Issues in Technology & Teacher Education*, *3*(1). Retrieved from http://www.citejournal.org/vol3/iss1/general/article5.cfm.

Kelly, A. E., & Lesh, R. A. (Eds.). (2000). *Handbook of research design in mathematics and science education*. Mahwah, NJ: Erlbaum.

Kent, A. (2007). Powerful preparation of preservice teachers using interactive video conferencing. *Journal of Literacy and Technology*, *8*(2), 42–58.

Kerin, R. (2009). Digital portraits: Teacher education and multiliteracies pedagogy. In Carrington, V., & Robinson, M. (Eds.), *Digital literacies: Social learning and classroom practices*. Thousand Oaks, CA: Sage Publications.

Kersten, F. (2006). Inclusion of technology resources in early childhood music education. *General Music Today*, *20*(1), 15–26. doi:10.1177/10483713060200010105

Kieran, C., & Saldanha, L. (2005). Computer algebra systems (CAS) as a tool for coaxing the emergence of reasoning about equivalence of algebraic expressions. In H. L. Chick & J. L. Vincent (Eds.), *Proceedings of the 29th Conference of the International Group for the Psychology of Mathematics Education*, (vol. 3, pp. 193-200). Melbourne, Australia: PME.

Kimball, W. H., Cohen, L. G., Dimmick, D., & Mills, R. (2003-04). No special equipment required. *Learning and Leading with Technology*, *31*(4), 12–15.

Kim, H., & Hannafin, M. (2008). Grounded design of web-enhanced case-based activity. *Educational Technology Research and Development*, *56*(2), 161–179. doi:10.1007/s11423-006-9010-9

Kim, H., & Hannafin, M. (2009). Web-enhanced case-based activity in teacher education: A case study. *Instructional Science*, *37*, 151–170. doi:10.1007/s11251-007-9040-7

Kim, K., Jain, S., Westhoff, G., & Rezabek, L. (2008). A quantitative exploration of preservice teachers' intent to use computer-based technology. *Journal of Instructional Psychology*, *35*(3), 275–287.

Kim, M. C., & Freemyer, S. (2011). Technology integration in science classrooms: Framework, principles, and examples. *Educational Technology, 51*(1), 25–29.

Kim, M. C., & Hannafin, M. J. (2007). Foundations and practice for Web-enhanced science inquiry: Grounded design perspectives. In Luppicini, R. (Ed.), *Online learning communities: A volume in perspectives in instructional technology and distance education* (pp. 53–72). Greenwich, CT: Information Age Publishing.

Kim, M. C., & Hannafin, M. J. (2011). Scaffolding problem solving in technology-enhanced learning environments (TELEs): Bridging research and theory with practice. *Computers & Education, 56*(2), 403–417. doi:10.1016/j.compedu.2010.08.024

Kim, M. C., Hannafin, M. J., & Bryan, L. A. (2007). Technology-enhanced inquiry tools in science education: An emerging pedagogical framework for classroom practice. *Science Education, 91*(6), 1010–1030. doi:10.1002/sce.20219

Kinzer, C. (2010). Considering literacy and policy in the context of digital environments. *Language Arts, 88*(1), 51–61.

Kirtman, L. (2008, March). Preservice teachers and mathematics: The impact of service-learning on teacher preparation. *School Science and Mathematics, 108*(3), 94–102. doi:10.1111/j.1949-8594.2008.tb17812.x

Kissel, B., Hathaway, J., & Wood, K. (2010). Digital collaborative literacy: Using wikis to promote social learning and literacy development. *Middle School Journal, 41*(5), 58–63.

Kleiner, B., Thomas, N., & Lewis, L. (2007). *Educational technology in teacher education programs for initial licensure (NCES 2008-040)*. Washington, DC: National Center for Education Statistics, Institute of Education Sciences, U.S. Department of Education.

Knapczyk, D. R., Hew, K., Frey, T. J., & Wall-Marencik, W. (2005). Evaluation of online mentoring of practicum experiences for limited licensed teachers. *Teacher Education and Special Education, 28*(4), 207–220. .doi:10.1177/088840640502800407

Koc, M., & Bakir, N. (2010). A needs assessment survey to investigate pre-service teachers' knowledge, experiences and perceptions about preparation to using educational technologies. *Turkish Online Journal of Distance Education, 9*(1), 13–22.

Koehler, M. J., & Mishra, P. (2008). Introducing TPACK. In American Association of Colleges for Teacher Education Committee on Innovation and Technology (Eds.), *Handbook of technological pedagogical content knowledge (TPACK) for educators* (pp. 3-29). New York, NY: Routledge.

Koehler, M. J., & Mishra, P. (2008). Introducing TPCK. AACTE Committee on Innovation and Technology (Ed.), *The handbook of technological pedagogical content knowledge (TPCK) for educators* (pp. 3-29). Mahwah, NJ: Lawrence Erlbaum Associates.

Koehler, M. J., & Mishra, P. (2010, June 1). *TPCK-Technological pedagogical content knowledge*. Retrieved from tpack.org

Koehler, M. J., & Mishra, P. (2008). Introducing TPCK. In Silverman, N. (Ed.), *Handbook of technological pedagogical content knowledge (TPCK) for educators* (pp. 1–20). New York, NY: Routledge.

Koehler, M. J., & Mishra, P. (2009). What is technological pedagogical content knowledge? [CITE Journal]. *Contemporary Issues in Technology & Teacher Education, 9*(1), 60–70.

Koehler, M. J., Mishra, P., & Kereluik, K. (2009). Looking back to the future of educational technology. *TechTrends, 53*, 48–53. doi:10.1007/s11528-009-0325-3

Koehler, M., Mishra, P., & Yahya, K. (2007). Tracing the development of teacher knowledge in a design seminar: Integrating content, pedagogy and technology. *Computers & Education, 49*(3), 740–762. doi:10.1016/j.compedu.2005.11.012

Kolodner, J. (1993). *Case-based reasoning*. San Mateo, CA: Morgan Kaufmann Publishers, Inc.

Konrad, M., Joseph, L. M., & Itoi, M. (2011). Using guided notes to enhance instruction for all students. *Intervention in School and Clinic, 46*(3), 131–140. .doi:10.1177/1053451210378163

Kopcha, T. (2008). *A systems-based approach to technology integration using mentoring and communities of practice.* Association for Educational Communications and Technology.

Kortering, L. J., McClannon, T. W., & Braziel, P. M. (2008). Universal design for learning: A look at what algebra and biology students with and without high incidence conditions are saying. *Remedial and Special Education, 29,* 352–363. .doi:10.1177/0741932507314020

Koshman, S. (2005). Testing user interaction with a prototype visualization-based information retrieval system. *Journal of the American Society for Information Science and Technology, 56*(8), 824–833. doi:10.1002/asi.20175

Kramarski, B., & Michalsky, T. (2010). Preparing preservice teachers for self-regulated learning in the context of technological pedagogical content knowledge. *Learning and Instruction, 20*(5), 14. doi:10.1016/j.learninstruc.2009.05.003

Krucli, T. E. (2004). Making assessment matter: Using the computer to create interactive feedback. *English Journal, 94,* 47–52. doi:10.2307/4128847

Krueger, K., Bobac, M., & Smaldino, S. (2004). InTime impact report: What was InTime's effectiveness and impact on faculty and preservice teachers? *Journal of Technology and Teacher Education, 12*(2), 185–210.

Krueger, K., Boboc, M., Smaldinom, S., Cocrnish, Y., & Callahan, W. (2004). InTime impact report: What was InTime's effectiveness and impact on faculty and preservice teachers? *Journal of Technology and Teacher Education, 12*(2), 185–210.

Krueger, K., Hansen, L., & Smaldino, S. (2000). Preservice teacher technology competencies. *TechTrends, 44*(3), 47–50. doi:10.1007/BF02778227

Kukulska-Hulme, A. (2010). Learning cultures on the move: Where are we heading? *Journal of Educational Technology & Society, 13*(4), 4–14.

Kulik, J. (2003). *Effects of using instructional technology in elementary and secondary schools: What controlled evaluation studies say.* Arlington, VA: SRI International. Retrieved February, 2011 from http://www.sri.com/policy/csted/reports/sandt/it/Kulik_ITinK-12_Main_Report.pdf

Kumtepe, A. T. (2006). The effects of computers on kindergarten children's social skills. *Online Submission, 5.*

Kundu, R., & Bain, C. (2006). WebQuests: Utilizing technology in a constructivist manner to facilitate meaningful preservice learning. *Art Education, 59*(2).

Kurtis, S. A., Matthews, C. E., & Smallwood, T. (2009). (Dis)solving the differences: A physical science lesson using universal design. *Intervention in School and Clinic, 44,* 151–159. doi:10.1177/1053451208326051

Labbo, L. (2005). From morning message to digital morning message: Moving from the tried and true to the new. *The Reading Teacher, 58*(8), 782–785. doi:10.1598/RT.58.8.9

Laffey, J., & Musser, D. (1998). Attitudes of preservice teachers about using technology in teaching. *Journal of Technology and Teacher Education, 6,* 223–242.

Lamb, A. (2003). Workshops that work! Building an effective, technology-rich faculty development program [Electronic version]. *Journal of Computing in Teacher Education, 21,* 77–83.

Lambert, J., & Gong, Y. (2010). 21st century paradigms for pre-service teacher technology preparation. *Computers in the Schools, 27*(1), 54–70. doi:10.1080/07380560903536272

Lambert, J., Gong, Y., & Cuper, P. (2008). Technology, transfer, and teaching: The impact of a single technology course on preservice teachers' computer attitudes and ability. *Journal of Technology and Teacher Education, 16*(4), 385–410.

Lam, Y. (2000). Technophilia vs. technophobia: A preliminary look at why second-language teachers do or do not use technology in their classrooms. *Canadian Modern Language Review, 56,* 390–420. doi:10.3138/cmlr.56.3.389

Land, S., & Hannafin, M. (2001). Student-centered Learning Environments. In Jonassen, D., & Land, S. (Eds.), *Theoretical foundations of learning environments* (pp. 1–23). Mahwah, NJ: Lawrence Erlbaum Associates.

Lankshear, C., & Knobel, M. (2003). *New literacies: Changing knowledge and classroom teaching.* Philadelphia, PA: Open University Press.

Lappan, G. (2000). The language of mathematics: The meaning and use of variable. *NCTM News Bulletin.* Retrieved from http://www.nctm.org/about/content. aspx?id=994

Larson, L. (2009). A descriptive study of mentoring and technology integration among teacher education faculty. *International Journal of Evidence Based Coaching and Mentoring, 7*(1).

Lasley, T. J., & Matczynski, T. J. (1995). Reflective teaching. In Ornstein, A. C. (Ed.), *Teaching: Theory into practice* (pp. 307–321).

Lathem, S., Parker, H., Morris, J., Deyo, A., & Agne, R. (2002). *Student as faculty mentors: Reversing the role of teacher and learner.* Retrieved from http://www.uvm.edu/pt3/exhibits/pdf/mentors.pdf

Lau, C., Higgins, K., Gelfer, J., Hong, E., & Miller, S. (2005). The effects of teacher facilitation on the social interactions of young children during computer activities. *Topics in Early Childhood Special Education, 25*(4), 208–217. doi :10.1177/02711214050250040201

Laurillard, D. (1993). *Rethinking university teaching: a framework for the effective use of educational technology.* London, UK: Routledge.

Lave, J., & Wenger, E. (1991). *Situated learning: Legitimate peripheral participation.* Cambridge, MA: Cambridge University Press.

Lawless, K. A., & Pellegrino, J. W. (2007). Professional development in integrating technology into teaching and learning: Knowns, unknowns, and ways to pursue better questions and answers. *Review of Educational Research, 77*(4), 575–614. doi:10.3102/0034654307309921

Leander, K., & Boldt, G. (2008). *New literacies in old literacy skins.* Paper presented at the Annual Meeting of the American Educational Research Association, New York.

Learn & Serve America. (2010). *What is service learning?* Retrieved September 28, 2010 from http://www.service-learning.org/what_is_service-learning/service-learning_is

Lee, H., & Hollebrands, K. (2008). Preparing to teach mathematics with technology: An integrated approach to developing technological pedagogical content knowledge. *Contemporary Issues in Technology & Teacher Education, 8*(4). Retrieved from http://www.citejournal.org/vol8/iss4/mathematics/article1.cfm.

Lee, J. (2008). *Visualizing elementary social studies methods.* Hoboken, NJ: Wiley and Sons.

Lee, J. S., Ginsburg, H. P., & Preston, M. D. (2009). Video interactions for teaching and learning (VITAL): Analyzing videos online to learn to teach early childhood mathematics. *Australian Journal of Early Childhood, 34*(2), 19–23.

Lee, M. R., & Lan, Y. (2007). From Web 2.0 to conversational knowledge management: Towards collaborative intelligence. *Journal of Entrepreneurship Research, 2*(2), 47–62.

Lehman, J. D., & Richardson, J. (2007). *Linking teacher preparation programs with K-12 schools via videoconferencing: Benefits and limitations.* Paper presented at American Educational Research association Annual Conference. Retrieved September 7, 2010, from http://p3t3.education.purdue.edu/AERA2007_Videoconf_Paper.pdf

Lehnart, A., Arafeh, S., Smith, A., & Macgill, A. R. (2008). *Writing, technology, and teens.* Washington, DC: Pew Internet and American Life Project.

Lehnart, A., Madden, M., & Hitlin, P. (2005). *Youth are leading the transition to a fully wired and mobile nation.* Washington, DC: Pew Internet and American Life Project.

Lehrer, R. (1993). Authors of knowledge: Patterns of hypermedia design. In Lajoie, S. P., & Derry, S. J. (Eds.), *Computers as cognitive tools.* Hillsdale, NJ: Lawrence Erlbaum.

Lei, J. (2009). Digital natives as preservice teachers: What technology preparation is needed? *Journal of Computing in Teacher Education, 25*(3), 87–97.

LeMaster, K., Williams, E., & Knop, N. (1998). Technology Implementation: Let's do it! *Journal of Physical Education, Recreation & Dance, 69*(9), 12–16.

Lemke, C., & Sweeney, J. F. (Eds.). (1999). *Transforming learning through technology: Policy roadmaps for the nation's governors.* Washington, DC: National Governors' Association.

Lenhart, A., Purcell, K., Smith, A., & Zickuhr, K. (2010). *Social media & mobile internet use among teens and young adults* [Electronic Version]. Retrieved June 6, 2010, from http://pewinternet.org/Reports/2010/Social Media and Young Adults.aspx

Lenski, S. D., Crumpler, T. P., Stallworth, C., & Crawford, K. M. (2005). Preparing culturally responsive PSTs. *Teacher Education Quarterly, 32*(2), 85–100.

Leont'ev, A. N. (1978). *Activity, consciousness, and personality*. Englewood Cliffs, NJ: Prentice Hall.

Leont'ev, A. N. (1981). *Problems of the development of the mind*. Moscow, Russia: Progress Publishers.

Lesar, S., Benner, S. M., Habel, J., & Coleman, L. (1997). Preparing general education teachers for inclusive settings: A constructivist teacher education program. *Teacher Education and Special Education, 20*, 204–220. doi:10.1177/088840649702000303

Leu, D. J. Jr. (2002). The new literacies: Research on reading instruction with the Internet and other digital technologies. In Samuels, J., & Farstrup, A. E. (Eds.), *What research has to say about reading instruction* (pp. 310–336). Newark, DE: International Reading Association.

Leu, D. J., Kinzer, C. K., Coiro, J. L., & Cammack, D. W. (2004). Toward a theory of new literacies emerging from the Internet and other information and communication technologies. In Unrau, N. J., & Ruddell, R. B. (Eds.), *Theoretical models and processes of reading* (5th ed., pp. 1570–1613). Newark, DE: International Reading Association.

Levin, D., Arafeh, S., Lenhart, A., & Rainie, L. (2002). *The digital disconnect: The widening gap between Internet-savvy students and their schools*. Washington, DC: Pew Internet and American Life Project.

Liang, G., Walls, R., Hicks, V., Clayton, L., & Yang, L. (2006). Will tomorrow's physical educators be prepared to teach in the digital age? *Contemporary Issues in Technology & Teacher Education, 6*(1), 143–156.

Lim, W.-Y., Lee, Y.-J., & Hung, D. (2008). "A prophet never accepted by their own town": A teacher's learning trajectory when using technology. *Asia-Pacific Journal of Teacher Education, 36*(3), 215–227. doi:10.1080/13598660802232605

Lin, C.-Y. (2008). Preservice teachers' beliefs about using technology in the mathematics classroom. *Journal of Computers in Mathematics and Science Teaching, 27*(3), 341–360.

Lindsay, J., & Davis, V. (2010). *Rubric assessment*. Flat Classroom Project. Retrieved September 30, 2010, from http://flatclassroomproject.wikispaces.com/Rubrics

Linnenbrink, E. A., & Pintrich, P. R. (2003). The role of self-efficacy beliefs in student engagement and learning in the classroom. *Reading & Writing Quarterly, 19*, 119–137. doi:10.1080/10573560308223

Linn, M. C. (2006). The knowledge integration perspective on learning and instruction. In Sawyer, R. K. (Ed.), *The Cambridge handbook of the learning sciences* (pp. 243–264). New York, NY: Cambridge University Press.

Lin, Q. (2008). Preservice teachers' learning experiences of constructing e-portfolios online. *The Internet and Higher Education, 11*(3-4), 194–200. doi:10.1016/j.iheduc.2008.07.002

Lipscomb, G. (2003). "I guess it was pretty fun": Using WebQuests in the middle school classroom. *Clearing House (Menasha, Wis.), 76*(3), 152–155. doi:10.1080/00098650309601993

Lipscomb, G. B., & Doppen, F. H. (2004/2005). Climbing the stairs: Pre-service social studies teachers' perceptions of technology integration. *The International Journal of Social Education, 9*(2), 70–87.

Lisenbee, P. (2009). Whiteboards and websites: Digital tools for the early childhood curriculum. *Young Children, 64*(6), 92–95.

Lohr, L. L. (2008). *Creating graphics for learning and performance: Lessons in visual literacy* (2nd ed.). Upper Saddle River, NJ: Pearson.

Lorenzo, G., & Ittelson, J. (2005). *An overview of eP-ortfolios*. The Educause Learning Initiative. Retrieved November 15, 2005, from http://www.educause.edu/ir/library/pdf/ELI3001.pdf.

Lorenzo, G., & Ittelson, J. G. (2005). *An overview of e-portfolios*. ELI Paper 1: 2005, EDUCAUSE Learning Initiative. Retrieved from http://net.educause.edu/ir/library/pdf/ELI3001.pdf

LoTi Connection. (2009). *About the LoTi digital age survey*. Retrieved from http://loticonnection.com/loti-take.html

Loucks-Horsley, S., Love, N., Stiles, K. E., Mundry, S., & Hewson, P. W. (2009). *Designing professional development for teachers of science and mathematics* (3rd ed.). Thousand Oaks, CA: Corwin Press.

Lowes, S. (2005, June). *Online teaching and classroom change: The impact of virtual high school on its teachers and their school*. A paper presented at the meeting of the North Central Regional Educational Laboratory, Chicago, IL. Retrieved from http://www.ilt.columbia.edu/publications/lowes_final.pdf

Lowther, D., & Inan, F., Strahl, & Ross, S. (2008). Does technology integration "work" when key barriers are removed? *Educational Media International, 45*(3), 195–213. doi:10.1080/09523980802284317

Ludwig, M., & Taymans, J. (2005). Teaming: Constructing high-quality faculty development in a PT3 project. *Journal of Technology and Teacher Education, 13*(3), 357–372.

Luehmann, A. (2008). Using blogging in support of teacher professional identity development: A case study. *Journal of the Learning Sciences, 17*, 287–337. doi:10.1080/10508400802192706

Luehmann, A., & Tinelli, L. (2008). Teacher professional identity development with social networking technologies: Learning reform through blogging. *Educational Media International, 45*(4), 323–333. doi:10.1080/09523980802573263

Luke, A., & Elkins, J. (1998). Reinventing literacy in "New Times". *Journal of Adolescent & Adult Literacy, 42*(1), 4–7.

Luria, A. R. (1932). *The nature of human conflicts*. New York, NY: Liveright.

Luria, A. R. (1966). *Higher cortical functions in man*. New York, NY: Basic Books.

Luria, A. R. (1979). *The making of mind*. Cambridge, MA: Harvard University Press.

MacLean, P., & Scott, B. (2007). Learning design: Requirements, practice and prospects. *Campus-Wide Information Systems, 24*(3), 187–198. doi:10.1108/10650740710762220

Maddox, C. (1984). Educational microcomputing: The need for research. *Computers in the Schools, 1*(1), 35–41. doi:10.1300/J025v01n01_04

Magliaro, J., & Ezeife, A. (2007). Pre-service teachers' preparedness to integrate computer technology into the curriculum. *Canadian Journal of Learning and Technology, 33*(3), 95.

Magliaro, J., & Ezeife, A. N. (2007). Preservice teachers' preparedness to integrate computer technology into the curriculum. *Canadian Journal of Learning and Technology, 33*(3), 95–111. Retrieved from http://www.cjlt.ca/content/vol33.3/Magliaro.html.

Ma, L. (1999). *Knowing and teaching elementary mathematics: Teachers understanding of fundamental mathematics in China and the United States*. Mahwah, NJ: Lawrence Erlbaum Associates.

Maloney, E. (2007). What can Web 2.0 teach us about learning? *The Chronicle of Higher Education, 25*(18), B26.

Marcaruso, P., & Walker, A. (2008). The efficacy of computer-assited instruction for advancing literacy skills in kindegraten children. *Reading Psychology, 29*(3), 266–287. doi:10.1080/02702710801982019

Margerum-Leys, J., & Marx, R. W. (2002). Teacher knowledge of educational technology: A case study of student/mentor teacher pairs. *Journal of Educational Computing Research, 26*(4), 427–462. doi:10.2190/JXBR-2G0G-1E4T-7T4M

Marino, M. T., Sameshima, P., & Beecher, C. C. (2009). Enhancing TPACK with assistive technology: Promoting inclusive practices in preservice teacher education. *Contemporary Issues in Technology & Teacher Education, 9*(2). Retrieved from http://www.citejournal.org/vol9/iss2/general/article1.cfm.

Marra, R. M. (2004). An online course to help teachers use technology to enhance learning: Successes and limitations. *Journal of Technology and Teacher Education, 12*(3), 411–430.

Martindale, T., & Dowdy, M. (2010). Personal learning environments. In Veletsianos, G. (Ed.), *Emerging technologies in distance education* (pp. 177–193). Edmonton, Canada: Athabasca University Press.

Martindale, T., & Wiley, D. A. (2005). Using weblogs in scholarship and teaching. *TechTrends, 49*(2), 55–61. doi:10.1007/BF02773972

Martorella, P. (1997). Technology and social studies or: Which way to the sleeping giant? *Theory and Research in Social Education, 25*(4), 511–514.

Marx, J. G., Honeycutt, K. A., Clayton, S. R., & Moreno, N. P. (2006). The Elizabeth Towns incident: An inquiry-based approach to learning anatomy developed through high school-university collaboration. *The American Biology Teacher, 68*(3), 7. doi:10.1662/0002-7685(2006)68[140:TETIAI]2.0.CO;2

Marzano, R. J. (2003). *What works in schools: Translating research into action.* Alexandria, VA: Association for Supervision and Curriculum Development.

Mason, C., Berson, M., Diem, R., Hicks, D., Lee, J., & Dralle, T. (2000). Guidelines for using technology to prepare social studies teachers. *Contemporary Issues in Technology and Teacher Education, 1*(1). Retrieved July 13, 2006, from http://www.citejournal.org/vol1/iss1/currentissues/socialstudies/article1.htm

Mason, C. (2001). Collaborative social studies teacher education across remote locations: Student experiences and perceptions. *The International Journal of Social Education, 15*(2), 46–61.

Mason, C., Berson, M., Diem, R., Hicks, D., Lee, J., & Dralle, T. (2000). Guidelines for using technology to prepare social studies teachers. *Contemporary Issues in Technology & Teacher Education, 1*(1), 1–14.

Mason, R., & Rennie, F. (2008). *E-learning and social networking handbook: Resources for higher education.* New York, NY: Routledge.

Massy, W. F., & Wilger, A. K. (1998). Technology's contribution to higher education productivity. *New Directions for Higher Education, 103*, 49–59. doi:10.1002/he.10304

McClain, K., & Cobb, P. (2001). Supporting students' ability to reason about data. *Educational Studies in Mathematics, 45*, 103–109. doi:10.1023/A:1013874514650

McClam, T., Diambra, J., Burton, B., Fuss, A., & Fudge, D. (2008). An analysis of a service learning project: Students' expectations, concerns, and reflections. *Journal of Experiential Education, 30*(3), 236–249. doi:10.5193/JEE.30.3.236

McCombs, B. L., & Whisler, J. S. (1997). *The learner-centered classroom and school: Strategies for increasing student motivation and achievement* (1st ed.). San Francisco, CA: Jossey-Bass.

McCormick, B., DeFanti, T., & Brown, M. (1987, November). Visualization in scientific computing. *Computer Graphics, 21*(6), 681–684.

McDougall, S. (2006). *One tablet or two? Opportunities for change in educational provision in the next 20 years.* Future Lab Publications. Retrieved from http://www.futurelab.org.uk/resources/documents/discussion_papers/One_tablet_or_two.pdf

McGee, P., & Diaz, V. (2007). Wikis and podcasts and blogs, oh my!: What is a faculty member supposed to do? *EDUCAUSE Review, 42*(5), 28–41.

McGuinness, C. (1993). Teaching thinking: New signs for theories of cognition. *Educational Psychology, 13*(3 & 4), 395–316.

Mcguire, J. M., Scott, S. S., & Shaw, S. F. (2006). Universal design and its applications in educational environments. *Remedial and Special Education, 27*, 166–175. doi:10.1177/07419325060270030501

McKenzie, J. (2001). How teachers learn technology best [Editorial]. *From Now On. The Teachers Technology Journal, 10*, 6.

McNamara, J. (2004). *Geocaching for dummies: A reference for the rest of us.* Hoboken, NJ: Wiley.

McPherson, S. (2009). "A dance with the butterflies:" A metamorphosis of teaching and learning through technology. *Early Childhood Education Journal, 37*(3), 229–236. doi:10.1007/s10643-009-0338-8

Meadows, M. (2004). Using technology in early childhood environments to strengthen cultural connections. *Information Technology in Childhood Education Annual, 2004*(1).

Meaney, K., Griffin, K., & Bohler, H. (2009). Service-learning: A venue for enhancing preservice educators' knowledge base for teaching. *International Journal for the Scholarship of Teaching and Learning, 3*(2), 1–17.

Means, B., Toyama, Y., Murphy, R., Bakia, M., & Jones, K. (2009) *Evaluation of evidence-based practices in online learning: A meta-analysis and review of online learning studies*. US Department of Education. Retrieved from http://www.ed.gov/rschstat/eval/tech/evidence-based-practices/finalreport.pdf

Means, B. (2010). Technology and education change: Focus on student learning. *Journal of Research on Technology in Education, 42*(3), 285–307.

Medina, A. L. (in press.). *Tri-perspective form for clinical observations.* Manuscript in preparation.

Medina, J. (2008). *Brain rules: 12 principles for surviving and thriving at work, home, and school.* Seattle, WA: Pear Press.

Medvin, M. B., Reed, D. M., & Behr, D. S. (2002, June 26-29, 2002). *Computer training for preschool teachers: Impact on computer self-efficacy and anxiety.* Paper presented at the Head Start National Research Conference, Washington, DC.

Meeus, W., Questier, F., & Derks, T. (2006). Open-source eportfolio: Development and implementation of an institution-wide electronic platform for students. *Educational Media International, 43*(2), 133–145. doi:10.1080/09523980600641148

Merrill, M. D. (2008). Reflections on a four decade search for effective, efficient and engaging instruction. In Allen, M. W. (Ed.), *Michael Allen's 2008 e-learning annual (Vol. 1,* pp. 141–167). Wiley Pfeiffer.

Meyer, D. (2005). *Math class needs a makeover.* TED: Ideas worth spreading. Retrieved September 21, 2010 from http://www.ted.com/talks/dan_meyer_math_curriculum_makeover.html

Mezirow, J. (1978). *Education for perspective transformation.* New York, NY: Teacher's College, Columbia University.

Michael, M. G., & Trezek, B. J. (2006). Universal design and multiple literacies: Creating access and ownership for students with disabilities. *Theory into Practice, 45,* 311–318. doi:10.1207/s15430421tip4504_4

Michigan Department of Education. (2006). *Michigan merit curriculum guidelines: Online learning.* Lansing, MI: Author. Retrieved from http://www.michigan.gov/documents/mde/Online10.06_final_175750_7.pdf

Michigan State Board of Education. (2008). *Standards for the preparation of teachers in educational technology: NP endorsement.* Retrieved from http://webcache.googleusercontent.com/search?q=cache:sW_hO6R1eQQJ:www.michigan.gov/documents/mde/EducTech_NP_SBEApprvl.5-13-08.A_236954_7.doc+Standards+for+the+Preparation+of+Teachers+in+Educational+Technology+(NP+Endorsement)&cd=2&hl=en&ct=clnk&gl=us&client=firefox-a

Miller, R. (2009a). *How we dream, part 1* [Video]. Retrieved from http://www.youtube.com/watch?v=PHvoBPjhsBA&feature=player_embedded

Miller, R. (2009b). *How we dream, part 2* [Video]. Retrieved from http://www.youtube.com/watch?v=6KsEQnOkTZ0&feature=player_embedded

Miller, K., Dunlap, C., & Gonzalez, A. (2007). The impact of a freshman-year service-learning experience on the achievement of standards articulated for teacher candidates. *School Community Journal, 17*(2), 111–121.

Millken Family Foundation. (2000). *How teaching matters: Bringing the classroom back into discussions of teacher quality.* Princeton, NJ: ETS. Retrieved from http://www.etc.org/research/pic

Milson, A. J., & LaComb, S. (2001). World-class sounds: Music, social studies, and the Internet. *Social Studies and the Young Learner, 13*(4), 1–2.

Mims, C., Polly, D., Shepherd, C. E., & Inan, F. (2006). Examining PT3 projects designed to improve preservice education. *TechTrends, 50*(3). doi:10.1007/s11528-006-7599-5

Mishra, P., & Koehler, M. J. (2008, March). *Introducing technological pedagogical content knowledge.* Paper presented the Annual Meeting of the American Educational Research Association, New York, March 24-28. (Conference Presentation)

Mishra, P., Koehler, M. J., Shin, T. S., Wolf, L. G., & DeSchryver, M. (2010). *Developing TPACK by design.* A part of the symposium titled Strategies for Teacher professional Development of TPACK presented at Society for Information Technology and Teacher Education Annual Conference in San Diego, CA.

Mishra, P., & Koehler, M. J. (2006). Technological pedagogical content knowledge: A framework for integrating technology in teacher knowledge. *Teachers College Record, 108*(6), 1017–1054. doi:10.1111/j.1467-9620.2006.00684.x

Mishra, P., & Koehler, M. J. (2009). Too cool for school? No way! Using the TPACK framework: You can have your hot tools and teach with them, too. *Learning and Leading with Technology, 36*(7), 14–18.

Mitra, S. (2010). *Sugata Mitra: The child-driven education* [Video] Retrieved from http://www.ted.com/talks/sugata_mitra_the_child_driven_education.html?awesm=on.ted.com_8YCW&utm_campaign=sugata_mitra_the_child_driven_education&utm_medium=on.ted.com-twitter&utm_source=direct-on.ted.com&utm_content=ted.com-talkpage

Moersch, C. (1995, November). Levels of technology implementation (LoTi): A framework for measuring classroom technology use. *Learning and Leading with Technology, 23*(3), 40–42.

Moersch, C. (2001). Next steps: Using LoTi as a research tool. *Learning and Leading with Technology, 29*(3), 22–27.

Mohnsen, B. (2004). *Using technology in physical education* (4th ed.). Cerritos, CA: Bonnie's Fitware.

Mohnsen, B. (2006). *Using technology in physical education* (5th ed.). Cerritos, CA: Bonnie's Fitware.

Mohnsen, B. (2010). *Using technology in physical education* (7th ed.). Cerritos, CA: Bonnie's Fitware.

Monk, S. (2003). Representation in school mathematics: learning to graph and graphing to learn. In Kilpatrick, J., Martin, W. G., & Schifter, D. (Eds.), *A research companion to principles and standards for school mathematics* (pp. 250–262). Reston, VA: NCTM.

Monsma, E. V. (2003). Using handheld technology for observational assessment in middle school physical education. *Teaching Elementary Physical Education, 14*(4), 35–37.

Moodle. (2011). *Statistics.* Retrieved from http://moodle.org/stats/

Moodle.org. (2010). *Moodle.org: Open-source community-based tools for learning.* Retrieved September 18, 2010, from http://moodle.org/

Moore, A. (1989). Testimony before the Senate Subcommittee on Education, Arts, Humanities of the Committee of Labor and Human Resources, field hearing, Jackson, MI. April 27, 1989, in U.S. Congress, Office of Technology Assessment, *Linking for Learning: A New 'Course for Education, OTA-SET-430* (Washington, DC: U.S. Government Printing Office, November, 1989). Retrieved from http://www.princeton.edu/~ota/disk1/1989/8921/8921.PDF

Moore, J. A., & Chae, B. (2007). Beginning teachers' use of online resources and communities. *Technology, Pedagogy and Education, 16*(2), 215–224. doi:10.1080/14759390701406844

Moore, M. G. (2007). The theory of transactional distance. In Moore, M. G. (Ed.), *The handbook of distance education* (2nd ed.). Mahwah, NJ: Lawrence Erlbaum Associates.

Moore, M. G., & Kearsley, G. (1996). The theoretical basis for distance education. In *Distance education: A systems view* (pp. 197–212). Belmont, CA: Wadsworth.

Morgan, A. (2010). Interactive whiteboards, interactivity and play in the classroom with children aged three to seven years. *European Early Childhood Education Research Journal, 18*(1), 93–104. doi:10.1080/13502930903520082

Morgan, B., & Smith, R. (2008). A Wiki for classroom writing. *The Reading Teacher, 62*(1), 80–82. doi:10.1598/RT.62.1.10

Morris, S. (2002). *Teaching and learning online: A step-by-step guide for designing an online K-12 school program.* Lanham, MD: Scarecrow Press Inc.

Mott, J. (2010). Envisioning the post-LMS era: The open learning network. *EDUCASE Quarterly, 33*(1). Retrieved from http://www.educause.edu/EDUCAUSE+Quarterly/EDUCAUSEQuarterlyMagazineVolum/EnvisioningthePostLMSEraTheOpe/199389

Mouza, C., & Wong, W. (2009). Student classroom practice: Case development for professional learning in technology integration. *Journal of Technology and Teacher Education, 17*(2), 175–202.

Mulcahy, D. M., Dibbon, D., & Norberg, C. (2008). *An investigation into the nature of education in a rural and remote region of Newfoundland and Labrador: The Straits.* St. John's, NL: The Harris Centre, Memorial University of Newfoundland.

Murphy, E., & Rodríguez-Manzanares, M. (2009a). Learner-centredness in high-school distance learning: Teachers' perspectives and research-validated principles. *Australasian Journal of Educational Technology, 25*(5), 597-610. Retrieved from http://www.ascilite.org.au/ajet/ajet25/murphy.html

Murphy, E. (2010). Online synchronous communication in the second-language classroom. *Canadian Journal of Learning and Technology., 35*(3). Retrieved from http://www.cjlt.ca/index.php/cjlt/article/view/539.

Murphy, E., & Coffin, G. (2003). Synchronous communication in a Web-based senior high school course: Maximizing affordances and minimizing constraints of the tool. *American Journal of Distance Education, 17*(4), 235–246. doi:10.1207/s15389286ajde1704_4

Murphy, E., & Rodríguez-Manzanares, M. (2009b). Sage without a stage: A cultural historical activity theory perspective on e-teaching in web-based, high-school classrooms. *International Review of Research in Open and Distance Learning, 10*(3). Retrieved from http://www.irrodl.org/index.php/irrodl/article/view/579/1300.

Murphy, E., & Rodríguez-Manzanares, M. (2009c). Teachers' perspectives on motivation in high-school distance education. *Journal of Distance Education, 23*(3), 1–24. Retrieved from http://www.jofde.ca/index.php/jde/article/view/602.

Murphy, E., Rodríguez-Manzanares, M., & Barbour, M. K. (2011). Asynchronous and synchronous teaching and learning in high-school distance education. *British Journal of Educational Technology, 42*(4). doi:10.1111/j.1467-8535.2010.01112.x

Murray, D. (2004). *A writer teaches writing.* Boston, MA: Heinle.

Murrow, E. (1951). *Introduction: This I believe* [radio broadcast]. Audio and written transcript: Specific quotation at 3:31-3:38. Retrieved from http://thisibelieve.org/essay/16844/

NAEYC. (1996). Position statement on technology and young children--Ages three through eight. *Young Children, 51*(6), 11–16.

National Assessment of Educational Progress Technology and Engineering Literacy Assessment. (n.d.). Retrieved from http://www.edgateway.net/cs/naepsci/print/docs/470

National Association of Professional Development Schools. (2007). *What it means to be a professional development school.* Columbia, SC: Author.

National Center for Academic Transformation. (2005). *The Buffet model.* Saratoga Springs, NY: Author. Retrieved from http://www.thencat.org/PlanRes/R2R_Model_Buffet.htm

National Center for Academic Transformation. (2005). *Who we are.* Saratoga Springs, NY: Author. Retrieved from http://www.thencat.org/whoweare.html

National Commission on Mathematics and Science Teaching (NCMST). (2000). *Before it's too late: A report to the nation from The National Commission on Mathematics and Science Teaching for the 21st century.* Jessup, MD: Author.

National Council for Accreditation of Teacher Education (NCATE). (Feb 2008). *Professional standards for the accreditation of teacher preparation institutions.* Washington, DC: NCATE.

National Council for Accreditation of Teacher Education. (2008). *Professional standards for the accreditation of teacher preparation institutions.* Washington, DC: NCATE.

National Council for Teachers of Mathematics. (2000). *Principles and standards for school mathematics.* Reston, VA: Author.

National Council for the Social Studies. (2006). *Technology position statement and guidelines.* Retrieved on August 10, 2009, from http://www.socialstudies.org/positions/technology

National Council for the Social Studies. (February 2009 r.). *NCSS position statement on media literacy.* Retrieved January 21, 2011, from http://www.socialstudies.org/positions/medialiteracy

National Council of Teachers of English. (2010). *The NCTE definition of 21st century literacies.* Retrieved from http://www.ncte.org/positions/statements/21stcentdefinition

National Council of Teachers of Mathematics. (2000). *Principles and standards for school mathematics.* Reston, VA: Author.

National Council on Disability. (May 31, 2001). *Federal policy barriers to assistive technology.* A report by the National Council. Washington, DC. [Online]. Retrieved from http://ned.gov.newroom/publications/assistivetechnology/html

National Education Technology Standards for Students. (2007). *International Society for Technology in Education.* Retrieved from http://www.iste.org/Libraries/PDFs/NETS_for_Student_2007_EN.sflb.ashx

National Partnership for Excellence and Accountability in Teaching (NPEAT). (2000). *Revisioning professional development: What learner-centered professional development looks like.* Oxford, OH: Author. Retrieved September 10, 2003, from http://www.nsdc.org/library/policy/npeat213.pdf

National Research Council (NRC). (2002). *How people learn.* Washington, DC: National Academy Press.

National Research Council. (1996). *National science education standards.* Washington, DC: National Academy Press.

National Research Council. (1999). *How people learn: Bridging research and practice* (M. S. Donovan, J. D. Bransford, & J. W. Pellegrino, Eds.). Committee on Learning Research and Educational Practice. Commission on Behavioral and Social Sciences and Education. Washington, DC: National Academy Press.

National Writing Project. (2010). *Because digital writing matters: Improving student writing in online and multimedia environments.* San Francisco: Jossey-Bass.

National Writing Project. (2010). *National Commission on Writing.* Retrieved on January 30, 2011, from http://www.nwp.org/cs/public/print/resource/2432

Nelson, J., Christopher, A., & Mims, C. (2009). TPACK and Web 2.0: Transformation of teaching and learning. *TechTrends*, *53*(5), 80–85. doi:10.1007/s11528-009-0329-z

New London Group. (1996). A pedagogy of multiliteracies: Designing social futures. *Harvard Educational Review*, *66*, 60–92.

New Zealand Council for Educational Research. (2010). *The knowledge age.* Retrieved September 27, 2010, from http://www.shiftingthinking.org/?page_id=58

Newby, T. J., Stepich, D. A., Lehman, J. D., Russell, J. D., & Ottenbreit-Leftwich, A. (2011). *Educational technology for teaching and learning* (4th ed.). Boston, MA: Pearson.

Newman, L., & Findlay, J. (2008). Communities of ethical practice: Using new technologies for ethical dialectical discourse. *Journal of Educational Technology & Society*, *11*(4), 16–28.

Nichols, R., Davis, K., McCord, T., Schmidt, D., & Slezak, A. (2009). The use of heart-rate monitors in physical education. *Strategies: A Journal for Physical and Sport Educators*, *22*(6), 19-23.

Niederhauser, D., & Lindstrom, D. (2006). Addressing the NETS for students through constructivist technology use in K-12 classrooms. *Journal of Educational Computing Research*, *34*(1), 91–128. doi:10.2190/E0X3-9CH0-EE2B-PLXG

Niess, M. L. (2008b). Knowledge needed for teaching with technologies – Call it TPACK. *AMTE Connections*, Spring, 9-10.

Niess, M. L. (2010, May). *Using classroom artifacts to judge teacher knowledge of reform-based instructional practices that integrate technology in mathematics and science classrooms.* Paper presentation for American Educational Research Association (AERA) Annual Conference, Denver, CO.

Niess, M. L., Lee, K., & Sadri, P. (2007, April). *Dynamic spreadsheets as learning technology tools: Developing teachers' technology pedagogical content knowledge (TPCK)* Paper presentation for the American Education Research Association Annual Conference, Chicago, IL.

Niess, M. L., Ronau, R. N., Driskell, S. O., Kosheleva, O., Pugalee, D., & Weinhold, M. W. (2009). Technological pedagogical content knowledge (TPCK): Preparation of mathematics teachers for 21st century teaching and learning. In F. Arbaugh & P. M. Taylor (Eds.), *Inquiry into mathematics teacher education. Association of Mathematics Teacher Educators (AMTE) Monograph Series, 5*, 143-156. January 2009.

Niess, M. L. (2001). Research into practice: A model for integrating technology in preservice science and mathematics content-specific teacher preparation. *School Science and Mathematics, 101*(2), 102–109. doi:10.1111/j.1949-8594.2001.tb18011.x

Niess, M. L. (2005). Preparing teachers to teach science and mathematics with technology: Developing a technology pedagogical content knowledge. *Teaching and Teacher Education, 21*(5), 509–523. doi:10.1016/j.tate.2005.03.006

Niess, M. L. (2006). Guest editorial: Preparing teachers to teach mathematics with technology. *Contemporary Issues in Technology & Teacher Education, 6*(2), 195–203.

Niess, M. L. (2008a). Guiding preservice teachers in developing TPCK. In Silverman, N. (Ed.), *Handbook of technological pedagogical content knowledge (TPCK) for educators* (pp. 223–250). New York, NY: Routledge.

Nikolopoulou, K. (2007). Early childhood educational software: Specific features and issues of localization. *Early Childhood Education Journal, 35*(2), 173–179. doi:10.1007/s10643-007-0168-5

Nikolov, R. (2007). Towards Web 2.0 schools: Rethinking the teachers professional development. In D. Benzie, & M. Iding (Eds.), *Proceedings of IFIP-Conference on Informatics, Mathematics and ICT: A golden triangle.* Boston, MA. Retrieved from http://dspace.ou.nl/bitstream/1820/1064/1/Nikolov-R-paper-IMICT07.pdf

Nippard, E., & Murphy, E. (2007). Social presence in the web-based synchronous secondary classroom. *Canadian Journal of Learning and Technology, 33*(1). Retrieved from http://www.cjlt.ca/content/vol33.1/nippard.html.

Nir-Gal, O., & Klein, P. S. (2004). Computers for cognitive development in early childhood--The teacher's role in the computer learning environment. *Information Technology in Childhood Education Annual,* 97–119.

Nixon, R. (1970). *Special message to the Congress on education reform.* Retrieved from http://www.presidency.ucsb.edu/ws/index.php?pid=2895

Nixon, A. (2009). Mediating social thought through digital storytelling. *Pedagogies: An International Journal, 4,* 63–76.

Norman, D. (1988). *The design of everyday things.* New York, NY: Doubleday.

Norman, M. (2000). The human side of school technology. *Education Digest, 65*(2), 45–52.

Norris, C., & Soloway, E. (2003). The viable alternative: Handhelds. *School Administrator, 60*(4), 26–28.

North American Council for Online Learning & Partnership for 21st Century Skills. (2006). *Virtual schools and 21st century skills.* Vienna, VA: Author. Retrieved 2008 from http://www.nacol.org/docs/NACOL_21CenturySkills.pdf

North American Council for Online Learning. (2008). *National standards for quality online teaching.* Vienna, VA: Author. Retrieved from http://www.nacol.org/nationalstandards/NACOL%20Standards%20Quality%20Online%20Teaching.pdf

North Carolina Professional Teaching Standards Commission. (2006). *North Carolina professional teaching standards.* Retrieved on October 10, 2008, from http://ncptsc.org/Final%20Standards%20Document.pdf.

North Carolina State Board of Education, Department of Public Instruction. (1997). *A strategic plan for reading literacy.* Retrieved from http://www.ncpublicschools.org/docs/curriculum/languagearts/elementary/strategicplanforreadingliteracy.pdf

Norton, P., & Farrell, N. (2001). When attitudes change, do changes in practice follow? In J. Price, et al. (Eds.), *Proceedings of Society for Information Technology & Teacher Education International Conference 2001* (pp. 959-964). Chesapeake, VA: AACE.

Norton, P., & Hathaway, D. (2008c). Reflections on the notion of community in online learning. In K. McFerrin, et al. (Eds.), *Proceedings of Society for Information Technology & Teacher Education International Conference 2008* (pp. 3097-3104). Chesapeake, VA: AACE.

Norton, P., & Schell, G. (2001). How much is enough? Comparing certificate and degree teacher education options. In J. Price, et al. (Eds.), *Proceedings of Society for Information Technology & Teacher Education International Conference 2001* (pp. 965-970). Chesapeake, VA: AACE.

Norton, P., & Sprague, D. (1999). Timber Lane tales: Problem-centered learning and technology integration. In J. Price, et al. (Eds.), *Proceedings of Society for Information Technology & Teacher Education International Conference 1999* (pp. 89-94). Chesapeake, VA: AACE.

Norton, P. (1994). Integrating technology in schools: a cohort process for graduate level inquiry. *Journal of Information Technology for Teacher Education, 3*(2), 163–174. doi:10.1080/0962029940030204

Norton, P. (1995). Integrating technology: Using telecommunications to augment graduate teacher education. *Journal of Technology and Teacher Education, 3*(1), 3–12.

Norton, P., & Hathaway, D. (2008a). On its way to K-12 classrooms: Web 2.0 goes to graduate school. *Computers in the Schools, 25*(3-4), 163–180. doi:10.1080/07380560802368116

Norton, P., & Hathaway, D. (2008b). Exploring two online learning environments: A classroom of one or many? *Journal of Technology on Research in Technology Education, 40*(4), 475–495.

Norton, P., & Hathaway, D. (2009). Exploring online learning through design and design-based research. In Maddux, C. (Ed.), *Research Highlights in Technology and Teacher Education 2009* (pp. 239–246). Chesapeake, VA: AACE.

Norton, P., & Hathaway, D. (2010a). Video production as an instructional strategy: Content learning and teacher practice. *Contemporary Issues in Technology & Teacher Education, 10*(1). Retrieved from http://www.citejournal.org/vol10/iss1/currentpractice/article2.cfm.

Norton, P., & Hathaway, D. (2010b). Online conversations with peers and with an expert mentor. In Maddux, C., Gibson, D., & Dodge, B. (Eds.), *Research Highlights in Technology and Teacher Education 2010* (pp. 239–246). Chesapeake, VA: AACE.

Norton, P., & Sprague, D. (1996). Changing teachers - Teachers changing schools: Assessing a graduate program in technology. *Journal of Information Technology and Teacher Education, 5*(1/2), 93–105.

Norton, P., & Sprague, D. (2002-2003). Timber Lane technology tales: A design experiment in alternative field experiences for preservice candidates. *Journal of Computing in Teacher Education, 19*(2), 40–46.

Norton, P., & Wiburg, K. M. (2004). *Teaching with technology: Designing opportunities to learn*. Toronto, Canada: Thomson Wadsworth.

Nussbaum, B. (2005, January 3). Getting schooled in innovation [Electronic version]. *Business Week Online*. Retrieved from http://www.businessweek.com/bwdaily/dnflash/jan2005/nf2005013_8303.htm

Nye, S. B. (2008). Teaching with technology resources in physical education. *VAHPERD Journal, 29*(4).

O'Brien, D. G., & Bauer, E. (2005). New literacies and the institution of old learning. *Reading Research Quarterly, 40*, 120–131. doi:10.1598/RRQ.40.1.7

O'Connor, K., Good, A., & Greene, H.C. (2006). Lead by example: The impact of tele-observation on social studies methods courses. *Social Studies Research and Practice, 1*(2).

O'Neill, L. M. (2001). Universal design for learning: Making education accessible to all learners. *Syllabus, April*, 31-32.

Oakley, G., & Jay, J. (2008). Making time for reading factors that influence the success of multimedia reading in the home. *The Reading Teacher, 62*(3), 246–255. doi:10.1598/RT.62.3.6

O'Bannon, B., Matthew, K. I., & Thomas, L. (1998). Faculty development: Key to the integration of technology in teacher preparation. *Journal of Computing in Teacher Education, 14*(4), 7–11.

Oblinger, D., & Oblinger, J. (2005). Is it age or IT: First steps toward understanding the Net Generation. In D. Oblinger & J. Obligner (Eds.), *Educating the Net Generation*, Educause 2005. Retrieved from http://www.educause.edu/educatingthenetgen/

Oblinger, D. (2003). Boomers, gen-xers, and millennials: Understanding the new students. *EDUCAUSE Review, 38*(4), 37–47.

O'Donnell, P., Weber, K. P., & McLaughlin, T. F. (2003). Improving correct and error rate and reading comprehension using key words and previewing: A case report with a language minority student. *Education & Treatment of Children, 26*, 237–254.

Office of Educational Technology. U.S. Department of Education (2010). *Transforming American education: Learning powered by technology. National Educational Technology Plan.* Retrieved on September 16, 2010 from www.ed.gov/technology.netp-2010

Office of Special Education Programs. (2006). *26ᵗʰ annual report to Congress on the implementation of the Individual with Disabilities Act, 2004* (Vols. 1, 2). Washington, DC: U.S. Department of Education.

Ohlund, B., & Yu, C. (2009). *Threats to validity of research design.* Retrieved on April 23, 2010, from http://www.creative-wisdom.com/teaching/WBI/threat.shtml

Okojie, M. C., & Olinzock, A. (2006). Developing a positive mind-set toward the use of technology for classroom instruction. *International Journal of Instructional Media, 33*(1), 33–41.

Oliver, K. (2007). Leveraging Web 2.0 in the redesign of a graduate-level technology integration course. *TechTrends, 51*(5), 55–61. doi:10.1007/s11528-007-0071-3

Oliver, K. (2009). An investigation of concept mapping to improve the reading comprehension of science texts. *Journal of Science Education and Technology, 18*(5), 402–414. doi:10.1007/s10956-009-9157-3

Oliver, K., & Raubenheimer, C. D. (2007a, June). Strategies for online concept mapping part 1. *Online Cl@ssroom. Ideas for Effective Instruction, 1*, 7–8.

Oliver, K., & Raubenheimer, C. D. (2007b, July). Strategies for online concept mapping part 2. *Online Cl@ssroom. Ideas for Effective Instruction, 1*, 3.

Oliver, M., & Trigwell, K. (2005). Can blended learning be redeemed? *E-learning, 2*(1), 17–26.

O'Reilly, T. (2007). What is Web 2.0: Design patterns and business models for the next generation of software. *Communications & Strategies, 1*, 17.

Ottenbreit-Leftwich, A., Glazewski, K., & Newby, T. (2010). Preservice technology integration course revision: A conceptual guide. [Chesapeake, VA: AACE.]. *Journal of Technology and Teacher Education, 18*(1), 5–33.

Ottenbreit-Leftwich, A., Glazewski, K., Newby, T., & Ertmer, P. (2010). Teacher value beliefs associated with using technology: Addressing professional and student needs. *Computers & Education, 55*(3), 1321–1335. doi:10.1016/j.compedu.2010.06.002

Ovando, C., Combs, M. C., & Collier, V. P. (2011). *Bilingual and ESL classrooms: Teaching in multicultural contexts* (5th ed.). New York, NY: McGraw-Hill.

Overbay, A., Patterson, A. S., Vasu, E. S., & Grable, L. L. (2010). Constructivism and technology use: Findings from the IMPACTing Leadership project. *Educational Media International, 47*(2), 103–120. doi:10.1080/09523987.2010.492675

Ozgun-Koca, S. A., Meagher, M., & Edwards, M. T. (2010). Preservice teachers' emerging TPACK in a technology-rich methods class. *Mathematics Educator, 19*(2), 10–20.

Ozgun-Koca, S. A., Meagher, M., & Todd, M. (2010). Preservice teachers' emerging TPACK in a technology-rich methods class. *Mathematics Educator, 19*(2), 10–20.

Pahl, R. (1996). Tech talk-for social studies teachers. *Social Studies, 87*(4), 186–187. doi:10.1080/00377996.1996.9958437

Palandro, D., Thoms, K., Kusek, K., Muller-Karger, F., & Greely, T. (2005). Satellite remote sensing of coral reefs: By learning about coral reefs, students gain an understanding of ecosystems and how cutting-edge technology can be used to study ecological change. *Science Teacher (Normal, Ill.), 72*(6), 51–55.

Pape, L., Adams, R., & Ribeiro, C. (2005). The virtual high school: Collaboration and online professional development. In Berge, Z. L., & Clark, T. (Eds.), *Virtual schools: Planning for success* (pp. 118–132). New York, NY: Teachers College Press.

Papert, S. (1998). *Child power: Keys to the new learning of the digital century*. Speech delivered at the eleventh Colin Cherry Memorial Lecture on Communication on June 2, 1998 at the Imperial College in London.

Papert, S. (1980). *Mindstorms: Children, computers, and powerful ideas*. Basic Books.

Papert, S. (1993). *The children's machine: Rethinking schools in the age of the computer*. New York, NY: Basic Books.

Parette, H. P., Quesenberry, A. C., & Blum, C. (2010). Missing the boat with technology usage in early childhood settings: A 21st century view of developmentally appropriate practice. *Early Childhood Education Journal, 37*(5), 335–343. doi:10.1007/s10643-009-0352-x

Parker, D. R. (1996). *Integrating faculty use of technology in teaching and teacher education*. Paper presented at the Annual Meeting of the Mid-South Educational Research Association.

Parker, M. A., Ndoye, A., & Ritzhaupt, A. D. (Manuscript submitted for publication). Qualitative analysis of ePortfolios in teacher education: Implications for successful integration. *Journal of Digital Learning in Teacher Education*.

Park, S. H., & Ertmer, P. A. (2008). Examining barriers in technology-enhanced problem-based learning; Using performance support systems approach. *British Journal of Educational Technology, 39*(4), 12. doi:10.1111/j.1467-8535.2008.00858.x

Partnership for 21st Century Skills. (2002). *Learning for the 21st century: A report and mile guide for 21st century skills*. Washington, DC: Author.

Partnership for 21st Century Skills. (n.d.). *Home page*. Retrieved from http://www.p21.org/index.php?option=com_content&task=view&id=254&Itemid=120

Pecheone, R. L., Pigg, M. J., Chung, R. R., & Souviney, R. J. (2005). Performance assessment and electronic portfolios: Their effect on teacher learning and education. *Clearing House (Menasha, Wis.), 78*(4), 164–176. doi:10.3200/TCHS.78.4.164-176

Peck, C., Cuban, L., & Kirkpatrick, H. (2002). Techno-promoter dreams, student realities. *Phi Delta Kappan, 83*(6), 472–480. Retrieved from http://www.pdkintl.org/kappan/k0202pec.htm.

Pellegrino, J. W., & Altman, J. E. (1997). Information technology and teacher preparation: Some critical issues and illustrative solutions. *Peabody Journal of Education, 72*(10), 89–121. doi:10.1207/s15327930pje7201_5

Pellegrino, J., Goldman, S., Bertenthal, M., & Lawless, K. (2007). Teacher education and technology: Initial results from the "what works and why" project. *Yearbook of the National Society for the Study of Education, 106*(2), 52–86. doi:10.1111/j.1744-7984.2007.00115.x

Penuel, W., Fishman, B., Yamaguchi, R., & Gallagher, L. (2007). What makes professional development effective? Strategies that foster curriculum implementation. *American Educational Research Journal, 44*(4), 921–958. doi:10.3102/0002831207308221

Persichiitte, K., Caffarella, E., & Fergusion-Pabst, D. (2003). A continuing journey toward technology infusion within teacher preparation. *TechTrends, 4*(3).

Persichitte, K., Caffarella, E. P., & Tharptitle, D. D. (1999). Technology integration in teacher preparation: A qualitative research study. *Journal of Technology and Teacher Education, 7*(3), 219–233.

Peterson, E. (2007). Incorporating screencasts in online teaching. *International Review of Research in Open and Distance Learning, 8*(3), 1–4.

Petty, T., & Heafner, T. (2009a). The remote observation of graduate interns: The missing piece of the puzzle. In G. Siemens & C. Fulford (Eds.), *Proceedings of World Conference on Educational Multimedia, Hypermedia and Telecommunications 2009* (pp. 4293-4297). Chesapeake, VA: AACE.

Petty, T., Heafner, T., & Hartshorne, R. (2009, March). Examining a pilot program for the remote observation of graduate interns. In R. Weber, K. McFerrin, R. Carlsen, & D. A. Willis, (Eds.), *2009 Society for Information Technology and Teacher Education Annual: Proceedings of SITE2009* (pp. 2658-2660). Norfolk, VA: Association for the Advancement of Computing in Education (AACE).

Petty, T., & Heafner, T. (2009b). What is ROGI? *Journal of Technology Integration in the Classroom, 1*(1), 21–27.

Picciano, A. G., & Seaman, J. (2009). K-12 online learning: A 2008 follow-up of the survey of US school district administrators. Sloan Consortium. Retrieved from http://sloanconsortium.org/publications/survey/pdf/k-12_online_learning_2008.pdf

Picciano, A. G., & Seaman, J. (2009). *K-12 online learning: A survey of U.S. school district administrators.* The Sloan Foundation. Retrieved from http://sloanconsortium.org/publications/survey/pdf/k-12_online_learning_2008.pdf

Pierson, M. (2001). Technology integration practice as a function of pedagogical expertise. *Journal of Research on Computing in Education, 33*(4), 413–430.

Pierson, M. (2005). Technology in the classroom: Thinking beyond machines. In Hughes, L. W. (Ed.), *Current issues in school leadership* (pp. 245–264). Mahwah, NJ: Lawrence Erlebaum Associates.

Pierson, M. E. (2001). Technology integration practices as function of pedagogical expertise. *Journal of Research on Computing in Education, 33*(4), 413–429.

Pierson, M. E., & McNeil, S. (2000). Preservice technology integration through collaborative action communities. *Contemporary Issues in Technology & Teacher Education, 1*(1), 189–199.

Pintrich, P. R. (2000). Multiple goals, multiple pathways: The role of goal orientation in learning and achievement. *Journal of Educational Psychology, 92*(3), 544–555. .doi:10.1037/0022-0663.92.3.544

Pisha, B., & Coyne, P. (2001). Smart from the start: The promise of universal design for learning. *Remedial and Special Education, 22*, 197–205. .doi:10.1177/074193250102200402

Pisha, B., & Stahl, S. (2005). The promise of new learning environments for students with disabilities. *Intervention in School and Clinic, 41*, 67–75. .doi:10.1177/1053451 2050410020601

Plourde, M. (2010). *Sakai @ UD progress report.* University of Delaware. Retrieved from http://www.slideshare.net/mathplourde/2232010-sakaiud-progress-report?from=ss_embed

Polly, D., Mims, C., Shepard, C., & Inan, F. (2010). Evidence of impact: Transforming teacher education with preparing tomorrow's teachers to teach with technology (PT3) grants. *Teaching and Teacher Education, 26*, 863–870. doi:10.1016/j.tate.2009.10.024

Polly, D., Mims, C., Shepherd, C. E., & Inai, F. (2010). Evidence of impact: Transforming teacher education with preparing tomorrow's teachers to teach with technology (PT3) grants. *Teaching and Teacher Education, 26*, 863–870. doi:10.1016/j.tate.2009.10.024

Pope, M., Hare, D., & Howard, E. (2002). Technology integration: Closing the gap between what preservice teachers are taught to do and what they can do. *Journal of Technology and Teacher Education, 10*(2), 191–203.

Porter, A. C., Garet, M. S., Desimone, L., Yoon, K. S., & Birman, B. F. (2000). *Does professional development change teaching practice? Results from a three-year study.* (U.S. Department of Education Report No. 2000–04). Retrieved September 23, 2010, from http://www.ed.gov/rschstat/eval/teaching/epdp/report.pdf

Porter, R., Buarienti, K., Brydon, B., Robb, J., Royston, A., & Painter, H. (2010). Writing better lab reports. *Science Teacher (Normal, Ill.), 77*(1), 6.

Potthoff, D. E., Dinsmore, J. A., Stirtz, G., Walsh, T., Ziebarth, J., & Eifler, K. (2000). Preparing for democracy and diversity: The impact of community-based field experiences on preservice teachers' knowledge, skills, and attitudes. *Action in Teacher Education, 22*(1), 79–92.

Preece, J., Rogers, Y., & Sharp, H. (2002). *Interaction design.* New York, NY: Wiley.

Prensky, M. (2001). Digital natives, digital immigrants. *On the Horizon, 9*(5). NCB University Press. Retrieved from http://pre2005.flexiblelearning.net.au/projects/resources/Digital_Natives_Digital_Immigrants.pdf

Prensky, M. (2006). *Shaping teach for the classroom.* Retrieved January 14, 2011,from http://www.edutopia.org/adopt-and-adapt-shaping-tech-for-classroom

Prensky, M. (2009). H. sapiens digital: From digital immigrants and digital natives to digital wisdom. *Innovate, 5*(3).

Prensky, M. (2001). Digital natives, digital immigrants. *Horizon, 9*(5). doi:10.1108/10748120110424816

Prensky, M. (2005). Listen to the natives. *Educational Leadership, 63*, 8–13.

Prensky, M. (2010). *Teaching digital natives: Partnering for real learning*. Thousand Oaks, CA: Corwin.

President's Committee of Advisors on Science and Technology. (2000). Report to the president on the use of technology to strengthen K-12 education in the United States. In Jossey-Bass Inc. (Eds.), *The Jossey-Bass reader on technology and learning*, (pp. 3-19). San Francisco, CA: Jossey-Bass Inc., Publishers.

Project Tomorrow. (2008). *21st century learners deserve a 21st century education: Selected national findings of the Speak up 2007 survey*. Retrieved March 28, 2009, from http://www.tomorrow.org/speakup/speakup_congress_2007.html

Project Tomorrow. (2009). *Speak up 2009: Creating our future: Students speak up about their vision for 21st century learning*. Retrieved from http://www.tomorrow.org/speakup/pdfs/SU09NationalFindingsStudents&Parents.pdf

Project Tomorrow. (2010). *Unleashing the future: Educators "Speak up" about the use of emerging technologies for learning*. Retrieved from http://www.tomorrow.org/speakup/pdfs/SU09UnleashingTheFuture.pdf

Project, S. U. C. C. E. E. D. (n.d.). *Project SUCCEED*. Retrieved from http://www.education.miami.edu/succeed/

Putnam, R. T., & Borko, H. (2000). What do new views of knowledge and thinking have to say about research on teacher learning? *Educational Researcher, 29*(1), 4–15.

Quillen, I. (2010). Analysis notes virtual ed. priorities in RTT winners. *Education Week, 30*(3).

Ragan, L. (2009). *How would you rank the critical competencies for teaching online?* Distance.

Rankin, E. (2001). *The work of writing: Insights and strategies for academics and professionals*. San Francisco, CA: Jossey-Bass.

Ravitz, J. L., Becker, H. J., & Wong, Y.-T. (2000). *Constructivist compatible beliefs and practices among U.S. teachers* (Teaching, Learning & Computing Report 4.) Irvine, CA: Center for Research on Information Technology and Organizations, University of California. Retrieved from http://www.crito.uci.edu/TLC/findings/report4/

Ravitz, J., & Hoadley, C. (2005). Supporting change and scholarship through review of online resources in professional development settings. *British Journal of Educational Technology, 36*(6), 957–974. doi:10.1111/j.1467-8535.2005.00567.x

Ray, B., & Coulter, G. A. (2010). Perceptions of the value of digital mini-games: Implications for middle school classrooms. *Journal of Digital Learning in Teacher Education, 26*(3), 92–100.

Ray, K. W. (2006). *Study driven: A framework for planning units of study in the writing workshop*. Portsmouth, NH: Heinemann.

Reed, A. (2008). Most states have technology standards for teachers. *edweek.org, 1*, 1.

Reeves, T. C. (2003). Storm clouds on the digital education horizon. *Journal of Computing in Higher Education, 15*(1), 3–26. doi:10.1007/BF02940850

Reeves, T. C. (2005). No significant differences revisited: A historical perspective on the research informing contemporary online learning. In Kearsley, G. (Ed.), *Online learning: Personal reflections on the transformation of education* (pp. 299–308). Englewood Cliffs, NJ: Educational Technology Publications.

Reeves, T. C., Herrington, J., & Oliver, R. (2002). Authentic activities and online learning. In Goody, A., Herrington, J., & Northcote, M. (Eds.), *Quality conversations: Research and development in higher education* (Vol. 25, pp. 562–567). Jamison, Australia: HERDSA.

Reeves, T. C., & Reeves, P. M. (1997). Effective dimensions of interactive learning on the World Wide Web. In Khan, B. H. (Ed.), *Web-based instruction* (pp. 59–66). Englewood Cliffs, NJ: Educational Technology Publications.

Remenyi, D. (2007). *Proceedings of the 6th European Conference on e-Learning*. London, UK: Academic Conferences Ltd.

Renyi, J. (1996). *Teachers take charge of their learning: Transforming professional development for student success*. Washington, DC: National Foundation for the Improvement of Education.

Repman, J., Zinskie, C., & Downs, E. (2010). Fulfilling the promise: Addressing institutional factors that impede the implementation of e-learning 2.0. In Yang, H. H., & Yuen, S. C.-Y. (Eds.), *Collective intelligence and e-learning 2.0: Implications of Web-based communities and networking* (pp. 44–60). New York, NY: Information Science Reference.

Resnick, L. B. (1985). Cognition and instruction: Recent theories of human competence. In Hammonds, B. L. (Ed.), *Psychology and learning* (*Vol. 4*, pp. 127–186). Washington, DC: American Psychological Association. doi:10.1037/10053-004

Rheingold, H. (2008). 'Using participatory media and public voice to encourage civic engagement. In B W. L. Bennett (Ed.), *Civic life online: Learning how digital media can engage youth*, (pp. 97-118). John D. And Catherine T. MacArther Foundation Series on Digital Media and Learning. Cambridge, MA: MIT Press.

Ribble, M. S., Bailey, G. D., & Ross, T. W. (2004). Digital citizenship: Addressing appropriate technology behavior. *Learning and Leading with Technology, 32*(1), 6–12.

Rice, K., & Dawley, L. (2007). *Going virtual! The status of professional development for K-12 online teachers*. Boise, ID: Boise State University. Retrieved from http://edtech.boisestate.edu/goingvirtual/goingvirtual1.pdf

Rice, E. H. (2002). The collaboration process in professional development schools: Results of a meta-ethnography, 1990-1998. *Journal of Teacher Education, 53*(1), 55–67. doi:10.1177/0022487102053001006

Rice, K. L. (2006). A comprehensive look at distance education in the K-12 context. *Journal of Research on Technology in Education, 38*(4), 425–448.

Richardson, W. (2006). *Blogs, wikis, podcasts, and other powerful web tools for classrooms*. Thousand Oaks, CA.

Rich, P. J., & Hannafin, M. J. (2008b). Decisions and reasons: Examining preservice teacher decision-making through video self-analysis. *Journal of Computing in Higher Education, 20*(1), 62–94. doi:10.1007/BF03033432

Rich, P., & Hannafin, M. (2008a). Capturing and assessing evidence of student teacher inquiry: A case study. *Teaching and Teacher Education, 24*, 1426–1440. .doi:10.1016/j.tate.2007.11.016

Rideout, V., Foehr, U. G., & Roberts, D. F. (2010). *Generation M2: Media in the lives of 8- to 18-year-olds*. Menlo Park, CA: Kaiser Family Foundation.

Riley, R. W., & Roberts, L. G. (2000, December). Putting a world-class education at the fingertips of all children: The national educational technology plan. *eLearning*. Washington, DC: U.S. Department of Education.

Rittel, H., & Webber, M. (1973). Dilemmas in a general theory of planning. *Policy Sciences, 4*(2), 155–169. doi:10.1007/BF01405730

Ritzhaupt, A. D., & Singh, O. (March, 2006). Student perspectives of ePortfolios in computing education. *Proceedings of the Association of Computing Machinery Southeast Conference*, Melbourne, FL, (pp. 152 - 157).

Ritzhaupt, A. D., Ndoye, A., & Parker, M. (2010). Validation of the electronic portfolio student perspective instrument (EPSPI): Conditions under a different integration initiative. *Journal of Digital Learning in Teacher Education, 26*(3), 111–119.

Ritzhaupt, A. D., Singh, O., Seyferth, T., & Dedrick, R. (2008). Development of the electronic portfolio student perspective instrument: An ePortfolio integration initiative. *Journal of Computing in Higher Education, 19*(2), 47–71. doi:10.1007/BF03033426

Ritzhaupt, A., Ndoye, A., & Parker, M. (2010). Validation of the electronic portfolio student perspective instrument (EPSPI): Conditions under a different integration initiative. *Journal of Digital Learning in Teacher Education, 26*(3), 111–119.

Robertson, C., & Lankford, D. (2010). Laboratory notebooks in the science classroom. *Science Teacher (Normal, Ill.), 77*(1), 5.

Roberts, T. (2008). What's going on in Room 13? *Art Education, 19*(6), 19–24.

Robin, B. (2008). Digital storytelling: A powerful technology tool for the 21st century classroom. *Theory into Practice, 47*, 220–228. doi:10.1080/00405840802153916

Roblyer, M. D., Freeman, J., Stabler, M., & Schneidmiller, J. (2007). *External evaluation of the Alabama ACCESS initiative: Phase 3 report*. Eugene, OR: International Society for Technology in Education. Retrieved from http://accessdl.state.al.us/2006Evaluation.pdf

Roblyer, M. D., & Doering, A. H. (2010). *Integrating educational technology into teaching* (5th ed.). Boston, MA: Allyn & Bacon.

Roblyer, M. D., & McKenzie, B. (2000). Distant but not out-of-touch: What makes an effective distance learning instructor? *Learning and Leading with Technology, 27*(6), 50–53.

Roblyer, M. K. (2003). *Integrating educational technology into teaching* (3rd ed.). Upper Saddle River, NJ: Merrill Prentice-Hall, Inc.

Roblyer, M., & Doering, A. (2010). *Integrating educational technology into teaching* (5th ed.). Boston, MA: Pearson Education.

Rock, T., Heafner, T., Oldendorf, S., Passe, J., O'Connor, K., Good, A., & Byrd, S. (2006). One state closer to a national crisis: A report on elementary social studies in North Carolina schools. *Theory and Research in Social Education, 34*(4), 455–483.

Rogers, E. (1995). *Diffusion of innovations*. New York, NY: Simon and Schuster Inc.

Rogers, E. M. (2003). *Diffusion of innovations*. New York, NY: Simon & Schuster, Inc.

Rorvig, M., & Lunin, L. F. (1999). Introduction and overview: Visualization, retrieval, and knowledge. *Journal of the American Society for Information Science American Society for Information Science, 50*(9), 790–793. doi:10.1002/(SICI)1097-4571(1999)50:9<790::AID-ASI7>3.0.CO;2-C

Rosaen, C., & Bird, T. (2005). Providing authentic contexts for learning information technology in teacher preparation. *Journal of Technology and Teacher Education, 13*(2), 211–231.

Roschelle, J., Pea, R., Hoadley, C., Gordin, D., & Means, B. (2001). Changing how and what children learn in schools with computer-based technologies. *The Future of Children, 10*(2), 76–101. doi:10.2307/1602690

Rose, D. H., & Meyer, A. (2002). *Teaching every student in the digital age*. Virginia: Association for Supervision and Curriculum Development.

Rose, D., & Meyer, A. (2000). Universal design for learning. *Journal of Special Education Technology, 15*(1), 67–70.

Rose, D., & Meyer, A. (2002). *Teaching every student in the digital age*. Alexandria, VA: ASCD.

Rosen, D. B., & Jaruszewicz, C. (2009). Developmentally appropriate technology use and early childhood teacher education. *Journal of Early Childhood Teacher Education, 30*(2), 162–171. doi:10.1080/10901020902886511

Rosen, D., & Nelson, C. (2008). Web 2.0: A new generation of learners and education. *Computers in the Schools, 25*(3), 211–225. doi:10.1080/07380560802370997

Rosenfeld, B., & Martinez-Pons, M. (2005). Promoting classroom technology use. *Quarterly Review of Distance Education, 6*(2), 145–153.

Rotherham, A. J., & Willingham, D. (2009). 21st century skills - The challenges ahead. *Educational Leadership, 67*(1), 16–21.

Rush, L. S. (2002). Taking a broad view of literacy: Lessons from the Appalachian Trail community. *Reading-Online*. Retrieved April 22, 2004 from http://www.readingonline.org/newliteracies/lit

Russel, M., Bebell, D., O'Dwyer, L., & O'Conner, K. (2003). Examining teacher technology use: Implications for pre-service and in-service teacher preparation. *Journal of Teacher Education, 54*, 2971–310. doi:10.1177/0022487103255985

Sadler, D. R. (1989). Formative assessment and the design of instructional systems. *Instructional Science, 18*(2), 119–144. doi:10.1007/BF00117714

Sakai Project. (n.d.). Retrieved from http://sakaiproject.org/

Saka, Y., Southerland, S., & Brooks, J. (2009). Becoming a member of a school community while working toward science education reform: Teacher induction from a cultural historical activity theory (CHAT) perspective. *Science Education, 93*, 996–1025. doi:10.1002/sce.20342

Salend, S. J. (2009). Technology-based classroom assessments: Alternatives to testing. *Teaching Exceptional Children, 41*(6), 49–58.

Sandholtz, J. H., Ringstaff, C., & Dwyer, D. C. (1997). *Teaching with technology: Creating student-centered classrooms*. New York, NY: Teachers College Press.

Sandholtz, J., Ringstaff, C., & Dwyer, C. D. (1997). *Teaching with technology: Creating student-centered classrooms*. New York, NY: Teachers College Press.

Sang, G., Valcke, M., van Braak, J., & Tondeur, J. (2010). Student teachers' thinking processes and ICT integration: Predictors of prospective teaching behaviors with educational technology. *Computers & Education, 54*(1), 103–112. doi:10.1016/j.compedu.2009.07.010

Scardamalia, M., & Bereiter, C. (2006). Knowledge building: Theory, pedagogy, and technology. In K. Sawyer (Ed.), *Cambridge handbook of the learning sciences* (pp. 97-118). New York, NY: Cambridge University Press. Retrieved from http://www.ikit.org/fulltext/2006_KBTheory.pdf

Scardamalia, M., & Bereiter, C. (1996). Computer support for knowledge-building communities. In Kotchmann, T. (Ed.), *CSCL: Theory and practice of an emerging paradigm*. Mahwah, NJ: Lawrence Erlbaum Associates.

Scardamalia, M., & Bereiter, C. (2006). Knowledge building: Theory, pedagogy, and technology. In Sawyer, K. (Ed.), *Cambridge handbook of the learning sciences* (pp. 97–118). New York, NY: Cambridge University Press.

Schaffhauser, D. (2009). Which came first--The technology or the pedagogy? *T.H.E. Journal, 36*(8), 27–32.

Schalock, H. D., & Myton, D. (2002). Connecting teaching and learning: An introduction to teacher work sample methodology. In Girod, G. (Ed.), *Connecting teaching and learning: A handbook for teacher educators on teacher work sample methodology*. Washington, DC: AACTE.

Schank, R. C. (1999). *Dynamic memory revisited*. New York, NY: Cambridge University Press. doi:10.1017/CBO9780511527920

Schell, L. (2004). Teaching learning styles with technology. *Journal of Physical Education, Recreation & Dance, 75*(1), 14–18.

Schifter, D., Bastable, V., & Russell, S. J. (2002). *Developing mathematical ideas: Measuring space in one, two, and three dimensions*. Parsippany, NJ: Dale Seymour.

Schlager, M., Farooq, U., Fusco, J., Schank, P., & Dwyer, N. (2009). Analyzing online social networking in professional learning communities: Cyber networks require cyber-research tools. *Journal of Teacher Education, 60*(1), 86–100. doi:10.1177/0022487108328487

Schlatter, B., & Hurd, A. (2005). Geocaching: The 21st century hide and seek. *Journal of Physical Education, Recreation & Dance, 76*(7), 28–32.

Schlechty, P. C. (1993). On the frontier of school reform with trailblazers, pioneers, and settlers. *Journal of Staff Development*, (Fall): 1993.

Schmidt, D. A., Baran, E., Thompson, A. D., Koehler, M. J., Mishra, P., & Shin, T. S. (2009). *Technological pedagogical content knowledge (TPACK): The development and validation of an assessment instrument for preservice teachers.* Paper presented at the annual meeting of the American Educational Research Association (AERA), San Diego, CA.

Schmidt, D. A., Baran, E., Thompson, A. D., Mishra, P., Koehler, M. J., & Shin, T. S. (2009). Technological pedagogical content knowledge (TPACK): The development and validation of an assessment instrument for preservice teachers. *Journal of Research on Technology in Education, 42*(2), 123–149.

Schofield, J. W., & Davidson, A. L. (2002). *Bringing the internet to school: Lessons from an urban district*. San Francisco, CA: Jossey-Bass.

Schon, D. A. (1996). *Educating the reflective practitioner: Toward a new design for teaching and learning in the professions*. San Francisco, CA: Jossey-Bass, Inc.

Schroeder, S. (2010). Web users now on Facebook longer than Google. *CNN Tech*. Retrieved September 10, 2010, from http://www.cnn.com/2010/TECH/social.media/09/10/facebook.google.time/

Schroeder, B. (2009). Within the wiki; Best practices for educators. *AACE Journal, 17*(3), 181–197.

Schrum, L. (1999). Technology professional development for teachers. *Educational Technology Research and Development, 47*(4), 83–90. doi:10.1007/BF02299599

Schrum, L., Thompson, A., Maddux, C., Sprague, D., Bull, G., & Bell, L. (2007). Editorial: Research on the effectiveness of technology in schools: The roles of pedagogy and content. *Contemporary Issues in Technology & Teacher Education, 7*(1), 456–460.

Schwartz, R. S., Lederman, N. G., & Crawford, B. A. (2004). Developing views of nature of science in an authentic context: An explicit approach to bridging the gap between nature of science and scientific inquiry. *Science Education, 88*(4), 36. doi:10.1002/sce.10128

Sclater, N. (2008). *(2008 June 24). Web 2.0, personal learning environments, and the future of learning management systems. EDUCAUSE* (p. 13). Center for Applied Research Bulletin.

Scribner-MacLean, M., Nikonchuk, A., Kaplo, P., & Wall, M. (2006). In sync with science teaching. *Science Teacher (Normal, Ill.), 73*(7), 26–29.

Seels, B., Campbell, S., & Talsma, V. (2003). Supporting excellence in technology through communities of learning. *Educational Technology Research and Development, 51*(1), 91–104. doi:10.1007/BF02504520

Senge, P. (1999). *The dance of change: The challenges of sustaining momentum in learning organizations*. New York, NY: Doubleday.

Severance, C., Hanss, T., & Hardin, J. (2010). IMS learning tools interoperability: Enabling a mash-up approach to teaching and learning tools. *Technology, Instruction. Cognition & Learning, 7*(3-4), 245–262.

Sewlyn, N. (2006). Exploring the digital disconnect between net-savvy students and their schools. *Learning, Media and Technology, 31*(1), 5–17. doi:10.1080/17439880500515416

Shaffer, D. W., & Resnick, M. (1999). Thick authenticity: New media and authentic learning. *Journal of Interactive Learning Research, 10*(2), 195–215.

Shanker, A. (1990). Staff development and the restructured school. In Joyce, B. (Ed.), *Changing school culture through staff development* (pp. 91–103). Alexandria, VA: ASCD.

Shapira, I. (2008). When young teachers go wild on the web. *Tech Policy*. Retrieved August 28, 2010, from http://www.washingtonpost.com/wp-dyn/content/article/2008/04/27/AR2008042702213.html

Sharpe, L., Hu, C., Crawford, L., Saravanan, G., Khine, M. S., Moo, S. N., & Wong, A. (2003). Enhancing multipoint desktop video conferencing (MDVC) with lesson video clips: Recent developments in pre-service teaching practice in Singapore. *Teaching and Teacher Education, 19*(3), 529–541. doi:10.1016/S0742-051X(03)00050-7

Sharpe, T., & Hawkins, A. (1998). Technology and the information age: A cautionary tale for higher education. *Quest, 50*(1), 19–32.

Shavelson, R., Ruiz-Primo, A., Li, M., & Ayala, C. (2003). *Evaluating new approaches to assessing learning (CSE Report 604)*. Los Angeles, CA: University of California National Center for Research on Evaluation.

Shaver, J. (1999). Electronic technology and the future of Social Studies in elementary and secondary schools. *Journal of Education, 181*(3), 13–41.

Shelton, M., & Jones, M. (1996). Staff development that works! A tale of four T's. *NASSP Bulletin, 80*(582), 99–105. doi:10.1177/019263659608058214

Sherry, L. (1995). Issues in distance learning. [Charlottesville, VA: AACE.]. *International Journal of Educational Telecommunications, 1*(4), 337–365.

Shin, T., Koehler, M., Mishra, P., Schmidt, D., Baran, E., & Thompson, A. (2009). *Changing technological pedagogical content knowledge (TPACK) through course experiences*. Paper presented at the Society for Information Technology & Teacher Education International Conference 2009, Charleston, SC, USA.

Shin, M., & Lee, Y.-J. (2009). Changing the landscape of teacher education via online teaching and learning. *Techniques: Connecting Education and Careers, 84*(1), 32–33.

Shneiderman, B. (1998). *Designing the user interface: Strategies for effective human-computer interaction* (3rd ed.). Menlo Park, CA: Addison Wesley.

Shoffner, M. (2009). Personal attitudes and technology: Implications for preservice teacher reflective practice. *Teacher Education Quarterly, 36*(2), 143–161.

Shreiter, B., & Ammon, P. (1989). *Teachers' thinking and their use of reading contracts*. Paper presented at the Annual Meeting of the American Educational Research Association, San Francisco, California.

Shulman, L. (1986). Those who understand: Knowledge growth in teaching. *Educational Researcher, 15*(2), 4–14.

Shulman, L. (1987). Knowledge and teaching: Foundations of the new reform. *Harvard Educational Review, 57*(1), 1–22.

Shulman, L. (1998). Teacher portfolios: A theoretical activity. In Lyons, N. (Ed.), *With portfolio in hand* (pp. 23–37). New York, NY: Teachers College Press.

Shulman, L. S. (1986). Those who understand: Knowledge growth in teaching. *Educational Research, 15*(4), 4–14.

Shulman, L. S. (1986). Those who understand: Knowledge growth in teaching. *Educational Researcher, 15*(2), 4–14.

Shulman, L. S. (1987). Knowledge and teaching: Foundations of the new reform. *Harvard Educational Review, 57*(1), 1–22.

Shulman, L. S. (1992). Toward a pedagogy of cases. In *Case methods in teacher education* (pp. 1–30). New York, NY: Teachers College Press.

Sibbet, D. (2008). Visual intelligence: Using the deep patterns of visual language to build cognitive skills. *Theory into Practice, 47*(2), 118–127. doi:10.1080/00405840801992306

Siegel, L. S. (2003). Basic cognitive processes and reading disabilities. In Swanson, H. L., Harris, K. R., & Graham, S. (Eds.), *Handbook of learning disabilities* (pp. 158–181). New York, NY: Guiliford Press.

Siegel, S., Haddock, B., & Wilken, L. (2009). Active video games (exergaming) and energy expenditure in college students. *International Journal of Exercise Science, 2*(3), 165–174.

Siemens, G. (2004). *eLearnSpace: Everything elearning.* ePortfolios. Retrieved June 27, 2005, from http://www.elearnspace.org/Articles/eportfolios.htm.

Sigala, M. (2007). Integrating Web 2.0 in e-learning environments: A socio-technical approach. *International Journal of Knowledge and Learning, 3*(6), 628–648. doi:10.1504/IJKL.2007.016837

Silverman, D. (1993). *Interpreting qualitative data: Methods for analyzing talk, text, and interaction.* London, UK: Sage.

Silverman, S. (1997). Technology and physical education: Present, possibilities, and potential problems. *Quest, 49*, 306–314.

Simões, L., & Gouveia, L. (2008). *Web 2.0 and higher education: Pedagogical implications.* Higher Education: New Challenges and Emerging Roles for Human and Social Development. 4th International Barcelona Conference on Higher Education Technical University of Catalonia (UPC).

Smerden, B., Cronen, S., Lanahan, L., Andersen, J., Iannotti, N., & Angeles, J. (2000). *Teachers' tools for the 21st Century: A report on teachers' use of technology.* Retrieved from http://nces.ed.gov/pubs2000/2000102A.pdf

Smith, R., Clark, T., & Blomeyer, R. L. (2005). *A synthesis of new research on K-12 online learning.* Naperville, IL: Learning Point Associates. Retrieved from http://www.ncrel.org/tech/synthesis/synthesis.pdf

Smith, H. J., Higgins, S., Wall, K., & Miller, J. (2005). Interactive whiteboards: Boon or bandwagon? A critical review of the literature. *Journal of Computer Assisted Learning, 21*, 91–101. doi:10.1111/j.1365-2729.2005.00117.x

Smith, L. K., Draper, R. J., & Sabey, B. L. (2005). The promise of technology to confront dilemmas in teacher education: The use of WebQuests in problem-based methods courses. *Journal of Computing in Higher Education, 21*(4), 99–108.

Snider, S. L., & Hirschy, S. (2009). A self-reflection framework for technology use by classroom teachers of young learners. *He Kupu, 2*(1), 31–44.

Snow, C. (2005). *Knowledge to support the teaching of reading: Preparing teachers for a changing world.* San Francisco, CA: Jossey-Bass.

Snow-Gerono, J. L. (2005). Professional development in a culture of inquiry: PDS teachers identify the benefits of professional learning communities. *Teaching and Teacher Education, 21*(3), 241–256. doi:10.1016/j.tate.2004.06.008

Snyder, J., Lippincott, A., & Bower, D. (1998). The inherent tensions in the multiple uses of portfolios in teacher education. *Teacher Education Quarterly, 25*(1), 45–60.

Sockman, B. R., & Sharma, P. (2007). Struggling toward a transformative model of instruction: It's not so easy! *Teaching and Teacher Education, 24*(4), 13.

So, H. J., Lossman, H., Lim, W., & Jacobson, M. J. (2009). Designing an online video based platform for teacher learning in Singapore. *Australasian Journal of Educational Technology, 25*(3), 440–457.

Solomon, G., & Schrum, L. (2007). *Web 2.0: New tools, new schools*. Washington, DC: International Society for Technology in Education.

Southworth, M., Mokros, J., Dorsey, C., & Smith, R. (2010). The case for cyberlearning: Genomics (and dragons!) in the high school biology classroom. *Science Teacher (Normal, Ill.), 77*(7), 28–33.

Sparks, D. (2002). *Designing powerful professional development for teachers and principals*. Oxford, OH: National Staff Development Council.

Spitz, B. (1996). Imagine the possibilities: Exploring the Internet with middle school students. In Valauskas, E. J., & Ertel, M. (Eds.), *The Internet for teachers and school library media specialists: Today's applications tomorrow's prospects* (pp. 181–191). New York, NY: Neal-Schuman.

Sprague, D., & Norton, P. (1999). Studying technology as a cohort: Teachers' reflections on the process. In J. Price, et al. (Eds.), *Proceedings of Society for Information Technology & Teacher Education International Conference 1999* (pp. 722-727). Chesapeake, VA: AACE.

Stancill, J. (2006, February 20). Tough task set for teacher training. *The Raleigh News & Observer*, A1.

Stein, M. K., Engle, R. A., Smith, M. S., & Hughes, E. K. (2006). Orchestrating productive mathematical discussions: Five practices for helping teachers move beyond show and tell. *Mathematical Thinking and Learning, 10*, 313–340. doi:10.1080/10986060802229675

Stein, M. K., Smith, M. S., Henningsen, M., & Silver, E. A. (2009). *Implementing standards-based mathematics instruction. A casebook for professional development*. New York, NY: Teachers College Press.

Stephens, L. C., & Ballast, K. H. (2010). *Using technology to improve adolescent writing: Digital make-overs for writing lessons*. Boston, MA: Pearson.

Strage, A. (2004). Long term academic benefits of service learning: Where and when do they manifest themselves? *College Student Journal, 38*(2), 257-262. ERIC Database (EJ704958).

Strage, A. (2000). Service learning: Enhancing student outcomes in a college level lecture course. *Michigan Journal of Community Service Learning, 7*, 5–13.

Strahan, D. (2003). Promoting a collaborative professional culture in three elementary schools that have beaten the odds. *The Elementary School Journal, 104*(2), 127–146. doi:10.1086/499746

Strange, J. (2009, November 5). *Kaia and room 10 – Why blogs and commenting on blogs are so important*. Retrieved from http://edm310fall2009.blogspot.com/2009/11/kaia-reads-book-and-her-father-skypes.html

Strange, J. (2009, September 23). *You are creating your intellectual trail – And it can and will be Googled*. Retrieved from http://edm310fall2009.blogspot.com/2009/09/required-reading-anthony-capps-m6-post.html

Strange, J. (2010, April 26). *ZZZ and the honest reflection post – Response to comments*. Retrieved from http://strangethoughtsbyjohn.blogspot.com/2010/04/zzz-and-honest-reflection-post-response.html

Strange, J. (2010, March 22). *Honest reflection is required*. Retrieved from http://edm310.blogspot.com/2010/03/honest-reflection-is-required-new.html

Strauss, A., & Corbin, J. (1998). *Basics of qualitative research. Techniques and procedures for developing grounded theory*. Thousand Oaks, CA: SAGE Publications, Inc.

Strawhecker, J., Messersmith, K., & Balcom, A. (2007). The role of electronic portfolios in the hiring of K–12 teachers. *Journal of Computing in Teacher Education, 24*(2), 65–71.

Strudler, N., Archambault, L., Bendixen, L., Anderson, D., & Weiss, R. (2003). Project THREAD: Technology helping restructure educational access and delivery. *Educational Technology Research and Development, 51*(1), 39–54. Retrieved from http://coe.nevada.edu/nstrudler/ETRD03.pdf. doi:10.1007/BF02504517

Strudler, N., Archambault, L., Bendixen, L., Anderson, D., & Weiss, R. (2003). Project THREAD: Technology helping restructure educational access and delivery. *Educational Technology Research and Development*, *51*(3), 41–56. doi:10.1007/BF02504517

Strudler, N., & Wetzel, K. (2005). The diffusion of electronic portfolios in teacher education: Issues of initiation and implementation. *Journal of Research on Technology in Education*, *37*(4), 411–433.

Strudler, N., & Wetzel, K. (2008). Costs and benefits of electronic portfolios in teacher education: Faculty perspectives. *Journal of Computing in Teacher Education*, *24*(4), 135–142.

Strudler, N., & Wetzel, L. (1999). Lessons from exemplary colleges of education: Factors affecting technology integration in preservice programs. *Educational Technology Research and Development*, *47*(4), 63–81. doi:10.1007/BF02299598

Sturm, M., Kennel, T., McBride, M., & Kelly, M. (2008). The pedagogical implications of Web 2.0. In Thomas, M. (Ed.), *Handbook of research on Web 2.0 and second language learning* (pp. 367–384). Hershey, PA: IGI Global. doi:10.4018/9781605661902.ch020

Subrahmanyam, K., Greenfield, P., Kraut, R., & Gross, E. (2001). The impact of computer use on children's and adolescents' development. *Applied Developmental Psychology*, *22*(1), 7–30. doi:10.1016/S0193-3973(00)00063-0

Sudzina, M. R. (1999). *Case study applications for teacher education: Cases of teaching and learning in the content areas*. Needham Heights, MA: Allyn & Bacon.

Suharwoto, G. (2006). *Secondary mathematics preservice teachers' development of technology pedagogical content knowledge in subject-specific, technology-integrated teacher preparation program*. (Unpublished doctoral dissertation.) Oregon State University.

Suharwoto, G., & Niess, M. L. (2006, March). *How do subject specific teacher preparation programs that integrate technology throughout the courses support the development of mathematics preservice teachers' TPCK (Technology Pedagogical Content Knowledge)?* Paper presentation for the Society of Information Technology and Teacher Education (SITE) Annual Conference, Orlando, Florida.

Sunstein, B. (1996). Assessing portfolio assessment: Three encounters of a close kind. *Voices from the Middle*, *3*(4), 13–22.

Surrey, D. W., & Ely, D. P. (2007). Adoption, diffusion, implementation, and institutionalization of instructional innovations. In Reiser, R. A., & Dempsey, J. V. (Eds.), *Trends and issues in instructional design and technology* (2nd ed., pp. 104–122). Upper Saddle River, NJ: Pearson Education, Inc.

Swaminathan, S. (2005, March). *Facilitating mathematical and scientific reasoning and reflection in young childen through digital documentation*. Paper presented at the Keefe-Bruyette Symposium, West Hartford, CT.

Swaminathan, S., & Gardner, P. (2008). *Digital video documentation as a reflective tool for enhancing children's mathematical and social understanding and reseasoning*. Paper presented at the National Institute for Early Childhood Professional Development, New Orleans, LA.

Swaminathan, S., & Rezai, N. (2010). *Documenting, reflecting, & teaching: Digital portfolios in the preschool classroom*. Paper presented at the International Society for Technology in Education, Denver, CO.

Swaminathan, S., Barbuto, L. M., Hines, N., Piquette, K. B., Trawick-Smith, J., & Wright, J. L. (2004). *Digital portfolios: Powerful tools for documenting and evaluating student learning*. Paper presented at the National Educational Computing Conference, New Orleans, LA.

Swaminathan, S., Barbuto, L. M., Trawick-Smith, J., & Wright, J. L. (2004). *Technology training for preschool teachers: Study of the training model, pedagogical changes and student learning*. Paper presented at the Annual Meeting of the American Educational Research Association, San Diego, CA.

Swaminathan, S. (2000). Integrating technology within the curriculum: Teachers' challenges and teacher educator's insights. *Journal of Early Childhood Teacher Education*, *21*(2), 289–294. doi:10.1080/0163638000210223

Swartz, R., & Costa, A. Beyer, B., Kallick, B., & Reagan, R. (2008). *Thinking based learning*. Norwood, MA: Christopher Gordon.

Tabak, I. (2004). Synergy: A complement to emerging patterns of distributed scaffolding. *Journal of the Learning Sciences, 13*(3), 305–335. doi:10.1207/s15327809jls1303_3

Taggart, K. G. (20100. *Technology in teacher preparation survey*. Retrieved from https://sites.google.com/site/technologyteachersurvey/home

Tapscott, D. (1998). *Growing up digital: The rise of the net generation*. New York, NY: McGraw-Hill Companies.

Taskstream. (2010). *Products and services*. Retrieved from http://www.taskstream.com/pub/ProductsAndServices.asp

Taylor, R. B. (2009). *Literacy integration unit assignment handout for READ 3255*. University of North Carolina at Charlotte, Department of Reading & Elementary Education.

Taylor, R. B. (2010a). *Syllabus for READ 6265*. University of North Carolina at Charlotte, Department of Reading & Elementary Education.

Taylor, R. B. (2010b). *Instructional service project assignment handout for READ 6265*. University of North Carolina at Charlotte, Department of Reading & Elementary Education.

Taylor, J. (2008). Tapping online professional development through communities of practice: Examples from the NIFL discussion lists. *Adult Basic Education and Literacy Journal, 2*(3), 182–196.

Temple, V., Allan, G., & Temple, B. (2003). *Employers' and students' perceptions of electronic employment portfolios*. Retrieved from http://www.aare.au/03pap/tem03523.pdf

Teo, T., Chai, C., Hung, D., & Lee, C. (2008). Beliefs about teaching and uses of technology among pre-service teachers. *Asia-Pacific Journal of Teacher Education, 36*(2), 163–174. doi:10.1080/13598660801971641

The Design-Based Research Collective. (2003). Design-based research: An emerging paradigm for educational inquiry. *Educational Researcher, 32*(1), 5–8. doi:10.3102/0013189X032001005

The IRIS Center for Preparing Enhancements. (n.d.). *Universal design for learning: Creating a learning environment that challenges and engages all students*. Retrieved from http://iris.peabody.vanderbilt.edu/udl/chalcycle.htm

The National Council of Teachers of Mathematics. (2009). *Guiding principles for mathematics curriculum and assessment*. Retrieved February, 2011 from http://www.nctm.org/standards/content.aspx?id=23273

Thompson, A. D., and Mishra, P. (2007). Breaking news: TPCK becomes TPACK! *Journal of Computing in Teacher Education, 24*, 38, 64.

Thompson, K. (2011). *University high school: Thompson's math homepage*. Retrieved from http://www.uhigh.ilstu.edu/math/thompson/thompsonbio.htm

Thompson, A. D. (2005). Scientifically based research: Establishing a research agenda for the technology in teacher education community. *Journal of Research on Technology in Education, 37*(4), 331–337.

Thompson, A. D., Schmidt, D. A., & Davis, N. E. (2003). Technology collaboratives for simultaneous renewal in teacher education. *Educational Technology Research and Development, 51*(1), 73–89. doi:10.1007/BF02504519

Tinker, R. (2001). Future technologies for special learners. *Journal of Special Education Technology, 16*(4).

Toledo, C. (2002). *Computer technology infusion: Three case studies of California university teacher education programs*. Unpublished Dissertation, United States International University, San Diego, CA.

Tomlinson, C. A. (1995). *How to differentiate instruction in mixed ability classrooms*. Alexandria, VA: ASCD.

Tomlinson, C. A. (1999). *The differentiated classroom: Responding to the needs of all learners*. Alexandria, VA: ASCD.

Topping, K. (2003). Self and peer assessment in school and university: Reliability, validity and utility. *Innovation and Change in Professional Education, 1*, 55–87. doi:10.1007/0-306-48125-1_4

Topp, N. W., Mortenson, R., & Grandgenett, N. (1995). Goal: Technology-using teachers- Key: Technology-using education faculty. In Willis, J., Robin, B., & Willis, D. (Eds.), *Technology and Teacher Education Annual 1995* (pp. 840–843). Charlottesville, VA: Association for the Advancement of Computing in Education.

Trawick-Smith, J. (2009). *Early child development: A multicultural perspective* (5th ed.). New York, NY: Prentice Hall.

Trilling, B., & Fadel, C. (2009). *21st century skills: Learning for life in our times*. San Francisco, CA: Jossey-Bass.

Trochim, W., & Donnelly, J. (2007). *The research methods knowledge base* (3rd ed.). Mason, OH: Atom Dog Publishing.

Trubowitz, S. (2005). Creating a culture for learning. *Educational Horizons, 83*(3), 171–176.

Tsoi, M. F., Goh, N. K., & Chia, L. S. (2005). Multimedia learning design pedagogy: A hybrid learning model. *US-China Education Review, 2*(9), 59–62.

Tucker, P. D., Stronge, J. H., Gareis, C. R., & Beers, C. S. (2003). The efficacy of portfolios for teacher evaluation and professional development: Do they make a difference? *Educational Administration Quarterly, 39*(5), 572–602. doi:10.1177/0013161X03257304

Twigg, C. (2002). Improving learning and reducing costs: new models for online learning. *EDUCAUSE, 38*(5), 28-38. http://net.educause.edu/ir/library/pdf/erm0352.pdf

Tyack, D., & Cuban, L. (1995). *Tinkering toward utopia: A century of public school reform*. Cambridge, MA: Harvard University Press.

U. S. Department of Education. (1997). *President Clinton's call to action for American education in the 21st Century: Technological literacy*. Retrieved from http://www2.ed.gov/updates/PresEDPlan/part11.html

U.S. Congress, Office of Technology Assessment. (1995). *Teachers and technology: Making the connections. OTA-HER 616*. Washington, DC: U.S. Government Printing Office.

U.S. Congress. (2001). *No Child Left Behind Act of 2001* (PL 107-110). Title II: Teacher Quality Enhancement. Retrieved from http://www.ed.gov/legislation/ESEA02/pg121.html

U.S. Department of Education (USDOE) & National Center for Education Statistics. (NCES). (2005). *Computer technology in the public school classroom: Teacher perspectives*. Washington, DC: NCES.

U.S. Department of Education Office of Educational Technology. (2010). *Transforming American education: Learning powered by technology*. Washington, D.C. Retrieved from http://www.ed.gov/technology/netp-2010

U.S. Department of Education, Office of Educational Technology. (2004). *Toward a new golden age in American education: How the internet, the law and today's students are revolutionizing expectations*. Washington, DC: U.S. Government Printing Office.

U.S. Department of Education. (2002). *Preparing tomorrow's teachers to use technology*. Retrieved October 5, 2010 from http://www.pt3.org/

U.S. Department of Education. (2004). *National educational technology plan. Toward a new golden age in American education: How the internet, the law and today's students are revolutionizing expectations*. Washington, DC: U.S. Department of Education. Retrieved from http://www2.ed.gov/about/offices/list/os/technology/plan/2004/plan.pdf

U.S. Department of Education. (2010). *National educational technology plan. Transforming American education: Learning powered by technology*. Washington, DC: U.S. Department of Education. Retrieved from http://www.ed.gov/sites/default/files/NETP-2010-final-report.pdf

UNESCO. (2008). *ICT competency standards for teachers – Policy framework*. Retrieved from http://cst.unesco-ci.org/sites/projects/cst/The%20Standards/ICT-CST-Policy%20Framework.pdf

United States Department of Education, Office of Innovation and Improvement. (2004). *Innovations in education: Alternative routes to teacher certification*. Washington, D.C.

University of Delaware. (2009). *Fall course sites in a learning management system at UD*. Retrieved from http://www.udel.edu/udlms/images/10-08-2009-UD-SakaiFallCourses.jpg

University of Delaware. (2010). *Minor in educational technology*. Retrieved from http://www.udel.edu/education/ed-tech-minor.html

Unnamed. (2009). *Welcome to my PLE*. Retrieved from http://www.ted.com/talks/sugata_mitra_the_child_driven_education.html?awesm=on.ted.com_8YCW&utm_campaign=sugata_mitra_the_child_driven_education&utm_medium=on.ted.com-twitter&utm_source=direct-on.ted.com&utm_content=ted.com-talkpage

US Census Bureau. (2010). *International database*. Retricved September 2, 2010, from http://www.census.gov/cgi-bin/broker

Uzunboylu, H. (2007). Teacher attitudes toward online education following an online inservice program. *International Journal on E-Learning*, *6*(2), 267–277.

Valli, L. (1992). *Reflective teacher education: Cases and critiques*. Albany, NY: State University of New York Press.

van den Heuvel-Panhuizen, M. (2003). The didactical use of models in realistic mathematics education: An example from a longitudinal trajectory on percentage. *Educational Studies in Mathematics*, *54*(1), 9–35. doi:10.1023/B:EDUC.0000005212.03219.dc

Van Es, E. A., & Sherin, M. G. (2008). Learning to notice in the context of a video club. *Teaching and Teacher Education*, *24*(2), 244–276. doi:10.1016/j.tate.2006.11.005

van Hover, S. D., Berson, M. J., Bolick, C. M., & Swan, K. O. (2006). Implications of ubiquitous computing for the social studies curriculum (Republished). *Contemporary Issues in Technology & Teacher Education*, *6*(2). Retrieved from http://www.citejournal.org/vol6/iss2/socialstudies/article3.cfm.

Van Learhoven, T. R., Munk, D. D., Lynch, K., Bosma, J., & Rouse, J. (2007). A model for preparing special and general education preservice teachers for inclusive education. *Journal of Teacher Education*, *58*, 440–455. doi:10.1177/0022487107306803

VanFossen, P. J., & Shiveley, J. M. (2000). Using the Internet to create primary source teaching packets. *Social Studies*, *91*(6), 244–252. doi:10.1080/00377990009602473

Venn, M., & Moore, R., L., & Gunter, P. L. (2001). Using audio/video conferencing to observe field based practices of rural teachers. *Rural Educator*, *22*(2), 24–27.

Vescio, V., Ross, D., & Adams, A. (2006). *A review of research on professional learning communities: What do we know?* Retrieved February 16, 2008, from http://www.nsrfharmony.org/research.vescio_ross_adams.pdf

Viegas, F. B., Wattenberg, M., & Feinberg, J. (2009). Participatory visualization with Wordle. *IEEE Transactions on Visualization and Computer Graphics*, *15*(6), 1137–1144. doi:10.1109/TVCG.2009.171

Vincent, J. (2007). The interactive whiteboard in an early years classroom: A case study in the impact of a new technology on pedagogy. *Australian Educational Computing*, *22*(1), 20–25.

Voithofer, R. (2007). *Web 2.0: What is it and how can it apply to teaching and teacher preparation?* Paper presented at the American Educational Research Association Conference, April 9-13, Chicago, IL.

Vygotsky, L. S. (1962). *Thought and language*. Cambridge, MA: MIT Press. doi:10.1037/11193-000

Vygotsky, L. S. (1978). Interaction between learning and development. In Cole, M., John-Steiner, V., Scribner, S., & Souberman, E. (Eds.), *Mind in society: The development of higher psychological processes*. Cambridge, MA: Harvard University Press.

Vygotsky, L. S. (1978). *Mind in society: The development of higher psychological functions*. Cambridge, MA: Harvard University Press.

Vygotsky, L. S. (1981). The development of higher forms of attention in childhood. In Wertsch, J. V. (Ed.), *The concept of activity in Soviet psychology* (pp. 189–240). Armonk, NY: Sharpe. doi:10.2753/RPO1061-0405180167

Wachira, P., & Keengwe, J. (2011). Technology integration barriers: Urban school mathematics teachers perspectives. *Journal of Science Education and Technology*, *20*(1), 17–25. doi:10.1007/s10956-010-9230-y

Waddoups, G. L., Wentworth, N., & Earle, R. (2004). Principles of technology integration and curriculum development: A faculty design team approach. *Computers in the Schools*, *21*, 15–23. doi:10.1300/J025v21n01_02

Wade, R. C., & Anderson, J. B. (1996). Community service learning: A strategy for preparing human service-oriented teachers. *Teacher Education Quarterly*, *23*. Retrieved June 13, 2008, from www.teqjournal.org/backvols/1996/23

Walizer, B. R., Jacobs, S. L., & Danner-Kuhn, C. L. (2007). The effectiveness of face-to-face vs. Web camera candidate observation evaluations. *Academic Leadership*, *5*(3), 1–9.

Wang, L., Ertmer, P., & Newby, T. (2004). Increasing pre-service teachers' self-efficacy beliefs for technology integration. *Journal of Research on Technology in Education*, *36*(3), 231–250.

Wang, M. (2007). Designing online courses that effectively engage learners from diverse cultural backgrounds. *British Journal of Educational Technology*, *38*(2), 294–311. doi:10.1111/j.1467-8535.2006.00626.x

Warlick, D. (2009). Grow your personal learning network. *Learning & Leading with Technology*. Retrieved from http://istelearning.org/wp-content/uploads/2010/04/Grow-Your-PLN.pdf

Warrick, W., & Norton, P. (2002). Graduate instruction combining online, on-site, and face-to-face: A study. In D. Willis, et al. (Eds.), *Proceedings of Society for Information Technology & Teacher Education International Conference 2002* (pp. 881-885). Chesapeake, VA: AACE.

Warrick, W., Connors, S., & Norton, P. (2004). E-mail, discussion boards, and synchronous chat: Comparing three modes of online collaboration. In R. Ferdig, et al. (Eds.), *Proceedings of Society for Information Technology & Teacher Education International Conference 2004* (pp. 2732-2738). Chesapeake, VA: AACE.

Warschauer, M., Knobel, M., & Stone, L. A. (2004). Technology and equity in schooling: Deconstructing the digital divide. *Educational Policy*, *18*(4), 562–588. doi:10.1177/0895904804266469

Wartella, E. A., & Nancy, J. (2000). Children and computers: New technology--old concerns. *Children and Computer Technology*, *10*(2), 31–43.

Watkins, S. C. (2009). *The young and the digital: What the migration to social network sites, games, and anytime, anywhere media means for our future*. Boston, MA: Beacon.

Watson, J. (2007). *A national primer on K-12 online learning*. Vienna, VA: North American Council for Online Learning. Retrieved from http://www.nacol.org/docs/national_report.pdf

Watson, J. F., Gemin, B., Ryan, J., & Wicks, M. (2009). *Keeping pace with K–12 online learning: A review of state-level policy and practice*. Naperville, IL: Learning Point Associates. Retrieved from http://www.kpk12.com/downloads/KeepingPace09-fullreport.pdf

Watson, J. F., Murin, A., Vashaw, L., Gemin, B., & Rapp, C. (2010). *Keeping pace with K–12 online learning: An annual review of policy and practice*. Naperville, IL: Learning Point Associates. Retrieved from http://www.kpk12.com/wp-content/uploads/KeepingPaceK12_2010.pdf

Watson, J., Murin, A., Vashaw, L., Gemin, B., & Rapp, C. (2010). *Keeping pace with k-12 online learning: An annual review of policy and practice*. Retrieved from http://www.flvs.net/areas/aboutus/Documents/Research/KeepingPaceK12_2010.pdf

Watson, W. R., & Watson, S. L. (2007). An argument for clarity: What are learning management systems, what are they not, and what should they become? *TechTrends*, *51*(2), 28–34. doi:10.1007/s11528-007-0023-y

Weinstein, C. E., & Mayer, R. E. (1986). The teaching of learning strategies. In Wittrock, M. (Ed.), *Handbook of research on teaching* (pp. 315–327). New York, NY: Macmillan.

Wenger, E., White, N., & Smith, J. D. (2009). *Digital habitats: Stewarding technology for communities*. Portland, OR: CPsquare.

Wenger, E. (1998). *Communities of practice: Learning, meaning, and identity*. New York, NY: Cambridge University Press.

Wenglinsky, H. (2005). *Using technology wisely: The keys to success in schools*. New York, NY: Teachers College Press.

Weston, C., McAlpine, L., & Bordonaro, T. (1995). A model for understanding formative evaluation in instructional design. *Educational Technology Research and Development*, *43*(3), 29–48. doi:10.1007/BF02300454

Wetzel, K., & Strudler, N. (2005). The diffusion of electronic portfolios in teacher education: Next steps and recommendations from accomplished users. *Journal of Research on Technology in Education*, *38*(2), 231–243.

Wetzel, K., & Strudler, N. (2006). Costs and benefits of electronic portfolios in teacher education: Student voices. *Journal of Computing in Teacher Education, 22*(3), 69–78.

Wexler, J., Waughn, S., Edmonds, M., & Reutebuch, C. K. (2008). A synthesis of fluency interventions for secondary struggling readers. *Reading and Writing, 21*, 317–347. doi:10.1007/s11145-007-9085-7

Wheeler, B. C. (2003). *EPortfolio project: Open source eportfolio release.* Andrew W. Mellon Foundation, Version 2.0, Retrieved from http://juicy.mellon.org/RIT/MellonO-SProjects/%20ePortfolio/Portfolio_Proposal_Public.doc.

Wheeler, S., Yeomans, P., & Wheeler, D. (2008). The good, the bad, and the wiki: Evaluating student-generated content for collaborative learning. *British Journal of Educational Technology, 39*(6), 987–995. doi:10.1111/j.1467-8535.2007.00799.x

White, B. Y., & Frederiksen, J. R. (1998). Inquiry, modeling, and metacognition: Making science accessible to all students. *Cognition and Instruction, 16*(1), 3–188. doi:10.1207/s1532690xci1601_2

White, C. (1997). Citizen participation and the Internet: Prospects for civic deliberation in the information age. *Social Studies, 88*(1), 23–28. doi:10.1080/00377999709603741

Whittier, D., & Lara, S. (2003). Preparing tomorrow's teachers to use technology (PT3) at Boston University through faculty development. *Estudios Sobre Educación, 5*, 47–60.

Wiggins, G. P., & McTighe, J. (2005). *Understanding by design.* Alexandria, VA: Association for Supervision & Curriculum Development.

Wiggins, G., & McTighe, J. (2006). *Understanding by design.* Upper Saddle River, NJ: Pearson Education, Inc.

Wiley, D. A. (2000). Connecting learning objects to instructional design theory: A definition, a metaphor, and a taxonomy. In D. A. Wiley (Ed.), *The instructional use of learning objects: Online version.* Retrieved January 23, 2006, from the http://reusability.org/read/chapters/wiley.doc

Wilhelm, L., Puckett, K., Beisser, S., Wishart, W., Merideth, E., & Sivakumaran, T. (2006). Lessons learned from the implementation of electronic portfolios at three universities. *TechTrends: Linking Research & Practice to Improve Learning, 50*(4), 62–82.

Wilkinson, C., Hiller, R. F., & Harrison, J. M. (1998). Technology tips: Improving computer literacy of preservice teachers. *Journal of Physical Education, Recreation & Dance, 69*(5), 10–13, 16.

Willett, R. (2009). Young people's video productions as new sites of learning. In Carrington, V., & Robinson, M. (Eds.), *Digital literacies: Social learning and classroom practices* (pp. 13–26). Thousand Oaks, CA: SAGE Publications.

Williams, K. S. (2007). *Using WebQuests to improve understanding of ecology.* Paper presented at the ESA/SER Joint Meeting, San Jose, CA.

Willingham, D. T. (Producer). (2008, September 8, 2010). *Learning styles don't exist.* Retrieved from http://www.youtube.com/watch?v=sIv9rz2NTUk

Wilson, C., Trautmann, R., Ma, N. M., Kinster, J. G., & Barker, B. J. (2010). Science pipes: A world of data at your fingertips. *Science Teacher (Normal, Ill.), 77*(7), 34–39.

Wilson, S. M., & Berne, J. (1999). Teacher learning and the acquisition of professional knowledge: An examination of research on contemporary professional development. *Review of Research in Education, 24*, 173–209.

Wimba. (n.d.). *Wimba, version 6* [Online Conferencing Software]. New York, NY: Wimba, Inc.

Windschitl, M., & Sahl, K. (2002). Tracing teachers' use of technology in a laptop computer school: The interplay of teacher beliefs, social dynamics, and institutional culture. *American Educational Research Journal, 39*(1), 165–205. doi:10.3102/00028312039001165

Wise, J. A., Thomas, J. J., Pennock, K., Lantrip, D., Pottier, M., Schur, A., & Crow, V. (1995) Visualizing the non-visual: Spatial analysis and interaction with information from text documents. *INFOVIS Proceedings of the 1995 IEEE Symposium on Information Visualization*, Atlanta, Georgia.

Wiske, M., Franz, K., & Breit, L. (2005). *Teaching for understanding with technology*. San Francisco, CA: Jossey Bass.

Wittrock, M. (1985). Teaching learner generative strategies for enhancing reading comprehension. *Theory into Practice, 24*(2), 123. doi:10.1080/00405848509543158

Wittrock, M. C. (1989). Generative processes of comprehension. *Educational Psychologist, 24*(4), 345–376. doi:10.1207/s15326985ep2404_2

Wittrock, M. C. (1992). Generative learning processes of the brain. *Educational Psychologist, 27*(4), 531–541. doi:10.1207/s15326985ep2704_8

Wolf, K., & Dietz, M. (1998). Teaching portfolios: Purposes and possibilities. *Teacher Education Quarterly, 25*(1), 9–22.

Wolfson, G. (2008). Using audio books to meet the needs of adolescent readers. *American Secondary Education, 36*(2), 105–114.

Wong, D., Mishra, P., Koehler, M. J., & Siebenthal, S. (2007). Teacher as filmmaker: iVideos, technology education, and professional development. In Girod, M., & Steed, J. (Eds.), *Technology in the college classroom*. Stillwater, OK: New Forums Press.

Wood, C. (2005). Highschool.com: The virtual classroom redefines education. *Edutopia, 1*(4), 31-44. Retrieved from http://www.edutopia.org/high-school-dot-com

Woodbridge, J. (2008). Technology integration as a transforming teaching strategy. *Tech Learning*. Retrieved on May 24, 2010, from www.techlearning.com/article/2022

Wood, E., Specht, J., Willoughby, T., & Mueller, J. (2008). Integrating computer technology in early childhood education environments: Issues raised by early childhood educators. *The Alberta Journal of Educational Research, 54*(2), 210–226.

Woods, M. L., Karp, G. G., Hui, M., & Perlman, D. (2008). Physical educators' technology competencies and usage. *Physical Educator, 65*(2), 82–99.

Wright, V. H. (2005). Bridging and closing technology gaps. In Vrasidas, C., & Glass, G. V. (Eds.), *Preparing teachers to teach with technology* (pp. 359–367). Greenwich, CT: Information Age Publishing.

Wright, V. H., & Wilson, E. K. (2005). From preservice to inservice teaching: A study of technology integration. *Journal of Computing in Teacher Education, 22*(2), 49–55.

Wright, V. H., Wilson, E. K., Gordon, W., & Stallworth, J. B. (2002). Master technology teacher: A partnership between preservice and inservice teachers and teacher educators. *Contemporary Issues in Technology & Teacher Education, 2*(3), 353–362.

Yancy, K. B. (2004). Postmodernism, palimpsest, and portfolios: Theoretical issues in the representation of student work. *College Composition and Communication, 55*, 738–761. doi:10.2307/4140669

Yancy, K. B. (2009). *Writing in the 21st Century*. Urbana, IL: National Council of Teachers of English.

Ying-Chen, L., & Kinzie, M. B. (2000). Computer technology training for prospective teachers: Computer attitudes and perceived self-efficacy. *Journal of Technology and Teacher Education (JTATE), 8*(4). Charlottesville, VA: Association for the Advancement of Computing in Education (AACE). ISSN 1059-7069.

Zawilinski, L. (2009). HOT blogging: A framework for blogging to promote higher order thinking. *The Reading Teacher, 62*, 650–660. doi:10.1598/RT.62.8.3

Zemelman, S., Daniels, H., & Hyde, A. (1998). *Best practice: New standards for teaching and learning in America's schools*. Portsmouth, NH: Heinemann.

Zhang, J. (2008). The implication of metaphors in information visualization. *Visualization for Information Retrieval, 23*, 215–237. doi:10.1007/978-3-540-75148-9_10

Zhao, Y. (2003). Introduction: What teachers need to know about technology? Framing the question. In Zhao, Y. (Ed.), *What should teachers know about technology: Perspectives and practices*. Greenwich, CT: Information Age Publishing.

Zhao, Y. (2003). *What teachers should know about technology: Perspectives and practices*. Greenwich, CT: Information Age Publishing.

Zhao, Y., Pugh, K., Sheldon, S., & Byers, J. L. (2002). Conditions for classroom technology innovations. *Teachers College Record, 104*(3), 485–515. doi:10.1111/1467-9620.00170

Ziemkiewicz, C., & Kosara, R. (2009). Preconceptions and individual differences in understanding visual metaphors. *Computer Graphics Forum, 28*(3), 911–918. doi:10.1111/j.1467-8659.2009.01442.x

Zucker, A., & Kozma, R. (2003). *The virtual high school: Teaching generation V.* New York, NY: Teachers College Press.

Zucker, T. A., & Invernizzi, M. (2008). My e-sorts and digital extensions of word study. *The Reading Teacher, 61*, 654–658. doi:10.1598/RT.61.8.7

About the Contributors

Drew Polly is an Assistant Professor in the Department of Reading and Elementary Education at the University of North Carolina at Charlotte. His research agenda focuses on examining how to support the implementation of technology and standards-based pedagogies. More information can be found at: http://education.uncc.edu/abpolly.

Clif Mims (http://clifmims.com) is an Associate Professor in the Department of Instructional Design and Technology at the University of Memphis and is the Executive Director of the Martin Institute for Teaching Excellence in Memphis, Tennessee. Mims is a teacher, researcher, author, speaker, and educational consultant specializing in the effective integration of technology with teaching and learning.

Kay Persichitte is the Dean of the College of Education at the University of Wyoming. Persichitte has extensive experience and background in curriculum and program development, accreditation, standards-based instruction, telecommunications systems and distance instruction, and preservice teacher technology integration.

* * *

Jennifer Banas is an Assistant Professor at Northeastern Illinois University. Previous to this appointment she served as an online course designer, faculty member, and Dean for the American College of Education. Other career experience includes teaching high school health education, working as a county health educator, training hospital employee and community members in CPR/first aid, and serving as a visiting research project coordinator for the Survey Research Laboratory at the University of Illinois-Chicago. Banas earned both her Doctorate in Instructional Design & Technology and Master of Education in Curriculum & Design at Northern Illinois University. She also holds a Master of Public Health from the University of Illinois-Chicago. She completed her Bachelor of Science in Community Health at the University of Illinois, Champaign-Urbana. Her areas of research include the application of learning, behavior, and communication models and theories to effectively, efficiently, and ethically teach and motivate learners.

Michael Barbour is an Assistant Professor at Wayne State University in Detroit, Michigan, where he teaches Instructional Technology and Qualitative Research Methodology. He completed his Ph.D. in Instructional Technology from the University of Georgia. Originally from Newfoundland and Labrador, Michael's interest in distance education for rural students began after accepting his first high school teaching position in a regional high school in a rural community of approximately 3,500 people. Having been educated in an urban area, Michael was troubled by the inequity of opportunity provided to his rural students and began a program to offer Advanced Placement (i.e., university-level) social studies courses over the Internet to students at his own school and other schools in the district. Michael has since works with numerous K-12 online learning programs in Canada, the United States, and worldwide as an online teacher, course developer, administrator, and evaluator. His current research interests focus on the effective design, delivery, and support of online learning to K-12 students in virtual school environments, particularly those in rural jurisdictions. Michael currently resides in Windsor, Ontario, Canada.

William Blanton is a Professor in the Department of Teaching and Learning at the University of Miami. He conducts research on learning-to-read, reading-to-learn, and thinking in subject matter areas, and the application of telecommunications, digital technology, videoconferencing, and instant messaging to learning to teach. The theoretical context in which he works is cultural-historical-activity theory, developed by Vygotsky, Luria, and Leontiev. He has been the editor of journals in reading education, served on editorial boards of major journals, and published widely in journals, such as *Journal of Educational Computing Research, Elementary School Journal, Reading Research Quarterly, Reading Psychology, Journal of Adolescent and Adult Literacy,* and *The Reading Teacher.*

Matt Bower, after beginning professional life as an actuary, soon decided that his true passion was education. After completing a Diploma of Education, he taught high school Mathematics for several years in Sydney, Alice Springs, and the UK. With an interest in applying IT to educational contexts, he completed a Bachelor of Science in Computing and a Master's degree in Education (online education) and soon after joined Macquarie University's Postgraduate Professional Development Programs to develop and teach in their online Graduate Diploma of IT program. During this time he completed his PhD thesis entitled "Designing for Interactive and Collaborative Learning in a Web-Conferencing Environment". Matt is now a Senior Lecturer in ICT for Macquarie University's School of Education, who specializes in developing pre-service teachers' ability to integrate technology into learning and teaching.

Carol Adamec Brown is Associate Professor in the Department of Mathematics, Science, and Instructional Technology at East Carolina University. Early research in computers in schools reported on collaborative practices between the classroom teacher, technology specialist, and the school library media specialist. Building on early career experiences as a classroom teacher and school media specialist, her work also includes best practices for the design of professional development for teachers and specialists in K12 environments. More recently Brown has investigated the use of digital resources to augment classroom instruction. She is Program Director for the MAEd in Instructional Technology, teaches in the College of Education at ECU.

David Buckner is an Assistant Professor of Social Studies Methodology at Oklahoma State University. He received his doctorate in Curriculum and Instruction at the University of Arkansas. Buckner was selected as a James Madison Fellow in 1999, and has received the 2010 Outstanding Higher Ed Educator of the Year Award from the Oklahoma Council for the Social Studies. He is a member of NCSS and CUFA, and serves on several national committees. Buckner's research interests include civics education, constitutional issues, and technology in the social studies classroom. Buckner and his wife Nita reside in Stillwater, OK.

Janice W. Butler is an Assistant Professor at the University of Texas at Brownsville in the Educational Technology graduate program. In education for 23 years, seventeen of which were spent in the K-12 environment, she continues to be interested in the potential impact of technology integrated into all classrooms. Butler continues to be actively involved in training teachers to in effective student-centered pedagogy and the use of technology to improve learning. Believing that systemic change must begin with higher education and teacher education programs, she has focused on the use of Web 2.0, low-threshold technology as a catalyst for change. These technologies with an additional emphasis on games and simulations comprise her research priorities.

Lina Lopez Chiappone is currently a Director of faculty and academic support, and TESOL program Professor at the Fischler School of Education and Human Services of Nova Southeastern University in Davie, Florida. Chiappone earned her doctorate in TESOL and Reading at the University of Miami (FL), where she taught in the department of teaching and learning, and conducted literacy research in Miami-Dade County Public Schools (M-DCPS) as part of several federal grants. She was also project director for a research study of best practices with English language learners in urban settings. Prior to that, Chiappone was a teacher for 10 years in M-DCPS, working primarily with the dropout prevention program at the elementary level. Her research and writing interests include computer-assisted language learning, multiple literacies, and vocabulary learning as they relate to students learning English as a second language.

Kenneth F. Clark has been at Georgia Southern University since 1988 and is a Professor of Instructional Technology where he teaches online graduate level courses in the Instructional Technology Program. He holds an EdD in Instructional Technology from the University of Florida, an Ed.S in Computer Science Education from Nova University, a M.Ed. in Mathematics Education from Florida Atlantic University, and a BS in Mathematics from Florida State University. Clark's major interest is in integrating technology into the instructional process.

Ann C. Cunningham is an Associate Professor of Instructional Design at Wake Forest University. She is currently the Director of Elementary Education and Interim Department Chair. Ann teaches undergraduate and graduate Instructional Design, Assessment, and Technology at the undergraduate and graduate levels. During her time at Wake Forest University, Ann has represented Wake Forest University in a PT3 grant partnership with two other universities, has served on the International Society for Technology in Education's Executive Board, and has been president of the SIG for Teacher Educators. Her research interests include the factors that influence teachers' instructional design choices, technology innovations appropriate for pK12 classrooms, professional learning communities, and electronic portfolio development. She has published research in technology journals in addition to several book chapters.

John H. Curry is an Assistant Professor of Educational Technology at Oklahoma State University. He earned his Ph.D. in Instructional Technology from Utah State University, and currently he teaches undergraduate courses in technology integration as well as graduate courses in Instructional Design and Performance Improvement Technology. He also serves as Communications Chair for the Multimedia Production division of the Association of Educational Communications and Technology and in the past twice coordinated the podcasting for the association's international conference. His research includes technology integration, applications of social networking, and various aspects of instructional design. He is honored by having been voted by students of Oklahoma State University as the Outstanding Faculty Member of the College of Education three years in a row. He and his wife have been married for nineteen years and are the proud parents of four children.

Gloria Gonzales-Dholakia is a doctoral student in the department of Curriculum and Instruction at the University of Texas at Austin. Her research focuses on instructional technology in the areas of PK-12 classroom technology integration, teacher education programs, and digital equity. Her dissertation research will focus on the relationship between teacher education and resulting novice teachers' conception of digital equity. She currently teaches for the School of Education and New College at St. Edward's University. Mrs. Gonzales-Dholakia holds an undergraduate degree in Biology and a Master's degree in Adult Education. Because service to community and education is of the upmost importance to Gloria, she currently serves on the board of directors for Leander Educational Excellence Foundation, is a Parent Teacher Association board member, and volunteers regularly at her children's school.

Elizabeth Downs is a Professor in the Instructional Technology program at Georgia Southern University. Elizabeth earned her Ph.D. in Instructional Technology from the University of Florida and M.Ed. in Educational Psychology also from the University of Florida. Elizabeth earned a B.S. degree in Elementary Education from Florida State University. Elizabeth's professional interests include cyberbullying, generational characteristics of learners, and applications of Web 2.0 tools in instruction.

Oliver Dreon is an Assistant Professor at Millersville University where he teaches Instructional Technology and supervises preservice science teachers. Dreon also coordinates the Digital Learning Studio, a technology integration and outreach center that serves the Millersville community. Prior to coming to Millersville in 2007, Dreon taught middle school math, science, and gifted classes and high school physics. He speaks locally and nationally on the integration of technology in classroom settings, the incorporation of 21st Century Skills across the PK-12 curriculum, and the ability of Web 2.0 applications to foster collaborative learning communities. His research interests include teacher development and professional teacher identity. Dreon also co-coordinates Millersville University's Professional Development School, which partners with local school districts to train new science teachers. He is a co-author of the book, *Authentic Instruction with Technology: a Student-Centered Approach*.

Sam Eneman is an Instructional Technology Consultant in the Center for Teaching and Learning at the University of North Carolina at Charlotte. He provides training and professional development support to faculty and staff. This includes developing workshops and Web-based video tutorials, meeting with faculty for one-on-one consultations, and producing the Center's podcast series, *Teaching and Learning Matters*. In addition to these and other related projects, Sam is also responsible for Wimba training.

Timothy Frey is an Associate Professor in the Department of Special Education, Counseling, and Student Affairs at Kansas State University. He teaches in both graduate and undergraduate teacher education programs at K-State. His research focuses on the use of technology to facilitate professional growth for teachers, studying the impact and effectiveness of professional development activities on K-12 students with disabilities. His recent projects have included: working with rural schools districts in Kansas on the collaborative design of on-line professional development activities, integrating UDL principles in the teacher education programs at K-State, and developing new strategies that utilize instructional and assistive technologies to improve outcomes for K-12 students with disabilities. Before pursuing his Ph.D. at Indiana University in Special Education with a minor in Instructional Systems Technology, he worked as a middle school special education teacher in Nebraska.

Adam M. Friedman is an Associate Professor, Director of Secondary Education and Director of Social Studies Education at Wake Forest University. He teaches undergraduate and graduate secondary social studies methods, undergraduate elementary social studies methods, as well as a course in descriptive research in social studies. His research interests include the factors that encourage and barriers that impede social studies teachers' technology use, the effect of technology use on student learning in social studies, and the Internet's impact on citizenship education. He has published his research in various social studies and technology journals and book chapters, and served as the co-chair of the technology committee of the National Council for the Social Studies.

Susan Gibson is a Professor in the Department of Elementary Education of the Faculty of Education at the University of Alberta, Edmonton Alberta, Canada. She teaches Social Studies Education in the Undergraduate Teacher Education Program and Curriculum Studies at the Master's and Doctoral levels. Her areas of research expertise include the preparation of social studies teachers, infusing technology into teaching and learning, and preparing preservice and practicing teachers for teaching in a digital age.

Amy J. Good is an Associate Professor in the Department of Reading and Elementary at the University of North Carolina at Charlotte. She teaches graduate and undergraduate social studies methods courses. Her research interests include social studies instruction, integration of technology, and teacher education.

Lucy Santos Green is an Assistant Professor of Instructional Technology in the department of Leadership, Technology & Human Development at Georgia Southern University. She holds an Ed.D. in Educational Instructional Technology from Texas Tech University, an MLS from Texas Woman's University and has a decade of K-12 teaching experience in Texas public schools. Her interests involve community-based research in K-12 settings, Web 2.0 integration in K-12 curriculum, school library media instructional partnerships and K-12 online learning.

Mark Gura, a native of New York City, taught in East Harlem public schools for 18 years. Afterwards, he spent 5 years as a staff and curriculum developer for the New York City Department of Education. He established the Office of Instructional Technology, for which he held the position of Director for 7 years, supervising professional development in the use of technology, citywide. After retiring, he joined Fordham University's Regional Educational Technology Center. He has taught Instructional Technology courses for both Fordham and Touro College. Mr. Gura has written books for ISTE, Information Age Books, Scarecrow Books, Corwin, and Teacher Created Materials. He has been an education writer for the New York Daily News and contributed numerous articles to *Converge, T.H.E. Journal,* and *EdTech Magazine.* He is the co-producer of the popular podcast The Teachers Podcast. Mr. Gura has spoken on the subject of Instructional Technology throughout the US.

Darci J. Harland is Assistant Director of Research at the Center for Mathematics, Science, and Technology (CeMaST) at Illinois State University. Her educational teaching experiences range from undergraduate and graduate education and biology courses to high school and middle school English and science courses. Her research interests include the influence of personality on online and face-to-face classroom participation, the use of digital media as a tool for reflection, the long-term impact of scientific research performed by high school and undergraduate students, and the level of inquiry in on-to-one laptop classrooms.

Lisa Harris is an Assistant Professor in the department of Counseling, Leadership, and Educational Studies at Winthrop University in Rock Hill, SC. Lisa teaches undergraduate educational technology courses, and graduate courses in assessment and educational research. Her research interests include computer assisted accommodations for students with disabilities, the development of effective course evaluation instruments, and Professional Development Schools.

Richard Hartshorne is an Associate Professor of Educational Technology at the University of Central Florida. He earned his Ph.D. in Curriculum and Instruction from the University of Florida. At the University of North Carolina at Charlotte, his teaching focuses on the integration of technology into the educational landscape, as well as instructional design and development. His research interests primarily involve the production and effective integration of instructional technology into the teaching and learning environment. The major areas of his research interest are rooted in online teaching and learning, technology and teacher education, and the integration of emerging technology into the k-post-secondary curriculum.

Dawn Hathaway is an Assistant Professor in the College of Education and Human Development, Graduate School of Education at George Mason University. Hathaway works with K-12 practicing teachers in a Master's program in Curriculum and Instruction with an emphasis on the Integration of Technology in Schools. She is also the coordinator of the Integration in Technology in Schools online certificate programs.

Tina L. Heafner is an Associate Professor of Social Studies Education in the Department of Middle, Secondary, and K-12 Education at the University of North Carolina at Charlotte. She earned his Ph.D. in Curriculum and Instruction from the University of North Carolina at Greensboro. At the University of North Carolina at Charlotte, her teaching focuses on the social studies methodology, curriculum studies, and content specific integration of technology. Her research interests primarily involve the state of social studies, best practices for social studies teaching and learning, with particular emphases on content area literacy and technology mediated learning. Her administrative responsibilities include coordinating both the M.Ed. in Secondary Education and the undergraduate Minor in Secondary Education.

Janice Hinson is a Professor and the Chair of the Department of Reading and Elementary Education at the University of North Carolina at Charlotte. Her research focuses on digital literacies, specifically in 1:1 laptop programs. She has a BA in Music Education from West Liberty University, a MSEd in Curriculum and Instruction from Old Dominion University, and an EdD in Curriculum and Instruction from the University of Virginia.

Charles B. Hodges earned a Ph.D. from the Learning Sciences and Technologies program at Virginia Tech and Mathematics degrees from Fairmont State College (B.S.) and West Virginia University (M.S.). His professional interests are self-efficacy and self-regulation in online learning environments, instructional software evaluation, and the preparation of instructional designers. He is an Assistant Professor of Instructional Technology at Georgia Southern University where he teaches in the online Instructional Technology Program. Recently, his research has appeared in the *Journal of Educational Computing Research, The Internet and Higher Education,* and *The International Journal of Teaching and Learning in Higher Education.*

Joan E. Hughes is an Associate Professor of Instructional Technology in the College of Education at The University of Texas at Austin. Her research examines preservice and inservice teachers' development of technological knowledge and practice of technology integration in content areas (see: http://www.techedges.org). She currently leads a longitudinal study of laptop computing in preservice teacher education and conducts case studies of school technology integration by examining the intersections of technology leadership, teacher knowledge, and technology use among students in and out of school. Her most recent publications are in *Educational Researcher, Educational Technology,* and *American Journal of Distance Education.* Hughes has 18 years of educational experience at elementary, middle school, and university levels. She worked previously as an Assistant and Associate Professor of Learning Technologies at the University of Minnesota, Twin Cities and earned her Ph.D. (Educational Psychology) at Michigan State University.

Thomas Jackson is an Assistant Professor in the College of Education at George Williams College of Aurora University. He began a career in teaching as "an essentialist teacher of the 1970s," but with instinctive progressive tendencies, he explored strategies to enrich student learning. After a second career as a corporate instructor and curriculum designer, Jackson returned to the elementary classroom, where the Principal of the school introduced him to a single computer classroom, but more importantly, supported the idea of student computer use. Four years later Jackson, through innovation and persistence, had reframed the classroom into a 16-station computer lab where his 4th grade students practiced content research, created improved educational products, and applied computer ingenuity. While Jackson coached and mentored, his students were invited to present learning products at several technology showcases. As a result, Jackson developed a consummate belief in the power of classroom integrated computer technology as a learning tool when implemented well.

Marshall G. Jones is an Associate Professor of Educational Technology and the Director of Graduate Studies in the Richard W. Riley College of Education at Winthrop University in Rock Hill, SC. Jones teaches graduate courses in Educational Technology and undergraduate courses in technology integration. His research interests and consulting experience includes project evaluation, instructional design, mobile learning, elearning, the design and development of constructivist learning environments, emerging technologies, and new media.

Stephanie A. Jones is an Assistant Professor in the online Instructional Technology program at Georgia Southern University, where she teaches future school librarians. She received a Ph.D. in Instructional Technology from the University of Georgia and a Master of Librarianship from Emory University. She began her professional library career in Georgia as a youth librarian in a public library and then worked as an elementary school librarian for fourteen years. Jones' current research interests include the career development of school librarians, the 21st century school library profession, collaboration, and storytelling pedagogy.

Kathryn Kennedy is an Assistant Professor at Georgia Southern University's College of Education in the Department of Leadership, Technology and Human Development. She holds a Ph.D. from the University of Florida (2010) in curriculum and instruction, with a concentration in educational technology, a Master's from the Florida State University (2005) in Library and Information Science, specializing in young adult literature, and a Bachelor of Arts from the University of Florida (2000) in English, with an emphasis in children's and adolescent literature. Her research interests and practical experience include pre-service and in-service teacher, technology specialist, and library/media center specialist professional development for technology integration and instructional design in traditional, blended, and online learning environments. She has a special interest in K-12 online learning. http://www.kathrynmkennedy.com/

Kristen Kereluik is a doctoral candidate in Educational Psychology and Educational Technology in the College of Education at Michigan State University. Her research focuses on the cognitive, contextual, and motivational variation in the use of multimedia tools for teaching and learning.

Minchi C. Kim is an Assistant Professor of Learning Design and Technology in the Department of Curriculum and Instruction at Purdue University. Professor Kim's research focuses on scaffolding students problem solving with technology-enhanced learning environments, advancing pedagogical frameworks for learning and teaching in technology-rich contexts, and integrating emergent technologies (simulations, games, Web 2.0) into classes. Kim's work has been published in numerous journals including *Instructional Science, Computers & Education,* and *Science Education.*

Brian Kissel is an Assistant Professor in the Department of Reading and Elementary Education at the University of North Carolina at Charlotte. Previously, he worked as an elementary school teacher, an elementary-based literacy coach, and a prekindergarten literacy coach. He teaches both graduate and undergraduate courses in writing development, writing instruction, and language arts. His current research interests include writing instruction and the integration of technology during writing instruction in elementary classrooms.

E. Ann Knackendoffel earned her Ph.D. at the University of Kansas, with a major in special education and minors in special education technology and school administration. She began in special education as a teacher of students with intellectual and learning disabilities as well as students with emotional and behavior disorders and taught at both the elementary and secondary levels. She is currently an Assistant Professor at Kansas State University and has taught courses related to assistive technology and special education and serves on various university committees related to technology implementation in education. She is a member of the Technology and Media Division of the Council for Exceptional Children and most recently co-author of a book with Drs. Peggy Dettmer and Linda Thurston entitled, *Collaboration, Consultation and Teamwork for Students with Special Needs,* 7th edition.

Matthew J. Koehler is an Associate Professor of Educational Technology and Educational Psychology at Michigan State University. His research and teaching focuses on understanding the affordances and constraints of new technologies; the design of technology-rich, innovative learning environments; and the professional development of teachers.

Joanne Leight teaches Instructional Technology to physical education majors at Slippery Rock University of Pennsylvania where she serves as Associate Professor and Assistant Department Chair. She earned her Doctorate degree in Education from Duquesne University. She has successfully published and presented many different topics in the area of technology use in physical education. She has also written many technology grants and has served as the technology editor of the *Journal of Physical Education, Recreation and Dance*.

Nanette Marcum-Dietrich is an Assistant Professor in the Department of Educational Foundations at Millersville University of Pennsylvania. She received her B.S. in Biology from Purdue University in 1995 and her Ph.D. in Science Education from the University of Delaware in 2005. Her research and teaching activities focus on the design of technology-rich curriculum for use in the secondary science classroom. Marcum-Dietrich is also the recipient of a National Science Foundation Grant to develop a cyber-learning game that allows students to model the hydrology of their neighborhoods using authentic data and a research grade hydrologic model (www.wikiwatershed.org). She has written numerous articles in both practitioner and peer reviewed scholarly journals that explore the intersection of technology and inquiry science teaching. Marcum-Dietrich also co-coordinates Millersville University's Professional Development School which partners with local school districts to train new science teachers and is a co-author of the book, *Authentic Instruction with Technology: a Student-Centered Approach*.

Adriana L. Medina is an Assistant Professor in the Department of Reading & Elementary Education at The University of North Carolina at Charlotte. Medina's areas of interest and research include adolescent literacy, teacher education, and educational program evaluation. Her primary teaching responsibilities include undergraduate and graduate courses in reading and content area literacy. Medina teaches a service learning course at Piedmont Open IB Middle School in Charlotte and works with the Center for Adolescent Literacies at UNC Charlotte on program evaluation projects including the evaluation of summer reading programs.

Punya Mishra is Professor of Educational Technology and Educational Psychology at Michigan State University. His scholarship lies at the intersection of technology, teaching, creativity and design. You can find out more about his work by going to http://punya.educ.msu.edu/

Abdou Ndoye is the Assessment Coordinator for the College of Arts and Sciences at Qatar University in Doha. Prior to his position he also served as the Assessment Director at the School of Education at the University of North Carolina Wilmington and also as the Director of the Online Master of Professional Studies at the University of Connecticut where he received his Ph.D. He is specialized in Learning Outcomes Assessment with research interests in building a culture of assessment, exploring faculty perspectives in learning outcomes, program assessment practices and assessing the impact of technology in education. He has experience teaching graduate and undergraduate courses in learning outcomes assessment, instructional design, and research methods.

Randy Nichols is an Associate Professor and Department Chair in the Physical Education Department at Slippery Rock University of Pennsylvania. Randy earned his doctorate in Physical Education Teacher Education from West Virginia University and has 21 years of teaching experience. He has presented and published numerous topics in the field of physical education including the use of technology in physical education. Randy teaches fitness and methods classes at Slippery Rock University.

Margaret (Maggie) L. Niess is Professor Emeritus of Mathematics Education at Oregon State University. Her research focuses on integrating technology in teaching science and mathematics and the knowledge teachers rely on for teaching with technologies –TPACK. She has authored multiple peer-reviewed works including a teacher preparation textbook, *Guiding Learning with Technology*. She is currently directing the design, implementation, and evaluation of a new online Master of Science program for K-12 mathematics and science teachers with an interdisciplinary science, mathematics, and technology emphasis. Research from this work has focused on developing a community of learners in online graduate coursework. She chaired the Technology Committee for the Association of Mathematics Teacher Educators (AMTE), served as Vice President of the Teacher Education Council for Society for Information Technology and Teacher Education (SITE), served on the Board of Directors for School Science and Mathematics (SSMA), and was an editor of *School Science and Mathematics Journal*.

Priscilla Norton has been involved with educational technology since the late 1970's, working with teachers to understand the role of the newer electronic technologies to support teaching and learning. Norton is Program Coordinator for the Integrating Technology in Schools Certificate, Master's, and Doctoral Programs. She specializes in technology integration, K-12 and is the author of numerous articles and two books – *Teaching with Technology* (2003) and *Technology for Teaching* (2001). More recently, Norton has been designing and developing e-learning environments for teachers and high school students resulting in part in *The Online Academy* – a virtual high school and *The Online Academy for Teachers* – an educational program to teach teachers to teach in virtual environments.

Chandra Hawley Orrill is an Assistant Professor in Mathematics Education at University of Massachusetts Dartmouth. She spent most of the last decade working as a research scientist at the University of Georgia where she was able to pursue a number of efforts, including the Technology Integration in Mathematics projects, related to helping teachers with their mathematics instruction. Chandra has also served as co-PI on an Institute for Educational Science project related to middle grades mathematics. Chandra's research interests focus on how teachers know and learn mathematics as well as how they use what they learn in their own classroom teaching. To this end, she has participated in and led numerous professional development, research, and measurement projects.

Anne Ottenbreit-Leftwich is an Assistant Professor of Instructional Systems Technology at Indiana University Bloomington. Ottenbreit-Leftwich's expertise lies in the areas of the design of digital curriculum resources, the use of technology to support pre-service teacher training, and development/implementation of professional development for teachers and teacher educators. Ottenbreit-Leftwich has experience working on large-scale funded projects, including projects supported by the U.S. Department of Education. Her current research focuses on teachers' value beliefs related technology and how those beliefs influence teachers' technology uses and integration. She is currently working on a project funded by the Fund for the Improvement of Postsecondary Education (FIPSE) investigating the technology tools teachers can use to support problem-based learning.

Michele A. Parker is an Assistant Professor of Educational Leadership at University of North Carolina at Wilmington. Her doctorate is in Research, Statistics, and Evaluation from the University of Virginia. She teaches an Instructional Technology course for undergraduates preparing to be teachers and research courses for graduate students. She examines the use of technology (e.g., ePortfolios, virtual classrooms, MUVEs) in K-12 and higher education, methodological issues such as the fidelity of implementation, and how to improve students' understanding of research methods.

Ydalisse Pérez is a Research Assistant of Mathematics Education in the Center for Mathematics, Science, and Technology (CeMaST) at Illinois State University. During the Master's program, she was involved in a study about secondary mathematics teachers' beliefs about English Language Learners (ELL) students' teaching and instruction; an article is currently in press. Currently, during the Ph.D. program, she is working with Darci Harland and Tami Martin in a study about the impact of technology use on educational reform in algebra classes. Her interests in mathematics education are: curriculum and teaching of algebra, Latino community in the mathematics classroom, cognitive thinking in math and how neuroscience contributes to understanding the learning of mathematics, students' aptitudes and mindsets in mathematics, and how to ignite students' interest in math, especially with logic argumentation and innovative technology.

Teresa M. Petty is an Assistant Professor and coordinator of online programs in the Department of Middle, Secondary, and K-12 Education at the University of North Carolina at Charlotte. She earned her Ed.D. in Curriculum and Instruction from the University of North Carolina at Chapel Hill. At the University of North Carolina at Charlotte, her teaching focuses on instructional design, secondary schools, and mathematics methods. Her research interests include teacher attraction/retention in high-need schools and online teaching/learning.

Paola Pilonieta is an Assistant Professor at the University of North Carolina at Charlotte. She taught first grade in an urban area for five years. She earned her PhD in the area of reading from the University of Miami. Her research interests revolve around comprehension instruction in the primary grades and teacher education.

Judi Repman earned a B.A. in History, a Master's Degree in Library Science and a Ph.D. in Educational Media from Louisiana State University, Baton Rouge. She began her faculty career at Texas Tech University in Lubbock, TX and is currently Professor and Coordinator of the online M.Ed. in Instructional Technology Program at Georgia Southern University, Statesboro, GA. Judi serves as the consulting Editor for *Library Media Connection* (*LMC*), a journal for school library and technology specialists. Her research interests include school library media programs, information literacy, and online teaching and learning.

Albert D. Ritzhaupt is an Assistant Professor of Educational Technology at the University of Florida in Gainesville, FL. His primary research areas focus on the development of technology-enhanced instruction, and technology integration in education. His publications have appeared in multiple venues, including the *Journal of Computing in Higher Education, Computers & Education, Journal of Educational Computing Research, Behavior Research Methods*, and *Computers in Human Behavior.* His primary teaching responsibilities include teaching graduate courses in project management, educational games and simulations, distance education, and foundations of educational technology.

Jeanne Samuel is an educational technologist with over 10 years experience as a teacher, trainer, and consultant. She is Microsoft and CompTIA certified in many areas including networking, security, and system administration. Last year Jeanne moved from full-time technology support and part time teaching to full-time teaching. This change allows Jeanne to explore the relationship between technology and pedagogy at a much deeper level. She continues to investigate ways to transparently use technology in the classroom to promote student academic performance while not creating time burdens on the classroom teacher. Jeanne teaches at Delgado Community College in New Orleans, LA. She is also an independent computer consultant/trainer for Anything PC.

John Strange is a Professor of Behavioral Studies and Education Technology in the College of Education at the University of South Alabama. Strange has been a faculty member at USA since 1988. Strange also served as the Founding Dean of the College of Public and Community Service at the University of Massachusetts at Boston from 1972-1979 and the Vice President of the Council for the Advancement of Experiential Learning from 1979-1983.

Sudha Swaminathan is Professor of Early Childhood Education at Eastern Connecticut State University, Willimantic, CT. Her primary teaching responsibilities include early childhood mathematics, science, and technology education classes. Her research interests include young children's developing mathematical abilities, early childhood educators' use of educational technology, and digital documentation as an assessment tool. To date, she has over 15 publications in several journals including the *Young Children* and *Childhood Education* and has made over 40 presentations at conferences. She is an active member of the National Association for the Education of Young Children, the International Society for Technology in Education, and the National Council of Teachers of Mathematics, and other national and international professional organizations. She is the recipient of several grants, including the 4-year $750,000 grant from the United Technologies Corporation for technology-based professional development efforts in the Hartford public preschools.

Kristen Taggart is a Doctoral Candidate at the University of Delaware in the Curriculum, Higher Education, and Technology program. She has worked for the Colonial School District in Delaware for the past seven years, both in instructional and administrative capacities. Her teaching career focused on high school geography, and her administrative experience is at the middle school level. Throughout her career, she has focused on using technology to improve student involvement and achievement in the classroom. Recently, Ms. Taggart also began teaching part-time at the University of Delaware in the Secondary Social Studies Education program in the Department of History. Her course introduces pre-service teacher candidates to various technologies they will encounter in their classrooms.

Bruce Taylor is an Associate Professor at the University of North Carolina at Charlotte in the Department of Reading and Elementary Education. He is director of the Center for Adolescent Literacies. His research and teaching focus on the social and cultural aspects of literacy and learning of adolescents and, in particular, ways to meet the academic learning needs of diverse and often marginalized students. His work explores the role of diverse texts—including digital texts—in content-area classrooms and the role of discourse in the lives of adolescents. Recently, he has begun to explore the role of inquiry and service learning as ways to advance literacy and promote agency among marginalized adolescents.

Maryann Tatum Tobin is a Professor of Reading Education at Nova Southeastern University's Fischler School of Education and Human Services. Prior to joining the faculty of NSU, Tobin was a high school English teacher and an online curriculum writer/editor. She is a graduate of the University of Miami, where she was an Adjunct Professor and Research Fellow for both the Digital Lessons Project and the Fifth Dimension Program. She was the University of Miami's Associate Teacher of the Year in 2001. Tobin also holds a Master's of Fine Arts in Motion Picture Screenwriting from the University of Miami. Her research focus is on Digital Storytelling and its uses as a comprehension activity in content area classrooms. She lives in Miami with her husband, their basset hound, and two horses.

Cheri Toledo, an Associate Professor in the Department of Curriculum and Instruction at Illinois State, specializes in educational technology. An educator for over 25 years, she has taught and coached on the K-12 and university levels, and been a junior high and high school academic counselor, and an Academic Dean. Cheri's research interests revolve around strategic uses of current and emerging technologies to increase effective teaching and learning, and issues and practices of Web-enhanced, blended, and online teaching and learning environments. She was a co-host for the Women of Web 2, an EdTechTalk Network webcast, and is a founding member and co-host of the new iteration, Women of Web 3. You can follow Cheri on Twitter (cheritoledo) and subscribe to her blog, Ed Tech Spin at http://drctedd.wordpress.com.

Monica W. Tracey is an Associate Professor of Instructional Technology in the College of Education at Wayne State University. Her teaching and research experience are on the theory of instructional design and its applications and preparing instructional designers. Tracey has over 20 publications including a book, book chapters, and journal articles in the area of instructional design and performance improvement. She is a recipient of a Faculty Recognition Award from Oakland University and the 2008 Design and Development Award for service from the international association in her field, the Association for Educational Communications and Technology (AECT). She serves on the editorial board for the *International Journal of Designs for Learning* and is a board member for AECT International. In 2008 Tracey directed a large scale cross-cultural customized instructional design and performance improvement project in Dubai, U.A.E.

Kelly L. Unger is a PhD Candidate of Instructional Technology in the College of Education at Wayne State University. Her practice and research experience center on designing and developing technology professional development for K-12 pre- and in-service teachers. Unger is also interested in implementing and researching various Web-based tools in multiple instructional and learning environments. At this time, she is working on her dissertation study, *Examining the Impact of Technology Professional Development on Secondary Education Teachers' Classroom Practice.* Selected as an AECT Intern in

2010, she was also an integral factor in starting the Michigan Chapter of AECT (MIAECT), where she currently serves as President of the Board. In 2004, Unger started her own educational technology consulting business, which provides K-12 school districts assistance with integrating various technologies into the curriculum.

Yu-Chi Wen is a Ph.D. student in the Instructional Technology program at The University of Texas at Austin. She is currently working with Dr. Hughes on the research project called Preservice Preparation and Practice in Laptop-Infused Teacher Education. She received her Master's degree in the same program in 2009. The title of her Master's report was "A Review of Using Weblogs for Teaching and Learning." Before entering the program, she taught English in an elementary school in Taiwan for four years. Her research interests include Web 2.0 technology in language learning and technology integration in preservice teacher education focusing on preservice teachers' technological pedagogical content knowledge (TPACK).

Patricia Wilkins is a full-time Lecturer of Instructional Systems Technology at the University of North Carolina at Charlotte. She earned her M. Ed. in Instructional Systems Technology and Curriculum and Instruction from the University of North Carolina at Charlotte. She is currently a Doctoral Candidate in the Educational Leadership program at the University of North Carolina at Charlotte. At the University of North Carolina at Charlotte, she primarily teaches pre-service teachers with a hands-on approach of integration of technology into the classroom environment. Her research interests include project-based learning, integrating technology into the curriculum, and utilizing Web 2.0 resources to enhance instructional practices into the learning environment. The areas of her research interest are K-12 teacher education and the integration of emerging technology into 21st Century classrooms.

Hyo-Jin Yoon is a Doctoral student in Curriculum and Instruction Department, specializing in Instructional Technology in the College of Education at The University of Texas at Austin. She is interested in research about preservice teacher technology preparation in teacher education programs. She is a member in the research group that studies a longitudinal study of laptop computing in preservice teacher education. She is currently conducting her dissertation, which is a study of technological preparation and practice through a cross-sectional case study design. She is also a Graduate Research Assistant in the IDEA Studio, which provides technology integration support to faculty in the College of Education at The University of Texas at Austin.

Andrea Zellner is a Doctoral Candidate in the hybrid program in Educational Psychology and Educational Technology in the College of Education at Michigan State University, and a teacher-consultant with the Red Cedar Writing Project. Her research focuses on social networks, teacher professional development, and digital writing.

Index